BLACKSTONE'S GUIDE TO

The Anti-Terrorism Legislation

SECOND EDITION

BLACKSTONE'S GUIDE TO

The Anti-Terrorism Legislation

SECOND EDITION

Clive Walker

OXFORD
UNIVERSITY PRESS

OXFORD
UNIVERSITY PRESS

Great Clarendon Street, Oxford OX2 6DP

Oxford University Press is a department of the University of Oxford.
It furthers the University's objective of excellence in research, scholarship,
and education by publishing worldwide in

Oxford New York

Auckland Cape Town Dar es Salaam Hong Kong Karachi
Kuala Lumpur Madrid Melbourne Mexico City Nairobi
New Delhi Shanghai Taipei Toronto

With offices in

Argentina Austria Brazil Chile Czech Republic France Greece
Guatemala Hungary Italy Japan Poland Portugal Singapore
South Korea Switzerland Thailand Turkey Ukraine Vietnam

Oxford is a registered trade mark of Oxford University Press
in the UK and in certain other countries

Published in the United States
by Oxford University Press Inc., New York

Crown copyright material is reproduced under Class Licence
Number C01P0000148 with the permission of OPSI
and the Queen's Printer for Scotland

First published 2002
Second edition published 2009

British Library Cataloguing in Publication Data

Data available

Library of Congress Cataloging-in-Publication Data

Walker, Clive, Dr.
    Blackstone's guide to the anti-terrorism legislation / Clive Walker.—2nd ed
        p. cm.
    Includes bibiliographical references and index.
    ISBN 978-0-19-954809-5 (pbk. : alk. paper) 1. Terrorism—Great Britain—
Prevention. 2. War and emergency legislation—Great Britain. I. Title. II. Title:
Anti-terrorism legislation.
    KD8039.W348 2009
    344.4105'32517—dc22   2009027863

Typeset by Cepha Imaging Private Ltd, Bangalore, India
Printed in Great Britain
on acid-free paper by
CPI Antony Rowe, Chippenham, Wiltshire

ISBN 978-0-19-954809-5

1 3 5 7 9 10 8 6 4 2

Preface

The predominance of terrorism as a generator of legal initiative and controversy is so palpable that justification for a second edition of this book hardly requires elaboration. The principal rationale resides in the major legislative and judicial developments since February 2002 (the date of the previous manuscript). As for legislative changes, only the Terrorism Act 2000 and the Anti-terrorism, Crime and Security Act 2001 then existed. A substantial body of extra legislation has now accrued: the Prevention of Terrorism Act 2005; the Terrorism Act 2006; the Terrorism (Northern Ireland) Act 2006; the Justice and Security (Northern Ireland) Act 2007; and the Counter-Terrorism Act 2008. Prolonged and, at times, bitter parliamentary debates lie in the background to these new Acts. In addition to this legislation, important judicial case law has emerged. As well as legal materials, many official reports have appeared, from the Home Office, parliamentary committees, and independent sources. Academic commentators have also grown markedly more prolific.

A prime purpose of this book is to explain the foregoing key legislative texts in detail, in context, and in combination. In keeping with the format of the Blackstone series, the bulk of the source legislation is also reproduced. Equally important is the enhanced and original analysis, which integrates considerations of policy and principle, while also exploring statistical data.

The commentaries so produced will be reflective of several themes. The first, evident from the potted history already related, is one of growing profusion, scope, and complexity. Aside from sheer bulk, there are equally noticeable transformations in content. One concerns the moving focus from Irish terrorism to international terrorism. Ever since the paramilitary ceasefires of 1996 and then the 'Good Friday' Agreement of 1998,[1] there has been a winding down of paramilitary violence in Northern Ireland, though splinter movements remain dangerous. Conversely, the dread engendered by Al-Qa'ida[2] and affiliated combinations have driven most subsequent legal and policy initiatives since the attacks on September 11, 2001. Whether called international terrorism, Islamist terrorism, or (preferably) *jihadist* terrorism,[3] this variant has placed terrorism at the centre-stage of British policy making and administration. A further change concerns the nature of threat. *Jihadist* terrorism is perceived as involving indiscriminate, substantial, and suicidal attacks on civilian targets. Consequently, policy goals have shifted further towards anticipatory responses. While criminal prosecution remains a desired goal, criminal justice has likewise been increasingly moulded towards early intervention. This trend finds its ultimate expression in the persistence of executive measures,

---

[1] British Irish Agreement reached in the multi-party negotiations (Cm 3883, 1998).
[2] Depictions of this Arabic name vary, but the above represents the form adopted in the Terrorism Act 2000 (Proscribed Organisations) (Amendment) Order 2001, SI 2001/1261.
[3] The latter will be preferred. '*Jihadist* terrorism' reflects the adaptation of the Qu'ranic concept of 'struggle' or 'striving' which is commonly invoked by such groups: see Rehman, J., *Islamic State Practices, International Law and the Threat from Terrorism* (Hart Publishing, Oxford, 2005).

which can respond to risk in ways which the due process of criminal justice will not countenance.

The legislature and judiciary must ensure accountability and respect for constitutionalism in these troubled times. Parliament has certainly expended growing attention to terrorism policy and legislation and has occasionally imposed limits, such as by rejecting forty-two or ninety days' detention. Other notable contributions have been made by select committees, especially the Home Affairs Committee and the Joint Committee on Human Rights. The judicial role has also become more prominent. The Human Rights Act 1998 has engendered less judicial deference and a more forthright platform for intervention in security matters.

A further marked trend is that the UK jurisdiction has become less distinct for its extensive legislative response to terrorism which has been a continuum for over two and a half centuries. Under the influence of the United Nations (especially Security Resolution 1373 of 28 September 2001), almost all jurisdictions have passed some comparable laws. This book will not engage in detailed comparative studies, but close parallels will be mentioned.

It remains a daunting task to keep pace with, and to derive meaning from, the often astonishing events and responses around terrorism which have unfolded during the past seven years. I am therefore grateful for the support of others. Aside from my colleagues at the School of Law in the University of Leeds (above all, Professors Crawford, Halson, and Wall), I thank especially Lord Carlile, Professor Robert Chesney (Wake Forest University), Murray Hunt (JCHR), Professor Andrew Lynch (UNSW), Eric Metcalf (JUSTICE), Professors Louise Richardson and Phillip Heymann (Harvard University), and Professor Max Taylor (St Andrew's University). I have also been substantially assisted by contacts in the Home Office, Northern Ireland Office, and the Police Counter-Terrorism Units. The Institute of Advanced Legal Studies and Stanford University afforded access to superb research facilities, as well as the National Archives. Jane Kavanagh and Katie Heath provided exceptional support on behalf of the publishers.

The book takes account of developments up to 31 March 2009. At that point, the Counter-Terrorism Act 2008 was not wholly in force. Consequently, its amendments to prior legislation have not all been consolidated in the Appendices.

Clive Walker
31 March 2009

Contents—Summary

Contents—Detailed

TABLE OF CASES

TABLE OF STATUTES

Statutes of Crown Dependencies

Guernsey

Isle of Man

Jersey

National Legislation

Canada

Ireland

New Zealand

US

TABLE OF STATUTORY INSTRUMENTS

TABLE OF EUROPEAN LEGISLATION

TABLE OF TREATIES AND CONVENTIONS

1

BACKGROUND AND INTRODUCTORY ISSUES

A. THE PHENOMENON OF TERRORISM

1. Concept of terrorism

'Terrorism' has endured as a term in political science since the French Revolution.[1]   **1.01**
Attempts at a precise definition will be considered next in this chapter. For the moment,
let us assume that terrorism means the application of violence for political ends. Whether
such action is justifiable historically, politically, or morally is a vital question. The commonplace mantra, indicating moral relativism, is that 'One man's terrorist is another
man's freedom fighter.' A more contemporary dictum notes that '. . . Osama bin Laden
was a freedom fighter for Reagan but a terrorist for Bush. One can change sides without
changing tactics . . .'[2] However, considerable progress has been made in international
law by distinguishing between political objectives, which remain forever contestable,
and specific techniques, such as the bombing of civilians, which have become depicted
as unpardonable wrongs.[3] Since this book is concerned with positive law, the moral vindication of terrorists or of the state which opposes them will not be considered. It follows
that the label 'terrorism' will be used to describe any action correlating to its legal description and is not meant to convey any pejorative implication.

---

[1] See Hoffman, B., *Inside Terrorism* (2nd edn, Columbia University Press, New York, 2006).
[2] Nielsen, K., 'On the moral justifiability of terrorism (state and otherwise)' (2003) 41 *Osgoode Hall Law
Journal* 427 at p 430. However, variant legal connotations arise between attacking a Russian tank in Afghanistan
and attacking civilians in New York.
[3] See International Convention for the Suppression of Terrorist Bombings, adopted by the General
Assembly of the United Nations on 15 December 1997 (37 I.L.M. 249).

2. Categories of terrorism

1.02 The categorization of terrorism often depends on the ends being pursued and can be depicted as: revolutionary and counter-revolutionary; sub-revolutionary; or statist. In all cases, the essence is a tripartite relationship whereby the actors (terrorists) seek to impact on a target (specific victims) with a view to influencing a political audience (typically the government or the general public).[4]

1.03 Revolutionary terrorism arises where a group or movement seeks to implement a change which can be counted as 'revolutionary'—a change in state allegiance or a fundamental constitutional change within that state. This tactic of terrorism may be adopted as an end in itself, for example, by anarchists or nihilists. However, terrorism is more frequently undertaken as a tactic based upon the conditions of endemic political and military weakness. There are two contexts in which the weak commonly resort to revolutionary terrorism: within independent states and as part of a campaign against decolonization.[5] The latter format seeks to increase the economic and political costs of retaining the external territory and to exert international pressure. Within independent states, the terrorists seek to trigger a spiral of governmental repression and consequent loss of popularity and authority.[6] It may be counted as a partial terrorist success if governmental victory is achieved at the expense of political fragmentation or deep unpopularity, thus paving the way for future conflict. Consequently, 'the issue is not merely survival, but the way in which society chooses to survive.'[7]

1.04 The United Kingdom can assuredly claim to have encountered more configurations and episodes of revolutionary terrorism than most other polities.[8] This thrasonical statement is founded upon several elements. The first relates to the bygone era of the British Empire, when there were multiple colonial campaigns of political violence. The second element of experience arises from the intermittent, irredentist campaigns of terrorism in Ireland against its incorporation within a predominantly British state over a period of more than three centuries. The Provisional Irish Republican Army announced a permanent end to violence in 2005, though splinter Republican groups remain active.[9]

1.05 The Irish context equally provides a good example of counter-revolutionary terrorism. Loyalists groups have resisted by force Nationalist demands for many centuries, with equally enduring paramilitary groups such as the Ulster Volunteer Force and Ulster Defence Association.[10]

1.06 Other sources of revolutionary terrorism generated from causes within the United Kingdom have been far less important until the past decade. Britain has been the locus for terrorism based on foreign or international causes, from the 1970s and onwards, when Palestinian groups sought to bring their campaign to the world through hijackings

---

[4] See Crelinsten, R.D., 'Analysing terrorism and counter-terrorism: a communication model' (2002) 14 *Terrorism & Political Violence* 77; Richardson, L., *What Terrorists Want* (John Murray, London, 2006).

[5] See White, J.R., *Terrorism* (4th edn, Wadsworth, Belmont, 2002) ch 12.

[6] Burton, A.M., *Urban Terrorism* (Leo Cooper, London, 1975) pp 5–6.

[7] Friedlander, R.A., *Terrorism: Documents of International and Local Control*, Vol I (Oceana, New York, 1979) p 108.

[8] See further Walker, C., 'Terrorism and criminal justice' [2004] *Criminal Law Review* 311.

[9] Neumann, P.G., *Britain's Long War* (Palgrave, Basingstoke, 2003); Independent Monitoring Commission, *Eighth Report* (2005–06 HC 870); Alonso, R., *The IRA and the Armed Struggle* (Routledge, Abingdon, 2007); Dingley, J., *Combating Terrorism in Northern Ireland* (Routledge, Abingdon, 2009).

[10] Wood, I.S., *Crimes of Loyalty* (Edinburgh University Press, Edinburgh, 2006).

and other attacks. Their tactics have since been emulated by other foreign-based groups, such as Sikh or Tamil independence movements.

The advent in Britain of Al-Qa'ida has developed a variant of revolutionary terrorism which cannot be depicted as entirely 'foreign' or 'international', since its political aims and membership contain domestic and foreign elements. Some relate to British involvement in Iraq and Afghanistan, some relate to Palestine, Middle Eastern governments, and the treatment of Muslims throughout the world. Thus, Al-Qa'ida is sometimes categorized as a wholly novel form of terrorism—'Third Millennium Terrorism'—with qualitatively distinct features, such as religious and cultural motivations alongside predominantly political aims, a networked configuration, the cataclysmic use of suicide attacks, a sophisticated reliance on technology, and global rather than nationalist aims.[11] Al-Qa'ida has been the banner under which some of the most destructive acts of terrorism in history have been committed. Notorious above all were the September 11, 2001 attacks, but the litany also includes bombings in New York in 1993, East Africa in 1998, Yemen in 2000, Bali in 2002, Jakarta in 2003 and 2004, Madrid in 2004, and London in 2005.[12]

Two further categories of 'terrorism' remain. Sub-revolutionary terrorism seeks a political end which does not involve a fundamental change to the existence or nature of the state but is confined to a particular policy or aspect of policy. Animal liberationists who have resorted to violence may provide an illustration, though their activities are not in practice treated under the rubric of terrorism. Next, terrorism as a tactic adopted by a state is the most prevalent and devastating form of all. Notable protagonists of terror tactics during the last century were Hitler and Stalin whose policies resulted in far more deaths than all revolutionary terrorism since that time.[13] Of course, state terrorism is not just the preserve of the great dictators. It is a distressingly commonplace accusation that even democracies are tempted to abandon restraints during terrorism emergencies. Engagement in 'Dirty Wars' is a charge made against the UK government not only during its historical colonial campaigns, but also in contemporary times, with the use of degrading and inhuman treatment against suspects,[14] policies of shoot-to-kill,[15] and collusion with counter-revolutionaries.[16]

1.07

1.08

---

[11] See Gunaratne, R., *Inside al Qaeda* (Columbia University Press, New York, 2002); Gray, J., *Al Qaeda and What It Means to Be Modern* (Faber and Faber, London, 2003); Sageman, M., *Understanding Terror Networks* (University of Pennsylvania Press, Pa., 2004); Greenberg, K.J., *Al Qaeda Now* (Cambridge University Press, Cambridge, 2005); Gerges, F.A., *The Far Enemy* (Cambridge University Press, New York, 2005); Wilkinson, P. (ed), *Homeland Security in the UK* (Routledge, Abingdon, 2007) chs 2, 3.

[12] See National Commission on Terrorist Attacks upon the United States, *The 9/11 Commission Report* (GPO, Washington, DC, 2004); Intelligence and Security Committee, *Inquiry into Intelligence, Assessments and Advice prior to the Terrorist Bombings on Bali 12 October 2002* (Cm 5724, London, 2002); *Report of the Official Account of the Bombings in London on the 7th July 2005* (2005–06 HC 1087).

[13] See Conquest, R., *The Great Terror* (Oxford University Press, Oxford, 2007).

[14] See *(Compton) Report of an Enquiry into allegations against the security forces of physical brutality in Northern Ireland arising out of arrests on the 9 August 1971* (Cmnd 4828, London, 1972); *(Parker) Report of the Committee of Privy Counsellors appointed to consider authorised procedures for the interrogation of persons suspected of terrorism* (Cmnd 4901, London, 1972); *(Bennett) Report of the Committee of Inquiry into Police Interrogation Procedures in Northern Ireland* (Cmnd 7497, London, 1979); *Ireland v United Kingdom* App no 5310/71, Ser A 25 (1978); *(Aitken) Investigation into cases of Deliberate Abuse and Unlawful Killing in Iraq in 2003 and 2004* (Ministry of Defence, 2008).

[15] See Bloody Sunday Inquiry (<http://www.bloody-sunday-inquiry.org.uk/>); Stevens Inquiry on UDA/RUC collusion (*The Times* 18 April 2003 pp 4, 5); de Menezes inquiries (IPCC, Stockwell One and Stockwell Two (London, 2007)).

[16] See Rolston, B., 'An effective mask for terror' (2005) 44 *Crime Law & Society* 181; Police Ombudsman for Northern Ireland, *Statement by the Police Ombudsman for Northern Ireland on her investigation into the circumstances surrounding the death of Raymond McCord Jr and related matters* (Belfast, 2007).

1.09   Whilst terrorism in all forms is seen as a security risk, often the prime threat of all, it is by no means the sole or most common threat. Contextualization is offered by the Civil Contingencies Act 2004.[17] For its purposes, 'emergencies' are defined in ss 1 and 19 as events or situations which threaten serious damage to human welfare or serious damage to the environment, or amount to war or terrorism which threatens serious damage to national security. Terrorism is thereby counted as just one potential emergency, with floods being in fact the most common source of emergency. The same panoply of potential disasters is listed in the Cabinet Office's paper, *The National Security Strategy of the United Kingdom*.[18] These broader conceptions of emergency may be redolent of a culture of fear which spawns increasing risk aversion, whereby public policy is determined by perceived risks which are disproportionate to our unprecedented levels of personal safety.[19] The allegation that governments overplay the risk of terrorism also reflects contemporary theoretical approaches to the centrality of risk, in particular, the management of diffuse and complex risks that even threaten the notion of 'modernity' itself. The 'risk society' (the idiom of Ulrich Beck) is therefore 'an epoch in which the dark sides of progress increasingly come to dominate social debate'.[20] Terrorism is one of these 'dark sides' in which the growth of Al-Qa'ida is a reflexive aspect of more positive features of late modernity such as globalized networks.

B. COUNTER-TERRORISM

1.10   The UK government published a clear, clever, and comprehensive counter-terrorism strategy ('CONTEST') in 2006 which was revised in 2009 as follows:[21]

Delivery of the strategy continues to be organised around four principal workstreams:
* Pursue: to stop terrorist attacks
* Prevent: to stop people becoming terrorists or supporting violent extremism
* Protect: to strengthen our protection against terrorist attack
* Prepare: where an attack cannot be stopped, to mitigate its impact.

1.11   The 'Protect' and 'Prepare' elements are very much the province of the Civil Contingencies Act 2004. The Act seeks to bolster through planning and networking the resilience of responders to potential emergencies.

1.12   'Prevent' has come to the fore since the July 2005 bombings, which forced the government and public to confront the unpalatable fact that the terrorism was not the work of alien foreigners but involved attacks by their erstwhile neighbours.[22] The concern is

---

[17] See Walker, C. and Broderick, J., *The Civil Contingencies Act 2004* (Oxford University Press, Oxford, 2006).
[18] Cm 7291, London, 2008.
[19] Furedi F., *Culture of Fear* (rev edn, Continuum, London, 2002), *Invitation to Terror* (Continuum, London, 2007). See further Mythen, G., and Walklate, S., 'Criminology and terrorism' (2006) 46 *British Journal of Criminology* 379.
[20] Beck, U., *Ecological Enlightenment* (Humanities Press, New Jersey, 1995) p 2.
[21] Home Office, *Countering International Terrorism* (Cm 6888, London, 2006), *Pursue, Prevent, Protect, Prepare: The United Kingdom's Strategy for Countering International Terrorism* (Cm 7547, London, 2009) para 7.07. See Gregory, F., 'National governance structures to manage the response to terrorist threats and attacks' in Wilkinson, P. (ed), *Homeland Security in the UK* (Routledge, Abingdon, 2007).
[22] See Walker, C., '"Know Thine Enemy as Thyself": Discerning Friend from Foe under Anti-Terrorism Laws' (2008) 32 *Melbourne Law Review* 275.

therefore to reduce this propensity, adding to the emphasis on anticipatory risk and averting attacks rather than picking up the pieces in their aftermath.[23]

As for 'Pursuit', an element often stressed is the importance of intelligence-gathering.[24] It can form the basis not only for pre-emptive action in general but also for the individual application of criminal justice disposals or alternative executive measures, or even for the application of a US-style 'war on terror'?[25] Which path to 'Pursuit' is preferable? Where there is sufficient evidence of criminal activity, then a criminal prosecution is the more legitimate response[26] A criminal justice path formed the core of the most important report on terrorism legislation, the Diplock Report in 1972.[27] This approach does not mean that criminal justice cannot adapt to allow for early intervention, and the very use of the term 'terrorism', interrogations under special arrest powers with special detention periods, special courts with no juries, and special 'precursor' offences have all been implemented. These changes can become so many and so deep that they endanger the legitimacy of the criminal justice process, and so produce political prisoners in the minds of defendants and their communities. The dangers were dramatized by the hunger strikes in the Maze Prison H Blocks in 1981 in resistance to the ascription of criminalization.[28] A further problem is that the criminal justice process, however modified, may remain unappealing to the security services who wish to avoid disclosure of methods and sources in a public courtroom. Hence, there emerge executive alternatives to prosecution such as internment and control orders. 1.13

British dalliance with a 'war model' has been confined to military operations in Afghanistan and Iraq. Even in this sphere, the operative rules have remained the regular international humanitarian and human rights laws. In this way, there has emerged no British 'legal black hole'[29] equivalent to the facilities and processes at Guantánamo Bay. Nor has there been a successful domestic application of executive powers to conduct surveillance or to override human rights safeguards through diplomatic assurances.[30] Instead the UK government has rejected even the terminology of the 'war on terror' and claims instead that 'prosecution is—first, second, and third—the government's preferred approach when dealing with suspected terrorists'.[31] 1.14

---

[23] See Dershowitz, A., *The Case for Preemption* (W.W. Norton, New York, 2006); Suskind, R., *The One Per Cent Doctrine* (Simon & Schuster, New York, 2007).

[24] Walker, C., 'Intelligence and anti-terrorism legislation in the United Kingdom' (2006) 44 *Crime, Law and Social Change* 387.

[25] See US Presidential Order, Detention, Treatment, and Trial of Certain Non-Citizens in the War Against Terrorism, 13 November 2001 (66 Federal Register 57831).

[26] Kentridge, S., 'The pathology of a legal system: criminal justice in South Africa' (1980) 128 *University of Pennsylvania Law Review* 603 at p 612; Zedner, L., 'Securing liberty in the face of terrorism' (2005) 32 *Journal of Law & Society* 507 at p 533; Gearty, C., *Can Human Rights Survive?* (Cambridge University Press, Cambridge, 2005) p 139.

[27] *Report of the Commission to consider Legal Procedures to Deal with Terrorist Activities in Northern Ireland* (Cmnd 5185, London, 1972).

[28] See Walker, C., 'Irish Republican Prisoners - Political Detainees, Prisoners of War or Common Criminals?' [1984] 19 *Irish Jurist*, 189; von Tangen Page, M., *Prisons, Peace and Terrorism* (Macmillan, Basingstoke, 1998); Williams, J., 'Hunger-Strikes: A Prisoner's Right or a "Wicked Folly"?' (2001) 40 *Howard Journal of Criminal Justice* 285.

[29] Steyn, J., 'Guantanamo Bay' (2003) 53 *International & Comparative Legal Quarterly* 1. See also Duffy, H., *The 'War on Terror' and the Framework of International Law* (Cambridge University Press, Cambridge, 2005); *R (Al-Skeini) v Secretary of State for Defence* [2007] UKHL 27.

[30] See Walker, C., 'The treatment of foreign terror suspects' (2007) 70 *Modern Law Review* 427.

[31] Hansard HC vol 472, col 561 (21 February 2008), Tony McNulty.

1.15   The CONTEST strategy is measured according to the related Public Service Agreement 26[32] and is overseen by a Cabinet Committee on National Security, International Relations and Development.[33] Alongside the Home Office, the Ministry of Defence is concerned with the overseas aspects of 'Prevent' and 'Pursue'.[34] Strictly speaking, CONTEST addresses international terrorism only, but the principles are wider in the National Policing Plan 2005–08 which depicts domestic counter-terrorism as 'an overarching imperative'.[35]

1.16   In a liberal democracy at least, the ultimate test of success or failure of strategies against terrorism is the maintenance of public support while at the same time respecting the fundamental values on which legitimacy and consensus cohere:[36]

Few things would provide a more gratifying victory to the terrorist than for this country to undermine its traditional freedoms, in the very process of countering the enemies of those freedoms.

1.17   The overall aim of CONTEST is not victory but 'to reduce the risk from international terrorism, so that people can go about their daily lives freely and with confidence'.[37] This modesty suggests that exit requires more elements. Governments do not relish negotiations with terrorists: 'The enemy of the moment always represented absolute evil, and it followed that any past or future agreement with him was impossible.'[38] Yet, the resolution of terrorism often resides in a concoction of security and political retorts.[39]

C. DEFINITION OF TERRORISM

1. Elements

1.18   The basic definition of 'terrorism' given earlier should now be examined more closely.[40] Arising from controversies engendered by the passage of the Terrorism Act 2006, the UK government initiated a review of the legal definition of 'terrorism', as set out in s 1 of the Terrorism Act 2000. The inquiry was conducted by Lord Carlile, who produced a comprehensive and thoughtful review in 2007.[41] However, the report proved to be of little consequence in accordance with the Home Office view that the definition remains 'comprehensive and effective'.[42] This recent debate has reignited longer-standing apprehensions about the span of special police powers and offences, as well the more deep-seated

---

[32] HM Treasury, *PSA Delivery Agreement 26: reducing the risk to the UK and its interests overseas from international terrorism* (<http://www.hm-treasury.gov.uk/d/pbr_csr07_psa26.pdf>, 2007).

[33] Home Office, *Pursue, Prevent, Protect, Prepare: The United Kingdom's Strategy for Countering International Terrorism* (Cm 7547, London, 2009) para 13.09.

[34] Ministry of Defence, *Defence Plan including the Government's Expenditure Plans 2008–2012* (Cm 7385, London, 2008) pp. 5, 6, 14, 15, 19.

[35] (Home Office, London, 2004) para 1.3.

[36] Hansard HC vol 833, col 634 (29 November 1974), Roy Jenkins.

[37] Home Office, *Pursue, Prevent, Protect, Prepare: The United Kingdom's Strategy for Countering International Terrorism* (Cm 7547, London, 2009) para 0.17.

[38] Orwell, G., *Nineteen Eighty-Four* (Penguin, Harmondsworth, 1954) p 31.

[39] Jones, S.G. and Libicki, M.C., *How Terrorist Groups End* (RAND, Santa Monica, 2008).

[40] See further Walker, C., 'The legal definition of "Terrorism" in United Kingdom law and beyond' [2007] *Public Law* 331.

[41] Lord Carlile, *The Definition of Terrorism* (Cm 7052, London, 2007).

[42] *Government Reply* (Cm 7058, London, 2007) p 5.

political quandary inherent in the task of defining 'terrorism'. Powerful polities have long sought to exercise hegemonic control over the ascription of legitimacy in emergencies.[43] One may recall the vehemence of Margaret Thatcher, commenting on the Republican hunger-strikes of 1981, that 'Crime is crime is crime. It is not political.'[44] In this way, the label can become an opportunistic and pejorative ascription rather than a simple description of a tactic. No doubt, 'counter-hegemonic political violence'[45] would not have the same ring to it, though it might reduce charges of acting as 'the rhetorical servant of the established order'.[46]

So what is meant by 'terrorism'? One author has surmised, 'Above the gates of hell is the warning that all that enter should abandon hope. Less dire but to the same effect is the warning given to those who try to define terrorism.'[47] Another author has compared the task to the search for the Holy Grail.[48] Nevertheless, wide currency is given to the following 'academic consensus' formula proffered by Schmid and Jongman:[49]   **1.19**

Terrorism is an anxiety-inspiring method of repeated violent action, employed by (semi-) clandestine individual, group, or state actors, for idiosyncratic, criminal, or political reasons, whereby—in contrast to assassination—the direct targets of violence are not the main targets.

Three common denominators might be distilled from this excerpt, relating to purpose, target, and method. Each warrants some elaboration.

As for purpose, it is asserted that a political end is in sight and that it can be facilitated   **1.20** through instilling terror, though terrorization is not the end in itself. Criminals such as armed bank robbers might also terrorize, but it is useful to distinguish by purpose those who instil fear on a grander scale through their ability to terrorize populations or their representatives rather than selected victims and for public rather than private gain.

The target element draws out the instrumentality, or communicative nature, of the   **1.21** violence. In this way, the victims of attack are not the sole objects in sight. The aim is to generate terror in a broader audience (often the general public). The broader audience may also differ from the target audience for the political end (often a government).

As regards method, the core is violence, and terrorism involves types of violence which   **1.22** cause terror, often amplified through devices such as media threats. Violence is usually conceived as perpetrating harm to human beings. Property destruction can also be 'violent' in common parlance and even in legal parlance,[50] though without accompanying human terror, one doubts it should qualify as 'terrorism'. By contrast, the UK government asserts that, excepting trivial damage such as graffiti,[51] 'people have lost their lives

---

[43] See Campbell, C., '"War on terrorism" and vicarious hegemons' (2005) 54 *International & Comparative Law Quarterly* 321 at p 353.

[44] Levin, B. and Donosky, L., 'Death wish in Ulster' (1981) *Newsweek* 40.

[45] Butko, T., 'Terrorism redefined' (2005) 18 *Peace Review* 145 at p 145.

[46] Gearty, C., 'Terrorism and morality' [2003] *European Human Rights Law Review* 377 at p 380.

[47] Tucker, D., *Skirmishes at the Edge of Empire* (Praeger, Westport, 1997) p 51.

[48] Levitt, G., 'Is "terrorism" worth defining?' (1986) 13 *Ohio Northern University Law Review* 97 at p 97.

[49] Schmid, A. and Jongman, A., *Political Terrorism* (North-Holland, Amsterdam, 1987) p 28. See further Schmid, A., '"Terrorism on trial": terrorism—the definitional problem' (2004) 36 *Case Western Reserve Journal of International Law* 375 and 'Frameworks for conceptualising terrorism' (2004) 16 *Terrorism & Political Violence* 197.

[50] See Public Order Act 1986, s 8.

[51] Hansard HL vol 613, col 235 (16 May 2000), Lord Bassam. The definition of terroristic attacks on property is narrower in s 57 since it expressly requires an endangerment of life.

in [property] attacks. It would be rash simply to exclude property, even though a terrorist organization could say that its intent was not to threaten life.'[52]

2. The roles of a legal definition

1.23 Before delineating what should be the legal definition of 'terrorism', one should first consider the roles that any definition might play. After all, why agonize over the word if it is not to be put to any significant use in counter-terrorism strategy?

1.24   Leaving aside any denunciatory function,[53] legal support can be a relevant tactic in all four aspects of the CONTEST formulation. There are two constant themes which conduce towards legal reliance upon the term 'terrorism'. One is that, in view of the serious threat posed by terrorism to the public and constitutional order, prevention often outweighs after-the-event pursuit.[54] This factor conduces towards widening the definition of 'terrorism' and dependent all-encompassing powers and offences so that early interventions become more possible than when dealing with 'ordinary decent criminals',[55] thereby allowing some margin of error.[56] The second theme is that preventive strategies require advance targeting of individuals, events, and places. Therefore, effective intelligence-gathering becomes vital so as to facilitate prevention, contingency planning, or even prosecution.[57] An abundance of information further allows a government to criticize rebels, to gauge the strength of political opposition, and to make cogent reforms.

1.25   Two conclusions about the legal definition of 'terrorism' flow from the foregoing discussion. The first is that, to secure its objectives, the legal definition of 'terrorism' should not depart far from what are accepted legitimate boundaries of criminal process and law. The second is that if indulgence through the use of the term 'terrorism' is to apply anywhere, then it is better utilized in the anticipatory aspects of criminal justice—the tasking of the police and security officials rather than during the criminal trial where process is meant to be solemn and where harm to others rather than motive is key.

3. The current legal formulation

1.26 The following version of the definition of 'terrorism' was advanced by s 20(1) of the Prevention of Terrorism (Temporary Provisions) Act 1989: '. . . "terrorism" means the use of violence for political ends and includes any use of violence for the purpose of putting the public or any section of the public in fear.'

---

[52] Hansard HC Standing Committee D, col 20 (18 January 2000), Charles Clarke. See also Lord Carlile, *The Definition of Terrorism* (Cm 7052, London, 2007) para 50 and *Government Reply* (Cm 7058, London, 2007) p 6.

[53] See Saul, B., *Defining Terrorism in International Law* (Oxford University Press, Oxford, 2006) ch 1.

[54] See further Joint Committee on Human Rights, *Counter-Terrorism Policy and Human Rights: Prosecution and Pre-Charge Detention* (2005–06 HL 240, HC 1576) para 6.

[55] *Review of the Operation of the Northern Ireland (Emergency Provisions) Act 1978* (Cmnd 9222, London, 1984) para 136.

[56] Hansard HC vol 346, col 410 (15 March 2000), Charles Clarke. See further Feldman, D., 'Human rights, terrorism risks: the roles of politicians and judges' [2006] *Public Law* 364.

[57] See Kitson, F., *Low Intensity Operations* (Faber, London, 1971) chs 6, 7; Kentridge, S., 'The pathology of a legal system: criminal justice in South Africa' (1980) 128 *University of Pennsylvania Law Review* 603 at p 612; Walker, C., 'Intelligence and anti-terrorism laws in the United Kingdom' (2006) 44 *Crime, Law and Social Change* 387.

The current definition (in s 1 of the Terrorism Act) states with much greater length   1.27
and detail as follows:[58]

(1) In this Act 'terrorism' means the use or threat of action where
    (a) the action falls within subsection (2),
    (b) the use or threat is designed to influence the government or an international govern-
        mental organization or to intimidate the public or a section of the public, and
    (c) the use or threat is made for the purpose of advancing a political, religious, racial or
        ideological cause.
(2) Action falls within this subsection if it
    (a) involves serious violence against a person,
    (b) involves serious damage to property,
    (c) endangers a person's life, other than that of the person committing the action,
    (d) creates a serious risk to the health or safety of the public or a section of the public, or
    (e) is designed seriously to interfere with or seriously to disrupt an electronic system.

The essence lies in s 1(1), which contains three conjunctive legs, all of which must normally be satisfied (subject to s 1(3) which designates the use of firearms or explosives as
terrorism regardless of s 1(1)(b)). Later legislation also largely relies upon this Terrorism
Act 2000 definition, though variants may arise in the enforcement of international law
or European Union obligations. It will be noted from s 1(1)(b) that terrorism may be
suffered either by the government (including its agents such as the police) or the
public.

Section 1 is purposefully wider than its predecessor in most respects, aside from two   1.28
points.[59] First, s 1 demands a 'serious'[60] level of violence (and also 'serious' damage or
risks to health and safety or electronic disruption). But s 1 does also encompass any
endangerment of life without qualification, 'other than that of the person committing
the action' (s 1(2)(c)).[61] Next, as originally drafted, the Terrorism Bill entirely dropped
the alternative objective in the previous definition of 'putting the public or any section
of the public in fear', which may sometimes result from non-political hooliganism or
individual acts of aggression. However, it is sufficient that the use or threat is 'to intimidate the public or a section of the public' (s 1(1)(b)).[62]

In more aspects, s 1 is significantly broader than its predecessor. A wider scope is given   1.29
to the word 'violence'.[63] Section 1(2) addresses (b) risks to property, (d) risks to safety,
and (e) interference with computer systems.[64] In a late modern society, the state is

---

[58] The Terrorism Act 2006, s 34 added the reference to international governmental organizations. See:
European Union Framework Decision on combating terrorism (2002/475/JHA, 13 June 2002) art. 1; the
International Convention for the Suppression of Acts of Nuclear Terrorism 2005 (Cm 7301, London, 2007)
art 1.5.

[59] See *Inquiry into Legislation against Terrorism* (Cm 3420, London, 1996) para 5.22; Home Office and
Northern Ireland Office, *Legislation against Terrorism* (Cm 4178, London, 1998) para 3.16; Hansard HL
vol 611, col 1484 (6 April 2000) and vol 614, col 1448 (4 July 2000), Lord Bassam; Hansard HC Standing
Committee D, col 31 (18 January 2000), Charles Clarke.

[60] This is equivalent to 'grievous': Hansard HL vol 614, col 166 (20 June 2000), Lord Bach.

[61] See Hansard HL vol 614, col 1451 (4 July 2000), Lord Bassam.

[62] The mention of a 'section of the public' may serve to protect minorities within groups or sects: Lord
Carlile, *The Definition of Terrorism* (Cm 7052, London, 2007) para 57.

[63] Home Office and Northern Ireland Office, *Legislation against Terrorism* (Cm 4178, London, 1998)
para 3.16.

[64] See Walker, C., 'Cyber-terrorism' (2006) 110 *Penn State Law Review* 625.

'hollowed out' and power is diffused across both public and private sectors. Power relates more to finance, knowledge, and security, and so the likely targets of terrorists shift in line with the new centres of power and the new power-holders. Next, as well as the listed actions, s 1 mentions the 'threat' of them, which correspondingly expands upon the use of violence.

1.30 Section 1 of the Terrorism Act next offers some widening of the relevant ends or motives of terrorism. The forbidden activities comprise, firstly, influencing the government and, secondly, religious or ideological causes. It could be argued that 'influence' is too wide, especially having regard to rights to political action under Arts 10 and 11 of the European Convention,[65] and a better word might be 'intimidate'.[66] Such an adjustment has been rejected by the government.[67] As for religious and ideological causes, whether these really amount to an extension again remains obscure.[68] The word 'religion' seems superfluous and might cause problems by blurring into personal disputes, such as family or clan disputes about an arranged marriage or a dowry.[69] Secondly, single issue ideological organizations, such as 'eco-terrorists' or anti-abortion groups, could also count as political campaigners even if their prime impact is upon private individuals (such as genetic crop farmers or abortionists) rather than the state, especially when their tactics fall within s 1(3). Rather than tightening the definition, the definition was extended by the Counter-Terrorism Act 2008 to allow for racial causes, to reflect recent international documents, as well as giving reassurance to minorities.[70]

1.31 The complaint being made here is that the definition is overbroad and should focus on the key mischief of terrorism which is its danger to political democracy. However, to go to the opposite extreme and remove all reference to motive would extend the special provisions to an over-broad range of circumstances.[71] The three conjunctive legs should all have relevance.[72]

1.32 As for the feared methods, these are limited in s 1(1) to actions, and so cannot include, for example, the omissions of going on strike (withdrawing labour or services) or passive forms of civil disobedience (a refusal to pay taxes). There is some room for doubt, however, on this score. For instance, the refusal to pay a tax is an omission, but it may also amount to the commission of an offence.

1.33 Assessing this definition against the prerequisites of purpose, target and method, the first and second aspects are largely secured by the Terrorism Act 2000, s 1(1)(b) and (c). As regards target, the terrorism violence should be an attack on the collective, subject to the exception of s 1(3). The idea behind this exception is to allow for the label of 'terrorism' to be ascribed in all cases to attacks by explosives or firearms upon political or public

---

[65] Tomkins, A., 'Legislating against terror' [2002] *Public Law* 205 at p 211.
[66] See Lord Carlile, *The Definition of Terrorism* (Cm 7052, London, 2007) para 59; (New Zealand) Terrorism Suppression Act 2002, s 5(2)(b).
[67] *Government Reply* (Cm 7058, London, 2007) p 6.
[68] Edge, P., 'Religious organisations and the prevention of terrorism legislation' (1999) 4 *Journal of Civil Liberties* 194 at p 198.
[69] These arguments were rejected by Lord Carlile, *The Definition of Terrorism* (Cm 7052, London, 2007) para 53.
[70] s 75. See Hansard HL vol 705, col 607 (11 November 2008), Lord West; Lord Carlile, *The Definition of Terrorism* (Cm 7052, London, 2007) para 65. See also Criminal Justice Act 2003 Sch 21 para 4(2)(c).
[71] Compare *R v Khawaja* (2006) 214 C.C.C. (3d) 399, [2008] Carswell Ont 6364. The defendant was linked with the Operation Crevice plot in London and was convicted: *The Times* 13 March 2009 p 39.
[72] See further Lord Carlile, *The Definition of Terrorism* (Cm 7052, London, 2007) para 55.

figures, even if the purpose of the assailant is not clear and may even be personal rather than political: '. . .we do not want the police to feel hindered in any way from acting in situations that most, if not all of us would regard as terrorism—such as assassinations—because it was not clear that either of those elements was present'.[73] However, this exception remains subject to the requirement of a purpose as in s 1(1)(c), and it is limited to attacks with explosives or firearms whereas attacks by drowning, poisoning, or strangulation would fall within s 1(1)(b).

As regards method, the core is violence of a kind which causes terror. It was argued 1.34 earlier that one more readily thinks in terms of attacks on humans than property (as allowed by s 1(2)(b) and (e)). But the prime problem here is that the core term, 'violence', is left unrefined and malleable. It is true that in many, perhaps most, cases, 'violence' can readily be translated into established offences. The European Court of Human Rights in *Brogan v United Kingdom* accepted 'terrorism' as within the Convention's notion of an 'offence' for the purposes of Art 5,[74] though that judgment must be read in the context of specific offences of membership of a proscribed organization founding the arrest of the applicant.[75] Nevertheless, one can still conceive of some situations where the current formulation goes further than necessary:[76]

One is where the person's action in committing suicide [as a form of protest] endangers other people's lives. One might call it the 'Emily Davison case', although no one, not even the horse, was seriously damaged except Emily herself. . . . The second issue relates to what one might call the 'Swampy case', where the protester may be thought to cause danger to other people because he tempts them to rescue him.

The point is that these actions may fall within s 1(2)(c) of the Terrorism Act 2000 by endangering a person's life, other than that of the person committing the action, as well as satisfying s 1(1)(a) and (c). Another example might be derived from the installation of the artist, Cornelia Parker, whose *Cold Dark Matter: An Exploded View*, is composed of the fragments of a garden shed.[77] Since the explosion was courtesy of the British Army's School of Ammunition, one might assume lawful authority for that particular detonation. But if another artist had undertaken a do-it-yourself explosion, as a representation not just as a parody of the creation of the universe and the subsequent human folly contained within it but also of the brutality of British military force, then s 1 might apply in a disproportionate way and reliance upon the good sense of prosecutors would not remove the chilling effect.[78]

An alternative approach (as adopted by the Northern Ireland (Emergency Provisions) 1.35 Acts 1973–96 and then in Pt VII of the Terrorism Act) is the 'scheduled offence' approach.[79] Counter-terrorism provisions can be designed by reference to a catalogue of

---

[73] Hansard HL vol 614, col 160 (20 June 2000), Lord Bach.
[74] App nos 11209, 11234, 11266/84, 11386/85, Ser A 145-B (1988) para 50. See also *Ireland v United Kingdom*, App no 5310/71, Ser A 25 (1978) para 196.
[75] Hansard HL vol 613, col 677 (16 May 2000), Lord Lloyd. In response, see Hansard HL vol 613, cols 681–2 (16 May 2000), Lord Bassam.
[76] Hansard HL vol 614, col 1446 (4 July 2000), Lord Beaumont.
[77] Lord Carlile, *The Definition of Terrorism* (Cm 7052, London, 2007) para 34.
[78] Compare Lord Carlile, *Report on the Operation in 2002 and 2003 of the Terrorism Act 2000* (Home Office, 2004) para 25.
[79] See further Walker, C., *The Anti-Terrorism Legislation* (Oxford University Press, Oxford, 2002) ch 7; Golder, B. and Williams, G., 'What is terrorism' (2004) 27 *University of New South Wales Law Journal* 270.

specified offences commonly involved in terrorism. This approach is emulated by the European Council Framework Decision on Terrorism.[80] A 'scheduled offence' approach better complies with fundamental requirements as to legal certainty and emphasizes the goal of responding with 'normal' laws rather than adopting a political, religious, ethnic, or racial framework.[81] Next, the scheduling approach can better differentiate between terrorism at home and abroad by devising different inventories of offences, the foreign list by reference to global international instruments which address aspects of terrorism.[82] Lord Carlile's preference was to structure more carefully the discretion of the Attorney General to allow prosecutions.[83] The Home Office view is that to limit the application of the definition of terrorism to actions contrary to the criminal law will not suffice.[84] It would hamper police discretion, and it would create uncertainties when dealing with international terrorism. It also alleges that there may be occurrences designed to terrify which are not unlawful—such as a refusal to perform a duty to keep others safe,[85] provided the refusal is for political rather than industrial motives.[86]

1.36   Lord Carlile's pronouncement in 2007 was that s 1 is 'practical and effective'.[87] However, in the absence of reform, the definition remains overbroad. Its breadth is often moderated by police and prosecution restraint. However, the definitional syntax will encourage the occasional excess, and it also has had the unfortunate consequence of setting a significant precedent for comparable jurisdictions.[88]

4. Context

1.37   Where the Terrorism Act 2000 may be condemned as particularly lax in comparison with its predecessor is not so much in the terms of its core elements of purpose, target, and method but in the circumstance of how these components are applied in the body of the legislation—the context. To cater for this broader context, there should be emphasis upon not only the types of seriously threatening and destabilizing offences being perpetrated but also the nature of the perpetrators, for it is that context which renders less capable 'normal' criminal justice processes and thereby justifies special laws. To put this another way, it is the decoupling of the legislation from its historical grounding in the undoubtedly serious conflict in Ireland that permits the overuse of draconian provisions in circumstances where ordinary policing and laws could suffice. The position is made much worse because s 1(4) makes explicit that the scope of the definition includes action

---

[80] European Union Council Framework Decision on Combating Terrorism (2002/475/ JHA), OJ L164/3, 13 June 2002. Compare the relevant United Nations documents and drafts: de Fillippo, M., 'Terrorist crimes and international cooperation' (2008) 19 *European Journal of International Law* 533.

[81] See Report of the Special Rapporteur on the promotion and protection of human rights and fundamental freedoms while countering terrorism (E/CN.4/2006/98, 2005) para 33; Cole, D., and Dempsey, J.X., *Terrorism and the Constitution* (3rd edn, New Press, New York, 2006) p 249.

[82] The broadest definition is the International Convention for the Suppression of the Financing of Terrorism (39 ILM 270, 1999), art 2.

[83] Lord Carlile, *The Definition of Terrorism* (Cm 7052, London, 2007) para 81.

[84] Hansard HL vol 611, col 1484 (6 April 2000), Lord Bassam.

[85] Hansard HL vol 614, col 1448 (4 July 2000), Lord Bassam.

[86] Hansard HC Standing Committee D, col 31 (18 January 2000), Charles Clarke.

[87] Lord Carlile, *Report on the Operation in 2005 of the Terrorism Act 2000* (Home Office, London, 2006) para 32.

[88] See Roach, K., 'Sources and trends in post 9/11 anti terrorism laws' in Goold, B.J., and Lazarus, L., *Security and Human Rights* (Hart, Oxford, 2007) p 244.

outside the United Kingdom against foreign governments. There were unsuccessful attempts in Parliament to confine the foreign coverage of the Terrorism Act 2000 to 'designated countries' rather than regimes which might be viewed as 'odious'.[89] But the implication of labelling some terrorism as officially acceptable was unpalatable to the government.

Consequently, if the legislation is to be disestablished from its Irish grounding, fur-   1.38
ther qualifications ought to be inserted to ensure that special measures really offer a proportionate response. A prime reason why special laws might be justifiable is where the political violence occurs in the context of a secretive and organized group—it is the collective paramilitary nature which makes the action so threatening and difficult to police. Therefore, s 1 should specify that the political violence must involve concerted action by a group of people acting in an organized and secretive way.

This context for violence is more clearly recognized in the alternative definition of   1.39
'terrorism' in s 2 of the Reinsurance (Acts of Terrorism) Act 1993, which establishes a scheme for reinsurance for commercial property damage resulting from terrorism:[90]

> (2) In this section 'acts of terrorism' means acts of persons acting on behalf of, or in connection with, any organisation which carries out activities directed towards the overthrowing or influencing, by force or violence, of Her Majesty's government in the United Kingdom or any other government de jure or de facto.
> (3) In subsection (2) above 'organisation' includes any association or combination of persons.

In practice, this need for context is recognized by the UK authorities[91] who have declined   1.40
to treat animal rights extremists as 'terrorists' even though they fit the definitional profile[92] and have been described as replicating 'a quasi-terrorist cellular structure'.[93] Conversely, the additional elements of definition would not fail to apply the bite of special laws to loose collectives inspired by a 'franchise' like Al-Qa'ida. For instance, the facts that the perpetration of the 7/7 London bombings involved at least four people, deploying sophisticated techniques and possibly with support from confederates abroad,[94] does raise elements of complexity and danger which defy the application of 'normal' law.

A further issue of context is the 'Kosovo problem'—the concern that British soldiers   1.41
in conflicts abroad could be labelled as terrorists. The government's response to this point unsatisfactorily relied on the alleged 'general principle in law that statutes do not bind the Crown unless by express provision or necessary implication'.[95] Since it is clear that the definition of terrorism can apply to state actors and that soldiers in Northern

---

[89] Hansard HC Standing Committee D, col 26 (18 January 2000), David Lidington. That s 1 protects the Libyan government was confirmed in *R v F* [2007] EWCA Crim 243 (see ch 6)

[90] See Walker, C., 'Political violence and commercial risk' (2004) 56 *Current Legal Problems* 531.

[91] *Government Reply* (Cm 7058, London, 2007) p 5.

[92] See Home Office, *Animal Rights Extremism* (London, 2001) para 3.75.

[93] Department of Trade and Industry, *Animal Welfare — Human Rights: protecting people from animal rights activists* (London, 2004) para 43.

[94] See Intelligence and Security Committee, *Report on the London Terrorist Attacks on 7 July 2005* (Cm 6785, London, 2005); *Report of the Official Account of the Bombings in London on 7 July 2005* (2005–06 HC 1087).

[95] Hansard HL vol 613, col 241 (16 May 2000), Lord Bach. See also *Re Lockerbie Air Disaster, The Times*, 20 May 1992 (CA).

Ireland have been treated under it,[96] a better approach might have been a more explicit statement about when force is 'lawful' under either domestic or international law.

5. Protest rights

1.42   An additional safeguard in the legal definition of 'terrorism' might be a proviso for the proportionate respect for individual freedoms of belief, expression, and of association (as in Arts 9 to 11 of the European Convention on Human Rights). Its purpose would be to offer 'symbolic reassurance'.[97] However, its practical utility is not evident.[98] It therefore remains a concern that the term, 'terrorism', is emotional and inimical to protesters, cranks, and fantasists as much as terrorists.

D. THE NEED FOR ANTI-TERRORISM LEGISLATION

1. Principles and policy

1.43   Implicit in the Terrorism Act 2000 is the claim that extensive legislation against political violence is needed now and forever after. Sunset clauses attached only to Pt VII and to some successor provisions in 2007. Most subsequent legislation never expires, though some is subject to annual renewal. Amongst the disadvantages of special laws are that they are unnecessary adjuncts to 'normal' laws relating to police powers, such as those in the Police and Criminal Evidence Act 1984, and regular criminal offences, that they engender abuses, and that they do damage to the country's international reputation.[99] Therefore, this claim to an ongoing need for distinct anti-terrorist laws should be examined. It can be answered at three levels which, for a century or so, have regularly convinced the ruling élites of many countries to react.[100]

1.44   The first level concerns the powers and duties of states. In principle, it is justifiable for liberal democracies to be empowered to defend their existence, and it might be claimed that 'The first priority of any Government is to ensure the security and safety of the nation and all members of the public.'[101] A democracy is not a suicide pact,[102] and exceptional measures have long been recognized as a legitimate reaction to clear and present dangers.[103] This approach is reflected in the European Convention on Human

---

[96] See further Lord Carlile, *The Definition of Terrorism* (Cm 7052, London, 2007) para 83.

[97] Roach, K., 'Canada's response to terrorism' in Ramraj, V.V., Hor, M., and Roach, K., *Global Anti-Terrorism Law and Policy* (Cambridge University Press, Cambridge, 2006) p 520.

[98] See Canadian Anti-terrorism Act 2002, s 83.01; New Zealand Terrorism Suppression Act 2001, s 5(5).

[99] *Inquiry into Legislation against Terrorism* (Cm 3420, London, 1996) paras 5.6–5.9.

[100] See Porter, B., *The Origins of the Vigilant State* (Weidenfeld & Nicolson, London, 1978) p 192; Walker, C., 'Clamping down on terrorism in the United Kingdom' (2006) 4 *Journal of International Criminal Justice* 1137.

[101] Home Office, *Pursue, Prevent, Protect, Prepare: The United Kingdom's Strategy for Countering International Terrorism* (Cm 7547, London, 2009) p 4.

[102] *Terminiello v Chicago* (1949) 337 US 1 at p 37 per Douglas J.

[103] See Schmitt, C., *Political Theology* (MIT Press, Cambridge, 1985); Chowdhury, S.R., *The Rule of Law in a State of Emergency* (Pinter, London, 1989); Finn, J.E., *Constitutions in Crisis* (Oxford University Press, Oxford, 1991); Oraa, J., *Human Rights in States of Emergency in International Law* (Clarendon Press, Oxford, 1992); Fitzpatrick, J.M., *Human Rights In Crisis* (University of Pennsylvania Press, Pa., 1994); Sajó, A. (ed),

Rights, Art 17 (prohibiting the engagement in any activity or performance of any act aimed at the destruction of rights and freedoms) and the power of derogation in time of emergency threatening the life of the nation under Art 15.[104] In the context of Northern Ireland terrorism, this derogation facility was repeatedly invoked—up to 1984, and from 1988 until 2001. It was upheld in relation to a scheme of seven days' police detention in *Brannigan and McBride v United Kingdom*.[105] One of the express purposes of the Terrorism Act 2000 was to allow the notice of derogation to be withdrawn (on 26 February 2001), though it continued in respect of the British Islands until 5 May 2006. A further derogation was entered in respect of the detention measures in Pt IV of the Anti-terrorism, Crime and Security Act 2001 but that in turn was withdrawn on 14 March 2005.[106] Aside from the power to take action, there is a state responsibility to act against violence in order to safeguard the protective right to life of citizens (as under Art 2 of the Convention).[107] In addition, states should more generally implement the enjoyment of rights and democracy (under Art 1) and, under United Nations instruments, must not harbour or condone terrorism.[108] In summary, security is valuable to society. However, it must not wholly subsume other values such as individual rights. Therefore, it may be viewed either as instrumental (as a condition for the securing of higher values)[109] or as a cipher for a bundle of rights, such as the right to life or liberty,[110] rather than an independent and conflicting value.

The second level of justification for special laws is more morally grounded. This argument points to the illegitimacy of terrorism as a form of political expression. Many of its emanations are almost certainly common crimes, crimes of war, or crimes against humanity, even if the political cause of the terrorist is deemed legitimate.[111]   1.45

Thirdly, terrorism may be depicted as a specialized form of criminality which presents peculiar complications in terms of policing and criminal process—such as its structure, capacity to intimidate, and sophistication. It therefore demands a specialist response to overcome the complications posed for normal detection methods and processes within criminal justice. Just as variations have been adopted against, for example, rapists, serious   1.46

Militant Democracy (Eleven International Publishing, Utrecht, 2004); Ferejohn, J., and Pasquino, P., 'The law of exception' (2004) 2 *International Journal of Constitutional Law* 210; Agamben, G., *The State of Exception* (University of Chicago Press, Chicago, 2005); Gross, O., and ní Aoláin, F., *Law in Times of Crisis* (Cambridge University Press, Cambridge, 2006); Dyzenhaus, D., *The Constitution of Law* (Cambridge University Press, Cambridge, 2006); Dyzenhaus, D., 'Schmitt v Dicey' (2006) 27 *Cardozo Law Review* 2005.

[104] Emergencies must be 'existential' in this sense, but Art 15 does not exhaust the range of legitimate anti-terrorism laws. Compare: Ackerman, B., *Before the Next Attack* (Yale University Press, New Haven, 2006) p 172.

[105] App nos 14553/89, 14554/89, Ser A 258-B. See further *Marshall v United Kingdom*, App no 41571/98, 10 July 2001; *Kerr v United Kingdom*, App no 40451/98, 10 July 2001.

[106] See Human Rights Act (Amendment Order) 2005, SI 2005/1071.

[107] See *Inquiry into Legislation against Terrorism* (Cm 3420, London, 1996) para 5.15; Hornle, T., 'Hijacked airplanes' (2007) 10 *New Criminal Law Review* 582. These duties are not absolute guarantees of safety: *X v Ireland*, App no 6040/73, 16 YB 388 (1973); *W v UK*, App no 9348/81, 32 DR 190 (1983); *X v UK*, App no 9825/82, 8 EHRR 49 (1985); *M v UK and Ireland*, App no 9837/82, 47 DR 27 (1986).

[108] See United Nations General Assembly Resolutions 40/61 of 9 December 1985; 49/60 of 9 December 1994; UN Security Council Resolution 1373 of 28 September 2001.

[109] Téson, F.R., 'Liberal security' in Wilson, R.A. (ed), *Human Rights in the 'War on Terror'* (Cambridge University Press, Cambridge, 2005).

[110] Lazarus, L., 'Mapping the right to security' in Goold, B.J. and Lazarus, L., *Security and Human Rights* (Hart, Oxford, 2007) p 344.

[111] See International Criminal Court Act 2001.

fraudsters, and drug traffickers,[112] so terrorists may warrant variant treatment because of their atypical organization, methods, and targets. As for organization, paramilitary groups can typically hinder the re-establishment of public safety and democratic processes because of their sophistication, the transnational scale of their activities, and the difficulty of obtaining assistance from paramilitary-affected communities because of the impact of intimidation or even popularity.

1.47   Whilst emergency laws have allure, they also entail dangers.[113] There arises pressure to respond quickly and decisively which can produce ill-considered 'panic' legislation. Secondly, fear is consciously or unconsciously amplified so as to justify reaction.[114] The ill-design arising from these two grounds may result in legislation which is ineffective and merely symbolic, or it may impact excessively or inappropriately. Thirdly, 'emergency' laws regularly linger beyond the original emergency. Fear and risk are endemic, not transitory, so normality is hard to reassert. The fourth point is that the executive branch of the state will become unduly dominant. People expect action not words, and the ability to take action is held by the executive not the courts or Parliament. In addition, the executive has the detailed information and intelligence and so appears better placed to act. Fifthly, emergencies are the time of greatest threat to individual and rights. Individual rights are often depicted as obstacles to public safety and security. Sixthly, even if Parliament does provide new laws, sweeping though they may be, there remains the grave danger that the executive or the security forces, will exceed them. Seventhly, emergency or special laws will provide a dangerous precedent which will result in contagion—that special powers will be adapted to unintended situations or the adoption within 'normal' laws of measures which become commonplace incursions onto liberty. This charge is commonly lodged against special powers in Northern Ireland becoming a proving ground for Britain,[115] but the evidence is equivocal and one can point to many instances of British distaste for any transfer.[116] Eighthly, security laws tend not to be applied fairly. Ethnic minorities or aliens will suffer most either through their discriminatory implementation or through the higher chances of abuse and error.[117] Thus, the legislation will trigger disaffection and discontent, such as among young Muslim males.[118] The causes of violent *jihadism* seem to be less dependent on the abusive exercise of security powers than was the position in Northern Ireland.[119] Nonetheless, the targeting of suspect communities still hinders the identification and detection of terrorists by encouraging sympathy for their cause and a reduction of voluntary assistance.

1.48   The cumulative outcomes of these features is an inclination towards overuse—that instead of a 'break glass in case of emergency' law model, there will be too much smashing

---

[112] Sexual Offences (Amendment) Act 1976; Drug Trafficking Offences Act 1994; Criminal Justice Act 1987.

[113] See Sunstein, C.R., *Worst-Case Scenarios* (Harvard University Press, Cambridge, 2007). Compare Posner, E.A. and Vermeule, A., *Terror in the Balance* (Oxford University Press, Oxford, 2007) ch 2.

[114] See Kahneman, D., Slovic, P., and Tversky, A., *Judgment under Uncertainty* (Cambridge University Press, New York, 1982).

[115] See Hillyard, P., 'The normalisation of special powers: From Northern Ireland to Britain' in Scraton, P. (ed), *Law, order and the authoritarian state* (Open University Press, Milton Keynes, 1987).

[116] See Mulcahy, A., ''The other lessons from Ireland' (2005) 2 *European Journal of Criminology* 185.

[117] Cole, D., *Enemy Aliens* (New Press, New York, 2006). Compare Posner, E.A. and Vermeule, A., 'Emergencies and democratic failure' (2006) 92 *Virginia Law Review* 1091.

[118] See Home Affairs Committee, *Terrorism and Community Relations* (2003–04 HC 165) para 43.

[119] See Hussein, E., *The Islamist* (Penguin, London, 2007).

of the glass to take out the special laws in preference to serviceable normal laws. A debate is thereby engendered about balance and limits.

2. Balance and limits

There has long been official and academic debate around the appropriate 'balance'   1.49
between security and liberty, with the assumption being that greater security demands lesser liberty. Thus, the Home Office paper, *Counter-Terrorism Powers: Reconciling Security and Liberty in an Open Society*, stated:[120]

There is nothing new about the dilemma of how best to ensure the security of a society, while protecting the individual rights of its citizens. Democratic governments have always had to strike a balance between the powers of the state and the rights of individuals.

It is rational to react to the consequences of terrorism and to the risks of upholding   1.50
rights in changed circumstances. It is rational to reassure the public in times of crisis.[121] What is less rational is the assertion that security and liberty can be 'balanced' in a causal 'hydraulic' relationship,[122] having regard also to the difficulties of cognitive measurement and the dubious validity of consequentialist arguments when weighing deontic values which cut across both liberty and security.[123]

In reality, experienced commentators in the field of anti-terrorism laws have long   1.51
eschewed any simplistic balance between security and rights and have sought to develop more intellectually rational, structured, and finely attuned mechanisms for choice even if there remains ultimately a 'tragic choice'.[124] An example is Lord Lloyd, who set four principles against which the legislation should be judged in his 1996 review:[125]

(i) Legislation against terrorism should approximate as closely as possible to the ordinary criminal law and procedure.[126]
(ii) Additional statutory offences and powers may be justified, but only if they are necessary to meet the anticipated threat. They must then strike the right balance between the needs of security and the rights and liberties of the individual;
(iii) The need for additional safeguards should be considered alongside any additional powers.
(iv) The law should comply with the UK's obligations in international law.

---

[120] (Cm 6147, London, 2004) p i. For earlier commentaries, see Rossiter, C.L., *Constitutional Dictatorship* (Harcourt, New York, 1948); Mathews, A.S., *Freedom, State Security and the Rule of Law* (Sweet & Maxwell, London, 1988).

[121] Ackerman, B., 'The emergency constitution' (2004) 113 *Yale Law Journal* 1029 at p 1037.

[122] Ashworth, A., 'Security, terrorism, and the value of human rights' in Goold, B.J., and Lazarus, L., *Security and Human Rights* (Hart, Oxford, 2007) p 208.

[123] See Waldron, J., 'Security and liberty: the image of balance' (2003) 11 *Journal of Political Philosophy* 191 at pp 194–8; Lustgarten, L., 'National security and political policy' in Brodeur, J.P., Gill, P., and Töllberg, D. (eds), *Democracy, Law and Security* (Ashgate, Aldershot, 2003); Zedner, L., 'Securing liberty in the face of terror' (2005) 32 *Journal of Law & Society* 507 at p 511; Donohue, L.K., *The Cost of Counterterrorism* (Cambridge University Press, Cambridge, 2007) ch 1.

[124] See Ackerman, B., 'The emergency constitution' (2004) 113 *Yale Law Journal* 1029 at p 1077; Lustgarten, L. 'National security and political policing' in Brodeur, J.P., Gill, P., and Töllborg, D. (eds), *Democracy, Law and Security: Internal security services in Europe* (Ashgate, Aldershot, 2003).

[125] Lloyd Report, *Inquiry into Legislation against Terrorism* (Cm 3420, London, 1996) para 3.1.

[126] See further Privy Counsellor Review Committee, *Anti-Terrorism, Crime and Security Act 2001, Review, Report* (2003–04 HC 100) para B1. Lloyd's principles are otherwise accepted: para C94.

Likewise, the 'guiding principles' behind the National Security Strategy comprise 'human rights, rule of law, legitimate and accountable government, justice, freedom, tolerance, and opportunity for all'.[127] Building upon these precepts and upon other formulations in these directions,[128] the normative setting should be delineated as 'constitutionalism' which can be understood according to three parameters.

1.52   There is first a need for a 'rights audit'.[129] Whilst there have been episodes of official angst about the imputed hindrance of rights on terrorism operations,[130] almost all official reviewers of the legislation, from Lord Diplock in 1972 onwards, have been enjoined to take account of human rights which have also proven resilient under the challenge of supreme emergencies.[131] Thus, the principle here advanced is that the rights of individuals must be respected according to traditions of the domestic jurisdictions and the demands of international law. For the United Kingdom, the two are largely assimilated by the Human Rights Act 1998.[132] The 1998 Act has had positive impacts in shaping and promoting political debate, in emboldening the courts, and in creating new pathways for rights discourse to become more explicit and prominent.[133]

1.53   Since rights values focus on the treatment of individuals, there is a special role for the courts as the prime deliberative forum. The concept of 'proportionality' will often be invoked to resolve the permissible incursions of security interests. In *A v Secretary of State for the Home Department*,[134] the House of Lords explained that when assessing whether an incursion into individual rights is arbitrary or excessive, the court must ask itself, 'whether: (i) the legislative objective is sufficiently important to justify limiting a fundamental right; (ii) the measures designed to meet the legislative objective are rationally connected to it; and (iii) the means used to impair the right or freedom are no more than is necessary to accomplish the objective.' A fourth test has sometimes been added: (iv) whether the measure strikes a proper balance between the gains for the policy purpose and the incursion into individual rights.[135] In *Huang and others v Secretary of State for the Home Department*, this formula was rendered as a balance between the interests of the community and the right of the individual.[136] These tests of proportionality

---

[127] (Cm 7291, London, 2008) para 2.1.

[128] See Walker, C.P., 'Constitutional governance and special powers against terrorism' (1997) 35 *Columbia Journal of Transnational Law* 1; Cotler, I., 'Terrorism, security and rights' (2002) 14 *National Journal of Constitutional Law* 13; Loader, I. and Walker, N., *Civilising Society* (Cambridge University Press, Cambridge, 2007).

[129] See Marks, J.H. , '9/11 + 3/11 + 7/7 = ? What counts in counterterrorism?' (2006) 37 *Columbia Human Rights Law Review* 559.

[130] See Department for Constitutional Affairs, *Review of the Implementation of the Human Rights Act* (London, 2006). Pending reforms are not intended to affect the anti-terrorism laws: Ministry of Justice, *Rights and Responsibilities* (Cm 7577, London, 2009) para 4.26.

[131] See Statman, D., 'Supreme emergencies revisited' (2006) 117 *Ethics* 58; Cole, D., 'Human rights and the challenge of terror' in Weinberg, L., *Democratic Responses to Terrorism* (Routledge, Abingdon, 2008) p 159.

[132] See Warbrick, C., 'The principles of the ECHR and the response of states to terrorism' [2002] *European Human Rights Law Review* 287; Sottioux, S., *Terrorism and the Limitation of Rights* (Hart, Oxford, 2008).

[133] See Gearty, C., '11 September 2001, counter-terrorism and the Human Rights Act' (2005) 32 *Journal of Law & Society* 18; Hiebert, J.L., 'Parliamentary review of terrorism measures' (2005) 65 *Modern Law Review* 676; Bonner, D., 'Responding to crisis' (2006) 122 *Law Quarterly Review* 602. Reference will be made primarily to the European Convention on Human Rights.

[134] [2004] UKHL 56 at para 30.

[135] *R v Oakes* (1986) 1 SCR 103 at p 139.

[136] [2007] UKHL 11 at para 19.

correspond to Lord Lloyd's initial three tests and can be elaborated further. In respect of (i), the perceived nature and level threat to security should be examined, with the expectation that it should be clear and present in order to warrant intervention. In respect of (ii), the question is whether the security measures are fit for the purpose addressing that particular threat at that particular level. As for (iii), one should ask whether there are 'adequate and effective guarantees against abuse'[137] and whether there are workable, less intrusive alternative responses. On (iv), are the drawbacks of the measure, for example in terms of success rate or impact on wider security concerns such as community cooperation, so great as to outweigh any benefits?

Proportionality in the context of terrorism laws must be appreciated in relation to different categories of rights. For those rights which are treated as absolute (such as Art 3) and despite continued academic debate, no balance or model of accommodation is suitable.[138] As is stated in *Chahal v United Kingdom*: 'in protecting their communities from terrorist violence . . ., the Convention prohibits in absolute terms torture or inhuman or degrading treatment or punishment, irrespective of the victim's conduct.'[139] Rights to liberty and due process under Arts 5 and 6 may be termed 'fundamental' rather than absolute. Here, the language of proportionality is recited[140] but applies only to the limited circumstances where these rights might be curtailed for the sake of the rights of others, such as victims or witnesses. Other rights (Arts 8 to 11) are provisional and may be proportionately balanced not only against rights but against wider societal interests. Here, the broad language of balance between security and rights finds some resonance. Proportionality inevitably demands a criminal justice approach to terrorism; as Lord Diplock demonstrated decades ago, even in direst circumstances, there is sufficient bite and invention within a criminal justice system to provide an effective response.[141]

1.54

When there is derogation under Art 15, consideration must be given to the existence of the emergency and to the need for any measure in pursuance of it, which should be 'strictly required' rather than proportionate.[142] The review of emergency causes acute problems both in terms of the standard of review and also as to the very justiciability of the question. Many have criticized undue judicial deference towards executive emergency decision-making.[143] The English judges have now accepted that review is proper, albeit that they have warned of the continuance of some 'deference'[144] to executive assessments in the implementation of counter-measures which is warranted by the superior information and expertise held by the executive. At the same time, the judges are no

1.55

---

[137] *Klass v Germany*, App no 5029/71, Ser A 28 (1978) para 50.

[138] See Dershowitz, A., *Why Terrorism Works* (Yale University Press, New Haven, 2002); Gross, O., 'Chaos and rules' (2003) 112 *Yale Law Journal* 1011; Ignatieff, M., *The Lesser Evil* (Edinburgh University Press, Edinburgh, 2005); Gross, O., 'Are torture warrants warranted?' (2004) 88 *Minnesota Law Review* 1481; Ginbar, V., *Why Not Torture Terrorists?* (Oxford University Press, Oxford, 2008).

[139] App no 22414/93, Reports 1996-V, para 79.

[140] See *Brogan v United Kingdom*, App nos 11209, 11234, 11266/84, 11386/85, Ser A 145-B, (1989) para 61; *R (on the application of Gillan) v Commissioner of Police for the Metropolis* [2006] UKHL 12 at para 64.

[141] Diplock Report, *Report of the Commission to consider legal procedures to deal with terrorist activities in Northern Ireland* (Cmnd 5185, London, 1972).

[142] See Ashworth, A., 'Security, terrorism, and the value of human rights' in Goold, B.J. and Lazarus, L., *Security and Human Rights* (Hart, Oxford, 2007) p 215.

[143] Dyzenhaus, D., *The Constitution of Law* (Cambridge University Press, Cambridge, 2006).

[144] See *Huang v Secretary of State for the Home Department* [2007] UKHL 11 at para 16; Lord Steyn, 'Deference: a tangled story' [2005] *Public Law* 346.

more 'amateurs' in the taking of complex security decisions than are the politicians who ultimately authorize them,[145] and the judges have advantages of focus and calm to balance against a relative deficit of information. Thus, Lord Bingham warned that 'While any decision made by a representative democratic body must of course command respect, the degree of respect will be conditioned by the nature of the decision.'[146] A more vivid formulation was offered by Lord Justice Laws in *International Transport Roth GmbH v Secretary of State for the Home Department*,[147] whose guideline is that 'greater deference will be due to the democratic powers where the subject-matter in hand is peculiarly within their constitutional responsibility, and less when it lies more particularly within the constitutional responsibility of the courts. . . . There are no tanks on the wrong lawns.' He posited the further useful guideline that 'greater deference is to be paid to an Act of Parliament than to a decision of the executive or subordinate measure'.[148]

1.56   The second aspect of constitutionalism demands 'accountability' which includes attributes such as information provision, open and independent debate, and an ability to participate in decision-making. These attributes conduce against contentions that a dictatorial regime is best fitted to respond to crisis and instead seek to ensure the continuance of parliamentary (in other words, public and partisan) scrutiny.[149] This process can be aided by stating explicitly some of the desirable limiting principles adduced earlier. So, for each part of anti-terrorism legislation, there should be expressed criteria by which to judge its value or dispensability and its proportionality, with a distinct vote on each part.

1.57   Vigilance through democratic accountability should be undertaken not simply by Parliament but also by an independent permanent standing committee.[150] The tailored need for special scrutiny contends against the mixing of 'normal' and 'special' provisions such as has occurred in the Anti-terrorism, Crime and Security Act 2001.[151] As well as democratic and expert accountability, the mechanism of judicial accountability can play an important role consistent with democracy.[152] The role of the judiciary will mainly arise on the basis of rights jurisprudence, as already described, but accountability to concepts such as legality should equally be applied.

1.58   The third and broadest aspect of constitutionalism demands 'constitutional governance'. This aspect includes the subjection of governmental action to a lawfulness requirement that terrorism laws 'indicate with reasonable clarity the scope and manner

---

[145] Compare Posner, E.A. and Vermeule, A., *Terror in the Balance* (Oxford University Press, Oxford, 2007) p 31.

[146] [2004] UKHL 56 at para 39.

[147] [2002] EWCA Civ 158 at paras 85, 86.

[148] *Ibid* at para 83.

[149] See House of Lords Constitution Committee, *Counter-Terrorism Bill: The role of ministers, Parliament, and the Judiciary* (2007–08 HL 167). The idea of escalating super-majorities in Ackerman, B., *Before the Next Attack* (Yale University Press, New Haven, 2006) p 80 wrongly assumes a chronologically finite threat and therefore entails successive, uncontrolled panics.

[150] Further consideration to scrutiny is given in ch 10.

[151] Privy Counsellor Review Committee, *Anti-Terrorism, Crime and Security Act 2001, Review, Report* (2003–04 HC 100) paras C111–13.

[152] [2004] UKHL 56 at para 42 per Lord Bingham.

of exercise of the relevant discretion conferred on the public authorities'.[153] Next, the 'constitutional' mode of governance demands respect for meta-norms—tenets of national constitutional law and also international law, as indicated by Lord Lloyd's fourth point, the impact of which ensures that the response to terrorism will be conducted within a liberal and democratic framework.[154] The norms must reflect the need for rationality and proportionality, including the overall purpose of the restoration of fundamental features of constitutional life. These considerations of constitutional governance also point towards the delineation of special powers in advance of an emergency. The repeal of all emergency laws is likely to abnegate the influence of the legislative and judicial branches and to gift absolute power to the executive. Contingent threats are also worthy of consideration but are already the subject of the Civil Contingencies Act 2004, Pt II, which entails a range of further restraints under the 'triple lock'. Contingent or precautionary risk, such as that detention without charge of suspects might be required for more than twenty-eight days, ought not to be the basis for measures in the terrorism legislation unless there is a willingness to match the safeguards in the 2004 Act.

As well as these three principled concerns, 'policy relevance and impact' must be considered. Legislation should meet demands of efficacy and efficiency, and these attributes should be judged in the light of the CONTEST strategy. Indeed, these tests ought to be the first to be applied, for if a measure does not sensibly advance the chosen strategy, there is no point in applying further tests.   1.59

3. Factual triggers

Is existing political or paramilitary violence in the United Kingdom of such severity as to warrant the severe departures from normal standards which are now perpetrated by anti-terrorism legislation? A precise econometric calculation of where the advantage lies is tricky.[155] For instance, there were 3,298 road deaths in the United Kingdom in 2006,[156] whereas the highest annual loss in the modern era from terrorism was 502 in 1972.[157] The legislative reactions to faulty driving and terrorism are very different. Yet, this comparison (which might also apply to diseases such as influenza) is facile, since there are significant qualitative differences. First, terrorists aim to terrorize, and this outcome can have a widespread, destabilizing impact, potentially causing deep social cleavages, the depression of economic activity, and political instability. Secondly, prevention is implemented both for the sake of road safety and security from terrorism, but the latter has secured an unusually generous allocation of resources which interdicted the   1.60

---

[153] *Malone v United Kingdom*, App no 8691/79, Ser A 82 (1984), para 79.

[154] Bell, C., *Peace Agreements and Human Rights* (Oxford University Press, Oxford, 2000) p 68.

[155] But see Posner, R.A., *Not a Suicide Pact* (Oxford University Press, New York, 2006); Enders, W. and Sandler, T., *The Political Economy of Terrorism* (Cambridge University Press, Cambridge, 2006).

[156] Department for Transport, *Road Casualties Great Britain 2006* (2007); PSNI, *Road Traffic Collision Statistics Annual Report 2006* (2007) p 7. See further Wolfendale, J., 'Terrorism, security and the threat of counter terrorism' (2007) 30 *Studies in Conflict and Terrorism* 75; Sunstein, C.R., *Worst-Case Scenarios* (Harvard University Press, Cambridge, 2007) ch 1.

[157] McKittrick, D., *et al*, *Lost Lives* (Mainstream, Edinburgh, 1999) p 1473.

plots, for example, of Dhiren Barot,[158] Omar Khyam,[159] and Abdulla Ahmed Ali,[160] thereby affecting the figures revealed in Table 1.1.

Table 1.1 Terrorism-related deaths in UK 2001–2007[161]

	2001	2002	2003	2004	2005	2006	2007
GB	0	0	0	0	57	1	1
N Ire.	18	17	15	7	4	6	4

The threat is also underlined by attacks abroad, especially in New York in 2001 (sixty-seven British victims) and Bali (twenty-four British deaths).

1.61   Overall, it is plausible to conclude that UK governments have been justified in invoking anti-terrorism laws for at least three reasons. Most important is the evidence just given of a clear and present danger, far more prescient than in February 2001 when the Terrorism Act 2000 came into force. The main focus is *jihadist* terrorism,[162] but dangers remain in Northern Ireland.[163] Conversely, other forms of terrorism originating within the United Kingdom, including animal rights violence, are not so severe or difficult as to warrant special laws.[164]

1.62   Secondly, total abolition of special legislation without replacement throws the baby out with the bath-water. In other words, safeguards and restraints, which have painstakingly been fought over, conceded, and honed over a period of years, will be lost alongside more reviled instruments of coercion.[165]

1.63   Thirdly, it is illogical to oppose all conceivable forms of special laws on a platform of concerns for human rights. Rather, our collective concern for human rights should lead to the utmost protection of citizens against either zombie-like paramilitary organizations or maddened security forces and that to vacate the field to either faction is to abdicate rather than to exercise responsibility for the governance of special powers. There is ample evidence to suggest that governments of wholly different complexions will, in a tight corner, wish to resort to much the same measures and react in much the same ways. Thus, if the legal field is left unattended, the power élite will very soon fill it with architecture which, in the circumstances of an emergency, will be rather ugly. One cannot coherently complain about 'panic' legislation but then deny to the state the principled and refined means to defend itself. The special rules for derogation will be considered further below.

---

[158] *The Times* 13 October 2006 p 1.

[159] *The Times* 1 May 2007 p 11.

[160] *The Times* 9 September 2008 p 6.

[161] Sources: PSNI Statistics on the Security Situation no 6 (2007) Table 6.1; IMC 17th 2007–08 HC 18 para 2.3; *Report of the Official Account of the Bombings in London on 7th July 2005* (2005–06 HC 1087) para 2. These totals include the deaths of Jean Charles de Menezes, Alexander Litvinenko, and five suicide bombers. The periods in Northern Ireland are from April 2000 to 31 March 2001 and onwards.

[162] The Prime Minister revealed there are 2,000 such suspects, and 75% have links to Pakistan: *The Times* 15 December 2008 p 33.

[163] Independent Monitoring Commission, *Seventeenth Report* (2007–08 HC 18).

[164] *Inquiry into Legislation against Terrorism* (Cm 3420, London, 1996) para 1.24; Home Office and Northern Ireland Office, *Legislation against Terrorism* (Cm 4178, London, 1998) para 3.10.

[165] Brennan, W.J., 'The American experience', in Shetreet, S., *Free Speech and National Security* (Nijhoff, Dordrecht, 1991) pp 16–17.

E. AN OUTLINE OF ANTI-TERRORISM LEGISLATION SINCE 2000

Special measures against terrorism have provided a constant feature of political and legal life within the United Kingdom for many years. However, this survey is confined to an outline of the legislation which forms the core of this book and will leave aside other domestic and international measures and organizational changes. **1.64**

1. Terrorism Act 2000

The Terrorism Bill potentially offered the opportunity for a new dispensation—a considered, comprehensive, and principled code rather than hastily drafted and fragmented emergency laws. The period of gestation took over four years and goes back to the Lloyd Report[166] as well as the government's broadly supportive response.[167] The passage of the Human Rights Act 1998 also made it advisable to conduct a more thorough and ethical statement. **1.65**

In the event, the Terrorism Act 2000 achieved a partial success. First, although an Act running to 131 sections and 16 Schedules appears comprehensive, its content is based largely on previous measures, and there was insufficient attempt to innovate. The Act was an occasion for clearer thinking rather than new thinking. Secondly, the Terrorism Act 2000 does not provide for the kind of structures to ensure accountability or the safeguards discussed above. Lord Lloyd's first principle of normalcy is not sufficiently expressed, nor are the structures of review sufficiently developed. Thirdly, compliance with the standards of the Human Rights Act 1998 was inadequately considered and has since been found to be wanting in several respects. The government claimed, pursuant to s 19 of the Human Rights Act 1998, that the Bill is compatible with European Convention rights. Its confidence may have been bolstered by the view of Lord Hope in *R v Director of Public Prosecutions, ex parte Kebilene*:[168] **1.66**

Then there is the nature of the threat which terrorism poses to a free and democratic society. It seeks to achieve its ends by violence and intimidation. It is often indiscriminate in its effects, and sophisticated methods are used to avoid detection both before and after the event. Society has a strong interest in preventing acts of terrorism before they are perpetrated—to spare the lives of innocent people and to avoid the massive damage and dislocation to ordinary life which may follow from explosions which destroy or damage property.

In terms of what it does deliver, the 2000 Act is divided into eight parts, with six of them reflecting its substantive themes: proscribed organizations; terrorist property; terrorist investigations; counter-terrorism powers; miscellaneous offences; and extra measures confined to Northern Ireland. These themes are detailed in Chapters 2 to 7 of this book. Amongst the innovations are a new definition of 'terrorism', an attempt to subject **1.67**

---

[166] *Inquiry into Legislation against Terrorism* (Cm 3420, London, 1996).
[167] *Legislation Against Terrorism* (Cm 4178, London, 1998).
[168] [2000] 2 AC 326 at p 387. This approach coheres with the view of the European Court of Human Rights: *Brogan v United Kingdom*, App nos 11209, 11234, 11266/84, 11386/85, Ser A 145-B, (1989) para 48; *Fox, Campbell and Hartley v United Kingdom*, App nos 12244, 12245, 12383/86, Ser A 182 (1990) para 44.

a wider range of measures to judicial or quasi-judicial oversight—such as through a new commission to consider proscription orders and the judicial scrutiny of detention following arrest. Next, the laws in Britain and Northern Ireland are largely harmonized—save for a temporary inventory (Pt VII) for Northern Ireland.[169]

1.68   Conversely, amongst the repeals were exclusion orders,[170] which had already lapsed in 1998. Another notable absentee was the power of internment without trial, which had been dormant since 1975,[171] and had been terminated by the Northern Ireland (Emergency Provisions) Act 1998.[172] The official Labour Party view was that 'internment is the terrorist's friend'.[173] Attempts to revive it were therefore firmly resisted by the Labour government. While 'It does not rule out for all time the introduction of the power to intern',[174] it would be 'a significant backward step at a time when we are normalising the security situation in Northern Ireland'.[175] The third non-appearance concerned the offence of withholding information.[176] Fourthly, the Criminal Justice (Terrorism and Conspiracy) Act 1998[177] provisions relating to specified organizations were renewed for Northern Ireland but were repealed in Britain.

1.69   The bulk of the Terrorism Act 2000 came into force on 19 February 2001 and remains the foremost code. The principal changes since then relate to Pt VII, which was confined to Northern Ireland. As related in Chapter 9, Pt VII was conceived as a temporary security longstop, renewable annually under s 112 and subject to a sunset of five years, pending the fate of the Peace Process. The final repeal of Pt VII[178] and its replacement by the Justice and Security (Northern Ireland) Act 2007 took effect on 1 August 2007.

1.70   Since the Terrorism Act 2000 is otherwise a permanent code, responding to a permanent threat to national security and the right to life of individuals, there is no requirement for periodic renewal or re-enactment.[179] According to government minister, Charles Clarke:[180]

We have had so-called temporary provisions on the statute book for 25 years. The time has come to face the fact of terrorism and be ready to deal with it for the foreseeable future. We need to make

---

[169] See Hogan, G., and Walker, C., *Political Violence and the Law in Ireland* (Manchester University Press, Manchester, 1989); Donohue, L.K., *Counter-Terrorism Law* (Irish Academic Press, Dublin, 2001).

[170] See Walker, C.P., *The Prevention of Terrorism in British Law* (2nd edn, Manchester University Press, Manchester, 1992) ch 5. *Inquiry into Legislation against Terrorism* (Cm 3420, London, 1996) paras 16.2–16.4; Home Office and Northern Ireland Office, *Legislation against Terrorism* (Cm 4178, London, 1998) para 5.7.

[171] See Spjut, R.J., 'Internment and detention without trial in Northern Ireland 1971–75' (1986) 49 *Modern Law Review* 712.

[172] *Inquiry into Legislation against Terrorism* (Cm 3420, London, 1996) para 16.8.

[173] Hansard HC Standing Committee A, col 73 (25 November 1997), Adam Ingram.

[174] Home Office and Northern Ireland Office, *Legislation against Terrorism* (Cm 4178, London, 1998) para 14.2.

[175] Hansard HL vol 613, col 1054 (16 May 2000), Lord Falconer.

[176] *Inquiry into Legislation against Terrorism* (Cm 3420, London, 1996) para 14.24), and the Home Office Consultation Paper (Home Office and Northern Ireland Office, *Legislation against Terrorism* (Cm 4178, London, 1998) para 7.17.

[177] See Walker, C., 'The bombs in Omagh and their aftermath' (1999) 62 *Modern Law Review* 879.

[178] A one-year stay had been allowed by the Terrorism (Northern Ireland) Act 2006. Note also the related measures in the Criminal Justice (Terrorism and Conspiracy) Act 1998, ss 1–4. The review under s 8 was formally abolished by the Criminal Justice and Immigration Act 2008, s 62.

[179] See Lord Lloyd, *Inquiry into Legislation against Terrorism* (Cm 3420, London, 1996) paras 1.20, 17.6.

[180] Hansard HC, vol 346, col 363 (15 March 2000).

the powers permanently available, although the fact that those powers are available does not mean that they have to be used.

While it is logical that there should be no requirement of renewal, the level of scrutiny applied otherwise to what are meant to be extreme incursions into the rights of individuals is disappointing. Section 126[181] simply requires that the Secretary of State shall lay before both Houses of Parliament at least once in every twelve months a report on the working of the legislation. This formulation pointed towards consideration of past application rather than future need. It also gave no promise as to Parliament's reaction to the report. There is no longer an annual debate on the floor of the House—the minister pointed rather to possible select committee scrutiny.[182]

The loss of the annual renewal mechanism is not decisive. There is not any serious 1.71
chance that any part of the legislation will be struck down or seriously analysed in an hour and a half debate. What is regrettable is the lack of initiative from Parliament to keep the legislation under systematic scrutiny. Yet, extraordinary powers should be subjected to extraordinary scrutiny. Select committees have not performed well, and the only major review has concerned stop and search powers,[183] though arrest powers have been scrutinized in the context of legislative proposals in 2006 and 2008. Proscription, financial measures, and criminal offences have largely been unnoticed. The annual report, which has been diligently compiled by Lord Carlile,[184] has been formalized by the Terrorism Act 2006, s 36, though without substantive change.

2. Anti-terrorism, Crime and Security Act 2001

There was no immediate rush to legislation following the 11 September attacks, and the 1.72
operation of the Terrorism Act did buy some time for reflection. Moreover, when the 2001 Bill did appear, it was in fair part constructed around the Terrorism Act, rather than striking out in wholly new and alarming directions such as a US-style 'war on terror'.[185] Yet, the overlapping Acts quickly produced a legislative morass, and the scrutiny was very limited. The Bill was outlined to Parliament on 15 October 2001,[186] was introduced on 12 November 2001, and was assented to a month later. The Home Affairs Select Committee[187] and Joint Committee on Human Rights[188] produced extensive reports, but parliamentary debate was curtailed by time-tabling motions.

By s 127, much of the Anti-terrorism, Crime and Security Act 2001 came into force 1.73
on the date of assent (14 December 2001) though Pt VII was triggered later (31 May 2002). The main change to the 2001 Act has been the repeal of detention without trial in Pt IV, which was secured by the Prevention of Terrorism Act 2005, which came into force on 11 March 2005.

---

[181] Hansard HC Standing Committee D col 312 (8 February 2000), Charles Clarke.
[182] *Ibid* col 315.
[183] Home Affairs Committee, *Terrorism and Community Relations* (2003–04 HC 165).
[184] See *Report on the Operation of the Terrorism Act 2000* (Home Office, London, 2002–09).
[185] See *US Presidential Order, Detention, Treatment, and Trial of Certain Non-Citizens in the War Against Terrorism*, 13 November 2001 (66 Federal Register 57831).
[186] Hansard HC vol 372, col 923.
[187] *Report on the Anti-terrorism, Crime and Security Bill 2001* (2001–02 HC 351).
[188] *Reports on the Anti-terrorism, Crime and Security Bill* (2001–02 HL 37, HC 372) and (2001–02 HL 51, HC 420).

1.74   The Bill was justified as the response to 'a terrorist threat that is quite different from anything that we have previously faced',[189] though, as a legislative vehicle, it also transported much else besides measures against terrorism and became a device to avoid scrutiny and opposition. The senses in which the attacks on 11 September 2001 were wholly novel has already been considered. There were strong apprehensions that Al-Qa'ida-related activities were beyond the scale previously imagined—out of the nineteen hijackers, eleven had links with the United Kingdom.[190]

1.75   A major distinction from the Terrorism Act was that the usual statement of compatibility with the Human Rights Act could only be issued[191] by invoking a derogation because of the non-compliance with Art 5(1)(f) of detention without trial under Pt IV. The derogation was issued domestically under the Human Rights Act 1998 (Designated Derogation) Order 2001[192] and was registered by the Council of Europe Secretariat on 18 December 2001. This claim of compatibility has been labelled 'disingenuous',[193] but it may be better understood as depicting derogation to be within the concept of human rights rather than in conflict with it, which its supervision within the 1998 Act scheme encourages.[194]

1.76   Justification for the notice was considered in *A v Secretary of State for the Home Department*. A majority found for the government on the basis of several arguments.[195] Quite simply, it had not been proven that the lower court (the Special Immigration Appeals Commission) had misdirected itself. Next, the jurisprudence of the European Court of Human Rights did not seem to require as a trigger the actual experience of widespread loss of life caused by an armed body dedicated to destroying the territorial integrity or other fundamental characteristics of the state. Lord Bingham was content to apply the Strasbourg approaches, including the recognition of a margin of appreciation for executive discretion even for the recognition of an emergency.[196] In addition, it was accepted that it would be sufficient that an emergency was 'imminent'.[197] Other judges argued that the European Court expected a more searching review in domestic courts,[198] though that contention is difficult to sustain. No judicial review was possible until the Human Rights Act 1998 came into force,[199] and yet the European Court had never condemned this legal omission. More trenchant domestic review would also require the development of a far more sophisticated jurisprudence than has yet been devised by the European Court.

---

[189] Hansard HL vol 629, col 142 (27 November 2001), Lord Goldsmith.

[190] See *The Times* 15 September 2001 p 1.

[191] *Home Office Explanatory Memorandum* (London, 2001) para 408.

[192] SI 2001/3644.

[193] Tomkins, A., 'Legislating against terror' [2002] *Public Law* 205 at p 217.

[194] Compare Hickman, T.R., 'Between human rights and the rule of law' (2005) 68 *Modern Law Review* 655.

[195] [2004] UKHL 56. See further Walker, C., 'Prisoners of "war all the time"' [2005] *European Human Rights Law Review* 50; Tierney, S., 'Determining the state of exception' (2005) 68 *Modern Law Review* 668; Bates, E., 'A "public emergency threatening the life of the nation"?' (2005) 76 *British Yearbook of International Law* 245.

[196] [2004] UKHL 56, para 29 (Lord Bingham).

[197] *Ibid* para 25 (Lord Bingham).

[198] For example, Lord Hope (paras 108, 131); Lord Rodger (paras 176, 178).

[199] Some judges were of the view that review of derogation is only possible because of the passage of the Anti-terrorism, Crime and Security Act 2001, s 30: Lord Rodger, para 164.

The notice was withdrawn on 16 March 2005. Subsequently, its validity was upheld in *A v United Kingdom*, the Strasbourg court reaching its conclusion in the context of the later attacks in 2005, and mindful of a standard which did not require the life of the nation to be threatened in its entirety, and of being 'acutely conscious of the difficulties faced by states in protecting their populations from terrorist violence'.[200] Might derogation still be available in the conditions prevailing in 2008?[201] It must be conceded that the factual situation has cohered towards the government's case. Compared to November 2001, when no Al-Qa'ida attack had ever taken place in the United Kingdom, it emerged that there were strong British links to the September 11 attacks, and these have been followed by attacks abroad by British citizens and several serious plots at home, one of which resulted in devastating loss of life in July 2005. The invasion of Iraq in 2003 has also provided an enduring rallying call for attack, but more terrorist incidents still regularly occur in France and Spain.[202]

1.77

Aside from Pt IV, the 2001 Act was a substantial legislative supplement, with 129 sections and 8 Schedules organized into 14 Parts. The first three parts deal with terrorist property (dealt with in Chapter 3). Chapter 8 will discuss the measures in Pts VI to X, dealing with dangerous substances and acute vulnerabilities, a recognition of the possible use of weapons of mass destruction. Other aspects of Pt X, as well as extracts from Pts XI and XIII, are translated into either Chapter 4 (terrorist investigations) or Chapter 5 (counter-terrorist powers). Next, there are various new criminal offences spread around the 2001 Act (covered within Chapter 6).

1.78

The claim that this catalogue amounts to 'the most draconian legislation Parliament has passed in peacetime in over a century'[203] rather underestimates the breadth and depth of the 2000 Act. It also underplays the constant history of alien internment in twentieth century Britain.[204] A more pertinent criticism of the 2001 Act was that it mixed 'normal' law with security law and allowed ill-considered changes to the former as if it was dealing with the dangers of the latter.[205]

1.79

The omissions from the 2001 legislation are again significant. One issue of interest was the criminalization of mercenary activities emanating from reports that British Muslims had travelled to Afghanistan intending to fight for the Taliban regime.[206] It took until 2006 for a partial response to emerge. Next, the introduction of identity cards was fleetingly raised. Their utility had been rejected by Lord Lloyd,[207] but, after the attacks in September 2001, the Home Secretary announced renewed support. However, the fear that such a controversial issue would unduly delay the Bill resulted in

1.80

---

[200] App no 3455/05, 19 February 2009, para 126. See further paras 177–81.

[201] A more extensive framework for invocation would help to limit use: Joint Committee on Human Rights, *Counter-Terrorism Policy and Human Rights: Counter-Terrorism Bill* (2007–08 HL 172/HC 1077) para 90.

[202] See Europol, TE-Sat: *European Situation and Trend Report 2007* (The Hague, 2007) p 13.

[203] Tomkins, A., 'Legislating against terror' [2002] *Public Law* 205 at p 205.

[204] See Cesarani, D., and Kushner, T., (eds), *The Internment of Aliens in Twentieth Century Britain* (Frank Cass, London, 1993).

[205] Privy Counsellor Review Committee, *Anti-terrorism, Crime and Security Act 2001, Review, Report* (2003–04 HC 100) B para 3.

[206] Walker, C. and Whyte, D., 'Contracting out war? Private military companies, law and regulation in the United Kingdom' (2005) 54 *International & Comparative Law Quarterly* 651.

[207] *Inquiry into Legislation against Terrorism* (Cm 3420, London, 1996) para 16.31.

the dropping of the idea.[208] A national system has now been enacted by the Identity Cards Act 2006, with the combating of terrorism as part of its rationale.[209]

1.81   A complex array of limits and reviews were inserted into the 2001 Act. By s 122, the Home Secretary was required to appoint a committee of no fewer than seven members, all Privy Counsellors, to conduct a review of the entire Act. But the government emphasized that the review was a one-off exercise which would report within two years[210] with a copy to be laid before Parliament.[211] In the event, the Newton Committee reported at the end of 2003.[212] Its thorough report recommended the end of detention without trial as well as detailed changes in other areas. The government's initial response was unenthusiastic. Its hand on detention without trial was forced by the House of Lords judgment in *A v Secretary of State for the Home Department*.[213] Otherwise, many other recommendations were rejected,[214] and no further review has taken place. The idea of a general two-year sunset clause was resisted: 'We are not convinced of the need for sunset clauses on . . . the bread-and-butter precautionary anti-terrorist measures in this Bill'.[215]

1.82   As for more limited reviews under the 2001 Act, Parliament insisted on limits in ss 28 and 29 on the duration of Pt IV by way of annual renewal by order and a review by an independent person (Lord Carlile was appointed).[216]

1.83   Another limit as to duration applied in Pt XI in connection with the retention of communications data, which was allowed to persist on a mandatory basis under s 104 for two years at a time. This scheme is now being replaced by permanent legislation, as detailed in Chapter 5.

1.84   The third limit, in s 111, allowed the implementation of European Union Third Pillar measures by order. The purpose of s 111 was to avoid legislative delay in the implementation of urgent, counter-measures. Rather than primary legislation, there could be secondary legislation, roughly equivalent to the precedent in Common Market matters to s 2(2) of the European Communities Act 1972. The power was hugely controversial, not least because it was not confined to anti-terrorism measures, and so was time-limited to 1 July 2002. In the event, while progress was made at European level, notably with the implementation of the European arrest warrant scheme,[217] it was implemented by the Extradition Act 2003 in line with the pace of European partners and the original intention of the government.[218] The other major development, the Council Framework

---

[208]   Hansard HC vol 374, cols 387–8 (8 November 2001), Angela Eagle.

[209]   Hansard HC vol 435, col 1165 (28 June 2005), Charles Clarke.

[210]   Hansard HL vol 629, col 1536 (13 December 2001), Lord Rooker.

[211]   Prompt attention was required by s 123.

[212]   Privy Counsellor Review Committee, *Anti-terrorism, Crime and Security Act 2001, Review, Report* (2003–04 HC 100).

[213]   [2004] UKHL 56.

[214]   Home Office, *Counter-Terrorism Powers: Reconciling Security and Liberty in an Open Society* (Cm 6147, London, 2004).

[215]   Hansard HL vol 629, col 634 (3 December 2001), Lord Rooker.

[216]   See Lord Carlile, *Anti-terrorism, Crime and Security Act 2001 Part IV Section 28, Reviews 2001–2005* (Home Office, London).

[217]   See Council Framework Decision 2002/584/JHA of 13 June 2002 on the European arrest warrant and the surrender procedures between member states. It was applied with success to obtain the surrender of Hussain Osman from Italy in 2005. See also *Boudhiba v Central Examining Court No 5 of the National Court of Justice Madrid Spain* [2006] EWHC 167 (Admin).

[218]   Hansard HL vol 629, col 1142 (10 December 2001), Baroness Symons.

Decision on Combating Terrorism of 2002[219] was not considered to require any immediate domestic response.

3. Prevention of Terrorism Act 2005

The policy of detention without trial under Pt IV of the 2001 Act came in for fierce criticism from the Privy Counsellor Review Committee set up under the 2001 Act. It viewed the system as objectionable because of the lack of safeguards, because it provided no protection against resident terrorists, and because viable alternatives existed in the forms of either a more aggressive criminal prosecution stance (aided by admissible electronic intercept evidence) or intrusive administrative restraints.[220] The Home Office Consultation Paper in response, regarded Pt IV as indispensable and depicted the alternative strategies as unworkable,[221] still based on the assumption that the threat remained predominantly from foreign nationals.[222]   1.85

There the matter might have rested were it not for the declaration of incompatibility under s 4 of the Human Rights Act 1998 issued by the House of Lords in *A v Secretary of State for the Home Department*.[223] As already noted, a majority of their Lordships did not condemn the use of the derogation notice. However, two features of the regime, that it was only directed against foreigners while ignoring threats from British citizens and that it comprised only a 'prison with three walls' (since those foreign detainees were entitled to leave the prison if willing to travel on to another country) meant it was condemned as disproportionate, discriminatory, and irrational.   1.86

After some hesitation, the government sought both to respond to the (non-binding) declaration of incompatibility under the Human Rights Act 1998, s 4, and to do so in a way which would not inevitably rely on a notice of derogation. The results are set out as 'control orders' in the Prevention of Terrorism Act 2005 (described in Chapter 7). This relatively short Act replaces Pt IV of the 2001 Act with executive restriction by way of control orders. The Act allows for two types of order, depending on their severity, namely derogating orders and non-derogating orders. The government has sought to rely solely upon non-derogating orders, but it has been condemned for overstepping the mark both in regard to the incursions into liberty and in regard to the 'thin veneer of legality'[224] in the procedures by which orders can be challenged. The legislative process was often bitter and suffered from the tight deadline for the expiration of Pt IV. Annual independent review is required under s 14,[225] and s 13 provides for expiration after one year whereupon there can be a renewal order and debate upon it.   1.87

---

[219] 2002/475/JHA of 13 June 2002. See further Council Framework Decision amending Framework Decision 2002/475/JHA on combating terrorism (6561/08); House of Commons European Scrutiny Committee, *Seventh Report* (2007–08 HC 16-vii).

[220] 30% of arrests under the Terrorism Act in 2003 affected British citizens: Privy Counsellor Review Committee, *Anti-terrorism, Crime and Security Act 2001 Review, Report* (2003–04 HC 100) para 193.

[221] Home Office, *Counter Terrorism Powers* (Cm 6147, London, 2004) Pt I paras 8, 34, Pt II para 31.

[222] *Ibid* paras 7, 10.

[223] [2004] UKHL 56.

[224] *Re MB* [2006] EWHC (Admin) 1000 at para 103.

[225] See *Reports of the Independent Reviewer pursuant to Section 14(3) of the Prevention of Terrorism Act 2005* (Home Office, London, 2006–09).

4. Terrorism Act 2006

1.88　The London bombings of 7 July 2005 'rightly and inevitably catalysed an earlier examination of potential additional legislation that had been envisaged at the time of the enactment of the Prevention of Terrorism Act 2005.'[226] Given that genesis, there is a heavy emphasis on dealing with the radicalization of 'neighbour terrorists',[227] though the Act was also motivated by the ratification the Council of Europe Convention on the Prevention of Terrorism 2005[228] which also gives impetus to the conferment of extra-jurisdictional coverage for terrorist-type offences.

1.89　The draft Terrorism Bill 2005 was made available by letters from the Home Secretary on 15 September 2005 and 5 October 2005. Great controversy ensued over two aspects—a new offence of the glorification of terrorism and a new maximum detention period of ninety days. In the face of considerable parliamentary opposition, the first measure was drafted out of the legislation, and the second was defeated. This Act was not 'a hurried piece of legislation',[229] since its inception to delivery occupied around seven months, a commendable reflective period given the backdrop of July 2005. The quality of debate was substantially aided by select committee reports.

1.90　Part I of the Act consists of a catalogue of offences which are designed to avert or penalize extremist messages or preparatory activities. The most controversial offences relate to the publication of statements that are likely to be understood by their audience as a direct or indirect encouragement (including 'glorification') to terrorism. These offences are described in Chapter 2, while the remaining offences, of training and preparations, are in Chapter 6. The most notable other change, amongst the miscellaneous changes in Pt II, is that the police powers of detention after arrest are also extended—by doubling the period to twenty-eight days. The opportunity was also taken to amend the definition of terrorism and to provide a statutory basis for the independent review of the legislation. The Terrorism Act 2006 commenced mainly on 13 April 2006, though the extension of detention provisions under s 23 were left until 25 July. Those provisions alone are subject to annual renewal under section 25. In addition, an independent review is required under s 36 for Pt I of the Act (much of Pt II being subject already to review as amendments to earlier legislation). Lord Carlile has duly obliged, with his reports rolled up in those for the Terrorism Act 2000.

5. Terrorism (Northern Ireland) Act 2006 and the Justice and Security (Northern Ireland) Act 2007

1.91　Part VII of the Terrorism Act 2000, which was subject to annual renewal but was also time-limited to 18 February 2006, was extended by the Terrorism (Northern Ireland) Act 2006 for up to two years. By that time, two factors were in play. First, the Joint

---

[226] Lord Carlile, *Proposals by Her Majesty's Government for changes to the laws against terrorism* (Home Office, London, 2005) para 6.

[227] See Walker, C., '"Know Thine Enemy as Thyself": Discerning Friend from Foe under Anti-Terrorism Laws' (2008) 32 *Melbourne Law Review* 275.

[228] Council of Europe Treaty Series No 196. For 'Convention offences', see Terrorism Act 2006, Sch 1.

[229] Jones, A., Bowers, R, and Lodge, H.D., *The Terrorism Act 2006* (Oxford University Press, Oxford, 2006) p v.

Declaration by the British and Irish Governments of 2003 had accepted a programme of security normalization, a change which had been foreseen by the Belfast ('Good Friday') Agreement.[230] This programme included the repeal of Pt VII of the Terrorism Act 2000. Secondly, the Provisional IRA had issued a statement on 28 July 2005 whereby its leadership had formally ordered an end to its armed campaign. At that point, the government sought to begin the implementation of the 2003 deal. The security situation in Northern Ireland had improved considerably, but there were still active paramilitary groups. So, the general reviews by Lord Carlile[231] and more specific reviews concerning the continuance of the non-jury 'Diplock' trials[232] advised a temporary extension to Pt VII. This extension was achieved by the 2006 Act, which enabled the Secretary of State to extend Pt VII by order up to 1 August 2008. The Act also allowed the Attorney General a discretionary power to deschedule any offence, and it repealed altogether some defunct measures in Pt VII.

A potentially longer lasting arrangement, replacing the 2006 Act arrangements, was installed by the Justice and Security (Northern Ireland) Act 2007. The Act implements arrangements to protect jurors from intimidation but retains for at least two further years the fail-safe of 'Diplock courts' on an amended basis though without any form of independent review. More startling is that the special police and army powers in Pt VII, many of which have the potential to breach Art 5, were continued with little debate and without specific time duration, albeit subject to a power to repeal by order and subject to annual review under s 40 (by Robert Whalley). The 2007 Act also adapts the Private Security Industry Act 2001 so as to establish permanent regulation of the private security industry in Northern Ireland. The latter change was the subject of detailed consultation by the Northern Ireland Office, which published a paper, *Regulating the Private Security Industry in Northern Ireland*, in 2006.

6. Counter-Terrorism Act 2008

In contrast to prior legislation since 2000, no overarching theme or trigger emerges for this substantial Act (of 102 sections and nine Schedules). It deepens and widens existing legal tactics, though executive measures remained static. The motivating themes are familiar—that the threat is 'very different in nature and scale' and that intervention is needed 'at a very early stage'.[233] Anti-terrorism laws are being worked into a comprehensive code, covering security administration, executive measures, police powers, criminal justice, and sentencing.[234] But the process remains unprincipled, incomplete, and fragmented.

The legislative process was notable for two reasons. One is the commendable breadth of scrutiny—lasting for some seventeen months between proposals and assent and incorporating the evidence of select witnesses before the Public Bill Committee stage.

1.92

1.93

1.94

---

[230] British Irish Agreement reached in the multi-party negotiations (Cm 3883, London, 1998).
[231] Lord Carlile, *Report on the Operation of Part VII of the Terrorism Act 2000* (Home Office, London, 2006) para 74.
[232] Northern Ireland Office, *Diplock Review Report* (Belfast, 2000) and *Replacement Arrangements for the Diplock Court System* (Belfast, 2006).
[233] Hansard HC vol 474, cols 647, 653 (1 April 2008), Jacqui Smith.
[234] See Home Office, *Possible Measures for Inclusion into a Future Counter-Terrorism Bill* (London, 2007); Lord Carlile, *Report on Proposed Measures for Inclusion in a Counter-Terrorism Bill* (Cm 7262, London, 2007).

Secondly, the parliamentary process did result in major alterations, with proposals to extend police detention from twenty-eight to forty-two days and also concerning special coronial hearings both being dropped.[235]

1.95   In line with this preamble, no single theme predominates. Part I enhances powers to gather and share information, especially by allowing the retention and use of fingerprints and DNA samples for counter-terrorism as well as criminal purposes. Next, and balancing the rejection of 42-day detention, many other criminal justice measures were passed, including post-charge questioning in Pt II, rules for extended venues for trials in Pt III, and also extended forfeiture and longer sentences for convicted terrorists. Post-sentence measures also make an appearance in Pt IV, whereby notification and foreign travel requirements can be applied to persons convicted of terrorism and since released. Parts V affords new powers to the Treasury to regulate terrorism financing, while Pt VI amends the procedures relating to Treasury-based powers over terrorism finances. A wide variety of miscellaneous reforms follows in Pt VII. There is no extra time limit or review scheme in this Act, which is a startling omission.

1.96   The Counter-Terrorism Act 2008 is partly in force. Sections 19-21 and Sch 1 commenced on 24 December 2008, ss 29 and 74 to 84 and Sch 8 on 16 February 2009, ss 62 to 73 and Sch 7 on 27 November 2008, ss 85 to 90 on 26 January 2009, ss 92 to 98 and 100 to 102 on 26 November 2008.

F. CONCLUSIONS

1.97   It would be a fine development if, having been fortified with these sweeping powers, the UK government and its security forces could have the confidence and ability to rely primarily on 'normal' policing powers and upon its extensive contingency planning and networks. However, as they perceive themselves to live in extraordinarily threatening times, the legislation can anticipate a long and active life. The emphasis should therefore be upon the standards of constitutionalism so that the persistence of special laws does not corrode the values of society and so that a return to normality is not lost from sight. With due regard for those values, attention will now be turned towards the detailed contents of the anti-terrorism legislation.

---

[235] For points of controversy, see Joint Committee on Human Rights, *Counter-Terrorism Policy and Human Rights: Counter-Terrorism Bill* (2007–08 HL 172/HC 1077).

2

EXTREMIST ORGANIZATIONS AND EXTREMIST SPEECH

A. PROSCRIPTION

1. Background

If terrorism is defined as 'violence for political ends', then the law must not only address 2.01
the 'violence' but also must consider the modes of mobilization of the 'political ends'.
The duality of the state's concerns may be illustrated by the pronouncement of the director of publicity for Sinn Féin, Danny Morrison, in 1981, that 'Who here really believes
we can win the war through the ballot box? But will anyone here object if, with a ballot
paper in this hand and an Armalite in the other, we take power in Ireland?'[1] In response,
the state measures to be discussed in this chapter might be viewed as particularly relevant
to the 'prevent' element of the CONTEST strategy. They seek to prevent the advance of
extreme ideologies by starving them of what Prime Minister Thatcher called the 'oxygen
of publicity'.[2] It is less certain that the 'pursue' strand is effectively secured, for few prosecutions have occurred.

Participation in organizations designated as concerned in Irish terrorism has long 2.02
been proscribed. Part II of the Terrorism Act 2000 builds upon the device in two ways.
First, it extends substantially the range of Northern Ireland groups proscribed in Britain.
Secondly, the scope of proscription is no longer confined to Northern Ireland groups
but covers foreign groups, as well as sub-state extremism. In addition, the Terrorism
Act 2006 extends the basis of proscription from deeds to words.

Under s 121, the interpretation of 'organization' includes any association or combin- 2.03
ation of persons, a phrase wide enough to encompass an affinity group or even an

---

[1] McAllister, I., '"The Armalite and the ballot box": Sinn Fein's electoral strategy in Northern Ireland'
(2004) 23 *Electoral Studies* 123 at p 124.
[2] <http://www.margaretthatcher.org/speeches/displaydocument.asp?docid=106096>.

33

anarchistic 'disorganization'. Diffuse networks such as Al-Qa'ida and self-generating combinations inspired by their ideologies could therefore qualify as 'organizations'. However, the looser the network, the more difficult will become proof of membership, rather than loyalty to personal confederates. In the signal prosecutions of Brahmin Benmerzouga and Baghdad Meziane, two Algerians were accused of Al-Qa'ida membership and funding offences, while the funding charges were sustained, the charges of membership under s 11 were dropped.[3]

2. Proscribed groups—Irish and other domestic

2.04   Under the Terrorism Act 2000, proscription in relation to Northern Ireland groups has been promulgated on a nationwide basis, which means that Loyalist groups are now banned in Britain. The listings under the 2000 Act are established in two ways. First, those Northern Ireland groups which were listed in prior legislation are listed afresh in Sch 2. Extra groups may be added under s 3(3) by statutory order. Because of the Peace Process, it has not proven necessary to exercise this power in the Irish context, though, equally, no group has been removed from the listings.

Table 2.1 Proscribed organizations relevant to Northern Ireland[4]

Continuity Army Council	A splinter group formed in 1994 as the armed wing of Republican Sinn Fein (RSF), following the Provisional IRA ceasefire. It also spawned the Continuity IRA.
Cumann na mBan	The 'Union of Women' was founded as an auxiliary to the IRA.
Fianna na hEireann	'Warriors of Ireland': the auxiliary youth section of the IRA.
Irish National Liberation Army	The INLA emerged in 1974 from former Official IRA members.
Irish People's Liberation Organisation	This name has been used by dissident INLA members.
Irish Republican Army	The leading Republican paramilitary group formed in 1918. A split in 1969 resulted in the Official IRA (observing a ceasefire since 1972) and the Provisional IRA which was the main source of Republican terrorism until a ceasefire in 1996. Splinters then appeared, producing the Real IRA and the Continuity IRA.
Loyalist Volunteer Force	The LVF was formed in 1996 out of the mid-Ulster Ulster Volunteer Force (UVF) unit.
Orange Volunteers	Several Loyalist groups have used this name intermittently since the early 1970s.
Red Hand Commando	A Loyalist group formed in 1972 and linked to the Ulster Volunteer Force (below).
Red Hand Defenders	A Loyalist paramilitary group, formed in 1998 from dissidents in other paramilitary groups who oppose the 'Peace Process'.
Saor Eire	'Free Ireland' has appeared intermittently since 1931.
Ulster Defence Association	The Loyalist paramilitary UDA was created in 1971 as a militant mass movement to support Unionism.
Ulster Freedom Fighters	The Loyalist UFF emerged from the Ulster Defence Association (below) in the early 1970s, often as a cover-name.
Ulster Volunteer Force	The Loyalist UVF was formed initially in 1912 but was reconstituted in 1966.

---

[3] *The Times* 2 April 2003 p 11.
[4] Source of listing: Terrorism Act 2000, Sch 2. For descriptions, see the reports of the Independent Monitoring Commission, acting under the Northern Ireland (Monitoring Commission etc) Act 2003.

It was admitted during debates on the 2000 Act that some of the foregoing are at any 2.05 one time dormant but that it was felt necessary to continue proscription so as to deny the use of historically resonant titles to dissidents.[5] Titles of organizations can indeed become both emotive and tricky in the Irish context. For example, the government hoped that the title, the 'Irish Republican Army', as it appears in Sch 2, should be considered sufficiently all-purpose to cover the Provisional IRA, the Official IRA, the Real IRA, and the Continuity IRA (also listed for the sake of comprehensive cover as the Continuity Army Council). In favour of the government's interpretation appears to be s 3(1)(b), by which an organization is proscribed if it operates under the same name as an organization listed in that Schedule. The interpretation was tested on charges of membership of the Real IRA and rejected by the Belfast Crown Court in *R v Mullen, Dillon, Murphy and O'Connor*; that judgment was quickly reversed in *R v Z* by the Northern Ireland Court of Appeal and House of Lords.[6]

There are two main grounds for supporting the House of Lords' decision. The first is 2.06 statutory interpretation. It was the settled intention of Parliament to cover all manifestations of Irish Republican paramilitary groups which chose to adopt a title resonating with the historical body, the Irish Republican Army—to cover 'the whole gambit'.[7] Furthermore, Parliament found it very convenient to express its intention in this global way since it thereby avoided easy circumvention both by the invention of new flags of convenience—'New IRA' or 'True IRA'—or by outlaw groups resorting to rebranding. Lords Bingham and Woolf treated s 3(1)(a) (an organization listed in Sch 2) and s 3(1)(b) as a composite whole (it being sufficient that a part or emanation of the group does in any event operate under the name of a scheduled organization). Lords Rodger, Carswell, and Brown treated paragraphs (a) and (b) of s 3(1) as mutually exclusive, whereby, if the Real IRA were not comprised within the name 'the IRA' and thus scheduled, they could not be said to be operating under 'the same name'. Paragraph (b) was seen as dealing only with an organization operating under an identical name to a listed group but asserting that it was independent. As for these different approaches, under Lord Bingham's view, it would seem that no organization at present falls directly under the term 'Irish Republican Army' in s 3(1)(a), but all those mentioned are within s 3(1)(b). Under Lord Brown's view, all must fall within s 3(1)(a). His view is based on an uncomfortably narrow reading of the phrase, 'the same name', in s 3(1)(b): 'Section 3(1)(b) seems to me intended and apt to cover only those cases where an organization operates under an identical name to that of an organization listed in Sch 2—say, for example, The Irish National Liberation Army—but asserts that it is completely independent of the listed organization.'[8] One should have thought that any organization using an identical name must fall within s 3(1)(a) (incidentally implying that any number of organizations can be affected—the single includes the plural according to the Interpretation Act 1978, s 6(c)). After all, the INLA is hardly in a position to register a trade mark and claim exclusivity over and above any upstarts. How are we to know when

---

[5] Hansard HC Standing Committee D, col 76 (25 January 2000), Adam Ingram.
[6] [2004] NICC 15, [2004] NICA 23, [2005] UKHL 35. See Walker, C., 'Commentary' [2005] *Criminal Law Review* 985; Bennion, F., 'Is the Real IRA a proscribed organization?' (2004) 168 *Justice of the Peace* 472, 'The Real IRA is proscribed after all' (2004) 168 *Justice of the Peace* 694.
[7] Hansard HC Standing Committee D (25 January 2000), Adam Ingram.
[8] [2005] UKHL 35 at para 68.

the 'genuine' INLA is involved? This problem in Lord Brown's interpretation is exacerbated in the case of Al-Qa'ida, a name which often represents a set of strategies and viewpoints and which can be assumed as a *nom de guerre* by whomsoever is stirred. All become Al-Qa'ida for legal purposes, whether Saudi compatriots headed by Osama bin Laden or autonomous bombers from Leeds. The views of Lord Bingham therefore seem more fitting, and one could argue that 'the same' does not mean 'identical' and that it is sufficient that the name mentioned in the proscribed list is exactly reproduced for all relevant groups, even if it does not comprise the full extent of the name actually used by those groups, a degree of flexibility which tessellates with ideas expressed to be behind the legislative intention.

2.07   Next, the Real IRA is specifically mentioned in UK legislation, not in the Terrorism Act 2000 but in the Northern Ireland (Sentences) Act 1998 (Specified Organisations) Order 1998.[9] The Sentences Act provides for the accelerated release of prisoners serving sentences of imprisonment for terrorist offences who fulfil various conditions, including the disavowal of violence and of support for any 'specified' organization. A specified organization is not here the same as a proscribed organization. By s 3(8) of the Sentences Act, a specified organization is defined as (a) concerned in terrorism connected with the affairs of Northern Ireland, or in promoting or encouraging it, and (b) has not established or is not maintaining a complete and unequivocal ceasefire. A listing in the Sentences Act does not undermine the foregoing assertions in relation to the 'global family' meaning of proscription under the Terrorism Act for the following reasons. The whole purpose of the Northern Ireland (Sentences) Act is to discern which factions are on ceasefire. It was recognized that the definition of 'proscribed' organization would not be fit for purpose on its own, hence the need for additional legislation. Thus, the legislative purpose is different and so the listings are different. The fact that some groups are not specified does not mean that the law distinguishes 'good' from 'bad' terrorists,[10] since groups such as the Irish Republican Army remain proscribed and otherwise criminalized. Thus, an absence of specification does not imply that proscription should fall away.

3. Proscribed groups—Other domestic

2.08   Beyond the Irish context, it was announced during the passage of the Terrorism Bill that there were no plans to proscribe any (non-Irish) domestic groups.[11] Aside from the sporadic activities of Welsh and Scottish nationalists,[12] animal rights and environmental militants were thought to be possible candidates for proscription, but they do not possess the sophistication, threat to persons, or overall strength to warrant suppression. In a paper in 2001, *Animal Rights Extremism*, the Home Office expressed itself as unpersuaded that proscription would assist[13] and recommended alternatives, including private law injunctions.[14]

---

[9] See now Northern Ireland (Sentences) Act 1998 (Specified Organisations) Order 2008, SI 2008/1975.
[10] Hansard HC vol 317, col 885 (2 September 1998), William Ross.
[11] Hansard HC vol 341, col 227 (14 December 1999), Charles Clarke.
[12] The Scottish National Liberation Army sent hoax bombs to 16 targets in 2002: *The Times* 4 March 2002 p 6. Wayne Cook and Steven Robinson were convicted of threats to kill English people (*The Times* 26 January 2008 p 2). The police's view was that 'these men are terrorists' (*Manchester Evening News* 18 January 2008 p 2), but terrorism legislation was not invoked.
[13] (London) para 3.7.5.
[14] *Ibid* para 3.4.2.

There are two exceptions to this general forbearance. First, two neo-Nazis have been arrested and convicted under anti-terrorism laws in 2008.[15] These reactions appear attractive in creating symmetry with the *jihadis*, but such individuals generally lack the sophistication, the scale, and the international complexities to make proportionate the application of anti-terrorism laws. Secondly, proscription has been applied under the Terrorism Act 2006 (discussed below) to two domestically based 'glorifiers' of *jihadi* terrorism.

4. Proscribed groups—Foreign

Reflecting warnings about the growing threat of international terrorism,[16] s 3 can also apply to groups primarily based abroad. In addition, this extension allows a more positive response to pressure from foreign governments to take action against émigré groups. It also offers an alternative to deportation which cannot be secured because of fears of torture[17] even when claims of terrorists to asylum can be rejected.[18] Extra-territorial focus was presaged first by the Criminal Justice (Terrorism and Conspiracy) Act 1998, under which UK authorities were given jurisdiction over acts of conspiracy and incitement in the United Kingdom relating to offences committed or intended to be committed abroad. Extradition law has also developed to allow for account to be taken of the impact of dissidents on friendly foreign states.[19]   2.09

Consequently, the Terrorism Act 2000, Pt II, can apply to foreign groups concerned in terrorism, and, by the Terrorism Act 2000 (Proscribed Organisations) (Amendment) Order 2001,[20] twenty-one organizations were listed when the Act came into force. This list has continued to grow, driven mainly by the threat of *jihadi* groups, but including also some nationalist movements and even a Marxist group (November 17). The list continues to grow (to forty-three) mainly because of conflicts in Afghanistan and Iraq.   2.10

Table 2.2 Proscription of international organizations[21]

Al-Qa'ida	'The Base' aims to unite Muslims, eliminate Western presence in the Middle East, and to replace Arab governments with a Caliphate. Usama bin Ladin, is the figurehead. The movement is responsible for the East African embassy bombings in 1998 and the September 11 2001 attacks, and had activities in the United Kingdom.[22] After the invasion of Afghanistan, it has operated more as a dispersed ideological vanguard.

---

[15] See Martyn Gilleard: *The Times* 26 June 2008 p 20; Nathan Worrell: *Grimsby Evening Telegraph* 13 December 2008 pp 1, 2, 3.

[16] Home Office and Northern Ireland Office, *Legislation against Terrorism* (Cm 4178, London, 1998) paras 4.14, 4.16.

[17] *Chahal v United Kingdom*, App no 22414/93, 1996-V.

[18] *T v Secretary of State for the Home Department* [1996] AC 742; *Al Fawwaz v Governor of Brixton Prison* [2001] UKHL 69.

[19] *Secretary of State for the Home Department v Rehman* [2001] 1 UKHL 47.

[20] SI 2001/1261.

[21] See Terrorism Act 2000 (Proscribed Organisations) (Amendment) Orders 2001–08, SI 2001/1261; SI 2002/2724; SI 2005/2892; SI 2006/1919; SI 2006/2016; SI 2007/2184, SI 2008/1931. Explanations are given at Hansard HC vol 391, col 875 (30 October 2002); vol 437, col 466 (13 October 2005) (covering 15 organizations); vol 462, col 1369 (10 July 2007); vol 479, col 193 (15 July 2008).

[22] See Home Office, *Pursue, Prevent, Protect, Prepare: The United Kingdom's Strategy for Countering International Terrorism* (Cm 7547, London, 2009) para 2.01.

Table 2.2 (Continued) Proscription of international organizations

Abu Nidal Organisation	This Palestinian group split from the PLO in 1974. Based variously in Libya, and Iraq, it has also spawned the Fatah Revolutionary Council.
Abu Sayyaf Group	The Abu Sayyaf Group ('Bearer of the Sword') has been active in the Mindanao, where it seeks an autonomous Islamic state. It has engaged in kidnapping and murder of foreign tourists.
Al-Ittihad Al-Islamia	The 'Islamic Union' is based in Somalia. The group is accused of bomb attacks as well as kidnapping of relief workers in 1998.
Al-Gama'at al-Islamiya	The Egyptian Islamic Group (GI) has been active since the late 1970s when it split from the EIJ (below). It conducts attacks on Egyptian and Western targets such as tourists (fifty-eight, including six British citizens, were killed in Luxor in 1997).
Ansar Al-Islam	The 'Supporters or Partisans of Islam' is a Kurdish Sunni Islamist group, based in northern Iraq.
Ansar Al-Sunna	Jamaat Ansar al-Sunna or Group of the Protectors of the Sunna is an Islamist group in Iraq.
Armed Islamic Group (Groupe Islamique Armée)	The GIA seeks to overthrow the Algerian regime and replace it with an Islamist state. The GIA began in early 1992 after the government prevented the election of the Islamic Salvation Front (FIS).
Asbat Al-Ansar	Asbat al-Ansar ('the League of the Partisans') consists of Sunni Islamists based in southern Lebanon.
Babbar Khalsa	The group fights for the liberation of Khalistan, the Sikh homeland in Punjab Province, which declared its independence in 1987. External attacks culminated in the bombing of Air India Flight 182 in 1985.
Baluchistan Liberation Army	The organization is dedicated to fighting for the independence of Baluchistan, currently split between Iran, Pakistan, and Afghanistan.
Basque Homeland & Liberty (Euskadi ta Askatasuna)	ETA was founded in 1959 to fight for an independent homeland principally in Spain's Basque region. There have been links through Irish Republican paramilitaries.
Egyptian Islamic Jihad	The group has existed since 1973 and concentrates on armed attacks against Egyptian officials but also is alleged to have bombed the US embassies in Dar es Salaam and Nairobi in August 1998.
Groupe Islamique Combattant Marocain	The Moroccan Islamic Combatant Group (Groupe Islamique Combattant Marocain, or GICM) is an Islamist group operating in North Africa. Activities include an attack in Casablanca in 2003 and involvement in the Madrid bombing of 2004.
HAMAS-Izz al-Din al-Qassem Brigades	Various groupings coalesced in the late 1980s to pursue the goal of establishing an Islamic Palestinian state. HAMAS is the acronym for Harakat al-Muqawama al-Islamiyya or Islamic Resistance Movement. The Izz el-Din al-Qassam (IDQ) Brigades are its military wing. HAMAS controls Gaza.
Harakat ul Mujahideen (HK)	HK is a group based in Pakistan and operating primarily in Kashmir, having formed in 1993 (as Harakat ul-Ansar). Its activities have been directed against the Indian security forces, civilians, and Western tourists.
Harakat-ul-Jihad-ul-Islami	The aim of HUJI is to achieve accession of Kashmir to Pakistan. HUJI has targeted Indian security positions in Kashmir and in India.
Harakat-ul-Jihad-ul-Islami (Bangladesh)	HUJI-B seeks the creation of an Islamist regime in Bangladesh. Three persons were convicted in 2008 of attempting to kill a British diplomat, Anwar Choudhury, in 2004.
Harakat-ul-Mujahideen/Alami	The aim of HuM/A seeks to establish a Caliphate based on *Sharia* law, and to incorporate Kashmir within Pakistan.
Hezb-e Islami Gulbuddin	The Hezb-e-Islami Gulbuddin is a fundamentalist faction of Afghanistan's Hezbi Islami Party. It was founded in 1977 by Gulbuddin Hekmatyar.
Hizballah Military Wing	Hizballah (The Party of God') is the Lebanese-based Islamist movement founded after the Israeli invasion in 1982. Since Hizballah is a major political party in Lebanon, proscription is confined to its military wing, including the Jihad Council and the Hizballah External Security Organization. Only the latter was listed up to 2008.

Table 2.2 (Continued) Proscription of international organizations

International Sikh Youth Federation	Also involved in the Khalistan conflict and drawing support from overseas Sikh communities. ISYF support is claimed to be spread across the UK.
Islamic Army of Aden	The group fights secularism in Yemen and other Arab countries. This has involved the formation of the Aden-Abyan Islamic Army and attacks on Western tourists.
Islamic Jihad Union	The Islamic Jihad Movement in Palestine (Harakat al-Jihād al-Islāmi fi Filastīn) is a Palestinian group. The PIJ's armed wing, the Al-Quds brigades, has claimed responsibility for numerous attacks in Israel.
Islamic Movement of Uzbekistan	The Islamic Movement of Uzbekistan (IMU), also known as the Islamic Movement of Turkestan (IMT) and the Islamic Party of Turkestan (IPT) aims to establish an Islamic State. The IMU kidnapped four US citizens in August 2000 and attempted to bomb embassies in 2004.
Jaish e Mohammed	The 'Army of Mohammed' is an Islamist group based in Pakistan and is concerned with attacks in Kashmir.
Jamaat ul-Furquan	The aim of JuF is to unite Kashmir with Pakistan and to establish a radical Islamist state in Pakistan.
Jammat-ul Mujahideen Bangladesh	The group has claimed responsibility for numerous fatal bomb attacks across Bangladesh in recent years, including suicide bomb attacks in 2005.
Jemaah Islamiyah	The 'Islamic Group' or 'Islamic Community' is based in South-east Asia and seeks to establish an Islamic State. It has also attacked Western targets, through bombings at Bali in 2002 (which killed twenty-four British tourists), the Marriott Hotel, Jakarta and then at the stock exchange in 2003, the Australian embassy in 2004, and a series of suicide bombings in Bali in 2005.
Jundallah	Jundallah ('Army of God') is an Islamist organization based in Waziristan, Pakistan and in Iran's Sistan and Baluchistan Province. The group seeks an independent Baluchistan under a Sunni Islamist government.
Khuddam ul-Islam	The aim of KuI is to unite Kashmir with Pakistan and to establish a radical Islamist state in Pakistan.
Kurdistan Workers' Party (Partiya Karkeren Kurdistan)	The PKK was founded in 1974 and seeks an independent Kurdish state in south-eastern Turkey. It engaged in armed attacks from 1984 until after the capture of its leader, Abdullah Öçalan, following which a ceasefire was called in 1999. The names Kongra Gele Kurdistan and KADEK are to be treated as other names for the group according to a further order in 2006.
Lashkar e Tayyaba	This Pakistani-based group (the 'Army of the Righteous') supports the decoupling of Kashmir from India. It also operates as Jama'at ud Da'wa.
Lashkar-e Jhangvi	Lashkar i Jhangvi (Army of Jhang) is a Sunni group in Pakistan. It attacked US oil workers in 1997, attempted to kill Pakistani Prime Minister Nawaz Sharif in 1999, and kidnapped and killed US journalist Daniel Pearl in January 2002. It is allied to the Taliban in Afghanistan.
Liberation Tigers of Tamil Eelam	The LTTE was founded in 1972 and is the most powerful group in Sri Lanka fighting for a distinct Tamil state. Armed conflict began in 1983.
Libyan Islamic Fighting Group	The LIFG opposes the regime of al-Qadhafi and aims to establish an Islamic state in Libya. Its attempted assassination in 1996 was allegedly part funded by the UK which has allowed a safe haven for the group.
Palestinian Islamic Jihad—Shaqaqi	A variety of Shia groups formed in the 1970s and based in the Gaza Strip committed to the creation of an Islamic Palestinian state and the destruction of Israel. Like HESO, PIJ is pro-Iranian.
Revolutionary Peoples' Liberation Party - Front	Te DHKP-C (Devrimci Halk Kurtulus Partisi-Cephesi) is a Marxist Turkish group which has origins going back to the 1970s whose operations have been mainly confined to Turkish targets in Turkey. The DHKP-C had an office in London which engaged in overt political activity.
Salafist Group for Call and Combat	The GSPC (Groupe Salafiste pour la Prédication et le Combat—also called the Hassan Hattab faction) emerged from the GIA in 1998, aims to create an Islamic state in Algeria.
Sipah-e Sahaba Pakistan	Sipah-e Sahaba Pakistan (renamed now as Millat-E Islami Pakistan) is a Wahabi group which targets the minority Shia Muslims in Pakistan. Lashkar i Jhangvi is a splinter group.

Table 2.2 (Continued) Proscription of international organizations

Tehrik Nefaz-e Shari'at Muhammadi.	Tehrik Nefaz-e Shari'at Muhammadi regularly attacks Coalition and Afghan government forces in Afghanistan and provides direct support to Al-Qa'ida and the Taliban.
Teyrebaz Azadiye Kurdistan	TAK is a Kurdish group which is suspected of killing UK nationals in a July 2005 minibus bombing in Kusadasi, Turkey.
17 November Revolutionary Organisation	A Marxist group established in 1975 in Greece and opposing the government and Western interests. In June 2000, N17 murdered Brigadier Stephen Saunders, the British Defence Attaché, which triggered several arrests.

2.11   There has been one de-proscription order—concerning the Mujaheddin e Khalq, which was founded in 1965 and became the largest and most active armed Iranian dissident group. It is also known as the People's Mujahedin of Iran ('PMOI'). It renounced violence in 2003, and, following litigation described below, was de-listed in 2008.[23]

2.12   The factors which originally shaped this list were enumerated by Lord Bassam:[24]

First, we would have to consider carefully the nature and scale of the group's activities; secondly, we would have to look at the specific threat that it posed to the United Kingdom and our citizens abroad, which is clearly a very important consideration, as well as the extent of its presence in this country. . . . Thirdly, we would also have to consider our responsibility to support other members of the international community in the global fight against terrorism.

They were then tabulated in the Home Office press release of 28 February 2001 which accompanied the first Order under the Act as follows:

(a) The nature and scale of an organisation's activities.
(b) The specific threat that it poses to the United Kingdom.
(c) The specific threat that it poses to British nationals overseas.
(d) The extent of the organisation's presence in the United Kingdom.
(e) The need to support other members of the international community in the global fight against terrorism.

The last factor allows a very wide discretion, but the UN Convention for the Suppression of Terrorist Bombings of 1997[25] demands under Art 15 that states take all practicable measures to prevent and counter terrorist preparations, including measures to prohibit in their territories illegal activities of persons, groups, and organizations that encourage, instigate, organize, knowingly finance, or engage in the perpetration of specified terrorist offences. This requirement is backed by UN Security Resolution 1373 of 28 September 2001: states are required by Art 2 to '(c) Deny safe haven to those who finance, plan, support, or commit terrorist acts, or provide safe havens; (d) Prevent those who finance, plan, facilitate or commit terrorist acts from using their respective territories for those purposes against other States or their citizens . . . .'. Nevertheless, it remains controversial that the cosmopolitan protection afforded to allies which can be relied upon to be liberal and democratic in responding to opposition and where the use of

---

[23] SI 2008/1645. See Hansard HC vol 478, col 98 (23 June 2008).
[24] Hansard HL vol 613, col 252 (16 May 2000).
[25] A/RES/52/164, Cm 4662, London, 1997.

violence for political ends may be said to be 'specious',[26] should equally benefit the 'axis of evil'.[27]

Another drawback with this policy is its apparent partiality, as the UK government attempts to turn itself into the arbiter between 'terrorist' and 'freedom fighter' and tries to keep pace with the fluidity of factions.[28] Examples of unproscribed groups which seem to fit the 'Bassam' criteria, include:

2.13

Table 2.3 International organizations escaping proscription

Al-Shabab	'The Youth' is a Somali group, arising after the removal of the Union of Islamic Courts in 2006 and responsible for the killing of journalist Kate Peyton in 2005 and two British teachers in 2008.
Fuerzas Armadas Revolucionarias de Colombia (FARC)	The Revolutionary Armed Forces of Colombia were formed in 1964 as the military wing of the Communist Party. James Monaghan, Niall Connolly, and Martin McCauley were convicted in 2004 for training FARC personnel in IRA bomb-making techniques. They returned to Ireland in 2005 in breach of bail.
Jaish al-Mahdi	The Mahdi Army is the principal Iraqi Shia militia, created by Muqtada al-Sadr in 2003. It has been active in Basra in attacks against British armed forces.

These difficulties reinforce Lord Carlile's assessment that the police remain 'equivocal' about the power of proscription.[29] One reason for scepticism concerns the very chimeral nature of some international groups. Nevertheless, the listings are ever widening, perhaps also serving the interests of healthy trade relations and smooth diplomacy.

5. Mechanisms and procedures of proscription within the anti-terrorism legislation

The Terrorism Act 2000 applies a steadfastly executive approach to the activation of proscription. By s 3(3), the Secretary of State may by order (a) add an organization to Sch 2; (b) remove an organization from that schedule; (c) amend that schedule in some other way (such as in relation to notes within it which may be used to explain or qualify the effects of proscription—this is done in relation to the 'Orange Volunteers'. Furthermore, the criteria remain subjectively worded—by s 3(4), orders can be made against a group if 'he believes that it is concerned in terrorism', a belief which may be derived under s 3(5) if an organization (a) commits or participates in acts of terrorism; (b) prepares for terrorism; (c) promotes or encourages terrorism; or (d) is otherwise concerned in terrorism. While subjective on paper, in *Lord Alton of Liverpool & others (In the Matter of The People's Mojahadeen Organisation of Iran) v Secretary of State for the Home Department* (hereinafter the '*Alton* case'),[30] the test in s 3(4) has been interpreted as

2.14

---

[26] *Inquiry into Legislation against Terrorism* (Cm 3420, London, 1996) vol II p 4.

[27] <http://georgewbush-whitehouse.archives.gov/news/releases/2002/01/20020129-11.html>, 2001.

[28] These difficulties were predicted in *Inquiry into Legislation against Terrorism* (Cm 3240, London, 1996) para 4.16.

[29] *Report on the Operation in 2001 of the Terrorism Act 2000* (2002) para 2.2; *Report on the Operation in 2002 and 2003 of the Terrorism Act 2000* (Home Office, 2004) para 29.

[30] PC/02/2006, 30 November 2007 at paras 67, 68; *Secretary of State for the Home Department v Lord Alton of Liverpool* [2008] EWCA Civ 443 at para 22.

applying in two stages. The first stage is whether the Secretary of State has an honest belief on reasonable grounds to satisfy the statutory test in s 3(4); then comes a second stage as to whether discretion should be used to apply proscription on policy grounds. An honest belief on reasonable grounds can only be formed through materials known to the decision-maker—the decision is personal and cannot be delegated.[31] That case also demanded 'current, active steps' by way of proof of being 'concerned in' terrorism; the mere contemplation of the possibility of some future violence is not enough.[32] Thus, the Court of Appeal distinguished between a group that has temporarily ceased terrorism 'for tactical reasons' with one that has decided to move away from violence, 'even if the possibility exists that it might decide to revert to terrorism in the future'.[33]

2.15 Once an order has been made, there is no statutory requirement that it be reviewed or renewed from time to time, though the Home Secretary has reassured that 'We do not put their names in a filing cabinet and forget about them'.[34] Proscription orders for international groups are kept under rolling review by a working group within government which includes the Foreign and Commonwealth Office.[35] The *Alton* case considered that regular review is a requirement of administrative law.[36]

2.16 Reflecting the worries caused by the title of the Real IRA, s 22 of the Terrorism Act 2006 inserts for the sake of 'important flexibility'[37] further powers into s 3(6), as a result of which where the Secretary of State believes that an organization listed in Sch 2 is operating wholly or partly under a name that is not specified in that Schedule but is for all practical purposes the same as an organization so listed, he may, by order, provide that the name that is not specified in that schedule is to be treated as another name for the listed organization. Adding a new name to the list may short-circuit the demands of the prosecution, but, of course, if it can be shown that the new activities are really committed under an alias on behalf of a proscribed organization, then a prosecution under that name could still be mounted.[38] An important difference between these adaptation orders and original proscription orders under s 3(3) is that the negative procedure is used for orders relating to the former and the affirmative procedure for the latter under s 123 of the Terrorism Act 2000. This power has been applied to add two aliases of the PKK and one for the Lashkar e Tayyabi[39]

2.17 While the Secretary of State retains the whip-hand, concern for the rights of those subjected to orders resulted in two procedures for challenge within the 2000 Act. One envisages an application to the Secretary of State for the setting aside of an order. If refused (and no application has ever been granted),[40] the second step is an application

---

[31] *Ibid* at para 130.

[32] *Ibid* at paras 124, 128.

[33] *Secretary of State for the Home Department v Lord Alton of Liverpool* [2008] EWCA Civ 443 at para 38.

[34] HC Standing Committee D, col 65 (18 January 2000), Charles Clarke.

[35] Lord Carlile, *Report on the Operation in 2007 of the Terrorism Act 2000* (Home Office, London, 2008) para 42.

[36] PC/02/2006, 30 November 2007 at para 73.

[37] Hansard HL vol 676, col 1144 (13 December 2005), Baroness Scotland.

[38] See Jones, A., Bowers, R, and Lodge, H.D., *The Terrorism Act 2006* (Oxford University Press, Oxford, 2006) para 6.40.

[39] Proscribed Organisations (Name Changes) Orders, SI 2006/1919 and SI 2009/578.

[40] The latest was an application by the LTTE: Lord Carlile, *Report on the Operation in 2007 of the Terrorism Act 2000* (Home Office, London, 2008) para 45.

for review by the Proscribed Organisations Appeal Commission ('POAC'). Direct application to POAC is not allowed—the government wishes to consider the matter first and also to save possible expense.[41] As well as contesting the initial order for proscription, the procedures may also be used to challenge the continuing propriety of an order.[42]

Applications to the Secretary of State for deproscription arise under s 4(1). The applicant may be either the proscribed organization or any person affected by the proscription order. The phrase, 'person affected', was interpreted in *R v Broadcasting Standards Commission, ex parte British Broadcasting Corporation*[43] to allow a complaint about an unwarranted infringement of the privacy of a body corporate on its own behalf arising from its employees being secretly filmed. Thus, one group member may bring an action under s 4 even if others (such as leaders) are more drastically affected. An action by a group leader would most evidently fall within s 4(1),[44] but a minority faction in a group may also conceivably bring an application, even where the majority favour a new group and prefer the old group to remain banned. The only successful deproscription application (after appeal), the *Alton* case,[45] was in the name of the Liberal Party peer, Lord Alton, joined by eighteen other members of the House of Lords (including a former Lord of Appeal in Ordinary) and sixteen members of the House of Commons, none of whom claimed to be a member of the PMOI. Their status as 'persons affected' derived simply from their wish to support the PMOI and was not contested.[46] While the great and the good were evidently sincere, such indulgence could allow busybodies to meddle, with attendant dangers of ill-argued or inappropriate disputes. The phrase has 'a wide and ill-defined catchment',[47] but it should not be applied with abandon.

2.18

Regulations relating to these proceedings must be made under s 4(3) and (4) and must include the giving of reasons. The Proscribed Organisations (Applications for Deproscription) Regulations 2001[48] require an application to be made in writing and with a statement of the grounds at any time after the organization in question has been proscribed (reg 3). Where the application is being made by the organization, the application must also state under reg 4 the name and address of the person submitting the application and the position which he holds in the organization or his authority to act on behalf of the organization. Where the application is made by a person affected by the organization's proscription, the application must detail, under reg 5, the manner in which the applicant is affected. By reg 8, the Secretary of State shall determine an application within a period of ninety days from (but excluding) the day on which he receives the application. Where the Secretary of State refuses an application, he shall under reg 9 immediately in writing inform the applicant.

2.19

---

[41] Hansard HL vol 613, col 262 (16 May 2000), Lord Bassam.

[42] *Ibid* at col 261.

[43] [2000] 3 WLR 1327.

[44] See *R v Broadcasting Complaints Commission, ex p Owen* [1985] 1 QB 1153.

[45] PC/02/2006, 30 November 2007. An application by the LTTE was refused in 2007: Lord Carlile, *Report on the Operation in 2007 of the Terrorism Act 2000* (Home Office, London, 2008) para 45.

[46] *Ibid* at para 20.

[47] *Huntingdon Life Sciences Group plc and others v Stop Huntingdon Animal Cruelty* [2007] EWHC 522 (QB) at para 43 per Holland J regarding the Civil Procedure Rules Pt 19.6.

[48] SI 2001/107, as amended by the Proscribed Organisations (Applications for Deproscription etc) Regulations 2006, SI 2006/2299.

2.20   The POAC is established under s 5 and is modelled on the Special Immigration Appeals Commission Act 1997, as suggested by the Lloyd Report.[49] By s 5(3), the POAC shall allow an appeal against a refusal to deproscribe if it considers that the decision to refuse was 'flawed when considered in the light of the principles applicable on an application for judicial review', a phrase which is meant to avoid review of the factual merits.[50] Where an order is made in favour of an applicant, the Secretary of State shall as soon as is reasonably practicable (a) lay before Parliament the draft of an order under s 3(3)(b) removing the organization from the list in Sch 2 or (b) make an order removing the organization from the list in that schedule. By s 9 and the Proscribed Organisations Appeal Commission (Human Rights Act Proceedings) Rules 2001,[51] the POAC becomes the appropriate tribunal for the purposes of s 7 of the Human Rights Act 1998, where such proceedings relate to a refusal by the Secretary of State to deproscribe an organization.

2.21   The constitution and procedures of the POAC are related in Sch 3 and in the supplementary Proscribed Organisations Appeal Commission (Procedure) Rules 2007.[52] By Sch 3 para 1, appointments shall be made by the Lord Chancellor. Given that members 'shall hold and vacate office in accordance with the terms of his appointment', there is no guarantee of statutory independence which may compromise the ability of the POAC to satisfy Art 6 of the European Convention.[53] Amongst the other terms and conditions, it is specified that each POAC panel must be three strong and must include at least one person who holds or has held high judicial office (within the meaning of the Appellate Jurisdiction Act 1876). The membership in 2008 consisted of two judicial members, Sir Harry Ognall (chair) and Sir Charles Mantell, plus four other legal members and five lay members. Under the supplementary r 6, an appeal must be lodged within forty-two days. By para 5, the Lord Chancellor shall make procedure rules, including by providing for proceedings before the Commission to be determined without an oral hearing in specified circumstances, for determining the burden of proof and admissibility of evidence, and for securing that information, including reasons for decisions,[54] is not disclosed contrary to the public interest. Though legal representation is to be allowed, the procedure rules may provide for full particulars to be withheld from the organization or applicant concerned and from any representative or even to enable the Commission to exclude persons (including representatives) from all or part of proceedings. Where proceedings are brought by an organization before the POAC, it may designate an individual to conduct those proceedings under para 6, so as to avoid rival factions causing duplication or confusion. In addition, under para 7, the relevant law officer may appoint a lawyer—a 'special advocate'—to represent the interests of an organization or other applicant.[55] No matter what is withheld from the appellant and his legal representative, the POAC and special advocate will be provided under supplementary rules 12 and 14 by the Secretary of State with a summary of the facts relating to the decision being

---

[49] *Inquiry into Legislation against Terrorism* (Cm 3420, London, 1996) para 13.32.
[50] See *Council of Civil Service Unions v Minister for the Civil Service* [1985] AC 374.
[51] SI 2001/127.
[52] SI 2007/1286 as amended by SI 2007/3377.
[53] See *Khan v United Kingdom*, App no 35394/97, 2000-V; *Millar v Dickson* [2001] UKPC D4.
[54] See Terrorism Act 2006, s 22(11).
[55] It is reported that they work vigorously in practice: Lord Carlile, *Report on the Operation in 2005 of the Terrorism Act 2000* (Home Office, London, 2006) para 55.

appealed against and the reasons for that decision, the grounds on which he opposes the appeal, and a statement of the evidence which he relies upon in support of those grounds. Surreptitious electronic surveillance is likely to be an important source of evidence, and it can exceptionally be led before the POAC according to the Regulation of Investigatory Powers Act 2000, s 18 but must not be disclosed to the applicant, the organization, or their representatives. Under supplementary r 25, the POAC may receive other evidence that would not be admissible in a court of law.

Section 6 of the Terrorism Act 2000 preserves a right of further appeal on a question of law to (depending on jurisdiction) the Court of Appeal, the Court of Session, or the Court of Appeal in Northern Ireland. An appeal may be brought only with the permission of the POAC or the appeal court.[56]   **2.22**

If an appeal under s 5 is successful, then by s 7 of the 2000 Act, any conviction which has been sustained in relation to activity which took place on or after the date of the refusal to deproscribe against which the appeal under s 5 was brought, the person affected may without leave bring an appeal which shall be granted and compensation shall be payable under s 133(5) of the Criminal Justice Act 1988.   **2.23**

The establishment of the POAC under s 5 of the Terrorism Act 2000 is in principle desirable and offers some antidote to executive dominance. However, the system suffers from considerable weaknesses.   **2.24**

First, it reflects the unwillingness to put sensitive security evidence before the courts[57] and thereby perpetrates the unfairness inherent in secret hearings which cannot necessarily be overcome by the device of special advocate.[58] Lord Carlile has suggested that the quality of review could improve were the POAC to be provided with a security-cleared case assistant.[59]   **2.25**

Next, though the wide interpretation given to 'person affected' has been helpful to encourage challenges, it will involve considerable courage to take a stance as a supporter and risk being labelled as a sympathizer or even a terrorist. Not surprisingly, few have been mounted. Aside from PMOI, notices of appeal have been lodged but not pursued by Lashkar e Tayyaba and the International Sikh Youth Federation. Immunity is granted by s 10 from criminal proceedings for an offence under any of ss 11 to 13, 15 to 19, and 56 of the 2000 Act arising from any submissions in an application. But this half-hearted concession does not relate to other offences or rule out other retribution such as immigration proceedings:[60]   **2.26**

The clause does not provide general immunity, and it would be wrong to do so. If, for instance, it emerged during proceedings that an individual had been involved in a bombing attack or had incited an act of terrorism abroad, immunity in respect of criminal proceedings would not apply. That strikes the right balance. Offences involving weapons, articles, information and so on are omitted from the immunity provided in the clause because they do not relate directly to proscription.

---

[56] r 30. See further Court of Appeal (Appeals from Proscribed Organisations Appeal Commission) Rules 2002, SI 2002/1843; Proscribed Organisations Appeal Commission (Procedure) (Amendment) Rules 2007, SI 2007/3377; Civil Procedure Rules Practice Direction 52 r 21.11.

[57] Hansard HC Standing Committee D, col 86 (25 January 2000), Charles Clarke.

[58] See *Secretary of State for the Home Department v MB* [2007] UKHL 46.

[59] Lord Carlile, *Report on the Operation in 2004 of the Terrorism Act 2000* (Home Office, London, 2005) para 47.

[60] Hansard HC Standing Committee D, col 111 (25 January 2000), Charles Clarke.

2.27 It would be preferable if the POAC took the role not only of appeal tribunal but also proactive review commission, so that all proscribed groups would undergo independent annual scrutiny.[61] There is overall scrutiny by Lord Carilile, the government's independent reviewer, but his focus is on the system rather than on every individual case. The Home Office review group's scrutiny is not public, not published and not independent, and the same might be said of the Joint Terrorism Analysis Centre.[62] The Independent Monitoring Commission comes close to performing this function, but for the Northern Ireland groups only.

2.28 Another problem with the POAC is that (contrary to the marginal note to s 5— 'Deproscription: appeal') it is confined to the principles of judicial review: s 5(3). Furthermore, under the rules of administrative law, POAC procedures will have to be exhausted before turning to the Divisional Court.[63] This point was sustained in *R (on the application of the Kurdistan Workers' Party and others) v Secretary of State for the Home Department; R (on the application of the People's Mojahedin Organisation of Iran and others) v Secretary of State for the Home Department; R (on the application of Ahmed) v Secretary of State for the Home Department*.[64] The PMOI, the Kurdistan Workers' Party ('PKK'), and Lashkar e Tayyabah ('LT') sought to challenge the lawfulness of their proscription by decision of the Secretary of State and the lawfulness of the regime of offences laid down by the 2000 Act. The grounds for challenge overlapped between the various organizations and were based on claims that the bans lacked due process and proportionality and breached rights to freedom of expression and association. The PMOI and LT had also applied to the POAC for review (no decision had by then been given), but the PKK had not challenged at POAC level. The challenges were viewed as arguable on the grounds of procedural fairness (since so many organizations had been outlawed together in one fell swoop, suggesting a lack of attention), on the grounds of proportionality (in the cases of the PMOI and LT) and on the ground of breach of rights. The High Court also took into account that the PMOI had successfully challenged its proscription in the USA on procedural grounds,[65] and it expressed some attraction for the idea that a group should be warned in advance before a ban comes into force.[66] However, all these arguable challenges failed on the threshold procedural ground that 'It is plain that Parliament, although not seeking to exclude the possibility of judicial review, intended the POAC to be the forum of first resort for the determination of claims relating to the lawfulness of proscription under the 2000 Act.'[67] The special features of the POAC—the secret hearings, the availability of intercept evidence, and its designation as the forum to hear arguments about the Human Rights Act 1998—provide a rationale for this viewpoint. Thus, there was 'no reason why POAC should be any less able than the Administrative Court to provide effective scrutiny of the matters under challenge'.[68] In fact, there are three advantages possessed by the Administrative Court. It can quash forthwith a proscription

---

[61] As suggested by the *Inquiry into Legislation against Terrorism* (Cm 3420, London, 1996) para 13.32.

[62] See <http://www.mi5.gov.uk/output/joint-terrorism-analysis-centre.html>.

[63] *R v Chief Constable of Merseyside, ex p Calveley* [1986] 2 WLR 144.

[64] [2002] EWHC 644 (Admin).

[65] This decision was later overturned: *People's Mojahedin Organisation of Iran v Department of State* (2003) 327 F.3d 1238.

[66] *Ibid* at para 65.

[67] *Ibid* at para 75 per Richards J.

[68] *Ibid* at para 84.

by statutory order (but probably not a listing under the original Sch 2), whereas the POAC can only demand a further deproscription order; but s 7 means that there is little practical impact. Secondly, POAC does not have the power to grant a declaration of incompatibility under s 4 of the Human Rights Act or to award damages under s 8. The POAC is also unable to entertain challenges to the proscription regime, such as the penalties under Part II (which formed part of the PKK's claim) or where there is no objection to the proscription of the group.

6. Standards of review in the POAC

Assuming the POAC is the prime remedy for those suffering a loss of rights because of proscription, will its standard of judicial review be sufficient to satisfy Arts 6, 10, and 13 of the European Convention? By and large, there is a long history of judicial deference to challenges to national security restrictions on organizations,[69] as demonstrated by cases such as *McEldowney v Forde* (a direct challenge)[70] and *R v Secretary of State for the Home Department, ex parte Brind* (concerning the more indirect issue of the broadcasting ban applied in 1988 to representatives of Irish paramilitaries).[71] Has the era of the Human Rights Act 1998 encouraged more adventure?   2.29

The first indication was negative. In *Re Williamson*,[72] the applicant, whose parents were killed in an IRA explosion, sought review of the decision in 1999 under the Northern Ireland (Sentences) Act 1998 by the Northern Ireland Secretary of State not to 'specify' the Provisional IRA as being connected with terrorism and not maintaining a complete ceasefire. The Secretary of State was satisfied that the Provisional IRA was involved in arms smuggling from the United States and a murder during 1999, and so the refusal thereafter to specify the Provisional IRA was claimed to be in breach of administrative law. The Northern Ireland Court of Appeal accepted that the Secretary of State possessed a high degree of knowledge and expertise and that decisions required political judgment as well as analytical skills. Lord Chief Justice Carswell concluded:[73]   2.30

> The area with which the 1998 Act is concerned is delicate and sensitive, and it is hardly surprising that strong views should be held on it or that decisions within this area should give rise to serious differences of opinion. It is part of the democratic process that such decisions should be taken by a minister responsible to Parliament, and so long as the manner in which they are taken is in accordance with the proper principles the courts should not and will not step outside their proper function of review.

---

[69] See Dyzenhaus, D., *The Constitution of Law* (Cambridge University Press, Cambridge, 2006).
[70] [1971] AC 632.
[71] [1991] AC 696. See further *Brind and McLaughlin v United Kingdom*, App nos 18714/91, 18759/91, (1994) 77-A DR 42; *Purcell v Ireland*, App no 15404/89, (1991) 70 DR 262; Weaver, R.I. and Bennett, G.J., 'The Northern Ireland broadcasting ban: some reflections on judicial review' (1989) 22 *Vanderbilt Journal of Transnational Law* 1119; Hogan, G., 'The demise of the Irish broadcasting ban' (1995) 1 *European Public Law* 69; Edgerton, G., 'Quelling the "Oxygen of Publicity"' (1996) 30 *Journal of Popular Culture* 115.
[72] [2000] NI 281.
[73] *Ibid* at p 304.

2.31　The second indication is the much more assertive outcome in the *Alton* case before the POAC. It was claimed that the PMOI had ceased all military activity and had handed over all weapons in 2003. While doubting the High Court's suggestion of a hearing before the order is made,[74] the POAC demanded regular Home Office reviews as a matter of law[75] and expressed itself as willing to apply 'intense scrutiny' to the material before it,[76] albeit that at the second stage of review of discretion based on national security and foreign policy considerations there would be a need for deference.[77] The Court of Appeal confirmed the need for an 'intense and detailed scrutiny'.[78] On the basis of that review (the open materials alone ran to fifteen volumes), the POAC concluded that the Home Secretary's decision had been flawed at the first stage and had confused current involvement in terrorism with 'a secret mental reservation' about eschewing violence for good as well as seeking explicit renunciation as an absolute requirement.[79] At the second stage, the POAC graciously accepted that the minister had not refused to deproscribe as a sop either to the Iraqis or the Iranians. But the Court of Appeal balanced this charity with some harsh words for the minister: 'It is a matter for comment and for regret that the decision-making process in this case has signally fallen short of the standards which our public law sets and which those affected by public decisions have come to expect.'[80] It is dangerous to rely on one case as being indicative of a wholesale change in judicial approaches in security cases, and another note of caution is that neither the fairness of the processes within the POAC nor the proportionality of proscription were seriously scrutinized. Nevertheless, the PMOI case displayed a willingness to grapple with the details of security matters almost without precedent in the field of proscription. Influential factors may include the Human Rights Act 1998[81] as well as the Terrorism Act 2000 itself, which offers a more open, less executive-dominated proscription process.

7. Proscription offences

2.32　There are three offences which complete Pt II of the Terrorism Act 2000, all closely derived from earlier legislation.[82] Within the context of these offences, proscription serves the purpose of short-circuiting the process of proof—the link is to the organization rather than to specific activities.[83]

2.33　By s 11(1) of the Terrorism Act 2000, a person commits an offence if he belongs or professes to belong to a proscribed organization. The term, 'profess' remains uncertain in its ambit according to Lord Bingham in *Sheldrake v Director of Public Prosecutions;*

---

[74] PC/02/2006, 30 November 2007 at para 63.
[75] *Ibid* at para 73.
[76] *Ibid* at para 113.
[77] *Ibid* at para 119.
[78] [2008] EWCA Civ 443 at para 43.
[79] *Ibid* at paras 338, 342.
[80] *Ibid* at para 57.
[81] See Gearty, C., '11 September 2001, counter-terrorism and the Human Rights Act 1998' (2005) 32 *Journal of Law & Society* 18.
[82] Prevention of Terrorism (Temporary Provisions) Act 1989, ss 2, 3; Northern Ireland (Emergency Provisions) Act 1996, ss 30, 31.
[83] See Home Office and Northern Ireland Office, *Legislation against Terrorism* (Cm 4178, London, 1998) para 4.6.

Attorney General's Reference (No 4 of 2002):[84] 'it is far from clear, in my opinion, whether it should be understood to denote an open affirmation of belonging to an organization or an acknowledgment of such belonging, and whether (in either case) such affirmation or acknowledgment, to fall within section 11(1), would have to be true.' However, the concerns about political stability and public order which provide foundations for this offence suggest that both affirmation and acknowledgment could be caught, and the truth of the assertion is beside the point since it is dangerous even to pretend that a proscribed organization is acceptable. At the same time, some expressions are uttered in circumstances of such frivolity or abstract debate that they should not be counted as an affirmation or acknowledgment at all, a possibility which was not, however, applied to the defendant in the *Reference* even though he was described as 'some latter day Walter Mitty or Billy Liar'.[85] Following the Terrorism Act 2006, s 17, where a person does anything outside the United Kingdom that would amount to an offence under s 11(1) if done in any part of it, liability will arise. The maximum penalties are: (a) on conviction on indictment, to imprisonment for a term not exceeding ten years, to a fine, or to both; or (b) on summary conviction, to imprisonment for a term not exceeding six months, to a fine not exceeding the statutory maximum, or to both.

A defence is provided in s 11(2) if it can be shown that membership has lapsed since the date of proscription. The prosecution must, of course, first establish membership,[86] but the defence is entirely for the defendant to prove on the balance of probabilities and s 118[87] does not apply here. In *R v Hundal; R v Dhaliwal*,[88] the relevant organization (the International Sikh Youth Federation, 'ISYF') was not proscribed in this country at the time that appellants joined it in Germany, but it was proscribed when they continued to undertake activities with the organization and arrived at Dover in 2002 with various ISYF paraphernalia. Both appellants admitted membership of the ISYF in Germany. Mr Hundal claimed that he had renounced membership in April 2001. Mr Dhaliwal claimed that he had not been a member of the ISYF since October 2000. It was accepted that neither appreciated that it was proscribed in the United Kingdom (a mistake of law), though that factor would affect sentence rather than conviction.[89] But the court was clear that, after proscription, activities anywhere in the world could incriminate, otherwise the device of joining a foreign branch would 'enable a coach and horses to be driven through the objects of the legislation'.[90]

2.34

The relationship of ss 11 and 118 was further considered in *Attorney General's Reference (No 4 of 2002)*, arising from a defendant who had been charged with being a member of, and professing to be a member of, the Hamas-Izz al-din al Qassem Brigades.[91] The most stark evidence against the accused was that on 28 September 2001, while attending college, he announced to his class that he was not afraid of any backlash following the events of 11 September because 'my family name is Bin Laden' and stated

2.35

---

[84] [2004] UKHL 43 at para 48. See also *R v Keogh* [2007] EWCA Crim 528.
[85] *Ibid.*
[86] Hansard HC Standing Committee D, col 117 (25 January 2000), Charles Clarke.
[87] See ch 6.
[88] [2004] EWCA Crim 389.
[89] *Ibid* at para 8. The sentence was reduced from 30 months to 12.
[90] *Ibid* at para 12.
[91] [2003] EWCA Crim 762 (regarding Adnan Abdelah, a Palestinian at N Tyneside College).

'I am a member of Hamas'.[92] After arrest, he admitted that he had been a member of Hamas from either 1997 or 1998 but said that he had left in 1999. At trial, the Crown conceded that s 11(2) imposed only an evidential burden on the defendant. However, the Court of Appeal viewed s 11(2) either as not relating to any element of the offence or as imposing a legal burden on the accused in proof of the defence.[93] This latter interpretation was reinforced by the omission of s 11(2) from s 118 and the fact that the defendant is 'peculiarly able to establish the date on which he became a member of a proscribed organization, or first professed membership.'[94] Nevertheless, the Court of Appeal upheld s 11(2) as consistent with Arts 6(2) and 10 of the European Convention on the basis that it is justified and proportionate. Both interpretations were reversed by the House of Lords in *Sheldrake v Director of Public Prosecutions; Attorney General's Reference (No 4 of 2002).*[95] Lord Bingham set out the parameter that 'Security concerns do not absolve member states from their duty to observe basic standards of fairness.'[96] The conclusion was that s 11(1) created a real risk that blameless conduct could be penalized, so s 11(2) was a necessary concomitant to it and should be read as involving an evidential burden only. Even though Parliament had intended to impose a legal burden by not listing it in s 118,[97] the words should be read down by reference to the Human Rights Act 1998, s 3. Bearing in mind that that participation in the activities of a proscribed organization was not an ingredient of the offence of belonging to or professing to belong to a proscribed organization, there could be substantial difficulties for a defendant to prove the elements of s 11(2) (amounting to proof of negative inactivity).[98] If s 11(2) were held to impose a legal burden, there would be much less room for the exercise of discretion to deal with conduct which was not of itself in furtherance of terrorism, unless the defendant proved beyond doubt the matters specified in s 11(2). As already noted, terms such as 'profess' were seen as dangerously wide. Therefore, the imposition of a legal burden upon the defendant was not a proportionate and justifiable legislative response to the threat of terrorism. This reading reduces the chance that purely passive membership can suffice for conviction, but Lord Bingham welcomed that outcome.[99] At the same time, and as a sting in the tail of the judgment, Lord Bingham ventured that s 11(2) is 'proportionate, for article 10 purposes, whether subsection (2) imposes a legal or an evidential burden'.[100]

2.36   Persons who cannot be shown directly to be members but have provided support commit an offence under s 12 of the 2000 Act. Amongst the distinct forms of involvement forbidden by s 12(1) is the act of inviting support. It is declared that the support is not, or is not restricted to, the provision of money or other property (since that activity is expressly within the meaning of s 15). Thus, the provision of labour and services (such as helping with money laundering or digging a hole for weapons) could fall into this category.

---

[92] *Ibid* para 6.
[93] *Ibid* at para 23.
[94] *Ibid* at para 42.
[95] [2004] UKHL 43.
[96] *Ibid* at para 21.
[97] *Ibid* at para 50.
[98] *Ibid* at para 51.
[99] *Ibid* at para 52.
[100] *Ibid* at para 54. Lords Rogers and Carswell dissented, since they preferred this reasoning.

Secondly, by s 12(2) of the 2000 Act, a person commits an offence if he arranges,   **2.37**
manages, or assists in arranging or managing a meeting which he knows is (a) to support
a proscribed organization; (b) to further the activities of a proscribed organization; or
(c) to be addressed by a person who belongs or professes to belong to a proscribed organization. There is a defence under s 12(4) to charges under sub-s (2)(c) if it can be shown
that he had no reasonable cause to believe that the address mentioned in sub-s (2)(c)
would support a proscribed organization or further its activities: 'That provides sufficient protection for arranging genuinely benign meetings while still ensuring that subsection (2)(c) will serve its basic purpose.'[101] 'Benign' meetings might include meetings
between government representatives and paramilitary leaders in order to end violence.
The defence under s 12(4) is expressly confined to private meetings. In the words of the
government minister:[102]

We accept that there could be a genuinely benign private meeting to be addressed by a member of
a proscribed organization . . . However, we cannot accept the arranging of public meetings to be
addressed by members of proscribed organizations, even when the person arranging the meeting
does not think that the address will support the organization.

Because of concerns about a breach of Art 6 of the European Convention, this defence
must be read subject to s 118(4): if evidence is adduced which is sufficient to raise an
issue, the court shall treat it as proved unless the prosecution disproves it beyond reasonable doubt. This express declaration is to secure that the burdens placed on the defendant are to be seen as evidential rather than legal burdens.[103]

Thirdly, by s 12(3) of the 2000 Act, a person commits an offence if he addresses a   **2.38**
meeting and the purpose of his address is to encourage support for a proscribed
organization or to further its activities. For these purposes, a 'meeting' means a meeting
of three or more persons, whether or not the public are admitted, and a meeting is
'private' if the public are not admitted.

The maximum penalties under s 12 are (a) on conviction on indictment, to imprison-   **2.39**
ment for a term not exceeding ten years, to a fine, or to both; or (b) on summary conviction, to imprisonment for a term not exceeding six months, to a fine not exceeding the
statutory maximum, or to both. The intention behind s 12 is to denounce debate in
public about any statement by an individual on behalf of a proscribed organization—'to
drive it down, drive it down, drive it down'.[104] However, a proposed wider offence of
addressing a meeting which a person knows is to be addressed by, 'a person who belongs
or professes to belong to a proscribed organization' was dropped in 2000.[105]

Perhaps the most flagrant breach of a proscription order (though not the most seri-   **2.40**
ous) is to display in public allegiance with, or support for, an impugned group. Under
s 13(1),[106] a person in a public place commits an offence if he (a) wears an item of
clothing; or (b) wears, carries, or displays an article, in such a way or in such circumstances as to arouse reasonable suspicion that he is a member or supporter of a proscribed

---

[101] Hansard HL vol 614, col 1453 (4 July 2000), Lord Bassam.
[102] Hansard HC vol 353, col 655 (10 July 2000), Charles Clarke.
[103] Hansard HL vol 613, col 754 (16 May 2000), Lord Bassam.
[104] Hansard HC Standing Committee D, col 137 (25 January 2000), Charles Clarke.
[105] Hansard HL vol 614, col 182 (20 June 2000), Lord Bach.
[106] In Scotland, breach of the peace might apply: Subhaan Younis (*The Times* 29 September 2005 p 3).

organization. In *Rankin v Murray*,[107] the defendant was convicted when embarking from the Belfast–Troon ferry terminal while wearing a ring inscribed with the initials, 'UVF'. The offence was felt to plug gaps in s 1 of the Public Order Act 1936 which is confined to the concept of a 'uniform'.[108] The offence can only be tried summarily and the maximum penalty is (a) imprisonment for a term not exceeding six months; (b) a fine not exceeding level 5 on the standard scale; or (c) both. As a result of these penalties, a distinct power to arrest without warrant is granted in Scotland.

2.41   Much of the purpose of proscription is symbolic—to express society's revulsion at violence as a political strategy as well as its determination to put a stop to it. This purpose is especially evident in Britain, where there were no convictions from 1990 to 2001.[109] In contrast, membership charges are more familiar in Northern Ireland, often as an added charge.[110] There were ninety convictions in Northern Ireland between 1991 and 1998. It remains the situation that most of those charged with the most serious terrorist offences in Britain are not charged with membership. Furthermore, many of the proscribed *mujahideen* groups conduct no activities in the United Kingdom.

Table 2.4 Charges under Part II of the Terrorism Act 2000[111]

Year	GB	NI
2001	5	2
2002	8	4
2003	13	34
2004	4	9
2005	3	11
2006	15	23
2007	7	n/a
Total	55	83

8. Assessment of proscription

2.42   Policy relevance to the CONTEST strategy and impact have now been considered. As for a rights audit, the objectives of security and the protection of life appear compelling, despite restrictions on expression and association which are provisional rights. Few have disputed the banning of Al-Qa'ida, though the activities within the United Kingdom of many other *jihadi* groups remain obscure. As for the Irish organizations, a distinction must be drawn between those observing ceasefires since 1998 and those dissenting from

---

[107] [2004] SCCR 422.

[108] See *O'Moran v DPP, Whelan v DPP* [1975] QB 864; Walker, C., 'Paramilitary displays and the PTA' [1992] *Juridical Review* 90.

[109] It was expressed as the main potential impact by Home Secretary, Roy Jenkins, *IRA Terrorism in Great Britain* (C(74)139, National Archives, London, 1974) para 3.

[110] See Hogan, G. and Walker C., *Political Violence and the Law in Ireland* (Manchester University Press, Manchester, 1989) ch 11.

[111] Sources: Home Office, Northern Ireland Office, *Reports of Lord Carlile*. Figures for 2001 are from 19 February 2001.

that stance. Regarding the former, there must come a time when their indisputable past involvement in violence becomes historical and deproscription becomes timely. The Independent Monitoring Commission has already documented a major transformation from 2004, when it was 'deeply concerned' about continuing paramilitary activity, to 2008, when it confirmed that the Provisional IRA has abandoned its terrorist structures and is being allowed to wither away.[112]

Next, the proportionality of banning an organization, as opposed to interdicting   2.43 its funding or prosecuting crimes by members, may be questioned. Proscription has often been of marginal utility in combating political violence, to which the survival of the IRA since 1918 in the teeth of almost continuous proscription bears ample testimony. Paramilitary organizations cannot be abolished by legislative fiat, and proscription actually increases the difficulties of infiltration and monitoring so as to achieve the criminalization of those members engaged in violence. Next, one might argue that the means used are disproportionate in extent and impact—for example, it should be possible to confine the ban to one territory, such as Northern Ireland (as applied in many cases before 2001). There should also be caution about the special offences, when similar outcomes can be achieved by ordinary offences such as the possession of weapons, conspiracy to carry out attacks, or public order offences,[113] such as paramilitary displays and management contrary to ss 1 and 2 of the Public Order Act 1936, sustained against IRA sympathizers in *O'Moran v DPP, Whelan v DPP*.[114] Doubt has also been cast on the guarantees against abuse and the absence of automatic periodic review.

In drawing up the overall balance, the rationale for proscription has sometimes shifted   2.44 to the 'presentational'[115]—that it expresses the condemnation of the community and 'averts the danger of public outrage being expressed in public disorder'.[116] But in view of the adequacy of regular public order laws, these presentational or public order grounds for proscription should be rejected. During the debates on the Terrorism Act 2000, the government called in aid other grounds for proscription—symbolism was one, but deterrence and prosecution were others:[117]

There are three principal reasons why we think proscription is important. First, it has been, and remains, a powerful deterrent to people to engage in terrorist activity. Secondly, related offences are a way of tackling some of the lower-level support for terrorist organisations. . . . Thirdly, proscription acts as a powerful signal of the rejection by the Government—and indeed by society as a whole—of organisations' claim to legitimacy. . . . The legislation is a powerful symbol of that censure and is important.

---

[112] *First Report* (2003–04 HC 516) para 2.1; *Nineteenth Report* (Cm 7464, London, 2008) ch 2.
[113] Public order law continues to be invoked in Scotland against Irish-related processions, resulting in the challenges: *Aberdeen Bon Accord Loyal Orange Lodge 701 v Aberdeen City Council* 2002 *Scots Law Times (Sh Ct)* 52; *Wishart Arch Defenders Loyal Orange Lodge 404 v Angus Council* 2002 *Scots Law Times (Sh Ct)* 43. The Public Processions (Northern Ireland) Act 1998 provides further regulatory powers.
[114] [1975] QB 864.
[115] *Report of the Operation of the Prevention of Terrorism (Temporary Provisions) Act 1976* (Cmnd 8803, London, 1983) para 207.
[116] *Review of the Operation of the Northern Ireland (Emergency Provisions) Act 1978* (Cmnd 9222, London, 1984) para 414.
[117] Hansard HC Standing Committee D, col 56 (18 January 2000), Charles Clarke.

Deterrence and prosecution should be tested against each listed group and in the light of the special protection accorded to political speech.[118] No such audit is made public.

2.45 Proscription powers under the Terrorism Act 2000 have been held to be compatible with the European Convention. In *R v Hundal; R v Dhaliwal*,[119] the fact that the membership had started before the organization was proscribed did not breach Art 7 (retrospective penalties). The bite of the offence was on arrival in the United Kingdom, in 2002, at which time evidence of membership persisted. A wider challenge was fleetingly raised in *O'Driscoll v Secretary of State for the Home Department*,[120] which concerned an offence under s 16 (and is therefore considered further in Chapter 3). Other arguments, that there is no lawful power, consistent with the European Convention on Human Rights, to proscribe an entire organization or to criminalize plain membership,[121] were not pursued. In *Sheldrake v Director of Public Prosecutions; Attorney General's Reference (No 4 of 2002)*,[122] it was stated in the House of Lords without argument that s 11(1) interferes with exercise of the right of free expression but that it is justifiable since it is directed to legitimate ends, it is prescribed by law, and it is necessary in a democratic society and proportionate, since the 'necessity of attacking terrorist organisations is . . . clear'. Those who espouse totalitarian views will find themselves disfavoured either under Art 17 or under the limitations to Arts 9 to 11.[123] As applied to Irish paramilitaries, the courts have accepted partial restrictions such as broadcast bans[124] and physical exclusion.[125] Likewise, the European Court of Human Rights Court has accepted the banning of bodies which seek, possibly by force, to impose *Sharia* law. Any association with violent methods will produce condemnation, even if the ultimate policy goals are acceptable.[126]

2.46 While the foregoing rights audit may produce no clear-cut condemnation, compliance with the precept of accountability is more uncertain. As mentioned above, there is no legislated system for the production of a detailed factual case for proscription (even if confined to overt attacks or crimes) nor for periodic review. A further problem concerns multiple proscriptions within a single order, meaning that the listed groups are offered by the government on an indiscriminate 'take it or leave it' basis.[127]

2.47 There is less to say about constitutional governance. The work of the POAC has improved on prior processes. But, reflecting upon the *Alton* case, the restoration of

---

[118] See, for example, *Lingens v Austria*, App no 9815/82, Ser A vol 103 (1986).
[119] [2004] EWCA Crim 389 at para 14.
[120] [2002] EWHC 2477 (Admin).
[121] *Ibid* at para 14.
[122] [2004] UKHL 43 at para 54 per Lord Bingham.
[123] *German Communist Party v Germany*, App no 350/57, 1 YBEC 222; *Retimag v Germany*, App no 712/60, 4 YBEC. Compare *United Communist Party of Turkey and Others v Turkey*, App no 19392/92, Reports 1998-I; *Socialist Party v Turkey*, App no 21237/93, Reports 1998-III; *Partidul Comunistilor (Nepeceristi) and Ungureanu v Romania*, App no 46626/99, 2005-I. See Brems, E., 'Freedom of political association and the question of party closures' in Sadurski, W. (ed), *Political Rights under Stress in 21ˢᵗ Century Europe* (Oxford University Press, Oxford, 2006).
[124] *R v Secretary of State for the Home Department, ex p Brind* [1991] AC 696; *Brind and McLaughlin v United Kingdom*, App nos 18714/91, 18759/91, 77-A DR 42 (1994); *Purcell v Ireland*, App no 15404/89, 70 DR 262 (1991).
[125] *Adams and Benn v United Kingdom*, App nos 28979/95, 30343/96, 88A D & R, 137 (1997).
[126] See further *Gündüz v Turkey*, App no 59745/00, 2003-XI.
[127] See the ongoing criticism at Hansard HC vol 462, col 1369 (10 July 2007), Tony McNulty.

normal constitutional life is not sufficiently pressing, as the government seems unwilling outside of Northern Ireland to engage with groups seeking to move away from violence.

B. EXTREMIST EXPRESSIONS

Following the London bombs of July 2005, the processes of radicalization of young   2.48
Muslim men became a pressing issue.[128] These events sparked the Prime Minister into presenting a 12-point plan which included the banning of organizations which encourage extremism.[129] In the background was the considerable official irritation with foreign extremists such as Abu Hamza and Omar Bakri Muhammed and Abu Qatada, who were seen as poisoning vulnerable minds.[130] In the wider background was a growing intolerance of foreign dissidents, marked after September 11, 2001, by UNSC Resolution 1373 which calls for action against asylum-seekers involved in terrorism.[131] International law took more definite shape, with Art 5 of the Council of Europe Convention on the Prevention of Terrorism of 2005 demanding domestic offences to outlaw the public provocation of terrorism offences.[132] A further plank of support for this initiative is the United Nations Security Council Resolution 1624 of 14 September 2005, also calling upon states to 'Prohibit by law incitement to commit a terrorist act or acts'. The delivery of the UK response is contained in the Terrorism Act 2006.

1. Proscription of group glorification

The first measure is to extend the device of proscription to group glorification. Though   2.49
s 3(5) already allows proscription where an organization (c) promotes or encourages terrorism, the link to action is even less direct under the 2006 Act since its emphasis is on speech and not deeds. Furthermore, the thrust of the power is aimed against domestic-based groups beyond the Irish context and has in fact been so applied.

The powers to proscribe organizations which glorify terrorism are inserted by the   2.50
Terrorism Act 2006, s 21. A new s 3(5A) to the Terrorism Act 2000 specifies that the power to proscribe any organization which 'promotes or encourages' terrorism under s 3(5)(c) shall extend its application to the situation of the 'unlawful glorification of the commission or preparation (whether in the past, in the future or generally) of acts of terrorism'. 'Glorification' requires the reasonable expectation that the audience will emulate terrorism in present circumstances (s 3(5B)), and it comprises any form of praise or celebration (s 3(5C)). The boundaries between incitement and glorification are difficult to draw and run the danger of infringing free speech. Parliament accepted that a ministerial

---

[128] See *Report of the Official Account of the Bombings in London on the 7ᵗʰ July 2005* (2005–06 HC 1087).
[129] *The Times* 6 August 2005 at p 1.
[130] See Walker, C., 'The treatment of foreign terror suspects' (2007) 70 *Modern Law Review* 427.
[131] (28 September 2001) art 3(f).
[132] CETS No 196. See further Committee of Experts on Terrorism, 'Apologie du Terrorisme' and 'Incitement to Terrorism' (CODEXTER, Strasbourg, 2004); Joint Committee on Human Rights, The Council of Europe Convention on the Prevention of Terrorism (2006–07 HL 26/HC 247); Hunt, A., 'The Council of Europe Convention on the Prevention of Terrorism' (2006) 4 *European Public Law* 603.

discretion to proscribe could be rightly broader than the formulation of a crime,[133] but changes made in the drafting to Pt I of the 2006 Act (considered below) were eventually reflected here too. As a result, the minister was sure that the formula would adequately distinguish 'cultural events or those that celebrate a part of our collective memory, such as Guy Fawkes and bonfire night, and people who glorify acts of terror to try to encourage similar acts here and now in existing circumstances.'[134] The same distinction would potentially apply to Irish celebrations of the past, whether the deeds of Michael Collins or William of Orange, depending on whether the praise is for an heroic history or for future emulation.

2.51   A potential problem in these cases is who or what represents the policy of the organization. Will every remark by every member be taken as adopted policy, or must impugned statements emanate from prominent or multiple members?[135] The same point could be made about attacks 'on behalf of an organization' which turn out to be unsanctioned operations, but acts of violence probably require greater joint planning and often are associated with formal claims of responsibility. It is far easier to make a wayward impulsive remark than to carry out an impromptu bombing.

2.52   Two groups were banned in July 2006 under these novel powers.[136]

Table 2.5 Proscription of group glorification

| Al-Ghurabaa | Al-Ghurabaa ('The Strangers') is an Islamist group. It succeeded Al-Muhajiroun ('The Emigrants'), founded by Omar Bakri Muhammad and others in Saudi Arabia in 1983 and disbanded in 2004. |
| The Saved Sect | With a similar background, The Saved Sect (formerly the Saviour Sect) pursues the mission of speaking out for proper standards for Muslims living in Western countries so as to ensure their salvation. |

One of the pieces of evidence against Al-Ghurabaa concerned comments by a representative about the London bombings of 2005 in the following terms: 'What I would say about those who do suicide operations or martyrdom operations is that they're completely praiseworthy. I have no allegiance to the Queen whatsoever or to British society; in fact if I see mujahideen attack the UK I am always standing with the Muslims.'[137] Other variants related to these two groups, such as Ahlus Sunnah wal Jamaah, have so far escaped proscription.[138] More controversial has been the continued legality of Hizb ut-Tahir,[139] a transnational political movement established in 1953 which advocates in Arab countries the establishment of a Caliphate and *Sharia* laws and in western countries the representation of Islamist viewpoints. Nevertheless, it 'remains an organization of concern and is kept under close review'.[140]

---

[133] Hansard HC vol 438, col 985 (2 November 2005).

[134] Hansard HC vol 438, col 994 (3 November 2005), Paul Goggins.

[135] See Saul, B., 'Speaking of terror' (2005) 28 *University of New South Wales Law Review* 868 at p 880.

[136] SI 2006/2016, Hansard HC vol 449, col 490 (20 July 2006).

[137] Hansard HC vol 449, col 493 (20 July 2006).

[138] Other candidates include the Muballigh, the Islamic Thinkers Society, the Society of Muslim Lawyers, the Supporters of Sharia, and Tablighi Jama'at (Hansard HC vol 449, col 496 (20 July 2006), Patrick Mercer).

[139] See Karajiannis, E. and McCauley, C., 'Hizb ut Tahir' (2006) 18 *Terrorism & Political Violence* 315.

[140] Hansard HC vol 472, col 588W (19 February 2008), Tony McNulty.

Lord Carlile predicted initially that there would be 'a significant number of additional   2.53
proscriptions'.[141] In response, the government has shown little enthusiasm for Lord
Carlile's view that this variant of proscription can play a role in 'reducing the opportunity for disaffected young people to become radicalized towards terrorism'.[142]

2. The offences of incitement of terrorism

The principal and highly controversial changes brought about by the Terrorism Act   2.54
2006 in relation to extremism concerned the new speech offences set out in ss 1 and
2.[143] Commitment to legislation on the glorification had been promised in the Labour
Party's 2005 election manifesto[144] but became acute after the bombings of July 2005.

(a) *Principal offences*
The principal offence in s 1(1) relates to the publication of statements that are 'likely to   2.55
be understood by some or all of the members of the public to whom it is published as a
direct or indirect encouragement or other inducement to them to the commission, preparation or instigation of acts of terrorism' or specified offences which are referred to as
'Convention offences'. The specified offences are listed in Sch 1 and can be changed by
affirmative order under s 20(9). Publication of one's statement is the core of the *actus reus*
(s 1(2)(a)). The 'statement' may take many formats under s 20(6), including words,
sounds, or images, and, by s 20(4), can be published 'in any manner' such as through an
electronic service.[145] A 'statement' may be part of a wider message and need not be confined to terrorism or offences in or with respect to the United Kingdom,[146] but s 1(4)
demands that account be taken of the contents as a whole and the circumstances and
manner of publication. For instance, 'there is a difference in how an academic thesis
on an issue and a radical and inflammatory pamphlet are likely to be understood.'[147]
The statement must be made to 'members of the public', who must be in the multiple
and are distinct from 'persons' who could comprise the respondents in a private conversation.[148] If the statement is made at a meeting, it must be a meeting or other group of
persons which is open to the public.[149] By s 20(3), the 'public' can include the public (or
any section of it) of any part of the United Kingdom or of a country or territory outside

---

[141] Lord Carlile, *Proposals by Her Majesty's Government for changes to the laws against terrorism* (Home Office, London, 2005) para 51. He now concludes it will make little difference: Lord Carlile, *Report on the Operation in 2007 of the Terrorism Act 2000* (Home Office, London, 2008) para 50.

[142] *Ibid* para 52.

[143] See Joint Committee on Human Rights, *Counter-Terrorism Policy and Human Rights: Terrorism Bill and related matters* (2005–06 HL 75, HC 561); Barnum, D., 'Indirect incitement and freedom of speech in Anglo-American law' [2006] *European Human Rights Law Review* 258; Leigh, L.H., 'The Terrorism Act 2006—a brief analysis' (2006) 170 *Justice of the Peace* 364; Jones, A., Bowers, R, and Lodge, H.D., *The Terrorism Act 2006* (Oxford University Press, Oxford, 2006); Hunt, A., 'Criminal prohibitions on direct and indirect encouragement of terrorism' [2007] *Criminal Law Review* 441.

[144] *Britain forward not back* (London, 2005) p 53: '. . . we will introduce new laws to help catch and convict those involved in helping to plan terrorist activity or who glorify or condone acts of terror.'

[145] By s 20(5), providing a service includes making a facility available.

[146] Leigh, L.H., 'The Terrorism Act 2006—a brief analysis' (2006) 170 *Justice of the Peace* 364 at p 364.

[147] Home Office Circular 8/2006, *The Terrorism Act 2006*, para 3.

[148] Hansard HL vol 676, col 435 (5 December 2005), Baroness Scotland.

[149] S 20(3). Compare Public Order Act 1986, s 16.

the United Kingdom. Furthermore, in so far as it relates to 'Convention offences', s 1 is within the parameters of s 17 of the Act (discussed below), which means that the offence could be committed by Palestinians in Gaza and Pakistanis in Peshawar.[150] The offence does not require that all the targeted members of the public are likely to be affected; the influenced subset must comprise 'some' which could suggest one or more affected recipients.[151] In applying the impact test, juries may face challenging calculations where the statement is confined to a section of the public consisting of 'small cohesive congregations'.[152] It is odd that the government should limit the offence to a public context, given the mischief of radicalization.[153]

2.56   As for the *mens rea*, in s 1(2)(b), the publisher must either intend members of the public to be directly or indirectly encouraged or otherwise induced by the statement to commit, prepare, or instigate acts of terrorism or specified offences, or be subjectively reckless as to whether members of the public will be so directly or indirectly encouraged by the statement. The original draft of the offence lacked this element of subjective specific intent—it was sufficient that there was intent as to publication and reasonable belief as to encouragement.[154] There was prolonged opposition to that version, including by seeking to revive the version of inadvertent recklessness in *Metropolitan Police Commissioner v Caldwell*[155] after it had been superseded by *R v G*[156] and even after *Caldwell* had been condemned as producing serious injustice.[157] The switch to subjective recklessness was accepted at committee stage in the House of Lords.[158] The other point to note about the *mens rea* is that the defendant must seek to affect multiple members of the public, so some of the questions about the extent of publication may become irrelevant. The requirement points again to a strong public order element in the offence.

2.57   By s 1(5), it is irrelevant whether the encouragement relates to one or more particular acts of terrorism or specified offences, or of a particular description or generally. This provision should not, however, excuse the prosecution from specifying the one or more acts or offences which were relevant.[159] It is also no defence under s 1(5)(b) to show that the dissemination fell on deaf ears—in other words, that no person was in fact encouraged or induced by the statement. The offence considers the objective tendency of the publication. However, where the allegation is of a recklessly made statement, it is a defence under s 1(6) to show that the statement neither expressed the originator's views nor had his

---

[150] See Jones, A., Bowers, R, and Lodge, H.D., *The Terrorism Act 2006* (Oxford University Press, Oxford, 2006) paras 1, 26–8. The fears of politically fraught prosecutions may be allayed by the hurdle of consent to prosecution under s 19(2).

[151] It has been suggested that 'some' requires more than a single person (and compare s 2(6)): Jones, A., Bowers, R, and Lodge, H.D., *The Terrorism Act 2006* (Oxford University Press, Oxford, 2006) para 2.18. But see further s 1(2)(b), as discussed below.

[152] Jones, A., Bowers, R., and Lodge, H.D., *The Terrorism Act 2006* (Oxford University Press, Oxford, 2006) para 2.35.

[153] Compare Public Order Act 1986, s 18. See *Review of Public Order Law* (Cmnd 9510, London, 1985) para 6.7.

[154] 2006–07 HC no 55. See Hansard HC vol 438, col 834 (2 November 2005), Dominic Grieve.

[155] [1982] AC 341.

[156] [2003] UKHL 50.

[157] *Ibid* para 45 per Lord Browne-Wilkinson.

[158] Hansard HL vol 676, col 430 (5 December 2005), Baroness Scotland.

[159] Compare Hunt, A., 'Criminal prohibitions on direct and indirect encouragement of terrorism' [2007] *Criminal Law Review* 441 at p 445.

endorsement and that it was clear, in all the circumstances of the statement's publication, that it did not express his views and (unless in receipt of a notice under s 3(3)) did not have his endorsement. Placing the burden of proof on defendants is felt to be justifiable since the facts are within their particular knowledge and they are best placed to lead relevant evidence on the point.[160] Thus, the government intended a legal rather than an evidential burden to be placed on the defendant,[161] though the precedent of *Sheldrake v Director of Public Prosecutions; Attorney General's Reference (No 4 of 2002)*[162] strongly suggests that the courts might take another view.

The most controversial aspect of the offence is indirect encouragement, and so Parliament sought to apply further clarifications and limits.[163] By sub-s (3), the indirect encouragement of terrorism includes a statement that 'glorifies' the commission or preparation of acts of terrorism or specified offences (either in their actual commission or in principle) but only if members of the public could reasonably be expected to infer that what is being glorified in the statement is being glorified as conduct that should be 'emulated by them in existing circumstances'. The continued reliance on 'glorification' represents an attempt to retain a vestige of a pre-parliamentary draft of the Bill, which included an offence of glorification distinct from the offence of encouragement.[164] It should be noted that the impact is on members of the public at large and not a particular audience, as under s 1(1). In this way, a predictive application of 'likely impact' is replaced by a wholly objective test where the jury can put themselves in the shoes of an audience.[165] It follows that it is no defence to show that an actual audience did not believe there was glorification, though this circumstance can be pleaded to direct incitement or other indirect incitements.

2.58

The notion of 'emulation' ensures that the words uttered should be understood as more than rhetorical. Consequently, praise for historical acts of violence, such as the taking over of the General Post Office, Dublin, in 1916, is not an offence, unless the statements can be readily understood to resonate with the present and to guide future action. The position may be clearer where the speaker glorifies ongoing or future (but not futuristic) acts of terrorism since the possibility of replication is then more palpable and practicable to the audience. Thus, a declaration that most devout British Muslims were 'over the moon' about the September 11 attacks refers to an historical act when uttered in 2005, but it must be close to falling within s 1(3) when allied to the statement that 'Ultimately, if your brothers and sisters were being killed in any part of the world, you would make your utmost effort to try to help them.'[166]

2.59

'Glorify' is partly defined in s 20(2) as including 'praise or celebration'. An all-embracing working (non-legal) definition was proffered by a Home Office Minister

2.60

---

[160] Hansard HL vol 676, cols 455 (5 December 2005), Baroness Scotland.
[161] Hansard HL vol 678, col 217 (1 February 2006), Lord Goldsmith.
[162] [2004] UKHL 43. See also Jones, A., Bowers, R, and Lodge, H.D., *The Terrorism Act 2006* (Oxford University Press, Oxford, 2006) para 2.52.
[163] See Hansard HL vol 679, col 136 (28 February 2006), vol 680, col 241 (22 March 2006).
[164] See Lord Carlile, *Proposals by Her Majesty's Government for changes to the laws against terrorism* (Home Office, London, 2005) para 21; Barendt, E., 'Threats to freedom of speech in the United Kingdom' (2005) 28 *University of New South Wales Law Journal* 895 at p 897.
[165] See Jones, A., Bowers, R, and Lodge, H.D., *The Terrorism Act 2006* (Oxford University Press, Oxford, 2006) para 2.41.
[166] These words were spoken by Hassan Butt in a published interview: Taseer, A., 'A British Jihadist' (2005) 113 *Prospect* (<http://www.prospect-magazine.co.uk/pdfarticle.php?id=6992>).

as follows: 'To glorify is to describe or represent as admirable, especially unjustifiably or undeservedly.'[167] Section 20(7) does clarify that references to conduct to be 'emulated in existing circumstances' include references to conduct that is illustrative of a type of conduct that should be so emulated. For example, a statement glorifying the bombing of a bus at Tavistock Square on 7 July 2005 and encouraging repeat performances may be interpreted as an encouragement to emulate by attacks on the transport network in general. The government's advice for speakers wishing to avoid glorification is that they should 'preface their remarks with the statement that they do not condone or endorse acts of terrorism or encouraging people to kill others. They could express sympathy and even support for the activity, but not in a way that encourages people to commit acts of terrorism.'[168] This 'love-hate' formula—love the cause but hate violent means—should not, however, be treated as a magic incantation which wards off all evil, for juries are entitled to consider the context of the words and the sincerity of the speaker, as made clear by s 1(4).

2.61   There is no illumination as to the meaning of 'indirect incitement' beyond the concept of glorification.[169] One notable distinction in the residue of indirect incitement is the absence of any requirement of emulation.

2.62   The penalties under s 1 are, on indictment, imprisonment for a term not exceeding seven years or a fine, or both; on summary conviction in England and Wales, imprisonment for a term not exceeding twelve months[170] (six months in Scotland or Northern Ireland) or a fine not exceeding the statutory maximum, or both.

2.63   The overall impact is to criminalize generalized and public encouragements—that terrorism would be a good thing, without stating where or when or against whom. In comparison, the 'normal' law of criminal encouragement in Pt II of the Serious Crime Act 2007 requires the encouragement of an act which would amount to one or more offence and at least with the belief that one or more offence would be committed as a consequence. Section 1 advances these normal boundaries, in the case of direct incitement, by specifying that it is an offence 'to incite people to engage in terrorist activities generally' and extra-territorially.[171] In the case of indirect incitement, it is an offence 'to incite them obliquely by creating the climate in which they may come to believe that terrorist acts are acceptable' such as by glorification or otherwise.[172] How this differs from 'normal' incitement remains uncertain since the 'normal' law does not use the terms 'direct' and 'indirect' but does occasionally accord a wide meaning to 'encourage', such as in cases of speed trap detection machines or books giving advice on the production of cannabis.[173] Perhaps the absence of any requirement of intended emulation outside of

---

[167] Hansard HL vol 677, col 583 (17 January 2006), Baroness Scotland.
[168] Hansard HC vol 439, col 429 (9 November 2005), Hazel Blears. See also Hansard HL vol 676, col 458 (5 December 2005), Baroness Scotland.
[169] See Hunt, A., 'Criminal prohibitions on direct and indirect encouragement of terrorism' [2007] *Criminal Law Review* 441 at p 452.
[170] Subject to the commencement of the Criminal Justice Act 2003, s 154(1).
[171] But see Criminal Justice (Terrorism and Conspiracy) Act 1998.
[172] Hansard HL vol 676, cols 432–3 (5 December 2005), Baroness Scotland. Compare Leigh, L.H., 'The Terrorism Act 2006—a brief analysis' (2006) 170 *Justice of the Peace* 364 at p 365; Cohen-Almagor, R., 'Boundaries of free expression before and after Prime Minister Rabin's assassination' in Cohen-Almagor, R., *Liberal Democracy and the Limits of Tolerance* (University of Michigan Press, Ann Arbor, 2000).
[173] *Invicta Plastics Ltd v Clare* [1976] RTR 251; *R v Marlow* [1998] 1 Cr App Rep (S) 273; Hunt, A., 'Criminal prohibitions on direct and indirect encouragement of terrorism' [2007] *Criminal Law Review* 441 at pp 453–5.

the realm of glorification could be one key difference, though the absence of actual audience reaction is less of a distinction under the 2007 Act.[174]

Having dealt with the originators of statements in s 1, s 2(1) deals with the secondary dissemination of terrorist publications with intent or recklessness as to direct or indirect encouragement to acts of terrorism.[175] Closely parallel to s 1(3), the meaning of indirect encouragement is explained in s 2(4). The offence may be committed in relation to a 'terrorist publication' by its distribution, circulation, giving, selling, lending, offering for sale or loan, provision of a service to others that enables them to access or acquire,[176] transmitting electronically, or possessing 'with a view' to the foregoing activities (s 2(2)).[177] Possession was added at the last stage of the Bill and reflects changes made in race hatred legislation.[178] It is sufficient that possession 'with a view' to the foregoing activities is one of the defendant's purposes and not necessarily the prime purpose. The publication may take many formats—it means an article or record[179] of any description which may be read, listened to, looked at, or watched (s 2(13)). In content, a 'terrorist publication' is defined in s 2(3) as containing matter of two distinct types. First, it covers matter likely to be understood, by some or all of the persons to whom it is or may become available as a consequence of that conduct, as a direct or indirect encouragement or other inducement to them to the commission, preparation, or instigation of acts of terrorism. Secondly, it covers matter likely to be useful in the commission or preparation of such acts and to be understood, by some or all of those persons, as contained in the publication, or made available to them, wholly or mainly for the purpose of being so useful to them. This second leg compensates for the fact that 'Convention offences' (as in Sch 1) are not mentioned under s 2(1). The explanation for this distinction is that s 1 is tied more closely to the terms in Art 5 of the Council of Europe Convention, namely, 'public provocations', whereas s 2 is more an artefact of British legislative design.[180] As a result, there is no application of extra-territorial effect under s 17. The effect of conduct in relation to a terrorist publication can be judged by reference to an effect of the publication on one or more persons to whom it is or may become available as a consequence of that conduct (s 2(6)). The possibility of affecting just one single person contrasts with the position under s 1. In contrast too is the possibility of judging likely impact not only on persons who either were exposed or may be exposed to the materials. In this way, the audience may in part be determined by the designs of the defendant, but it might also be affected by the choice of medium. For example, it will be

2.64

---

[174] See Law Commission, *Inchoate Liability for Assisting and Encouraging Crime* (Report no 300, Cm 6878, London, 2006) para 1.3.

[175] Subjective recklessness was inserted in line with s 1: Hansard HL vol 677, col 551 (17 January 2006), Baroness Scotland.

[176] An example might be the running of a market stall: Leigh, L.H., 'The Terrorism Act 2006—a brief analysis' (2006) 170 *Justice of the Peace* 364 at p 364.

[177] This definition is exclusive to s 2 and so s 20(4) does not apply.

[178] See Hansard HL vol 678, col 197 (1 February 2006); Public Order Act 1986, s 23 (as suggested by the *Review of Public Order Law* (Cmnd 9510, London, 1985) para 6.8). Lord Carlile also suggested an analogy with paedophile offences as in Criminal Justice Act 1988, s 160 (*Proposals by Her Majesty's Government for changes to the laws against terrorism* (Home Office, London, 2005) para 25), but possession *per se* is not an offence under s 2.

[179] See further s 20(2), (8).

[180] Hunt, A., 'Criminal prohibitions on direct and indirect encouragement of terrorism' [2007] *Criminal Law Review* 441 at pp 444, 445.

difficult to delimit the audience for an internet posting. It is also notable that the offence mentions 'persons' and not members of the public as in s 1, which means that private circulations of public statements could be prohibited. A possible explanation for the distinction is again that s 2 is less dependent on Art 5 of the Council of Europe Convention.

2.65 The concept of 'terrorist publication' is explained further by s 2(5) which directs that the nature of the publications must be determined at the time of the conduct in s 2(2) and having regard both to the contents of the publication as a whole and to the circumstances in which that conduct occurs. It is also irrelevant whether the dissemination relates to materials disseminated relate to particular acts of terrorism, of acts of terrorism of a particular description, or of acts of terrorism generally (s 2(7)).

2.66 The *mens rea* presumably requires intention as to the forms of dissemination in s 2(2)(a) to (e) while for the possession offence under s 2(2)(f), there must be an intent to possess with the future intent to disseminate. In addition, it is specified in sub-s (1) that the person must intend or be reckless that an effect of his conduct (not necessarily the sole or prime effect) will be a direct or indirect encouragement or other inducement to the commission, preparation, or instigation of acts of terrorism or the provision of assistance in the commission or preparation of such acts.

2.67 Parallel to s 1(6), it is a defence under s 2(9) to show that the statement neither expressed the publisher's views nor had his endorsement and that it was clear, in all the circumstances of the statement's publication, that it did not express his views and (unless in receipt of a notice under s 3(3)) did not have his endorsement.[181] By s 2(10), the defence is again confined to reckless and not intentional actions, and is also confined to encouragement offences and not offences relating to useful materials. Of course, it is conceivable that materials will be prosecuted as relating to both types of offence in s 2(3), and if the defence is raised in those circumstances, the jury might find it difficult to disentangle liability.[182] The defence can benefit 'all legitimate librarians, academics and booksellers' (and the same applies to news broadcasters) who may have examined the article but still do not endorse the contents.[183] Nevertheless, where, for example, an academic officer suspects or believes that a student intends to use the available materials for terrorist purposes rather than scholastic endeavour, she should 'as a good citizen' inform the security authorities.[184] This injunction was taken to heart by the University of Nottingham when a student, Rizwaan Sabir, was arrested in 2008 for downloading materials in connection with his postgraduate research, together with his friend and ex-student, Hicham Yezza, to whom he had passed the materials.[185] The offending materials were an Al-Qa'ida training manual which had been published in redacted form on the US Department of Justice website.[186] The Vice Chancellor, Sir Colin Campbell,

---

[181] The government intended that the defendant carries a legal burden of proof: Hansard HL vol 678, col 218 (1 February 2006), Lord Goldsmith. Lord Carlile viewed it as an evidential burden: *Proposals by Her Majesty's Government for changes to the laws against terrorism* (Home Office, London, 2005) para 25. There is also a strong possibility that the courts will impose an evidential burden: *Sheldrake v Director of Public Prosecutions; Attorney General's Reference (No 4 of 2002)* [2004] UKHL 43.

[182] See Jones, A., Bowers, R, and Lodge, H.D., *The Terrorism Act 2006* (Oxford University Press, Oxford, 2006) para 2.87.

[183] Hansard HL vol 676, col 465 (5 December 2005), Baroness Scotland. See also Hansard HL vol 677, col 554 (17 January 2006), Baroness Scotland; *Explanatory Notes to the Terrorism Act 2006* (HMSO, London, 2006) para 27.

[184] Hansard HL vol 676, col 629 (7 December 2005), Baroness Scotland.

[185] See *The Guardian* 24 May 2008 p 8;<http://freehicham.co.uk/>.

[186] <http://www.usdoj.gov/ag/manualpart1_1.pdf>, 2005.

warned, without much regard for the defences in ss 1 and 2, that it is illegitimate to study the operational or tactical aspects of terrorism, as opposed to its political dimensions.[187] Lord Carlile had rightly warned before enactment that there was a danger that academic research into terrorism might be 'turned into samizdat activity'.[188]

As in s 1, there is no defence that the dissemination fell on deaf ears. By sub-s (8) it is irrelevant whether any person is in fact encouraged or induced or makes use of the materials. However, where under sub-s (10) the offence is one of direct or indirect encouragement only (and so this is not applicable to matter useful to terrorists) and the person was not acting intentionally within sub-s (1)(a), there is a defence of unauthorized dissemination under sub-s (9) by which it is a defence to show that the terrorist publication neither expressed the defendant's views nor had his endorsement and that it was clear, in all the circumstances of the conduct, that that matter did not express his views and (subject to receiving a notice under s 3(3)) did not have his endorsement.   2.68

Section 2 goes beyond the 'normal' law of incitement in many respects, though much of its potential impact on third party publishers is moderated by s 2(9). Thus, the important impact is upon sympathetic disseminators or possessors of materials, where the accused is one step away from the original incitement and where it might be difficult to prove the sharing of the same *mens rea* as the author.[189]   2.69

The penalties as the same as under s 1. In *R v Rahman, R v Mohammed*,[190] the conviction of Rahman under s 2(2)(f) arose from an instruction to disseminate to six named persons a letter containing instructions for the distribution of Al-Qa'ida propaganda and a description of fighting. Mohammed sold Islamic material at stalls in the North of England, and a small part of his stock fell foul of the tighter laws when the 2006 Act came into force. The Court of Appeal gave guidance that: any reduction in sentence for recklessness rather than intention would be small; the volume and content of the material disseminated would be relevant; s 2 offences are likely to be less serious than breaches of ss 57 and 58 of the Terrorism Act 2000.[191] The conviction under s 2 of Shella Roma seems to underline this point, as she was sentenced to a three-year community order for seeking to print and distribute an extremist pamphlet.[192]   2.70

(b) *Internet materials*

Section 3 seeks to apply these offences in the context of unlawfully terrorist-related articles or records[193] on the internet and to devise a short-circuit enforcement power. It is claimed that 'extremist' websites have grown from 12 in 1998 to over 4,000 in 2008.[194]   2.71

---

[187] *Times Higher Educational Supplement* 24 July 2008.

[188] Lord Carlile, *Proposals by Her Majesty's Government for changes to the laws against terrorism* (Home Office, London, 2005) para 28.

[189] See further Hunt, A., 'Criminal prohibitions on direct and indirect encouragement of terrorism' [2007] *Criminal Law Review* 441 at p 445.

[190] [2008] EWCA Crim 1465. Note also *R v Malcolm Hodges*, who was convicted in 2008 of reckless encouragement of *jihadis* to attack accountancy organizations: <http://www.dailymail.co.uk/news/article-516448/Man-urged-terror-attacks-accountancy-institutes-10-years-failing-professional-exams.html>.

[191] *Ibid* at paras 5, 7, 41. The sentences were five and a half years (Rahman) and two years (Mohammed).

[192] *The Times* 31 March 2009 p 17.

[193] s 3(7). The meaning is by reference to the two categories of matter within s 2(3), with the usual definition of 'indirect incitement' in s 3(8).

[194] Home Office, *Pursue, Prevent, Protect, Prepare: The United Kingdom's Strategy for Countering International Terrorism* (Cm 7547, London, 2009) para 5.14.

Section 3(1) applies where the original publication under s 1 or the dissemination under s 2 was produced in the course of, or in connection with, the provision or use of a service provided electronically. The impugned materials are those which are 'unlawfully terrorism-related', which means, under s 3(7), that a statement or an article or record constitutes either a direct or indirect encouragement or other inducement to the commission, preparation, or instigation of acts of terrorism or Convention offences; or information which is likely to be useful to any one or more of those persons in the commission or preparation of such acts.[195] In this way, s 3 covers a combination of the wrongful activities in s 1 (acts of terrorism and Convention offences) and 2 (acts of terrorism and useful materials). As in ss 2 and 3, indirect encouragement is refined in sub-s (8) to include glorification provided that there is a suggestion of emulation in existing circumstances.

2.72 The gist of the process is that, under s 3(3), where a constable forms the opinion that a statement, article, or record held on the system of the service provider is 'unlawfully terrorism-related', a notice can be issued which requires the provider to arrange for the material to become unavailable to the public and also warns the provider that a failure to comply with the notice within two working days[196] will result in the matter being regarded as having his endorsement, and explains the possible liability under sub-s (4). More detailed rules about notices are set out under s 4.

2.73 It is specified in s 3(2) that a failure to comply with the notice without reasonable excuse within two working days is to be regarded as an endorsement of the matter. Furthermore, a failure to comply under sub-s (4) can equally arise where a person initially complies with the notice but subsequently publishes or causes to be published a statement which is, or is for all practical purposes, the same or to the same effect as the statement to which the notice related (known as a 'repeat statement'), for the person is treated as already having received a notice. There is a defence under sub-ss (5) and (6) if the person can demonstrate to a legal burden of proof[197] that he has taken 'taken every step he reasonably could' to prevent a repeat statement from becoming available to the public and to ascertain whether it does and was not aware of the publication of the repeat statement or took 'every step he reasonably could' to deal with it when he did become aware. The phrase, 'every step he reasonably could' is meant to impose a higher duty of attention that 'taking reasonable steps', a standard which may be satisfied overall without taking some reasonable steps. The threat regarding failure to comply is not tantamount to the commission of an offence through endorsement under s 1 or 2 since other elements of those offences must be proven nor are all Convention offences covered by s 2. Other limits on impact are that the refusal to comply with a notice is not itself an offence, nor even is there any police power to force the take-down of materials.

---

[195] The phrase in sub-s (7)(a), 'likely to be understood' demands a higher standard of proof than 'capable of being understood': Hansard HL vol 676, col 700 (7 December 2005), Baroness Scotland.

[196] See s 3(9).

[197] Hansard HL vol 678, col 217 (1 February 2006), Lord Goldsmith. This burden of proof is said to be fair and reasonable: Hansard HL vol 676, col 709 (7 December 2005), Baroness Scotland. Lord Carlile viewed it as an evidential burden: *Proposals by Her Majesty's Government for changes to the laws against terrorism* (Home Office, London, 2005) para 25. There is also a strong possibility that the courts will impose an evidential burden: *Sheldrake v Director of Public Prosecutions; Attorney General's Reference (No 4 of 2002)* [2004] UKHL 43.

It was felt by critics to be unpalatable that these restrictions on freedom of expression do not engage a judicial officer at any stage, who, far more than a commercial service provider, could be expected to stand up for the principle of rights.[198] The government retort was that judicial process would create the danger of undue delay in a 'fast moving world'.[199] However, the possibility that an over-enthusiastic local police officer might tread too heavily is taken up by the *Home Office Guidance on Notices Issued under Section 3 of the Terrorism Act 2006*, which was promised in response to parliamentary apprehensions.[200] The Guidance advises that these notices can be initiated by any constable but in practice ought to be confined to officers of the Metropolitan Police Service Counter-Terrorist Command (SO15) who are trained and experienced in electronic policing; they will apply in writing or electronically, setting out reasons, for the giving of the notice, to an authorizing officer of superintendent rank or above in the Metropolitan Police Counter-Terrorism Command; there should also be consultation with the Association of Chief Police Officers Terrorism and Allied Matters policy lead.[201] Whether this relatively obscure Guidance saves the scheme from challenge by the publishers of web pages under Arts 6, 10, and 13 of the European Convention, remains to be seen, but the statutory scheme does not require reasons to be given, does not pay express regard to free expression, and does not set any scheme for objections.

2.74

The potential operation of s 3 has to be curtailed by the impact of the Electronic Commerce Directive.[202] In particular, liability must be curtailed where an information society service provider acts as an automatic 'conduit' of information (Art 12), provider of a cache for information (Art 13), or host of information without actual knowledge of illegal activity (Art 14). It is also forbidden under Art 15 to impose a general obligation on providers, when providing the services covered by Arts 12, 13, and 14, to monitor the information which they transmit or store, nor a general obligation actively to seek facts or circumstances indicating illegal activity. The government conceded during debates on the 2006 Act that UK-based providers who are blocked from taking action against information held on a computer in a third country by the laws of that land will be viewed as having a reasonable excuse under s 3(2).[203] It was also conceded that s 3(5), as applied to repeat statements, should not be interpreted as imposing a duty of general monitoring or prevention.[204] There was also the promise that the police should first act against the webmaster rather than the service provider.[205] The Electronic Commerce Directive (Terrorism Act 2006) Regulations 2007[206] further clarify the relationship to the Electronic Commerce Directive. The government resisted any further, domestic exemption for common carrier services.[207]

2.75

[198] See Hansard HL vol 679, col 168 (28 February 2006); Lord Carlile, *Proposals by Her Majesty's Government for changes to the laws against terrorism* (Home Office, London, 2005) para 27.

[199] Hansard HL vol 676, col 677 (7 December 2005), Baroness Scotland.

[200] Hansard HC vol 442, col 1472 (15 February 2006), Hazel Blears.

[201] Paras 13–16.

[202] 2000/31/EC. See Electronic Commerce (European Communities Directive) Regulations 2002, SI 2002/2013.

[203] Hansard HL vol 676, col 671 (7 December 2005), Baroness Scotland.

[204] *Ibid* at col 672. See also Guidance, para 42.

[205] *Ibid* at col 612. This point is not reflected in the Guidance, para 10.

[206] SI 2007/1550.

[207] Hansard HL vol 677, col 611 (17 January 2006), Baroness Scotland. 'Electronic communications networks' is defined in the Communications Act 2003, s 32.

2.76   No use has yet been made of s 3 since service providers are responsive to police 'advice'.[208] Indeed, the Guidance suggests contact between police and provider before any notice is issued and that a 'voluntary approach' should be taken where the provider is not viewed as encouraging publication.[209]

(c) Search, seizure, and forfeiture of terrorist publications

2.77   Section 28 provides for an alternative mode of disposal of s 2 materials, modelled on Sch 3 of the Customs and Excise Management Act 1979. A justice of the peace (or sheriff in Scotland), if satisfied that there are reasonable grounds for suspecting that articles falling within s 2(2)(a) to (e)[210] are likely to be found on any premises, may issue a search and seizure warrant. Proceedings for forfeiture may then be taken on an information laid by or on behalf of the Director of Public Prosecutions or the Director of Public Prosecutions for Northern Ireland.[211]

2.78   The details as to the forfeiture procedures in relation to seized materials are set out in Sch 2. By para 2, the relevant constable must give notice to owners or, in default, occupiers of the premises where the article was seized. Any person claiming that the seized article is not liable to forfeiture may give notice under para 3 of that claim to a constable at any police station in the police area in which the premises where the seizure took place are located; the notice must be in writing and issued within one month of the date of the constable's notice or (if not an owner or occupier) of the date of the seizure. If no such counter-claim is issued, the article can be treated under para 5 as automatically forfeited at the end of the relevant periods. If there is a counter-claim, under para 6, the relevant constable must decide whether to take proceedings to ask the court to condemn the article as forfeited; the court can so order if it finds that the article was liable to forfeiture at the time of its seizure, and it is not satisfied that its forfeiture would be inappropriate. Otherwise, if either the constable does not take proceedings or the court is not convinced to order forfeiture, the article must be returned to the person who appears to the court to be entitled to it.[212] The venues for these civil proceedings can be, in England or Wales, either in the High Court or in a magistrates' court (with appeal to the Crown Court), in Scotland, either in the Court of Session or in the sheriff court, and in Northern Ireland, either in the High Court or in a court of summary jurisdiction (with appeal to the county court).[213]

2.79   Disposal by this route follows in the pattern of s 3 of the Obscene Publications Act 1959.[214] However, the danger is that this form of administrative justice underplays the value of free expression. In the context of terrorism-related proceedings, it is entirely conceivable that an owner or occupier will not wish to take on the forces of the state and gain a dubious reputation for themselves. Lord Carlile argued that the jurisdiction

---

[208] See Lord Carlile, *Report on the Operation in 2007 of the Terrorism Act 2000* (Home Office, London, 2008) para 297.
[209] Paras 20, 27, Annex C.
[210] The private possession covered by s 2(2)(f) is thereby excluded. There is also a saving for legally privileged materials under the Police and Criminal Evidence Act 1984 s 19(6): Hansard HL vol 676, col 1244 (7 December 2005), Baroness Scotland.
[211] s 28(5), (10).
[212] It can be disposed of if it is not practicable within 12 months: para 13.
[213] Paras 7, 10.
[214] See Robertson, G., *Obscenity* (Weidenfeld & Nicolson, London, 1979) ch 4.

should be exercised by professional district judges (magistrates' courts) and not magistrates,[215] though a lay element seems desirable in principle.

(d) *Assessment*

The new offences cross a number of important philosophical boundaries in the delimitation of state power.[216] Based on a rights audit, speech which encourages violence in any circumstances is harmful and should be stopped.[217] In *Zana v Turkey*,[218] the applicant's statement of sympathy for the PKK had to be regarded as likely to exacerbate an already violent situation and unprotected by Art 10, even though the applicant was a mayor in the region. In *Gündüz v Turkey*,[219] the leader of Tarikat Aczmendi (an Islamic sect) criticized moderate Islamic intellectuals and called his supporters to have 'one brave man among the Muslims to plant a dagger in their soft underbelly and run them through twice with a bayonet'. Even as a metaphor, such language did not rouse any support from the European Court of Human Rights, nor did a cartoon in praise of the September 11 attacks published in the Basque country in *Leroy v France*.[220] But where, as in *Arslan v Turkey*,[221] the Court was sure that the words used did not constitute an incitement to violence, armed resistance, or an uprising, then it defended statements, such as those in a book which alleged that the Turkish state oppressed the Kurds and so explained the consequent 'resistance' and 'Kurdish intifada'. As made clear in *Gerger v Turkey*,[222] words such as 'resistance', 'struggle' and 'liberation' do not necessarily constitute an incitement to violence. The more neutral reporting of declarations or interviews of terrorist representatives by media professionals will also tend to attract the protection of the Court, as in *Sürek and Özdemir v Turkey*,[223] and latitude is given to artistic and academic speech.[224] Being one step removed from any direct incitement to violence or the certainty that anyone is actually affected by the incitement may cast more doubt on the compliance of ss 1 and 2.[225]

2.80

---

[215] Lord Carlile, *Proposals by Her Majesty's Government for changes to the laws against terrorism* (Home Office, London, 2005) para 75.

[216] See Gross, H., *A Theory of Criminal Justice* (Oxford University Press, Oxford, 1979) p 128; Ashworth, A., *Principles of Criminal Law* (5th edn, Oxford University Press, Oxford, 2006) pp 49–50; Australian Law Reform Commission, *Fighting Words* (Report 104, Canberra, 2006) ch 6.

[217] For further discussion, see Davis, H., 'Lessons from Turkey: anti-terrorism legislation and the protection of free speech' [2005] *European Human Rights Law Review* 75.

[218] App no 18954/91, 1997-VII. See also *Sürek v Turkey (No 1)*, App no 26682/95, 1999-IV (calling for bloody revenge); *Sürek v Turkey (No 3)*, App no 24735/94, 8 July 1999 (encouragement to wage a war of national liberation), *Falakaoglu and Saygili v Turkey*, App nos 22147/02, 24972/03, 23 January 2007.

[219] App no 59745/00, 2003-XI.

[220] App no 36109/03, 2 October 2008.

[221] App no 23462/94, 8 July 1999, para 48. See also *Ceylan v Turkey*, App no 23556/94, 1999-IV; *Erdoğdu v Turkey* App no 25723/94, 2000-VI.

[222] App no 24919/94, 8 July 1999, para 50. See also *Erdogdu and Ince v Turkey*, App nos 25067/94; 25068/94, 8 July 1999; *Okçuoglu v Turkey*, App no 24246/94, 8 July 1999; *Polat v Turkey*, App no 23500/94, 8 July 1999.

[223] App nos 23927/94, 24277/94, 8 July 1999. See also *Sürek v Turkey (No 2)*, App no 24122/94, 8 July 1999; *Sürek v Turkey (No 4)*, App no 24762/94, 8 July 1999.

[224] *Başkaya and Okçuoğlu v Turkey*, App nos 23536/94, 24408/94, 1999-IV; *Karataş v Turkey*, App no 23168/94, 1999-IV.

[225] See Joint Committee on Human Rights, *Counter-Terrorism Policy and Human Rights: Terrorism Bill and related matters* (2005–06 HL 75, HC 561) para 34; Hunt, A., 'Criminal prohibitions on direct and indirect encouragement of terrorism' [2007] *Criminal Law Review* 441 at p 452.

2.81   While the general objective may be supportable, a major criticism of the legislation is its vagueness,[226] and there are also apparent inconsistencies and therefore unexpected complexities. However, the English courts have viewed as compatible with Art 10 words such as 'insulting'.[227] The European Court of Human Rights has upheld, at least for some purposes, the term 'breach of the peace'.[228]

2.82   The third test of proportionality is more contestable, since there exists already a myriad of clearer and less contentious offences which already circumscribe extremist speech such as emanating from the glorifiers of terrorism. The common law offence of seditious libel should not be counted as amongst the preferred alternatives, though it has been clarified.[229] However, statutory alternatives do exist, although they do not precisely replicate the 2006 Act and so the Joint Committee on Human Rights accepted the need for these developments.[230] Most directly relevant are the offences in the Terrorism Act 2000, Pt II and also in ss 59 to 61, which deal with incitements of terrorism abroad, invoked, for instance, against 'cyberterrorist' 'Irhabi 007', Younis Tsouli.[231] Abu Izzadeen was convicted of terrorist fundraising and inciting terror abroad but cleared of encouraging terrorism.[232] Beyond the Terrorism Act 2000, there is the offence of soliciting murder under the Offences against the Person Act 1861, s 4.[233] Public order offences can be invoked for lesser outrages, such as showing a video of a beheading in Iraq[234] or organizing without notice vituperative protests outside an embassy.[235] In summary, there are no clear gaps in the law where harm can be caused with impunity. The possibility of alternative charges was illustrated by the first recorded conviction under the 2006 Act. Arising from videos and CDs in his possession when arrested at Glasgow Airport, plus computer materials and a website (Al Battar), Mohammed Atif Siddique was convicted not only of collecting and distributing terrorist propaganda, but also of offences under the Terrorism Act 2000, ss 54, 57, and 58 (which were viewed as most serious), plus breach of the peace.[236]

2.83   As for the overall balance in the fourth test of proportionality, the European Court of Human Rights has little sympathy for extreme speech which flirts with violence, as

---

[226] Joint Committee on Human Rights, *Counter-Terrorism Policy and Human Rights: Terrorism Bill and related matters* (2005–05 HL 75, HC 561) paras 27–8. See also Report of the Special Rapporteur on the promotion and protection of human rights and fundamental freedoms while countering terrorism (A/61/267, 2006) para 7.

[227] *Hammond v DPP* [2004] EWHC 69 (Admin) at para 27.

[228] Compare *Steel and others v United Kingdom*, App no 24838/94, 1998-VII; *Hashman and Harrup v United Kingdom*, App no 25594/94, 1999-VIII.

[229] See *R v Bow Street Magistrates Court, ex p Choudhury* [1991] 1 QB 429. For application to terrorism, see Walker, C., *The Prevention of Terrorism in British Law* (2nd edn, Manchester University Press, Manchester, 1992) ch 11.

[230] Joint Committee on Human Rights, *Counter-Terrorism Policy and Human Rights: Terrorism Bill and related matters* (2005–05 HL 75, HC 561) para 25.

[231] *Attorney General's References (Nos 85, 86, and 87 of 2007) R v Tsouli and others* [2007] EWCA Crim 3300.

[232] *The Times* 19 April 2008 p 25.

[233] See *R v el-Faisal* [2004] EWCA Crim 456; *R v Hamza* [2006] EWCA Crim 2918; *R v Saleem, Javed, and Muhid* [2007] EWCA Crim 2692; cases of Attila Ahmet and Mohammed Hamid, *The Times* 8 March 2008 p 26; O'Donoghue, T., 'Glorification, Irish terror and Abu Hamza' (2006) 170 *Justice of the Peace* 291.

[234] See the case of Subhann Younis (Glasgow District Court, *The Times* 29 September 2005 p 3).

[235] See the case of Anjem Choudary (*The Guardian* 22 July 2006 p 14).

[236] *The Times* 18 September 2007 p 31; *The Scotsman* 24 October 2007 p 7. For the views of his lawyer, see *Re Anwar* [2008] HCJAC 36.

already explained. It was readily rejected even in *O'Driscoll v Secretary of State for the Home Department*[237] in connection with a magazine which was said to contain no incitement to violence. The justification of s 1 and 2 may be easier to achieve since there is mention of the emulation of action except in the case of non-glorifying indirect incitement.[238] Therefore, with that exception, these are not pure speech crimes,[239] but they do seek to intervene before one extreme speaker generates multiple extreme actors.[240] Nevertheless, there may be three important qualifications to be considered.

One is the application of these offences in the context of foreign regimes (by reference to s 17).[241] For example, there were furious debates about whether this offence might criminalize anyone who glorified armed opposition to the Apartheid regime in South Africa (such as the revered Nelson Mandela), and there were calls for the future prosecution of Cherie Booth, the wife of British Prime Minister Tony Blair, for stating that 'in view of the illegal occupation of Palestinian land I can well understand how decent Palestinians become terrorists'.[242] What if Saddam Hussein were still in power and called upon the British government to take action against any surviving 'terrorists' of Dujail who, in 1982, had attempted to assassinate him (reprisals against whom eventually resulted in a death sentence against him)? Plots against the Libyan regime were possibly encouraged years ago,[243] but now there is rapprochement. Conversely, plots against Syria are openly tolerated.[244] The offences lead onto a slippery slope into passing judgment upon all manner of foreign disputes and chance remarks. 2.84

The second qualification is that the policy of closing down channels of political discourse may be counter-productive when applied to political actors and speech. Surely, the Northern Ireland experience should have taught the UK government the folly of freezing out political fronts. Whilst much of what the political sympathizers of violent groups have to say is unpalatable or even reprehensible, their views must be debated so that the extremists, government, and public can be educated and respond with intelligence,[245] rather than receiving only the hateful instrument of martyrdom statements.[246] In line with these concerns, the European Court of Human Rights has been particularly wary of restraints on the speech of politicians.[247] 2.85

The third qualification is that the offences in the 2006 Act go beyond what is required by international law, especially as represented by the Council of Europe Convention on the 2.86

---

[237] [2002] EWHC 2477 (Admin).

[238] See Hunt, A., 'Criminal prohibitions on direct and indirect encouragement of terrorism' [2007] *Criminal Law Review* 441 at pp 455–6.

[239] *Ibid* at p 450.

[240] See Fiss, O., 'Freedom of speech and political violence' in Cohen-Almagor, R., *Liberal Democracy and the Limits of Tolerance* (University of Michigan Press, Ann Arbor, 2000) p 75.

[241] Joint Committee on Human Rights, *Counter-Terrorism Policy and Human Rights: Terrorism Bill and related matters* (2005–06 HL 75, HC 561) para 12.

[242] Hansard HC vol 438, col 844 (2 November 2005), Bob Marshall-Andrews.

[243] Allegations were made by David Shayler: <http://cryptome.org/shayler-gaddafi.htm>.

[244] See the activities of the 'National Salvation Front': *The Times* 5 June 2006 p 30.

[245] Hansard HC vol 438, col 326 (26 October 2005), Charles Clarke.

[246] For excerpts of the video of Mohammed Sidique Khan, see <http://news.bbc.co.uk/1/hi/uk/4206800.stm>, 2005.

[247] *Castells v Spain*, App No 11798/85, Ser A, vol 236 (1992). See also *Association Ekin v France*, App no 39288/98, 2001-VIII; Ribbelink, O., *'Apologie du Terrorisme' and 'Incitement to Terrorism'* (Council of Europe, Strasbourg, 2004).

Prevention of Terrorism of 2005.[248] The government views this discrepancy as unproblematic,[249] but it does raise questions as to whether the curtailments of rights will be seen as legitimate when subjected to international scrutiny.

2.87 Democratic accountability has been adequately engaged during the passage of these controversial offences, though the potential impact on internet expression is not being adequately monitored so as to facilitate future policy debate.

2.88 Constitutional governance might also be said to be deficient because of the vague nature of incitement. This commentary has demonstrated that the offences in ss 1 and 2 are riddled with uncertainties and unexplained anomalies.

C. OTHER MEASURES AGAINST EXTREMISM

1. Racial and religious hatred

2.89 Part V of the Anti-terrorism, Crime and Security Act 2001 addresses racial and religious hatred in order to give reassurance to home and foreign audiences.[250] It is an offence under ss 37 and 38 to stir up hatred against racial groups abroad. In addition, ss 40 and 41 increase the maximum penalties for race hatred offences from two to seven years. As for religious hatred, s 39 of the Anti-terrorism, Crime and Security Act allows a religious motivation to be treated as an aggravating factor in charging offenders under the Crime and Disorder Act 1998, s 28 and then sentencing them under s 153 of the Powers of Criminal Courts (Sentencing) Act 2000. The view of the Newton Committee was that broader reform should be considered in a context other than the terrorism legislation.[251] An offence of religious hatred has emerged in the Racial and Religious Hatred Act 2006, as well as the abolition of blasphemy.[252]

2. Measures against extremism beyond the terrorism legislation

2.90 It is also beyond the scope of this book to explain laws against political extremism beyond the anti-terrorism legislation. But mention might be made of those most closely allied. They include electoral restraints, often designed to curtail Sinn Féin, in the Representation of the People Act 1981,[253] the Elected Authorities (Northern Ireland) Act 1989,[254] plus

---

[248] See Joint Committee on Human Rights, *Counter-Terrorism Policy and Human Rights: Terrorism Bill and related matters* (2005–06 HL 75, HC 561) para 41; Joint Committee on Human Rights, *The Council of Europe Convention on the Prevention of Terrorism* (2006–07 HL 26/HC 247) paras 26–39.

[249] Government Response to the Joint Committee on Human Rights, *Counter-Terrorism Policy and Human Rights: Terrorism Bill and related matters* (2005–06 HL 114, HC 888) p 7.

[250] Hansard HC vol 375, col 703 (26 November 2001), David Blunkett. See further Idriss, M.M., 'Religion and the Anti-terrorism, Crime and Security Act 2001' [2002] *Criminal Law Review* 890; House of Lords Select Committee on Religious Offences in England and Wales (2002–03 HL 95) chs 8, 9; Allen, C. and Nielsen, J., *Summary report on Islamophobia in the EU after 11 September 2001* (European Union Monitoring Centre on Racism and Xenophobia, Vienna, 2002); Stone, R., *Islamophobia* (Trentham Books, Stoke, 2004).

[251] Privy Counsellor Review Committee, *Anti-terrorism, Crime and Security Act 2001 Review, Report* (2003–04 HC 100) para 270.

[252] Criminal Justice and Immigration Act 2008, s 79.

[253] Walker, C., 'Prisoners in Parliament—another view' [1982] *Public Law* 389.

[254] Walker, C., 'Elected representatives and the democratic process in Northern Ireland' (1988) 51 *Modern Law Review* 605.

restraints on the broadcast media[255] and threats against cyberspace.[256] Other specialist laws have addressed animal rights extremists.[257] Added to this legislative catalogue, the bombings of July 2005 were the signal for comprehensive community policies under the programme 'Preventing Extremism Together'.[258]

D. EXTREMISM—CONCLUSIONS

The anti-terrorism legislation reflects a long-standing notion of 'militant democracy' in which a state based on legitimate foundations should avoid 'suicidal lethargy' in the face of opponents who abuse its tolerance by destroying its values.[259] Even if this stance of militancy is legitimate, and Art 17 of the European Convention suggests approval, consideration should be given as to whether, on a rights audit, less intrusive measures than proscription or speech offences would better distinguish the legitimacy of extreme speech which seeks the overthrow of the constitutional order and the encouragement of violence. On the basis of democratic accountability and constitutional governance, significant improvements in proscription processes have been noted. But these must be set alongside the vast expansion in the invocation of the powers, often unexplained and against foreign groups fighting against dire oppression. As for the offences in the 2006 Act, the breadth of the definition of terrorism, including its indiscriminate extra-territorial application, compounds the latitude of these measures, especially as insufficient weight is assigned to the human rights value of political speech. These criticisms do not, however, imply that activists in groups such as Al-Qa'ida should be treated as irregular combatants rather than terrorists;[260] the application of the laws of war in the wrong circumstances, as in Guantánamo Bay, may achieve maximum freedom of action for the executive but also the maximum opprobrium and human rights abuses.

2.91

---

[255] See BBC editorial guidelines (<www.bbc.co.uk/guidelines/editorialguidelines/edguide/war>); Butler, D., *The Trouble with Reporting Northern Ireland* (Avebury, Aldershot, 1995); Edgerton, G., 'Quelling the "Oxygen of Publicity"' (1996) 30 *Journal of Popular Culture* 115.

[256] Walker, C., 'Cyber-terrorism' (2006) 110 *Penn State Law Review* 625.

[257] Criminal Justice and Public Order Act 1994, ss 68, 69; Criminal Justice and Courts Services Act 2000, s 46; Criminal Justice and Police Act 2001, s 42; Serious Organised Crime and Police Act 2005, ss 145, 146. See Home Office, *Animal Rights Extremism* (London, 2001); Home Office, *Animal Welfare—Human Rights* (London, 2004).

[258] See Home Office, *Pursue, Prevent, Protect, Prepare: The United Kingdom's Strategy for Countering International Terrorism* (Cm 7547, London, 2009) para 9.04.

[259] Lowenstein, K., 'Militant democracy and human rights' (1937) 31 *Am Pol Sci Rev* 417, at p 432. See also Sajó, A. (ed), *Militant Democracy* (Eleven International Publishing, Utrecht, 2004).

[260] See Meltzer, D., 'Al Qa'ida: terrorists or irregulars?' in Strawson, J., *Law After Ground Zero* (Glasshouse Press, London, 2002).

3
TERRORIST FUNDING
AND PROPERTY

A. BACKGROUND

A constant refrain is that 'money is a crucial factor in the continuance of terrorism'[1] and   3.01
that '[m]oney underpins all terrorist activity . . . ',[2] though these statements rather
downplay the personal commitment which drives individuals to volunteer for high
odds of death. Attempts to formulate a legislative rejoinder began in 1989[3] but were
estimated to have produced limited impact by the Lloyd Report.[4]

The most significant innovations in Pt III of the Terrorism Act 2000 embark tenta-   3.02
tively on the road of civil forfeiture through cash seizures and extend the financial
offences and criminal forfeiture to foreign terrorism through the operation of s 1.[5] Part
III begins with a definition of 'terrorist property' in s 14 which exceeds the demands of

---

[1] Jellicoe Report, *Report of the Operation of the Prevention of Terrorism (Temporary Provisions) Act 1976*
(Cmnd 8803, London, 1983) para 213.
[2] Home Office, *Possible Measures for Inclusion into a Future Counter-Terrorism Bill* (London, 2007) para 54.
[3] See Prevention of Terrorism (Temporary Provisions) Act 1989, Pt III; Northern Ireland (Emergency
Provisions) Act 1991, Pt VII.
[4] See *Inquiry into Legislation against Terrorism* (Cm 3420, London, 1996) ch 13; Home Office and Northern
Ireland Office, *Legislation against Terrorism* (Cm 4178, London, 1998) ch 6.
[5] See further (A/RES/54/109, Cm 4663, London, 1999) art 7.

the United Nations Convention for the Suppression of the Financing of Terrorism since it extends beyond assets and funds into resources.[6]

3.03   These strategies are supplemented by the Anti-terrorism, Crime and Security Act 2001. Part I replaces the cash seizure powers in the Terrorism Act 2000. The main variance is that the exercise of the power is no longer confined to internal or external borders. Section 3 and Sch 2 also amend other Parts of the Terrorism Act 2000 to extend the scope of investigative and freezing powers. More original ideas in the 2001 Act concern the introduction of account monitoring and customer information orders, and extra powers to freeze the assets of overseas bodies or residents.

3.04   The strategy behind these measures (and other besides) was set out in an *Action Plan on Terrorist Financing of 2001*[7] and also involved structural developments as well as a shift in emphasis upon underground banking systems and money service businesses.[8]

B. OFFENCES

3.05   All stages of tangible support for terrorism are covered by a series of offences in ss 15 to 18 of the Terrorism Act 2000. Initial fund-raising or donations are forbidden by three offences in s 15 of the Terrorism Act 2000, involving (1) the invitation of a contribution, (2) receiving such a contribution, or (3) providing a contribution.[9] The aid can be provided by money or other property being solicited, received, or made available, whether or not for consideration. In this way, a loan would be covered whether it was intended to be repaid or not.

3.06   The *mens rea* for the offences requires, as alternatives, intention as to terroristic purposes or reasonable (rather than subjective) suspicion of them. The most straightforward instance of reasonable suspicion is where the person knows of the primary facts from which reasonable suspicion can be inferred. More difficult is where the person is ignorant of the primary facts founding the reasonable suspicion, whether because of negligence or otherwise. Section 15 does appear to require that the person really does harbour a reasonable suspicion and so has knowledge of the primary facts. A more objective standard to cater for the wilfully or carelessly ignorant should not apply in the absence of wording such as that the defendant 'ought to' reasonably suspect or where 'there is' a reasonable suspicion.[10]

---

[6] (A/RES/54/109, Cm 4663, London, 1999) art 1. See Legal Department of the IMF, *Suppressing the Financing of Terrorism: A Handbook for Legislative Drafting* (IMF, Washington DC, 2003) p 5. Such a wider approach may be warranted by the UN Security Council Resolution 1373 (2001), art 1(c).

[7] Hansard HC vol 372, col 940 (15 October 2001), Gordon Brown.

[8] See HM Treasury, *The Financial Challenge to Crime and Terrorism* (London, 2007) para 3.66; Money Laundering Regulations 2007, SI 2007/2157; HMRC, The Money Service Business Action Plan (<http://www.hmrc.gov.uk/mlr/money-service-busplan.pdf>, 2008).

[9] Compare the Terrorism Financing Convention, art 2 which requires the involvement to be conducted wilfully and has no equivalent to s 15(1)(a): Legal Department of the IMF, *Suppressing the Financing of Terrorism: A Handbook for Legislative Drafting* (IMF, Washington, DC, 2003) p 7; Davis, K.E., 'The financial war on terrorism' in Ramraj, V.V. *et al*, *Global Anti-Terrorism Law and Policing* (Cambridge University Press, Cambridge, 2005) p 182.

[10] Compare Smith, I., Owen, T., and Bodnar, A., *Asset Recovery* (Oxford University Press, Oxford, 2007) para I.3.349.

An example of a s 15 offence in action (combined with s 17) was *R v McDonald, Rafferty, and O'Farrell*.[11] Three members of the Real IRA were convicted of seeking weapons and money from a person whom they believed to be an Iraqi government agent but who was an agent of the CIA and British Security Service. **3.07**

The next stage involves the processing or laundering of the proceeds. By s 16 of the 2000 Act, a person commits an offence by using money or other property for the purposes of terrorism or possesses money or other property, if there is intent that it should be used, or reasonable cause to suspect that it may be used, for the purposes of terrorism. The alternative *actus reus* of possession seems to create an offence dependent entirely on *mens rea*.[12] **3.08**

The offence in s 16 was tested in *O'Driscoll v Secretary of State for the Home Department*.[13] The claimant, a British citizen, arrested at Dover for possession of a magazine associated with a proscribed Turkish organization, DHKP-C, argued that s 16 was incompatible with Arts 10 and 11 of the European Convention on Human Rights. The Divisional Court noted that in order to prove an offence, it was necessary to show that the defendant had a specific intent, and the same mental element was also important in assessing proportionality.[14] The question then was whether the organization had been properly proscribed. If so, and the proscription was not disputed, then a narrowly conceived offence to enforce some of the financial aspects of proscription could not be regarded as disproportionate. There are two points of weakness for s 16 in this reasoning. The first is that it assumes a close linkage between a publication and the funding of a proscribed organization. In this case, the applicant had not been convicted of an offence of membership. The second weakness is that s 16 can also relate to 'the purposes of terrorism'. This formulation does not founder on grounds of vagueness,[15] but the absence of proscription undermines the assumption that 'there is no question about the terrorist nature of the organization'[16] no longer applies. **3.09**

A less controversial example concerns Kazi Nurur Rahman, who was convicted of attempting to possess weapons, including missiles, offered in a sting operation.[17] This example also illustrates the potential overlap between the offences in Pt III.[18] **3.10**

More indirect involvement is covered by ss 17 and 18. By s 17 ('Funding arrangements'), a person commits an offence by entering into (in other words, is part of the initiation of), or becoming concerned in (in other words, joins in some existing relationship or transaction), an arrangement as a result of which money or other property is made available or is to be made available to another, with knowledge or reasonable cause to suspect that it will or may be used for the purposes of terrorism. **3.11**

The application of s 17 was illustrated by the convictions in 2003 of Benmerzouga and Meziane.[19] These two Algerians raised money through skimming credit card details **3.12**

---

[11] [2005] EWCA Crim 1945.

[12] It exceeds the Convention: Davis, K.E., 'The financial war on terrorism' in Ramraj, V.V. *et al*, *Global Anti-Terrorism Law and Policing* (Cambridge University Press, Cambridge, 2005) p 182.

[13] [2002] EWHC 2477 (Admin).

[14] *Ibid* at paras 26, 27.

[15] *Ibid* at para 24.

[16] *Ibid* at para 26.

[17] <http://news.bbc.co.uk/1/hi/uk/6206886.stm>, 2007.

[18] See Practice Direction (Criminal Proceedings: Consolidation) [2002] 2 Cr App Rep 533 at para IV.34.3.

[19] *R v Meziane* [2004] EWCA Crim 1768. See also *R v Khan* [2007] EWCA Crim 2331.

and sending them to associates, who raised over £200,000. Detection arose not through suspicious financial transactions but through monitored associates.

3.13   By s 18 ('Money laundering'), a person commits an offence by entering into, or becoming concerned in, an arrangement which facilitates the retention or control by or on behalf of another person of terrorist property. The 'arrangements' can involve concealment, by removal from the jurisdiction, by transfer to nominees, or otherwise. By use of the term 'terrorist property', the section catches funding purposes which do not directly relate to terrorism, such as payments to the relatives of paramilitary prisoners.[20] Under s 18(2), proof of *mens rea* is even easier: the burden is switched to the defendant to prove on balance that he did not know and had no reasonable cause to suspect that the arrangement related to terrorist property. Reasonable cause to suspect may be based on information then available, though wilful reluctance to investigate suspicious circumstances will not provide absolution.[21] Section 118 does not apply to this defence. It is submitted that this switch in the burden of proof is unfair outside the regulated sector or even professional actors and should be interpreted as an evidentiary.[22]

3.14   According to s 22, the maximum penalties for the foregoing offences are: (a) on conviction on indictment, imprisonment not exceeding fourteen years, a fine, or both; (b) on summary conviction, imprisonment not exceeding six months, a fine not exceeding the statutory maximum, or both. The maximum was applied in *R v McDonald, Rafferty, and O'Farrell*, discounted by a guilty plea.[23] An increased maximum of life imprisonment has been mooted,[24] but the courts have already warned that 'substantial deterrent sentences' will be imposed.[25]

3.15   The jurisdiction over these offences is extended by s 63 of the Terrorism Act 2000, which is detailed in Chapter 6.

3.16   Alongside these special offences sit relevant 'normal' offences, such as extortion or demanding money with menaces under the Theft Act 1968, s 21. The crime is treated with severity in a terrorism context,[26] though there are calls for an aggravated penalty to be stated in statute.[27]

C. FORFEITURE

3.17   As demanded by the United Nations Convention for the Suppression of the Financing of Terrorism,[28] the Terrorism Act 2000, s 23, contains compendious provisions which allow criminal forfeiture predicated upon an *ad personam* conviction under ss 15 to 18 of

---

[20] Compare and distinguish *R v Loizou* [2005] EWCA Crim 1579.

[21] Compare Elagab, O., 'Control of terrorist funds and the banking system' (2006) 21 *Journal of Banking Law & Regulation* 38 at p 39.

[22] See further Smith, I., Owen, T., and Bodnar, A., *Asset Recovery* (Oxford University Press, Oxford, 2007) para I.3.626.

[23] [2005] EWCA Crim 1945 and [2005] EWCA Crim 1970.

[24] HM Treasury, *The Financial Challenge to Crime and Terrorism* (London, 2007) para 2.9.

[25] *Ibid* at para 74 per Lord Justice Tuckey. Note also *R v Khan: The Times* 18 March 2006 p 41.

[26] See *Attorney General's Reference (No 5 of 2006) (Potts)* [2004] NICA 27; *Attorney General's Reference No 5 of 2006 (O'Donnell)* [2006] NICA 38; *R v Lowey and Bennett* [2007] NICA 9.

[27] Northern Ireland Affairs Select Committee, *Organised Crime in Northern Ireland* (2005–06 HC 886) para 192.

[28] (A/RES/54/109, Cm 4663, London, 1999) art 8.

the 2000 Act. Several changes are made by Sch 2, Pt II, to the Anti-terrorism, Crime and Security Act 2001 and the Counter-Terrorism Act 2008 (s 34 substitutes a new version of s 23) in order to broaden and clarify the powers. Next, since s 23 only applies to offences under ss 15 to 18,[29] the Counter-Terrorism Act 2008, s 35, inserts s 23A so as to extend forfeiture to any terrorist-type offence, as an alternative to the Proceeds of Crime Act 2002.

1. Powers

Where a forfeiture order is imposed under s 23 regarding an offence under ss 15(1), 15(2), or 16, it may extend to money or other property which the convict, at the time of the offence, possessed or controlled, and which, at that time, has in fact been used for terrorism or where there is intent or reasonable cause to suspect its use for the purposes of terrorism. This wording is altered in relation to s 15(3)—it is sufficient that there has in fact been use for terrorism or that the person subjectively knew or had reasonable cause to suspect the use for the purposes of terrorism. Under ss 17 and 18, there must be proof that there has in fact been use for terrorism or that the person intended such use. For s 18, there is no burden on the prosecution to show that the money or property was in the possession of the convicted person or even that he had reasonable cause to suspect that it might be used for the purposes of terrorism, though the person may have sought to contest these matters under s 18(2).[30] The changes in 2008 allow for the forfeiture of property which had been used for the purposes of terrorism whether envisaged to any degree or not. A case in point might be the forfeiture of a rented flat where bombs are made. The property of an unwitting landlord is thus put in jeopardy.

3.18

The new s 23A, as inserted in 2008, arises when there is a conviction for specified offences which comprise further specified terrorism legislation offences beyond ss 15 to 18 (in sub-s (2)), or offences ancillary (as defined by s 94 of the 2008 Act), or 'normal' offences beyond the terrorism legislation falling within Sch 2 of the 2008 Act[31] where the court determines under s 30 or 31 there exists a terrorist connection (as defined in s 93). The property must be in the possession or control of the convict where it had been used for the purposes of terrorism, or it was intended for such use, or where the court believes that it will be used for such use.

3.19

This extension is derived from s 111 of the Terrorism Act 2000 (formerly s 4 of the Criminal Justice (Terrorism and Conspiracy) Act 1998), which, before repeal in 2007, had applied an extended version of forfeiture to persons convicted of membership of specified organizations and related offences. However, s 23A applies in much broader circumstances, though only where the court believe the property will be used in terrorism, rather than may be used.[32]

3.20

---

[29] *Inquiry into Legislation against Terrorism* (Cm 3420, London, 1996) para 13.24; Home Office and Northern Ireland Office, *Legislation against Terrorism* (Cm 4178, London, 1998) para 6.21; HM Treasury, *The Financial Challenge to Crime and Terrorism* (London, 2007) para 2.9.

[30] Compare Mitchell, A.R., Taylor, S.M.E., and Talbot, K., *Mitchell, Taylor and Talbot on Confiscation and the Proceeds of Crime* (3rd edn, Sweet & Maxwell. London, 2002) para 12.005.

[31] The list can be amended by affirmative order for offences committed after the order: s 23A(5), (6); Delegated Powers and Regulatory Reform Committee, *Counter-Terrorism Bill* (2007–08 HL 133) para 5.

[32] HC Hansard Public Bill Committee on the Counter-Terrorism Bill, cols 394–5 (13 May 2008), Tony McNulty. Compare *Inquiry into Legislation against Terrorism* (Cm 3420, London, 1996) para 13.24. The more

3.21   The court may order under s 23(7) the forfeiture of any money or property which wholly or partly, and directly or indirectly, is received by any person as a payment or reward in connection with offences under ss 15 to 18. So, while a terrorist finance offence must have been committed, it need not have been committed by the person holding the money or property. Thus, where an accountant prepared accounts on behalf of a proscribed organization and was recompensed, the payment can be forfeited even though it was not intended or suspected for use in terrorism.[33] By s 23B (inserted by s 36 of the 2008 Act), when considering whether to make an order, a court shall have regard to (a) the value of the property; and (b) the likely financial and other effects on the convicted person.

2. Procedures

3.22   Section 23B (replacing s 23(7) in the 2000 version) allows the court to hear property claims by third parties such as family relatives. Third parties in the guise of victims of terrorism are considered for the first time in the anti-terrorism legislation by s 37 of the 2008 Act. By Sch 4, para 4A, the court making a forfeiture order can order that an amount is to be paid to the victim out of the proceeds of forfeiture (after deduction of the costs of disposal, third party property rights, and the fees of a receiver). This type of compensation can be made where the court is satisfied that it would have made an order under s 130 of the Powers of Criminal Courts (Sentencing) Act 2000, if it had not been for the inadequacy of the offender's means.

3.23   Remaining procedural details are set out at great length in Sch 4 to the Terrorism Act 2000,[34] Pt I relating to England and Wales, Pt II to Scotland, and Pt III to Northern Ireland. These provisions will be described primarily by reference to England and Wales.

3.24   Forfeiture orders will normally be made by the Crown Court, since most prosecutions under Pt III will arise in that venue. Schedule 4, para 2 sets out the ancillary powers of the courts, such as physical handover to a designated court officer[35] or to a designated police officer, directions for sale or disposal, the appointment of receivers, and payments to third party claimants under s 23(7). The costs and liabilities from the process are covered by para 3.

3.25   Given that the criminal trial and also the forfeiture proceedings may take some time to transact, para 5 seeks to avert the interim dissipation of assets. Accordingly, the High Court may make a restraint order where a forfeiture order has already been made, or it appears to the High Court that a forfeiture order may arise in ongoing proceedings for the offence.[36] The Anti-terrorism, Crime and Security Act 2001 amends para 5 to bring forward the bite of restraint orders. An application may also apply when a criminal

---

general Powers of the Criminal Court (Sentencing) Act 2000, s 143 does not cover land: *R v Khan* (1982) 76 Cr App Rep 29.

[33] See Home Office, *Explanatory Notes to the Terrorism Act 2000* (London, 2000) para 33.
[34] As amended by the Counter-Terrorism Act 2008, s 39 and sch 3 to account for ss 23A, 23B.
[35] As specified under para 4, and amended by the Courts Act 2003.
[36] See further: Civil Procedure Rules RSC Ord 115 Pt III; Practice Direction: Restraint orders and appointment of receivers in connection with criminal proceedings and investigations; *Re G (restraint order)* [2001] EWHC Admin 606.

investigation has been started with regard to s 15 to 18 offences and it appears to the High Court that a forfeiture order may be made in subsequent proceedings.[37] Prosecutors may wish to avail themselves of the facility under para 5(4) to apply for a restraint order to a judge in chambers without notice.[38] Lord Lloyd suggested that the restraint order procedure should be handled by the Crown Court so as to reduce the procedural complications for police and prosecutors.[39] But the power remains confined to the more remote High Court. The trial judge should be notified of the proceedings but should not mention them at trial.[40]

The effect of a restraint order is to prohibit a person to whom notice of it is given 3.26 from dealing with the relevant property. To reinforce the powers of restraint, para 7 allows a constable a summary power of seizure of any property subject to a restraint order for the purpose of preventing it from being removed from the jurisdiction, though the seizure should be notified to the High Court which will give directions. The consequences of restraint orders on registered land are covered by para 8.

Once a restraint order is issued,[41] notice must be given to any person affected by the 3.27 order, and such persons can apply for variation or discharge which must be granted when the criminal proceedings are completed (para 6). A restraint order shall also be discharged on such an application if the proceedings for the offence are not instituted within such time as the High Court considers reasonable, or, in any event, if the proceedings for the offence have been 'concluded' as defined by para 11 (though there may then be imposed a final forfeiture order). The court rules also allow for the indemnification of third parties against expenses incurred in complying with the order, and for living and legal expenses of the defendant.[42] On the latter aspect, the related Practice Direction[43] provides these expenses will be allowed 'normally, unless it is clear that a person restrained has sufficient assets which are not subject to the order . . . '.

Where a restraint order is discharged because criminal proceedings are not instituted 3.28 within a reasonable time, or do not result in conviction, or result in conviction which is subsequently pardoned or quashed, any person who had an interest in any property which was subject to restraint may apply under para 9 to the High Court for compensation (payable by the police or Director of Public Prosecutions). However, the right to compensation is strictly confined by para 9(4), by which the High Court must be satisfied: (a) that there was a 'serious default' on the part of a person concerned in the investigation or prosecution of the offence; (b) that the default is attributable to the police or Crown Prosecution Service; (c) that the applicant has suffered loss in consequence of the forfeiture order or restraint order; and (d) that, having regard to all the circumstances, it

---

[37] Lord Lloyd had sought a limit of five days before any arrest: *Inquiry into Legislation against Terrorism* (Cm 3420, London, 1996) paras 13.26, 13.27.

[38] See sch 4 para 5(4); RSC Ord 115 r 26. See *Jennings v Crown Prosecution Service* [2005] EWCA Civ 746; *Customs and Excise Commissioners v S* [2004] EWCA Crim 2374.

[39] See *Inquiry into Legislation against Terrorism* (Cm 3420, London, 1996) para 13.26.

[40] There is no set rule, unlike under the Criminal Procedure Rules 2005 r 61.14.

[41] It is argued that an order might be resisted by an offer of an undertaking (see Smith, I., Owen, T., and Bodnar, A., *Asset Recovery* (Oxford University Press, Oxford, 2007) para II.134), but the public interest in preventing terrorism financing is even higher than that in anti-money laundering.

[42] Civil Procedure Rules RSC Ord 115 r 27; Practice Direction r 4.

[43] Practice Direction, para 4.4.

is appropriate to order compensation to be paid.[44] Furthermore, by para 9(5), the High Court shall not order compensation to be paid where it appears to it that proceedings for the offence would have been instituted even if the serious default had not occurred. A slightly more generous compensation provision is set out in para 10, which applies where a forfeiture order or a restraint order is made in, or in relation to, proceedings for an offence, where the conviction is subsequently quashed on an appeal under s 7(2) or (5) and without proof of serious default. A person who had an interest in any property which was subject to the order may receive compensation if the High Court is satisfied the applicant has suffered loss and it is appropriate to order compensation to be paid (in this case by the Secretary of State).[45]

3.29   Forfeiture or restraint orders made in other jurisdictions in the British Islands and in external jurisdictions specified by order may be enforced in England and Wales under paras 13 and 14. The Terrorism Act 2000 (Enforcement of External Orders) Order 2001[46] includes all European Union and G7 states (plus India). These arrangements have been replaced for European Union states by the addition of paras 11A to 11G to Sch 4 via the Crime (International Co-operation) Act 2003.[47] The 2003 Act implements the Framework Decision on the execution in the European Union of orders freezing property or evidence adopted by the Council of the European Union on 22 July 2003.[48] When overseas freezing orders are received into the High Court, the Director of Public Prosecutions must be notified and given an opportunity to be heard, and the court may decline enforcement if its impact would be incompatible with the Human Rights Act 1998 (para 11E) or it would prejudice domestic proceedings (para 11F).

3.30   Corresponding powers for Scotland are set out in Pt II of Sch 4. The powers are conferred principally upon the Court of Session.[49] Applications for restraint orders shall be made by the Lord Advocate. Forfeiture in Northern Ireland is related by Pt III. An additional pathway for restraint orders used to be provided by para 36, whereby the Secretary of State could make an order. With doubts about consistency with Art 6 of the European Convention,[50] para 36 was repealed by the Terrorism (Northern Ireland) Act 2006. One special feature which persists is that it is a specific offence under para 37 to contravene a restraint order. This offence is additional to the contempt power of the High Court (as would apply elsewhere) and allows special pre-trial and trial processes to be applied (now under the Justice and Security (Northern Ireland) Act 2007). It is a defence to prove that there was a reasonable excuse for the contravention; s 118 does not apply.

---

[44] Much of the phraseology derives from the *ex gratia* system of payment of compensation for miscarriages of justice (Hansard HC vol 87, cols 689W (29 November 1985), Douglas Hurd) which was abolished in 2006. These restraints are not considered arbitrary: *Andrews v United Kingdom*, App no 49584/99, 26 September 2002; *Capewell v CCE* [2005] EWCA Civ 964.

[45] There may also be a residual discretion to protect the property rights of third parties under the Human Rights Act 1998: *Re A* [2002] EWHC 611.

[46] SI 2001/3927.

[47] s 90 and Sch 4. For other offences, see Serious Organised Crime and Police Act 2005, s 96.

[48] 2003/577/JHA, art 3. For implementation, see Council Document 5937/2/06.

[49] See Act of Sederunt (Rules of the Court of Session Amendment No 6) (Terrorism Act 2000) 2001, SSI 2001/494.

[50] See *Inquiry into Legislation against Terrorism* (Cm 3420, London, 1996) para 13.22.

Finally, Sch 4, Pt IV (which applies throughout the United Kingdom), relates to the   3.31
impact of forfeiture in the case of 'qualifying insolvency proceedings'. The effect is that an
application can be made by an insolvency practitioner within six months of the making
of a forfeiture order to remove the property from the impact of the forfeiture order and
allow it to be dealt with in the insolvency proceedings. Nevertheless, under para 48, the
Secretary of State shall be a creditor in those proceedings to the amount or value of the
forfeited property, albeit ranking after all other creditors.

D. SEIZURE OF CASH

The most eye-catching change introduced in the Terrorism Act 2000 is the power to   3.32
seize cash—a form of *in rem* civil forfeiture which is not dependent on criminal conviction. This change is based around the recommendations of the Lloyd Report,[51] but the
Report called for powers to apply only to cash being taken out of the country and subject
to a lower limit of £2,500 and with authorization to hold for more that forty-eight hours
being tested by a circuit judge. The seizure power assumes that the 'criminal economy is
much more cash intensive than the legitimate economy', based around the needs for
liquidity and anonymity.[52] The powers initially in the Terrorism Act 2000 were confined
to borders (including between Britain and Northern Ireland) because of the historical
precedents in the Drug Trafficking Act 1994, Pt II, and because borders provide effective
choke-points. Mainly because of the desire to remove this limitation,[53] but also to extend
the definition of 'cash', s 1 and Sch 1 of the Anti-terrorism, Crime and Security Act 2001
replaced wholesale ss 24 to 31 of the Terrorism Act 2000.

According to s 1(1) of the 2001 Act, the powers of seizure are to enable 'terrorist cash'   3.33
which (a) is intended to be used for terrorism purposes; (b) consists of resources of
a proscribed organization; or (c) is, or represents, property obtained through terrorism,
to be forfeited in civil proceedings before a magistrates' court or (in Scotland) the sheriff.
It is emphasized by s 1(2) that the seizure is exercisable whether or not any criminal
proceedings have been brought. Under Sch 1, para 1, 'terrorist cash' means cash within
sub-s (1)(a) or (b) of s 1, or property earmarked as terrorist property. For these purposes,
'cash' includes coins and notes in any currency, postal orders, cheques of any kind,
including travellers' cheques, bankers' drafts, bearer bonds and bearer shares, and
such other kinds of monetary instrument as the Secretary of State may specify by order.
Any amount, no matter how small, may be seized.[54] Counterfeit 'cash' is not within para
1 but could be held on import and export under ss 20 and 21 of the Forgery and
Counterfeiting Act 1981.[55]

By para 2, an 'authorised officer' may seize and detain terrorist cash on the basis of   3.34
reasonable grounds for suspecting its presence, even if it is not reasonably practicable to

---

[51] *Inquiry into Legislation against Terrorism* (Cm 3420, London, 1996) para 13.33.
[52] Bell, R.E., 'The seizure, detention and forfeiture of cash in the UK' (2003) 11 *Journal of Financial Crime*
134 at p 134.
[53] Compare *Webb v Chief Constable of Merseyside Police* [2000] QB 427.
[54] See Home Office and Northern Ireland Office, *Legislation against Terrorism* (Cm 4178, London, 1998)
para 6.28. Compare Proceeds of Crime Act 2002, s 303 (currently, £1,000 is specified).
[55] Hansard HL vol 629, col 1049 (6 December 2001), Lord Rooker.

split it from a larger stash.[56] The Code of Practice for authorised officers under the Terrorism Act 2001[57] gives guidance as to the exercise of para 2:[58]

'Reasonable grounds for suspecting' are likely to depend upon particular circumstances and the authorised officer should take into account such factors as how the cash was discovered, the amount involved, its origins, intended movement, destination, reasons given for a cash as opposed to normal banking transaction, whether the courier(s) and/or the owners of the cash (if different) have any links with terrorists or terrorist groups, whether here or overseas. Where the authorised officer has suspicions about the cash he/she should give the person who has possession of it a reasonable opportunity to provide an explanation on the details of its ownership, origins, purpose, destination, and reasons for moving the amount in this way and to provide the authorised officer with supporting documentation. The authorised officer should make clear to the person that anything said will be noted and used in the event that the cash is seized and an application made to the court for its detention or forfeiture.

Authorised officers are advised under para 15 to give written notification to the possessor (including a statement of powers exercised, value seized, and rights to challenge in court). The person should also be asked to sign the copy kept by the officer.

3.35   The cohort of 'authorised officers' comprises constables, customs officers, and immigration officers, but the Code of Practice (para 6) advises that the powers should normally be exercised by the police.

3.36   Once seized, the cash must be released not later than forty-eight hours from seizure (counting only working days).[59] An authorised officer or the Commissioners of Customs and Excise (or in Scotland a procurator fiscal) may apply under para 3 to a magistrates' court (or in Scotland, the sheriff) for an extension order. The court must be satisfied that the assets are terrorist cash and that the continued detention of the cash is justified pending investigation or pending a determination whether to institute criminal proceedings; up to three months' extra time can be allowed from the date of the order.[60] On the first application for extension, the hearing may take place without notice and in the absence of the affected persons and their representative (para 3A).[61] The provisional nature of this hearing, the pressing social need of combating terrorism, and the involvement of a judicial officer may perhaps avert a breach of rights to due process, privacy, or property under the European Convention.[62] A court detention order may be renewed further but not beyond two years beginning with the date when the first extension order was made.

---

[56] See Home Office Circular 30/2002: *Guidance for the Police and Public on the implementation of Sections 1–2 of the Anti-terrorism Crime and Security Act 2001*, para 17.

[57] Para 11 (the Code is issued under the Terrorism Act 2000 (Code of Practice for Authorised Officers) Order 2001, SI 2001/425). See Delegated Powers and Regulatory Reform Select Committee, *Report on the Anti-terrorism, Crime and Security Bill* (2001–02 HL 45) para 15.

[58] Compare Bell, R.E., 'The seizure, detention and forfeiture of cash in the UK' (2003) 11 *Journal of Financial Crime* 134 at p 138.

[59] See Counter-Terrorism Act 2008, s 83; Home Office, *Possible Measures for Inclusion in a Future Counter-Terrorism Bill* (London, 2007) para 70.

[60] See Magistrates' Courts (Detention and Forfeiture of Terrorist Cash) (No 2) Rules 2001, SI 2001/4013; Magistrates' Courts (Detention and Forfeiture of Terrorist Cash) Rules (Northern Ireland) 2002, SR 2002/12.

[61] Inserted by Terrorism Act 2006, s 35(1).

[62] Compare *Crémieux v France*, App no 11471/85, A256-B (1993); *Chappell v United Kingdom*, App no 10461/83, A152-A (1989) para 57; *Murray v United Kingdom*, App no 14310/88, A300-A (1994).

During its detention, the cash shall, under para 4, unless required as evidence of an offence, be held in an interest bearing account.

Under para 5, any person may apply to the court for a direction that seized cash be released. An authorised officer, or, in Scotland, the procurator fiscal, may themselves take the initiative to release cash if satisfied that its detention is no longer justified (with notice to the magistrates' court or sheriff). But no cash may be released while proceedings on an application for its forfeiture under para 6 (below) or proceedings anywhere which relate to the cash are pending.   3.37

The next stage will normally involve forfeiture procedures under para 6. This process is quite distinct from that under s 23. An authorised officer or the Commissioners of Customs and Excise may apply to a magistrates' court, or, in Scotland, the Scottish Ministers (formerly the procurator fiscal) may apply to the sheriff, for an order forfeiting detained cash. The court may grant an application only if satisfied on the balance of probabilities that the cash is terrorist cash. The forfeiture can apply not only against the seized cash, but also in relation to any accrued profits (para 15). The proceedings are to be treated as civil under s 1(1) of the Anti-terrorism, Crime and Security Act 2001.   3.38

Parties with a claim to ownership of detained cash may apply for release of the cash (or their share of it) under para 9. Furthermore, the forfeiture will not apply against an excepted joint owner—a joint tenant who obtained the property in circumstances in which it would not (as against him) be earmarked as terrorist property (paras 6, 17). This idea of earmarking is explained further in paras 11 and 12 which ensure that forfeiture can capture property obtained through terrorism and property which represents property obtained through terrorism. By para 11, a person obtains property through terrorism if he obtains property by, or in return for, acts of terrorism (such as carrying out a killing or explosion in return for payment) or acts carried out for the purposes of terrorism (for example, leasing a house to a terrorist cell). It is immaterial whether or not any money, goods, or services were provided. Thus, property still counts as having been obtained through terrorism regardless of any investment in it: 'So if a person buys guns with honestly come by money, and sells them at a profit, the whole of the proceeds of the sale will count as having been obtained through terrorism, and not just the profit.'[63] It is also unnecessary to show that the property was obtained through a particular act of terrorism if it is proven that the property was obtained through a range of terrorist acts. Therefore, it will not matter, for example, if it cannot be established whether funds are attributable to extortion, customs evasion, or armed robbery, provided that all those are acts of terrorism or acts for the purposes of terrorism.   3.39

Having established that the property is obtained through terrorism in these ways, it is then 'earmarked as terrorist property' under para 12. If earmarked terrorist property is disposed of (as defined by para 18), it remains earmarked only if the recipient obtained it on a disposal from the person who obtained the property through terrorism or if the recipient himself is a person from whom the cash could be directly seized. Conversely, anyone who obtains terrorist property on disposal and does so in good faith, for value, and without notice that it was earmarked is immune from forfeiture (para 16). Thus, a purchaser who paid full value for a car used in terrorism but who was unaware of its terrorist origins escapes forfeiture and the property is no longer earmarked, though   3.40

---

[63] Home Office, *Explanatory Notes on the Anti-terrorism, Crime and Security Bill* (London, 2001) para 340.

the cash paid for the car then becomes earmarked. This immunity also applies to civil damages paid out of terrorist property or to payments of compensation or restitution. But if the property remains earmarked, it can be traced through to property which represents the original terrorist cash (para 13). Thus, if a person is given a car in return for carrying out an act of terrorism and then sells it, the cash so obtained will be property earmarked as terrorist property, as will property secured when the cash is spent. Mixed property can also be apportioned, and only the terrorist cash element forfeited (para 14). Paragraph 15 provides that any profits accruing from property obtained through terrorism or traceable property are also to be treated as relevant property. All these provisions on earmarked terrorist property apply under para 18 to events occurring before commencement of the Act. This retrospective application does not breach Art 7 of the European Convention since these are civil *in rem* proceedings.[64]

3.41   Paragraphs 7 and 7A[65] afford an appeal by a party to the original hearing within thirty days in England and Wales, to the Crown Court, or in Scotland to the Court of Session, or in Northern Ireland, to the county court. The appeal court does not have to hold a full rehearing and may make any order it thinks appropriate, including the release of part of the cash to meet reasonable legal expenses in connection with the appeal. The grant of public legal services (authorized by s 2(1) of the Anti-terrorism, Crime and Security Act 2001) is also important in the achievement of fair process.[66]

3.42   If the cash is subjected to a forfeiture order, then, para 8 requires that it shall be paid into central government coffers. If the cash is not ultimately subjected to a forfeiture order (or where there was a failure to put the cash into an interest-bearing account), the person to whom it belongs or from whom it was seized may apply for compensation under para 10 but only where there are 'exceptional' circumstances.

3.43   Further enforcement rules concerning the roles of authorised officers are set out in s 115 and Sch 14 to the Terrorism Act 2000. By paras 2 and 3 of Sch 14, an officer may enter a vehicle or use reasonable force. By para 4, information acquired by an officer may be supplied: (a) to the Secretary of State for use in relation to immigration; (b) to the Commissioners of Customs and Excise or a customs officer; (c) to a constable; (d) to the Serious Organised Crime Agency (SOCA); (e) to a person specified by order of the Secretary of State.

3.44   Detailed rules of court[67] are provided for under the Magistrates' Courts (Detention and Forfeiture of Terrorist Cash) (No 2) Rules 2001[68] and the Magistrates' Courts (Detention and Forfeiture of Terrorist Cash) Rules (Northern Ireland) 2002.[69] The Crown Court (Amendment) Rules 2001[70] establish appeal procedures. Procedures in the Sheriff Court are dealt with by the Act of Sederunt (Summary Applications, Statutory Applications and Appeals etc Rules) Amendment (Detention and Forfeiture of Terrorist Cash) 2002.[71]

---

[64] Compare *Welch v United Kingdom*, App no 17440/90, Ser A 307-A (1995). See further *Phillips v United Kingdom*, App no 41087/98, 2001-VII; *McIntosh v Lord Advocate* [2001] UKPC D1.

[65] As substituted by the Counter-Terrorism Act 2008, s 84. See *Home Office, Possible Measures for Inclusion in a future Counter-Terrorism Bill* (London, 2007) para 70.

[66] Compare *Benham v United Kingdom*, App no 19380/92, 1996-III.

[67] The Terrorism Act 2000, s 31 was not replaced in 2001 so general rule-making powers apply.

[68] SI 2001/4013, replacing SI 2001/194, and further amended by the Magistrates' Courts (Miscellaneous Amendments) Rules 2003, SI 2003/1236.

[69] SR 2002/12, replacing SR 2001/65.

[70] SI 2001/193.

[71] SSI 2002/129.

Should the magistrates' courts handle this complex civil forfeiture litigation?[72]   3.45
Attempts to switch proceedings to Crown Court were defeated in the House of Lords on
the basis that the corresponding jurisdiction in respect of drugs-related cash had not
encountered any problems.[73] The Newton Committee also deprecated hearings in magistrates' courts, albeit more because of their openness than their level of expertise.[74]

E. ASSESSMENT OF DOMESTIC MEASURES

The legal responses to terrorism financing fall within the 'Prevent' and 'Pursuit' strands of   3.46
CONTEST. Two broad gains may flow from a financial approach to terrorism. First, if
finance can be limited, then terrorist groups are forced into choices between violent activities or political and social activities. Secondly, greater monitoring and criminal and civil law
interventions will constrain and detect the activities of terrorists. There may be direct detection at points of acquisition or dealing or through charging preparatory offences under the
Terrorism Act 2000 or 2006. More indirect action arises through the forfeiture of equipment, materials, or finance, sometimes as a civil rather than criminal action. For example,
Thomas 'Slab' Murphy, an alleged quartermaster for the IRA,[75] forfeited (in conjunction
with his brothers) €1.2m to agencies in Ireland and Britain and awaits tax evasion charges.[76]

It may be questioned whether this scheme to 'follow the money' is worthwhile.[77]   3.47
Terrorism may not incur major outlay, and self-benefit is not their ultimate objective, so
that techniques applicable to avaricious or ostentatious gangsters will not have the same
impact on idealistic terrorists. The hope is that this distinction is not unambiguous and
that terrorists commit acquisitive crimes, and thereby amplify their visibility, either out
of necessity or because of abuse of power. The evidence is equivocal. Many paramilitary
groups in Northern Ireland have engaged in extensive racketeering:[78]

The phenomenon of non-terrorist paramilitary crime is a complex one and is not confined to
those activities at the top end of the scale, such as the smuggling of drugs, oil and other high value

---

[72] Binning, P., 'In safe hands?' Striking the balance between privacy and security—Anti-terrorist finance
measures' (2002) 6 *European Human Rights Law Review* 734 at p 743.
[73] Hansard HL vol 629, col 305 (28 November 2001), col 1047 (6 December 2001), Lord Rooker.
[74] Privy Counsellor Review Committee, *Anti-terrorism, Crime and Security Act 2001, Review, Report* (2003–
04 HC 100) para B15. The idea of a transfer was welcomed: Home Office, *Counter-Terrorism Powers:
Reconciling Security and Liberty in an Open Society* (Cm 6147, London, 2004) para 114.
[75] See *Murphy v Times Newspapers* [2000] 1 IR 522.
[76] See *The Times* 18 October 2008 p 28.
[77] See Gilmore, W.S., *Dirty Money* (3rd edn, Council of Europe, Strasbourg, 2004) pp 2, 119; Zagaris, B.,
'The merging of the anti-money laundering and counter-terrorism financial enforcement regimes after Sept.
11, 2001' (2004) 22 *Berkeley Journal of International Law* 123; Levi, M., and Reuter, P., 'Money Laundering'
in Tonry, M. (ed), *Crime and Justice* (vol 34, Chicago University Press, Chicago, 2006).
[78] Independent Monitoring Commission, Third Report (2003–04 HC 1218) para 5.2. See further First
Report (2003–04 HC 516) para 6.5, Fourth Report (2004–05 HC 308), Fifth Report (2005–06 HC 46) chap 6,
Seventh Report (2005–06 HC 546) ch 5, Tenth Report (2005–06 HC 1066) ch 4; Northern Ireland Select
Committee, *The Financing of Terrorism in Northern Ireland* (2001–02 HC 978), *Organised Crime in Northern
Ireland* (2005–06 HC 886); Organised Crime Task Force, *Annual Report and Threat Assessment 2008* (Belfast,
2008) p 27; Silke, A., 'In defense of the realm' (1998) 21 *Studies in Conflict and Terrorism* 331, and 'Drink, Drugs
and Rock'n'Roll' (2000) 23 *Studies in Conflict and Terrorism* 107; Horgan, J. and Taylor, M., 'Playing the "Green
Card"' (1999) 11 *Terrorism & Political Violence* 1 and (2003) 15 *Terrorism & Political Violence* 1; Moran, J.,
Policing the Peace in Northern Ireland (Manchester University Press, Manchester, 2008) chs 3, 4, 6.

goods, large scale counterfeiting and bank robbery. It includes all those activities in which groups of paramilitaries are working together for their criminal benefit. These activities include drugs smuggling and robbery. They also include others lower down the scale, such as the retail end of larger operations, like the supply of smuggled alcohol to individual pubs.

3.48　　At the same time, terrorist operations may entail surprisingly modest outlays and may derive their funding from lawful sources. Thus, the ambitious attacks on September 11, 2001, did require substantial funds—up to $500,000 in travel and accommodation expenses.[79] However, the 7 July 2005 London bombers left a small financial footprint:[80]

Current indications are that the group was self-financed. There is no evidence of external sources of income. Our best estimate is that the overall cost is less than £8,000. The overseas trips, bomb making equipment, rent, car hire and UK travel being the main cost elements. The group appears to have raised the necessary cash by methods that would be extremely difficult to identify as related to terrorism or other serious criminality.

3.49　　The financial base of Al-Qa'ida, in terms of strength and derivation, remains a matter of controversy,[81] but some of the features seem to include reliance upon culturally embedded practices such as alms-giving (*zakat*)[82] or informal funds transfer systems, notably the *hawala* system of money remittances.[83]

3.50　　As for policy effectiveness, Pt III has experienced modest deployments:

Table 3.1 Application of Terrorism Act Part III[84]

	GB		NI	
Year	Offences ss 15–19	Cash seized £ (cases)	Offences ss 15–19	Cash seized £ (cases)
2001	10	18500 (n/a)	4	n/a
2002	12	90170 (8)	9	n/a
2003	7	269396 (14)	7	n/a
2004	7	16312 (3)	4	n/a
2005	11	9318 (1)	7	n/a
2006	5	81818 (n/a)	11	n/a
2007	19	9155 (n/a)	n/a	n/a
Total	71	494699	42	n/a

[79] National Commission on Terrorist Attacks Upon the United States, Final Report (USGPO, Washington, DC, 2004) p 172.

[80] Home Office, *Report of the Official Account of the Bombings in London on the 7th July 2005* (2005–06 HC 1087) paras 63, 64.

[81] See Napoleoni, L., *Modern Jihad* (Pluto, London, 2003); Ehrenfeld, R., *Funding Evil* (Bonus Books, Santa Monica, 2003); Burr, J.M. and Collins, R.O., *Alms for Jihad* (Cambridge University Press, New York, 2006); Naylor, R.T., *Satanic Purses* (McGill-Queen's University Press, Montreal, 2006).

[82] Several charities are listed under UN Security Council Resolution 1267 of 1999.

[83] See IMF/World Bank, Informal Funds Transfer Systems (Washington, DC, 2003); National Commission on Terrorist Attacks Upon the United States, Final Report (GPO, Washington, DC, 2004) pp 171, 533; McCulloch, J. and Pickering, S., 'Suppressing the financing of terrorism' (2005) 45 *British Journal of Criminology* 470; Razavi, M., 'Hawala' (2006) 44 *Crime, Law and Social Change* 277; Payment Services Directive 2007/64/EC; Passas, N. and Maimbo, S.M., 'The design, development and implementation of regulatory and supervisory frameworks for informal funds transfer system' in Biersteker, T.J., and Eckert, S.E (eds), *Countering the Financing of Terrorism* (Routledge, London, 2008).

[84] Sources: Carlile Reports; NIO Statistics & Research Branch. 2001 is from 19 February.

No sustained statistics are disclosed as to forfeiture either following criminal conviction or cash seizure. The Organised Crime Task Force, a multi-agency partnership which sets strategic priorities in Northern Ireland,[85] has revealed that during 2005/06 in Northern Ireland assets worth £30m were restrained, confiscated, or seized.[86] Since April 2006, the lead policing group, the National Terrorist Financial Investigation Unit, has seized £1,344,271 in cash.[87] The most publicized cash seizure was from Loyalist paramilitary leader, Johnny Adair, who, on relocating from Northern Ireland to Britain in February 2003 was relieved of £70,000 in cash at the Cairnryan ferry terminal.[88]

Moving from a policy to a rights audit, the courts have been less solicitous of provi- 3.51
sional property and family rights compared to liberty and due process.[89] Criminal forfeiture is treated as 'a financial penalty (with a custodial penalty in default of payment) but it is a penalty imposed for the offence of which he has been convicted and involves no accusation of any other offence'.[90] The result is that Art 6(2) does not apply since the person is not 'charged'. However, Art 6(1) remains applicable and may require some moderation of the operation of the measures, most likely under ss 15(3), 17, and 18 where there can be a reverse onus presumption, though the extent of these burdens may be viewed as proportionate.[91] The trial judge must remain 'astute to avoid injustice'.[92] Another aspect where the trial judge should remain guarded concerns the standard of proof. Given that forfeiture of property linked to terrorism involves a serious imputation against personal reputation, the courts should set a heightened civil standard in cash seizures.[93] The UK courts have likewise held forfeiture proceedings to be civil in nature,[94] and they have also found them to be a 'precise, fair and proportionate response to the important need to protect the public'.[95] However, less attention has been paid to the impact on family members without property rights.[96]

The European Court of Human Rights in *Butler v United Kingdom*[97] found that the 3.52
civil forfeiture of cash presumed to be derived from drug trafficking was a preventative measure and not a criminal sanction. The Court also accepted the proportionality of the intervention, influenced by the judicial supervision, and also the possibility of appeal by way of complete rehearing at the Crown Court.

---

[85] Moran, J., *Policing the Peace in Northern Ireland* (Manchester University Press, Manchester, 2008) ch 7.
[86] Organised Crime Task Force, *Annual Report and Threat Assessment 2006* (Belfast, 2006) p 6.
[87] Hansard HC vol 473, col 938w (18 March 2008). Other seizures under Sch 5 amount to £650k: HM Treasury, *The Financial Challenge to Crime and Terrorism* (London, 2007) para 2.52.
[88] See Wood, I.S., *Crimes of Loyalty* (Edinburgh University Press, Edinburgh, 2006) p 292.
[89] See Donohue, L.K., *The Cost of Counterterrorism* (Cambridge University Press, Cambridge, 2007) ch 3.
[90] *McIntosh v Lord Advocate* [2001] UKPC D1 at para 25. See also *Phillips v United Kingdom*, App no 41087/98, 2001–VII.
[91] See *R v Rezvi* [2002] UKHL 1 at para 15; Trechsel, S., *Human Rights in Criminal Proceedings* (Oxford University Press, Oxford, 2005) pp 34–5.
[92] *R v Benjafield* [2002] UKHL 2 at para 8.
[93] See *R (on the application of McCann) v Crown Court at Manchester* [2002] UKHL 39 at para 83; *Assets Recovery Agency v He & Chen* [2004] EWHC 3021 (Admin) at para 66.
[94] *Butt v HM Customs & Excise* [2001] EWHC Admin 1066; *Re the Director of the Assets Recovery Agency* [2004] NIQB 21; *Walsh v Director of the Assets Recovery Agency* [2005] NICA 6. See Kennedy, A., 'Justifying the civil recovery of criminal proceeds' (2005) 26 *Company Lawyer* 137.
[95] *R v Rezvi* [2002] UKHL 1 at para 17.
[96] See *Director of Assets Recovery Agency v Jackson* [2007] EWHC 2553 (QB) at para 221.
[97] App no 41661/98, 2002-VI. Compare Performance & Innovation Unit, *Recovering the Proceeds of Crime* (Cabinet Office, London, 2000) para 5.12; Joint Committee on Human Rights, *Proceeds of Crime Bill: Further Report* (2001–02 HL 75/HC 475) para 24.

3.53   Turning attention to democratic accountability, there is a dearth of information about the operation of forfeiture, and not much detail even regarding the Pt III offences. These aspects of the terrorism legislation are largely ignored during debates in Parliament and concerning the desirable structures for responding to financial crimes in general, including the transfer of responsibilities from the Assets Recovery Agency.[98]

3.54   As for constitutional governance, the main criticism is too many overlapping and complex codes rather than an absence of regulation.[99] The complexity of the terrorism legislation is compounded by the fact that it confusingly overlaps with, and often appears deficient alongside, the Proceeds of Crime Act 2002. That Act contains an impressive array of money laundering offences in Pt VII. In *R v Silcock*,[100] the defendants, said to be linked to the Official IRA, pleaded guilty to conspiring to import $4.25m in counterfeit notes. Next, criminal confiscation is covered by the Proceeds of Crime Act, Pts II to IV, and seizures to a total of £534,000 have been made by the National Terrorist Financial Unit under that legislation.[101] The 2002 Act scheme is more ambitious than the terrorism legislation in several respects, such as by providing for presumptions about benefit over six prior years from 'general criminal conduct' as well as 'particular criminal conduct' where a 'criminal lifestyle' can be established.[102] These presumptions may not breach Art 6(2) since they are 'essential to the preventive scheme'.[103] However, the broad definition of 'benefit' can operate disproportionately or even as an abuse of process.[104]

3.55   More radical still, civil recovery going well beyond cash seizure is allowed by the 2002 Act, Pt V. There is no counterpart in the terrorism legislation,[105] nor is it demanded by international law.[106] The applicability to terrorism is demonstrated by the action against Thomas Murphy, already described, and against figures associated with Loyalist groups, including Stephen Warnock,[107] Jim Gray,[108] Jim Johnston,[109] and Colin Armstrong,[110] Alongside this civil confiscation, s 317 allows for the issuance of tax demands in relation to gains reasonably believed to derive from crime.[111]

---

[98] See National Audit Office, *The Assets Recovery Agency* (2006–07 HC 253); Home Office, *One Step Ahead: a 21st Century Strategy to Defeat Organised Crime* (Cm 6167, London, 2004) para 5.1. See now the Serious Crimes Act 2007, Pt III.

[99] Complexity can be gauged from the extensive guidance given by Joint Money Laundering Steering Group, *Guidance on the Prevention of Money Laundering and the Financing of Terrorism for the Financial Services Industry* (British Bankers' Association, London, 2006).

[100] [2004] EWCA Crim 408.

[101] Lord Carlile, *Report on the Operation in 2007 of the Terrorism Act 2000* (Home Office, London, 2008) para 80.

[102] Proceeds of Crime Act 2002, ss 6, 75, sch 2.

[103] *Welch v United Kingdom*, App no 17440/90, Ser A 307-A (1995) para 33. See further Joint Committee on Human Rights, *Proceeds of Crime Bill: Further Report* (2001–02 HL 75/HC 475) para 8 and *Further Report* (2001–02 HL 75/HC 475) para 6.

[104] *R v Shabir* [2008] EWCA Crim 1809.

[105] Compare the Proceeds of Crime Act 1996 in Ireland (see McCutcheon, J.P. and Walsh, D.P.J., *The Confiscation of Criminal Assets* (Round Hall, Dublin, 1999)) and the Racketeering and Corrupt Organisations Act 1970 (18 USC ss 1961–8).

[106] Legal Department of the IMF, *Suppressing the Financing of Terrorism: A Handbook for Legislative Drafting* (IMF, Washington, DC, 2003) p 38.

[107] *Re Warnock* [2005] NIQB 16.

[108] *The Daily Telegraph* 16 January 2007 p 8. See also *R v Benson* [2005] NICC 31.

[109] *The Independent* 25 November 2004 p 28. See also *R v Benson* [2005] NICC 31.

[110] *Re Armstrong* [2007] NIQB 20; *Irish News* 18 January 2008 p 5.

[111] See Cory, R., 'Taxing the proceeds of crime' [2007] *British Tax Review* 356.

It is not possible simply to abolish the terrorism legislation and rely solely on the 2002   **3.56**
Act. In the case of terrorist finance, 'It is not their criminal origins that makes them
"tainted" but their use . . . '.[112] However, the Proceeds of Crime Act 2002 offers a blue-
print for thorough revision for three reasons. First, it contains provisions which are more
familiar to policing agencies. Secondly, as shown by the foregoing survey, the 2002 Act
is more comprehensive and sophisticated in several respects. As a result, it is already used
in terrorism cases. Thirdly, a consolidated set of anti-money laundering and terrorism
finance measures would be more coherent and provide fewer loopholes. As well as learning from the 2002 Act, more emphasis could be put on private governance in order to
reduce funds at source, as is being tested in Northern Ireland through the Independent
Private Sector Inspector General concept.[113]

F. INTERNATIONAL FINANCIAL MEASURES AGAINST TERRORISM

The admixture of international and state-sponsored terrorism has prompted the United   **3.57**
Nations and European Union to undertake a direct role against terrorist finances. It has
produced twin tracks of general international treaty law and specific sanctions. The general measures include the United Nations Convention for the Suppression of the
Financing of Terrorism,[114] which has shaped Pt III. The devices of embargoes against
states and 'smart' sanctions have also been invoked. The latter format is remarkable in
that it applies a new form of international financial outlawry against specified persons
and organizations.[115] Responsibility for enforcement shifted to the Asset Freezing Unit
of the Financial Crime Team in the Treasury in 2007.[116]

1. Al-Qa'ida and Taliban international sanctions

The process began with the UN Security Council Resolution Sanctions Order 1267 on   **3.58**
15 October 1999.[117] The sanctions include a freeze of Taliban funds, as well as financial
assets of bin Laden and listed individuals and entities. In the United Kingdom, these
measures were implemented under the United Nations Act 1946, s 1, by the Afghanistan
(United Nations Sanctions) Orders of 1999 and 2001.[118] Around £90m was seized, but
much of it was returned to the successor Afghan government.[119]

---

[112] See Legal Department of the IMF, *Suppressing the Financing of Terrorism: A Handbook for Legislative Drafting* (IMF, Washington, DC, 2003) p 49.
[113] See Goldstock, R., *Organised Crime in Northern Ireland* (Northern Ireland Office, Belfast, 2004).
[114] A/RES/54/109, Cm 4663, London, 1999.
[115] See Davis, K.E., 'The financial war on terrorism' in Ramraj, V.V. *et al*, *Global Anti-Terrorism Law and Policing* (Cambridge University Press, Cambridge, 2005) p 183.
[116] See <http://www.hm-treasury.gov.uk/fin_sanctions_alqaida.htm; http://www.hm-treasury.gov.uk/fin_sanctions_terrorist.htm>.
[117] S/RES/1267. S/RES/1333, 19 December 2000, which extended the regime to Al-Qa'ida. See Legal Department of the IMF, *Suppressing the Financing of Terrorism: A Handbook for Legislative Drafting* (IMF, Washington, DC, 2003) p 22.
[118] SI 1999/3133; SI 2001/396 and 2557.
[119] Binning, P., 'In safe hands?' Striking the balance between privacy and security—Anti-terrorist finance measures' (2002) 6 *European Human Rights Law Review* 734 at p 741.

3.59   After the 11 September attacks, further accounts were frozen, and mechanisms were also strengthened. There is the Al-Qaida and Taliban Sanctions Committee (the 1267 Committee) which is supported by its Analytical Support and Sanctions Monitoring Team.[120] The 1267 Committee can designate or remove persons at the request of governments,[121] but the Committee does not appraise the information and the process is secretive and executive-dominated.

3.60   This regime is now implemented in the United Kingdom by the Al-Qaida and Taliban (United Nations Measures) Orders 2002 and 2006 made under the United Nations Act 1946.[122] The Orders apply within the United Kingdom and to actions anywhere by British citizens (Art 1 of both Orders). Affected persons or organizations comprise anyone who is or may be: Usama bin Laden; anyone designated by the Sanctions Committee; or anyone designated by a Treasury direction based on reasonable grounds for suspecting. The 2002 Order restricts the supply and export of restricted goods.[123] The 2006 Order prohibits dealings with 'funds' and 'economic resources' or making assets available to listed persons, subject to a licensing procedure to enable humanitarian and other purposes.[124] Breach of these prohibitions is a criminal offence under Art 10. A variety of enforcement powers are also granted.

3.61   The system has barely been mentioned in Parliament or by the reviews by Lord Carlile. The evidence from a few reported cases and from the bare listings themselves[125] suggests three circumstances of usage. One concerns foreigners who are mainly abroad and stand convicted of offences, charged or simply suspected. The second element is the listing of organizations connected with Al-Qa'ida, some of which are proscribed. The third category concerns those arrested for terrorist non-financial offences (so that restraint orders are not readily applicable); it was reported that the Treasury froze the assets of persons implicated in the liquid bomb plot on aircraft in August 2006.[126]

3.62   Added to this complex picture, the European Union has underwritten these provisions so as to ensure uniformity in application.[127] Regulation (EC) 881/2002 of 27 May 2002 is directly enforceable under the European Communities Act 1972, though the Al-Qa'ida and Taliban (United Nations Measures) Order 2006 is also viewed as having legality under the 1946 Act, so as to make twin track claims to legality.[128]

---

[120] See <http://www.un.org/sc/committees/1267/index.shtml>.

[121] See 1267 Committee, Guidelines of the Committee for the Conduct of its Work, (<http://www.un.org/sc/committees/1267/pdf/1267_guidelines.pdf, 2002–07>); Fassbender, B., *Targeted Sanctions and Due Process* (United Nations Office of Legal Affairs, New York, 2006); Radicati di Brocolo, L.G., and Meghani, M., Freezing the assets of international terrorist organisations' in Bianchi, A., *Enforcing International Norms Against Terrorism* (Hart, Oxford, 2004) p 398.

[122] SI 2002/111, 251; SI 2006/2952. See Hansard HC vol 450, col 11WS (10 October 2006).

[123] See Export Control (Security and Para-military Goods) Order 2006, SI 2006/1696.

[124] Six households and two individuals are affected for the payment of state benefits under UN Orders: HM Treasury, *The Financial Challenge to Crime and Terrorism* (London, 2007) para. 2.33.

[125] See <http://www.hm-treasury.gov.uk/fin_sanctions_alqaida.htm>. At the end of October 2008, there were 142 Taliban-related listings, and 363 (including 249 individuals) Al-Qa'ida listings, with 37 de-listings.

[126] Hansard HC vol 450, col 11WS (10 October 2006).

[127] See further de Cesari, P., 'The European Union' and Nalin, E., 'The European Union and Human Rights' in Nesi, G. (ed), *International Co-operation in Counter-Terrorism* (Ashgate, Aldershot, 2006); O'Neill, M., 'A critical analysis of the European Union legal provisions on terrorism' (2008) 20 *Terrorism & Political Violence* 26.

[128] See *R (on the application of M and others) v HM Treasury* [2006] EWHC (Admin) 2328 at para 41.

2. General international sanctions

Responding to the events of 11 September 2001, the UN Security Council Resolution   3.63
1373 of 28 September 2001[129] demands that states should curtail the financing of terrorism and sets up a Counter-Terrorism Committee to inspect and chivvy state action.
These measures apply to terrorism in general but without a specific list to guide state
reactions.[130] The ferocity and breadth of this promulgation has again been problematic,
with later attempts to offer a counter-balancing regard for human rights.[131]

Once again, the European Union augmented this initiative, and Council Common   3.64
Position 2001/931/CFSP has required a further listing and asset freezing system to
address terrorism extending beyond the borders of one member state.[132] However, there
is no published fact-finding by which the threats are established in Council. Further
details of the European scheme are imparted by Council Regulation (EC) No 2580/2001
of 27 December 2001,[133] updated by a succession of Council Decisions.

The UK government reacted to Security Council Resolution 1373 by the passage of   3.65
the Terrorism (United Nations Measures) Order 2001,[134] issued under the authority of
the United Nations Act 1946. The European legislation began to be implemented by the
Terrorism (United Nations Measures) Order 2001 (Amendment) Regulations 2003,[135]
under the authority of s 2(2) of the European Communities Act 1972. There was an
attempt to consolidate these two strands by the Terrorism (United Nations Measures)
Order 2006, issued under the United Nations Act 1946.[136] Article 2 contains the definitions of 'economic resources', 'financial services', 'financial trading', 'funds', and of
'terrorism'. The measures which follow affect designated persons as identified either by a
Council Decision or by a Treasury direction (Arts 3 and 4). In this way, the Treasury can
act in advance of the Council or even beyond European Community competence and in
pursuance of the spirit of Resolution 1373. The requirements to freeze are in Arts 7 and
8, subject to a licence under Art 11. Circumvention is an offence under Art 10.

In the consolidated list of 2008, there are ninety-six individuals and sixty-one groups,   3.66
including several Basque and Greek groups, specified Irish organizations, Aum Shinrikyo,
the Communist Party of the Philippines, HAMAS (in addition to the al-Qassem
Brigades), the Revolutionary Armed Forces of Colombia (FARC), and the Shining Path
(Sendero Luminoso), plus persons associated. The list is not intended to duplicate those
covered by Resolution 1267, but there is some repetition.[137]

---

[129] S/RES/1373. See Legal Department of the IMF, *Suppressing the Financing of Terrorism: A Handbook for Legislative Drafting* (IMF, Washington, DC, 2003) p14.
[130] See Clunan, A.L., 'US and international responses to terrorist financing' in Giraldo, J.K., and Trinkunas, H.A., (eds), *Terrorism Financing and State Responses* (Stanford University Press, Palo Alto, 2007) p 280.
[131] See S/RES/1456, 20 January 2003; S/RES/1617, 29 July 2005; S/RES/1566, 8 October 2004; S/2005/789, 16 December 2005; S/RES/1624, 14 September 2005. The UN Commission on Human Rights Resolution 2005/80 appointed the Special Rapporteur on the promotion and protection of human rights and fundamental freedoms while countering terrorism.
[132] See 2001/930/CPSP, 27 December 2001.
[133] See Reinisch, A., 'The actions of the European Union to combat international terrorism' in Bianchi, A., *Enforcing International Norms Against Terrorism* (Hart, Oxford, 2004).
[134] SI 2001/3365.
[135] SI 2003/1297. See further the amending orders at SI 2003/2209, SI 2003/2430, SI 2004/2309, SI 2005/1525.
[136] SI 2006/2657.
[137] See *A, K, M, Q and G v HM Treasury* [2008] EWHC 869 (Admin) at para 1.

3. Other freezing orders

(a) *2001 Act scheme*

3.67   Part II of the Anti-terrorism, Crime and Security Act 2001 allows for unilateral action by the UK government, though 'If a decision to impose sanctions is taken at European Community level or under a United Nations Security Council resolution, it would not be appropriate to use the power.'[138] By s 4 of the Anti-terrorism, Crime and Security Act 2001, the Treasury may make a freezing order: either to deny funds and assets to foreign terrorists where they may pose a threat to the life or property of UK nationals or residents; or, to prohibit financial transactions by foreign governments or persons who are deemed to be threatening the national economy.[139] 'Nationals' and 'residents' are defined by s 9.

3.68   It was made clear at enactment that the breadth of the second leg went beyond terrorism into other emergencies and thereby replaced pre-existing powers derived from wartime regulations.[140] The previous recorded instance of their use was against the Iraqi government after its invasion of Kuwait in 1990.[141] The future applications within official contemplation included 'kleptocrats', rogue states, and illegal funds from the proceeds of crime.[142] Attempts in the Lords to confine the clause to terrorism were rebuffed for the government by Baroness Symons as impractical,[143] while Lord McIntosh argued that international obligations would guard against s 4 'being used as an illegitimate tool to protect UK businesses' while still asserting that 'the power is intended to provide wide-ranging protection against threats to national security'.[144]

3.69   The power is exercisable under s 10 by statutory instrument which must be laid before Parliament after being made and is subject to the requirement of affirmative resolution within twenty-eight days. The Bank of England will draw the attention of banks to such orders.[145] Orders can be amended or revoked under ss 11 and 12.

3.70   The contents of freezing orders are related in ss 5, 6, and Sch 3. A freezing order is an order which prohibits persons from making funds available to, or for the benefit of, persons specified in the order. 'Funds' are defined as 'financial assets and economic benefits of any kind'. By Sch 3, para 4, the order must allow for the granting of licences authorizing funds to be made available, such as for basic living expenses or legal fees. Paragraph 7 envisages a range of offences. By para 10, an order may include provision for the award of compensation on the grounds that a person has suffered loss as a result of an order or the refusal of a licence.

3.71   The legislation does not as such provide for substantive challenge or appeal or review, though, by para 11, the specified person can demand written reasons from the Treasury.[146]

---

138   Hansard HL vol 629, col 353 (28 November 2001), Lord McIntosh.
139   See further Lennon, G. and Walker, C., 'Hot money in a cold climate' [2008] *Public Law* 37.
140   See Emergency Laws (Re-enactments and Repeals) Act 1964, s 2; Finance Act 1968, s 55.
141   Hansard HL vol 704, col 1054 (21 October 2008).
142   Hansard HC vol 375, col 34 (19 November, 2001), David Blunkett.
143   Hansard HL vol 629, col 600 (3 December, 2001).
144   Hansard HL vol 629, col 353 (28 November, 2001).
145   Hansard HL vol 629, col 362 (28 November 2001), Lord McIntosh.
146   These are qualified by the Counter-Terrorism Act 2008, s 70, by which the Treasury shall not be obliged to disclose any information which it would not be required to disclose under Pt VI (especially s 67) of that Act.

An application for judicial review would be possible.[147] The Treasury announced in 2007 that it would wish to use closed source evidence and that it would not object to the use of special advocates.[148] These processes are now formalized by the Counter-Terrorism Act 2008, Pt VI. By s 7, the Treasury must keep a freezing order under review, and, in any event, by s 8, it must cease after two years.

The power in s 4 rested in obscurity for some years, but its invocation in 2008 was spectacular. Concerned at the severe banking crisis in Iceland and a threat by the Icelandic government to leave British depositors at the back of the queue for compensation, the Landsbanki Freezing Order 2008[149] prevented the British branch of the bank from 'repatriating' assets back to Iceland.[150] The Icelandic Prime Minister, Geir Haarde, complained that Britain had performed an 'unfriendly act'.[151]   3.72

As for other possible challenges aside from *vires*, the Landsbanki Order may be challenged on the basis of Art 6 and Art 1 of Protocol 1. Perhaps with the looming threat of litigation by the Icelandic authorities, the government tabled amendments to the Counter-Terrorism Bill so that an application to set aside an order may be made to the High Court which will apply the principles of judicial review.[152] Given that judicial review was already available, the main impact will be to apply the procedures of what became Pt V of the Counter-Terrorism Act 2008 (including the involvement of intercept evidence and special advocates).   3.73

Whilst strictly lawful, s 4 constitutes a dangerous use of terrorism legislation. In consequence of the ghosting of s 4 aboard the 2001 Act, the Newton Committee recommended that the measures should be translated into the Civil Contingencies Act 2004.[153] The proposal was rejected by the government on the basis that s 4 allowed 'rapid emergency action if and when UK interests are, or could be threatened'.[154]   3.74

(b) *2008 Act scheme*

Added as an afterthought to Pt V of the 2008 Act[155] in the form of '23 pages of fresh legislation that is only tangentially related'[156] is a further platform for financial restrictions. As happened in 2001, these measures were piteously explained and debated, even though they apply beyond terrorism and overlap with the 2001 scheme. The addition is introduced by s 62, with copious details in Sch 7. The rationale is the wish to provide a platform for the rapid translation into action of demands from the Financial Action Task Force ('FATF'), an emanation of the G8 and otherwise without legal recognition in UK law.[157] The Treasury is empowered to direct, regulate, or prohibit transactions by   3.75

---

[147] Hansard HL vol 629, col 1060 (6 December 2001), Lord McIntosh.

[148] HM Treasury, *The Financial Challenge to Crime and Terrorism* (London, 2007) para 2.33.

[149] SI 2008/2668, as amended by SI 2008/2766.

[150] See Hansard HL vol 704, col 1548 (28 October 2008); Hansard HC vol 481, col 775w (27 October 2008).

[151] *The Times* (London) 10 October 2008 p 7.

[152] Hansard HL vol 704, col 1048 (21 October 2008).

[153] Privy Counsellor Review Committee, *Anti-terrorism, Crime and Security Act 2001, Review, Report* (2003–04 HC 100) para B20.

[154] Home Office, *Counter-terrorism Powers* (Cm 6147, London, 2004) paras 12–13.

[155] Hansard HL vol 705, col 576 (11 November 2008).

[156] Hansard HL vol 705, col 936 (17 November 2008), Lord Marksford.

[157] See Gilmore, W.S., *Dirty Money* (3rd edn, Council of Europe, Strasbourg, 2004) ch 5.

financial and credit institutions with persons in non-EEA countries in order to stop criminal money laundering, terrorist financing, or weapons proliferation. The Schedule then provides for a supervisory regime and for civil and criminal penalties in the event of non-compliance. Exactly why Sch 7 was rushed through in this way, unless simply to avoid close scrutiny, remains obscure. The government called in aid an FATF statement on 16 October 2008 which warned of the involvement of Iran in terrorism financing and of Uzbekistan in money laundering.[158] However, neither danger was wholly novel, other FATF missives have been ignored,[159] and other regulatory powers already existed to ensure restraints.[160]

3.76   The core condition for the exercise of powers in Sch 7, para 1 are that (a) the FATF has called for measures to be taken against a country because of the risk it presents of money laundering or terrorist financing; (b) the Treasury reasonably believe a country poses a significant risk to national interests because of the risk of money laundering or terrorist financing there; or (c) the Treasury reasonably believe a country poses a significant risk to national interests because of involvement with nuclear, radiological, biological, or chemical weapons.

3.77   Directions may be issued under para 3 to designated persons in the financial sector (which is defined in paras 4 to 7, subject to change by affirmative order) on an individual, categorical, or universal basis.

3.78   The contents of directions are delineated by para 9. The Treasury can impose requirements or restraints over transactions or relationships with private businesses, governmental bodies, or individual residents. Some of the kinds of directions which may be imposed are set out in paras 10 (customer due diligence), 11 (ongoing monitoring), 12 (systematic reporting), and 13 (limiting or ceasing business). In all instances, the direction must be proportionate to the risks or national interests (para 9(6)). Paragraph 17 allows for the issuance of licences to exempt acts.

3.79   The procedures governing directions to all persons in the sector demand issuance by a statutory order which must be affirmative if it curtails business transactions; a direction to a particular person need not be contained in an order (para 14). Directions expire after one year (renewable) and notice of directions issued to a particular person should be served on them, while general directions should be publicized (paras 15, 16, and 42).

3.80   In the exercise of their functions, enforcement authorities (which means, under s 18, the Financial Services Authority, the Commissioners for Her Majesty's Revenue and Customs, the Office of Fair Trading, and the Department of Enterprise, Trade and Investment in Northern Ireland—but not the police) may demand information or documents (para 19), and may enter and inspect with and without warrant (paras 20 and 21). Paragraph 22 seeks to protect legal professional privilege.

3.81   Civil penalties may be imposed for default or breach by the enforcement authorities under paras 25 to 27, subject to appeal under para 28. Criminal offences for non-compliance or false information are set out in paras 30 and 31, with coverage under paras 32 and 34 of conduct outside the United Kingdom.

---

[158] Hansard HL vol 705, col 577 (11 November 2008), Lord Myners.
[159] Hansard HL vol 705, col 587 (11 November 2008), Baroness Miller.
[160] The Money Laundering Regulations 2007, SI2007/2157, were claimed to be too limited (*ibid* col 578), but no mention was made of the Export Control Act 2002 or sectoral regulatory powers.

As the responsible ministry, the Treasury must report annually to Parliament on their   3.82
exercise of powers (para 38). Enforcement authorities must also must take appropriate
measures to monitor persons operating in their financial sectors, and the Treasury shall
assist by drawing up guidance (paras 39 and 40).

4. Assessment and procedures relating to international measures

These international measures are consistent with the 'Prevent' strategy and allow inter-   3.83
vention on low levels of proof. Another notable strategic gain for the UK government is
the ability to foist upon European or even global audiences its own condemnation of
domestic groupings, allowing several Irish groups to become European pariahs.

In grave doubt are the accountability and the constitutional governance of these   3.84
measures. Those affected are left beyond legal and democratic governance and are subject primarily to political spheres of influence at international level.

Next, these measure fail any rights audit and lack almost any scintilla of due process   3.85
or proportionate concern for property or family life.[161] These rights deficiencies have
been evident in profuse litigation against the European implementation. The Grand
Chamber of the Court of Justice has latterly concluded in *Kadi and Al Barakaat
International Foundation v Council of the EU* that the obligations implementing Resolution 1267 improperly contradict European law constitutional principles, which include
respect for fundamental rights.[162] Article 6 rights have also been applied to the listing
and the procedures pursuant to Resolution 1373.[163]

As for challenges in domestic courts, the regulations were held to be 'deliberately   3.86
draconian' in *R (on the application of M and others) v HM Treasury*,[164] but not unduly
vague, unfair, or disproportionate. The House of Lords has made a preliminary reference
to the European Court of Justice on their meaning. Further complaints, in *A, K, M, Q,
and G v HM Treasury*,[165] produced wholesale condemnation in the High Court on
grounds of breach of the fundamental principles of European Union law, disproportionality in comparison to Resolution 1373, and also *ultra vires* the parent United Nations
Act 1946 since the Order was not 'necessary and expedient'. The Court of Appeal
reversed in part, with Lord Justice Sedley in dissent. The Order implementing Resolution
1373 was only *ultra vires* in so far as it allowed Treasury designation of those who 'may
be' involved in terrorism.[166] However, procedural safeguards could be sufficiently
achieved on a case-by-case basis,[167] and the criminal sanctions under Arts 7 and 8 were

---

[161] See Eden, P., 'International measures to prevent and suppress the financing of terrorism' in Eden, P. and
O'Donnell, T., *September 11, 2001: A Turning Point in International and Domestic Law?* (Transnational
Publishers, New York, 2005); Report of the Special Rapporteur on the promotion and protection of human
rights and fundamental freedoms while countering terrorism (A/61/267, 2006) paras 31–41; Almqvist, J., 'A
human rights critique of European judicial review: counter-terrorism sanctions' (2008) 57 *International &
Comparative Law Quarterly* 303.

[162] (T-315/01, 21 September 2005, C-402/05, 415/05. 3 September 2008) at paras 348, 349, 352, 370.

[163] See especially *Organisation des Modjahedines du Peuple d'Iran v Council* (T-228/02, 12 December 2006,
T-157/07, T-256/07, 23 October 2008, T-284/08, 4 December 2008).

[164] [2006] EWHC (Admin) 2328 at para 64. See also [2007] EWCA Civ 173; [2008] UKHL 26.

[165] [2008] EWHC 869 (Admin); [2008] EWCA Civ 1187.

[166] [2008] EWCA Civ 1187 at para 53.

[167] *Ibid* at para 78.

also adequately certain and proportionate, including by the licensing scheme under Art 11 and the operation of the *de minimis* principle.[168] On similar reasoning, the 1267 Order and the designation under it were also upheld, though only by implying a 'merits based review'.[169]

3.87   The procedural deficiencies at domestic level, remedies for which were promised in 2006,[170] have belatedly been addressed for both schemes by Pt VI of the Counter-Terrorism Act 2008.[171] Discomfort during the foregoing litigation with HM Treasury provided a spurt of action. An application to set aside financial restrictions, whether under the wholly domestic 2001 or 2008 Act schemes or under the United Nations Orders (defined by s 64), can be made under s 63. Any person affected by the order (which could include relations through family or business) must apply to the Queen's Bench Division of the High Court (under s 71) or the Court of Session in Scotland which shall apply judicial review principles to what are depicted as 'financial restrictions proceedings' (ss 65, 67). The proceedings will be governed by special rules of court which must under s 66 take account of two predominant interests: the need for a proper review of the decision subject to challenge, and the need to ensure that disclosures are not made where this would be contrary to the public interest. It is regrettable that no priority is set between these two interests. In the absence of any derogation notice, there is a fundamental level of procedural justice which must be observed, even if the effect is to curtail the available evidence or to terminate the financial order.[172] The rule-making powers under ss 66, 67, and 72 envisage the use of special advocates (explained further in s 68),[173] limited disclosure and reasons, and exclusion from hearings. As far as the rules of disclosure are concerned, s 67(6) provides that nothing in s 67 is to be read as requiring the court to act in a manner inconsistent with Art 6 of the European Convention on Human Rights, though the same point does not appear in s 66. Pending the implementation of the Chilcot Report,[174] s 69 does, however, enable the disclosure of intercepted communications in these proceedings.

3.88   Whether these procedures are sufficient to meet the demands of Art 6 will be decided on a case-by-case basis, since the impact of suppression or exclusion can only be determined in the light of the nature of the restriction and its impact on proceedings. To take an example, s 67(3)(d) states that 'if permission is given by the court not to disclose material, it must consider requiring the Treasury to provide a summary of the material' to parties. Even if a summary is provided, it may not be enough; if it is not, then objections will surely be raised.[175] The government did give an assurance that the rules of court will ensure that the special advocate is never excluded.[176]

---

[168]   *Ibid* at paras 87–101.
[169]   *Ibid* at paras 119, 121. See Gearty, C., *Civil Liberties* (Oxford University Press, Oxford, 2007) ch 9.
[170]   See Hansard HC vol 450, col 11WS (10 October 2006).
[171]   Hansard HL vol 704, col 1048 (21 October 2008).
[172]   See *Re MB* [2007] UKHL 46.
[173]   This office will be explained in connection with control orders in ch 7.
[174]   *Privy Council Review of intercept as evidence: report to the Prime Minister and the Home Secretary* (Cm 7324, London, 2008).
[175]   See HC Hansard Public Bill Committee on the Counter-Terrorism Bill, *Memorandum from JUSTICE*, para 108.
[176]   HC Hansard Public Bill Committee on the Counter-Terrorism Bill, cols 439, 446 (13 May 2008), Tony McNulty.

G. FINANCIAL INVESTIGATIONS

In order to assist the detection process, professional financial intermediaries are encour- **3.89** aged to report their suspicions to the authorities.[177] By s 19(1) of the 2000 Act, where a person believes or suspects that another person has committed an offence under any of ss 15 to 18 on the basis of information which comes to his attention in the course of a trade, profession, business, or employment, an offence is committed if he does not disclose the information to a police officer or member of the Serious Organised Crime Agency ('SOCA') as soon as reasonably practicable. The width of the duty is striking; it is sufficient to have a subjective belief or suspicion which can only be safely suppressed if the intermediary has a 'reasonable excuse' under sub-s (3). This defence is not subject to s 118, but it is arguable that this switch is fair in the context of professionals who are trained to be on guard and should keep records; the extension to any other business is more dubious.[178] Under s 19(7), the duty has a global reach to equivalent actions overseas.

Exceptions are accorded to legally privileged information or the making of a disclo- **3.90** sure by an employee to an established higher authority, and the officials in regulatory authorities are also excused.[179] The disclosure defence allows for professional bodies to perform collating and channelling functions for police organizations by means of a 'Suspicious Activity Report'. The number of reports has increased substantially—from 18,408 in 2000 to 210,524 in 2007–08, though just 956 were terrorist-related and were referred to the National Terrorist Finance Investigation Unit.[180] It remains a problem to sort the wheat from the chaff, to discourage defensive reporting, and to encourage a more cooperative attitude from the security authorities.[181] The Privy Counsellor Review Committee argued for the destruction of reports unless an investigation is ongoing,[182] but the idea was rejected by the Home Office Consultation Paper.[183]

The government was at pains to emphasize the confinement of s 19 to professionals **3.91** handling finance. However, family and business relations may overlap in the situation of small businesses. Another concern arises from the fact that journalism is considered a 'profession' for these purposes, so a reporter with knowledge of the preparations for an explosion might have relevant information for the purposes of s 19,[184] which may chill inclinations towards investigative journalism.[185] The government minister (Lord Bassam) refused to accept any specific exemption for journalists.[186]

---

[177] As amended by the Terrorism Act 2000 and Proceeds of Crime Act 2002 (Amendment) Regulations 2007, SI 2007/3398.

[178] See also Smith, I., Owen, T., and Bodnar, A., *Asset Recovery* (Oxford University Press, Oxford, 2007) para I.3.634.

[179] Terrorism Act 2000 (Crown Servants and Regulators) Regulations 2001, SI 2001/192 (made under s 119).

[180] SOCA, *The Suspicious Activity Reports Regime Annual Report 2008* (London, 2008) p 9.

[181] KPMG, Review of the Regime for Handling Suspicious Activity Reports (London, 2003); Privy Counsellor Review Committee, *Anti-terrorism, Crime and Security Act 2001, Review, Report* (2003–04 HC 100) paras D134; Lander, S., Review of the Suspicious Activity Reports Regime (Home Office, London, 2006); HM Treasury, *The Financial Challenge to Crime and Terrorism* (London, 2007) paras 2.39, 2.60.

[182] *Anti-terrorism, Crime and Security Act 2001 Review, Report* (2003–04 HC 100) para D136.

[183] Home Office and Northern Ireland Office, *Legislation against Terrorism* (Cm 4178, London, 1998) Pt II para 10.

[184] Hansard HC Standing Committee D, col 155 (25 January 2000), Charles Clarke.

[185] See *Goodwin v United Kingdom*, App no 17488/90, Reports 1996-II.

[186] Hansard HL vol 613, col 653 (16 May 2000).

3.92　　The government's original justifications for the confinement of s 19 were largely for-gotten during the enactment of the Counter-Terrorism Act 2008, s 77. The background to this measure was concern since 9/11 that charities are being misused as a vehicle for raising or transferring money to terrorists.[187] Section 77 therefore inserts as s 22A of the 2000 Act a new definition of 'employment' which encompasses both paid and unpaid employment and can even include voluntary work. In this way, the unpaid volunteers who are the trustees of a charity must act with the same insight as professional forensic accountants. The Home Office describes the amendment as 'a very minor change to close a possible gap in the current provisions'.[188] But this statement grossly misrepre-sents the reformulated width of the duty. The result is to deter and penalize community-spirited individuals. Furthermore, those who take on duties such as trusts should be warned specifically about their new duties, and there should be readily available advice given to them (including a hotline) furnished by the Charity Commissioners.

3.93　　An even stricter duty to disclose is imposed on the 'regulated sector'[189] by Sch 2, Part III of the Anti-terrorism, Crime and Security Act 2001. This duty is applied instead of, and not additional to, s 19. Most businesses handling substantial financial activity are cov-ered. Under s 21A (as inserted into the Terrorism Act 2000), a person in that sector commits an offence if he knows or suspects[190] or has reasonable grounds for knowing or suspecting, that another person has attempted or committed an offence under any of ss 15 to 18 (including with extra-territorial effect), unless the information is disclosed to a constable, officer of SOCA, or a nominated officer of his employer as soon as practic-able. The duty is subject to a reasonable excuse not to disclose and to exceptions for legal privilege or legal advice. The objective standard, whereby the person can be liable without subjective awareness of any suspicion, is said to be justified by the '[g]reater awareness and higher standards of reporting in the financial sector'.[191] Given the object-ive standard, the court must consider whether the person followed any guidance by the relevant supervisory authority or professional body. Though the guidelines can be helpful,[192] they do not answer criticisms that the impact of s 21A unfairly applies equally to junior and senior staff,[193] and there are also difficulties in distinguishing between the regulated sector and the non-regulated sector when some businesses (lawyers and accountants) operate in both sectors. Nevertheless, only one offence is recorded up to the end of 2005,[194] suggesting that the offence mainly operates to guide

---

[187] See HM Treasury, *The Financial Challenge to Crime and Terrorism* (London, 2007); Home Office and HM Treasury, *Review of Safeguards to Protect the Charitable Sector (England and Wales) from Terrorist Abuse* (London, 2007).

[188] Home Office, *Possible Measures for Inclusion into a Future Counter-Terrorism Bill* (London, 2007) para 22.

[189] See Terrorism Act 2000, Sch 3A; Terrorism Act 2000 (Business in the Regulated Sector and Supervisory Authorities) Order 2007, SI 2007/3288.

[190] See 'Knowledge and suspicion under the Terrorism Act' (2003) 6 *Journal of Money Laundering Control* 255.

[191] Home Office, *Regulatory Impact Assessment: Terrorist Property* (2001) para 8

[192] See Law Society, *Anti-terrorism practice note: The conflicting duties of maintaining client confidentiality and reporting terrorism* (London, 2007). International guidance is given by the nine Special Recommendations of the Financial Action Task Force (<http://www.fatf-gafi.org>).

[193] See Lord Carlile, *Report on the Operation in 2002 and 2003 of the Terrorism Act 2000* (Home Office, 2004) para 50.

[194] Hansard HL vol 687, col 264wa (18 December 2006).

procedures and as a threat. Under section 21B, any disclosure within s 21A does not breach legal restraints on disclosure.

As well as disclosure duties, s 21D forbids tipping off in the regulated sector, subject **3.94** to s 21E (disclosures within an undertaking or group), s 21F (other permitted disclosures between institutions or professionals for the purpose only of preventing offences), and s 21G (disclosure to a supervisory authority or for the purpose of dissuading a client from unlawful conduct).[195] The measures place advisers within the regulator sector in a difficult position if their client becomes curious or angry as to why their contractually enforceable instructions are not transacted.[196] There is no set period for SOCA to reach a decision.[197]

Alongside a duty to disclose, s 20 of the Terrorism Act 2000 adopts a more permissive **3.95** path. A person may choose to disclose to a suitable authority a suspicion or belief (and its basis) that any money or other property is terrorist property or is derived from terrorist property or a belief or suspicion that arises in the course of a trade, profession, business, or employment that a person has committed an offence under ss 15 to 18. The disclosure may be made notwithstanding any legal restriction on disclosure. This provision is said to be used frequently.[198]

The next strategy to assist law enforcement is contained in s 21 of the Terrorism **3.96** Act 2000, which allows for more ongoing cooperation with the police. A person avoids an offence under ss 15 to 18 if acting within their scope with express police consent or even where the person acts on his own initiative but makes a disclosure as soon as is reasonably practicable.[199] Consent is often sought by professional advisers and financial bodies so as to avoid incurring tipping off penalties. If the police intervene before contact is made, s 21(5) provides for a defence to the effect that the person intended to make a disclosure of the kind mentioned and there is reasonable excuse for his failure to do so up to that point. Section 118 does not apply to this defence. In some instances, consent should also be sought under Pt II of the Regulation of Investigatory Powers Act 2000 for covert human intelligence sources or even intrusive surveillance.[200]

The same two provisions in s 21 are applied to contacts with SOCA under ss 21ZA **3.97** and 21ZB. Next, s 21ZC grants a defence to anyone with a reasonable excuse for non-disclosure under s 21ZA or 21ZB at any stage. It is also made clear by s 21C that any disclosure to a constable (including by the non-regulated sector) must be relayed to SOCA.

Aside from financial bodies, charities have come under closer scrutiny. In their report, **3.98** *Review of Safeguards to Protect the Charitable Sector (England and Wales) from Terrorist Abuse*,[201] the Home Office and HM Treasury regard the channelling of funds by charities to terrorists as 'extremely rare'. Nevertheless, they urge the Charity Commission to

---

[195] See Shenton, V., 'Tipping a loser' (2008) 105/19 *Law Society Gazette* 29.
[196] See *K Ltd v National Westminster Bank* [2006] EWCA Civ 1039.
[197] Compare Proceeds of Crime Act 2002, s 335.
[198] (*Rowe*) *Report of the Operation in 1998 of the Prevention of Terrorism (Temporary Provisions) Acts* (Home Office, London, 1999) para 66.
[199] There were 13,223 applications for consent in 2007–08: SOCA, *The Suspicious Activity Reports Regime Annual Report 2008* (London, 2008) p 15.
[200] See *Teixeira da Castro v Portugal*, App no 25829/94, 1998-IV; *Lambert v France*, App no 23618/94, 1998-V.
[201] (London, 2007) para 2.10.

reinforce awareness of risk factors, and extra finance has allowed the Commission to establish a Faith and Social Cohesion Unit.

H. CROWN SERVANTS AND REGULATORS

3.99 By s 119(1) of the Terrorism Act 2000, the Secretary of State may make regulations providing for any of ss 15 to 23A and 39 to apply to persons in the public service of the Crown. In other words, civil servants and employees of semi-autonomous state agencies may be subjected to financial offences, restraints, and investigations and may not assert a defence of Crown privilege.[202] In pursuance of this power, the Terrorism Act 2000 (Crown Servants and Regulators) Regulations 2001,[203] reg 3, apply ss 15 to 23A and 39 to the Director of Savings and any person employed by the Director in carrying on relevant financial business. On the other hand, reg 4 disapplies s 19 from the persons in the following bodies: the Bank of England; the Financial Services Authority; a designated professional body within the meaning of section 326(2) of the Financial Services and Markets Act 1986; the Council of Lloyd's; the Registrar and Assistant Registrar of Credit Unions for Northern Ireland; any person who is employed by, or otherwise engaged in, the service of any person referred to above for the purpose of performing such functions.

3.100 The Secretary of State may also under s 119(2) choose to exempt from duties of disclosure under s 19 persons who are in his opinion performing regulatory, supervisory, investigative, or registration functions of a public nature. Those persons are of course expected to tip off where appropriate, but do not require the sanction of a possible offence to encourage them to do so, nor, perhaps, would it be appropriate for them to answer in public for slip-ups.[204]

I. CONCLUSIONS

3.101 The suppression of terrorism finance is a worthy ambition, but the current regime has not evidently delivered more than meagre results. Causality cannot be attributed to legislative inattention but may reside in problems of under-valuation in policing cultures, under-resourcing, and obstacles to inter-agency cooperation.[205] International efforts are also of uncertain impact and involve processes which are an affront to the rule of law. Concerted action has been hampered either because of technical shortcomings or because of lack of will from countries which do not perceive themselves as threatened.[206] Part of

---

[202] Hansard HC Standing Committee D col 297 (3 February 2000), Charles Clarke.

[203] SI 2001/192, as amended by the Financial Services and Markets Act 2000 (Consequential Amendments) Order 2002, SI 2002/1555, art 43.

[204] See Hansard HC Standing Committee D col 297 (3 February 2000), Charles Clarke.

[205] Cabinet Office Performance and Innovation Office, *Recovering the Proceeds of Crime* (London, 2000). See further Northern Ireland Affairs Select Committee, *The Financing of Terrorism in Northern Ireland* (2001–02 HC 978) paras 50, 129, 140, 157; Bell, R.E., 'The confiscation, forfeiture and disruption of terrorist finances' (2003) 7 *Journal of Money Laundering Control* 105 at p 121.

[206] See Enders, W. and Sanders, T., *The Political Economy of Terrorism* (Cambridge University Press, New York, 2006) p 158.

the problem lies in the conditions of late modern terrorism, whereby the movement of finance within globalized networks is unremarkable yet complex.

Yet, it may be mistaken to emphasize quantitative measures.[207] Small sums are seized because small sums are involved. If the authorities turned a blind eye, larger sums would become available. Measures against finance can reduce the scale of operations and deter financiers. Funding for Islamist movements is said to be in sharp decline.[208] There may also be a disruptive function. Maybe the finance will offer the intelligence lead to more substantial evidence before or after the fact. For example, it was alleged that Rashid Rauf, whose arrest in Pakistan sparked the arrests of those in the 'liquid bomb' airline plot in 2006, was placed under surveillance, following alerts from the National Terrorist Financial Investigation Unit about money transfers from a British charity.[209]   3.102

The Treasury remains determined to persevere, according to its 2007 paper, *The Financial Challenge to Crime and Terrorism*.[210] Nevertheless, on current data, 'following the money' usually leads participants on a merry dance   3.103

---

[207] Levi, M., 'Lessons for countering terrorist finances from the war on serious and organised crime' in Biersteker, T.J., and Eckert, S.E. (eds), *Countering the Financing of Terrorism* (Routledge, London, 2008) p 264.

[208] Burr, J.M. and Collins, R.O., *Alms for Jihad* (Cambridge University Press, New York, 2006) p 302.

[209] Acharya, A., and Husin, G., 'Countering terrorist financing' *The Business Times Singapore* 25 August 2006.

[210] HM Treasury, *The Financial Challenge to Crime and Terrorism* (London, 2007).

4

TERRORIST INVESTIGATIONS

A. BACKGROUND

A definition of 'terrorist investigations' appears in s 32 as a peg on which to hang the   4.01
various provisions within Pt IV:

> . . . terrorist investigation' means an investigation of—
> (a) the commission, preparation or instigation of acts of terrorism,
> (b) an act which appears to have been done for the purposes of terrorism,
> (c) the resources of a proscribed organisation,
> (d) the possibility of making an order under section 3(3), or
> (e) the commission, preparation or instigation of an offence under this Act or under Part 1
>   of the Terrorism Act 2006 other than an offence under section 1 or 2 of that Act.[1]

The concept does not require the authorities to await the occurrence of any proven
crime or proven link to terrorism and will allow investigations not only into completed
criminal offences but also into preparatory work relevant to terrorism, such as in relation
to future proscription or transnational activities which are not yet outlawed within the
jurisdiction.

---

[1] As amended by the Terrorism Act 2006, s 37(1). The exclusion of the Terrorism Act 2006, ss 1 and 2 was
to delimit those controversial offences: Hansard HL vol 677, col 1242 (25 January 2006), Lord Bassam.

B. CORDONS

1. Powers

4.02   Part IV first turns its attention to the setting up of cordons and reproduces powers first enacted after the 1996 Docklands bombings.[2] The typical scenario will be where the police suspect that a bomb has been planted or wish to take control over the vicinity of an actual explosion or arrest operation.

4.03   By s 33 of the 2000 Act, a police officer can designate a 'cordoned area' if considered 'expedient for the purposes of a terrorist investigation'.[3] The acting officer must by s 34 be of at least the rank of superintendent, unless there is urgency, in which case any constable may step in. An amendment under the Anti-terrorism, Crime and Security Act 2001[4] allows a superintendent (but not other officers even in an emergency) in the British Transport Police[5] and Ministry of Defence Police to designate cordon areas in places within their jurisdiction.

4.04   The power is unusually broad and is expressed in terms of 'expedience' to cater for confused situations:[6]

An example might be where a bomb warning was imprecise, or the police believed it was inaccurate—deliberately or otherwise. In such a case the necessity for a cordon might be debatable, but it makes good sense to have one. Similarly, in the case of stop and search or parking restriction powers, there could be cases where a cordon might not be considered 'reasonably necessary' but could be to the general advantage.

4.05   Because of the circumstances of grave emergency in which such operations arise, the designation may be oral in the first instance (ss 33(3) and 34(3)), but it must be confirmed in writing as soon as reasonably practicable. Once an order has been issued under s 33, the police must demarcate the cordoned area, so far as is reasonably practicable, by means of tape marked with the word 'police' or in such other manner as a constable considers appropriate.

4.06   By s 35, a designation has effect as specified in the order, but it must not endure longer than the end of the period of fourteen days beginning with the day on which the designation is made, renewable for up to a further fourteen days. While an area remains designated, any constable in uniform may, under s 36(1) order physical evacuation of persons and vehicles, arrange for the removal of parked vehicles, and prohibit or restrict access to a cordoned area by pedestrians or vehicles.

4.07   A person commits a summary only offence under s 36(4) by failing to comply with an order, prohibition or restriction.[7] It is a defence under s 36(3) for a person to prove a reasonable excuse for the failure; lack of clear specification of the designated area might be one ground. Section 118 does not apply to this defence.

---

[2] See Prevention of Terrorism (Additional Powers) Act 1996, ss 4, 5.
[3] 'Expedient' should be interpreted as in *R (on the application of Gillan) v Commissioner of Police for the Metropolis* [2006] UKHL 12.
[4] Sch 7, para 30.
[5] This power does not apply in Northern Ireland: Railways and Transport Safety Act 2003, s 31.
[6] Hansard HL vol 613, col 660 (16 May 2000), Lord Bassam.
[7] Note the pending changes as to penalty: Criminal Justice Act 2003, s 280, Sch 26 para 55.

2. Assessment

The imposition of cordons is a sensible adjunct to the strategies of 'Prevent' and 'Pursuit'. **4.08**
As for efficiency and efficacy, police activities overwhelmingly converge upon London.
When invoked elsewhere, the practices appear erratic.

Table 4.1 Cordon powers[8]

Year	Met Police		City London		Other Eng/Wales		Scot		NI	
	No.	Ave. mins.	No	Ave. mins.	No. (forces)	Ave. mins.	No	Ave. mins.	No.	Ave. mins.
2001	30	118	0	0	1 (1)	4320	0	0	62	n/a
2002	14	184	0	0	12 (2)	260	0	0	239	n/a
2003	16	158	0	0	8 (4)	2295	0	0	175	n/a
2004	4	60	17	47	0	0	0	0	126	n/a
2005	68	408	11	40	0	0	0	0	72	n/a
2006	13	67	8	30	8 (1)	4716	0	0	46	287
2007	52	81	22	43	0	0	0	0	n/a	n/a

Accountability for cordons is under-developed. It is not specified what detail must be **4.09**
given in the written confirmation nor to whom the confirmation is to be given nor
where the written document is to be lodged. Unlike under s 44,[9] no ministerial oversight
is required nor review by a senior police officer. There is no requirement to mediate with
the community. There is no guidance akin to that for s 44. Judicial review is available as
an avenue for challenge, though many cordons will have been lifted by the time the lawyers assemble in court. Given current divergent practices, a limit of, say, twenty-four
hours, should apply beyond which judicial authorization should be obtained.

Moving to a rights audit, the fleeting and incidental nature of the impact on liberty is **4.10**
probably not sufficient to incur the restraints of Art 5.[10] Freedom of movement is certainly affected but is not yet recognized under the Human Rights Act 1998. As for rights
to family life and enjoyment of property, a court is more ready to find proportionality.[11]
Most vulnerable to challenge is the initial trigger of 'expedience', which may be deemed
to be inadequate to ensure necessity and proportionality related to terrorism rather than
police convenience.[12]

As for alternative methods of achieving the same goal, common law powers were **4.11**
invoked against Alan Clark, MP,[13] who was convicted of obstruction of the police in the

---

[8] Sources: Carlile Reports: note the duration prior to 2004 is expressed only in full hours; NIO Statistics
& Research Branch: the statistics start from 1 April 2001; 2006 from the PSNI.
[9] See ch 5.
[10] See *R (on the application of Gillan) v Commissioner of Police for the Metropolis* [2006] UKHL 12; *R (on the
application of Laporte) v Chief Constable of Gloucestershire* [2006] UKHL 55; *Austin v Commissioner of Police of
the Metropolis* [2009] UKHL 9.
[11] *(Margaret) Murray v United Kingdom*, App no 14310/88 Ser A 300A (1994) para 90.
[12] Compare *Fox, Hartley and Campbell v United Kingdom*, App nos 12244/86, 12245/86, 12383/86,
Ser A 182 (1990).
[13] *The Times* 14 June 1996 p 5.

execution of their duty at Bow Street Magistrates' Courts for breaching a police cordon during a bomb alert. In addition to common law protective powers, common law forensic protection powers have since been developed. In *DPP v Morrison*,[14] police officers were held to be entitled to erect a cordon to investigate a crime and to preserve evidence. They could even assume that that there was always consent to do so on private land over which a public right of way existed, such as a shopping mall.[15] Another relevant power is s 22(3)(d) of the Civil Contingencies Act 2004, by which regulations may prohibit, or enable the prohibition of, movement to or from a specified place. Thus, a cordon can be imposed around an area affected by, say, a 'dirty' bomb, assuming an emergency can be established to activate Pt II of the Act.[16] In summary, alternative powers do exist and should be considered, but the common law does not have the clarity of the terrorism legislation, and the Civil Contingencies Act applies only to catastrophic incidents.

C. COMPULSORY OBTAINING OF TESTIMONY AND EVIDENCE

1. Powers

4.12 Section 37 of the Terrorism Act 2000[17] introduces several measures in Sch 5 by which testimony and documentary evidence may be obtained under compulsion. The schedule offers variants upon Sch 1 of the Police and Criminal Evidence Act 1984 ('PACE') or the Police and Criminal Evidence (Northern Ireland) Order 1989. The main differences are the triggering criteria, which relate to 'terrorist investigations' rather than to specified offences, and the powers so triggered. However, in many details, the terminology of the PACE legislation is followed.[18] In so far as these powers (or any others in the Terrorism Act 2000) involve the search of premises, then, by s 116(1), a power to search premises allows the search of any container within it. In so far as they involve judicial proceedings, a small pool of judges hear these cases, located in court buildings with secure storage facilities.[19]

4.13 The first search power, to enter premises, to search the premises or any person found there, and to seize and retain any relevant material, is in Sch 5, para 1(1): 'A constable may apply to a justice of the peace for the issue of a warrant under this paragraph for the purposes of a terrorist investigation.' The premises to be targeted may be particular (for a 'specific premises warrant') or, following amendment by the Terrorism Act 2006, s 26,[20] they may comprise any or sets of premises occupied or controlled by a person specified in the application (an 'all premises warrant').[21] To make an application, the constable

---

[14] [2003] EWHC Admin 683.

[15] The assumption is also made in PACE Code B para 2.3.

[16] See Walker, C. and Broderick, J., *The Civil Contingencies Act 2004* (Oxford University Press, Oxford, 2006) ch 5.

[17] Compare Prevention of Terrorism (Temporary Provisions) Act 1989, s 17 and sch 7.

[18] See further the direct application of PACE ss 21, 22: Sch 5 para 17.

[19] Lord Carlile, *Report on the Operation in 2001 of the Terrorism Act 2000* (Home Office, London, 2002) para 4.5.

[20] This was inspired by the Serious Organised Crime and Police Act 2005, ss 113, 114.

[21] A warrant may incorporate both formats: *Redknapp v Metropolitan Police Commissioner* [2008] EWHC 1177 (Admin).

must have reasonable grounds under para 1(3) for believing that the evidence is likely to be of substantial value to a terrorist investigation, and that it must be seized in order to prevent it from being concealed, lost, damaged, altered, or destroyed. In turn, the justice may grant an application only if 'satisfied' under para 1(5): (a) that the warrant is sought for the purposes of a terrorist investigation; (b) that there are reasonable grounds for believing that there is material on the premises which is likely to be of substantial value to a terrorist investigation; (c) that the issue of a warrant is likely to be necessary in the circumstances of the case; and (d) in the case of an all premises warrant, that it is not reasonably practicable to specify all the premises. 'Excepted material' may not be the subject of an application. Paragraph 1 includes in the definition of 'terrorist investigation' anything likely to be of substantial value to 'a', and not 'the', terrorist investigation so that where material relevant to a different terrorist investigation is discovered, there is no need to return to court for another warrant.

Additional powers to seize and sift elsewhere materials are generally enabled under the Criminal Justice and Police Act 2001, ss 50, 51, and 55. These powers have been expanded by the Counter-Terrorism Act 2008 which allows for the removal of documents[22] for examination in the context of a police search under existing terrorism legislation search powers.[23] Now, there is power, backed by the deterrence of an offence of obstruction under s 2,[24] to remove a document from premises so that the police can examine it elsewhere, where it is not possible to examine it effectively at the search site because of its bulk or inextricable link to other material.[25] Before this amendment, the sifting power applied only in relation to the search powers in the Terrorism Act 2000 Sch 5 in relation to paras 1, 3, 11, and 15.[26] Section 1 of the 2008 Act grants this power in relation to a much wider range of search powers[27] in order that the police can examine back at base materials such as foreign language documents and computer data so as to ascertain whether they may be seized. The other major change brought about by s 1 is that it lowers the threshold for seizure. Reliance on the 2001 Act scheme required reasonable suspicion that the extra seized materials were relevant evidence in relation to the offence justifying the search. The standard of reasonable suspicion is removed by s 1—it is sufficient that an officer might merely 'think' that what appears to be a restaurant bill from Peshawar is in fact an Al-Qa'ida document.[28] Thus, s 1 provides aid where the document is 'entirely obscure', though it is not to encourage 'fishing expeditions' as will be clarified by PACE Code B.[29] The Act also more clearly regulates the seizures without reference back to the 2001 Act. In particular, the power is subject to the protection

4.14

---

[22] Only documents can be taken and not, for example, computers: Hansard HL vol 704, col 344 (9 October 2008), Lord West.

[23] There were 347 seizures in the last five years: Hansard HL vol 704, col 358 (9 October 2008), Lord West. Powers to examine documents in the Terrorism Act 2000, s 87 expired in 2007.

[24] Compare Police Act 1996 s 89.

[25] It is promised that PACE Codes will explain further: Hansard HC Public Bill Committee on the Counter-Terrorism Bill, col 177 (29 April 2008), Tony McNulty.

[26] Criminal Justice and Police Act 2001, sch 1 para 70.

[27] It adds: Terrorism Act 2000 s 43, sch 5 paras 28, 31, Prevention of Terrorism Act 2005, ss 7A, 7B or 7C, and Terrorism Act 2006, s 28.

[28] Hansard HC Public Bill Committee on the Counter Terrorism Bill, col 169 (29 April 2008), Tony McNulty.

[29] Hansard HL vol 704, cols 339, 343 (9 October 2008), Lord West.

under s 3[30] of documents that are, or may be, legally privileged, where the constable has reasonable cause to believe the item has that status. If it is discovered that a document that has been removed is an item subject to legal privilege, it must be returned immediately unless they cannot be separated from other parts. By s 4, there must be a written record of the removal as soon as is reasonably practicable and in any event within twenty-four hours of the removal. Section 5 limits the retention for examination to forty-eight hours unless further retention for an extra forty-eight hours is authorized by a chief inspector. Supervised access or a copy may be granted to the owner under s 6. Copying of the material is restricted under s 7.

4.15   Greater latitude is allowed in the second search power in Sch 5, in para 2, because the application does not relate to residential premises.[31] There is no equivalent to this power in PACE 1984. Here, the application is made by a police officer of at least the rank of superintendent, and the justice of the peace need not be concerned that the issue of a warrant is likely to be necessary in the circumstances of the case. The purpose is to facilitate mass searches, such as of lock-up premises in a given area where it is suspected that bomb-makers are active but without sufficient knowledge as to the precise location of their premises. Such a warrant is exercisable only within twenty-four hours of issuance of the warrant. Under para 2, the premises must be specified, but there is an 'all premises' variant under para 2A.[32]

4.16   The third search power relates to cordoned areas, including residential premises. There is no equivalent in PACE 1984. Schedule 5, para 3 empowers a police officer of at least the rank of superintendent, on reasonable grounds for believing that there is material to be found on the premises, to authorize by a written and signed authority a search of specified premises which are wholly or partly within a cordoned area. To cater for dire emergencies, perhaps within the first few minutes after cordoning off, any constable may give an authorization (presumably to himself) if he considers it necessary by reason of urgency. The search may be repeated at any time during designation. The limitations as to materials which may be seized are the same as in para 1, and the power to seize and sift elsewhere under the Criminal Justice and Police Act 2001 also apply. It is a summary offence wilfully to obstruct a search under para 3.[33]

4.17   The fourth investigative power, under para 5, deals with the production of, or access to, excluded and special procedure material which are defined together (along with legally privileged materials) as 'excepted materials' in para 4 for the whole of the first part of Sch 5 by reference to PACE 1984. These materials are excepted from the objectives of the foregoing three powers, though it is only legally privileged materials which may not be seized and retained under those powers if found by chance rather than design. The potential search power under para 5 for excluded material is in sharp contrast with the PACE legislation. By para 8, only legally privileged material is exempt from the clutches of para 5 which overrides all other statutory restrictions, even, according to para 9, to material held by government departments.

---

[30] Compare Criminal Justice and Police Act 2001, s 54.
[31] Classification as 'non-residential' depends on the reasonable belief of a police officer: para 2(4), 2A(4).
[32] See Terrorism Act 2006, s 26.
[33] The penalty will increase to 51 weeks: Criminal Justice Act 2003, s 280, Sch 26 para 55.

By para 5(1), a constable may apply to a circuit judge[34] for an order to access 4.18
excluded or special procedure material (including, under para 7, material coming into
existence within twenty-eight days) for the purposes of a terrorist investigation. There
is no requirement that notice be given to the possessor of the materials or that the
material must be potential 'evidence' for a court case. An application may also relate to
a person who is likely to have possession of such material within twenty-eight days. If
granted, the order may require under para 5(3) a specified person normally within seven
days: (a) to produce to a constable within a specified period for seizure and retention
any relevant material; (b) to give a constable access to relevant material within a
specified period; and (c) to state to the best of his knowledge and belief the location of
relevant material if it is not in, and will not come into, his possession, custody, or power
within the period specified under (a) or (b). An order may also require any other
person who appears to the judge to be entitled to grant entry to the premises to allow
entry and access.

The circuit judge may grant an order[35] if 'satisfied' of two criteria in para 6. The first 4.19
condition relates to the relevance to the purposes of a terrorist investigation as well as the
need for 'reasonable grounds for believing that the material is likely to be of substantial
value'. The second condition demands reasonable grounds for believing that it is in the
public interest that the material should be produced.

Much of the consequent litigation has considered excluded or special procedure jour- 4.20
nalistic materials. In *R v Middlesex Guildhall Crown Court, ex parte Salinger*,[36] the police
sought from prominent US journalist, Pierre Salinger, and his employers records of
interviews conducted in Libya with the two prime suspects of the Lockerbie bombing in
1988. It was held by the High Court that on the initial *ex parte* application, the police
should provide to the judge a written statement of the material evidence, including
the nature of the available information subject to secrecy and sensitivity, and the police
officer should appear before the judge to provide oral evidence. The judge could then
decide on the grant of the order and also on what information might be served on
the recipients. In turn, the recipients are entitled to be given, preferably in writing and
at the time of service of the order, as much information as could properly be provided as
to the grounds for the order but it would rarely be appropriate or necessary for disclosure
of the source or details. Their subsequent application to discharge or vary should be
made to the same judge with the same police officer who gave oral evidence being
present. On this application, the judge will reconsider the order afresh on its merits,
and there is no onus on the recipient to satisfy the judge that the order was wrongly
made. The processes were further clarified in *Re Morris*.[37] Appearance at the *ex parte*
stage by the possessors should be rare but could be allowed at the discretion of the court

---

[34] A district judge (magistrates' courts) may also act once the Courts Act 2003, s 65, sch 4, para 9(a) comes
into force; this change will affect all the powers in sch 5. In Northern Ireland, a Crown Court judge acts in this
capacity (substituted for a county court judge by the Anti-terrorism, Crime and Security Act 2001, s 121, to
bring it in line with the Proceeds of Crime Act 2002, s 343). This switch to Crown Court removed the availability of judicial review in Northern Ireland, but a process to discharge or vary is still implied: *Re Morris* [2003]
NICC 11.
[35] Under para 10, it is treated as if it were an order of the Crown Court.
[36] [1993] QB 564.
[37] [2003] NICC 11 at para 35.

where it did not impede the investigation and could be of assistance to the court, which might be especially true in difficult and complex cases involving the media.[38]

4.21 Journalistic material was again investigated in 1991 when Box Productions compiled a programme, broadcast by Channel 4, which alleged that there was collusion between members of the Royal Ulster Constabulary and Loyalist terrorists which was presided over by a secret committee of prominent people.[39] The police sought the production of documents connected with the programme. A redacted dossier of material was handed to the police, but it was claimed that further sensitive material had either been destroyed or removed from the jurisdiction and that the only person who knew the whereabouts of the material was a researcher employed by Box Productions. The judge then directed that the material sent abroad should be brought back and produced to the police. The respondents refused to comply and thereby put themselves in contempt of court. The Divisional Court could not review the judge's exercise of his discretion to make the order, and it therefore proceeded to impose a fine of £75,000 for the contempt.[40]

4.22 In *Re Moloney's Application*,[41] the Northern Ireland editor of the *Sunday Tribune* newspaper was required to produce any notes of an interview with William Stobie, who was later accused of the murder of lawyer Patrick Finucane. Quashing the Recorder's order, the High Court stated:[42]

. . . the police have in our view to show something more than a possibility that the material will be of some use. They must establish that there are reasonable grounds for believing that the material is likely to be of substantial value to the investigation.

4.23 In *Re Jordan*,[43] the police sought materials from a BBC *Panorama* programme, 'Gangsters at War', which showed an announcement by a masked man on behalf of the Ulster Freedom Fighters. He was identified through voice analysis as Dennis Cunningham.[44] Any arguments about the chilling effect of disclosure on the ability to carry out investigative journalism were outweighed in the view of the Crown Court in Belfast by 'the unmasking of terrorists and bringing them to justice'.[45]

4.24 In *Malik v Manchester Crown Court*,[46] a production order was granted under para 6 in connection with a book manuscript written about Hassan Butt, entitled, *Leaving Al-Qaeda*. The police believed materials possessed by Malik, who helped to write the book, might disclose evidence of crimes by Butt. It was held that 'likely' under para 6(2)(b) demanded a high standard—'probable'; but 'substantial value' required only a value more than minimal.[47] Being 'satisfied' required a firm belief rather than a suspicion.[48] On review, it was determined that the grant of the order could not be faulted,

[38] *Ibid* at para 35.
[39] See further McPhilemey, S., *The Committee* (Roberts Rinehart, Boulder, 1999).
[40] *DPP v Channel 4 & Box Productions* [1993] 2 All ER 517. See further Costigan, R., 'Further dispatches' (1992) 142 *New Law Journal* 1417.
[41] [2000] NIJB 195.
[42] *Ibid* at p 207.
[43] [2003] NICC 1.
[44] He was later convicted on this evidence: *R v Cunningham* [2005] NICC 45.
[45] [2003] NICC 1 at para 21 per Judge Hart.
[46] [2008] EWHC 1362 (Admin).
[47] *Ibid* at para 36.
[48] *Ibid* at para 37.

though the terms were altered. The High Court indicated that a court could of its own motion appoint a special advocate to appear at the *ex parte* hearing or on an application for variation or discharge, but only in exceptional cases.[49]

Two issues not yet adequately litigated are, first whether compliance with the production order might involve forcible self-incrimination contrary to Art 6 of the European Convention. The offences of withholding information about terrorism offences committed by another under ss 19 or 38B of the Terrorism Act 2000 (both described later in this chapter) might be engaged by production orders. It was indicated in *R v Central Criminal Court, ex parte Bright*[50] that the statutory powers of production override the right against self-incrimination. The production of physical materials with an existence independent of the will of the defendant has been treated as distinct from demanding information from the knowledge of the defendant.[51] The second factor yet to be fully rehearsed is the impact of s 12(4) of the Human Rights Act 1998, which requires particular regard for the importance of freedom of expression before any order is granted.

Should a production order under para 5 be viewed as inappropriate for the purposes of the investigation (perhaps because it would tip off a potential collaborator), then under para 11, a constable may apply to a circuit judge (or in Northern Ireland, a Crown Court judge) for the issuance of a warrant to permit entry, search, and seizure. This variant procedure may be selected where, under para 12, a circuit judge is satisfied that a production order (whether on specified premises or an 'all premises' type) has not been complied with (para 12(1)) or where satisfied (under para 12(2)–(4)) that there are reasonable grounds for believing there is present material likely to be of substantial value but that it is not appropriate to proceed by way of production order. The power to seize and retain materials attracts additional powers to seize and retain articles for sifting elsewhere enabled under the Criminal Justice and Police Act 2001.

The fifth type of investigative power is ancillary to the foregoing. By Sch 5, para 13, a constable may apply to a circuit judge (or in Northern Ireland, a Crown Court judge) for an order requiring any person specified in the order to provide an explanation of any material seized, produced, or made available under paras 1, 5, or 11. There is no equivalent to this invasive power in PACE 1984. Though the usual exception as to legal privilege applies, a lawyer may be required to provide the name and address of his client. There is no immunity against revealing information concerning other excepted materials. It is an offence under para 14 knowingly or recklessly to make a false or misleading statement. By para 13(4)(b), and in deference to Art 6, a statement in response to a requirement imposed by an order under this paragraph may be used in evidence against the maker only on a prosecution for an offence under para 14 but not for any other offence.[52]

4.25

4.26

4.27

---

[49] *Ibid* at para 99.

[50] [2001] 2 All ER 244. Compare *Inner West London Coroner v Channel 4 Television Corporation* [2007] EWHC 2513 (QB).

[51] See *Brown v Stott* [2000] UKPC D3; *R v Allen* [2001] UKHL 45; *O'Halloran and Francis v United Kingdom*, App nos 15809/02, 25624/02, 29 June 2007; *R v S* [2008] EWCA Crim 2177.

[52] See *Saunders v United Kingdom*, App no 19187/91, 1996-VI; *I.J.L. v United Kingdom*, App nos 29522/95, 30056/96, 30574/96, 2000-IX; Munday, R, 'Inferences from silence and the European Human Rights law' [1996] *Criminal Law Review* 370; Sedley, S., 'Wringing out the fault' (2001) 52 *Northern Ireland Legal Quarterly* 107; Berger, M., 'Compelled self-reporting and the principle against compelled self incrimination' [2006] *European Human Rights Law Review* 25.

4.28   The sixth investigative power, under Sch 5, para 15, deals with cases of urgency. A police officer of at least the rank of superintendent may give written authority equivalent to a warrant or order under para 1 or 11. The officer must have reasonable grounds for believing that the case is one of great emergency and that immediate action is necessary. Particulars of the case shall then be notified as soon as is reasonably practicable to the Secretary of State, though no particular response is then required. Wilful obstruction of a search is a summary offence.[53] There is no defence of reasonable excuse, but the requirement that the obstruction be 'wilful' performs part of its job. The power to seize and retain materials attracts additional powers to seize and sift under the Criminal Justice and Police Act 2001.

4.29   There is a corresponding emergency equivalent to the compulsory disclosure power under Sch 5, para 13 for materials under para 15. By para 16, if a police officer of at least the rank of superintendent has reasonable grounds for believing that the case is one of great emergency he may by a written notice require any person specified in the notice to provide an explanation of any material seized in pursuance of an order under para 15. It is a summary offence to fail to comply with a notice. It is a defence for a person charged with such an offence to show that he had a reasonable excuse for his failure (perhaps relating to the difficulty of accessing or amassing information within a required time scale); s 118 does not apply.

4.30   Finally, there are some variants for Northern Ireland and Scotland. The adaptations for Northern Ireland are minor,[54] since erstwhile executive powers of the Secretary of State by Sch 5, paras 19, 20, and 21, have now been repealed.[55]

4.31   Part II of Sch 5 provides for Scottish powers equivalent (but not extra) to those in England and Wales. Powers corresponding to the first category are in para 28; the procurator fiscal may apply to the sheriff to grant a warrant for the purposes of a terrorist investigation.[56] There is no direct equivalent to the second or third search powers. However, similar to the fourth power, by para 22, the procurator fiscal may apply to the sheriff for a production order which can relate to material of any specified description (the concepts of special procedure and excluded materials not being part of Scottish law). Explanations, as in the fifth power, can be required under para 30 on application by the procurator fiscal to the sheriff. Police powers, dealing with urgent situations in the sixth category, are granted by paras 31 and 32.

2. Assessment

4.32   These powers seek cumulatively to enable the 'Pursuit' of terrorists but achieve their goal by lowering safeguards normally available in PACE and without consideration of whether the 'normal' powers in PACE could instead get the job done. In so far as reliance is deemed unavoidable, whether because of the additional powers offered by the Terrorism Act or because of its broader notion of 'terrorist investigation', three departures from PACE cause most disquiet. One is that the powers under paras 1, 5, and 11 are subjectively

---

[53] The penalty is to increase to 51 weeks: Criminal Justice Act 2003, s 280, sch 26, para 55.
[54] See Sch 5 para 18.
[55] Terrorism (Northern Ireland) Act 2006, s 5, sch
[56] All premises warrants are provided for by the Terrorism Act 2006, s 27.

worded.[57] Secondly, the police can issue their own authorizations under para 15, without subsequent reporting and confirmation by a judicial officer. The third departure concerns the extension of powers to excepted material under paras 5 and 13. It is arguable that insufficient attention has been accorded to investigative journalism. In *Goodwin v United Kingdom*, the European Court recognized that '[p]rotection of journalist sources is one of the basic conditions for press freedom'.[58] The interests of the administration of justice, including the need to identify offenders, may result in an order for disclosure if the countervailing interests are clear.[59] But even when competing rights are in play, free expression has importance,[60] but the vigour of the courts in applying strictly Sch 5 has not been adequate.

Various criticisms may be mounted of specific measures in Sch 5. The idea that non-residential premises should attract virtually no privacy protection misreads the European Convention.[61] Therefore, the power in paras 2 and 3 should be confined to emergencies and should be strictly limited in time.   4.33

The necessity for the powers should also be scrutinized. As well as PACE, the field of financial criminal investigations is also occupied by the Proceeds of Crime Act 2002, Pt VIII. Part VIII investigations are narrower since they relate to whether someone has derived 'benefit from his criminal conduct' (s 341), but the enforcement measures otherwise closely resemble Sch 5, including production orders (ss 345 and 380, but not extending to excluded material by ss 348 and 383), search warrants (ss 352 and 387), and disclosure orders (ss 357 and 391). The criteria for issuance under s 358 are notably stricter, and the courts have imposed sensible limits when dealing with external activities on behalf of the foreign authorities who had deliberately chosen not to seek an order in their own country.[62] Consolidation would be beneficial to ensure unity of terminology and coverage of the 2002 Act's extensive guidance,[63] and to improve constitutional governance.   4.34

The attribute of accountability is woefully weak in Sch 5. A total of 694 production orders were issued in 2006,[64] and few applications are denied.[65] Otherwise, scrutiny in Parliament and by the independent reviewers is minimal. As for constitutional governance, the codes are detailed, and the possibility of judicial challenge does exist.   4.35

---

[57] Compare PACE, sch 1.

[58] App No 17488/90, 1996-II para 39.

[59] *Secretary of State for Defence v Guardian Newspapers* [1984] 3 WLR 986; *Maxwell v Pressdram* [1987] 1 WLR 298; *In re an Inquiry under the Company Securities (Insider Dealing) Act 1985* [1988] 2 WLR 33; *X v Y* [1988] 2 All ER 648; *X Ltd v Morgan-Grampian (Publishers) Ltd* [1991] 1 AC 1; *Camelot Group plc v Centaur Communications Ltd* [1999] QB 124; *Ashworth Hospital Authority v MGN Ltd* [2002] UKHL 29.

[60] *Re S (A Child)* [2004] UKHL 47 at para 17.

[61] Compare *Chappell v United Kingdom*, App no 10461/83, Ser A 152-A (1989); *Halford v United Kingdom*, App no 20605/92, 1997-III.

[62] According to *Serious Fraud Office v King* [2008] EWCA Crim 530 at para 59.

[63] See Proceeds of Crime Act 2002 (Investigations in England, Wales and Northern Ireland: Code of Practice) Order 2008, SI 2008/946.

[64] HM Treasury, *The Financial Challenge to Crime and Terrorism* (London, 2007) para 2.64. The figure used to be around 100: *(Rowe) Report of the Operation in 1998 of the Prevention of Terrorism (Temporary Provisions) Acts* (Home Office, London, 1999) para 70.

[65] Lord Carlile, *Report on the Operation in 2001 of the Terrorism Act 2000* (Home Office, London, 2002) para 4.6.

D. ADDITIONAL DISCLOSURE POWERS

4.36   Further powers to assist financial investigations are granted by Pt IV.[66] The tactic of enforced disclosure in complex cases has been advanced from financial investigations to terrorist investigations by s 33 of the Terrorism Act 2006. Disclosure to the security services is encouraged by the Counter-Terrorism Act 2008.

1. Customer information

4.37   At the core of Sch 6 to the Terrorism Act 2000 is the disclosure order. The application is made under para 2, in England and Wales or Northern Ireland, by a police officer holding at least the rank of superintendent, or, in Scotland, by the procurator fiscal. The order can be authorized under para 3 by, in England and Wales, a circuit judge, in Scotland, by the sheriff, or, in Northern Ireland, a Crown Court judge.[67] They must be satisfied (not to any objective standard) under para 5 that: (a) the order is sought for the purposes of a terrorist investigation, (b) the tracing of terrorist property is desirable for the purposes of the investigation, and (c) the order will enhance the effectiveness of the investigation.

4.38   If an order is granted, then by para 1, a constable may require the affected financial institution to provide 'customer information' for the purposes of a terrorist investigation, notwithstanding any restriction on the disclosure of information imposed by statute or common law. An institution which fails to comply with a requirement under this paragraph shall be liable to summary conviction. But it is a defence to prove that the information required was not in the institution's possession or that it was not reasonably practicable to comply with the requirement (such as where there would be an enormous amount of information to convey[68]). 'Customer information' is defined in para 7 to include information whether a business relationship exists or existed between the financial institution and a particular person and then, assuming that there is a relationship, relevant dates and identifying data. Most of the applications have related to bank and credit card details[69] and arise where the police have a name (and perhaps an address) but are unsure of accounts held.[70]

4.39   In line with the requirements of Art 6 of the European Convention, Sch 6, para 9 provides that customer information provided by a financial institution under this schedule shall not be admissible in evidence in criminal proceedings against the institution or any of its officers or employees (save for a prosecution for an offence of non-compliance under para 1 or 8).

---

[66] The basis is the Proceeds of Crime (Northern Ireland) Order 1996, SI 1996/1299, sch 2.

[67] The Criminal Procedure Rules r 62.1 cover variation and discharge but not application, so it is suggested that r 62.3 for the Proceeds of Crime Act 2002 should be followed: Smith, I., Owen, T., and Bodnar, A., *Asset Recovery* (Oxford University Press, Oxford, 2007) para I.2.514.

[68] Hansard HC vol 346, col 331 (15 March 2000), Charles Clarke.

[69] Lord Carlile, *Report on the Operation in 2001 of the Terrorism Act 2000* (Home Office, London, 2002) para 4.7.

[70] There was just one order sought by the Metropolitan Police in 2007.

Orders can apply against specified financial institutions or as a collective,[71] the latter reflecting operational practice of so-called general bank circulars in Northern Ireland.[72] The financial institution only has to say whether it holds accounts in the names given but cannot be required to provide any details of what is in the account. If the police want such information, they would need to seek a production order under Sch 5 or an account monitoring order under Sch 6A. Perhaps because Sch 6 might obviate more costly investigations, the banks were 'generally supportive' of the device.[73] It is arguable that a collective authorization, especially without independent oversight, does not proportionately protect privacy under Art 8 of the European Convention.[74]

4.40

2. Account monitoring information

The Anti-terrorism, Crime and Security Act 2001, s 3 and Sch 3, inserted a new s 38A and Sch 6A into the Terrorism Act 2000 and thereby allows for account monitoring orders. These powers can be activated in relation to 'financial institutions', a category which can be added to by order.[75] They differ from Sch 6 in two major effects: they relate to transactions rather than identity, and they can allow for real-time disclosure rather than a disclosure of records.[76] There are no limits on the information so gathered, including accounts relating to legal matters, for 'we cannot see any occasion when such information would be legally privileged'.[77]

4.41

By Sch 6A, para 2, a judge may, on an application by an appropriate officer, make an account monitoring order if satisfied that the order is sought for the purposes of a terrorist investigation, the tracing of terrorist property is desirable for the purposes of the investigation, and the order will enhance the effectiveness of the investigation. If an order is made, then the financial institution specified in the application for the order will be notified with a copy of the order.[78] Subsequently, it must for the period specified in the order (which cannot exceed ninety days) provide information of the description specified in the application to an appropriate officer. These proceedings will (by para 1) be conducted before a circuit judge sitting in the Crown Court or, in Scotland, the sheriff. The judge may hear the application *ex parte* in chambers (para 3). The 'appropriate officer' will be a police officer or, in Scotland, the procurator fiscal. In view of the intrusiveness of the powers, it is surprising that a police officer of any rank can apply, though in practice, senior detectives are the likely participants. Applications to vary or

4.42

---

[71] Sch 6 para 1(1A), inserted by the Anti-terrorism, Crime and Security Act 2001, sch 2 para 6(1), (3). See Home Office Circular 30/2002: *Guidance for the Police and Public on the implementation of Sections 1–2 of the Anti-terrorism, Crime and Security Act 2001*, para 72.

[72] See the *(Rowe) Review of the Northern Ireland (Emergency Provisions) Act 1991* (Cm 2706, London, 1995) para 145. There were 23 general bank circulars issued between August 1996 and December 2000: Donohue, L.K., *The Cost of Counterterrorism* (Cambridge University Press, Cambridge, 2007) p 140.

[73] Hansard HC vol 346, col 329 (15 March 2000), Charles Clarke.

[74] Compare *Chappell v United Kingdom*, App no 10461/83, Ser A 152-A (1989).

[75] See Terrorism Act 2000, sch 6 para 6, sch 6A para 1(5), as amended. The definition was based on the Money Laundering Regulations 1993, SI 1993/1933. See now the Money Laundering Regulations 2003, SI 2003/3075, art 2(2).

[76] See Home Office Circular 30/2002: *Guidance for the Police and Public on the implementation of Sections 1–2 of the Anti-terrorism, Crime and Security Act 2001*, para 45.

[77] Hansard HL vol 629, col 345 (28 November 2001), Lord Rooker.

[78] Criminal Procedure Rules r 62.1.

discharge may be made by an authorized officer or by any person affected by the order, and notice must be given to the police forty-eight hours before the hearing (para 4).

4.43   Though it is reassuring that a judge is the arbiter over such orders, the test for an order is subjectively worded.[79] An amendment to require reasonable suspicion was rejected in the House of Lords on the grounds that 'the requirement to have reasonable grounds would preclude the use of this investigatory tool at an early stage in the investigation when it might not be possible to establish such reasonable grounds'.[80]

4.44   If an order is granted,[81] then by para 6, it takes effect as if an order of the court (so its breach would be a contempt of court), and it overrides any legal restriction on the disclosure of information. Because of its compulsory nature, a statement made by a financial institution in response to an account monitoring order may not be used in evidence against it in criminal proceedings (para 7), save for proceedings for contempt of court, or for forfeiture under s 23, or for a prosecution for an offence where the financial institution makes a statement inconsistent with a prior statement.

3. Terrorist investigation disclosure

4.45   The Serious Organised Crime and Police Act 2005[82] provides for investigating authorities (defined in s 60 as the Director of Public Prosecutions, the Director of Revenue and Customs Prosecutions, and the Lord Advocate) to be granted powers to compel individuals to produce documents, to answer questions, and to provide information in connection with specified crimes related to organized crime, terrorism finance, or revenue offences. Section 61 defines the terrorism offences as those in the Terrorism Act 2000, ss 15 to 18. In these circumstances, the investigating authority can issue a disclosure notice under s 62, subject to the restrictions in ss 64 and 65. No judicial authorization is required, except where it is decided to proceed by way of forceful entry and seizure, as when a person has failed to comply with a disclosure notice, or where it is not practicable to give a disclosure notice, or where giving such a notice might seriously prejudice the investigation (s 66).

4.46   The narrow focus on terrorism finance investigations was transformed under s 33 of the Terrorism Act 2006. The disclosure notice powers are thereby extended to any 'terrorist investigation', defined in narrower terms than section 32 as 'an investigation of (a) the commission, preparation or instigation of acts of terrorism, (b) any act or omission which appears to have been for the purposes of terrorism and which consists in or involves the commission, preparation or instigation of an offence, or (c) the commission, preparation or instigation of an offence under the Terrorism Act 2000 . . . or under Part 1 of the Terrorism Act 2006 other than an offence under section 1 or 2 . . .'. There was virtually no debate on these new powers in Parliament to explain their purpose as distinct from existing powers such as under Sch 5, para 13. The judicial oversight in that provision more accords with constitutional governance than the unchecked powers

---

[79] Compare *Chappell v United Kingdom*, App no 10461/83, Ser A 152-A (1989), para 60.
[80] Hansard HL vol 629, col 344, (28 November 2001), Lord Rooker.
[81] For the first seven months of 2008 there were less than 10 orders granted to the Metropolitan Police.
[82] See Home Office, *One Step Ahead: A 21st Century Strategy to Defeat Organised Crime* (Cm 6167, London, 2004) para 6.2.1.

under the 2005 Act. Older precedents, such as judicial examination under the Explosive Substances Act 1883, s 6,[83] likewise impose tighter oversight.

4. Security and intelligence services disclosure

To ensure that information may be passed on to the intelligence services regardless of legal duties of confidentiality, the Counter-Terrorism Act 2008, s 19 permits the transmission of information.[84] People may do so on a whim without worrying about whether a public interest defence can be established under common law duties of confidentiality, though there is no obligation so created.[85] Information thus obtained can be used for any of the purposes of the security services or for crime-related purposes.[86] Some restraints apply under s 20: the directors of the agencies must strive to ensure observance of their general duties not to act excessively in the collection or disclosure of information; there is particular regard in s 20 to the Data Protection Act 1998 and the Regulation of Investigatory Powers Act 2000, Pt I, so these cannot be overridden. Of course, whether the Data Protection Act is a restraint depends on what purposes are registered, and there is no equivalent to s 35 of the Serious Organised Crime and Police Act 2005 which restrains onward disclosure from SOCA. The government also firmly rejected as unworkable ongoing review of information held or received by the intelligence services based on whether its collection infringed Art 3.[87] Apparently the security services look at these matters in a 'generic fashion' having regard to country and agency provenance.[88]   4.47

5. Assessment

As with sch 5, these powers cumulatively enable the 'Pursuit' of terrorists, as well as disruption to 'Prevent' terrorism. As for accountability, scrutiny and information provision is largely absent. Statistics are not issued as to the numbers of orders. As for constitutional governance, there has been no case law, and the guides are patchy. The relevant Criminal Procedure Rule, r 62, covers only certain aspects of the procedures.[89]   4.48

Amongst the issues arising on a rights audit are the subjectively worded powers, the ability of any police officer to apply for an account monitoring order, and the absence of any requirement to consider the impact on third parties on account monitoring, all of which are relevant to rights of privacy under Art 8. The next point concerns workable   4.49

---

[83] See Walker, C., 'Post-charge questioning of suspects' [2008] *Criminal Law Review* 509.

[84] The power to hold such information is considered to lie within the Security Service Act 1989 s 2(2)(a) and the Intelligence Services Act 1994 ss 2(2)(a), 4(2)(a), but this is confirmed by s 19(2) and disclosure is for the wider purposes covered by s 19(3)–(5): Hansard HC Public Bill Committee on the Counter Terrorism Bill, col 234 (29 April 2008), Tony McNulty.

[85] HL Hansard vol 704, col 402 (9 October 2008), Lord West.

[86] As a result, sch1 amends a number of specific information-sharing gateways so that the more general rule in s 19 can apply.

[87] Joint Committee on Human Rights, *Government Responses to the Committee's 20th and 21st Reports and other correspondence* (2007–08 HL 127, HC 756) p 28.

[88] HL Hansard vol 704, col 408 (9 October 2008), Baroness Manning Buller.

[89] See also Act of Adjournal (Criminal Procedural Rules Amendment No 2) (Terrorism Act 2000 and Anti-terrorism, Crime and Security Act 2001) 2001, SSI 2001/486.

alternatives, which revisits the overlapping Proceeds of Crime Act 2002, wherein both customer information (ss 363 and 397) and account monitoring (ss 370 and 404) orders duly make their appearances.[90] There are also Financial Reporting Orders in the Serious Organised Crime and Police Act 2005, so as to allow long-term monitoring as part of sentence at conviction.[91] As with production orders, consolidation could ensure unity of terminology and better guidance.

4.50 Specific orders are at least preferable to global and blanket data mining of financial information, such as takes place under the US Terrorist Finance Tracking Program in relation to 'SWIFT'—the Society for Worldwide Interbank Financial Telecommunication, based in Brussels. It has been making available information in an unregulated and promiscuous basis, probably in breach of privacy and data protection laws. Even a US–EU compromise arrangement agreed in 2007 limits only the purposes of the information and the length of retention, rather than imposing further oversight.[92]

E. ADDITIONAL DISCLOSURE POWERS FOR PUBLIC AUTHORITIES

1. Disclosure by public authorities

(a) *Background*

4.51 Just as financial institutions hold potentially valuable information about terrorism, so public authorities are another pre-eminent source of data. The belief is that any notable terrorist group cannot avoid resort to financial institutions nor avoid providing information to public bodies, whether for national insurance, social security, driving licence, or other purposes. Therefore, Pt III of the Anti-terrorism, Crime and Security Act 2001 authorizes the disclosure of information held by public authorities[93] for law enforcement and intelligence purposes. Though welcomed at the time by the Home Affairs Committee,[94] it should be emphasized that these powers are not directly linked, nor confined, to 'terrorist investigations'.

4.52 The Pt III powers are, by ss 17(6) and 19(10), additional to existing legal powers of disclosure, such as the powers of disclosure allowed by the Data Protection Act 1998. Section 29 of the 1998 Act provides an exemption to non-disclosure where the disclosure

---

[90] Their relevance is confirmed, for example, by s 364(5). The customer information orders are actually wider under the Proceeds of Crime Act 2002, ss 364(2), 398(2) (covering, for example, information about other accounts).

[91] See HM Treasury, *The Financial Challenge to Crime and Terrorism* (London, 2007) para 2.17. But the only specified triggering terrorism offence is directing under the Terrorism Act 2000, s 56.

[92] See Council of the EU, Processing of EU Originating Personal Data by United States Treasury Department for Counter Terrorism Purposes—SWIFT (10741/2/07 Rev 2, 2007); Connorton, P., 'Tracking terrorist financing through SWIFT' (2007) 76 *Fordham Law Review* 283; Fuster, G.G., De Hert, P., and Gutwirth, S., 'SWIFT and the vulnerability of transatlantic data transfers' (2008) 22 *International Review of Law Computers & Technology* 191.

[93] By s 20(1), 'public authority' has the same meaning as in the Human Rights Act 1998, s 6. See further Joint Committee on Human Rights, *The meaning of public authority under the Human Rights Act* (2003–04 HL 39/HC382), (2006–07 HL 77/HC 410).

[94] *Report on the Anti-terrorism, Crime and Security Bill 2001* (2001–02 HC 351) para 55.

is for the prevention or detection of crime or the apprehension or prosecution of offenders. This exemption was considered inadequate for anti-terrorism purposes for two reasons. First, it requires a pre-disclosure assessment of the legality of disclosing the information on the part of the possessor of data, whereas, sometimes, the full picture is held by the requesting authority which is reluctant to reveal it. Secondly, the Data Protection Act 1998 restrains transfers of data outside the European Economic Area unless the receiving state ensures an adequate level of data protection, whereas terrorism engages several countries which may have inadequate data protection regimes. Whether evasion of this second problem is an effect of s 17 is not clear. The government emphasized during debate that the Data Protection Act 1998 did apply under s 17.[95] However, s 17 itself is silent (unlike s 19(7) below). In so far as overseas recipients are encountered, one hopes that adequate data protection assurances will be in place. This expectation is not always matched by reality, as illustrated by the exchange of data with the United States relating to air passengers and other carrier information[96] which has probably been the most voluminous use of the Pt III powers.[97]

As well as the Data Protection Act 1998, there are several other statutory sharing arrangements which operate in two directions. The first direction starts with the data holder who is then allowed to transfer data. Thus, the Commissioners for Revenue and Customs Act 2005, ss 17 to 21, grant several powers to transfer information, including for the purposes of the prevention or detection of crime or in relation to public safety or for national security. The handling of information by the social welfare authorities is likewise facilitated under the Social Security Administration Fraud Act 1997 and the Finance Act 1997, s 110. By s 68 of the Serious Crime Act 2007, a public authority may, for the purposes of preventing fraud, disclose information as a member of a specified anti-fraud organization. Otherwise, official bodies must abide by the restraints of the Data Protection Act 1998 as well as the Official Secrets Act 1989.   4.53

The second direction of transfer empowers the potential data receiver. For example, the Serious Organised Crime and Police Act 2005 ensures that SOCA can use information obtained in connection with any one of its functions to assist in exercising other functions (s 32), while s 33 allows SOCA to disclose information for criminal justice purposes, whether in the United Kingdom or elsewhere, and the exercise of any functions of any intelligence service. Section 34 allows disclosure of information to SOCA. Section 36 even imposes a duty on UK police forces to pass on relevant information. Information obtained under Pts V and VIII of the Proceeds of Crime Act 2002 may also be recycled for other prosecution purposes (s 435).   4.54

---

[95] Hansard HL vol 629, col 418 (28 November 2001), Lord McIntosh.

[96] See Council Directive 2004/82/EC on the obligation of carriers to communicate passenger data; ECJ in *European Parliament v Council of the European Union and European Parliament v Commission of the European Communities*, C-317/04 and C-318/04, 2006; Draft Framework Decision on the Use of Passenger Name Records for Law Enforcement Purposes (MEMO/07/449, 2007); Ravich, T.M., 'Is Airline Passenger Profiling Necessary?' (2007) 62 *University of Miami Law Review* 1; Ntouvas, I., 'Air passenger data transfer to the USA: the decision of the ECJ and latest developments' (2008) 16 *International Journal of Law & Information Technology* 73.

[97] This basis is cited by Performance and Innovations Unit of the Cabinet Office, *Privacy and Data-Sharing: The Way Forward For Public Services* (<http://www.cabinetoffice.gov.uk/media/cabinetoffice/strategy/assets/piu%20data.pdf >, 2002) para 4.30.

(b) *Provisions*

4.55   The Anti-terrorism, Crime and Security Act 2001, s 17, reinterprets a range of provisions, listed in Sch 4,[98] to have effect in relation to the disclosure of information by or on behalf of a public authority, as if the purposes for which the disclosure of information is authorized by that provision includes the purposes of any criminal investigation, actual or contemplated and whether in the United Kingdom or elsewhere. The information may have been created or gathered before the commencement of the Act (s 17(7)). The list in Sch 4 to the 2001 Act includes fifty-three provisions, and, by s 17(3), may be altered by statutory instrument.[99]

4.56   Because s 17 authorizes domestic public authorities to aid foreign investigations and proceedings, a restraint is inserted by s 18. The implication is that UK national security interests may not invariably be served by entrusting information to every foreign power that seeks it. The restraint will take the form of a direction from the Secretary of State, who can specify any overseas proceedings or any description of overseas proceedings and can prohibit a disclosure either absolutely or on conditions. It must appear to the Secretary of State that the overseas proceedings relate or would relate to a matter which could more appropriately be carried out by a court or other authority within the United Kingdom or of a third country. Directions cannot apply to any disclosure by a minister of the Crown or by the Treasury—they have concurrent authority to make their own decisions as to the public interest. Any person who, knowing of any direction under this section, discloses any information in contravention of that direction shall be guilty of an offence under s 18(6). No direction has been published to date.

2. Disclosure by revenue authorities

4.57   Even more sweeping disclosure powers are granted by s 19 in respect of information held by the Commissioners of Inland Revenue or the Commissioners of Customs and Excise within their records of around 32 million individuals and 1.1 million companies or organizations.[100] Rather than relaxing specific prohibitions on disclosure, s 19(2) simply asserts that 'No obligation of secrecy imposed by statute or otherwise prevents the disclosure' for the purpose of facilitating the functions of the intelligence services (not mentioned in s 17) or the purposes of criminal investigation, whether in the United Kingdom or elsewhere. The House of Lords' attempt to confine the power to terrorism and security matters[101] was rebuffed.

4.58   Because of privacy concerns, the disclosure must be proportionate to what is sought to be achieved by it (s 19(3)).[102] In addition, there is senior administrative oversight; by s 19(4), the information must be disclosed by the General or Special Commissioners. The Commissioners should also ensure under s 19(5) that there will not be further

---

[98]   As amended by later amendments including the Equality Act 2006 and the National Health Service Act 2006. Note also the Wireless Telegraphy Act 2006, s 111.

[99]   Orders are subject to affirmative resolution, a procedure which was inserted after criticism from the Delegated Powers and Regulatory Reform Select Committee, *Report on the Anti-terrorism, Crime and Security Bill* (2001–02 HL 45), para 17. No order has been issued.

[100]   House of Commons Library, Research Paper 01/98, London, 2001, p 12.

[101]   Hansard HL vol 629, col 976 (6 December 2001).

[102]   See further 'Confidentiality and the duty of disclosure' (2003) 6 *Journal of Money Laundering Control* 248.

disclosure except for a purpose mentioned (which does not include intelligence purposes) or by express consent of the Commissioners. There is also a reminder in s 19(7) that nothing in this section authorizes the making of any disclosure that is prohibited by the Data Protection Act 1998. The absence of this reminder from s 17 should not be viewed as a green light for disclosure but reflects its more restrained ambit, though there was a similar phrase in the failed clause 45 of the Criminal Justice and Police Bill.

According to HM Revenue and Customs guide of 2002, *Anti-terrorism, Crime and Security Act 2001: Code of Practice on the Disclosure of Information*,[103] memorandums of understanding will be put in place with correspondent policing organizations. Amongst the guidelines are that organizations which receive information from the Revenue Departments under the criminal investigations and proceedings provisions must not pass that information on to others except with the consent of the relevant Revenue Department and that their ultimate purpose must not be for assisting intelligence-gathering.[104] There should be no disclosure of information to overseas jurisdictions which do not offer an adequate level of protection along the lines of the Data Protection Act 1998 and the Human Rights Act 1998.[105] Only a limited number of staff will be authorized to send or receive requests.[106] Whilst the Code says relatively little about standards of proof for the establishment of 'a legitimate interest'[107] to trigger disclosure, the Code signals greater concern for privacy than under s 17.[108]

4.59

3. Assessment

These disclosure powers fall within the 'Prevent' and 'Pursue' elements of CONTEST. Their efficiency and effectiveness is impossible to judge. Little information is revealed about the costs of operations nor their operational impact. The only insight into operation has come from the Newton Committee which divulged that between January 2002 and September 2003 there were 20,705 disclosures under s 19 of which 870 (4 per cent) related to terrorism.[109] The absence of information equally raises criticisms on the grounds of accountability and constitutional governance. The mixing of 'normal' and security situations reduces scrutiny and safeguards across the board.[110] The Newton Committee called for greater oversight by the Information Commissioner and the publication of statistics, while authorizations should be granted by a judge except in terrorist cases.[111]

4.60

---

[103] <http://www.hmrc.gov.uk/pdfs/cop_at.htm>. See also IDG60150—Procedure for disclosing to others (government): Anti-terrorism, Crime and Security Act 2001 (ATCSA).

[104] *Ibid* paras 2.10, 2.11.

[105] *Ibid* para 3.9.

[106] *Ibid* paras 3.11, 3.12.

[107] *Ibid* para 3.11.

[108] See Law Society, *A Memorandum of Evidence to the Committee of Privy Counsellors, Anti-terrorism, Crime and Security Act 2001 Review* (2002) p 4. There is no mention of the 2001 Act by the Department for Constitutional Affairs in Public Sector Data Sharing: *Guidance on the Law* (London, 2003).

[109] Privy Counsellor Review Committee, *Anti-terrorism, Crime and Security Act 2001, Review, Report* (2003–04 HC 100) D paras 157, 158.

[110] *Ibid* B para 3. See Lyon, D., *Surveillance After September 11* (Polity, Cambridge, 2005).

[111] *Ibid* B paras 21–3. This proposal was rejected by the Home Office, *Counter-Terrorism Powers: Reconciling Security and Liberty in an Open Society* (Cm 6147, London, 2004) Pt II para 25.

4.61   The Information Commissioner has commented generally that:[112]

In a world of rapid change—political, social, economic, and technological—it is vital that we articulate the values of personal privacy and public openness. These values cannot simply be abandoned in the face of threats—whether from terrorism, serious crime, international instability or anti-social conduct on our streets. . . . Equally, the values of privacy and openness are not absolutes. Both require delicate and proportionate balances to be drawn in the face of both threat and opportunity.

4.62   Likewise, the Surveillance Studies Network has warned that 'surveillance, especially that associated with high technology and antiterrorism, distracts from alternatives and from larger and more urgent questions' as well as being applied to an ever-increasing circle of applications away from terrorism.[113] The measures have evident impact on privacy rights under Art 8.[114] Part III covers a very wide range of highly confidential information which is often provided under compulsion (a distinction from the financial information dealt with elsewhere in Pt III). Sections 17 and 19 may therefore be questioned on grounds of proportionality as follows.

4.63   First, the legislative objective is too widely expressed in terms of 'any criminal investigation whatever' or 'any criminal proceedings whatever', and also without any level of suspicion or belief being reached. How can minor regulatory offences, which may not actually have occurred,[115] warrant serious intrusions into personal informational privacy? The Sch 4 list includes, for example, the Merchant Shipping (Liner Conferences) Act 1982 and the Diseases of Fish Act 1983. An attempt at Commons Committee stage to confine the power to terrorism rather than crime failed,[116] since the government wanted 'to make it simple for public officials to understand what they are supposed to disclose' by the expedient of allowing disclosure in virtually all circumstances.[117] Reversing a later Lords' amendment,[118] the Home Secretary, David Blunkett, sought to illustrate the need for breadth:[119]

Take an employment agency that is being inspected. The inspectors come across information relating to an individual seeking to take up a particular, sensitive job. It is discovered that that person has claimed large amounts of benefit. Let us call him Mr AQ, just as an example of someone who might seek to do that. According to the framing of the House of Lords proposal [to restrict the power to terrorism], it would not be possible for that information to be shared. No one outside the House would thank us if we so restrained information giving and the sharing of concerns that Mr AQ continued to draw benefits. It would be illegal to pass on the information required.

---

[112] Information Commissioner, *Annual Report 2003* (2002–03 HC 727) p 7.
[113] *A Report on the Surveillance Society* (Information Commissioner, Wilmslow, 2006) paras 2.8.3, 9.9.4. See further Thomas, R. and Walport, M., *Data Sharing Review* (<http://www.justice.gov.uk/docs/data-sharing-review.pdf>, Ministry of Justice, 2008); Home Affairs Committee, *A Surveillance Society?* (2007–08 HC 58, and Government Reply, Cm 7449, 2008).
[114] The storing and release of information is within Art 8: *Leander v Sweden*, App no 9248/81, Ser A 116 (1987) para 69.
[115] See s 20.
[116] Hansard HC vol 375, col 791 (26 November 2001).
[117] *Ibid* col 794, Ruth Kelly.
[118] Hansard HL vol 629, col 972 (6 December 2001); col 1432 (13 December 2001).
[119] Hansard HC vol 376, col 898 (12 December 2001).

Of course, it may turn out that Mr AQ is a terrorist and that benefit fraud is a precursor to terrorism and part of the jigsaw of evidence against him, but that is a very long shot and is no more likely than for any motorist stopped for defective tyres or a TV licence defaulter.

Measures very similar to Pt III were encouraged in 2000 by the Performance and Innovations Unit of the Cabinet Office (later published as *Privacy and Data-Sharing*)[120] and by proposals in relation to the proceeds of crime by the Inland Revenue.[121] Yet, these proposals were removed from the Criminal Justice and Police Bill 2000–01.[122] Part III may have made some sense if designed around the concept of 'terrorist investigations' under s 32, but the current wording is explicitly wider and betrays another legislative history and purpose which the 2001 Act should not have been commandeered to serve.

4.64

Other aspects of over-breadth are that information might be disclosed to assist foreign investigations (such as about price fixing)[123] which are not crimes within the United Kingdom, that there is no judicial oversight, no requirement of senior administrative authorization, and an insufficient evidential standard of proof.[124] Some attempt has been made to answer the first concern by s 20(2) and (3), which requires the foreign proceedings to involve criminal conduct which has equivalence to the law in the relevant part of the United Kingdom.

4.65

Next, Pt III installs no added measures against abuse.[125] Without notification to those affected,[126] how can existing mechanisms such as the Data Protection Act 1998 or an action for breach of privacy under s 7 of the Human Rights Act 1998 be viable?[127] As a nod in the direction of concerns for privacy, s 17(5) provides that 'No disclosure of information shall be made by virtue of this section unless the public authority by which the disclosure is made is satisfied that the making of the disclosure is proportionate to what is sought to be achieved by it.' This wording was added under pressure from the House of Lords.[128] But there is no requirement that the disclosure be considered necessary in the public interest[129] or that it be subjected to prior or subsequent independent oversight. An attempt in the House of Lords to impose prior judicial control was firmly resisted on grounds of practicality.[130] As a result, the Joint Committee on Human Rights condemned these measures.[131]

4.66

Finally, there may be unwanted side-effects, such as reluctance to cooperate with authorities over legitimate information-gathering and their careless handling of data

4.67

---

[120] <http://www.cabinetoffice.gov.uk/media/cabinetoffice/strategy/assets/piu%20data.pdf>, 2002) para 4.28.

[121] Recovering the Proceeds of Crime, <http://www.cabinetoffice.gov.uk/media/cabinetoffice/strategy/assets/crime.pdf>, 2000, p 95

[122] 2000–01 HC 31. See Hansard HL vol 625, col 1036 (9 May 2001).

[123] See *Norris v Government of the United States of America* [2008] UKHL 16.

[124] See Hansard HC Standing Committee F, col 412 *et seq* (6 March 2001).

[125] See *Malone v United Kingdom*, App no 8691/79, Ser A 82 (1984) at para 81.

[126] See Binning, P., 'In safe hands? Striking the balance between privacy and security—anti-terrorism finance measures' (2002) 6 *European Human Rights Law Review* 734 at p 749.

[127] Compare *Peck v United Kingdom*, App no 44647/98, 2003-I at para 103.

[128] Hansard HL vol 376, col 1108 (13 December 2001).

[129] Compare the Data Protection Act 1998, s 59.

[130] Hansard HL vol 629, col 390 (28 November 2001), Lord McIntosh.

[131] *Report on the Anti-terrorism, Crime and Security Bill* (2001–02 HL 51, HC 420), para 24.

transfers. Another problem is the issue of self-incrimination. Some of the measures listed in Sch 4, as amended by the Youth Justice and Criminal Evidence Act 1999, ss 58 and 59, do provide restraint on the use of evidence obtained under threat of prosecution but only in respect of those financial offences. The problem does not, however, apply to the disclosing officials since 'There is no question of public officials being obliged to make disclosures. It is up to them to decide whether to do so.'[132]

F. OFFENCE OF WITHHOLDING INFORMATION

1. Offence

4.68   One of the vaunted reforms secured by the Terrorism Act 2000 was the dropping of the offence of withholding information (formerly in s 18 in the Prevention of Terrorism (Temporary Provisions) Act 1989). In the light of persistent unease about the imposition of a legal duty to help the police, the offence had been recommended for repeal by the Inquiry into Legislation against Terrorism[133] and the subsequent Home Office Consultation Paper.[134] A more focused offence dealing with financial institutions, formerly at s 18A of the 1989 Act, is replicated as s 19 of the Terrorism Act 2000. Despite this considered and principled outcome, the offence of withholding information was soon revived in almost identical terms (but applicable to all forms of terrorism and not just Northern Ireland) by s 117 of the Anti-terrorism, Crime and Security Act 2001, which inserts s 38B into the Terrorism Act 2000.

4.69   The offence is committed under s 38B(2) of the 2000 Act if a person, without reasonable excuse, fails to disclose information falling within s 38B(1), which is information which he knows or believes might be of material assistance in preventing the commission by another person of an act of terrorism, or in securing the apprehension, prosecution, or conviction of another person, in the United Kingdom, for an offence involving the commission, preparation, or instigation of an act of terrorism. The definition of 'an act of terrorism' is that laid out in s 1 of the Terrorism Act 2000. As a result, the 'action' in relation to terrorism may take place outside the United Kingdom, and it may be of a passive nature for the benefit of a proscribed organization. Section 38B(3) lists the officials to whom disclosure should be made—to a constable, or in Northern Ireland to a constable or a member of Her Majesty's forces.

4.70   As for the *actus reus*, a person may commit this offence through total inactivity (by not answering police questions or by not volunteering information), through the partial suppression of information, or by relating a false account when the true facts are known. The information must be of a kind which is, or is believed to be, 'of material assistance'. This means that a person reasonably aware of their situation would consider that it ought to be disclosed, whereas information garnered through vague rumour or gossip would not trigger the duty. To prove this issue of fact, the police may have to describe their investigations up to that point, which obviously limits the attractiveness of s 38B until their inquiries are exhausted.

---

[132] Hansard HL vol 629, col 367 (28 November 2001), Lord McIntosh.
[133] (Cm 3420, London, 1996) para 14.24.
[134] Home Office and Northern Ireland Office, *Legislation against Terrorism* (Cm 4178, 1998) para 12.7.

The *mens rea*, 'knows or believes', means that it is not enough that the defendant   4.71
strongly suspects the possession of material information or thinks it probable or that a
reasonable person would have been put on inquiry. Belief as an alternative to knowledge
is relevant only to the materiality of the assistance which the withheld information might
have given.[135] Provided the defendant does genuinely believe the information is relevant,
an offence can be committed even if it is neither material nor accurate. However, there
really must be an act of terrorism somewhere in the background, whatever the belief of
the defendant. In *Attorney General's Reference (No 3 of 1993)*,[136] the defendant, while
believing that a murder by shooting was an act of terrorism, was acquitted on the ground
that the Crown had failed to prove that the murder was an offence of a terrorist nature.
The Northern Ireland Court of Appeal held that the intention of Parliament was that
the Crown had to prove that an actual terrorist offence had in fact been committed. The
difference in wording from that in s 5(1) of the Criminal Law Act (Northern Ireland)
1967 (which imposes a duty to inform where a person has committed an arrestable
offence) was explained by the fact that s 18 applied to the withholding of information
which might help to prevent the commission of a (future) terrorist offence as well as
information about a perpetrated offence. There appears to be some inconsistency in reasoning between these two points. If s 38B can apply in aid of future prevention of terrorism as well as the apprehension, prosecution, or conviction of an offender, which is
certainly an expressed aim, then it is not true that the Crown always must show an
offence has actually been committed. This apparent inconsistency can be resolved in two
ways. First, one might argue that the *Attorney General's Reference* was argued on the basis
of the defendant's information securing apprehension, prosecution, or conviction under
s 38(1)(b) and not prevention under s 38(1)(a). In that context, it is consistent to establish an actual offence, otherwise the exercise becomes futile. The demand for upfront
information is not futile to prevention under s 38(1)(a) where no offence has yet been
committed. However, one might delimit this draconian offence by still interpreting the
section as requiring evidence that, subsequently, an offence related to the knowledge or
belief was committed.[137] Without that link, there is a danger of turning s 38B into a
crime for the paranoid and fantasists. This interpretation does, however, considerably
reduce the scope of the offence and turns it more into a sanction *ex post facto* than a
threat *ex ante*. Alternatively, the vagueness of the knowledge or belief and uncertainty as
to linked action might be a matter left to the defence under s 38B(4) if the paranoid are
ever prosecuted.

2. Defence

By s 38B(4), it is a defence for a person charged with an offence under sub-s (2) to   4.72
prove that he had a reasonable excuse for not making the disclosure. The defence of
reasonable excuse will often relate to fears of reprisal or reaction going beyond the
defence of duress. The operation of this defence gives rise to considerable controversies
in four contexts.

---

[135] *R v Rock* (NICA, 1990).
[136] [1993] NI 50.
[137] *R v Rock* (NICA, 1990).

4.73   The first is where there is a close personal relationship between the person involved in terrorism and the person with knowledge of it, such as a husband and wife. Though the prospect caused some anguish in Parliament, the uncompromising view of the sponsor of the original section 18[138] and of the government was that 'when dealing with foul and disgusting deeds, someone who knows that someone else is likely to be threatened and imperilled has not only a moral duty to tell the police, but a legal one as well'.[139] The current Home Office Circular 7/2002 also makes no allowance: 'having a legal or familial relationship with someone does not constitute immunity from the obligation to disclose information . . . '.[140] Several recent prosecutions have concerned the spouses or siblings of terrorists.

4.74   Following the suicide attack of Omar Sharif in Tel Aviv in 2003, his wife, Tahira Tabassum, his sister, Parveen, and his brother, Zahid, were accused of withholding his plan but were all acquitted in 2004.[141] Next, Yeshi Girma, wife of 21 July bomber, Hussein Osman, Mulu Girma (Yeshi's sister) and her former partner Mohammed Kabashi, and Essaya Girma (Yeshi's brother) were all convicted of withholding information, assisting his escape, and destroying evidence.[142] Next, Sabeel Ahmed, brother of Kafeel Ahmed who planted car bombs outside London nightclubs and then died following the failed car bombing of Glasgow Airport in 2007, was convicted under s 38B for failing to disclose e-mails which he discovered the evening after the attack.[143] Next, Abdul Sherif and five others were convicted in connection with the attempted bombings on 21 July 2005.[144] The applicants were held to have known or believed that the bombings were to take place and failed to give information under s 38B and even in one case impeded arrest by offering a safe house (contrary to s 4(1) of the Criminal Law Act 1967). The convictions were upheld. In the case of Ali, the judge was fully entitled in his direction to make it plain 'that it was not sufficient for the prosecution to establish that a defendant had closed his eyes, but that the jury was entitled to conclude, if satisfied that he had deliberately closed his eyes to the obvious because he did not wish to be told the truth, that that fact was capable of being evidence to support a conclusion that that defendant either knew or believed the fact in question.'[145] There were also aspects of the treatment of Abdurahman which were 'undoubtedly troubling'.[146] The defendant was at first treated as a cooperative witness, but it seems to be up to the defendant to make a full and frank disclosure and not up to the police to cajole, threaten, or tease out every detail.

4.75   Sherif and others also appealed against sentence, but the Court of Appeal upheld the application of the maximum of five years. The Court held that 'it will be the seriousness of the terrorist activity about which a defendant has failed to give information which will determine the level of criminality, rather that the extent of the information which could

---

[138] Hansard HC vol 882, col 929 (28 November 1974), George Cunningham.
[139] Hansard HC Standing Committee D, col 243 (24 November 1983), David Waddington.
[140] At p 5. Compare Home Office Circular No 90/1983, para 9; see also Home Office Circular No 27/1989, para 7.4.
[141] See *The Times* 29 November 2005 p 6.
[142] *R v Girma* [2009] EWCA Crim 912.
[143] *The Times* 12 April 2008 p 9.
[144] [2008] EWCA Crim 2653.
[145] *Ibid* para 27.
[146] *Ibid* para 38.

be provided which will affect the sentence.'[147] This approach is troubling. While the sentence should take account of the harm which could have been prevented, the main focus should remain on the culpability of the accused. A harsh outcome also applied since consecutive sentences were imposed on the basis that both limbs of s 38B (silence before, and after, the crime) were involved. One may again argue that, concentrating on the actions of the defendant rather than the other protected criminals, the culpability was continuous — misplaced loyalty or fear of involvement. The only concession was in the case of Fardosa Abdullahi, who was seen as the vulnerable fiancée of one of the suicide bombers, whereas the others were young men without remorse.

The second problem area for the s 38B(4) defence concerns the impact of potentially   4.76
privileged relationships, such as between a lawyer and terrorist client. In *Sykes v Director of Public Prosecutions*,[148] the defendant was convicted of the analogous offence of misprision of felony (abolished in 1967) in connection with the supply of firearms to the IRA. In the House of Lords, Lord Denning's view was that a solicitor, doctor, or clergyman who received information in confidence would have a defence but that close personal ties would not suffice.[149] The position adopted in *Sykes* should be reproduced in regard to legal privilege under s 38B, having regard to the importance of the independent legal advice in litigation.[150] The government sought in 1989 to distinguish between (unprivileged) information which may prevent terrorism and (privileged) information which may assist the prosecution of terrorists.[151] This contrast is unwarranted by the wording of s 38B, though it is reflected in guidance in 1999 from the Law Society that a solicitor could reveal information which 'he believes necessary to prevent the client from committing a criminal act that the solicitor believes on reasonable grounds is likely to result in serious bodily harm', but otherwise 'a solicitor is not obliged to disclose confidential or privileged information under this provision other than in wholly exceptional circumstances'.[152] The 1999 Guidance was replaced in 2007 by the Solicitors' Code of Conduct, which refers only to financial provisions in relation to money laundering.[153] However, the Law Society has at the same time issued the Anti-terrorism Practice Note, which advises that legal privilege does apply under s 38B but that disclosure contrary to client confidentiality is required where the information concerns pending serious bodily harm.[154]

The third situation to cause misgivings is whether a suspect's own privilege against   4.77
self-incrimination provides a reasonable excuse for remaining silent. This issue was partly settled for the former s 18 by an amendment which provided that the information being suppressed must concern terrorist involvement by 'any other person'.[155] This wording is replicated in s 38B. However, if a person's evidence implicates both himself and another, must it be disclosed when the self-damning details cannot be severed? A broad view in

---

[147] *Ibid* para 45.
[148] [1962] AC 528.
[149] *Ibid* at p 564.
[150] See *R v Derby Magistrates, ex p B* [1996] AC 487.
[151] Hansard HL vol 504, cols 980–1 (28 February 1989).
[152] *The Guide to the Professional Conduct of Solicitors* (8th edn, London, 1999) paras 16.02.3, 16.02.13.
[153] (Solicitors' Regulatory Authority, London, 2007) para 4.06.11.
[154] <http://www.lawsociety.org.uk/documents/downloads/dynamic/practicenote_terrorismact2000.pdf>, p 11.
[155] See Jellicoe Report, *Review of the Operation of the Prevention of Terrorism (Temporary Provisions) Act 1976* (Cmnd 8803, London, 1983) para 233.

favour of protection against self-incrimination was expressed in relation to the former s 18 in *HM Advocate v Von*.[156] This prosecution arose out of fund-raising activities on behalf of the UVF in Scotland. The reasons for favouring the privilege were based on some unconvincing distinctions from what is now s 172 of the Road Traffic Act 1988. The further argument which now arises is the impact of Art 6 of the European Convention. Based on the precedent of *Brown v Stott* (*Procurator Fiscal, Dunfermline*),[157] there may be important distinctions concerning the extent of questioning (which is viewed as limited to 'a single, simple question' in the case of s 172),[158] the degree of compulsion (where in the context of s 172, there is voluntary submission in the first place to a regulatory regime) and the severity of the penalty (which is non-custodial under s 172). On balance, the danger of self-incrimination was probably not envisaged by the architects of the former s 18 as a reasonable excuse. However, given the precedent of *Von's* case, the courts should not curtail the normal right to silence of a witness just because the person's knowledge also implicates others.

4.78   A related complication concerns the inter-relationship between s 38B and the laws allowing inferences to be drawn from silence in response to police questioning, the Criminal Evidence (Northern Ireland) Order 1988,[159] and the Criminal Justice and Public Order Act 1994. The inter-relationship is complex. When the suspect has committed an offence and remains silent, there is no infringement of s 38B, but Art 3 of the 1988 Order/s 34 of the 1994 Act may penalize silence if a criminal prosecution is mounted. Thus, the statutory provisions do not overlap, but the police's incantation of a complex caution under the other legislation together with a recitation of s 38B may sow confusion. Conversely, where the subject knows about another's wrongdoing but is not personally implicated, an offence may be committed under s 38B. It follows that silence in response to questioning about that offence may also trigger adverse inferences. Consequently, silence could be damning twice over: it forms the *actus reus* of s 38B and then leads to the adverse inference that the person has suppressed relevant information and is guilty of the offence. It is regrettable that clear advice is absent from the Home Office Circular 7/2002 or PACE Code H.[160]

4.79   The fourth area of doubt around 'reasonable excuse' arises from the consequences for the media. A reporter may discover information about terrorism by interviewing a terrorist leader or by witnessing a paramilitary display. Arranging, attending, or reporting such events may implicate the journalist in various offences (especially under the Terrorism Act 2006, s 8), but s 38B can involve two further impacts. Firstly, the offence contributes to a 'chilling' effect on the reporting of terrorism. Correspondents can expect close attention from the police and hostility and special restrictions from their own superiors. Thus, coverage of Irish terrorism abounded with difficulties and was to some extent suppressed as 'guilty secrets'.[161] The second effect is the direct threat of prosecution where insufficient weight is given in s 38B to investigative journalism.[162]

---

[156] 1979 SLT (Notes) 62

[157] [2003] 1 AC 681. See further *O'Halloran and Francis v United Kingdom*, App nos 15809/02; 25624/02, 29 June 2007.

[158] *Ibid* at p 705 per Lord Bingham.

[159] SI 1988/1987.

[160] Compare Home Office Circular No 90/1983, para 9.

[161] Curtis, L., *Ireland: the Propaganda War* (Pluto Press, London, 1984) p 275.

[162] See Walker, C.P., *The Prevention of Terrorism in British Law* (2nd edn, Manchester University Press, Manchester, 1992) pp 141–3.

3. Process

The penalties for the offence are, on indictment, imprisonment for up to five years, or a fine or both; or on summary conviction, imprisonment for up to six months or a fine or both. In the *Girma* case, the sentences (not confined to s 38B offences) ranged up to fifteen years, which Judge Worsley described as 'woefully inadequate'.[163]   **4.80**

Section 38B(6) allows proceedings for an offence to be taken in any place where the person to be charged is or has at any time been since he first knew or believed that the information might be of material assistance. This provision as to venue allows a person present in the United Kingdom to be charged with the offence even if he was outside the United Kingdom at the time he became aware of the information:[164]   **4.81**

For example, information about an act to be carried out in Greece could come to the attention of a UK resident while that person was in Spain—if the information were not disclosed and the act took place, that person could be charged in the UK or elsewhere, if evidence of deliberate non-disclosure were established.

4. Assessment

In Great Britain, from 1984 until 2001, only fifteen charges were brought, with one conviction.[165] By contrast, the offence figured much more prominently in Northern Ireland, with 140 charges between 1974 and 2001; there were a further 308 charges of withholding information, presumably under s 5(1) of the Criminal Law Act (Northern Ireland) 1967.[166] The greater level of terrorist activity probably accounts for its higher use there. In addition, there was greater familiarity with the concept through the operation of s 5(1). Section 38B remains distinct in that the information must relate to 'terrorism' rather than an 'arrestable offence' and may concern future as well as past activities. However, there is considerable duplication between the two offences.   **4.82**

Claims that the offence will 'play an important role in countering terrorism and bringing terrorists to justice by reminding the public of their obligation to help protect their fellow citizens'[167] are at best unproven: **4.83**

Table 4.2 Withholding information[168]

	Terrorism Acts charges: GB	Terrorism Acts charges: NI	CLA s.5 charges: NI
2000	0	0	4
2001	0	0	1
2002	0	0	2

---

[163] *The Times* 13 June 2008 p 11.
[164] Home Office Circular 7/2002, p 5.
[165] *Home Office Statistics on the Operation of the Prevention of Terrorism Legislation 16/01* (2001) p 12.
[166] *Northern Ireland Office Research and Statistical Bulletin 6/2001* (Belfast, 2001) pp 5, 6.
[167] Hansard HL vol 629, col 625 (3 December 2001), Lord Rooker.
[168] Sources: *Home Office Statistics on the Operation of the Prevention of Terrorism Legislation 16/01* (2001); Lord Carlile, *Annual Reports on the Terrorism Act; Northern Ireland Office Statistics and Research Branch, Northern Ireland Statistics on the Operation of the Terrorism Act 2000.*

Table 4.2 (Continued) Withholding information

	Terrorism Acts charges: GB	Terrorism Acts charges: NI	CLA s.5 charges: NI
2003	6	0	3
2004	0	0	0
2005	10	0	2
2006	6	0	0
2007	5	n/a	n/a

4.84   Charges under s 38B can be germane in five situations. The first is that, where the evidence of involvement in terrorism as an accomplice, conspirator, or member of a proscribed organization is relatively weak, s 38B may be used as an additional, 'back-stop' count, a practice adopted in Northern Ireland though less prevalent now in Britain. Next, where the police have successfully detected active terrorists, peripheral offenders may be prosecuted under s 38B. The third category is where a police investigation into a terrorist plot has largely failed, but evidence against some minor participants has been unearthed. The fourth target, active bystanders who have been coerced into aiding terrorists (especially by loaning their cars),[169] arose in Northern Ireland. The fifth situation affects passive bystanders—persons not accused of terrorism involvement in any degree but who became aware of the plans of terrorists. This category has risen to the fore in Britain and affects family members of a prime offender.

4.85   Justification for s 38B must turn on practice and principle. In practice, the main advantage is that it will 'create an atmosphere in which it [is] respectable to provide . . . information'.[170] Information can then be used to prevent, protect, and pursue. Given this objective, rates of prosecution are not decisive. The real value of the measure is to influence people to volunteer information; the prosecution of recalcitrant minor participants after violence is a second-best. There is no clear evidence that the offence has achieved its central goal of increasing the flow of information, and it seems improbable that it will ever do so. It is presumably not claimed that s 38B carries much clout with hardened terrorists, so it must be primarily aimed against those on the periphery of terrorism, most likely as passive bystanders. Yet, even such soft targets are likely either to be more intimidated by terrorists or by concern for the plight of their kinfolk. Seemingly, the police have likewise recognized there is often little advantage in prosecuting bystanders after the event. There is a great deal more to be gained by surveillance and winning the cooperation of communities. Yet, any encouragement through s 38B must be set against the coercive features of the anti-terrorism legislation which can create fear and community apprehension to such a degree that one firm of lawyers allegedly advises non-cooperation with the police as a matter of routine.[171] The Jellicoe Report concluded that 'the section is of significant value to the police service, but that service could operate without it if required to do so'.[172]

---

[169] R v Rock (NICA, 1990).

[170] Hansard HC vol 882, cols 928–9 (28 November 1974), George Cunningham.

[171] See Home Affairs Committee, Terrorism Detention Powers (2005–06 HC 910) para 83. See <http://www.aranisolicitors.com/know_your_rights.pdf>,<http://www.aranisolicitors.com/know_your_rights_2.pdf>.

[172] Review of the Operation of the Prevention of Terrorism (Temporary Provisions) Act 1976 (Cmnd 8803, London, 1983) para 222.

The drawbacks in principle were most highlighted by Lord Shackleton[173] who recommended abolition at least in Britain, since, 'there are genuine doubts about its implications in principle and about the way it might be used in the course of interviewing someone . . . it has an unpleasant ring about it in terms of civil liberties'. His verdict was rightly attacked in Parliament as hardly 'persuasive rationally',[174] but more precise arguments for and against may be formulated.   4.86

The first justification for s 38B might be that offences involving withholding information are familiar to our legal system. As well as s 5(1) in Northern Ireland, other closely related provisions include s 6(2) of the Explosive Substances Act 1883, s 6(1) of the Official Secrets Act 1920, and misprision of treason. Consequently, in exceptionally dangerous situations, society regularly compels its citizenry to provide succour, and 'in the case of terrorism, which is almost by definition criminal activity aimed at society as a whole, it seems . . . reasonable that there should be more than a merely moral duty to assist the police'.[175]   4.87

Section 38B conforms to established precedents, but those precedents might themselves be unsound because they conflict with the accepted policy of policing by consent. Thus, the offence can be decried for creating the sort of 'informer's society which exists in totalitarian states'.[176] Another theoretical objection to s 38B is that the harmful action and the dishonest intent are not primarily those of the defendant under s 38B and so the offence should not form part of the criminal law. In reply, if it is acceptable to impose a legal, as well as a moral, duty to help the police to combat terrorism, it follows that an omission to fulfil that duty properly incurs legal sanctions.   4.88

In conclusion, there is value in maintaining an offence of withholding information.[177] However, to achieve proportionality to other rights, s 38B should be further limited to specified serious offences, and it should deal more explicitly and generously with persons suspected of other offences, with lawyers, and with journalists.   4.89

G. OFFENCES OF DISCLOSURE OF INFORMATION

Section 39 of the Terrorism Act 2000 provides for two sets of offences to discourage or penalize disclosures that may damage the effectiveness of ongoing terrorist investigations. The offences may affect both those conducting the investigations, including civilian aids of the security authorities, and also outsiders such as journalists. Disclosures within the regulated sector are exempted from s 39 since they fall under the corresponding strict liability offence of tipping off under s 21D.[178] These offences under s 39 add to those   4.90

---

[173] *Review of the Operation of the Prevention of Terrorism (Temporary Provisions) Acts 1974 and 1976* (Cmnd 7324, London, 1978) paras 132, 133.

[174] Hansard HC vol 969, col 1662 (21 March 1979), George Cunningham.

[175] Jellicoe Report, loc cit para 101. See also Ministry of Justice, *Rights and Responsibilities* (Cm 7577, London, 2009) para 2.28.

[176] Hansard HC vol 904, col 475 (28 January 1976), Ian Mikardo.

[177] The Newton Committee was in favour of the measure: Privy Counsellor Review Committee, *Anti-terrorism, Crime and Security Act 2001, Review, Report* (2003–04 HC 100) B2 para 57.

[178] s 39(6A). See Terrorism Act 2000 and Proceeds of Crime Act 2002 (Amendment) Regulations 2007, SI 2007/3398. The regulated sector is as defined by sch 3A: s 39(9).

under the Official Secrets Act 1989, s 4 of which was raised against the disclosure of a Joint Terrorism Analysis Centre document in *R v Thomas Lund-Lack*.[179] Comparison may next be drawn with the offences of prejudicing investigations contrary to ss 342 and 333A (for the regulated sector) of the Proceeds of Crime Act 2002. No charges were brought under s 39 between 2001 and the end of 2007.

H. CONCLUSIONS

4.91   Information-sharing was depicted by the Home Office in 2007 as one of the great advances to be achieved by the Counter-Terrorism Act 2008.[180] This claim is dubious. There is already a wide range of intelligence-sharing, sanctioned by prior legislation. Most of the limitations on the exercise are not legal but, as found by the 9/11 Commission, arise from institutional rivalries and suspicions,[181] or as the Bichard Report[182] also found, arise from the technical incompatibilities of different databases or the failure to invest in compatibility. The other general comment is that much of the information-sharing and the special investigative techniques is unregulated by judicial supervision which not only threatens individual rights but also diminishes the opportunity for the production of evidence in a prosecution.[183]

---

[179] *The Times* 28 July 2007 p 32.
[180] *Possible Measures For Inclusion In A Future Counter-Terrorism Bill* (Home Office, 2007) para 3.
[181] See National Commission on Terrorist Attacks upon the United States, *The 9/11 Commission Report* (2004) ch 11.
[182] Bichard Inquiry, *Report* (2003–04 HC 653). See further: Home Office, *Bichard Inquiry Recommendations: Progress Report* (Home Office, London, 2004); Bichard Inquiry, *Final Report* (HMSO, London, 2005).
[183] See Report of the Special Rapporteur on the promotion and protection of human rights and fundamental freedoms while countering terrorism (A/HRC/10/3. 2009) para 29.

5

COUNTER-TERRORIST POWERS

A. INTRODUCTION

Part V of the Terrorism Act 2000 contains the anti-terrorism legislation's most endur-   5.01
ingly controversial measures. The catalogue in Pt V overlaps considerably with Pt IV but
more often involves action against individuals. The personalized nature of Pt V is
reflected in reliance on the term 'terrorist'. By s 40(1), 'terrorist' means a person who
(a) has committed an offence under any of ss 11, 12, 15 to 18, 54, and 56 to 63, or
(b) is or has been concerned in the commission, preparation, or instigation of acts of
'terrorism' (as defined by s 1). By referring to 'preparation or instigation' as well as 'commission', the statutory term covers terrorism which is either 'active' or 'passive' (such as
membership of a proscribed organization).[1] The breadth of s 40(1)(b) means that the
failure to update this definition to take in the offences under the Terrorism Act 2006 is
not so noteworthy.

The powers granted in Pt V are not exclusive, but, by s 114, are additional to common   5.02
law or statutory policing powers such as under the Police and Criminal Evidence Act
1984 ('PACE').[2] However, terrorism suspects arrested under PACE cannot then be
rearrested under s 41 unless further offences are disclosed.[3] Police officers may therefore
be minded to opt for the Terrorism Act powers. There is no express principle of normality
which requires the enforcement officer to prefer 'normal' powers.

Another general statement under s 114 is that a constable may, if necessary, use rea-   5.03
sonable force for the purpose of exercising a power conferred on him under the Act (with

---

[1] *McKee v Chief Constable for Northern Ireland* [1984] 1 WLR 1358. See Walker, C.P., 'Emergency arrest
powers' (1985) 36 *Northern Ireland Legal Quarterly* 145.
[2] See also Police and Criminal Evidence (Northern Ireland) Order 1989, SI 1989/1341.
[3] See PACE s 41(9).

the exception of the powers to question someone at a port or border area under Sch 7, paras 2 and 3). These extra 'special' powers are cited since not all security operations are conducted in relation to specified criminal offences. The common law powers to prevent crime or to act in self-defence or the statutory powers under se 3 of the Criminal Law Act 1967 and s 117 of PACE (and their equivalents elsewhere) are much more commonly invoked in terrorist operations, and their application has proven constantly contentious. The most recent dispute concerned the shooting of Jean Charles de Menezes in 2005,[4] and there is a lengthy and bitter anthology of shootings in Northern Ireland.[5]

5.04　　The counter-terrorism policing powers in Pt V and elsewhere have become so voluminous that not all can be covered in detail. Exposition will be reserved for the most prominent: arrest; post-charge questioning; stop and search; and port controls. This list leaves out: search powers (ss 42 and 43); parking restrictions (ss 48 to 52); and electronic surveillance, including data retention. The principal reason for omission of the latter is not relative unimportance but because Pt XI of the Anti-terrorism, Crime and Security Act 2001 is now being replaced by mainstream legislation.[6]

B. ARREST

1. The arrest power

5.05　　The controversy surrounding Pt V of the Terrorism Act 2000 reaches its apogee in s 41, which deals with arrest without warrant. The lineage of these special arrest provisions dates back to 1974.[7] There may be three reasons for a special power of arrest of this kind.

5.06　　The traditional purpose is to interrogate suspects so as to uncover admissible evidence sufficient to put before a court, to gather background intelligence information, or simply to disrupt. These objectives are aided by an extraordinarily lengthy period of detention and by the fact that no detailed reasons need be offered at the point of arrest.[8] This purpose is allied to the idea that the threat of terrorism demands an anticipatory police intervention.

5.07　　A second and mounting reason for the special arrest and detention powers is to facilitate the carrying out of searches. These are of two types. One is the search of premises. The other relates to forensic testing. Despite its occasional disastrous lapses in standards,[9] testing for explosive substances, DNA profiling, and the examination of CCTV footage has become the stock-in-trade of terrorism investigations.

---

[4] See Independent Police Complaints Commission, *Stockwell One* (London, 2007) and *Stockwell Two* (London, 2007); Kennison, P. and Loumanksy, A., 'Shoot to kill' (2007) *Crime, Law & Social Change* 151.

[5] See *Reference under s.48A Criminal Appeal (Northern Ireland) Act 1968 (No 1 of 1975)* [1977] AC 105; *R v Clegg* [1995] 1 AC 482; *McCann v United Kingdom*, App No 18984/91, Ser A 324 (1995); Bloody Sunday Inquiry (<http://www.bloody-sunday-inquiry.org.uk>).

[6] See Data Retention (EC Directive) Regulations 2007, SI 2007/2199, and 2009, SI 2009/589; Home Office, *Transposition of Directive 2006/24/EC* (London, 2008).

[7] See Walker, C.P., *The Prevention of Terrorism in British Law* (2nd edn, Manchester University Press, Manchester, 1992) ch 8.

[8] See *Forbes v HM Advocate* 1990 SC (JC) 215; *Brady v Chief Constable for the RUC* [1991] 2 NIJB 22; *Oscar v Chief Constable of the RUC* [1992] NI 290.

[9] See (May Inquiry), *Reports of the Inquiry into the circumstances surrounding the convictions arising out of the bomb attacks in Guildford and Woolwich in 1974* (1989–90 HC 556), (1992–93 HC 296), (1993–94 HC 449);

The third reason for s 41 is to deal with the special problems posed by international 5.08
terrorism. Not only might there be dangerous and cohesive groups, but the police have
long faced complications over proof of identity, translation, and liaison with foreign
security agencies.[10]

The actual arrest power is provided for by s 41(1): 'A constable may arrest without a 5.09
warrant a person whom he reasonably suspects to be a terrorist.' The standard of reasonable suspicion in this context has been explored in *O'Hara v United Kingdom*.[11] While
'the "reasonableness" of the suspicion on which an arrest must be based forms an essential part of the safeguard against arbitrary arrest and detention', it is accepted that 'facts
which raise a suspicion need not be of the same level as those necessary to justify a conviction, or even the bringing of a charge'.[12] In *O'Hara*, the information from four separate informers, who had proved previously reliable and whose information concerning
the murder was consistent amounted to sufficient albeit 'sparse materials'.[13] As for the
components of reasonable suspicion, the House of Lords in *O'Hara* decided that its
components involve both a genuine and subjective suspicion in the mind of the arrestor
that the arrestee has been concerned in acts of terrorism and also objectively reasonable
grounds for forming such a suspicion.[14] Many such arrests will arise in the context of
second-hand information via briefings rather than events or information received first-
hand by the arresting officer. So long as the two components are present, the arrest can
be lawful,[15] but Lord Steyn in *O'Hara* was of the view that, no matter how trusting the
arresting officer might be of a briefing officer with an impeccable record of providing
good faith and reliable information, 'a mere request to arrest without any further information by an equal ranking officer, or a junior officer, is incapable of amounting to reasonable grounds for the necessary suspicion. How can the badge of the superior officer,
and the fact that he gave an order, make a difference?'[16]

A recurrent feature associated with s 41 is multiple arrests. These extra arrests might be 5.10
described as 'precautionary'.[17] For example, in *Commissioner of Police of the Metropolis v
Raissi*,[18] Lofti Raissi was arrested under s 41 on the basis of information from the FBI
which alleged that he had links to one of the September 11 hijackers and had been involved
in flight training in Arizona. Also arrested were his brother and wife on the basis of their
close relations and physical proximity. His wife also had been in Arizona and had worked
at an airline check-in. It was held that it was reasonable to suspect that the wife was com-
plicit, but the suspicions against the brother did not meet a sufficient standard.[19]

(Caddy Report), *Assessment and Implications of centrifuge Contamination in the Trace Explosive Section of the
Forensic Explosives Laboratory at Fort Halstead* (Cm 3491, London, 1996).

[10] See *(Jellicoe) Report of the Operation of the Prevention of Terrorism (Temporary Provisions) Act 1976* (Cmnd
8803, London, 1983) paras 13, 23, 75–8.

[11] App no 37555/97, 2001-X.

[12] *Ibid* paras 34, 36.

[13] *Ibid* paras 40, 42.

[14] *O'Hara v Chief Constable of the RUC* [1997] AC 286.

[15] See further Walker, C., 'Emergency arrest powers' (1985) 36 *Northern Ireland Legal Quarterly* 145;
Hunt, A., 'Terrorism and reasonable suspicion by "proxy"' (1997) 113 *Law Quarterly Review* 540.

[16] *O'Hara v Chief Constable of the RUC* [1997] AC 286 at p 293.

[17] See Metropolitan Police Authority, *Counter-Terrorism: The London Debate* (London, 2007) p 25.

[18] [2008] EWCA Civ 1237. See also *R (Raissi) v Secretary of State for the Home Department* [2008] EWCA
Civ 72; Leigh, L., 'Arrest: reasonable grounds for suspicion' (2008) 172 *Justice of the Peace* 180.

[19] *Ibid* at paras 47, 48.

5.11   The s 41 formulation differs from normal arrest powers in that no specific offence need be in the mind of the arresting officer. The result is to afford wider discretion in carrying out investigations. It follows that, though still required to state that an arrest is being imposed and the ground for the arrest, the police are not required to give detailed reasons.[20] To go further could disclose police methods or informers or may bolster the anti-interrogation training of suspects. Thus, in *Ex parte Lynch*, a constable arrested Lynch and told him that, 'I was arresting him under [the specified statutory power] as I suspected him of being involved in terrorist activities. . .'.[21] Lynch complained that this recital was inadequate (he was actually suspected of membership of the IRA and the murder of a policeman). Lord Chief Justice Lowry was wary of committing himself to enforcing the recital of substantial reasons, so no specific offence or act need ever be mentioned.[22] However, a bare reference to the section in the terrorism legislation was held to be inadequate in *Van Hout v Chief Constable of the Royal Ulster Constabulary.*[23] Article 5(2) of the European Convention allows a few hours' delay and for reasons to be deduced from a later interrogation.[24]

5.12   The definition of 'terrorism' relevant to s 40(1)(b) is that in s 1. Before 2001, Irish arrests provided the mainstay.[25] Since then, the vast majority of arrests in Britain relate to international origins. There are isolated reports of arrests for domestic causes such as animal rights and ecological protestors, or Scottish and Welsh nationalism,[26] or racist activities. Thus, proportionality applies in practice if not on paper. However, in the cases of Martyn Gilleard and Nathan Worrell, two successive neo-Nazis were arrested under s 41 (and then charged and convicted under ss 57 and 58).[27] Their situations could easily have been countered by non-terrorist arrest powers and offences, but a spurious equality with *jihadis* seems to have been sought.

5.13   Terrorist plots and attacks usually do entail serious offences, and this convergence has prompted the European Court of Human Rights in *Brogan* to accept 'terrorism' as within the European Convention's notion of an 'offence' for the purposes of Art 5(1)(c).[28] At the same time, that decision was delivered in the context of indications that specific offences of membership of a proscribed organization were in mind. This point was emphasized by Lord Lloyd in debates on the Terrorism Bill,[29] and his solution to ensure compliance with Art 5(1)(c) was to enact an offence of 'terrorism'.[30] In response, the

---

[20] See *R v Officer in charge of Police Office, Castlereagh, ex p Lynch* [1980] NI 126; Walker, C.P., 'Arrest and rearrest' (1984) 35 *Northern Ireland Legal Quarterly* 1.

[21] [1980] NI 126 at p 128. Compare *Re McElduff* [1972] NI 1.

[22] *Ibid*, at p 137. The same arguments did not apply to arrests based on s 40(1)(a): *ibid* at pp 130–1; *Forbes v H.M. Advocate* 1990 SCCR 69.

[23] (1984) 28 June (QBD).

[24] *Fox, Hartley, and Campbell v United Kingdom*, App no Ser A 182 (1990) paras 41–3; *(Margaret) Murray v United Kingdom*, App no 14310/88 Ser A 300-A (1994) para 77.

[25] See Brown, D., *Detention under the Prevention of Terrorism Act* (Home Office Research and Planning Unit paper 75, London, 1993) p 6.

[26] There were 26 arrests between 1980 and 1984 (Colville Report, *Review of the Operation of the Prevention of Terrorism (Temporary Provisions) Act 1984* (Cm 264, London, 1987) para 7.92.

[27] See (Gilleard) *The Times* 26 June 2008 p 20; (Worrell) *Grimsby Evening Telegraph*, 13 December 2008 pp 1, 2, 3.

[28] *Brogan v United Kingdom*, App nos 11209, 11234, 11266/84, 11386/85, Ser A 145-B (1988) para 50. See also *Ireland v United Kingdom*, App no 5310/71, Ser A. 25 (1978) para 196.

[29] Hansard HL vol 613, col 677 (16 May 2000).

[30] *Inquiry into Legislation against Terrorism* (Cm 3420, London, 1996) para 8.16. See also Lord Carlile, *Report on the Operation in 2001 of the Terrorism Act 2000* (Home Office, London, 2002) para 5.4.

government was content to rely upon the authority of *Brogan* for the proposition that 'a terrorist arrest power, without an explicit link to a specific offence, is compatible with the ECHR and Article 5(1)(c) in particular.'[31] Overall, the precedents are not favourable to Lord Lloyd's contention, and the tide of legislative development represented by the passage of broad offences, such as encouragement and preparation of terrorism (under the Terrorism Act 2006, ss 1 and 5), is also adverse.

A further difference from 'normal' arrest powers is that there is no need to comply with the requirement of necessity which applies under PACE s 24(4) (as amended in 2005). However, the looser administrative law standard that the power is being used for proper purposes applies.[32]   5.14

A final broad feature of the arrest power is that, by s 41(9), a constable in one part of the United Kingdom may exercise the power in any other part.[33]   5.15

2. The detention power

The detention allowed subsequent to arrest under s 41 seeks to afford the police the widest opportunities for investigations and so departs considerably from the PACE norms (Scottish laws are less precise but are more restrictive still). Section 41(3) allows for police-sanctioned detention of up to forty-eight hours. The detention period may then be extended for further judicially-authorized periods which can last up to twenty-eight days from arrest, as laid down in Sch 8. The person can be detained pending the relevant applications: s 41(5), (6). A refusal of an extension (unless no grounds then exist for arrest) does not mean immediate release if there is unexpired time already allowed: s 41(8). Lord Lloyd recommended that four days should be the maximum.[34] The maximum period stood at seven days from 1974 until 2003, since when it has quadrupled.   5.16

(a) *Judicial scrutiny at forty-eight hours—warrant of further detention*

The first important waypoint in the process of review of the need for prolonged detention arises at forty-eight hours. The authorization rules are set out in Pt III of Sch 8; whenever successful, the person's detention may continue for the full period as specified (s 41(7)). The process involves an application for a 'warrant of further detention' under para 29 of Sch 8 which may be made by a police officer of at least the rank of superintendent or, following amendments in the Terrorism Act 2006, s 23, a Crown Prosecutor in England and Wales, the Lord Advocate or a procurator fiscal in Scotland, or the Director of Public Prosecutions for Northern Ireland. Even before the changes in the 2006 Act, there existed in Scotland a protocol between police and prosecution whereby applications are made only with the agreement of the procurator fiscal who will also attend the relevant hearing and speak to the application.[35] However, applications elsewhere within fourteen days are left to the police,[36] and prosecutors take the   5.17

---

[31] Hansard HL vol 613, cols 681–2 (16 May 2000), Lord Bassam. See also Home Office and Northern Ireland Office, *Legislation against Terrorism* (Cm 4178, London, 1998) para 7.16.

[32] *Holgate-Mohammed v Duke* [1984] AC 437.

[33] Compare Criminal Justice and Public Order Act 1994, ss 137, 140. See Walker, C., 'Internal cross-border policing' (1997) 56 *Cambridge Law Journal* 114.

[34] Inquiry into Legislation against Terrorism (Cm. 3420, London, 1996) paras 9.10, 9.22.

[35] Hansard HL vol 677, cols 1206–1207 (25 January 2006), Baroness Scotland.

[36] Crown Prosecution Service, *Scrutiny of Pre-Charge Detention in Terrorist Cases* (London, 2007) para 11.

lead after fourteen days.[37] Just two applications under the Terrorism Act 2000 have been refused in England and Wales; seven others were granted for a period shorter than requested.[38]

5.18   If granted, a warrant of further detention shall expire not later than the end of the period of seven days from arrest or a lesser specified period.[39] If a lesser period is granted and more time is needed, the next application should be under para 36 (below) rather than a repeat application under para 29 (as used to be case under the formulation of para 36(1) before amendment in 2006). The form of warrant is set out in the Magistrates' Courts (Forms) (Amendment) Rules 2001.[40]

5.19   The definition of a 'judicial authority' is (a) in England and Wales, a designated district judge (magistrates' court); (b) in Scotland, the sheriff; and (c) in Northern Ireland, a county court judge, or a designated resident magistrate. The involvement of judicial personnel represents a major departure from the position under the Prevention of Terrorism (Temporary Provisions) Act 1989, pursuant to which the Home Secretary or Northern Ireland Secretary reviewed these applications. This absence of judicial oversight sparked a successful challenge under Art 5(3) before the European Court of Human Rights in *Brogan and others v United Kingdom*.[41] Even the shortest of the four periods of detention concerned, namely four days and six hours, fell outside the requirement of being 'brought promptly before a judge'. The legal consequence was recourse to a derogation under Art 15 which was upheld in *Brannigan and McBride v United Kingdom*.[42]

5.20   The desire to avoid continued reliance upon the palliative of derogation was resolved by the Terrorism Act 2000 with the judicial involvement at forty-eight hours.[43] The notice of derogation for the United Kingdom was withdrawn. A less heralded outcome of the withdrawal has been to extend the permissible period of detention for international terrorist suspects. Since the derogation notice was justifiable only in the case of the situation of Northern Ireland, it was the practice not to detain international suspects for more than four days.[44] However, given the insertion of judicial oversight, the seven-day detention power can be applied to all categories of suspects.

5.21   The insertion of independent judicial scrutiny and the determination to live without derogation should be welcomed, but not all applauded the change. The Official Opposition felt:[45]

> . . . unconvinced that it is legitimately a judicial function, rather than an Executive one. The decision to extend detention under existing legislation is usually based on intelligence material in the hands of the Executive that cannot be considered appropriate for judicial consideration. The information

---

[37] Hansard HC vol 478, col 81 (23 June 2008), Tony McNulty.
[38] Crown Prosecution Service, *Scrutiny of Pre-Charge Detention in Terrorist Cases* (London, 2007) para 12.
[39] See Terrorism Act 2006, s 23.
[40] SI 2001/166.
[41] *Brogan v United Kingdom*, App nos 11209, 11234, 11266/84, 11386/85, Ser A 145-B (1988). See further *McEldowney and others v United Kingdom*, App no 14550/89, Res DH(94) 31; *O'Hara v United Kingdom*, App no 37555/97, 2001-X; Livingstone, S., 'A week is a long time in detention' (1989) 40 *Northern Ireland Legal Quarterly* 288.
[42] App nos 14553/89, 14554/89, Ser A 258-B (1994). See further *Marshall v United Kingdom*, App no 41571/98, 10 July 2001; *Kerr v United Kingdom*, App no 40451/98, 10 July 2001; Marks, S., 'Civil liberties at the margins' (1995) 15 *Oxford Journal of Legal Studies* 69.
[43] *Inquiry into Legislation against Terrorism* (Cm 3420, London, 1996) para 9.20.
[44] Hansard HC Standing Committee D, cols 182, 183 (25 January 2000), Charles Clarke.
[45] Hansard HC vol 341, col 172 (14 December 1999), Ann Widdecombe.

is often of such a sensitive nature that it cannot be disclosed to a detainee or his legal adviser without compromising the source of the intelligence, thus endangering lives or impeding an investigation. By giving that power to a judicial authority, the judiciary would inevitably be seen as part of the investigation and prosecution process, which could bring its independence into question.

These views correlate closely with the arguments of the UK government in *Marshall v United Kingdom*,[46] when it was seeking to oppose a challenge to the then executive-based system of detention review. However, the proposition that judges cannot handle sensitive intelligence evidence and cannot operate without full disclosure to the accused is belied by their deployment as reviewers in other security contexts (especially under the Special Immigration Appeal Commission Act 1997) and by the compromises made everyday in the courts under the doctrine of public interest immunity. 5.22

The mechanisms by which a warrant of further detention at this first stage may be obtained, are further related in Pt III of Sch 8. By para 30, an application for a warrant, which may be written or oral, must be made within the initial forty-eight hours or within six hours of the end of that period (if not reasonably practicable to make it within forty-eight hours). The consideration by the judicial authority must likewise take place within those time limits save for adjournments to enable the person to whom the application relates to obtain legal representation (para 35), so in practice an application will often commence well within the 48-hour mark. When making an application, a notice must be given to the detainee, and it must state the grounds upon which further detention is sought (para 31). The reference to 'grounds' rather than 'reasons' means that set formulae are used which do not go into the details of an individual investigation.[47] The discretion of the judicial authority to grant an extension is limited by para 32. The judicial authority must be satisfied that (a) there are reasonable grounds for believing that the further detention of the person to whom the application relates is necessary to obtain relevant evidence (relating to proof that he is a 'terrorist' within s 40) whether by questioning him or otherwise or to preserve relevant evidence or pending the result of an examination or analysis of any relevant evidence or of anything the examination or analysis of which is to be or is being carried out with a view to obtaining relevant evidence;[48] and (b) the investigation in connection with which the person is detained is being conducted diligently and expeditiously. The statement of these criteria is a development over the predecessor legislation (which contained none). However, they remain opaque compared to the 'Colville criteria'—a listing of reasons originally appearing in the Colville Report of 1987[49] and then promulgated to police forces as a guide.[50] They were never comprehensive (interrogation of the detainee is not mentioned)[51] but include: 5.23

1. Checking of fingerprints.
2. Forensic tests.

---

[46] App no 41571/98, 10 July 2001, p 8.

[47] See *R v Officer in charge of Police Office, Castlereagh, ex p Lynch* [1980] NI 126.

[48] The ground relating to forensic testing added under the Terrorism Act 2006, s 24, was added in response to challenge by judicial review in Northern Ireland: Hansard HC vol 832, col 918 (2 November 2005), Charles Clarke.

[49] *Review of the Operation of the Prevention of Terrorism (Temporary Provisions) Act 1984* (Cm 264, London, 1987) para 5.16.

[50] Home Office Circular No 27/1989: *Prevention of Terrorism (Temporary Provisions) Act 1989*, para 4.11.

[51] For techniques of interrogation in terrorist cases, see Williamson, T. (ed), *Investigative Interviewing* (Willan, Cullompton, 2006) chs 2, 4.

3. Checking the detainee's replies against intelligence.
4. New lines of enquiry.
5. Interrogation to identify accomplices.
6. Correlating information obtained from one or more other detained person in the same case.
7. Awaiting a decision by the DPP.
8. Finding and consulting other witnesses.
9. Identification parade.
10. Checking an alibi.
11. Translating documents.
12. Obtaining an interpreter and carrying out the necessary interview with his assistance.
13. Communications with foreign police forces sometimes across time zones and language difficulties.
14. Evaluation of documents once translated and further investigated.

5.24   A further procedural improvement in the 2000 Act, and one again in keeping with Art 5(3) of the European Convention, is that by para 33, the detainee shall be given an opportunity to make oral or written representations to the judicial authority and shall be entitled to be legally represented at the hearing, if necessary following an adjournment.[52] However, the right to make representations does not necessarily entail a hearing and, under para 33(3), the judicial authority may exclude the detainee or any representative from any part of the hearing. The judicial authority may also, if there are reasonable grounds established under para 34, on an application from the police or prosecution, withhold information from either or both of the detainee or any representative. On this occasion at least, the power is structured and relevant grounds are that disclosure could lead to evidence being interfered with or harmed, relevant property (subject to possible investigation or forfeiture or confiscation) being removed or lost, other suspects being alerted, and other persons being interfered with or injured. These grounds are broadly the same as in PACE, but the same does not apply to two further grounds: the prevention of an act of terrorism becoming more difficult as a result of a person being alerted, or the gathering of information about the commission, preparation, or instigation of an act of terrorism being interfered with. Yet more grounds relate to the possibility that the detained person has benefited from his criminal conduct, and that the recovery of the value of the property constituting the benefit would be hindered if the information were disclosed.[53] The detainee and any representative are automatically excluded from the hearing of an application under para 34. This blanket rule may be inconsistent with an effective judicial hearing under Art 5(3) whereby the judicial officer has 'the obligation of hearing himself the individual brought before him'.[54]

---

[52] See Legal Advice and Assistance (Scope) Regulations 2001, SI 2001/179; Legal Advice and Assistance (Amendment) Regulations 2001, SI 2001/191; Criminal Defence Service (General) (No 2) Regulations 2001, SI 2001/1437 para 4(k); Criminal Defence Service (General) (No 2) (Amendment) Regulations 2002, SI 2002/712; Advice and Assistance (Assistance by Way of Representation) (Scotland) Amendment (No 2) Regulations 2001, SSI 2001/43, as consolidated in the Advice and Assistance (Assistance by Way of Representation) (Scotland) Regulations 2003, SSI 2003/179.
[53] As amended by the Proceeds of Crime Act 2002, Sch 11 para 39.
[54] *Schiesser v Switzerland*, App no 7710/76, Ser A 34 (1979) para 31.

The courts take seriously the right to make representations. In *Re Quigley's Application*,[55] the Northern Ireland High Court warned that failure to take account of representations might result in the quashing of a decision to extend detention. In *Ward v Police Service for Northern Ireland*,[56] the House of Lords upheld the exercise of the power under para 33 to exclude the detainee and lawyer from sensitive aspects of police representations—such as an indication of the issues they wanted next to explore or the formulation of questions. Even so, their Lordships warned that judges who allow exclusion in this way take upon themselves an enhanced duty to check what the police are demanding. However, the judges have no independent means of scrutiny of case data.

The prospect of appearance in person was further reduced by s 75 of the Criminal Justice and Police Act 2001. The judicial authority may direct that the hearing and all representations be effected by suitable communications links and not in the physical presence of the detainee or of any legal representative. Video links are now used in 80 per cent of cases[57] and are firmly encouraged by para 33(9), whereby, 'If in a case where it has power to do so a judicial authority decides not to give a direction under sub-paragraph (4), it shall state its reasons for not giving it.' This presumption should be reversed. A video link is not as effective a safeguard for discerning oppression or physical welfare as appearance in person.[58]

(b) *Judicial reviews of extensions beyond seven days—extensions of warrants*

The second waypoint in the detention power occurs at seven days. To authorize detention beyond this point, a warrant of further detention must be issued under para 36, two versions of which have prevailed since 2003. By the Criminal Justice Act 2003, s 306, the specified period could be extended by the same judicial authorities as under para 29 to a period ending not later than the end of the period of fourteen days beginning with the arrest. This extension, which came into force on 20 January 2004, was barely debated in Parliament. The main arguments for the change were marshalled by Lord Carlile[59] and related to the difficulties of identifying foreigners and interpreting what they say as well as arranging specialist legal advice and attending to their spiritual welfare, plus the delays in forensic testing and computer analysis.

The provisions in s 306 were trumped by the extension to twenty-eight days by s 23 of the Terrorism Act 2006 which came into force on 25 July 2006. For applications which take the detention period up to fourteen days, there remains an echo of s 306 since the decision is by the same judicial authority as under para 29 provided no application has previously been made to a senior judge in respect of that period. However, whenever the application for extension takes the period beyond fourteen days, it must

5.25

5.26

5.27

5.28

---

[55] [1997] NI 202.

[56] [2007] UKHL 50.

[57] Joint Committee on Human Rights, *Counter-Terrorism Policy and Human Rights: 28 days, intercept and post-charge questioning* (2006–07 HL 157/HC 394) para 75.

[58] See *R v Chief Constable of Kent Constabulary, ex p Kent Police Federation Joint Branch Board* (1999) *The Times* 1 December; *Report to the United Kingdom Government on the Visit to the United Kingdom carried out by the European Committee for the Prevention of Torture and Inhuman and Degrading Treatment* (CPT/Inf (2008) 27) para 8 and *Response of the United Kingdom Government* (CPT/Inf (2008) 28) para 14; Joint Committee on Human Rights, *Counter-Terrorism Policy and Human Rights: 28 days, intercept and post-charge questioning* (2006–07 HL 157/HC 394) para 79.

[59] Hansard HL vol 653, cols 957–9 (15 October 2003); Lord Carlile, *Report on the Operation in 2002 and 2003 of the Terrorism Act 2000* (Home Office, London, 2004) para 111. Since 2001, 16 out of 212 detentions had lasted for 6 days or more: Hansard HL vol 654, col 1296 (11 November 2003).

be heard by 'a senior judge', meaning a judge of the High Court or of the High Court of Justiciary (para 36(7)).[60] At this point, the Crown Prosecution Service's Counter-Terrorism Division will become involved in the application process.[61] The application will involve open source and sensitive material, and the defendant will be given a summary of lines of inquiry to date and in the future, subject to sensitivity.[62] The court should consider the lines of inquiry, the timetable, the nexus to the charging decision, and evidence of due diligence such as hours being worked.[63] There were again variant views as to the wisdom of judicial involvement.[64]

5.29   Such grants of further detention cannot endure more than seven days (subject to the 28-day maximum) from the expiration of the previously granted period (para 36(3)(b)). A shorter period than seven days may either be requested or imposed by the senior judge, but it must be inappropriate for the normal seven days to apply (para 36(3AA)). The procedural rules in paras 30 to 34 apply here.

5.30   A further safeguard instituted in 2006 is that the extraordinary extra power of detention was granted for just one year under s 25 of the Terrorism Act 2006, but it has so far been renewed by affirmative order.[65] In default of the tabling or approval of an order, the maximum period will revert to fourteen days.

5.31   Challenges to decisions to extend detention might be possible by way of judicial review or habeas corpus within fourteen days. Thereafter, a decision of a High Court judge cannot be reviewed in these ways.[66]

(c) *Police reviews*

5.32   As well as the judicial forms of authorization, the police themselves keep the validity of the detention under constant review. There are parallels with PACE, s 40, but also some key differences.

5.33   The process is introduced by Pt II of Sch 8. Paragraph 21 requires periodic checks by a 'review officer'.[67] By para 24, the review officer shall be an officer who has not been directly involved in the investigation. For reviews within the first 24-hour period, the review officer shall be an officer of at least the rank of inspector (but, under para 25, if an investigative officer of a higher rank gives disputed directions, the matter of review shall be referred to a superintendent or higher rank). After twenty-four hours, a superintendent or higher rank must act as reviewer. The reviews must be carried out in person by an officer present at the police station where the detainee is held.[68]

5.34   By para 21, the first police review shall be carried out as soon as is reasonably practicable after the time of the person's arrest. Subsequent reviews shall be carried out at intervals of not more than twelve hours. The reviews may be postponed where an interviewing

---

[60] See Hansard HC vol 439, col 326 (9 November 2005), Charles Clarke.
[61] See Crown Prosecution Service, *Scrutiny of Pre-Charge Detention in Terrorist Cases* (London, 2007) para 1.
[62] *Ibid* para 6.
[63] *Ibid* paras 8, 9.
[64] Compare Lord Carlile, *Proposals by Her Majesty's Government for Changes to the Laws against Terrorism* (Home Office, London, 2005) paras 64, 67; Hansard HL vol 676, col 1157 (13 December 2005), Lord Lloyd.
[65] SI 2007/2181, SI 2008/1745. See Joint Committee on Human Rights, *Counter-Terrorism Policy and Human Rights: Annual Renewal of 28 days* (2007-08 HL 32/HC 825).
[66] See *R (on the application of Hussain) v Collins* [2006] EWHC 2467 (Admin).
[67] See further PACE Code H para 14.
[68] There is no equivalent in the Criminal Justice and Police Act 2001, s 73.

officer is satisfied that an interruption would prejudice the inquiry, or while no review officer is readily available, or while it is otherwise not practicable for any other reason to carry out the review (para 22).

To authorize continued detention, the officer review must be satisfied that it is neces- 5.35 sary under para 23: (a) to obtain relevant evidence (that the person is a 'terrorist') whether by questioning him or otherwise; (b) to preserve relevant evidence; (ba) to await the result of an examination or analysis of any relevant evidence;[69] (c) pending a decision whether to apply to the Secretary of State for a deportation notice to be served on the detained person; (d) pending the making of an application to the Secretary of State for a deportation notice to be served on the detained person; (e) pending consideration by the Secretary of State whether to serve a deportation notice on the detained person; or (f) pending a decision whether the detained person should be charged with an offence. The review officer must also be sure that the investigations (under (a) or (b)) or the processes (under (c) to (f)) are being conducted diligently and expeditiously. Grounds (a) and (b) have in the past been in practice the most common.[70] By s 41(4), if the review officer does not authorize continued detention, the person shall be released, unless detained under any other power and subject to any application for judicial extension.

In conducting the review, various procedural rights must be observed. First, a review 5.36 officer shall grant an opportunity to make representations (para 26).[71] Secondly, by para 27, where a review officer decides to authorize continued detention, the detained person shall be informed of rights to legal advice and to notify an outsider of his whereabouts. By para 28, the review officer shall make a written record of the outcome of the review and other relevant details in the presence of the detained person and inform him whether continued detention has been authorized, and, if so, of his grounds. There are exceptions when the detainee is incapable of understanding what is said to him, violent, or in urgent need of medical attention.

Formal police reviews terminate under para 21(4) after a judicial warrant extending 5.37 detention has been issued under Pt III of Sch 8. It is regrettable that the Terrorism Act 2000 does not recognize the need for formal police vigilance beyond forty-eight hours. However, it is considered good practice that police 'welfare' checks, usually by a custody officer, should continue after forty-eight hours.[72] Furthermore, in view of lengthier detention times now possible, para 37 (inserted by the Terrorism Act 2006, s 23) requires that, beyond the 48-hour limit, where it appears to the custody officer in charge of the detained person's case that any of the grounds in para 32 which were relied upon by the judicial authority or senior judge who last authorized his further detention no longer apply, the officer must arrange for the immediate release of the detainee.

(d) Other PACE rules

Several important PACE rules do not apply under the Terrorism Act detention, as is 5.38 made clear by PACE s 51(b). Some negative consequences flow.

---

[69] See Terrorism Act 2006, s 24.
[70] 88% according to Brown, D., *Detention under the Prevention of Terrorism Act* (Home Office Research and Planning Unit paper 75, London, 1993) p 47.
[71] 6% of detainees had a solicitor: *ibid*.
[72] See *ibid* p 46.

5.39   First, ss 34 and 37 of PACE are not applicable since s 41 does not involve arrest for an offence. One result is that there is no power for the police to release on bail.[73] Given that the range of offences of terrorism now range to peripheral involvement, it would be helpful to make such a power of police bail available.[74] In *R (on the application of I) v City of Westminster Magistrates' Court*,[75] Mr Justice Collins considered whether this absence of bail breached Art 5 of the European Convention. Formal reviews at, and after, forty-eight hours were considered to meet the requirements of Art 5. It was even suggested that a police review officer could impose conditions on continued detention for specific terrorist offences,[76] though it is not clearly explained how this squares with PACE, s 51, or with a judicial decision that continued detention is necessary.

5.40   A clearer analysis was offered in *McKay v United Kingdom*.[77] The applicant had been arrested for terrorism activities in Northern Ireland. The Resident Magistrate who considered his remand had no power to grant bail, a power reserved to a High Court judge under the (repealed) Terrorism Act 2000, s 67). Consequently, he had to make a separate application for bail, entailing an extra day in custody. The European Court accepted that different authorities could be tasked to deal with the legality and necessity of detention and the distinct issue of grant of bail. The lawfulness issue was analysed along *Brogan* lines. As for the grant of bail, Art 5(3) requires opportunities for release pending trial so as to reflect the independence of the judiciary, and these opportunities must be provided with 'due diligence' but not necessarily even at the first (judicial) review hearing.[78] There had been sufficient expedition to arrange a bail hearing.

5.41   Another result of s 51(b) is that there is no need to end pre-charge detention because there is sufficient evidence for a charge—as is made further clear by s 41(7). However, any detention which goes beyond that point may breach Art 5(1)(c) of the European Convention.

5.42   Next, difficulties might arise with terrorist detainees who are ill. One example is Dr Kafeel Ahmed who was severely burnt (and later died) in the attack on Glasgow airport in 2007.[79] Another concerns Mohammed Abdul Kahar who was shot by police in an arrest operation in 2006.[80] If the person is so ill that there is no formal police arrest, the clock does not run, but the police will usually arrest so as to restrict access. Another scenario is where a suspect is arrested but becomes unfit for interview. Rules allowing the suspension of the detention clock while in hospital, under PACE, s 41(6), do not apply. Assimilation of PACE and the Terrorism Act would seem worthwhile.

---

[73] PACE Code H para 1.6. After 14 days, a High Court judge has common law powers to grant bail: *R v Spilsbury* [1892] 2 QB 615.

[74] Joint Committee on Human Rights, *Counter-Terrorism Policy and Human Rights, Counter-Terrorism Bill* (2007–08 HL 108/HC 554) para 54. Compare HL Hansard vol 704, col 585 (13 October 2008).

[75] [2008] EWHC 2146 (Admin).

[76] *Ibid* paras 9, 22.

[77] App no 543/03, 3 October 2006.

[78] *Ibid* paras 36, 39, 46, 47.

[79] Lord Carlile, *Report on Proposed Measures for Inclusion in a Counter-Terrorism Bill* (Cm 7262, London, 2007) para 43.

[80] IPCC, *Independent Investigations into Complaints made following the Forest Green counter-terrorist operation on 2 June 2006* (London, 2007).

3. The treatment of detainees

(a) *Codes*

The humane and fair treatment of terrorist suspects has long generated bitter contro-   5.43
versy and litigation, whether in Northern Ireland[81] or in Guantánamo Bay.[82] In the light
of the experience in Northern Ireland, the UK government asserted in 1972 that any
methods contrary to Art 3 of the European Convention were not to be countenanced.[83]
It would be naïve to assume this statement commands universal observance, but the
gradual refinement of laws and administrative rules and procedures, especially those
rolled out first in Northern Ireland pursuant to the Bennett Report,[84] did eventually
achieve the reduction of physical malpractices within police stations. Further safeguards
have followed in the wake of PACE and its emulation in Scotland.

Part I of Sch 8 of the Terrorism Act 2000 provides the principal framework for the   5.44
treatment of detainees. Alongside, there are more detailed guides[85] which have been
largely consolidated as a specialist PACE Code H in Connection with the Detention,
Treatment and Questioning by Police Officers of Persons under Section 41 of, and
Schedule 8 to, the Terrorism Act 2000.[86] PACE Code D (identification) can also apply to
terrorism cases.[87] Next, there are some special codes issued under the Terrorism Act 2000.
For Northern Ireland, the codes were issued pursuant to s 99 of the Terrorism Act 2000
and were then consolidated in 2006 as the Terrorism Act 2000 (Section 99) Code of
Practice which covered both detention and identification.[88] But s 99 and its codes
expired with Pt VII in 2007.[89] Pending a wider review of police powers,[90] the Northern
Ireland Office then issued 'Interim Administrative Guidance' to the police. These interim

---

[81] See *Ireland v UK*, App no 5310/71, Ser A 25 (1978); *Report of the Committee of Inquiry into Police Interrogation Procedures in Northern Ireland* (Cmnd 9497, London, 1979).

[82] See Duffy, H., *The 'War on Terror' and the Framework of International Law* (Cambridge University Press, New York, 2005).

[83] See *(Compton) Report of an Enquiry into allegations against the security forces of physical brutality in Northern Ireland arising out of arrests on the 9 August 1971* (Cmnd 4828, London, 1972); *(Parker) Report of the Committee of Privy Counsellors appointed to consider authorised procedures for the interrogation of persons suspected of terrorism* (Cmnd 4901, London, 1972); *(Aitken) Investigation into cases of Deliberate Abuse and Unlawful Killing in Iraq in 2003 and 2004* (Ministry of Defence, London, 2008).

[84] *Report of the Committee of Inquiry into Police Interrogation Procedures in Northern Ireland* (Cmnd 9497, London, 1979). See also Body of Principles for the Protection of All Persons under Any Form of Detention or Imprisonment (UNGA res 43/173 of 9 December 1988).

[85] See Hansard HL vol 684, col 311 (5 July 2006), Baroness Scotland.

[86] See Home Office Circular 23/2006. The Code does not apply to detainees under the Prevention of Terrorism Act 2005, s 5 (likely to result in short detentions only); detainees for examination under sch 7 (a separate code under sch 14 applies), or to detainees under stop and search powers (PACE Code A applies): para 1.4.

[87] But see para 2.17(iii).

[88] <http://www.nio.gov.uk/terrorism_act_2000_(section_99)_code_of_practice.pdf>, as brought into force by 2006, SI 2006/1330. See previously Terrorism Act 2000 (Code of Practice on the Exercise of Police Powers) (Northern Ireland) Order 2001, SI 2001/401, as revised by Terrorism Act 2000 (Revised Code of Practice for the Identification of Persons by Police Officers) (Northern Ireland) Order 2006, SI 2006/1330; *In the matter of an application by JR10 for judicial review* [2007] NIQB 56).

[89] See Terrorism (Northern Ireland) Act 2006 (Transitional Provisions and Savings) Order 2007, SI 2007/2259.

[90] Police and Criminal Evidence (Northern Ireland) Order 1989, Modernising Police Powers (Northern Ireland Office, Belfast, 2007).

arrangements ended in November 2008 when a Code H for Northern Ireland was instituted.[91]

5.45   In the absence of an equivalent to PACE in Scotland, the details are contained in the Terrorism (Interviews) (Scotland) Order 2001.[92] The Lord Advocate and the Minister for Justice issued further guidelines in 2006 to Scottish Chief Constables about the detention of terrorist suspects.[93]

5.46   The regime under the codes is largely redolent of PACE, and there is a commitment to apply PACE rules more fully.[94] Particular features include special emphasis upon the need to facilitate reading materials, religious observances, visits, and exercise, special efforts to explain when there are extended periods without interviews, a heightened need to allow visits, exercise, and reading materials if the intermission is twenty-four hours or more.[95]

(b) *Location*

5.47   The permissible places of detention are designated under para 1. In England and Wales, the designated places comprise any police station[96] or prison or (additionally for persons under 18) any young offender institution, secure training centre or other place of safety.[97] In practice, Paddington Green Police Station in London and Govan in Scotland have been specially adapted.[98] High security prisons are now used outside Scotland for those held for more than fourteen days, unless the detainee specifically requests otherwise and that request can be accommodated, or the transfer would hinder the investigation.[99] In Northern Ireland, a custom-built Serious Crime Suite in Antrim Police Station serves as the prime venue. Persons may be removed from the designated place only for the purposes of examination (or to establish nationality or to arrange removal from the country) under Sch 7.

(c) *Identification and searches*

5.48   Most of the relevant identification and search powers are those set out in Pt V of the PACE legislation or equivalents.[100] The power to take steps reasonably necessary to identify the individual (Sch 8, para 2) may be accomplished by photographing, measuring, or otherwise identifying the detained person. The 'other steps' could include, for example, voice recognition tests, but expressly do not include fingerprints, non-intimate samples, or intimate sampling since they are dealt with in para 10 (with records being required under para 11). Fingerprints and non-intimate samples may be taken with the appropriate consent given in writing, or, without consent where a superintendent authorizes the

---

[91] Police and Criminal Evidence (Northern Ireland) Order 1989 (Codes of Practice) (No 4) Order 2008, SRNI 2008/408. Other PACE Codes are authorized by SRNI 2007/58. The authority is the Police and Criminal Evidence (Northern Ireland) Order 1989, art 65.

[92] SI 2001/428.

[93] *Guidelines on the detention, treatment and questioning by police officers of persons arrested under s 41 and sch 8 of the Terrorism Act 2000* (Crown Office, Edinburgh, 2006).

[94] See Home Office and Northern Ireland Office, *Legislation against Terrorism* (Cm 4178, London, 1998) para 8.50.

[95] PACE Code H paras 8, 11, 12.

[96] The same applies in Scotland: Guidelines 2006, para 3.

[97] Terrorism Act 2000 (Places of Detention) Designation 2006.

[98] Hansard HL vol 684, col 314 (5 July 2006), Baroness Scotland.

[99] PACE Code H para 14.5. Persons transferred are treated according to the Prison Rules.

[100] PACE Code H paras 4, 16.

fingerprints or samples to be taken or where the person has been convicted of a recordable offence. The fingerprints must be taken by a constable—civilian support officers may not act in these cases.[101] In the case of intimate samples, there must be written consent from the detainee,[102] as well as authorization by a superintendent under para 10. The intimate sample (aside from urine) must be taken by a registered medical practitioner or, for dental impressions, a registered dentist (para 13). Under para 12, if two or more non-intimate samples taken for the same means of analysis prove insufficient for forensic purposes, an authorization for an additional intimate sample may be given in respect of a person since released from detention, provided again that the person also consents to the sampling. Under para 11, the detainee shall be informed of the purposes of the process and the reasons for taking it by consent or the grounds on which an authorization has been given. Where appropriate consent is refused without good cause, adverse inferences may be drawn from the refusal in later proceedings (para 13).

The establishment of identity is also addressed by the Anti-terrorism, Crime and Security Act 2001, s 89 which specifies that fingerprints can be taken from those detained under the Terrorism Act 2000 in order to ascertain their identity for a wider range of purposes than those already specified in Sch 8, para 10, such as other, non-criminal, forms of disposal. Accordingly, sub-paras (6A) and (6B) to Sch 8 allow a superintendent or higher rank to authorize the taking of fingerprints without consent if the person has refused to identify himself or the officer reasonably believes that he has given a false identity. Subsection (3) also allows the police under sub-s (4) to examine fingerprints or DNA samples retained under Terrorism Act 2000 powers when investigating a crime that is apparently non-terrorist. 'For example, a van may be stolen for use as a bomb, but recovered without any evidence of its intended terrorist use'.[103] Before this change, those records could be searched by the police for terrorism purposes, so there arose 'a risk that they will miss connections between ordinary criminal offences, which may be committed as precursors to terrorist activity, and terrorist suspects'.[104]

Along the same lines, ss 90 (England and Wales) and 91 (Northern Ireland) extend other 'normal' search powers under PACE s 54 to establish identity.[105] By an added s 54A, such searches may also relate to 'any mark that would tend to identify him' or 'for the purpose of facilitating the ascertainment of his identity' where the person has refused to identify himself or the officer has reasonable grounds for suspecting that a false identity has been provided. Photographs may be taken of such marks (meaning bodily features and injuries). In effect, what might otherwise have been considered an intimate search (a search of body orifices other than the mouth) under s 55 of PACE 1984 can now be undertaken for purposes of identification rather than the investigatory or safety purposes allowed under s 55. It is expressly forbidden to use s 54A for the purposes of intimate searches within s 55 (s 54A(8)), but then it is expressly permitted under

5.49

5.50

---

[101] See Lord Carlile, *Report on the Operation in 2004 of the Terrorism Act 2000* (Home Office, London, 2005) para 82.

[102] See British Medical Association and the Faculty of Forensic and Legal Medicine, *Guidelines and Advice: Doctors asked to perform intimate body searches* (London, 2007).

[103] Hansard HL vol 629, col 711 (4 December 2001), Lord Rooker.

[104] Hansard HC vol 375, col 742 (26 November 2001), Beverley Hughes.

[105] The use of anti-terrorism legislation for this purpose was criticized by the Newton Committee: Privy Counsellor Review Committee, *Anti-terrorism, Crime and Security Act 2001, Review, Report* (2003–04 HC 100) para C334.

s 54A(9) to use or disclose a photograph taken under this section for any purpose related to the prevention or detection of crime, the investigation of an offence, or the conduct of a prosecution. There is no corresponding power for Scotland.

5.51   Next, s 90(2) amends PACE ss 27 and 61 regarding fingerprints taken from an arrested person to establish or check their identity.[106] Once taken, these fingerprints can be retained whether or not the person is proceeded against or convicted,[107] but can be used only for the purposes of the prevention or detection of crime, the investigation of an offence, or the pursuit of a prosecution.

5.52   In further pursuance of the establishment of identity, s 92 (s 93 in Northern Ireland) inserts a new s 64A after s 64 of PACE 1984 which affords a power to photograph a person who is detained at a police station with or without consent. Section 92(2) expressly allows the police to require the removal of any item or substance, such as face paint, worn on or over the whole or any part of that person's face or head and if the person does not comply, may use force under s 117 of PACE 1984. While the purpose of the measure is mainly identification, sub-s (4) does allow for photographs to be used for criminal justice purposes and for them subsequently to be retained and used for a related purpose. The taking of photographs for these purposes does not infringe Art 8.[108]

5.53   The photographing of suspects outside a police station or otherwise is not closely regulated. Suspects targeted for surveillance may fall within the Regulation of Investigatory Powers Act 2000, Pt II, otherwise only the loose protections of 'private life' apply under Art 8 of the European Convention.[109] In line with ss 92 and 93 inside the police station, ss 94 and 95 (in Northern Ireland) replace s 60(4A) of the Criminal Justice and Public Order Act 1994 allowing the removal of face coverings worn for the purpose of concealing identity. Sections 94 and 95 provide that in relation to the power to require the removal of face coverings only, an authorization (in the form required by sub-s (6)) may be given (under s 60AA) where an inspector reasonably believes offences may take place in that locality and that it is expedient to give such an authorization. The authorization lasts for twenty-four hours, extendable for twenty-four hours by a superintendent. It is an offence to refuse to comply.

5.54   The police will be expected[110] to conform to the warning not to confuse the wearing of coverings intended as disguises with the fact that 'Many people customarily cover their heads or faces for religious reasons—for example, Muslim women, Sikh men, Sikh or Hindu women, or Rastafarian men or women.' The Forum against Islamophobia and

---

[106] Presumably because of the lesser threat from international terrorism, the measure no longer applies in Northern Ireland: Criminal Justice (Northern Ireland) Order 2004, SI 2004/1500 Sch 3. Police, Public Order and Criminal Justice (Scotland) Act 2006, s 82 also allows the taking of fingerprints to establish identity but they may not be retained.

[107] The blanket retention of samples breaches Art 8: *Rotaru v Romania*, App no 28341/95, 2000-V; *S and Marper v United Kingdom*, App no 30562/04; 30566/04, 4 December 2008. See also Privy Counsellor Review Committee, *Anti-terrorism, Crime and Security Act 2001, Review, Report* (2003–04 HC 100) paras B44, B45, C345; *Home Office Counter-Terrorism Powers* (Cm 6147, London, 2004) paras II.111, II.114.

[108] See *(Margaret) Murray v United Kingdom*, App no 14310/88, Ser A 300A (1994); *Kinnunen v Finland*, App no 24950/94, 15 May 1996 (Comm).

[109] See *Friedl v Austria*, App no 15225/89, Ser A 305B (1995); *Wood v Commissioner of Police of the Metropolis* [2009] EWCA Civ 414.

[110] PACE Code A, note 4. See Hansard HC vol 375, col 761 (26 November 2001), Beverley Hughes; Hansard HL vol 629, col 736 (4 December 2001), Lord Rooker; Home Office Circular 32/2002: *Anti-terrorism, Crime and Security Act 2001: Section 94 Removal of Disguises*.

Racism was not reassured and objected to these powers.[111] The Newton Committee argued that these extra powers to remove disguises should be confined to terrorism cases.[112] It is admitted that the motivation behind the legislation is not terrorism but 'because the police believe that the tactic of wearing face coverings has become increasingly widespread during all kinds of events that could lead to public disorder'.[113] There is also no equivalent in Scotland.[114] Thus, the 2001 Act was used as a sly vehicle of more general public order law reform, though the Minister of State argued that it would be impractical to categorize in advance trespassers as terrorists or otherwise. [115]

(d) *Information sharing*

Though the powers to take and retain fingerprints and samples are wider than under the PACE legislation, the purposes for which they can be utilized were originally limited by para 14 in that they could be used only for the purpose of a terrorist investigation and not for routine criminal checks under s 63A(1) of PACE 1984. However, the position was changed by s 84 of the Criminal Justice and Police Act 2001 which allows the subsequent use not only for the purposes of a terrorist investigation but also for purposes related to the prevention or detection of crime, the investigation of an offence, or the conduct of a prosecution. Secondly, the exclusion of checks against the fingerprints or samples under s 63A or its Northern Ireland equivalent is diminished since the purposes of the prevention or detection of crime, the investigation of an offence, or the conduct of a prosecution are again allowed. Thirdly, the relevant criminal investigations may relate to offences outside the United Kingdom.

5.55

Further data-sharing is facilitated by the Counter-Terrorism Act 2008 both by further allowing exchanges of data and also by providing legality for the collection of certain types of data. In pursuance of the latter objective, s 18 brings the personal identification data held by law enforcement organizations, such as on the Counter-Terrorism DNA Database though not confined to it, within legal regulation in regard to fingerprints or DNA samples. Without this basis, there is a ground for challenge under Art 8.[116] These samples derive from discarded cigarettes or drinks containers while acting under Pt III of the Police Act 1997, while conducting surveillance under Pt II of the Regulation of Investigatory Powers Act 2000, or otherwise lawfully obtained (such as from international partners).[117] Once legally grounded in this way, the materials can be used for national security, criminal justice, or identification purposes.

5.56

Having brought all material within a legal footing whether in police criminal databases, the Counter-Terrorism DNA Database, or security services databases, the next step measure is to allow disclosure between these databases and with foreign agencies. This goal is achieved by ss 14 to 18 of the 2008 Act.

5.57

---

[111] Submission to the Home Affairs Committee, London, 2001, para 6. See also Joint Committee on Human Rights, *Report on the Anti-terrorism, Crime and Security Bill* (2001–02 HL 37, HC 372) para 62.

[112] Privy Counsellor Review Committee, *Anti-terrorism, Crime and Security Act 2001, Review, Report* (2003–04 HC 100) paras B47, C352. The reform proposal was rejected: Home Office, *Counter-Terrorism Powers* (Cm 6147, London, 2004) para II.127.

[113] Hansard HC vol 375, col 760 (26 November 2001), Beverley Hughes.

[114] *Ibid* col 764.

[115] *Ibid* col 749.

[116] HC Hansard Public Bill Committee on the Counter-Terrorism Bill, col 225 (29 April 2008), Tony McNulty.

[117] Hansard HL vol 704, cols 396, 397 (9 October 2008), Lord West.

5.58   Section 14 allows for samples and prints obtained under PACE (s 15 applies in Northern Ireland, but Scotland awaits devolved legislation) to be utilized beyond the current purposes in ss 63A and 64 of PACE in the interests of national security,[118] or for criminal justice, or identification purposes. The police will thereby be allowed to check their PACE material, or counter-terrorism material, against the databases of the security services and vice versa.

5.59   The same trick is applied by s 16 to the counter-terrorism police who take samples under Sch 8 of the Terrorism Act 2000. The wording of para 14 is amended to allow cross-checking against PACE material, security service material, or material under s 18 (s 16). This means that police Terrorism Act samples can be entered on the NDNAD.[119] It remains unlikely, however, that the security database materials will be used in court since that would require explanations of the provenance of the materials, much of which was not governed by PACE codes.[120] Section 17 applies the same rules to Scotland.

5.60   The final aspect of the changes takes us back to s 18. The material covered there can be utilized by allowing a check against it or disclosing it between UK law enforcement or security agencies or indeed to 'any person' (s 18(4)), so long as used for proper purposes. The effect is to allow exchanges of this data with foreign policing or security agencies.[121]

5.61   Information-sharing was depicted in the Home Office, *Possible Measures* paper as one of the great advances to be achieved by the Counter-Terrorism Act.[122] This claim is dubious. Most of the limitations are not legal but, as found by the US 9/11 Commission, arise from institutional rivalries and suspicions,[123] or as the Bichard Report[124] also found, arise from the technical incompatibilities or the failure to invest.

5.62   Nevertheless, there are important advances brought about by Pt I of the Counter-Terrorism Act 2008. Its measures represent a worthy attempt at imparting legality within the principle of constitutionalism. However, the accountability of the police and, even more so, the security services, for policies made about the direction of resources in data collection and the retention of data samples remains weak.[125] The absence of regulation of retention is so acute as to amount to a breach of Art 8 of the European Convention, as confirmed by *S and Marper v United Kingdom*.[126] Oversight is by the Information Commissioner and the Forensic Science Regulator,[127] but the former is essentially responsive while the latter deals with systems, not people. There may also be overreach in terms

---

[118] See Security Service Act 1989, s 1.

[119] House of Commons Public Bill Committee on the Counter Terrorism Bill, col 222 (29 April 2008), Tony McNulty.

[120] *Ibid* col 220.

[121] Arrangements are being made for the sharing of police data under the Prüm Convention 2005 which was signed by the UK government in 2007 and is being further implemented by the Prüm Council Decision: 2008/615/JHA, Decision 2008/616/2008.

[122] Home Office, *Possible Measures for Inclusion into a Future Counter-Terrorism Bill* (London, 2007) paras 3, 23.

[123] See National Commission on Terrorist Attacks upon the United States, *The 9/11 Commission Report* (Washington, DC, 2004).

[124] See Bichard Inquiry, *Report* (2003–04 HC 653) and *Final Report* (Home Office, London, 2005).

[125] See ACPO, *Retention Guidelines for Nominal Records on the Police National Computer* (London, 2006). No policy statement has been issued by the security services.

[126] App nos 30562/04, 30566/04, 4 December 2008.

[127] Hansard HL vol 704, col 384 (9 October 2008), Lord West.

of the failure to regulate the weeding out of information which might have been obtained in breach of Art 3.[128]

(e) *Records*

The keeping of full and accurate records of the treatment of a detainee is a vital element of ensuring propriety and humanity. Reflecting PACE rules, a custody record must be kept for every detainee,[129] though individual police officer identification data[130] and the enhanced risk assessments do not form part of the custody record.[131]

As for records of interviews, Sch 8, para 3 deals with the audio and video recording provided they take place in a designated police station (which means that interviews at ports will not necessarily be taped). Statutory orders and codes of practice must be issued to ensure the implementation of audio recording, but the making of an order and code requiring the video recording is a matter of discretion. The Terrorism Act 2000 (Code of Practice on Audio Recording of Interviews) Order 2001[132] allows for a code of practice in connection with the audio recording. The Terrorism Act 2000 (Code of Practice on Audio Recording of Interviews) (No 2) Order 2001[133] demands that any interview shall be audio recorded in accordance with the audio code. By para 2.1 of the issued Code, the audio recording of interviews shall be carried out openly. By para 3.3, the whole of each interview shall be audio recorded, including the taking and reading back of any statement. In this way, there is no provision for 'off-the-record' conversations, though there is no definition of 'interview' and 'public safety interviews' apparently do not count.[134] Under para 5, an accurate record must also be made of each interview with a detained person, and the person interviewed must be given the opportunity under tape-recorded conditions to read the interview record and to sign it as correct or to indicate the respects in which he considers it inaccurate. By para 8, at the conclusion of criminal proceedings, or in the event of a direction not to prosecute, the contents of a working copy of the tape shall be completely erased.

In response to the history of abuses of prisoners, video recording first applied in Northern Ireland, beginning with overhead silent videos under the Northern Ireland (Emergency Provisions) Act 1996, s 53. A power in relation to full video recording in Northern Ireland subsisted in s 100 of the Terrorism Act 2000, but this power was never activated and has now been repealed.[135] The Terrorism Act 2000 (Video Recording of Interviews) Order 2000[136] provides for interviews only in Northern Ireland to be recorded by video with sound, and then the current Terrorism Act 2000 (Code of Practice on Video Recording of Interviews) (Northern Ireland) Order 2003[137] allows for a detailed code of practice. The source for these orders is paras 3 and 4 of Sch 8, and

5.63

5.64

5.65

---

[128] See Joint Committee on Human Rights, *Counter-Terrorism Policy and Human Rights: 42 days and public emergencies* (2007–08 HL 116, HC 635) paras 67, 73.
[129] PACE Code H para 2.
[130] *Ibid* para 2.8.
[131] PACE Code H para 3.8.
[132] SI 2001/159. See Home Office, *Code of Practice for the audio recording of interviews under the Terrorism Act 2000* (Stationery Office, London, 2001).
[133] SI 2001/189. PACE Code E is not applicable: para 3.2.
[134] *R v Ibrahim* [2008] EWCA Crim 880.
[135] Terrorism (Northern Ireland) Act 2006, s 2.
[136] SI 2000/3179.
[137] SI 2003/110, replacing SI 2001/402.

not s 100. There is no requirement for routine video recording of interviews elsewhere in Britain, though custody areas may be recorded,[138] and the police now often favour the video recording of interviews in terrorism cases.[139]

(f) Access to outsiders

5.66 Aspects of the PACE regime are applied without significant change to s 41 detainees, including the rules about appropriate adults[140] and persons responsible for the welfare of juveniles,[141] as well as interpreters.[142] Foreigners (including, for these purposes, Irish citizens detained in Britain) also have rights to contact and consult with consular officials.[143] Some consulates will even be informed automatically.[144] These rights arise pursuant to the Vienna Convention on Consular Relations 1963,[145] Art 36.1, as implemented by the Consular Relations Act 1968.[146]

5.67 Code H requires a medical check to be carried out at least daily after ninety-six hours.[147] The Scottish Guidelines of 2006 demand that there must be a medical check 'Towards the end of the initial 48 hour or any extended period of detention, or where the senior investigating officer indicates that s/he is considering releasing a detainees from a period of detention'.[148] The strictest rules are in Northern Ireland where medical checks are arranged on arrival, before any interview, every twenty-four hours, and on release.[149] In a study in England and Wales before 2001, it was found that 46 per cent of terrorism detainees saw a doctor; delay was authorized in 26 per cent of cases.[150] Doctors should consider not only medical fitness for interview and any signs of injury but also diet and exercise.[151]

5.68 Independent custody visitors may attend under the usual rules,[152] a scheme extended to Northern Ireland in 2005.[153] Code H also envisages the possibility of other 'official' visitors, including accredited faith representatives, members of either House of

---

[138] PACE Code H para 3.11; PACE Code F para 3.2.

[139] Joint Committee on Human Rights, *Counter-Terrorism Policy and Human Rights: 28 days, intercept and post-charge questioning* (2006–07 HL 157/HC 394) para 81.

[140] PACE Code H paras 1.13, 3.17.

[141] *Ibid* para 3.15.

[142] *Ibid* para 13.

[143] See *ibid* paras 3.3, 7; *(Colville) Review of the Operation of the Prevention of Terrorism (Temporary Provisions) Act 1984* (Cm. 264, London, 1987), paras 6.2.1, 6.2.2; *Colville Annual Report on the Operation in 1990 of the Prevention of Terrorism (Temporary Provisions) Acts* (Home Office) para 4.2.

[144] PACE Code H Annex F.

[145] Cmnd 2113, London, 1963.

[146] See Brown, D., *Detention under the Prevention of Terrorism Act* (Home Office Research and Planning Unit paper 75, London, 1993) pp 38–39.

[147] PACE Code H para 9.

[148] PACE Code H para 23.

[149] *Ibid* paras 9.2, 9.3. See Joint Committee on Human Rights, *Counter-Terrorism Policy and Human Rights: 28 days, intercept and post-charge questioning* (2006–07 HL 157/HC 394) paras 88, 91.

[150] Brown, D., *Detention under the Prevention of Terrorism Act* (Home Office Research and Planning Unit paper 75, London, 1993) p 35.

[151] Faculty of Forensic and Legal Medicine, Medical Care of Persons Detained under the Terrorism Act 2000 (<https://fflm.ac.uk/upload/documents/1189093340.pdf>, 2004).

[152] Police Reform Act 2002, s 51; Code of Practice on Independent Custody Visiting (Home Office, 2003).

[153] See Patten Report (Patten Commission (The Independent Commission on Policing for Northern Ireland), *A New Beginning: Policing in Northern Ireland* (Northern Ireland Office, Belfast, 1999) para 8.16.

Parliament, and public officials (such as from the security services) needing to interview the prisoner in the course of their duties.[154] There is no right of access in these cases.

Drawing further upon the PACE precedents,[155] rights to have a person informed of 5.69 the detention and to have access to a legal adviser are granted by paras 6 and 7 of Sch 8 of the Terrorism Act 2000.[156] The detainee must also be told clearly about the existence of these rights, but risk assessments will be carried out by the police of those to be contacted.[157] Guidance as to the right not to be held incommunicado places greater emphasis than normal on the grant of family visits which should be allowed where possible or, if not possible, more visits from independent custody visitors.[158]

The primary legal right of access comprises not only private consultation but also 5.70 securing the presence of the lawyer during the interview (para 7).[159] In Scotland, the relevant rights are set out in paras 16 and, in the absence of previous legislation or case law on presence of a lawyer at interview, para 19. The details have appeared as the Terrorism (Interviews) (Scotland) Order 2001.[160]

Delays to the exercise of these rights may be authorized by a superintendent under 5.71 para 8 for up to forty-eight hours. The grounds for doing so are equivalent to those in the PACE legislation, save that extra grounds are added to take account of the basis of the arrest in terrorism and not crime.[161] Writing materials and access to the telephone may be refused on similar grounds.[162] In Northern Ireland, the courts had set their face against the provision of writing materials,[163] so writing materials are allowed in the Code of Practice[164] only for the purpose of making representations about continued detention. Where delay is authorized, the detained person shall be told the reason for the delay as soon as is reasonably practicable, and the reason shall be recorded. Any decision to delay should be considered in the light of an actual request and the circumstances then prevailing; it would be wrong to lay down any blanket policy of denial or to deny in anticipation of a request.[165] To deny family notification even within the 48-hour limit may breach Art 8.[166]

A lawyer who is considered to impede the interviewing process by preventing proper 5.72 questioning of the detainee may be excluded under PACE Code H, though such a 'serious step' should probably be reported to the Law Society.[167] Other concerns about the presence of a given lawyer, either through intentional collusion or the relaying of

---

[154] PACE Code H para 5C.

[155] See PACE ss 56 and 58.

[156] See PACE Code H paras 5, 6.

[157] *Ibid* para 3.8. See further Home Office Circular 32/2000 *Detainee Risk Assessment & Revised Prisoner Escort Request (PER) Form.*

[158] PACE Code H paras 5.4, 5B. Compare Joint Committee on Human Rights, *Counter-Terrorism Policy and Human Rights: 28 days, intercept and post-charge questioning* (2006–07 HL 157/HC 394) para 101, and Government Reply (Cm 7215, London, 2007) p 8.

[159] Compare at common law: *R v Chief Constable of the Royal Ulster Constabulary, ex p Begley* [1997] 1 WLR 1475.

[160] SI 2001/428.

[161] Amended by the Proceeds of Crime Act 2002 and the Serious Organised Crime and Police Act 2005.

[162] PACE Code H para 5.6.

[163] *Re Floyd's Application and related applications* [1997] NI 414.

[164] See Terrorism Act 2000 (s 99) Code of Practice 2006 para 3G.

[165] *Cullen v Chief Constable of the Royal Ulster Constabulary* [2003] UKHL 39.

[166] 45 hours' delay was a breach in *McVeigh, O'Neill, and Evans v United Kingdom*, App nos 8022, 8025, 8027/77; DR 25 p 15 (1981).

[167] PACE Code H paras 6.10–6.12.

unwitting messages may give rise to a further residual power, unrelated to the Terrorism Act 2000, to exclude that lawyer. In *Malik v Chief Constable of Greater Manchester*,[168] the police excluded Malik's solicitor because of evidence from a video of a public meeting relating to recruitment for a terrorist organization. The video made reference to the solicitor's presence at the event. The police justifiably excluded that solicitor on the basis that he could be called as a witness to the nature of the meeting. The action could perhaps be explained as falling with para 8 as amounting to an interference with, or harm to, evidence. After forty-eight hours, the arguments would have to rest on broad common law powers to prevent interferences with the administration of justice. By contrast, the court emphasized that issues such as conflicts of interest in representing multiple defendants were for the solicitor to address rather than the police.

5.73   Legal advice was declared in *Cullen v Chief Constable of the Royal Ulster Constabulary*[169] to be 'a quasi-constitutional right of fundamental importance in a free society'. The establishment of this quasi-right did not, however, found any action for damages. However, its breach may impact on the fairness of any later trial. In *(John) Murray v United Kingdom*,[170] the European Court of Human Rights concluded that it would be incompatible with the right to a fair trial to base a conviction solely or mainly on the accused's silence. In addition, inferences drawn in unfair circumstances, such as where there had been a denial of access to a lawyer for forty-eight hours, would contravene Art 6(1) in conjunction with Art 6(3)(c).[171] In line with this warning, the government expects deferment to be limited to 'exceptional cases'.[172] PACE Code H further advises that the total exclusion of legal advice means that adverse inferences from silence cannot be drawn.[173]

5.74   Another qualification to the exercise of the right of access to a lawyer, particular to the Terrorism Act 2000, is that a direction may be given under para 9 (para 17 in Scotland) that a detained person may consult a solicitor only in the sight and hearing of a 'qualified officer' (an inspector).[174] This serious intrusion must be authorized by an officer of at least the rank of Commander or Assistant Chief Constable and only if the officer giving it has reasonable grounds for believing that, unless the direction is given, the exercise of the right by the detained person will have any of the consequences specified as for delay. Even with these restraints, it is very doubtful whether access to legal advice under these circumstances can ever meet the standards of Art 6 of the European Convention. In *Brennan v United Kingdom*,[175] the presence of the police during a consultation session with the detainee's solicitor triggered a breach of Art 6: '. . . the Court cannot but conclude that the presence of the police officer would have inevitably prevented the applicant from speaking frankly to his solicitor and given him reason to hesitate before

---

[168] [2006] EWHC 2396 (Admin).
[169] [2003] UKHL 39 at para 67 per Lord Millett.
[170] App no 18731/91, Reports 1996-I. See further Flaherty, M.S., 'Interrogation, legal advice and human rights in Northern Ireland' (1997) 27 *Columbia Human Rights Law Review* 1.
[171] *Ibid* at para 66. See also *Averill v United Kingdom,* App no 36408/97, 2000-VI; *Magee v United Kingdom*, App no 28135/95, 2000-VI.
[172] Hansard HC vol 346, col 375 (15 March 2000), Charles Clarke.
[173] PACE Code H para 6.7(b).
[174] As amended by the Counter-Terrorism Act 2008, s 82.
[175] App no 39846/98, 2001-X, para 62. The Body of Principles for the Protection of All Persons under Any Form of Detention or Imprisonment (UNGA res 43/173 of 9 December 1988) principle 18.4 does not allow for hearing in any circumstances.

broaching questions of potential significance to the case against him.' Covert surveillance may also be conducted under the Regulation of Investigatory Powers Act 2000, Pt II, according to *McE v Prison Service of Northern Ireland*, with some regret from the House of Lords that the Home Secretary had not yet taken steps by order to assimilate the directed surveillance to the scrutiny level required for intrusive surveillance.[176]

Subsequent to *Brennan*, the Home Office issued Circular 42/2003,[177] in which it is emphasized that para 9 remains viable only in 'limited circumstances'. Two factors considered to be of particular relevance to indicating the need for legal advice are whether the suspect has been cooperative and answering questions and whether the suspect could be considered vulnerable, not only in terms of mental or physical attributes but also because of restricted language ability and cultural differences or even 'overwhelming or prolonged emotional distress'.[178] It may have been more straightforward to abolish para 9. Instead, any unacceptable lawyer should be excluded, and this action should be justified in court, as in *Malik*. 5.75

As well as the express powers under para 9, it was accepted in *Re C*[179] that the police can lawfully refuse to give assurances not to engage in covert surveillance, but it was emphasized that confidentiality of legal advice is a fundamental right, and it was also accepted that the process of surveillance might be subject to the Regulation of Investigatory Powers Act 2000, s 28. Objections may also arise when the surveillance captures members of Parliament who talk with constituents who have been arrested or charged. The interception of their communications under the Regulation of Investigatory Powers Act 2000, Pt I, is subject to prime ministerial oversight under the Wilson Doctrine, and the surveillance of their prison visits can be exempted under the Approved Visitors Scheme.[180] 5.76

Deferment of rights to legal advice is becoming uncommon.[181] The reasons for the trend relate to pressure from legal challenges and reviews by national and international bodies.[182] A possible third reason is the influence of 'normal' practices under PACE 1984 and the police acceptance of the compatibility of solicitors within the police working environment. This attitude did not always prevail in Northern Ireland,[183] where there are allegations of police collusion in the murders of two prominent Northern Ireland lawyers, Pat Finucane in 1989[184] and Rosemary Nelson in 1999,[185] though most problems relate to police actions before 2000.[186] 5.77

---

[176] [2009] UKHL 15 at para 52.

[177] (Home Office, London, 2003) paras 9, 12.

[178] *Ibid* para 15.

[179] [2007] NIQB 101.

[180] See Chief Surveillance Commissioner, *Report on Two Visits by Sadiq Khan, MP, to Babar Ahmed at HM Prison Woodall* (Cm 7336, London, 2008).

[181] Compare Brown, D., *Detention under the Prevention of Terrorism Act* (Home Office Research and Planning Unit paper 75, London, 1993) pp 9–10, 17–18, 21–23, 28.

[182] See, for example, United Nations Committee against Torture, *4th Report under Article 19 by the United Kingdom of Great Britain and Northern Ireland* (CAT/C/67/Add.2, 2004) para 85.

[183] See Stevens Enquiry 3, *Overview and Recommendations* (Metropolitan Police Service, London, 2003).

[184] See Cory Collusion Inquiry Report, *Pat Finucane* (2003–04 HC 470); Rolston, B., 'An effective mask for terror' (2005) 44 *Crime, Law & Social Change* 181.

[185] See Cory Collusion Inquiry Report, *Rosemary Nelson* (2003–04 HC 473) and Rosemary Nelson Inquiry (<http://www.rosemarynelsoninquiry.org/>).

[186] Police Ombudsman for Northern Ireland, *A Study of the Treatment of Solicitors and Barristers by the Police in Northern Ireland* (Belfast, 2003).

Table 5.1 **Access to lawyers and family in Northern Ireland**[187]

	Lawyer		Family	
	Granted (% of detainees)	Delayed	Granted (% of detainees)	Delayed
2001	124 (69%)	1	32 (18%)	0
2002	232 (98%)	0	130 (55%)	0
2003	354 (99%)	0	167 (47%)	1
2004	223 (97%)	4	102 (44%)	3
2005	246 (99%)	0	81 (33%)	0
2006	213 (99%)	0	114 (53%)	3

4. Assessment

(a) *Evaluation of the power to arrest*

5.78 The arguments favouring exceptionally broad powers to arrest must principally reside in the effectiveness of the opportunity which is afforded to gather information or to disrupt dangerous activities.[188] The gathering of intelligence is said to be a 'crucial' strategy in dealing with terrorism,[189] and it may in any event be difficult to disentangle intelligence-gathering from forensic interrogation.[190] The low ratio of arrests to ensuing criminal charges in terrorism cases compared to 'normal' arrests does seem to corroborate that intelligence-gathering is an important objective. In this way, special arrest powers evidently are meant to serve the interests of 'Pursuit', but by allowing pre-emptive or speculative arrests, 'Prevent' may also be achieved through deterrence and disruption.

5.79 The police view is that special arrest powers have proven the most 'critical' measure in successive anti-terrorist legislation.[191] The data as to usage shows constant and discerning invocation, though the validity of the police endorsement could only be proven through in-depth studies of the uniqueness of the s 41 power in given cases.

Table 5.2 **Arrests under s 41 in Britain**[192]

Year	Arrests			Charges (% of arrests)	Other action (eg deport) (% of arrests)
	Arrests	(i) Intern't'l (ii) Irish (iii) Domestic	At port/other place		
2001	131	92 / 37 / 2	34 / 97	41 (31%)	22 (17%)

---

[187] Source: NIO Statistics & Research Branch.

[188] See Walker, C., 'Intelligence and Anti-terrorism Legislation in the United Kingdom' (2006) 44 *Crime, Law & Social Change* 387.

[189] Wilkinson, P., *Terrorism versus Democracy* (Frank Cass, London, 2000), p 105.

[190] *Review of the Northern Ireland (Emergency Provisions) Act 1991* (Cm 2706 London, 1995) para 126.

[191] *Inquiry into Legislation against terrorism* (Cm 3420, London, 1996) para 4.14.

[192] Source: Carlile Reports. The figures for 2001 are from 19 February, and '2001' covers until the end of February 2002.

Table 5.2 (continued) Arrests under s 41 in Britain

2002	193	141 / 37 / 15	30 / 163	74 (38%)	42 (22%)
2003	275	213 / 40 / 22	23 / 252	94 (34%)	31 (11%)
2004	162	137 / 16 / 9	11 / 151	40 (25%)	30 (19%)
2005	266	237 / 21 / 8	16 / 250	35 (13%)	10 (4%)
2006	185	not disclosed	not disclosed	85 (46%)	6 (3%)
2007	257	not disclosed	not disclosed	92 (36%)	9 (4%)
Total	**1469**	**n/a**	**n/a**	**461 (31%)**	**150 (10%)**

In 2006, the data for 'arrests' include twenty-nine cases which are described as effected under other legislation where the investigation was conducted as a terrorist investigation. This inclusion may have inflated the charging rate.

Table 5.3 Arrests under s 41 in Northern Ireland[193]

Year	Arrests	Extended detention (% of arrests)	Extended detention (days)			Charges (% of arrests)	Time of charge (a) <48 hrs (b) 48hrs–7 days (c) 7–14 days (d) 15–28 days
			48 hrs –7 days	7–14 days	14–28 days		
2001	179	12 (7%)	9	n/a	n/a	50 (28%)	(a) 45 (b) 5
2002	236	12 (5%)	12	n/a	n/a	80 (34%)	(a) 74 (b) 6
2003	359	23 (6%)	23	n/a	n/a	121 (34%)	(a) 112 (b) 9
2004	230	16 (7%)	16	0	n/a	69 (30%)	(a) 60 (b) 9
2005	249	24 (10%)	24	0	n/a	73 (29%)	(a) 61 (b) 12
2006	215	14 (7%)	14	0	0	62 (29%)	(a) 54 (b) 8
Total	**1468**	**101(7%)**	**98**	**0**	**0**	**455 (31%)**	**(a) 406 (b) 49**

The returns in Northern Ireland are notably more settled compared to Britain, probably a reflection both of greater experience in handling the powers and also greater knowledge about the terrorist threat. Extensions of detentions are becoming relatively uncommon at this stage of the conflict (25 per cent was the rate before this decade) and are below the British level. Nevertheless, the rate of charging remains at the low British level. Very few applications for extension are refused. One notable exception related to Colin Duffy and others, arrested in 2009 for the murder of two soliders in Antrim;[194] Duffy was immediately rearrested and charged.

An alternative view of s 41 is that it affords excessive and oppressive powers. Several disadvantages can flow. First, there is damage is to the legitimacy of the criminal justice system through miscarriages of justice over thirty years.[195] A direct causal effect might be traced through those cases which depended on confessions. The May Inquiry Final Report, following the case of the Guildford Four, acutely observed that, 'If all the safe

5.80

---

[193] Source: NIO Statistics & Research Branch. Note: 2001 from 19 February (ie commencement of Terrorism Act 2000). There is no record of 'other disposals' (such as deportation) in Northern Ireland.

[194] Re Duffy [2009] NIQB 31

[195] See Walker, C. (ed), Miscarriages of Justice (Oxford University Press, Oxford, 1999) ch 2.

guards of PACE are necessary to avoid miscarriages of justice then it must be recognized that in terrorist cases greater risks of injustice are accepted than in the ordinary course of criminal cases.'[196]

5.81   The second danger is to community relations, which derives from concern about how suspects from a given community are treated in detention and also the targeting of vulnerable minorities for arrest. The perception of too many detainees is that they are detained 'primarily because they are Irish'[197] or, one might say now, because they are perceived as 'Muslim', though the two phenomena cannot be exactly equated.[198] The Equality Impact Assessment carried out in relation to the Counter-Terrorism Bill[199] unearthed strong impressions that the powers were unfairly targeted against Muslims, as a result of which they were less willing to volunteer help to the police.

5.82   Adopting a rights audit, the justification of s 41 under Art 5(1)(c) of the European Convention must rest on the rational connection and success of the power for the purpose of gathering intelligence against terrorism, as already assessed. There are some guarantees against abuse—a basis in reasonable suspicion and extensions which require 'relevant evidence' which is formulated in terms of offences.[200] Furthermore, the European Court of Human Rights has acceded to the use of the term 'terrorism' so far as its substance remains close to the concept of crimes. In other respects, the guarantees against abuse are not as extensive as possible. There is no code equivalent to PACE Code G (for the statutory power of arrest by police officers). Another deficiency is that s 41 is not limited by the 'necessity criteria', as specified by PACE, s 24(4).[201] 'Necessity' here should also require a prioritization of PACE powers ahead of terrorism legislation. In the light of these features, one might uphold as proportionate a special initial power to arrest so as to allow for a broad inquiry and for intelligence-gathering, which may lead to further criminal investigations or may trigger executive disposals such as control or deportation orders. Nevertheless, it is arguable that the power could be easily limited in ways which avoided vagueness and such a high rate of release without charge—such as being limited to lists of 'scheduled' offences, as was argued in Chapter 1. Even more radical would be the abolition of s 41 as a power to arrest, leaving only special extensions to PACE periods of detention.

5.83   On the standard of accountability, there are many deficiencies. The level of information provision about what is crucial for charging or extended detention is very limited. There is more reassurance that Parliament has applied close scrutiny, as has the Independent Police Complaints Commission, which has called in all complaints relating to terrorism arrests and also suggested that they be filmed.[202] The performance of the judiciary is more variable, though *Raissi* suggests a willingness to delve deeper.

---

[196] May, Sir John, Report of the Inquiry into the circumstances surrounding the convictions arising out of the bomb attacks in Guildford and Woolwich in 1974, *Final Report* (1993–94 HC 449) para 21.8.

[197] Hillyard, P., *Suspect Community* (Pluto Press, London, 1993) at p 7.

[198] Greer, S., 'Human Rights and the struggle against terrorism in the United Kingdom' [2008] *European Human Rights Law Review* 163.

[199] (Home Office, London, 2008) pp 4, 5.

[200] sch 8 para 32.

[201] See Serious Organised Crime and Police Act 2005, s 110; Police and Criminal Evidence (Amendment) (Northern Ireland) Order 2007 SI 2007/288 art 15.

[202] See <http://www.ipcc.gov.uk/news/pr250105_antiterror.htm>; *The Times* 18 January 2005 p 2.

(b) *Evaluation of the detention powers*

Accountability and constitutional governance for the attendant detention power pre- 5.84
sents a mixed picture. On the one hand, the debates in 2000, 2006, and 2008 (though
not in 2003) about the length of detention were exhaustive. On the other hand, the level
of information—statistics on arrest and detention—is not as detailed nor as accessible as
existed under the pre-Terrorism Act 2000 legislation.[203]

The key criticisms within a rights audit are based on incursion upon liberty, and 5.85
assessments may be conducted on grounds of productivity in terms of results, proportionality, the wider drawbacks to society, and the sufficiency of safeguards.

The general picture as to use is that most detentions in Britain are for less than seven 5.86
days and all have done so in Northern Ireland (see Table 5.3). Thus, the main criticism
should focus on detentions between four to seven days, which have a high rate of non-
charging but still involve exceptional incursion into liberty.

Table 5.4 Detention periods in Britain 2001–2007[204]

Detention less than 24 Hours (% within this period)		*% of total detentions*
Released without charge	353 (70%)	
Other disposal ie charge, caution, bailed, immigration, etc	151 (30%)	
Total	**504**	**43%**
Detention between 1 day and 7 days		
Released without charge	272 (49%)	
Other disposal ie charge, caution, bailed, immigration, etc	278 (51%)	
	550	47%
Detention between 7 and 14 days		
Released without charge	23 (23%)	
Other disposal ie charge, caution, bailed, immigration, etc	75 (75%)	
	98	9%
Detention beyond 14 days		
Released without charge	3	
Other disposal ie charge, caution, bailed, immigration, etc	8	
	11	1%

---

[203] See Joint Committee on Human Rights, *Counter-Terrorism Policy and Human Rights: 28 days, intercept and post-charge questioning* (2006–07 HL 157/HC 394) paras 32–42; Joint Committee on Human Rights, *Counter-Terrorism Policy and Human Rights: Annual Renewal of 28 days* (2007–08 HL 32/HC 825) para 19.

[204] Source: Counter-Terrorism Command, Metropolitan Police Service, 2008.

Table 5.4 (continued) Detention periods in Britain 2001–2007

Overall		
Released without charge	651 (56%)	
Other disposal ie charge, caution, immigration etc	512 (44%)	
No detention time recorded	3	
	1166	100%

5.87   Before the era of the Terrorism Act 2000, and mainly therefore focused upon Irish terrorist suspects, the total average interviewing time was around 3 hours 8 minutes and the total average detention length was 28 hours 23 minutes,[205] with 22 per cent being held for more than 48 hours. These rates are much longer than PACE 1984, where the average detention is around six hours and where around 95 per cent of detentions are less than 24 hours.

5.88   The controversy over the extended periods under the Terrorism Act 2006 elicited the following more detailed information, which shows a restrained usage and a high rate of charging. All occurred in Britain in relation to international terrorism. No detention beyond fourteen days has occurred since renewal of the power in 2007.[206]

Table 5.5 Detentions beyond fourteen days from 25 July 2006 to 19 February 2008[207]

Period of detention	*No of detainees*	*Charged*
14 to 15 days	1	1
18 to 19 days	1	1
19 to 20 days	3	3
27 to 28 days	6	3
Total	11	8

5.89   As for productivity, though the claim that an increase on detention powers 'has enabled suspects to be charged who may otherwise have had to be released',[208] hard evidence that the rate of charging is increased by the choice of special powers or by the elongation of detention periods could only be discerned by detailed case studies. Following PACE arrests, 52 per cent are charged and 17 per cent are cautioned.[209] The ratios have remained significantly lower for terrorism arrests, despite their exhaustive investigations and enhanced resources.[210] At the same time, it has already been argued that one of the

---

[205] Brown, D., *Detention under the Prevention of Terrorism Act* (Home Office Research and Planning Unit paper 75, London, 1993) pp 31, 50.
[206] Joint Committee on Human Rights, *Counter-Terrorism Policy and Human Rights: Annual Renewal of 28 days* (2007–08 HL 32/HC 825) para 24.
[207] Hansard HC vol 477, col 685W (16 June 2008), Tony McNulty.
[208] Home Office, *Options for Pre-Charge Detention in Terrorist Cases* (London, 2007) p 5.
[209] Phillips, C. and Brown, D., Entry into the Criminal Justice System: A Study of Police Arrests and their Outcomes (Home Office Research Study 185, 1998) p 82.
[210] But the rate has risen from 31%: Brown, D., *Detention under the Prevention of Terrorism Act* (Home Office Research and Planning Unit paper 75, London, 1993) p 49.

main purposes of s 41 arrests is intelligence-gathering, and so the lower rate of charging may be expected. This claim makes it yet more complex to judge 'productivity'. Intelligence is not made public in courts, and the police do not disclose the amount or quality of intelligence gathered from each arrest.

A more specific justification offered is that these detention periods are required   5.90
because of the amount of evidence generated by the complex and multiple attacks such as on 21 July 2005 (when there were 38,000 exhibits, 80,000 CCTV videos, 1,400 finger-prints, and 160 crime scenes)[211] or in the case of Barot.[212] But the generation of a large amount of evidence does not demonstrate that it was impossible within fourteen days to show sufficient evidence for a prosecution to succeed on the basis of serious charges. A surfeit of evidence is not a reason for more detention time. Charges were brought against the 21/7 bombers and against Barot which resulted in convictions and lengthy sentences. Another case which might be considered is the 2006 airline plot,[213] which did result in acquittals on some of the most serious charges—does that show more time was needed? The problem raised at the time was the early police intervention being precipi-tated by the arrest of Rashid Rauf in Pakistan.[214] Any amount of extra time in detention could not make up for lost covert evidence-gathering pre-arrest. Nor has it been alleged that other arrestees have been released and have gone on to engage in further terrorism.

In summary, the extension of detention beyond the four-day norm is yet to be empiric-   5.91
ally justified, and there is no compelling factual case for an extension beyond fourteen days. Probably the best one can say is that police experience does show that arrest up to fourteen days is constantly valued. Of course, it is always possible that more incriminat-ing evidence may turn up if more time were to be given.[215] It is always possible that any person released, whether suspected criminal or suspected terrorist, might commit a future offence. But on that logic, police detention should be unlimited, and liberty should be abolished. Any residual risk might also be alleviated by resort to control orders for those who are released without charge or even acquitted in court. In the case of Rauf Abdullah Mohammad, having been acquitted under the Terrorism Act 2000, s 57, he was immediately subjected to a control order, dubbed a 'conviction lite'.[216]

Regarding the proportionality of any gains to the objectives of Pursuit or Prevent set   5.92
against the infringement of liberty, it might first be noted that persons suspected of seri-ous arrestable offences can only be detained for up to ninety-six hours under the PACE legislation, so why should terrorists pose more difficulty? Despite several recent reviews of PACE, there has been no movement towards extended detention periods. As for pro-portionality to the practices of other democratic societies, no other country within Western Europe, nor comparable common law jurisdiction elsewhere, matches the United Kingdom's limit of 28 days' police detention.[217] However, this finding is subject to the civil law practice of lengthy judicial investigation and to common law substitute

---

[211] Hansard HC vol 438, col 341 (26 October 2005), Charles Clarke.
[212] See Carlisle, D., 'Dhiren Barot' (2007) 30 *Studies in Conflict & Terrorism* 1057.
[213] Home Office, *Options for Pre-Charge Detention in Terrorist Cases* (London, 2007) p 5.
[214] See *The Guardian* 10 September 2008 p 11.
[215] Home Office, *Options for Pre-Charge Detention in Terrorist Cases* (London, 2007) pp 6, 7.
[216] See *The Times* 30 August 2006 p 4 (quoting Gareth Crossman, Liberty).
[217] See further Foreign & Commonwealth Office, *Counter-Terrorism Legislation and Practice: A Survey of Selected Countries* (London, 2005); JUSTICE, *From Arrest To Charge In 48 Hours: Complex terrorism cases in the US since 9/11* (London, 2007); Russell, J., *Charge or release: Terrorism Pre-Charge Detention Comparative Law Study* (Liberty, London, 2007).

approaches extending even to the extremes of military detention at Guantánamo Bay and extraordinary rendition for surrogate interrogation elsewhere.

5.93   The wider drawbacks to society relate again to the generation of miscarriages of justice and also community distrust, as already discussed.

5.94   Given the extraordinary elongation of detention periods since 2003, more safeguards could be conceived to keep these periods within bounds. For example, it could be specified that a warrant should not last more than forty-eight hours at a stretch up to seven days and perhaps no more than ninety-six hours between seven and fourteen days. Another important safeguard would be a presumption of presence at hearings and that evidence will be revealed. The greater structuring of hearings beyond fourteen days would also be helpful with more explicit checklists to encourage judicial involvement.[218] If hearings are to be held in the absence of the accused, then judges should be able to appoint special advocates. There should also be verification of any application beyond seven days by a higher police officer such as an Assistant Chief Constable.[219] Finally, police reviews should formally continue after forty-eight hours, and police bail should be available.

5.95   These debates around the practices of special detention must next be set in the context of Art 5 of the European Convention. No absolute time limit is set in Art 5(1)(c) of the European Convention. Nevertheless, the detainee remains in police hands under Sch 8 rather than under the auspices of the 'competent legal authority'. The indulgence to test out reasonable suspicions is surely not endless if liberty is to be meaningful. Where the tolerance for genuine police endeavours ends will be determined on a case-by-case basis and more time will certainly be allowed in the context of terrorism investigations.[220]

5.96   The detention powers are more vulnerable to challenge under the remainder of Art 5. Article 5(2) requires prompt disclosure of the reasons for the arrest and the charges against the detainee.[221] If the latter is taken literally, as requiring charges to be laid promptly, then the reasoning in *Brogan* might suggest that police detention without charge for more than a few days cannot be acceptable, despite longer judicially directed detentions in civil law systems. Even under Art 5(3), the European Court in *McKay v United Kingdom*,[222] emphasized the need for a review which is prompt, automatic, and without requiring action by the detainee, conducted by an independent officer who can order release, and examining the lawfulness of the detention as well as due diligence. The mechanisms under Sch 8 go a long way to meeting these criteria. However, whether the judicial inquiry in a context going on well beyond seven days is sufficiently regular, sufficiently extensive, and sufficiently open[223] remains to be tested. Other problems arise under Art 5(4). The form of judicial hearings are not fully adversarial since disclosure is limited and there might

---

[218] See Lord Carlile, *Report on the Operation in 2007 of the Terrorism Act 2000* (Home Office, London, 2008) para 105.

[219] Joint Committee on Human Rights, *Counter-Terrorism Policy and Human Rights: Terrorism Bill and related matters* (2005–05 HL 75, HC 561) para 102.

[220] The Joint Committee on Human Rights, Criminal Justice Bill (2002–03 HC 724, HL 119) advised that the extended period did not *per se* breach Art 5 of the European Convention (para 102).

[221] Joint Committee on Human Rights, *Counter-Terrorism Policy and Human Rights: Counter-Terrorism Bill* (2007–08 HL 50, HC 199) para 18.

[222] App no 543/03, 3 October 2006, paras 33–5, 40, 46.

[223] See Joint Committee on Human Rights, *Counter-Terrorism Policy and Human Rights: 42 days* (2007–08 HL 23/HC 156) paras 83, 84 (in 3 out of 17 cases of detention beyond 14 days the suspect was excluded); Joint Committee on Human Rights, *Counter-Terrorism Policy and Human Rights, Counter-Terrorism Bill* (2007–08 HL 108/HC 554) paras 31–3.

even be *ex parte* hearings,[224] nor are they based on a full review of the merits of the detention,[225] although the terms of para 32 are broad enough for the matter to be raised, and the decision by the Northern Ireland High Court in *Re Duffy* asserts that it would amount to 'neglect' if the lawfulness of the basis for the arrest was not considered.[226]

Given the doubts raised about the proportionality or even legality of existing deten- 5.97
tion powers, would it be possible to justify a period of forty-two days (as embodied in the Counter-Terrorism Bill 2007–08)[227] or ninety days (as in the Terrorism Bill 2005–06)?[228] Since both versions were defeated in Parliament, it is not intended to examine the details of the proposals or every counter-argument. The only further point which is worth raising and which proved influential in debates is that more apposite reforms should be undertaken. Concentration should be upon widening the available charges so that they can fit evidence of preparations rather than completed plots, a notion which has largely been achieved by the offences of engaging in preparatory actions just passed under the Terrorism Act 2006. Next, there could be a widening of admissible evidence through changes in the rules relating to intercept evidence, again taken up following the Chilcot Report,[229] even though official reports downplay its future impact.[230] Thirdly, there should be encouragement to rely upon the Threshold Test for prosecutions which demands only reasonable suspicion at the point of charge where a complex investigation is continuing and there is a reasonable expectation of further evidence becoming available to meet the Full Code Test.[231] It is frequently used in terrorist cases.[232] Fourthly, there should be greater opportunities for post-charge questioning. The Counter-Terrorism Act 2008 has now implemented this tactic. Fifthly, beyond the extraordinary detention powers in

---

[224] See HC Hansard Public Bill Committee on the Counter-Terrorism Bill, Evidence from Susan Hemming, col 56 (22 April 2008). The use of *ex parte* hearings is said to be very limited: col 56.

[225] See *Garcia Alva v Germany*, App no 23541/94, 13 February 2001 para 39; Joint Committee on Human Rights, *Counter-Terrorism Policy and Human Rights, Counter-Terrorism Bill* (2007–08 HL 108/HC 554) para 21.

[226] [2009] NIQB 31 at para 26. Compare *R (on the application of Hussain) v Collins* [2006] EWHC 2467 (Admin) at para 16.

[227] No 63 cl 22. See Home Office, *Options for Pre-Charge Detention in Terrorist Cases* (London, 2007); Joint Committee on Human Rights, *Counter-Terrorism Policy and Human Rights: 42 days* (2007–08 HL 23/HC 156); Joint Committee on Human Rights, *Counter-Terrorism Policy and Human Rights: 42 days and public emergencies* (2007–08 HL 116/HC 635); House of Commons Home Affairs Committee, *The Government's Counter-Terrorism Proposals* (2007–08 HC 43); House of Lords Constitution Committee, *Counter-Terrorism Bill: The role of ministers, Parliament and the judiciary* (2007–08 HL 167).

[228] HC no 55 cl 23. See Joint Committee on Human Rights, *Counter-Terrorism Policy and Human Rights: Terrorism Bill and related matters* (2005–06 HL 75, HC 561) and *Government Response* (2005–06 HL114/HC 888); House of Commons Home Affairs Committee, *Terrorism Detention Powers* (2005–06 HC 910); Lord Carlile, *Proposals by Her Majesty's Government for Changes to the Laws against Terrorism* (Home Office, 2005). For the substitution of 28 days, see Hansard HC vol 439, col 357 (9 November 2005), David Winnick.

[229] *Privy Council Review of intercept as evidence: report to the Prime Minister and the Home Secretary* (Cm 7324, London, 2008).

[230] *Ibid* paras 53, 58. Compare Joint Committee on Human Rights, *Counter–Terrorism Policy and Human Rights: 28 days, intercept and post-charge questioning* (2006–07 HL 157/HC 394) paras 120, 123.

[231] Code for Prosecutors (Crown Prosecution Service, London, 2004) para 6. See House of Commons Home Affairs Committee, *Detention Powers* (2005–06 HC 910) para 112; Joint Committee on Human Rights, *Counter-Terrorism Policy and Human Rights: Prosecution and Pre-Charge Detention* (2005–06 HL 240, HC 1576) para 131.

[232] See Joint Committee on Human Rights, *Counter-Terrorism Policy and Human Rights: Counter-Terrorism Bill* (2007–08 HL 50, HC 199) para 77; House of Commons Home Affairs Committee, *The Government's Counter-Terrorism Proposals* (2007–08 HC 43) para 67.

the Terrorism Act 2000 are precautionary measures such as control orders and the extensive powers in the Civil Contingencies Act 2004 which might be invoked in an emergency.[233]

5.98   The government's conclusion to this debate was the petulant reaction by the Home Secretary[234] who flourished a draft Bill within hours of defeat of the 42-day proposal in the House of Lords.[235] The Counter-Terrorism (Temporary Provisions) Bill 2008, reviving 42-day detention but embodying few of the previous safeguards,[236] will be tabled as and when necessary.

(c) Evaluation of the conditions of detention

5.99   During a period of lengthy police detention, augmented safeguards for the prisoner are essential to avert the enhanced opportunities for abuse and ill-treatment or 'a significant risk of psychological forms of ill-treatment'.[237] One should question whether the Terrorism Act 2000 has achieved sufficient progress to meet its inherent challenge to the right to humane treatment under Art 3 and due process under Art 6.

5.100   Several other safeguards can be conceived which are currently lacking and would aid claims to proportionality. One of the more radical would be a special rule of inadmissibility of any statements or silences if made after the normal PACE period of four days. After that point,[238] the inherent oppression in the suppression of liberty warrants protection of the suspect, regardless of time needed for forensic examinations or checks with foreign agencies.[239] The second suggestion, floated during debates on forty-two and ninety days, is to pay compensation to anyone held for more than four days and not charged. Thirdly, more detailed rules are needed as to living conditions, such as clothing, reading and writing materials, exercise, natural light, and clocks. PACE Code H's brutal solution is simply a transfer to prison detention after fourteen days.[240] The government has stalled on refurbishment of detention facilities.[241] Fourthly, the 'safety interview', an off-the-record discussion in order to protect life or against serious property damage, as revealed in R v Ibrahim,[242] should never be the basis for any incriminating statement or silence. In that case, the police had warned that his statements would be recorded and used in evidence and the statements did not constitute the prime evidence of the offence. Thus, the court was cautious but set too little store by the fact that legal advice had been

---

[233] See Home Office, *Options for Pre-Charge Detention in Terrorist Cases* (London, 2007) pp 7, 11; Joint Committee on Human Rights, *Counter-Terrorism Policy and Human Rights: 42 days* (2007–08 HL 23/HC 156) paras 54–5.

[234] See HC Hansard vol 480, col 620 (13 October 2008).

[235] See HL Hansard vol 704, col 491 (13 October 2008), Lord Dear.

[236] HL Hansard vol 703, col 687 (8 July 2008), Lord Steyn.

[237] European Committee for the Prevention of Torture in regard to the Castlereagh Holding Centre in Belfast (CPT/Inf(94) 17, 1994) para 109.

[238] Before that point, the courts can assess the impact on Art 6 case-by-case: *Latimer v United Kingdom*, App no 12141/04, 31 May 2005.

[239] Lord Carlile, *Proposals by Her Majesty's Government for Changes to the Laws against Terrorism* (Home Office, London, 2005) para 60.

[240] Joint Committee on Human Rights, *Counter-Terrorism Policy and Human Rights: 28 days, intercept and post-charge questioning* (2006-07 HL 157/HC 394) para 73. Most are in fact transferred, but the Council of Europe Committee for the Prevention of Torture and Inhuman and Degrading Treatment argues that transfer should be compulsory: *Report to the United Kingdom Government on the Visit to the United Kingdom carried out by the European Committee for the Prevention of Torture and Inhuman and Degrading Treatment* (CPT/Inf (2008) 27, para 7) and *Response of the United Kingdom Government* (CPT/Inf (2008) 28, paras 6, 9).

[241] *Government Reply* (Cm 7429, London, 2008) p 6.

[242] [2008] EWCA Crim 880.

improperly refused.[243] Fifthly, the continuous independent oversight of detention conditions should involve the revival of the office of the Independent Commissioner for Detained Terrorist Suspects which was discontinued in 2005.[244] The work was taken up by the Northern Ireland Policing Board (including its Independent Custody Visiting Scheme), but it suffers shortcomings in comparison to the previous system.[245] A revival is now in prospect in response to an amendment to the Counter-Terrorism Bill.[246]

The most fundamental rethink would involve the institution of an examining magistrate system, which has been favoured by Lord Carlile.[247] However, the difficulties of transplantation and the doubts concerning efficacy based on experiences abroad[248] have weighed against this change. Concentration should be on building up of expertise in the CPS Counter-Terrorism Division.[249]   5.101

C. POST-CHARGE QUESTIONING AND DETENTION

1. Provisions

Policy-makers in two contexts have recently alighted upon the post-charge questioning of   5.102
suspects as a device to achieve important policy goals. The first such occasion concerned a proposal to change the rules in PACE by the Home Office in *Modernising Police Powers: Review of the Police and Criminal Evidence Act (PACE) 1984*.[250] PACE Code C, para 16.5, does allow questioning 'in the interests of justice for the detainee to have put to them, and have an opportunity to comment on, information concerning the offence which has come to light since they were charged or informed they might be prosecuted'. But it does not permit detention for this purpose nor for adverse inferences to be drawn from silence. The arguments in favour of change in the terrorism context seek to build upon the Threshold Test by Crown Prosecutors,[251] recognizing at the same time that post-charge questioning 'very rarely' at present,[252] even though much new evidence becomes available after charge.[253]

---

[243] *Ibid* para 104. Compare *Report to the United Kingdom Government on the Visit to the United Kingdom carried out by the European Committee for the Prevention of Torture and Inhuman and Degrading Treatment* (CPT/Inf (2008) 27) para 12 and *Response of the United Kingdom Government* (CPT/Inf (2008) 28) para 19.

[244] See Walker, C. and Fitzpatrick, B., 'Holding Centres in Northern Ireland, the Independent Commissioner and the rights of detainees' [1999] *European Human Rights Law Review* 27; *A New Beginning: Policing in Northern Ireland* (Northern Ireland Office, Belfast, 1999) para 8.16.

[245] See *Human Rights Annual Report 2006* (Belfast, 2006) pp 116–24; Lay Visitors' Reports Order 2005 SR (NI) 420.

[246] HL Hansard vol 705, col 158 (4 November 2008), Lord Lloyd.

[247] See Home Office, *Terrorist Investigations and the French Examining Magistrates System* (London, 2007).

[248] See Home Office, *Options for Pre-Charge Detention in Terrorist Cases* (London, 2007) p 11; Joint Committee on Human Rights, *Counter-Terrorism Policy and Human Rights: Prosecution and Pre-Charge Detention* (2005–06 HL 240, HC 1576) paras 72, 76, 117.

[249] Home Office, *Terrorist Investigations and the French Examining Magistrates System* (London, 2007) p 11.

[250] (London, 2007) para 3.51.

[251] See Crown Prosecution Service, *Code for Crown Prosecutors* (London, 2004) para 6. The test has been invoked against 4 out of 8 detainees charged after detention for more than 14 days: Joint Committee on Human Rights, Counter-Terrorism Policy and Human Rights: Counter-Terrorism Bill (2007–08 HL 50, HC 199) para 77.

[252] Lord Carlile, *Report on Proposed Measures for Inclusion in a Counter-Terrorism Bill* (Cm 7262, London, 2007) para 22.

[253] Joint Committee on Human Rights, *Counter-terrorism Policy and Human Rights: 42 Days* (2007–08 HL23 HC156) q 210; HC Hansard Public Bill Committee on the Counter-Terrorism Bill, Evidence from Sir Ken MacDonald, col 49 (22 April 2008).

5.103   The model of post-charge questioning transcribed into the Counter-Terrorism Act 2008 experienced major amendments during passage which improved the safeguards considerably. Early versions envisaged police authorizations, with a check by the prison governor holding the detainee[254] or, later, by a justice of the peace. Five-day periods of detention were envisaged. The Act now adopts judicial scrutiny and shorter time limits.

5.104   Section 22 provides that a Crown Court judge may authorize questioning if the person has been charged with a terrorist offence (as defined by reference to a fixed list of offences in s 27)[255] or an offence with a terrorist connection (as defined by s 93). The latter possibility creates uncertainty—it must be shown that the offence is, or takes place in the course of, an act of terrorism, or is committed for the purposes of terrorism. Lengthy preliminary hearings might be entailed where terrorist suspects are charged with ancillary offences such as fraud. The matter would naturally arise at the order for a preparatory hearing,[256] but the section does not forbid applications before then for fear of creating a potential gap.[257] The result is to encourage the police to charge a listed terrorist offence to avoid these arguments.[258] Applications may be made by police or prosecutors. The wording of s 22(2) strongly suggests that the application must relate only to 'the offence' which has been charged. If novel offences are uncovered, then a further pre-charge arrest would be possible.

5.105   The judge must be satisfied under s 22(6) that further questioning is necessary in the interests of justice, that the investigation is being conducted diligently and expeditiously, and that questioning will not interfere unduly with the preparation of the person's defence. The judge must specify the period for questioning, but there is an absolute limit of forty-eight hours for any given authorization, though there may be repeated authorizations. Aside from the time limit, the judge may also impose conditions as appear to be necessary in the interests of justice. They may include conditions as to the place where the questioning is to be carried out, including removal from prison to a police station. It is not expressly ruled out that there can be questioning after the trial commences, but the second criterion for the grant suggests strongly that it would not normally be allowed and it could be viewed as unfair under PACE s 78.[259] In any event, a failure to respond in the courtroom to the evidence for the prosecution will allow adverse inferences under s 35 of the Criminal Justice and Public Order Act 1994.[260] Whether the judge should be able to direct the questioning was doubted by the government as too redolent of the mantle of an investigative magistrate as well as creating practical problems in oversight.[261] It would be in keeping with legislative intention for a judge to specify as a condition in the interests of justice what cannot be raised at interview.

---

[254] Crime (Sentences) Act 1997 Schedule 1 and Prison Service Order 1801: Production of Prisoners at the request of the Police (2000).

[255] See HC Hansard Public Bill Committee on the Counter-Terrorism Bill, col 355 (8 May 2008), Tony McNulty.

[256] Criminal Procedure and Investigations Act 1996, s 29.

[257] HL Hansard vol 705, col 171 (4 November 2008), Lord West.

[258] See Joint Committee on Human Rights, *Government Responses to the Committee's 20th and 21st Reports and other correspondence* (2007–08 HL 127, HC 756) p 5.

[259] House of Commons Public Bill Committee on the Counter Terrorism Bill, col 341 (8 May 2008), Tony McNulty.

[260] For the impact, see Jackson, J., Wolfe, M., and Quinn, K., *Legislating Against Silence* (NIO Research and Statistical Series: report no.1, Belfast, 2000).

[261] HL Hansard vol 705, cols 171, 172 (4 November 2008), Lord West.

Given that many terrorist suspects are expected to remain silent, s 22(9) applies   5.106
s 34(1) of the Criminal Justice and Public Order Act 1994 to allow for adverse inferences, and ss 36 and 37 can also apply. As for the legitimacy of drawing adverse inferences from post-charge questioning, the European Court of Human Rights in *Murray
(John) v United Kingdom* held that the privilege against self-incrimination under Art 6 is
not absolute[262] but can be overborne provided there is a strong element of judicial supervision of the questioning and warnings at trial to the jury. However, the fraught circumstances of terrorist detentions and prosecutions will often raise issues as to fairness,
especially so near to trial.

The PACE Codes will be amended to explain further the proper treatment of the   5.107
post-charge detainee, including the dangers of questioning after the commencement of
trial.[263] The code will also cover access to lawyers, but this important safeguard was not
put on the face of the Act for the odd reason that it would give a veto to the suspect.[264]
In Scotland, the Lord Advocate will publish guidelines.[265]

By s 25, there must also be a code of practice under the 2008 Act itself to take account   5.108
of the requirement for the recording of post-charge interviews by video recording with
sound. This code is not made under PACE since it must apply in Scotland.[266] As with
pre-charge questioning, it is regrettable that there is no attempt to regulate the evasive
safety interviews as seen in *Ibrahim*.[267] Another side-effect which will be encouraged by
post-charge questioning is plea-bargaining—it offers a golden opportunity for such dis-
cussions, which have been also encouraged by the courts.[268]

These rules apply in Northern Ireland, except that a district judge (magistrates' court)   5.109
will take the decision (s 24). However, there are significant variations in Scotland under
s 23. The application for post-charge questioning is to be by a prosecutor and is made to
a sheriff. No inference from silence can be drawn. These selections of judges were made
before the switch to Crown Court judges in England and Wales.[269]

2. Assessment

A striking feature of the debate for change is that it is bereft of detailed argument or   5.110
detailed consideration of relevant principles or practicalities.

In principle, any move towards post-charge questioning is troubling, essentially   5.111
because the point of charge should represent a switch in responsibility for the prisoner
from the police to the courts and should reflect the heightened need for fair treatment
when a trial is pending.[270]

The first point is now better reflected by the requirement of judicial management   5.112
under s 22. But the scheme falls short of a system of judicial examination in which the

---

[262] App no 18731/91, 1996-I, at para 47. See also *Saunders v United Kingdom*, App no 19187/91, 1996-VI;
Shannon v United Kingdom, App no 6563/03, 4 October 2005.
[263] HC Hansard Public Bill Committee on the Counter-Terrorism Bill, col 341 (8 May 2008), Tony McNulty.
[264] HC Hansard vol 476, col 196 (10 June 2008), Tony McNulty.
[265] HL Hansard vol 705, col 183 (4 November 2008), Lord West.
[266] *Ibid* col 186.
[267] *R v Ibrahim* [2008] EWCA Crim 880.
[268] See *R v Goodyear* [2005] EWCA Crim 888.
[269] Hansard HL vol 704, col 768 (15 October 2008), Lord West.
[270] See further Walker, C., 'Post-charge questioning of suspects' [2008] *Criminal Law Review* 509.

judge remains wholly in charge.[271] It could directly avoid questioning which falls within the process of disclosure, which infringes upon legal privilege, or descends into 'dry run for cross-examination by the prosecution'.[272]

5.113   The second points awaits delineation in the new PACE Codes. So, it is impossible to complete a rights audit until the details are revealed. The ruling out of incriminating statements and inferences from silence would be the clearest signal of the exceptionally oppressive nature of this power, but Parliament has now agreed otherwise.

D. STOP AND SEARCH

1. Provisions[273]

5.114   The powers of stop and search in s 44 of the Terrorism Act 2000 can be more randomly exercised than the foregoing. These powers were said to be required to afford a chance to intercept munitions or to thwart plans[274] and followed Irish Republican Army truck bombs in the City of London in 1992 and 1993 and then in Docklands in 1996.

5.115   Any police constable in uniform can stop a vehicle and search the vehicle, the driver, or any passenger, and also stop and search a pedestrian, if located within an area or at a place specified in an authorization. It is made clear in s 45(1)(b) that there can be a random or blanket search—the power 'may be exercised whether or not the constable has grounds for suspecting the presence of articles of that kind'. Subsequent amendments allow the British Transport Police, Ministry of Defence Police, and Civil Nuclear Constabulary to exercise these powers.[275] By amendment in the Terrorism Act 2006, s 30, the powers extend to internal waters.[276] There are three different offences under s 47(1) for non-compliance with stops and searches.

5.116   There are some limits to the exercise of the powers. By s 45, powers must be exercised only for the purpose of 'searching for articles of a kind which could be used in connection with terrorism' (s 45(1)(a)). They may not involve a person being required 'to remove any clothing in public except for headgear, footwear, an outer coat, a jacket or gloves' (s 45(3)). A further safeguard is that a driver or pedestrian may apply within twelve months for a written statement as to the legal basis for the stop (s 45(5)). Next, when exercising stop and search powers, police officers must have regard to PACE Code A. First, according to para 1.1 of Code A, powers to stop and search must be used 'fairly, responsibly, with respect for people being searched and without unlawful discrimination'. Secondly, para 1.2 of Code A provides that the 'intrusion on the liberty of the person stopped or searched' has to be brief and that any detention 'must take place at or near the location of the stop'.

---

[271] See Explosive Substances Act 1883, s 6. The idea is rejected by Lord Carlile, *Report on Proposed Measures for Inclusion in a Counter-Terrorism Bill* (Cm 7262, London, 2007) para 23.

[272] Joint Committee on Human Rights, *Counter-Terrorism Policy and Human Rights: 42 Days* (2007–08 HL23 HC156) q 222 (Ali Bajwa).

[273] See further Walker, C., '"Know Thine Enemy as Thyself": Discerning Friend from Foe under Anti-Terrorism Laws' (2008) 32 *Melbourne Law Review* 275.

[274] Lord Lloyd of Berwick, *Inquiry into Legislation against Terrorism* (Cm 3420, London, 1996) paras 10.14, 10.21.

[275] Anti-terrorism, Crime and Security Act 2001, sch 7, paras 29, 31; Energy Act 2004, sch 23. See further Home Office Circulars 24/2002 and 25/2002 (London, 2002).

[276] For the definition, see Home Office Circular 8/2006 (London, 2006) para 69.

On the other hand, since the power is not applied on the basis of reasonable suspicion, there may be some doubts as to the applicability of the warning in para 2.2 not to exercise the powers based on 'generalisations or stereotypical images [or] A person's religion'. The Stop and Search Manual published in 2005 by the Stop and Search Action Team in the Home Office makes clear that reasonable suspicion does not apply to s 44.[277]

The precondition for exercise, an authorization, may be granted only if the senior police officer giving it considers it 'expedient' for the prevention of acts of terrorism (s 44(3)). An authorization, which may be valid for up to 28 days under s 46 and can be renewed, may be given by an Assistant Chief Constable or a Commander of a London force. Section 46 requires the police to inform the Secretary of State as soon as is reasonably practicable. The authorization must be confirmed (or amended or rejected) within forty-eight hours. Forces are encouraged by Home Office guidance to be specific and limited on area coverage.[278] Though the authorization processes are clear, they have been breached in at least six cases.[279]   5.117

2. Application

The powers had been used twenty-nine times in five police areas (twenty-two in London alone) from 1994 to 1996.[280] There seems to have been a dwindling after that date, but then a revival after 9/11. Five manifest patterns have occurred: a sustained increase in the use of this power, a low rate of consequent terrorist arrests, a higher rate of non-terrorist arrests, a disproportionate impact on Asian ethnic minorities, and uneven geographical delivery.   5.118

Table 5.6 Usage of s 44[281]

Year	Stops (n)			Terrorism/other arrests (n)			Ethnicity (n)[282]			Location %		
	Vehicle	Pedestrian	Total	Vehicle	Pedestrian	Totals	White	Black	Asian	Metropolitan Police	City (London)	Other
2001/2	7604	946	8550	20/149	0/20	20/169	6629	529	744	49	32	19
2002/3	16761	4774	21577	11/280	7/79	18/359	14429	1745	2989	61	21	18
2003/4	21287	8120	29407	14/358	5/112	19/470	20637	2704	3668	53	25	23
2004/5	21121	10941	32062	35/240	24/153	59/393	23389	2511	3485	40	20	40
2005/6	25479	19064	44543	46/246	59/212	105/458	30837	4155	6805	51	15	35

The incidence of usage has increased substantially over the five-year period, more so in relation to pedestrians than vehicles. Resultant arrests of relevance to terrorism are secured at a very low rate (well under one per cent). Concentration upon this figure alone discounts the greater number of non-terrorist arrests, on the ground that these   5.119

---

[277] (Home Office, London, 2005) para 66.
[278] Home Office, Circular 03/01 (London, 2001) para 5.6.2.
[279] Lord Carlile, *Report on the Operation in 2007 of the Terrorism Act 2000* (Home Office, London, 2008) para 126 and *Government Reply* (Cm 7429, London, 2008) p 8.
[280] *Inquiry into Legislation against Terrorism* (Cm 3420, London, 1996) para 10.16.
[281] Ministry of Justice, *Statistics on Race and the Criminal Justice System—2006* (London, 2007).
[282] Some are not recorded.

extraneous impacts cannot possibly justify the existence and invocation of s 44 powers. However, Assistant Chief Constable Beckley defended (on behalf of the Association of Chief Police Officers) the lack of consequent arrests by stressing that 'this is a power to be used to put people off their plans, hence it is used in a pretty random way'.[283] In this way, the disruptive potential is more important than its interdictory potential, a claim which is very difficult to test in empirical terms.

5.120   One can appreciate that arrests for non-terrorist offences can arise from the genuinely unexpected detection of drugs or offensive weapons. But there is a fear of the transposition of terrorism powers more widely than is proper. Some notable instances include Walter Wolfgang, an 82-year old party activist, who was ejected from the Labour Party's 2005 annual conference after he heckled Foreign Secretary Jack Straw and then was stopped under s 44 when he tried to re-enter the venue.[284] A woman in Dundee was stopped for walking along a cycle path.[285] Another example might be Nicholas Gaubert, who was disabled by a Taser after acting 'strangely' on a Leeds bus shortly after the July 7 bombings. Police thought he might be a suicide bomber, but he was a diabetic who was entering a coma.[286]

5.121   Analysis in terms of ethnicity reveals an over-representation of minorities,[287] given the overall composition of the UK's population which comprises 92 per cent white, 4 per cent Asian, and 2 per cent black.[288] The extent of these racial inequalities, also in non-terrorism stop and search powers, is disputed because of the inaccuracy of recording practices and the nature of the users of public spaces.[289] In addition, 'Asian' should not be translated as 'Muslim', since only half of those belonging to this ethnic group are in fact Muslims, though this proportion rises to 92 per cent for those of Pakistani or Bangladeshi origins.[290]

5.122   The power is also exercised selectively in terms of location. Overwhelmingly, its usage has been concentrated in London, where it has been in force on a rolling basis since 2001.[291] Over a given year, only a minority of force areas issue authorizations.[292]

3. Evaluation

5.123   The exercise of s 44 has been considered at length by the Court of Appeal,[293] and the House of Lords,[294] in *R (on the application of Gillan) v Metropolitan Police Commissioner*.

---

[283] Home Affairs Committee, *Terrorism and Community Relations* (2003–04 HC 165) para 54.

[284] *The Guardian* 29 September 2005 p 1.

[285] *The Times* 17 October 2005 p 8.

[286] *Yorkshire Post* 7 July 2008.

[287] It is not considered seriously disproportionate in London: Metropolitan Police Authority, *Counter-Terrorism: The London Debate* (London, 2007) p 49.

[288] See Office for National Statistics, *National Statistics: Ethnicity* (London, 2003).

[289] See Bowling, B. and Phillips, C., 'Disproportionate and discriminatory' (2007) 70 *Modern Law Review* 936.

[290] Home Affairs Committee, *Terrorism and Community Relations* (2005–06, HC 165-I) para 63.

[291] Lord Carlile, *Report on the Operation in 2007 of the Terrorism Act 2000* (Home Office, London, 2008) paras 125, 129.

[292] *Ibid* at para 99.

[293] *R (on the application of Gillan) v Metropolitan Police Commissioner* [2005] 1 QB 388 ('*Gillan CA*').

[294] *R (on the application of Gillan) v Metropolitan Police Commissioner* [2006] 2 AC 307 ('*Gillan HL*'). See Moeckli, D., 'Stop and search under the Terrorism Act' (2007) 70 *Modern Law Review* 659; Edwards, R.A., 'Stop and search, terrorism and the human rights deficit' (2008) 37 *Common Law World Review* 211.

The facts were that an Assistant Commissioner of the Metropolitan Police gave an authorization under s 44(4) covering the whole of the Metropolitan Police District. That authorization was confirmed (without any publicity) and was then renewed on a continuous basis since February 2001 and is still persisting today. Both applicants were stopped near an arms fair being held at the ExCel Centre, Docklands. Nothing incriminating was found; the length of the transaction was up to thirty minutes.

Both appellants unsuccessfully challenged the police action. The first argument was that s 44, as an incursion into liberties, should be construed restrictively and had been used excessively. The House of Lords determined that the use of the word 'expedient' in s 44(3) was significant parliamentary language,[295] set alongside the incorporation of other constraints. Taking these contexts together, s 44(3) was taken to mean that an authorization might be expedient if, and only if, the person giving it considered it likely that the stop and search powers would be 'of significant practical value and utility in seeking to achieve . . . the prevention of acts of terrorism'.[296] By contrast, the Home Office's Circular, *Authorisations of Stop and Search Powers under Section 44 of the Terrorism Act 2000*, emphasizes more strictly that: 'Powers should only be authorized where they are absolutely necessary to support a forces [sic] anti-terrorism operations.'[297] Lord Bingham was satisfied that the authorization and confirmation processes had not become a 'routine bureaucratic exercise'[298] though one might argue that their Lordships too easily accepted evidence of vulnerabilities as equivalent to evidence of threats.

5.124

The next challenges were that the commander in charge of the police operation had wrongly invoked the powers in that place and time and that there was excessive action by the operational officers against the appellants. Lord Bingham emphasized that the implementing constable is not free to act arbitrarily and must not stop and search people who are 'obviously not terrorist suspects'.[299] The lower courts were more pointedly critical of police practices on this score because of lack of direction and briefing.[300] Guidance has since been promulgated, whereby officers are required 'to review fully the intelligence on each authorization and clearly show the link between that intelligence and the geographic extent of the location in which the powers will be used', though a force-wide authorization is still permitted.[301]

5.125

Turning to implementation questions, though the applicants were not from an ethnic minority, some of their Lordships were troubled by the dangers of discrimination inherent in these powers. The police approach was starkly described in 2005 by Ian Johnston, Chief Constable of the British Transport Police: 'We should not waste time searching old white ladies. It is going to be disproportionate. It is going to be young men, not exclusively, but it may be disproportionate when it comes to ethnic groups.'[302]

5.126

The Home Office Minister, Hazel Blears, concurred that sources of the terrorist threat 'inevitably means that some of our counter-terrorist powers will be disproportionately

5.127

---

[295] *Gillan HL* at paras 14 and 60.
[296] *Ibid* at para 15.
[297] Home Office, *Authorizations of Stop and Search Powers under Section 44 of the Terrorism Act* (Circular 038/2004, 2004) para 9.
[298] *Ibid* at para 18.
[299] *Ibid* para 35.
[300] See Lord Carlile, *Report on the Operation in 2002 and 2003 of the Terrorism Act 2000* (London, 2004) para 86.
[301] See Home Office, Circular 038/2004 (London, 2004), Circular 22/2006 (London, 2006).
[302] *The Guardian* 17 August 2005 p 6.

experienced by people in the Muslim community'.[303] The apparent conserving of resources and selection as targets of the politically marginal may explain this resort to profiling.[304] But are these forms of racial or ethnic profiling a lawful tactic?

5.128 Returning to *Gillan*, in Lord Hope's view, 'the mere fact that the person appears to be of Asian origin is not a legitimate reason for its exercise.'[305] While an appearance which suggests that the person is of Asian origin may attract the constable's initial attention, a further factor must be in the mind of the constable. Yet, this resolution lacks precision as to prominence of racial considerations and too easily accepts that race or ethnicity is by its nature sufficiently connected to a terrorist suspect benchmark description and that it does not unduly divert attention from more pertinent criteria, such as behavioural and antecedent information. It also remains troublesome to reconcile even this partial reliance upon racial origins as a basis for official action with the absolute ban in the Race Relations Act 1976.[306] Even on the more flexible standard under Art 14 of the European Convention, whether racial or ethnic origins can be said to provide an 'objective and reasonable' justification for official action[307] may be doubted since many terrorists do not fit the paradigm of Asian and since 'Asian' does not betoken 'Muslim'.

5.129 Aside from issues of construction and implementation, the House of Lords concentrated heavily on human rights issues. Reflecting a continuing trend in English case law, the House of Lords denied the applicability of Art 5 to police operation where detention is not the primary aim. However, to depict in this way the stop and search process as akin to waiting to board a bus or waiting until the light turns green at a pedestrian crossing,[308] is wholly unconvincing for two important reasons. Firstly, s 45 involves the exercise of an official coercive power not a directive power—the person waiting for the bus or for the green light can give up and try another route. Nor is the time of 'non-detention detention' as momentary as suggested.

5.130 As for Art 8 rights to privacy, the stop and search was readily justified as necessary in a democratic society and proportionate in response to the clear and present danger of terrorism. Indeed, in parallel to his treatment of Art 5, Lord Bingham was 'doubtful whether an ordinary superficial search of the person can be said to show a lack of respect for private life'.[309] Similar arguments applied to Arts 10 and 11.

5.131 As for the standard of legality, relevant to both Arts 5 and 8, their Lordships viewed s 44 as passing the test. Lord Bingham was further seduced into this stance by arguments of security—that 'publishing the details of authorisations . . . would by implication reveal those places where such measures had not been put in place, thereby identifying vulnerable targets'.[310] These latter views confuse legal availability with strategies or

---

[303] Home Affairs Committee, *Terrorism and Community Relations* (2003–04 HC 165) para 46.

[304] See Report of the Special Rapporteur on the promotion and protection of human rights and fundamental freedoms while countering terrorism (A/HRC/4/26, 2007); Moeckli, D., *Human Rights and Non-Discrimination in the 'War on Terror'* (Oxford University Press, Oxford, 2008) pp 198, 200.

[305] *Gillan HL* at para 45.

[306] See *R (on the application of European Roma Rights Centre) v Immigration Officer at Prague Airport (United Nations High Commissioner for Refugees Intervening)* [2005] 2 AC 1.

[307] See *Belgian Linguistics case*, App nos 1474/62; 1677/62; 1691/62 ; 1769/63 ; 1994/63 ; 2126/64 Ser A 6 (1968) para 10. The same standard has been applied to nationality: *Gaygusuz v Austria*, App no 17371/90, 1996-IV, para 42.

[308] *Gillan HL* at para 25.

[309] *Ibid* at para 28.

[310] *Ibid* at paras 33, 34.

tactics of operational implementation across an area as large as London. Given that court cases (and Lord Carlile) have revealed that the sections have been in continuous force throughout London since 2001, only a dim-witted terrorist would be unaware of these powers in general terms. By contrast, the Association of Chief Police Officers emphasize, in their *Practice Advice on Stop and Search Powers*, issued in 2006,[311] community involvement under s 44, since it will increase confidence, reassure the public, and encourage the flow of intelligence.[312] Home Office Circular 27/2008 also recommends that a community impact assessment be carried out before any s 44 authorization.[313]

Some dismiss the perceptions or realities of discrimination as hot air, on the basis that racial profiling is 'among the most misunderstood and emotionally laden terms in the modern vocabulary of law enforcement and politics'.[314] Nevertheless, the hard facts render the s 44 powers of stop and search hard to defend on grounds of proportionality. The application of 'all-risks' policing powers, by which the police will treat anyone and everyone as a risk, and the reason for their attention is not so much the individual but the target, has become commonplace. However, if terrorists can be both neighbours and aliens, the indicators of involvement must be drawn in very vague terms, including age, gender, and race, all of which are poor predictors. As a result, many false positives and false negatives are created, thereby creating miscarriages of justice which damage the legitimacy of the legal system as well as diverting resources from more promising investigative leads.[315] It is no use being 'data rich but intelligence poor'.[316]   5.132

Aside from individual discomforts, there is also the potential to divide minority communities from police because the quest for terrorists impacts unevenly. The House of Commons Home Affairs Select Committee found 'a clear perception among all our Muslim witnesses that Muslims are being stigmatized by the operation of the Terrorism Act: this is extremely harmful to community relations.'[317] Not only does this create social tensions, but it will also hamper the flow of assistance to the police from minority communities. As a result, Lord Carlile has called for much more restrained usage,[318] a call endorsed by senior police officers[319] and backed by more detailed demands for information before authorizations can be confirmed by the Home Office.[320]   5.133

Added to these national criticisms must be the statements of non-discrimination in international law.[321]   5.134

---

[311] (National Centre for Policing Excellence, Wyborton, 2006).

[312] *Ibid* p 12.

[313] Replacing Home Office Circular 22/2006.

[314] Dershowitz, A.M., *Why Terrorism Works* (Yale University Press, New Haven, 2002) p 207.

[315] See Harris, D.A., 'New Risks, New Tactics' [2004] *Utah Law Review* 913.

[316] Metropolitan Police Authority, *Report of the MPA Scrutiny on MPS Stop and Search Practice* (London, 2004) p 9. A pertinent example is that two of the 9/11 hijackers were subject to US traffic stops and one even received a speeding ticket: National Commission on Terrorist Attacks upon the United States, *The 9/11 Commission Report* (GPO, Washington, DC, 2004) pp 231, 253.

[317] Home Affairs Committee, *Terrorism and Community Relations* (2003–04 HC 165) para 153. See also Metropolitan Police Authority, *Report of the MPA Scrutiny on MPS Stop and Search Practice* (London, 2004) paras 150–78.

[318] Lord Carlile, *Report on the Operation in 2006 of the Terrorism Act 2000* (Home Office, London, 2007) para 114.

[319] *The Guardian* 17 February 2006 p 4.

[320] Home Office Circular 27/2008: *Authorisation of Stop and Search Powers under Section 44 of the Terrorism Act 2000*.

[321] Report of the Special Rapporteur on the promotion and protection of human rights and fundamental freedoms while countering terrorism (A/HRC/4/26, 2007) Pt II.

5.135　In conclusion, s 44 exemplifies the proliferation of all-risks policing, including the growth of racial profiling in its application, a technique which has increased in acceptability since 11 September 2001. Yet, because of the exigencies of the situation (especially limited policing resources), all-risks cannot be applied literally. Thereupon, choice will be based on professional or sectarian cultures as much as rational choice and may well mask unpalatable or unlawful considerations. As a result, like the imaginary American crimes shaped by racial profiling or racial prejudice, such as 'driving while Black'[322] or 'flying while Arab',[323] s 44 may have created the nasty British equivalent of 'perambulating while Muslim'.

5.136　To remedy this situation, a redesigned power should replace s 44 which is inherently hard to regulate.[324] The first step is to apply stop and search only to the protection of listed vulnerable targets. For this much more select list of targets, a policy of blanket stops and searches is a more sustainable way forward, is one which can monitor and disrupt,[325] and is one which avoids by racially driven discretion.

5.137　The second step is to instil more statutory structuring. Code A and the ACPO guidance could be augmented, for example, by clearer narrative about profiling and about the choice of 'special' or 'normal' powers to stop and search.

5.138　A third consideration is accountability. Invocation should become subject to confirmation by a judge *ab initio*.[326] There should be a statutory obligation to explain the results, including in local meetings. The police might also be encouraged to invite community representatives to shadow them in the exercise of powers. Nationally, Parliament must keep under review the need for the continued existence of s 44.

E.　PORT AND BORDER CONTROLS

1. Provisions

5.139　Another example of the all-risks approach to the policing of terrorism is the universal screening of passengers at airports, based on international standards.[327] There are corresponding

---

[322] See Harris, D.A., *Racial Profiling on Our Nation's Highways* (ACLU, New York, 1999).

[323] See Baker, E., 'Flying while Arab—Racial profiling and air travel security' (2002) 67 *Journal of Air Law and Commerce* 1375.

[324] See Bowling, B. and Phillips, C., 'Disproportionate and discriminatory' (2007) 70 *Modern Law Review* 936 at p 961. Compare the weaker remedies of de Schutter, O. and Ringelheim, J., 'Ethnic profiling' (2008) 71 *Modern Law Review* 358.

[325] Report of the Special Rapporteur on the promotion and protection of human rights and fundamental freedoms while countering terrorism (A/HRC/4/26, 2007) para 61. Compare a random search pattern which would still entail discretion as well as ignoring the possibility of intelligent direction (see Moeckli, D., *Human Rights and Non-Discrimination in the 'War on Terror'* (Oxford University Press, Oxford, 2008) p 220).

[326] See Privy Counsellor Review Committee, *Anti-terrorism, Crime and Security Act 2001, Review, Report* (2003–04 HC 100) para 86; Lord Carlile, *Report on the Operation in 2007 of the Terrorism Act 2000* (Home Office, London, 2008) and *Government Reply* (Cm 7429, London, 2008) para 128.

[327] See (Hague) Convention for the Suppression of Unlawful Seizure of Aircraft (10 ILM 133, 1970); (Montreal) Convention for the Suppression of Unlawful Acts against the Safety of Civil Aviation (10 ILM 1151, 1971); (Montreal) Protocol on the Suppression of Unlawful Acts of Violence at Airports Serving International Civil Aviation (27 ILM 627, 1988); International Civil Aviation Organisation, Annex 17 to its Standards and Recommended Practices.

measures in place relating to maritime security.[328] These international measures are supplemented in the United Kingdom by the port controls under Pt V and Sch 7 of the Terrorism Act 2000, which replaced the measures in place since 1974 within the 'Common Travel Area' between the United Kingdom and the Republic of Ireland, where passport controls do not apply.[329] Their purpose is to disrupt possible terrorist planning and logistics and also to gather low-level intelligence about movements. The controls also deter attacks on the travel facilities themselves. Further controls were implemented by s 118 of the Anti-terrorism, Crime and Security Act 2001, which allows an examining officer to exercise the port controls in relation to persons travelling on any internal or external route. The port controls add to the regulation of entry under the Immigration Act 1971, with Sch 2 of that Act acting as a blue-print for Sch 7.

Alongside Sch 7, Sch 14, para 6, envisages the issuance of a code of practice for authorized officers.[330] The Code issued pursuant to the Terrorism Act 2000 (Code of Practice for examining officers under the Terrorism Act 2000) Order 2001 was revised in 2007.[331]   5.140

By Sch 1, para 1, an 'examining officer' (meaning a constable, an immigration officer, or a designated customs officer) may question a person for the purpose of determining whether he appears to be a 'terrorist'.[332] Reflecting the 'all-risks' nature of these powers, it is made clear under para 2 that examining officers may exercise their powers whether or not they have grounds for suspicion against any individual. In this way, the 'copper's nose'[333] for wrongdoing may be used, based on intuition rather than rational indicators, and resulting again in overuse.[334] This power can be applied to a person entering or leaving Great Britain or Northern Ireland at a port or airport or (under para 3) within one mile of border between Northern Ireland and the Republic of Ireland or wherever is the first stop of a train from the Republic. By s 118 of the Anti-terrorism, Security and Crime Act 2001, an examining officer may also exercise the port controls in relation to persons whose presence at a port is believed to be connected with their travelling on a flight within Great Britain or Northern Ireland or to a person on a ship or aircraft that has arrived at any place in Great Britain or Northern Ireland whether from within or outside Great Britain or Northern Ireland. In addition, the travel controls can apply in the Channel Tunnel system by the Channel Tunnel (International Arrangements) (Amendment) Order 2001.[335] Under s 114, a constable may not use reasonable force for   5.141

---

[328] See (Rome) Convention for the Suppression of Unlawful Acts against the Safety of Maritime Navigation (27 ILM 668, 1988); (Rome) Protocol for the Suppression of Unlawful Acts Against the Safety of Fixed Platforms Located on the Continental Shelf (27 ILM 685, 1988).

[329] See Home Office and Northern Ireland Office, *Legislation against Terrorism* (Cm 4178, London, 1998) para 11.17.

[330] Home Office and Northern Ireland Office, *Legislation against Terrorism* (Cm 4178, London, 1998) para 11.14.

[331] SI 2001/427; <http://www.homeoffice.gov.uk/documents/cons-2007-tact-cop-exam-officers/cons-2007-code-of-practice?view=Binary>.

[332] Soldiers can no longer act since the repeal of s 97.

[333] Lord Carlile, *Report on the Operation in 2006 of the Terrorism Act 2000* (Home Office, London, 2007) para 33. See further Norris, C. and Armstrong, G., *The Maximum Surveillance Society* (Berg, Oxford, 1999) pp 118–19.

[334] Lord Carlile, *Report on the Operation in 2004 of the Terrorism Act 2000* (Home Office, London, 2005) para 17.

[335] SI 2001/178.

the purpose of exercising a power under paras 2 and 3. Presumably, those who fail to cooperate will often give rise to suspicion sufficient for a s 41 arrest.

5.142 To check for persons falling within para 2, an examining officer may under para 7 search a ship or aircraft, or anything on it or to be loaded or just unloaded. In order to carry out an examination, an examining officer may under para 6 stop a person or vehicle, authorize the person's removal from a ship, aircraft, or vehicle, or detain a person. The conditions of detention are covered by Sch 8, save that the length of detention must not exceed nine hours; further detention may then be authorized by an arrest but not for the port control purposes.[336] Nine hours represents a reduction from twelve in the previous regime, though Lord Lloyd had recommended six hours,[337] and most persons are released within four hours.

5.143 A person who is questioned under paras 2 or 3 must, under para 5: (a) give the examining officer any information in his possession which the officer requests; (b) give the examining officer on request either a valid passport or another document which establishes his identity; (c) declare whether he has with him documents of a kind specified by the examining officer; or (d) give the examining officer on request any document which he has with him and which is of a kind specified by the officer. The Code of Practice may unduly extend these powers by including within 'information' passwords to data but not if the data is located elsewhere than in an article in possession of the traveller.[338] No reference is made to the Regulation of Investigatory Powers Act 2000, s 49 by which the revelation of 'protected information' should only be required under judicial authority.

5.144 The compulsory nature of these powers was attacked in *R v Hundal; R v Dhaliwal*,[339] where the defendants, accused of membership of the International Sikh Youth Federation, were questioned and searched when held at Dover. The search of their vehicle, which turned up incriminating documents, was held not to breach Art 6 because of the 'clear distinction between requiring someone to answer questions and requiring a person to produce either documents or other information to the prosecution and a case where what the person concerned is compelled to do is to allow the relevant authority to conduct a search.'[340]

5.145 The person, and any ship or aircraft carrying him (or vehicle in Northern Ireland), may also be searched under para 8 by an examining officer (or a person authorized under para 10). By amendment under the Terrorism Act 2006, s 29, there may also be searches within transported vehicles, a power previously confined to the Northern Ireland border. There is also a wide power to search unaccompanied baggage and goods under para 9. Section 118(4) of the 2001 Act amends para 9 by applying the powers to examine goods which have arrived in or are about to leave Great Britain or Northern Ireland whether the place they have come from or are going to is within or outside Great Britain or Northern Ireland. Property may be seized for further investigation for a period of seven days under para 11.

---

[336] Compare *Breen v Chief Constable of Dumfries and Galloway*, 1997 SLT 826.
[337] *Inquiry into Legislation against Terrorism* (Cm 3420, London, 1996) para 10.57.
[338] Para 20.
[339] [2004] EWCA Crim 389 at para 14.
[340] *Ibid* at para 18 per Lord Woolf.

To aid the process of scrutiny of traffic, Sch 7 regulates entry and exit points within   5.146
the Common Travel Area (augmenting corresponding restrictions on external ports of
entry under the Immigration Act 1971). In this way, it becomes more manageable to
impose port controls. By para 12, carriers of passengers for reward involved in journeys
to or from Great Britain, the Republic of Ireland, Northern Ireland, or any of the Islands,
must call at a designated port or in circumstances specifically approved by an examining
officer. Aircraft which are not carrying passengers for reward must either call at a designated port or give at least twelve hours' notice in writing to the police,[341] arrangements
viewed as lax by Lord Carlile.[342] No regulations apply to non-passenger boat movements, though coastguard monitoring does pertain. A list of designated ports is scheduled. Within designated ports, the Secretary of State may order ship or aircraft operators
to allocate 'control areas' (para 13) in which passengers are expected to embark or disem-
bark and may order port managers to provide specified facilities within them (para 14).
In practice, formal notice is avoided, and facilities for examining and examination officers are negotiated.[343]

Operators must routinely ensure that passengers and crew are subject to examination   5.147
(para 15) and must provide passenger information if an examining officer makes a written request (para 17).[344] Under Sch 7, this provision only applied to the Common
Travel Area, but s 119 of the 2001 Act extends the duty to external travel. An order-
making power requires the Secretary of State to define the information required, and
details are given in Sch 7 to the Terrorism Act 2000 (Information) Order 2002.[345]

'Carding' is currently allowed under para 16, so that passengers may be required   5.148
by an examining officer to complete and produce a card containing information about
their identity. The designs of the cards are set out in the Terrorism Act 2000 (Carding)
Order 2001.[346] It was hoped that the routine provision of extensive passenger
information,[347] plus the desire to encourage the Northern Ireland Peace Process by
reducing burdens on Irish travellers, would remove the need for carding.[348] Section
53(2) therefore allows the Secretary of State to order the repeal of 'carding'. If applied,
carding must be activated by affirmative order. In the event, the Terrorism Act 2000
(Carding) Order 2001[349] maintains carding in force. Moreover, it is surprising that the
facility of low-level intelligence-gathering involved in carding should be given up so

---

[341] Compare *Inquiry into Legislation against Terrorism* (Cm 3420, London, 1996) para 10.57.

[342] Lord Carlile, *Report on the Operation in 2007 of the Terrorism Act 2000* (Home Office, London, 2008)
paras 148, 149.

[343] Home Office, Circular 03/01 (London, 2001) para 16.18.

[344] Specified information must not duplicate information under the Immigration Act 1971, sch 2
paras 27(2), 27B. This limit has been criticized (Lord Carlile, *Report on the Operation in 2001 of the Terrorism
Act 2000* (Home Office, London, 2002) para 5.18). The police have independent powers to demand
passenger and crew information for international journeys (Immigration, Asylum and Nationality Act 2006,
s 32), and there is a scheme of information sharing between agencies (ss 36–8; Immigration, Asylum
and Nationality Act 2006 (Duty to Share Information and Disclosure of Information for Security Purposes)
Order 2008, SI 2008/539). For domestic journeys, see Police and Justice Act 2006, s 14 (not yet
implemented).

[345] SI 2002/1945.

[346] SI 2001/426.

[347] Home Office and Northern Ireland Office, *Legislation against Terrorism* (Cm 4178, London, 1998)
para 11.20.

[348] Hansard HL vol 613, cols 736–7 (23 May 2000), Lord Bassam.

[349] SI 2001/426.

readily, given that 'The police have found it to be an extremely useful tool in tackling terrorism' and that there are 'sound strategic reasons to carry out checks at ports'.[350] The possibility of 'back-door' entry by international terrorists is another reason for retention.

5.149   Further details of the exercise of functions by examining officers are set out in s 115 and Sch 14 to the 2000 Act. By para 2 of Sch 14, an officer may enter a vehicle and may, by para 3, use reasonable force for the purpose of exercising an examining power (apart from paras 2 and 3 of Sch 7). By para 4, any information acquired by an examining officer may be supplied to immigration, tax, and police authorities or to a person specified by order of the Secretary of State. Conversely, under para 4(2), information acquired by a customs officer or an immigration officer may be supplied to an examining officer. No similar powers exist for freight manifests, and Lord Carlile has long been critical of the accuracy of freight manifest records under para 17.[351]

5.150   Amongst the further regulations under the Terrorism Act 2000 (Code of Practice for Examining Officers) Order 2007, para 6 specifies that only in exceptional circumstances should an immigration officer or customs officer exercise functions under the Act and only when a police officer is not readily available; or if specifically requested to do so by a police sergeant or higher rank. Pursuant to a recommendation of the Lloyd Report,[352] contact with the public is handled in para 10 as follows:

Examining officers should therefore make every reasonable effort to exercise the power in such a way as to minimise causing embarrassment or offence to a person who has no terrorist connections. The powers to stop and question a person should not be exercised in a way which unfairly discriminates against a person on the grounds of race, colour, religion, creed, gender or sexual orientation. When deciding whether to question a person the examining officer should bear in mind that the primary reason for doing so is to maximise disruption of terrorist movements into and out of the United Kingdom.

Note for guidance on paragraph 10: . . . Examining officers should take particular care not to discriminate unfairly against minority ethnic groups in the exercise of these powers.

5.151   It is a summary offence under Sch 7, para 18, wilfully to fail to comply with a duty, to contravene a prohibition, or to obstruct or to frustrate a search or examination under the port controls. To give reassurance to hard-pressed commercial operators, the offence was amended during passage to require wilful default.[353]

2. Evaluation

5.152   Compared to the numbers of passengers passing through the relevant ports, very few detentions are made. For example, in 1995, out of around 170 million travellers, just 720,000 were examined, 60 per cent in the Common Travel Area.[354] During 2000, only

---

[350] Hansard HL vol 613, cols 736, 746 (16 May 2000), Lord Bassam.
[351] See Lord Carlile, *Report on the Operation in 2007 of the Terrorism Act 2000* (Home Office, London, 2008) para 156. The police now have extra powers to access freight information: Immigration, Asylum and Nationality Act 2006, s 33.
[352] *Inquiry into Legislation against Terrorism* (Cm 3420, London, 1996) para 10.57.
[353] Hansard HL vol 614, col 1457 (4 July 2000), Lord Bach.
[354] *Inquiry into Legislation against Terrorism* (Cm 3420, London, 1996) paras 10.26, 10.38.

521 persons (mostly Irish) were examined for more than one hour.[355] At the same time, many of the resultant arrests relate to non-terrorist matters which have been discovered incidentally—such as the possession of stolen goods or drugs or the execution of an outstanding arrest warrant.[356] This suggests that, if there is utility in the exercise at all, it must be to gather low-level intelligence[357] or to maximize disruptions, as the Code of Practice for Examining Officers states above.

Physical controls at ports and airports could promote the 'protect' strand of CONTEST. However, the evidence in terms of arrests is not convincing, so faith has to be placed in the value of intelligence and disruption which are very hard to assess. In any event, there are considerable costs in terms of the dislocation of transport links. In addition, there may have been displacement of targeting to other transport links, illustrated by attacks in London in 2005.   5.153

As for a rights audit, these checks probably fall within the exception to the right to liberty for a stated legal 'obligation' under Art 5(1)(b) of the European Convention. This verdict was reached by the European Commission in regard to travellers from the Irish Republic in the *McVeigh* case.[358] The same view was adopted in regard to passengers between Britain and Northern Ireland in *Harkin, X, Lyttle, Gillen, and McCann v United Kingdom*.[359] While these decisions can be doubted both for their reasoning and level of authority, it is notable that the Terrorism Act 2000 now provides a shorter initial period of detention, though the maximum is considerably more than for stops and searches. It is doubtful that the attempted restrictions in the foregoing code of practice will make much difference, since they are not 'law' under the Convention.[360]   5.154

The Code is silent about community consultation. The concerns expressed about s 44 apply here also.   5.155

F. CONCLUSIONS

The maxim of UK Prime Minister, Tony Blair, in response to the 7 July 2005 London bombing was to '[l]et no one be in any doubt, the rules of the game are changing.'[361] He correctly identifies that many jurisdictions are embarking upon new regimes against terrorism which depart from the hallowed principles of criminal justice. Yet the pursuit of this 'game' will inevitably entail damage to the legitimacy and fairness of criminal justice systems and will prove counter-productive in trying to engage the support of communities. All-risks policing, so prominent in this chapter, may come to threaten the very goal   5.156

---

[355] Home Office Statistics.

[356] *Inquiry into Legislation against Terrorism* (Cm 3420, London, 1996) para 10.40.

[357] See Home Office, *Regulatory Impact Assessment: Terrorism Act 2000 Passenger Information* (2001) para 3.

[358] *McVeigh, O'Neill, and Evans v United Kingdom*, App nos 8022, 8025, 8027/77; DR 18 p 66 (admissibility), DR 25 p 15 (final report). See Warbrick, C., 'The Prevention of Terrorism (Temporary Provisions) Act 1976 and the European Convention on Human Rights: the McVeigh case' (1983) 32 *International & Comparative Law Quarterly* 757; Clayton, R. and Tomlinson, H., *The Law of Human Rights* (2nd edn, Oxford University Press, Oxford, 2009) para 10.183.

[359] App nos 11539, 11641, 11650, 11651, 11652/85, (1981) 9 EHRR 381.

[360] Compare Rowe, J.J., 'The Terrorism Act 2000' [2000] *Criminal Law Review* 527 at p 536.

[361] *The Times* 6 August 2005 p 1.

of the government's stated counter-terrorism strategy ('CONTEST'), which is 'to reduce the risk from international terrorism, so that people can go about their daily lives freely and with confidence.'[362] Freedom cannot be delivered by legislation which substantially diminishes civil, political, economic, or social life. Confidence cannot be secured if people are fearful of the arbitrary and ineffective impact of security measures.

---

[362] Home Office, *Pursue, Prevent, Protect, Prepare: The United Kingdom's Strategy for Countering International Terrorism* (Cm 7547, London, 2009) para 0.17.

6

CRIMINAL OFFENCES AND
THE PROCESSING OF OFFENDERS

A. INTRODUCTION

Ever since the implementation of the Diplock Report,[1] the government has reiterated   6.01
that 'prosecution is—first, second and third—the government's preferred approach
when dealing with suspected terrorists'.[2] Consistent with this policy, many offences
levelled against terrorists are not in the anti-terrorism legislation. The criminalization
approach logically demands that terrorists should not be treated as offenders or prisoners
with political motivations which mark them out as extraordinary or afford them special
status.[3] Accordingly, homicides, offences against the person, and offences under the
Explosive Substances Act 1883 are the common diet of major terrorist trials.[4] An offence
of terrorism has been resisted.[5]

Yet, leaving aside the special case of Northern Ireland which is covered in Chapter 9,   6.02
this forbearance from interference with the solemn stages of criminal justice is crum-
bling. A constant theme in this book has been the escalating emphasis upon anticipatory

---

[1] *Report of the Commission to consider legal procedures to deal with terrorist activities in Northern Ireland*
(Cmnd 5185, London, 1972).

[2] Hansard HC vol 472, col 561 (21 February 2008), Tony McNulty.

[3] See Walker, C.P., 'Irish Republic prisoners, political detainees, prisoners of war or common criminals?'
(1984) 19 *Irish Jurist* 189.

[4] See *R v Bourgass* [2005] EWCA Crim 1943, [2006] EWCA Crim 3397; *R v Barot* [2007] EWCA Crim
1119; *R v Khyam* [2008] EWCA Crim 1612; *R v Ibrahim* [2008] EWCA Crim 880; *R v Asiedu* [2008] EWCA
Crim 1725; *R v Sherif* [2008] EWCA Crim 2653; *R v Ali The Times* 9 September 2008 p 1; *R v Abdulla
The Times* 17 December 2008 p 1.

[5] See Gardiner Report, *Report of a Committee to consider, in the context of civil liberties and human rights,
measures to deal with terrorism in Northern Ireland* (Cmnd 5847, London, 1975) para 70; Hansard HL vol 611,
col 1487 (6 April 2000), Lord Bassam.

risk, and it has applied within criminal justice as elsewhere. It is reflected in net-widening through the use of the term 'terrorism' and the fabrication of precursor crimes.[6] These extend the reach of the criminal law to a point where, often based on equivocal evidence, the prospect of harm is uncertain and where the only immorality has been the imagining of wickedness rather than its infliction or a fair imputation that it will occur. Other policies of risk management relate to the disposal of convicted terrorists—by punishment and post-punishment.

6.03   A criminal justice approach, assuming it entails individual responsibility, equality, and system legality and due process, should be considered preferable to executive or administrative disposals or to any full-blown 'war on terror'. Thus, successive governments have been right to seek to maximize criminal justice and to reject the contention that 'it is not enough to serve our enemies with legal papers'.[7]

B. CRIMINAL OFFENCES

1. Training for terrorism

6.04   Section 54 is the first 'precursor offence' listed in Pt VI of the Terrorism Act 2000 and deals with weapons training. A person commits an offence if he provides instruction or training in the making or use of (a) firearms, (aa) radioactive material or weapons designed or adapted for the discharge of any radioactive material,[8] (b) explosives, or (c) chemical, biological or nuclear weapons. The penalty is up to ten years' imprisonment, and the court may also forfeit items connected with the offence.[9] The offence was extended from Northern Ireland to the whole country, despite the recommendation otherwise by Lord Lloyd.[10] Perhaps the conviction of David Copeland, who carried out bombings in London in 1999 out of racist and homophobic motives, strengthened the case for extension.[11] He had obtained bomb-making information from the internet, though he could not actually assemble the necessary ingredients.[12] Library books have long supplied such data.[13]

6.05   Fearful of incidents such as the use of sarin by the Aum Shinrikyo cult in Tokyo in 1995 as well as scares about anthrax following the 11 September attacks, the offence has been extended beyond conventional munitions. The enlargement was envisaged by the Home Office Consultation Paper,[14] and these new terms are described in s 55 of the Terrorism Act 2000, as amended by s 120(2) of the Anti-terrorism, Crime and Security

---

[6] Zedner, L., 'Seeking security by eroding rights' in Goold, B.J. and Lazarus, L., *Security and Human Rights* (Hart, Oxford, 2007) p 259.

[7] President Bush, State of the Union Address 2004 (*The Washington Post* 21 January 2004 p A18).

[8] Amended by the Anti-terrorism, Crime and Security Act 2001, s 120.

[9] See further s 120A, inserted by the Terrorism Act 2006, s 37 to ensure consistency with s 7.

[10] *Inquiry into Legislation against Terrorism* (Cm 3420, London, 1996) para 14.28.

[11] *The Times* 1 July 2000 p 1.

[12] Wolkind, M. and Sweeney, N., '*R v David Copeland*' (2001) 41 *Medicine Science and Law* 185 at p 190.

[13] See Grivas-Dighenis, G., *Guerrilla Warfare and EOKA's Struggle* (Longmans, London, 1964).

[14] Home Office and Northern Ireland Office, *Legislation against Terrorism* (Cm 4178, London, 1998) para 12.13.

Act 2001. The offence applies to training in any 'biological weapon', 'chemical weapon', and 'radioactive material'. The definition of 'nuclear weapon', which used to appear in s 55 (by reference to the Nuclear Material (Offences) Act 1983) is now omitted, presumably because the meaning of 'radioactive material' is wider still.

Quite why this offence could not be translated into the regular explosives and fire- 6.06
arms codes is not clear, save for one reference to 'terrorism'. This appears in s 54(5), by which it is a defence to prove that one's action or involvement was wholly for a purpose other than assisting, preparing for, or participating in terrorism. This formulation is curiously wide. The defence would seem to apply, for example, to a non-terrorist gang-ster who trains confederates how to blow off a safe door.[15] Section 118 applies an evidential burden of proof to the defence, as explained more fully later in this chapter.

It is correspondingly an offence under s 54(2) to receive instruction or training, or, under 6.07
s 54(3) to invite another to receive instruction or training contrary to sub-s (1) or (2) even if the activity is to take place outside the United Kingdom. In this way, the offence also now pertains to recruitment for training as well as the training itself, a response to groups seeking to recruit British Muslims for military training in Afghanistan, Pakistan, and elsewhere.[16] Under s 54(4), 'instructions' and 'invitations' can be general (such as by a pamphlet or via the internet) or to specific persons, but no identifiable recipient is needed.

Offences around training are amplified by the Terrorism Act 2006, ss 6 and 8. These 6.08
relate to techniques other than specified weaponry. Section 6 (but not s 8) reflects the Council of Europe Convention on the Prevention of Terrorism 2005,[17] Art 7. The maxi-mum penalty is ten years, and materials under s 6 can be forfeited under s 7.

By s 6(1), an offence arises through providing instruction or training with knowledge 6.09
that the person receiving it intends to use the skills in terrorism. The intention of the recipient is important—an earlier version included suspicion of future use, which could have closed down university classes in chemistry and military studies collections of public libraries.[18] It is forbidden under s 6(2) to receive instruction or training. Aside from the overlap with s 54, similar conduct may fall within ss 1 or 2 of the 2006 Act.

Section 6(3) describes the relevant skills which are the subject of the instruction or 6.10
training. They must relate to: (a) the making, handling, or use of a noxious substance;[19] (b) the use of any method or technique for doing anything else that is capable of being done for the purposes of terrorism, in connection with terrorism or Convention offences;[20] or (c) the design or adaptation, for the purposes of terrorism or Convention offences, of any method or technique. Illustrations of each include:[21] (a) instruction about a bomb to disperse a virus; (b) a technique for causing a stampede in a crowd; or (c) giving instructions about the placing of a bomb to cause maximum disruption. The skills them-selves might have a lawful purpose, especially under (b) (training in anti-surveillance techniques to avoid a stalker) and (c) (learning to fly an aircraft). The absence of a

---

[15] See *R v G* [2008] EWCA Crim 922. Compare *R v G* [2009] UKHL 13.
[16] See further Walker, C. and Whyte, D., 'Contracting out war?' (2005) 54 *International & Comparative Law Quarterly* 651.
[17] ETS 196.
[18] See Hansard HL vol 676, col 716 (7 December 2005), Baroness Scotland.
[19] For 'noxious substance', see s 6(7).
[20] 'Convention offences' are those listed in sch 1.
[21] See Home Office Circular 8/2006 (London, 2006) para 17.

defence of reasonable excuse or lawful purpose comparable to s 54(5) reduces the pretexts which can be raised.[22]

6.11   Under s 6(4), the instruction or training can be provided to a target audience or to the world in general (such as through the internet) where even the identities of the recipients are not known. However, it will then be difficult to prove *mens rea* since the intention of the recipient will also be hard to gauge.[23] By s 6(4)(b), the forms of terrorism or Convention offences can be specific or agglomerations.

6.12   A s 8(1) offence arises when a person attends at any place, whether in the United Kingdom or abroad, where instruction or training within s 6 or s 54(1) of the 2000 Act is being provided. This broad *actus reus* does not require participation by the person (confirmed by s 8(3)(a)), nor does it require the delineation of specific offences (confirmed in s 8(3)(b)), but it does require the instruction or training to be 'live'. Visiting a camp during vacation periods to talk with instructors or participants would not be an offence. By s 8(6), there need be no evidence of anyone paying heed, but there should be participants other than the instructors. As for the *mens rea*, by s 8(2), the person in attendance must know or believe that instruction or training is being provided for purposes connected with terrorism or Convention offences, or the circumstances are such that a reasonable person would have realized the nature of the activity. Under the second, objective formula, innocents abroad may breach this standard if the penny drops after a reasonable person would have realized what was going on and would have left beforehand. It is also not part of the *mens rea* that the offender intends or condones the training. There is guilt by association rather than involvement.

6.13   The main debate on s 8 was whether there should be a reasonable excuse for mere observation such as by an investigative journalist.[24] The government was steadfast against creating exceptions and viewed such investigative journalism or research as a step too far.[25] The same would apply to the deliverers of groceries.[26]

6.14   Given the allegation that 75 per cent of *jihadi* training occurs in Pakistan,[27] s 8 could be invoked to cast suspicions on persons attending madrasses and other independent foreign institutes. A more beneficial effect might be to displace control orders (described in Chapter 7) which have been repeatedly applied to those seeking to join *jihadi* groups.[28] One case to emerge in England concerned Mohammed Hamid (the self-styled 'Osama bin London') who was convicted with six others for military-style training which included paint-balling.[29]

---

[22] See Joint Committee on Human Rights, *Counter-Terrorism Policy and Human Rights: Prosecution and Pre-Charge Detention* (2005–06 HL 240/HC 1576) para 59.

[23] See Leigh, L.H., 'The Terrorism Act 2006—a brief analysis' (2006) 170 *Justice of the Peace* 364.

[24] Lord Carlile, *Proposals by Her Majesty's Government for Changes to the Laws against Terrorism* (Home Office, 2005) para 39.

[25] Hansard HC vol 438, col 1015 (3 November 2005), Paul Goggins; *Government Reply to the Joint Committee on Human Rights* (2005–06 HL 114/HC 888) p 10.

[26] Jones, A., Bowers, R, and Lodge, H.D., *The Terrorism Act 2006* (Oxford University Press, Oxford, 2006) para 3.20.

[27] Gordon Brown, *The Times* 15 December 2008 p 33.

[28] See the case of Habib Ahmed, *The Times* 21 September 2006 p 11.

[29] *The Times* 27 February 2008 pp 1, 2, 6, 7.

2. Threats and hoaxes relating to dangerous substances

Just as the offence of weapons training has been extended to cover chemical, biological,   6.15
and nuclear weapons and materials, so ss 113 to 115 of the Anti-terrorism, Crime and
Security Act 2001 extend offences relating to threats and hoaxes from firearms and
explosives to chemical, biological, and nuclear weapons and materials.

By s 113(1), it becomes an offence for a person to use a noxious substance or thing to   6.16
cause serious harm in a manner designed to influence the government or to intimidate
the public. The serious harm is defined further by sub-s (2), in terms which reflect
s 1(2)(a) to (d) (but not disruption to electronic systems) of the Terrorism Act 2000,
including by the induction of fear of serious danger or risk. The latter caters for the situation where the attack has been disrupted, 'for example, where the police intercept a
package of anthrax spores designed to kill the recipient before it reaches its target'.[30] By
s 113(3), it is an offence to threaten an action which constitutes an offence under
sub-s (1) with the intention of inducing fear in a person anywhere in the world. Conduct
of these kinds outside the United Kingdom may fall within s 113A, as described later.

Section 113 has not displaced the common law offence of conspiracy to cause a   6.17
public nuisance. The manufacture of ricin and cyanide was the basis for this charge in
R v Bourgass.[31] The Court of Appeal rejected the argument that s 113 should be used in
preference and also held that its maximum penalty (fourteen years) was not an appropriate yardstick sentence for the common law offence (up to life).

Section 114 deals with hoaxes with reference to 'a noxious substance or other noxious   6.18
thing'. It is an offence to place or send 'any substance or article intending to make others
believe that it is likely to be or contain a noxious substance or thing which could endanger human life or health'. Relevant actions might include 'scattering white powder in a
public place or spraying concentrated water droplets around in an Underground train'.[32]
By sub-s (2), it is an offence for a person falsely to communicate any information to
another person anywhere in the world that a noxious substance or thing is or will be in
a place and so likely to cause harm or to endanger human life or health.

Section 114 adds to s 51 of the Criminal Law Act 1977 (as amended), which makes   6.19
it an offence for someone to place or send any article intending to make another person
believe that it is likely to explode or ignite and thereby cause personal injury or damage
to property. It is also an offence under s 51 to communicate any hoax information along
these lines. Corresponding offences exist in Scotland (s 63) and in Northern Ireland.[33]
A related offence is contamination or interference with goods or by making it appear, or
making threats or claims, that goods have been contaminated or interfered with,
contrary to s 38 of the Public Order Act 1986. These offences were considered too limited
after the anthrax attacks in the USA in late 2001. Section 51 relates only to hoax devices
which are 'likely to explode or ignite'. Section 38 protects only the integrity of goods;
it was felt that the criminal law should be expanded. The penalty for s 114 is up to
seven years' imprisonment as under s 51, but less than the ten years of s 38.

---

[30] Hansard HL vol 629, col 1162 (10 December 2001), Lord Rooker.
[31] *R v Bourgass* [2005] EWCA Crim 1943, [2006] EWCA Crim 3397.
[32] Home Office Circular 7/2002, p 4. There is no retrospective effect: Home Affairs Committee, *Report on the Anti-terrorism, Crime and Security Bill 2001* (2001–02 HC 351) para 64.
[33] Criminal Law (Amendment) (Northern Ireland) Order 1977, SI 1977/1249, art 3.

6.20   For the purposes of both ss 113 and 114, s 115 makes clear that 'substance' includes any biological agent and any other natural or artificial substance. The word 'noxious' is not defined. The meaning under s 23 of the Offences against the Person Act 1861 (to administer a noxious thing to endanger life) requires the jury to consider 'quality and quantity' and to decide as a question of fact and degree whether that thing was noxious.[34] Section 115 also specifies that no particular victim need be in mind. So, threats and hoaxes issued at large, such as via the internet, can be penalized.

6.21   Few prosecutions have been recorded,[35] and more effective counteractions against hoaxes have comprised sophisticated telephonic tracing and packaging technology.

3. Directing a terrorist organization

6.22   Returning to precursor offences, s 56(1) of the Terrorism Act 2000 makes it an offence to direct, at any level, the activities of an organization which is concerned in the commission of acts of terrorism. Section 56 derives from the mounting apprehension in Northern Ireland in the late 1980s about terrorist 'godfathers' who avoided involvement at the sharp end of death and destruction.[36] The offence began as the Northern Ireland (Emergency Provisions) Act 1991, s 27, but s 56 now applies to all forms of terrorism (and not even just proscribed organizations) and throughout the United Kingdom. However, the offender must occupy some level within a terrorist organization. Section 56 also imposes a severer penalty (up to life imprisonment) than those in Pt II of the 2000 Act.

6.23   All 'directions' are penalized, even if lawful and, indeed, desirable. For example, it would be an offence for an IRA commander to direct others to surrender, to observe a ceasefire, or to help in fund-raising for prisoners' wives. Another example might be the IRA commander who orders the IRA quartermaster to buy a gross of balaclavas. The underling might commit a Pt II or III offence under the Terrorism Act 2000; the director would additionally commit an offence under s 56. Evidence of 'predicate crimes' such as these will be powerful aids to prosecution under s 56 but are not essential.

6.24   It has been emphasized that 'directing' has its ordinary, common-sense meaning and that the reference to 'any level' is designed to catch not so much minor members of the terrorist group as regional and local (as well as headquarters) leaders.[37] Thus, it is not a fair criticism that the concept, 'directs', is contradicted by the qualification, 'at any level', or that the IRA's kitchen staff would be guilty under s 56 by 'directing' the washing up of the IRA's dirty dishes.[38] In law, to 'direct' has been defined more narrowly than is implied by such examples and seems to embody the attributes of being able to order other people and of commanding some obedience from them.[39] Thus, direction 'embraces the notion of a controlling influence on the activities in question'.[40]

---

[34] Archbold, *Criminal Pleading Evidence and Practice* (56th edn, Sweet & Maxwell, London, 2008) para 19–230.

[35] See Privy Counsellor Review Committee, *Anti-terrorism, Crime and Security Act 2001, Review, Report* (2003–04 HC 100) para 428.

[36] See Walker, C. and Reid, K., 'The offence of directing terrorist organisations' [1993] *Criminal Law Review* 669.

[37] Hansard HC vol 187, col 404 (6 March 1991).

[38] Hansard HL vol 528, col 1394 (13 May 1991).

[39] See *Bolton Engineering v T.J. Graham* [1957] 1 QB 159; *Dudderidge v Rawlings* (1912) 108 LT 802.

[40] Hansard HL vol 528, col 1396 (13 May 1991), Lord Belstead.

Very few convictions have been secured, but the Home Office Consultation Paper   6.25
maintained that they did have 'a major impact'.[41] The most notable prosecution in
Northern Ireland involved Johnny Adair, the Loyalist gang leader.[42] The only reported
British case concerned Rangzieb Ahmed,[43] who was linked to Harakat-ul-Mujahideen.

4. Possession for terrorist purposes

There are two further precursor offences of possession for terrorist purposes in the   6.26
Terrorism Act 2000, one relating to items (s 57) and one to information (s 58).

(a) *Possession of items—s 57*

The offence of possession of items for terrorist purposes began life as s 30 of the Northern   6.27
Ireland (Emergency Provisions) Act 1991, though the notion was there confined to
possession in public places.[44] Then, the Criminal Justice and Public Order Act 1994,
s 63, enacted the offence in Britain by way of the Prevention of Terrorism (Temporary
Provisions) Act 1989, s 16A. Continuance was supported by Lord Lloyd.[45] Section 57
now applies throughout the United Kingdom. The level of maximum penalty was
increased by the Terrorism Act 2006, s 13, from ten years to fifteen years, following criticisms in the trial of Andrew Rowe.[46]

Section 57(1) is contravened by possession of an article in circumstances which give   6.28
rise to a reasonable suspicion that the possession is for a purpose connected with terrorism. The 'terrorism' is not confined to the activities of proscribed organizations. 'Article'
is further defined in s 121 to include 'substance and any other thing'. The articles possessed will often be lawful in themselves and even commonplace. Section 57 thereby differs markedly from those caught red-handed in possession of explosives and firearms,
offensive weapons, or equipment for theft where more specific offences apply.[47] Rather,
items such as wires, batteries, rubber gloves, scales, electronic timers, overalls, balaclavas,
agricultural fertilizer, and gas cylinders, especially in conjunction, form the fare of s 57.
The collection may be highly equivocal—persons with overalls and balaclavas may be preparing for an attack on a police patrol or on a rabbit warren. Regarding multiple-use articles
such as computer disks or cars, which might be possessed for several purposes, it is submitted
that s 57(1) only requires 'a' purpose to be nefarious, not a main or sole purpose.[48]

The intent required for s 57 means basically that the defendant has knowledge of   6.29
presence, and control over, the article.[49] Based on that possession and control, the Crown
must prove beyond reasonable doubt that those circumstances give rise to a reasonable

---

[41] Home Office and Northern Ireland Office, *Legislation against Terrorism* (Cm 4178, London, 1998)
para 12.9.
[42] See *The Irish Times* 7 September 1994 p 8.
[43] *The Times* 19 December 2008 p 8.
[44] See *Review of the Northern Ireland (Emergency Provisions) Acts 1978 and 1987* (Cm 1115, London, 1990)
para 2.9.
[45] *Inquiry into Legislation against Terrorism* (Cm. 3420, London, 1996) para 14.6.
[46] *The Guardian* 24 September 2005 p 7.
[47] See Explosive Substances Act 1883 s 4; Firearms Act 1968 ss 16–21; Prevention of Crime Act 1953 s 1;
Theft Act 1968 s 25.
[48] Compare *R v Zafar* [2008] EWCA Crim 184 at para 22.
[49] *R v G* [2009] UKHL 13 at para 53.

suspicion of a terrorist purpose. Proof of possession for a terrorist purpose requires examination of the circumstances of possession, but the Crown does not need to prove the precise, subjective purpose harboured by the defendant—'something which might well be impossible to prove'[50] and which delays anticipatory intervention.

6.30   The connection between the content of the article and the implementation of terrorism was clarified in *R v Zafar*[51] and *R v K*.[52] In *Zafar*, the prosecution had sought a guilty verdict under s 57 on the basis that the relevant purposes of the articles related to travelling to Pakistan, training in Pakistan, and fighting in Afghanistan. At the time, only the last item on the list was deemed relevant, which suggests a requirement of not only a link to terrorism in some passive sense but a link to active terrorist offending. There must be proven 'a direct connection between the objects possessed and the acts of terrorism. The section should be interpreted as if it reads . . . he intends it to be used for the purpose . . . '.[53] But there was nothing inherent in travel to Pakistan which directly connected to the incitement amongst the group to engage in terrorism. Any further actions in Pakistan were conditional on later intentions and actions.[54] Thus, the convictions were unsound.

6.31   Proof of 'possession' is aided by sub-s (3): if it is proved that an article (a) was on any premises at the same time as the accused; or (b) was on premises of which the accused was the occupier or which he habitually used otherwise than as a member of the public, the court may assume that the accused possessed the article.

6.32   Recognizing the possible overreach, s 57(2) offers a defence by proof that possession of the article was not for a purpose connected with the commission, preparation, or instigation of an act of terrorism. The defence does not nullify the elements already proven but provides an excuse for them, which the prosecution can then challenge beyond reasonable doubt.[55] This switch does not, however, then require the Crown to prove beyond reasonable doubt that the defendant's possession of the article was for a purpose connected with terrorism—that would be to go beyond the defence and add elements to the formulation of the offence.[56] For example, if the evidence concerns the possession of fertilizer, and the defendant shows, sufficiently under s 118, a non-terrorist purpose connected with gardening, the prosecution must show beyond reasonable doubt that the defence is untrue:[57]

. . . for instance, by leading evidence that the garden had been consistently neglected, that there were no gardening tools in the house, and that the quantity of fertiliser was more than would be required for the garden in question. . . . There is no need whatever for the Crown to go further . . . and prove, beyond reasonable doubt, that the defendant actually possessed the fertiliser for a purpose connected with the commission etc of an act of terrorism. That would be to impose on the Crown a requirement that is not to be found in section 57(1).

6.33   In addition, under s 57(3), it is open to the defendant to show he did not know of the presence of the item on the premises or had no control over it. It has been argued

---

[50]   *Ibid* at para 55.
[51]   [2008] EWCA Crim 184.
[52]   [2008] EWCA Crim 185.
[53]   *Ibid* at para 29.
[54]   *Ibid* at para 45.
[55]   *R v G* [2009] UKHL 13 at paras 63, 66.
[56]   *Ibid* at para 67.
[57]   *Ibid* at para 68.

that these defences do not alleviate the unfairness of the offence and in fact perpetrate another by switching the burden of proof to the defence, contrary to the presumption of innocence under Art 6(2) of the European Convention.

The meaning of the offence and its possible breach of Art 6(2) have been considered in *R v Director of Public Prosecutions, ex parte Kebilene*.[58] The Divisional Court felt that there was a 'blatant and obvious' breach of Art 6(2).[59] The House of Lords ultimately decided the case on the technical ground of the non-reviewability of prosecution decisions, but, drawing upon s 3 of the Human Rights Act 1998, Lord Hope devised a modified meaning which complied with Art 6(2):[60]   6.34

> It is necessary in the first place to distinguish between the shifting from the prosecution to the accused . . . the 'evidential burden', or the burden of introducing evidence in support of his case, on the one hand and the 'persuasive burden,' or the burden of persuading the jury as to his guilt or innocence, on the other. A 'persuasive' burden of proof requires the accused to prove, on a balance of probabilities, a fact which is essential to the determination of his guilt or innocence. It reverses the burden of proof by removing it from the prosecution and transferring it to the accused. An 'evidential' burden requires only that the accused must adduce sufficient evidence to raise an issue before it has to be determined as one of the facts in the case. The prosecution does not need to lead any evidence about it, so the accused needs to do this if he wishes to put the point in issue. But if it is put in issue, the burden of proof remains with the prosecution. The accused need only raise a reasonable doubt about his guilt.

Flowing from this distinction, an 'evidential' burden, as under s 57, does not necessarily breach the presumption of innocence under Art 6(2), which, though a fundamental right, does seem to allow some manipulation where important social concerns are involved and where the defendant has ready access to the information required for the defence.[61] Once the issue is raised, the burden is taken up by the prosecution to disprove any defence and to discharge the final burden of proof of guilt beyond reasonable doubt of all essential facts (possession and reasonable suspicion of a terrorist purpose). By contrast, statutory presumptions which transfer the legal or 'persuasive' burden to the accused, or, even more starkly, a 'mandatory' presumption of guilt relating to an essential element of the offence would more probably breach Art 6(2).   6.35

In reaction to *Kebilene*, the Government sought to re-enact the offence without change. However, in the light of the onslaught from critics, s 118 was added to the 2000 Act and affects both ss 57(2) and 57(3). By s 118, if evidence is adduced which is sufficient to raise an issue, the court shall treat it as proved unless the prosecution disproves it beyond reasonable doubt. This formula was intended to be merely declaratory.[62] It certainly prevents s 57 from placing any 'legal' or 'persuasive' burden upon the defendant. It may also slightly ease the 'evidential' burden placed on the defendant by requiring simply the issue to be raised for it to negate the presumption in the statute unless the   6.36

---

[58] [2000] 2 AC 326.

[59] *Ibid* at p 344 per Lord Bingham.

[60] [2000] 2 AC 326 at pp 378–9.

[61] See *Salabiaku v France*, App no 10519/83 Ser A 141-A (1988). See further *Sheldrake v Director of Public Prosecutions; Attorney General's Reference (No 4 of 2002)* [2004] UKHL 43; Treschel, S., *Human Rights in Criminal Proceedings* (Oxford University Press, Oxford, 2005) pp 168–71.

[62] Hansard HL vol 613, col 754 (16 May 2000), Lord Bassam.

prosecution can prove otherwise.[63] Certainly, the courts have been receptive to defendants. In *R v Boutrab*,[64] a bare claim that 'curiosity' was the reason for possession was sufficient to switch the burden back to the prosecution, though in *Kebilene*, Lord Hope warned that 'It should not be thought that proof to this standard will be a formality.'[65]

6.37   Some commentators suggest that the dispute was misconceived on the grounds that the prosecution must prove beyond reasonable doubt not only the possession of the items relevant to s 57 but also reasonable suspicion of the terroristic purpose, so that the burden of proof is not shifted at all.[66] Yet, the presence of items under s 57 is far less suggestive of blameworthy conduct than under comparable precursor offences. Being in charge of false identity documents, counterfeit credit cards, and a three band radio, as in the case of *Meziane*,[67] is much less determinative of terrorism purpose than is possession of a knife or a jemmy suggestive of an offence against the person or against property. If it takes no great effort to prove the offence at the outset by the prosecution, then the real task in court is for the defence, which of course was always the intention of the legislation. In this way, the argument does fall within Art 6(2), even though, ostensibly, one might think that the real dispute is about the formulation of criminal offences.[68]

6.38   Adding to the debate is the decision in *Sheldrake v Director of Public Prosecutions; Attorney General's Reference (No 4 of 2002)*.[69] Here, the reverse burden of proof in s 11(2) of the 2000 Act was again read down as an evidential and not legal burden, even though Lord Bingham believed that Parliament's intention was otherwise, especially because it was not listed in s 118.[70] The result would seem to be three levels of reactions to reverse burdens. First, the measure might be interpreted on its face or by reference to s 118 as imposing an evidential burden. Secondly, where s 118 does not apply and even where the burden is expressed to be legal, then unless the offence is also expressed to overrule Art 6(2), the *Attorney General's Reference (No 4 of 2002)* will ride to the rescue where it is felt that the legal burden would be unfair, which will be judged according to the effects of the reverse burden, including how easily the accused can discharge the burden or how difficult it would be for the prosecution to establish the facts, bearing in mind the seriousness of the offences and the level of penalties.

(b) *Collection of information—s 58*

6.39   Offences of collecting or recording or possessing information in a document or record of a kind likely to be useful to terrorism have existed in Northern Ireland for some time (latterly in the Northern Ireland (Emergency Provisions) Act 1996, s 33). They were also translated into Britain by the Criminal Justice and Public Order Act 1994, s 63, as s 16B

---

[63] See Rowe, J.J., 'The Terrorism Act 2000' [2000] *Criminal Law Review* 527 at p 540.

[64] [2005] NICC 30 at paras 80, 84.

[65] [2000] 2 AC 326 at p 387.

[66] Roberts, P., 'The presumption of innocence brought home?' (2002) 118 *Law Quarterly Review* 41 at p 54. See also Buxton, R., 'The Human Rights Act and the substantive criminal law' [2000] *Criminal Law Review* 331 at p 332.

[67] *The Times* 2 April 2003 p 11. See *R v Meziane* [2004] EWCA Crim 1768.

[68] Compare *(John) Murray v United Kingdom* App no 18731/91, 1996-I, at paras 45, 47. See Treschel, S., *Human Rights in Criminal Proceedings* (Oxford University Press, Oxford, 2005) pp 356–7.

[69] [2004] UKHL 43. See also *R v Keogh* [2007] EWCA Crim 528.

[70] *Ibid* at para 50.

of the Prevention of Terrorism (Temporary Provisions) Act 1989. Now they are set out in s 58 of the Terrorism Act 2000.

Section 58(1) contains two variants of *actus reus*: collecting or making a record of 6.40 information likely to be useful in terrorism or possessing a document or record containing information of that kind. A 'record' includes photographic or electronic formats as well as writings and drawings (s 58(2)), but mental notes and knowledge which are not recorded are not covered. It is unnecessary to show that the information was obtained or held in breach of law. The possession of army manuals was the basis for conviction in *R v Lorenc*.[71]

As for *mens rea*, s 58 does not contain any equivalent to s 57(3), regarding the assump- 6.41 tion of possession of the articles in certain circumstances. Therefore, the Crown must prove beyond a reasonable doubt that there is knowledge as to the presence of, and control over, the document or record.[72] A further element is that the defendant must be aware of the nature of the information—measures of concealment will be good evidence of such knowledge.[73]

There is no element in s 58(1) that requires the Crown to show that the defendant had 6.42 a terrorist purpose. In *R v K*, the defendant, Khalid Khaliq, mounted the bold argument that s 58 was insufficiently certain to comply with Art 7 of the European Convention. In response, the Court of Appeal sought to remedy any imprecision by reading in the requirement of a purpose useful to terrorism. In this case, it is the purpose of the information rather than the possessor at stake—it intrinsically 'calls for an explanation'.[74] The information (without regard to its surrounding circumstances, unlike under s 57) must be of an intrinsic kind which gives rise to a reasonable suspicion on its face that it is likely to provide practical assistance to a person committing or preparing terrorism rather than simply encouraging the commission of terrorism. To illustrate, the A–Z of London could be of use to a terrorist in order to find a target, but that use would not place it within s 58 since that document does not intrinsically arouse suspicion unless one looked at the circumstances of its usage. The ruling in *R v K* was applied in *R v Samina Malik*.[75] The defendant, known by her pen-name as the 'Lyrical Terrorist', was convicted under s 58, not for her crass poetry such as 'How to Behead', but for her possession of documents about military techniques, along with other documents of a propagandist nature. She was acquitted on appeal on the grounds that the judge's summing up had failed to isolate those documents capable of founding a conviction under s 58 by satisfying the test of inherent practical utility. The House of Lords in *R v G*[76] endorsed that 'the aim was to catch the possession of information which would typically be of use to terrorists, as opposed to ordinary members of the population . . . the information must, of its very nature, be designed to provide practical assistance.' The usage need not be unique to terrorists—a manual on explosives might also benefit bank robbers but would still raise suspicions of a terrorist purpose.

---

[71] [1988] NI 96.
[72] *R v G* [2009] UKHL 13 at para 46.
[73] *Ibid* at paras 47, 48.
[74] [2008] EWCA Crim 185 at para 14. See further *R v G* [2009] UKHL 13 at para 44 on reliance upon extrinsic explanations.
[75] [2008] EWCA Crim 1450.
[76] [2009] UKHL 13 at para 43. The terrorist may be the defendant or a third party: para 49.

6.43   By s 58(3), it is a defence when the prosecution has proven all elements of the offence[77] for the defendant to prove a 'reasonable excuse'. As with s 57(2), the defence does not nullify the elements already proven but provides an excuse for them, which the prosecution can then challenge beyond reasonable doubt but without also proving beyond reasonable doubt that the defendant's possession of the article was for a purpose connected with terrorism.[78] Suppose, a defendant raises a defence of reasonable excuse regarding the possession of a computer disk containing the Al-Qa'ida Training Manual that he had found it on a train minutes earlier and was going to hand it in to the police when stopped under s 44.[79] If the Crown proved beyond a reasonable doubt that the defendant's story was untrue—maybe he had phoned a contact to pass on the disk—the defence is defeated, but the Crown does not also have to show the precise terrorist purpose for which the information was to be used. In *R v McLaughlin*,[80] a hobby radio enthusiast had a reasonable excuse for possessing a list of police radio frequencies, though the Court of Appeal in that case did seem to take account of purpose, which is not sound law under s 58.

6.44   The penalties equate to those for s 54. According to *R v Mansha*,[81] 'a person convicted of a terrorist offence must expect a substantial sentence . . . to serve as a deterrent to others and to mark the extreme seriousness of the criminality'. Forfeiture may be ordered of any document or record containing the impugned information.

6.45   Once again, the main controversy surrounding s 58 concerns the equivocal nature of the actions involved and the fact that the defendant shoulder the burden of proof of reasonable excuse under sub-s (3), subject to s 118. The indeterminate range of the offence causes alarm for journalists: 'What journalist worth his or her salt does not have a contacts book? A cuttings file? A file on the activities and personal details of prominent public figures?'[82] Scholars who study terrorism might also skirt s 58.

(c) *Litigation about ss 57 and 58*

6.46   Two principal disputes have arisen in recent litigation which cut across both offences. The first controversy is whether ss 57 and 58 are mutually exclusive, which was the unexpected result in *R v M*.[83] The defendants (Malik, Zafar, and others) were subject to three sets of 'mirror image' counts under ss 57 and 58. The prosecution sought to justify the dual charges on two grounds: that s 57 refers to an 'instigation' which is not covered by s 58; and that s 58 criminalizes the collection of information or the making of a record of information, which is 'likely to be useful' to terrorism, whereas s 57 demands a reasonable suspicion that that is the case. The foregoing differences are real enough but were not sufficient to convince Lord Justice Hooper to accept the duality on the basis that it had rendered redundant s 58 since any 'document or record' will be an 'article' under s 57.[84]

---

[77]   *Ibid* at para 60.
[78]   *R v G* [2009] UKHL 13 at paras 63, 69.
[79]   *Ibid* at para 69.
[80]   [1993] NI 28. See further *R v G* [2009] UKHL 13 at para 84.
[81]   [2006] EWCA Crim 2051 at para 11 per Forbes J.
[82]   Hickman, L., 'Press freedom and new legislation' (2001) 151 *New Law Journal* 716.
[83]   [2007] EWCA Crim 218. See 'Comment' [2007] *Criminal Law Review* 72.
[84]   *Ibid* at paras 33, 34.

These conclusions were rightly rejected shortly afterwards by the Court of Appeal in 6.47
R v Rowe.[85] Rowe had been convicted under s 57 for the possession of notes on mortar bombs and of a code about possible targets, but he argued that he should have been prosecuted under s 58. However, the earlier decision was rejected. It was accepted that vaguely worded anti-terrorism laws overlap, an intended feature of the sweeping legislation. The overlapping provisions do not become redundant since there remain important differences between ss 57 and 58.[86] First, s 57 applies to possession, while s 58 applies not only to possession but also to collecting or making. Secondly, s 57 covers 'articles' which are widely defined, whereas s 58 covers only 'documents or records' which are a subset of articles. Thirdly, s 57 applies where the circumstances give rise to a reasonable suspicion of a terrorist purpose, whereas s 58 focuses on the nature of the information without regard to circumstances or purpose. This ruling was applied to Malik, Zafar, and others in *R v M (No 2)*.[87] Nevertheless, while overlapping offences are possible, there must be regard to the possible confusion of juries if both are run together.[88]

The second principal dispute relates to the bounds of 'reasonable excuse'. Can plot- 6.48
ting terrorism aggressively against a tyrannical regime or by way of defence against the regime's aggression be excused as the noble cause of 'freedom fighters' or 'defenders of the people'? The point was raised in *R v F*,[89] concerning a refugee from Libya who was charged under s 58. The Court of Appeal concluded, correctly in technical terms, that, as a matter of legislative history of s 1, Parliament had decided to restrict political freedoms even in the context of the enemies of foreign despots.[90] Next, the Court of Appeal did not accept that its line of interpretation was contrary to the democracy in Art 3 of Protocol 1 of the European Convention. Rather, a wider definition of terrorism supported the right to life under Art 2.[91] Just as the challenge to the interpretation of s 1 failed, so the related argument under s 58(3) was rejected as incoherent.[92]

The Court of Appeal maintained its hostility to this line of defence in the context of 6.49
s 57(2) in *R v Rowe*, where the defendant's purpose in the possession of the materials was claimed to be the lawful defence of Muslims in Croatia and Chechnya.[93] A more general defence beyond ss 57 and 58, to resist unlawful attack by state forces on one's co-religionists or one's tribe, may also be doubted,[94] unless perhaps it can be shown that the objective was the private protection of kith and kin rather than any broader political purpose.

The meaning of 'reasonable excuse' under s 58 was next examined in *R v G*,[95] where 6.50
the Court of Appeal rejected the prosecution contention that a 'reasonable excuse' under s 58(3) could not be based on an 'illegitimate reason' (such as to 'wind up' prison officers by collecting materials about munitions). This indulgence might appear startling, but it

---

[85] [2007] EWCA Crim 635, as applied in *R v Boutrab* [2007] NICA 23.
[86] See further *R v G* [2009] UKHL 13 at paras 57–9.
[87] [2007] EWCA Crim 970.
[88] *R v Samina Malik* [2008] EWCA Crim 1450 at para 43.
[89] [2007] EWCA Crim 243. See further 'Comment' [2007] *Criminal Law Review* 160.
[90] *Ibid* at para 11.
[91] *Ibid* at para 29.
[92] *Ibid* at para 38.
[93] [2007] EWCA Crim 635 at paras 46, 48.
[94] See *R v Jones* [2006] UKHL 16.
[95] [2008] EWCA Crim 922.

rules out only charges under s 58 and not prison disciplinary charges for possessing objectionable materials.[96] The House of Lords reversed this interpretation and emphasized that the excuse must be reasonable under the wording of s 58(3), based on the intrinsic nature of the information.[97] Collections to cause annoyance to prison officers were not reasonable. The court would not accept within the defence claims that the information was for the purpose of burgling for private gain, rather than bombing for public purposes, the Home Secretary's house could amount to a reasonable excuse. The effect is to draw into the scope of the anti-terrorism legislation actions which are probably 'ordinary decent criminality' rather than terrorism. The House of Lords has thus extended the boundaries of s 58 and has subjected criminals to a wider net of criminality and of severer penalties than would otherwise apply because society is not prepared to take the risk of discerning for sure between crime and terrorism. The defendant is thrown back on arguments about the intrinsic nature of the information and whether it relates to terrorism, handicapped by not being able to show wider circumstances or purposes or even mental delusions.

6.51   The same interpretation against nefarious purposes does not apply under s 57(2) since its focus is the purpose of the defendant without reference to its reasonableness: 'So it would indeed be a defence to a section 57(1) charge for a defendant to show, for instance, that his actual purpose for having an explosive was to blow open a bank vault.'[98] The court could feel sanguine about this outcome because an offence under the Explosive Substances Act 1883, s 4, would then be made out, suggesting that prosecutors should invoke this provision rather more than at present.

6.52   Looking at recent litigation more generally, the courts have stopped a trend whereby ss 57 and 58 were becoming akin to offences of the possession of 'terrorism pornography'[99] by revelling in the notion of terrorism. Following these judicial revisions, there also seems to have been some toning down in the severity of sentences for the possession of written or computer extremist materials. For example, the court applied a 9-month suspended sentence and community service to Samina Malik (who was later acquitted on appeal).[100] However, more substantive articles (such as a car loaned for terrorist purposes)[101] or more specific information (such as how to attack the royal family)[102] will still incur more severe sentences. Furthermore, though these judgments reduce the scope of ss 57 and 58, the offences are far from 'almost redundant'.[103]

(d) *Information about the security forces—s 58A*

6.53   The Counter-Terrorism Act 2008, s 76, inserted s 58A into the 2000 Act. It concerns eliciting, publishing, or communicating information about members of the security forces. The enactment was prompted by two recent convictions for collecting information

---

[96] See Prison Rules 1999, SI 1999/728 r 43.
[97] [2009] UKHL 13 at paras 75, 77.
[98] *Ibid* at para 74.
[99] Criminal Justice Act 1988, s 160.
[100] *The Times* 6 December 2007 p 31.
[101] See *R v Harkness* [2008] NICA 51 (seven years).
[102] See Aabid Khan, *The Times* 20 September 2008 p 15 (12 years).
[103] Tadros, V., 'Crime and security' (2008) 71 *Modern Law Review* 940 at p 968.

about soldiers, of Mohammed Abu Bakr Mansha[104] and of Parviz Khan.[105] Also in the background was the expiration in Northern Ireland of s 103 of the 2000 Act.[106]

By s 58A(1),[107] it is an offence to elicit or attempt to elicit information about a member of Her Majesty's forces, a member of any of the intelligence services, or a constable, which is of a kind likely to be useful to a person committing or preparing an act of terrorism, or to publish or communicate such information. Section 103 applied to soldiers, police officers, judges, and court officers, and prison staff, but not members of the intelligence services. Under s 58A(2) (which is subject to s 118), it is a defence for a person charged with an offence to prove that they had a reasonable excuse for their action. Recent judicial interpretations of s 58 should apply here too, so that the isolated media photographing of overt security operations should escape criminalization.[108]

6.54

How does s 58A add to s 58? As for *actus reus*, all that appears exclusive to s 58A(1)(a) is eliciting or attempting to elicit, though attempting to collect under s 58 could already be an offence. Publishing or communicating under s 58A(1)(b) could fall within s 39 of the 2000 Act or ss 1, 2, and 5 of the Terrorism Act 2006.

6.55

(e) *Acts preparatory*

The culmination of the trend favouring precursor offences is the Terrorism Act 2006, s 5. Support for such an offence has long been mooted,[109] though, as the Newton Committee Report remarked, the absence of available offences was not highlighted as problematic.[110] In part, s 5 might also be said to respond to Art 6 of the European Convention for the Prevention of Terrorism 2005, by which action should be taken against 'recruitment for terrorism', including to solicit another person to participate in the commission of a terrorist offence. However, the correspondence is partial, and it is notable that s 5 does not mention Convention offences.

6.56

By s 5(1), an offence arises if, with the intention of (a) committing acts of terrorism; or (b) assisting another to commit such acts, a person engages in any conduct in preparation for giving effect to that intention. The penalty is up to life imprisonment.[111]

6.57

The scope of the preparatory acts is deliberately broad, save that the object of attention must be 'acts' rather than, say, the continued existence of a proscribed organization. Acts of terrorism are also distinct from acts of terrorists, the assistance of whom might comprise, say, shopping. The modes of involvement in connection with those 'acts' can be distinct from conspiracies (requiring an agreement with others)[112] or attempts

6.58

---

[104] *R v Mansha* [2006] EWCA Crim 2051.

[105] *The Times* 19 February 2008 p 3.

[106] See Home Office, *Possible Measures for Inclusion into a Future Counter-Terrorism Bill* (London, 2007) para 32.

[107] Note also Sch 8 of the 2008 Act regarding jurisdiction over information society services.

[108] Hansard HL vol 704, col 1072 (21 October 2008) Lord West; case of Malcolm Sleath (*The Times* 16 April 2009 p 23).

[109] Home Office, *Counter-Terrorism Powers: Reconciling Security and Liberty in an Open Society* (Cm 6147, London, 2004) para 48; Lord Carlile, *Anti-terrorism, Crime and Security Act 2001 Part IV Section 28, Review 2003* (Home Office, 2004) para 101.

[110] Privy Counsellor Review Committee, *Anti-terrorism, Crime and Security Act 2001, Review, Report* (2003–04 HC 100) para 207.

[111] As under s 56, it is not mandatory: Hansard HL vol 676, col 715 (7 December 2005).

[112] See Joint Committee on Human Rights, *Counter-Terrorism Policy and Human Rights: Prosecution and Pre-Charge Detention* (2005–06 HL 240/HC 1576) para 54.

(the very definition of which demands action which is 'more than merely preparatory').[113] In addition, attempts and conspiracies are in relation to specific 'normal' offences rather than 'terrorism'.

6.59   There must be intent to commit or assist the acts or to assist acts. The person must have the further intent that the act or assistance must further terrorism. By s 5(2), it is expressly irrelevant whether the intention and preparations relate to one or more particular acts of terrorism, acts of terrorism of a particular description, or acts of terrorism generally.

6.60   It is difficult to pin down which activities might fall distinctly within s 5. The Explanatory Memorandum for the 2006 Act gave as an example the possession of items that could be used for terrorism even if not immediately[114]—a fair recital of s 57. Lord Carlile more cogently mentions the provision of accommodation or credit card fraud to raise living expenses,[115] though offences of withholding information, helping proscribed organizations, and terrorism financing may also apply. As for the latter, the government minister contended that 'simply making a financial donation would not be caught by the offence' and went on to claim that the true meaning of the *actus reus* demands 'active engagement in planning to carry out an act of terrorism'.[116] This reasoning does not sit easily with s 5(2) but may perhaps be justified by reference to the word 'engages' and its higher sense of activity than, say, a donation or simply agreeing to belong to a group.

6.61   Section 5 fits with the 'Prevent' and 'Pursue' strands of CONTEST and might displace some control orders,[117] but it sits less happily with the demands of a rights audit. The breadth of the offence fails to guide the citizen. The broad nature of 'preparations' come close to penalizing bad intentions rather than harms and leaving no possibility for withdrawal. It is not just that the 'exact plans are unknown'[118] but that the offence approximates to 'having criminal thoughts'.[119] There is no list of outlawed activities, no set level of commitment to the enterprise nor as to its viability. Acts of charity, such as by providing accommodation or transport, could become viewed as guilt by association or inadvertence after a guest is found to be involved in terrorism.[120]

6.62   An illustration might be the case of Saajid Badat.[121] He entered a guilty plea to charges of conspiring to destroy aircraft and the possession of explosives, when the police discovered in 2003 the parts for a shoe bomb in a box in his bedroom. Badat had withdrawn from the enterprise two years earlier, but the presence of explosives remains a danger to life and a temptation to later use. Changing these facts, what if Badat had withdrawn before collecting the explosives from Pakistan, at a point when his 'preparation' had been to designate a suitable box to house the explosive materials and to write 'Danger: Explosives!' on the lid? Here are acts preparatory, but without harm or even potential harm.

---

[113] Criminal Attempts Act 1981, s 1(1).

[114] (Home Office, London, 2006) para 49.

[115] Lord Carlile, *Proposals by Her Majesty's Government for Changes to the Laws against Terrorism* (Home Office, London, 2005) para 30.

[116] Hansard HC vol 438, cols 1000–1001 (3 November 2005), Paul Goggins.

[117] See Mohammed Abushamma, *The Times* 29 November 2008 p 24.

[118] Hansard HC vol 438, col 999 (3 November 2005), Paul Goggins.

[119] Jones, A., Bowers, R, and Lodge, H.D., *The Terrorism Act 2006* (Oxford University Press, Oxford, 2006) para 3.05.

[120] See Joint Committee on Human Rights, *Counter-Terrorism Policy and Human Rights: Prosecution and Pre-Charge Detention* (2005–06 HL 240/HC 1576) para 94.

[121] *The Times* 1 March 2005 p 1.

An actual illustration of s 5 concerned Sohail Anjum Qureshi, who pleaded guilty to   6.63
preparing for the commission of terrorist acts.[122] He had been arrested at Heathrow
Airport, en route to Pakistan. His luggage included night-vision binoculars, medical
provisions, two British passports, and nearly £9,000 in cash. Another notable conviction
was that of Martyn Gilleard, charged under s 5 and also under s 58 of the 2000 Act in
connection with possession of nail bombs and *The Anarchist Cookbook* in pursuit of his
neo-Nazi activities.[123] Nicholas Roddis was convicted for leaving a hoax bomb on a bus
in Rotherham and collecting items and materials to make explosives.[124] It is notable that
other offences were available in every case.

(f) *Internal jurisdiction*

Under common law, a substantial part of the activities constituting a criminal offence   6.64
must take place within that jurisdiction in which the court trying the offence is located.
Following the Glasgow airport bombing in 2007, committed by a group which also
planted two car bombs in London the previous day, there was concern that the attacks
could not be tried together in either Scotland or England, with consequent inconveni-
ence and expense.[125]

Therefore, s 28 of the Counter-Terrorism Act 2008 states that in respect of specified   6.65
terrorism offences committed in the United Kingdom, proceedings may be taken at 'any
place'. The substantial list of terrorism legislation offences (including even relatively low-
level offences)[126] may be amended by affirmative statutory order. This power will be
applied only to offences committed on or after the coming into force of s 28.[127]

Safeguards were added to deal with the application of this provision in Scotland and   6.66
Northern Ireland. Regarding Scotland, the Act is silent on how to arbitrate between possible court venues, but it was promised during passage that there will always be consultation as well as a formal protocol.[128] Scotland's stricter pre-trial custody limit[129] and the
absence of inferences from silence at trial will result in transfers south rather than north.

As regards Northern Ireland, the fear was that ceding an English or Scottish case to   6.67
Northern Ireland could excessively trigger non-jury trials under s 1 of the Justice and
Security (Northern Ireland) Act 2007. Section 28(6) therefore specifies that the Director
of Public Prosecutions for Northern Ireland may not issue a certificate in respect of
transferred proceedings on the basis that the offence was committed in circumstances of
religious or political hostility. Rather, there can only be a non-jury trial when the offence
bears a connection to a terrorist organization proscribed in connection with the affairs
of Northern Ireland and there is a risk that the administration of justice might be
impaired by jury trial.

---

[122] [2008] EWCA Crim 1054.
[123] *The Times* 26 June 2008 p 22.
[124] *Yorkshire Post* 19 July 2008.
[125] Lord Carlile, *Report on Proposed Measures for Inclusion in a Counter-Terrorism Bill* (Cm 7262, London, 2007) para 9.
[126] Hansard HC Public Bill Committee on the Counter Terrorism Bill, col. 361 (8 May 2008), Tony McNulty.
[127] Hansard HC vol 477, cols 226–7 (10 June 2008), Tony McNulty.
[128] Hansard HL vol 704, col 776 (15 October 2008), Lord West.
[129] Criminal Procedure (Amendment) (Scotland) Act 2004 s 6. See Hansard HC Public Bill Committee on the Counter-Terrorism Bill, cols 89–90 (22 April 2008), Elish Angiolini.

(g) *External jurisdiction*

6.68 (i) *Inciting terrorism overseas* The remaining offences in Pt VI of the Terrorism Act 2000 relate to the establishment or extension of jurisdiction over criminal offences rather than the extension of the formulation of offences or the creation of new offences. This notion of extended jurisdiction follows in the footsteps of Victorian-era foreign dissidents who were subjected to the offence of solicitation of murder under the Offences against the Person Act 1861, s 4.[130] Sections 5 to 7 of the Criminal Justice (Terrorism and Conspiracy) Act 1998 latterly conferred jurisdiction over acts of conspiracy in the United Kingdom relating to offences committed or intended to be committed abroad.[131]

6.69 Sections 59 to 61 of the Terrorism Act 2000 grant in turn English, Northern Irish, and Scottish courts jurisdiction over offences of incitement of terrorism abroad where the act would, if committed within jurisdiction, constitute any offence listed in sub-s (2).[132] The listed offences are meant to equate roughly to s 1 of the Terrorism Act, but are inevitably more precise than that term. However, the government minister, Lord Bach, denied that there is any substantial difference: 'It is not a case of one definition of "terrorism" for here and a narrower one for abroad; it is the same definition for all acts, whether here or abroad.'[133] By sub-s (4), it is immaterial whether or not the person incited is in the United Kingdom at the time of the incitement. By sub-s (5), any person acting on behalf of, or holding office under, the Crown cannot be liable—members of the security services are still allowed to foment rebellion.[134] The penalty is to correspond to that applicable on conviction of such an incitement if it occurred in the United Kingdom.[135]

6.70 Sections 59 to 61 turn certain offences into universal crimes even when they are not so recognized in international conventions or under the Suppression of Terrorism Act 1978. The official aim is to deter those who seek to use the United Kingdom as a base from which to promote terrorist acts abroad.[136] The Suppression of Terrorism Act 1978 already grants extra-territorial jurisdiction over a number of serious offences, and, in the official view, this prohibition should extend universally: 'There is no obvious justification for incitement to commit murder in Turkey or India to be an offence in the UK, whereas incitement to commit murder in Japan or Australia is not an offence'.[137] But the incitement of many designated terrorist offences (hijacking and so on) already carry universal jurisdiction. Further, no cases of incitements have resulted in prosecution instead of extradition under the 1978 Act.[138] There will also arise evidential difficulties

---

[130] *R v Most* (1881) 7 QBD 244; *R v Antonelli and Barberi* (1905) 70 JP 4. For more recent cases, see *R v El-Faisal* [2004] EWCA Crim 343 and [2004] EWCA Crim 456; *R v Abu Hamza* [2006] EWCA Crim 2918; *R v Saleem, Muhid, and Javed* [2007] EWCA Crim 2692; *R v Rahman* [2008] EWCA Crim 2290.

[131] See *Inquiry into Legislation against Terrorism* (Cm 3420, London, 1996) para 12.39.

[132] Home Office and Northern Ireland Office, *Legislation against Terrorism* (Cm 4178, London, 1998), paras 4.18, 4.19.

[133] Hansard HL vol 613, col 760, 16 May 2000.

[134] See Home Office, Circular 03/01: *Terrorism Act 2000* (Home Office, London, 2001) para 6.7. Otherwise, the Criminal Justice Act 1948, s 31 might apply.

[135] See *Attorney General's References (Nos 85, 86, and 87 of 2007) R v Tsouli* [2007] EWCA Crim 3300 para 35.

[136] Home Office and Northern Ireland Office, *Legislation against Terrorism* (Cm 4178, London, 1998) para 4.19.

[137] Hansard HC vol 341, col 163 (14 December 1999), Jack Straw.

[138] Hansard HC Standing Committee D, col 262 (1 February 2000), Charles Clarke.

for dissident groups who are seeking to establish their true nature and intentions.[139] On the other hand, despotic regimes can seek protection alongside liberal democracies.

An illustration is the case of Younis Tsouli who, under the tag of 'Irhabi007', was con- 6.71 victed of inciting terrorism abroad (as well as fraud) arising from his websites which carried praise for beheadings and other terrorist violence.[140] Abu Izzadeen was prosecuted for a speech in Birmingham which called for the beheading of British Muslim soldiers and praised the July 7 bombers; further charges followed in 2007 concerning his speech at the London Central Mosque in 2004, when money was collected to finance terrorist activity in Iraq, and he was recorded as saying 'Jihad with money, jihad with money. The jihad is to give money for weapons, for tanks, for RPGs, for M16s.'[141] He was convicted of terrorist fundraising and inciting terrorism overseas but cleared of encouraging terrorism.

(ii) *United Nations terrorist bombing and finance offences*   Over several decades, inter- 6.72 national treaties have developed to respond to specific forms of terrorism such as hijacking.[142] That list has been augmented by two broader UN treaties, the UN Convention for the Suppression of Terrorist Bombings[143] and the UN Convention for the Suppression of the Financing of Terrorism.[144] Sections 62 to 64 allow for prosecution in the United Kingdom for, or the extradition in respect of, terrorism activities committed abroad and which fall within the terms of these Conventions.

By s 62, if a person does anything outside the United Kingdom as an act of terrorism 6.73 or for the purposes of terrorism, and his action would have constituted the commission of a specified offence (under the Explosive Substances Act 1883, ss 2, 3, or 5, the Biological Weapons Act 1974, s 1, or the Chemical Weapons Act 1996, s 2) if it had been done in the United Kingdom, he shall be guilty of the offence of terrorist bombing. As a limit on s 62, it is expressed government policy that extradition should be preferred to extra-territorial prosecution wherever possible.[145] Section 62 exceeds the mandatory terms of the UN Bombing Convention, which, by Art 2, relates to bombings in official or specified public places, though Art 6(5) does not preclude wider domestic law.

Section 62 can be illustrated by the case of McDonald, Rafferty, and O'Farrell who 6.74 were convicted in 2002 of attempting to acquire weaponry for the Real IRA after being lured to a meeting in Slovakia with security service agents, pretending to represent the Iraqi government.[146]

Pursuant to the UN Terrorism Financing Convention, s 63 allows for jurisdiction 6.75 over forms of financial activities which would fall under ss 15 to 18 if they had been perpetrated in the United Kingdom but are actually performed outside the jurisdiction. Section 63 exceeds the confines of the UN Terrorism Financing Convention in that the

---

[139] See JUSTICE, *Response to Legislation against Terrorism* (London, 1999) paras 3.6, 3.7.

[140] *Attorney General's References (Nos 85, 86, and 87 of 2007) R v Tsouli* [2007] EWCA Crim 3300.

[141] *The Guardian* 9 February 2007 p 4, 25 April 2007 p 4, *The Times* 18 April 2008 p 21.

[142] Aviation Security Act 1982; Aviation and Maritime Security Act 1990. See also Internationally Protected Persons Act 1978; Taking of Hostages Act 1982; Nuclear Material (Offences) Act 1983; Marking of Plastic Explosives for Detection Regulations 1996, SI 1996/890.

[143] A/RES/52/164 Cm 4662, London, 1997.

[144] A/RES/54/ 109 Cm 4663, London, 1999.

[145] Hansard HC Standing Committee D, col 309 (8 February 2000), Charles Clarke.

[146] [2005] EWCA Crim 1945, [2005] EWCA Crim 1970.

definition of 'terrorism' used in ss 15 to 18 is wider than the definition in Art 2 of the Convention.

6.76   By s 64 of the 2000 Act, and reflecting Art 9 of the UN Bombing Convention and Art 11 of the UN Terrorism Financing Convention, extradition for these offences is facilitated.[147]

6.77   (iii) *Bribery and corruption abroad*   The opportunity was taken in Pt XII of the Anti-terrorism, Crime and Security Act 2001 to address the laws relating to bribery and corruption of foreign governments and officials.[148] The Minister of State (Beverley Hughes) valiantly argued that there was a link to terrorism because 'corrupt Governments help to create the conditions that engender terrorism'.[149] In truth, the 2001 Act provided a convenient vessel for proposals too troublesome to enact alone. The Newton Committee concurred in the need for a more thorough overhaul than possible in the anti-terrorism legislation.[150] Given the tenuous link to terrorism and the voluminous official reports into future reform now pending,[151] the issue will not be further explored.

6.78   (iv) *Other rules on external jurisdiction*   The Criminal Justice (International Cooperation) Act 2003, Pt II, amends various offences in the Terrorism Act and Anti-terrorism, Crime and Security Act 2001. Section 52 inserts a new s 63A into the 2000 Act—the effect is to bring within jurisdiction offences under ss 54 and 56 to 61 if committed outside the United Kingdom by a UK national or resident. This extension reflects the Council Framework Decision of 13 June 2002 on Combating Terrorism.[152]

6.79   A new s 63B covers various non-terrorist legislation offences against the person and property if committed by a UK national or resident for the purposes of terrorism. If those offences are committed by a non-national/resident against a UK national/resident or a 'protected person' related to British diplomatic services, then criminal jurisdiction can again be assumed under s 63C. The welfare of diplomatic 'protected persons' linked to the United Kingdom is the subject of s 63D. Attacks on their property or vehicles anywhere in the world fall within jurisdiction (attacks on the person already contravene the Internationally Protected Persons Act 1978).

6.80   Section 53 of the 2003 Act inserts a new s 113A, relating to the use of noxious substances for the purpose of advancing a political, religious, or ideological cause. There is universal jurisdiction if (i) an act is done by a United Kingdom national/resident; or (ii) perpetrated against them or a protected person; or (iii) against the premises or vehicle of a protected person.

6.81   Next, the Terrorism Act 2006, s 17, provides a further extension of jurisdiction. for offences contained in ss 1, 6, and 8 to 11 of the 2006 Act and ss 11(1) and 54 in the

---

[147] See also Extradition (Terrorist Bombings) Order 2002, SI 2002/1831.

[148] See Home Office, *Raising Standards and Upholding Integrity: the Prevention of Corruption* (Cm 4759, London, 2000); Home Office Circular 2/2002: *International application of the UK law on corruption*.

[149] Hansard HC vol 375, col 418, (21 November 2001).

[150] Privy Counsellor Review Committee, *Anti-terrorism, Crime and Security Act 2001, Review, Report* (2003–04 HC 100) para 421. By then, there had been no charges: para 414.

[151] Law Commission, *Reforming Bribery* (Consultation Paper 185, 2007, and Report LC313 (2007–08 HC 928); Ministry of Justice, *Bribery* (Cm 7570, London, 2009). See also *R (on the application of Corner House Research) v Director of the Serious Fraud Office* [2008] UKHL 60.

[152] 2002/475/JHA, OJ L164, art 9.

2000 Act. Section 17 gives effect to Art 14 of the Council of Europe Convention on the Prevention of Terrorism in regard to the offences in ss 1 and 6. Section 8 is included since it is notorious that much terrorist training occurs in Pakistan. Article 9 of the International Convention for the Suppression of Acts of Nuclear Terrorism[153] is the basis for the extension in respect of the offences in ss 9 to 11.

The offence of conspiring to cause explosions or possessing explosives with intent to endanger life or to cause serious injury to property under s 3 of the Explosive Substances Act 1883, a common charge in terrorist cases, is also amended by s 17.[154] The activities, if committed by a foreigner, must still take place in the United Kingdom or its dependencies (for British citizens, there is already universal jurisdiction), but instead of requiring the explosion to be intended to occur in the United Kingdom or the Republic of Ireland, it may be planned for anywhere. The amendment applies in terrorism or non-terrorism cases, but in Scotland, as a reserved matter, it relates to terrorism alone.[155]   **6.82**

(h) *Consent to prosecution*

Given the sensitivity and potential oppression relating to the special offences in the anti-terrorism legislation, by s 117 of the Terrorism Act 2000, the consent of the relevant Director of Public Prosecutions is required in England and Wales or Northern Ireland for the prosecution of any offence under the Act (save for specified less serious offences under ss 36 and 51 and some of the schedules). This appointment represents a departure from the Prevention of Terrorism (Temporary Provisions) Act 1989, s 19, which relied upon the Attorney General.   **6.83**

By amendments in s 37 of the Terrorism Act 2006 (which reflects s 19 below) and s 29 of the Counter-Terrorism Act 2008,[156] the Attorney General (or Advocate General for Northern Ireland) must act where it appears to the Director of Public Prosecutions that relevant prosecutions relate to offences committed either outside the United Kingdom or for a purpose connected with the affairs of a foreign country. Proceedings for an offence by reference to ss 63B, 63C, or 63D (which are necessarily extra-territorial) also require the consent of the Attorney General under s 63E. These filters are next applied by the Terrorism Act 2006, s 19,[157] to the offences in Pt I of that Act. In addition, the intention is that the Director of Public Prosecutions will consult the Attorney General more widely.[158]   **6.84**

In Scotland, the Lord Advocate will always be engaged, so filters are unnecessary.[159]   **6.85**

The involvement of law officers is a 'safety valve'[160] and some antidote to the trend, evident in *R v F*, that the UK government values friendship with oil-owning despots more highly than the political freedoms of refugee underdogs. But the breadth of the offences will require assessments of all manner of delicate disputes, such as the   **6.86**

---

[153] A/59/766, Cm 7301, London, 2008.
[154] See also Terrorism Act 2000, s 62.
[155] Hansard HL vol 676, col 732 (7 December 2005), Baroness Scotland.
[156] See Lord Carlile, *The Definition of Terrorism* (Cm 7052, London, 2007) para 81.
[157] As amended by the Counter-Terrorism Act 2008, s 29.
[158] Hansard HC Standing Committee D, col 295 (3 February 2000), Charles Clarke.
[159] Hansard HL vol 676, col 736 (7 December 2005), Baroness Scotland.
[160] Lord Carlile, *Proposals by Her Majesty's Government for Changes to the Laws against Terrorism* (Home Office, London, 2005) para 49.

decision not to prosecute Boris Beresovsky for invoking revolution in Russia, considered not to be equivalent to a s 59 offence.[161] There can be comity with Council of Europe and related states, already achieved by the Suppression of Terrorism Act 1978, s 4. Otherwise, universal jurisdiction is better serviced by offences within international conventions[162] or by international courts.[163] Beyond those grounds, the imposition of British domestic values may blunder into overseas situations where justification for some crimes may be strong.[164]

(i) *Assessment of offences*

6.87 The policy relevance and impact of these special offences is based primarily upon 'Pursuit', though the predominance of precursor offences also addresses 'Prevent'. As to the achievement of these goals, the statistics in Tables 6.1 and 6.2 reveal the frequent use of ss 57 and 58 but the desuetude of other offences in the Terrorism Act 2000. It is too early to judge the 2006 Act offences, but there is considerable prosecutorial interest. The statistics in Table 6.3 reveal that the sustaining of convictions in comparison to the effort of arrest and charge is modest, even when account is taken of not only principal and precursor terrorism and terrorism-connected offences but also 'pretext charges' such as frauds and immigration breaches.[165]. This quantitative data tells us less about their deterrent effect or the gains for public safety through the imposition of long sentences of imprisonment, both of which must be set against the motivation towards terrorism from perceptions of illegitimacy.

Table 6.1 Terrorism legislation: charges in Great Britain[166]

Date of charge	Possessing materials s 57	Possessing information s 58	Weapons training s 54	Directing terrorism s 56	2006 Act	Total
2001	3	0	0	0	n/a	3
2002	22	6	0	0	n/a	28
2003	29	9	4	0	n/a	42
2004	3	5	0	0	n/a	8
2005	13	8	0	2	n/a	23
2006			39		32	71
2007			59		17	76
Total			202 (total for ss 54–58)		49	251

[161] <http://www.cps.gov.uk/news/press_releases/138_07/index.html>.

[162] *R v Bow Street Metropolitan Stipendiary Magistrate, ex p Pinochet Ugarte (No 3)* [2000] 1 AC 147.

[163] Compare Lord Carlile, *Proposals by Her Majesty's Government for Changes to the Laws against Terrorism* (Home Office, 2005) para 46.

[164] Hansard HC vol 438, col 1045 (3 November 2005), Dominic Grieve.

[165] See Chesney, R., 'The sleeper scenario' (2005) 42 *Harvard Journal on Legislation* 1 at p 32.

[166] Source: Reports of Lord Carlile.

Table 6.2 'Terrorist' charges: Northern Ireland[167]

Date of charge	Homicide related	Offences against person, kidnap, intimidation	Property, blackmail, arson, drugs offences	Munitions offences	Possessing materials s 57	Possessing information s 58	Weapons training s 54	Directing terrorism s 56	Information s 103	Hoax	Other	Total
2001	14	0	5	43	6	7	0	0	0	1	5	81
2002	10	3	18	61	17	17	0	0	6	1	23	156
2003	21	17	49	104	32	10	1	0	5	1	44	284
2004	3	26	23	90	24	1	0	0	1	0	15	183
2005	19	20	32	46	10	3	0	0	3	0	25	158
2006	7	8	6	47	7	0	0	0	0	1	30	106
Totals	**74**	**74**	**133**	**391**	**96**	**38**	**1**	**0**	**15**	**4**	**142**	**968**

[167] Source: Reports of Lord Carlile; Northern Ireland Office Statistics & Research.

Table 6.3 'Terrorist' prosecutions in Great Britain 11 September 2001 to 31 March 2008[168]

Date	Arrests				Charges				Convictions			Other action				
	Arrests Terrorism Acts	Arrests other	Arrests total	Release without charge	Charges – terrorism Acts crimes	Charges – Other terrorism crimes	Charges – non-terrorism crimes	Charges total (% of arrests)	Terrorism Acts crimes	Other crimes	Totals (% of charges)	Police caution	Immigration	Mental health	Transfer to other police	Other total (% of arrests)
2001/2	94	14	108	58	15	7	16	38 (35%)	6	6	12 (32%)	0	13	0	0	13 (12%)
2002/3	237	38	275	141	38	26	30	94 (34%)	9	25	34 (36%)	3	34	2	0	39 (14%)
2003/4	178	13	191	81	34	18	38	90 (47%)	6	15	21 (23%)	3	9	5	2	21 (11%)
2004/5	157	11	168	109	15	20	12	47 (28%)	2	16	18 (38%)	4	5	1	1	13 (8%)
2005/6	273	12	285	193	36	14	25	75 (26%)	24	14	38 (51%)	1	11	2	1	16 (6%)
2006/7	191	22	213	101	60	21	22	103 (48%)	33	12	45 (44%)	0	5	1	1	10 (5%)
2007/8	156	75	231	136	43	12	19	74 (32%)	22	6	28 (38%)	2	11	5	0	19 (8%)
Total	1286	185	1471	819	241	118	162	521 (35%)	102	94	196 (38%)	13	88	16	5	131 (9%)

[168] Source: Home Office, Statistics on Terrorism Arrests and Outcomes Great Britain 11 September 2001 to 31 March 2008 (04/09, Home Office, London, 2009). There were an additional 38 arrests following a terrorist investigation from 19 February 2001 to 10 September 2001.

Applying a rights audit, there are three foremost areas of disharmony. The first relates   6.88
to the uncertainty inherent in many special offences, which struggle to meet a standard
of 'lawfulness' set by the European Convention.[169] The issue was raised directly in *R v K*,
as already related, and the legal clarifications provided by the Court of Appeal in that
and other cases have certainly improved the lucidity of ss 57 and 58. However, new
indeterminacies are raised by the offences enacted in 2006.

The second concern is whether the right to fair trial under Art 6 of the European   6.89
Convention has been adequately respected.[170] This point has already been examined in
the context of reverse burdens of proof.

A third concern is that insufficient attention has been given to the impact on other   6.90
rights, especially free speech. One wonders whether some of the scribblings or internet
downloads which founded prosecutions described hitherto could have been forgiven
or at most cautioned, not only for the sake of avoiding miscarriages of justice and community disharmony but also in the belief that a marketplace of ideas will render an overwhelming rejection of political violence.

As for constitutional governance and accountability, the fact that the criminal justice   6.91
system is the province of the courts means that scrutiny through challenge is intense.
The treatment of ss 57 and 58 show that the courts are aware of some of the dangers of
uncertainty and unfairness which these offences create. Rather less care has been shown
by Parliament, and neither the initial design of the legislation nor its subsequent review
has been accorded anywhere near as much attention as paid to police detention powers,
even though rights to liberty and fair trial are equally fundamental. Nor has the release
of information about the application of offences been adequate.

C. PROCESSING OF OFFENDERS

1. The penology of terrorism

(a) *Deterrence and security*

To date, most laws affecting the deterrence and security of terrorist prisoners were found   6.92
outside the anti-terrorism legislation in either policy statements about tariffs in life sentences[171] or in court sentencing decisions.[172] These have affirmed on many occasions

---

[169] See *Steel v United Kingdom*, App no 24838/94, 1998-VII, para 54.

[170] Report of the Special Rapporteur on the promotion and protection of human rights and fundamental
freedoms while countering terrorism (A/63/223, 2008) para 12.

[171] See Criminal Justice Act 2003, sch 21; Amendment No 6 to the Consolidated Criminal Practice
Direction [2004] All ER (D) 256 (May) IV.49.33; *R v Hindawi* (1988) 10 Cr App R (S) 104; *R v Secretary of
State for the Home Department, ex p McCartney* (1994) *The Times* 25 May 1994; *R v Martin* [1999] 1 Cr App
R (S) 477; *R (Anderson) v Secretary of State for the Home Department* [2002] UKHL 46; *R v Larmour* [2004]
NICC 4; *R v Riaz* [2004] EWHC 74 (QB); *R (Nejad) v Secretary of State for the Home Department* [2004]
EWCA Civ 33; *R v Barot* [2007] EWCA Crim 1119; *Attorney General's References (Nos 85, 86, and 87 of 2007)
R v Tsouli* [2007] EWCA Crim 3300; *R v Timlin* [2007] EWHC 1225 (QB).

[172] See for example *R v McDonald, Rafferty, and O'Farrell* [2005] EWCA Crim 1945; *R v Mansha* [2006]
EWCA Crim 2051; *R v Asiedu* [2008] EWCA Crim 1725.

that terrorism deserves exceptionally severe sentences. Extended sentences for public protection can be imposed under the Criminal Justice Act 2003, s 224.[173]

6.93   Despite the sustained absence of any scintilla of leniency, several reviewers have sought clearer statements of deterrence in terrorist sentences.[174] Their recommendations have now been reflected in the Counter-Terrorism Act 2008. Section 30 contains a procedure for enhanced sentencing in England and Wales for a specified offence which has or may have a 'terrorist connection'. The specified offences in Sch 2, which can be amended by affirmative order under s 33, are those outside the terrorism legislation and include homicides, offences under the Explosives Substances Act 1883, and offences relating to weapons of mass destruction. The Explanatory Notes suggest that such offences account for around 40 per cent of terrorist cases. Section 31 applies in Scotland (and without requiring more than one witness); service cases fall under s 32. However, the measures do not affect Northern Ireland, presumably because of political sensitivity about terrorism sentencing.

6.94   In applying s 30, the court must first determine whether there is a terrorist connection. This consideration is treated as a sentencing issue (s 30(3)), so the criminal standard of proof will apply[175] and any dispute over evidence will entail further consideration of the trial evidence or evidence adduced in a Newton hearing[176] following a guilty plea, with the decision taken by the judge. If the court rules that a terrorist connection is established, then the court must treat it as an aggravating factor and must so state in open court.

6.95   Given the history adduced earlier, this provision is of marginal impact. The Home Office somehow believed that the fact that many terrorists are charged with offences other than those under the anti-terrorism legislation prevented enhanced sentences.[177] It is arguable that the non-appearance of an offence in Sch 2 might in future dissuade the court from an enhanced sentence. Perhaps the objective was also to forestall any judicial reversal of the policy of draconian sentences, a sign of which was given in *R v Rahman, R v Mohammed*,[178] where it was feared that excessive sentences would 'inflame rather than deter extremism'.

6.96   Another criticism is that the designation of a case as 'terrorist connected' is a matter for the judge rather than the jury. But the reason why a 'pretext' offence is charged rather than a terrorism offence is because of doubts over whether it can be proven to a satisfactory level that the person is involved in terrorism. Thus, it may be unfair to apply an extra penalty where a terrorist connection cannot be sustained beyond reasonable doubt before a jury.[179]

---

[173] Applied to Mohammed Hamid *The Times* 8 March 2008 p 26. See Wattad, M., 'Is terrorism a crime or an aggravating factor in sentencing?' (2006) 4 *Journal of International Criminal Justice* 1017.

[174] Lord Lloyd, *Inquiry into Legislation against Terrorism* (Cm 3420, London, 1996) ch 5; Privy Counsellor Review Committee, *Anti-terrorism, Crime and Security Act 2001, Review, Report* (2003–04 HC 100) para 218; Lord Carlile, *The Definition of Terrorism* (Cm 7052, London, 2007) para 44.

[175] Hansard HC Public Bill Committee on the Counter-Terrorism Bill, col 381 (8 May 2008), Tony McNulty.

[176] *R v Newton* (1982) 77 Cr App R 13. See Lord Carlile, *Report on Proposed Measures for Inclusion in a Counter-Terrorism Bill* (Cm 7262, London, 2007) para 27.

[177] Home Office, *Possible Measures for Inclusion into a Future Counter-Terrorism Bill* (London, 2007) para 38. The measure also links to notification (para 39) but does not have to be dependent.

[178] [2008] EWCA Crim 1465 at para 8.

[179] Home Affairs Committee, *The Government's Counter-Terrorism Proposals* (2007–08 HC 43) para 97.

(b) *Incentives*

Sentencing law and policy can also be used as an incentive to end terrorism. This tactic   6.97
was crucial to the Northern Ireland 'Peace Process', where the grant of early release under
the Northern Ireland (Remission of Sentences) Act 1995 and the Northern Ireland
(Sentences) Act 1998 aided the success of the enterprise, allied to immunity from prosecution under the Northern Ireland Arms Decommissioning Act 1997. The operation
of these measures goes well beyond the anti-terrorism legislation and so will not be taken
further here. Likewise, proposals[180] for discounts for cooperative offenders who give
information about terrorist confederates have been implemented in the general context
of the Serious Organised Crime and Police Act 2005, Pt II.

2. Post-punishment

Part IV of the Counter-Terrorism Act 2008 moves back into the territory of risk man-   6.98
agement. Though 'administrative justice', its requirements are backed by criminal
offences under s 54.

(a) *Notification*

Notification is modelled on sex offenders registration under the Sex Offenders Act 1997   6.99
(now the Sexual Offences Act 2003, Pt II).[181] This same idea applies to 'dangerous' violent and sexual offenders by the Criminal Justice Act 2003, s 325.[182] More schemes of
notification, for violent offenders and persons with designated special immigration
status, are in the Criminal Justice and Immigration Act 2008, Pts VII and X.

Notification applies to a person aged over 16 and sentenced to imprisonment for one   6.100
year or more (ss 44, 45, and 46) for a terrorism legislation offence (as listed in s 41) or
for an offence with a terrorism connection (as described in s 42 and relying on the list in
Sch 2).[183] In Northern Ireland, only offences under s 41 are relevant. Service court
sentences fall under Sch 6. The obligation of notification is automatically imposed,
though the existence of a terrorist connection can be appealed against under s 42(2).

Initial notification under s 47 demands the transmission of details about identity,   6.101
residence, and travel to the police, to be delivered in person within three days of release
from detention (s 50). There follow two subsequent duties—notification of changes
(s 48) and periodic re-notification (s 49). Changes are defined to include staying at an
address in the United Kingdom for a period of seven days or for a combined period of
seven days within twelve months. Periodic re-notification is annual, regardless of changes.
Complex rules under ss 55 and 56 deal with the impact of absence abroad. The police
must issue a written acknowledgment of receipt of the details and, on attendance, may
take fingerprints and photographs.[184]

---

[180] Lord Lloyd, *Inquiry into Legislation against Terrorism* (Cm 3420, London, 1996) ch 15; Joint Committee
on Human Rights, *Counter-Terrorism Policy and Human Rights: Prosecution and Pre-Charge Detention*
(2005–06 HL 240/HC 1576) para 110.

[181] Hansard HC Public Bill Committee on the Counter-Terrorism Bill, col 408 (13 May 2008), Tony
McNulty.

[182] See National MAPPA Team, MAPPA Guidance 2007.

[183] See s 43 for offences committed before commencement.

[184] It is not clear whether 'photograph' includes an iris scan. Compare Immigration and Asylum Act 1999
s 144; Nationality, Immigration and Asylum Act 2002 s 126; Asylum and Immigration (Treatment of

6.102   The duration of notification is regulated by s 53. For persons over 18 at the time of conviction and sentenced to life imprisonment or imprisonment for ten years or more, the period is thirty years. A period of fifteen years applies to those sentenced to five to 10 years. Otherwise, the period is ten years (including for all offenders aged 16 and 17). These lengthy periods arise because the government believed that it would not secure renewals of orders: 'The fact that a person has not reoffended is not sufficient to establish the absence of such a risk.'[185] A Kafkaesque world thus arises in which a person cannot prove contrition or rehabilitation. Even the executive device of control orders embodies periodic review.

6.103   Notification can also be applied under s 57 and Sch 4 to persons convicted of terrorism offences abroad. Under para 4, applications to apply notification may be made by the chief police officer for the area where the individual resides or is landing. The system applies to British nationals and to foreign nationals, in their case in addition to powers to refuse entry under the Immigration Act 1971, Sch 2, para 21 or the enhanced controls of special immigration status under the Criminal Justice and Immigration Act 2008, Pt X. Schedule 4, para 2(4) deems that the foreign offence corresponds to an offence to which Pt IV applies unless disputed by the defendant. If the conditions are met, then the High Court must make an order (para 3). It is denied that this requires proof to a criminal standard;[186] one might argue in response that notification denounces the character of the person and paves the way for prohibition and so should be proven to a high standard. No appeal route is offered, but para 3(3) excepts notification where the foreign conviction involved a flagrant denial of the right to a fair trial.[187]

(b) *Overseas travel restrictions*

6.104   As a subset of measures within notification, compulsory foreign travel notification can arise under s 52.[188] The power is to be triggered by statutory order. It will be easier to apply the power in all cases of notification so as to firm up the impression that these orders are regulatory rather than selectively punitive and therefore within Art 6(3). If applicable, the person must notify to the police details of departure, destination, and return.

6.105   Next, foreign travel restriction orders are delivered by s 58 and Sch 5.[189] A court can prohibit a person from travelling abroad to any specified country or all countries where it is necessary to prevent engagement in terrorism abroad. The conditions to be met are in para 2: the person must be subject to the notification requirements and must, since being sentenced, have behaved in a way that makes it necessary to prevent him from taking part in terrorism abroad. As under Sch 4, the application must be made by a chief officer of police but in this case to a magistrates' or sheriff court. The standard of proof in respect of the behaviour will be the heightened civil standard described in *R v Crown*

Claimants, etc) Act 2004 s 35; Identity Cards Act 2006 s 42.

[185] Hansard HL vol 704, col 795 (13 October 2008), Lord West.
[186] Hansard HC Public Bill Committee on the Counter-Terrorism Bill, col 425 (13 May 2008), Tony McNulty.
[187] See *EM (Lebanon) v Secretary of State for the Home Department* [2008] UKHL 64.
[188] Home Office, *Possible Measures for Inclusion into a Future Counter-Terrorism Bill* (London, 2007) para 50.
[189] *Ibid* para 51.

Court of Manchester, ex parte McCann.[190] The magistrates' court has discretion as to its response (para 2(5)) and is subject to appeal (paras 12 to 14). Breach of an order is an offence under para 15. A person subject to an order prohibiting all foreign travel must surrender all their passports to the police (whether UK or foreign, under s 60). The order lasts for a fixed period of up to six months at a time (para 7).

The device of travel restriction is increasingly accepted[191] and has been imposed on   6.106
football hooligans,[192] sex offenders,[193] drug traffickers,[194] and violent offenders.[195] It may even be consistent with Magna Carta of 1215, s 42, which excepts from free movement persons 'that have been imprisoned or outlawed'. It might also avoid disproportionate resort to control orders, but the measure is more likely to have a net-widening impact since it involves far less scrutiny than is accorded to control orders. Since the measure falls more within freedom of movement rather than liberty, human rights challenges are hampered.

Notification seeks to aid the detection of crime and to act as a deterrent.[196] But its   6.107
automatic application will create extra workload for the police, takes no proportionate heed of individual circumstances of privacy,[197] and signals the failure of criminal justice penal process to avert risk.[198] Notification and especially travel restrictions may also breach European Union law as applied to foreigners since the restrictions are based wholly on previous convictions.[199] A prolonged order is simply an admission that there is no specific suspicion of involvement at any given point. The extension to overseas convicts is especially problematic. Different countries have very different conceptions of terrorism.

D. CRIMINAL JUSTICE PROCESS

Whilst the criminal law has experienced radical changes at the hands of the anti-terror-   6.108
ism legislation, criminal process has been less emphasized in the anti-terrorism legislation, subject to experiences in Northern Ireland (which will be described in Chapter 9). One of the few special procedural measures is s 16 of the Terrorism Act 2006 which ensures that preparatory hearings are mandatory in terrorism cases under s 29 of the Criminal Procedure and Investigations Act 1996.[200] The objective is to ensure that there is enhanced judicial management of terrorism indictments. The rule applies not only

---

[190] [2002] UKHL 39.

[191] See Lord Carlile, *Report on Proposed Measures for Inclusion in a Counter-Terrorism Bill* (Cm 7262, London, 2007) para 38.

[192] Football Spectators Act 1989; Football (Offences and Disorder) Act 1999.

[193] Sexual Offences Act 2003, s 114.

[194] Criminal Justice and Police Act 2001, s 33.

[195] Criminal Justice and Immigration Act 2008, Pt VII.

[196] Home Office, *Possible Measures for Inclusion into a Future Counter-Terrorism Bill* (London, 2007) paras 47, 48.

[197] Compare *R (on the application of F) v Secretary of State for Justice* [2008] EWHC 3170; *R (on the application of Wright) v Secretary of State for Health* [2009] UKHL 3.

[198] Compare Northern Ireland (Sentences) Act 1998, s 9.

[199] See European Parliament and Council Directive 2004/38/EC of 29 April 2004, art 28, as implemented by Immigration (European Economic Area) Regulations 2006, SI 2006/1003.

[200] See s 16(3) for the variant impact on serious fraud cases under Criminal Justice Act 1987.

where at least one person in the case is charged with a terrorism offence (as defined in s 16(5)) but also where at least one person in the case is charged with an offence that carries a penalty of a maximum of at least ten years' imprisonment and it appears to the judge that the offence has a terrorist connection (defined in s 16(8)). Section 16 has been implemented further through the Protocol on the Management of Terrorism Cases issued by the President of the Queen's Bench Division.[201]

6.109   This attention to detail and the imposition of centralized and senior judicial active involvement is generally to be welcomed.[202] But it dilutes the principle of trial by peers and could threaten further if concerns about cost and delay become overweening. It is also not clear whether it will be sufficient to avert the allure of more risky reforms such as the appointment of investigative magistrates[203] or even special non-jury security courts, as applied in the Lockerbie trial[204] and as have been mooted for sensitive inquests.[205]

E. CONCLUSIONS

6.110   The agenda of the anti-terrorism legislation has expanded within criminal justice. The consequent dangers to individual rights to fair trial and to collective perceptions of legitimacy have been delineated. Nevertheless, this focus on the Old Bailey rather than Belmarsh is still welcomed. A criminal justice response serves not only the neutralization of individual threats but also symbolic, denunciatory functions which should strengthen faith in societal values.[206] The idea that justice can be better achieved in the context of executive measures is implausible.[207] Yet, there is the danger that the policy of criminalization will be jeopardized because the siren voice of security will demand convergence between executive measures and criminal justice and a slide towards minimum standards of due process.

6.111   To avoid undermining the criminalization project, four checks are suggested. First, prosecutors should consider in priority charges under 'normal' offences. Secondly, there should be much closer monitoring of the results of the prosecution process, so that its impact can be better understood. Thirdly, the security services should be trained further to produce evidence and to expect to make court appearances as often as executive hearings.[208] Finally, the courts should recognize that they are on their own patch where their expertise exceeds that of the minister. They must act as prime guardians against miscarriages of justice, prisoner hunger strikes, and community disenchantment.

---

[201] (2nd edn, Courts Service, London, 2007).

[202] See *R v Khyam* [2008] EWCA Crim 1612 at paras 24, 152; Lord Carlile, *Report on the Operation in 2007 of the Terrorism Act 2000* (Home Office, London, 2008) and *Government Reply* (Cm 7429, London, 2008) para 309.

[203] See Joint Committee on Human Rights, *Counter-Terrorism Policy and Human Rights: Prosecution and Pre-Charge Detention* (2005–06 HL 240/HC 1576) paras 76, 109, 138.

[204] *HM Advocate v Al-Megrahi* 2002 JC 99, [2008] HCJAC 58.

[205] Counter-Terrorism Bill 2007–08, Pt VI; Coroners and Justice Bill 2008–09 cl 11.

[206] See Roach, K., 'The criminal law and terrorism' in Ramraj, V.V., Hor, M., and Roach, K., *Global Anti-terrorism Law and Policy* (Cambridge University Press, Cambridge, 2005) p 136.

[207] Tadros, V., 'Justice and terrorism' (2007) 10 *New Criminal Law Review* 658 at p 688.

[208] See Starmer, K., 'Setting the record straight: human rights in an era of international terrorism' [2007] *European Human Rights Law Review* 123 at p 131.

7
EXECUTIVE CONTROL ORDERS

A. BACKGROUND

1. Policy background

The resort to executive control orders in the Prevention of Terrorism Act 2005 is attrib-   7.01
utable to two dynamics. The first relates to the growing willingness to react to the anticipatory risk of mass terrorism casualties which conduces towards pre-emptive or
preventative interventions.[1] Therefore, despite every modification to criminal justice
processes and offences and despite the expressed priority for prosecution, described in
Chapter 6, hurdles persist to the criminalization of terrorists. They include evidential
and procedural obstacles to the use of sensitive information, as well as the exacting
standard of proof. Furthermore, the deterrence of punishment is distrusted.[2]

The second dynamic is the increasing threat of 'neighbour' terrorism[3]—reflecting the   7.02
gradual recognition that terrorism derives not only by alien outlaws, as represented
by Osama bin Laden, but also, and more ominously, from the insidious threat of our
neighbours. This trend was epitomized by the three British citizens and one long-term
British resident who were responsible for the London bombings of 7 July 2005.[4] These
were Yorkshire folk whose mundane backgrounds set at naught many of the tactics of the
security forces hunting for cells of crazed foreigners. The profile of the perpetrators
was not, on reflection, an isolated aberration, and antecedents included Richard Reid

---

[1] See further Dershowitz, A., *Preemption: A Knife that Cuts Both Ways* (W.W. Norton, New York, 2006).
The emphasis upon 'anticipatory action' is not a new concept: see Chief of Staff, Palestine—imposition of
martial law (CP(47) 107, National Archives, London, 1947) p 3.
[2] *Report of the Official Account of the Bombings in London on 7 July 2005* (2005–06 HC 1087) para 7.
[3] See Walker, C., '"Know thine enemy as thyself"' (2008) 32 *Melbourne Law Review* 275.
[4] See Intelligence and Security Committee, *Report on the London Terrorist Attacks on 7 July 2005* (Cm 6785,
London, 2005); *Report of the Official Account of the Bombings in London on 7 July 2005* (2005–06 HC 1087).

(the shoe bomber on a transatlantic flight in 2001),[5] Ahmad Omar Saeed Sheikh (sentenced to death in Hyderabad in 2002 for the murder of Daniel Pearl),[6] suicide bombings in Tel Aviv in 2003 by Asif Mohammed Hanif and Omar Khan Sharif,[7] and, subject to denials, the dozen or so British citizens or residents detained in Guantánamo Bay.[8]

7.03   Turning to appropriate responses, an inevitable consequence of the risk dynamic and the net-widening to 'neighbours' is an intelligence-led approach.[9] As distinct from the strategy of criminalization, the outcomes sought are to prevent, disrupt, and counter, thereby engaging in 'control'. Most states have resorted to these executive-based risk management alternatives. In the United Kingdom, measures such as proscription, detention without trial, control orders, port controls, data-mining, and the seizure of assets evidently fall into this category. In addition, several powers such as special policing powers could legitimately be included in either strategy, though their tactical use tends towards the control strategy. The pursuit of 'control' has been evident in all anti-terrorism legislation, including the Terrorism Act 2000, which contains extensive police powers. 'Control' is also recognized in the 'Prevent' strand of the CONTEST strategy.

7.04   Control is arguably even more controversial than criminalization in design and implementation. The techniques of control are practically difficult to handle and to collate.[10] Their impacts are corrosive of constitutionalism, since individual rights are diminished or eliminated without the convincing and legitimating public spectacle of a trial and proof beyond reasonable doubt. Instead, the ultimate decision-making rests in the hands of untrained and more politically-motivated government ministers as opposed to detached judges.[11]

2. Legislative background

7.05   The notion of executive restraint orders so as to avert terrorism is nothing new in British law. The UK government has long honed them not only at home but also abroad in colonial campaigns.[12]

7.06   The most direct forerunner was the Prevention of Violence (Temporary Provisions) Act 1939, which reacted to Irish Republican Army attacks in Britain with measures of exclusion, prohibition, and registration with the police.[13] Some of the regulations under the Civil Authorities (Special Powers) Act 1922 (Northern Ireland) also permitted

---

[5] *US v Reid* 369 F 3d 619 (2004).

[6] See *The Guardian* 16 July 2002 p 10.

[7] See *Daily Telegraph* 20 May 2003 p 2.

[8] See Center for Constitutional Rights, *Composite Statement: Detention in Afghanistan and Guantánamo Bay* (New York, 2004).

[9] See Walker, C., 'Intelligence and anti-terrorism laws in the United Kingdom' (2005) 44 *Crime Law & Social Change* 387.

[10] Bichard Inquiry, *Report* (2003–04 HC 653); Home Office, *Bichard Inquiry Recommendations: Progress Report* (Home Office, London, 2004); Bichard Inquiry, *Final Report* (HMSO, London, 2005).

[11] See Committee of Privy Counsellors, *Review of Intelligence on Weapons of Mass Destruction* (2003–04 HC 898) ch 4.

[12] See Simpson, A.W.B., *In the Highest Degree Odious* (Oxford University Press, Oxford, 1994); Simpson, A.W.B., *Human Rights and the End of Empire* (Oxford University Press, Oxford, 2004); Bonner, D., *Executive Measures, Terrorism and National Security* (Ashgate, Aldershot, 2007).

[13] See Walker, C., *The Prevention of Terrorism in British Law* (2nd edn, Manchester University Press, Manchester, 1992) ch 4.

residence orders or requirements to report to the police.[14] Exclusion orders were revived under the Prevention of Terrorism Acts from 1974 to 1998.[15]

These precedents had little apparent influence over the policies and designs which resulted in the Prevention of Terrorism Act 2005. Instead, control orders grew in the shadow of the latest incarnation of detention without trial, which was erected by Pt IV of the Anti-terrorism, Crime and Security Act 2001 and persisted until 2005. Its details have been fully related elsewhere.[16] The 2001 Act was in turn shaped by the judgment of the European Court of Human Rights in *Chahal v United Kingdom*,[17] wherein the government was warned that the expulsion of a terrorist suspect to a jurisdiction where torture was a substantial possibility would contravene Art 3 of the European Convention on Human Rights. Since total freedom for terrorist suspects is not an unacceptable alternative,[18] detention under Pt IV was enacted once the danger became acute after September 11. In this way, anticipatory risk was addressed, but the policy failed to cover 'neighbour' terrorism since Pt IV was drafted within immigration powers and so could only apply to persons liable to deportation.

Just seventeen detention orders were issued under Pt IV. Nevertheless, the emergence of detention without trial and the accompanying derogation under Art 15 of the European Convention were politically unpalatable. Opposition culminated in the report in 2003, under s 122 of the 2001 Act, of a review committee of Privy Counsellors, chaired by Lord Newton.[19] The immediate Home Office response[20] anticipated no urgent reform. However, this insouciance was terminally shaken because of the intervention of the House of Lords in *A v Secretary of State for the Home Department* in late 2004.[21] While a majority deferentially accepted that a public emergency existed sufficient to warrant a derogation notice under Art 15, Pt IV was incompatible with measures which could be said to be 'strictly necessary' on the grounds of disproportionality and discrimination. The 'greater intensity of review'[22] applying to the test of 'strict requirement' under Art 15 picked on two troubling features of Pt IV. One was that it only applied to deportable aliens. The other was that the creation of a 'prison with three walls'—the absent fourth wall allowing foreign terrorists to depart the jurisdiction and plot abroad—likewise made no sense in security terms. The former feature additionally

7.07

7.08

---

[14] See Donohue, L.K., *Counter-Terrorism Law* (Irish Academic Press, Dublin, 2001).

[15] See Walker, C., 'Constitutional governance and special powers against terrorism' (1997) 35 *Columbia Journal of Transnational Law* 1.

[16] See the 1st edn of this book (ch 8). For reviews see Joint Committee on Human Rights, *Continuance in Force of Sections 21 to 23 of the Anti-terrorism, Crime and Security Act 2001* (2002–03 HC 462/HL 59), *Statutory Review: Continuance of Pt.IV* (2003–04 HL 38/HC 381); Lord Carlile, *Reviews of Pt. IV of the Anti-terrorism, Crime and Security Act 2001–2005* (Home Office, London, 2002–06).

[17] *Chahal v United Kingdom*, App no 22414/93, Reports 1996-V. See also *Saadi v Italy*, App no 37201/06, 28 February 2008; *NA v United Kingdom*, App no 25904/07, 24 June 2008; *Ramzy v Netherlands*, App no 25424/05.

[18] Home Office, *Counter-Terrorism Powers* (Cm 6147, London, 2004) p ii.

[19] Privy Counsellor Review Committee, *Anti-terrorism, Crime and Security Act 2001 Review, Report* (2003–04 HC 100).

[20] Home Office, *Counter-Terrorism Powers* (Cm 6147, London, 2004).

[21] [2004] UKHL 56. See Dickson, B., 'Law versus terrorism: can law win?' [2005] *European Human Rights Law Review* 1; Walker, C., 'Prisoners of "war all the time"' [2005] *European Human Rights Law Review* 50; Tomkins, A., 'Readings of A *v* Secretary of State for the Home Department' [2005] *Public Law* 259; Feldman, D., 'Proportionality and discrimination in anti-terrorism legislation' (2005) 64 *Cambridge Law Journal* 271.

[22] [2004] UKHL 56 at paras 42, 44.

breached Art 14 of the Convention. This House of Lords judgment was endorsed by the Strasbourg court in 2009. According to *A v United Kingdom*,[23] the government has acted properly in resorting to derogation. But the measures adopted could not be strictly necessary in view of the features noted by the House of Lords.

7.09   Following that judgment, the detention under Pt IV (ss 21 to 32) was repealed and replaced by control orders under the Prevention of Terrorism Act 2005. Control orders avoid the identified shortcomings. However, they remain controversial because they avoid the hallowed safeguards inherent in prosecution and yet still impact severely on individual rights to liberty, privacy, property, and association.

7.10   There remains in force under Pt IV of the 2001 Act a rump of measures which block the consideration of the substance of an asylum claim made by persons whose removal from the United Kingdom has already been deemed to be conducive to the public good (ss 33 and 34). Section 36 allows the Secretary of State to retain fingerprints taken in asylum and certain immigration cases. Section 33 has since been repealed and overtaken by further measures under the Immigration, Asylum and Nationality Act 2006 and the Criminal Justice and Immigration Act 2008, Pt X. Since these laws are located outside the anti-terrorism legislation, they will not be considered further here.[24]

B. CONTROL ORDERS—THE SYSTEM

1. Outline

7.11   The Prevention of Terrorism Act 2005 came into force on 11 March 2005, just seventeen days after its introduction into Parliament. This rapid legislative delivery was the subject of highly rancorous debate which 'demeaned' Parliament[25] as well as becoming the catalyst for the most severe bout of disagreement between the Houses of Commons and Lords in modern history. The opposition complained about the lack of time for debate, the lack of safeguards, the failure to boost prosecution, and the limited future review. These disagreements were, however, subdued on later renewals.

7.12   The essence of the legislation is to permit the government to issue 'control orders' which regulate and restrict individuals suspected of being involved in terrorism. They fit the pattern of dealing with anticipatory risk, and so the basis for the orders is intelligence-led[26] and the mechanism for trigger is executive-based. Many of the former detainees were subjected to control orders, though, following the July 2005 bombings in London, the government redoubled its efforts to impose forced removal. Nine control orders issued against former detainees were then revoked, and they were detained pending deportation and litigation about deportation.[27]

7.13   The mechanisms for review draw from Pt IV, though the inclusion of suspect citizens within the scheme meant that the Special Immigration Appeals Commission

---

[23] App no 3455/05, 19 February 2009, para 190.

[24] See Walker, C., 'The treatment of foreign terror suspects' (2007) 70 *Modern Law Review* 427.

[25] Hansard HC vol 431, col 774 (28 February 2005), Dominic Grieve.

[26] Lord Carlile, *First Report of the Independent Reviewer pursuant to Section 14(3) of the Prevention of Terrorism Act 2005* (Home Office, London, 2006) para 36.

[27] See *Q v Secretary of State for the Home Department* [2006] EWHC (Admin) 2690; *RB and OO v Secretary of State for the Home Department* [2009] UKHL 10.

('SIAC') Act 1997, which was the mechanism for review under Part IV, was no longer an appropriate venue. Jurisdiction has instead been vested in the High Court or Court of Session (for Scotland) under s 15 under similar terms.[28] Lord Carlile voiced a preference for initial reliance upon the district judges (magistrates' courts), resident magistrates (in Northern Ireland), or Scottish sheriffs who have experience of applications for extension of detention under s 41 of the Terrorism Act 2000.[29] The government's view was that the seriousness of the process merited High Court attention.[30] A more fundamental objection was that judicial involvement would bring disrepute because control orders were said to involve 'a risk assessment' and 'not a decision'.[31] These views were shared by some senior judges[32] but should be rejected. The precedent of SIAC has been firmly established, and it was categorized as a 'court of record' under the Anti-terrorism, Crime and Security Act 2001, s 35. In addition, judges are involved every day in risk assessment when taking bail and sentencing decisions.

Besides extending to citizens as well as foreigners, control orders are distinct from Pt IV in that they do not necessarily rely upon a derogation notice. Derogation from rights to liberty (within the terms of Art 5 of the European Convention) remains possible, and those orders would require a corresponding derogation notice to be issued and can only be made by the courts (s 4). Non-derogating control orders (expected to be the norm) must be confirmed by the courts (s 3). This distinction between derogating and non-derogating should be understood in light of the jurisprudence of the European Court of Human Rights in *Guzzardi v Italy*, where the Court declared that Art 5:[33] 7.14

. . . is not concerned with mere restrictions on liberty of movement. . . . In order to determine whether someone has been 'deprived of his liberty' within the meaning of Art 5, the starting point must be his concrete situation and account must be taken of a whole range of criteria such as the type, duration, effects and manner of implementation of the measure in question.

Thus, there is no 'bright line' between liberty and restriction.[34] An important further implication of non-derogating control powers is that they can address sources of terrorism which are not specific to a derogation notice.[35]

2. Control orders—contents

A control order is defined under s 1(1) as 'an order against an individual that imposes obligations on him for purposes connected with protecting members of the public from a risk of terrorism.' By s 1(3), the obligations imposed must be considered 'necessary 7.15

---

[28] But note the Prevention of Terrorism Act 2005, sch 1 para 4, which imposes a duty of full disclosure of relevant material. Another difference is suggested to be the absence of the prospect of deportation (*AR* [2008] EWHC 3164 (Admin) para 4), though the prospect of prosecution is in play.

[29] Hansard HL vol 670, col 372 (3 March 2005), Lord Carlile.

[30] Hansard HL vol 670, col 671 (8 March 2005), Lord Falconer.

[31] Hansard HL vol 670, col 163 (1 March 2005), Lord Lloyd.

[32] Hansard HC vol 431, col 1576 (9 March 2005), Charles Clarke.

[33] App no 7367/76, Ser A vol 39 (1980) at para 91. See further *Raimondo v Italy*, App no 12954/87, Ser A vol 281-A, (1994); *Mancini and Mancini v Italy*, App no 44955/98, 2001-IX; *Labita v Italy*, App no 26772/95, 2000-IV.

[34] *JJ* [2007] UKHL 45 at para 17 per Lord Bingham. Note that the other party in control order cases is always the Secretary of State for the Home Department (not cited in this chapter).

[35] Compare *AU* [2009] EWHC 49 (Admin).

for purposes connected with preventing or restricting involvement by that individual in terrorism-related activity.' Under s 1(5), the meaning of 'terrorism' is taken from the Terrorism Act 2000, s 1. Section 1(9) defines 'involvement in terrorism-related activity' (which may relate to specific acts or to terrorism in general) as comprising: (a) the commission, preparation, or instigation of acts of terrorism; (b) conduct which facilitates or is intended to facilitate such acts; (c) conduct which gives encouragement or is intended to give encouragement to such acts; or (d) conduct which gives support or assistance to others known or believed to be involved in terrorism-related activity. The final leg (d) differs from the others in that it demands an element of *mens rea* as to outcomes. The government resisted an amendment to insert 'knowingly' in (a) to (c), suggesting that the need to protect the public would not be triggered by the unwitting.[36]

7.16   The original formulation of s 1(9) was excessive. It could encompass individuals who, while not knowingly assisting terrorism, had intentionally provided, say, accommodation to someone who was believed by the government to be supporting terrorism. There could be any number of links in this chain of association.[37] Therefore, the Counter-Terrorism Act 2008, s 79, reformulated the wording by referring in (d) to activity 'by the individual concerned' which it defines by reference to (a) to (c).

7.17   The meaning of terrorism-related 'activity' in s 1(9) was considered further in *AR*.[38] The control order was based on membership of a proscribed organization, the Libyan Islamic Fighting Group, but the contention was sustained that membership had not been active since proscription. The control order could not stand, since, by s 1(5) of the Terrorism Act 2000, 'a reference to action taken for the purposes of terrorism includes a reference to action taken for the benefit of a proscribed organization', excused prior activity. However, a control order could be established on a more general view of past activity if membership could raise an inference of a future propensity to engage in terrorism. In *AT and AW*,[39] the Home Secretary was entitled to take a cautious view as to future involvement, though reports on the suspects could not mislead the Home Secretary by implying that activities are occurring in the present rather than the past. In *AU*, a control order based wholly on prior convictions would not be sufficient to show current 'activity', but an order was valid where there was also evidence of a continuing propensity to commit terrorism.[40] The court was not, in any event, bound by findings in the criminal prosecution except for the fact of conviction itself.[41] In *GG and NN*,[42] well-founded suspicions of involvement in terrorism two years previously were balanced against evidence of one suspect settling down with a family, and his order was quashed.

7.18   Section 1(4) next sets out an extensive list of obligations that may be imposed pursuant to a control order. It includes: (a) a prohibition or restriction on the possession or use of specified articles or substances (such as a computer); (b) a prohibition or restriction on the use of specified services or facilities (banking facilities or a telephone will be in

---

[36] Hansard HC vol 670, cols 459–60 (3 March 2005), Lord Falconer.
[37] Hansard HC Public Bill Committee on the Counter-Terrorism Bill, col 493 (15 May 2008), Tony McNulty.
[38] [2008] EWHC 3164 (Admin).
[39] [2009] EWHC 512 (Admin) at para 29.
[40] [2009] EWHC 49 (Admin) at para 6.
[41] *Ibid* at paras 7, 8 (as required by the Civil Evidence Act 1968, s 11(2)).
[42] [2009] EWHC 142 (Admin) at para 23.

mind here); (c) a restriction with respect to work, occupation, or business; (d) a restriction on associations or communications; (e) restrictions in respect of place of residence or on visitors to it; (f) a prohibition on presence at specified places or areas at specified times or days; (g) a prohibition or restriction on movements; (h) a requirement to comply with prohibitions or restrictions on movements as may be imposed, for a period not exceeding twenty-four hours; (i) a requirement to surrender a passport or other documents or things; (j) a requirement to give access to a place of residence or to other premises; (k) a requirement to allow searches for the purpose of checking on the contravention of obligations; (l) a requirement to allow specified persons to remove objects and to subject them to tests or to retain them; (m) a requirement to submit to photographing; (n) a requirement to cooperate with arrangements for monitoring by electronic or other means; (o) a requirement to comply with a demand to provide information; (p) a requirement to report to a specified person at specified times and places. Under s 1(8), an obligation may be worded so that it can be waived by the authorities provided prior approval is sought.

The foregoing list appears comprehensive, and most requirements are actually applied in combination.[43] An exception in practice is the prohibition on leaving the country which is often not applied to foreigners in the hope that they might opt for self-deportation. Claims of disproportionality, along the lines raised against the 'prison with three walls' under the 2001 Act, are reduced by the fact that the Home Office usually seizes travel documents such as passports and so can still determine their destination.   **7.19**

The Counter-Terrorism Act 2008 has responded to a need for further non-consensual powers of entry into premises.[44] The deficiency relates to the wording of s 1(4)(j) which allows the imposition of a requirement on the controlled person to give access to specified persons to his place of residence or to other premises to which he has power to grant access. On the original wording, it is arguable that if a controlled person is out of the residence or has gone missing, the police cannot require him to grant access. Arguably, the power should be restricted in this way—to offer a safeguard that the suspect should always be aware of intrusions into privacy unless the police wish to revert to entry under the Terrorism Act 2000. However, the 2008 Act grants new powers, which even affect persons subject to control orders made before 2008. Obstruction is an offence under s 9.   **7.20**

So, by s 7A, where a police officer reasonably suspects that the controlled person has absconded, the constable may enter (if necessary by force) and search relevant premises[45] for the purpose of determining whether the person has absconded or for material that may assist in the pursuit and arrest of the controlled person. There is no statutory definition of 'abscond', which suggests that ordinary meanings such as 'to hide oneself, to go away hurriedly and secretly' should apply.[46] Aside from absconding, other facets of breach of a control order can be checked by entry and search under s 7B. As an alternative to the use of these summary powers, under s 7C, the constable may apply to a justice   **7.21**

---

[43] See Lord Carlile, *Fourth Report of the Independent Review Pursuant to Section 14(3) of the Prevention of Terrorism Act 2005* (Home Office, London, 2009) Annexes 1, 3–5.

[44] See Home Office, *Possible Measures for Inclusion into a Future Counter-Terrorism Bill* (London, 2007) para 57.

[45] The formula seeks to protect subsequent owners or tenants: Hansard HL vol 705, col 935 (17 November 2008), Lord West.

[46] See *Re M* [2001] EWCA Civ 458 at para 28.

of the peace or sheriff for the issue of a warrant to check whether the controlled person is complying with obligations under a control order.

7.22   The 2008 Act has also amended s 1(4)(m), in line with the general policy in Pt I of the Counter-Terrorism Act 2008 of expanding the storage and sharing of forensic data. Sections 10 to 12 grant a power for a constable to take, as well as photographs, fingerprints and non-intimate samples from individuals subject to control orders. The sampling can also be for security or criminal investigative purposes as well as preventative purposes.[47] In Scotland, samples from controlled persons may be used only for the purposes of a terrorist investigation or in the interests of national security and not crime detection, and the sampling must be authorized by an inspector in the case of non-intimate samples of non-pubic hair or nail samples and external body fluid samples (but not fingerprints).[48]

7.23   As for s 1(4)(p), it was held in *R v AD*,[49] that the Home Office may involve a third party in monitoring the reporting obligations, and the third party is not confined to a 'passive role'. Thus, a police inspector could act as an assigned 'contact officer' and be conferred with the power to vary the reporting hours, though there was also a specified 'Control Order Contact Officer' at the Home Office to deal with queries.

7.24   Section 1(4) still does not expressly mention submission to a personal search. Though the section is worded in permissive terms, the court in *GG and NN* was unwilling to read in such an imposition on personal liberty.[50] It could also be argued that if obligations are imposed outside the express headings of s 1(4), then they will not be 'prescribed by law' for the purposes of the European Convention.[51] Other attempts during legislative passage to curtail the discretion in s 1(4) (such as through restraints on the taking of legal advice or being required to provide self-incriminating or confidential information) were resisted. However, the government accepted that imposing an obligation to leave the United Kingdom would be an improper usurpation of deportation powers and that legal privilege could only be taken away by express words.[52] The legislators also posited a distinction between the improper asking for information for the purposes of securing a conviction and legitimately asking for information to prevent terrorism. This distinction is not convincing. If a person refuses to answer the question, 'Where is the bomb?,' then an offence under s 9(1) might arise for contravening an obligation under s 1(4)(o) to provide information.

7.25   Obligations are further explained in s 1(5), which emphasizes the restriction of movements, and thereby allows curfews or exclusion zones. Controlled persons may also be required under s 1(6) to cooperate with practical arrangements for monitoring control orders, such as wearing and maintaining apparatus as directed. The controlled person may further be required under s 1(7) to provide information under a control order, including advance information about proposed movements or other activities.

---

[47] Hansard HL vol 704, col 393 (9 October 2008), Lord West.
[48] See Criminal Procedure (Scotland) Act 1995.
[49] [2007] EWCA Crim 1009.
[50] [2009] EWHC 142 (Admin) at para 59.
[51] Joint Committee on Human Rights, *Prevention of Terrorism Bill: Preliminary Report* (2004–05 HL 61/HC 389) para 17.
[52] Hansard HL vol 670, cols 444–50 (3 March 2005), Lord Falconer.

3. Control orders—issuance

There are two types of control orders. The issuance of a 'non-derogating' control order 7.26
is by the Home Secretary and with the confirmation of a court under ss 2 and 3. If an
order involves any obligation which is incompatible with the right to liberty under Art 5
of the European Convention on Human Rights—a 'derogating obligation'—it can be
made only by the court on an application by the Secretary of State under s 4. Such an
order must be justified by reference to a designation order (under s 14(1) of the Human
Rights Act 1998). The derogation should relate under ss 1(2)(a) and 1(10) to rights to
liberty under Art 5, and no power is granted to issue obligations that derogate from
other rights. In any event, some rights are non-derogable, such as rights against torture
under Art 3. A derogation cannot relate to Art 6 if it would negate any possibility of
complaint about the enjoyment of non-derogable rights.[53]

(a) *Non-derogating control orders*

Section 15 provides the unhelpful definition that a non-derogating control order 'means 7.27
a control order made by the Secretary of State'. This formulation made sense in the initial
drafts of the Act (before there was court involvement). In contrast, under s 15, a derogating control order is defined as 'a control order imposing obligations that are or include
derogating obligations' (which are defined by s 1(10)). One might better define a non-
derogating control order as an order which does not contain derogating obligations.

The Home Secretary may make a non-derogating control order under s 2(1) if she: 7.28
(a) has reasonable grounds for suspecting that the individual is or has been involved in
terrorism-related activity; and (b) considers that it is necessary, for purposes connected
with protecting members of the public from a risk of terrorism, to make a control order
imposing obligations on that individual. The procedures under s 2(2) allow the Secretary
of State to impose a control order on an individual already subject to a control order
imposed by the court where the court has decided to revoke a control order (under s 3
below) but has postponed that revocation in order to allow the Secretary of State to
decide whether to impose a new order. A new order can also be issued after a previous
order has expired or has been quashed without postponement by the courts.

Examining in further detail the meanings of the two tests in s 2(1), the first test is expressly 7.29
objective, though 'activity' can cover a wide range. In *AL*,[54] a British citizen was subjected
to a control order since he intended to travel to Afghanistan to engage in radicalization
activities. The control order was upheld by the High Court. Any net-widening towards the
encouragement, rather than the doing, of terrorism might be said to be the fault of the
Terrorism Act 2006, s 1. A more restrictive view was taken by Mr Justice Collins in *Bullivant*,
whereby 'Expressions of support for Islamic extremists . . . the sharing of extremist views or
keeping company with extremists will not suffice, but will obviously provide support for
suspicion of intended involvement in such activities.'[55] The Joint Committee on Human
Rights has suggested that there should be evidence of direct support for terrorism activity.[56]

---

[53] Weissbrodt, D.S., *The Right to a Fair Trial* (Kluwer, Hague, 2001) ch 5.
[54] [2007] EWHC 1970 (Admin).
[55] [2008] EWHC (Admin) 337 at para 14.
[56] Joint Committee on Human Rights, *Counter-Terrorism Policy and Human Rights: Counter-Terrorism Bill*
(2007–08 HL 50/HC 199) para 39.

7.30   The second test of necessity is apparently subjective, though the modern practice is to set an objective standard.[57] Necessity will arise from the seriousness and persistence of activity and also the inability of other techniques of surveillance to avert danger.

7.31   The proof threshold is set at a low level, consistent with the dynamic of anticipatory risk and lower even than required for the issuance of a civil injunction.[58] In response to demands that the legislature adopt a balance-of-probabilities test, the Home Secretary made clear that to accede would mean that 'potentially dangerous individuals could simply slip away'.[59] In assessing the level of proof, consideration may be given to the statement of Lord Hoffmann in *Secretary of State for the Home Department v Rehman* (a deportation case), in which he stated that 'the question in the present case is not whether a given event happened but the extent of future risk. This depends upon an evaluation of the evidence of the appellant's conduct against a broad range of facts with which they may interact'.[60] This position was echoed in cases decided under Pt IV. In *Secretary of State for the Home Department v M*, Lord Woolf stated, 'Although, therefore, the test is an objective one, it is also one which involves a value judgment as to what is properly to be considered reasonable in those circumstances.' [61] In *A v Secretary of State for the Home Department (No 2)* (dealing principally with the admissibility of evidence of torture), the court regarded as 'unfortunate' a statement by SIAC that the formula was 'not a demanding standard'.[62] Nevertheless, Lord Justice Laws concluded that, 'The nature of the subject-matter is such that it will as I have indicated very often, usually, be impossible to prove the past facts which make the case that A is a terrorist.'[63]

7.32   By s 2(4), a non-derogating control order expires after twelve months but may be renewed. The date must be specified under s 2(5), but it appears that there is no power to vary the period from twelve months. On renewal under s 2(6), the Secretary of State must find that the order would protect members of the public from a risk of terrorism and must deem necessary any obligations imposed by the renewed order. These grounds differ from those pertaining to the original imposition in that there is no need to review the evidence for the original suspicion that the individual is or has been involved in terrorism-related activity. In this way, the case for renewal may differ entirely from the case for imposition.

7.33   In the original draft of the legislation, non-derogating control orders could be instituted by the Secretary of State without any involvement of the courts. This feature was one of the major bones of contention in Parliament.[64] After much jousting on the issue, a compromise was reached that there should be an early judicial check by way of an *ex parte* application for leave to make the order. Consequently, the Home Secretary, and not the court, remains the author of the order but only if an application

---

[57] See *R v Ministry of Defence* [1996] QB 517 at p 538; *Youssef v Home Office* [2004] EWHC 1884 at para 62.

[58] Hansard HL vol 670, col 371 (3 March 2005), Lord Carlile.

[59] Hansard HC vol 431, col 1588 (9 March 2005), Charles Clarke.

[60] [2001] UKHL 47 at para 56.

[61] [2004] EWCA (Civ) 324 at para 16.

[62] [2004] EWCA (Civ) 1123 at para 49 per Pill LJ.

[63] *Ibid* at para 231.

[64] See Joint Committee on Human Rights, *Prevention of Terrorism Bill: Preliminary Report* (2004–05 HL 61/HC 389).

has been made to the court for permission to issue it under s 3(1)(a). There are two exceptional procedures. By s 3(1)(b), the Secretary of State can state in the control order that the urgency of the case requires the making of an order without court permission. Alternatively, s 3(1)(c) allows an order to be made on the Secretary of State's authority alone if issued before 14 March 2005 against a detainee under Pt IV of the 2001 Act. For these exceptional cases, the Secretary of State must still refer the control order to the court immediately under s 3(3) and (4).

On application under s 3(1)(a), provided the court concludes that the relevant decisions are not 'obviously flawed', directions will be given for a full hearing as soon as reasonably practicable. The same rule applies under s 3(3) and (6) after a referral under (b) and (c), but there are two added possibilities for court intervention (again on the 'obviously flawed' standard) in those situations. 7.34

First, s 3(6)(b) allows (in relation to orders issued under sub-ss (3)(1)(b) and (3)(1)(c)) the court to quash a particular obligation within the order, whereas an order under (a) is on an all-or-nothing basis—s 3(2)(a) mentions review only of the grounds of the order and not its obligations. However, it is possible that the same review power applies to an order under (a) pursuant to s 2(9). If treated as a proviso guiding action at the later stage of court hearings, it makes sense that obligations can then be imposed as the court considers necessary to prevent involvement in any terrorism activity and not just the activity which originally gave rise to the grounds for the Secretary of State's suspicion. 7.35

Secondly, in relation to (b) only, the court may quash the 'certificate' of urgency under s 3(8). The wording here betrays the haste of drafting, for a 'certificate' is relevant to a referral under (c) and not under (b). While the 'certificate' can be quashed if flawed, the order itself is not expressly quashed as a result, and the phrase 'certificate contained in the order' suggests a severance of the issues. However, if there was no power under s 3(1)(b) to issue the order in the first place, then the provisions of (a) should have been followed. Thus, in that case, without a court's permission, there can be no valid order, and the Secretary of State must immediately apply to the court for a decision under s 3(2). 7.36

By contrast, it would appear that a case under (a) entails more court discretion in one aspect. Section 3(2)(b) states that the court 'may' grant permission for an order which is not obviously flawed—'may' suggests some residual discretion, perhaps based on an abuse of process or some other fundamental defect. Under s 3(6)(c), the court 'must' confirm the order if it is not obviously flawed. 7.37

The sensitive nature of these intelligence-led procedures in court is exemplified by s 3(5). The initial hearings in connection with non-derogating control orders, in which the court will decide whether to grant permission for the order to be made under procedure (a) or will consider the Secretary of State's decision to impose the order without the court's permission under procedure (b) or (c) may be made in the absence of, without the knowledge of, and without representation for the subject of the order. However, the court must ensure under s 3(9) that the controlled person is notified of its decision on a reference under sub-s (3)(a). Furthermore, when the court orders a full hearing, the court must make arrangements under s 3(7) within seven days of the court's decision for the suspect to be given an opportunity to make representations *inter partes* about the directions already given or the making of further directions. This time limit of seven days has caused problems in practice because delays sometimes occur so that 7.38

arrangements can be put in place to enforce the order.[65] The Counter-Terrorism Act 2008, s 80, therefore recalibrates the clock to run from the service of the order on the suspect.

7.39   Assuming there is a full hearing on a non-derogating control order and the suspect does not ask for desistance of proceedings under s 3(14), the court must determine under s 3(10) whether the decisions of the Secretary of State were 'flawed' in terms of the factual grounds or of the necessity for each obligation. Though the term 'flawed' rather than 'obviously flawed' is used here, there is no legal difference: s 3(11) defines both by reference to 'the principles applicable on an application for judicial review'. Hence, the full hearing is not a *de novo* consideration, and the courts should not substitute their own judgment on the merits.[66] However, the boundary of review has been pushed in one respect—in *Bullivant*,[67] evidence which becomes available in time for a s 3(11) hearing but after an order is imposed must still be considered by the court.

7.40   As well as the limited basis for review, the court's scrutiny must reflect that the decision only requires a 'reasonable suspicion'. Parliamentary challenges to this lowly level of proof, and attempts to insert a balance-of-probabilities test or even the criminal standard of proof were all rebuffed.[68]

7.41   If the court decides in a full hearing order that a decision of the Secretary of State was flawed, it must under s 3(12): (a) quash the control order; (b) quash one or more of the obligations contained in the order; or (c) give directions to the Secretary of State to revoke or modify the order. Otherwise, under s 3(13), it must uphold the order, and no residual discretion is mentioned. The quashing of an order may be stayed pending appeal under s 15(2); alternatively, the Secretary of State may proceed to make a new order (Sch, para 8). Lord Carlile has suggested that the courts should be granted a power to amend orders which are obviously flawed so as to avoid the complications of making and serving a new order.[69] However, it would conflict with the intentions of Parliament (and the Home Office) to allow a judicial power of this kind.

(b) *Derogating control orders*

7.42   Section 4 envisages orders which are so draconian in their intrusion into liberty that they can only be justified by reference to a derogation notice under Art 15. The most palpable obligation will be 'house arrest'—confinement within a specified place for an intolerable length of time. Whether a derogating order could even allow internment may be doubted. Section 1(4) only allows restrictions in respect of a 'place of residence' and restrictions on movement only for up to twenty-four hours. Furthermore, s 1(2)(a) only envisages derogations in relation to Art 5, and internment will inevitably negate other rights such as family life.

---

[65] Compare Lord Carlile, *First Report of the Independent Reviewer pursuant to Section 14(3) of the Prevention of Terrorism Act 2005* (Home Office, London, 2006) para 49; Joint Committee on Human Rights, *Counter-Terrorism Policy and Human Rights: Counter-Terrorism Bill* (2007–08 HL 50/HC 199) para 39.

[66] *MB* [2006] EWHC (Admin) 1000 at para 79.

[67] [2008] EWHC 337 (Admin) at para 11.

[68] Hansard HL vol 670, col 152 (1 March 2005) and col 482 (7 March 2005).

[69] Lord Carlile, *Special Report of the Independent Reviewer in relation to Quarterly Reports under section 14(1) of the Prevention of Terrorism Act 2005* (Home Office, London, 2006) para 24.

Reflecting the fact that 'the right to liberty is in play',[70] the courts are more heavily   7.43
involved in the issuance of derogating control orders, though the standard of proof and
procedures still respond to anticipatory risk and thereby diverge significantly from criminal trials. In contrast with non-derogating orders, the courts issue the s 4 order, there is
automatic subsequent referral to the court, and the civil standard of proof applies. The
next difference is that the issuance of these orders must be predicated upon the lawful
issuance of a notice of derogation under Art 15 and a designation order under s 14(1)(b)
of the Human Rights Act 1998.

As mentioned, under s 4(1), the order must be made by the court. The court must   7.44
hold an immediate preliminary hearing on an application from the Secretary of State to
decide whether to make a derogating control order against an individual. No time limit
is specified for what is to count as 'immediate'. If the court decides to make the order, it
then must give directions for a full hearing. Once again, this preliminary hearing may
occur under s 4(2) in the absence of, without the knowledge of, and without representation for, the subject of the order. At the preliminary hearing, the court may make the
order if, by s 4(3), it appears that: (a) there is material which is capable of establishing
involvement in terrorism-related activity; (b) reasonable grounds for believing that the
imposition of obligations is necessary to protect the public; (c) the risk is linked to a
public emergency in respect of which there is a designated derogation in respect of
Art 5; and (d) the obligations being imposed are derogating obligations. The test in
(a) is suggestive of a *prima facie* case, rather more searching than for a non-derogating
order, and intentionally so. Even the test in (b) requires the court positively to satisfy
itself rather than asking in the negative whether the Secretary of State is obviously wrong.
As with s 3(2)(b), there is also some suggestion of a residual discretion.

Pending a full hearing, the court may impose interim obligations under s 4(4), no   7.45
doubt on promptings from the Home Office. At the full hearing, the court may confirm,
modify, or revoke the control order under s 4(5) and (13). The tests to be applied by the
court are much more searching than the 'flawed' test under s 3. Under s 4(7), the court
may confirm the order only if: (a) it is satisfied, on the balance of probabilities, of
involvement in terrorism-related activity; (b) it considers that the imposition of obligations is necessary to protect the public; (c) the risk is linked to a designated derogation
from Art 5; and (d) the obligations include derogating obligations. At the same time,
there is no explicit basis on which to review the necessity for the derogation order itself.
In *A v Secretary of State for the Home Department*, some judges were of the view that
review of derogation in the context of detention without trial was only possible because
of the express grounds for review in s 30 of the 2001 Act.[71] Another limitation concerns
the standard of proof, set at the 'balance of probabilities'. Here, however, the courts
might be expected to adapt the civil standard to the circumstances, and, where the
allegations are serious, the standard of proof rises.[72]

The mechanics of a derogating control order include that it will last for six months   7.46
under s 4(8), unless revoked or because it would otherwise continue beyond the period

---

[70] Hansard HL vol 670, col 121 (3 March 2005), Lord Falconer.
[71] [2004] UKHL 56 at para 164 per Lord Rodger.
[72] *Re H* [1996] AC 563 at pp 586–7; *R (on the application of McCann) v Manchester Crown Court* [2002]
UKHL 39 at para 83. Their relevance to control orders is confirmed at Hansard HL vol 670, col 507
(7 March 2005), Lord Falconer.

provided for in s 6 (linking it to the persistence of the relevant derogation notice). Under s 6, the Secretary of State declares that it remains necessary for him to have the power to impose derogating obligations under the original derogation. Assuming the derogation remains operative, a derogating control order can be renewed under s 4(10). Its wording subtly differs from the criteria for the original order. The balance-of-probabilities standard is not repeated; instead, a test of necessity is applied. It is likely, however, that courts will apply the same standard of proof as before. A temporary extension pending the decision in the renewal hearing can be allowed under s 4(11) and (12).

7.47   The government made it clear from the outset that derogating orders were an embellishment to the legislation which will be, and have in fact been, locked in the trophy cabinet. The Home Office views non-derogating notices as proportionate to the operational needs of the security forces. As for the political and legal reasons for this reticence, derogating notices involve the bother of proof of an emergency which might be disputed if based on the threat from just one or two individuals, and the debates about them would also raise evident conflicts of constitutional interest and dangers of prejudice to individual rights. Nevertheless, the government asserted that as a matter of principle the 'threat that we currently face' allowed for a derogation.[73] The Joint Committee on Human Rights' contention that it is a breach of human rights law to sponsor a provision dependent upon a derogation when no derogation is in force[74] is mistaken in principle and contrary to European practice.

(c) *Processes*

7.48   Jurisdiction is conferred under the Schedule, para 10, on the Queen's Bench Division of the High Court or the Outer House of the Court of Session in Scotland. This contrasts with the involvement of the Special Immigration Appeals Commission for detentions without trial, but the sensitivity of the hearings persists. The control order will involve not only open materials, relating facts about the suspect such as movements and meetings, but also closed material, such as intercept data, intelligence assessments, and statements from security sources or third parties. The 2005 Act therefore carves out a process within the High Court which is equivalent to that pertaining to SIAC. Accordingly, s 11(1) and (2) provide that control order decisions and derogation matters are not to be questioned in any legal proceedings, including for Human Rights Act purposes. The scope of appeals is reduced by s 11(3), which states that appeals can only be on a question of law. Lord Carlile has expressed the view that an appeal court should be able to raise factual error or factual change of circumstances.[75] A further restriction is set out in s 11(4), whereby only the Secretary of State can appeal against a judgment on an application under s 3(1)(a) (seeking permission to impose a non-derogating control order) or on a reference under s 3(3)(a) (seeking confirmation of a non-derogating control order made without court permission). In these cases, the controlled person is still able to challenge the decision in the full hearing following directions.

---

[73] Hansard HC vol 431, col 153 (22 February 2005), Charles Clarke.

[74] Joint Committee on Human Rights, *Prevention of Terrorism Bill: Preliminary Report* (2004–05 HL 61, HC 389) para 9.

[75] Lord Carlile, *Third Report of the Independent Review Pursuant to Section 14(3) of the Prevention of Terrorism Act 2005* (Home Office, London, 2008) para 82.

Additional procedural issues are addressed in the Act's Schedule.[76] More detailed court rules can be devised by the normal channels, though, by para 3, outside of Scotland, the first set of rules was delivered by the Lord Chancellor.[77]   7.49

Under para 2, there is a general duty on persons exercising the relevant powers to have regard to the need to secure the proper review of control orders. At the same time, there is equally a duty to have regard to the need to ensure that disclosures of information are not made contrary to the public interest.   7.50

By para 4(2), the rules may provide for proceedings in the absence of the controlled person or his legal representative (though there may be provided a summary of the evidence taken in closed proceedings) and for the withholding of full particulars of the reasons for decisions. At the same time, under para 4(3), all 'relevant material' (as defined in sub-para (5)) must be disclosed; thus, exculpatory material must be disclosed even if the Home Office does not wish to rely on it.[78] However, application may be made (always in the absence of the controlled person and his legal representative) for evidence to be treated as 'closed' and so be disclosed only to the court and to a person appointed under para 7 as the special advocate. If the Secretary of State elects not to disclose relevant material, or provide a summary, the court may prevent the Secretary of State from relying on that material. The court may also require the Secretary of State to withdraw any allegation or argument to which that material relates.   7.51

Paragraph 5 deals with an application by the controlled person or the Secretary of State for an order mandating the anonymity of the controlled person. Anonymity has become the normal practice and is worthwhile to avoid harassment and prejudice to any subsequent trial.[79] It was held in *Times Newspapers*[80] that even though the principles of open justice could encompass control orders, anonymity was justified, though should not be applied automatically, primarily to secure the effective operation of the control order. Monitoring and enforcement could become more difficult through intrusive media and community involvement. Privacy and family rights under Art 8 could also be affected by the stigma of being labelled a terrorist. The application for anonymity may be made even before the relevant court proceedings have commenced, such as following an arrest under s 5. The Counter-Terrorism Act 2008, se 81, also allows for anonymity provided, under para 5 to the Schedule, an application for a control order has been made to the High Court.[81]   7.52

Paragraph 6 allows for the court to call for assistance from lay advisers, appointed for this purpose by the Lord Chancellor.[82] These advisers are likely to be experts in security and terrorism.   7.53

---

[76] For legal assistance, see Community Legal Service (Financial) (Amendment No 2) Regulations 2005, SI 2005/1097, reg 2. For legal costs, see *E* [2009] EWHC 597 (Admin).

[77] See Delegated Powers and Regulatory Reform Committee, *Twelfth Report* (2004–05 HL 63) para 14, *Thirteenth Report* (2004–5 HL 80) annex 4.

[78] See Hansard HL vol 670, col 692 (8 March 2005).

[79] Lord Carlile, *Special Report of the Independent Reviewer in relation to Quarterly Reports under section 14(1) of the Prevention of Terrorism Act 2005* (Home Office, London, 2006) paras 10, 11, 22; Lord Carlile, *Third Report of the Independent Review Pursuant to Section 14(3) of the Prevention of Terrorism Act 2005* (Home Office, London, 2008) para 20.

[80] [2008] EWHC 2455.

[81] Joint Committee on Human Rights, *Counter-Terrorism Policy and Human Rights: Counter-Terrorism Bill* (2007–08 HL 50, HC 199) para 39.

[82] This allows for payment: Hansard HL vol 670, col 702 (8 March 2005), Lord Falconer.

7.54　　A key safeguard for the controlled person is the appointment of qualified lawyers as 'special advocates' under para 7. Their role is to 'represent the interests' of a relevant party in control order proceedings where that party and his legal representative are excluded from the proceedings. This role will comprise, first, the normal representation work of an advocate as applied here in closed sessions. The second aspect relates to disclosure and the testing of the need for closed sessions and closed evidence. There may be a further facet of the disclosure role, which is to ensure that all material evidence has been disclosed, whether closed or not.[83]

7.55　　The impact of the fifty or so special advocates, experienced barristers who are appointed in practice by the Solicitor General,[84] is the subject of much debate.[85] Lord Carlile has expressed approbation.[86] Some judges have also given positive verdicts, especially Lord Hoffmann in *MB*, who viewed their work as decisive.[87] In *A v United Kingdom*, the European Court of Human Rights accepted that the device provides an important safeguard, but special advisers are not a panacea to remedy the loss of process rights.[88]

7.56　　A more critical view, expressed by Lord Steyn, is that 'the special advocate procedure undermines the very essence of elementary justice'.[89] Certainly the special advocate works under added hindrances compared to normal advocates. First, the special advocate is not 'responsible' under para 7(5) of the Schedule to the controlled person. Consequently, the advocate cannot be instructed by, or be legally liable to, the suspect.[90] Perhaps a code of ethics would be helpful.[91] Secondly, and the most serious hindrance, is their limited ability to consult with the suspect which is only allowed before they have inspected closed materials, unless authorized on application to the court. Applications are rare since they would reveal confidential tactics to the Home Office. The possibility of an *ex parte* application to the High Court would be helpful.[92] Suspects should also be encouraged to give evidence before the closed sessions to keep open the channels of communication as long as possible.[93] A third disadvantage is lack of support in that special advocates do not have instructing solicitors. To remedy this deficiency, the special advocates are supported by the Special Advocates Support Office, established in 2005 within the Treasury Solicitor's Office.[94] Its

---

[83] Not all material is automatically disclosed to the special adviser under CPR r 76.27: see Constitutional Affairs Committee, *The Operation of the Special Immigration Appeals Commission (SIAC) and the Use of Special Advocates* (2004–5 HC 323-I) para 61.

[84] *Ibid* at para.69.

[85] See *ibid*; Metcalf, E., 'Representative but not responsible: the use of special advocates in English law' (2004) 1 *JUSTICE Journal* 11; Bonner, D., *Executive Measures, Terrorism and National Security* (Ashgate, Aldershot, 2007) ch 8; Ip, J., 'The rise and spread of the special advocate' [2008] *Public Law* 717.

[86] Lord Carlile, *Second Report of the Independent Review Pursuant to Section 14(3) of the Prevention of Terrorism Act 2005* (Home Office, London, 2007) para 49.

[87] *MB and AF* [2007] UKHL 46 at paras 51, 54.

[88] App no 3455/05, 19 February 2009, paras 219, 220.

[89] *R v Roberts* [2005] UKHL 45 at para 88 (dissenting).

[90] See Bonner, D., *Executive Measures, Terrorism and National Security* (Ashgate, Aldershot, 2007) p 280.

[91] Boon, A. and Nash, S., 'Special advocacy' (2006) 9 *Legal Ethics* 101 at p 121.

[92] Joint Committee on Human Rights, *Counter-Terrorism Policy and Human Rights, Counter-Terrorism Bill* (2007–08 HL 108/HC 554) para 104.

[93] *Bullivant* [2007] EWHC 2938 (Admin).

[94] Constitutional Affairs Committee, *The Operation of the Special Immigration Appeals Commission (SIAC) and the Use of Special Advocates* (2004–5 HC, 323-I) paras 108, 109, 112. See A Guide to the Role of Special Advocates and the Special Advocates Support Office, <http://www.attorneygeneral.gov.uk/attachments/Special_Advocates.pdf>, 2006.

small band of lawyers play the role of instructing solicitors, but there is no research cadre as the government felt they would be bureaucratic and expensive.[95] Fourthly, special advocates are limited in their ability to cross-examine[96] or to call expert security witnesses.[97] The government will not permit other serving security agents to offer another narrative, though has no objections to independent experts.[98]

The special court rules are contained in Pt 76 of the Civil Procedure Rules.[99] Rule 76.2 requires the court to give effect to the overriding objective in para 2 of the Schedule to 'ensure that information is not disclosed contrary to the public interest', and the public interest is defined broadly by r 76.1(4). A stark illustration of the impact of this rule is *AH*.[100] The applicant sought to present evidence of twelve meetings with security service agents who were to be called as witnesses. The Home Secretary objected to this manoeuvre by reference to the NCND (Neither Confirm Nor Deny) policy in regard to security information.[101] Given that the Home Office was not relying upon the meetings as adverse evidence, the court had little difficulty in translating NCND to mean that the security agents would, if called, have no obligation to answer questions about the meetings. 7.57

Rule 76.22 enables the court to conduct hearings in private and to exclude the controlled person and his representatives. The controlled person may choose not to provide evidence, but silence should not result in adverse inferences though it might affect the weight of evidence.[102] Rule 76.24 describes the functions of the special advocate. Rule 76.26 enables the court to 'receive evidence that would not, but for this rule, be admissible'. One controversy arising here was whether the rules should exclude evidence arising from torture. The Lord Chancellor stated that there is no intention to rely upon such evidence where there is knowledge or belief of the application of torture.[103] In *A v Secretary of State for the Home Department (No 2)*,[104] the House of Lords directed that SIAC could not receive evidence obtained by the use of torture. The majority of their Lordships held that the appellant should raise a plausible reason as to why evidence adduced might have been procured by torture, before the burden passed to the tribunal to consider the suspicion, investigate it, and determine whether the evidence should be admitted on a balance of probabilities. The same rules can be expected to apply to control orders. Less controversial is the submission of evidence previously submitted in 7.58

---

[95] *Reply to the Constitutional Affairs Committee* (Cm 6596, London, 2005) para 12.

[96] The government has promised to amend the rules: Joint Committee on Human Rights, *Counter-Terrorism Policy and Human Rights: Annual Renewal of Control Orders Legislation 2009* (2008–09 HL37/HC382) para 23.

[97] Joint Committee on Human Rights, *Counter-Terrorism Policy and Human Rights, Counter-Terrorism Bill* (2007–08 HL108/HC 554) para 110; Government Reply (Cm 7344, London, 2008) p 8.

[98] Constitutional Affairs Committee, *The Operation of the Special Immigration Appeals Commission (SIAC) and the Use of Special Advocates* (2004–5 HC, 323-I) paras 29, 77, 93; *Reply to the Constitutional Affairs Committee* (Cm 6596, London, 2005) para 10.

[99] Civil Procedure (Amendment No 2) Rules, 2005, SI 2005/656, pt 76.

[100] [2008] EWHC 1045 (Admin).

[101] See *Re Scappaticci* [2003] NIQB 56.

[102] *GG* [2009] EWHC 142 (Admin) at para 29.

[103] Hansard HL vol 670, col 610 (7 March 2005), Lord Falconer.

[104] [2005] UKHL 71 at para 52. See Grief, N., 'The exclusion of foreign torture evidence' (2006) *European Human Rights Law Review* 200.

a criminal trial. In *Bullivant*,[105] Mr Justice Collins felt uneasy about any attempt to refute evidence accepted at a criminal trial, but this approach was rightly not followed in *AU*, aside from the fact of conviction.[106] Other rules about evidence are in r 76.27, by which the Secretary of State is required to make a reasonable search for relevant material and to file and serve that material. By Rules 76.28 and 76.29, the Secretary of State must apply to the court for permission to withhold closed material and file a statement explaining the reasons for withholding that material. The material is then scrutinized by the special advocate who may challenge the need to withhold all or any of the closed material. If the court finds in favour of the Secretary of State, it must next consider whether to direct the Secretary of State to serve a summary of that material.

4. Criminal prosecution

7.59   Despite the dynamic of anticipatory risk, the government claimed that prosecution is 'our preferred approach'.[107] Section 8 reflects this assertion and applies where it appears to the Secretary of State that (a) an individual's suspected involvement in terrorism-related activity may have involved the commission of an offence relating to terrorism, and (b) that the commission of that offence is being or would fall to be investigated by a police force. The latter prong presumably rules out criminal consideration where a foreign offence is alleged which is of a nature alien to the English legal system (such as slandering the state or officials) or where the foreign offence would not fall within any extra-jurisdictional provision. Before making a control order, s 11(2) requires the Secretary of State to consult with the relevant chief police officer (as defined in s 8(7)) to consider whether evidence is available that could realistically be used for the purposes of a prosecution. If a control order is made, sub-s (3) requires the Secretary of State to inform that chief police officer, and, thereafter, sub-s (4) requires the chief police officer to keep the feasibility of prosecution under review. It has been argued that the formula in s 8 may exclude cases where public interest grounds have predetermined that there should be no investigation with a view to prosecution.[108] However, the better view is that s 8 requires consideration, no matter how hopeless the prospects.

7.60   The Act's reliance on the police (and not the Crown Prosecution Service) as the agency empowered to make judgments about prosecution seems obtuse. Admittedly, s 11(5) requires the chief police officer to consult the relevant prosecuting authority, but only when a control order has been made and only to the extent that is considered appropriate to do so. Subsection (6) even provides that the chief police officer's duty to consult the relevant prosecuting authority may be satisfied by a consultation that took place before the Act was passed. The government sought to justify the secondary role of the prosecution by reference to the need to maintain its independence.[109] Why the prosecution should be more deserving than the constabulary of symbolic independence is not

---

[105] [2008] EWHC 337 (Admin) at para 8.
[106] [2009] EWHC 49 (Admin) at paras 7, 8 (as required by the Civil Evidence Act 1968, s 11(2)).
[107] Hansard HC vol 431, col 339 (23 February 2005), Charles Clarke.
[108] Lord Carlile, *First Report of the Independent Reviewer pursuant to Section 14(3) of the Prevention of Terrorism Act 2005* (Home Office, London, 2006) para 55.
[109] Hansard HL vol 670, cols 442, 539 (3 March 2005), Baroness Scotland.

apparent. It is equally unclear why prosecutors sacrifice independence when their professional judgment is reported to the Home Secretary rather than a court.

Other ideas for the facilitation of prosecution (and therefore the reduction or avoidance of reliance on control orders) occupied lengthy debates on the Bill. Most prominent was the proposal that evidence from the interception of communications should be available in criminal proceedings, thereby amending the current exclusionary rule in s 17 of the Regulation of Investigatory Powers Act 2000 and bringing it into line with the inclusionary rule for control order proceedings (Sch, para 9). The Newton Committee favoured intercept evidence as one solution to reliance upon detention without trial.[110] After long Home Office resistance, a change has now been signalled by the Chilcot Report.[111] Nevertheless, that Report continues to downplay its future consequence for terrorist cases,[112] and Lord Carlile concurs that any impact will be 'rare'.[113] 7.61

An array of other ideas for encouraging prosecution was examined by the Joint Committee on Human Rights.[114] They include: inter-agency protocols for the sharing of information, firmer judicial pre-trial management, and incentives for witnesses. Another important factor is the development of the Threshold Test as part of the Code for Crown Prosecutors.[115] 7.62

Further assurance to the security authorities should be taken from the fact that the prioritization of prosecution does not preclude later resort to control orders. For example, Rauf Abdullah Mohammad was charged under the Terrorism Act 2000, s 57, with making a video which extolled the killing of Western political leaders. The jury returned a not-guilty verdict, but he was immediately subjected to a control order or 'conviction lite,' according to one commentator.[116] 7.63

5. Ancillary issues

Section 5(1) allows for arrest and detention pending the issuance of a derogating control order where the Secretary of State has applied to the court. The power has several unusual features (including up to ninety-six hours of detention), which probably breach Art 5 of the European Convention. Section 5(9) admits this breach but authorizes it by reference to the designated derogation which will thereby serve a dual purpose. By contrast, there is no specific power to arrest and detain in connection with non-derogating control orders. The prime explanation is that a control order may be made as a matter of urgency by the Home Secretary under s 3(1)(b). In many cases, arrest will already have taken place under s 41 of the Terrorism Act 2000. 7.64

---

[110] Privy Counsellor Review Committee, *Anti-terrorism, Crime and Security Act 2001, Review, Report* (2003–04 HC 100) para 208.

[111] *Privy Council Review of intercept as evidence* (Cm 7324, London, 2008).

[112] *Ibid* paras 53, 58. Compare Joint Committee on Human Rights, *Counter-Terrorism Policy and Human Rights*: 28 days, intercept and post-charge questioning (2006–07 HL 157/HC 394) paras 120, 123.

[113] *Third Report of the Independent Reviewer pursuant to Section 14(3) of the Prevention of Terrorism Act 2005* (Home Office, London, 2008) para 38.

[114] *Counter-Terrorism Policy and Human Rights: Prosecution and Pre-Charge Detention* (2005–06 HL 240/HC 1576).

[115] (London, 2004) para 6.

[116] *The Times* 30 August 2006 p 4 (quoting Gareth Crossman).

7.65   Modification or revocation of orders is dealt with under s 7. Appeals relating to non-derogating control orders are covered by s 10. Paragraph 8(2) to the Schedule allows the Secretary of State to make a new control order to the same or similar effect and can rely on the same matters.

7.66   The next ancillary issue concerns breaches of orders under s 9, which cites offences of (1) contravening an obligation without reasonable excuse, (2) failing without reasonable excuse to report on entering or leaving the country, and (3) intentionally obstructing the delivery of a notice (the latter is a summary only offence). Indulgence is often shown in the application of s 9, and numerous minor infractions are not prosecuted.[117] In *Bullivant*, a prosecution under s 9 for failure to report at the police station failed on the basis the defendant was mentally ill.[118] Where a control order or obligation is quashed, s 12 allows a person convicted of a related offence under s 9(1) or (2) to obtain the quashing of the conviction. This result follows from para 8(1) of the Schedule, whereby where an order or obligation is quashed, it shall be treated as never having been made. In consequence, s 12(8) permits compensation to be awarded.

C. CONTROL ORDERS—REVIEW MECHANISMS

1. Review by Parliament and the executive

7.67   So as to aid future parliamentary review, s 13 provides that ss 1 to 9 expire after twelve months (from 11 March 2005). They may then be renewed for a period not exceeding one year at a time by affirmative order (unless urgent), subject to the Secretary of State consulting with the independent reviewer appointed under s 14 (discussed below), the Intelligence Services Commissioner, and the Director-General of the Security Service. Only the views of the independent reviewer are published. Opponents of the legislation asked for a sunset deadline to be imposed, as well as a review by Privy Counsellors. The government rejected these demands and even offered the disquieting anti-democratic interpretation that sunset clauses would in fact 'send the message to terrorists . . . that we are uncertain'.[119] The government also promised that another anti-terrorism Bill would be forthcoming in the following session when amendments or repeals could be tabled.[120] In fact, when the Terrorism Act 2006 emerged, no changes were made to the 2005 Act and it was barely debated.

7.68   Further assistance to parliamentary scrutiny is secured under s 14, by which the Secretary of State must report to Parliament on a tri-monthly basis on the exercise of the powers. In practice, the Secretary of State has lodged a ministerial written answer, thereby foreclosing debate.[121]

7.69   As mentioned, also under s 14, the Secretary of State must appoint an independent person to review the operation of the Act after nine months and every twelve months

---

[117] Lord Carlile, *First Report of the Independent Reviewer pursuant to Section 14(3) of the Prevention of Terrorism Act 2005* (Home Office, London, 2006) para 63.

[118] [2008] EWHC 337 (Admin).

[119] Hansard HC vol 431, col 1626 (9 March 2005), Hazel Blears.

[120] Hansard HL vol 670, col 1058 (10 March 2005), Lord Falconer.

[121] See Lord Carlile, *Special Report of the Independent Reviewer in relation to Quarterly Reports under section 14(1) of the Prevention of Terrorism Act 2005* (Home Office, London, 2006) para 27; Hansard HC vol 454, col 40ws (11 December 2006), John Reid.

thereafter. These reports must be laid before Parliament. Lord Carlile was appointed as independent reviewer. He has accepted that all control orders to date were properly made but has raised a number of important systemic deficiencies.

In his First Report, Lord Carlile criticized the severity of curfew obligations which 'fall not very far short of house arrest, and certainly inhibit normal life considerably'.[122] This prescient hint was not taken by the Home Office, and excesses had to be resolved in court (as described later).   7.70

Lord Carlile next called for the establishment of a Home Office-led procedure whereby officials and representatives of the control authorities meet to monitor each case.[123] Consequently, the government established a Home Office Review Group, including law enforcement and intelligence representatives (but there is again no mention of prosecutors). It considers quarterly and in private all extant orders.[124]   7.71

As regards s 8, Lord Carlile has revealed that letters from chief officers of police in relation to each controlled person are woefully thin on explanations. Accordingly, he has repeatedly asked for more detail and also suggested that the letters be disclosed to the suspects.[125]   7.72

In his Second Annual Report in 2007, Lord Carlile argued that the Control Order Review Group should give more attention to proactive measures to achieve exit from the regime.[126] The idea was later underlined by a proposal that orders should normally expire after two years,[127] a proposal which will be considered later.   7.73

This review process has been very thorough but also relatively conservative, concentrating mainly on finer detail. By contrast, the Joint Committee on Human Rights has delivered more policy-oriented scrutiny, covering compliance with Arts 5 and 6 of the European Convention, greater judicial involvement, higher standards of proof,[128] and, as already detailed, the boosting of prosecution.   7.74

2. Judicial review

Based on a survey of the forerunners to control orders, such as exclusion orders under the Prevention of Terrorism Acts 1974–96,[129] the prospects for effective court intervention   7.75

---

[122] Lord Carlile, *First Report of the Independent Reviewer pursuant to Section 14(3) of the Prevention of Terrorism Act 2005* (Home Office, London, 2006) para 43.

[123] *Ibid* para 46.

[124] Letter from the Home Secretary (London, 26 April 2006). See *Third Report of the Independent Reviewer pursuant to Section 14(3) of the Prevention of Terrorism Act 2005* (Home Office, London, 2008) para 47; *Fourth Report of the Independent Review Pursuant to Section 14(3) of the Prevention of Terrorism Act 2005* (Home Office, London, 2009) para 56.

[125] *Ibid* at para 58; *Third Report of the Independent Review Pursuant to Section 14(3) of the Prevention of Terrorism Act 2005* (Home Office, London, 2008) para 74; *Fourth Report of the Independent Review Pursuant to Section 14(3) of the Prevention of Terrorism Act 2005* (Home Office, London, 2009) para 78. The government claims that more is being demanded: Government Reply (Cm 7367, London, 2008) p 6.

[126] *Second Report of the Independent Review Pursuant to Section 14(3) of the Prevention of Terrorism Act 2005* (Home Office, London, 2007) para 43.

[127] *Third Report of the Independent Reviewer pursuant to Section 14(3) of the Prevention of Terrorism Act 2005* (Home Office, London, 2008) para 50; *Fourth Report of the Independent Review Pursuant to Section 14(3) of the Prevention of Terrorism Act 2005* (Home Office, London, 2009) para 58.

[128] Joint Committee on Human Rights, *Counter-Terrorism Policy and Human Rights: Draft Prevention of Terrorism Act 2005 (Continuance in force of sections 1 to 9) Order 2006* (2005–06 HL 122, HC 915).

[129] See Walker, C., 'Constitutional governance and special powers against terrorism' (1997) 35 *Columbia Journal of Transnational Law* 1.

appeared dim. National security considerations hobbled any litigation because of the sensitive evidence, the disclosure of which involved 'unacceptable risks'.[130] This judicial stance altered substantially during the review of detention without trial from 2001 until 2005. Two prominent factors affected this modification. The first was the terms of the 2001 legislation, which gave SIAC the primary review role and even designates it as an authoritative 'court of record'. The second change is the Human Rights Act 1998, which fosters a culture of rights. The impact of the review resulted in few detention orders being set aside. Nevertheless, the willingness to test the fine details went well beyond earlier practices.

7.76   Judicial review of control orders has continued these trends. Further operative influences include the strong signal of activism imparted by the House of Lords in *A v Secretary of State for the Home Department*, which was the undoing of the 2001 Act. Secondly, judicial interference with control orders seems less dramatic than springing a suspected terrorism from Belmarsh Prison. Thirdly, the legislative scheme gives yet more encouragement to judicial intervention.[131] The power is vested in the High Court or Court of Session and thus has been placed in the mainstream of the legal system. The results of the judicial review will now be explored,[132] especially three judgments from the House of Lords, which were delivered together on 31 October 2007.

(a) *Contents and impact on liberty*

7.77   Control order obligations might impact in many potential ways upon even the flexibly defined right to liberty in *Guzzardi*. The other aspect of the rights context of relevance is that the United Kingdom has not ratified the right to freedom of movement in Art 2 of Protocol 4, so the operative standards are limited.[133]

7.78   In *Secretary of State for the Home Department v JJ*,[134] the control orders demanded that the respondents observed an 18-hour curfew confined to their small flats, that they wore electronic tags, and that visitors had to be authorized. Beyond their residences, they were confined to movements within 72 square kilometres, not including any area in which they had previously lived before, and were not allowed to meet unauthorized persons. There were prohibitions on communications equipment.

7.79   The House of Lords held that the cumulative effect of these obligations breached Art 5 since their lives were 'wholly regulated by the Home Office'.[135] The majority even opined that an analogy with detention in an open prison was apt, though the fate of the suspects was even more bleak since 'controlled persons did not enjoy the association with others and the access to entertainment facilities which a prisoner in an open prison

---

[130] Shackleton Report, *Review of the Operation of the Prevention of Terrorism (Temporary Provisions) Acts 1974 and 1976* (Cmnd 7324, London, 1978) para 52.
[131] But note that SIAC could reach its own conclusions on evidence rather than being confined to review: *A* [2005] EWHC 1669 (Admin) at paras 15, 16.
[132] See Foster, S., 'Control orders, human rights and the House of Lords' (2007) 171 *Justice of the Peace* 863; Sandhill, A., 'Liberty, fairness and UK control order cases' [2008] *European Human Rights Law Review* 119; Walker, C., 'Commentary' [2008] *Criminal Law Review* 493; McGoldrick, D., 'Security detention— United Kingdom practice' (2009) 40 *Case Western Reserve Journal of International Law* 507.
[133] See Bates, E., 'Anti-terrorism control orders' (2009) 29 *Legal Studies* 99 at p 126.
[134] [2007] UKHL 45. See also [2006] EWHC 1623 (Admin); [2006] EWCA Civ 1141.
[135] *Ibid* at para 24.

would expect to enjoy'.[136] It was emphasized by Lord Bingham that the line between compliance and non-compliance with Art 5 could not be treated as mechanical and that operative factors went beyond physical restraints.[137] Compatibility with Art 5 must therefore embrace the type, duration, effects, and manner of implementation of the obligations. Other cases have suggested that account must also be taken of the impact of the restrictions in the light of the mental state of the affected individual.[138] This broad interpretation was justified by the jurisprudence of the European Court, and the subsequent decision in *A v United Kingdom*[139] likewise urges a strict interpretation of exceptions to Art 5 which also seems consistent with Lord Bingham's approach.

The Home Secretary sought to salvage the situation by arguing that if the control orders breached Art 5, then the courts should not quash the orders but only the offending obligations or should even direct modification of them. However, the majority in the House of Lords took the line that that was effectively a nullity by amounting to that the derogating order could not be cured, and new orders were required. One suspect went 'on the run', thereby avoiding the service of the amended control order.[140]   7.80

By comparison, a similar complaint raised by *AF*, who was subject to a curfew for fourteen hours in a flat occupied with his father, was rejected. Likewise, controlled person *E*, subject to a curfew for twelve hours which he had to spend with his wife and family, was determined not to have been subjected to a breach of his liberty.   7.81

Despite Lord Bingham's stricture against mechanical tests, Lord Brown in *JJ* took pity on the practical difficulties facing the Home Office and pronounced that sixteen hours would be an acceptable maximum limit, though warned that it could be excessive in given circumstances.[141] Since then, orders have been reissued with 16-hour curfews as a maximum[142] and with an average of thirteen hours.[143] The courts have continued to insist on looking at all restrictions—the degree of social isolation has emerged as important, and orders which impose 'internal exile' will be quashed.[144]   7.82

This outcome suggests that the Home Office does not view *JJ* as fundamentally undermining the viability of control orders, albeit that modified arrangements entail greater expenditure on surveillance. The Home Office has resisted a legislative restatement, preferring the nuanced House of Lords' judgment.[145]   7.83

---

[136] [2007] UKHL 45 at para 24.

[137] *Ibid* at para.16. Lords Hoffmann and Carswell dissented.

[138] *E* [2007] EWCA Civ 459 para 55; *Rideh* [2007] EWHC 2237 (Admin) para 60.

[139] App No 3455/05, 19 February 2009 para 171.

[140] *The Times* 17 October 2006 p 2, 18 October 2006 pp 3, 4.

[141] [2007] UKHL 45 at paras 105, 106.

[142] Hansard HC vol 469, col 38ws (12 December 2007), Tony McNulty.

[143] Lord Carlile, *Fourth Report of the Independent Review Pursuant to Section 14(3) of the Prevention of Terrorism Act 2005* (Home Office, London, 2009) para 15.

[144] *AP* [2008] EWHC 2001 (Admin) at para 97. A curfew of nine hours pertained in *Guzzardi*: App no 7367/76, Ser A vol 39 at para 91.

[145] Joint Committee on Human Rights, *Terrorism Policy and Human Rights: Annual Review of Control Orders Legislation 2008* (2007–08 HL 57/HC 356) paras 44, 48; *Counter-Terrorism Policy and Human Rights, Counter-Terrorism Bill* (2007–08 HL 108/HC 554) para 87; *Government Reply* (Cm 7368, London, 2008) p 4.

(b) *Processes and fairness*

7.84 The House of Lords considered issues of process under the standard of Art 6 in *MB and AF*.[146] The material which justified MB's control order included open and closed statements. The open statement contained specific allegations as follows:[147]

MB is an Islamist extremist who, as recently as March 2005, attempted to travel to Syria and then Yemen. . . . The Security Service is confident that prior to the authorities preventing his travel, MB intended to go to Iraq to fight against coalition forces. Despite having been stopped from travelling once, MB showed no inclination to cancel his plans. . . . However, given that SHAREB is an experienced facilitator with the ability to acquire false documentation, the Security Service assesses that his lack of passport will not prevent MB from travelling indefinitely.

These open allegations were admitted to be 'relatively thin' so that 'it is difficult to see how, in reality [MB] could make any effective challenge'.[148] The position of AF was even worse. AF was suspected of active links with the proscribed Libyan Islamic Fighting Group. The essence of the Secretary of State's case against AF was in the closed material.[149]

7.85 The House of Lords accepted that these proceedings fell within the less demanding civil limb of Art 6(1) since they did not involve the determination of a criminal charge. The Secretary of State's suspicion of conduct did not have to disclose any criminal offence, and the order was preventative in purpose, not punitive or retributive.[150] Next, the disclosure of relevant evidence was not an absolute right even in criminal proceedings against terrorism.[151] Applying these general principles, neither suspect had enjoyed a substantial measure of procedural justice, and so there was a breach of Art 6. Yet, there was no declaration of incompatibility since the legislation did not oblige a fatal level of suppression or exclusion. A majority of their Lordships read down under s 3 of the Human Rights Act 1998 so that the procedures take effect 'except where to do so would be incompatible with the right of the controlled person to a fair trial'.[152]

7.86 The outcome was not wholly in favour either of the controlled persons or the Home Office. The Home Office secured two clear victories—acceptance of the lower civil standard under Art 6(1) with the prediction that breaches of it would be 'wholly exceptional'[153] and the avoidance of a declaration of incompatibility under s 4 of the Human Rights Act 1998. At the same time, Lord Bingham accepted that 'the application of the civil limb of art 6(1) does in my opinion entitle such person to such measure of procedural protection as is commensurate with the gravity of the potential consequences'.[154] Therefore, whether a control order process satisfies Art 6(1) depends on the severity of the accusations and obligations and the nature of the process. By the time the case had been fully argued, taking into account open material, closed material, and the impact of the special advocate, the High Court will have to assess whether 'a substantial measure

---

[146] [2007] UKHL 46. See also [2006] EWHC (Admin) 1000; [2006] EWCA (Civ) 1140.

[147] *Ibid* at para 20.

[148] *Ibid* at paras 39, 66.

[149] *Ibid* at para 42.

[150] *Ibid* at para 24. Compare Joint Committee on Human Rights, *Counter-Terrorism Policy and Human Rights: Draft Prevention of Terrorism Act 2005 (Continuance in force of sections 1 to 9) Order* 2006 (2005–06 HL 122/HC 915) para 50.

[151] See *Botmeh and Alami v United Kingdom*, App No 15187/03, 7 June 2007.

[152] [2007] UKHL 46 at para 72 per Baroness Hale.

[153] *Ibid* at para 90 per Lord Brown.

[154] *Ibid* at para 24.

or degree of procedural justice'[155] has been accorded. Article 6 involves fundamental rights, and so any obstacles for the defence have to be counterbalanced by the procedures adopted by the judicial authorities, such as special advocates. However, aside from Lord Hoffmann,[156] the majority concluded that the special advocate system is not a panacea which can automatically wipe the slate clean of any grave disability under Art 6.

In this way, the outcome on Art 6 is inherently more uncomfortable for the Home Office than the position on liberty. The Home Office now faces a stark decision as to whether to compromise compelling security arguments in favour of disclosure, or whether to avoid reliance on the sensitive information and hope that less sensitive submissions will carry the day, or to abandon altogether the control order option. The result may be described as a teasing dance involving the shedding of intelligence and evidential veils, as the coy Home Office seeks to reveal tantalizing flashes of its dossier but will not lay everything bare from the outset. It is fortunate that the dance can be played out in the High Court which has offered to allow the Home Office to remedy any defect by further revelation after the close of the arguments in both open and closed hearings.[157] The courts have also assisted by offering to assume the validity of findings made on an earlier hearing under s 3(10), subject to any differences in the evidence relevant to those issues before the court on each of those hearings.[158] The courts have also assisted the Home Office by allowing it to impose confidentiality undertakings in relation to disclosed materials, so long as they do not hamper the legitimate pursuit of the suspect's case.[159]

This process of to and fro has raised another complaint of unfairness, namely, whether a judge who had decided issues in relation to detainees under the 2001 Act should then sit under the 2005 Act in relation to the same suspects.[160] Lord Justice Kennedy stated that no 'sweeping conclusion'[161] could be reached either to disqualify or to affirm competence. He noted that issues decided previously were not binding. In *AF (No 2)*,[162] it was questioned whether a High Court judge who had previously rejected the Arts 5 and 6 submissions, which had been reversed by the House of Lords and remitted back, should hear the case again. The Court of Appeal held that there was no appearance of bias and justice was served by having a judge who was familiar with the case.

The courts have, as expected, found it tricky to apply the *MB* judgement.[163] The most notable dispute returned to the House of Lords in *AF (No 3)*.[164] The question was whether suppression of even the gist of evidence meets Art 6 standards where, as stated by Lord Brown in *AF*,[165] 'no possible challenge could conceivably have succeeded'. The House of Lords concluded in *AF (No 3)* that *MB* had not set any 'core irreducible

7.87

7.88

7.89

---

[155] *Ibid* at para 32.
[156] [2007] UKHL 46 at paras 51, 54.
[157] *Bullivant* [2007] EWHC 2938 (Admin).
[158] *AF* [2007] EWHC 2828 (Admin) para 17. But findings of SIAC are not binding: *AR* [2008] EWHC 3164 (Admin) at para 4.
[159] *M* [2009] EWHC 425 (Admin).
[160] *A* [2005] EWHC 1669 (Admin).
[161] *Ibid* at para 22.
[162] [2008] EWCA Civ 117. See further [2008] EWHC 453 (Admin).
[163] See *Abu Rideh* [2008] EWHC 1993 (Admin); *AE* [2008] EWHC 132 (Admin); *AH* EWHC 1018 (Admin); *AN* [2008] EWHC 372 (Admin).
[164] [2009] UKHL 28. For prior decisions, see [2008] EWHC 689 (Admin), [2008] EWCA Civ 1148.
[165] [2007] UKHL 46 at para 90.

minimum' for the level of disclosure.[166] However, any complacency about this outcome was dispelled by the Strasbourg Court. In *A v United Kingdom*, a decision delivered just weeks previously, it endorsed that there can be restrictions upon adversarial process in the interests of national security,[167] but it sustained breaches of Art 6 where disclosure had been insubstantial or non-existent.[168] The House of Lords treated this judgment as a damning definitive resolution to the Home Office's advocacy of total suppression. The crucial test is now that 'the controlee must be given sufficient information about the allegations against him to enable him to give effective instructions in relation to those allegations. Provdided that this requirement is satisfied there can be a fair trial notwithstanding that the controlee is not provided with the detail or the sources of the evidence forming the basis of the allegations. Where, however, the open material consists purely of general assertions and the case against the controlee is based solely or to a decisive degree on closed materials the requirements of a fair trial will not be satisfied. . .'.[169] Paragraph 4(3)(d) of the Schedule to the 2005 Act was therefore 'read down' under the Human Rights Act.

7.90   This judgment causes further discomfort for the Home Office, but control is not rendered unworkable since substantial non-disclosure is still flexibly allowed. More positively, it recognizes the human agency of suspects and their potential to correct error, the potential feelings of resentment of their relatives and community, and the need for public confidence in the application of draconian powers. It also avoids a confusion of process and outcomes, recognizing that common law doctrines of natural law and of Art 6 demand fair process no matter whether the outcome is supportable or not. The outcome also encourages through disclosure some degree of adversarial contest, as intended by the Schedule to the 2005 Act.

(c) *Prosecution*

7.91   In contrast to the achievements of review under the prior headings, the courts have been less insistent upon the prioritization of prosecution. In *E*,[170] a non-derogating control order was challenged because the Secretary of State breached s 8. E, a Tunisian and former detainee under the 2001 Act, was suspected of involvement in the Tunisian Fighting Group, though it was not a proscribed organization and there was no evidence that E had directly engaged in violence. His claim that the realistic prospects of prosecuting him had not been properly pursued under s 8 arose from criminal prosecutions of associates in Belgium in 2003 and 2005. Yet, so far as the English authorities were concerned, no serious inquiry appeared to have been conducted, and E had not been interviewed by the police.[171]

7.92   The House of Lords agreed that the control order regime was not intended to avert the ordinary processes of criminal justice. However, their Lordships accepted that the duty to consider prosecution under s 8(2) before an initial control order is imposed was not a mandatory precondition to the initial making of a control order; to require

---

[166] [2009] UKHL 28 at paras 21, 38.
[167] App no 3455/05, 19 February 2009, para 205.
[168] *Ibid* at paras 223, 224. See further Joint Committee on Human Rights, *Counter-Terrorism Policy and Human Rights: Annual Renewal of Control Orders Legislation 2009* (2008–09 HL37/HC382) para 27.
[169] [2009] UKHL 28 para 59. Compare *A v United Kingdom*, App no 3455/05, 19 February 2009, para 220.
[170] [2007] UKHL 47. See also [2007] EWHC 233 (Admin); [2007] EWCA Civ 459.
[171] [2007] EWHC (Admin) 233 at para 124.

otherwise could emasculate the preventative intent behind control orders. Nevertheless, s 8(2) was found to be 'expressed in strong mandatory terms. . . . Plainly this duty is to be taken seriously.'[172] Furthermore, if prosecution was not properly considered, then the High Court could find the making of the order to be unnecessary or to be flawed under s 3. In this case the Secretary of State had consulted the chief officer of police, who had consulted the Crown Prosecution Service, and the advice had been negative.

The next argument was that the Secretary of State failed under s 8(4) to ensure that prosecution was kept under effective review after the control order was first made. The expressed view of the Home Office, that s 8(4) required no more than asking the police from time to time whether the prospect of successful prosecution had increased, was wrong, and Lord Bingham demanded a meaningful continuing review. Moreover, the Home Office must fulfil its duty to supply any relevant materials which came into its possession.[173] Adverse findings similar to s 8(2) could flow under s 3 in the event of non-observance of these duties. **7.93**

After all these warnings, the case ended with a whimper, for the House of Lords dismissed the materiality of the new information about E. Rather like the position on Art 5, the more diligent consideration of prosecution might require more resources to be expended but does not present any insuperable practical security problem for the Home Office or police. Therefore, this judgment was a mere shot across the bows of the Home Office. It is not evident whether efforts to comply have been more than perfunctory, as evidenced by Lord Carlile's concerns,. The government claims that more careful scrutiny has been instituted,[174] but no person subject to a control order has ever been prosecuted (aside from breaches of the order). The ruling out of prosecution should be a legal precondition, and the legislation should specify the frequency of review, the duty on relevant agencies to share information, and the duty on the police (and the DPP) to give reasons.[175] **7.94**

(d) Other legal challenges

Challenges were also raised in lower court litigation in *E* about the impact of control orders on family life (Art 8), an issue which was also taken up at one stage by his wife and children as third parties. The restrictions on computers and telephones raised issues under Art 10 (freedom of expression) but were not pursued. A further complaint was the damage to the mental health of his children (Art 3). **7.95**

In considering both Arts 3 and 8, the courts paid close attention to the psychological impacts, which caused depression for E himself and stress for his children. There was also information about hindrances to religious observances and child-care arrangements and, more generally, social isolation and stresses of police scrutiny. On Art 8, there was evidence of national security interests to provide justification within Art 8(2), and the obligations enjoyed sufficient certainty to be 'in accordance with the law'. As for Art 3, the **7.96**

---

[172] *Ibid* at para 15 per Lord Bingham.
[173] *Ibid* at para 18.
[174] *Government reply* (Cm 7194, London, 2007) p 12.
[175] Joint Committee on Human Rights, *Terrorism Policy and Human Rights: Annual Review of Control Orders Legislation 2008* (2007–08 HL 57/HC 356) paras 67, 72, 73; Joint Committee on Human Rights, *Counter-Terrorism Policy and Human Rights, Counter-Terrorism Bill* (2007–08 HL 108/HC 554) paras 73, 80. Compare Hansard HL vol 705, col 611 (11 November 2008), Lord West; *Government Reply* (Cm 7368, London, 2008) p 9.

control order restrictions were held not to pose a risk of such significant impact on the children's mental health that they were sufficiently 'humiliating and debasing them and possibly breaking their moral resistance'.[176] No specific conclusion was reached about E himself as the complaint was not pursued. It seems unlikely that control orders will regularly breach Art 3, given the requirement of a 'high threshold' of damaging treatment.[177]

7.97   Mental health issues were also considered in *Abu Rideh*.[178] The applicant experienced a particular aversion to the process of reporting to the police. The court accepted that the mental stress did not remove the need for a control order—mentally disturbed people can still commit terrorism. But the Home Secretary was ordered to find alternatives to the mechanism of reporting to the police in person and, in a second hearing, was ordered to reduce the frequency of reporting by telephone.

7.98   Challenges are of course regularly made both to the evidential sufficiency for the suspicion of terrorism activity or the necessity of an obligation and as to the formulation of an obligation.[179]

(e) *Conclusions*

7.99   This morass of cases reveals an 'intense'[180] and sustained level of judicial vigilance and regular defeats for the government despite intermittent professions of deference. But, unlike in the detention case, their Lordships avoided a declaration of incompatibility. Perhaps they wished to avoid another spectacular show-down with the politicians. Perhaps control orders are of a lower order of threat to basic rights and can be compatible, as Arts 5 and 6 jurisprudence suggests.[181] Either way, the subtle effect of the judgments is to return the disputes to High Court level for case-by-case resolution. Thus, the control order system may be 'largely unscathed' but the courts have hardly 'beaten a retreat' or confined their role to 'major irritant'.[182] There are now over thirty hearings per year, they are heard in primary courts of justice and not hidden away in a tribunal, and their superintendence has required justification and regular reassessment by the Home Office.

7.100   As an initial reaction to some of the first instance judgments, the then Home Secretary, John Reid, reportedly bemoaned that control orders 'have got holes all through them'.[183] However, for the most part, the Home Office has put a brave face on the impact of these judgments. Nevertheless, the combination of review mechanisms, especially of the judicial variety, has created a dynamic towards prosecution and towards the reduction of dependence on control orders. Continual judicial sniping has put a brake on the proliferation of the control order system.

---

[176] [2007] EWHC 233 (Admin) at para 309; [2007] EWCA Civ 459 at para 121.

[177] *A v United Kingdom*, App no 3455/05, 19 February 2009, para 134.

[178] *A* [2008] EWHC 1382 (Admin); *Rideh* [2008] EWHC 2019 (Admin). See further Liberty, *Renewing the Prevention of Terrorism Act 2005 Annex 2: Redacted Witness Statement by Gareth Peirce* (Liberty, London, 2006).

[179] See for example: *E* [2007] EWHC 2232 (Admin); *AR* [2008] EWHC 2789 (Admin) and [2008] EWHC 3164 (Admin); *AE* [2008] EWHC 1743 (Admin); *AP* [2008] EWHC 2001 (Admin); *M* [2009] EWHC 572 (Admin).

[180] *M* [2009] EWHC 572 (Admin) at para 7.

[181] In *Guzzardi v Italy*, Art 6(2) and (3) was inapplicable: App no 7367/76, Ser A vol 39 (1980) at para 108.

[182] Ewing, K.D. and Tham, J-C., 'The continuing futility of the Human Rights Act' [2008] *Public Law* 668 at pp 668, 691.

[183] *The Times* 25 January 2007 p 2.

At the same time, the system is not as just as it could be. For the sake of clarity, the 7.101
case law should be codified, but attempts to do so during the passage of the Counter-
Terrorism Bill failed since the government remains content to work with the more flexible guidance given by the judgments.[184] Some substantive changes would also be
worthwhile—changing the standard of proof to make it commensurate with restrictions
imposed, setting a minimum standard of disclosure, and issuing reasons for making an
order.[185]

D. CONTROL ORDERS—ASSESSMENT

The practical imposition of control orders evidences three trends in Table 7.1. First, the 7.102
absolute numbers are low. The number of orders in force has averaged 13.5, a rate
similar to detention without trial even though there is no requirement of a derogation
notice. The second feature is that orders against British citizens have become a regular
feature, in vindication of the House of Lords' judgment. A third feature is that all
subjects are male and suspected of international terrorism; Irish dissidents may yet prove
to be candidates.

Table 7.1 Control orders in force and by nationality[186]

Year end to 10 Dec	Control orders in force at year end		
	British citizen	Foreigner	Total
2005	1	8	9
2006	7	9	16
2007	8	6	14
2008	4	9	15
Ave total	5.0	8.0	13.5

Table 7.2 Control orders issued and persons affected[187]

Year end to 10 Dec	Control order issued	Cumulative total persons affected
2005	18	18
2006	19	19
2007	7	31
2008	9	38
Total	53	38

---

[184] Joint Committee on Human Rights, *Counter-Terrorism Policy and Human Rights, Counter-Terrorism Bill* (2007–08 HL 108/HC 554) para 97; *Government Reply* (Cm 7344, London, 2008) p 5 and (Cm 7368, London, 2008) p 1.

[185] Joint Committee on Human Rights, *Counter-Terrorism Policy and Human Rights: Counter-Terrorism Bill* (2007–08 HL 50, HC 199) para 64; Joint Committee on Human Rights, *Counter-Terrorism Policy and Human Rights, Counter-Terrorism Bill* (2007–08 HL 108/HC 554) paras 101, 107.

[186] Sources: Home Office Statements to Parliament; Carlile Reports.

[187] Sources: Home Office Statements to Parliament; Carlile Reports.

7.103   Table 7.2 qualifies the picture just presented. The cumulative total of orders issued and persons affected far exceeds the figure for detention without trial. In fact, the number of control orders in force would have been higher and more oriented towards foreigners had it not been for an aggressive policy of deportations after July 2005.[188] At the same time, even if the figure for control orders is higher than for detention without trial, it is much lower than the rate of prosecution for terrorist-related offences; from 2005 to 2008, over 100 prosecutions have been mounted.

7.104   Another quantitative indicator which has sparked comment is the rate of breaches and absconders. A seventh subject was reported as missing in 2007.[189] One problem is the more limited curfew hours after *JJ*, but the rate is also attributed to the inability to take fingerprints or DNA which was dealt with by the 2008 Act.

7.105   Turning to qualitative assessments, accountability has already been assessed in regard to reviews by Parliament and by the independent assessor. Levels of constitutional governance are good, with detailed rules as to the working of the system and no shortage of possibilities for oversight in the courts.

7.106   As the analysis of judicial review has demonstrated, audit on the basis of individual rights has been prominent. However, there remains a broader question of relevance to a rights audit—whether executive control measures, with their heavy reliance on security intelligence, can comply with constitutional values. An initial objection that decisions affecting individual rights should only be based on 'pure' evidence is belied by trenchant domestic changes to the rules of admissibility in criminal proceedings, such as Pt XI of the Criminal Justice Act 2003. This issue must also take account of the laissez-faire attitude of the European Court of Human Rights, which, while accepting that pre-trial and evidential rules can impact on fair process under Art 6,[190] has emphasized the primacy of national law in determining evidential issues.[191] Nevertheless, fairness demands that intelligence must be properly assessed. The legal regulation of intelligence is at a more nascent stage compared to rules about evidence, but it could be effectively developed.

7.107   First, there should be legal guidance about targeting, given the known dangers of skewing the objects of investigative attention through police cultures.[192]

7.108   Secondly, what is counted as 'quality' or 'valid' intelligence is not sufficiently structured. As for quality in intelligence, it is possible to apply objective standards of reliability, such as used by the police in criminal intelligence.[193] The decision-maker should be able to assess: what are the qualifications of the person who generated the intelligence and what were the methods used to generate analysis acceptable to a wider community? This idea was summarily rejected in *GG and NN*.[194] Next, what constitutes 'valid' intelligence raises normative issues. Is it acceptable, for instance, to use intelligence obtained by

---

[188] Up to the end of 2008, 153 persons were deported on national security grounds and 87 for unacceptable behaviour: Home Office, *Pursue, Prevent, Protect, Prepare: The United Kingdom's Strategy for Countering International Terrorism* (Cm 7547, London, 2009) para 8.19.

[189] *The Times* 22 June 2007 p 32.

[190] See *(John) Murray v United Kingdom*, App no 14310/88, Ser A vol 300 para 47 (1993); *Shannon v United Kingdom*, App no 6563/03, 4 October 2005.

[191] *Schenk v Switzerland*, App no 10862/84, Ser A vol 140 (1988) para 46.

[192] See Gill, P., *Rounding Up the Usual Suspects?* (Ashgate, Aldershot, 2000) pp 130, 249.

[193] See National Centre for Policing Excellence, Guidance on the National Intelligence Model (<http://www.acpo.police.uk/asp/policies/Data/nim2005.pdf>, 2005).

[194] [2009] EWHC 142 (Admin) at para 41.

torture, inhuman or degrading treatment, or obtained by illegal means such as an unlawful search or unlawful capture into jurisdiction? Only torture has yet been considered.

Processes must next be considered. There should be a safeguard of internal oversight by way of pre-authorization and based on the intrusiveness rather than the sensitivity. In addition, decision-makers should be able to see all original data. 7.109

Outcomes must next be delimited. In particular, without the high standard of proof as in judicial contexts, there should be time limits on orders. In this way, there should be an exit strategy both for individuals out of their personal plight and for the Home Office to move away from executive measures. To this end, it might be specified that an executive order should persist for no more than twelve months, without the possibility of renewal on the same grounds.[195] A time limit could transform the situation by turning a control order into a kind of provisional-charge or a provisional-deportation bail order. Either way, the Home Office would be under notice that it cannot rely on control orders for what one minister called (with inimitable logic) 'an identifiable, limited period . . . on a continuous basis'.[196] The order would afford sufficient time for the collection of evidence through intense surveillance and monitoring that will either prove or dispel the state's suspicions. Where evidence cannot be found, then the authorities face a decision as to whether the person remains suspect in which case they can still be subjected to intense surveillance. Lord Carlile has endorsed this proposal, though with a modified period of two years and without specifying it as an absolute rule.[197] As at the end of 2008, five suspects had been controlled for longer than two years.[198] The Joint Committee on Human Rights is also in favour, and it also suggests a duty to review every three months.[199] The government's response is that there is nothing 'magical' about any set period,[200] though an indefinite control order is equally said to be 'probably not appropriate'.[201] The judicial line is that an order can continue indefinitely so long as the terrorist activity persists.[202] However, one wonders how it is that persons subject to such strict management can maintain active links to terrorism and, if they do, how it is that prosecution cannot be mounted. 7.110

Beyond control orders, Lord Carlile has suggested that anti-social behaviour orders or civil injunctions might be considered,[203] though the government is doubtful, presumably because of their limited impact and their open procedures.[204] The Counter-Terrorism 7.111

---

[195] See Gil-Robles, A., Report by Mr Alvaro Gil-Robles Commissioner for Human Rights on his visit to the United Kingdom CommDH (2005) 6 (Council of Europe, Strasbourg, 2005) para 25; House of Lords Constitution Committee, The Prevention of Terrorism Bill (2004–05 HL 66) para 13; Walker, C., 'Keeping control of terrorists without losing control of constitutionalism' (2007) 59 Stanford Law Review 1395 at p 1458.

[196] Hansard HL vol 670, col 515 (7 March 2005), Baroness Scotland.

[197] See Third Report of the Independent Reviewer pursuant to Section 14(3) of the Prevention of Terrorism Act 2005 (Home Office, London, 2008) para 50; Fourth Report of the Independent Review Pursuant to Section 14(3) of the Prevention of Terrorism Act 2005 (Home Office, London, 2009) para 58.

[198] Hansard HC vol 488, col 738 (3 March 2009).

[199] Joint Committee on Human Rights, Terrorism Policy and Human Rights: Annual Review of Control Orders Legislation 2008 (2007–08 HL 57/HC 356) para 84.

[200] Hansard HC vol 477, col 211 (10 June 2008), Tony McNulty. See further Government Reply (Cm 7367, London, 2008) p 4.

[201] Hansard HC vol 472, cols 566, 584 (21 February 2008), Tony McNulty.

[202] Rideh [2008] EWHC 2019 (Admin) at para 24; GG and NN [2009] EWHC 142 (Admin) at para 50.

[203] Lord Carlile, Third Report of the Independent Review Pursuant to Section 14(3) of the Prevention of Terrorism Act 2005 (Home Office, London, 2008) para 26.

[204] Government Reply (Cm 7367, London, 2008) p 2; Hansard HC vol 472, col 566 (21 February 2008), Tony McNulty.

Act 2008, Pt IV, allows for 'notification' restraints which can be imposed post-sentence, and these might reduce further the need for control orders. As well as considering alternatives to control orders, the opposite trend has also emerged with the advent of the 'serious crime prevention order'.[205] This civil order can be imposed via the Serious Crime Act 2007 by the High Court under s 1 or the Crown Court under s 19 on the balance of probabilities if satisfied that the subject has been involved in serious crime and it has reasonable grounds to believe that the order would protect the public from further serious crime.

E. CONTROL ORDERS—CONCLUSIONS

7.112 Responses, such as control orders, which address anticipatory risk and 'neighbour' terrorism, will continue to have cogency in a risk-preoccupied society. Control orders at least seek more tailored responses than the blunter instrument of detention without trial. Control orders also reflect a more judicialized approach than prior executive models but fail abysmally by the standards of criminal process.

7.113   It is almost certain that the notion of control orders will persist for some time, just as registration orders lingered from 1939 to 1954 and exclusion orders lasted from 1974 until 1998. The prospects for Parliament calling time on control orders will strengthen when the number of extant orders has been suffiently depressed through a combination of factors—a statutory limitation period, an increase in prosecutions with intercept evidence, and the use of notification orders.

7.114   In the meantime, the drawbacks of control orders should not be ignored. Alongside their attempted assessment of future risk comes uncertainty and unfair process, which impinge on the rights of the individual. A criminal justice approach as the core response to terrorism remains preferable as it is founded on the moral platform of legitimacy and fairness[206] whilst also offering a practical response to danger. As stated by Roy Jenkins, the Home Secretary who sponsored the first British counter-terrorism bill in the contemporary era, 'Few things would provide a more gratifying victory to the terrorist than for this country to undermine its traditional freedoms in the very process of countering the enemies of those freedoms.'[207] The point was echoed by Lord Hoffmann in *A v Secretary of State for the Home Department*:[208]

Terrorist violence, serious as it is, does not threaten our institutions of government or our existence as a civil community. . . . The real threat to the life of the nation, in the sense of a people living in accordance with its traditional laws and political values, comes not from terrorism but from laws such as these. That is the true measure of what terrorism may achieve. It is for Parliament to decide whether to give the terrorists such a victory.

The prospect of minimizing the role of control orders should be taken more seriously if freedoms, such as the right to due process in para 39 of Magna Carta in 1215, are to mean more than historical artefacts.

---

[205] Home Office, *New Powers Against Organised and Financial Crime* (Cm 6875, London, 2006).

[206] Zedner, L., 'Securing liberty in the face of terror' (2005) 32 *Journal of Law & Society* 507.

[207] Hansard HC vol 882, col 634 (29 November 1974). But compare *Secretary of State for the Home Department v Rehman* [2001] UKHL 47 at para 62.

[208] [2004] UKHL 56 at paras 96, 97.

8

DANGEROUS SUBSTANCES AND ACUTE VULNERABILITIES

A. INTRODUCTION

Dangerous substances and acute vulnerabilities are reflected in Pts VI to IX of the Anti- 8.01
terrorism, Crime and Security Act 2001. They react to the exploitation of aircraft as
weapons on September 11, alongside intelligence about Al-Qa'ida interest in weapons of
mass destruction ('WMD').[1] The threat became more pressing, after letters containing
anthrax were posted in the US during late 2001[2] and several alleged plots to develop
ricin were uncovered in Britain. It later transpired that the American anthrax attacks
were probably the work of an insider scientist,[3] while British prosecutions have confirmed the intention but not the proximity of infliction. The terrorist interest in WMD
is not unique to Al-Qa'ida. Even nineteenth century anarchists devised designs to spread
diseases.[4] In contemporary times, Georgi Markov was killed by Bulgarian agents in
London in 1978 by ricin poisoning, and the Aum Shinrikyo sect in Japan inflicted sarin
gas attacks on Matsumoto in 1994 and the Tokyo underground in 1995.[5] Nevertheless,

---

[1] See National Commission on Terrorist Attacks upon the United States, *The 9/11 Commission Report*
(GPO, Washington DC, 2004) pp 117, 128, 151; Levi, M., *On Nuclear Terrorism* (Harvard University Press,
Cambridge, 2007) ch 3.
[2] See Sarasin, P., *Anthrax: Bioterror as Fact and Fantasy* (Harvard University Press, Cambridge, 2006); Cole,
L.A., 'The US anthrax letters' in Clunan, A.L., Lavoy, P.R., and Martin, S.B. (eds), *Terrorism, War, or Disease?*
(Stanford University Press, Stanford, 2008).
[3] The FBI's chief suspect, Bruce Ivins, committed suicide: *The Times* 2 August 2008 p 37.
[4] Quail, J., *The Slow Burning Fuse* (Paladin, London, 1978) pp 169–70.
[5] Bereanu, V. and Todorov, K., *The Umbrella murder* (TEL, Bury St Edmunds, 1994). See Lifton, R.,
Destroying the World to Save It (Henry Holt, New York, 1999); Reader, I., *Religious Violence in Contemporary
Japan* (University of Hawaii Press, Honolulu, 2000).

the perception of risk has remained heightened,[6] as affirmed by the demand under the UN Security Council Resolution 1540 of 28 April 2004 to take action against non-state actors seeking WMD.

8.02   Accordingly, the anti-terrorism laws tighten the laws relating to WMD and also improves the security of the nuclear and the aviation sectors. These anti-terrorism laws now sit alongside 'normal' laws which deal with firearms and explosives controls. Firearms are highly restricted under the Firearms Acts 1968–97.[7] Explosives are controlled through the Manufacture and Storage of Explosives Regulations 2005.[8] Offences are contained in the Explosive Substances Act 1883, which responded to Fenian and anarchist attacks.

B. OFFENCES RELATING TO WEAPONS OF MASS DESTRUCTION

8.03   Part VI of the Anti-terrorism, Crime and Security Act 2001 tightens offences relating to possession and transfer.[9] Threats and hoaxes about these types of materials have already been explored in Chapter 6.

1. Biological agents and toxins and chemical weapons[10]

8.04   The Anti-terrorism, Crime and Security Act 2001 builds upon controls already set out in the Biological Weapons Act 1974 and the Chemical Weapons Act 1996. This legislation is based on international treaties, namely the Convention on the Prohibition of the Development, Production and Stockpiling of Bacteriological (Biological) and Toxin Weapons and on their Destruction 1972 ('BWC')[11] and the Convention on the Prohibition of the Development, Production, Stockpiling and Use of Chemical Weapons and on their Destruction 1993 ('CWC').[12]

8.05   The Biological Weapons Act 1974 implements domestically the BWC. The BWC is generally considered to be weak since it contains no verification mechanisms. Even the blunders in relation to WMD in Iraq[13] have not altered the stance of the United States which has rejected any protocol on grounds that inspection could compromise biotechnology trade secrets and security. This stance was affirmed in the Fifth Review

---

[6] See Home Office, *Pursue, Prevent, Protect, Prepare: The United Kingdom's Strategy for Countering International Terrorism* (Cm 7547, London, 2009) p 126.

[7] Challenges failed in the multiple judgments on 26 September 2000; see for example: *Ian Edgar (Liverpool) Ltd v United Kingdom*, App no 37683/97, 2000–I.

[8] SI 2005/1082. See also Marking of Plastic Explosives for Detection Regulations 1996, SI 1996/890.

[9] See further Home Office Circular 16/2002: *Part 6 of the Anti-terrorism, Crime & Security Act 2001— Weapons of Mass Destruction*.

[10] See especially Bothe, M., Ronzitti, N., and Rosas, A. (eds), *The New Chemical Weapons Convention* (Kluwer, Hague, 1998); Allison, G., *Nuclear Terrorism* (Henry Holt, New York, 2004); Kellman, B., *Bioviolence* (Cambridge University Press, New York, 2007); Bellany, I. (ed), *Terrorism and Weapons of Mass Destruction* (Routledge, Abingdon, 2007); Levi, M., *On Nuclear Terrorism* (Harvard University Press, Cambridge, 2007); Clunan, A.L., Lavoy, P.R., and Martin, S.B. (eds), *Terrorism, War, or Disease?* (Stanford University Press, Stanford, 2008); Fidler, D.P. and Goston, L.O., *Biosecurity in the Global Age* (Stanford University Press, Stanford, 2008).

[11] Cmnd 5053, London 1972.

[12] Cm 2331, London 1993.

[13] See *(Butler) Review of Intelligence on Weapons of Mass Destruction* (2003–04 HC 898) ch 5.

Conference in 2001[14] and at the Sixth Review Conference in 2006, though it was agreed then to establish an Implementation Support Unit.[15] Otherwise, the United Nations Security Council can order expert investigations on request of a state,[16] and a 1540 Committee is mandated to promote implementation.[17] The World Health Organization also assists states.[18] Domestically, the Department of Energy and Climate Change takes responsibility.[19]

The CWC bans the development, production, stockpiling, transfer, and use of chemical weapons, as overseen by an inspection and verification regime through the Organisation for the Prohibition of Chemical Weapons.[20] At national level, regulation is by the Chemical Weapons Convention National Authority within the Department for Business, Innovation and Skills[21] which reports annually.[22]   8.06

Turning to the Anti-terrorism, Crime and Security Act 2001, the Biological Weapons Act 1974 is amended by s 43 to make it an offence to transfer biological agents or toxins outside the United Kingdom or to assist another person to do so, provided the biological agent or toxin is likely to be kept or used (whether by the transferee or any other person) otherwise than for prophylactic, protective, or other peaceful purposes and he knows or has reason to believe that that is the case. This offence is added as s 1(1A), and it supplements offences already in s 1:   8.07

(1) No person shall develop, produce, stockpile, acquire or retain—
 (a) any biological agent or toxin of a type and in a quantity that has no justification for prophylactic, protective or other peaceful purposes; or
 (b) any weapon, equipment or means of delivery designed to use biological agents or toxins for hostile purposes or in armed conflict.
(2) In this section 'biological agent' means any microbial or other biological agent; and 'toxin' means any toxin, whatever its origin or method of production.

There is no corresponding alteration to the Chemical Weapons Act 1996 because that Act already makes it an offence to 'participate in the transfer of a chemical weapon' under s 2:   8.08

(1) No person shall—
 (a) use a chemical weapon;
 (b) develop or produce a chemical weapon;
 (c) have a chemical weapon in his possession;
 (d) participate in the transfer of a chemical weapon;
 (e) engage in military preparations, or in preparations of a military nature, intending to use a chemical weapon.

---

[14] See Foreign and Commonwealth Office, *Strengthening the Biological and Toxin Weapons Convention* (Cm 5484, London, 2002); *Foreign Affairs Committee Biological Weapons Green Paper* (2002–03 HC 671); Foreign and Commonwealth Office, *The Biological Weapons Green Paper* (Cm 5713 and 5857, London, 2003).
[15] See <http://www.unog.ch/bwc/isu>.
[16] BWC, art 6.
[17] See <http://www.un.org/sc/1540/>; S/2008/493.
[18] See <http://www.who.int/csr/outbreaknetwork/en/>.
[19] <http://www.berr.gov.uk/energy/non-proliferation/page40872.html>.
[20] <http://www.opcw.org/>.
[21] <http://www.berr.gov.uk/energy/non-proliferation/cbw/national-authority/page40746.html>.
[22] See *Annual Report for 2007: operation of the Chemical Weapons Act 1996* (2007–08 HC 968).

By s 1 of that Act, 'chemical weapons' are (a) toxic chemicals and their precursors; (b) munitions and other devices designed to cause death or harm through the toxic properties of toxic chemicals released by them; (c) equipment designed for use in connection with munitions and devices falling within para (b). In turn, a toxic chemical is 'a chemical which through its chemical action on life processes can cause death, permanent harm or temporary incapacity to humans or animals', and a precursor is 'a chemical reactant which takes part at any stage in the production (by whatever method) of a toxic chemical'.

8.09   Next, s 44 extends UK jurisdiction over offences under s 1 of the Biological Weapons Act 1974 carried out overseas by a United Kingdom person (defined by s 56). The corresponding measure in relation to chemical weapons already exists under s 3 of the 1996 Act. In addition, under s 50, it becomes an offence (with a sentence of up to life imprisonment) for a United Kingdom person outside the United Kingdom to assist a foreigner to do an act which would (for a United Kingdom person) be contrary to s 1 of the Biological Weapons Act 1974 or s 2 of the Chemical Weapons Act 1996. This phraseology would not extend to a United Kingdom-resident foreigner, who, while abroad, commits an act that, if committed by a British person, would be an offence.[23] However, the Terrorism Act 2000, s 62, would seem to cover this deficiency.[24]

8.10   Further incidental matters are dealt with in ss 45 and 46 (except in Scotland), by which the Customs and Excise Commissioners can enforce offences under the Biological Weapons Act 1974 and the Chemical Weapons Act 1996 (or under s 50 of the Anti-terrorism, Crime and Security Act 2001 relating to biological weapons), in cases involving the development or production outside the United Kingdom of relevant materials or the movement of a biological or chemical weapon across a border. The Attorney General must grant consent under s 2 of the 1974 Act and s 31 of the 1996 Act.

2. Nuclear weapons

8.11   The possession and proliferation of nuclear materials have always been the subject of the utmost international attention, with the International Atomic Energy Agency to the fore.[25] Domestically, the Department for Business, Innovation and Skills oversees nuclear regulation,[26] while the executive authority is the United Kingdom Atomic Energy Authority (UKAEA) which delivers the UK Safeguards Programme. Compliance with the international regimes is vested in the UK Safeguards Office at the Nuclear Directorate of the Health and Safety Executive.[27]

8.12   Whilst the terrorist use of nuclear weapons would undoubtedly entail offences against the person and against property on a huge scale, technically crude devices—'dirty bombs'—the preparatory stages of manufacturing a weapon were not so clearly covered by any offence prior to the 2001 Act. Consequently, by s 47(1), it becomes an offence (punishable by life imprisonment) if a person (a) knowingly causes a nuclear weapon

---

[23] Hansard HC vol 375, col 719 (26 November 2001), Ben Bradshaw.

[24] See Privy Counsellor Review Committee, *Anti-terrorism, Crime and Security Act 2001, Review, Report* (2003–04 HC 100) para 280.

[25] <http://www.iaea.org/>.

[26] <http://www.berr.gov.uk/energy/non-proliferation/nuclear/index.html>.

[27] <http://www.hse.gov.uk/nuclear/safeguards/index.htm>.

explosion; (b) develops or produces, or participates in the development or production of, a nuclear weapon; (c) has a nuclear weapon in his possession; (d) participates in the transfer of a nuclear weapon; or (e) engages in military preparations, or in preparations of a military nature, intending to use, or threaten to use, a nuclear weapon. Section 48 makes exceptions for actions carried out in the course of an armed conflict or for actions authorized by the Secretary of State.[28] Section 49 sets out defences for the absence of knowledge that an object was a nuclear weapon or for an attempt to inform the Secretary of State or a police officer as soon as practicable after discovering that an object was a nuclear weapon. The term, 'nuclear weapons', a phrase based on international law, does not readily cover radiological or 'dirty' bombs.[29] However, by s 47(6), 'nuclear weapon' is defined to include nuclear explosive devices not intended for use as a weapon—for example, nuclear material from the nuclear power industry may be released as a 'dirty' bomb where the explosive material is non-nuclear and the nuclear material is a contaminant. The offences under s 47 apply to acts outside the United Kingdom by a United Kingdom person. Furthermore, s 50 applies to a s 47 offence, so it becomes an offence for a United Kingdom person outside the United Kingdom to assist a foreigner to do an act which would (for a United Kingdom person) contravene s 47.

By s 47(9), the offence of knowingly causing a nuclear weapon explosion will cease to have effect on the coming into force of the Nuclear Explosions (Prohibitions and Inspections) Act 1998. Because it contains a similar, internationally approved offence, it will replace s 47(1)(a). The relevant offence is in s (1) of the 1998 Act and applies to 'Any person who knowingly causes a nuclear weapon test explosion or any other nuclear explosion. . .'. The 1998 Act will become operative following the entry into force of the Comprehensive Test Ban Treaty.[30] Though ratified by the United Kingdom in 1998, the Treaty awaits ratification by China and the USA.[31] The Comprehensive Nuclear-Test-Ban Treaty Organization Preparatory Commission[32] engages in remote monitoring but not site monitoring.   **8.13**

The Terrorism Act 2006 has added further offences involving radioactive devices and materials and nuclear facilities and sites. The inspiration is the UN Convention for the Suppression of Acts of Nuclear Terrorism, which the United Kingdom signed in 2005.[33] These add to, and overlap with, a wide array of existing offences, not only those under the 2001 Act but also under the Nuclear Material (Offences) Act 1983, the Radioactive Substances Act 1993, and even under the common law offence of causing a public nuisance.   **8.14**

So as to allow early intervention in terrorism situations alone against someone who possesses the material for a weapon rather than a weapon itself (as under s 47 of the 2001 Act), s 9 forbids the making or possession of radioactive devices or materials with the intention of use in terrorism. The 'terrorism' may be a particular act or an unformulated   **8.15**

---

[28] See Hansard HC vol 375, col 721 (26 November 2001), Ben Bradshaw. See further s 54.

[29] Hansard HL vol 629, col 643 (3 December 2001), Baroness Symons.

[30] *Comprehensive Nuclear-Test-Ban Treaty adopted in New York on 10 September 1996 and the Protocol to that Treaty* (Cm 3665 and 4675, London, 1997, 2000).

[31] *An Additional Protocol* (Cm 4282, London, 1999) is implemented by the Nuclear Safeguards Act 2000.

[32] <http://www.ctbto.org/>.

[33] Cm 7301, London, 2008. See Joyner, C.C., 'Countering nuclear terrorism' (2007) 18 *European Journal of International Law* 225.

general inclination. The penalty is up to life imprisonment.[34] The meaning of a 'radioactive device' can range under s 9(4) from a nuclear weapon through to radioactive dispersal or radiation emission devices. Radioactive material must be of sufficient strength to cause a serious danger to personal life or injury (presumably, including the possessor's own life or bodily integrity), serious damage to property, or danger to the health or safety of the public (including a foreign public under s 20(3)). Thus, very low-level radioactive material, which might otherwise be covered by the 'radiation-emitting device' mentioned in s 9(4), cannot give rise to the offence, even if a scientifically challenged terrorist believes, for example, that a handful of lithium batteries or ionizing-based smoke detectors can cause harm.[35] On the meaning of 'public', s 20(3)(b) states that 'except in s 9(4)', that term can extend to 'a meeting or other group of persons which is open to the public (whether unconditionally or on the making of a payment or the satisfaction of other conditions)'. The result is that the court should be satisfied that the threat from radioactivity is to the public at large, including innocent victims at a public meeting, and not just to a gathering of plotters.[36]

8.16   Section 10 deals with the misuse of radioactive devices or materials (s 10(1)), or the misuse or damage of nuclear facilities (including reactors, plant, transportation, or storage) so as to cause release of radioactive material or its risk (s 10(2)). In either case, the action must be for the purposes of terrorism. But this attendant condition could conceivably be met by protestors who engineer damage resulting in the release of radioactivity; there would occur property damage designed to influence a government under s 1 of the Terrorism Act 2000. The penalty is up to life imprisonment.

8.17   Section 11(1) relates to demands backed by the threat of action for supply or access relating to radioactive devices or materials or to nuclear facilities for the purposes of terrorism. This offence is akin to demanding with menaces.[37] Section 11(2) relates to threats alone not backed by 'menaces', covering also the ground of hoax offences. In both cases, the *actus reus* must relate to existing acts of terrorism or more broadly for the purposes of terrorism which might include preparatory stages.[38]

8.18   By s 11A (added by the Counter-Terrorism Act 2008, s 38, as a simpler alternative to s 23A of the Terrorism Act 2000), when a conviction is sustained under ss 9 to 10, the court may order forfeiture.

8.19   Section 14 increases the penalty from fourteen years to up to life imprisonment for s 2 of the Nuclear Material (Offences) Act 1983 (offences involving preparatory acts and threats).

8.20   Further changes to the Nuclear Material (Offences) Act 1983 are implemented by the Criminal Justice and Immigration Act 2008, s 75 and Sch 17. The choice of this Act as the vehicle for change, rather than the Counter-Terrorism Act 2008, shows how arbitrary the agenda of the anti-terrorism legislation sometimes becomes. Section 75 is in furtherance of the ratification of the Amendment to the Convention on the Physical Protection

---

[34] See Hansard HL vol 676, col 723 (7 December 2005).

[35] But see Silverstein, K., *The Radioactive Boy Scout* (Random House, New York, 2004).

[36] Hansard HL vol 676, col 723 (7 December 2005) and *ibid* col 725 and vol 677, col 1200 (25 January 2006), Lord Bassam.

[37] See Theft Act 1968, s 21.

[38] Compare Jones, A., Bowers, R, and Lodge, H.D., *The Terrorism Act 2006* (Oxford University Press, Oxford, 2006) para 4.11.

of Nuclear Material 2005,[39] which amends the Convention on the Physical Protection of Nuclear Material 1980,[40] as implemented mainly by the Nuclear Material (Offences) Act 1983. The main impact of the amendment is to create extra criminal offences with universal jurisdiction within the 1983 Act, and the opportunity has also been taken to increase penalties to life imprisonment in that Act and under the Customs and Excise Management Act 1979. In accordance with the Convention, the 1983 Act is not to apply to nuclear materials or facilities for military or non-peaceful purposes.[41]

As for the body of Sch 17, s 1 offences in relation to nuclear material are added to by s 1(1A) (causing death, injury, or damage resulting from the emission of ionizing radiation or the release of radioactive material or an act interfering with the operation of, a nuclear facility), s 1B (receiving, holding, or dealing nuclear material or doing an act in relation to a nuclear facility for the purpose of causing damage to the environment), and s 1C (unlawfully importing or exporting nuclear material). Section 2 offences involving preparatory acts and threats are reworked and are added to by s 2A (providing for extended jurisdiction for inchoate and secondary offences). **8.21**

3. Supplemental matters

Section 51 of the Anti-terrorism, Crime and Security Act 2001 allows the venue for trial for offences under ss 47 and 50 to be anywhere in the United Kingdom. **8.22**

By s 52, there are granted powers of entry under a justice's or sheriff's warrant to officers of the Secretary of State to search for evidence for the commission of an offence under ss 47 and 50. The police cannot obtain a warrant directly (presumably these are considered to be matters beyond their expertise), but they may be permitted to accompany authorized officers. It was intended to preserve legal privilege under the order-making power in s 124,[42] but no order has been made. **8.23**

By s 53, the Customs and Excise Commissioners can enforce ss 47 and 50 in cases involving offences outside the United Kingdom or the movement of a nuclear weapon across a border. Officers of the Commissioners can institute offences in England and Wales and Northern Ireland (assuming the Attorney General gives consent under s 54). This section does not apply to Scotland. **8.24**

By s 55, the Attorney General's consent is required for prosecutions under ss 47 and 50 in England and Wales and Northern Ireland. **8.25**

Trade in these materials can also be restricted. Importation can be forbidden under the Import of Goods (Control) Order 1954.[43] The Export Control Act 2002[44] imposes corresponding controls (by way of licensing) on exports, including for the purpose of preventing terrorism anywhere in the world (Sch, para 3(2)E). **8.26**

---

[39] <http://www.iaea.org/Publications/Documents/Conventions/cppnm.html>.
[40] Cmnd 8112, London, 1983.
[41] See further ss 3A, 6.
[42] Hansard HL vol 629, col 640 (3 December 2001), Baroness Symons.
[43] SI 1954/23, amended by SI 1954/627, SI 1975/2117, SI 1978/806. See Export and Customs Powers (Defence) Act 1939; Import and Export Control Act 1990.
[44] See Export Control Order 2008, SI 2008/3231; Department for Trade and Industry, *Export Control Act 2002. 2007 Review of export control legislation* (London, 2007); Yihdego, Z. and Savage, A., 'The UK arms export regime' [2008] *Public Law* 546.

4. Comment on offences

8.27   Individual liberty does not wield a strong normative pull in this field. The state has a duty to protect the right to life under Art 2 of the European Convention, whereas there can be no conceivable right to dabble with substances which are horrendously dangerous to fellow humans.

8.28   What is more at doubt is the utility of the domestic effort beyond symbolism and reassurance. One is struck by the complexity and duplication of the changes. There have been some post-2001 charges—the first since enactment of the WMD legislation—but no convictions. For instance, the 'Wood Green plot' comprised an alleged chemical attack on the London tube, and castor oil beans were found with recipes (but no ricin). The arrests in London, Bournemouth, Norfolk, and Manchester incidentally involved the killing of Detective Constable Stephen Oake in 2003. Kamel Bourgass was convicted of murder and public nuisance, but the charges under the Chemical Weapons Act 1993 were not sustained.[45] Public nuisance through chemical and radiological attacks was alleged against Dhiren Barot but seemingly not pursued.[46] In the next case, Abdurahman Kanyare was acquitted of conspiracy to possess terrorism materials through the attempted purchase of 'red mercury' from an undercover *News of the World* journalist.[47] Allegations against two brothers, Mohammed Abdul Kahar and Abdul Koyair, arrested in Forest Green in June 2006, likewise came to naught. Given the modest record of prosecution, it might be helpful to consider the alternative approach of *in rem* forfeiture on grounds of reasonable suspicion, as applies under the Chemical Weapons Act 1993, ss 4 to 10.

8.29   The other major deficiency is the weakness of international measures against biological weapons. It has been suggested that the UN Security Council should build upon its powers to intervene and also the precedent of the 1540 Committee to set up further structures around biological security.[48]

C. SECURITY OF PATHOGENS AND TOXINS

1. Laboratory controls

8.30   There are reasons to be especially fearful of biological weapons.[49] The materials can be more readily obtained or produced than, say, radiological material. The modern urban environment, with high concentrations of highly mobile populations, facilitates transmission and hinders containment. Detection of the perpetrators is difficult when, unlike a bomb, there is no immediate impact.

8.31   Part VII of the Anti-terrorism, Crime and Security Act 2001 is more self-contained than Pt VI, for it imparts a novel domestic scheme of regulation unrelated to international

---

[45] See *R v Bourgass* [2005] EWCA Crim 1943, [2006] EWCA Crim 3397.
[46] See *R v Barot* [2007] EWCA Crim 1119; Carlisle, D., 'Dhiren Barot' (2007) 30 *Studies in Conflict & Terrorism* 1057.
[47] *The Times* 26 July 2006 p 14.
[48] Kellman, B., *Bioviolence* (Cambridge University Press, New York, 2007) p 226; Fidler, D.P. and Goston, L.O., *Biosecurity in the Global Age* (Stanford University Press, Stanford, 2008) p 253.
[49] See Clunan, A.L., Lavoy, P.R., and Martin, S.B. (eds), *Terrorism, War, or Disease?* (Stanford University Press, Stanford, 2008) p 1.

prerequisites. However, as one would expect with deadly pathogens and toxins, it follows plenty of other official attention from several sources.[50]

The Advisory Committee on Dangerous Pathogens (ACDP),[51] based within the Department of Health, advises the Health and Environment Ministers, the Health and Safety Executive, and their devolved counterparts, on all aspects of hazards to workers and others from exposure to pathogens. Its guides, which cover the running of laboratories and healthcare premises, apply the Control of Substances Hazardous to Health Regulations 2002.[52]   8.32

The Home Office has issued guidance about decontamination procedures in response to deliberate release,[53] while the Department of Health has formulated its broad-ranging NHS Emergency Planning Guidance 2005. The Health Protection Authority (HPA)[54] also provides a service through its Centre for Emergency Preparedness and Response. The HPA also includes a Centre for Infections and a Centre for Radiation, Chemical, and Environmental Hazards. Plans to deal with more specific crises are also in place, including smallpox and anthrax.[55]   8.33

Implementing the advisory standards in the workplace is the Health and Safety Executive (HSE). There is guidance on laboratories from its Health Services Advisory Committee.[56] Laboratories handling pathogens must first notify the HSE (2002 Regulations, Sch 3) and must then have suitable facilities for containment under reg 7. The Regulations (Sch 3, para 2) define four levels of hazard: 8.34

(a) Group 1—unlikely to cause human disease;
(b) Group 2—can cause human disease and may be a hazard to employees; it is unlikely to spread to the community and there is usually effective prophylaxis or treatment available;
(c) Group 3—can cause severe human disease and may be a serious hazard to employees; it may spread to the community, but there is usually effective prophylaxis or treatment available;
(d) Group 4—causes severe human disease and is a serious hazard to employees; it is likely to spread to the community and there is usually no effective prophylaxis or treatment available.

There are corresponding containment levels for laboratory work (Sch 3, para 3), which are matched to the hazard levels in the Approved List of Biological Agents, published by the ACDP.[57]

---

[50] See further Walker, C. and Broderick, J., *The Civil Contingencies Act 2004* (Oxford University Press, Oxford, 2006) ch 4.

[51] See <http://www.advisorybodies.doh.gov.uk/acdp/>.

[52] SI 2002/2677, as amended by SI 2004/3386.

[53] Home Office, *The Decontamination of People Exposed to Chemical, Biological, Radiological or Nuclear (CBRN) Substances or Material* (London, 2003).

[54] <http://www.hpa.org.uk/>.

[55] *Smallpox Mass Vaccination* (Department of Health, London, 2005); *Aide-Memoires on the Deliberate Release of Anthrax* (Department of Health, London, 2004).

[56] *Safe Working and the Prevention of Infection in Clinical Laboratories and Similar Facilities* (HSE Books, Sudbury, 2003).

[57] (HSE, Norwich, 2004), made under the Health and Safety at Work etc Act 1974, s15. See further Importation of Animal Pathogens Order 1980, SI 1980/212; Specified Animal Pathogens Order 1998, SI 1998/463; Plant Health (England) and (Scotland) Orders 2005, SI 2005/2530 and SSI 2005/613.

8.35   While seemingly extensive, these workplace controls focus on health and safety, especially of laboratory employees. Safe containment carries implications for defence from attack and the exclusion of disreputable handlers and suppliers. But there is little said about physical security of access or the vetting of workers.[58]

8.36   These security concerns lie at the heart of Pt VII of the Anti-terrorism, Crime and Security Act 2001. Its scheme proceeds not by licensing but by compulsory audit.[59] The dangerous pathogens and toxins which are within its scheme are defined as 'dangerous substances' in s 58 and Sch 5, and they include anything which consists of, or includes, or is infected by, or carries, a listed substance. The list of 'Pathogens and Toxins' in Sch 5 was chosen by reference to their degree of hazard as well as their availability and usefulness to terrorists. As well as natural substances, the Schedule covers micro-organisms which have been 'genetically modified by any means' (Notes 1(b)).[60] Orders in 2002 and 2007 exclude substances held as a medicine, or for clinical or diagnostic purposes (provided there is disposal after the diagnosis), or in a form that will not allow propagation, or as food or feeding stuff, or where toxins are held in very small quantities.[61] Though no specific exemption is granted, the listing is not considered to include vaccine strains derived from listed micro-organisms, such as attenuated Yellow Fever virus vaccine strain 17D, since they are not seriously harmful to health.[62] If listed material is stably modified by the deletion of genes involved in pathogenicity, then it can be exempted.[63] The possession of a gene library or viral replicons derived from listed materials would not be covered so long as they could not generate an infectious agent.[64]

8.37   The Secretary of State may, by affirmative order,[65] modify the list provided the material is not simply dangerous but 'could be used in an act of terrorism to endanger life or cause serious harm to human health' (s 58(3)).

8.38   As well as the power to amend the list of dangerous substances in Sch 5, s 75 allows the Secretary of State to apply Pt VII by affirmative order to a much wider range of substances, namely: (a) toxic chemicals (within the meaning of the Chemical Weapons Act 1996), provided the Secretary of State is satisfied that the chemical could be used in an act of terrorism to endanger life or cause serious harm to human health; or (b) animal pathogens, plant pathogens, and pests, provided the Secretary of State is satisfied that there is a risk that the pathogen or pest is of a description that could be used in an act of terrorism to cause widespread damage to property, significant disruption to the public, or significant alarm to the public.

8.39   The initial 2001 version of Sch 5 derived from the intergovernmental 'Australia Group' which had worked since 1985 to control state proliferation of chemical and

---

[58] See Home Office, *Regulatory Impact Assessment: Security of Pathogens and Toxins* (2001), para 2.
[59] Hansard HL vol 629, col 650 (3 December 2001), Lord Bassam.
[60] Some guidance will be derived from the Genetically Modified Organisms (Contained Use) Regulations 2000, SI 2000/2831; National Counter-Terrorism Security Office, *Pathogens and Toxins Guidance* (London, 2007) para 19.
[61] Security of Pathogens and Toxins (Exceptions to Dangerous Substances) Regulations 2002, SI 2002/1281; Security of Animal Pathogens (Exceptions to Dangerous Substances) Regulations 2007, SI 2007/932.
[62] National Counter-Terrorism Security Office, *Pathogens and Toxins Guidance* (London, 2007) para 12.
[63] *Ibid* para 13.
[64] *Ibid* paras 16, 17.
[65] See s 73(2).

biological materials.[66] The government was not satisfied with the Australia list[67] and circulated after 2001 a wider 'Salisbury Group' list with which it sought to encourage voluntary compliance and which it intended to enforce by order.[68] The changes followed in two steps but not until 2007. First, there was the addition of animal pathogens by order under s 75 in 2007.[69] Secondly, changes were issued to the original list,[70] urged not only by the cross-governmental 'Salisbury Group review',[71] but also by the Science and Technology Select Committee and the Newton Report. The relevant considerations for inclusion on the list are as follows:[72]

- The extent to which the UK population is vulnerable to infection by the pathogen;
- How infectious the pathogen is when spread by the airborne route or through contamination of food or water supplies;
- The extent to which the disease caused by the pathogen is transmitted from person-to-person;
- Availability of measures, such as vaccines, to deal with potential incidents;
- The severity and duration of illness caused by the pathogen, including the availability of treatment;
- How long the pathogen is able to survive in the environment
- How easy it is to grow, and store, the pathogen.

The animal pathogens were added in a distinct Sch 5, with the strange result that there are two discrete Sch 5s to the Act, one for 'Pathogens and Toxins' and the new one for 'Animal Pathogens'. The reason for this convoluted drafting is to allow separate 'Notes' sections for each schedule.

Table 8.1 Examples of dangerous substances under Pt VII[73]

Nature	Substance	Hazard group
VIRUS (an organism that can only reproduce within other organisms' cells which are affected by the process)	Dengue fever virus	3
	Ebola virus	4
	Herpes simiae (B virus)	4
	Influenza viruses (pandemic strains)	3
	Lassa fever virus	4
	Polio virus	2
	Rabies virus	3
	Variola virus (smallpox)	4
	Yellow fever virus	3
RICKETTSIAE (bacteria which cannot survive outside the cells of animals)	Rickettsia prowazeki (typhus)	3
	Rickettsia rickettsii (typhus)	3

---

[66] See <http://www.australiagroup.net/>.

[67] Hansard HL vol 690, col 914 (15 March 2007), Lord Bassam.

[68] Home Office, *Counter-Terrorism Powers: Reconciling Security and Liberty in an Open Society* (Cm 6147, London, 2004) Pt II para 68. The Group is based on the Centre for Applied Microbiology and Research, Porton Down.

[69] Pt 7 of the Anti-terrorism, Crime and Security Act 2001 (Extension to Animal Pathogens) Order 2007, SI 2007/926.

[70] Sch 5 to the Anti-terrorism, Crime and Security Act 2001 (Modification) Order 2007, SI 2007/929.

[71] See Regulatory Impact Assessment, para 10.1.

[72] *Ibid* para.1.3.

[73] See Zubay, G. *et al* (eds), *Agents of Bioterrorism* (Columbia University Press, New York, 2005).

Table 8.1 (Continued) Examples of dangerous substances under Pt VII

Nature	Substance	Hazard group
BACTERIA (single celled organisms that multiply by cell division and do not possess a nucleus)	Bacillus anthracis (anthrax)	3
	Clostridium botulinum	2
	Mycobacterium tuberculosis	3
	Salmonella paratyphi A, B, C and typhi	3
	Shigella boydii, dysenteriae and flexneri	2, 3, 2
	Vibrio cholerae	2
	Yersinia pestis (Plague)	3
FUNGI (organisms which share some characteristics of animals as well as plants)	Cladophialophora bantiana	3
	Cryptococcus neoformans	2
TOXIN (a poisonous agent or substance, such as proteins from bacteria, produced by a living organism)	Botulinum toxins (Botulism)	2
	Ricin	None
	Staphylococcus aureus toxins	2
ANIMAL PATHOGENS (biological agents which cause diseases in animals derived from animals)	Foot and mouth disease virus	None
	Highly pathogenic avian influenza (HPAI)	None
	Rabies and rabies-related Lyssaviruses	3

8.40   Having set the parameters, s 59 obliges the occupiers of premises to notify the Secretary of State within one month before keeping or using any dangerous substance. Further information can be demanded by the police under ss 60 and 61 about the substances, the security arrangements, and the personnel involved. Section 61 also requires occupiers to exclude others. Where occupiers intend to give access to anyone else, notification must be given to the police, and access must be denied until thirty days following the notification unless otherwise agreed by the police. The police can also, under s 65, enter relevant premises, following at least two days' notice, with any other persons, to assess security measures. In addition (for example, when there is urgency), under s 66, a justice of the peace or sheriff may issue a search warrant where the police believe that dangerous substances are kept or used on premises for which no notification has been given, or where it is believed that the occupier may not be compliant with directions.

8.41   Having carried out their checks on the premises and relevant persons, the police can, under s 62, require the occupier to improve the security arrangements. More drastic enforcement powers are given to the Secretary of State, who, under s 63, can require the disposal of any dangerous substances where security arrangements are unsatisfactory, and, under s 64, can require that any specified person be denied access to dangerous substances or the premises where exclusion is necessary in the interest of national security or public safety. It is assumed that 'national security' embraces 'international security'.[74]

8.42   By s 67 of the 2001 Act, it is an offence (punishable by up to five years' imprisonment) for occupiers of premises to fail, without reasonable excuse, to comply with any duty or directions. Sections 68 and 69 deal with offences by bodies corporate, partnerships, and unincorporated associations.

8.43   In view of the constraints on personal property and privacy imposed by these measures, a number of appeal mechanisms have been founded though to date have stood idle. First, s 70 of the 2001 Act establishes the Pathogens Access Appeal Commission

---

[74] Hansard HL vol 629, col 676 (3 December 2001), Lord Rooker. See *Secretary of State for the Home Department v Rehman* [2001] 1 UKHL 47.

(PAAC) to receive appeals made by any person denied access on the direction of the Secretary of State under s 64. By s 70(3), the Commission must allow an appeal if it considers that the decision to give the directions was flawed when considered on the basis of judicial review principles. A further appeal on law may be made with permission under s 70(4) to the Court of Appeal or Court of Session.

Schedule 6 to the 2001 Act deals with the constitution and procedures of the PAAC. **8.44** The Commissioners are appointed by the Lord Chancellor and shall hold and vacate office in accordance with the terms of the appointment (para 1); whether this is sufficient independence for European Convention purposes is doubtful.[75] The PAAC shall normally sit as a panel of three, including one person who holds or has held high judicial office (defined by para 4). By para 5, in line with the Proscribed Organisations Appeal Commission (described in Chapter 2), the rules of procedure may provide for the denial of reasons and evidence from the applicant and from any representative or their exclusion from all or part of proceedings. Where evidence is kept secret in this way, Sch 6 follows the pattern established in the Special Immigration Appeals Commission Act 1997. More detailed rules are in the Pathogens Access Appeal Commission (Procedure) Rules 2002[76] and the Court of Appeal (Appeals from Pathogens Access Appeal Commission) Rules 2002.[77]

Appeals aside from persons denied access (such as from occupiers of premises against **8.45** directions relating to compliance with security directions, the disposal of dangerous substances, or the provision of information about security arrangements) are provided for by s 71. The person may appeal within one month to a magistrates' court (with a further appeal to the Crown Court) on the ground that, having regard to all the circumstances of the case, it is unreasonable to be required to do that act. In Scotland, the route is the sheriff court, to sheriff principal, to Court of Session.

2. Comment

Initial surveys suggested that around a half of the relevant laboratories required some **8.46** work.[78] No prosecutions or closures have been reported, but health and safety legislation transgressions have occurred.[79] Some 395 laboratories have been identified as falling under the Vulnerable Sites and Sectors Programme of the National Counter-Terrorism Security Office, a police unit which is now located in the Centre for the Protection of the National Infrastructure.[80] Those within the scheme will be visited by Counter-Terrorism Security Advisers. Their security assessments will be informed by two Home Office guidelines (which have restricted access), Security of Pathogens and Toxins and Personnel Security Measures for Laboratories. Much emphasis is rightly placed on

---

[75] The position was preserved by the Tribunals, Courts and Enforcement Act 2007, s 59, by removing both PAAC and POAC members from the Judicial Appointments Commission selection process. But note the requirement to consult the Lord Chief Justice (Constitutional Reform Act 2005, Sch 4 para 300).

[76] SI 2002/1845.

[77] SI 2002/1844 r 4.

[78] Hansard HC vol 375, col 723 (26 November 2001), Beverley Hughes.

[79] See *HSE v Imperial College* (Blackfriars Crown Court, 2 March 2001, Health and Safety Executive Press Release E031:01–2 March 2001).

[80] See <http://www.nactso.gov.uk/pathogens.php>.

'personnel security and the insider threat',[81] but no individual has been barred from access.[82] Of the 310 sites under the Act,[83] around 100 (diagnostic laboratories) are exempted under the 2002 Order,[84] though they will still receive visits; an extra 10 sites holding animal pathogens were added in 2007.[85]

8.47   The scheme works passably well within its terms, especially as just fifty laboratories were known to the Health and Safety Executive. Yet, there are still vulnerabilities. First, no security standards are set in Pt VII, so the Counter-Terrorist Security Advisers lack waypoints[86] and must rely upon either general guidance[87] or even on the advice of the technicians being audited. Secondly, it is futile to impose increasingly strict physical protection in the United Kingdom while the measures are not replicated by any international convention about laboratory standards.[88] A third potential gap is that the regulations do not apply to substances in post or transit[89] or to the suppliers of DNA part sequences of pathogens.[90]

8.48   The House of Commons Foreign Affairs Committee has proffered the idea of a central authority for the control of dangerous pathogens,[91] covering not only laboratories but the proliferation of human expertise. The real threat lurks not so much in known laboratories, which often have just a few microgrammes of toxins, but the transfer of knowledge to dangerous individuals who can obtain their materials from uncontrolled sources. The spectre of unethical scientists on the loose may be exemplified by Huda Salih Mahdi Ammash (designated as 'Mrs Anthrax' in the popular press) who, after studying in US universities, became the head of the Iraqi biological weapons programme. Next, Rihab Taha ('Dr Germ') obtained a doctorate in plant toxins from the University of East Anglia in 1984. Dr Taha's team produced several pathogens and toxins in Iraq. Both women were detained in Iraq by US forces from 2003 to 2005.

8.49   The dangers of the subversion of research have become recognized in several ways. First, a voluntary vetting scheme of potential students in higher education institutes within the United Kingdom was introduced in 1994. The scheme applies whenever an applicant emanates from one of ten target countries and is interested in one of twenty-one

---

[81] *Explanatory Memorandum to Part 7 of the Anti-terrorism, Crime and Security Act 2001 (Extension to Animal Pathogens) Order 2007*, para 4.1.

[82] House of Commons Science and Technology Committee, *The Scientific Response to Terrorism* (2003–04 HC 415) para 289.

[83] Privy Counsellor Review Committee, *Anti-terrorism, Crime and Security Act 2001, Review, Report* (2003–04 HC 100) para 287.

[84] The Newton Committee opposed this exemption: *ibid* para 295. A change was promised by the Home Office, *Counter-Terrorism Powers* (Cm 6147, London, 2004) para 70.

[85] *Explanatory Memorandum to Part 7 of the Anti-terrorism, Crime and Security Act 2001 (Extension to Animal Pathogens) Order 2007*, paras 4.2, 4.3.

[86] See House of Commons Science and Technology Committee, *The Scientific Response to Terrorism* (2003–04 HC 415) para 191; Privy Counsellor Review Committee, *Anti-terrorism, Crime, and Security Act 2001 Report* (2003–04 HC 100) Pt D. para 288.

[87] See Home Office, *Counter-Terrorism Powers* (Cm 6147, London, 2004) Pt II para 71.

[88] Foreign Affairs, Committee, *Biological Weapons*, Green Paper (2003–04 HC 150) para 34. Note the non-binding World Health Organization, *Laboratory Biosafety Manual* (3rd edn, Geneva, 2004).

[89] See Privy Counsellor Review Committee, *Anti-terrorism, Crime and Security Act 2001, Review, Report* (2003–04 HC 100) para 296; Home Office, *Counter-Terrorism Powers* (Cm 6147, London, 2004) Pt II para 75.

[90] See Aldhous, P., 'The bioweapon is in the post' (2005) *New Scientist* 9 November p 8; *The Guardian* 14 June 2006 pp 1, 6.

[91] Foreign Affairs Committee, *Biological Weapons*, Green Paper (2003–04 HC 150) para 32.

disciplines.[92] But not all higher education institutes take part, and the scheme does not apply to the National Health Service or commercial laboratories. Furthermore, it is tricky to apply these rules, which were devised with state weaponry and spying in mind, to the more amorphous concept of terrorism.[93] The Foreign and Commonwealth Office recognizes a need to review the scheme[94] but rejects a central authority for the control of dangerous pathogens.

A second academic restriction was announced by the Medical Research Council, the **8.50** Wellcome Trust, and the Biotechnology and Biological Sciences Research Council in 2005.[95] Their policy statement demands that applications for research funding and their assessment should specifically consider risks of misuse. There has also been heightened vigilance by scientific journals to filter out information which might harbour dual uses.[96]

Whatever the utility of audit, the laboratory owner's rights to property can readily be **8.51** overridden by concern for the protection of life and health. Thus, the debates on Pt VII barely mentioned the intrusion into private property and the costs to businesses. At the same time, the threats of bioterrorism should not become 'a political obsession . . . a phantasm',[97] since excessive restraints will affect not only rights to privacy and property but also benign technological development.

D. SECURITY OF NUCLEAR SITES

Part VIII of the Anti-terrorism, Crime and Security Act 2001 deals with the security of **8.52** the nuclear industry. Like the offences in Pt VI, it builds upon existing measures. Its focus is organizations, installations, and information rather than the materials themselves, as under Pt VII.

1. Organizations

The Civil Nuclear Constabulary ('CNC') is the lead security force. As constituted by the **8.53** Energy Act 2004, s 52, it succeeds the Atomic Energy Authority Constabulary, formed in 1954 and formalized by the AEA (Special Constabulary) Act 1976.[98] CNC officers, who have the full constabulary powers under s 56, are tasked to provide physical protection at non-defence nuclear sites and at non-designated defence sites. The largest contingent (out of a total of around 800 officers and staff) is based at Sellafield. In practice, its jurisdiction is confined to fifteen civil nuclear sites (out of thirty-two civil licensed

---

[92] House of Commons Science and Technology Committee, *The Scientific Response to Terrorism* (2003–04 HC 415) para 200.
[93] *Government Reply to the House of Commons Science and Technology Committee* (Cm 6108, London, 2004) para 141.
[94] *Biological Weapons*, Green Paper (Cm 5713, London, 2003) p 2.
[95] <http://www.mrc.ac.uk/Utilities/Documentrecord/index.htm?d=MRC002538>.
[96] See Aldhous, P, 'The accidental terrorists' *New Scientist* 10 June 2006 p 24; Lindes, M.S., 'Censuring science' in Gerstmann, E. and Streb, M.J., *Academic Freedom at the Dawn of a New Century* (Stanford University Press, Stanford, 2006) at p 90.
[97] Sarasin, P., *Anthrax: Bioterror as Fact and Fantasy* (Harvard University Press, Cambridge, 2006) p 6.
[98] See Department for Trade and Industry, Managing the Nuclear Legacy (Cm 5552, London, 2002); Simpson, J., 'The UK and the threat of nuclear terrorism' in Wilkinson, P. (ed), *Homeland Security in the UK* (Routledge, Abingdon, 2007).

nuclear sites), a five-kilometre radius around them, plus the transportation of nuclear materials. 'Nuclear material' is defined in s 71 as including only fissile material in the form of uranium or plutonium or as prescribed,[99] but not other radioactive material. Aside from its remote system of accountability and the fact that it is funded by the industry, the other notable feature of the CNC is its officers are routinely armed.

8.54   The arrangements under the Energy Act 2004 in terms of jurisdiction and constabulary powers now reflect changes originally made by s 76 of the 2001 Act (which has been repealed). Furthermore, s 57 of the 2004 Act confers on the CNC the power to stop and search under s 44 of the Terrorism Act 2000. The Home Office Circular 26/2005, Coordinated Policing Protocol between the Civil Nuclear Constabulary and Home Office Police Forces/Scottish Police Forces, deals with policing cooperation. It directs notice of external armed patrols, confers prime authority for the policing of anti-nuclear and environmental protests on the local Chief Constable, and requires consultation before s 44 is used.[100]

2. Installations

8.55   By s 77 of the 2001 Act,[101] the civil nuclear industry is subjected to added security obligations, and these replace some earlier powers in the Nuclear Installations Act 1965 and the Atomic Energy Authority Act 1971. The Secretary of State may make regulations under s 77(1) (after consultation with the HSE and subject to negative resolution) for the security of nuclear sites, premises, material, and equipment, including material in transport, other radioactive material, and sensitive nuclear information. The regulations may require under s 77(2) the production of satisfactory security plans, compliance with any directions from the Secretary of State, and the creation of criminal offences. They can apply under s 77(4) to acts done outside the United Kingdom by United Kingdom persons. For these purposes, 'sensitive nuclear information' means under s 77(7)(a) information relating to, or capable of use in connection with, the enrichment of uranium; or (b) information relating to activities carried out on or in relation to nuclear sites or other nuclear premises which appears to the Secretary of State to be information which needs to be protected in the interests of national security.

8.56   The Nuclear Industries Security Regulations 2003[102] are partly based on the authority of s 77, especially Pt III (transportation arrangements and the use of approved carriers) and Pt IV (sensitive information), and partly on the Health and Safety at Work etc Act 1974. Part II requires an approved Site Security Plan, covering the physical installations for each site and also the suitability of staff. For other nuclear sites, directions can be issued under the Atomic Energy Act 1954, s 3, and the Nuclear Installations Act 1965.

8.57   The Office of Civil Nuclear Security (OCNS), made part of the Health and Safety Executive's Nuclear Directorate in 2007, is the principal security regulator, though non-security aspects are for the Nuclear Installations Inspectorate, which is the enforcement

---

[99] See Nuclear Industries Security Regulations 2003, SI 2003/403 Art 3.
[100] Paras 14, 18, 29. See Civil Nuclear Police Authority, *Annual Report and Accounts 2007/08* (2007–08 HC 817) p 14.
[101] As amended by the Energy Act 2004, s 77.
[102] SI 2003/403, as amended by SI 2006/2815.

arm of the Nuclear Directorate.[103] Within the setting of the 2003 Regulations, the OCNS is responsible for setting security standards and for enforcing compliance through inspections. It covers site, transport, information, and personnel security, the latter through a Vetting Office.[104] It works with policy officials in the Department for Business, Innovation and Skills' Nuclear Consultations and Liabilities Directorate. There is less regulation for non-licensed sites, such as universities and hospitals, which the Newton Committee asked to be addressed.[105]

Further oversight and standard-setting is provided at an international level by the Convention on the Physical Protection of Nuclear Material[106] which came into force in 1987 under the sponsorship of the UN's International Atomic Energy Agency.[107] The UK Safeguards Office, also within the Nuclear Directorate, handles compliance with its international safeguards obligations.   8.58

The next special measure regarding nuclear security is in the Terrorism Act 2006, s 12, dealing with trespass upon nuclear sites. Section 12 amends ss 128 and 129 (for Scotland) of the Serious Organised Crime and Police Act 2005 so as to extend that legislation to include all licensed nuclear sites (both civil and defence).[108] It becomes an offence to enter or to be on a nuclear site as a trespasser. These 'protected sites' do not have to be designated by order, unlike others already within the 2005 Act. The 'protected' nuclear site is defined, in s 128(1B), as (a) so much of premises in respect of which a nuclear site licence (within the meaning of the Nuclear Installations Act 1965) is in force as lies within the outer perimeter of the protection provided for those premises (meaning the outermost fences, walls, or other obstacles provided or relied on for protecting those premises from intruders); and (b) so much of any other premises of which premises fall within that outer perimeter of protection. In this way, where the area covered by the outer perimeter fence goes beyond the area of the licensed site, it is still an offence to be inside the outer perimeter fence. Conversely, where there is land that is part of a licensed nuclear site, but which falls beyond the outer perimeter fence, it is not an offence to trespass; if it is not a secure area, then trespass is not an immediate threat. Extra powers arise under s 130 to arrest a person suspected of committing the offence. It is a defence for trespassers to prove that they did not know, nor had reasonable cause to suspect, that the site was a protected site (s 128(4)); but ignorance of the designation as trespass is no defence.   8.59

The 2005 Act has been criticized as an undue brake on public protest,[109] and equivalent powers which affect the vicinity of Parliament are to be removed.[110] However, such   8.60

---

[103] <http://www.hse.gov.uk/nuclear/ocns>. See Simpson, J., 'The UK and the threat of nuclear terrorism' in Wilkinson, P. (ed), *Homeland Security in the UK* (Routledge, Abingdon, 2007).

[104] See The State of Security in the Civil Nuclear Industry and the Effectiveness of Security Regulation April 2007 to March 2008 (<http://www.hse.gov.uk/nuclear/ocns/ocns0708.pdf>, 2008) para 5.

[105] See Privy Counsellor Review Committee, *Anti-terrorism, Crime and Security Act 2001, Review, Report* (2003–04 HC 100) para 310; Home Office, *Counter-Terrorism Powers: Reconciling Security and Liberty in an Open Society* (Cm 6147, London, 2004) para 76.

[106] Cm 2945, London, 1995.

[107] See The Physical Protection of Nuclear Material and Nuclear Facilities (INFCIRC/225/Rev4, <http://www.iaea.org/Publications/Documents/Infcircs/1999/infcirc225r4c/rev4_content.html>).

[108] For a listing, see Home Office Circular 018/2007: *Trespass on Protected Sites—Sections 128–131 of the Serious Organised Crime and Police Act 2005*, Annex B.

[109] See especially *DPP v Haw* [2007] EWHC 1931. Compare Lord Carlile, *Proposals by Her Majesty's Government for Changes to the Laws against Terrorism* (Home Office, London, 2005) para 42.

[110] See Ministry of Justice, *The Governance of Britain: Constitutional Renewal* (Cm 7342, London, 2008) para 29.

controls have withstood past challenge under Arts 10 and 11, even when applicable to more obviously suitable venues than a nuclear site.[111] The government claims justification on the basis that protest might be used as a cover for entry by terrorists or to distract guards.[112]

8.61   Beyond the anti-terrorism legislation, other measures taken after the September 11 attacks to enhance nuclear safety related to aircraft overflight.[113] It was announced[114] that aircraft were to be prohibited from flying below a specified height and within a specified radius of Sellafield. Similar restrictions had operated around Magnox reactors on five sites. The restrictions for all sites are now set out in the Air Navigation (Restriction of Flying) (Nuclear Installations) Regulations 2007.[115]

3. Information

8.62   It is vital to keep secure not only nuclear material itself but also information about nuclear technology. Licensed companies working in the nuclear industry are already subject to safety and security regimes. The Nuclear Industries Security (Amendment) Regulations 2006[116] substitute a new reg 22 within the 2003 Regulations. The licensed operators must maintain appropriate security standards to minimize risk of loss, theft, or unauthorized disclosure of nuclear information or uranium enrichment equipment or software. They must also ensure that their officers, employees, contractors, and consultants observe the relevant security standards. The Secretary of State can issue specific directions about security and should be informed of any loss or threat. OCNS Information Security Inspectors advise operators.[117]

8.63   Section 79 of the 2001 Act[118] adds to the regulations by making it an offence for anyone, whether falling under the regulations or not,[119] to disclose any information or thing where disclosure might prejudice the security of any nuclear site or of any nuclear material either with the intention of prejudicing security or being reckless as to prejudice. Section 79 extends to activities committed outside the United Kingdom if done by a United Kingdom person. For these purposes, the relevant nuclear material is that held on a nuclear site within the United Kingdom or nuclear material anywhere in the world which is being transported to or from a nuclear site or carried on board a British ship. The penalty on conviction is up to seven years' imprisonment. This broad offence makes no reference to whether the information is in the public domain or whether it might be in the public interest to disclose it. Battles fought over the Official Secrets Act 1989

---

[111] See *Christian against Fascism and Racism v United Kingdom*, App no 8440/78, DR 21, p 138 (1980); *Kent v Metropolitan Police Commissioner*, *The Times*, 14 May 1981.

[112] Hansard HC vol 438, col 1027 (3 November 2005), Paul Goggins.

[113] See Edwards, E., 'What would happen if a passenger jet ploughed into a nuclear plant', *New Scientist*, 13 October 2001 p 1010.

[114] Hansard HC vol 374, col 540w, 12 November 2001.

[115] SI 2007/1929.

[116] SI 2006/2815.

[117] See The State of Security in the Civil Nuclear Industry and the Effectiveness of Security Regulation April 2007 to March 2008 (<http://www.hse.gov.uk/nuclear/ocns/ocns0708.pdf>, 2008) para 45.

[118] As amended by the Energy Act 2004, s 69.

[119] See Home Office, *Regulatory Impact Assessment: Security of Nuclear Industry, Security of Pathogens and Toxins (2001)* para 41.

might have to be resumed here,[120] and explicit defences of public interest should have been included. However, the government minister gave the following reassurance:[121]

... there is a great deal of information on nuclear transport that has no security implications. This is not in any way intended to be an attack on monitoring by environmental groups on where nuclear matter is moved around the country. People standing and observing on bridges and railway lines can hardly be prejudicing security because they are collecting public information. The same applies to the disclosure of information already in the public domain. The dissemination of that information is very unlikely to fall within the offence here.. . . I reiterate that it will not cover environmental monitoring or whistle-blowing on health and safety matters. It is about giving advance notice of transport movements that leaves them open to attack.

Next, s 80 of the 2001 Act allows the Secretary of State to make regulations (subject to the affirmative procedure) to prohibit the disclosure of information about the 'enrichment' of uranium (meaning any treatment of uranium that increases the proportion of the isotope 235 in the uranium). Like s 79, s 80 extends to individuals as well as regulated companies.[122] The regulations may provide for any prohibition to apply to acts done outside the United Kingdom by United Kingdom persons. This wider jurisdiction is taken since 'this technology is highly attractive to proliferators'.[123] Breach of the regulations is an offence under sub-s (3), and the penalty is again up to seven years' imprisonment. The Enrichment Technology (Prohibition on Disclosure) Regulations 2004[124] prohibit the disclosure of equipment, software, and information. Regulation 2 applies to both intentional and reckless disclosures and to disclosures within the United Kingdom as well as disclosures by United Kingdom persons abroad. The test of recklessness replicates the formulation of inadvertent recklessness in *Metropolitan Police Commissioner v Caldwell*[125] even though it has been superseded for most purposes by *R v G*.[126] Some exemptions are granted in reg 3, while the Secretary of State has various override powers in regs 4 and 5. **8.64**

Section 80A is inserted by the Energy Act 2008, s 101. It allows the Secretary of State to designate as a prohibited place for the purposes of s 3(c) of the Official Secrets Act 1911 a site which holds equipment, software, or information connected to the enrichment of uranium, no matter whether it is Crown property or not. Two issues are addressed by this amendment. First, following the restructuring of the nuclear industry under the Energy Act 2004, sensitive nuclear information about uranium enrichment may be stored away from licensed sites (for example, at research facilities). Secondly, the only offences protecting information at premises that are not licensed to undertake uranium enrichment are 'normal' offences such as burglary, theft, or receiving. So as to impose more severe sanctions, s 80A brings the Official Secrets Act 1911, s 1, into play, along with its penalty of not less than three years' and not more than fourteen years' **8.65**

---

[120] See also Joint Committee on Human Rights, *Report on the Anti-terrorism, Crime and Security Bill* (2001–02 HL 51/HC 420) para 26.
[121] Hansard HL vol 629, cols 1277, 1279 (11 December 2001), Lord Rooker.
[122] Home Office, *Regulatory Impact Assessment: Security of Nuclear Industry, Security of Pathogens and Toxins (2001)* para 25.
[123] Hansard HL vol 629, col 685 (3 December 2001), Lord Sainsbury.
[124] SI 2004/1818.
[125] [1982] AC 341.
[126] [2003] UKHL 50.

imprisonment.[127] Further, s 1(2) of the Official Secrets Act 1911 allows conviction without proof that a person entered a 'prohibited place' for a purpose which would adversely affect the security interests of the state.[128]

8.66   Finally, s 81 defines the meaning of a 'United Kingdom person' and also provides that the offences under ss 79 and 80 may only be prosecuted by, or with the consent of, the relevant Attorney General. The same applies to s 80A under the Official Secrets Act 1911, s 8.

4. Comment

8.67   Overall, the system is 'comprehensive and incisive'.[129] It would appear to work reasonably well, though much must be taken on trust because of the suppression of information and because the OCNS lacks the independence of other inspectorates and does not comprehensively cover the whole field. There should also be statutory recognition of public interest in publications and protest about the nuclear industry.

E. SECURITY OF AVIATION AND PORTS

1. Aviation

8.68   Part IX of the Anti-terrorism, Crime and Security Act 2001 supplements the substantial body of internationally inspired laws relating to aviation security.[130] In the light of the hijackings on 11 September, aviation was depicted as a prime vulnerability to terrorist attack, because of its complex operations, its need for public access, its emblematic representation of state interests and Western modernity, and the arousal of media interest in spectacular events with mass casualties. The Lockerbie attack of 1988 remains the most murderous terrorist attack on British territory.[131] The failed attempt by the 'shoe bomber', Richard Reid, in late 2001 illustrates the enduring allure of this target.[132]

8.69   As far as domestic law is concerned, the most relevant measures are the Tokyo Convention Act 1967[133] which was replaced by the Civil Aviation Act 1982, s 92 (as supplemented by the Civil Aviation (Amendment) Act 1996), the Hijacking Act 1971,[134] the Protection

---

[127] Official Secrets Act 1920, s 8(1).

[128] See further *Chandler v DPP* [1964] AC 763.

[129] Simpson, J., 'The UK and the threat of nuclear terrorism' in Wilkinson, P. (ed), *Homeland Security in the UK* (Routledge, Abingdon, 2007) p 177.

[130] See Tan, A.K-J., 'Recent developments relating to terrorism and aviation security' in Ramraj, V.V., Hor, M., and Roach, K., *Global Anti-terrorism Law and Policy* (Cambridge University Press, Cambridge, 2005); Clarke, R.V. and Newman, G.R., *Outsmarting the Terrorists* (Praeger, Westport, 2006) ch 4; Wilkinson, P., 'Enhancing UK aviation security post 9/11' in Wilkinson, P., (ed), *Homeland Security in the UK* (Routledge, Abingdon, 2007).

[131] *HM Advocate v Al-Megrahi* 2002 JC 99, [2008] HCJAC 58. See Grant, J.P., *The Lockerbie Trial* (Oceana, Dobbs Ferry, 2004).

[132] *US v Reid* 369 F 3d 619 (2004).

[133] *Convention on Offences and certain other Acts committed on board aircraft* (Cmnd 2261, London, 1961).

[134] *Convention for the Suppression of Unlawful Seizures of Aircraft* (Cmnd 4577, London, 1971).

of Aircraft Act 1973,[135] and the Policing of Airports Act 1974, all three replaced by the Aviation Security Act 1982, and the Aviation and Maritime Security Act 1990.[136] Their impacts fall into three parts.

First, Pt I of the Aviation Security Act 1982 contains broad offences with wide juris-   8.70
diction dealing with hijacking, the destruction or endangerment of aircraft, and the possession of dangerous articles. These offences are supplemented by s 1 of the Aviation and Maritime Security Act 1990, which forbids the endangerment of life or property at aerodromes. Secondly, protective measures for aircraft and aerodromes may be required by directive from the Secretary of State for Transport or the Director of the Transport Security and Contingencies Directorate (TRANSEC)[137] under Pt II of the 1982 Act (as amended in 1990). These reflect the International Civil Aviation Organisation's Standards and Recommended Practices (SARPs). The SARPs relating to civil aviation security are contained in Annex 17[138] to the (Chicago) Convention on International Civil Aviation 1944. The emphasis is rightly upon ground security through the detection of explosives and firearms, the scrutiny of passengers, and passenger-baggage matching.[139] The policing of airports is implemented by Pt III of the 1982 Act. Airports may be 'designated' under s 25 so that the local police force may freely enter what is otherwise private property. Nine major British airports are designated. Section 28 confers extra powers to stop and question, and bylaws under the Airports Authority Act 1972 can also restrict or prohibit access to airports.

Aviation security arrangements are overseen by the Department of Transport's   8.71
National Aviation Security Committee. The Department of Transport issues the National Aviation Security Programme and Handbook,[140] which is applied locally at each airport by an Airport Security Committee, using a Multi-Agency Threat and Risk Assessment (MATRA) methodology.

After the attacks of September 11, increased security involved the random searching   8.72
of hold baggage, increased searching of passengers, and an expanded list of prohibited articles.[141] Sky marshals were insisted upon by US authorities in late 2003, despite opposition from British pilots.[142] There has been much debate about the sharing of passenger data. The United States government demanded in November 2001, pursuant to the Aviation and Transportation Security Act,[143] full supply of the passenger name record (PNR)—the airline's reservation file for each passenger journey. This automatic transfer of data raised objections under the European Data Protection Directive 95/46/EC.

---

[135] *Convention for the Suppression of Unlawful Acts against the Safety of Civil Aviation* (Cmnd 4822, London, 1971).
[136] *Protocol for the Suppression of Unlawful Acts of Violence at Airports Serving International Civil Aviation* (Cm 378, London, 1988).
[137] See <http://www.dft.gov.uk/pgr/security/about/>.
[138] (8th edn, Montreal, 2006), as subject to Amendment 10 (ICAO Doc 7300/8, 2001).
[139] See also EU Regulations 2320/2002 and 300/2008; Commission Regulations (EC) 622/2003, 1217/2003, 1486/2003, 68/2004, 849/2004, 1138/2004, 781/2005, 857/2005, 65/2006, 1546/2006, 358/2008, 820/2008.
[140] See *Wheeler Report on Airport Security* (<http://www.dft.gov.uk/pgr/security/aviation/airport/airportsecurityreport.pdf>, 2002) paras.1.3, 3.28.
[141] See *ibid* para 1.19.
[142] See Air Navigation Order 2005, SI 2005/1970 Art 69; Hansard HC vol 416, col 161 (6 January 2004).
[143] US Code 49, s 44909(c)(3).

Consequently, the bilateral agreement for transfer in 2004[144] was called into question before the European Court of Justice.[145] A further bilateral agreement was devised in 2006.[146] The idea of passenger data transfer for air travel between Europe and destinations other than the US is now being advanced further by the draft Framework Decision on the Use of Passenger Name Records for Law Enforcement Purposes 2007.[147] The UK government is critical of the draft as not going far enough, preferring it to apply to all travel formats (including rail) and to journeys inside the European Union.[148]

8.73   The changes effected by Pt IX of the Anti-terrorism, Crime and Security Act 2001 mainly relate to the policing and protective measures.[149] As regards policing, extra powers of summary arrest were granted in s 82 for offences relating to unauthorized presence in the restricted zone of an airport or on an aircraft (the Aviation Security Act 1982, ss 21C(1) and 21D(1)) and trespassing on a licensed aerodrome (the Civil Aviation Act 1982, s 39(1)). These powers were replaced by the Police Reform Act 2002, Sch 6, which in turn has been overtaken by the Serious Organized Crime and Police Act 2005, s 110.[150] In Scotland, a statutory power of arrest without warrant remains in force under s 82(3), and a further Scottish summary power is granted[151] for offences relating to the contravention of an offence under an order in council made under the Civil Aviation Act 1982, s 60, where the offence relates to specified behaviour by a person in an aircraft towards a crew member or which is likely to endanger an aircraft, or a person in an aircraft, and also the prohibition of drunkenness.[152]

8.74   Other relatively minor policing changes include, by s 83, an increase in the penalty (from level 1 to level 3) for the offence of trespass on an aerodrome contrary to s 39(1) of the Civil Aviation Act 1982,[153] and by s 84, the conferment of a specific power for the police or aviation authority employees to use force to remove intruders whose presence is unauthorized under s 21C of the Aviation Security Act 1982 (equivalent to s 31(4) of the Aviation and Maritime Security Act 1990, as amended, for ports areas and under Art 31 of the Channel Tunnel Security Order 1994).[154] While the purported aim of these measures is to ensure the security of airports, they could be used against environmental protesters. It was also threatened that they would be used against journalists who 'probe'

---

[144] See Council Decision 2004/496/EC of May 17th, 2004 on the conclusion of an Agreement between the European Community and the United States of America on the processing and transfer of PNR data by Air Carriers to the United States Department of Homeland Security, Bureau of Customs and Border Protection.

[145] See *European Parliament v Council of the European Union and European Parliament v Commission of the European Communities*, C-317/04 and C-318/04, 2006.

[146] Agreement between the European Union and the United States of America on the processing and transfer of passenger name record (PNR) data by air carriers to the United States Department of Homeland Security (13668/06) and Annexes (see Processing and transfer of passenger name record data by air carriers to the United States Department of Homeland Security—'PNR', 11304/07); House of Lords European Union Committee, *The EU/US Passenger Name Record (PNR) Agreement* (2007–08 HL 108).

[147] COM (2007) 654 final.

[148] See House of Lords European Union Committee, *The Passenger Name Record (PNR) Framework Decision* (2007–08 HL 106) and *Government Reply* (Cm 7461, London, 2008); House of Commons European Scrutiny Committee, *Seventh Report* (2007–08 HC 16-vii).

[149] Beyond the anti-terrorism legislation, see also the Police and Justice Act 2006, ss 12, 14.

[150] See also Police and Criminal Evidence (Amendment) (Northern Ireland) Order 2007, SI 2007/288 Art 15.

[151] Added by the Aviation (Offences) Act 2003, s 1(3).

[152] See especially Air Navigation Order 2005, SI 2005/1970, Arts 73–8.

[153] It must be an aerodrome licensed under the Air Navigation Order 2005, SI 2005/1970, Art 128.

[154] SI 1994/570.

airport security,[155] though these stunts have continued to go unpunished.[156] There are
around seventy incidents per year,[157] but the Newton Committee recorded just one
conviction under ss 82 to 84.[158]

Next, s 86 of the 2001 Act extends powers of 'authorized persons' (meaning officials   8.75
in TRANSEC) to bring them in line with provisions for the detention of ships and
Channel Tunnel trains.[159] They may issue a written direction to detain aircraft, if necessary by force, not solely to carry out an inspection of airworthiness (as permitted by s 60
of the Civil Aviation Act 1982 and Art 24 of the Air Navigation Order 2005)[160] but also
if 'of the opinion' that the standard of security uncovered by the inspection is inadequate
because of a failure to comply with the statutory directions or an enforcement notice or
because of threats or potential acts of violence. These powers are granted through an
added s 20B to the Aviation Security Act 1982. There are corresponding offences of failing to comply or obstruction. The operator may appeal to the Secretary of State and
must be allowed to make representations under s 86(5). There are no recorded uses of
s 86,[161] but flights have been grounded by operators on security advice.[162]

Further protective security measures are contained in ss 85 and 87 of the 2001 Act.   8.76
Section 85 inserts s 20A into the Aviation Security Act 1982 in order to grant the
Secretary of State extra powers under s 21F of the 1982 Act. Under s 21F, the Secretary
of State for Transport maintains a list of approved air cargo agents who meet the condition of compliance with security standards pursuant to the Aviation Security (Air Cargo
Agents) Regulations 1993.[163] These arrangements are applied by s 85 to other parts of
the industry which provide security services to civil aviation—'for example companies
contracted by airports and airlines to provide passenger and baggage screening services,
and companies and individuals who provide aviation security training services'.[164]
Section 87 tightens the regulations relating to air cargo agents themselves to prevent
fraud.[165] Section 87 enacts a new s 21F, to create a level 5 summary offence of issuing a
document which falsely claims to come from a security-approved air cargo agent. Three
cases have arisen, resulting in a caution and warnings.[166]

---

[155] Home Office, *Regulatory Impact Assessment: Aviation Security* (2001) para 8.
[156] See *The Independent* 3 November 2001 p 5 (*The Mirror*); *The Independent* 7 January 2002 p 9 (*Sunday People*); *Daily Telegraph* 6 January 2004 p 9 (BBC).
[157] Home Office, *Regulatory Impact Assessment: Aviation Security* (London, 2001) para 9.
[158] Privy Counsellor Review Committee, *Anti-terrorism, Crime and Security Act 2001, Review, Report* (2003–04 HC 100) para 316. There were 13 arrests.
[159] Aviation and Maritime Security Act 1990, s 21; Channel Tunnel (Security) Order 1994, SI 1994/570, Art 27.
[160] SI 2005/1970.
[161] Privy Counsellor Review Committee, *Anti-terrorism, Crime and Security Act 2001, Review, Report* (2003–04 HC 100) para 319.
[162] See *The Times* 2 January 2004 p 1 (Washington), 3 January 2004 p 1 (Riyadh), 13 February 2004 p 1 (Washington and Riyadh).
[163] SI 1993/1073, as amended by SI 1996/1607, SI 1998/1152.
[164] Home Office, *Explanatory Notes to the Anti-terrorism, Crime and Security Bill* (London, 2001) para 189.
[165] Home Office, *Regulatory Impact Assessment: Aviation Security* (London, 2001) para 36.
[166] Privy Counsellor Review Committee, *Anti-terrorism, Crime and Security Act 2001, Review, Report* (2003–04 HC 100) para 325.

8.77   It would be difficult to devise on paper a more stringent security system.[167] Several plots to attack aviation or airports have been uncovered,[168] but, aside from the Glasgow airport attack in 2007 when a car bomb reached the terminus doors,[169] no major infractions have occurred since 1984.[170] Of course, just outside the security fence was the mortaring of Heathrow by the Provisional IRA in 1994 and the attempted car bomb at Glasgow Airport in 2007 which resulted in wider vehicle exclusion zones.[171] For air travel to grind to a halt because of security restrictions would itself be a victory for terrorism, and the initial responses to the 'liquid bomb' threat in 2006 almost had this impact.[172]

8.78   The main criticism is not the achieved levels of air security but the limited accountability and constitutional governance. The Anti-terrorism, Crime and Security Act 2001 did not offer the occasion for thorough review. Piecemeal reviews have included the Wheeler Review of 2002. In 2006, the (Boys-Smith) Independent Review of Airport Policing in 2006[173] was critical of the system of designation because it made airports divorced from mainstream policing. The Independent Review of Personnel Security Across the Transport Sector[174] demanded greater attention to this aspect of risk through greater use of identity checks and vetting. In response, the Department of Transport paper, *Airport Policing Funding and Security Planning*,[175] promises to implement these changes, some of which are in the Transport Security Bill 2008–09.

2. Ports and shipping

8.79   The security of ports and shipping has been laggardly compared to aviation security.[176] As for domestic laws, port controls have been described in Chapter 5, but these are confined largely to the scrutiny of passenger transits rather than the security of ports. As for international laws, following the *Achille Lauro* incident in 1985,[177] the (Rome) Convention for the Suppression of Unlawful Acts against the Safety of Maritime Navigation,[178] and the (Rome) Protocol for the Suppression of Unlawful Acts Against the Safety of Fixed Platforms Located on the Continental Shelf[179] were agreed. They have been implemented by the Aviation and Maritime Security Act 1990. Part II contains a series of offences, such as hijacking, while Pt III deals with protective security—restricted access, searches, and enforcement measures.

---

[167] See Hainmuller, J. and Lemnitzer, J.M. 'Why do Europeans fly safer?' (2003) 15 *Terrorism and Political Violence* 1.

[168] See the cases of Mohammed Afroz (*The Express* 23 July 2005 p 9), Mohammed Naeem Noor Khan (*The Times* 24 November 2004 p 4, 21 August 2007 p 15), and Saajid Badat (*The Times* 1 March 2005 p 1).

[169] See *R v Abdulla The Times* 17 December 2008 p 3.

[170] See Malik, O., *The Analysis of Terrorist Attacks on Aviation* (RIIA, London, 2000) p 26.

[171] Hansard HC vol 467, col 667 (14 November 2007) Gordon Brown.

[172] See House of Commons Transport Committee, *Passengers' experience of air travel* (2006–07 HC 435).

[173] Department for Transport, London, 2006.

[174] Department for Transport, London, 2008.

[175] Department for Transport, London, 2008.

[176] See Beckman, R.C., 'International responses to combat maritime terrorism' in Ramraj, V.V., Hor, M., and Roach, K., *Global Anti-terrorism Law and Policy* (Cambridge University Press, Cambridge, 2005); Greenberg, M.D. *et al*, *Maritime Terrorism* (RAND, Santa Monica, 2006); Lehr, P., 'Port security in the UK' in Wilkinson, P., (ed), *Homeland Security in the UK* (Routledge, Abingdon, 2007).

[177] See Cassese, A., *Terrorism, Politics, and Law* (Blackwell, Oxford, 1989).

[178] 27 ILM 668, 1988.

[179] 27 ILM 685, 1988.

After the September 11 attacks and the bombings of the *USS Cole* in 2000 and the 8.80
French tanker, *Limburg*, in 2002 and wider allegations of Al-Qa'ida use of shipping,[180] the
International Maritime Organisation produced an International Ship and Port Facility
Security Code 2004 as the amending Chapter XI-2 to the Safety of Life at Sea Convention
1974.[181] The Code requires ports and specified ships to be certified as having adequate
security plans, training, personnel, and equipment.[182] TRANSEC oversees the application
of the Code to UK ports. The Department for Transport has established the National
Maritime Security Committee to enable consultation on maritime security. There is also a
Shipping Panel and a Ports Panel for consultation on specific matters. Ferries might be considered particularly vulnerable, as evidenced by the attack on the Philippine SuperFerry 14
by the Abu Sayyaf Group in 2004,[183] but TRANSEC has conducted training exercises.[184]

Other domestic measures include the Home Office's Programme Cyclamen—radi- 8.81
ation screening at ports and airports.[185] A more comprehensive Container Security
Initiative was launched in 2002 by the US Department for Homeland Security which
includes the pre-screening of containers;[186] British agencies cooperate in this programme. The US has also pursued an aggressive policy of the boarding at sea of suspect
vessels; British boardings have also occurred,[187] and the government is party to the
Proliferation Security Initiative[188] which seeks to intercept banned weapons and weapons technology. The government is next planning to ratify the 2005 Protocols to the
Convention for the Suppression of Unlawful Acts against the Safety of Maritime
Navigation. The Transport Security Bill 2008–09 contains new offences of using ships
to cause death or serious injury or to transport weapons of mass destruction.

F. POLICING VULNERABLE SITES

The existence of the Civil Nuclear Constabulary as a specialist force tasked to protect a 8.82
vulnerable site has already been detailed. Other specialist police forces, the Ministry of
Defence Police (MDP) and British Transport Police (BTP), are likewise given extra
responsibility by Pt X of the Anti-terrorism, Crime and Security Act 2001 so as to maximize their expertise and capabilities.[189] The Police National CBRN Centre is responsible
for the specialist training of personnel.[190]

---

[180] See Mintz, J., '15 freighters believed to be linked to Al Qaeda' *Washington Post* 31 December 2002 p A01.
[181] See EC Reg 725/2004 on enhancing ship and port facility security [2004] OJ L129/6; Ship and Port
Facility (Security) Regulations 2004, SI 2004/1495 (as amended by SI 2005/1434).
[182] Note the Automatic Identification Systems for ships under SOLAS ch V r 19 and the Long Range
Identification and Tracking of ships by satellite (r 19–1).
[183] Greenberg, M.D. *et al*, *Maritime Terrorism* (RAND, Santa Monica, 2006) ch 6.
[184] See Transport Security Directive, *Annual Report 2006–2007* (London, 2007) p 10.
[185] <http://security.homeoffice.gov.uk/science-innovation/radiation-screening1>.
[186] See now Security and Accountability For Every Port Act 2006 (6 U.S.C. s 945). There is also the voluntary Customs-Trade Partnership Against Terrorism (C-TPAT) scheme: s 961.
[187] The *MV Nisha* was boarded but released: *The Independent* 28 December 2001 p 5.
[188] See <http://www.state.gov/t/isn/c10390.htm>; Byers, M., 'Policing the High Seas: The Proliferation
Security Initiative' (2004) 98 *American Journal of International Law* 526; Guilfoyle, D., 'Maritime interdiction
of weapons of mass destruction' (2007) 12 *Journal of Conflict and Security Law* 1.
[189] See further Walker, C., 'The governance of the Critical National Infrastructure' [2008] *Public Law* 323
at p 337.
[190] See Madill, K., 'Central role' *Police Review* 26 September 2008 at p 28.

1. Ministry of Defence Police

8.83   The MDP was formed in 1971 from the unification of distinct service constabularies and now subsists under the Ministry of Defence Police Act 1987. The MDP is a civilian police force with around 3,500 officers in five divisions and exercising full constabulary powers.[191] The MDP has limited public accountability, and its jurisdiction is confined to around 200 Ministry of Defence establishments. All uniformed officers are trained to use firearms. The MDP is part of the Ministry of Defence Police and Guarding Agency which was created by the merger in 2004 with the Ministry of Defence Guard Service, which was formed in 1992 after Irish Republican attacks on military targets in England, the most serious being the bombing of the Royal Marines' School of Music, Deal, in 1989.[192] The unarmed Guard Service has 3,900 personnel and remains administratively distinct. Other Ministry of Defence security needs are met by armed services bodies, especially the Military Provost Guard Service, and by private security firms.[193]

8.84   The role of the MDP in anti-terrorism work is enhanced by s 98 of the 2001 Act, which amends s 2 of the Ministry of Defence Police Act 1987. By s 98(3), the MDP jurisdiction in relation to defence personnel (which applies anywhere in the United Kingdom) is extended from the alleged commission of offences by defence personnel to offences against defence personnel (such as any attempt to incite or bribe defence personnel into committing offences revealing confidential information).

8.85   By s 98(4), the MDP is enabled to operate beyond defence-related property and with full 'normal' constabulary powers whenever a constable of a Home Department police force, the Police Service of Northern Ireland, the British Transport Police, or the Civil Nuclear Constabulary has asked for assistance. The intervention must relate to 'a particular incident, investigation or operation', and the powers will then be exercisable within the police area of the requesting police force. In an emergency, an MDP officer in uniform (or with proof of office, such as a warrant card), may act on reasonable suspicion of an offence or where he reasonably believes that action is necessary to save life or prevent or minimize personal injury, and on the reasonable belief that waiting for a request would frustrate or seriously prejudice the purpose of the action. It is expected that such emergency circumstances will be narrowly conceived: 'Given the availability of modern radio communications, the effect will restrict its use to circumstances of genuine emergency when a virtually instant reaction is needed'.[194] Examples might be where:[195]

Intelligence is received that a possible terrorist is near a defence base—perhaps a US base. The suspect is believed to be a member of an illegal organisation, or to have with him a stolen passport or a weapon. There may be no immediate threat of violence; the suspect is only scouting—carrying out reconnaissance. Under the Terrorism Act 2000, the MDP have the power to arrest members of illegal organizations. They have powers of arrest and stop and search related to stolen articles, but at present they could act only if two requirements are met: the suspect is 'in the vicinity' of the base on which the police are operating, and the local force agrees. The new powers in the Bill will

---

[191] The Guard Service (and the Northern Ireland Security Guard Service) can be given special constable status under the Emergency Laws (Miscellaneous Provisions) Act 1947, sch 2.
[192] See Walker, C.P., *The Prevention of Terrorism in British Law* (2nd edn, Manchester University Press, Manchester, 1992) ch 11.
[193] See Ministry of Defence Police and Guarding (1995–96) HC 189.
[194] Hansard HC vol 375, col 775 (26 November 2001), Lewis Moonie.
[195] *Ibid* col 776.

allow the MDP to act if there is no time to bring in the local police—in other words, if there is an emergency.

To take a second case—an MDP officer in a street adjacent to defence property is approached by a woman who says, 'Stop that man, he has taken my purse'. That could happen up the road at the Ministry of Defence—our own officers patrol outside. The officer sees a man running away. Should he say, 'Sorry, can't help. Although I may look like a police officer, I am in the MDP and I have no jurisdiction'? Should the officer try to establish whether the man had or had not used violence in taking the purse—by which time the man will have made off? Should the officer try to contact the local police station to seek instruction? The result would be the same.

Additional to s 98, s 99 (inserting a new s 2A into the 1987 Act) envisages that the MDP may also swing into action where another police force requires extra resources to meet a special burden. If offering such inter-force assistance (similar to the Police Act 1996, s 24(3)), the MDP officers come under the direction of the chief officer of the force with which they are serving for the time being and have full powers of a constable of that force. Corresponding Scottish measures are in Sch 7, paras 1 to 7.   **8.86**

One aspect of counter-terrorism deployment of the MDP since 2001 has involved the exercise of stop and search powers under s 44. These arise from patrols carried out in the Government Security Zone in Whitehall and Westminster under Metropolitan Police authority (and often involving joint patrols).[196] There were 5,236 such searches during 2007–08. Similar assistance has also been given to the British Transport Police and at demonstration sites, such as Menwith Hill.[197]   **8.87**

Another aspect of deployment has comprised protective security for parts of the critical national infrastructure, especially gas processing sites under Operation Vintage.[198] Nuclear power stations and North Sea gas terminals were mentioned as potential targets of those tried for the 'liquid bomb' conspiracy.[199] The MDP's national coverage and armed capability make it ideal for these purposes, and this role, which presumably falls within s 99 rather than amounting to 'a particular incident' under s 98(4), has become semi-permanent by 2008 even though Home Office guidelines state that assistance should not be 'routinely requested'.[200]   **8.88**

So as to avoid confusion, especially when firearms are involved, a protocol has been agreed between the MDP and local police. They must inform the local chief constable of any crime of terrorism, so that the investigation can be taken over, and any armed deployment should be the subject of prior notification in the case of escorts and agreement in the case of patrols.[201] There should also be consultation before any authorization under s 44.[202]   **8.89**

---

[196] See Ministry of Defence Police and Guarding Agency, *Annual Report and Accounts 2007–2008* (2007–08 HC 699) p 29. The total for all sites was 6,127, all on the basis of non-MDP authorizations: p 40.

[197] During 2007–08, 415 stops were made under s.44: *ibid* p 31.

[198] See Ministry of Defence Police and Guarding Agency, *Annual Report and Accounts 2007–2008* (2007–08 HC 699) p 5; Walker, C., 'The governance of the Critical National Infrastructure' [2008] *Public Law* 323 at p 338.

[199] See *The Times* 5 April 2008 p 10.

[200] Home Office Circular 24/2002: *A protocol between the Ministry of Defence Police and Home Office Police Forces*, para 11.

[201] *Ibid* paras 4, 22, 24.

[202] *Ibid* para 14.

8.90   This constant demand on MDP resources was recognized by the Home Office in Possible Measures for Inclusion in a Future Counter-Terrorism Bill 2007.[203] However, the Counter-Terrorism Act 2008, ss 85 to 90, modestly confine themselves to allowing recovery from gas transporters of the costs of the 'extra police services' incurred by the Ministry of Defence Police or local forces at gas installations where their deployment is considered by the Secretary of State to be: '(a) . . . necessary because of a risk of loss of or disruption to the supply of gas connected with it, and (b) that the loss or disruption would have a serious impact on the United Kingdom or any part of it.' It is notable that the necessity is not confined to terrorism risk.[204] The gas transporter can then recoup its costs from customers.

8.91   In this way, the Ministry of Defence Police is stumbling towards the assumption of the mantle of default CNI police, though there is apparently some competition from the CNC.[205] A more comprehensive vision, encompassing the entire CNI infrastructure and the security structures necessary to protect it, including accountability, is lacking.

2. British Transport Police

8.92   The British Transport Police (BTP), the successor to Victorian railway police forces, was established under the Transport Acts 1962–92 under the British Railways Board (BRB). The Railways Act 1993 transferred these powers direct to the Secretary of State who acted through the BRB. The Strategic Rail Authority inherited the authority of the BRB under the Transport Act 2000. The BTP was reconstituted under the Railways and Transport Safety Act 2003, Pt III.[206] The Act brings the BTP further into line with Home Office police forces by establishing a police authority and tidying the policing powers and jurisdiction. The BTP remains under s 31 primarily confined to railway property but can venture beyond for a purpose connected to the railway. The BTP does not extend to Northern Ireland but does take responsibility for some light railways, including the London Underground. There are around 2,800 officers, spread across seven divisions. Other than its national basis, specialist jurisdiction, and lack of local accountability, the BTP is very similar to Home Office-maintained police forces. Its prime focus remains on public order, assaults, and property offences, but terrorism has become a headline activity.

8.93   Section 100 makes stipulations for the BTP to act outside their normal railways jurisdiction corresponding to those for the MDP. According to the government memorandum accompanying the 2001 Bill:[207]

BTP constables already have jurisdiction on, and in the vicinity of, the railways and elsewhere on railways matters. They need however to move between railway sites and often have a presence in city centres, and BTP officers are frequently called upon to intervene in incidents outside their 'railways' jurisdiction. It is estimated that some such 8,000 incidents occur each year. In these circumstances BTP officers only have the powers of an ordinary citizen, despite being police officers

---

[203] Para 67.
[204] Hansard HC Public Bill Committee on the Counter-Terrorism Bill, col 497 (15 May 2008), Tony McNulty.
[205] See *Mail on Sunday* 10 August 2008 p 30.
[206] See Department for Transport, *Modernising the British Transport Police* (London, 2001).
[207] (London, 2001) para 254.

fully trained to the standards of a Home Office force, and despite routinely dealing with the same range of incidents in the course of their railway activities.

Therefore, similar to s 98(4), s 100(1) allows a BTP officer to assist other forces (and with the full powers of that force) on request in relation to a 'particular' incident, investigation, or operation. The power can be exercised without request in an emergency, as under s 98(4).

As with the MDP, a protocol deals with relations with local police. It is again stated   **8.94** that they must inform the local chief constable of any crime of terrorism, that there should also be consultation before any authorization under s 44, and that their assistance should not be routinely requested.[208]

Since 2001, the BTP has engaged in high visibility policing and continuous security   **8.95** checks through 'sniffer' dogs and the widespread use of stop and search powers under s 44.[209] The BTP has also encountered many bomb threats and seeks to handle them with a minimum of disruption; out of over 10,000 threats from 2000 onwards, fewer than 70 station closures have resulted.[210]

3. Both forces

Both the MDP and BTP are vested with a range of further policing powers by Sch 7 of   **8.96** the 2001 Act. Most apply to the BTP and follow the review of its status by the Department of Transport in 2001.[211] Those of relevance are in paras 29 to 33 which amend the Terrorism Act 2000. Section 34 is amended (by para 30) to allow the BTP and the MDP, in certain circumstances, to designate areas in which cordons may be erected for the purposes of terrorist investigations. Section 44 of the Terrorism Act 2000 is amended (by para 31) to allow the BTP and MDP, through an assistant chief constable, themselves to authorize its use.

4. Comment

Many of the proposals relating to the extension of the jurisdiction of the specialist police   **8.97** revive earlier plans for reform. Consequently, the familiar criticism arises of the 2001 Act being used as a vehicle to push through unpalatable changes without time for proper consideration or for the insertion of effective safeguards for human rights.[212] The refusal to tie down the extensions to direct terrorism connections was valiantly addressed by the Defence Minister, Lord Bach:[213]

. . . what is it reasonable to assume is terrorism? . . . Perhaps I may cite as an example an individual acting suspiciously and tampering with a vehicle. He may be attempting simply to steal it, which

---

[208] Home Office Circular 25/2002: *A protocol between British Transport Police and Home Office Police Forces*, paras 4, 12, 15.

[209] For example, 66,000 stops were carried out in 2007–08: British Transport Police, *Annual Report 2007–08* (London, 2008) p 3.

[210] *Ibid* p 25.

[211] See Department for Transport, *Modernising the British Transport Police* (London, 2001) ch 6.

[212] Joint Committee on Human Rights, *Report on the Anti-terrorism, Crime and Security Bill* (2001–02 HL 37/HC 372) para 68.

[213] HL Debs vol 629, col 643 (4 December 2001); see also cols 1466, 1533 (13 December 2001).

would not be an act of terrorism. Alternatively, he may be seeking to place a bomb under the car. Clearly that would be such an act.

Yet, if it is so impossible to distinguish terrorism from crime, one wonders what is the value of the arrest power in s 41 at the heart of the Terrorism Act 2000?

8.98   As regards the MDP, similar ideas had appeared in the Armed Forces Bill 2000–01 but were withdrawn.[214] The Select Committee was keen to avoid the pre-emption of local police forces and sought clearer local protocols.[215] Their hostility was based on the criticisms that the MDP lacked training to interface with the public, that they could be used as a mobile paramilitary police, and that they had a limited degree of local public accountability.[216] None of these concerns was addressed by the Anti-terrorism, Crime and Security Act 2001. Nevertheless, the Defence Select Committee supported much of the legislation as sensible and practicable though recognized defects regarding accountability, complaints, and inspection.[217] Subsequently, three independent members have been added to the Ministry of Defence Police Committee.[218] and complaints and inspection have been addressed by the Police Reform Act 2002, Pt V.[219]

8.99   As for the BTP, the government announced its intention to introduce legislation about the BTP in 1998 in order, *inter alia*, to create an independent national police authority and to give the BTP jurisdiction outside the railways in certain circumstances. Pursuant to the Department of Transport's consultation document of 2001, *Modernising the British Transport Police*,[220] the Railways and Transport Safety Act 2003 has, as already noted, implemented these undertakings.

8.100   The government has generally asserted that the MDP and other specialist forces should be entrusted with wider policing duties:[221]

Anyone would think that members of the MDP police only ever deal with people in uniform. That is simply not the case; they police housing estates . . . They undergo the same basic training as any other constable. Their primary role is, in fact, to deal with civilians, dependants, contractors, trades people and visitors to our sites. The MDP police service football and rugby matches. They police public events, garrison areas, such as Colchester, Salisbury Plain, Aldershot and Catterick, and public roads open to and widely used by the general public. They run community initiatives in defence areas. . . . They are not amateurs; they are highly trained civilian police officers. They are not a military police force.

8.101   As well as debate about the roles of the MDP and BTP, other concerns have been expressed about the effectiveness of policing institutions at ports and airports. First, there is long-standing criticism that the police Special Branches are unduly disjointed and under-resourced.[222] One response has been a form of regionalization.[223] The second

---

[214] Select Committee on the Armed Forces Bill (2000–01 HC 154-I), xvi.
[215] *Ibid* paras 36, 39, 46.
[216] *Ibid* paras 40, 52.
[217] Defence Select Committee, *The Ministry of Defence Police* (2001–02 HC 382) paras 23, 28, 34, 36.
[218] Hansard HC vol 375, col 779 (26 November 2001), Lewis Moonie.
[219] See for Scotland, Police, Public Order and Criminal Justice (Scotland) Act 2006 (Consequential Provisions and Modifications) Order 2007, SI 2007/1098 Art 4.
[220] See para 5.1.
[221] Hansard HC vol 375, cols 778–9 (26 November 2001), Lewis Moonie.
[222] See Lord Carlile, *Report on the Operation in 2001 of the Terrorism Act 2000* (Home Office, London, 2002) para 5.27.
[223] See Her Majesty's Inspectorate of Constabulary, *A Need to Know* (Home Office, London, 2003) para 2.95.

criticism relates to the fragmentation of borders policing, which has generated in 2008 the UK Border Agency, which takes over from the Border and Immigration Agency, UK visas, and the port of entry functions of HM Revenue and Customs.[224] But policing remains distinct.[225]

G. CONCLUSIONS

Most of the measures discussed in this chapter serve the strategic purposes of 'Prevent' and 'Protect'. On these terms, the measures have achieved mixed success. The security of air travel has seemingly interdicted or deterred all but the most ingenious attacks upon British airlines or within British airports. Sadly, other transportation systems and crowded places are less secure, as evidenced by the bombings on London transport systems on 7 July 2005, and as acknowledged by the Security Minister in 2007.[226]

8.102

Despite the July 2005 incidents, mass transit systems and public venues more generally cannot successfully operate if treated like airlines. Therefore, much of the emphasis must be on 'prepare' as represented by the Civil Contingencies Act 2004. A great deal of activity has been undertaken in that direction,[227] though the July bombings also identified shortcomings, especially in communications systems.[228]

8.103

Issues of human rights appear less prominently in this chapter. One reason is that some of the counter-measures, especially those dealing with WMD, are remote from ordinary lives, and the impact falls on select constituencies which operate under more corporatist relationships with security agencies. The second, less excusable, reason is that the threat to rights is insidious. Thus, target-hardening through mass surveillance does impact on rights, especially privacy rights, but it is imposed without individual notice or judicial oversight.[229] Where intrusions are justiciable, then the courts should demand the showing of 'an undoubted pressing social need'.[230]

8.104

Issues of accountability have already been considered in relation to the specialist policing forces. These forces may also be too small and too disjointed to offer protection of the critical national infrastructure in total.[231] Next, there has been meagre accountability for the WMD measures, the only comprehensive and open exception being the Newton Committee. Transport policies have also been under-explored, with TRANSEC guilty of 'Spartan' reports on its activities,[232] and no wider consideration of governing

8.105

---

[224] See Cabinet Office, *Security in a Global Hub* (London, 2007).

[225] See further ACPO and UKBA, *Memorandum of Understanding: Police and UK Border Agency Engagement to Strengthen the UK Border (2008)*.

[226] Hansard HL vol 467, col 44ws (14 November 2007), Lord West. One response has been training sessions for business, hotel, and retail staff under Project Argus: <http://www.nactso.gov.uk/argus.php>.

[227] See further Walker, C. and Broderick, J., *The Civil Contingencies Act 2004* (Oxford University Press, Oxford, 2006) ch 4.

[228] See Home Office, *Addressing Lessons from the Emergency Response to the 7 July 2005 London Bombings* (London: 2006), paras 64–72; Home Affairs Committee, *Policing in the 21st Century* (2007–08 HC 364) para 285.

[229] Report of the Special Rapporteur on the promotion and protection of human rights and fundamental freedoms while countering terrorism (A/HRC/10/3. 2009).

[230] *Tabernacle v Secretary of State for Defence* [2009] EWCA Civ 23 at para 39

[231] See Walker, C., 'The governance of the Critical National Infrastructure' [2008] *Public Law* 323 at pp 348–50; Home Affairs Committee, *Policing in the 21st Century* (2007–08 HC 364) para 265.

[232] House of Commons Transport Committee, *UK Transport Security* (2005–06 HC 637) para 37.

structures.[233] Even the reviews of the transport attacks on 7 July 2005 were uncritical or partial in range.[234]

8.106   Regarding constitutional governance, Parliament performed feebly in 2001, and its inattention has largely persisted. The reviews by Lord Carlile do not extend to these Parts of the 2001 Act. The Newton Committee argued for regular reports to the Home Affairs Committee for Pt VII and to the Science and Technology Committee for Pt VIII.[235] Only in that last couple of years has serious thought been given to the laws and policies about terrorism risk management in relation to the critical national infrastructure. There is now evidence of 'a concerted effort',[236] including work pursuant to the Civil Contingencies Act 2004 regime, and institutional reform in the shape of the Health Protection Agency[237] and the Centre for the Protection of the National Infrastructure.[238] Further evidence of the more systematic approach came in a series of reviews, the Review of the Protection of Crowded Places, Critical National Infrastructure and Transport Infrastructure, and the Protective Security Review relating to Hazardous Substances, conducted by Lord West in 2007 and 2008.[239] It is difficult to gauge their impact since they have not been published.

8.107   Progress will depend to a greater extent than for other areas covered in this book upon resource allocation and also international cooperation. How a liberal democracy cohabits with the endemic risk created by the dark side of its technological progress is a challenge yet to be fully resolved.

---

[233] See Gregory, F., 'National governance structures to manage the response to terrorist threats and attacks' in Wilkinson, P., (ed), *Homeland Security in the UK* (Routledge, Abingdon, 2007).

[234] See *Report of the Official Account of the Bombings in London on the 7th July 2005* (2005–06 HC 1087); Intelligence and Security Committee, *Inquiry into Intelligence, Report into the London Terrorist Attacks on 7 July 2005* (Cm 6785, London, 2005) and *Government Reply* (Cm 6786, London, 2006); London Resilience Forum, *Looking Back, Moving Forward* (London, 2006); London Assembly, *Report of the 7 July Review Committee* (London, 2006); Home Office, *Addressing Lessons from the Emergency Response to the 7 July 2005 London Bombings* (London, 2006).

[235] Privy Counsellor Review Committee, *Anti-terrorism, Crime and Security Act 2001, Review, Report* (2003–04 HC 100) paras 295, 311.

[236] House of Commons Science and Technology Committee, *The Scientific Response to Terrorism* (2003–04 HC 415) para 245.

[237] See Walker, C., 'Biological attack, terrorism and the law' (2004) 17 *Terrorism and Political Violence* 175 at p 193.

[238] <http://www.cpni.gov.uk/>. See Walker, C., 'The governance of the Critical National Infrastructure' [2008] *Public Law* 323 at p 338.

[239] See Hansard HC vol 467, col 44ws (14 November 2007); Hansard HL vol 703, col 153ws (22 July 2008).

9
NORTHERN IRELAND SPECIAL MEASURES

A. INTRODUCTION

'They haven't gone away, you know.'[1] This reassurance to his constituents about the   **9.01** protective arms of the Provisional IRA came from Sinn Féin President Gerry Adams in the aftermath of its ceasefire in 1994. The same sentiment applies to the anti-terrorism legislation in Northern Ireland. The Peace Process was heralded by Provisional IRA ceasefire (suspended in 1996 but reinstated in 1997) and matching moves by leading Loyalist groups. It was cemented by the Belfast Agreement 1998.[2] A permanent cessation on 28 July 2005 by the Provisional IRA has followed. The security situation has dramatically improved, as evidenced below.

---

[1] *The Guardian* 14 August 1995 p 1. See Tonge, J., 'They haven't gone away, you know' (2004) 16 *Terrorism & Political Violence* 671.

[2] Cm 3883, London, 1998. See Wilford, R., (ed), *Aspects of the Belfast Agreement* (Oxford University Press, Oxford, 2001).

Table 9.1 Security trends in Northern Ireland 1968–2008[3]

Year period	Shootings		Bombings		Deaths				
	Incidents	Incidents ave. p.a.	Devices	Devices ave. p.a.	Police	Military	Civilian	Total	Ave. p.a.
1969–1979	27175	2470	9740	885	131	429	1445	2005	182
1980–1994	7883	526	5143	343	165	223	795	1183	79
1995–1998	611	153	585	117	6	3	92	101	25
1999–2008	1868	187	1267	127	0	0	82	82	8
Whole period	37537	1251	16735	558	302	655	2414	3371	112

Yet, this data reveals that the most dramatic reduction is in the shooting match between security forces and paramilitaries, while other violence persists and with no promise of disbandment. Furthermore, there persist groups of dissidents who do not accept any settlement. As shown by the killings of two soldiers and one police officer in February 2009,[4] they retain the capacity to commit serious acts of terrorism. Therefore, anti-terrorism laws have also remained.

9.02   As a result, the essence of the Northern Ireland (Emergency Provisions) Acts 1973–98, which trace their lineage back to the Civil Authorities (Special Powers) Acts (Northern Ireland) 1922–43 and beyond, were translated into the Terrorism Act 2000.[5] However, they were kept distinct in Pt VII and made subject to annual renewal by s 112,[6] to an expiry date (18 February 2006), and to review by Lord Carlile.[7]

9.03   The British government gave a commitment in the Belfast Agreement to 'normal security arrangements'.[8] The most marked impact has been the progressive dismantling of British Army presence.[9] The process has been documented by the Independent Monitoring Commission[10] which, just a few years ago, viewed law enforcement as 'far from normal'[11] and remained 'deeply concerned' about paramilitary activity.[12]

9.04   These events formed a backdrop to the drafting of the Terrorism (Northern Ireland) Act 2006, which adopted a cautious approach to the permanent ceasefire while at the same time emitting positive signals of normalization. On the one hand, the overall time limit in Pt VII was extended by the Terrorism (Northern Ireland) Act 2006 to

[3] Source: Police Service of Northern Ireland.

[4] The Times 9 March 2009 p 1, 11 March 2009 p 1. See also Lord Carlile, First Annual Review of Arrangements for National Security in Northern Ireland (Northern Ireland Office, Belfast, 2008) para 44.

[5] See Hogan, G., and Walker C., Political Violence and the Law in Ireland (Manchester University Press, Manchester, 1989); Donohue, L.K., Counter-Terrorism Law (Irish Academic Press, Dublin, 2001); Inquiry into Legislation against Terrorism (Cm 3420, London, 1996) para 14.11.

[6] See SI 2002/365, 2003/427, 2004/431, 2005/350.

[7] See Lord Carlile, Report on the Operation in 2001 of Part VII of the Terrorism Act 2000 (Home Office, London, 2001).

[8] (Cm 3883, London, 1998) Security para 2.

[9] See Independent Monitoring Commission, Ninth Report (2005–06 HC 969).

[10] Northern Ireland (Monitoring Commission etc) Act 2003. The mechanism and agenda were based on the Joint Declaration by the British and Irish governments, 13 April 2003.

[11] Second Report (2003–04 HC 913) para 3.1.

[12] See Independent Monitoring Commission, First Report (2003–04 HC 516) para 2.1; Re Sinn Fein [2005] NIQB 10.

31 July 2007, extendable further to 1 August 2008. On the other hand, there was a time limit, despite some Unionist calls for a much longer period of exception.[13] Furthermore, several sections in Pt VII were repealed or modified. Nevertheless, the essentials of Pt VII survived intact.

A further tranche of normalization measures was notified to the Independent Monitoring Commission in early 2006, including a commitment to repeal Pt VII in 2007.[14] The Justice and Security (Northern Ireland) Act 2007 has duly replaced Pt VII.[15] Its advent was marked by the end of Operation Banner—intervention in support of the civil authorities in Northern Ireland, which began in 1969 and terminated on 31 July 2007.[16] Now, the British Army provides only specialist support under Operation Helvetic. **9.05**

Several important aspects of the former regime have now terminated, including the special offences of collecting information under s 103 (though it has since been revived in s 58A, as described in Chapter 6) and the offence of wearing a hood in public places under s 35 (subject again to new powers to remove face coverings, as dealt with in Chapter 5). **9.06**

A more major omission concerns the rules about 'specified organizations'. This code was originally contained in the Criminal Justice (Terrorism and Conspiracy) Act 1998, passed after the Omagh bombing on 15 August 1998.[17] The 'specified organizations' were comprised of recalcitrant paramilitaries who challenged the Peace Process. These measure were incorporated as ss 107 to 111 of the Terrorism Act 2000 and included evidential changes to assist with proof of membership and special rules as to the forfeiture of property. Much of the legislation was a dead-letter and did not assist with prosecutions for the Omagh bombing.[18] **9.07**

Within the sphere of pre-trial criminal justice process, special restrictions on bail (under s 67 of the 2000 Act) have slipped away,[19] alongside special rules about the pre-trial detention of young persons under ss 70 and 71. Rules about time limits on the length of the pre-trial process, under ss 72 and 73 of the 2000 Act,[20] were in any event never activated because of the dire consequences of failure to meet the deadlines and have now expired.[21] Delay remains a serious problem.[22] Special evidential rules have also been culled, namely **9.08**

---

[13] Hansard HC Standing Committee E, col 4 (8 November 2005).

[14] Independent Monitoring Commission, *Ninth Report* (2005–06 HC 969) para 5.1.

[15] See also Terrorism (Northern Ireland) Act 2006 (Transitional Provisions and Savings) Order 2007, SI 2007/2259.

[16] Independent Monitoring Commission, *Sixteenth Report* (London, 2007) para 4.32. For the continued role of the army, see Bass, C., and Smith, M.L.R., 'The war continues?' in Dingley, J. (ed), *Combating Terrorism in Northern Ireland* (Routledge, Abingdon, 2009).

[17] See further Walker, C.P., 'The bombs in Omagh and their aftermath: the Criminal Justice (Terrorism and Conspiracy) Act 1998' (1999) 62 *Modern Law Review* 879; Campbell, C., 'Two steps backwards' [1999] *Criminal Law Review* 941; Kent, K.D., 'Basic rights and anti-terrorism legislation' (2000) 33 *Vanderbilt Journal of Transnational Law* 221.

[18] See *R v Hoey* [2007] NICC 49; Police Ombudsman for Northern Ireland, *Investigation of Matters relating to the Omagh Bombing on August 15 1998* (Belfast, 2007); Policing Board for Northern Ireland, *Omagh Bomb Investigation* (Belfast, 2008); *A Review of the Science of Low Template DNA Analysis* (Home Office, London, 2008).

[19] See also *McKay v United Kingdom*, App no 543/03, 3 October 2006; *Re McKay* [2002] NIQB 31; *R v McAuley* [2004] NIQB 5.

[20] See *Re Shaw* [2003] NIQB 68.

[21] See now Criminal Justice (Northern Ireland) Order 2003, SI 2003/1247 Pt III (not in force).

[22] The average for the period 2001 to the end of June 2007 from remand to trial is 68 weeks: source: Northern Ireland Office Statistics & Research Agency; Carlile Reports.

those under s 76 relating to the admissibility of confessions[23] and the switching of proof under section 77 in cases of the possession of munitions.[24] Post-conviction, a variety of special penal measures in ss 78 to 80 of the 2000 Act are also defunct.

9.09   While much has changed, the 2007 Act ensures that the past is not forgotten. There remain, for at least two further years, juryless courts, as well as several special police and army powers and continued special regulation of the private security industry. Thus, normalization is subject to the further withering of paramilitarism.

B. SPECIAL CRIMINAL PROCESS

9.10   Between 1973 until 2007, a distinct special criminal process was maintained for terrorism. The centrepiece was the non-jury trial but arranged around it were special rules as to pre-trial process, special evidential rules, and special penal measures. The 2007 Act maintains the core feature of juryless trials, but most of the outliers have been discarded, as already noted. More constant are the rules in 'normal' law which have been readily applied to terrorist trials. These include the drawing of adverse inferences from silence under the Criminal Evidence (Northern Ireland) Order 1988.[25] Likewise, the use of informant evidence is vital, but, unlike during the period from 1981 to 1985 when the testimony of 'supergrasses' dominated the criminal justice scene,[26] this type of evidence has receded again into the background.

1. Trial without jury

(a) *Background*

9.11   The major modification brought about by the Northern Ireland (Emergency Provisions) Act 1973 was the pursuance of a policy of criminalization through a special court. The device was championed by the Report of the Commission to consider legal procedures to deal with terrorist activities in Northern Ireland,[27] and, taking its name from the report's chairman, began life in 1973 as the 'Diplock courts'. The reasons for removing the jury were based upon, first, the sectarian bias which might arise or be perceived to arise from what were then juries composed mainly of Protestants and, second, the fear of intimidation of juries by paramilitaries.[28]

9.12   There has been a commitment to phase out the Diplock courts since 1998,[29] and it was reaffirmed by the Northern Ireland Office's consultation paper, *Diplock Review: Report*,

---

[23] See Terrorism Act 2000 (Cessation of Effect of Section 76) Order 2002, SI 2141; Diplock Trials Review Group (Northern Ireland Office, Belfast, 2000).

[24] See *R v Shoukri* [2003] NICA 53.

[25] SI 1988/1987. See Jackson, J.D., 'Curtailing the right to silence' [1991] *Criminal Law Review* 404, 'Inferences from silence' (1993) 44 *Northern Ireland Legal Quarterly* 103, 'Interpreting the silence provisions' [1995] *Criminal Law Review* 587; *Murray (John)* v *United Kingdom*, App no 18731/91, Reports 1996-I; *Averill* v *United Kingdom*, App no 36408/97, 2000-VI; *Magee* v *United Kingdom*, App no 28135/95, 2000-VI.

[26] See Greer, S.C., *Supergrasses* (Clarendon Press, Oxford, 1995).

[27] Cmnd 5185, London, 1972. See Twining, W.L., 'Emergency powers and the criminal process' [1973] *Criminal Law Review* 406.

[28] See also Donohue. L., 'Terrorism and trial by jury' (2007) 59 *Stanford Law Review* 1321 at p 1329.

[29] Home Office and Northern Ireland Office, *Legislation against Terrorism* (Cm 4178, London, 1998) para 13.8.

published in May 2000.[30] Yet, the time was not then considered ripe for change.[31] Three factors were eventually persuasive in favour of alteration.

First, the number of Diplock trials declined sharply.[32] By 2006, just 91 out of 1543   9.13 (6 per cent) defendants in Crown Court that year fell within the Diplock system, down from a rate of around 20 per cent during the previous decade.[33]

Table 9.2 Trials without a jury 2001–2007[34]

Year	Total defendants disposed of	Found guilty or guilty plea to at least one count	Not guilty all charges	Other, eg not proceed
2001	62	52	8	2
2002	113	97	11	5
2003	111	101	10	0
2004	77	52	23	2
2005	90	66	18	6
2006	91	83	8	0
2007	113	101	12	0
Total	**657**	**552**	**90**	**15**

Second, there arose a viable alternative after the passage in England and Wales of the   9.14 Criminal Justice Act 2003, Pt VII.[35] The Crown Court judge may decide to proceed without a jury where satisfied under s 44 that there is a real and present danger of jury tampering and the likelihood that such tampering would take place is so substantial as to make it necessary in the interests of justice to dispense with a jury.[36] However, respect for legal traditions and the improved care for victims and witnesses in court buildings mean that the measure has never been invoked. Nevertheless, s 50 applies the Act to Northern Ireland,[37] albeit on a basis which is mutually exclusive with Diplock trials. It was applied in *R v Mackle*, a case of evasion of duty where a juror had been approached by two partly masked men.[38] While the Criminal Justice Act 2003 is workable, the government did not view it as a wholly suitable model for Northern Ireland,[39] primarily because of the levels of information required for triggering the measures and also the relatively open processes by which the transfer is considered. The government has accepted that the 2003 Act can be used where tampering arises after the trial has started, a situation where the evidence will be clear, whereas the 2007 Act will be used proactively to

---

[30] (Belfast, 2000) p 2.

[31] *Ibid*, pp 6, 16.

[32] See Northern Ireland Office, *Replacement Arrangements for the Diplock Court System* (Belfast, 2006) para 2.5.

[33] Source: Northern Ireland Court Service, Judicial Statistics 2006, Table C.6.

[34] Source: Northern Ireland Court Service, Judicial Statistics.

[35] See Home Office White Paper, *Justice for All* (Cm 5563, London, 2002) paras 4.32, 4.33.

[36] Compare (Auld) *Review of the Criminal Courts in England and Wales* (London, 2001) para 118; Home Affairs Committee, *Criminal Justice Bill* (2002–03 HC 83) para 88.

[37] It commenced on 7 January 2007: SI 2006/3422. See Criminal Appeal (Trial without jury where danger of jury tampering and trial by jury of sample counts only) Rules (Northern Ireland) 2006, SR (NI) 2006/487.

[38] [2007] NICA 37.

[39] Lord Carlile, *Report on the Operation in 2004 of Part VII of the Terrorism Act 2000* (Home Office, London, 2005) para 2.7.

deal with earlier risk.[40] This demarcation is reflected in s 2 of the 2007 Act, which requires intervention before arraignment.

9.15   The third factor impelling a return to jury trials was the ongoing policy of security normalization. Thus, the commitment to jury trial was repeated in 2006 in a Northern Ireland Office paper, *Devolving Police and Justice in Northern Ireland*.[41] The government also rebuffed the absolute rejection of jury trials by the Northern Ireland Affairs committee.[42] The Northern Ireland Office then formulated its considered views in a consultation paper, *Replacement Arrangements for the Diplock Court System*.[43] The government pledged itself to a commendable presumption in favour of jury trial but recognized the need for a fall-back position in the context of a close-knit community where it remains implausible that jurors can be made invisible.[44] The opportunity would also be taken to reform jury practices to offer more protection,[45] including proactive criminal record checks, restricted access to juror information, the abolition of peremptory challenge and the restriction of the Crown's right to stand by, and the physical screening and separation of the jury from other court users and the public.[46] All are rationally linked and are sensible.[47] They have largely been enacted by the Justice and Security (Northern Ireland) Act 2007, ss 10 to 13 for all cases and not just terrorist cases. But the Crown's right to stand by survives, an apparent breach of equality of arms though one which persists in England too.[48] Under Attorney General guidelines now issued[49] (which closely mirror the English version),[50] routine background checks will not be confined to criminal convictions but will also consider whether potential jurors can be entrusted with *in camera* evidence and whether their political beliefs are unacceptably biased.[51]

9.16   The resulting treatment of the defence and prosecution under the 2007 Act was considered in *Re McPartland*.[52] The complaint was that the removal of the protections afforded by peremptory challenge and the right to know the identity of jurors compromised the fairness of the trial contrary to Art 6, especially having regard to the continued rights of the prosecution. Lord Chief Justice Kerr endorsed the Act's policy of protection against 'malevolent individuals'.[53] The court considered that anonymization did reduce

---

[40] Hansard HC vol 454, col 896 (13 December 2006), Peter Hain.

[41] (Belfast, 2006) para 18.10.

[42] Northern Ireland Affairs Committee, *Organised Crime in Northern Ireland* (2005–06 HC 886) para 222 and Government Reply (2005–06 HC 1642) para 59.

[43] Belfast, 2006.

[44] *Ibid* paras 1.2, 2.7, 2.8.

[45] Protection for witness is contained in the Criminal Evidence (Northern Ireland) Order 1999, SI 1999/2789 Pts II–IV.

[46] *Ibid* paras 3.5, 3.7, 3.11, 3.16, 3.18, 3.19.

[47] Such suggestions were also made in the *Review of the Northern Ireland (Emergency Provisions) Act* 1991 (Cm 2706, London, 1995), ch 14.

[48] See Joint Committee on Human Rights, Legislative Scrutiny: *Third Progress Report* (2006–07 HL 46/HC 303) para 1.51; Attorney General's Guidelines, *Exercise by the Crown of its Right of Stand-By* [1989] 88 Cr App R 123.

[49] Hansard HL vol 690, col GC138 (19 March 2007), Lord Goldsmith.

[50] *Attorney General's Guidelines on Jury Checks on the Use of the Prosecution of Stand-By* (London, 2007).

[51] Joint Committee on Human Rights, Legislative Scrutiny: *Third Progress Report* (2006–07 HL 46/HC 303) para 1.42; Attorney General's Guidelines, *Exercise by the Crown of its Right of Stand-By* [1989] 88 Cr App R 123 para 4.

[52] [2008] NIQB 1.

[53] *Ibid* at para 38.

the value of challenge for cause but was an essential mechanism to reassure jurors and preserve the integrity of trials.[54]

At the same time, these reforms do not eradicate with sufficient certainty all cases of paramilitary pressure. Though proven cases of jury tampering are few,[55] the ability to threaten and the perception of threat are appreciably greater than in Britain. Therefore, the consultation paper proposed a system whereby the Director of Public Prosecutions should be able to apply for a non-jury trial on defined statutory grounds, with challenge via judicial review.[56] This system would remain in priority over the Criminal Justice Act 2003.[57] 9.17

Lord Carlile largely endorsed this blueprint but argued that certification should be reviewed by a High Court judge on application[58] and that the English reforms on eligibility for service, which have seen police officers and prosecutors appearing in juries,[59] should extend to Northern Ireland,[60] contrary to the Northern Ireland Office's queasiness about 'perception issues'.[61] 9.18

Aside from Lord Carlile's variations, these proposals were largely enacted as the Justice and Security (Northern Ireland) Act 2007. The Independent Monitoring Commission implausibly sought to distance the new arrangements from the past, claiming 'a very different focus'.[62] In reality, there is a continuum, which the government recognizes by placing a two-year time limit under s 9, though this period can be extended by affirmative order for further two-year periods. 9.19

(b) *Certification*

Section 1 of the 2007 Act allows discretion for the Director of Public Prosecutions for Northern Ireland to issue a certificate affecting any trial on indictment so that the trial of a defendant (and anyone tried with that defendant) can be conducted in the Crown Court without a jury. Thus, the default position is jury trial, though there is no expressed presumption, just as there is not under the Criminal Justice Act 2003. The choice of Director rather than Attorney General (as under Pt VII) signals a more judicial process and one which is locally based.[63] Under s 2, the certificate must be lodged with the magistrates' court prior to committal or, prior to arraignment, the Crown Court—after that time, the Criminal Justice Act 2003 comes into play, as already described. 9.20

There is a two-part statutory test under s 1 for the exercise of the power. The formulae are more explicit and comprehensive than under Pt VII but set a lower standard of proof and take account of factors other than direct jury tampering compared to the 2003 Act. 9.21

---

[54] *Ibid* at paras 41, 43.

[55] See Joint Committee on Human Rights, Legislative Scrutiny: *Third Progress Report* (2006–07 HL 46/HC 303) para 1.11.

[56] Northern Ireland Office, *Replacement Arrangements for the Diplock Court System* (Belfast, 2006) paras 4.5, 4.12.

[57] *Ibid* para 4.21.

[58] *Ibid* app A para 23; Lord Clyde, *6th Report of the Justice Oversight Commissioner* (NIO, Belfast, 2006) para 8.51.

[59] Criminal Justice Act 2003, sch 33. See *R v Abdroikov* [2007] UKHL 37; *R v Khan* [2008] EWCA Crim 531.

[60] Northern Ireland Office, *Replacement Arrangements for the Diplock Court System* (Belfast, 2006) app A para 32.

[61] *Ibid* para 3.25.

[62] Independent Monitoring Commission, *Sixteenth Report* (London, 2007) para 5.8.

[63] Hansard HL vol 690, col GC108 (19 March 2007), Lord Goldsmith.

9.22   First, any one of four conditions must be suspected by the Director under s 1(3) to (6). Condition 1 is that the defendant has a link to a proscribed organization as an existing or former member or through an 'associate' (defined in s 1(9) as an existing or former spouse, civil partner, enduring family partner, friend, or relative). The term 'associate' is very broad, and the government accepted that the spirit of the legislation demands that the Director will consider the quality of relationships going beyond formal blood ties in the case of relatives. After all, 'one could be estranged from one's parents but very close to a second cousin'.[64] Condition 2 is that an offence is committed with involvement by, or on behalf of, a proscribed organization. Condition 3 is that an attempt is made to interfere with the investigation or prosecution with involvement by, or on behalf of, a proscribed organization. The intimidation of witnesses might be a ready indication of a willingness to threaten a juror. Equally, interference with physical evidence, such as trying to burn down buildings containing relevant samples,[65] would be relevant. It should be noted that Conditions 3 and 4 do not require paramilitary membership to be proven.[66] Condition 4 is that the indictable offence occurred as a result of, or in connection with, sectarianism (defined in s 1(7) as hostility based to any extent on religious belief or political opinion, whether real, supposed, or its absence, and applying under s 1(8) even if the sectarianism was not shared by the defendant or was viewed as the fault of the victims). Only proscribed groups connected to Northern Ireland are relevant to any condition (s 1(10)).

9.23   Second, because of one of the foregoing conditions being satisfied, the Director must also under s 1(2) be 'satisfied that . . . there is a risk that the administration of justice might be impaired if the trial were to be conducted with a jury'. The Director is not asked also to consider whether lesser restrictions (including under ss 10 to 13 or in addition under the Contempt of Court Act 1981 or the Criminal Evidence (Northern Ireland) Order 1999, would suffice.[67]

9.24   This system of certification is undoubtedly superior to the Pt VII scheme (in Sch 9), which relied upon the trigger of an offence within the indictment falling within a listed schedule—the 'scheduled offence' approach. The relevant conditions under s 1 embody a more direct connection to interferences with trials. The relevant conditions in the 2007 Act are also explicit and clear. By contrast, under Pt VII, the mechanism was a presumption for juryless trial, subject to certifying out by the Attorney General. The Attorney General applied a non-statutory test which, as approved in *Re Shuker*,[68] stated 'that it is his policy not to deschedule an offence unless he is satisfied that it is not connected with the emergency'.[69] The Attorney General's decision was based on materials, often including background intelligence information and a recommendation about de-scheduling, submitted by the Director of Public Prosecutions.[70] Between 2001 and the

---

[64] See Hansard HL vol 689, col 1056 (20 February 2007), Lord Rooker.
[65] The buildings of the Forensic Science Service of Northern Ireland were damaged by a van bomb: *The Guardian* 25 September 1992 p 25. There was forensic cleansing following the murder of Robert McCartney in 2005: Independent Monitoring Commission, *Fifth Report* (2004–05 HC 46) ch 4.
[66] Hansard HC vol 456, col 757 (6 February 2007), Paul Goggins.
[67] Joint Committee on Human Rights, Legislative Scrutiny: *Third Progress Report* (2006–07 HL 46/HC 303) para 1.26.
[68] [2004] NIQB 20 at para 14.
[69] *Explanatory Memorandum to the Justice & Security Act 2007* (Stationery Office, London, 2007) para 5.
[70] *Ibid* at para 15.

end of June 2007, the rate of certifying out was 84 per cent.[71] The same bundle will now appear before the Director of Public Prosecutions.

The lack of certain connection between the scheduled offence and terrorism became **9.25** acute where the scheduled offence was an ancillary offence such as robbery which might be committed by paramilitaries or 'ordinary decent criminals'.[72] The result was the over-use of the Diplock courts,[73] especially as the certifying out power did not apply to all offences until the Terrorism (Northern Ireland) Act 2006, s 3 was passed. By contrast, the 2007 Act system allows for flexibility—it can allocate to juryless trials what the Counter-Terrorism Act 2008, s 93, refers to as offences with a terrorism connection. This switch to certifying in may incidentally assist with the ability to leave aside cases involving international terrorism which otherwise would be tried by jury in Britain but not Northern Ireland. Earlier objections to certifying in fell away by 2007, especially as cases were few and the rate of de-scheduling had risen up to 90 per cent.[74]

The main point of contention remaining about certification under the 2007 Act **9.26** relates to limits on challenge. Certification is presented as no more than a mode of trial decision.[75] But if it is maintained that jury trial is superior, as is contended by 77 per cent of the Northern Ireland population,[76] then those who are being selected for non-jury trial are suffering a detriment. They should only suffer this detriment if their fate is demonstrably proportionate to the interests of a fair trial. But how will fairness be demonstrated if the decision of the DPP is taken, even if with the advice of counsel,[77] behind closed doors and taking account of 'national security interests'[78] and not just those of immediate parties to the trial? Consequently, there is much to commend Lord Carlile's suggestion of the involvement of special advocates and the testing of the certificate before a High Court judge in procedures similar to the Special Immigration Appeal Commission.[79] That process would allow full consideration of the issues by a senior judge but without threat to national security or prejudice to a future trial. This check would still fall well short of the process in the Criminal Justice Act 2003, by which an application is made to the judge at a preparatory hearing at which both parties can make representations (s 50(3)). In the format actually adopted, the 2007 Act affords neither hearings nor reasons because of fears about intelligence 'spilling out'[80] and about delays[81] under a judicial model.

---

[71] Sources: Northern Ireland Office Statistics & Research Agency; Carlile Reports.
[72] *Review of the Operation of the Northern Ireland (Emergency Provisions) Act 1978* (Cmnd 9222, London, 1984) para 136.
[73] See Walsh, D.P.J., *The Use and Abuse of Emergency Legislation in Northern Ireland* (Cobden Trust, London, 1983); *Review of the Northern Ireland (Emergency Provisions) Act 1991* (Cm 2706, London, 1995), para 36; *Inquiry into Legislation against Terrorism* (Cm 3420, London, 1996) para 16.16.
[74] Northern Ireland Office, *Replacement Arrangements for the Diplock Court System* (Belfast, 2006) para 2.5.
[75] *Replacement Arrangements for the Diplock Court System* (Belfast, 2006) para 4.5.
[76] *Review of the Criminal Justice System in Northern Ireland* (NIO, Belfast, 2000) para 7.62.
[77] Northern Ireland Office, *Replacement Arrangements for the Diplock Court System* (Belfast, 2006) para 4.18. Lord Carlile also suggested that there should be an automatic referral for an opinion by a special advocate: app A para 20.
[78] *Ibid* para 4.12.
[79] *Ibid* app A para 23.
[80] Hansard HC vol 454, col 969 (13 December 2006), Paul Goggins.
[81] HC Hansard Public Bill Committee on the Justice and Security Bill, col 18 (16 January 2007), Paul Goggins.

9.27   Section 7(1) allows challenges confined to the grounds of dishonesty, bad faith, or other exceptional circumstances.[82] The courts will decide what constitutes 'exceptional circumstances', a phrase taken from *Kebilene*.[83] In addition, s 7(1)(c) interprets the phrase as 'including in particular exceptional circumstances . . . lack of jurisdiction or error of law'.[84] In this way, the grounds are similar to judicial review, save that procedural challenges in natural justice do not lie. There may also be challenge under the Human Rights Act 1998 (s 7(2)). The government justified s 7(1) as at least equivalent to what the judges had considered appropriate for review of the Attorney General's decision not to de-schedule a Diplock case under Pt VII in *Re Shuker*,[85] which rejected the full range of judicial review and accepted review only within limited categories of exceptions.[86] It should also be noted that, being a matter of public law rather than 'civil rights', there is no direct right to due process within Art 6(1).[87] Where the operation of the process raises issues of discrimination, then Art 6 is engaged,[88] and it remains to be seen whether the s 7 review categorizes discrimination as an exceptional circumstance. It could in any event fall within the Human Rights Act 1998. A further certificate under the Northern Ireland Act 1998, s 90, might then arise, diverting the litigation into the s 91 tribunal.

(c) *Trial process*

9.28   When a certificate is issued, the key feature under s 5 is trial by Crown Court judge sitting without a jury. Otherwise, the court can exercise the same powers and jurisdiction as if a jury were present, including conviction on alternative lesser charges. An exception, under s 8, is that a jury must still decide issues of fitness for trial, even if a certificate has been issued. Rules of court can be made under s 6.

9.29   As under the previous regime, there are some subsidiary special features. First, by s 5(4), the trial court may not draw any adverse inferences from the fact that a certificate has been issued. Secondly, s 5(6) requires the court to provide a reasoned verdict for conviction (but not acquittal) on any count. This requirement, also present in Pt VII, facilitates the bringing of an appeal. Thirdly, as under Pt VII again, s 5(7) and (9) remove restrictions on the right of appeal that would otherwise apply under ss 1 and 10(1) of the Criminal Appeal (Northern Ireland) Act 1980. A defendant can appeal against sentence or conviction, and the prosecution can appeal against sentence directly to the Court of Appeal, without seeking the leave of the Court of Appeal or a certificate of the trial judge. Fourthly, the juryless trial will normally be held in the Crown Court buildings in Belfast, but, as under Pt VII, s 4 allows the Lord Chief Justice of Northern Ireland to

---

[82] The absence of a full appeal is criticized by the UN Human Rights Committee, Concluding Observations (CCPR/C/GBR/CO/6, 2008) para 18.

[83] *R v DPP, ex p Kebilene* [2000] 2 AC 326 at p 371 per Lord Steyn.

[84] These meanings were viewed as already implicit: Hansard HL vol 690, col GC125 (19 March 2007), Lord Goldsmith.

[85] [2004] NIQB 20. See also *Re Rooney* [1995] NI 398; *Re Adams* [2001] NI 1.

[86] The House of Lords Constitution Committee, *Justice and Security (Northern Ireland) Bill* (2006–07 HL 54) paras 4 and 5 viewed s 7 as unnecessary and preferred a case-based approach.

[87] *Ibid* at para 34.

[88] *Tinnelly and McElduff v United Kingdom*, App nos 20390/92; 21322/92, 1998-IV, para 61. See also *Devlin v United Kingdom*, App no 29545/95, 30 October 2001; *Devenney v United Kingdom*, App no 24265/94, 19 March 2002.

direct other venues. Terrorist trials have always been centred in Belfast, which offers a highly secure and relatively convenient location for lawyers and security force witnesses. However, alternatives or additions were devised with a view to reducing delays.[89]

(d) *Comment*

The continuance of juryless trials seeks to secure the 'Pursuit' of terrorists in a way which does not inherently breach Art 6 of the European Convention, since no jury trial is guaranteed therein. Nor does a distinct system amount to unreasonable discrimination—reasons can readily be found for objective and reasonable divergence in terms of local conditions.[90] The further assessment of Diplock courts depends principally upon delivery in practice through the performance of the judge and the practical impact of the absence of the jury.

9.30

There can be little misgiving about independence or legal competence of assigned judges. Regular county court or High Court judges will preside. It is some forty years since military officers have sat in trials in either part of Ireland.[91] Next, some defendants may even prefer the more reasoned verdict of a judge to that of the Delphic jury verdict. Moreover, there have been few claims of miscarriages of justice.[92] The government's view is that 'there is nothing to show that the system has produced perverse judgments or that it has lowered standards'.[93]

9.31

Amongst the possible discontents arising from non-jury trials are the prejudice to the defendant from the enhanced role of 'case-hardened' judges.[94] Given the preponderance of non-Catholic judges, these misgivings have been more keenly felt by Republican defendants. The effective acquittal rate (percentage pleading not guilty found not guilty) has been variable (ranging from 29 per cent in 1993 to 100 per cent in 1998, reflecting low numbers of defendants who plead not guilty). It has generally fallen below the rate for non-scheduled trials. Another detriment is the loss of enhanced community confidence and understanding through jury service.[95] Thirdly, there is the problem of over-reach—that non-terrorist cases are drawn into the system for reasons of convenience rather than necessity.[96]

9.32

The absence of the jury has other impacts which may be viewed by some as beneficial and others as detriments. Judicial primacy seems to encourage more interventions and focuses more on legal issues rather than on advocacy.[97] There is also a heightened reliance upon silence as evidence.[98]

9.33

---

[89] See *Review of the Operation of the Northern Ireland (Emergency Provisions) Act 1978* (Cmnd 9222, London, 1984) paras 173–87.

[90] See *Magee v United Kingdom*, App No 28135/95, 2000-VI, para 50.

[91] See *Eccles v Ireland* [1985] IR 545.

[92] See Dickson, B., 'Miscarriages of justice in Northern Ireland' in Walker, C., and Starmer, K., *Miscarriages of Justice* (Blackstone Press, London, 1999).

[93] Hansard HC vol 301, col 173 (18 November 1997), Adam Ingram. See also Ministry of Justice, *Rights and Responsibilities* (Cm 7577, London, 2009) para 3.28.

[94] *Inquiry into Legislation against Terrorism* (Cm 3420, London, 1996) paras 16.16–16.18.

[95] Matthews, R., Hancock, L., and Briggs, D., Jurors' perceptions, understanding, confidence and satisfaction in the jury system (Findings 277, Home Office, London, 2004).

[96] Walsh, D.P.J., *The Use and Abuse of Emergency Legislation in Northern Ireland* (Cobden Trust, London, 1983).

[97] See Jackson, J.D. and Doran, S., *Judge without Jury* (Clarendon Press, Oxford, 1995).

[98] Jackson, J.D., Quinn, K., and Wolfe, M., *Legislating against Silence* (Northern Ireland Office, Belfast, 2001).

9.34   Given that there are at least some perceived drawbacks, could they be avoided by alternative designs?[99] One compromise would be to employ a judge to deal with legal issues accompanied by three lay assessors of fact, who would retain the elements of common sense and freshness normally imparted by a jury.[100] There is less enthusiasm for a three-judge court because of staffing difficulties[101] and because in principle, it is no nearer to a jury.[102] During the current period of normalization, any interim reforms could even be seen as 'provocative' or 'mere tinkering'.[103] The preference is simply for the existing model to 'wither on the vine'.[104] Early indications are promising. From 1 August 2007 to 31 July 2008, twenty-nine certificates were issued, relating to twenty-eight cases.[105] Nonetheless, there might be a lingering tail of business produced by the police's Historical Enquiries Team (for deaths from 1969 until 1998) and the Retrospective Murder Review Unit (1998 to 2004, when the Crime Operations Division was established).[106]

9.35   During the passage of the 2007 Act, ministers undertook to make a statement to Parliament each year on the volume of non-jury trial cases. Otherwise, accountability is signally lacking. There is no ongoing review. Consequently, the next parliamentary review will be bereft of hard data or expert guidance. Constitutional governance is, however, much better secured under the certain terms of this scheme than under Pt VII, subject to the limits of s 7.

2. Pre-trial special processes

9.36   One enduring pre-trial special rule under s 3 (previously s 66 in Pt VII) concerns requests for a preliminary inquiry before a magistrates' court[107] rather than a preliminary investigation. When a s 1 certificate is being returned, the court must grant the request unless a preliminary investigation is considered to be in the interests of justice (sub-s (4)(b)) or there is an extra-territorial offence under the Criminal Jurisdiction Act 1975 (sub-s (4)(c)). The normal need for agreement from the defence can be dispensed with so as to avoid delays by the non-recognition of the court system by Republican defendants[108] or, more pertinent nowadays, to avoid the calling of witnesses who could then be subject to intimidation.

9.37   This measure inflicts a lost opportunity for the defence to challenge evidence. Whether unfair in the context of a trial will depend on the extent of later disclosure and

---

[99] See Jackson, J.D., Quinn, K., and O'Malley, T., 'The jury system in contemporary Ireland' (1999) 62 *Law & Contemporary Problems* 203.

[100] See Greer, S., and White, A., *Abolishing the Diplock Courts* (Cobden Trust, London, 1986); *Review of the Operation of the Northern Ireland (Emergency Provisions) Act 1978* (Cmnd 9222, London, 1984) paras 108–29.

[101] It is estimated that a further 10 judges would be needed: Hansard HC Standing Committee E, col 25 (8 November 2005), Shaun Woodward.

[102] *Review of the Northern Ireland (Emergency Provisions) Act 1991* (Cm 2706, London, 1995), paras 62–4.

[103] Lord Carlile, *Report on the Operation in 2002 of Part VII of the Terrorism Act 2000* (Home Office, London, 2003) para 5.16.

[104] Hansard HL vol 689, col 1052 (20 February 2007), Lord Rooker.

[105] Hansard HL vol 705, col WS143 (25 November 2008).

[106] See Northern Affairs Committee, *Policing and Criminal Justice in Northern Ireland* (2007–08 HC 335); Moran, J., *Policing the Peace in Northern Ireland* (Manchester University Press, Manchester, 2008) ch 6.

[107] See Magistrates' Courts (Northern Ireland) Order 1981, SI 1981/1675.

[108] See *Report of a Committee to consider, in the context of civil liberties and human rights, measures to deal with terrorism in Northern Ireland* (Cmnd 5847, London, 1975).

cross-examination.[109] Nevertheless, it is surely wrong for the courts to extend preliminary inquiries for the sake of convenience (such as where soldier-witnesses are in Afghanistan) or to allow anonymity for such witnesses under the Criminal Evidence (Witness Anonymity) Act 2008.[110]

C. SPECIAL POLICING POWERS

The Northern Ireland (Emergency Provisions) Acts contained a startling array of special powers granted to soldiers as well as police officers. Most continued to find a berth in Pt VII of the Terrorism Act 2000, and now vestiges remain in the Justice and Security (Northern Ireland) Act 2007. Their retention was far less debated than the juryless trials, though they affect many thousands more people. The commitment to normalization and the post-1975 policy of police primacy[111] does, however, pertain. But its progress is curtailed by a recognition that the British Army might still be involved in munitions disposals and manpower reinforcement at the policing of parades.[112] So, special powers for soldiers are required.[113] Fewer police powers remain, though some have alternatively been translated from Pt VII into permanent laws or into similar measures in the Counter-Terrorism Act 2008.   9.38

Several powers were dropped entirely in 2007. The departed include s 81, by which a constable could enter and search any premises to look for a 'terrorist'.[114] The police power of arrest for scheduled offences in s 82 is also dropped, leaving them to apply the Police and Criminal Evidence (Northern Ireland) Order 1989 ('PACE').[115] Both powers were in a state of disuse before repeal.[116]   9.39

Reasonable force may be used in the execution of the powers which follow, according to s 33. This extra power is necessary since not all circumstances will involve crime prevention or enforcement for the purposes of the Criminal Law Act (Northern Ireland) 1967, s 3. The application of this rule to lethal force and plastic baton rounds has been an enduring controversy.[117]   9.40

These special policing powers (and also the powers to undertake security operations described in the next part of the chapter) are additional under s 33(2) to any under the royal prerogative[118] or under the common law.   9.41

---

[109] See *Re Kerr* [1997] NI 225.

[110] See *DPP v McKenna* [2008] NI MAG 1.

[111] See Walker, C., 'The Role and Powers of the Army in Northern Ireland' in Hadfield, B., (ed) *Northern Ireland Politics and the Constitution* (Open University Press, Buckingham, 1992) pp 112, 114–15.

[112] See Northern Ireland Office, *Devolving Police and Justice in Northern Ireland* (Belfast, 2006) para 18.10; Public Processions (Northern Ireland) Act 1998; *Strategic Review of Parading in Northern Ireland, Interim Consultative Report* (Northern Ireland Office, Belfast, 2008).

[113] The minister claimed just 8 out of 48: Hansard HC vol 454, col 899 (13 December 2006), Peter Hain.

[114] See Hansard HC Standing Committee B, col 162 (30 January 1996), Sir John Wheeler.

[115] See SI 2007/288 art 15. Compare Hansard HC Standing Committee B, col 169 (30 January 1996), Sir John Wheeler.

[116] In 2006, there were 19 entries under s 81, 6 arrests and 7 searches under s 82: sources: Northern Ireland Office Statistics & Research Agency, Carlile Reports, PSNI.

[117] See especially *Reference under s 48A Criminal Appeal (Northern Ireland) Act 1968 (No 1 of 1975)* [1977] AC 105; *R v Clegg* [1995] 1 AC 482; *Re McBride*, 17 April 2002 (QBD); *McCann v United Kingdom*, App no 18984/91, Ser A vol 324 (1995).

[118] See Walker, C., and Broderick, J., *The Civil Contingencies Act 2004* (Oxford University Press, Oxford, 2006) para 2.24.

1. Stop and question

9.42 Broad powers are granted both to soldiers and police officers under s 21 (formerly s 89 in Pt VII) to stop and question any person, including the power to stop a vehicle. The purpose under s 21(1) is to ascertain 'his identity and movements'. Additional powers are granted under s 21(2) to soldiers to question the person about what he knows about a recent explosion or another recent incident endangering life, or what he knows about a person killed or injured in a recent explosion or incident. These additional powers are no longer granted to the police, presumably because they are conferred with sufficient other powers to engage the public, including under s 44 of the 2000 Act. The incidental detention may persist 'for so long as is necessary'. It will normally amount to a matter of minutes, such as at a vehicle check-point, but a detention of one hour twenty-five minutes was deemed lawful in *Mooney v Ministry of Defence*.[119] This phrase must be read as subject to reasonably connected purposes, but an attempt to impose a specific time limit (such as fifteen minutes) has failed during successive parliamentary debates.[120] It is an offence (punishable only by fine) to fail to stop or to refuse to answer a question or to fail to answer to the best of his knowledge and ability.[121]

9.43 The breadth of the power to stop and detain—without any requirement of reasonable suspicion or necessity[122]—appears to fall foul of Art 5 of the European Convention, but the relatively modest length of the detention will probably evade any liability.[123] In addition, the breadth of the possible questioning, the absence of any legal advice, and the possible seriousness of the issues involved would surely cast doubt on whether the reliance in court upon answers produced under s 21(2) could withstand challenge under Art 6(2).[124] However, the more likely scenario for questioning is where the military undertake explosive ordnance disposal work and seek information to clear the area rather than to detect crime.[125]

2. Military arrest

9.44 Normally, soldiers have no special legal powers but are, literally, citizens in uniform. Given their enhanced policing function in Northern Ireland, it has been necessary to bolster their legal status. So, s 22 (based on s 83 in Pt VII) provides that a member of the

---

[119] [1994] 8 BNIL n28.

[120] Hansard HC Standing Committee D, col 282 (3 February 2000), Adam Ingram; Hansard (HL) vol 690 col GC216 (21 March 2007).

[121] As suggested by the *Review of the Northern Ireland (Emergency Provisions) Act 1991* (Cm 2706, London, 1995) para 93.

[122] The government resisted such conditions as unnecessary and creating uncertain change from the Part VII formulae and possible delay: Joint Committee on Human Rights, Legislative Scrutiny: *Third Progress Report* (2006–07 HL 46/HC 303) para1.79; HC Hansard Public Bill Committee on the Justice and Security Bill cols 107–8 (18 January 2007), Paul Goggins.

[123] See *R (on the application of Gillan) v Commissioner of the Police of the Metropolis* [2006] UKHL 12; *Austin v Commissioner of Police of the Metropolis* [2009] UKHL 5. Compare: *McVeigh, O'Neill and Evans v United Kingdom*, App nos 8022, 8025, 8027/77, DR 25 p 15 (1981); *Murray (Margaret) v United Kingdom*, App no 14310/88, Ser A. 300A (1995).

[124] See *Murray (John) v United Kingdom*, App no 18731/91, Reports 1996-I.

[125] *Explanatory Memorandum to the Justice and Security (Northern Ireland) Act 2007* (Stationery Office, London, 2007) para 61.

armed forces on duty may arrest and detain a person for up to four hours if reasonably suspected of committing, being about to commit, or having committed any offence. The detention power of four hours is to afford sufficient time for a handover to a police officer who can then arrest under, say, s 41. Premises (as defined by s 42) where that person is or is reasonably suspected to be may be entered and searched for the purposes of the arrest. This broad power can apply even to trivial offences, but wide latitude is afforded because of the lack of legal training of soldiers. At the same time, the design lacks proportionality. While an individual arrest would be too fleeting to be within Art 5 of the European Convention, repeated arrests might breach Arts 5 or 8.

Equally reflecting a lack of legal training is s 22(2), by which a soldier making an arrest is deemed to comply with any rule of law requiring him to state the ground of arrest 'if he states that he is making the arrest as a member of Her Majesty's forces'. But the requirements of Art 5(2) of the European Convention are preserved under s 22(5).[126] This requirement on first glance negates s 22(2). However, the European Court in *Fox* accepted that reasons can be inferred from questions put to a suspect; in other words, it might still be possible to comply with Art 5(2) without giving a formal recitation of reasons. The House of Lords also accepted in *Murray v Ministry of Defence*[127] that the reason-giving process can be postponed until the scene is made secure. It should have been possible to require the recitation of the facts triggering (as is the common practice),[128] even if legal reasons (in terms of offences) would be more difficult for untutored soldiers.[129]

9.45

There are supplementary powers of entry and search for the purpose of making an arrest under s 22(3) (theoretically narrower than the previous version because entry is on the basis of an offence rather than a 'terrorist'). There is also granted by s 22(3) a power of seizure of items for a period not exceeding four hours of anything which he reasonably suspects is being, has been, or is intended to be used in the commission of an offence under ss 31 and 32 (described below).

9.46

Military arrests have virtually died out since 1998. Between 1990 and 1994, there were 362 arrests; from 1995 to 2000, there were just 49. Single figures were recorded from 2002 onwards, with none in 2007.[130]

9.47

3. Powers of entry

Section 23(1) (formerly provided for by s 90 of Pt VII) allows police officers or soldiers a power of entry onto premises, including vehicles under s 42, if considered necessary in the course of operations for the preservation of peace or the maintenance of order. Because of the need for a rapid response to unfolding events, this wording does little to discourage disproportionate intrusions into property and privacy by specifying

9.48

---

[126] As explained in *Fox, Campbell, and Hartley v United Kingdom*, App nos 12244, 12245, 12383/86, Ser A. 182 (1990) paras 40–2. See Finnie, W., 'Anti-terrorist legislation and the European Convention on Human Rights' (1991) 54 *Modern Law Review* 288.

[127] [1988] 2 All ER 521. See Walker, C.P., 'Army special powers on parade' (1989) 40 *Northern Ireland Legal Quarterly* 1; *Murray (Margaret) v United Kingdom*, App no 14310/88, Ser A. 300A (1994).

[128] Hansard HL vol 690, col GC223 (21 March 2007), Lord Rooker.

[129] Joint Committee on Human Rights, Legislative Scrutiny: *Third Progress Report* (2006–07 HL 46/HC 303) paras 1.88, 1.89.

[130] Source: Northern Ireland Office.

an objective standard or requiring a link to terrorism.[131] The absence of reasonable suspicion and judicial oversight must render the power vulnerable to challenge under Art 8 of the European Convention.

9.49   Some preconditions do apply, an advance on the position under s90. Under s 23(2), a constable may not enter a building without written authorization from an officer of the rank of superintendent or above. However, oral authorization from an inspector or above will suffice where it is not reasonably practicable to obtain written authorization. If it is not reasonably practicable to obtain either written or oral authorization, then the constable may still lawfully enter. A record shall be made of each entry as soon as reasonably practicable, with details as specified in s 23(6). Copies of records or authorizations must be given to the owners or occupiers as soon as is reasonably practicable.

9.50   There are no corresponding demands for authorization or record-keeping for soldiers. To require formalities was viewed as endangering operations.[132]

4. Search powers

9.51   Searches for unlawful munitions and transmitters are covered by s 24 and Sch 3 (formerly in s 84 and Sch 10[133] of Pt VII). Any materials found may be seized, retained, and destroyed under Sch 3, para 5.

9.52   By para 2 of Sch 3, police officers or soldiers may enter property to conduct searches on a random or routine basis. In the case of the police only, they can be accompanied by other persons, such as civilian Scenes of Crime Officers. Authorization of team members must be explicit, if not precise.[134] Dwellings may only be entered on foot on a reasonable suspicion that there are munitions or wireless apparatus unlawfully present. There must also be prior authorization: for soldiers by a commissioned officer; for police officers by an officer of inspector rank or above.

9.53   Paragraph 3 bestows on the police and military supplementary powers which may be exercised if reasonably believed to be necessary in order for the search to be carried out or to stop the search from being frustrated. These measures react to case law in which preventative tactics were challenged.[135] The officer may require any occupier or visitor to remain in the building in general or in a specified part or to go from one part to another. An officer may also stop someone who does not live in the building from entering it. No requirement can last for more than four hours, unless it is extended for up to a further four hours (which is only allowed once) by a superintendent (in the case of the police) or a major (in the case of the army). An extension may only be granted on grounds of reasonable necessity to carry out the search or to prevent the search being frustrated. It is an offence under para 8 knowingly to fail to comply with requirements under para 3 or to wilfully obstruct or to seek to frustrate searches of premises. The

---

[131] See HC Hansard Public Bill Committee on the Justice and Security Bill, col 126 (18 January 2007), Paul Goggins.

[132] HC Hansard Public Bill Committee on the Justice and Security Bill, col 127 (18 January 2007), Paul Goggins.

[133] Powers in s 85 for explosives inspectors have been repealed.

[134] *Kirkpatrick v Chief Constable of the Royal Ulster Constublary* [1988] NI 421.

[135] See *Murray v Ministry of Defence* [1988] 2 All ER 521; *Murray (Margaret)* v *United Kingdom*, App no 14310/88, Ser A. 300A (1995). See also *Connor v Chief Constable of Merseyside Police* [2006] EWCA Civ 1549.

detention may be justified, if at all, under Art 5(1)(b) of the European Convention by reference to the offence in Sch 3 para 8.[136] Paragraph 4 allows persons found in dwellings (as defined by s 42) entered under para 2 to be searched.

Unless it is not reasonably practicable, records must be made of searches of premises   9.54
under para 6, and, under para 7, a copy shall be supplied as soon as possible to the occupier. In practice, records are also made of any damage caused by the search, and the owner is asked to sign these records.[137]

Paragraph 4 also allows stop and search powers in a public place on a random or rou-   9.55
tine basis in order to establish whether a person unlawfully possesses munitions or wireless apparatus. For individuals not in a public place, the officer must have reasonable suspicion. Failure to stop is an offence under para 9.

Search powers under s 25 (formerly in s 86 of Pt VII) are granted to soldiers to enter   9.56
and search any premises in which they reasonably believe a person has been unlawfully detained and whose life is endangered. No warrant or authorization is normally required because of the critical danger to life. However, if entry is into a dwelling, there must be a prior authorization by a commissioned officer. There is still no requirement for reasonable suspicion in relation to the detained person being located in the premises to be searched—it follows that area searches are possible. There are no corresponding police powers because the PACE (Northern Ireland) Order 1989, Art 19(1)(e), allows a constable to enter and search any premises for the purpose of 'saving life or limb'. The absence of reasonable suspicion or judicial oversight raises questions under Art 8 of the European Convention.

Powers to search premises in ss 24 and 25 also include, under s 42, vehicles, which   9.57
may be stationary or may be stopped by order. Section 26 explains further that, where necessary or expedient, the vehicle may be taken away for searching. An offence of failing to stop a vehicle is contained in s 26. When searching a vehicle for munitions and transmitters, under s 26(5) the officer may require a person to remain with the vehicle or to go to any place the vehicle is taken where the searcher reasonably believes it necessary for carrying out the search. The requirement as to presence may only last as long as the search, or for four hours (extendable to eight hours as under Sch 3), whichever is shorter. A record must be made and a copy given to the owner or driver of the vehicle.

These powers have been used on an enormous scale, though the operations have now   9.58
been scaled back. Section 24 is additional to police powers under s 44 of the Terrorism Act 2000. Section 44 is invoked around ten times more frequently than ss 21 and 24, and its rapidly increasing usage now outstrips every other police area except London.[138] It was not questioned during debates why extra stop and search powers were needed for the police in addition to s 44. The police claim that authorization procedures under s 44 would be an 'inhibition',[139] but, in an era of normalization, inhibitory mechanisms are a blessing. It is further suggested that s 21 allows questioning in a way which s 44

---

[136] Hansard HL vol 69, col GC227 (21 March 2007), Lord Rooker. See Joint Committee on Human Rights, *Legislative Scrutiny: Third Progress Report* (2006–07 HL 46/HC 303) para 1.96.

[137] See Walker, C.P., 'Army special powers on parade' (1989) 40 *Northern Ireland Legal Quarterly* 1.

[138] In 2006, there were 1,739 stops, rising to 6,882 in 2008 (sources: NIO, PSNI). Data is not kept about the religion of those stopped nor whether multiple stops are experienced.

[139] Whalley, R., *Report of the Independent Reviewer: Justice and Security (Northern Ireland) Act 2007* (Northern Ireland Office, Belfast, 2007) para 84.

does not.[140] However, as the main purpose is disruption, it seems doubtful that the loss of interrogatory powers would imperil the success of the powers and it also wrongly suggests that the police stand mute during s 44 searches and do not routinely ask about identity and movements.

5. Document examinations

9.59 Exceptional powers are granted under s 27 (formerly s 87 of Pt VII and applying to both police and soldiers) for soldiers only, who are conducting a search under ss 24 to 26 in order to ascertain whether the information contained in documents or records is likely to be useful for terrorism, and if necessary or expedient, to remove them to another place for up to forty-eight hours. There is an exemption where there is reasonable cause to believe legal privilege applies. It is an offence to obstruct the soldier. Under s 28, the documents may not be photographed or copied. A written record of examinations must be made as soon as reasonably practicable, and a copy supplied to the person who had custody or to the occupier of the building.

9.60 The absence of any requirement of reasonable suspicion or judicial oversight may again give rise to challenges under Art 8, though it may be more doubtful that the use in court of seized documentary evidence would be deemed unfair under Art 6.[141] The power is now wider than the version in s 87, which was confined to evidence under ss 58 or 103 of the 2000 Act.

9.61 Section 27 does not extend to the police because they are granted permanent powers under the Policing (Miscellaneous Provisions) (Northern Ireland) Order 2007,[142] Art 13, to examine documents and electronic records in order to establish whether or not they contain evidence of a serious crime. The documents and records can be taken away and examined for up to forty-eight hours (extendable to ninety-six hours). It has already been noted in Chapter 4 that further powers have been granted to the police to remove documents for examination under the Counter-Terrorism Act 2008, s 1.

6. Statistics as to use

9.62 The following table evidences the dwindling of special powers, save for powers to stop and search.

Table 9.3 Special powers[143]

Year	Army arrest s 83 and s 22	Army search s 83 and s 22	Munitions etc search s 84 and s 24 (police/army)	Stop and search s 84 and s 24	Documents s 87 and s 27	Stop and question s 89 and s 21 (police/army)
2001 (part)	44	6	266/359	166	46	99/6223

---

[140] *Ibid.*
[141] See *Funke v France*, App no 10828/84, Ser A 256-A (1993).
[142] SI 2007/912.
[143] Sources: Northern Ireland Office Statistics & Research Agency, Carlile Reports, PSNI.

Table 9.3 (Continued) Special powers

Year	Army arrest s 83 and s 22	Army search s 83 and s 22	Munitions etc search s 84 and s 24 (police/army)	Stop and search s 84 and s 24	Documents s 87 and s 27	Stop and question s 89 and s 21 (police/army)
2002	23	106	591/283	3957	51	2448/9873
2003	5	72	565/1686	2621	101	1368/10921
2004	6	22	322/361	2984	83	1962/5156
2005	6	79	388/239	3925	106	2473/3101
2006	1	125	232/104	2071	36	1104/24
2007	0	96 (to 30 Sept)	101/40 (to 30 Sept)	134 (from 1 July)	8 (to 30 Sept)	403/0

D. SECURITY OPERATIONS

The Justice and Security (Northern Ireland) Act 2007 next preserves various provisions   9.63
which range well beyond the scope of what would normally be conceived as policing
powers. Their purpose is to permit security operations, as well as more permanent installations relating to the offensive or defensive capabilities of the security forces. Most of
the powers have been translated from Pt VII, but some have been allowed to fall away
(including a regulation-making power under s 96).[144]

Section 29 (formerly s 91 of Pt VII) allows the Secretary of State, if considered neces-   9.64
sary for the preservation of the peace or the maintenance of order, to authorize a person
to take possession of land or other property or to carry out works on land (or even to
destroy property). No local planning or judicial oversight is required. This power allows
the building of military structures (such as watchtowers), the dismantling of structures
which threaten military bases, the provision of protection for residents at sectarian inter-
faces, and the reinforcement of security barriers at contentious parades.[145] Rights to
private property under Art 1 of Protocol 1 of the European Convention are notoriously
subject to limitations for public goods,[146] and so it is unlikely that the rational use of this
power could be impugned.

More specific powers are granted by s 30 (formerly s 92) to implement road restric-   9.65
tions, diversions, and closures. The diversion or closure may be ordered by any soldier or
person authorized by the Secretary of State for the immediate preservation of the peace
or the maintenance of order. Directions for closure in calmer circumstances must be
issued by the Secretary of State under s 32 (formerly s 94). These interventions are
undertaken for defensive purposes (both to benefit the security forces and vulnerable
communities) or to make movement m\ore detectable, such as around the border with
the Republic. In that setting, there has been considerable discord, because of inconven-
ience for local inhabitants. Some residents have therefore sought physically to remove

---

[144] See Northern Ireland (Emergency Provisions) Regulations 1991, SI 1991/1759; Lord Carlile, *Report on the Operation in 2005 of Part VII of the Terrorism Act 2000* (Home Office, London, 2006) para 99.

[145] See Lord Carlile, *Report on the Operation in 2002 of Part VII of the Terrorism Act 2000* (Home Office, London, 2003) para 11.4.

[146] See Çoban, A.R., *Protection of Property Rights within the European Convention on Human Rights* (Ashgate, Aldershot, 2004).

the barriers or to fill in cratered roads. An array of offences relating to interferences and the creation of bypasses is therefore set out in ss 31 and 32 (formerly ss 93 and 94). Section 31 deals with interferences to works under ss 29 and 31. It is a defence to show reasonable excuse, but s 118 does not apply. Section 32(2) deals with interferences with closures, and s 32(3) forbids the execution of bypasses and even the possession of construction equipment within 200 metres of road closure works, unless, under s 32(4), with reasonable excuse (again, s 118 does not apply).

9.66   Section 30 mentions soldiers since police officers have alternative and permanent powers under the Policing (Miscellaneous Provisions) (Northern Ireland) Order 2007, Art 12. Article 12 allows police to wholly or partly close or divert roads or prohibit or restrict the exercise of a right of way or the use of a waterway, if considered necessary for the preservation of the peace or the maintenance of public order. It also makes it an offence to interfere with works, apparatus, or equipment used in connection with the exercise of the power.

E. COMPENSATION

9.67   Compensation is provided under s 38 and Sch 4, para 1, whenever '(a) real or personal property is taken, occupied, destroyed or damaged, or (b) any other act is done which interferes with private rights of property' in exercising powers under ss 21 to 32. The nature of 'private rights' has been explained in *R (McCreesh) v County Court Judge of Armagh*[147] and in *R (Secretary of State for Northern Ireland) v County Court Judge for Armagh*.[148] The cases demonstrate that special loss (such as to business profits) arising from interference with a public right (such as a road closure) is not recoverable. Under para 3, claims must be brought within twenty-eight days, subject to a discretion to allow applications within six months on written request. When the Secretary of State refuses to exercise this discretion, there can be an appeal to the county court. Claims are determined at the first instance by the Secretary of State (para 4); no reasons need be given.[149] There is an appeal against refusal to pay or the amount of payment to the county court (para 5), where there is a full hearing.[150] Where a claim is allowed, then costs can also be paid under para 7. Compensation may be refused or reduced where false statements are made or there is not full disclosure (para 6—these actions may also be offences of deception under para 12). In addition, compensation may be refused on public policy grounds under para 9 in respect of an act done in connection with, or revealing evidence of, an offence for which the claimant is convicted.[151] Those whose houses are damaged in searches which reveal hidden explosives or firearms should attract no sympathy. But the width of this disqualification is not proportionate to the needs of public policy under Art 1 of Protocol 1 of the European Convention. For example, why should a person who has been convicted of an offence of attempting to create a bypass be refused compensation for land occupied as a result of the road blocks? Is not the fine for the offence sufficient?

---

[147] [1978] NI 164.
[148] [1981] NI 19.
[149] See *Adam v Secretary of State for Northern Ireland* [1990] NI 183 (criminal injuries rules).
[150] *Ibid.*
[151] Compare (under criminal injuries rules) *Re McCallion* [2001] NI 401; *Re Creighton*, 23 April 2001, (QB).

Pursuant to the Peace Process, military and security installations are being dismantled, **9.68** and many border crossings have been reopened. Thus, requisitions and compensation payments are also being wound down:

Table 9.4 Requisition and compensation[152]

Year	Requisition order	De-requisition order	Compensation (£m)
2001	12	13	1.833
2002	14	15	4.027
2003	14	22	1.886
2004	14	14	0.426
2005	15	16	0.164
2006	2	2	0.194
2007 (to 30 Sept)	0	18	0.077

F. CONTROLS AND COMMENTS ON SPECIAL POWERS

In terms of the CONTEST strategy, these measures perform similar roles to s 44 of the **9.69** Terrorism Act 2000. Though 'Pursuit' may result, the main impact is to 'Prevent' through disruption and intelligence-gathering.[153] Some assert great success,[154] but intelligence impacts remain too shadowy to assess with certainty. As for drawbacks, several design aspects pay insufficient consideration to individual rights, though actual challenges have been relatively few and have produced 'a relatively easy ride',[155] probably reflecting the street level of their application. There is also a question-mark against the entire existence of some powers as unnecessary duplications, especially the police stop and search powers. As for the remaining military powers, others have suggested that military aid should be replaced by mutual police aid.[156] However, given that the military are 'highly unlikely'[157] to be needed to assist with public order (with no call out since 2006), the remaining focus on munitions points towards continuing specialist military involvement but with special powers confined to that purpose.

As for accountability, the Justice and Security (Northern Ireland) Act 2007 reflects **9.70** the oversight mechanisms in the main body of the Terrorism Act 2000. Thus, unlike Pt VII, there is no fixed life span, on the basis that the threat may remain 'for a considerable time'.[158] But there is annual review. By s 40, the Secretary of State must appoint a

---

[152] Source: Northern Ireland Office Statistics & Research Agency, Carlile Reports.

[153] Whalley, R., *Report of the Independent Reviewer: Justice and Security (Northern Ireland) Act 2007* (Northern Ireland Office, Belfast, 2007) para 82.

[154] Dingley, J. (ed), *Combating Terrorism in Northern Ireland* (Routledge, Abingdon, 2009) pp 3, 188.

[155] Morgan, A., 'Northern Ireland terrorism' in Dingley, J. (ed), *Combating Terrorism in Northern Ireland* (Routledge, Abingdon, 2009) p 172.

[156] Whalley, R., *Report of the Independent Reviewer: Justice and Security (Northern Ireland) Act 2007* (Northern Ireland Office, Belfast, 2007) para 100.

[157] *Ibid* para 191.

[158] HC Hansard Public Bill Committee on the Justice and Security Bill, col 147 (18 January 2007), Paul Goggins.

reviewer to report annually on the operation of ss 21 to 32, and the report must be laid before Parliament. This review is markedly less effective than under Pt VII, since the remit does not extend to juryless trials, even though they are the most temporary and exceptional of all.

9.71   To assist the review, and accountability in general, s 37 (formerly s 104) requires the police to keep records of the exercise of the powers in ss 21 to 26. This requirement follows a recommendation of the Patten Commission,[159] but it is subject to the proviso that it must be reasonably practicable to implement in the circumstances.

9.72   The reviewer under s 40 must additionally report on the procedures adopted by the armed forces in Northern Ireland for receiving, investigating, and responding to complaints, a function formerly exercised by the Independent Assessor of Military Complaints Procedures (first instituted on a non-statutory basis following Viscount Colville's report in 1990[160] and latterly under s 98 and Sch 11 of Pt VII). The first annual report appeared in 1993.[161] The reviewer may not receive or investigate complaints, but stands one step back and audits the process. The closest to direct intervention is that the reviewer may require the General Officer Commanding to review a particular case (under s 40(6)(d)). The reviewer's impact cannot therefore match that of the Ombudsman under the Police (Northern Ireland) Act 2000, Pt VIII. Most complaints nowadays relate to helicopter overflights.[162] The decline in military patrolling makes the absence of more interventionist powers less important and justifies the elimination of a distinct office.

9.73   The Secretary of State may also under s 40 direct the reviewer to conduct a review into other specified matters. No request has yet been made.

9.74   The first review, by Robert Whalley, appeared in late 2008.[163] It is apparent in the report that the reviewer is not only confined to ss 21 to 32 but also lacks information about the interplay with Terrorism Act 2000 powers (especially s 44).[164] The statistical information is more limited than that given under Pt VII. The review also lacks any firm grounding in principle. There is recitation of the usual notion of 'balance'[165] between operational effectiveness and the need for a transition to normality, but no detailed consideration of issues, for example, under the European Convention on Human Rights. On balance, this review should have been combined with those of Lord Carlile. Review models will be considered further in Chapter 10.

9.75   The review and the impetus towards normalization are reflected in s 41, by which the Secretary of State may by affirmative order repeal ss 21 to 40.

9.76   Remaining aspects of constitutional governance rely upon the trend set by the PACE legislation. Thus, the various security powers may be subjected under s 34 to regulation by codes of practice. The affirmative procedure for issuance is required under s 36. According to s 35 (formerly s 101), the status of the codes is the same as in PACE.

---

[159] Independent Commission on Policing for Northern Ireland, *A New Beginning: Policing in Northern Ireland* (Northern Ireland Office, Belfast 1999), para 8.14.

[160] *Review of the Northern Ireland (Emergency Provisions) Acts 1978 and 1987* (Cm 1115, London, 1990) ch 5.

[161] 1993–94 HC 369.

[162] Whalley, R., *Report of the Independent Reviewer: Justice and Security (Northern Ireland) Act 2007* (Northern Ireland Office, Belfast, 2007) para 131.

[163] *Ibid.*

[164] *Ibid* paras 30, 183.

[165] *Ibid* para 17.

A failure to comply shall not create criminal or civil liability, but it shall be admissible in evidence and shall be taken into account. The hesitant 'may' appears because the government may conclude that PACE codes are sufficient.[166] Prior codes were latterly[167] made under ss 99 and 100 of Pt VII. No specific 2007 Act code has appeared, in breach of a ministerial promise.[168]

Another control is that any offence arising under ss 21 to 32 (except under Sch 4, para 12) can only be prosecuted with the consent of the Director of Public Prosecutions under s 39, with the added permission of the Attorney General where the offence has been committed for a purpose wholly or partly connected with the affairs of a country other than the United Kingdom. This extra restraint is in line with the Counter-Terrorism Act 2008, s 29.   9.77

Accountability for Northern Ireland special powers has been poor compared to the main body of the Terrorism Acts. Pre-legislation consultation papers were confined to juryless trials and private security services. Debates in the parliamentary chambers have been shorter and poorly attended. These codes have been largely ignored by select committees, including even the Northern Ireland Affairs Committee. Detailed scrutiny has been left to the Northern Ireland Human Rights Commission,[169] but its influence in Westminster and Whitehall seems to be limited.   9.78

G. PRIVATE SECURITY SERVICES

The fund-raising activities of paramilitary groups in Northern Ireland have included the proffering of private security services, sometimes amounting to little more than extortion.[170] To ensure that terrorist-connected firms or individuals could be filtered out of the industry, the Northern Ireland (Emergency Provisions) Act 1987 required providers of private security services to be licensed by the Northern Ireland Office, so that backgrounds could be vetted. These measures were continued by Pt VII (s 106 and Sch 13), despite the government commitment to translate them into normal laws.[171]   9.79

Further debate at the time of the expiration of Pt VII suggested that the simple solution would be to apply the Private Security Industry Act 2001. The government was concerned that the process of vetting and of Enhanced Criminal Records Checks would reveal sensitive intelligence to applicants.[172] Nevertheless, the Northern Ireland Office   9.80

---

[166] Hansard HC Standing Committee D, col 284 (3 February 2000), Adam Ingram.

[167] See the Northern Ireland Office *Guide to the Emergency Powers* in 1990 which was superseded by codes issued in 1994 and 1996 (SI 1993/ 2788, SI 1996/1698) under the Northern Ireland (Emergency Provisions) Act 1991, s 61.

[168] Hansard HL vol 689, col 1058 (20 February 2007), Lord Rooker.

[169] See Northern Ireland Act 1998, s 68.

[170] See Independent Monitoring Commission, *Fifth Report* (2005–06 HC 46) para 6.11; Northern Ireland Affairs Committee, *Organized Crime in Northern Ireland* (2005–06 HC 886) para 203; Organized Crime Task Force, *Annual Report* (Belfast, 2008) p 50; Moran, J., *Policing the Peace in Northern Ireland* (Manchester University Press, Manchester, 2008) p 65.

[171] Home Office and Northern Ireland Office, *Legislation against Terrorism* (Cm 4178, London, 1998) para13.16.

[172] Lord Carlile, *Report on the Operation in 2002 of Part VII of the Terrorism Act 2000* (Home Office, London, 2003) para 17.4.

accepted in 2006 that adapting the Security Industry Authority ('SIA') to Northern Ireland would be the best option.[173]

9.81 This application is secured by the Justice and Security (Northern Ireland) Act 2007, ss 48, 49, and Sch 6. The Act amends the Private Security Industry Act 2001 to give the SIA future control over regulation. Only technical changes are made in the adaptation under s 49. There is, however, to be an unspecified transition period to allow for preparations. Once the SIA is ready to commence operations in Northern Ireland, the relevant provisions of the 2001 Act will be brought into effect in Northern Ireland by order, which will at the same time terminate an interim scheme under Sch 6.

9.82 The interim scheme in Sch 6 builds on, and expands, the Pt VII version. By para 1, 'security services' means the services of one or more individuals as security guards (whether or not provided together with other services relating to the protection of property or persons). To enforce the regulatory system, it is an offence to provide or offer (para 4) or to advertise (para 5) unlicensed services, or to pay for them (para 6). There is a defence under paras 5 and 6 to the effect that the person reasonably believed the other party was in fact licensed (s 118 does not apply).

9.83 The Northern Ireland Office remains the licensing authority (para 8) for the interim scheme. The basis for the grant or refusal of licences is considerably expanded compared to the Pt VII scheme which focused entirely on connections to a proscribed organization.[174] Instead, by para 9, four considerations are taken into account. Condition 1 is that a proscribed organization or a closely connected organization would benefit from the granting of that licence. Condition 2 is that there are reasonable grounds to suspect that the applicant's security services business or any of the applicant's partners, employees, or officers are engaged in criminal activity. Condition 3 deals with a persistent failure to comply with the regulations. Condition 4 deals with a failure to comply with conditions imposed on a licence. Those conditions, under para 10, must relate to the prevention of paramilitary or criminal connections; they still do not allow for the imposition of ongoing training requirements or other professional standards, unlike the 2001 Act scheme. Individual security guards must also be notified to the Secretary of State, as well as other change of personnel within the business, no less than fourteen days before employment is to commence (paras 16 to 19). It is an offence to fail to give requested information.

9.84 A refusal to issue a licence shall be notified (para 11). Once issued, the licence is valid for twelve months (para 12), but it can be revoked if any of the Conditions apply (para 13), subject to allowing representations to be made. Where a licence is refused or revoked or where conditions imposed are unacceptable, the applicant may appeal to the High Court under para 14. The appeal mechanism was not available until the 2000 Act and reflects concerns about the impact of the European Convention, Art 6 and Art 1 of Protocol 1.[175] To protect sensitive information where the grounds relate to a proscribed organization or criminal activity, the Secretary of State may simply issue a certificate to that effect. The appellant shall be notified of the Secretary of State's decision to issue a certificate. Appeal against the certificate lies to the Tribunal established by the Northern Ireland Act 1998, s 91.

---

[173] Northern Ireland Office, *Regulating the Private Security Industry in Northern Ireland* (Belfast, 2006) para 36.
[174] *Ibid* para 10.
[175] Home Office, Circular 03/01: *Terrorism Act 2000* (Home Office, London, 2001) para 22.10.

The police may carry out inspections to check records, if necessary by force (para 20). It is an offence to fail to produce the records demanded. Paragraph 21 also provides for an offence of keeping knowingly false or misleading records. **9.85**

Between 1990 and 2000, 2,674 certificates were issued or renewed, with just 23 refused, cancelled or revoked.[176] The system operates, therefore, by way of deterrent rather than filter. This pattern has continued between 2001 and the end of September 2007: 652 out of 669 applications were granted. **9.86**

Lord Lloyd called for the abolition of the special licensing regime, subject to the proven establishment of peace in Northern Ireland.[177] However, the reforms now being undertaken are preferable in terms of upholding the rule of law. **9.87**

H. CONCLUSIONS

The resolution of political violence in Northern Ireland during the period 2001 to 2008 has engaged a wide range of policies. Anti-terrorism legislation has certainly played a part, with the delivery of criminalization through juryless trials being the key achievement. Special powers represent a more contested blessing, with militarization being part of the reason for conflict by stimulating violent reaction[178] as well as a method of limiting paramilitarism.[179] The legislation has been driven by history as well as pragmatism,[180] therefore real innovations have occurred elsewhere. **9.88**

Within criminal justice, innovations have included immunity for those who hand over weaponry[181] or provide information about the graves of victims.[182] More vital have been a new sentencing regime to allow the early release of paramilitary prisoners,[183] redesigns to policing[184] and criminal justice institutions,[185] inquiries into collusion[186] and contested events,[187] and fumbling efforts to help victims.[188] An attempt to deal with the 'on the runs'—fugitives from Northern Ireland who had long settled abroad—proved **9.89**

---

[176] Source: Northern Ireland Office.

[177] *Inquiry into Legislation against Terrorism* (Cm 3420, London, 1996) para 16.27.

[178] See Campbell, C. and Connelly, I., 'Making war on terror?' (2006) 69 *Modern Law Review* 935 at p 956.

[179] Irwin, A. and Maloney, M., 'The military response' and Morgan, A., 'Northern Ireland terrorism' in Dingley, J. (ed), *Combating Terrorism in Northern Ireland* (Routledge, Abingdon, 2009) pp 215, 223

[180] Compare Morgan, A., 'Northern Ireland terrorism' in Dingley, J. (ed), *Combating Terrorism in Northern Ireland* (Routledge, Abingdon, 2009) p 157.

[181] Northern Ireland Arms Decommissioning Act 1997.

[182] Northern Ireland (Location of Victims' Remains) Act 1999.

[183] Northern Ireland (Sentences) Act 1998.

[184] Police (Northern Ireland) Act 2000. See Mulcahy, A., *Policing Northern Ireland* (Willan, Cullompton, 2006).

[185] See Justice (Northern Ireland) Act 2002; Justice (Northern Ireland) Act 2004.

[186] See, for example, Stevens Inquiry on UDA/RUC collusion (*The Times* 18 April 2003 pp 4, 5); Police Ombudsman for Northern Ireland, *The Circumstances surrounding the death of Raymond McCord Junior and related Matters* (Belfast, 2007).

[187] See currently Bloody Sunday Inquiry (<http://www.bloody-sunday-inquiry.org.uk>); Billy Wright Inquiry (<http://www.billywrightinquiry.org>); Robert Hamill Inquiry (<http://www.roberthamillinquiry. org>); Rosemary Nelson Inquiry (<http://www.rosemarynelsoninquiry.org>).

[188] See Northern Ireland Affairs Committee, *Ways of Dealing with Northern Ireland's Past* (2005–06 HC 530); Victims and Survivors (Northern Ireland) Order 2006, SI 2006/2953; Commission for Victims and Survivors Act (Northern Ireland) 2008; *Report of the Consultative Group on the Past* (Belfast, 2009).

abortive.[189] Beyond criminal justice, there is an even wider agenda in terms of economic and social reform to deal with the consequences of violence and to reduce tension.[190]

Wider lessons from 'The Troubles' in Northern Ireland are also contested, but two might be ventured. One is that human rights abuses tend to occur in severe situations of terrorism, whereupon their occurrence fuels further conflict.[191] It is vital, therefore, to instil the values of rights, accountability, and constitutionalism. The 2007 Act represents the latest effort. It is an improvement on its predecessors, but several opportunities were missed to advance further. The second lesson is that the reduction of such bitter conflict demands attention be paid to the political aspects of terrorism at least as much as security aspects. The willingness to talk constructively with sworn enemies is an unpalatable but necessary precondition. The Provisional IRA might be withering away,[192] but Northern Ireland remains a deeply fissured society,[193] and the Peace Process is far from its journey's end.[194]

---

[189] See Northern Ireland Office, *Proposal in Relation to On the Runs* (Belfast, 2003); Northern Ireland (Offences) Bill 2005–06 HC 81.

[190] See Northern Ireland Affairs Committee, *Relocation following paramilitary intimidation* (2000–01 HC 59) and *Reply of the Northern Ireland Executive* (2001–02 HC 461).

[191] See Committee on the Administration of Justice, *War on Terror* (Belfast, 2007).

[192] Independent Monitoring Commission, *Nineteenth Report* (Cm 7464, London, 2008) para 2.12.

[193] For physical segregation, see <http://www.belfastinterfaceproject.org>.

[194] See also Neumann, P.G., *Britain's Long War* (Palgrave, Basingstoke, 2003) p 188.

10

OTHER MATTERS AND CONCLUSIONS

A. LEGISLATIVE STRUCTURE AND REVIEW

The consolidation of the anti-terrorism legislation has long been mooted as a desirable goal, but, with the propensity for fresh measures, its achievement appears a forlorn ambition. The consolidation of previous distinct codes for Britain and Northern Ireland represented one of the undoubted benefits of the Terrorism Act 2000. However, any gain has been dissipated with the later passage of four major anti-terrorism Acts and several other non-terrorism legislative amendments. **10.01**

Independent review schemes are equally muddled. The coverage is beset by 'pragmatic incrementalism'.[1] The Terrorism Act 2000 is fully reviewed, though there was a spin-off added review for Pt VII, now replaced by review of ss 21 to 32 of the Justice and Security (Northern Ireland) Act 2007. The reviewer can also be commissioned to undertake thematic reviews and has reported on proposals in 2005 and 2007 for extended detention of ninety days and then forty-two days under s 41, and on the definition of terrorism.[2] There is currently no review specific to the Anti-terrorism, Crime and Security Act 2001, the Justice and Security (Northern Ireland) Act 2007, ss 1 to 9 (non-jury trials), or the Counter-Terrorism Act 2008. **10.02**

To some extent the obstacles thus presented are overcome by appointing the same person to undertake virtually all reviews. Thus, Lord Carlile was appointed on 11 September 2001 under the Terrorism Act and has subsequently shouldered almost all the later reviews.[3] The only exercise beyond his orbit relates to the 2007 Act which is handled by Robert Whalley. The review reports are always accurate and helpful, but more **10.03**

---

[1] Lord Carlile, Conference on the Regulation of Criminal Justice (Manchester, 9 April 2008).
[2] See Bibliography for details.
[3] See also Lord Carlile, *First Annual Review of Arrangements for National Security in Northern Ireland* (Northern Ireland Office, Belfast, 2008).

could be achieved by a structure which relied less upon happenstance and the capacity of just one person, no matter how able.

10.04   The reviews should be strengthened in order to meet standards of accountability and to improve the audit of the treatment of rights and constitutional governance.[4] First, the invocation of powers should be subject to pre-announced and expressly invoked criteria, in order that the reviewers and Parliament can make judgments as to the desirability of the provisions. Secondly, there should be an independent review panel, not just one or two persons, so as to incorporate a range of views, to cope with the burgeoning workload, and to adopt a rolling system of appointments so as to infuse fresh ideas to avoid institutional capture. Lord Carlile views himself as a watchdog and commentator whose main constituency is Parliament and the government; he seeks success principally in terms of relevance to, and improvement of, debates. One implication of the target audience is that reports must be short and relatively shorn of arguments and data. However, a panel could address different audiences—Parliament and government may arguably be the prime audience, but the communities most affected by the legislation, the lawyers who work with it, and even the general public, all have legitimate interests in greater knowledge about the legislation. The panel should investigate and report on any proposed institution of anti-terrorism legislation, its working while in force, its renewal, and its compatibility with policy and standards. It should be able to draw upon the resources of specialists. Thirdly, there should be a specialist review committee in Parliament as its chief correspondent.[5] Under the current disposition of parliamentary committees, the function of reviewing anti-terrorism legislation is clearly either of insufficient priority or of excessive bulk.

B. ANCILLARY MATTERS

1. Interpretations

10.05 Various terms are given specific meanings, starting with 'terrorism' itself in s 1 of the 2000 Act (described in Chapter 1). A list of other interpretations is furnished by s 121 of the Terrorism Act 2000. One is that 'property' includes property wherever situated and whether real or personal, heritable or moveable, and things in action and other intangible or incorporeal property. Another, already noted (in Chapter 2), is that an 'organization' includes any association or combination of persons, a phrase wide enough to encompass an affinity group or even an anarchistic 'disorganization'. The interpretations provided elsewhere in the Act are indexed at s 122. Further interpretative lists are set out in the Prevention of Terrorism Act 2005, s 15, and the Terrorism Act 2006, s 20.

2. Evidence

10.06 One of the most contentious issues in debates on the Terrorism Act 2000 concerned the several offences which shifted onto the defence a significant element of the burden of

---

[4] These ideas were rejected by the government: Joint Committee on Human Rights, *Government Responses to the Committee's 20th and 21st Reports and other correspondence* (2007–08 HL 127, HC 756) p 20. Compare *Independent Reviewer of Terrorism Laws Bill 2008* (House of Representatives, Canberra, 2008).

[5] See Joint Committee on Human Rights, *Terrorism Policy and Human Rights: Annual Review of Control Orders Legislation 2008* (2007–08 HL 57/HC 356) para 33.

proof (as detailed already in Chapter 6). In response, s 118 of the Terrorism Act 2000 declares that these formulations impose an evidential burden but that the final burden of proof remains on the prosecution.

There are two situations where s 118 is utilized in the Act. One relates to provisions where 'it is a defence for a person charged with an offence to prove a particular matter' (s 118(1) and (2)—such as ss 12(4) or 39(5)(a)). The other are provisions where a court '(a) may make an assumption in relation to a person charged with an offence unless a particular matter is proved, or (b) may accept a fact as sufficient evidence unless a particular matter is proved' (s 118(3) and (4)—such as s 57(1) and (3)). In total, s 118 is applicable to the following provisions: ss 12(4), 39(5)(a), 54, 57, and 58. It follows that s 118 does not affect: s 11(2) (membership); s 18(2) (money laundering); s 19(3) (disclosure); s 21(5) (cooperation with the police); s 36(3) (breach of cordons); s 51(3) (breach of parking restrictions); Sch 5, paras 16 and 32 (explanation orders); Sch 6, para 1 (financial disclosures). **10.07**

A further point of evidence is dealt with by s 120 of the Terrorism Act 2000, by which notices and directions from the Secretary of State are deemed to be valid until the contrary is proved, while certificates shall be evidence (or, in Scotland, sufficient evidence) of the document in legal proceedings. **10.08**

3. Secondary legislation

The Terrorism Act 2000 serves as the parent legislation for various possible orders and regulations. Section 123 describes the processes for issuance. Most statutory instruments will, under s 123(2), be subject to the 'negative' procedure, but affirmative resolution is required under s 123(3) and (4) for orders relating to more important measures, such as proscription (subject to cases of urgency for those powers under sub-s (4)). There is no set process for 'directions', but, by s 124, a direction given under the Act may be varied or revoked by a further direction. **10.09**

There are many powers to make secondary legislation in the Anti-terrorism, Crime and Security Act 2001 but no central signpost equivalent to s 123 of the 2000 Act. The most wide-ranging power is in s 124, which reflects a sometimes chaotic legislative process and the concern that mistakes would later need correction. By s 124(1), a minister of the Crown 'may by order make such incidental, consequential, transitional or supplemental provision as he thinks necessary or expedient' in relation to the 2001 Act. By s 124(2), the power can even extend to primary legislation, by amending, repealing, or revoking any legislative provision before the 2001 Act or passed in the same session. Despite their breadth, such orders are subject only to negative resolution. The Privy Counsellor Review Committee called for the repeal of s 124.[6] The Home Office rejected this restraint[7] but has never resorted to the power. **10.10**

4. Jurisdiction

The Terrorism Act 2000 generally extends to the whole of the United Kingdom (under s 130), as does the Prevention of Terrorism Act 2005 and virtually all of the Terrorism **10.11**

---

[6] *Anti-terrorism, Crime and Security Act 2001 Review, Report* (2003–04 HC 100) para 4.42.
[7] Home Office, *Counter-Terrorism Powers: Reconciling Security and Liberty in an Open Society* (Cm 6147, London, 2004) para 175.

Act 2006 (excepting s 17). The Anti-terrorism, Crime and Security Act 2001 contains some exceptions for Scotland, including Pt V (race and religion—disapplied because of the breadth of Scottish public order offences) and Pt XII (bribery and corruption—a devolved matter). As regards Northern Ireland, measures regarding the Civil Nuclear Constabulary and the British Transport Police are irrelevant since those forces have no local representation. The Counter-Terrorism Act 2008 applies throughout the United Kingdom, but with variations under s 28 and exemption under s 30 for Northern Ireland. The Justice and Security (Northern Ireland) Act 2007 only affects Northern Ireland.

10.12   The jurisdictions of Jersey, Guernsey, and the Isle of Man are not subject to the Terrorism Act 2000. Instead, their equivalent laws largely rest on the model of the Terrorism Act 2000 and are based on local legislation, namely: the Anti-terrorism and Crime Act 2003 (Isle of Man);[8] the Terrorism (Jersey) Law 2002 and the Terrorism (Amendment) (Jersey) Law 2006; and the Terrorism and Crime (Bailiwick of Guernsey) Law 2002. By contrast, the Anti-terrorism, Crime and Security Act 2001 envisages several impacts. By s 57, an order in council may direct that any of the provisions of Pt VI shall extend to any of the Channel Islands, the Isle of Man, or to any British overseas territory.[9] By s 88, Pt IX of the Act can be applied by order to the Channel Islands, the Isle of Man, or any colony. Under both the Prevention of Terrorism Act 2005, s 16(8) and the Terrorism Act 2006, s 39, an order in council may direct that any provisions shall extend, with such modifications as appear appropriate, to any of the Channel Islands or the Isle of Man.

C. COVERAGE

10.13   Though this book is not the appropriate place to explore them in detail, many other facets of anti-terrorism-related laws remain beyond the special legislation and some pertinent issues have not been tackled at all.

10.14   In the category of laws beyond the anti-terrorism legislation might be cited the Civil Contingencies Act 2004, which addresses the 'Protect' strand of the CONTEST strategy, as well as many other potential emergencies.[10] However, that legislation has not provided for effective central inspection, nor has it adequately addressed the policing of the critical national infrastructure, as discussed in Chapter 8.[11] Explosive and firearms legislation has been updated from time to time but has not been openly reviewed with reference to terrorism.[12] Offences against the state, such as treason, though less pressing concerns, have been the subject of official attention.[13] The application of lethal force and inquisitions into its use are surely worthy of further legal attention, as mentioned in Chapter 5. It is extraordinary that guidelines for shooting suicide bombers, Operation

---

[8] Note that maximum detention pursuant to s 30 is now seven days. Compare the position under prior legislation: Walker, C.P., 'The detention of suspected terrorists in the British Islands' (1992) 12 *Legal Studies* 178.

[9] See Chemical Weapons (Overseas Territories) Order 2005, SI 2005/854.

[10] See Walker, C. and Broderick, J., *The Civil Contingencies Act 2004: Risk, Resilience and the Law in the United Kingdom* (Oxford University Press, Oxford, 2006); Roach, K., 'Must we trade rights for security?' (2006) 27 *Cardozo Law Review* 2157 at p 2158; Clarke, R.V., and Newman, G.R., *Outsmarting the Terrorists* (Praeger, Westport, 2006); Cabinet Office, *Security in a Global Hub* (London, 2007).

[11] See also Walker, C., 'The governance of the Critical National Infrastructure' [2008] *Public Law* 323.

[12] See Home Office, *Pursue, Prevent, Protect, Prepare: The United Kingdom's Strategy for Countering International Terrorism* (Cm 7547, London, 2009) para 10.35.

[13] Lord Goldsmith, *Citizenship: Our Common Bond* (Ministry of Justice, London, 2008) para 43.

Kratos, should be devised in secret by the police and never formally debated in Parliament.[14] Attempts to hold secretive and juryless inquests,[15] or to evade any inquiry at all,[16] are also highly problematic. Finally, enhanced sentencing has been addressed by the Counter-Terrorism Act 2008, but other sentencing aspects, such as accelerated release and social reinsertion, apply only in Northern Ireland.[17]

Regarding pertinent issues which await legislative attention, one of the most import-ant concerns the treatment of the victims of terrorism. Good reasons exist for special recognition of the plight of terrorism victims—they are attacked for public rather than private causes, there is a need for public solidarity, and it is public policy to instil restor-ation in the face of terrorism especially as private insurance or normal security measures may offer no protection.[18] Only one piece of nationwide legislation, the Reinsurance (Acts of Terrorism) Act 1993, is designed to address some of these problems by ensuring the continued availability of insurance for commercial properties.[19] The rich tenants of the towers of the City of London are hardly the most deserving cases, but no legal action has been taken to make generous provision for compensation for personal injury (espe-cially if inflicted overseas)[20] or, outside of legal schemes, to provide advice and counsel-ling.[21] Lack of such practical support was suffered after the 7 July bombings.[22] Though 141 British citizens have been killed abroad by terrorism since 2001,[23] the government refused to support the further assistance offered by the Victims of Terrorism (Compensation) Bill 2006–07,[24] though it has donated to the British Red Cross Relief Fund for UK Victims of Terrorism Overseas[25] and also offers exceptional assistance by embassies.[26]

10.15

Victims have been considered more fully in Northern Ireland, starting with the report in 1998 by Sir Kenneth Bloomfield, *We Will Remember Them*.[27] Debates are continuing

10.16

---

[14] See Independence Police Complaints Commission, *Stockwell One: Investigation into the shooting of Jean Charles de Menezes at Stockwell underground station on 22 July 2005* (London, 2007) ch 9.

[15] See Coroners and Justice Bill 2008–09 cl 11; Joint Committee on Human Rights, *Legislative Scrutiny: Coroners and Justice Bill* (2008–09 HL 57/HC 362).

[16] See *Jordan, McKerr, Kelly, Shanaghan v United Kingdom*, App nos 24746/94, 28883/95, 30054/96, 37715/97, 4 May 2001; *McShane v United Kingdom*, App no 43290/98, 28 May 2002; *Finucane v United Kingdom*, App no 29178/95, 1 July 2003; *Reavey v United Kingdom*, App no 34640/04, 27 November 2007. See Requa, M., and Anthony, G., 'Coroners, controversial deaths, and Northern Ireland's past conflict' [2008] *Public Law* 443.

[17] See Northern Ireland (Remission of Sentences) Act 1995 and the Northern Ireland (Sentences) Act 1998. Compare Lord Lloyd, *Inquiry into Legislation against Terrorism* (Cm 3420, London, 1996) paras 15.4, 15.11.

[18] See further Rabin, R.L. and Sugarman, S.D., 'The case for specially compensating the victims of terrorist attacks' (2007) 35 *Hofstra Law Review* 901 at p 914.

[19] See Walker, C., 'Political violence and commercial risk' (2004) 56 *Current Legal Problems* 531; Walker, C., 'Liability for acts of terrorism' in Koch, B.A. (ed), *Liability for Acts of Terrorism* (Springer, Vienna, 2004). There was also assistance for airline operators in 2001, but the Trioka system discontinued the issuance of new policies after September 2002: HM Treasury, *Reserve Accounts* (2003–04 HC 920) p 35.

[20] Few countries have criminal compensation schemes beyond Europe. See European Convention on the Compensation of Victims of Violent Crimes of 1983 (ETS 116, 1983); Council Directive 2004/80/EC of 29 April 2004 relating to compensation to crime victims.

[21] See Silke, A. (ed), *Terrorists, Victims and Society* (Wiley, Chichester, 2003).

[22] See London Resilience Forum, *Looking Back, Moving Forward* (London, 2006); London Assembly, *Report of the 7 July Review Committee* (London, 2006); Home Office, *Addressing Lessons from the Emergency Response to the 7 July 2005 London Bombings* (London, 2006).

[23] Hansard HC vol 481, col 249WH (29 November 2008), Tessa Jowell.

[24] See *ibid*.

[25] See <http://www.redcross.org.uk/news.asp?id=70137>.

[26] Hansard HC vol 481, col 253WH (29 November 2008), Tessa Jowell.

[27] (Northern Ireland Office, Belfast, 1998).

as to concrete, rather than symbolic, support. The Good Friday Agreement looked towards a Victims Commissioner to deliver the substantive ideas,[28] though few have subsequently emerged.[29] The issue has now been taken on by the Commission for Victims and Survivors Act (Northern Ireland) 2008.[30] The independent Consultative Group on the Past has also sparked interest and controversy with its report in 2009.[31] A broader theme of truth and reconciliation is also reflected in some of these initiatives, as well as in the inquiries into past contentious events, notably Bloody Sunday.[32] However, its inability to draw out more than partial and self-serving accounts or to deliver any insight within a decade casts a shadow over such devices.

10.17   Another area which awaits proper scrutiny concerns state organizational structures. The configuration of anti-terrorism policing has changed substantially since 2001, but no public inquiry has been held into the overall disposition not just of bodies such as the Counter-Terrorism Units,[33] but also of the security services, and agencies such as the Joint Terrorism Analysis Centre.[34] Does the United Kingdom have the appropriate organizational structures to attain its strategic goals against terrorism? Are the reforms within the police and the Home Office, which includes the establishment of an Office for Security and Counter-Terrorism,[35] working as expected? Do the functional divisions between Home Office and Cabinet Office and between intelligence agencies enhance efficiency and effectiveness?[36]

10.18   Finally, the 'Deportation with Assurances' of terrorism suspects has been widely condemned, though the House of Lords finally accepted the concept in *RB and OO v Secretary of State for the Home Department*.[37] These devices may eventually prove to be worthwhile, but, in any event, there should be much stronger and clearer legislation to set standards for such arrangements, as well as review mechanisms.[38]

D. FINAL REMARKS

10.19   It was asserted in Chapter 1 that the generation of permanent anti-terrorism legislation is a worthwhile exercise in practical and ethical terms. Validations for distinct anti-terrorist laws can be mounted on the basis of the requirements of constitutional and

---

[28] See *Rights, Safeguards and Equality of Opportunity* (Cm 3883, London, 1998) paras 6.11–6.13.

[29] Tangible measures include the Victims Unit of the Northern Ireland Executive (<http://www.ofmdfmni.gov.uk/victims.htm>), and the rights of victims to information in the Northern Ireland (Sentence) Act 1998, s 15, and of relatives under the Northern Ireland (Location of Victims' Remains) Act 1999 s 5(2).

[30] It replaced the Victims and Survivors (Northern Ireland) Order 2006, SI 2006/2953.

[31] See <http://www.cgpni.org/>.

[32] See <http://www.bloody-sunday-inquiry.org.uk/>; Ní Aoláin, F., *The Politics of Force* (Blackstaff, Belfast, 2000); Walsh, D., *Bloody Sunday and the Rule of Law in Northern Ireland* (Gill & MacMillan, Dublin, 2000).

[33] See Home Office, *Pursue, Prevent, Protect, Prepare: The United Kingdom's Strategy for Countering International Terrorism* (Cm 7547, London, 2009) paras 8.10, 8.50, 14.30.

[34] See Intelligence and Security Committee, *Annual Report 2002–03* (Cm 5837, London, 2003) para 62 and *Annual Report 2003–04* (Cm 6240, London, 2004) para 92.

[35] See Home Office, *Pursue, Prevent, Protect, Prepare: The United Kingdom's Strategy for Countering International Terrorism* (Cm 7547, London, 2009) para 7.22.

[36] See *ibid* paras 8.04, 11.23.

[37] [2009] UKHL 10.

[38] See further Walker, C., 'The treatment of foreign terror suspects' (2007) 70 *Modern Law Review* 427; Tooze, J., 'Deportation with assurance' (2009) 159 *New Law Journal* 419.

international law, the illegitimacy of terrorism, the problems posed by specialized criminality, and the timeliness of legislating in advance of an emergency. Any such code must,
nonetheless, observe the standards set out in Chapter 1, involving 'policy relevance and
impact', a 'rights audit', 'accountability', and 'constitutional governance'. As delivered,
some commentators view the anti-terrorism laws in the United Kingdom as 'an unmiti-
gated disaster' for 'the motherland of liberty'.[39] Even the Archbishop of York, John
Sentamu, has warned about the development of a police state.[40] Though Lord Carlile
dismissed this language as 'extravagant',[41] terrorism policing certainly extends into political life, with proscription and new offences about the encouragement of terrorism. It
impinges on civil life, with restrictions on liberty through arrest, stop and search, port
controls, and for the few, control orders. Economic life has also been affected by the
surveillance of financial transactions. At the same time, the UK government counter-
terrorism strategy does emphasize that its overall goal should be 'to reduce the risk
from international terrorism, so that people can go about their daily lives freely and with
confidence'.[42] Have those desirable ends been secured? With an emphasis upon prevention and the management of risk, where non-occurrence is the desired result, quantitative measures are problematic. Though statistics have been presented throughout this
book, they do not give a full sense of motivation, achievement, or public support.[43] So,
qualitative impressions will now be added.

The survey in this book suggests that, what others might call a legislative model of   **10.20**
accommodation[44] has been shown to be worthwhile in two senses. One is that there can
be tangible impacts in terms of policy objectives from legal intervention. The legislation
has been scored in this book against CONTEST. While many claims are not sustained
and while others are exaggerated, neither is a universal finding. The other sense in which
the exercise is worthwhile is that the policy outcomes can be achieved without always
sacrificing societal values. Once again, it is not claimed that there is entire normative
compliance, but there are many instances of genuine attempts to secure protection for
rights and to avoid undue usage of anti-terrorism laws. This imperfect model of accommodation is surely, for reasons outlined in Chapter 1, preferable to a 'business as usual'
model which pretends law cannot help against the modes of attack presented by terrorism. Equally, it is preferable to the 'extra-legal measures model' of *ex post facto* reckoning
and possible punishment or indemnity, which presents an endless vista of officials who
are more likely to lie about their misdeeds and have then to cover over misdeeds in solidarity with colleagues than to face any reckoning. Even when a public reckoning is
applied, the model assumes absolution and so becomes a 'business as usual model' with
institutional indulgence.

---

[39] Ackerman, B., *Before the Next Attack* (Yale University Press, New Haven, 2006) p 70.

[40] *The Times* 5 February 2007 p 26.

[41] Lord Carlile, *Report on the Operation in 2006 of the Terrorism Act 2000* (Home Office, London, 2007)
para 30.

[42] Home Office, *Pursue, Prevent, Protect, Prepare: The United Kingdom's Strategy for Countering International
Terrorism* (Cm 7547, London, 2009) para 0.17.

[43] Compare Home Affairs Committee, *Policing in the 21st Century* (2007–08 HC 364-I) para 40; Gearty,
C., *Civil Liberties* (Oxford University Press, Oxford, 2007) pp 50–7.

[44] Gross, O. and ní Aoláin, F., *Law in Times of Crisis* (Cambridge University Press, Cambridge, 2006) chs
1–4. Terrorism law is also depicted as 'vicious virus': Gearty, C., *Civil Liberties* (Oxford University Press,
Oxford, 2007) p 44.

10.21   Moving from general assessments to specific legislation, the Terrorism Act 2000 represents a valuable attempt to fulfil the role of a code against terrorism, though it fails to meet the desired standards in every respect. Certainly, the Privy Counsellor Review Committee Review found the model of the Terrorism Act 2000 'compelling'—it is desirable to have on a permanent basis, 'considered, properly regulated counter-terrorism legislation' with its own 'tailored safeguards'.[45]

10.22   The 2001 and 2005 Acts have proven much less satisfactory either in substance or as polished legislative performances. Part IV of the 2001 Act was a dubious artifice which rightly foundered. Many other parts of that Act owe more to opportunism than terrorism, as admitted in this candid statement of Lord Rooker:[46]

> I fully admit that, as we prepared the Bill, we trawled Whitehall. . . . We are seeking to close the loopholes and fill the gaps. Frankly, there is no good cause for giving future Home Secretaries extra work when the matter can be dealt with now.

10.23   For its part, the 2005 Act fosters the abhorrent process of allowing the executive to sit in judgment over individual freedoms. Perhaps the best that can be said of control is that it avoids worse outcomes—either another variant of detention without trial or the emulation of the American concept of the 'war on terror'. That approach misconceives not only the threat of terrorism but also the most appropriate response.[47] The 'war' approach is conducive to a lack of accountability and proportionality and threatens an everlasting departure from civil society.[48] There is a 'war' element to UK responses to terrorism, and it suffers from these unpalatable attributes, but it is primarily confined to overseas activities in situations of armed conflict (where it is termed 'counter-insurgency')[49] and therefore goes beyond the terms of this book. Yet, even the alternative to the war model still delivers an extensive security state.

10.24   The 2006 and 2008 Acts have at least reverted to a more calculated approach in which criminalization is prioritized. But their accretion underlines the sobering thought, proffered by the Home Affairs Committee, that the overall result is that 'this country has more anti-terrorist legislation on its statute books than almost any other developed democracy'.[50]

10.25   Aside from the extension of the anti-terrorism legislation, other persistent trends are manifest. One is the permanence of the special provisions against terrorism. This permanence is increasingly unremarkable. The 21st century concept of normality in criminal justice embodies the contingency and reality of 'special' powers dealing with 'special'

---

[45]   Report (2003–04 HC 100) paras 14, 107, 111.

[46]   Hansard HL vol 629, col 633 (3 December 2001), Lord Rooker.

[47]   See Scraton, P. (ed), *Beyond September 11* (Pluto, Cambridge, 2002) p 8; Strawson, J. (ed), *Law After Ground Zero* (Glasshouse Press, London, 2002) p xi; Greenwood, C., 'War, terrorism and international law' (2003) 56 *Current Legal Problems* 505; Lowe, V., '"Clear and present danger": Response to terrorism' (2005) 54 *International and Comparative Law Quarterly* 185; Campbell, C., '"War in terror" and vicarious hegemons' (2005) 54 *International and Comparative Law Quarterly* 321; Duffy, H., *The 'War on Terror' and the Framework of International Law* (Cambridge University Press, Cambridge, 2005).

[48]   See Allen, F.A., *The Habits of Legality* (Oxford University Press, New York, 1996) pp 37–40; see Walker, C., 'Terrorism and criminal justice' [2004] *Criminal Law Review* 311.

[49]   See Home Office, *Pursue, Prevent, Protect, Prepare: The United Kingdom's Strategy for Countering International Terrorism* (Cm 7547, London, 2009) para 7.15.

[50]   *Report on the Anti-terrorism, Crime and Security Bill 2001* (2001–02 HC 351) para 1.

situations or risks,[51] whether terrorism, serious frauds, sex offenders, or the anti-social. This trend towards fragmentation and specialization may be warranted, provided sensible safeguards and scrutiny are secured. One should not confuse the construction of such a specialist code in modern democracies with a bout of transient 'emergency law' in a Roman dictatorship.[52] In addition, permanence is not the same as the 'normalization' of special powers or the 'contamination' of 'normal' laws.[53] It is true that special laws are difficult to confine in temporal, geographical, or functional terms,[54] and there is overlap with 'normal' laws, such as in regard to asset confiscation and restrictions on the right against self-incrimination. Nonetheless, one can equally point to many instances of British distaste for Northern Irish anti-terrorism legislation and efforts to curtail their excesses.

The second trend concerns the emphasis upon anticipatory risk and the proactive   10.26
countering of terrorism, whereby it is felt to be unacceptably dangerous to allow the terrorists to move towards their objectives if the results are mass casualties or the use of weapons of mass destruction.[55] The result is an emphasis on intelligence-gathering, demonstrated not only by the perseverance with executive measures such as detention without trial and control orders but also by the proliferation of precursor criminal offences. This trend is encouraged by the more holistic approach to terrorism represented by the CONTEST doctrine, which gives greater prominence to 'Prevent', 'Protect, and 'Prepare' alongside the more traditional 'Pursuit'.

A third trend concerns the symbolic role of anti-terrorism laws. For instance, some   10.27
offences which were the subject of intense debate, such as indirect incitement, have hardly been used. This feature may also betray the difficulties of gathering intelligence which is translatable into public action and also the sensitivities of imposing every conceivable legislative burden upon communities which are suspicious in equal measure to their being suspect.[56] It is not certain that the public always appreciates the assurance being offered by symbolic legislation. Polling on the 42-day proposal suggested scepticism about the gain from the loss of liberty and suspicion of the motives of politicians.[57]

A fourth trend concerns the growing influence of international law. As terrorism is   10.28
successfully depicted by western states as a universal scourge, so it is increasingly possible to base state action on international accords.[58] Only glimpses of this trend have been

---

[51] See Gross, O., and Ni Aolain, F., 'To know where we are going we need to know where we are' in Hegarty, A. and Leonard, S., *Human Rights* (Cavendish, London, 1999) p 82.

[52] See Ferejohn, J., and Pasquino, P., 'The law of the exception' (2004) 2 *International Journal of Constitutional Law* 210.

[53] See Hillyard, P., 'The normalisation of special powers: From Northern Ireland to Britain' in Scraton, P. (ed), *Law, order and the authoritarian state* (Open University Press, Milton Keynes, 1987).

[54] See Gross, O., 'Chaos and rules' (2003) 112 *Yale Law Journal* 1011.

[55] Walker, C., 'Intelligence and Anti-Terrorism Legislation in the United Kingdom' (2006) 44 *Crime, Law & Social Change* 387.

[56] See Fenwick, H., *Civil Liberties and Human Rights* (4th edn, Routledge-Cavendish, Abingdon, 2007) p 1233.

[57] Only 36% supported the extension: Joseph Rowntree, British Policies Survey (http://www.jrrt.org.uk/uploads/ICM%20Poll%20Detention%20of%20Terrorist%20Suspects.pdf>, 2008). Compare the ICM poll in 2006 which found 73% favoured the more abstract proposition of loss of rights in return for greater security: Landman, T., 'The continuity of terror and counterterror' in Brysk, A., and Shafir, G., *National Insecurity and Human Rights* (University of California Press, Berkeley, 2007).

[58] See Bowring, B., 'The degradation of international law?' in Strawson, J., (ed), *Law After Ground Zero* (Glasshouse Press, London, 2002).

evidenced in this book, since it focuses on domestic law, but, aside from the international crimes mentioned in Chapter 8 and the more pervasive influence of the European Convention on Human Rights, the European Union and United Nations have been conspicuously busy since September 11, 2001.[59]

10.29   A fifth unrelenting theme has been the troublesome relationship between anti-terrorism laws and human rights. Almost all official reviewers of the legislation, from Lord Diplock in 1972 onwards, have been enjoined to take account of human rights, and so the concept has been to the fore, even though its application has often failed to satisfy human rights advocates. It follows that the Human Rights Act 1998 was never destined to have a major impact in this area, given that legislation had been 'Strasbourg-proofed' for some years and given that the European Convention on Human Rights shows considerable indulgence towards anti-terrorism legislation.[60] Indeed, the application of human rights discourse has been a two-edged sword, with failed challenges resulting sometimes in entrenchment and legitimation and the insertion of human rights safeguards encouraging the grant of more extreme powers.[61] Nevertheless, human rights have become the pre-eminent standard for review.

10.30   This point leads to the sixth, more positive, trend—the rising assertion of decisive judicial and parliamentary review. The judges have been prominent in the field of executive orders, whereby they condemned detention without trial and have curtailed control orders, whereas arrest and search powers have emerged largely unscathed.[62] Parliament stood out against the wilder claims to increase detention after arrest but did sanction a 28-day period which is well beyond the norm of four days.[63] This trend towards greater assertiveness in security disputes challenges the assertion that anti-terrorism legislation represents naked power—rule by law and not the rule of law.[64] There is evidence in this book of a growing disposition on the part of legislature, judiciary, and even the executive to adopt a principled approach. The approach towards anti-terrorism legislation adopted by the United Kingdom is far from a totalitarian state of exception which operates in a legal vacuum [65]—the government has not declared an all-encompassing 'war on terror' which rivals or replaces regular laws. Nor has it produced a 'zone of anomie in which all legal determinations are deactivated'.[66] Those commentators who peddle such a picture appear ignorant of the effort of the international community since 1945 to determine that no such state of anomie or Hobbesian state of savagery can be allowed again under the contemporary codes of humanitarian law and the international laws of human rights which apply to emergencies. The modern rulers of liberal democracies who seek to draw

---

[59] See Bianchi, A., *Enforcing International Norms Against Terrorism* (Hart, Oxford, 2004); Duffy, H., *The 'War on Terror' and the Framework of International Law* (Cambridge University Press, Cambridge, 2005); Eden, P., and O'Donnell, T. (eds), *September 11, 2001* (Transnational Publishers, Ardsley, New York, 2005); Gregory, F., 'The EU's response to 9/11' (2005) 17 *Terrorism & Political Violence* 105; O'Neill, M., 'A critical analysis of the European Union legal provisions on terrorism' (2008) 20 *Terrorism & Political Violence* 26.

[60] See Council of Europe, *The Fight against Terrorism* (3rd edn, Strasbourg, 2005); Warbrick, C., 'The principles of the ECHR and the response of states to terrorism' [2002] *European Human Rights Law Review* 287.

[61] For example, judicial review of Terrorism Act 2000, s 41, detentions paved the way for doubling the post-review period of detention by the Criminal Justice Act 2003, s 306.

[62] See Gearty, C., 'Human rights in an age of counter-terrorism' (2005) 58 *Current Legal Problems* 25.

[63] Police and Criminal Evidence Act 1984, Pt IV.

[64] See Agamben, G., *The State of Exception* (University of Chicago Press, Chicago, 2005).

[65] Compare Schmitt, C., *Political Theology* (MIT Press, Cambridge, 1985).

[66] Agamben, G., *The State of Exception* (University of Chicago Press, Chicago, 2005) p 50.

upon the poisonous old doctrines of executive authority have rightly faced concerted legal opposition and unprecedented unpopularity. Most norms have not at any time been suspended, but society has adapted to a new normality of terrorism. As the Foreign Secretary, David Miliband, has declared, 'We must respond to terrorism by championing the rule of law, not by subordinating it, for it is the cornerstone of the democratic society.'[67] There is much room for disagreement on the outcomes, but the trend towards strategic action and constitutionalism at least demonstrates that the principles set out in Chapter 1 are becoming 'not a mask but the true image of our nation'[68] and offer protection from naked state power.[69] The law thereby has demonstrated some capacity through its normative power and through the independence of its institutions to respond to executive claims to power.[70]

The impact of anti-terrorism legislation is often largely peripheral in effect. More important factors in dealing with terrorism will comprise normal police powers and criminal offences and regular techniques of investigation and securitization. These must operate alongside cooperation and vigilance on the part of the public who provide, even in terrorist cases where there is an emphasis on proactive intelligence-gathering, much of the policing capability of society. International cooperation is also of growing importance in response to more fluid and global vulnerabilities. Above all, there must be a vibrant and inclusive democracy which can discern the difference between vituperative and politically immature hot air and violence with the potential to spill blood and which holds its nerve and its cherished values in the face of the heat and light of the terrorist spectacular. That democracy must even remain willing to speak to its enemies. More campaigns of political violence end because of political processes than through defeat or degradation via a security response, though the point here is that both are important.[71] One must expect that 'democracies respond when there is blood on the streets',[72] and there is righteous justification for them to do so based on the international law duties to combat terrorism and the duty in national and international law to protect individual life.[73] At the same time, in an asymmetric conflict, the terrorists cannot destroy western polities.[74] But they may be able to provoke western polities to destroy their own spirits and cultures through the politics and practices of fear, discrimination, and the intolerance of dissent and liberty.

10.31

---

[67] *The Guardian* 15 January 2009 p 29.

[68] Ignatieff, M., *The Lesser Evil* (Edinburgh University Press, Edinburgh 2005) p 144.

[69] See Marks, S., 'State centrism, international law and the anxieties of influence' (2006) 19 *Leiden Journal of International Law* 339; Campbell, C., and Connelly, I., 'Making war on terror? (2006) 69 *Modern Law Review* 935 at p 939; Vaughan, B., and Kilcommins, S., *Terrorism, Rights and the Rule of Law* (Willan, Cullompton, 2008) p 13.

[70] Campbell, C., and Connelly, I., 'Making war on terror? (2006) 69 *Modern Law Review* 935 at p 939.

[71] The figures are 43% and 40%: Jones, G.G., and Libecki, M.C., *How Terrorist Groups End* (Rand, Santa Monica, 2008).

[72] Collins, J.M. 'And the walls came tumbling down' (2002) 39 *American Criminal Law Review* 1261 at p 1261. See also Sajó, A. (ed), *Militant Democracy* (Eleven International Publishing, Utrecht, 2004).

[73] See Walker, C., 'Clamping Down on Terrorism in the United Kingdom' (2006) 4 *Journal of International Criminal Justice* 1137.

[74] Ignatieff, M., *The Lesser Evil* (Edinburgh University Press, Edinburgh 2005) p 80.

APPENDIX 1

Terrorism Act 2000[1]

An Act to make provision about terrorism; and to make temporary provision for Northern Ireland about the prosecution and punishment of certain offences, the preservation of peace and the maintenance of order.

(20th July 2000)

PART I
INTRODUCTORY

1 Terrorism: interpretation

(1) In this Act "terrorism" means the use or threat of action where
    (a) the action falls within subsection (2),
    (b) the use or threat is designed to influence the government [or an international governmental organisation][2] or to intimidate the public or a section of the public, and
    (c) the use or threat is made for the purpose of advancing a political, religious [,racial][3] or ideological cause.

(2) Action falls within this subsection if it
    (a) involves serious violence against a person,
    (b) involves serious damage to property,
    (c) endangers a person's life, other than that of the person committing the action,
    (d) creates a serious risk to the health or safety of the public or a section of the public, or
    (e) is designed seriously to interfere with or seriously to disrupt an electronic system.

(3) The use or threat of action falling within subsection (2) which involves the use of firearms or explosives is terrorism whether or not subsection (1)(b) is satisfied.

(4) In this section
    (a) "action" includes action outside the United Kingdom,
    (b) a reference to any person or to property is a reference to any person, or to property, wherever situated,
    (c) a reference to the public includes a reference to the public of a country other than the United Kingdom, and
    (d) "the government" means the government of the United Kingdom, of a Part of the United Kingdom or of a country other than the United Kingdom.

---

[1] In these appendices, legislation not yet in force is represented in italics and square brackets (except for the Counter-Terrorism Act 2008), and repeals not yet in force are represented in italics. Provisions are consolidated up to 31 March 2009.

[2] Inserted by the Terrorism Act 2006, s 34(a).

[3] Inserted by the Counter-Terrorism Act 2008, s 75(1), (2)(a).

(5) In this Act a reference to action taken for the purposes of terrorism includes a reference to action taken for the benefit of a proscribed organisation.

2 Temporary legislation *(omitted)*

PART II
PROSCRIBED ORGANISATIONS

Procedure

3 Proscription

(1) For the purposes of this Act an organisation is proscribed if
   (a) it is listed in Schedule 2, or
   (b) it operates under the same name as an organisation listed in that Schedule.
(2) Subsection (1)(b) shall not apply in relation to an organisation listed in Schedule 2 if its entry is the subject of a note in that Schedule.
(3) The Secretary of State may by order
   (a) add an organisation to Schedule 2;
   (b) remove an organisation from that Schedule;
   (c) amend that Schedule in some other way.
(4) The Secretary of State may exercise his power under subsection (3)(a) in respect of an organisation only if he believes that it is concerned in terrorism.
(5) For the purposes of subsection (4) an organisation is concerned in terrorism if it
   (a) commits or participates in acts of terrorism,
   (b) prepares for terrorism,
   (c) promotes or encourages terrorism, or
   (d) is otherwise concerned in terrorism.
[(5A) The cases in which an organisation promotes or encourages terrorism for the purposes of subsection (5)(c) include any case in which activities of the organisation
   (a) include the unlawful glorification of the commission or preparation (whether in the past, in the future or generally) of acts of terrorism; or
   (b) are carried out in a manner that ensures that the organisation is associated with statements containing any such glorification.
(5B) The glorification of any conduct is unlawful for the purposes of subsection (5A) if there are persons who may become aware of it who could reasonably be expected to infer that what is being glorified, is being glorified as
   (a) conduct that should be emulated in existing circumstances, or
   (b) conduct that is illustrative of a type of conduct that should be so emulated.
(5C) In this section
   'glorification' includes any form of praise or celebration, and cognate expressions are to be construed accordingly;
   'statement' includes a communication without words consisting of sounds or images or both.][4]
[(6) Where the Secretary of State believes
   (a) that an organisation listed in Schedule 2 is operating wholly or partly under a name that is not specified in that Schedule (whether as well as or instead of under the specified name), or

---

[4] Inserted by the Terrorism Act 2006, s 21.

(b) that an organisation that is operating under a name that is not so specified is otherwise for all practical purposes the same as an organisation so listed,

he may, by order, provide that the name that is not specified in that Schedule is to be treated as another name for the listed organisation.

(7) Where an order under subsection (6) provides for a name to be treated as another name for an organisation, this Act shall have effect in relation to acts occurring while

(a) the order is in force, and

(b) the organisation continues to be listed in Schedule 2,

as if the organisation were listed in that Schedule under the other name, as well as under the name specified in the Schedule.

(8) The Secretary of State may at any time by order revoke an order under subsection (6) or otherwise provide for a name specified in such an order to cease to be treated as a name for a particular organisation.

(9) Nothing in subsections (6) to (8) prevents any liability from being established in any proceedings by proof that an organisation is the same as an organisation listed in Schedule 2, even though it is or was operating under a name specified neither in Schedule 2 nor in an order under subsection (6).][5]

4 Deproscription: application

[(1) An application may be made to the Secretary of State for an order under section 3(3) or (8)

(a) removing an organisation from Schedule 2, or

(b) providing for a name to cease to be treated as a name for an organisation listed in that Schedule.][6]

(2) An application may be made by

(a) the organisation, or

(b) any person affected by the organisation's proscription [or by the treatment of the name as a name for the organisation.][7]

(3) The Secretary of State shall make regulations prescribing the procedure for applications under this section.

(4) The regulations shall, in particular

(a) require the Secretary of State to determine an application within a specified period of time, and

(b) require an application to state the grounds on which it is made.

5 Deproscription: appeal

(1) There shall be a commission, to be known as the Proscribed Organisations Appeal Commission.

(2) Where an application under section 4 has been refused, the applicant may appeal to the Commission.

(3) The Commission shall allow an appeal against a refusal to deproscribe an organisation [or to provide for a name to cease to be treated as a name for an organisation][8] if it considers that the decision to refuse was flawed when considered in the light of the principles applicable on an application for judicial review.

(4) Where the Commission allows an appeal under this section [...],[9] it may make an order under this subsection.

---

[5] Inserted by the Terrorism Act 2006, s 22(1), (2).

[6] Substituted by the Terrorism Act 2006, s 22(1), (3).

[7] Inserted by the Terrorism Act 2006, s 22(1), (4).

[8] Inserted by the Terrorism Act 2006, s 22(1), (5)(a).

[9] Repealed by the Terrorism Act 2006, ss 22(1), (5)(b), 37(5), Sch 3.

(5)   Where an order is made under subsection (4) [in respect of an appeal against a refusal to deproscribe an organisation],[10] the Secretary of State shall as soon as is reasonably practicable
  (a) lay before Parliament, in accordance with section 123(4), the draft of an order under section 3(3)(b) removing the organisation from the list in Schedule 2, or
  (b) make an order removing the organisation from the list in Schedule 2 in pursuance of section 123(5).
[(5A) Where an order is made under subsection (4) in respect of an appeal against a refusal to provide for a name to cease to be treated as a name for an organisation, the Secretary of State shall, as soon as is reasonably practicable, make an order under section 3(8) providing that the name in question is to cease to be so treated in relation to that organisation.][11]
(6)   Schedule 3 (constitution of the Commission and procedure) shall have effect.

6 Further appeal

(1) A party to an appeal under section 5 which the Proscribed Organisations Appeal Commission has determined may bring a further appeal on a question of law to
  (a) the Court of Appeal, if the first appeal was heard in England and Wales,
  (b) the Court of Session, if the first appeal was heard in Scotland, or
  (c) the Court of Appeal in Northern Ireland, if the first appeal was heard in Northern Ireland.
(2) An appeal under subsection (1) may be brought only with the permission
  (a) of the Commission, or
  (b) where the Commission refuses permission, of the court to which the appeal would be brought.
(3) An order under section 5(4) shall not require the Secretary of State to take any action until the final determination or disposal of an appeal under this section (including any appeal to the *House of Lords*[12] [*Supreme Court*].[13]

7 Appeal: effect on conviction, &c

(1)   This section applies where
  (a) an appeal under section 5 has been allowed in respect of an organisation,
  (b) an order has been made under section 3(3)(b) in respect of the organisation in accordance with an order of the Commission under section 5(4) (and, if the order was made in reliance on section 123(5), a resolution has been passed by each House of Parliament under section 123(5)(b)),
  (c) a person has been convicted of an offence in respect of the organisation under any of sections 11 to 13, 15 to 19 and 56, and
  (d) the activity to which the charge referred took place on or after the date of the refusal to deproscribe against which the appeal under section 5 was brought.
[(1A) This section also applies where
  (a) an appeal under section 5 has been allowed in respect of a name treated as the name for an organisation,
  (b) an order has been made under section 3(8) in respect of the name in accordance with an order of the Commission under section 5(4),
  (c) a person has been convicted of an offence in respect of the organisation under any of sections 11 to 13, 15 to 19 and 56, and

---

[10] Inserted by the Terrorism Act 2006, s 22(1), (5)(c).
[11] Inserted by the Terrorism Act 2006, s 22(1), (6).
[12] Repealed by the Constitutional Reform Act 2005, s 40(4), Sch 9, Pt 1, para 71, not yet in force.
[13] Substituted by the Constitutional Reform Act 2005, s 40(4), Sch 9, Pt 1, para 71, not yet in force.

(d) the activity to which the charge referred took place on or after the date of the refusal, against which the appeal under section 5 was brought, to provide for a name to cease to be treated as a name for the organisation.][14]

(2) If the person mentioned in subsection (1)(c) [or (1A)(c)][15] was convicted on indictment
    (a) he may appeal against the conviction to the Court of Appeal, and
    (b) the Court of Appeal shall allow the appeal.

(3) A person may appeal against a conviction by virtue of subsection (2) whether or not he has already appealed against the conviction.

(4) An appeal by virtue of subsection (2)
    (a) must be brought within the period of 28 days beginning with the date on which the order mentioned in subsection (1)(b) [or (1A)(b)][16] comes into force, and
    (b) shall be treated as an appeal under section 1 of the Criminal Appeal Act 1968 (but does not require leave).

(5) If the person mentioned in subsection (1)(c) [or (1A)(c)][17] was convicted by a magistrates' court
    (a) he may appeal against the conviction to the Crown Court, and
    (b) the Crown Court shall allow the appeal.

(6) A person may appeal against a conviction by virtue of subsection (5)
    (a) whether or not he pleaded guilty,
    (b) whether or not he has already appealed against the conviction, and
    (c) whether or not he has made an application in respect of the conviction under section 111 of the Magistrates' Courts Act 1980 (case stated).

(7) An appeal by virtue of subsection (5)
    (a) must be brought within the period of 21 days beginning with the date on which the order mentioned in subsection (1)(b) [or (1A)(b)][18] comes into force, and
    (b) shall be treated as an appeal under section 108(1)(b) of the Magistrates' Courts Act 1980.

(8) In section 133(5) of the Criminal Justice Act 1988 (compensation for miscarriage of justice) after paragraph (b) there shall be inserted
    "or
    (c) on an appeal under section 7 of the Terrorism Act 2000."

8 Section 7: Scotland and Northern Ireland *(omitted)*

9 Human Rights Act 1998

(1) This section applies where rules (within the meaning of section 7 of the Human Rights Act 1998 (jurisdiction)) provide for proceedings under section 7(1) of that Act to be brought before the Proscribed Organisations Appeal Commission.

(2) The following provisions of this Act shall apply in relation to proceedings under section 7(1) of that Act as they apply to appeals under section 5 of this Act
    (a) section 5(4)[, (5) and (5A)][19],
    (b) section 6,
    (c) section 7, and
    (d) paragraphs 4 to [7][20] of Schedule 3.

(3) The Commission shall decide proceedings in accordance with the principles applicable on an application for judicial review.

---

[14] Inserted by the Terrorism Act 2006, s 22(1), (7).
[15] Inserted by the Terrorism Act 2006, s 22(1), (8)(a).
[16] Inserted by the Terrorism Act 2006, s 22(1), (8)(b).
[17] Inserted by the Terrorism Act 2006, s 22(1), (8)(c).
[18] Inserted by the Terrorism Act 2006, s 22(1), (8)(d).
[19] Substituted by the Terrorism Act 2006, s 22(1), (9)(a).
[20] Substituted by the Regulation of Investigatory Powers Act 2000, s 82(1), Sch 4, para 12 (1).

(4) In the application of the provisions mentioned in subsection (2)

    (a) a reference to the Commission allowing an appeal shall be taken as a reference to the Commission determining that an action of the Secretary of State is incompatible with a Convention right, [...][21]

    (b) a reference to the refusal to deproscribe against which an appeal was brought shall be taken as a reference to the action of the Secretary of State which is found to be incompatible with a Convention right[, and

    (c) a reference to a refusal to provide for a name to cease to be treated as a name for an organisation shall be taken as a reference to the action of the Secretary of State which is found to be incompatible with a Convention right.][22]

10 Immunity

(1) The following shall not be admissible as evidence in proceedings for an offence under any of sections 11 to 13, 15 to 19 and 56

    (a) evidence of anything done in relation to an application to the Secretary of State under section 4,

    (b) evidence of anything done in relation to proceedings before the Proscribed Organisations Appeal Commission under section 5 above or section 7(1) of the Human Rights Act 1998,

    (c) evidence of anything done in relation to proceedings under section 6 (including that section as applied by section 9(2)), and

    (d) any document submitted for the purposes of proceedings mentioned in any of paragraphs (a) to (c).

(2) But subsection (1) does not prevent evidence from being adduced on behalf of the accused.

Offences

11 Membership

(1) A person commits an offence if he belongs or professes to belong to a proscribed organisation.

(2) It is a defence for a person charged with an offence under subsection (1) to prove

    (a) that the organisation was not proscribed on the last (or only) occasion on which he became a member or began to profess to be a member, and

    (b) that he has not taken part in the activities of the organisation at any time while it was proscribed.

(3) A person guilty of an offence under this section shall be liable

    (a) on conviction on indictment, to imprisonment for a term not exceeding ten years, to a fine or to both, or

    (b) on summary conviction, to imprisonment for a term not exceeding six months, to a fine not exceeding the statutory maximum or to both.

(4) *(omitted)*

12 Support

(1) A person commits an offence if

    (a) he invites support for a proscribed organisation, and

    (b) the support is not, or is not restricted to, the provision of money or other property (within the meaning of section 15).

(2) A person commits an offence if he arranges, manages or assists in arranging or managing a meeting which he knows is

    (a) to support a proscribed organisation,

---

[21] Repealed by virtue of the Terrorism Act 2006, s 37(5), Sch 3.

[22] Inserted by the Terrorism Act 2006, s 22(1), (9)(b).

(b) to further the activities of a proscribed organisation, or

(c) to be addressed by a person who belongs or professes to belong to a proscribed organisation.

(3) A person commits an offence if he addresses a meeting and the purpose of his address is to encourage support for a proscribed organisation or to further its activities.

(4) Where a person is charged with an offence under subsection (2)(c) in respect of a private meeting it is a defence for him to prove that he had no reasonable cause to believe that the address mentioned in subsection (2)(c) would support a proscribed organisation or further its activities.

(5) In subsections (2) to (4)

(a) "meeting" means a meeting of three or more persons, whether or not the public are admitted, and

(b) a meeting is private if the public are not admitted.

(6) A person guilty of an offence under this section shall be liable

(a) on conviction on indictment, to imprisonment for a term not exceeding ten years, to a fine or to both, or

(b) on summary conviction, to imprisonment for a term not exceeding six months, to a fine not exceeding the statutory maximum or to both.

13 Uniform

(1) A person in a public place commits an offence if he

(a) wears an item of clothing, or

(b) wears, carries or displays an article,

in such a way or in such circumstances as to arouse reasonable suspicion that he is a member or supporter of a proscribed organisation.

(2) A constable in Scotland may arrest a person without a warrant if he has reasonable grounds to suspect that the person is guilty of an offence under this section.

(3) A person guilty of an offence under this section shall be liable on summary conviction to

(a) imprisonment for a term not exceeding six months,

(b) a fine not exceeding level 5 on the standard scale, or

(c) both.

PART III
TERRORIST PROPERTY

Interpretation

14 Terrorist property

(1) In this Act "terrorist property" means

(a) money or other property which is likely to be used for the purposes of terrorism (including any resources of a proscribed organisation),

(b) proceeds of the commission of acts of terrorism, and

(c) proceeds of acts carried out for the purposes of terrorism.

(2) In subsection (1)

(a) a reference to proceeds of an act includes a reference to any property which wholly or partly, and directly or indirectly, represents the proceeds of the act (including payments or other rewards in connection with its commission), and

(b) the reference to an organisation's resources includes a reference to any money or other property which is applied or made available, or is to be applied or made available, for use by the organisation.

Offences

15 Fund-raising

(1) A person commits an offence if he
   (a) invites another to provide money or other property, and
   (b) intends that it should be used, or has reasonable cause to suspect that it may be used, for the purposes of terrorism.
(2) A person commits an offence if he
   (a) receives money or other property, and
   (b) intends that it should be used, or has reasonable cause to suspect that it may be used, for the purposes of terrorism.
(3) A person commits an offence if he
   (a) provides money or other property, and
   (b) knows or has reasonable cause to suspect that it will or may be used for the purposes of terrorism.
(4) In this section a reference to the provision of money or other property is a reference to its being given, lent or otherwise made available, whether or not for consideration.

16 Use and possession

(1) A person commits an offence if he uses money or other property for the purposes of terrorism.
(2) A person commits an offence if he
   (a) possesses money or other property, and
   (b) intends that it should be used, or has reasonable cause to suspect that it may be used, for the purposes of terrorism.

17 Funding arrangements

A person commits an offence if
(a) he enters into or becomes concerned in an arrangement as a result of which money or other property is made available or is to be made available to another, and
(b) he knows or has reasonable cause to suspect that it will or may be used for the purposes of terrorism.

18 Money laundering

(1) A person commits an offence if he enters into or becomes concerned in an arrangement which facilitates the retention or control by or on behalf of another person of terrorist property
   (a) by concealment,
   (b) by removal from the jurisdiction,
   (c) by transfer to nominees, or
   (d) in any other way.
(2) It is a defence for a person charged with an offence under subsection (1) to prove that he did not know and had no reasonable cause to suspect that the arrangement related to terrorist property.

19 Disclosure of information: duty

(1) This section applies where a person
   (a) believes or suspects that another person has committed an offence under any of sections 15 to 18, and
   (b) bases his belief or suspicion on information which [comes to his attention
      (i) in the course of a trade, profession or business, or
      (ii) in the course of his employment (whether or not in the course of a trade, profession or business)].[23]

---

[23] Substituted by the Counter-Terrorism Act 2008, s 77(1), (2).

[(1A) But this section does not apply if the information came to the person in the course of a business in the regulated sector.][24]

(2) The person commits an offence if he does not disclose to a constable as soon as is reasonably practicable
  (a) his belief or suspicion, and
  (b) the information on which it is based.

(3) It is a defence for a person charged with an offence under subsection (2) to prove that he had a reasonable excuse for not making the disclosure.

(4) Where
  (a) a person is in employment,
  (b) his employer has established a procedure for the making of disclosures of the matters specified in subsection (2), and
  (c) he is charged with an offence under that subsection,
  it is a defence for him to prove that he disclosed the matters specified in that subsection in accordance with the procedure.

(5) Subsection (2) does not require disclosure by a professional legal adviser of
  (a) information which he obtains in privileged circumstances, or
  (b) a belief or suspicion based on information which he obtains in privileged circumstances.

(6) For the purpose of subsection (5) information is obtained by an adviser in privileged circumstances if it comes to him, otherwise than with a view to furthering a criminal purpose
  (a) from a client or a client's representative, in connection with the provision of legal advice by the adviser to the client,
  (b) from a person seeking legal advice from the adviser, or from the person's representative, or
  (c) from any person, for the purpose of actual or contemplated legal proceedings.

(7) For the purposes of subsection (1)(a) a person shall be treated as having committed an offence under one of sections 15 to 18 if
  (a) he has taken an action or been in possession of a thing, and
  (b) he would have committed an offence under one of those sections if he had been in the United Kingdom at the time when he took the action or was in possession of the thing.

[(7A) The reference to a business in the regulated sector must be construed in accordance with Schedule 3A.

(7B) The reference to a constable includes a reference to a [member of the staff of the Serious Organised Crime Agency][25] authorised for the purposes of this section by the Director General of [that Agency][26][27]

(8) A person guilty of an offence under this section shall be liable
  (a) on conviction on indictment, to imprisonment for a term not exceeding five years, to a fine or to both, or
  (b) on summary conviction, to imprisonment for a term not exceeding six months, or to a fine not exceeding the statutory maximum or to both.

20 Disclosure of information: permission

(1) A person may disclose to a constable
  (a) a suspicion or belief that any money or other property is terrorist property or is derived from terrorist property;
  (b) any matter on which the suspicion or belief is based.

---

[24] Inserted by the Anti-terrorism, Crime and Security Act 2001, s 3, Sch 2, Pt 3, para 5(1), (3).
[25] Substituted by the Serious Organised Crime and Police Act 2005, s 59, Sch 4, paras 125, 126(a).
[26] Substituted by the Serious Organised Crime and Police Act 2005, s 59, Sch 4, paras 125, 126(b).
[27] Inserted by the Anti-terrorism, Crime and Security Act 2001, s 3, Sch 2, Pt 3, para 5(1)(4).

(2) A person may make a disclosure to a constable in the circumstances mentioned in section 19(1) and (2).

(3) Subsections (1) and (2) shall have effect notwithstanding any restriction on the disclosure of information imposed by statute or otherwise.

(4) Where

(a) a person is in employment, and

(b) his employer has established a procedure for the making of disclosures of the kinds mentioned in subsection (1) and section 19(2),

subsections (1) and (2) shall have effect in relation to that person as if any reference to disclosure to a constable included a reference to disclosure in accordance with the procedure.

[(5) References to a constable include references to a [member of the staff of the Serious Organised Crime Agency][28] authorised for the purposes of this section by the Director General of [that Agency][29].][30]

21 Cooperation with police

(1) A person does not commit an offence under any of sections 15 to 18 if he is acting with the express consent of a constable.

(2) Subject to subsections (3) and (4), a person does not commit an offence under any of sections 15 to 18 by involvement in a transaction or arrangement relating to money or other property if he discloses to a constable

(a) his suspicion or belief that the money or other property is terrorist property, and

(b) the information on which his suspicion or belief is based.

(3) Subsection (2) applies only where a person makes a disclosure

(a) after he becomes concerned in the transaction concerned,

(b) on his own initiative, and

(c) as soon as is reasonably practicable.

(4) Subsection (2) does not apply to a person if

(a) a constable forbids him to continue his involvement in the transaction or arrangement to which the disclosure relates, and

(b) he continues his involvement.

(5) It is a defence for a person charged with an offence under any of sections 15(2) and (3) and 16 to 18 to prove that

(a) he intended to make a disclosure of the kind mentioned in subsections (2) and (3), and

(b) there is reasonable excuse for his failure to do so.

(6) Where

(a) a person is in employment, and

(b) his employer has established a procedure for the making of disclosures of the same kind as may be made to a constable under subsection (2),

this section shall have effect in relation to that person as if any reference to disclosure to a constable included a reference to disclosure in accordance with the procedure.

(7) A reference in this section to a transaction or arrangement relating to money or other property includes a reference to use or possession.

[21ZA Arrangements with prior consent

(1) A person does not commit an offence under any of sections 15 to 18 by involvement in a transaction or an arrangement relating to money or other property if, before becoming involved, the person

---

[28] Substituted by the Serious Organised Crime and Police Act 2005, s 59, Sch 4, paras 125, 127(a).

[29] Substituted by the Serious Organised Crime and Police Act 2005, s 59, Sch 4, paras 125, 127(b).

[30] Inserted by the Anti-terrorism, Crime and Security Act 2001, s 3, Sch 2, Pt 3, para 5(1)(5).

(a) discloses to an authorised officer the person's suspicion] or belief that the money or other property is terrorist property and the information on which the suspicion or belief is based, and

(b) has the authorised officer's consent to becoming involved in the transaction or arrangement.

(2) A person is treated as having an authorised officer's consent if before the end of the notice period the person does not receive notice from an authorised officer that consent is refused.

(3) The notice period is the period of 7 working days starting with the first working day after the person makes the disclosure.

(4) A working day is a day other than a Saturday, a Sunday, Christmas Day, Good Friday or a day that is a bank holiday under the Banking and Financial Dealings Act 1971 (c 80) in the part of the United Kingdom in which the person is when making the disclosure.

(5) In this section "authorised officer" means a member of the staff of the Serious Organised Crime Agency authorised for the purposes of this section by the Director General of that Agency.

(6) The reference in this section to a transaction or arrangement relating to money or other property includes a reference to use or possession.][31]

[21ZB Disclosure after entering into arrangements

(1) A person does not commit an offence under any of sections 15 to 18 by involvement in a transaction or an arrangement relating to money or other property if, after becoming involved, the person discloses to an authorised officer

(a) the person's suspicion or belief that the money or other property is terrorist property, and

(b) the information on which the suspicion or belief is based.

(2) This section applies only where

(a) there is a reasonable excuse for the person's failure to make the disclosure before becoming involved in the transaction or arrangement, and

(b) the disclosure is made on the person's own initiative and as soon as it is reasonably practicable for the person to make it.

(3) This section does not apply to a person if

(a) an authorised officer forbids the person to continue involvement in the transaction or arrangement to which the disclosure relates, and

(b) the person continues that involvement.

(4) In this section "authorised officer" means a member of the staff of the Serious Organised Crime Agency authorised for the purposes of this section by the Director General of that Agency.

(5) The reference in this section to a transaction or arrangement relating to money or other property includes a reference to use or possession.][32]

[21ZC Reasonable excuse for failure to disclose

It is a defence for a person charged with an offence under any of sections 15 to 18 to prove that

(a) the person intended to make a disclosure of the kind mentioned in section 21ZA or 21ZB, and

(b) there is a reasonable excuse for the person's failure to do so.][33]

[21A Failure to disclose: regulated sector

(1) A person commits an offence if each of the following three conditions is satisfied.

(2) The first condition is that he

(a) knows or suspects, or

---

[31] Inserted by SI 2007/3398, reg 2, Sch 1, paras 1, 2.
[32] Inserted by SI 2007/3398, reg 2, Sch 1, paras 1, 2.
[33] Inserted by SI 2007/3398, reg 2, Sch 1, paras 1, 2.

    (b) has reasonable grounds for knowing or suspecting,

that another person has committed [or attempted to commit][34] an offence under any of sections 15 to 18.

   (3) The second condition is that the information or other matter

    (a) on which his knowledge or suspicion is based, or

    (b) which gives reasonable grounds for such knowledge or suspicion,

came to him in the course of a business in the regulated sector.

   (4) The third condition is that he does not disclose the information or other matter to a constable or a nominated officer as soon as is practicable after it comes to him.

   (5) But a person does not commit an offence under this section if

    (a) he has a reasonable excuse for not disclosing the information or other matter;

    (b) he is a professional legal adviser [or relevant professional adviser][35] and the information or other matter came to him in privileged circumstances[; or

    (c) subsection (5A) applies to him][36].

[(5A) This subsection applies to a person if

    (a) the person is employed by, or is in partnership with, a professional legal adviser or relevant professional adviser to provide the adviser with assistance or support,

    (b) the information or other matter comes to the person in connection with the provision of such assistance or support, and

    (c) the information or other matter came to the adviser in privileged circumstances.][37]

   (6) In deciding whether a person committed an offence under this section the court must consider whether he followed any relevant guidance which was at the time concerned

    (a) issued by a supervisory authority or any other appropriate body,

    (b) approved by the Treasury, and

    (c) published in a manner it approved as appropriate in its opinion to bring the guidance to the attention of persons likely to be affected by it.

   (7) A disclosure to a nominated officer is a disclosure which

    (a) is made to a person nominated by the alleged offender's employer to receive disclosures under this section, and

    (b) is made in the course of the alleged offender's employment and in accordance with the procedure established by the employer for the purpose.

   (8) Information or other matter comes to a professional legal adviser [or relevant professional adviser][38] in privileged circumstances if it is communicated or given to him

    (a) by (or by a representative of) a client of his in connection with the giving by the adviser of legal advice to the client,

    (b) by (or by a representative of) a person seeking legal advice from the adviser, or

    (c) by a person in connection with legal proceedings or contemplated legal proceedings.

   (9) But subsection (8) does not apply to information or other matter which is communicated or given with a view to furthering a criminal purpose.

 (10) Schedule 3A has effect for the purpose of determining what is

    (a) a business in the regulated sector;

    (b) a supervisory authority.

 (11) For the purposes of subsection (2) a person is to be taken to have committed an offence there mentioned if

    (a) he has taken an action or been in possession of a thing, and

---

[34] Inserted by SI 2007/3398, reg 2, Sch 1, paras 1, 3(1), (2).

[35] Inserted by SI 2007/3398, reg 2, Sch 1, paras 1, 3(1), (3)(a).

[36] Inserted by SI 2007/3398, reg 2, Sch 1, paras 1, 3(1), (3)(b).

[37] Inserted by SI 2007/3398, reg 2, Sch 1, paras 1, 3(1), (4).

[38] Inserted by SI 2007/3398, reg 2, Sch 1, paras 1, 3(1), (5).

(b) he would have committed the offence if he had been in the United Kingdom at the time when he took the action or was in possession of the thing.

(12) A person guilty of an offence under this section is liable

    (a) on conviction on indictment, to imprisonment for a term not exceeding five years or to a fine or to both;

    (b) on summary conviction, to imprisonment for a term not exceeding six months or to a fine not exceeding the statutory maximum or to both.

(13) An appropriate body is any body which regulates or is representative of any trade, profession, business or employment carried on by the alleged offender.

(14) The reference to a constable includes a reference to a [member of the staff of the Serious Organised Crime Agency][39] authorised for the purposes of this section by the Director General of [that Agency][40].

[(15) In this section "relevant professional adviser" means an accountant, auditor or tax adviser who is a member of a professional body which is established for accountants, auditors or tax advisers (as the case may be) and which makes provision for

    (a) testing the competence of those seeking admission to membership of such a body as a condition for such admission; and

    (b) imposing and maintaining professional and ethical standards for its members, as well as imposing sanctions for non-compliance with those standards.][41][42]

[21B Protected disclosures

(1) A disclosure which satisfies the following three conditions is not to be taken to breach any restriction on the disclosure of information (however imposed).

(2) The first condition is that the information or other matter disclosed came to the person making the disclosure (the discloser) in the course of a business in the regulated sector.

(3) The second condition is that the information or other matter

    (a) causes the discloser to know or suspect, or

    (b) gives him reasonable grounds for knowing or suspecting,

that another person has committed [or attempted to commit][43] an offence under any of sections 15 to 18.

(4) The third condition is that the disclosure is made to a constable or a nominated officer as soon as is practicable after the information or other matter comes to the discloser.

(5) A disclosure to a nominated officer is a disclosure which

    (a) is made to a person nominated by the discloser's employer to receive disclosures under this section, and

    (b) is made in the course of the discloser's employment and in accordance with the procedure established by the employer for the purpose.

(6) The reference to a business in the regulated sector must be construed in accordance with Schedule 3A.

(7) The reference to a constable includes a reference to a [member of the staff of the Serious Organised Crime Agency][44] authorised for the purposes of this section by the Director General of [that Agency][45].][46]

---

[39] Substituted by the Serious Organised Crime and Police Act 2005, s 59, Sch 4, paras 125, 128(a).

[40] Substituted by the Serious Organised Crime and Police Act 2005, s 59, Sch 4, paras 125, 128(b).

[41] Inserted by SI 2007/3398, reg 2, Sch 1, paras 1, 3(1), (6).

[42] Inserted by the Anti-terrorism, Crime and Security Act 2001, s 3, Sch 2, Pt 3, para 5(1), (2).

[43] Inserted by SI 2007/3398, reg 2, Sch 1, paras 1, 4.

[44] Substituted by the Serious Organised Crime and Police Act 2005, s 59, Sch 4, paras 125, 129(a).

[45] Substituted by the Serious Organised Crime and Police Act 2005, s 59, Sch 4, paras 125, 128(b).

[46] Inserted by the Anti-terrorism, Crime and Security Act 2001, s 3, Sch 2, Pt 3, para 5(1)(2).

[21C Disclosures to SOCA

(1) Where a disclosure is made under a provision of this Part to a constable, the constable must disclose it in full as soon as practicable after it has been made to a member of staff of the Serious Organised Crime Agency authorised for the purposes of that provision by the Director General of that Agency.

(2) Where a disclosure is made under section 21 (cooperation with police) to a constable, the constable must disclose it in full as soon as practicable after it has been made to a member of staff of the Serious Organised Crime Agency authorised for the purposes of this subsection by the Director General of that Agency.][47]

[21D Tipping off: regulated sector

(1) A person commits an offence if
   (a) the person discloses any matter within subsection (2);
   (b) the disclosure is likely to prejudice any investigation that might be conducted following the disclosure referred to in that subsection; and
   (c) the information on which the disclosure is based came to the person in the course of a business in the regulated sector.

(2) The matters are that the person or another person has made a disclosure under a provision of this Part
   (a) to a constable,
   (b) in accordance with a procedure established by that person's employer for the making of disclosures under that provision,
   (c) to a nominated officer, or
   (d) to a member of staff of the Serious Organised Crime Agency authorised for the purposes of that provision by the Director General of that Agency,
of information that came to that person in the course of a business in the regulated sector.

(3) A person commits an offence if
   (a) the person discloses that an investigation into allegations that an offence under this Part has been committed is being contemplated or is being carried out;
   (b) the disclosure is likely to prejudice that investigation; and
   (c) the information on which the disclosure is based came to the person in the course of a business in the regulated sector.

(4) A person guilty of an offence under this section is liable
   (a) on summary conviction to imprisonment for a term not exceeding three months, or to a fine not exceeding level 5 on the standard scale, or to both;
   (b) on conviction on indictment to imprisonment for a term not exceeding two years, or to a fine, or to both.

(5) This section is subject to
   (a) section 21E (disclosures within an undertaking or group etc),
   (b) section 21F (other permitted disclosures between institutions etc), and
   (c) section 21G (other permitted disclosures etc).][48]

[21E Disclosures within an undertaking or group etc

(1) An employee, officer or partner of an undertaking does not commit an offence under section 21D if the disclosure is to an employee, officer or partner of the same undertaking.

(2) A person does not commit an offence under section 21D in respect of a disclosure by a credit institution or a financial institution if

---

[47] Inserted by SI 2007/3398, reg 2, Sch 1, paras 1, 5.
[48] Inserted by SI 2007/3398, reg 2, Sch 1, paras 1, 5.

(a) the disclosure is to a credit institution or a financial institution,

(b) the institution to whom the disclosure is made is situated in an EEA State or in a country or territory imposing equivalent money laundering requirements, and

(c) both the institution making the disclosure and the institution to whom it is made belong to the same group.

(3) In subsection (2) "group" has the same meaning as in Directive 2002/87/EC of the European Parliament and of the Council of 16th December 2002 on the supplementary supervision of credit institutions, insurance undertakings and investment firms in a financial conglomerate.

(4) A professional legal adviser or a relevant professional adviser does not commit an offence under section 21D if

(a) the disclosure is to a professional legal adviser or a relevant professional adviser,

(b) both the person making the disclosure and the person to whom it is made carry on business in an EEA state or in a country or territory imposing equivalent money laundering requirements, and

(c) those persons perform their professional activities within different undertakings that share common ownership, management or control.][49]

[21F Other permitted disclosures between institutions etc

(1) This section applies to a disclosure

(a) by a credit institution to another credit institution,

(b) by a financial institution to another financial institution,

(c) by a professional legal adviser to another professional legal adviser, or

(d) by a relevant professional adviser of a particular kind to another relevant professional adviser of the same kind.

(2) A person does not commit an offence under section 21D in respect of a disclosure to which this section applies if

(a) the disclosure relates to

(i) a client or former client of the institution or adviser making the disclosure and the institution or adviser to whom it is made,

(ii) a transaction involving them both, or

(iii) the provision of a service involving them both;

(b) the disclosure is for the purpose only of preventing an offence under this Part of this Act;

(c) the institution or adviser to whom the disclosure is made is situated in an EEA State or in a country or territory imposing equivalent money laundering requirements; and

(d) the institution or adviser making the disclosure and the institution or adviser to whom it is made are subject to equivalent duties of professional confidentiality and the protection of personal data (within the meaning of section 1 of the Data Protection Act 1998).][50]

[21G Other permitted disclosures etc

(1) A person does not commit an offence under section 21D if the disclosure is

(a) to the authority that is the supervisory authority for that person by virtue of the Money Laundering Regulations 2007 (SI 2007/2157); or

(b) for the purpose of

(i) the detection, investigation or prosecution of a criminal offence (whether in the United Kingdom or elsewhere),

(ii) an investigation under the Proceeds of Crime Act 2002, or

(iii) the enforcement of any order of a court under that Act.

---

[49] Inserted by SI 2007/3398, reg 2, Sch 1, paras 1, 5.
[50] Inserted by SI 2007/3398, reg 2, Sch 1, paras 1, 5.

(2) A professional legal adviser or a relevant professional adviser does not commit an offence under section 21D if the disclosure

(a) is to the adviser's client, and

(b) is made for the purpose of dissuading the client from engaging in conduct amounting to an offence.

(3) A person does not commit an offence under section 21D(1) if the person does not know or suspect that the disclosure is likely to have the effect mentioned in section 21D(1)(b).

(4) A person does not commit an offence under section 21D(3) if the person does not know or suspect that the disclosure is likely to have the effect mentioned in section 21D(3)(b).][51]

[21H Interpretation of sections 21D to 21G

(1) The references in sections 21D to 21G

(a) to a business in the regulated sector, and

(b) to a supervisory authority,

are to be construed in accordance with Schedule 3A.

(2) In those sections

"credit institution" has the same meaning as in Schedule 3A;

"financial institution" means an undertaking that carries on a business in the regulated sector by virtue of any of paragraphs (b) to (i) of paragraph 1(1) of that Schedule.

(3) References in those sections to a disclosure by or to a credit institution or a financial institution include disclosure by or to an employee, officer or partner of the institution acting on its behalf.

(4) For the purposes of those sections a country or territory imposes "equivalent money laundering requirements" if it imposes requirements equivalent to those laid down in Directive 2005/60/EC of the European Parliament and of the Council of 26th October 2005 on the prevention of the use of the financial system for the purpose of money laundering and terrorist financing.

(5) In those sections "relevant professional adviser" means an accountant, auditor or tax adviser who is a member of a professional body which is established for accountants, auditors or tax advisers (as the case may be) and which makes provision for

(a) testing the competence of those seeking admission to membership of such a body as a condition for such admission; and

(b) imposing and maintaining professional and ethical standards for its members, as well as imposing sanctions for non-compliance with those standards.][52]

22 Penalties

A person guilty of an offence under any of sections 15 to 18 shall be liable

(a) on conviction on indictment, to imprisonment for a term not exceeding 14 years, to a fine or to both, or

(b) on summary conviction, to imprisonment for a term not exceeding six months, to a fine not exceeding the statutory maximum or to both.

[22A Meaning of "employment"

In sections 19 to 21B

(a) "employment" means any employment (whether paid or unpaid) and includes

(i) work under a contract for services or as an office-holder,

---

[51] Inserted by SI 2007/3398, reg 2, Sch 1, paras 1, 5.
[52] Inserted by SI 2007/3398, reg 2, Sch 1, paras 1, 5.

   (ii) work experience provided pursuant to a training course or programme or in the course of training for employment, and

   (iii) voluntary work;

(b) "employer" has a corresponding meaning.][53]

23 Forfeiture

(1) *The court by or before which a person is convicted of an offence under any of sections 15 to 18 may make a forfeiture order in accordance with the provisions of this section.*

(2) *Where a person is convicted of an offence under section 15(1) or (2) or 16 the court may order the forfeiture of any money or other property*

   (a) *which, at the time of the offence, he had in his possession or under his control, and*

   (b) *which, at that time, he intended should be used, or had reasonable cause to suspect might be used, for the purposes of terrorism.*

(3) *Where a person is convicted of an offence under section 15(3) the court may order the for-feiture of any money or other property*

   (a) *which, at the time of the offence, he had in his possession or under his control, and*

   (b) *which, at that time, he knew or had reasonable cause to suspect would or might be used for the purposes of terrorism.*

(4) *Where a person is convicted of an offence under section 17 the court may order the forfeiture of the money or other property*

   (a) *to which the arrangement in question related, and*

   (b) *which, at the time of the offence, he knew or had reasonable cause to suspect would or might be used for the purposes of terrorism.*

(5) *Where a person is convicted of an offence under section 18 the court may order the forfeiture of the money or other property to which the arrangement in question related.*

(6) *Where a person is convicted of an offence under any of sections 15 to 18, the court may order the forfeiture of any money or other property which wholly or partly, and directly or indirectly, is received by any person as a payment or other reward in connection with the commission of the offence.*

(7) *Where a person other than the convicted person claims to be the owner of or otherwise interested in anything which can be forfeited by an order under this section, the court shall give him an opportunity to be heard before making an order.*

(8) *A court in Scotland shall not make an order under this section except on the application of the prosecutor*

   (a) *in proceedings on indictment, when he moves for sentence, and*

   (b) *in summary proceedings, before the court convicts the accused,*

   and for the purposes of any appeal or review, an order under this section made by a court in Scotland is a sentence.

(9) *Schedule 4 (which makes further provision in relation to forfeiture orders under this section) shall have effect.*[54]

[23 Forfeiture: terrorist property offences

(1) *The court by or before which a person is convicted of an offence under any of sections 15 to 18 may make a forfeiture order in accordance with the provisions of this section.*

(2) *Where a person is convicted of an offence under section 15(1) or (2) or 16, the court may order the forfeiture of any money or other property which, at the time of the offence, the person had in their possession or under their control and which*

   (a) *had been used for the purposes of terrorism, or*

   (b) *they intended should be used, or had reasonable cause to suspect might be used, for those purposes.*

---

[53] Inserted by the Counter-Terrorism Act 2008, s 77(1), (3).

[54] Repealed by the Counter-Terrorism Act 2008, s 34, not yet in force.

(3) *Where a person is convicted of an offence under section 15(3) the court may order the forfeiture of any money or other property which, at the time of the offence, the person had in their possession or under their control and which*

    (a) *had been used for the purposes of terrorism, or*

    (b) *which, at that time, they knew or had reasonable cause to suspect would or might be used for those purposes.*

(4) *Where a person is convicted of an offence under section 17 or 18 the court may order the forfeiture of any money or other property which, at the time of the offence, the person had in their possession or under their control and which*

    (a) *had been used for the purposes of terrorism, or*

    (b) *was, at that time, intended by them to be used for those purposes.*

(5) *Where a person is convicted of an offence under section 17 the court may order the forfeiture of the money or other property to which the arrangement in question related, and which*

    (a) *had been used for the purposes of terrorism, or*

    (b) *at the time of the offence, the person knew or had reasonable cause to suspect would or might be used for those purposes.*

(6) *Where a person is convicted of an offence under section 18 the court may order the forfeiture of the money or other property to which the arrangement in question related.*

(7) *Where a person is convicted of an offence under any of sections 15 to 18, the court may order the forfeiture of any money or other property which wholly or partly, and directly or indirectly, is received by any person as a payment or other reward in connection with the commission of the offence.]*[55]

[23A Forfeiture: other terrorism offences and offences with a terrorist connection

(1) *The court by or before which a person is convicted of an offence to which this section applies may order the forfeiture of any money or other property in relation to which the following conditions are met*

    (a) *that it was, at the time of the offence, in the possession or control of the person convicted; and*

    (b) *that*

        (i)   *it had been used for the purposes of terrorism,*

        (ii) *it was intended by that person that it should be used for the purposes of terrorism, or*

        (iii) *the court believes that it will be used for the purposes of terrorism unless forfeited.*

(2) *This section applies to an offence under*

    (a) *any of the following provisions of this Act*

        section 54 (weapons training);

        section 57, 58 or 58A (possessing things and collecting information for the purposes of terrorism);

        section 59, 60 or 61 (inciting terrorism outside the United Kingdom);

    (b) *any of the following provisions of Part 1 of the Terrorism Act 2006 (c 11)*

        section 2 (dissemination of terrorist publications);

        section 5 (preparation of terrorist acts);

        section 6 (training for terrorism);

        sections 9 to 11 (offences involving radioactive devices or materials).

(3) *This section applies to any ancillary offence (as defined in section 94 of the Counter-Terrorism Act 2008) in relation to an offence listed in subsection (2).*

(4) *This section also applies to an offence specified in Schedule 2 to the Counter-Terrorism Act 2008 (offences where terrorist connection to be considered) as to which*

    (a) *in England and Wales, the court dealing with the offence has determined, in accordance with section 30 of that Act, that the offence has a terrorist connection;*

---

[55] Substituted by the Counter-Terrorism Act 2008, s 34, not yet in force.

(b) in Scotland, it has been proved, in accordance with section 31 of that Act, that the offence has a terrorist connection.

(5) The Secretary of State may by order amend subsection (2).

(6) An order adding an offence to subsection (2) applies only in relation to offences committed after the order comes into force.]⁵⁶

[23B Forfeiture: supplementary provisions

(1) Before making an order under section 23 or 23A, a court must give an opportunity to be heard to any person, other than the convicted person, who claims to be the owner or otherwise interested in anything which can be forfeited under that section.

(2) In considering whether to make an order under section 23 or 23A in respect of any property, a court shall have regard to
   (a) the value of the property, and
   (b) the likely financial and other effects on the convicted person of the making of the order (taken together with any other order that the court contemplates making).

(3) A court in Scotland must not make an order under section 23 or 23A except on the application of the prosecutor
   (a) in proceedings on indictment, when the prosecutor moves for sentence, and
   (b) in summary proceedings, before the court sentences the accused;
   and for the purposes of any appeal or review, an order under either of those sections made by a court in Scotland is a sentence.

(4) Schedule 4 makes further provision in relation to forfeiture orders under section 23 or 23A.]⁵⁷

24 to 31 [...]⁵⁸

PART IV
TERRORIST INVESTIGATIONS

Interpretation

32 Terrorist investigation

In this Act "terrorist investigation" means an investigation of
(a) the commission, preparation or instigation of acts of terrorism,
(b) an act which appears to have been done for the purposes of terrorism,
(c) the resources of a proscribed organisation,
(d) the possibility of making an order under section 3(3), or
(e) the commission, preparation or instigation of an offence under this Act [or under Part 1 of the Terrorism Act 2006 other than an offence under section 1 or 2 of that Act]⁵⁹.

Cordons

33 Cordoned areas

(1) An area is a cordoned area for the purposes of this Act if it is designated under this section.

(2) A designation may be made only if the person making it considers it expedient for the purposes of a terrorist investigation.

---

⁵⁶ Inserted by the Counter-Terrorism Act 2008, s 35(1), not in force.
⁵⁷ Inserted by the Counter-Terrorism Act 2008, s 36, not in force.
⁵⁸ Repealed by the Anti-terrorism, Crime and Security Act 2001, ss 1(4), 125, Sch 8, Pt 1.
⁵⁹ Inserted by the Terrorism Act 2006, s 37(1).

(3) If a designation is made orally, the person making it shall confirm it in writing as soon as is reasonably practicable.

(4) The person making a designation shall arrange for the demarcation of the cordoned area, so far as is reasonably practicable

    (a) by means of tape marked with the word "police", or

    (b) in such other manner as a constable considers appropriate.

34 Power to designate

(1) Subject to [subsections (1A), (1B) and (2)],[60] a designation under section 33 may only be made

    (a) where the area is outside Northern Ireland and is wholly or partly within a police area, by an officer for the police area who is of at least the rank of superintendent, and

    (b) where the area is in Northern Ireland, by a [member of the Police Service of Northern Ireland][61] who is of at least the rank of superintendent.

[[(1A) A designation under section 33 may be made in relation to an area (outside Northern Ireland) which is in a place specified in section 31(1)(a) to (f) of the Railways and Transport Safety Act, by a member of the British Transport Police Force who is of at least the rank of superintendent.][62]

(1B) A designation under section 33 may be made by a member of the Ministry of Defence Police who is of at least the rank of superintendent in relation to an area outside or in Northern Ireland

    (a) if it is a place to which subsection (2) of section 2 of the Ministry of Defence Police Act 1987 (c 4) applies,

    (b) if a request has been made under paragraph (a), (b) or (d) of subsection (3A) of that section in relation to a terrorist investigation and it is a place where he has the powers and privileges of a constable by virtue of that subsection as a result of the request, or

    [(c) if a request has been made under paragraph (c) of that subsection in relation to a terrorist investigation and it is a place described in subsection 1A of this section.][63]

(1C) But a designation under section 33 may not be made by

    (a) a member of the British Transport Police Force, or

    (b) a member of the Ministry of Defence Police,

in any other case.][64]

(2) A constable who is not of the rank required by subsection (1) may make a designation if he considers it necessary by reason of urgency.

(3) Where a constable makes a designation in reliance on subsection (2) he shall as soon as is reasonably practicable

    (a) make a written record of the time at which the designation was made, and

    (b) ensure that a police officer of at least the rank of superintendent is informed.

(4) An officer who is informed of a designation in accordance with subsection (3)(b)

    (a) shall confirm the designation or cancel it with effect from such time as he may direct, and

    (b) shall, if he cancels the designation, make a written record of the cancellation and the reason for it.

35 Duration

(1) A designation under section 33 has effect, subject to subsections (2) to (5), during the period

    (a) beginning at the time when it is made, and

    (b) ending with a date or at a time specified in the designation.

---

[60] Substituted by the Anti-terrorism, Crime and Security Act 2001, s 101, Sch 7, paras 29, 30(1), (2).
[61] Substituted by the Police (Northern Ireland) Act 2000, s 78(2)(c).
[62] Substituted by SI 2004/1573, art 12(6)(a).
[63] Substituted by SI 2004/1573, art 12(6)(b).
[64] Inserted by the Anti-terrorism, Crime and Security Act 2001, s 101, Sch 7, paras 29, 30(1), (3).

(2) The date or time specified under subsection (1)(b) must not occur after the end of the period of 14 days beginning with the day on which the designation is made.

(3) The period during which a designation has effect may be extended in writing from time to time by
    (a) the person who made it, or
    (b) a person who could have made it (otherwise than by virtue of section 34(2)).

(4) An extension shall specify the additional period during which the designation is to have effect.

(5) A designation shall not have effect after the end of the period of 28 days beginning with the day on which it is made.

36 Police powers

(1) A constable in uniform may
    (a) order a person in a cordoned area to leave it immediately;
    (b) order a person immediately to leave premises which are wholly or partly in or adjacent to a cordoned area;
    (c) order the driver or person in charge of a vehicle in a cordoned area to move it from the area immediately;
    (d) arrange for the removal of a vehicle from a cordoned area;
    (e) arrange for the movement of a vehicle within a cordoned area;
    (f) prohibit or restrict access to a cordoned area by pedestrians or vehicles.

(2) A person commits an offence if he fails to comply with an order, prohibition or restriction imposed by virtue of subsection (1).

(3) It is a defence for a person charged with an offence under subsection (2) to prove that he had a reasonable excuse for his failure.

(4) A person guilty of an offence under subsection (2) shall be liable on summary conviction to
    (a) imprisonment for a term not exceeding *three months*[65] *(51 weeks)*,[66]
    (b) a fine not exceeding level 4 on the standard scale, or
    (c) both.

Information and evidence

37 Powers

Schedule 5 (power to obtain information, &c) shall have effect.

38 Financial information

Schedule 6 (financial information) shall have effect.

[38A Account monitoring orders

Schedule 6A (account monitoring orders) shall have effect.][67]

[38B Information about acts of terrorism

(1) This section applies where a person has information which he knows or believes might be of material assistance
    (a) in preventing the commission by another person of an act of terrorism, or
    (b) in securing the apprehension, prosecution or conviction of another person, in the United Kingdom, for an offence involving the commission, preparation or instigation of an act of terrorism.

---

[65] Repealed by the Criminal Justice Act 2003, s 280(2), (3), Sch 26, para 55(1), (2), not yet in force.
[66] Substituted by the Criminal Justice Act 2003, s 280(2), (3), Sch 26, para 55(1), (2), not yet in force.
[67] Inserted by the Anti-terrorism, Crime and Security Act 2001, s 3, Sch 2, Pt 1, para 1(1), (2).

(2) The person commits an offence if he does not disclose the information as soon as reasonably practicable in accordance with subsection (3).

(3) Disclosure is in accordance with this subsection if it is made
   (a) in England and Wales, to a constable,
   (b) in Scotland, to a constable, or
   (c) in Northern Ireland, to a constable or a member of Her Majesty's forces.

(4) It is a defence for a person charged with an offence under subsection (2) to prove that he had a reasonable excuse for not making the disclosure.

(5) A person guilty of an offence under this section shall be liable
   (a) on conviction on indictment, to imprisonment for a term not exceeding five years, or to a fine or to both, or
   (b) on summary conviction, to imprisonment for a term not exceeding six months, or to a fine not exceeding the statutory maximum or to both.

(6) Proceedings for an offence under this section may be taken, and the offence may for the purposes of those proceedings be treated as having been committed, in any place where the person to be charged is or has at any time been since he first knew or believed that the information might be of material assistance as mentioned in subsection (1).][68]

39 Disclosure of information, &c

(1) Subsection (2) applies where a person knows or has reasonable cause to suspect that a constable is conducting or proposes to conduct a terrorist investigation.

(2) The person commits an offence if he
   (a) discloses to another anything which is likely to prejudice the investigation, or
   (b) interferes with material which is likely to be relevant to the investigation.

(3) Subsection (4) applies where a person knows or has reasonable cause to suspect that a disclosure has been or will be made under any of sections 19 [to 21B][69] [or 38B.][70]

(4) The person commits an offence if he
   (a) discloses to another anything which is likely to prejudice an investigation resulting from the disclosure under that section, or
   (b) interferes with material which is likely to be relevant to an investigation resulting from the disclosure under that section.

(5) It is a defence for a person charged with an offence under subsection (2) or (4) to prove
   (a) that he did not know and had no reasonable cause to suspect that the disclosure or interference was likely to affect a terrorist investigation, or
   (b) that he had a reasonable excuse for the disclosure or interference.

(6) Subsections (2) and (4) do not apply to a disclosure which is made by a professional legal adviser
   (a) to his client or to his client's representative in connection with the provision of legal advice by the adviser to the client and not with a view to furthering a criminal purpose, or
   (b) to any person for the purpose of actual or contemplated legal proceedings and not with a view to furthering a criminal purpose.

[(6A) Subsections (2) and (4) do not apply if
   (a) the disclosure is of a matter within section 21D(2) or (3)(a) (terrorist property: tipping off), and
   (b) the information on which the disclosure is based came to the person in the course of a business in the regulated sector.][71]

---

[68] Inserted by the Anti-terrorism, Crime and Security Act 2001, s 117(1), (2).
[69] Substituted by SI 2007/3398, reg 2, Sch 1, paras 1, 6(1), (2).
[70] Inserted by the Anti-terrorism, Crime and Security Act 2001, s 117(1), (3).
[71] Inserted by SI 2007/3398, reg 2, Sch 1, paras 1, 6(1), (3).

(7) A person guilty of an offence under this section shall be liable

  (a) on conviction on indictment, to imprisonment for a term not exceeding five years, to a fine or to both, or

  (b) on summary conviction, to imprisonment for a term not exceeding six months, to a fine not exceeding the statutory maximum or to both.

(8) For the purposes of this section

  (a) a reference to conducting a terrorist investigation includes a reference to taking part in the conduct of, or assisting, a terrorist investigation, and

  (b) a person interferes with material if he falsifies it, conceals it, destroys it or disposes of it, or if he causes or permits another to do any of those things.

[(9) The reference in subsection (6A) to a business in the regulated sector is to be construed in accordance with Schedule 3A.][72]

PART V
COUNTER-TERRORIST POWERS

Suspected terrorists

40 Terrorist: interpretation

(1) In this Part "terrorist" means a person who

  (a) has committed an offence under any of sections 11, 12, 15 to 18, 54 and 56 to 63, or

  (b) is or has been concerned in the commission, preparation or instigation of acts of terrorism.

(2) The reference in subsection (1)(b) to a person who has been concerned in the commission, preparation or instigation of acts of terrorism includes a reference to a person who has been, whether before or after the passing of this Act, concerned in the commission, preparation or instigation of acts of terrorism within the meaning given by section 1.

41 Arrest without warrant

(1) A constable may arrest without a warrant a person whom he reasonably suspects to be a terrorist.

(2) Where a person is arrested under this section the provisions of Schedule 8 (detention: treatment, review and extension) shall apply.

(3) Subject to subsections (4) to (7), a person detained under this section shall (unless detained under any other power) be released not later than the end of the period of 48 hours beginning

  (a) with the time of his arrest under this section, or

  (b) if he was being detained under Schedule 7 when he was arrested under this section, with the time when his examination under that Schedule began.

(4) If on a review of a person's detention under Part II of Schedule 8 the review officer does not authorise continued detention, the person shall (unless detained in accordance with subsection (5) or (6) or under any other power) be released.

(5) Where a police officer intends to make an application for a warrant under paragraph 29 of Schedule 8 extending a person's detention, the person may be detained pending the making of the application.

(6) Where an application has been made under paragraph 29 or 36 of Schedule 8 in respect of a person's detention, he may be detained pending the conclusion of proceedings on the application.

---

[72] Inserted by SI 2007/3398, reg 2, Sch 1, paras 1, 6(1), (4).

(7) Where an application under paragraph 29 or 36 of Schedule 8 is granted in respect of a person's detention, he may be detained, subject to paragraph 37 of that Schedule, during the period specified in the warrant.

(8) The refusal of an application in respect of a person's detention under paragraph 29 or 36 of Schedule 8 shall not prevent his continued detention in accordance with this section.

(9) A person who has the powers of a constable in one Part of the United Kingdom may exercise the power under subsection (1) in any Part of the United Kingdom.

42 Search of premises

(1) A justice of the peace may on the application of a constable issue a warrant in relation to specified premises if he is satisfied that there are reasonable grounds for suspecting that a person whom the constable reasonably suspects to be a person falling within section 40(1)(b) is to be found there.

(2) A warrant under this section shall authorise any constable to enter and search the specified premises for the purpose of arresting the person referred to in subsection (1) under section 41.

(3) In the application of subsection (1) to Scotland
   (a) "justice of the peace" includes the sheriff, and
   (b) the justice of the peace or sheriff can be satisfied as mentioned in that subsection only by having heard evidence on oath.

43 Search of persons

(1) A constable may stop and search a person whom he reasonably suspects to be a terrorist to discover whether he has in his possession anything which may constitute evidence that he is a terrorist.

(2) A constable may search a person arrested under section 41 to discover whether he has in his possession anything which may constitute evidence that he is a terrorist.

(3) A search of a person under this section must be carried out by someone of the same sex.

(4) A constable may seize and retain anything which he discovers in the course of a search of a person under subsection (1) or (2) and which he reasonably suspects may constitute evidence that the person is a terrorist.

(5) A person who has the powers of a constable in one Part of the United Kingdom may exercise a power under this section in any Part of the United Kingdom.

Power to stop and search

44 Authorisations

(1) An authorisation under this subsection authorises any constable in uniform to stop a vehicle in an area or at a place specified in the authorisation and to search
   (a) the vehicle;
   (b) the driver of the vehicle;
   (c) a passenger in the vehicle;
   (d) anything in or on the vehicle or carried by the driver or a passenger.

(2) An authorisation under this subsection authorises any constable in uniform to stop a pedestrian in an area or at a place specified in the authorisation and to search
   (a) the pedestrian;
   (b) anything carried by him.

(3) An authorisation under subsection (1) or (2) may be given only if the person giving it considers it expedient for the prevention of acts of terrorism.

(4)   An authorisation may be given
    (a) where the specified area or place is the whole or part of a police area outside Northern Ireland other than one mentioned in paragraph (b) or (c), by a police officer for the area who is of at least the rank of assistant chief constable;
    (b) where the specified area or place is the whole or part of the metropolitan police district, by a police officer for the district who is of at least the rank of commander of the metropolitan police;
    (c) where the specified area or place is the whole or part of the City of London, by a police officer for the City who is of at least the rank of commander in the City of London police force;
    (d) where the specified area or place is the whole or part of Northern Ireland, by a [member of the Police Service of Northern Ireland][73] who is of at least the rank of assistant chief constable.

[(4ZA) The power of a person mentioned in subsection (4) to give an authorisation specifying an area or place so mentioned includes power to give such an authorisation specifying such an area or place together with
    (a) the internal waters adjacent to that area or place; or
    (b) such area of those internal waters as is specified in the authorisation.][74]

[[(4A) In a case (within subsection (4)(a), (b) or (c)) in which the specified area or place is in a place described in section 34(1A), an authorisation may also be given by a member of the British Transport Police Force who is of at least the rank of assistant chief constable.][75]

(4B)   In a case in which the specified area or place is a place to which section 2(2) of the Ministry of Defence Police Act 1987 applies, an authorisation may also be given by a member of the Ministry of Defence Police who is of at least the rank of assistant chief constable.

[(4BA) In a case in which the specified area or place is a place in which members of the Civil Nuclear Constabulary have the powers and privileges of a constable, an authorisation may also be given by a member of that Constabulary who is of at least the rank of assistant chief constable.][76]

(4C)   But an authorisation may not be given by
    (a) a member of the British Transport Police Force, [...][77]
    (b) a member of the Ministry of Defence Police, [or
    (c) a member of the Civil Nuclear Constabulary,][78]
    in any other case.][79]

(5)   If an authorisation is given orally, the person giving it shall confirm it in writing as soon as is reasonably practicable.

[(5A)   In this section
    'driver', in relation to an aircraft, hovercraft or vessel, means the captain, pilot or other person with control of the aircraft, hovercraft or vessel or any member of its crew and, in relation to a train, includes any member of its crew;
    'internal waters' means waters in the United Kingdom that are not comprised in any police area.][80]

---

[73] Substituted by the Police (Northern Ireland) Act 2000, s 78(2)(c).
[74] Inserted by the Terrorism Act 2006, s 30(1), (2).
[75] Substituted by SI 2004/1573, art 12(6)(c).
[76] Inserted by the Energy Act 2004, s 57(1), (2)(a).
[77] Repealed by the Energy Act 2004, s 197(9), Sch 23, Pt 1.
[78] Inserted by the Energy Act 2004, s 57(1), (2)(b).
[79] Inserted by the Anti-terrorism, Crime and Security Act 2001, s 101, Sch 7, paras 29, 31.
[80] Inserted by the Terrorism Act 2006, s 30(1), (3).

45 Exercise of power

(1) The power conferred by an authorisation under section 44(1) or (2)

    (a) may be exercised only for the purpose of searching for articles of a kind which could be used in connection with terrorism, and

    (b) may be exercised whether or not the constable has grounds for suspecting the presence of articles of that kind.

(2) A constable may seize and retain an article which he discovers in the course of a search by virtue of section 44(1) or (2) and which he reasonably suspects is intended to be used in connection with terrorism.

(3) A constable exercising the power conferred by an authorisation may not require a person to remove any clothing in public except for headgear, footwear, an outer coat, a jacket or gloves.

(4) Where a constable proposes to search a person or vehicle by virtue of section 44(1) or (2) he may detain the person or vehicle for such time as is reasonably required to permit the search to be carried out at or near the place where the person or vehicle is stopped.

(5) Where

    (a) a vehicle or pedestrian is stopped by virtue of section 44(1) or (2), and

    (b) the driver of the vehicle or the pedestrian applies for a written statement that the vehicle was stopped, or that he was stopped, by virtue of section 44(1) or (2),

the written statement shall be provided.

(6) An application under subsection (5) must be made within the period of 12 months beginning with the date on which the vehicle or pedestrian was stopped.

[(7) In this section 'driver' has the same meaning as in section 44.][81]

46 Duration of authorisation

(1) An authorisation under section 44 has effect, subject to subsections (2) to (7), during the period

    (a) beginning at the time when the authorisation is given, and

    (b) ending with a date or at a time specified in the authorisation.

(2) The date or time specified under subsection (1)(b) must not occur after the end of the period of 28 days beginning with the day on which the authorisation is given.

[(2A) An authorisation under section 44(4BA) does not have effect except in relation to times when the specified area or place is a place where members of the Civil Nuclear Constabulary have the powers and privileges of a constable.][82]

(3) The person who gives an authorisation shall inform the Secretary of State as soon as is reasonably practicable.

(4) If an authorisation is not confirmed by the Secretary of State before the end of the period of 48 hours beginning with the time when it is given

    (a) it shall cease to have effect at the end of that period, but

    (b) its ceasing to have effect shall not affect the lawfulness of anything done in reliance on it before the end of that period.

(5) Where the Secretary of State confirms an authorisation he may substitute an earlier date or time for the date or time specified under subsection (1)(b).

(6) The Secretary of State may cancel an authorisation with effect from a specified time.

(7) An authorisation may be renewed in writing by the person who gave it or by a person who could have given it; and subsections (1) to (6) shall apply as if a new authorisation were given on each occasion on which the authorisation is renewed.

---

[81] Inserted by the Terrorism Act 2006, s 30(1), (4).
[82] Inserted by the Energy Act 2004, s 57(1), (3).

47 Offences

(1) A person commits an offence if he
  (a) fails to stop a vehicle when required to do so by a constable in the exercise of the power conferred by an authorisation under section 44(1);
  (b) fails to stop when required to do so by a constable in the exercise of the power conferred by an authorisation under section 44(2);
  (c) wilfully obstructs a constable in the exercise of the power conferred by an authorisation under section 44(1) or (2).
(2) A person guilty of an offence under this section shall be liable on summary conviction to
  (a) imprisonment for a term not exceeding six months,
  (b) a fine not exceeding level 5 on the standard scale, or
  (c) both.

Parking

48 Authorisations

(1) An authorisation under this section authorises any constable in uniform to prohibit or restrict the parking of vehicles on a road specified in the authorisation.
(2) An authorisation may be given only if the person giving it considers it expedient for the prevention of acts of terrorism.
(3) An authorisation may be given
  (a) where the road specified is outside Northern Ireland and is wholly or partly within a police area other than one mentioned in paragraphs (b) or (c), by a police officer for the area who is of at least the rank of assistant chief constable;
  (b) where the road specified is wholly or partly in the metropolitan police district, by a police officer for the district who is of at least the rank of commander of the metropolitan police;
  (c) where the road specified is wholly or partly in the City of London, by a police officer for the City who is of at least the rank of commander in the City of London police force;
  (d) where the road specified is in Northern Ireland, by a [member of the Police Service of Northern Ireland][83] who is of at least the rank of assistant chief constable.
(4) If an authorisation is given orally, the person giving it shall confirm it in writing as soon as is reasonably practicable.

49 Exercise of power

(1) The power conferred by an authorisation under section 48 shall be exercised by placing a traffic sign on the road concerned.
(2) A constable exercising the power conferred by an authorisation under section 48 may suspend a parking place.
(3) Where a parking place is suspended under subsection (2), the suspension shall be treated as a restriction imposed by virtue of section 48
  (a) for the purposes of section 99 of the Road Traffic Regulation Act 1984 (removal of vehicles illegally parked, &c) and of any regulations in force under that section, and
  (b) for the purposes of Articles 47 and 48 of the Road Traffic Regulation (Northern Ireland) Order 1997 (in relation to Northern Ireland).

---

[83] Substituted by the Police (Northern Ireland) Act 2000, s 78(2)(c).

50 Duration of authorisation

(1) An authorisation under section 48 has effect, subject to subsections (2) and (3), during the period specified in the authorisation.

(2) The period specified shall not exceed 28 days.

(3) An authorisation may be renewed in writing by the person who gave it or by a person who could have given it; and subsections (1) and (2) shall apply as if a new authorisation were given on each occasion on which the authorisation is renewed.

51 Offences

(1) A person commits an offence if he parks a vehicle in contravention of a prohibition or restriction imposed by virtue of section 48.

(2) A person commits an offence if
   (a) he is the driver or other person in charge of a vehicle which has been permitted to remain at rest in contravention of any prohibition or restriction imposed by virtue of section 48, and
   (b) he fails to move the vehicle when ordered to do so by a constable in uniform.

(3) It is a defence for a person charged with an offence under this section to prove that he had a reasonable excuse for the act or omission in question.

(4) Possession of a current disabled person's badge shall not itself constitute a reasonable excuse for the purposes of subsection (3).

(5) A person guilty of an offence under subsection (1) shall be liable on summary conviction to a fine not exceeding level 4 on the standard scale.

(6) A person guilty of an offence under subsection (2) shall be liable on summary conviction to
   (a) imprisonment for a term not exceeding *three months*[84] *(51 weeks)*,[85]
   (b) a fine not exceeding level 4 on the standard scale, or
   (c) both.

52 Interpretation

In sections 48 to 51

"disabled person's badge" means a badge issued, or having effect as if issued, under any regulations for the time being in force under section 21 of the Chronically Sick and Disabled Persons Act 1970 (in relation to England and Wales and Scotland) or section 14 of the Chronically Sick and Disabled Persons (Northern Ireland) Act 1978 (in relation to Northern Ireland);

"driver" means, in relation to a vehicle which has been left on any road, the person who was driving it when it was left there;

"parking" means leaving a vehicle or permitting it to remain at rest;

"traffic sign" has the meaning given in section 142(1) of the Road Traffic Regulation Act 1984 (in relation to England and Wales and Scotland) and in Article 28 of the Road Traffic Regulation (Northern Ireland) Order 1997 (in relation to Northern Ireland);

"vehicle" has the same meaning as in section 99(5) of the Road Traffic Regulation Act 1984 (in relation to England and Wales and Scotland) and Article 47(4) of the Road Traffic Regulation (Northern Ireland) Order 1997 (in relation to Northern Ireland).

---

[84] Repealed by the Criminal Justice Act 2003, s 280(2), (3), Sch 26, para 55(1), (3), not yet in force.
[85] Substituted by the Criminal Justice Act 2003, s 280(2), (3), Sch 26, para 55(1), (3), not yet in force.

Port and border controls

53 Port and border controls

(1) Schedule 7 (port and border controls) shall have effect.

(2) The Secretary of State may by order repeal paragraph 16 of Schedule 7.

(3) The powers conferred by Schedule 7 shall be exercisable notwithstanding the rights conferred by section 1 of the Immigration Act 1971 (general principles regulating entry into and staying in the United Kingdom).

PART VI
MISCELLANEOUS

Terrorist offences

54 Weapons training

(1) A person commits an offence if he provides instruction or training in the making or use of
  (a) firearms,
  [(aa) radioactive material or weapons designed or adapted for the discharge of any radioactive material,][86]
  (b) explosives, or
  (c) chemical, biological or nuclear weapons.

(2) A person commits an offence if he receives instruction or training in the making or use of
  (a) firearms,
  [(aa) radioactive material or weapons designed or adapted for the discharge of any radioactive material,][87]
  (b) explosives, or
  (c) chemical, biological or nuclear weapons.

(3) A person commits an offence if he invites another to receive instruction or training and the receipt
  (a) would constitute an offence under subsection (2), or
  (b) would constitute an offence under subsection (2) but for the fact that it is to take place outside the United Kingdom.

(4) For the purpose of subsections (1) and (3)
  (a) a reference to the provision of instruction includes a reference to making it available either generally or to one or more specific persons, and
  (b) an invitation to receive instruction or training may be either general or addressed to one or more specific persons.

(5) It is a defence for a person charged with an offence under this section in relation to instruction or training to prove that his action or involvement was wholly for a purpose other than assisting, preparing for or participating in terrorism.

(6) A person guilty of an offence under this section shall be liable
  (a) on conviction on indictment, to imprisonment for a term not exceeding ten years, to a fine or to both, or
  (b) on summary conviction, to imprisonment for a term not exceeding six months, to a fine not exceeding the statutory maximum or to both.

(7) *A court by or before which a person is convicted of an offence under this section may order the forfeiture of anything which the court considers to have been in the person's possession for purposes connected with the offence.*

---

[86] Inserted by the Anti-terrorism, Crime and Security Act 2001, s 120(1).
[87] Inserted by the Anti-terrorism, Crime and Security Act 2001, s 120(1).

(8) Before making an order under subsection (7) a court must give an opportunity to be heard to any person, other than the convicted person, who claims to be the owner of or otherwise interested in anything which can be forfeited under that subsection.

(9) An order under subsection (7) shall not come into force until there is no further possibility of it being varied, or set aside, on appeal (disregarding any power of a court to grant leave to appeal out of time).[88]

55 Weapons training: interpretation

In section 54

["biological weapon" means a biological agent or toxin (within the meaning of the Biological Weapons Act 1974) in a form capable of use for hostile purposes or anything to which section 1(1)(b) of that Act applies,][89]

"chemical weapon" has the meaning given by section 1 of the Chemical Weapons Act 1996, and

["radioactive material" means radioactive material capable of endangering life or causing harm to human health][90]

[. . .][91]

56 Directing terrorist organisation

(1) A person commits an offence if he directs, at any level, the activities of an organisation which is concerned in the commission of acts of terrorism.

(2) A person guilty of an offence under this section is liable on conviction on indictment to imprisonment for life.

57 Possession for terrorist purposes

(1) A person commits an offence if he possesses an article in circumstances which give rise to a reasonable suspicion that his possession is for a purpose connected with the commission, preparation or instigation of an act of terrorism.

(2) It is a defence for a person charged with an offence under this section to prove that his possession of the article was not for a purpose connected with the commission, preparation or instigation of an act of terrorism.

(3) In proceedings for an offence under this section, if it is proved that an article

    (a) was on any premises at the same time as the accused, or

    (b) was on premises of which the accused was the occupier or which he habitually used otherwise than as a member of the public,

the court may assume that the accused possessed the article, unless he proves that he did not know of its presence on the premises or that he had no control over it.

(4) A person guilty of an offence under this section shall be liable

    (a) on conviction on indictment, to imprisonment for a term not exceeding [15 years][92] to a fine or to both, or

    (b) on summary conviction, to imprisonment for a term not exceeding six months, to a fine not exceeding the statutory maximum or to both.

---

[88] Repealed by the Counter-Terrorism Act 2008, ss 39, 99, Sch 3, para 2, Sch 9, Pt 3, not yet in force.

[89] Substituted by the Anti-terrorism, Crime and Security Act 2001, s 120(2)(a).

[90] Inserted by the Anti-terrorism, Crime and Security Act 2001, s 120(2)(b).

[91] Repealed by the Anti-terrorism, Crime and Security Act 2001, ss 120(2)(c), 125, Sch 8, Pt 7.

[92] Substituted by the Terrorism Act 2006, s 13(1).

58 Collection of information

(1) A person commits an offence if
  (a) he collects or makes a record of information of a kind likely to be useful to a person committing or preparing an act of terrorism, or
  (b) he possesses a document or record containing information of that kind.
(2) In this section "record" includes a photographic or electronic record.
(3) It is a defence for a person charged with an offence under this section to prove that he had a reasonable excuse for his action or possession.
(4) A person guilty of an offence under this section shall be liable
  (a) on conviction on indictment, to imprisonment for a term not exceeding 10 years, to a fine or to both, or
  (b) on summary conviction, to imprisonment for a term not exceeding six months, to a fine not exceeding the statutory maximum or to both.
(5) *A court by or before which a person is convicted of an offence under this section may order the forfeiture of any document or record containing information of the kind mentioned in subsection (1)(a).*
(6) *Before making an order under subsection (5) a court must give an opportunity to be heard to any person, other than the convicted person, who claims to be the owner of or otherwise interested in anything which can be forfeited under that subsection.*
(7) *An order under subsection (5) shall not come into force until there is no further possibility of it being varied, or set aside, on appeal (disregarding any power of a court to grant leave to appeal out of time).*[93]

[58A Eliciting, publishing or communicating information about members of armed forces &c

(1) A person commits an offence who
  (a) elicits or attempts to elicit information about an individual who is or has been
    (i) a member of Her Majesty's forces,
    (ii) a member of any of the intelligence services, or
    (iii) a constable,
    which is of a kind likely to be useful to a person committing or preparing an act of terrorism, or
  (b) publishes or communicates any such information.
(2) It is a defence for a person charged with an offence under this section to prove that they had a reasonable excuse for their action.
(3) A person guilty of an offence under this section is liable
  (a) on conviction on indictment, to imprisonment for a term not exceeding 10 years or to a fine, or to both;
  (b) on summary conviction
    (i) in England and Wales or Scotland, to imprisonment for a term not exceeding 12 months or to a fine not exceeding the statutory maximum, or to both;
    (ii) in Northern Ireland, to imprisonment for a term not exceeding 6 months or to a fine not exceeding the statutory maximum, or to both.
(4) In this section "the intelligence services" means the Security Service, the Secret Intelligence Service and GCHQ (within the meaning of section 3 of the Intelligence Services Act 1994 (c 13)).
(5) Schedule 8A to this Act contains supplementary provisions relating to the offence under this section.][94]

---

[93] Repealed by the Counter-Terrorism Act 2008, ss 39, 99, Sch 3, para 3, Sch 9, Pt 3, not yet in force.
[94] Inserted by the Counter-Terrorism Act 2008, s 76(1).

Inciting terrorism overseas

59 England and Wales

(1) A person commits an offence if
    (a) he incites another person to commit an act of terrorism wholly or partly outside the United Kingdom, and
    (b) the act would, if committed in England and Wales, constitute one of the offences listed in subsection (2).

(2) Those offences are
    (a) murder,
    (b) an offence under section 18 of the Offences against the Person Act 1861 (wounding with intent),
    (c) an offence under section 23 or 24 of that Act (poison),
    (d) an offence under section 28 or 29 of that Act (explosions), and
    (e) an offence under section 1(2) of the Criminal Damage Act 1971 (endangering life by damaging property).

(3) A person guilty of an offence under this section shall be liable to any penalty to which he would be liable on conviction of the offence listed in subsection (2) which corresponds to the act which he incites.

(4) For the purposes of subsection (1) it is immaterial whether or not the person incited is in the United Kingdom at the time of the incitement.

(5) Nothing in this section imposes criminal liability on any person acting on behalf of, or holding office under, the Crown.

60 Northern Ireland *(omitted)*

61 Scotland *(omitted)*

Terrorist bombing and finance offences

62 Terrorist bombing: jurisdiction

(1) If
    (a) a person does anything outside the United Kingdom as an act of terrorism or for the purposes of terrorism, and
    (b) his action would have constituted the commission of one of the offences listed in subsection (2) if it had been done in the United Kingdom,
he shall be guilty of the offence.

(2) The offences referred to in subsection (1)(b) are
    (a) an offence under section 2, 3 or 5 of the Explosive Substances Act 1883 (causing explosions, &c),
    (b) an offence under section 1 of the Biological Weapons Act 1974 (biological weapons), and
    (c) an offence under section 2 of the Chemical Weapons Act 1996 (chemical weapons).

63 Terrorist finance: jurisdiction

(1) If
    (a) a person does anything outside the United Kingdom, and
    (b) his action would have constituted the commission of an offence under any of sections 15 to 18 if it had been done in the United Kingdom,
he shall be guilty of the offence.

(2) For the purposes of subsection (1)(b), section 18(1)(b) shall be read as if for "the jurisdiction" there were substituted "a jurisdiction".

[Extra-territorial jurisdiction for other terrorist offences &c][95]

[63A Other terrorist offences under this Act: jurisdiction

(1) If

    (a) a United Kingdom national or a United Kingdom resident does anything outside the United Kingdom, and

    (b) his action, if done in any part of the United Kingdom, would have constituted an offence under [. . .][96] any of sections 56 to 61,

he shall be guilty in that part of the United Kingdom of the offence.

(2) For the purposes of this section and sections 63B and 63C a "United Kingdom national" means an individual who is

    (a) a British citizen, a British overseas territories citizen, a British National (Overseas) or a British Overseas citizen,

    (b) a person who under the British Nationality Act 1981 is a British subject, or

    (c) a British protected person within the meaning of that Act.

(3) For the purposes of this section and sections 63B and 63C a "United Kingdom resident" means an individual who is resident in the United Kingdom.][97]

[63B Terrorist attacks abroad by UK nationals or residents: jurisdiction

(1) If

    (a) a United Kingdom national or a United Kingdom resident does anything outside the United Kingdom as an act of terrorism or for the purposes of terrorism, and

    (b) his action, if done in any part of the United Kingdom, would have constituted an offence listed in subsection (2),

he shall be guilty in that part of the United Kingdom of the offence.

(2) These are the offences

    (a) murder, manslaughter, culpable homicide, rape, assault causing injury, assault to injury, kidnapping, abduction or false imprisonment,

    (b) an offence under section 4, 16, 18, 20, 21, 22, 23, 24, 28, 29, 30 or 64 of the Offences against the Person Act 1861,

    (c) an offence under any of sections 1 to 5 of the Forgery and Counterfeiting Act 1981,

    (d) the uttering of a forged document or an offence under section 46A of the Criminal Law (Consolidation) (Scotland) Act 1995,

    (e) an offence under section 1 or 2 of the Criminal Damage Act 1971,

    (f) an offence under Article 3 or 4 of the Criminal Damage (Northern Ireland) Order 1977,

    (g) malicious mischief,

    (h) wilful fire-raising.][98]

[63C Terrorist attacks abroad on UK nationals, residents and diplomatic staff &c: jurisdiction

(1) If

    (a) a person does anything outside the United Kingdom as an act of terrorism or for the purposes of terrorism,

    (b) his action is done to, or in relation to, a United Kingdom national, a United Kingdom resident or a protected person, and

    (c) his action, if done in any part of the United Kingdom, would have constituted an offence listed in subsection (2),

he shall be guilty in that part of the United Kingdom of the offence.

---

[95] Inserted by the Crime (International Co-operation) Act 2003, s 52.
[96] Repealed by the Terrorism Act 2006, sc 37(s), Sch 3.
[97] Inserted by the Crime (International Co-operation) Act 2003, s 52.
[98] Inserted by the Crime (International Co-operation) Act 2003, s 52.

(2) These are the offences
  (a) murder, manslaughter, culpable homicide, rape, assault causing injury, assault to injury, kidnapping, abduction or false imprisonment,
  (b) an offence under section 4, 16, 18, 20, 21, 22, 23, 24, 28, 29, 30 or 64 of the Offences against the Person Act 1861,
  (c) an offence under section 1, 2, 3, 4 or 5(1) or (3) of the Forgery and Counterfeiting Act 1981,
  (d) the uttering of a forged document or an offence under section 46A(1) of the Criminal Law (Consolidation) (Scotland) Act 1995.
(3) For the purposes of this section and section 63D a person is a protected person if
  (a) he is a member of a United Kingdom diplomatic mission within the meaning of Article 1(b) of the Vienna Convention on Diplomatic Relations signed in 1961 (as that Article has effect in the United Kingdom by virtue of section 2 of and Schedule 1 to the Diplomatic Privileges Act 1964),
  (b) he is a member of a United Kingdom consular post within the meaning of Article 1(g) of the Vienna Convention on Consular Relations signed in 1963 (as that Article has effect in the United Kingdom by virtue of section 1 of and Schedule 1 to the Consular Relations Act 1968),
  (c) he carries out any functions for the purposes of [the European Medicines Agency][99] or
  (d) he carries out any functions for the purposes of a body specified in an order made by the Secretary of State.
(4) The Secretary of State may specify a body under subsection (3)(d) only if
  (a) it is established by or under the Treaty establishing the European Community or the Treaty on European Union, and
  (b) the principal place in which its functions are carried out is a place in the United Kingdom.
(5) If in any proceedings a question arises as to whether a person is or was a protected person, a certificate
  (a) issued by or under the authority of the Secretary of State, and
  (b) stating any fact relating to the question,
  is to be conclusive evidence of that fact.][100]

[**63D Terrorist attacks or threats abroad in connection with UK diplomatic premises &c: jurisdiction**

(1) If
  (a) a person does anything outside the United Kingdom as an act of terrorism or for the purposes of terrorism,
  (b) his action is done in connection with an attack on relevant premises or on a vehicle ordinarily used by a protected person,
  (c) the attack is made when a protected person is on or in the premises or vehicle, and
  (d) his action, if done in any part of the United Kingdom, would have constituted an offence listed in subsection (2),
  he shall be guilty in that part of the United Kingdom of the offence.
(2) These are the offences
  (a) an offence under section 1 of the Criminal Damage Act 1971,
  (b) an offence under Article 3 of the Criminal Damage (Northern Ireland) Order 1977,
  (c) malicious mischief,
  (d) wilful fire-raising.

---

[99] Substituted by SI 2004/3224, reg 4.
[100] Inserted by the Crime (International Co-operation) Act 2003, s 52.

(3) If
   (a) a person does anything outside the United Kingdom as an act of terrorism or for the purposes of terrorism,
   (b) his action consists of a threat of an attack on relevant premises or on a vehicle ordinarily used by a protected person,
   (c) the attack is threatened to be made when a protected person is, or is likely to be, on or in the premises or vehicle, and
   (d) his action, if done in any part of the United Kingdom, would have constituted an offence listed in subsection (4),

he shall be guilty in that part of the United Kingdom of the offence.

(4) These are the offences
   (a) an offence under section 2 of the Criminal Damage Act 1971,
   (b) an offence under Article 4 of the Criminal Damage (Northern Ireland) Order 1977,
   (c) breach of the peace (in relation to Scotland only).

(5) "Relevant premises" means
   (a) premises at which a protected person resides or is staying, or
   (b) premises which a protected person uses for the purpose of carrying out his functions as such a person.][101]

[63E   Sections 63B to 63D: supplementary

(1) Proceedings for an offence which (disregarding the Acts listed in subsection (2)) would not be an offence apart from section 63B, 63C or 63D are not to be started
   (a) in England and Wales, except by or with the consent of the Attorney General,
   (b) in Northern Ireland, except by or with the consent of the Advocate General for Northern Ireland.

(2) These are the Acts
   (a) the Internationally Protected Persons Act 1978,
   (b) the Suppression of Terrorism Act 1978,
   (c) the Nuclear Material (Offences) Act 1983,
   (d) the United Nations Personnel Act 1997.

(3) For the purposes of sections 63C and 63D it is immaterial whether a person knows that another person is a United Kingdom national, a United Kingdom resident or a protected person.

(4) In relation to any time before the coming into force of section 27(1) of the Justice (Northern Ireland) Act 2002, the reference in subsection (1)(b) to the Advocate General for Northern Ireland is to be read as a reference to the Attorney General for Northern Ireland.][102]

64   [. . .][103]

PART VII
NORTHERN IRELAND

65–113 [. . .][104]

---

[101] Inserted by the Crime (International Co-operation) Act 2003, s 52.
[102] Inserted by the Crime (International Co-operation) Act 2003, s 52.
[103] Repealed by the Extradition Act 2003, ss 219(1), 220, Sch 3, paras 1, 11, Sch 4.
[104] Ceased to have effort by virtue of the Terrorism (Northern Ireland) Act 2006.

PART VIII

GENERAL

114 Police powers

(1) A power conferred by virtue of this Act on a constable
   (a) is additional to powers which he has at common law or by virtue of any other enactment, and
   (b) shall not be taken to affect those powers.
(2) A constable may if necessary use reasonable force for the purpose of exercising a power conferred on him by virtue of this Act (apart from paragraphs 2 and 3 of Schedule 7).
(3) Where anything is seized by a constable under a power conferred by virtue of this Act, it may (unless the contrary intention appears) be retained for so long as is necessary in all the circumstances.

115 Officers' powers

Schedule 14 (which makes provision about the exercise of functions by authorised officers for the purposes of sections 25 to 31 and examining officers for the purposes of Schedule 7) shall have effect.

116 Powers to stop and search

(1) A power to search premises conferred by virtue of this Act shall be taken to include power to search a container.
(2) A power conferred by virtue of this Act to stop a person includes power to stop a vehicle (other than an aircraft which is airborne).
(3) A person commits an offence if he fails to stop a vehicle when required to do so by virtue of this section.
(4) A person guilty of an offence under subsection (3) shall be liable on summary conviction to
   (a) imprisonment for a term not exceeding six months,
   (b) a fine not exceeding level 5 on the standard scale, or
   (c) both.

117 Consent to prosecution

(1) This section applies to an offence under any provision of this Act other than an offence under
   (a) section 36,
   (b) section 51,
   (c) paragraph 18 of Schedule 7,
   (d) paragraph 12 of Schedule 12, or
   (e) Schedule 13.
(2) Proceedings for an offence to which this section applies
   (a) shall not be instituted in England and Wales without the consent of the Director of Public Prosecutions, and
   (b) shall not be instituted in Northern Ireland without the consent of the Director of Public Prosecutions for Northern Ireland.
[(2A) But if it appears to the Director of Public Prosecutions or the Director of Public Prosecutions for Northern Ireland that an offence to which this section applies has been committed [outside the United Kingdom][105] or for a purpose wholly or partly connected with the affairs of a country other than the United Kingdom, his consent for the purposes of this section may be given only with the permission

---

[105] Inserted by the Counter-Terrorism Act 2008, s 29.

(a) in the case of the Director of Public Prosecutions, of the Attorney General; and

(b) in the case of the Director of Public Prosecutions for Northern Ireland, of the Advocate General for Northern Ireland.

(2B) In relation to any time before the coming into force of section 27(1) of the Justice (Northern Ireland) Act 2002, the reference in subsection (2A) to the Advocate General for Northern Ireland is to be read as a reference to the Attorney General for Northern Ireland.][106]

118 Defences

(1) Subsection (2) applies where in accordance with a provision mentioned in subsection (5) it is a defence for a person charged with an offence to prove a particular matter.

(2) If the person adduces evidence which is sufficient to raise an issue with respect to the matter the court or jury shall assume that the defence is satisfied unless the prosecution proves beyond reasonable doubt that it is not.

(3) Subsection (4) applies where in accordance with a provision mentioned in subsection (5) a court

(a) may make an assumption in relation to a person charged with an offence unless a particular matter is proved, or

(b) may accept a fact as sufficient evidence unless a particular matter is proved.

(4) If evidence is adduced which is sufficient to raise an issue with respect to the matter mentioned in subsection (3)(a) or (b) the court shall treat it as proved unless the prosecution disproves it beyond reasonable doubt.

(5) The provisions in respect of which subsections (2) and (4) apply are

(a) sections 12(4), 39(5)(a), 54, 57, 58, [58A][107], 77 and 103 of this Act, and

(b) sections 13, 32 and 33 of the Northern Ireland (Emergency Provisions) Act 1996 (possession and information offences) as they have effect by virtue of Schedule 1 to this Act.

119 Crown servants, regulators, &c

(1) The Secretary of State may make regulations providing for any of sections 15 to 23[108] [(*sections 15 to 23A*)][109] and 39 to apply to persons in the public service of the Crown.

(2) The Secretary of State may make regulations providing for section 19 not to apply to persons who are in his opinion performing or connected with the performance of regulatory, supervisory, investigative or registration functions of a public nature.

(3) Regulations

(a) may make different provision for different purposes,

(b) may make provision which is to apply only in specified circumstances, and

(c) may make provision which applies only to particular persons or to persons of a particular description.

120 Evidence

(1) A document which purports to be

(a) a notice or direction given or order made by the Secretary of State for the purposes of a provision of this Act, and

(b) signed by him or on his behalf,

shall be received in evidence and shall, until the contrary is proved, be deemed to have been given or made by the Secretary of State.

---

[106] Substituted, for sub-s (3) as originally enacted, by the Terrorism Act 2006, s 37(2).

[107] Inserted by the Counter-Terrorism Act 2008, s 76(3).

[108] Repealed by the Counter-Terrorism Act 2008, s 39, Sch 3, para 4, not yet in force.

[109] Substituted by the Counter-Terrorism Act 2008, s 39, Sch 3, para 4, not yet in force.

(2) A document bearing a certificate which
- (a) purports to be signed by or on behalf of the Secretary of State, and
- (b) states that the document is a true copy of a notice or direction given or order made by the Secretary of State for the purposes of a provision of this Act,

shall be evidence (or, in Scotland, sufficient evidence) of the document in legal proceedings.

(3) In subsections (1) and (2) a reference to an order does not include a reference to an order made by statutory instrument.

(4) The Documentary Evidence Act 1868 shall apply to an authorisation given in writing by the Secretary of State for the purposes of this Act as it applies to an order made by him.

[120A *Supplemental powers of court in respect of forfeiture orders*

(1) Where the court makes an order under section 54, 58 or 103 for the forfeiture of anything, it may also make such other provision as appears to it to be necessary for giving effect to the forfeiture.

(2) That provision may include, in particular, provision relating to the retention, handling, disposal or destruction of what is forfeited.

(3) Provision made by virtue of this section may be varied at any time by the court that made it.][110]

[120A Supplementary powers of forfeiture

(1) A court by or before which a person is convicted of an offence under a provision mentioned in column 1 of the following table may order the forfeiture of any item mentioned in column 2 in relation to that offence.

Offence	Items liable to forfeiture
Section 54 (weapons training)	Anything that the court considers to have been in the possession of the person for purposes connected with the offence.
Section 57 (possession for terrorist purposes)	Any article that is the subject matter of the offence.
Section 58 (collection of information)	Any document or record containing information of the kind mentioned in subsection (1)(a) of that section.
Section 58A (eliciting, publishing or communicating information about members of armed forces etc)	Any document or record containing information of the kind mentioned in subsection (1)(a) of that section.

(2) Before making an order under this section, a court must give an opportunity to be heard to any person, other than the convicted person, who claims to be the owner or otherwise interested in anything which can be forfeited under this section.

(3) An order under this section does not come into force until there is no further possibility of it being varied, or set aside, on appeal (disregarding any power of a court to grant leave to appeal out of time).

(4) Where a court makes an order under this section, it may also make such other provision as appears to it to be necessary for giving effect to the forfeiture, including, in particular, provision relating to the retention, handling, disposal or destruction of what is forfeited.

(5) Provision made by virtue of subsection (4) may be varied at any time by the court that made it.

(6) The power of forfeiture under this section is in addition to any power of forfeiture under section 23A.][111]

---

[110] Substituted by the Counter-Terrorism Act 2008, s 38(1), not yet in force.
[111] Inserted by the Terrorism Act 2006, s 37(3).

121 Interpretation

In this Act

"act" and "action" include omission,

"article" includes substance and any other thing,

["British Transport Police Force" means the constables appointed under section 53 of the British Transport Commission Act 1949 (c xxix),][112]

["customs officer" means an officer of Revenue and Customs,][113]

"dwelling" means a building or part of a building used as a dwelling, and a vehicle which is habitually stationary and which is used as a dwelling,

"explosive" means

(a) an article or substance manufactured for the purpose of producing a practical effect by explosion,

(b) materials for making an article or substance within paragraph (a),

(c) anything used or intended to be used for causing or assisting in causing an explosion, and

(d) a part of anything within paragraph (a) or (c),

"firearm" includes an air gun or air pistol,

"immigration officer" means a person appointed as an immigration officer under paragraph 1 of Schedule 2 to the Immigration Act 1971,

"the Islands" means the Channel Islands and the Isle of Man,

"organisation" includes any association or combination of persons,

. . .[114] "premises"[, except in section 63D,][115] includes any place and in particular includes

(a) a vehicle,

(b) an offshore installation within the meaning given in section 44 of the Petroleum Act 1998, and

(c) a tent or moveable structure,

"property" includes property wherever situated and whether real or personal, heritable or moveable, and things in action and other intangible or incorporeal property,

"public place" means a place to which members of the public have or are permitted to have access, whether or not for payment,

"road" has the same meaning as in the Road Traffic Act 1988 (in relation to England and Wales), the Roads (Scotland) Act 1984 (in relation to Scotland) and the Road Traffic Regulation (Northern Ireland) Order 1997 (in relation to Northern Ireland), and includes part of a road, and

"vehicle", except in sections 48 to 52 and Schedule 7, includes an aircraft, hovercraft, train or vessel.

---

[112] Inserted by the Anti-terrorism, Crime and Security Act 2001, s 101, Sch 7, para 29, 32(a).

[113] Substituted by the Commissioners for Revenue and Customs Act 2005, s 50(6), Sch 4, para 78.

[114] Inserted by the Anti-terrorism, Crime and Security Act 2001, s 101, Sch 7, paras 29, 32(b); repealed by SI 2004/1573, art 12(6)(d).

[115] Inserted by the Crime (International Co-operation) Act 2003, s 91(1), Sch 5, paras 75, 76.

122 Index of defined expressions

In this Act the expressions listed below are defined by the provisions specified.

Expression	Interpretation provision
Act	Section 121
Action	Section 121
Action taken for the purposes of terrorism	Section 1(5)
Article	Section 121
[. . .]116	[. . .]
British Transport Police Force	Section 121117
[. . .]118	[. . .]
Cordoned area	Section 33
Customs officer	Section 121
Dwelling	Section 121
Examining officer	Schedule 7, paragraph 1
Explosive	Section 121
Firearm	Section 121
Immigration officer	Section 121
The Islands	Section 121
Organisation	Section 121
[Policed Premises	Section 121]119
Premises	Section 121
Property	Section 121
Proscribed organisation	Section 3(1)
Public place	Section 121
Road	Section 121
Scheduled offence (in Part VII)	Section 65
Terrorism	Section 1
Terrorist (in Part V)	Section 40
Terrorist investigation	Section 32
Terrorist property	Section 14
Vehicle	Section 121
Vehicle (in sections 48 to 51)	Section 52

123 Orders and regulations *(omitted)*

124 Directions *(omitted)*

125 Amendments and repeals *(omitted)*

126 [. . .]120

127 Money *(omitted)*

128 Commencement *(omitted)*

129 Transitional provisions *(omitted)*

130 Extent *(omitted)*

131 Short title *(omitted)*

---

116 Repealed by the Anti-terrorism, Crime and Security Act 2001, s 125, Sch 8, Pt1.
117 Inserted by the Anti-terrorism, Crime and Security Act 2001, s 101, Sch 7, paras 29, 33(a).
118 Repealed by the Anti-terrorism, Crime and Security Act 2001, s 125, Sch 8, Pt 1.
119 Inserted by the Anti-terrorism, Crime and Security Act 2001, s 101, Sch 7, paras 29, 33(b).
120 Repealed by the Terrorism Act 2006, s 37(5), Sch 3.

SCHEDULE 1
NORTHERN IRELAND (EMERGENCY PROVISIONS) ACT 1996
(omitted)

SCHEDULE 2 Section 3
PROSCRIBED ORGANISATIONS

(The listed organisations are related in Chapter 2)

Note

The entry for The Orange Volunteers refers to the organisation which uses that name and in the name of which a statement described as a press release was published on 14th October 1998.

The entry for Jemaah Islamiyah refers to the organisation using that name that is based in south-east Asia, members of which were arrested by the Singapore authorities in December 2001 in connection with a plot to attack US and other Western targets in Singapore.

SCHEDULE 3 Section 5
THE PROSCRIBED ORGANISATIONS APPEAL COMMISSION

Constitution and administration

1 (1) The Commission shall consist of members appointed by the Lord Chancellor.
 (2) The Lord Chancellor shall appoint one of the members as chairman.
 (3) A member shall hold and vacate office in accordance with the terms of his appointment.
 (4) A member may resign at any time by notice in writing to the Lord Chancellor.
2 The Lord Chancellor may appoint officers and servants for the Commission.
3 The Lord Chancellor
 (a) may pay sums by way of remuneration, allowances, pensions and gratuities to or in respect of members, officers and servants,
 (b) may pay compensation to a person who ceases to be a member of the Commission if the Lord Chancellor thinks it appropriate because of special circumstances, and
 (c) may pay sums in respect of expenses of the Commission.

Procedure

4 (1) The Commission shall sit at such times and in such places as the Lord Chancellor may direct [*after consulting the following*
 (a) *the Lord Chief Justice of England and Wales;*
 (b) *the Lord President of the Court of Session;*
 (c) *the Lord Chief Justice of Northern Ireland.*[121]
 (2) The Commission may sit in two or more divisions.]
 (3) At each sitting of the Commission
 (a) three members shall attend,

---

[121] Inserted by the Constitutional Reform Act 2005, s 15(1), Sch 4, Pt 1, paras 287, 289(1), (2), not yet in force.

(b) one of the members shall be a person who holds or has held high judicial office (within the meaning of *the Appellate Jurisdiction Act 1876*)[122] [*Part 3 of the Constitutional Reform Act 2005) or is or has been a member of the Judicial Committee of the Privy Council*],[123] and

(c) the chairman or another member nominated by him shall preside and report the Commission's decision.

[(4) The Lord Chief Justice may nominate a judicial office holder (as defined in section 109(4) of the Constitutional Reform Act 2005) to exercise his functions under this paragraph.

(5) The Lord President of the Court of Session may nominate a judge of the Court of Session who is a member of the First or Second Division of the Inner House of that Court to exercise his functions under this paragraph.

(6) The Lord Chief Justice of Northern Ireland may nominate any of the following to exercise his functions under this paragraph

(a) the holder of one of the offices listed in Schedule 1 to the Justice (Northern Ireland) Act 2002 (c 26);

(b) a Lord Justice of Appeal (as defined in section 88 of that Act).][124]

5 (1) The Lord Chancellor may make rules

(a) regulating the exercise of the right of appeal to the Commission;

(b) prescribing practice and procedure to be followed in relation to proceedings before the Commission;

(c) providing for proceedings before the Commission to be determined without an oral hearing in specified circumstances;

(d) making provision about evidence in proceedings before the Commission (including provision about the burden of proof and admissibility of evidence);

(e) making provision about proof of the Commission's decisions.

(2) In making the rules the Lord Chancellor shall, in particular, have regard to the need to secure

(a) that decisions which are the subject of appeals are properly reviewed, and

(b) that information is not disclosed contrary to the public interest.

(3) The rules shall make provision permitting organisations to be legally represented in proceedings before the Commission.

(4) The rules may, in particular

(a) provide for full particulars of the reasons for proscription or refusal to deproscribe to be withheld from the organisation or applicant concerned and from any person representing it or him;

[(aa) provide for full particulars of the reasons for

(i) the making of an order under section 3(6), or

(ii) a refusal to provide for a name to cease to be treated as a name for an organisation, to be withheld from the organisation or applicant concerned and from any person representing it or him;][125]

(b) enable the Commission to exclude persons (including representatives) from all or part of proceedings;

(c) enable the Commission to provide a summary of evidence taken in the absence of a person excluded by virtue of paragraph (b);

---

[122] Repealed by the Constitutional Reform Act 2005, s 145(1), Sch 17, Pt 2, para 29, not yet in force.

[123] Substituted by the Constitutional Reform Act 2005, s 145(1), Sch 17, Pt 2, para 29, not yet in force.

[124] Inserted by the Constitutional Reform Act 2005, s 15(1), Sch 4, Pt 1, paras 287, 289(1), (3).

[125] Inserted by the Terrorism Act 2006, s 22(1), (11).

(d) permit preliminary or incidental functions to be discharged by a single member;

(e) permit proceedings for permission to appeal under section 6 to be determined by a single member;

(f) make provision about the functions of persons appointed under paragraph 7;

(g) make different provision for different parties or descriptions of party.

(5) Rules under this paragraph

(a) shall be made by statutory instrument, and

(b) shall not be made unless a draft has been laid before and approved by resolution of each House of Parliament.

(6) In this paragraph a reference to proceedings before the Commission includes a reference to proceedings arising out of proceedings before the Commission.

6 (1) This paragraph applies to

(a) proceedings brought by an organisation before the Commission, and

(b) proceedings arising out of proceedings to which paragraph (a) applies.

(2) Proceedings shall be conducted on behalf of the organisation by a person designated by the Commission (with such legal representation as he may choose to obtain).

(3) In [paragraph 5][126] of this Schedule a reference to an organisation includes a reference to a person designated under this paragraph.

7 (1) The relevant law officer may appoint a person to represent the interests of an organisation or other applicant in proceedings in relation to which an order has been made by virtue of paragraph 5(4)(b).

(2) The relevant law officer is

(a) in relation to proceedings in England and Wales, the Attorney General,

(b) in relation to proceedings in Scotland, the Advocate General for Scotland, and

(c) in relation to proceedings in Northern Ireland, the *Attorney General for Northern Ireland*[127] *[(Advocate General for Northern Ireland)].*[128]

(3) A person appointed under this paragraph must

(a) have a general qualification for the purposes of section 71 of the Courts and Legal Services Act 1990 (qualification for legal appointments),

(b) be an advocate or a solicitor who has rights of audience in the Court of Session or the High Court of Justiciary by virtue of section 25A of the Solicitors (Scotland) Act 1980, or

(c) be a member of the Bar of Northern Ireland.

(4) A person appointed under this paragraph shall not be responsible to the organisation or other applicant whose interests he is appointed to represent.

(5) In [paragraph 5][129] of this Schedule a reference to a representative does not include a reference to a person appointed under this paragraph.

8 [. . .][130]

---

[126] Substituted by the Regulation of Investigatory Powers Act 2000, s 82(1), Sch 4, para 12(2).

[127] Repealed by the Counter-Terrorism Act 2008, s 91(1), (2), not yet in force.

[128] Counter-Terrorism Act 2008, s 91(1), (2), not yet in force.

[129] Substituted by the Regulation of Investigatory Powers Act 2000, s 82(1), Sch 4, para 12(2).

[130] Repealed by the Regulation of Investigatory Powers Act 2000, s 82(2), Sch 5.

SCHEDULE 3A
REGULATED SECTOR AND SUPERVISORY AUTHORITIES *(omitted)*

SCHEDULE 4   Section 23
FORFEITURE ORDERS

PART I
ENGLAND AND WALES

Interpretation

1 In this Part of this Schedule
"forfeiture order" means an order made by a court in England and Wales under section 23
[*or 23A*],[131] and
"forfeited property" means the money or other property to which a forfeiture order applies.
[*"relevant offence" means*
(a) an offence under any of sections 15 to 18,
(b) an offence to which section 23A applies, or
(c) in relation to a restraint order, any offence specified in Schedule 2 to the Counter-Terrorism Act
2008 (offences where terrorist connection to be considered).][132]

Implementation of forfeiture orders

2 (1) Where a court in England and Wales makes a forfeiture order it may make such other provision as appears to it to be necessary for giving effect to the order, and in particular it may
(a) require any of the forfeited property to be paid or handed over to the proper officer or
to a constable designated for the purpose by the chief officer of police of a police force
specified in the order;
(b) direct any of the forfeited property other than money or land to be sold or otherwise
disposed of in such manner as the court may direct and the proceeds (if any) to be paid
to the proper officer;
(c) appoint a receiver to take possession, subject to such conditions and exceptions as may
be specified by the court, of any of the forfeited property, to realise it in such manner
as the court may direct and to pay the proceeds to the proper officer;
(d) direct a specified part of any forfeited money, or of the proceeds of the sale, disposal or
realisation of any forfeited property, to be paid by the proper officer to a specified
person falling within *section 23(7)*[133] *[section 23B(1)]*.[134]
(2) A forfeiture order shall not come into force until there is no further possibility of it being
varied, or set aside, on appeal (disregarding any power of a court to grant leave to appeal
out of time).
(3) In sub-paragraph (1)(b) and (d) a reference to the proceeds of the sale, disposal or realisation of property is a reference to the proceeds after deduction of the costs of sale, disposal
or realisation.
(4) Section 140 of the Magistrates' Courts Act 1980 (disposal of non-pecuniary forfeitures)
shall not apply.

[131] Inserted by the Terrorism Act 2008, s 39, Sch 3, para 5(1), (2)(a), not yet in force.
[132] Inserted by the Terrorism Act 2008, s 39, Sch 3, para 5(1), (2)(b), not yet in force.
[133] Repealed by the Terrorism Act 2008, s 39, Sch 3, para 5(1), (3), not yet in force.
[134] Substituted by the Terrorism Act 2008, s 39, Sch 3, para 5(1), (3), not yet in force.

3 (1) A receiver appointed under paragraph 2 shall be entitled to be paid his remuneration and expenses by the proper officer out of the proceeds of the property realised by the receiver and paid to the proper officer under paragraph 2(1)(c).

(2) If and so far as those proceeds are insufficient, the receiver shall be entitled to be paid his remuneration and expenses by the prosecutor.

(3) A receiver appointed under paragraph 2 shall not be liable to any person in respect of any loss or damage resulting from action

(a) which he takes in relation to property which is not forfeited property, but which he reasonably believes to be forfeited property,

(b) which he would be entitled to take if the property were forfeited property, and

(c) which he reasonably believes that he is entitled to take because of his belief that the property is forfeited property.

(4) Sub-paragraph (3) does not apply in so far as the loss or damage is caused by the receiver's negligence.

4 (1) In paragraphs 2 and 3 "the proper officer" means

(a) where the forfeiture order is made by a magistrates' court, the [designated officer][135] for that court,

(b) where the forfeiture order is made by the Crown Court and the defendant was committed to the Crown Court by a magistrates' court, the [designated officer][136] for the magistrates' court, and

(c) where the forfeiture order is made by the Crown Court and the proceedings were instituted by a bill of indictment preferred by virtue of section 2(2)(b) of the Administration of Justice (Miscellaneous Provisions) Act 1933, the [designated officer][137] for the magistrates' court for the place where the trial took place.

(2) The proper officer shall issue a certificate in respect of a forfeiture order if an application is made by

(a) the prosecutor in the proceedings in which the forfeiture order was made,

(b) the defendant in those proceedings, or

(c) a person whom the court heard under *section 23(7)*[138] [*section 23B(1)*][139] before making the order.

(3) The certificate shall state the extent (if any) to which, at the date of the certificate, effect has been given to the forfeiture order.

Application of proceeds to compensate victims

[4A (1) *Where a court makes a forfeiture order in a case where*

(a) *the offender has been convicted of an offence that has resulted in a person suffering personal injury, loss or damage, or*

(b) *any such offence is taken into consideration by the court in determining sentence,*

the court may also order that an amount not exceeding a sum specified by the court is to be paid to that person out of the proceeds of the forfeiture.

(2) *For this purpose the proceeds of the forfeiture means the aggregate amount of*

(a) *any forfeited money, and*

(b) *the proceeds of the sale, disposal or realisation of any forfeited property, after deduction of the costs of the sale, disposal or realisation,*

reduced by the amount of any payment under paragraph 2(1)(d) or 3(1).

---

135 Substituted by the Courts Act 2003, s 109(1), Sch 8, para 388(1), (2).
136 Substituted by the Courts Act 2003, s 109(1), Sch 8, para 388(1), (2).
137 Substituted by the Courts Act 2003, s 109(1), Sch 8, para 388(1), (2).
138 Repealed by the Counter-Terrorism Act 2008, s 39, Sch 3, para 5(1), (4), not yet in force.
139 Substituted by the Counter-Terrorism Act 2008, s 39, Sch 3, para 5(1), (4), not yet in force.

(3) *The court may make an order under this paragraph only if it is satisfied that but for the inadequacy of the offender's means it would have made a compensation order under section 130 of the Powers of Criminal Courts (Sentencing) Act 2000 under which the offender would have been required to pay compensation of an amount not less than the specified amount.*][140]

Restraint orders

5 (1) The High Court may make a restraint order under this paragraph where
  (a) proceedings have been instituted in England and Wales for *an offence under any of sections 15 to 18*[141] *(a relevant offence)*,[142]
  (b) the proceedings have not been concluded,
  (c) an application for a restraint order is made to the High Court by the prosecutor, and
  (d) a forfeiture order has been made, or it appears to the High Court that a forfeiture order may be made, in the proceedings for the offence.
 [(2) The High Court may also make a restraint order under this paragraph where
  (a) a criminal investigation has been started in England and Wales with regard to *an offence under any of sections 15 to 18*[143] *(a relevant offence)*,[144]][145]
  (b) an application for a restraint order is made to the High Court by the person who the High Court is satisfied will have the conduct of any proceedings for the offence, and
  (c) it appears to the High Court that a forfeiture order may be made in any proceedings for the offence.
 (3) A restraint order prohibits a person to whom notice of it is given, subject to any conditions and exceptions specified in the order, from dealing with property in respect of which a forfeiture order has been or could be made in [any proceedings][146] referred to in sub-paragraph (1) or (2).
 (4) An application for a restraint order may be made to a judge in chambers without notice.
 (5) In this paragraph a reference to dealing with property includes a reference to removing the property from Great Britain.
 [(6) In this paragraph "criminal investigation" means an investigation which police officers or other persons have a duty to conduct with a view to it being ascertained whether a person should be charged with an offence.][147]
6 (1) A restraint order shall provide for notice of it to be given to any person affected by the order.
 (2) A restraint order may be discharged or varied by the High Court on the application of a person affected by it.
 [(3) A restraint order made under paragraph 5(1) shall in particular be discharged on an application under sub-paragraph (2) if the proceedings for the offence have been concluded.
 (4) A restraint order made under paragraph 5(2) shall in particular be discharged on an application under sub-paragraph (2)
  (a) if no proceedings in respect of *offences under any of sections 15 to 18*[148] [*relevant offences*],[149] are instituted within such time as the High Court considers reasonable, and

---

[140] Inserted by the Counter-Terrorism Act 2008, s 37(1), not yet in force.
[141] Repealed by the Counter-Terrorism Act 2008, s 39, Sch 3, para 5(1), (5), not yet in force.
[142] Substituted by the Counter-Terrorism Act 2008, s 39, Sch 3 ,para 5(1), (5), not yet in force.
[143] Repealed by the Counter-Terrorism Act 2008, s 39, Sch 3, para 5(1), (5), not yet in force.
[144] Substituted by the Counter-Terrorism Act 2008, s 39, Sch 3 ,para 5(1), (5), not yet in force.
[145] Substituted by the Anti-terrorism Crime and Security Act 2001, s 3, Sch 2, Pt 2, para 2(1), (1).
[146] Substituted by the Anti-terrorism Crime and Security Act 2001, s 3, Sch 2, Pt 2, para 2(1), (3).
[147] Inserted by the Anti-terrorism Crime and Security Act 2001, s 3, Sch 2, Pt 2, para 2(1), (4).
[148] Repealed by the Counter-Terrorism Act 2008, s 39, Sch 3, para 5(1), (6), not yet in force.
[149] Substituted by the Counter-Terrorism Act 2008, s 39, Sch 3, para 5(1), (6), not yet in force.

(b) if all proceedings in respect of *offences under any of sections 15 to 18*[150] [*relevant offences*],[151] have been concluded.][152]

7 (1) A constable may seize any property subject to a restraint order for the purpose of preventing it from being removed from Great Britain.

(2) Property seized under this paragraph shall be dealt with in accordance with the High Court's directions.

8 (1) The Land Charges Act 1972 and the [Land Registration Act 2002][153]

(a) shall apply in relation to restraint orders as they apply in relation to orders affecting land made by the court for the purpose of enforcing judgments or recognizances[, except that no notice may be entered in the register of title under the Land Registration Act 2002 in respect of such orders],[154] and

(b) shall apply in relation to applications for restraint orders as they apply in relation to other pending land actions.

(2)–(3) [. . .][155]

Compensation[156]

9 (1) This paragraph applies where a restraint order is discharged under [paragraph 6(4)(a)][157]

(2) This paragraph also applies where a forfeiture order or a restraint order is made in or in relation to proceedings for *an offence under any of sections 15 to 18*[158] [*a relevant offence*],[159] which

(a) do not result in conviction for *an offence under any of those sections*[160] [*a relevant offence*),[161]

(b) result in conviction for *an offence under any of those sections*[162] [*a relevant offence*][163] in respect of which the person convicted is subsequently pardoned by Her Majesty, or

(c) result in conviction for *an offence under any of those sections*[164] [*a relevant offence*][165] which is subsequently quashed.

(3) A person who had an interest in any property which was subject to the order may apply to the High Court for compensation.

(4) The High Court may order compensation to be paid to the applicant if satisfied

(a) that there was a serious default on the part of a person concerned in the investigation or prosecution of the offence,

(b) that the person in default was or was acting as a member of a police force, or was a member of the Crown Prosecution Service or was acting on behalf of the Service,

(c) that the applicant has suffered loss in consequence of anything done in relation to the property by or in pursuance of the forfeiture order or restraint order, and

---

[150] Repeated by the Counter-Terrorism Act 2008, s 39, Sch 3, para 5(1), (6), not yet in force.
[151] Substituted by the Counter-Terrorism Act 2008, s 39, Sch 3, para 5(1), (6), not yet in force.
[152] Substituted, for sub-para(3) as originally ended, by the Anti-terrorism, Crime and Security Act 2001 s 3.
[153] Substituted by the Land Registration Act 2002, s 133, Sch 11, para 38(a).
[154] Inserted by the Land Registration Act 2002, s 133, Sch 11, para 38(b)
[155] Repealed by the Land Registration Act 2002, s 135, Sch 13.
[156] Heading replaced by the Counter-Terrorism Act 2008, s 39, Sch 3, para 5(1), (7) not yet in force.
[157] Substituted by the Anti-terrorism, Crime and Security Act 2001, s 3, Sch 2, Pt 2, para 2(1), 7.
[158] Repealed by the Counter-Terrorism Act 2008, s 39, Sch 3, para 5(1), (8)(a), not yet in force.
[159] Substituted by the Counter-Terrorism Act 2008, s 39, Sch 3, para 5(1), (8)(a), not yet in force.
[160] Repealed by the Counter-Terrorism Act 2008, s 39, Sch 3, para 5(1), (8)(b), not yet in force.
[161] Substituted by the Counter-Terrorism Act 2008, s 39, Sch 3, para 5(1), (8)(b), not yet in force.
[162] Repealed by the Counter-Terrorism Act 2008, s 39, Sch 3, para 5(1), (8)(b), not yet in force.
[163] Substituted by the Counter-Terrorism Act 2008, s 39, Sch 3, para 5(1), (8)(b), not yet in force.
[164] Repealed by the Counter-Terrorism Act 2008, s 39, Sch 3, para 5(1), (8)(b), not yet in force.
[165] Substituted by the Counter-Terrorism Act 2008, s 39, Sch 3, para 5(1), (8)(b), not yet in force.

(d) that, having regard to all the circumstances, it is appropriate to order compensation to be paid.

(5) The High Court shall not order compensation to be paid where it appears to it that proceedings for the offence would have been instituted even if the serious default had not occurred.

(6) Compensation payable under this paragraph shall be paid

    (a) where the person in default was or was acting as a member of a police force, out of the police fund out of which the expenses of that police force are met, and

    (b) where the person in default was a member of the Crown Prosecution Service, or was acting on behalf of the Service, by the Director of Public Prosecutions.

10 (1) This paragraph applies where

    (a) a forfeiture order or a restraint order is made in or in relation to proceedings for *an offence under any of sections 15 to 18*[166] *[a relevant offence]*,[167] and

    (b) the proceedings result in a conviction which is subsequently quashed on an appeal under section 7(2) or (5).

(2) A person who had an interest in any property which was subject to the order may apply to the High Court for compensation.

(3) The High Court may order compensation to be paid to the applicant if satisfied

    (a) that the applicant has suffered loss in consequence of anything done in relation to the property by or in pursuance of the forfeiture order or restraint order, and

    (b) that, having regard to all the circumstances, it is appropriate to order compensation to be paid.

(4) Compensation payable under this paragraph shall be paid by the Secretary of State.

Proceedings for an offence: timing

11 (1) For the purposes of this Part of this Schedule proceedings for an offence are instituted

    (a) when a justice of the peace issues a summons or warrant under section 1 of the Magistrates' Courts Act 1980 in respect of the offence;

    [*(aa) when a public prosecutor issues a written charge and requisition in respect of the offence;*][168]

    (b) when a person is charged with the offence after being taken into custody without a warrant;

    (c) when a bill of indictment charging a person with the offence is preferred by virtue of section 2(2)(b) of the Administration of Justice (Miscellaneous Provisions) Act 1933.

(2) Where the application of sub-paragraph (1) would result in there being more than one time for the institution of proceedings they shall be taken to be instituted at the earliest of those times.

[*(2A) In sub-paragraph (1) "public prosecutor", "requisition" and "written charge" have the same meaning as in section 29 of the Criminal Justice Act 2003.*][169]

(3) For the purposes of this Part of this Schedule proceedings are concluded

    (a) when a forfeiture order has been made in those proceedings and effect has been given to it in respect of all the forfeited property, or

    (b) when no forfeiture order has been made in those proceedings and there is no further possibility of one being made as a result of an appeal (disregarding any power of a court to grant leave to appeal out of time).

---

[166] Repealed by the Counter-Terrorism Act 2008, s 39, Sch 3, para 5(1), (9), not yet in force.

[167] Substituted by the Counter-Terrorism Act 2008, s 39, Sch 3, para 5(1), (9), not yet in force.

[168] Inserted by the Criminal Justice Act 2003, s 331, Sch 36, Pt 2, para 14(1), (2), not yet in force.

[169] Inserted by the Criminal Justice Act 2003, s 331, Sch 36, Pt 2, para 14(1), (3), not yet in force.

Domestic and overseas freezing orders

[**11A** (1) This paragraph has effect for the purposes of paragraphs 11B to 11G.

(2) The relevant Framework Decision means the Framework Decision on the execution in the European Union of orders freezing property or evidence adopted by the Council of the European Union on 22nd July 2003.

(3) A listed offence means

(a) an offence described in Article 3(2) of the relevant Framework Decision, or

(b) a prescribed offence or an offence of a prescribed description.

(4) An order under sub-paragraph (3)(b) which, for the purposes of paragraph 11D, prescribes an offence or a description of offences may require that the conduct which constitutes the offence or offences would, if it occurred in a part of the United Kingdom, constitute an offence in that part.

(5) Specified information, in relation to a certificate under paragraph 11B or 11D, means

(a) any information required to be given by the form of certificate annexed to the relevant Framework Decision, or

(b) any prescribed information.

(6) In this paragraph, "prescribed" means prescribed by an order made by the Secretary of State.

(7) A participating country means

(a) a country other than the United Kingdom which is a member State on a day appointed for the commencement of Schedule 4 to the Crime (International Co-operation) Act 2003, and

(b) any other member State designated by an order made by the Secretary of State.

(8) "Country" includes territory.

(9) Section 14(2)(a) applies for the purposes of determining what are the proceeds of the commission of an offence.

Domestic freezing orders: certification

11B (1) If any of the property to which an application for a restraint order relates is property in a participating country, the applicant may ask the High Court to make a certificate under this paragraph.

(2) The High Court may make a certificate under this paragraph if

(a) it makes a restraint order in relation to property in the participating country, and

(b) it is satisfied that there is a good arguable case that the property is likely to be used for the purposes of a listed offence or is the proceeds of the commission of a listed offence.

(3) A certificate under this paragraph is a certificate which

(a) is made for the purposes of the relevant Framework Decision, and

(b) gives the specified information.

(4) If the High Court makes a certificate under this paragraph

(a) the restraint order must provide for notice of the certificate to be given to the person affected by it, and

(b) paragraph 6(2) to (4) applies to the certificate as it applies to the restraint order.

Sending domestic freezing orders

11C (1) If a certificate is made under paragraph 11B, the restraint order and the certificate are to be sent to the Secretary of State for forwarding to

(a) a court exercising jurisdiction in the place where the property is situated, or

(b) any authority recognised by the government of the participating country as the appropriate authority for receiving orders of that kind.

(2) *The restraint order and the certificate must be accompanied by a forfeiture order, unless the certificate indicates when the court expects a forfeiture order to be sent.*

(3) *The certificate must include a translation of it into an appropriate language of the participating country (if that language is not English).*

(4) *The certificate must be signed by or on behalf of the court and must include a statement as to the accuracy of the information given in it. The signature may be an electronic signature.*

(5) *If the restraint order and the certificate are not accompanied by a forfeiture order, but a forfeiture order is subsequently made, it is to be sent to the Secretary of State for forwarding as mentioned in sub-paragraph (1).*

Overseas freezing orders

11D (1) *Paragraph 11E applies where an overseas freezing order made by an appropriate court or authority in a participating country is received by the Secretary of State from the court or authority which made or confirmed the order.*

(2) *An overseas freezing order is an order prohibiting dealing with property*

    (a) *which is in the United Kingdom,*

    (b) *which the appropriate court or authority considers is likely to be used for the purposes of a listed offence or is the proceeds of the commission of such an offence, and*

    (c) *in respect of which an order has been or may be made by a court exercising criminal jurisdiction in the participating country for the forfeiture of the property,*

and in respect of which the following requirements of this paragraph are met.

(3) *The action which the appropriate court or authority considered would constitute or, as the case may be, constituted the listed offence is action done as an act of terrorism or for the purposes of terrorism.*

(4) *The order must relate to*

    (a) *criminal proceedings instituted in the participating country, or*

    (b) *a criminal investigation being carried on there.*

(5) *The order must be accompanied by a certificate which gives the specified information; but a certificate may be treated as giving any specified information which is not given in it if the Secretary of State has the information in question.*

(6) *The certificate must*

    (a) *be signed by or on behalf of the court or authority which made or confirmed the order,*

    (b) *include a statement as to the accuracy of the information given in it,*

    (c) *if it is not in English, include a translation of it into English (or, if appropriate, Welsh). The signature may be an electronic signature.*

(7) *The order must be accompanied by an order made by a court exercising criminal jurisdiction in that country for the forfeiture of the property, unless the certificate indicates when such an order is expected to be sent.*

(8) *An appropriate court or authority in a participating country in relation to an overseas freezing order is*

    (a) *a court exercising criminal jurisdiction in the country,*

    (b) *a prosecuting authority in the country,*

    (c) *any other authority in the country which appears to the Secretary of State to have the function of making such orders.*

(9) *References in paragraphs 11E to 11G to an overseas freezing order include its accompanying certificate.*

Enforcement of overseas freezing orders

11E (1) *Where this paragraph applies the Secretary of State must send a copy of the overseas freezing order to the High Court and to the Director of Public Prosecutions.*

(2) The court is to consider the overseas freezing order on its own initiative within a period prescribed by rules of court.

(3) Before giving effect to the overseas freezing order, the court must give the Director an opportunity to be heard.

(4) The court may decide not to give effect to the overseas freezing order only if, in its opinion, giving effect to it would be incompatible with any of the Convention rights (within the meaning of the Human Rights Act 1998).

11F The High Court may postpone giving effect to an overseas freezing order in respect of any property

(a) in order to avoid prejudicing a criminal investigation which is taking place in the United Kingdom, or

(b) if, under an order made by a court in criminal proceedings in the United Kingdom, the property may not be dealt with.

11G (1) Where the High Court decides to give effect to an overseas freezing order, it must

(a) register the order in that court,

(b) provide for notice of the registration to be given to any person affected by it.

(2) For the purpose of enforcing an overseas freezing order registered in the High Court, the order is to have effect as if it were an order made by that court.

(3) Paragraph 7 applies to an overseas freezing order registered in the High Court as it applies to a restraint order under paragraph 5.

(4) The High Court may cancel the registration of the order, or vary the property to which the order applies, on an application by the Director of Public Prosecutions or any other person affected by it, if or to the extent that

(a) the court is of the opinion mentioned in paragraph 11E(4), or

(b) the court is of the opinion that the order has ceased to have effect in the participating country.

(5) Her Majesty may by Order in Council make further provision for the enforcement in England and Wales of registered overseas freezing orders.

(6) An Order in Council under this paragraph

(a) may make different provision for different cases,

(b) is not to be made unless a draft of it has been laid before and approved by resolution of each House of Parliament.][170]

Enforcement of orders made elsewhere in the British Islands

12 In the following provisions of this Part of this Schedule

"a Scottish order" means

(a) an order made in Scotland under section 23 [or 23A][171] ("a Scottish forfeiture order"),

(b) an order made under paragraph 18 ("a Scottish restraint order"), or

(c) an order made under any other provision of Part II of this Schedule in relation to a Scottish forfeiture or restraint order;

"a Northern Ireland order" means

(a) an order made in Northern Ireland under section 23 [or 23A][172] ("a Northern Ireland forfeiture order"),

(b) an order made under paragraph 33 ("a Northern Ireland restraint order"), or

(c) an order made under any other provision of Part III of this Schedule in relation to a Northern Ireland forfeiture or restraint order;

---

[170] Inserted by the Crime (International Co-Operation) Act 2003, s 90, Sch 4, paras 1, 3, not yet in force.

[171] Inserted by the Counter-Terrorism Act 2008, s 39, Sch 3, para 5(1), (10), not yet in force.

[172] Inserted by the Counter-Terrorism Act 2008, s 39, Sch 3, para 5(1), (10), not yet in force.

"an Islands order" means an order made in any of the Islands under a provision of the law of that Island corresponding to

(a) section 23 [*or 23A*][173] ("an Islands forfeiture order"),

(b) paragraph 5 ("an Islands restraint order"), or

(c) any other provision of this Part of this Schedule.

13 (1) Subject to the provisions of this paragraph, a Scottish, Northern Ireland or Islands order shall have effect in the law of England and Wales.

(2) But such an order shall be enforced in England and Wales only in accordance with

(a) the provisions of this paragraph, and

(b) any provision made by rules of court as to the manner in which, and the conditions subject to which, such orders are to be enforced there.

(3) On an application made to it in accordance with rules of court for registration of a Scottish, Northern Ireland or Islands order, the High Court shall direct that the order shall, in accordance with such rules, be registered in that court.

(4) Rules of court shall also make provision

(a) for cancelling or varying the registration of a Scottish, Northern Ireland or Islands forfeiture order when effect has been given to it, whether in England and Wales or elsewhere, in respect of all or, as the case may be, part of the money or other property to which the order applies;

(b) for cancelling or varying the registration of a Scottish, Northern Ireland or Islands restraint order which has been discharged or varied by the court by which it was made.

(5) If a Scottish, Northern Ireland or Islands forfeiture order is registered under this paragraph the High Court shall have, in relation to that order, the same powers as a court has under paragraph 2(1) to give effect to a forfeiture order made by it and

(a) paragraph 3 shall apply accordingly,

(b) any functions of [the designated officer for a magistrates' court][174] shall be exercised by the appropriate officer of the High Court, and

(c) after making any payment required by virtue of paragraph 2(1)(d) or 3, the balance of any sums received by the appropriate officer of the High Court by virtue of an order made under this sub-paragraph shall be paid by him to the Secretary of State.

(6) If a Scottish, Northern Ireland or Islands restraint order is registered under this paragraph

(a) paragraphs 7 and 8 shall apply as they apply to a restraint order under paragraph 5, and

(b) the High Court shall have power to make an order under section 33 of the *Supreme Court Act 1981*[175] [*Senior Courts Act 1981*][176] (extended power to order inspection of property, &c) in relation to proceedings brought or likely to be brought for a Scottish, Northern Ireland or Islands restraint order as if those proceedings had been brought or were likely to be brought in the High Court.

(7) In addition, if a Scottish, Northern Ireland or Islands order is registered under this paragraph

(a) the High Court shall have, in relation to its enforcement, the same power as if the order had originally been made in the High Court,

(b) proceedings for or with respect to its enforcement may be taken as if the order had originally been made in the High Court, and

---

[173] Inserted by the Counter-Terrorism Act 2008, s 39, Sch 3, para 5(1), (10), not yet in force.

[174] Substituted by the Courts Act 2003, s 109(1), Sch 8, para 388(1), (3), not yet in force.

[175] Repealed by the Constitutional Reform Act 2005, s 59(5), Sch 11, Pt 1, para 1(2), not yet in force.

[176] Substituted by the Constitutional Reform Act 2005, s 59(5), Sch 11, Pt 1, para 1(2), not yet in force.

(c) proceedings for or with respect to contravention of such an order, whether before or after such registration, may be taken as if the order had originally been made in the High Court.

(8) The High Court may also make such orders or do otherwise as seems to it appropriate for the purpose of

(a) assisting the achievement in England and Wales of the purposes of a Scottish, Northern Ireland or Islands order, or

(b) assisting a receiver or other person directed by a Scottish, Northern Ireland or Islands order to sell or otherwise dispose of property.

(9) The following documents shall be received in evidence in England and Wales without further proof

(a) a document purporting to be a copy of a Scottish, Northern Ireland or Islands order and to be certified as such by a proper officer of the court by which it was made, and

(b) a document purporting to be a certificate for purposes corresponding to those of paragraph 4(2) and (3) and to be certified by a proper officer of the court concerned.

Enforcement of orders made in designated countries

14 (1) Her Majesty may by Order in Council make provision for the purpose of enabling the enforcement in England and Wales of external orders.

(2) An "external order" means an order [*(other than an overseas freezing order within the meaning of paragraph 11D)*][177]

(a) which is made in a country or territory designated for the purposes of this paragraph by the Order in Council, and

(b) which makes relevant provision.

(3) "Relevant provision" means

(a) provision for the forfeiture of terrorist property ("an external forfeiture order"), or

(b) provision prohibiting dealing with property which is subject to an external forfeiture order or in respect of which such an order could be made in proceedings which have been or are to be instituted in the designated country or territory ("an external restraint order").

(4) An Order in Council under this paragraph may, in particular, include provision

(a) which, for the purpose of facilitating the enforcement of any external order that may be made, has effect at times before there is an external order to be enforced;

(b) for matters corresponding to those for which provision is made by, or can be made under, paragraph 13(1) to (8) in relation to the orders to which that paragraph applies;

(c) for the proof of any matter relevant for the purposes of anything falling to be done in pursuance of the Order in Council.

(5) An Order in Council under this paragraph may also make provision with respect to anything falling to be done on behalf of the United Kingdom in a designated country or territory in relation to proceedings in that country or territory for or in connection with the making of an external order.

(6) An Order in Council under this paragraph

(a) may make different provision for different cases, and

(b) shall not be made unless a draft of it has been laid before and approved by resolution of each House of Parliament.

---

[177] Inserted by the Crime (International Cooperation) act 2003, s 90, Sch 4, paras 1, 4, not yet in force.

PART II

SCOTLAND *(omitted)*

PART III

NORTHERN IRELAND *(omitted)*

Domestic and overseas freezing orders (omitted)

PART IV

INSOLVENCY: UNITED KINGDOM PROVISIONS *(omitted)*

SCHEDULE 5   Section 37

TERRORIST INVESTIGATIONS: INFORMATION

PART I

ENGLAND AND WALES AND NORTHERN IRELAND

Searches

1 (1)   A constable may apply to a justice of the peace for the issue of a warrant under this paragraph for the purposes of a terrorist investigation.

(2)   A warrant under this paragraph shall authorise any constable

     (a)   to enter [premises mentioned in sub-paragraph (2A)],[178]

     (b)   to search the premises and any person found there, and

     (c)   to seize and retain any relevant material which is found on a search under paragraph (b).

[(2A) The premises referred to in sub-paragraph (2)(a) are

     (a)   one or more sets of premises specified in the application (in which case the application is for a 'specific premises warrant'); or

     (b)   any premises occupied or controlled by a person specified in the application, including such sets of premises as are so specified (in which case the application is for an 'all premises warrant').][179]

(3)   For the purpose of sub-paragraph (2)(c) material is relevant if the constable has reasonable grounds for believing that

     (a)   it is likely to be of substantial value, whether by itself or together with other material, to a terrorist investigation, and

     (b)   it must be seized in order to prevent it from being concealed, lost, damaged, altered or destroyed.

(4)   A warrant under this paragraph shall not authorise

     (a)   the seizure and retention of items subject to legal privilege, or

     (b)   a constable to require a person to remove any clothing in public except for headgear, footwear, an outer coat, a jacket or gloves.

(5)   Subject to paragraph 2, a justice may grant an application under this paragraph if satisfied

     (a)   that the warrant is sought for the purposes of a terrorist investigation,

---

[178] Substituted by the Terrorism Act 2006, s 26(1), (2).

[179] Inserted by the Terrorism Act 2006, s 26(1), (3).

(b) that there are reasonable grounds for believing that there is material on [premises to which the application relates][180] which is likely to be of substantial value, whether by itself or together with other material, to a terrorist investigation and which does not consist of or include excepted material (within the meaning of paragraph 4 below), [. . .][181]

(c) that the issue of a warrant is likely to be necessary in the circumstances of the case, [and][182]

[(d) in the case of an application for an all premises warrant, that it is not reasonably practicable to specify in the application all the premises which the person so specified occupies or controls and which might need to be searched.][183]

2 (1) This paragraph applies where an application [for a specific premises warrant][184] is made under paragraph 1 and

(a) the application is made by a police officer of at least the rank of superintendent,

(b) the application does not relate to residential premises, and

(c) the justice to whom the application is made is not satisfied of the matter referred to in paragraph 1(5)(c).

(2) The justice may grant the application if satisfied of the matters referred to in paragraph 1(5)(a) and (b).

(3) Where a warrant under paragraph 1 is issued by virtue of this paragraph, the powers under paragraph 1(2)(a) and (b) are exercisable only within the period of 24 hours beginning with the time when the warrant is issued.

(4) For the purpose of sub-paragraph (1) "residential premises" means any premises which the officer making the application has reasonable grounds for believing are used wholly or mainly as a dwelling.

[2A (1) This paragraph applies where an application for an all premises warrant is made under paragraph 1 and

(a) the application is made by a police officer of at least the rank of superintendent, and

(b) the justice to whom the application is made is not satisfied of the matter referred to in paragraph 1(5)(c).

(2) The justice may grant the application if satisfied of the matters referred to in paragraph 1(5)(a), (b) and (d).

(3) Where a warrant under paragraph 1 is issued by virtue of this paragraph, the powers under paragraph 1(2)(a) and (b) are exercisable only

(a) in respect of premises which are not residential premises, and

(b) within the period of 24 hours beginning with the time when the warrant is issued.

(4) For the purpose of sub-paragraph (3) 'residential premises', in relation to a power under paragraph 1(2)(a) or (b), means any premises which the constable exercising the power has reasonable grounds for believing are used wholly or mainly as a dwelling.][185]

3 (1) Subject to sub-paragraph (2), a police officer of at least the rank of superintendent may by a written authority signed by him authorise a search of specified premises which are wholly or partly within a cordoned area.

(2) A constable who is not of the rank required by sub-paragraph (1) may give an authorisation under this paragraph if he considers it necessary by reason of urgency.

(3) An authorisation under this paragraph shall authorise any constable

(a) to enter the premises specified in the authority,

---

[180] Substituted by the Terrorism Act 2006, s 26(1), (4)(a).
[181] Repealed by the Terrorism Act 2006, s 37(5), Sch 3.
[182] Inserted by the Terrorism Act 2006, s 26(1), (4)(b).
[183] Inserted by the Terrorism Act 2006, s 26(1), (4)(c).
[184] Inserted by the Terrorism Act 2006, s 26(1), (5).
[185] Inserted by the Terrorism Act 2006, s 26(1), (6).

    (b) to search the premises and any person found there, and

    (c) to seize and retain any relevant material (within the meaning of paragraph 1(3)) which is found on a search under paragraph (b).

(4) The powers under sub-paragraph (3)(a) and (b) may be exercised

    (a) on one or more occasions, and

    (b) at any time during the period when the designation of the cordoned area under section 33 has effect.

(5) An authorisation under this paragraph shall not authorise

    (a) the seizure and retention of items subject to legal privilege;

    (b) a constable to require a person to remove any clothing in public except for headgear, footwear, an outer coat, a jacket or gloves.

(6) An authorisation under this paragraph shall not be given unless the person giving it has reasonable grounds for believing that there is material to be found on the premises which

    (a) is likely to be of substantial value, whether by itself or together with other material, to a terrorist investigation, and

    (b) does not consist of or include excepted material.

(7) A person commits an offence if he wilfully obstructs a search under this paragraph.

(8) A person guilty of an offence under sub-paragraph (7) shall be liable on summary conviction to

    (a) imprisonment for a term not exceeding *three months*[186] *[51 weeks]*,[187]

    (b) a fine not exceeding level 4 on the standard scale, or

    (c) both.

Excepted material

4 In this Part

    (a) "excluded material" has the meaning given by section 11 of the Police and Criminal Evidence Act 1984,

    (b) "items subject to legal privilege" has the meaning given by section 10 of that Act, and

    (c) "special procedure material" has the meaning given by section 14 of that Act;

and material is "excepted material" if it falls within any of paragraphs (a) to (c).

Excluded and special procedure material: production & access

5 (1) A constable may apply to a Circuit judge [*or a District Judge (Magistrates' Courts)*][188] for an order under this paragraph for the purposes of a terrorist investigation.

(2) An application for an order shall relate to particular material, or material of a particular description, which consists of or includes excluded material or special procedure material.

(3) An order under this paragraph may require a specified person

    (a) to produce to a constable within a specified period for seizure and retention any material which he has in his possession, custody or power and to which the application relates;

    (b) to give a constable access to any material of the kind mentioned in paragraph (a) within a specified period;

    (c) to state to the best of his knowledge and belief the location of material to which the application relates if it is not in, and it will not come into, his possession, custody or power within the period specified under paragraph (a) or (b).

---

[186] Repealed by the Criminal Justice Act 2003, s 280(2), Sch 26, para 55(1), (4)(a), not yet in force.

[187] Substituted by the Criminal Justice Act 2003, s 280(2), Sch 26, para 55(1), (4)(a), not yet in force.

[188] Inserted by the Courts Act 2003, s 65, Sch 4, para 9(a), not yet in force.

(4) For the purposes of this paragraph
- (a) an order may specify a person only if he appears to the Circuit judge [*or the District Judge (Magistrates' Courts)*][189] to have in his possession, custody or power any of the material to which the application relates, and
- (b) a period specified in an order shall be the period of seven days beginning with the date of the order unless it appears to the judge that a different period would be appropriate in the particular circumstances of the application.

(5) Where a [*a District Judge (Magistrates' Courts)*][190] makes an order under sub-paragraph (3)(b) in relation to material on any premises, he may, on the application of a constable, order any person who appears to the judge to be entitled to grant entry to the premises to allow any constable to enter the premises to obtain access to the material.

6 (1) A Circuit judge [*or a District Judge (Magistrates' Courts)*][191] may grant an application under paragraph 5 if satisfied
- (a) that the material to which the application relates consists of or includes excluded material or special procedure material,
- (b) that it does not include items subject to legal privilege, and
- (c) that the conditions in sub-paragraphs (2) and (3) are satisfied in respect of that material.

(2) The first condition is that
- (a) the order is sought for the purposes of a terrorist investigation, and
- (b) there are reasonable grounds for believing that the material is likely to be of substantial value, whether by itself or together with other material, to a terrorist investigation.

(3) The second condition is that there are reasonable grounds for believing that it is in the public interest that the material should be produced or that access to it should be given having regard
- (a) to the benefit likely to accrue to a terrorist investigation if the material is obtained, and
- (b) to the circumstances under which the person concerned has any of the material in his possession, custody or power.

7 (1) An order under paragraph 5 may be made in relation to
- (a) material consisting of or including excluded or special procedure material which is expected to come into existence within the period of 28 days beginning with the date of the order;
- (b) a person who the Circuit judge [*or the District Judge (Magistrates' Courts)*][192] thinks is likely to have any of the material to which the application relates in his possession, custody or power within that period.

(2) Where an order is made under paragraph 5 by virtue of this paragraph, paragraph 5(3) shall apply with the following modifications
- (a) the order shall require the specified person to notify a named constable as soon as is reasonably practicable after any material to which the application relates comes into his possession, custody or power,
- (b) the reference in paragraph 5(3)(a) to material which the specified person has in his possession, custody or power shall be taken as a reference to the material referred to in paragraph (a) above which comes into his possession, custody or power, and
- (c) the reference in paragraph 5(3)(c) to the specified period shall be taken as a reference to the period of 28 days beginning with the date of the order.

(3) Where an order is made under paragraph 5 by virtue of this paragraph, paragraph 5(4) shall not apply and the order
- (a) may only specify a person falling within sub-paragraph (1)(b), and

---

[189] Inserted by the Courts Act 2003, s 65, Sch 4, para 9(b), not yet in force.
[190] Inserted by the Courts Act 2003, s 65, Sch 4, para 9(a), not yet in force.
[191] Inserted by the Courts Act 2003, s 65, Sch 4, para 9(a), not yet in force.
[192] Inserted by the Courts Act 2003, s 65, Sch 4, para 9(b), not yet in force.

(b) shall specify the period of seven days beginning with the date of notification required under sub-paragraph (2)(a) unless it appears to the judge that a different period would be appropriate in the particular circumstances of the application.

8 (1) An order under paragraph 5

    (a) shall not confer any right to production of, or access to, items subject to legal privilege, and

    (b) shall have effect notwithstanding any restriction on the disclosure of information imposed by statute or otherwise.

(2) Where the material to which an application under paragraph 5 relates consists of information contained in a computer

    (a) an order under paragraph 5(3)(a) shall have effect as an order to produce the material in a form in which it can be taken away and in which it is visible and legible, and

    (b) an order under paragraph 5(3)(b) shall have effect as an order to give access to the material in a form in which it is visible and legible.

9 (1) An order under paragraph 5 may be made in relation to material in the possession, custody or power of a government department.

(2) Where an order is made by virtue of sub-paragraph (1)

    (a) it shall be served as if the proceedings were civil proceedings against the department, and

    (b) it may require any officer of the department, whether named in the order or not, who may for the time being have in his possession, custody or power the material concerned, to comply with the order.

(3) In this paragraph "government department" means an authorised government department for the purposes of the Crown Proceedings Act 1947.

10 (1) An order of a Circuit judge [*or a District Judge (Magistrates' Courts)*][193] under paragraph 5 shall have effect as if it were an order of the Crown Court.

(2) [Criminal Procedure Rules][194] may make provision about proceedings relating to an order under paragraph 5.

(3) In particular, the rules may make provision about the variation or discharge of an order.

Excluded or special procedure material: search

11 (1) A constable may apply to a Circuit judge [*or a District Judge (Magistrates' Courts)*][195] for the issue of a warrant under this paragraph for the purposes of a terrorist investigation.

(2) A warrant under this paragraph shall authorise any constable

    (a) to enter [premises mentioned in sub-paragraph (3A)],[196]

    (b) to search the premises and any person found there, and

    (c) to seize and retain any relevant material which is found on a search under paragraph (b).

(3) A warrant under this paragraph shall not authorise

    (a) the seizure and retention of items subject to legal privilege;

    (b) a constable to require a person to remove any clothing in public except for headgear, footwear, an outer coat, a jacket or gloves.

[(3A) The premises referred to in sub-paragraph (2)(a) are

    (a) one or more sets of premises specified in the application (in which case the application is for a 'specific premises warrant'); or

---

[193] Inserted by the Courts Act 2003, s 65, Sch 4, para 9(a), not yet in force.
[194] Substituted by the Courts Act 2003, Sch 109(1), Sch 8, para 389(1), (2).
[195] Inserted by the Courts Act 2003, s 65, Sch 4, para 9(a), not yet in force.
[196] Substituted by the Terrorism Act 2006, s 26(1), (7).

(b) any premises occupied or controlled by a person specified in the application, including such sets of premises as are so specified (in which case the application is for an 'all premises warrant').][197]

(4) For the purpose of sub-paragraph (2)(c) material is relevant if the constable has reasonable grounds for believing that it is likely to be of substantial value, whether by itself or together with other material, to a terrorist investigation.

12 (1) A Circuit judge [or a District Judge (Magistrates' Courts)][198] may grant an application [for a specific premises warrant][199] under paragraph 11 if satisfied that an order made under paragraph 5 in relation to material on the premises specified in the application has not been complied with.

(2) A Circuit judge [or a District Judge (Magistrates' Courts)][200] may also grant an application [for a specific premises warrant][201] under paragraph 11 if satisfied that there are reasonable grounds for believing that

(a) there is material on premises specified in the application which consists of or includes excluded material or special procedure material but does not include items subject to legal privilege, and

(b) the conditions in sub-paragraphs (3) and (4) are satisfied.

[(2A) A Circuit judge or a District Judge (Magistrates' Courts) may grant an application for an all premises warrant under paragraph 11 if satisfied

(a) that an order made under paragraph 5 has not been complied with, and

(b) that the person specified in the application is also specified in the order.

(2B) A Circuit judge or a District Judge (Magistrates' Courts) may also grant an application for an all premises warrant under paragraph 11 if satisfied that there are reasonable grounds for believing

(a) that there is material on premises to which the application relates which consists of or includes excluded material or special procedure material but does not include items subject to legal privilege, and

(b) that the conditions in sub-paragraphs (3) and (4) are met.][202]

(3) The first condition is that

(a) the warrant is sought for the purposes of a terrorist investigation, and

(b) the material is likely to be of substantial value, whether by itself or together with other material, to a terrorist investigation.

(4) The second condition is that it is not appropriate to make an order under paragraph 5 in relation to the material because

(a) it is not practicable to communicate with any person entitled to produce the material,

(b) it is not practicable to communicate with any person entitled to grant access to the material or entitled to grant entry to [premises to which the application for the warrant relates],[203] or

(c) a terrorist investigation may be seriously prejudiced unless a constable can secure immediate access to the material.

---

[197] Inserted by the Terrorism Act 2006, s 26(1), (8).
[198] Inserted by the Courts Act 2003, s 65, Sch 4, para 9(a), not yet in force.
[199] Inserted by the Terrorism Act 2006, s 26(1), (9).
[200] Inserted by the Courts Act 2003, s 65, Sch 4, para 9(a), not yet in force.
[201] Inserted by the Terrorism Act 2006, s 26(1), (9).
[202] Inserted by the Terrorism Act 2006, s 26(1), (10).
[203] Substituted by the Terrorism Act 2006, s 26(1), (11).

Explanations

13 (1) A constable may apply to a Circuit judge [*or a District Judge (Magistrates' Courts)*]²⁰⁴ for an order under this paragraph requiring any person specified in the order to provide an explanation of any material
   (a) seized in pursuance of a warrant under paragraph 1 or 11, or
   (b) produced or made available to a constable under paragraph 5.
   (2) An order under this paragraph shall not require any person to disclose any information which he would be entitled to refuse to disclose on grounds of legal professional privilege in proceedings in the High Court.
   (3) But a lawyer may be required to provide the name and address of his client.
   (4) A statement by a person in response to a requirement imposed by an order under this paragraph
   (a) may be made orally or in writing, and
   (b) may be used in evidence against him only on a prosecution for an offence under paragraph 14.
   (5) Paragraph 10 shall apply to orders under this paragraph as it applies to orders under paragraph 5.

14 (1) A person commits an offence if, in purported compliance with an order under paragraph 13, he
   (a) makes a statement which he knows to be false or misleading in a material particular, or
   (b) recklessly makes a statement which is false or misleading in a material particular.
   (2) A person guilty of an offence under sub-paragraph (1) shall be liable
   (a) on conviction on indictment, to imprisonment for a term not exceeding two years, to a fine or to both, or
   (b) on summary conviction, to imprisonment for a term not exceeding six months, to a fine not exceeding the statutory maximum or to both.

Urgent cases

15 (1) A police officer of at least the rank of superintendent may by a written order signed by him give to any constable the authority which may be given by a search warrant under paragraph 1 or 11.
   (2) An order shall not be made under this paragraph unless the officer has reasonable grounds for believing
   (a) that the case is one of great emergency, and
   (b) that immediate action is necessary.
   (3) Where an order is made under this paragraph particulars of the case shall be notified as soon as is reasonably practicable to the Secretary of State.
   (4) A person commits an offence if he wilfully obstructs a search under this paragraph.
   (5) A person guilty of an offence under sub-paragraph (4) shall be liable on summary conviction to
   (a) imprisonment for a term not exceeding *three months*²⁰⁵ [*51 weeks*],²⁰⁶
   (b) a fine not exceeding level 4 on the standard scale, or
   (c) both.

16 (1) If a police officer of at least the rank of superintendent has reasonable grounds for believing that the case is one of great emergency he may by a written notice signed by him require any person specified in the notice to provide an explanation of any material seized in pursuance of an order under paragraph 15.

---

²⁰⁴ Inserted by the Courts Act 2003, s 65, Sch 4, para 9(a), not yet in force.
²⁰⁵ Repealed by the Criminal Justice Act 2003, s 280(2), Sch 26, para 55(1), (4)(b), not yet in force.
²⁰⁶ Substituted by the Criminal Justice Act 2003, s 280(2), Sch 26, para 55(1), (4)(b), not yet in force.

(2) Sub-paragraphs (2) to (4) of paragraph 13 and paragraph 14 shall apply to a notice under this paragraph as they apply to an order under paragraph 13.

(3) A person commits an offence if he fails to comply with a notice under this paragraph.

(4) It is a defence for a person charged with an offence under sub-paragraph (3) to show that he had a reasonable excuse for his failure.

(5) A person guilty of an offence under sub-paragraph (3) shall be liable on summary conviction to
  (a) imprisonment for a term not exceeding six months,
  (b) a fine not exceeding level 5 on the standard scale, or
  (c) both.

Supplementary

17 *(omitted)*

Northern Ireland

18 *(omitted)*
19–21 [. . .][207]

PART II
SCOTLAND *(omitted)*

SCHEDULE 6   Section 38
FINANCIAL INFORMATION

Orders

1 (1) Where an order has been made under this paragraph in relation to a terrorist investigation, a constable named in the order may require a financial institution [to which the order applies][208] to provide customer information for the purposes of the investigation.

[(1A) The order may provide that it applies to
  (a) all financial institutions,
  (b) a particular description, or particular descriptions, of financial institutions, or
  (c) a particular financial institution or particular financial institutions.][209]

(2) The information shall be provided
  (a) in such manner and within such time as the constable may specify, and
  (b) notwithstanding any restriction on the disclosure of information imposed by statute or otherwise.

(3) An institution which fails to comply with a requirement under this paragraph shall be guilty of an offence.

(4) It is a defence for an institution charged with an offence under sub-paragraph (3) to prove
  (a) that the information required was not in the institution's possession, or
  (b) that it was not reasonably practicable for the institution to comply with the requirement.

(5) An institution guilty of an offence under sub-paragraph (3) shall be liable on summary conviction to a fine not exceeding level 5 on the standard scale.

---

[207] Repealed by the Terrorism (Northern Ireland) Act 2006, s 5(2), Schedule.
[208] Inserted by the Anti-terrorism, Crime and Security Act 2001, s 3, Sch 2, Pt 4, para 6(1), (2).
[209] Inserted by the Anti-terrorism, Crime and Security Act 2001, s 3, Sch 2, Pt 4, para 6(1), (3).

Procedure

2 An order under paragraph 1 may be made only on the application of
  (a) in England and Wales or Northern Ireland, a police officer of at least the rank of superintendent, or
  (b) in Scotland, the procurator fiscal.
3 An order under paragraph 1 may be made only by
  (a) in England and Wales, a Circuit judge [*or a District Judge (Magistrates' Courts)*,]²¹⁰
  (b) in Scotland, the sheriff, or
  (c) in Northern Ireland, a [Crown Court judge].²¹¹
4 *(omitted)*

Criteria for making order

5 An order under paragraph 1 may be made only if the person making it is satisfied that
  (a) the order is sought for the purposes of a terrorist investigation,
  (b) the tracing of terrorist property is desirable for the purposes of the investigation, and
  (c) the order will enhance the effectiveness of the investigation.

Financial institution

6 (1) In this Schedule "financial institution" means
  [(a) a person who has permission under Part 4 of the Financial Services and Markets Act 2000 to accept deposits,]²¹²
  (b) [. . .]²¹³
  (c) a credit union (within the meaning of the Credit Unions Act 1979 or the Credit Unions (Northern Ireland) Order 1985),
  [(d) a person carrying on a relevant regulated activity,]²¹⁴
  (e) the National Savings Bank,
  (f) a person who carries out an activity for the purposes of raising money authorised to be raised under the National Loans Act 1968 under the auspices of the Director of National Savings,
  (g) a European institution carrying on a home regulated activity (within the meaning of [Directive 2006/48/EC of the European Parliament and of the Council of 14 June 2006]²¹⁵ relating to the taking up and pursuit of the business of credit institutions),
  (h) a person carrying out an activity specified in any of points 1 to 12 and 14 of [Annex 1]²¹⁶ to that Directive, and
  (i) a person who carries on an insurance business in accordance with an authorisation pursuant to [Article 4 or 51 of Directive 2002/83/EC of the European Parliament and of the Council of 5th November 2002 concerning life assurance].²¹⁷

---

²¹⁰ Inserted by the Courts Act 2003, s 65, Sch 4, para 10, not yet in force.
²¹¹ Substituted by the Anti-terrorism, Crime and Security Act 2001, s 121(1), (4).
²¹² Substituted by SI 2001/3649, art 361(1), (2)(a).
²¹³ Repealed by SI 2001/3649, art 361(1), (2)(b).
²¹⁴ Substituted by SI 2001/3649, art 361(1), (2)(c).
²¹⁵ Substituted by SI 2006/3221, reg 29(2), Sch 4, para 6(1), (3).
²¹⁶ Substituted by SI 2000/2952, reg 9(b).
²¹⁷ Substituted by SI 2004/3379, reg 7.

[(1A)For the purposes of sub-paragraph (1)(d), a relevant regulated activity means
    (a) dealing in investments as principal or as agent,
    (b) arranging deals in investments,
    [(ba) operating a multilateral trading facility,][218]
    (c) managing investments,
    (d) safeguarding and administering investments,
    (e) sending dematerialised instructions,
    (f) establishing etc collective investment schemes,
    (g) advising on investments.
(1B) Sub-paragraphs (1)(a) and (1A) must be read with
    (a) section 22 of the Financial Services and Markets Act 2000;
    (b) any relevant order under that section; and
    (c) Schedule 2 to that Act.][219]
(2) The Secretary of State may by order provide for a class of person
    (a) to be a financial institution for the purposes of this Schedule, or
    (b) to cease to be a financial institution for the purposes of this Schedule.
(3) An institution which ceases to be a financial institution for the purposes of this Schedule (whether by virtue of sub-paragraph (2)(b) or otherwise) shall continue to be treated as a financial institution for the purposes of any requirement under paragraph 1 to provide customer information which relates to a time when the institution was a financial institution.

Customer information

7 (1) In this Schedule "customer information" means (subject to sub-paragraph (3))
    (a) information whether a business relationship exists or existed between a financial institution and a particular person ("a customer"),
    (b) a customer's account number,
    (c) a customer's full name,
    (d) a customer's date of birth,
    (e) a customer's address or former address,
    (f) the date on which a business relationship between a financial institution and a customer begins or ends,
    (g) any evidence of a customer's identity obtained by a financial institution in pursuance of or for the purposes of any legislation relating to money laundering, and
    (h) the identity of a person sharing an account with a customer.
(2) For the purposes of this Schedule there is a business relationship between a financial institution and a person if (and only if)
    (a) there is an arrangement between them designed to facilitate the carrying out of frequent or regular transactions between them, and
    (b) the total amount of payments to be made in the course of the arrangement is neither known nor capable of being ascertained when the arrangement is made.
(3) The Secretary of State may by order provide for a class of information
    (a) to be customer information for the purposes of this Schedule, or
    (b) to cease to be customer information for the purposes of this Schedule.

---

[218] Inserted by SI 2006/3384, art 33.
[219] Inserted by SI 2001/3649, art 361(1), (3).

Offence by body corporate, &c

8 *(omitted)*

Self-incrimination

9 (1) Customer information provided by a financial institution under this Schedule shall not be admissible in evidence in criminal proceedings against the institution or any of its officers or employees.

   (2) Sub-paragraph (1) shall not apply in relation to proceedings for an offence under paragraph 1(3) (including proceedings brought by virtue of paragraph 8).

[SCHEDULE 6A
ACCOUNT MONITORING ORDERS

Introduction

1 (1) This paragraph applies for the purposes of this Schedule.

   (2) A judge is

     (a) *a Circuit judge,*[220] [*a Circuit judge or a District Judge (Magistrates' Courts),*][221] in England and Wales;

     (b) the sheriff, in Scotland;

     (c) a Crown Court judge, in Northern Ireland.

   (3) The court is

     (a) the Crown Court, in England and Wales or Northern Ireland;

     (b) the sheriff, in Scotland.

   (4) An appropriate officer is

     (a) a police officer, in England and Wales or Northern Ireland;

     (b) the procurator fiscal, in Scotland.

   (5) "Financial institution" has the same meaning as in Schedule 6.

Account monitoring orders

2 (1) A judge may, on an application made to him by an appropriate officer, make an account monitoring order if he is satisfied that

     (a) the order is sought for the purposes of a terrorist investigation,

     (b) the tracing of terrorist property is desirable for the purposes of the investigation, and

     (c) the order will enhance the effectiveness of the investigation.

   (2) The application for an account monitoring order must state that the order is sought against the financial institution specified in the application in relation to information which

     (a) relates to an account or accounts held at the institution by the person specified in the application (whether solely or jointly with another), and

     (b) is of the description so specified.

   (3) The application for an account monitoring order may specify information relating to

     (a) all accounts held by the person specified in the application for the order at the financial institution so specified,

     (b) a particular description, or particular descriptions, of accounts so held, or

     (c) a particular account, or particular accounts, so held.

---

[220] Repealed by the Courts Act 2003, s 65, Sch 4, para 11, not yet in force.
[221] Inserted by the Courts Act 2003, s 65, Sch 4, para 11, not yet in force.

(4) An account monitoring order is an order that the financial institution specified in the application for the order must

    (a) for the period specified in the order,

    (b) in the manner so specified,

    (c) at or by the time or times so specified, and

    (d) at the place or places so specified,

provide information of the description specified in the application to an appropriate officer.

(5) The period stated in an account monitoring order must not exceed the period of 90 days beginning with the day on which the order is made.

Applications

3 (1) An application for an account monitoring order may be made ex parte to a judge in chambers.

   (2) The description of information specified in an application for an account monitoring order may be varied by the person who made the application.

   (3) If the application was made by a police officer, the description of information specified in it may be varied by a different police officer.

Discharge or variation

4 (1) An application to discharge or vary an account monitoring order may be made to the court by

    (a) the person who applied for the order;

    (b) any person affected by the order.

   (2) If the application for the account monitoring order was made by a police officer, an application to discharge or vary the order may be made by a different police officer.

   (3) The court

    (a) may discharge the order;

    (b) may vary the order.

Rules of court

5 *(omitted)*

Effect of orders

6 (1) In England and Wales and Northern Ireland, an account monitoring order has effect as if it were an order of the court.

   (2) An account monitoring order has effect in spite of any restriction on the disclosure of information (however imposed).

Statements

7 (1) A statement made by a financial institution in response to an account monitoring order may not be used in evidence against it in criminal proceedings.

   (2) But sub-paragraph (1) does not apply

    (a) in the case of proceedings for contempt of court;

    (b) in the case of proceedings under section 23 where the financial institution has been convicted of an offence under any of sections 15 to 18;

    (c) on a prosecution for an offence where, in giving evidence, the financial institution makes a statement inconsistent with the statement mentioned in sub-paragraph (1).

(3) A statement may not be used by virtue of sub-paragraph (2)(c) against a financial institution unless

(a) evidence relating to it is adduced, or

(b) a question relating to it is asked,

by or on behalf of the financial institution in the proceedings arising out of the prosecution.][222]

SCHEDULE 7
PORT AND BORDER CONTROLS

Section 53

Interpretation

1 (1) In this Schedule "examining officer" means any of the following

(a) a constable,

(b) an immigration officer, and

(c) a customs officer who is designated for the purpose of this Schedule by the Secretary of State and the Commissioners of Customs and Excise.

(2) In this Schedule

"the border area" has the meaning given by paragraph 4,

"captain" means master of a ship or commander of an aircraft,

"port" includes an airport and a hoverport,

"ship" includes a hovercraft, and

"vehicle" includes a train.

(3) A place shall be treated as a port for the purposes of this Schedule in relation to a person if an examining officer believes that the person

(a) has gone there for the purpose of embarking on a ship or aircraft, or

(b) has arrived there on disembarking from a ship or aircraft.

Power to stop, question and detain

2 (1) An examining officer may question a person to whom this paragraph applies for the purpose of determining whether he appears to be a person falling within section 40(1)(b).

(2) This paragraph applies to a person if

(a) he is at a port or in the border area, and

(b) the examining officer believes that the person's presence at the port or in the area is connected with his entering or leaving Great Britain or Northern Ireland [or his travelling by air within Great Britain or within Northern Ireland][223].

(3) This paragraph also applies to a person on a ship or aircraft which has arrived [at any place in Great Britain or Northern Ireland (whether from within or outside Great Britain or Northern Ireland)][224].

(4) An examining officer may exercise his powers under this paragraph whether or not he has grounds for suspecting that a person falls within section 40(1)(b).

3 An examining officer may question a person who is in the border area for the purpose of determining whether his presence in the area is connected with his entering or leaving Northern Ireland.

---

[222] Inserted by the Anti-terrorism, Crime and Security Act 2001, s 3, Sch 2, Pt 1, para 1(1), (3).

[223] Inserted by the Anti-terrorism, Crime and Security Act 2001, s 118(1), (2).

[224] Substituted by the Anti-terrorism, Crime and Security Act 2001, s 118(1), (3).

4 (1) A place in Northern Ireland is within the border area for the purposes of paragraphs 2 and 3 if it is no more than one mile from the border between Northern Ireland and the Republic of Ireland.

(2) If a train goes from the Republic of Ireland to Northern Ireland, the first place in Northern Ireland at which it stops for the purpose of allowing passengers to leave is within the border area for the purposes of paragraphs 2 and 3.

5 A person who is questioned under paragraph 2 or 3 must

(a) give the examining officer any information in his possession which the officer requests;

(b) give the examining officer on request either a valid passport which includes a photograph or another document which establishes his identity;

(c) declare whether he has with him documents of a kind specified by the examining officer;

(d) give the examining officer on request any document which he has with him and which is of a kind specified by the officer.

6 (1) For the purposes of exercising a power under paragraph 2 or 3 an examining officer may

(a) stop a person or vehicle;

(b) detain a person.

(2) For the purpose of detaining a person under this paragraph, an examining officer may authorise the person's removal from a ship, aircraft or vehicle.

(3) Where a person is detained under this paragraph the provisions of Part 1 of Schedule 8 (treatment) shall apply.

(4) A person detained under this paragraph shall (unless detained under any other power) be released not later than the end of the period of nine hours beginning with the time when his examination begins.

Searches

7 For the purpose of satisfying himself whether there are any persons whom he may wish to question under paragraph 2 an examining officer may

(a) search a ship or aircraft;

(b) search anything on a ship or aircraft;

(c) search anything which he reasonably believes has been, or is about to be, on a ship or aircraft.

8 (1) An examining officer who questions a person under paragraph 2 may, for the purpose of determining whether he falls within section 40(1)(b)

(a) search the person;

(b) search anything which he has with him, or which belongs to him, and which is on a ship or aircraft;

(c) search anything which he has with him, or which belongs to him, and which the examining officer reasonably believes has been, or is about to be, on a ship or aircraft;

(d) search a ship or aircraft for anything falling within paragraph (b);

[(e) search a vehicle which is on a ship or aircraft;

(f) search a vehicle which the examining officer reasonably believes has been, or is about to be, on a ship or aircraft.][225]

(2) Where an examining officer questions a person in the border area under paragraph 2 he may (in addition to the matters specified in sub-paragraph (1)), for the purpose of determining whether the person falls within section 40(1)(b)

(a) search a vehicle;

(b) search anything in or on a vehicle;

(c) search anything which he reasonably believes has been, or is about to be, in or on a vehicle.

(3) A search of a person under this paragraph must be carried out by someone of the same sex.

---

[225] Inserted by the Terrorism Act 2006, s 29.

9 (1) An examining officer may examine goods to which this paragraph applies for the purpose of determining whether they have been used in the commission, preparation or instigation of acts of terrorism.

   [(2) This paragraph applies to

      (a) goods which have arrived in or are about to leave Great Britain or Northern Ireland on a ship or vehicle, and

      (b) goods which have arrived at or are about to leave any place in Great Britain or Northern Ireland on an aircraft (whether the place they have come from or are going to is within or outside Great Britain or Northern Ireland).][226]

   (3) In this paragraph "goods" includes

      (a) property of any description, and

      (b) containers.

   (4) An examining officer may board a ship or aircraft or enter a vehicle for the purpose of determining whether to exercise his power under this paragraph.

10 (1) An examining officer may authorise a person to carry out on his behalf a search or examination under any of paragraphs 7 to 9.

   (2) A person authorised under this paragraph shall be treated as an examining officer for the purposes of

      (a) paragraphs 9(4) and 11 of this Schedule, and

      (b) paragraphs 2 and 3 of Schedule 14.

Detention of property

11 (1) This paragraph applies to anything which

      (a) is given to an examining officer in accordance with paragraph 5(d),

      (b) is searched or found on a search under paragraph 8, or

      (c) is examined under paragraph 9.

   (2) An examining officer may detain the thing

      (a) for the purpose of examination, for a period not exceeding seven days beginning with the day on which the detention commences,

      (b) while he believes that it may be needed for use as evidence in criminal proceedings, or

      (c) while he believes that it may be needed in connection with a decision by the Secretary of State whether to make a deportation order under the Immigration Act 1971.

Designated ports

12 (1) This paragraph applies to a journey

      (a) to Great Britain from the Republic of Ireland, Northern Ireland or any of the Islands,

      (b) from Great Britain to any of those places,

      (c) to Northern Ireland from Great Britain, the Republic of Ireland or any of the Islands, or

      (d) from Northern Ireland to any of those places.

   (2) Where a ship or aircraft is employed to carry passengers for reward on a journey to which this paragraph applies the owners or agents of the ship or aircraft shall not arrange for it to call at a port in Great Britain or Northern Ireland for the purpose of disembarking or embarking passengers unless

      (a) the port is a designated port, or

      (b) an examining officer approves the arrangement.

---

[226] Substituted by the Anti-terrorism, Crime and Security Act 2001, s 118(1), (4).

(3) Where an aircraft is employed on a journey to which this paragraph applies otherwise than to carry passengers for reward, the captain of the aircraft shall not permit it to call at or leave a port in Great Britain or Northern Ireland unless

    (a) the port is a designated port, or

    (b) he gives at least 12 hours' notice in writing to a constable for the police area in which the port is situated (or, where the port is in Northern Ireland, to a [member of the Police Service of Northern Ireland).][227]

(4) A designated port is a port which appears in the Table at the end of this Schedule.

(5) The Secretary of State may by order

    (a) add an entry to the Table;

    (b) remove an entry from the Table.

Embarkation and disembarkation

13 (1) The Secretary of State may by notice in writing to the owners or agents of ships or aircraft

    (a) designate control areas in any port in the United Kingdom;

    (b) specify conditions for or restrictions on the embarkation or disembarkation of passengers in a control area.

(2) Where owners or agents of a ship or aircraft receive notice under sub-paragraph (1) in relation to a port they shall take all reasonable steps to ensure, in respect of the ship or aircraft

    (a) that passengers do not embark or disembark at the port outside a control area, and

    (b) that any specified conditions are met and any specified restrictions are complied with.

14 (1) The Secretary of State may by notice in writing to persons concerned with the management of a port in the United Kingdom ("the port managers")

    (a) designate control areas in the port;

    (b) require the port managers to provide at their own expense specified facilities in a control area for the purposes of the embarkation or disembarkation of passengers or their examination under this Schedule;

    (c) require conditions to be met and restrictions to be complied with in relation to the embarkation or disembarkation of passengers in a control area;

    (d) require the port managers to display, in specified locations in control areas, notices containing specified information about the provisions of this Schedule in such form as may be specified.

(2) Where port managers receive notice under sub-paragraph (1) they shall take all reasonable steps to comply with any requirement set out in the notice.

15 (1) This paragraph applies to a ship employed to carry passengers for reward, or an aircraft, which

    (a) arrives in Great Britain from the Republic of Ireland, Northern Ireland or any of the Islands,

    (b) arrives in Northern Ireland from Great Britain, the Republic of Ireland or any of the Islands,

    (c) leaves Great Britain for the Republic of Ireland, Northern Ireland or any of the Islands, or

    (d) leaves Northern Ireland for Great Britain, the Republic of Ireland or any of the Islands.

(2) The captain shall ensure

    (a) that passengers and members of the crew do not disembark at a port in Great Britain or Northern Ireland unless either they have been examined by an examining officer or they disembark in accordance with arrangements approved by an examining officer;

---

[227] substituted by the Police (Northern Ireland) Act 2000, s 78(2)(c).

(b) that passengers and members of the crew do not embark at a port in Great Britain or Northern Ireland except in accordance with arrangements approved by an examining officer;

(c) where a person is to be examined under this Schedule on board the ship or aircraft, that he is presented for examination in an orderly manner.

(3) Where paragraph 27 of Schedule 2 to the Immigration Act 1971 (disembarkation requirements on arrival in the United Kingdom) applies, the requirements of sub-paragraph (2)(a) above are in addition to the requirements of paragraph 27 of that Schedule.

Carding

16 (1) The Secretary of State may by order make provision requiring a person to whom this paragraph applies, if required to do so by an examining officer, to complete and produce to the officer a card containing such information in such form as the order may specify.

(2) An order under this paragraph may require the owners or agents of a ship or aircraft employed to carry passengers for reward to supply their passengers with cards in the form required by virtue of sub-paragraph (1).

(3) This paragraph applies to a person

(a) who disembarks in Great Britain from a ship or aircraft which has come from the Republic of Ireland, Northern Ireland or any of the Islands,

(b) who disembarks in Northern Ireland from a ship or aircraft which has come from Great Britain, the Republic of Ireland, or any of the Islands,

(c) who embarks in Great Britain on a ship or aircraft which is going to the Republic of Ireland, Northern Ireland or any of the Islands, or

(d) who embarks in Northern Ireland on a ship or aircraft which is going to Great Britain, the Republic of Ireland, or any of the Islands.

Provision of passenger information

17 [(1) This paragraph applies to a ship or aircraft which

(a) arrives or is expected to arrive in any place in the United Kingdom (whether from another place in the United Kingdom or from outside the United Kingdom), or

(b) leaves or is expected to leave the United Kingdom.][228]

(2) If an examining officer gives the owners or agents of a ship or aircraft to which this paragraph applies a written request to provide specified information, the owners or agents shall comply with the request as soon as is reasonably practicable.

(3) A request to an owner or agent may relate

(a) to a particular ship or aircraft,

(b) to all ships or aircraft of the owner or agent to which this paragraph applies, or

(c) to specified ships or aircraft.

(4) Information may be specified in a request only if it is of a kind which is prescribed by order of the Secretary of State and which relates

(a) to passengers,

(b) to crew, [. . .][229]

(c) to vehicles belonging to passengers or crew, [or

(d) to goods][230].

(5) A passenger or member of the crew on a ship or aircraft shall give the captain any information required for the purpose of enabling the owners or agents to comply with a request under this paragraph.

---

[228] Substituted by the Anti-terrorism, Crime and Security Act 2001, s 119(1), (2).
[229] Repealed by the Anti-terrorism, Crime and Security Act 2001, s 119(1), (3)(a).
[230] Inserted by the Anti-terrorism, Crime and Security Act 2001, s 119(1), (3)(b).

(6) Sub-paragraphs (2) and (5) shall not require the provision of information which is required to be provided under or by virtue of paragraph 27(2) or 27B of Schedule 2 to the Immigration Act 1971.

Offences

18 (1) A person commits an offence if he

(a) wilfully fails to comply with a duty imposed under or by virtue of this Schedule,

(b) wilfully contravenes a prohibition imposed under or by virtue of this Schedule, or

(c) wilfully obstructs, or seeks to frustrate, a search or examination under or by virtue of this Schedule.

(2) A person guilty of an offence under this paragraph shall be liable on summary conviction to

(a) imprisonment for a term not exceeding *three months*[231] [*51 weeks,*][232]

(b) a fine not exceeding level 4 on the standard scale, or

(c) both.

Table
Designated Ports
Great Britain

Seaports	Airports
Ardrossan	Aberdeen
Cairnryan	Biggin Hill
Campbeltown	Birmingham
Fishguard	Blackpool
Fleetwood	Bournemouth (Hurn)
Heysham	Bristol
Holyhead	Cambridge
Pembroke Dock	Cardiff
Plymouth	Carlisle
Poole Harbour	Coventry
Port of Liverpool	East Midlands
Portsmouth Continental Ferry Port	Edinburgh
Southampton	Exeter
Stranraer	Glasgow
Swansea	Gloucester/Cheltenham (Staverton)
Torquay	Humberside
Troon	Leeds/Bradford
Weymouth	Liverpool
	London-City
	London-Gatwick
	London-Heathrow
	Luton

[231] Repealed by the Criminal Justice Act 2003, s 280(2), (3), Sch 26, para 55(1), (5), not yet in force.

[232] Substituted by the Criminal Justice Act 2003, s 280(2), (3), Sch 26, para 55(1), (5), not yet in force.

Great Britain (Cont.)

Seaports	Airports
	Lydd
	Manchester
	Manston
	Newcastle
	Norwich
	Plymouth
	Prestwick
	Sheffield City
	Southampton
	Southend
	Stansted
	Teesside

Northern Ireland

Seaports	Airports
Ballycastle	Belfast City
Belfast	Belfast International
Larne	City of Derry
Port of Londonderry	
Warrenpoint	

SCHEDULE 8   Section 41 and Schedule 7, para 6
DETENTION

PART I
TREATMENT OF PERSONS DETAINED UNDER
SECTION 41 OR SCHEDULE 7

Place of detention

1 (1) The Secretary of State shall designate places at which persons may be detained under Schedule 7 or section 41.

(2) In this Schedule a reference to a police station includes a reference to any place which the Secretary of State has designated under sub-paragraph (1) as a place where a person may be detained under section 41.

(3) Where a person is detained under Schedule 7, he may be taken in the custody of an examining officer or of a person acting under an examining officer's authority to and from any place where his attendance is required for the purpose of

(a) his examination under that Schedule,

(b) establishing his nationality or citizenship, or

(c) making arrangements for his admission to a country or territory outside the United Kingdom.

(4) A constable who arrests a person under section 41 shall take him as soon as is reasonably practicable to the police station which the constable considers the most appropriate.

(5) In this paragraph "examining officer" has the meaning given in Schedule 7.

(6) Where a person is arrested in one Part of the United Kingdom and all or part of his detention takes place in another Part, the provisions of this Schedule which apply to detention in a particular Part of the United Kingdom apply in relation to him while he is detained in that Part.

Identification

2 (1) An authorised person may take any steps which are reasonably necessary for

(a) photographing the detained person,

(b) measuring him, or

(c) identifying him.

(2) In sub-paragraph (1) "authorised person" means any of the following

(a) a constable,

(b) a prison officer,

(c) a person authorised by the Secretary of State, and

(d) in the case of a person detained under Schedule 7, an examining officer (within the meaning of that Schedule).

(3) This paragraph does not confer the power to take

(a) fingerprints, non-intimate samples or intimate samples (within the meaning given by paragraph 15 below), or

(b) relevant physical data or samples as mentioned in section 18 of the Criminal Procedure (Scotland) Act 1995 as applied by paragraph 20 below.

Audio and video recording of interviews

3 (1) The Secretary of State shall

(a) issue a code of practice about the audio recording of interviews to which this paragraph applies, and

(b) make an order requiring the audio recording of interviews to which this paragraph applies in accordance with any relevant code of practice under paragraph (a).

(2) The Secretary of State may make an order requiring the video recording of

(a) interviews to which this paragraph applies;

(b) interviews to which this paragraph applies which take place in a particular Part of the United Kingdom.

(3) An order under sub-paragraph (2) shall specify whether the video recording which it requires is to be silent or with sound.

(4) Where an order is made under sub-paragraph (2)

(a) the Secretary of State shall issue a code of practice about the video recording of interviews to which the order applies, and

(b) the order shall require the interviews to be video recorded in accordance with any relevant code of practice under paragraph (a).

(5) Where the Secretary of State has made an order under sub-paragraph (2) requiring certain interviews to be video recorded with sound

(a) he need not make an order under sub-paragraph (1)(b) in relation to those interviews, but

(b) he may do so.

(6) This paragraph applies to any interview by a constable of a person detained under Schedule 7 or section 41 if the interview takes place in a police station.

(7) A code of practice under this paragraph

    (a) may make provision in relation to a particular Part of the United Kingdom;

    (b) may make different provision for different Parts of the United Kingdom.

4 (1) This paragraph applies to a code of practice under paragraph 3.

(2) Where the Secretary of State proposes to issue a code of practice he shall

    (a) publish a draft,

    (b) consider any representations made to him about the draft, and

    (c) if he thinks it appropriate, modify the draft in the light of any representations made to him.

(3) The Secretary of State shall lay a draft of the code before Parliament.

(4) When the Secretary of State has laid a draft code before Parliament he may bring it into operation by order.

(5) The Secretary of State may revise a code and issue the revised code; and sub-paragraphs (2) to (4) shall apply to a revised code as they apply to an original code.

(6) The failure by a constable to observe a provision of a code shall not of itself make him liable to criminal or civil proceedings.

(7) A code

    (a) shall be admissible in evidence in criminal and civil proceedings, and

    (b) shall be taken into account by a court or tribunal in any case in which it appears to the court or tribunal to be relevant.

Status

5 A detained person shall be deemed to be in legal custody throughout the period of his detention.

Rights: England, Wales and Northern Ireland

6 (1) Subject to paragraph 8, a person detained under Schedule 7 or section 41 at a police station in England, Wales or Northern Ireland shall be entitled, if he so requests, to have one named person informed as soon as is reasonably practicable that he is being detained there.

(2) The person named must be

    (a) a friend of the detained person,

    (b) a relative, or

    (c) a person who is known to the detained person or who is likely to take an interest in his welfare.

(3) Where a detained person is transferred from one police station to another, he shall be entitled to exercise the right under this paragraph in respect of the police station to which he is transferred.

7 (1) Subject to paragraphs 8 and 9, a person detained under Schedule 7 or section 41 at a police station in England, Wales or Northern Ireland shall be entitled, if he so requests, to consult a solicitor as soon as is reasonably practicable, privately and at any time.

(2) Where a request is made under sub-paragraph (1), the request and the time at which it was made shall be recorded.

8 (1) Subject to sub-paragraph (2), an officer of at least the rank of superintendent may authorise a delay

    (a) in informing the person named by a detained person under paragraph 6;

    (b) in permitting a detained person to consult a solicitor under paragraph 7.

(2) But where a person is detained under section 41 he must be permitted to exercise his rights under paragraphs 6 and 7 before the end of the period mentioned in subsection (3) of that section.

(3) Subject to sub-paragraph (5), an officer may give an authorisation under sub-paragraph (1) only if he has reasonable grounds for believing
  (a) in the case of an authorisation under sub-paragraph (1)(a), that informing the named person of the detained person's detention will have any of the consequences specified in sub-paragraph (4), or
  (b) in the case of an authorisation under sub-paragraph (1)(b), that the exercise of the right under paragraph 7 at the time when the detained person desires to exercise it will have any of the consequences specified in sub-paragraph (4).

(4) Those consequences are
  (a) interference with or harm to evidence of a [serious offence,][233]
  (b) interference with or physical injury to any person,
  (c) the alerting of persons who are suspected of having committed a [serious offence][234] but who have not been arrested for it,
  (d) the hindering of the recovery of property obtained as a result of a [serious offence][235] or in respect of which a forfeiture order could be made under section 23 (*or section 23A*),[236]
  (e) interference with the gathering of information about the commission, preparation or instigation of acts of terrorism,
  (f) the alerting of a person and thereby making it more difficult to prevent an act of terrorism, and
  (g) the alerting of a person and thereby making it more difficult to secure a person's apprehension, prosecution or conviction in connection with the commission, preparation or instigation of an act of terrorism.

[(5) An officer may also give an authorisation under sub-paragraph (1) if he has reasonable grounds for believing that
  (a) the detained person has benefited from his criminal conduct, and
  (b) the recovery of the value of the property constituting the benefit will be hindered by
    (i) informing the named person of the detained person's detention (in the case of an authorisation under sub-paragraph (1)(a)), or
    (ii) the exercise of the right under paragraph 7 (in the case of an authorisation under sub-paragraph (1)(b)).

(5A) For the purposes of sub-paragraph (5) the question whether a person has benefited from his criminal conduct is to be decided in accordance with Part 2 of the Proceeds of Crime Act 2002.][237]

(6) If an authorisation under sub-paragraph (1) is given orally, the person giving it shall confirm it in writing as soon as is reasonably practicable.

(7) Where an authorisation under sub-paragraph (1) is given
  (a) the detained person shall be told the reason for the delay as soon as is reasonably practicable, and
  (b) the reason shall be recorded as soon as is reasonably practicable.

(8) Where the reason for authorising delay ceases to subsist there may be no further delay in permitting the exercise of the right in the absence of a further authorisation under sub-paragraph (1).

---

[233] Substituted by the Serious Organised Crime and Police Act 2005, s 111, Sch 7, Pt 3, para 48(1)(a), (2).

[234] Substituted by the Serious Organised Crime and Police Act 2005, s 111, Sch 7, Pt 3, para 48(1)(a), (2).

[235] Substituted by the Serious Organised Crime and Police Act 2005, s 111, Sch 7, Pt 3, para 48(1)(a), (2).

[236] Inserted by the Counter-Terrorism Act 2008, Sch 3, para 6, not yet in force.

[237] Substituted, for sub-para (5) as originally enacted, by the Proceeds of Crime Act 2000, s 456, Sch 11, paras 1, 39(1), (2).

(9) [In this paragraph, references to a "serious offence" are (in relation to England and Wales) to an indictable offence, and (in relation to Northern Ireland) to a serious arrestable offence within the meaning of Article 87 of the Police and Criminal Evidence (Northern Ireland) Order 1989; but also include][238]

(a) an offence under any of the provisions mentioned in section 40(1)(a) of this Act, and

(b) an attempt or conspiracy to commit an offence under any of the provisions mentioned in section 40(1)(a).

9 (1) A direction under this paragraph may provide that a detained person who wishes to exercise the right under paragraph 7 may consult a solicitor only in the sight and hearing of a qualified officer.

(2) A direction under this paragraph may be given

(a) where the person is detained at a police station in England or Wales, by an officer of at least the rank of Commander or Assistant Chief Constable, or

(b) where the person is detained at a police station in Northern Ireland, by an officer of at least the rank of Assistant Chief Constable.

[(3) A direction under this paragraph may be given only if the officer giving it has reasonable grounds for believing

(a) that, unless the direction is given, the exercise of the right by the detained person will have any of the consequences specified in paragraph 8(4), or

(b) that the detained person has benefited from his criminal conduct and that, unless the direction is given, the exercise of the right by the detained person will hinder the recovery of the value of the property constituting the benefit.][239]

(4) In this paragraph "a qualified officer" means a police officer who

(a) is of at least the rank of inspector,

(b) is of the uniformed branch of the force of which the officer giving the direction is a member, and

(c) in the opinion of the officer giving the direction, has no connection with the detained person's case.

(5) A direction under this paragraph shall cease to have effect once the reason for giving it ceases to subsist.

10 (1) This paragraph applies where a person is detained in England, Wales or Northern Ireland under Schedule 7 or section 41.

(2) Fingerprints may be taken from the detained person only if they are taken by a constable

(a) with the appropriate consent given in writing, or

(b) without that consent under sub-paragraph (4).

(3) A non-intimate sample may be taken from the detained person only if it is taken by a constable

(a) with the appropriate consent given in writing, or

(b) without that consent under sub-paragraph (4).

(4) Fingerprints or a non-intimate sample may be taken from the detained person without the appropriate consent only if

(a) he is detained at a police station and a police officer of at least the rank of superintendent authorises the fingerprints or sample to be taken, or

(b) he has been convicted of a recordable offence and, where a non-intimate sample is to be taken, he was convicted of the offence on or after 10th April 1995 (or 29th July 1996 where the non-intimate sample is to be taken in Northern Ireland).

---

[238] Substituted by the Serious Organised Crime and Police Act 2005, s 111, Sch 7, Pt 3, part 48(1)(b), (2).

[239] Substituted by the Counter-Terrorism Act 2008, s 82 (1).

(5) An intimate sample may be taken from the detained person only if

    (a) he is detained at a police station,

    (b) the appropriate consent is given in writing,

    (c) a police officer of at least the rank of superintendent authorises the sample to be taken, and

    (d) subject to paragraph 13(2) and (3), the sample is taken by a constable.

(6) [Subject to sub-paragraph (6A)][240] an officer may give an authorisation under sub-paragraph (4)(a) or (5)(c) only if

    (a) in the case of a person detained under section 41, the officer reasonably suspects that the person has been involved in an offence under any of the provisions mentioned in section 40(1)(a), and the officer reasonably believes that the fingerprints or sample will tend to confirm or disprove his involvement, or

    (b) in any case, the officer is satisfied that the taking of the fingerprints or sample from the person is necessary in order to assist in determining whether he falls within section 40(1)(b).

[(6A) An officer may also give an authorisation under sub-paragraph (4)(a) for the taking of fingerprints if

    (a) he is satisfied that the fingerprints of the detained person will facilitate the ascertainment of that person's identity; and

    (b) that person has refused to identify himself or the officer has reasonable grounds for suspecting that that person is not who he claims to be.

(6B) In this paragraph references to ascertaining a person's identity include references to showing that he is not a particular person.][241]

(7) If an authorisation under sub-paragraph (4)(a) or (5)(c) is given orally, the person giving it shall confirm it in writing as soon as is reasonably practicable.

11 (1) Before fingerprints or a sample are taken from a person under paragraph 10, he shall be informed

    (a) that the fingerprints or sample may be used for the purposes of paragraph 14(4), section 63A(1) of the Police and Criminal Evidence Act 1984 and Article 63A(1) of the Police and Criminal Evidence (Northern Ireland) Order 1989 (checking of fingerprints and samples), and

    (b) where the fingerprints or sample are to be taken under paragraph 10(2)(a), (3)(a) or (4)(b), of the reason for taking the fingerprints or sample.

(2) Before fingerprints or a sample are taken from a person upon an authorisation given under paragraph 10(4)(a) or (5)(c), he shall be informed

    (a) that the authorisation has been given,

    (b) of the grounds upon which it has been given, and

    (c) where relevant, of the nature of the offence in which it is suspected that he has been involved.

(3) After fingerprints or a sample are taken under paragraph 10, there shall be recorded as soon as is reasonably practicable any of the following which apply

    (a) the fact that the person has been informed in accordance with sub-paragraphs (1) and (2),

    (b) the reason referred to in sub-paragraph (1)(b),

    (c) the authorisation given under paragraph 10(4)(a) or (5)(c),

    (d) the grounds upon which that authorisation has been given, and

    (e) the fact that the appropriate consent has been given.

---

[240] Inserted by the Anti-terrorism, Crime and Security Act 2001, s 89(1), (2).
[241] Inserted by the Anti-terrorism, Crime and Security Act 2001, s 89(1), (2).

12 (1) This paragraph applies where
    (a) two or more non-intimate samples suitable for the same means of analysis have been taken from a person under paragraph 10,
    (b) those samples have proved insufficient, and
    (c) the person has been released from detention.
  (2) An intimate sample may be taken from the person if
    (a) the appropriate consent is given in writing,
    (b) a police officer of at least the rank of superintendent authorises the sample to be taken, and
    (c) subject to paragraph 13(2) and (3), the sample is taken by a constable.
  (3) Paragraphs 10(6) and (7) and 11 shall apply in relation to the taking of an intimate sample under this paragraph; and a reference to a person detained under section 41 shall be taken as a reference to a person who was detained under section 41 when the non-intimate samples mentioned in sub-paragraph (1)(a) were taken.

13 (1) Where appropriate written consent to the taking of an intimate sample from a person under paragraph 10 or 12 is refused without good cause, in any proceedings against that person for an offence
    (a) the court, in determining whether to commit him for trial or whether there is a case to answer, may draw such inferences from the refusal as appear proper, and
    (b) the court or jury, in determining whether that person is guilty of the offence charged, may draw such inferences from the refusal as appear proper.
  (2) An intimate sample other than a sample of urine or a dental impression may be taken under paragraph 10 or 12 only by a registered medical practitioner acting on the authority of a constable.
  (3) An intimate sample which is a dental impression may be taken under paragraph 10 or 12 only by a registered dentist acting on the authority of a constable.
  (4) Where a sample of hair other than pubic hair is to be taken under paragraph 10 the sample may be taken either by cutting hairs or by plucking hairs with their roots so long as no more are plucked than the person taking the sample reasonably considers to be necessary for a sufficient sample.

14 (1) This paragraph applies to
    (a) fingerprints or samples taken under paragraph 10 or 12, and
    (b) information derived from those samples.
  [(2) The fingerprints and samples may be retained but shall not be used by any person except for the purposes of a terrorist investigation *or for purposes related to the prevention or detection of crime, the investigation of an offence or the conduct of a prosecution.*[242] [*or as mentioned in sub-paragraph (2A)*][243][244]
  (2A) The fingerprints or samples may be used
    (a) in the interests of national security,
    (b) for purposes related to the prevention or detection of crime, the investigation of an offence or the conduct of a prosecution, or
    (c) for purposes related to the identification of a deceased person or of the person from whom the material came.
  (3) *In particular, a check may not be made against them under*
    (a) *section 63A(1) of the Police and Criminal Evidence Act 1984 (checking of fingerprints and samples), or*

---

[242] Repealed by the Counter-Terrorism Act 2008, s 16(1), (2), not yet in force.
[243] Substituted by the Counter-Terrorism Act 2008, s 16(1), (2), not yet in force.
[244] Substituted by the Criminal Justice and Police Act 2001, s 84(1), (2).

    (b) *Article 63A(1) of the Police and Criminal Evidence (Northern Ireland) Order 1989 (checking of fingerprints and samples),*

except for the purpose of a terrorist investigation [or for purposes related to the prevention or detection of crime, the investigation of an offence or the conduct of a prosecution.][245, 246]

(4)   The fingerprints, samples or information may be checked, subject to sub-paragraph (2), against

    (a) other fingerprints or samples taken under paragraph 10 or 12 or information derived from those samples,

    (b) relevant physical data or samples taken by virtue of paragraph 20, [*(ba) material to which section 18 of the Counter-Terrorism Act 20088 applies*][247]

    (c) any of the fingerprints, samples and information mentioned in section 63A(1)(a) and (b) of the Police and Criminal Evidence Act 1984 (checking of fingerprints and samples),

    (d) any of the fingerprints, samples and information mentioned in Article 63A(1)(a) and (b) of the Police and Criminal Evidence (Northern Ireland) Order 1989 (checking of fingerprints and samples), and

    (e) fingerprints or samples taken under section 15(9) of, or paragraph 7(5) of Schedule 5 to, the Prevention of Terrorism (Temporary Provisions) Act 1989 or information derived from those samples.

[(4A) In this paragraph

    (a) a reference to crime includes a reference to any conduct which

       (i) constitutes one or more criminal offences (whether under the law of a part of the United Kingdom or of a country or territory outside the United Kingdom); or

      (ii) is, or corresponds to, any conduct which, if it all took place in any one part of the United Kingdom, would constitute one or more criminal offences;

      and

    (b) the references to an investigation and to a prosecution include references, respectively, to any investigation outside the United Kingdom of any crime or suspected crime and to a prosecution brought in respect of any crime in a country or territory outside the United Kingdom.][248]

(5)   This paragraph (other than sub-paragraph (4)) shall apply to fingerprints or samples taken under section 15(9) of, or paragraph 7(5) of Schedule 5 to, the Prevention of Terrorism (Temporary Provisions) Act 1989 and information derived from those samples as it applies to fingerprints or samples taken under paragraph 10 or 12 and the information derived from those samples.

15 (1) In the application of paragraphs 10 to 14 in relation to a person detained in England or Wales the following expressions shall have the meaning given by section 65 of the Police and Criminal Evidence Act 1984 (Part V definitions)

    (a) "appropriate consent",

    (b) "fingerprints",

    (c) "insufficient",

    (d) "intimate sample",

    (e) "non-intimate sample",

    (f) "registered dentist", and

    (g) "sufficient".

---

[245] Inserted by the Criminal Justice and Police Act 2001, s 84(1), (3).
[246] Repealed by the Counter-Terrorism Act 2008, ss 16(1), (4), 99, Sch 9, Pt 1, not yet in force.
[247] Inserted by the Counter-Terrorism Act 2008, s 16(1), (5), not yet in force.
[248] Inserted by the Criminal Justice and Police Act 2001, s 84(1), (4).

(2) In the application of paragraphs 10 to 14 in relation to a person detained in Northern Ireland the expressions listed in sub-paragraph (1) shall have the meaning given by Article 53 of the Police and Criminal Evidence (Northern Ireland) Order 1989 (definitions).

(3) In paragraph 10 "recordable offence" shall have

    (a) in relation to a person detained in England or Wales, the meaning given by section 118(1) of the Police and Criminal Evidence Act 1984 (general interpretation), and

    (b) in relation to a person detained in Northern Ireland, the meaning given by Article 2(2) of the Police and Criminal Evidence (Northern Ireland) Order 1989 (definitions).

Rights: Scotland

16 (1) A person detained under Schedule 7 or section 41 at a police station in Scotland shall be entitled to have intimation of his detention and of the place where he is being detained sent without delay to a solicitor and to another person named by him.

(2) The person named must be

    (a) a friend of the detained person,

    (b) a relative, or

    (c) a person who is known to the detained person or who is likely to take an interest in his welfare.

(3) Where a detained person is transferred from one police station to another, he shall be entitled to exercise the right under sub-paragraph (1) in respect of the police station to which he is transferred.

(4) A police officer not below the rank of superintendent may authorise a delay in making intimation where, in his view, the delay is necessary on one of the grounds mentioned in paragraph 17(3) or where paragraph 17(4) applies.

(5) Where a detained person requests that the intimation be made, there shall be recorded the time when the request is

    (a) made, and

    (b) complied with.

(6) A person detained shall be entitled to consult a solicitor at any time, without delay.

(7) A police officer not below the rank of superintendent may authorise a delay in holding the consultation where, in his view, the delay is necessary on one of the grounds mentioned in paragraph 17(3) or where paragraph 17(4) applies.

(8) Subject to paragraph 17, the consultation shall be private.

(9) Where a person is detained under section 41 he must be permitted to exercise his rights under this paragraph before the end of the period mentioned in subsection (3) of that section.

17 (1) An officer not below the rank of Assistant Chief Constable may direct that the consultation mentioned in paragraph 16(6) shall be in the presence of a uniformed officer not below the rank of inspector if it appears to the officer giving the direction to be necessary on one of the grounds mentioned in sub-paragraph (3).

(2) A uniformed officer directed to be present during a consultation shall be an officer who, in the opinion of the officer giving the direction, has no connection with the case.

(3) The grounds mentioned in paragraph 16(4) and (7) and in sub-paragraph (1) are

    (a) that it is in the interests of the investigation or prevention of crime;

    (b) that it is in the interests of the apprehension, prosecution or conviction of offenders;

    (c) that it will further the recovery of property obtained as a result of the commission of an offence or in respect of which a forfeiture order could be made under section 23 [*or 23A*;][249]

---

[249] Inserted by the Counter-Terrorism Act 2008, s.39, Sch 3, para 6, not yet in force.

(d) that it will further the operation of [Part 2 or 3 of the Proceeds of Crime Act 2002][250] or the Proceeds of Crime (Northern Ireland) Order 1996 (confiscation of the proceeds of an offence).

[(4) This sub-paragraph applies where an officer mentioned in paragraph 16(4) or (7) has reasonable grounds for believing that

(a) the detained person has benefited from his criminal conduct, and

(b) the recovery of the value of the property constituting the benefit will be hindered by

   (i) informing the named person of the detained person's detention (in the case of an authorisation under paragraph 16(4)), or

   (ii) the exercise of the entitlement under paragraph 16(6) (in the case of an authorisation under paragraph 16(7)).

(4A) For the purposes of sub-paragraph (4) the question whether a person has benefited from his criminal conduct is to be decided in accordance with Part 3 of the Proceeds of Crime Act 2002.][251]

(5) Where delay is authorised in the exercising of any of the rights mentioned in paragraph 16(1) and (6)

(a) if the authorisation is given orally, the person giving it shall confirm it in writing as soon as is reasonably practicable,

(b) the detained person shall be told the reason for the delay as soon as is reasonably practicable, and

(c) the reason shall be recorded as soon as is reasonably practicable.

18 (1) Paragraphs 16 and 17 shall have effect, in relation to a person detained under section 41 or Schedule 7, in place of any enactment or rule of law under or by virtue of which a person arrested or detained may be entitled to communicate or consult with any other person.

(2) But, where a person detained under Schedule 7 or section 41 at a police station in Scotland appears to a constable to be a child

(a) the other person named by the person detained in pursuance of paragraph 16(1) shall be that person's parent, and

(b) section 15(4) of the Criminal Procedure (Scotland) Act 1995 shall apply to the person detained as it applies to a person who appears to a constable to be a child who is being detained as mentioned in paragraph (b) of section 15(1) of that Act,

and in this sub-paragraph "child" and "parent" have the same meaning as in section 15(4) of that Act.

19 The Secretary of State shall, by order, make provision to require that

(a) except in such circumstances, and

(b) subject to such conditions,

as may be specified in the order, where a person detained has been permitted to consult a solicitor, the solicitor shall be allowed to be present at any interview carried out in connection with a terrorist investigation or for the purposes of Schedule 7.

20 (1) Subject to the modifications specified in sub-paragraphs (2) and (3), section 18 of the Criminal Procedure (Scotland) Act 1995 (procedure for taking certain prints and samples) shall apply to a person detained under Schedule 7 or section 41 at a police station in Scotland as it applies to a person arrested or a person detained under section 14 of that Act.

(2) For subsection (2) of section 18 there shall be substituted

---

[250] Substituted by the Proceeds of Crime Act 2002, s 456, Sch 11, paras 1, 39(1), (3).
[251] Substituted for sub-para (40) as originally enacted, by the Proceeds of Crime Act 2002, s 456, Sch 11, paras 1, 39(1), (4).

["(2) Subject to subsection (2A), a constable may take from a detained person or require a detained person to provide relevant physical data only if

    (a) in the case of a person detained under section 41 of the Terrorism Act 2000, he reasonably suspects that the person has been involved in an offence under any of the provisions mentioned in section 40(1)(a) of that Act and he reasonably believes that the relevant physical data will tend to confirm or disprove his involvement; or

    (b) in any case, he is satisfied that it is necessary to do so in order to assist in determining whether the person falls within section 40(1)(b).

(2A) A constable may also take fingerprints from a detained person or require him to provide them if

    (a) he is satisfied that the fingerprints of that person will facilitate the ascertainment of that person's identity; and

    (b) that person has refused to identify himself or the constable has reasonable grounds for suspecting that that person is not who he claims to be.

(2B) In this section references to ascertaining a person's identity include references to showing that he is not a particular person."][252]

[(3) Subsections (3) to (5) shall not apply, but any relevant physical data or sample taken in pursuance of section 18 as applied by this paragraph may be retained but shall not be used by any person *except for the purposes of a terrorist investigation or for purposes related to the prevention or detection of crime, the investigation of an offence or the conduct of a prosecution*[253] *(except*

    (a) for the purposes of a terrorist investigation,

    (b) in the interests of national security, or

    (c) for purposes related to the prevention or detection of crime, the investigation of an offence or the conduct of a prosecution).[254]

(4) In this paragraph

    (a) a reference to crime includes a reference to any conduct which

        (i) constitutes one or more criminal offences (whether under the law of a part of the United Kingdom or of a country or territory outside the United Kingdom); or

        (ii) is, or corresponds to, any conduct which, if it all took place in any one part of the United Kingdom, would constitute one or more criminal offences; and

    (b) the references to an investigation and to a prosecution include references, respectively, to any investigation outside the United Kingdom of any crime or suspected crime and to a prosecution brought in respect of any crime in a country or territory outside the United Kingdom.][255]

20A (1) *Section 20 of the Criminal Procedure (Scotland) Act 1995 applies to relevant physical data or samples taken from a person detained under Schedule 7 or section 41 at a police station in Scotland with the following modifications.*

    (2) *Omit the references to impressions.*

    (3) *For the words from "against other such data" to the end substitute", subject to paragraph 20(3) of Schedule 8 to the Terrorism Act 2000, against—*

        (a) other such data, samples and information,

---

[252] Substituted, for sub-s (2) as originally enacted, by the Anti-terrorism, Crime and Security Act 2001, s 89(1), (3).

[253] Repealed by the Counter-Terrorism Act 2008, s 17(1), (2), not yet in force.

[254] Substituted by the Counter-Terrorism Act 2008, s 17(1), (2), not yet in force.

[255] Substituted, for sub-para (3) as originally enacted, by the Anti-terrorism, Crime and Security Act 2001, s 89 (1), (4).

(b) *any of the fingerprints, samples and information mentioned in section 63A(1)(a) and (b) of the Police and Criminal Evidence Act 1984 (c 60) (checking of fingerprints and samples), and*

(c) *material to which section 18 of the Counter-Terrorism Act 2008 applies.]²⁵⁶"*

PART II
REVIEW OF DETENTION UNDER SECTION 41

Requirement

21 (1) A person's detention shall be periodically reviewed by a review officer.

(2) The first review shall be carried out as soon as is reasonably practicable after the time of the person's arrest.

(3) Subsequent reviews shall, subject to paragraph 22, be carried out at intervals of not more than 12 hours.

(4) No review of a person's detention shall be carried out after a warrant extending his detention has been issued under Part III.

Postponement

22 (1) A review may be postponed if at the latest time at which it may be carried out in accordance with paragraph 21

(a) the detained person is being questioned by a police officer and an officer is satisfied that an interruption of the questioning to carry out the review would prejudice the investigation in connection with which the person is being detained,

(b) no review officer is readily available, or

(c) it is not practicable for any other reason to carry out the review.

(2) Where a review is postponed it shall be carried out as soon as is reasonably practicable.

(3) For the purposes of ascertaining the time within which the next review is to be carried out, a postponed review shall be deemed to have been carried out at the latest time at which it could have been carried out in accordance with paragraph 21.

Grounds for continued detention

23 (1) A review officer may authorise a person's continued detention only if satisfied that it is necessary

(a) to obtain relevant evidence whether by questioning him or otherwise,

(b) to preserve relevant evidence,

[(ba) pending the result of an examination or analysis of any relevant evidence or of anything the examination or analysis of which is to be or is being carried out with a view to obtaining relevant evidence,]²⁵⁷

(c) pending a decision whether to apply to the Secretary of State for a deportation notice to be served on the detained person,

(d) pending the making of an application to the Secretary of State for a deportation notice to be served on the detained person,

(e) pending consideration by the Secretary of State whether to serve a deportation notice on the detained person, or

(f) pending a decision whether the detained person should be charged with an offence.

---

²⁵⁶ Inserted by the Counter-Terrorism Act 2008, s 17(3), not yet in force.
²⁵⁷ Inserted by the Terrorism Act 2006, s 24(1).

(2) The review officer shall not authorise continued detention by virtue of sub-paragraph (1)(a) or (b) unless he is satisfied that the investigation in connection with which the person is detained is being conducted diligently and expeditiously.

(3) The review officer shall not authorise continued detention by virtue of sub-paragraph (1)(c) to (f) unless he is satisfied that the process pending the completion of which detention is necessary is being conducted diligently and expeditiously.

(4) In [this paragraph]²⁵⁸ "relevant evidence" means evidence which
   (a) relates to the commission by the detained person of an offence under any of the provisions mentioned in section 40(1)(a), or
   (b) indicates that the detained person falls within section 40(1)(b).

(5) In sub-paragraph (1) "deportation notice" means notice of a decision to make a deportation order under the Immigration Act 1971.

Review officer

24 (1) The review officer shall be an officer who has not been directly involved in the investigation in connection with which the person is detained.

(2) In the case of a review carried out within the period of 24 hours beginning with the time of arrest, the review officer shall be an officer of at least the rank of inspector.

(3) In the case of any other review, the review officer shall be an officer of at least the rank of superintendent.

25 (1) This paragraph applies where
   (a) the review officer is of a rank lower than superintendent,
   (b) an officer of higher rank than the review officer gives directions relating to the detained person, and
   (c) those directions are at variance with the performance by the review officer of a duty imposed on him under this Schedule.

(2) The review officer shall refer the matter at once to an officer of at least the rank of superintendent.

Representations

26 (1) Before determining whether to authorise a person's continued detention, a review officer shall give either of the following persons an opportunity to make representations about the detention
   (a) the detained person, or
   (b) a solicitor representing him who is available at the time of the review.

(2) Representations may be oral or written.

(3) A review officer may refuse to hear oral representations from the detained person if he considers that he is unfit to make representations because of his condition or behaviour.

Rights

27 (1) Where a review officer authorises continued detention he shall inform the detained person
   (a) of any of his rights under paragraphs 6 and 7 which he has not yet exercised, and
   (b) if the exercise of any of his rights under either of those paragraphs is being delayed in accordance with the provisions of paragraph 8, of the fact that it is being so delayed.

(2) Where a review of a person's detention is being carried out at a time when his exercise of a right under either of those paragraphs is being delayed

---

²⁵⁸ Substituted by the Terrorism Act 2006, s 24(4).

(a) the review officer shall consider whether the reason or reasons for which the delay was authorised continue to subsist, and

(b) if in his opinion the reason or reasons have ceased to subsist, he shall inform the officer who authorised the delay of his opinion (unless he was that officer).

(3) In the application of this paragraph to Scotland, for the references to paragraphs 6, 7 and 8 substitute references to paragraph 16.

(4) The following provisions (requirement to bring an accused person before the court after his arrest) shall not apply to a person detained under section 41

(a) section 135(3) of the Criminal Procedure (Scotland) Act 1995, and

(b) Article 8(1) of the Criminal Justice (Children) (Northern Ireland) Order 1998.

(5) Section 22(1) of the Criminal Procedure (Scotland) Act 1995 (interim liberation by officer in charge of police station) shall not apply to a person detained under section 41.

Record

28 (1) A review officer carrying out a review shall make a written record of the outcome of the review and of any of the following which apply

(a) the grounds upon which continued detention is authorised,

(b) the reason for postponement of the review,

(c) the fact that the detained person has been informed as required under paragraph 27(1),

(d) the officer's conclusion on the matter considered under paragraph 27(2)(a),

(e) the fact that he has taken action under paragraph 27(2)(b), and

(f) the fact that the detained person is being detained by virtue of section 41(5) or (6).

(2) The review officer shall

(a) make the record in the presence of the detained person, and

(b) inform him at that time whether the review officer is authorising continued detention, and if he is, of his grounds.

(3) Sub-paragraph (2) shall not apply where, at the time when the record is made, the detained person is

(a) incapable of understanding what is said to him,

(b) violent or likely to become violent, or

(c) in urgent need of medical attention.

PART III
EXTENSION OF DETENTION UNDER SECTION 41

Warrants of further detention

29 (1) [Each of the following

(a) in England and Wales, a Crown Prosecutor,

(b) in Scotland, the Lord Advocate or a procurator fiscal,

(c) in Northern Ireland, the Director of Public Prosecutions for Northern Ireland,

(d) in any part of the United Kingdom, a police officer of at least the rank of superintendent,

may][259] apply to a judicial authority for the issue of a warrant of further detention under this Part.

(2) A warrant of further detention

(a) shall authorise the further detention under section 41 of a specified person for a specified period, and

(b) shall state the time at which it is issued.

---

[259] Substituted by the Terrorism Act 2006, s 23(1), (2).

(3) [Subject to sub-paragraph (3A) and paragraph 36,]²⁶⁰ the specified period in relation to a person shall [be]²⁶¹ the period of seven days beginning

    (a) with the time of his arrest under section 41, or

    (b) if he was being detained under Schedule 7 when he was arrested under section 41, with the time when his examination under that Schedule began.

[(3A) A judicial authority may issue a warrant of further detention in relation to a person which specifies a shorter period as the period for which that person's further detention is authorised if

    (a) the application for the warrant is an application for a warrant specifying a shorter period; or

    (b) the judicial authority is satisfied that there are circumstances that would make it inappropriate for the specified period to be as long as the period of seven days mentioned in sub-paragraph (3).]²⁶²

(4) In this Part "judicial authority" means

    (a) in England and Wales, [. . .]²⁶³ a District Judge (Magistrates' Courts) who is designated for the purpose of this Part [by the Lord Chief Justice of England and Wales [. . .]²⁶⁴]²⁶⁵

    (b) in Scotland, the sheriff, and

    (c) in Northern Ireland, a county court judge, or a resident magistrate who is designated for the purpose of this Part [by the Lord Chief Justice of Northern Ireland. [. . .]²⁶⁶]²⁶⁷

[(5) The Lord Chief Justice may nominate a judicial office holder (as defined in section 109(4) of the Constitutional Reform Act 2005) to exercise his functions under sub-paragraph (4)(a).

(6) The Lord Chief Justice of Northern Ireland may nominate any of the following to exercise his functions under sub-paragraph (4)(c)

    (a) the holder of one of the offices listed in Schedule 1 to the Justice (Northern Ireland) Act 2002;

    (b) a Lord Justice of Appeal (as defined in section 88 of that Act).]²⁶⁸

Time limit

30 (1) An application for a warrant shall be made

    (a) during the period mentioned in section 41(3), or

    (b) within six hours of the end of that period.

(2) The judicial authority hearing an application made by virtue of sub-paragraph (1)(b) shall dismiss the application if he considers that it would have been reasonably practicable to make it during the period mentioned in section 41(3).

(3) For the purposes of this Schedule, an application for a warrant is made when written or oral notice of an intention to make the application is given to a judicial authority.

²⁶⁰ Substituted (for words as inserted by the Criminal Justice Act 2003, s 306(1), (3)(a)) by the Terrorism Act 2006, s 23(1), (3)(a).

²⁶¹ Substituted by the Terrorism Act 2006, s 23(1), (3)(b).

²⁶² Inserted by the Terrorism Act 2006, s 23(1), (4).

²⁶³ Repealed by the Courts Act 2003, s 109(1), (3), Sch 8, para 391, Sch 10.

²⁶⁴ Repealed by the Counter-Terrorism Act 2008, ss 82(2), 99, Sch 9, Pt 6.

²⁶⁵ Substituted by the Constitutional Reform Act 2005, s 15(1), Sch 4, Pt 1, paras 287, 290 (1), (2)(a).

²⁶⁶ Repealed by the Counter-Terrrorism Act 2008, ss 82(2), 99, Sch 9, Pt 6.

²⁶⁷ Substituted by the Constitutional Reform Act 2005, s 15(1), Sch 4, Pt 1, paras 287, 290(1), (2)(b).

²⁶⁸ Inserted by the Constitutional Reform Act 2005, s 15(1), Sch 4, Pt 1, paras 287, 290(1)(2)(c).

Notice

31 An application for a warrant may not be heard unless the person to whom it relates has been given a notice stating
   (a) that the application has been made,
   (b) the time at which the application was made,
   (c) the time at which it is to be heard, and
   (d) the grounds upon which further detention is sought.

Grounds for extension

32 (1) A judicial authority may issue a warrant of further detention only if satisfied that
   (a) there are reasonable grounds for believing that the further detention of the person to whom the application relates is necessary [as mentioned in sub-paragraph (1A),][269] and
   (b) the investigation in connection with which the person is detained is being conducted diligently and expeditiously.
   [(1A) The further detention of a person is necessary as mentioned in this sub-paragraph if it is necessary
   (a) to obtain relevant evidence whether by questioning him or otherwise;
   (b) to preserve relevant evidence; or
   (c) pending the result of an examination or analysis of any relevant evidence or of anything the examination or analysis of which is to be or is being carried out with a view to obtaining relevant evidence.][270]
   (2) In [this paragraph][271] "relevant evidence" means, in relation to the person to whom the application relates, evidence which
   (a) relates to his commission of an offence under any of the provisions mentioned in section 40(1)(a), or
   (b) indicates that he is a person falling within section 40(1)(b).

Representation

33 (1) The person to whom an application relates shall
   (a) be given an opportunity to make oral or written representations to the judicial authority about the application, and
   (b) subject to sub-paragraph (3), be entitled to be legally represented at the hearing.
   (2) A judicial authority shall adjourn the hearing of an application to enable the person to whom the application relates to obtain legal representation where
   (a) he is not legally represented,
   (b) he is entitled to be legally represented, and
   (c) he wishes to be so represented.
   (3) A judicial authority may exclude any of the following persons from any part of the hearing
   (a) the person to whom the application relates;
   (b) anyone representing him.
   [(4) A judicial authority may, after giving an opportunity for representations to be made by or on behalf of the applicant and the person to whom the application relates, direct
   (a) that the hearing of the application must be conducted, and

---

[269] Substituted by the Terrorism Act 2006, s 24(2).
[270] Inserted by the Terrorism Act 2006, s 24(3).
[271] Substituted by the Terrorism Act 2006, s 24(5).

(b) that all representations by or on behalf of a person for the purposes of the hearing must be made,

by such means (whether a live television link or other means) falling within sub-paragraph (5) as may be specified in the direction and not in the presence (apart from by those means) of the applicant, of the person to whom the application relates or of any legal representative of that person.

(5) A means of conducting the hearing and of making representations falls within this sub-paragraph if it allows the person to whom the application relates and any legal representative of his (without being present at the hearing and to the extent that they are not excluded from it under sub-paragraph (3))

(a) to see and hear the judicial authority and the making of representations to it by other persons; and

(b) to be seen and heard by the judicial authority.

(6) If the person to whom the application relates wishes to make representations about whether a direction should be given under sub-paragraph (4), he must do so by using the facilities that will be used if the judicial authority decides to give a direction under that sub-paragraph.

(7) Sub-paragraph (2) applies to the hearing of representations about whether a direction should be given under sub-paragraph (4) in the case of any application as it applies to a hearing of the application.

(8) A judicial authority shall not give a direction under sub-paragraph (4) unless

(a) it has been notified by the Secretary of State that facilities are available at the place where the person to whom the application relates is held for the judicial authority to conduct a hearing by means falling within sub-paragraph (5); and

(b) that notification has not been withdrawn.

(9) If in a case where it has power to do so a judicial authority decides not to give a direction under sub-paragraph (4), it shall state its reasons for not giving it.][272]

Information

34 (1) The [person][273] who has made an application for a warrant may apply to the judicial authority for an order that specified information upon which he intends to rely be withheld from

(a) the person to whom the application relates, and

(b) anyone representing him.

(2) Subject to sub-paragraph (3), a judicial authority may make an order under sub-paragraph (1) in relation to specified information only if satisfied that there are reasonable grounds for believing that if the information were disclosed

(a) evidence of an offence under any of the provisions mentioned in section 40(1)(a) would be interfered with or harmed,

(b) the recovery of property obtained as a result of an offence under any of those provisions would be hindered,

(c) the recovery of property in respect of which a forfeiture order could be made under section 23 [*or 23A*][274] would be hindered,

(d) the apprehension, prosecution or conviction of a person who is suspected of falling within section 40(1)(a) or (b) would be made more difficult as a result of his being alerted,

---

[272] Inserted, in relation to England, Wales and Northern Ireland, by the Criminal Justice and Police Act 2001, s 75.

[273] Substituted by the Terrorism Act 2006, s 23(1),(5).

[274] Inserted by the Counter-Terrorism Act 2008, s 39, Sch 3, para 6, not yet in force.

(e) the prevention of an act of terrorism would be made more difficult as a result of a person being alerted,

(f) the gathering of information about the commission, preparation or instigation of an act of terrorism would be interfered with, or

(g) a person would be interfered with or physically injured.

[(3) A judicial authority may also make an order under sub-paragraph (1) in relation to specified information if satisfied that there are reasonable grounds for believing that

(a) the detained person has benefited from his criminal conduct, and

(b) the recovery of the value of the property constituting the benefit would be hindered if the information were disclosed.

(3A) For the purposes of sub-paragraph (3) the question whether a person has benefited from his criminal conduct is to be decided in accordance with Part 2 or 3 of the Proceeds of Crime Act 2002.][275]

(4) The judicial authority shall direct that the following be excluded from the hearing of the application under this paragraph

(a) the person to whom the application for a warrant relates, and

(b) anyone representing him.

Adjournments

35 (1) A judicial authority may adjourn the hearing of an application for a warrant only if the hearing is adjourned to a date before the expiry of the period mentioned in section 41(3).

(2) This paragraph shall not apply to an adjournment under paragraph 33(2).

Extensions of warrants

36 (1) [Each of the following

(a) in England and Wales, a Crown Prosecutor,

(b) in Scotland, the Lord Advocate or a procurator fiscal,

(c) in Northern Ireland, the Director of Public Prosecutions for Northern Ireland,

(d) in any part of the United Kingdom, a police officer of at least the rank of superintendent,

may][276] apply [. . .][277] for the extension or further extension of the period specified in a warrant of further detention.

(1A) The person to whom an application under sub-paragraph (1) may be made is

(a) in the case of an application falling within sub-paragraph (1B), a judicial authority; and

(b) in any other case, a senior judge.

(1B) An application for the extension or further extension of a period falls within this sub-paragraph if

(a) the grant of the application otherwise than in accordance with sub-paragraph (3AA)(b) would extend that period to a time that is no more than fourteen days after the relevant time; and

(b) no application has previously been made to a senior judge in respect of that period.][278]

---

[275] Substituted, for sub-para (3) as originally enacted, by the proceeds of Crime Act 2002, s 456, Sch 11, paras 1, 39(1), (5).

[276] Substituted by the Terrorism Act 2006, s 23(1), (2).

[277] Repealed by the Terrorism Act 2006, ss 23(1), (6), 37(5), Sch 3.

[278] Inserted by the Terrorism Act 2006, s 23(1), (6).

(2) Where the period specified is extended, the warrant shall be endorsed with a note stating the new specified period.

[(3) Subject to sub-paragraph (3AA), the period by which the specified period is extended or further extended shall be the period which

(a) begins with the time specified in sub-paragraph (3A); and

(b) ends with whichever is the earlier of

(i) the end of the period of seven days beginning with that time; and

(ii) the end of the period of 28 days beginning with the relevant time.

(3A) The time referred to in sub-paragraph (3)(a) is

(a) in the case of a warrant specifying a period which has not previously been extended under this paragraph, the end of the period specified in the warrant, and

(b) in any other case, the end of the period for which the period specified in the warrant was last extended under this paragraph.

(3AA) A judicial authority or senior judge may extend or further extend the period specified in a warrant by a shorter period than is required by sub-paragraph (3) if

(a) the application for the extension is an application for an extension by a period that is shorter than is so required; or

(b) the judicial authority or senior judge is satisfied that there are circumstances that would make it inappropriate for the period of the extension to be as long as the period so required.]279

[(3B) In this paragraph "the relevant time", in relation to a person, means

(a) the time of his arrest under section 41, or

(b) if he was being detained under Schedule 7 when he was arrested under section 41, the time when his examination under that Schedule began.]280

(4) Paragraphs 30(3) and 31 to 34 shall apply to an application under this paragraph as they apply to an application for a warrant of further detention [but, in relation to an application made by virtue of sub-paragraph (1A)(b) to a senior judge, as if

(a) references to a judicial authority were references to a senior judge; and

(b) references to the judicial authority in question were references to the senior judge in question.]281

(5) A judicial authority [or senior judge]282 may adjourn the hearing of an application under sub-paragraph (1) only if the hearing is adjourned to a date before the expiry of the period specified in the warrant.

(6) Sub-paragraph (5) shall not apply to an adjournment under paragraph 33(2).

[(7) In this paragraph and paragraph 37 'senior judge' means a judge of the High Court or of the High Court of Justiciary.]283

Detention conditions

[37 (1) This paragraph applies where

(a) a person ('the detained person') is detained by virtue of a warrant issued under this Part of this Schedule; and

---

279 Substituted, for sub-paras (3), (3A) (sub-para (3) as originally enacted and sub-para (3A) as inserted by the Criminal Justice Act 2003, s 306(1), (4)), by the Terrorism Act-2006, s 23(1), (7).

280 Inserted by the Criminal Justice Act 2003, s 306(1), (4).

281 Inserted by the Terrorism Act 2006, s 23(1), (8).

282 Inserted by the Terrorism Act 2006, s 23(1), (9).

283 Inserted by the Terrorism Act 2006 s 23(1), (10); paras 36+37 modified, in relation to any further extension under the said para 36 for a period begining on 25 July 2006, by the Terrorism Act 2006, s 25 and SI 2006/1936, art 2(1), (2)(a).

(b) his detention is not authorised by virtue of section 41(5) or (6) or otherwise apart from the warrant.

(2) If it at any time appears to the police officer or other person in charge of the detained person's case that any of the matters mentioned in paragraph 32(1)(a) and (b) on which the judicial authority or senior judge last authorised his further detention no longer apply, he must

  (a) if he has custody of the detained person, release him immediately; and

  (b) if he does not, immediately inform the person who does have custody of the detained person that those matters no longer apply in the detained person's case.

(3) A person with custody of the detained person who is informed in accordance with this paragraph that those matters no longer apply in his case must release that person immediately.][284]

[SCHEDULE 8A
OFFENCE UNDER SECTION 58A: SUPPLEMENTARY PROVISIONS

Introduction

1 (1) This Schedule makes supplementary provision relating to the offence in section 58A (eliciting, publishing or communicating information about members of the armed forces etc).

(2) The purpose of this Schedule is to comply with Directive 2000/31/EC of the European Parliament and of the Council of 8 June 2000 on certain legal aspects of information society services, in particular electronic commerce, in the Internal Market ("the E-Commerce Directive").

2–7 *(omitted)*][285]

SCHEDULE 9–13

[. . .][286]

SCHEDULE 14   Section 115
EXERCISE OF OFFICERS' POWERS

General

1 In this Schedule an "officer" means

  (a) an authorised officer within the meaning given by [the terrorist cash provisions],[287] and

  (b) an examining officer within the meaning of Schedule 7

[and "the terrorist cash provisions" means Schedule 1 to the Anti-terrorism, Crime and Security Act 2001.][288]

2 An officer may enter a vehicle (within the meaning of section 121) for the purpose of exercising any of the functions conferred on him by virtue of this Act [or the terrorist cash provisions][289].

---

[284] Substituted by the Terrorism Act 2006, s 23(1), (11).
[285] Inserted by the Counter-Terrorism Act 2008, s 76(4), Sch 8.
[286] Ceased to have effect by virtue of the Terrorism (Northern Ireland) Act 2006, s 1(1), (2)(b).
[287] Substituted by the Anti-terrorism, Crime and Security Act 2001, s 2(4), (5)(a).
[288] Inserted by the Anti-terrorism, Crime and Security Act 2001, s 2(4), (5)(b).
[289] Inserted by the Anti-terrorism, Crime and Security Act 2001, s 2(4), (4), (6).

3 An officer may if necessary use reasonable force for the purpose of exercising a power conferred on him by virtue of this Act (apart from paragraphs 2 and 3 of Schedule 7) [or the terrorist cash provisions.][290]

Information

4 (1) Information acquired by an officer may be supplied
  (a) to the Secretary of State for use in relation to immigration;
  (b) to the Commissioners of Customs and Excise or a customs officer;
  (c) to a constable;
  [(d) to the Serious Organised Crime Agency;][291]
  (e) to a person specified by order of the Secretary of State for use of a kind specified in the order.
  (2) Information acquired by a customs officer or an immigration officer may be supplied to an examining officer within the meaning of Schedule 7.

Code of practice

5 An officer shall perform functions conferred on him by virtue of this Act [or the terrorist cash provisions][292] in accordance with any relevant code of practice in operation under paragraph 6.
6 (1) The Secretary of State shall issue codes of practice about the exercise by officers of functions conferred on them by virtue of this Act [or the terrorist cash provisions.][293]
  (2) The failure by an officer to observe a provision of a code shall not of itself make him liable to criminal or civil proceedings.
  (3) A code
  (a) shall be admissible in evidence in criminal and civil proceedings, and
  (b) shall be taken into account by a court or tribunal in any case in which it appears to the court or tribunal to be relevant.
  (4) The Secretary of State may revise a code and issue the revised code.
7 *(omitted)*

SCHEDULE 15
CONSEQUENTIAL AMENDMENTS *(omitted)*

SCHEDULE 16
REPEALS AND REVOCATIONS *(omitted)*

---

[290] Inserted by the Anti-terrorism, Crime and Security Act 2001, s 2(4), (4), (6).
[291] Substituted by the Serious Organised and Police Act 2005, s 89, Sch 4, paras 125, 130.
[292] Inserted by the Anti-terrorism, Crime and Security Act 2001, s 2(4), (7).
[293] Inserted by the Anti-terrorism, Crime and Security Act 2001, s 2(4), (6).

Anti-terrorism, Crime and Security Act 2001

An Act to amend the Terrorism Act 2000; to make further provision about terrorism and security; to provide for the freezing of assets; to make provision about immigration and asylum; to amend or extend the criminal law and powers for preventing crime and enforcing that law; to make provision about the control of pathogens and toxins; to provide for the retention of communications data; to provide for implementation of Title VI of the Treaty on European Union; and for connected purposes.

(14th December 2001)

PART I
TERRORIST PROPERTY

1 Forfeiture of terrorist cash

(1) Schedule 1 (which makes provision for enabling cash which
 (a) is intended to be used for the purposes of terrorism,
 (b) consists of resources of an organisation which is a proscribed organisation, or
 (c) is, or represents, property obtained through terrorism,
 to be forfeited in civil proceedings before a magistrates' court or (in Scotland) the sheriff) is to have effect.

(2) The powers conferred by Schedule 1 are exercisable in relation to any cash whether or not any proceedings have been brought for an offence in connection with the cash.

(3) Expressions used in this section have the same meaning as in Schedule 1.

(4) Sections 24 to 31 of the Terrorism Act 2000 (c 11) (seizure of terrorist cash) are to cease to have effect.

(5) An order under section 127 bringing Schedule 1 into force may make any modifications of any code of practice then in operation under Schedule 14 to the Terrorism Act 2000 (exercise of officers' powers) which the Secretary of State thinks necessary or expedient.

2 Amendments relating to section 1 *(omitted)*

3 Terrorist property: amendments *(omitted)*

PART II
FREEZING ORDERS

Orders

4 Power to make order

(1) The Treasury may make a freezing order if the following two conditions are satisfied.

(2) The first condition is that the Treasury reasonably believe that

   (a) action to the detriment of the United Kingdom's economy (or part of it) has been or is likely to be taken by a person or persons, or

   (b) action constituting a threat to the life or property of one or more nationals of the United Kingdom or residents of the United Kingdom has been or is likely to be taken by a person or persons.

(3) If one person is believed to have taken or to be likely to take the action the second condition is that the person is

   (a) the government of a country or territory outside the United Kingdom, or

   (b) a resident of a country or territory outside the United Kingdom.

(4) If two or more persons are believed to have taken or to be likely to take the action the second condition is that each of them falls within paragraph (a) or (b) of subsection (3); and different persons may fall within different paragraphs.

5 Contents of order

(1) A freezing order is an order which prohibits persons from making funds available to or for the benefit of a person or persons specified in the order.

(2) The order must provide that these are the persons who are prohibited

   (a) all persons in the United Kingdom, and

   (b) all persons elsewhere who are nationals of the United Kingdom or are bodies incorporated under the law of any part of the United Kingdom or are Scottish partnerships.

(3) The order may specify the following (and only the following) as the person or persons to whom or for whose benefit funds are not to be made available

   (a) the person or persons reasonably believed by the Treasury to have taken or to be likely to take the action referred to in section 4;

   (b) any person the Treasury reasonably believe has provided or is likely to provide assistance (directly or indirectly) to that person or any of those persons.

(4) A person may be specified under subsection (3) by

   (a) being named in the order, or

   (b) falling within a description of persons set out in the order.

(5) The description must be such that a reasonable person would know whether he fell within it.

(6) Funds are financial assets and economic benefits of any kind.

6 Contents: further provisions

Schedule 3 contains further provisions about the contents of freezing orders.

7 Review of order

The Treasury must keep a freezing order under review.

8 Duration of order

A freezing order ceases to have effect at the end of the period of 2 years starting with the day on which it is made.

Interpretation

9 Nationals and residents *(omitted)*

Orders: procedure etc

10 Procedure for making freezing orders

(1) A power to make a freezing order is exercisable by statutory instrument.

(2) A freezing order

    (a) must be laid before Parliament after being made;

    (b) ceases to have effect at the end of the relevant period unless before the end of that period the order is approved by a resolution of each House of Parliament (but without that affecting anything done under the order or the power to make a new order).

(3) The relevant period is a period of 28 days starting with the day on which the order is made.

(4) In calculating the relevant period no account is to be taken of any time during which Parliament is dissolved or prorogued or during which both Houses are adjourned for more than 4 days.

(5) If the Treasury propose to make a freezing order in the belief that the condition in section 4(2)(b) is satisfied, they must not make the order unless they consult the Secretary of State.

11 Procedure for making certain amending orders *(omitted)*

12 Procedure for revoking orders *(omitted)*

13 De-hybridisation *(omitted)*

14 Orders: supplementary *(omitted)*

Miscellaneous

15 The Crown *(omitted)*

16 Repeals *(omitted)*

PART III
DISCLOSURE OF INFORMATION

17 Extension of existing disclosure powers

(1) This section applies to the provisions listed in Schedule 4, so far as they authorise the disclosure of information.

(2) Each of the provisions to which this section applies shall have effect, in relation to the disclosure of information by or on behalf of a public authority, as if the purposes for which the disclosure of information is authorised by that provision included each of the following

    (a) the purposes of any criminal investigation whatever which is being or may be carried out, whether in the United Kingdom or elsewhere;

    (b) the purposes of any criminal proceedings whatever which have been or may be initiated, whether in the United Kingdom or elsewhere;

    (c) the purposes of the initiation or bringing to an end of any such investigation or proceedings;

    (d) the purpose of facilitating a determination of whether any such investigation or proceedings should be initiated or brought to an end.

(3) The Treasury may by order made by statutory instrument add any provision contained in any subordinate legislation to the provisions to which this section applies.

(4) The Treasury shall not make an order under subsection (3) unless a draft of it has been laid before Parliament and approved by a resolution of each House.

(5) No disclosure of information shall be made by virtue of this section unless the public authority by which the disclosure is made is satisfied that the making of the disclosure is proportionate to what is sought to be achieved by it.

(6) Nothing in this section shall be taken to prejudice any power to disclose information which exists apart from this section.

(7) The information that may be disclosed by virtue of this section includes information obtained before the commencement of this section.

18 Restriction on disclosure of information for overseas purposes

(1) Subject to subsections (2) and (3), the Secretary of State may give a direction which
  (a) specifies any overseas proceedings or any description of overseas proceedings; and
  (b) prohibits the making of any relevant disclosure for the purposes of those proceedings or, as the case may be, of proceedings of that description.

(2) In subsection (1) the reference, in relation to a direction, to a relevant disclosure is a reference to a disclosure authorised by any of the provisions to which section 17 applies which
  (a) is made for a purpose mentioned in subsection (2)(a) to (d) of that section; and
  (b) is a disclosure of any such information as is described in the direction.

(3) The Secretary of State shall not give a direction under this section unless it appears to him that the overseas proceedings in question, or that overseas proceedings of the description in question, relate or would relate
  (a) to a matter in respect of which it would be more appropriate for any jurisdiction or investigation to be exercised or carried out by a court or other authority of the United Kingdom, or of a particular part of the United Kingdom;
  (b) to a matter in respect of which it would be more appropriate for any jurisdiction or investigation to be exercised or carried out by a court or other authority of a third country; or
  (c) to a matter that would fall within paragraph (a) or (b)
    (i) if it were appropriate for there to be any exercise of jurisdiction or investigation at all; and
    (ii) if (where one does not exist) a court or other authority with the necessary jurisdiction or functions existed in the United Kingdom, in the part of the United Kingdom in question or, as the case may be, in the third country in question.

(4) A direction under this section shall not have the effect of prohibiting
  (a) the making of any disclosure by a Minister of the Crown or by the Treasury; or
  (b) the making of any disclosure in pursuance of a Community obligation.

(5) A direction under this section
  (a) may prohibit the making of disclosures absolutely or in such cases, or subject to such conditions as to consent or otherwise, as may be specified in it; and
  (b) must be published or otherwise issued by the Secretary of State in such manner as he considers appropriate for bringing it to the attention of persons likely to be affected by it.

(6) A person who, knowing of any direction under this section, discloses any information in contravention of that direction shall be guilty of an offence and liable
  (a) on conviction on indictment, to imprisonment for a term not exceeding two years or to a fine or to both;
  (b) on summary conviction, to imprisonment for a term not exceeding three months or to a fine not exceeding the statutory maximum or to both.

(7) The following are overseas proceedings for the purposes of this section
  (a) criminal proceedings which are taking place, or will or may take place, in a country or territory outside the United Kingdom;
  (b) a criminal investigation which is being, or will or may be, conducted by an authority of any such country or territory.

(8) References in this section, in relation to any proceedings or investigation, to a third country are references to any country or territory outside the United Kingdom which is not the country or territory where the proceedings are taking place, or will or may take place or, as the case may be, is not the country or territory of the authority which is conducting the investigation, or which will or may conduct it.

(9) In this section "court" includes a tribunal of any description.

19 Disclosure of information held by revenue departments

(1) This section applies to information which is held by or on behalf of the Commissioners of Inland Revenue or by or on behalf of the Commissioners of Customs and Excise, including information obtained before the coming into force of this section.

(2) No obligation of secrecy imposed by statute or otherwise prevents the disclosure, in accordance with the following provisions of this section, of information to which this section applies if the disclosure is made

    (a) [...][1]

    (b) for the purposes of any criminal investigation whatever which is being or may be carried out, whether in the United Kingdom or elsewhere;

    (c) for the purposes of any criminal proceedings whatever which have been or may be initiated, whether in the United Kingdom or elsewhere;

    (d) for the purposes of the initiation or bringing to an end of any such investigation or proceedings; or

    (e) for the purpose of facilitating a determination of whether any such investigation or proceedings should be initiated or brought to an end.

(3) No disclosure of information to which this section applies shall be made by virtue of this section unless the person by whom the disclosure is made is satisfied that the making of the disclosure is proportionate to what is sought to be achieved by it.

(4) Information to which this section applies shall not be disclosed by virtue of this section except by the Commissioners by or on whose behalf it is held or with their authority.

(5) Information obtained by means of a disclosure authorised by subsection (2) shall not be further disclosed except

    (a) for a purpose mentioned in that subsection; and

    (b) with the consent of the Commissioners by whom or with whose authority it was initially disclosed;

and information so obtained otherwise than by or on behalf of any of the intelligence services shall not be further disclosed (with or without such consent) to any of those services, or to any person acting on behalf of any of those services, except for a purpose mentioned in paragraphs (b) to (e) of that subsection.

(6) A consent for the purposes of subsection (5) may be given either in relation to a particular disclosure or in relation to disclosures made in such circumstances as may be specified or described in the consent.

(7) Nothing in this section authorises the making of any disclosure which is prohibited by any provision of the Data Protection Act 1998 (c 29).

(8) References in this section to information which is held on behalf of the Commissioners of Inland Revenue or of the Commissioners of Customs and Excise include references to information which

    (a) is held by a person who provides services to the Commissioners of Inland Revenue or, as the case may be, to the Commissioners of Customs and Excise; and

    (b) is held by that person in connection with the provision of those services.

---

[1] Repealed by the Counter-Terrorism Act 2008, ss 20(4), 99, Sch 1, para 1, Sch 9, Pt 2.

(9) In this section "intelligence service" has the same meaning as in the Regulation of Investigatory Powers Act 2000 (c 23).

(10) Nothing in this section shall be taken to prejudice any power to disclose information which exists apart from this section.

20 Interpretation of Part III

(1) In this Part

"criminal investigation" means an investigation of any criminal conduct, including an investigation of alleged or suspected criminal conduct and an investigation of whether criminal conduct has taken place;

"information" includes

(a) documents; and

(b) in relation to a disclosure authorised by a provision to which section 17 applies, anything that falls to be treated as information for the purposes of that provision;

"public authority" has the same meaning as in section 6 of the Human Rights Act 1998 (c 42); and

"subordinate legislation" has the same meaning as in the Interpretation Act 1978 (c 30).

(2) Proceedings outside the United Kingdom shall not be taken to be criminal proceedings for the purposes of this Part unless the conduct with which the defendant in those proceedings is charged is criminal conduct or conduct which, to a substantial extent, consists of criminal conduct.

(3) In this section

"conduct" includes acts, omissions and statements; and

"criminal conduct" means any conduct which

(a) constitutes one or more criminal offences under the law of a part of the United Kingdom; or

(b) is, or corresponds to, conduct which, if it all took place in a particular part of the United Kingdom, would constitute one or more offences under the law of that part of the United Kingdom.

PART IV
IMMIGRATION AND ASYLUM

21–33 *(repealed)*

34–36 *(omitted)*

PART V
RACE AND RELIGION *(omitted)*

37–42 *(omitted)*

PART VI
WEAPONS OF MASS DESTRUCTION

Amendment of the Biological Weapons Act 1974 and the Chemical Weapons Act 1996

43 Transfers of biological agents and toxins

In section 1 of the Biological Weapons Act 1974 (c 6) (restriction on development etc of certain biological agents and toxins and of biological weapons), after subsection (1) insert

"(1A) A person shall not
  (a) transfer any biological agent or toxin to another person or enter into an agreement to do so, or
  (b) make arrangements under which another person transfers any biological agent or toxin or enters into an agreement with a third person to do so,
  if the biological agent or toxin is likely to be kept or used (whether by the transferee or any other person) otherwise than for prophylactic, protective or other peaceful purposes and he knows or has reason to believe that that is the case."

44 Extraterritorial application of biological weapons offences

After section 1 of the Biological Weapons Act 1974 insert

"1A Extraterritorial application of section 1

  (1) Section 1 applies to acts done outside the United Kingdom, but only if they are done by a United Kingdom person.
  (2) Proceedings for an offence committed under section 1 outside the United Kingdom may be taken, and the offence may for incidental purposes be treated as having been committed, in any place in the United Kingdom.
  (3) Her Majesty may by Order in Council extend the application of section 1, so far as it applies to acts done outside the United Kingdom, to bodies incorporated under the law of any of the Channel Islands, the Isle of Man or any colony.
  (4) In this section "United Kingdom person" means a United Kingdom national, a Scottish partnership or a body incorporated under the law of a part of the United Kingdom.
  (5) For this purpose a United Kingdom national is an individual who is
    (a) a British citizen, a British Dependent Territories citizen, a British National (Overseas) or a British Overseas citizen;
    (b) a person who under the British Nationality Act 1981 (c 61) is a British subject; or
    (c) a British protected person within the meaning of that Act.
  (6) Nothing in this section affects any criminal liability arising otherwise than under this section."

45 Customs and Excise prosecutions for biological weapons offences

Before section 2 of the Biological Weapons Act 1974 (c 6) insert

"1B Customs and Excise prosecutions

  (1) Proceedings for a biological weapons offence may be instituted by order of the Commissioners of Customs and Excise if it appears to them that the offence has involved
    (a) the development or production outside the United Kingdom of any thing mentioned in section 1(1)(a) or (b) above;
    (b) the movement of any such thing into or out of any country or territory;
    (c) any proposal or attempt to do anything falling within paragraph (a) or (b) above.
  (2) In this section "biological weapons offence" means an offence under section 1 of this Act or section 50 of the Anti-terrorism, Crime and Security Act 2001 (including an offence of aiding, abetting, counselling, procuring or inciting the commission of, or attempting or conspiring to commit, such an offence).
  (3) Any proceedings for an offence which are instituted under subsection (1) above shall be commenced in the name of an officer, but may be continued by another officer.
  (4) Where the Commissioners of Customs and Excise investigate, or propose to investigate, any matter with a view to determining
    (a) whether there are grounds for believing that a biological weapons offence has been committed, or

(b) whether a person should be prosecuted for such an offence,

that matter shall be treated as an assigned matter within the meaning of the Customs and Excise Management Act 1979.

(5) Nothing in this section affects any power of any person (including any officer) apart from this section.

(6) In this section "officer" means a person commissioned by the Commissioners of Customs and Excise.

(7) This section does not apply to the institution of proceedings in Scotland."

46 Customs and Excise prosecutions for chemical weapons offences

Before section 31 of the Chemical Weapons Act 1996 (c 6) insert

"30A Customs and Excise prosecutions

(1) Proceedings for a chemical weapons offence may be instituted by order of the Commissioners of Customs and Excise if it appears to them that the offence has involved

(a) the development or production outside the United Kingdom of a chemical weapon;

(b) the movement of a chemical weapon into or out of any country or territory;

(c) any proposal or attempt to do anything falling within paragraph (a) or (b).

(2) In this section "chemical weapons offence" means an offence under section 2 above or section 50 of the Anti-terrorism, Crime and Security Act 2001 (including an offence of aiding, abetting, counselling, procuring or inciting the commission of, or attempting or conspiring to commit, such an offence).

(3) Any proceedings for an offence which are instituted under subsection (1) shall be commenced in the name of an officer, but may be continued by another officer.

(4) Where the Commissioners of Customs and Excise investigate, or propose to investigate, any matter with a view to determining

(a) whether there are grounds for believing that a chemical weapons offence has been committed, or

(b) whether a person should be prosecuted for such an offence,

that matter shall be treated as an assigned matter within the meaning of the Customs and Excise Management Act 1979.

(5) Nothing in this section affects any power of any person (including any officer) apart from this section.

(6) In this section "officer" means a person commissioned by the Commissioners of Customs and Excise.

(7) This section does not apply to the institution of proceedings in Scotland."

Nuclear weapons

47 Use etc of nuclear weapons

(1) A person who

(a) knowingly causes a nuclear weapon explosion;

(b) develops or produces, or participates in the development or production of, a nuclear weapon;

(c) has a nuclear weapon in his possession;

(d) participates in the transfer of a nuclear weapon; or

(e) engages in military preparations, or in preparations of a military nature, intending to use, or threaten to use, a nuclear weapon,

is guilty of an offence.

(2) Subsection (1) has effect subject to the exceptions and defences in sections 48 and 49.

(3) For the purposes of subsection (1)(b) a person participates in the development or production of a nuclear weapon if he does any act which

    (a) facilitates the development by another of the capability to produce or use a nuclear weapon, or

    (b) facilitates the making by another of a nuclear weapon,

knowing or having reason to believe that his act has (or will have) that effect.

(4) For the purposes of subsection (1)(d) a person participates in the transfer of a nuclear weapon if

    (a) he buys or otherwise acquires it or agrees with another to do so;

    (b) he sells or otherwise disposes of it or agrees with another to do so; or

    (c) he makes arrangements under which another person either acquires or disposes of it or agrees with a third person to do so.

(5) A person guilty of an offence under this section is liable on conviction on indictment to imprisonment for life.

(6) In this section "nuclear weapon" includes a nuclear explosive device that is not intended for use as a weapon.

(7) This section applies to acts done outside the United Kingdom, but only if they are done by a United Kingdom person.

(8) Nothing in subsection (7) affects any criminal liability arising otherwise than under that subsection.

(9) Paragraph (a) of subsection (1) shall cease to have effect on the coming into force of the Nuclear Explosions (Prohibition and Inspections) Act 1998 (c 7).

48 Exceptions

(1) Nothing in section 47 applies

    (a) to an act which is authorised under subsection (2); or

    (b) to an act done in the course of an armed conflict.

(2) The Secretary of State may

    (a) authorise any act which would otherwise contravene section 47 in such manner and on such terms as he thinks fit; and

    (b) withdraw or vary any authorisation given under this subsection.

(3) Any question arising in proceedings for an offence under section 47 as to whether anything was done in the course of an armed conflict shall be determined by the Secretary of State.

(4) A certificate purporting to set out any such determination and to be signed by the Secretary of State shall be received in evidence in any such proceedings and shall be presumed to be so signed unless the contrary is shown.

49 Defences

(1) In proceedings for an offence under section 47(1)(c) or (d) relating to an object it is a defence for the accused to show that he did not know and had no reason to believe that the object was a nuclear weapon.

(2) But he shall be taken to have shown that fact if

    (a) sufficient evidence is adduced to raise an issue with respect to it; and

    (b) the contrary is not proved by the prosecution beyond reasonable doubt.

(3) In proceedings for such an offence it is also a defence for the accused to show that he knew or believed that the object was a nuclear weapon but, as soon as reasonably practicable after he first knew or believed that fact, he took all reasonable steps to inform the Secretary of State or a constable of his knowledge or belief.

Assisting or inducing weapons-related acts overseas

50 Assisting or inducing certain weapons-related acts overseas

(1) A person who aids, abets, counsels or procures, or incites, a person who is not a United Kingdom person to do a relevant act outside the United Kingdom is guilty of an offence.

(2) For this purpose a relevant act is an act that, if done by a United Kingdom person, would contravene any of the following provisions
  (a) section 1 of the Biological Weapons Act 1974 (offences relating to biological agents and toxins);
  (b) section 2 of the Chemical Weapons Act 1996 (offences relating to chemical weapons); or
  (c) section 47 above (offences relating to nuclear weapons).

(3) Nothing in this section applies to an act mentioned in subsection (1) which
  (a) relates to a relevant act which would contravene section 47; and
  (b) is authorised by the Secretary of State;
  and section 48(2) applies for the purpose of authorising acts that would otherwise constitute an offence under this section.

(4) A person accused of an offence under this section in relation to a relevant act which would contravene a provision mentioned in subsection (2) may raise any defence which would be open to a person accused of the corresponding offence ancillary to an offence under that provision.

(5) A person convicted of an offence under this section is liable on conviction on indictment to imprisonment for life.

(6) This section applies to acts done outside the United Kingdom, but only if they are done by a United Kingdom person.

(7) Nothing in this section prejudices any criminal liability existing apart from this section.

Supplemental provisions relating to sections 47 and 50

51 Extraterritorial application

(1) Proceedings for an offence committed under section 47 or 50 outside the United Kingdom may be taken, and the offence may for incidental purposes be treated as having been committed, in any part of the United Kingdom.

(2) Her Majesty may by Order in Council extend the application of section 47 or 50, so far as it applies to acts done outside the United Kingdom, to bodies incorporated under the law of any of the Channel Islands, the Isle of Man or any colony.

52 Powers of entry

(1) If
  (a) a justice of the peace is satisfied on information on oath that there are reasonable grounds for suspecting that evidence of the commission of an offence under section 47 or 50 is to be found on any premises; or
  (b) in Scotland the sheriff is satisfied by evidence on oath as mentioned in paragraph (a),
  he may issue a warrant authorising an authorised officer to enter the premises, if necessary by force, at any time within one month from the time of the issue of the warrant and to search them.

(2) The powers of a person who enters the premises under the authority of the warrant include power
  (a) to take with him such other persons and such equipment as appear to him to be necessary;
  (b) to inspect, seize and retain any substance, equipment or document found on the premises;
  (c) to require any document or other information which is held in electronic form and is accessible from the premises to be produced in a form
  (i) in which he can read and copy it; or
  (ii) from which it can readily be produced in a form in which he can read and copy it;

(d) to copy any document which he has reasonable cause to believe may be required as evidence for the purposes of proceedings in respect of an offence under section 47 or 50.

(3) A constable who enters premises under the authority of a warrant or by virtue of subsection (2)(a) may

(a) give such assistance as an authorised officer may request for the purpose of facilitating the exercise of any power under this section; and

(b) search or cause to be searched any person on the premises who the constable has reasonable cause to believe may have in his possession any document or other thing which may be required as evidence for the purposes of proceedings in respect of an offence under section 47 or 50.

(4) No constable shall search a person of the opposite sex.

(5) The powers conferred by a warrant under this section shall only be exercisable, if the warrant so provides, in the presence of a constable.

(6) A person who

(a) wilfully obstructs an authorised officer in the exercise of a power conferred by a warrant under this section; or

(b) fails without reasonable excuse to comply with a reasonable request made by an authorised officer or a constable for the purpose of facilitating the exercise of such a power,

is guilty of an offence.

(7) A person guilty of an offence under subsection (6) is liable

(a) on summary conviction, to a fine not exceeding the statutory maximum; and

(b) on conviction on indictment, to imprisonment for a term not exceeding two years or a fine (or both).

(8) In this section "authorised officer" means an authorised officer of the Secretary of State.

53 Revenue and Customs prosecutions *(omitted)*

54 Offences

(1) A person who knowingly or recklessly makes a false or misleading statement for the purpose of obtaining (or opposing the variation or withdrawal of) authorisation for the purposes of section 47 or 50 is guilty of an offence.

(2) A person guilty of an offence under subsection (1) is liable

(a) on summary conviction, to a fine of an amount not exceeding the statutory maximum;

(b) on conviction on indictment, to imprisonment for a term not exceeding two years or a fine (or both).

(3) Where an offence under section 47, 50 or subsection (1) above committed by a body corporate is proved to have been committed with the consent or connivance of, or to be attributable to any neglect on the part of

(a) a director, manager, secretary or other similar officer of the body corporate; or

(b) any person who was purporting to act in any such capacity,

he as well as the body corporate shall be guilty of that offence and shall be liable to be proceeded against and punished accordingly.

(4) In subsection (3) "director", in relation to a body corporate whose affairs are managed by its members, means a member of the body corporate.

55 Consent to prosecutions

Proceedings for an offence under section 47 or 50 shall not be instituted

(a) in England and Wales, except by or with the consent of the Attorney General;

(b) in Northern Ireland, except by or with the consent of the *Attorney General for Northern Ireland*[2] [*Advocate General for Northern Ireland*].[3]

---

[2] Repealed by the Justice (Northern Ireland) Act 2002, s 28(2), Sch 7, para 36(a), not yet in force.

[3] Substituted by the Justice (Northern Ireland) Act 2002, s 28(2), Sch 7, para 36(a), not yet in force.

56 Interpretation of Part VI

(1) In this Part "United Kingdom person" means a United Kingdom national, a Scottish partnership or a body incorporated under the law of a part of the United Kingdom.

(2) For this purpose a United Kingdom national is an individual who is

   (a) a British citizen, a [British overseas territories citizen][4], a British National (Overseas) or a British Overseas citizen;

   (b) a person who under the British Nationality Act 1981 (c 61) is a British subject; or

   (c) a British protected person within the meaning of that Act.

57 Power to extend Part VI to dependencies *(omitted)*

PART VII
SECURITY OF PATHOGENS AND TOXINS

58 Pathogens and toxins in relation to which requirements under Part VII apply

(1) Schedule 5 (which lists the pathogens and toxins in relation to which the requirements of this Part apply) has effect.

(2) The Secretary of State may by order modify any provision of Schedule 5 (including the notes).

(3) The Secretary of State may not add any pathogen or toxin to that Schedule unless he is satisfied that the pathogen or toxin could be used in an act of terrorism to endanger life or cause serious harm to human health.

(4) In this Part "dangerous substance" means

   (a) anything which consists of or includes a substance for the time being mentioned in Schedule 5; or

   (b) anything which is infected with or otherwise carries any such substance.

(5) But something otherwise falling within subsection (4) is not to be regarded as a dangerous substance if

   (a) it satisfies prescribed conditions; or

   (b) it is kept or used in prescribed circumstances.

59 Duty to notify Secretary of State before keeping or using dangerous substances

(1) The occupier of any premises must give a notice to the Secretary of State before any dangerous substance is kept or used there.

(2) Subsection (1) does not apply to premises in respect of which a notice has previously been given under that subsection (unless it has been withdrawn).

(3) The occupier of any premises in respect of which a notice has been given may withdraw the notice if no dangerous substance is kept or used there.

(4) A notice under this section must

   (a) identify the premises in which the substance is kept or used;

   (b) identify any building or site of which the premises form part; and

   (c) contain such other particulars (if any) as may be prescribed.

(5) The occupier of any premises in which any dangerous substance is kept or used on the day on which this section comes into force must give a notice under this section before the end of the period of one month beginning with that day.

(6) Where

   (a) a substance which is kept or used in any premises becomes a dangerous substance by virtue of a modification of Schedule 5, but

---

[4] Substituted by virtue of the British Overseas Territories Act 2002, s 2(3).

(b) no other dangerous substance is kept or used there,

the occupier of the premises must give a notice under this section before the end of the period of one month beginning with the day on which that modification comes into force.

60 Information about security of dangerous substances

(1) A constable may give to the occupier of any relevant premises a notice requiring him to give the chief officer of police such information as is specified or described in the notice by a time so specified and in a form and manner so specified.

(2) The required information must relate to
  (a) any dangerous substance kept or used in the premises; or
  (b) the measures taken (whether by the occupier or any other person) to ensure the security of any such substance.

(3) In this Part references to measures taken to ensure the security of any dangerous substance kept or used in any relevant premises include
  (a) measures taken to ensure the security of any building or site of which the premises form part; and
  (b) measures taken for the purpose of ensuring access to the substance is given only to those whose activities require access and only in circumstances that ensure the security of the substance.

(4) In this Part "relevant premises" means any premises
  (a) in which any dangerous substance is kept or used, or
  (b) in respect of which a notice under section 59 is in force.

61 Information about persons with access to dangerous substances

(1) A police officer of at least the rank of inspector may give to the occupier of any relevant premises a notice requiring him to give the chief officer of police a list of
  (a) each person who has access to any dangerous substance kept or used there;
  (b) each person who, in such circumstances as are specified or described in the notice, has access to such part of the premises as is so specified or described;
  (c) each person who, in such circumstances as are specified or described in the notice, has access to the premises; or
  (d) each person who, in such circumstances as are specified or described in the notice, has access to any building or site of which the premises form part.

(2) A list under subsection (1) must be given before the end of the period of one month beginning with the day on which the notice is given.

(3) Where a list under subsection (1) is given, the occupier of the premises for the time being
  (a) must secure that only the persons mentioned in the list are given the access identified in the list relating to them; but
  (b) may give a supplementary list to the chief officer of police or other persons to whom it is proposed to give access.

(4) Where a supplementary list is given under subsection (3)(b), the occupier of the premises for the time being must secure that persons mentioned in that list do not have the proposed access relating to them until the end of the period of 30 days beginning with the day on which that list is given.

(5) The chief officer of police may direct that a person may have such access before the end of that period.

(6) The Secretary of State may by order modify the period mentioned in subsection (4).

(7) Any list under this section must
  (a) identify the access which the person has, or is proposed to have;
  (b) state the full name of that person, his date of birth, his address and his nationality; and
  (c) contain such other matters (if any) as may be prescribed.

62 Directions requiring security measures

(1) A constable may give directions to the occupier of any relevant premises requiring him to take such measures to ensure the security of any dangerous substance kept or used there as are specified or described in the directions by a time so specified.

(2) The directions may
   (a) specify or describe the substances in relation to the security of which the measures relate; and
   (b) require the occupier to give a notice to the chief officer of police before any other dangerous substance specified or described in the directions is kept or used in the premises.

63 Directions requiring disposal of dangerous substances

(1) Where the Secretary of State has reasonable grounds for believing that adequate measures to ensure the security of any dangerous substance kept or used in any relevant premises are not being taken and are unlikely to be taken, he may give a direction to the occupier of the premises requiring him to dispose of the substance.

(2) The direction must
   (a) specify the manner in which, and time by which, the dangerous substance must be disposed of; or
   (b) require the occupier to produce the dangerous substance to a person specified or described in the notice in a manner and by a time so specified for him to dispose of.

64 Directions requiring denial of access

(1) The Secretary of State may give directions to the occupier of any relevant premises requiring him to secure that the person identified in the directions
   (a) is not to have access to any dangerous substance kept or used there;
   (b) is not to have, in such circumstances (if any) as may be specified or described in the directions, access to such part of the premises as is so specified or described;
   (c) is not to have, in such circumstances (if any) as may be specified or described in the directions, access to the premises; or
   (d) is not to have, in such circumstances (if any) as may be specified or described in the directions, access to any building or site of which the premises form part.

(2) The directions must be given under the hand of the Secretary of State.

(3) The Secretary of State may not give the directions unless he believes that they are necessary in the interests of national security.

65 Powers of entry

(1) A constable may, on giving notice under this section, enter any relevant premises, or any building or site of which the premises form part, at a reasonable time for the purpose of assessing the measures taken to ensure the security of any dangerous substance kept or used in the premises.

(2) The notice must be given to the occupier of the premises, or (as the case may be) the occupier of the building or site of which the premises form part, at least 2 working days before the proposed entry.

(3) The notice must set out the purpose mentioned in subsection (1).

(4) A constable who has entered any premises, building or site by virtue of subsection (1) may for the purpose mentioned in that subsection
   (a) search the premises, building or site;
   (b) require any person who appears to the constable to be in charge of the premises, building or site to facilitate any such inspection; and
   (c) require any such person to answer any question.

(5) The powers of a constable under this section include power to take with him such other persons as appear to him to be necessary.

66 Search warrants

(1) If, in England and Wales or Northern Ireland, on an application made by a constable a justice of the peace is satisfied that there are reasonable grounds for believing
  (a) that a dangerous substance is kept or used in any premises but that no notice under section 59 is in force in respect of the premises, or
  (b) that the occupier of any relevant premises is failing to comply with any direction given to him under section 62 or 63,
and that any of the conditions mentioned in subsection (4) apply, he may issue a warrant authorising a constable to enter the premises, if necessary by force, and to search them.
(2) If, in Scotland, on an application made by the procurator fiscal the sheriff is satisfied as mentioned in subsection (1), he may issue a warrant authorising a constable to enter the premises, if necessary by force, and to search them.
(3) A constable may seize and retain anything which he believes is or contains a dangerous substance.
(4) The conditions mentioned in subsection (1) are
  (a) that it is not practicable to communicate with any person entitled to grant entry to the premises;
  (b) that it is practicable to communicate with a person entitled to grant entry to the premises but it is not practicable to communicate with any person entitled to grant access to any substance which may be a dangerous substance;
  (c) that entry to the premises will not be granted unless a warrant is produced;
  (d) that the purpose of a search may be frustrated or seriously prejudiced unless a constable arriving at the premises can secure immediate entry to them.

67 Offences

(1) An occupier who fails without reasonable excuse to comply with any duty or direction imposed on him by or under this Part is guilty of an offence.
(2) A person who, in giving any information to a person exercising functions under this Part, knowingly or recklessly makes a statement which is false or misleading in a material particular is guilty of an offence.
(3) A person guilty of an offence under this section is liable
  (a) on conviction on indictment, to imprisonment for a term not exceeding five years or a fine (or both); and
  (b) on summary conviction, to imprisonment for a term not exceeding six months or a fine not exceeding the statutory maximum (or both).

68 Bodies corporate *(omitted)*

69 Partnerships and unincorporated associations *(omitted)*

70 Denial of access: appeals

(1) There shall be a commission, to be known as the Pathogens Access Appeal Commission.
(2) Any person aggrieved by directions given under section 64 may appeal to the Commission.
(3) The Commission must allow an appeal if it considers that the decision to give the directions was flawed when considered in the light of the principles applicable on an application for judicial review.
(4) A party to any appeal under this section which the Commission has determined may bring a further appeal on a question of law to
  (a) the Court of Appeal, if the first appeal was heard in England and Wales;

    (b) the Court of Session, if the first appeal was heard in Scotland; or

    (c) the Court of Appeal in Northern Ireland, if the first appeal was heard in Northern Ireland.

(5) An appeal under subsection () may be brought only with the permission of

    (a) the Commission; or

    (b) where the Commission refuses permission, the court to which the appeal would be brought.

(6) Schedule 6 (constitution of the Commission and procedure) has effect.

71 Other appeals

(1) Any person who is required to do any act in response to

    (a) any notice under section 60, or

    (b) any directions under section 62 or 63,

may appeal to a magistrates' court against the requirement on the ground that, having regard to all the circumstances of the case, it is unreasonable to be required to do that act.

(2) An appeal may not be brought after the end of the period of one month beginning with the day on which the notice or directions were given.

(3) If the magistrates' court allows the appeal, it may

    (a) direct that the required act need not be done; or

    (b) make such modification of the requirement as it considers appropriate.

(4) An appeal shall lie to the Crown Court against any decision of the magistrates' court.

(5) Subsections (1) to (3) apply to Scotland with the substitution for references to the magistrates' court of references to the sheriff.

(6) The appeal to the sheriff is by way of summary application.

(7) A further appeal shall lie

    (a) to the sheriff principal from the decision of the sheriff; and

    (b) with the leave of the sheriff principal, to the Court of Session from the decision of the sheriff principal.

(8) In the application of this section to Northern Ireland references to a magistrates' court are to a court of summary jurisdiction.

72 Giving of directions or notices

Any direction or notice under this Part may be given by post.

73 Orders and regulations *(omitted)*

74 Interpretation of Part 7

(1) In this Part

"act of terrorism" has the same meaning as in the Terrorism Act 2000 (c 11);

"chief officer of police" means

    (a) in relation to any premises in Great Britain, the chief officer of police for the area in which the premises are situated; and

    (b) in relation to any premises in Northern Ireland, the Chief Constable of the Police Service of Northern Ireland;

"dangerous substance" has the meaning given in section 58;

"direction" means a direction in writing;

"notice" means a notice in writing;

"occupier" includes a partnership or unincorporated association and, in relation to premises that are unoccupied, means any person entitled to occupy the premises;

"prescribed" means prescribed in regulations made by the Secretary of State; and

"relevant premises" has the meaning given in section 60.

(2) In this Part references to measures taken to ensure the security of any dangerous substance are to be construed in accordance with section 60.

75 Power to extend Part VII to animal or plant pathogens, pests or toxic chemicals

(1) The Secretary of State may, in relation to anything to which this section applies, make an order applying, or making provision corresponding to, any provision of this Part, with or without modifications.

(2) This section applies to
   (a) toxic chemicals (within the meaning of the Chemical Weapons Act 1996 (c 6));
   (b) animal pathogens;
   (c) plant pathogens; and
   (d) pests.

(3) The power under this section may be exercised in relation to any chemical only if the Secretary of State is satisfied that the chemical could be used in an act of terrorism to endanger life or cause serious harm to human health.

(4) The power under this section may be exercised in relation to any pathogen or pest only if the Secretary of State is satisfied that there is a risk that the pathogen or pest is of a description that could be used in an act of terrorism to cause
   (a) widespread damage to property;
   (b) significant disruption to the public; or
   (c) significant alarm to the public.

(5) An order under this section may
   (a) provide for any reference in the order to an instrument or other document to take effect as a reference to that instrument or document as revised or re-issued from time to time;
   (b) make different provision for different purposes; and
   (c) make such incidental, supplementary and transitional provision as the Secretary of State thinks fit.

(6) A statutory instrument containing an order under this section shall not be made unless a draft of it has been laid before and approved by a resolution of each House of Parliament.

PART VIII
SECURITY OF NUCLEAR INDUSTRY

76 [...][5]

77 Regulation of security of civil nuclear industry

(1) The Secretary of State may make regulations for the purpose of ensuring the security of
   (a) nuclear sites and other nuclear premises;
   (b) nuclear material used or stored on nuclear sites or other nuclear premises and equipment or software used or stored on such sites or premises in connection with activities involving nuclear material;
   (c) other radioactive material used or stored on nuclear sites and equipment or software used or stored on nuclear sites in connection with activities involving other radioactive material;
   [(ca) equipment or software in the United Kingdom which
      (i) is capable of being used in, or in connection with, the enrichment of uranium; and
      (ii) is in the possession or control of a person involved in uranium enrichment activities;][6]

---

[5] Repealed with savings by the Energy Act 2004, s 197(9), (10), Sch 23, Pt 1, Pt 2, para 3.
[6] Inserted by the Energy Act 2004, ss 77(1), (2).

[(d) sensitive nuclear information which is in the possession or control in the United Kingdom of
  (i) a person who is involved in activities on or in relation to a nuclear site or nuclear premises or who is proposing or likely to become so involved;
  (ii) a person involved in uranium enrichment activities; or
  (iii) a person who is storing, transporting or transmitting the information for or on behalf of a person falling within sub-paragraph (i) or (ii);][7]

(e) nuclear material which is being (or is expected to be)
  (i) transported within the United Kingdom or its territorial sea;
  (ii) transported (outside the United Kingdom and its territorial sea) to or from any nuclear site or other nuclear premises in the United Kingdom; or
  (iii) carried on board a United Kingdom ship;

(f) information relating to the security of anything mentioned in paragraphs (a) to (e).

(2) The regulations may, in particular
  (a) require a person to produce for the approval of the Secretary of State a plan for ensuring the security of anything mentioned in subsection (1) and to comply with the plan as approved by the Secretary of State;
  (b) require compliance with any directions given by the Secretary of State;
  (c) impose requirements in relation to any activities by reference to the approval of the Secretary of State;
  (d) create summary offences or offences triable either way;
  (e) make provision for the purposes mentioned in subsection (1) corresponding to any provision which may be made for the general purposes of Part 1 of the Health and Safety at Work etc Act 1974 (c 37) by virtue of section 15(2), (3)(c) and (4) to (8) of that Act (health and safety regulations);
  (f) make provision corresponding to any provision which may be made by virtue of section 43(2) to (5), (8) and (9) of that Act (fees), in connection with the performance by or on behalf of the Secretary of State or any other specified body or person of functions under the regulations; and
  (g) apply (with or without modifications), or make provision corresponding to, any provision contained in sections 19 to 42 and 44 to 47 of that Act.

(3) An offence under the regulations may be made punishable
  (a) in the case of an offence triable either way
    (i) on conviction on indictment, with imprisonment for a term not exceeding two years or a fine (or both); and
    (ii) on summary conviction, with imprisonment for a term not exceeding six months or a fine not exceeding the statutory maximum (or both); or
  (b) in the case of a summary offence, with imprisonment for a term not exceeding six months or a fine not exceeding level 5 on the standard scale (or both).

(4) The regulations may make
  (a) provision applying to acts done outside the United Kingdom by United Kingdom persons;
  (b) different provision for different purposes; and
  (c) such incidental, supplementary and transitional provision as the Secretary of State considers appropriate.

(5) Before making the regulations the Secretary of State shall consult
  (a) [the Health and Safety Executive;][8] and
  (b) such other persons as he considers appropriate.

(6) The power to make the regulations is exercisable by statutory instrument subject to annulment in pursuance of a resolution of either House of Parliament.

---

[7] Substituted by the Energy Act 2004, s 77(1), (3).
[8] Substituted by SI 2008/960, art 22, Sch 3.

[(6A) References in this section to a person involved in uranium enrichment activities are references to a person who is or is proposing to become involved in any of the following activities (whether in the United Kingdom or elsewhere)

(a) the enrichment of uranium;

(b) activities carried on with a view to, or in connection with, the enrichment of uranium;

(c) the production, storage, transport or transmission of equipment or software for or on behalf of persons involved in uranium enrichment activities; or

(d) activities that make it reasonable to assume that he will become involved in something mentioned in paragraphs (a) to (c).][9]

(7) In this section

["enrichment of uranium" means a treatment of uranium that increases the proportion of isotope 235 contained in the uranium;

"equipment" includes equipment that has not been assembled and its components;][10]

["nuclear material" has the same meaning as in Chapter 3 of Part 1 of the Energy Act 2004;

"nuclear site" means a licensed nuclear site within the meaning of that Chapter;][11]

"other nuclear premises" means premises other than a nuclear site on which nuclear material is used or stored;

"sensitive nuclear information" means

(a) information relating to, or capable of use in connection with, [the enrichment of][12] uranium; or

(b) information relating to activities carried out on or in relation to nuclear sites or other nuclear premises which appears to the Secretary of State to be information which needs to be protected in the interests of national security;

"United Kingdom ship" means a ship registered in the United Kingdom under Part 2 of the Merchant Shipping Act 1995 (c 21)

(8) Any sums received by virtue of provision made under subsection (2)(f) shall be paid into the Consolidated Fund.

78 Repeals relating to security of civil nuclear installations *(omitted)*

79 Prohibition of disclosures relating to nuclear security

(1) A person is guilty of an offence if he discloses any information or thing the disclosure of which might prejudice the security of any nuclear site or of any nuclear material

(a) with the intention of prejudicing that security; or

(b) being reckless as to whether the disclosure might prejudice that security.

(2) The reference in subsection (1) to nuclear material is a reference to

(a) nuclear material which is being held on any nuclear site, or

(b) nuclear material anywhere in the world which is being transported to or from a nuclear site or carried on board a British ship,

(including nuclear material which is expected to be so held, transported or carried).

(3) A person guilty of an offence under subsection (1) is liable

(a) on conviction on indictment, to imprisonment for a term not exceeding seven years or a fine (or both); and

(b) on summary conviction, to imprisonment for a term not exceeding six months or a fine not exceeding the statutory maximum (or both).

(4) In this section

"British ship" means a ship (including a ship belonging to Her Majesty) which is registered in the United Kingdom;

---

[9] Inserted by the Energy Act 2004, s 77(1), (4).

[10] Inserted by the Energy Act 2004, s 77(1), (5)(a).

[11] Substituted, for definitions as originally enacted, by the Energy Act 2004, s 69(1) sch 14, para 10(1).

[12] Substituted by the Energy Act 2004, s 77(1), (5)(b).

"disclose" and "disclosure", in relation to a thing, include parting with possession of it;

["nuclear material" has the same meaning as in Chapter 3 of Part 1 of the Energy Act 2004;][13] and

"nuclear site" means a site in the United Kingdom (including a site occupied by or on behalf of the Crown) which is (or is expected to be) used for any purpose mentioned in section 1(1) of the Nuclear Installations Act 1965 (c 57).

(5) This section applies to acts done outside the United Kingdom, but only if they are done by a United Kingdom person.

(6) Proceedings for an offence committed outside the United Kingdom may be taken, and the offence may for incidental purposes be treated as having been committed, in any place in the United Kingdom.

(7) Nothing in subsection (5) affects any criminal liability arising otherwise than under that subsection.

80 Prohibition of disclosures of uranium enrichment technology

(1) This section applies to
  (a) any information about the enrichment of uranium; or
  (b) any information or thing which is, or is likely to be, used in connection with the enrichment of uranium;
  and for this purpose "the enrichment of uranium" means any treatment of uranium that increases the proportion of the isotope 235 contained in the uranium.

(2) The Secretary of State may make regulations prohibiting the disclosure of information or things to which this section applies.

(3) A person who contravenes a prohibition is guilty of an offence and liable
  (a) on conviction on indictment, to imprisonment for a term not exceeding seven years or a fine (or both); and
  (b) on summary conviction, to imprisonment for a term not exceeding six months or a fine not exceeding the statutory maximum (or both).

(4) The regulations may, in particular, provide for
  (a) a prohibition to apply, or not to apply
    (i) to such information or things; and
    (ii) in such cases or circumstances,
    as may be prescribed;
  (b) the authorisation by the Secretary of State of disclosures that would otherwise be prohibited; and
  (c) defences to an offence under subsection (3) relating to any prohibition.

(5) The regulations may
  (a) provide for any prohibition to apply to acts done outside the United Kingdom by United Kingdom persons;
  (b) make different provision for different purposes; and
  (c) make such incidental, supplementary and transitional provision as the Secretary of State thinks fit.

(6) The power to make the regulations is exercisable by statutory instrument.

(7) The regulations shall not be made unless a draft of the regulations has been laid before and approved by each House of Parliament.

(8) In this section
  "disclosure", in relation to a thing, includes parting with possession of it;
  "information" includes software; and
  "prescribed" means specified or described in the regulations.

---

[13] Substituted by the Energy Act 2004, s 69(1), Sch 14, para 10(2).

[80A Extension of Official Secrets Acts to certain places

(1) A place to which subsection (2) applies is deemed to be a place belonging to or used for the purposes of Her Majesty for the purposes of section 3(c) of the Official Secrets Act 1911 (c 28) (power of Secretary of State to declare a place belonging to or used for the purposes of Her Majesty a prohibited place).

(2) This subsection applies to a place if

    (a) equipment or software which is designed or adapted for use in, or in connection with, the enrichment of uranium (or which is not so designed or adapted but is likely to be of exceptional use in that connection) is held at the place, or

    (b) information relating to, or capable of use in connection with, the enrichment of uranium is held at the place.

(3) In this section

    "enrichment of uranium" means a treatment of uranium which increases the proportion of isotope 235 contained in the uranium, and

    "equipment" includes equipment which has not yet been assembled and a component of equipment.][14]

81 Part VIII: supplementary

(1) Proceedings for an offence under section 79 or 80 shall not be instituted

    (a) in England and Wales, except by or with the consent of the Attorney General; or

    (b) in Northern Ireland, except by or with the consent of the *Attorney General for Northern Ireland*[15] [*Advocate General for Northern Ireland*][16].

(2) In this Part "United Kingdom person" means a United Kingdom national, a Scottish partnership or a body incorporated under the law of any part of the United Kingdom.

(3) For this purpose a United Kingdom national is an individual who is

    (a) a British citizen, a [British overseas territories citizen][17], a British National (Overseas) or a British Overseas citizen;

    (b) a person who under the British Nationality Act 1981 (c 61) is a British subject; or

    (c) a British protected person within the meaning of that Act.

PART IX
AVIATION SECURITY

82–88 *(omitted)*

PART X
POLICE POWERS

Identification

89 Fingerprinting of terrorist suspects

(1) Schedule 8 to the Terrorism Act 2000 (c 11) (persons detained under terrorism provisions) is amended as follows.

(2) In paragraph 10, at the beginning of sub-paragraph (6) (grounds on which officer may authorise fingerprinting or taking of sample), insert "Subject to sub-paragraph (6A)"; and after that sub-paragraph insert

---

[14] Inserted by the Energy Act 2008, s 101.

[15] Repealed by the Justice (Northern Ireland) Act 2002, s 28(2), Sch 7, para 36(b), not yet in force.

[16] Substituted by the Justice (Northern Ireland) Act 2002, s 28(2), Sch 7, para 36(b), not yet in force.

[17] Substituted by virtue of the British Overseas Territories Act 2002, s 2(3).

"(6A) An officer may also give an authorisation under sub-paragraph (4)(a) for the taking of fingerprints if

    (a) he is satisfied that the fingerprints of the detained person will facilitate the ascertainment of that person's identity; and

    (b) that person has refused to identify himself or the officer has reasonable grounds for suspecting that that person is not who he claims to be.

(6B)   In this paragraph references to ascertaining a person's identity include references to showing that he is not a particular person."

(3)   In paragraph 20(2), for the subsection (2) substituted by way of modification of section 18 of the Criminal Procedure (Scotland) Act 1995 (c 46) substitute

"(2)   Subject to subsection (2A), a constable may take from a detained person or require a detained person to provide relevant physical data only if

    (a) in the case of a person detained under section 41 of the Terrorism Act 2000, he reasonably suspects that the person has been involved in an offence under any of the provisions mentioned in section 40(1)(a) of that Act and he reasonably believes that the relevant physical data will tend to confirm or disprove his involvement; or

    (b) in any case, he is satisfied that it is necessary to do so in order to assist in determining whether the person falls within section 40(1)(b).

(2A)   A constable may also take fingerprints from a detained person or require him to provide them if

    (a) he is satisfied that the fingerprints of that person will facilitate the ascertainment of that person's identity; and

    (b) that person has refused to identify himself or the constable has reasonable grounds for suspecting that that person is not who he claims to be.

(2B)   In this section references to ascertaining a person's identity include references to showing that he is not a particular person."

(4)   For paragraph 20(3) substitute

"(3)   Subsections (3) to (5) shall not apply, but any relevant physical data or sample taken in pursuance of section 18 as applied by this paragraph may be retained but shall not be used by any person except for the purposes of a terrorist investigation or for purposes related to the prevention or detection of crime, the investigation of an offence or the conduct of a prosecution.

(4)   In this paragraph

    (a) a reference to crime includes a reference to any conduct which

        (i) constitutes one or more criminal offences (whether under the law of a part of the United Kingdom or of a country or territory outside the United Kingdom); or

        (ii) is, or corresponds to, any conduct which, if it all took place in any one part of the United Kingdom, would constitute one or more criminal offences; and

    (b) the references to an investigation and to a prosecution include references, respectively, to any investigation outside the United Kingdom of any crime or suspected crime and to a prosecution brought in respect of any crime in a country or territory outside the United Kingdom."

90 Searches, examinations and fingerprinting: England and Wales

(1)   After section 54 of the Police and Criminal Evidence Act 1984 (c 60) (searches of detained persons) insert

"54A Searches and examination to ascertain identity

    (1) If an officer of at least the rank of inspector authorises it, a person who is detained in a police station may be searched or examined, or both

        (a) for the purpose of ascertaining whether he has any mark that would tend to identify him as a person involved in the commission of an offence; or

        (b) for the purpose of facilitating the ascertainment of his identity.

(2) An officer may only give an authorisation under subsection (1) for the purpose mentioned in paragraph (a) of that subsection if

    (a) the appropriate consent to a search or examination that would reveal whether the mark in question exists has been withheld; or

    (b) it is not practicable to obtain such consent.

(3) An officer may only give an authorisation under subsection (1) in a case in which subsection (2) does not apply if

    (a) the person in question has refused to identify himself; or

    (b) the officer has reasonable grounds for suspecting that that person is not who he claims to be.

(4) An officer may give an authorisation under subsection (1) orally or in writing but, if he gives it orally, he shall confirm it in writing as soon as is practicable.

(5) Any identifying mark found on a search or examination under this section may be photographed

    (a) with the appropriate consent; or

    (b) if the appropriate consent is withheld or it is not practicable to obtain it, without it.

(6) Where a search or examination may be carried out under this section, or a photograph may be taken under this section, the only persons entitled to carry out the search or examination, or to take the photograph, are

    (a) constables; and

    (b) persons who (without being constables) are designated for the purposes of this section by the chief officer of police for the police area in which the police station in question is situated;

and section 117 (use of force) applies to the exercise by a person falling within paragraph (b) of the powers conferred by the preceding provisions of this section as it applies to the exercise of those powers by a constable.

(7) A person may not under this section carry out a search or examination of a person of the opposite sex or take a photograph of any part of the body of a person of the opposite sex.

(8) An intimate search may not be carried out under this section.

(9) A photograph taken under this section

    (a) may be used by, or disclosed to, any person for any purpose related to the prevention or detection of crime, the investigation of an offence or the conduct of a prosecution; and

    (b) after being so used or disclosed, may be retained but may not be used or disclosed except for a purpose so related.

(10) In subsection

    (a) the reference to crime includes a reference to any conduct which

        (i) constitutes one or more criminal offences (whether under the law of a part of the United Kingdom or of a country or territory outside the United Kingdom); or

        (ii) is, or corresponds to, any conduct which, if it all took place in any one part of the United Kingdom, would constitute one or more criminal offences;

    and

    (b) the references to an investigation and to a prosecution include references, respectively, to any investigation outside the United Kingdom of any crime or suspected crime and to a prosecution brought in respect of any crime in a country or territory outside the United Kingdom.

(11) In this section

    (a) references to ascertaining a person's identity include references to showing that he is not a particular person; and

    (b) references to taking a photograph include references to using any process by means of which a visual image may be produced, and references to photographing a person shall be construed accordingly.

(12) In this section "mark" includes features and injuries; and a mark is an identifying mark for the purposes of this section if its existence in any person's case facilitates the ascertainment of his identity or his identification as a person involved in the commission of an offence."

(2) In section 61(4) of that Act (grounds on which fingerprinting of person detained at a police station may be authorised)

(a) in paragraph (b), after "his involvement" insert "or will facilitate the ascertainment of his identity (within the meaning of section 54A), or both";

(b) after that paragraph insert

"but an authorisation shall not be given for the purpose only of facilitating the ascertainment of that person's identity except where he has refused to identify himself or the officer has reasonable grounds for suspecting that he is not who he claims to be."

91 Searches, examinations and fingerprinting: Northern Ireland *(omitted)*

92 Photographing of suspects etc: England and Wales

After section 64 of the Police and Criminal Evidence Act 1984 (c 60) insert

"64A Photographing of suspects etc

(1) A person who is detained at a police station may be photographed

(a) with the appropriate consent; or

(b) if the appropriate consent is withheld or it is not practicable to obtain it, without it.

(2) A person proposing to take a photograph of any person under this section

(a) may, for the purpose of doing so, require the removal of any item or substance worn on or over the whole or any part of the head or face of the person to be photographed; and

(b) if the requirement is not complied with, may remove the item or substance himself.

(3) Where a photograph may be taken under this section, the only persons entitled to take the photograph are

(a) constables; and

(b) persons who (without being constables) are designated for the purposes of this section by the chief officer of police for the police area in which the police station in question is situated;

and section 117 (use of force) applies to the exercise by a person falling within paragraph (b) of the powers conferred by the preceding provisions of this section as it applies to the exercise of those powers by a constable.

(4) A photograph taken under this section

(a) may be used by, or disclosed to, any person for any purpose related to the prevention or detection of crime, the investigation of an offence or the conduct of a prosecution; and

(b) after being so used or disclosed, may be retained but may not be used or disclosed except for a purpose so related.

(5) In subsection (4)

(a) the reference to crime includes a reference to any conduct which

(i) constitutes one or more criminal offences (whether under the law of a part of the United Kingdom or of a country or territory outside the United Kingdom); or

(ii) is, or corresponds to, any conduct which, if it all took place in any one part of the United Kingdom, would constitute one or more criminal offences; and

(b) the references to an investigation and to a prosecution include references, respectively, to any investigation outside the United Kingdom of any crime or suspected crime and to a prosecution brought in respect of any crime in a country or territory outside the United Kingdom.

(6) References in this section to taking a photograph include references to using any process by means of which a visual image may be produced; and references to photographing a person shall be construed accordingly."

93 Photographing of suspects etc: Northern Ireland *(omitted)*

94 Powers to require removal of disguises: England and Wales

(1) After section 60 of the Criminal Justice and Public Order Act 1994 (c 33) insert

"60AA Powers to require removal of disguises

(1) Where
(a) an authorisation under section 60 is for the time being in force in relation to any locality for any period, or
(b) an authorisation under subsection (3) that the powers conferred by subsection (2) shall be exercisable at any place in a locality is in force for any period,
those powers shall be exercisable at any place in that locality at any time in that period.

(2) This subsection confers power on any constable in uniform
(a) to require any person to remove any item which the constable reasonably believes that person is wearing wholly or mainly for the purpose of concealing his identity;
(b) to seize any item which the constable reasonably believes any person intends to wear wholly or mainly for that purpose.

(3) If a police officer of or above the rank of inspector reasonably believes
(a) that activities may take place in any locality in his police area that are likely (if they take place) to involve the commission of offences, and
(b) that it is expedient, in order to prevent or control the activities, to give an authorisation under this subsection,
he may give an authorisation that the powers conferred by this section shall be exercisable at any place within that locality for a specified period not exceeding twenty-four hours.

(4) If it appears to an officer of or above the rank of superintendent that it is expedient to do so, having regard to offences which
(a) have been committed in connection with the activities in respect of which the authorisation was given, or
(b) are reasonably suspected to have been so committed,
he may direct that the authorisation shall continue in force for a further twenty-four hours.

(5) If an inspector gives an authorisation under subsection, he must, as soon as it is practicable to do so, cause an officer of or above the rank of superintendent to be informed.

(6) Any authorisation under this section
(a) shall be in writing and signed by the officer giving it; and
(b) shall specify
(i) the grounds on which it is given;
(ii) the locality in which the powers conferred by this section are exercisable;
(iii) the period during which those powers are exercisable;
and a direction under subsection (4) shall also be given in writing or, where that is not practicable, recorded in writing as soon as it is practicable to do so.

(7) A person who fails to remove an item worn by him when required to do so by a constable in the exercise of his power under this section shall be liable, on summary conviction, to imprisonment for a term not exceeding one month or to a fine not exceeding level 3 on the standard scale or both.

(8) The preceding provisions of this section, so far as they relate to an authorisation by a member of the British Transport Police Force (including one who for the time being has the same powers and privileges as a member of a police force for a police area),

shall have effect as if references to a locality or to a locality in his police area were references to any locality in or in the vicinity of any policed premises, or to the whole or any part of any such premises.

(9) In this section "British Transport Police Force" and "policed premises" each has the same meaning as in section 60.

(10) The powers conferred by this section are in addition to, and not in derogation of, any power otherwise conferred.

(11) This section does not extend to Scotland."

(2) In section 60A(1) of that Act (retention of things seized under section 60), after "section 60" insert "or 60AA".

(3) [...][18]

95 Powers to require removal of disguises: Northern Ireland *(omitted)*

Powers of stop, search and seizure in Northern Ireland

96–97 *(omitted)*

MoD and transport police

98 Jurisdiction of MoD police *(omitted)*

99 Provision of assistance by MoD police *(omitted)*

100 Jurisdiction of transport police *(omitted)*

101 Further provisions about transport police and MoD police *(omitted)*

PART XI
RETENTION OF COMMUNICATIONS DATA *(omitted)*

PART XII
BRIBERY AND CORRUPTION *(omitted)*

PART XIII
MISCELLANEOUS

111–112 *(expired)*

Dangerous substances

113 Use of noxious substances or things to cause harm and intimidate

(1) A person who takes any action which
  (a) involves the use of a noxious substance or other noxious thing;

---

[18] Repealed by the Police Reform Act 2002, s 107(2), Sch 8.

(b) has or is likely to have an effect falling within subsection (2); and

(c) is designed to influence the government [or an international governmental organisation][19] or to intimidate the public or a section of the public,

is guilty of an offence.

(2) Action has an effect falling within this subsection if it

(a) causes serious violence against a person anywhere in the world;

(b) causes serious damage to real or personal property anywhere in the world;

(c) endangers human life or creates a serious risk to the health or safety of the public or a section of the public; or

(d) induces in members of the public the fear that the action is likely to endanger their lives or create a serious risk to their health or safety;

but any effect on the person taking the action is to be disregarded.

(3) A person who

(a) makes a threat that he or another will take any action which constitutes an offence under subsection (1); and

(b) intends thereby to induce in a person anywhere in the world the fear that the threat is likely to be carried out,

is guilty of an offence.

(4) A person guilty of an offence under this section is liable

(a) on summary conviction, to imprisonment for a term not exceeding six months or a fine not exceeding the statutory maximum (or both); and

(b) on conviction on indictment, to imprisonment for a term not exceeding fourteen years or a fine (or both).

(5) In this section

"the government" means the government of the United Kingdom, of a part of the United Kingdom or of a country other than the United Kingdom; and

"the public" includes the public of a country other than the United Kingdom.

[113A Application of section 113

(1) Section 113 applies to conduct done

(a) in the United Kingdom; or

(b) outside the United Kingdom which satisfies the following two conditions.

(2) The first condition is that the conduct is done for the purpose of advancing a political, religious, [racial][20] or ideological cause.

(3) The second condition is that the conduct is

(a) by a United Kingdom national or a United Kingdom resident;

(b) by any person done to, or in relation to, a United Kingdom national, a United Kingdom resident or a protected person; or

(c) by any person done in circumstances which fall within section 63D(1)(b) and (c) or (3)(b) and (c) of the Terrorism Act 2000.

(4) The following expressions have the same meaning as they have for the purposes of sections 63C and 63D of that Act

(a) "United Kingdom national";

(b) "United Kingdom resident";

(c) "protected person".

(5) For the purposes of this section it is immaterial whether a person knows that another is a United Kingdom national, a United Kingdom resident or a protected person.][21]

---

[19] Inserted by the Terrorism Act 2006, s 34(b).
[20] Inserted by the Counter-Terrorism Act 2008, s 75(1), (2)(b).
[21] Inserted by the Crime (International Co-operation) Act 2003, s 53.

[113B Consent to prosecution for offence under section 113

(1) Proceedings for an offence committed under section 113 outside the United Kingdom are not to be started
   (a) in England and Wales, except by or with the consent of the Attorney General;
   (b) in Northern Ireland, except by or with the consent of the Advocate General for Northern Ireland.
(2) Proceedings for an offence committed under section 113 outside the United Kingdom may be taken, and the offence may for incidental purposes be treated as having been committed, in any part of the United Kingdom.
(3) In relation to any time before the coming into force of section 27(1) of the Justice (Northern Ireland) Act 2002, the reference in subsection (1)(b) to the Advocate General for Northern Ireland is to be read as a reference to the Attorney General for Northern Ireland.][22]

114 Hoaxes involving noxious substances or things

(1) A person is guilty of an offence if he
   (a) places any substance or other thing in any place; or
   (b) sends any substance or other thing from one place to another (by post, rail or any other means whatever);
   with the intention of inducing in a person anywhere in the world a belief that it is likely to be (or contain) a noxious substance or other noxious thing and thereby endanger human life or create a serious risk to human health.
(2) A person is guilty of an offence if he communicates any information which he knows or believes to be false with the intention of inducing in a person anywhere in the world a belief that a noxious substance or other noxious thing is likely to be present (whether at the time the information is communicated or later) in any place and thereby endanger human life or create a serious risk to human health.
(3) A person guilty of an offence under this section is liable
   (a) on summary conviction, to imprisonment for a term not exceeding six months or a fine not exceeding the statutory maximum (or both); and
   (b) on conviction on indictment, to imprisonment for a term not exceeding seven years or a fine (or both).

115 Sections 113 and 114: supplementary

(1) For the purposes of sections 113 and 114 "substance" includes any biological agent and any other natural or artificial substance (whatever its form, origin or method of production).
(2) For a person to be guilty of an offence under section 113(3) or 114 it is not necessary for him to have any particular person in mind as the person in whom he intends to induce the belief in question.

Intelligence Services Act 1994

116 Amendments of Intelligence Services Act 1994 *(omitted)*

Terrorism Act 2000

117 Information about acts of terrorism

(1) The Terrorism Act 2000 (c 11) is amended as follows.
(2) After section 38 insert

---

[22] Inserted by the Crime (International Co-operation) Act 2003, s 53.

"38B Information about acts of terrorism (omitted)

118 Port and airport controls for domestic travel *(omitted)*

119 Passenger information *(omitted)*

120 Weapons training for terrorists *(omitted)*

121 Crown Court judges: Northern Ireland *(omitted)*

PART XIV

SUPPLEMENTAL

122–123 […]²³

124 Consequential and supplementary provision

(1) A Minister of the Crown may by order make such incidental, consequential, transitional or supplemental provision as he thinks necessary or expedient for the general purposes, or any particular purpose, of this Act or in consequence of any provision made by or under this Act or for giving full effect to this Act or any such provision.

(2) An order under this section may, in particular, make provision
   (a) for applying (with or without modifications) or amending, repealing or revoking any provision of or made under an Act passed before this Act or in the same Session,
   (b) for making savings, or additional savings, from the effect of any repeal or revocation made by or under this Act.

(3) Amendments made under this section are in addition, and without prejudice, to those made by or under any other provision of this Act.

(4) No other provision of this Act restricts the powers conferred by this section.

(5) An order under this section may make different provision for different purposes.

(6) An order under this section shall be made by statutory instrument which shall be subject to annulment in pursuance of a resolution of either House of Parliament.

(7) In this Part, "Minister of the Crown" has the same meaning as in the Ministers of the Crown Act 1975 (c 26).

125 Repeals and revocation *(omitted)*

126 Expenses *(omitted)*

127 Commencement *(omitted)*

128 Extent *(omitted)*

129 Short title *(omitted)*

SCHEDULE 1   Section 1

FORFEITURE OF TERRORIST CASH

PART 1

INTRODUCTORY

1 Terrorist cash

(1) This Schedule applies to cash ("terrorist cash") which
   (a) is within subsection (1)(a) or (b) of section 1, or
   (b) is property earmarked as terrorist property.

---

²³ Repealed by the Statute Law (Repeals) Act 2008, s 1(1), Sch 1 Pt 3.

(2) "Cash" means
  (a) coins and notes in any currency,
  (b) postal orders,
  (c) cheques of any kind, including travellers' cheques,
  (d) bankers' drafts,
  (e) bearer bonds and bearer shares,
found at any place in the United Kingdom.

(3) Cash also includes any kind of monetary instrument which is found at any place in the United Kingdom, if the instrument is specified by the Secretary of State by order.

(4) The power to make an order under sub-paragraph (3) is exercisable by statutory instrument, which is subject to annulment in pursuance of a resolution of either House of Parliament.

PART 2
SEIZURE AND DETENTION

2 Seizure of cash

(1) An authorised officer may seize any cash if he has reasonable grounds for suspecting that it is terrorist cash.

(2) An authorised officer may also seize cash part of which he has reasonable grounds for suspecting to be terrorist cash if it is not reasonably practicable to seize only that part.

3 Detention of seized cash

(1) While the authorised officer continues to have reasonable grounds for his suspicion, cash seized under this Schedule may be detained initially for a period of 48 hours.

[(1A) In determining the period of 48 hours specified in sub-paragraph (1) there shall be disregarded
  (a) any Saturday or Sunday;
  (b) Christmas Day;
  (c) Good Friday;
  (d) any day that is a bank holiday under the Banking and Financial Dealings Act 1971 in the part of the United Kingdom in which the cash is seized;
  (e) any day prescribed under section 8(2) of the Criminal Procedure (Scotland) Act 1995 as a court holiday in the sheriff court district in which the cash is seized.][24]

(2) The period for which the cash or any part of it may be detained may be extended by an order made by a magistrates' court or (in Scotland) the sheriff; but the order may not authorise the detention of any of the cash
  (a) beyond the end of the period of three months beginning with the date of the order, and
  (b) in the case of any further order under this paragraph, beyond the end of the period of two years beginning with the date of the first order.

(3) A justice of the peace may also exercise the power of a magistrates' court to make the first order under sub-paragraph (2) extending the period.

[(3A) An application to a justice of the peace or the sheriff for an order under sub-paragraph (2) making the first extension of the period
  (a) may be made and heard without notice of the application or hearing having been given to any of the persons affected by the application or to the legal representative of such a person, and
  (b) may be heard and determined in private in the absence of persons so affected and of their legal representatives.][25]

(4) An order under sub-paragraph (2) must provide for notice to be given to persons affected by it.

---

[24] Inserted by the Counter-Terrorism Act 2008, s 83(1), (2).
[25] Inserted by the Terrorism Act 2006, s 35(1).

(5) An application for an order under sub-paragraph (2)

    (a) in relation to England and Wales and Northern Ireland, may be made by the Commissioners of Customs and Excise or an authorised officer,

    (b) in relation to Scotland, may be made by a procurator fiscal,

and the court, sheriff or justice may make the order if satisfied, in relation to any cash to be further detained, that one of the following conditions is met.

(6) The first condition is that there are reasonable grounds for suspecting that the cash is intended to be used for the purposes of terrorism and that either

    (a) its continued detention is justified while its intended use is further investigated or consideration is given to bringing (in the United Kingdom or elsewhere) proceedings against any person for an offence with which the cash is connected, or

    (b) proceedings against any person for an offence with which the cash is connected have been started and have not been concluded.

(7) The second condition is that there are reasonable grounds for suspecting that the cash consists of resources of an organisation which is a proscribed organisation and that either

    (a) its continued detention is justified while investigation is made into whether or not it consists of such resources or consideration is given to bringing (in the United Kingdom or elsewhere) proceedings against any person for an offence with which the cash is connected, or

    (b) proceedings against any person for an offence with which the cash is connected have been started and have not been concluded.

(8) The third condition is that there are reasonable grounds for suspecting that the cash is property earmarked as terrorist property and that either

    (a) its continued detention is justified while its derivation is further investigated or consideration is given to bringing (in the United Kingdom or elsewhere) proceedings against any person for an offence with which the cash is connected, or

    (b) proceedings against any person for an offence with which the cash is connected have been started and have not been concluded.

4 Payment of detained cash into an account

(1) If cash is detained under this Schedule for more than 48 hours [(determined in accordance with paragraph 3(1A))],[26] it is to be held in an interest-bearing account and the interest accruing on it is to be added to it on its forfeiture or release.

(2) In the case of cash seized under paragraph 2(2), the authorised officer must, on paying it into the account, release so much of the cash then held in the account as is not attributable to terrorist cash.

(3) Sub-paragraph (1) does not apply if the cash is required as evidence of an offence or evidence in proceedings under this Schedule.

5 Release of detained cash

(1) This paragraph applies while any cash is detained under this Schedule.

(2) A magistrates' court or (in Scotland) the sheriff may direct the release of the whole or any part of the cash if satisfied, on an application by the person from whom it was seized, that the conditions in paragraph 3 for the detention of cash are no longer met in relation to the cash to be released.

(3) A authorised officer or (in Scotland) a procurator fiscal may, after notifying the magistrates' court, sheriff or justice under whose order cash is being detained, release the whole or any part of it if satisfied that the detention of the cash to be released is no longer justified.

(4) But cash is not to be released

---

[26] Inserted by the Counter-Terrorism Act 2008, s 83(1), (3).

(a) if an application for its forfeiture under paragraph 6, or for its release under paragraph 9, is made, until any proceedings in pursuance of the application (including any proceedings on appeal) are concluded,

(b) if (in the United Kingdom or elsewhere) proceedings are started against any person for an offence with which the cash is connected, until the proceedings are concluded.

PART 3
FORFEITURE

6 Forfeiture

(1) While cash is detained under this Schedule, an application for the forfeiture of the whole or any part of it may be made
  (a) to a magistrates' court by the Commissioners of Customs and Excise or an authorised officer,
  (b) (in Scotland) to the sheriff by the Scottish Ministers.

(2) The court or sheriff may order the forfeiture of the cash or any part of it if satisfied that the cash or part is terrorist cash.

(3) In the case of property earmarked as terrorist property which belongs to joint tenants one of whom is an excepted joint owner, the order may not apply to so much of it as the court or sheriff thinks is attributable to the excepted joint owner's share.

(4) An excepted joint owner is a joint tenant who obtained the property in circumstances in which it would not (as against him) be earmarked; and references to his share of the earmarked property are to so much of the property as would have been his if the joint tenancy had been severed.

[7 Appeal against decision in forfeiture proceedings

(1) A party to proceedings for an order under paragraph 6 ("a forfeiture order") who is aggrieved by a forfeiture order made in the proceedings or by the decision of the court or sheriff not to make a forfeiture order may appeal
  (a) in England and Wales, to the Crown Court;
  (b) in Scotland, to the sheriff principal;
  (c) in Northern Ireland, to a county court.

(2) The appeal must be brought before the end of the period of 30 days beginning with the date on which the order is made or, as the case may be, the decision is given.
This is subject to paragraph 7A (extended time for appealing in certain cases of deproscription).

(3) The court or sheriff principal hearing the appeal may make any order that appears to the court or sheriff principal to be appropriate.

(4) If an appeal against a forfeiture order is upheld, the court or sheriff principal may order the release of the cash.

7A Extended time for appealing in certain cases where deproscription order made

(1) This paragraph applies where
  (a) a successful application for a forfeiture order relies (wholly or partly) on the fact that an organisation is proscribed,
  (b) an application under section 4 of the Terrorism Act 2000 for a deproscription order in respect of the organisation is refused by the Secretary of State,
  (c) the forfeited cash is seized under this Schedule on or after the date of the refusal of that application,
  (d) an appeal against that refusal is allowed under section 5 of that Act,
  (e) a deproscription order is made accordingly, and
  (f) if the order is made in reliance on section 123(5) of that Act, a resolution is passed by each House of Parliament under section 123(5)(b).

(2) Where this paragraph applies, an appeal under paragraph 7 above against the forfeiture order may be brought at any time before the end of the period of 30 days beginning with the date on which the deproscription order comes into force.

(3) In this paragraph a "deproscription order" means an order under section 3(3)(b) or (8) of the Terrorism Act 2000.][27]

8 Application of forfeited cash

(1) Cash forfeited under this Schedule, and any accrued interest on it
  (a) if forfeited by a magistrates' court in England and Wales or Northern Ireland, is to be paid into the Consolidated Fund,
  (b) if forfeited by the sheriff, is to be paid into the Scottish Consolidated Fund.

(2) But it is not to be paid in
  (a) before the end of the period within which an appeal under paragraph 7 may be made, or
  (b) if a person appeals under that paragraph, before the appeal is determined or otherwise disposed of.

PART 4
MISCELLANEOUS

9 Victims

(1) A person who claims that any cash detained under this Schedule, or any part of it, belongs to him may apply to a magistrates' court or (in Scotland) the sheriff for the cash or part to be released to him.

(2) The application may be made in the course of proceedings under paragraph 3 or 6 or at any other time.

(3) If it appears to the court or sheriff concerned that
  (a) the applicant was deprived of the cash claimed, or of property which it represents, by criminal conduct,
  (b) the property he was deprived of was not, immediately before he was deprived of it, property obtained by or in return for criminal conduct and nor did it then represent such property, and
  (c) the cash claimed belongs to him,
the court or sheriff may order the cash to be released to the applicant.

10 Compensation

(1) If no forfeiture order is made in respect of any cash detained under this Schedule, the person to whom the cash belongs or from whom it was seized may make an application to the magistrates' court or (in Scotland) the sheriff for compensation.

(2) If, for any period after the initial detention of the cash for 48 hours [(determined in accordance with paragraph 3(1A))],[28] the cash was not held in an interest-bearing account while detained, the court or sheriff may order an amount of compensation to be paid to the applicant.

(3) The amount of compensation to be paid under sub-paragraph (2) is the amount the court or sheriff thinks would have been earned in interest in the period in question if the cash had been held in an interest-bearing account.

(4) If the court or sheriff is satisfied that, taking account of any interest to be paid under this Schedule or any amount to be paid under sub-paragraph (2), the applicant has suffered loss

---

[27] Replaces para 7 as originally enacted, by the Counter-Terrorism Act 2008, s 84(1).
[28] Inserted by the Counter-Terrorism Act 2008, s 83(1), (3).

as a result of the detention of the cash and that the circumstances are exceptional, the court or sheriff may order compensation (or additional compensation) to be paid to him .

(5) The amount of compensation to be paid under sub-paragraph (4) is the amount the court or sheriff thinks reasonable, having regard to the loss suffered and any other relevant circumstances.

(6) If the cash was seized by a customs officer, the compensation is to be paid by the Commissioners of Customs and Excise.

(7) If the cash was seized by a constable, the compensation is to be paid as follows

(a) in the case of a constable of a police force in England and Wales, it is to be paid out of the police fund from which the expenses of the police force are met,

(b) in the case of a constable of a police force in Scotland, it is to be paid by the police authority or joint police board for the police area for which that force is maintained,

(c) in the case of a police officer within the meaning of the Police (Northern Ireland) Act 2000 (c 32), it is to be paid out of money provided by the Chief Constable.

(8) If the cash was seized by an immigration officer, the compensation is to be paid by the Secretary of State.

(9) If a forfeiture order is made in respect only of a part of any cash detained under this Schedule, this paragraph has effect in relation to the other part.

(10) This paragraph does not apply if the court or sheriff makes an order under paragraph 9.

PART 5
PROPERTY EARMARKED AS TERRORIST PROPERTY

11 Property obtained through terrorism

(1) A person obtains property through terrorism if he obtains property by or in return for acts of terrorism, or acts carried out for the purposes of terrorism.

(2) In deciding whether any property was obtained through terrorism

(a) it is immaterial whether or not any money, goods or services were provided in order to put the person in question in a position to carry out the acts,

(b) it is not necessary to show that the act was of a particular kind if it is shown that the property was obtained through acts of one of a number of kinds, each of which would have been an act of terrorism, or an act carried out for the purposes of terrorism.

12 Property earmarked as terrorist property

(1) Property obtained through terrorism is earmarked as terrorist property.

(2) But if property obtained through terrorism has been disposed of (since it was so obtained), it is earmarked as terrorist property only if it is held by a person into whose hands it may be followed.

(3) Earmarked property obtained through terrorism may be followed into the hands of a person obtaining it on a disposal by

(a) the person who obtained the property through terrorism, or

(b) a person into whose hands it may (by virtue of this sub-paragraph) be followed.

13 Tracing property

(1) Where property obtained through terrorism ("the original property") is or has been earmarked as terrorist property, property which represents the original property is also earmarked.

(2) If a person enters into a transaction by which

(a) he disposes of earmarked property, whether the original property or property which (by virtue of this Part) represents the original property, and

(b) he obtains other property in place of it,

the other property represents the original property.

(3) If a person disposes of earmarked property which represents the original property, the property may be followed into the hands of the person who obtains it (and it continues to represent the original property).

14 Mixing property

(1) Sub-paragraph (2) applies if a person's property which is earmarked as terrorist property is mixed with other property (whether his property or another's).

(2) The portion of the mixed property which is attributable to the property earmarked as terrorist property represents the property obtained through terrorism.

(3) Property earmarked as terrorist property is mixed with other property if (for example) it is used
   (a) to increase funds held in a bank account,
   (b) in part payment for the acquisition of an asset,
   (c) for the restoration or improvement of land,
   (d) by a person holding a leasehold interest in the property to acquire the freehold.

15 Accruing profits

(1) This paragraph applies where a person who has property earmarked as terrorist property obtains further property consisting of profits accruing in respect of the earmarked property.

(2) The further property is to be treated as representing the property obtained through terrorism.

16 General exceptions

(1) If
   (a) a person disposes of property earmarked as terrorist property, and
   (b) the person who obtains it on the disposal does so in good faith, for value and without notice that it was earmarked,
   the property may not be followed into that person's hands and, accordingly, it ceases to be earmarked.

(2) If
   (a) in pursuance of a judgment in civil proceedings (whether in the United Kingdom or elsewhere), the defendant makes a payment to the claimant or the claimant otherwise obtains property from the defendant,
   (b) the claimant's claim is based on the defendant's criminal conduct, and
   (c) apart from this sub-paragraph, the sum received, or the property obtained, by the claimant would be earmarked as terrorist property,
   the property ceases to be earmarked.
   In relation to Scotland, "claimant" and "defendant" are to be read as "pursuer" and "defender"; and, in relation to Northern Ireland, "claimant" is to be read as "plaintiff".

(3) If
   (a) a payment is made to a person in pursuance of a compensation order under Article 14 of the Criminal Justice (Northern Ireland) Order 1994 (SI 1994/2795 (NI 15)), section 249 of the Criminal Procedure (Scotland) Act 1995 (c 46) or section 130 of the Powers of Criminal Courts (Sentencing) Act 2000 (c 6)[, *or in pursuance of a service compensation order under the Armed Forces Act 2006*],[29] and
   (b) apart from this sub-paragraph, the sum received would be earmarked as terrorist property,
   the property ceases to be earmarked.

(4) If
   (a) a payment is made to a person in pursuance of a restitution order under section 27 of the Theft Act (Northern Ireland) 1969 (c 16 (NI)) or section 148(2) of the Powers of Criminal

---

[29] Inserted by the Armed Forces Act 2006, s 378(1), Sch 16, para 196, parts of which not yet in force.

Courts (Sentencing) Act 2000 or a person otherwise obtains any property in pursuance of such an order, and

(b) apart from this sub-paragraph, the sum received, or the property obtained, would be earmarked as terrorist property,

the property ceases to be earmarked.

(5) If

(a) in pursuance of an order made by the court under section 382(3) or 383(5) of the Financial Services and Markets Act 2000 (c 8) (restitution orders), an amount is paid to or distributed among any persons in accordance with the court's directions, and

(b) apart from this sub-paragraph, the sum received by them would be earmarked as terrorist property,

the property ceases to be earmarked.

(6) If

(a) in pursuance of a requirement of the Financial Services Authority under section 384(5) of the Financial Services and Markets Act 2000 (c 8) (power of authority to require restitution), an amount is paid to or distributed among any persons, and

(b) apart from this sub-paragraph, the sum received by them would be earmarked as terrorist property,

the property ceases to be earmarked.

(7) Where

(a) a person enters into a transaction to which paragraph 13(2) applies, and

(b) the disposal is one to which sub-paragraph (1) applies,

this paragraph does not affect the question whether (by virtue of paragraph 13(2)) any property obtained on the transaction in place of the property disposed of is earmarked.

PART 6
INTERPRETATION

17 Property

(1) Property is all property wherever situated and includes

(a) money,

(b) all forms of property, real or personal, heritable or moveable,

(c) things in action and other intangible or incorporeal property.

(2) Any reference to a person's property (whether expressed as a reference to the property he holds or otherwise) is to be read as follows.

(3) In relation to land, it is a reference to any interest which he holds in the land.

(4) In relation to property other than land, it is a reference

(a) to the property (if it belongs to him), or

(b) to any other interest which he holds in the property.

18 Obtaining and disposing of property

(1) References to a person disposing of his property include a reference

(a) to his disposing of a part of it, or

(b) to his granting an interest in it,

(or to both); and references to the property disposed of are to any property obtained on the disposal.

(2) If a person grants an interest in property of his which is earmarked as terrorist property, the question whether the interest is also earmarked is to be determined in the same manner as it is on any other disposal of earmarked property.

(3) A person who makes a payment to another is to be treated as making a disposal of his property to the other, whatever form the payment takes.

(4) Where a person's property passes to another under a will or intestacy or by operation of law, it is to be treated as disposed of by him to the other.

(5) A person is only to be treated as having obtained his property for value in a case where he gave unexecuted consideration if the consideration has become executed consideration.

19 General interpretation

(1) In this Schedule
"authorised officer" means a constable, a customs officer or an immigration officer,
"cash" has the meaning given by paragraph 1,
"constable", in relation to Northern Ireland, means a police officer within the meaning of the Police (Northern Ireland) Act 2000 (c 32),
"criminal conduct" means conduct which constitutes an offence in any part of the United Kingdom, or would constitute an offence in any part of the United Kingdom if it occurred there,
"customs officer" means an officer commissioned by the Commissioners of Customs and Excise under section 6(3) of the Customs and Excise Management Act 1979 (c 2),
"forfeiture order" has the meaning given by paragraph 7,
"immigration officer" means a person appointed as an immigration officer under paragraph 1 of Schedule 2 to the Immigration Act 1971 (c 77),
"interest", in relation to land
   (a) in the case of land in England and Wales or Northern Ireland, means any legal estate and any equitable interest or power,
   (b) in the case of land in Scotland, means any estate, interest, servitude or other heritable right in or over land, including a heritable security,
"interest", in relation to property other than land, includes any right (including a right to possession of the property),
"part", in relation to property, includes a portion,
"property obtained through terrorism" has the meaning given by paragraph 11,
"property earmarked as terrorist property" is to be read in accordance with Part 5,
"proscribed organisation" has the same meaning as in the Terrorism Act 2000 (c 11),
"terrorism" has the same meaning as in the Terrorism Act 2000,
"terrorist cash" has the meaning given by paragraph 1,
"value" means market value.

(2) Paragraphs 17 and 18 and the following provisions apply for the purposes of this Schedule.

(3) For the purpose of deciding whether or not property was earmarked as terrorist property at any time (including times before commencement), it is to be assumed that this Schedule was in force at that and any other relevant time.

(4) References to anything done or intended to be done for the purposes of terrorism include anything done or intended to be done for the benefit of a proscribed organisation.

(5) An organisation's resources include any cash which is applied or made available, or is to be applied or made available, for use by the organisation.

(6) Proceedings against any person for an offence are concluded when
   (a) the person is convicted or acquitted,
   (b) the prosecution is discontinued or, in Scotland, the trial diet is deserted simpliciter, or
   (c) the jury is discharged without a finding [otherwise than in circumstances where the proceedings are continued without a jury.][30]

---

[30] Inserted by the Criminal Justice Act 2003, s 331, Sch 36, Pt 4, para 77.

SCHEDULE 2   Section 3
TERRORIST PROPERTY: AMENDMENTS

PART 1
ACCOUNT MONITORING ORDERS

1

(1) The Terrorism Act 2000 is amended as follows.

(2) The following section is inserted after section 38

"38A Account monitoring orders

Schedule 6A (account monitoring orders) shall have effect."

(3) The following Schedule is inserted after Schedule 6

"SCHEDULE 6A
ACCOUNT MONITORING ORDERS

1 Introduction

(1) This paragraph applies for the purposes of this Schedule.

(2) A judge is

    (a) a Circuit judge, in England and Wales;

    (b) the sheriff, in Scotland;

    (c) a Crown Court judge, in Northern Ireland.

(3) The court is

    (a) the Crown Court, in England and Wales or Northern Ireland;

    (b) the sheriff court, in Scotland.

(4) An appropriate officer is

    (a) a police officer, in England and Wales or Northern Ireland;

    (b) the procurator fiscal, in Scotland.

(5) "Financial institution" has the same meaning as in Schedule 6.

2 Account monitoring orders

(1) A judge may, on an application made to him by an appropriate officer, make an account monitoring order if he is satisfied that

    (a) the order is sought for the purposes of a terrorist investigation,

    (b) the tracing of terrorist property is desirable for the purposes of the investigation, and

    (c) the order will enhance the effectiveness of the investigation.

(2) The application for an account monitoring order must state that the order is sought against the financial institution specified in the application in relation to information which

    (a) relates to an account or accounts held at the institution by the person specified in the application (whether solely or jointly with another), and

    (b) is of the description so specified.

(3) The application for an account monitoring order may specify information relating to

    (a) all accounts held by the person specified in the application for the order at the financial institution so specified,

    (b) a particular description, or particular descriptions, of accounts so held, or

    (c) a particular account, or particular accounts, so held.

442

(4) An account monitoring order is an order that the financial institution specified in the application for the order must

    (a) for the period specified in the order,

    (b) in the manner so specified,

    (c) at or by the time or times so specified, and

    (d) at the place or places so specified,

provide information of the description specified in the application to an appropriate officer.

(5) The period stated in an account monitoring order must not exceed the period of 90 days beginning with the day on which the order is made.

3 Applications

(1) An application for an account monitoring order may be made ex parte to a judge in chambers.

(2) The description of information specified in an application for an account monitoring order may be varied by the person who made the application.

(3) If the application was made by a police officer, the description of information specified in it may be varied by a different police officer.

4 Discharge or variation

(1) An application to discharge or vary an account monitoring order may be made to the court by

    (a) the person who applied for the order;

    (b) any person affected by the order.

(2) If the application for the account monitoring order was made by a police officer, an application to discharge or vary the order may be made by a different police officer.

(3) The court

    (a) may discharge the order;

    (b) may vary the order.

5 Rules of court *(omitted)*

6 Effect of orders

(1) In England and Wales and Northern Ireland, an account monitoring order has effect as if it were an order of the court.

(2) An account monitoring order has effect in spite of any restriction on the disclosure of information (however imposed).

7 Statements

(1) A statement made by a financial institution in response to an account monitoring order may not be used in evidence against it in criminal proceedings.

(2) But sub-paragraph (1) does not apply

    (a) in the case of proceedings for contempt of court;

    (b) in the case of proceedings under section 23 where the financial institution has been convicted of an offence under any of sections 15 to 18;

    (c) on a prosecution for an offence where, in giving evidence, the financial institution makes a statement inconsistent with the statement mentioned in sub-paragraph (1).

(3) A statement may not be used by virtue of sub-paragraph (2)(c) against a financial institution unless

    (a) evidence relating to it is adduced, or

    (b) a question relating to it is asked,

by or on behalf of the financial institution in the proceedings arising out of the prosecution."

PART 2
RESTRAINT ORDERS

2–4 *(omitted)*

PART 3
DISCLOSURE OF INFORMATION

5 *(omitted)*

SCHEDULE 3   Section 6
FREEZING ORDERS

1 Interpretation

References in this Schedule to a person specified in a freezing order as a person to whom or for whose benefit funds are not to be made available are to be read in accordance with section 5(4).

2 Funds

A freezing order may include provision that funds include gold, cash, deposits, securities (such as stocks, shares and debentures) and such other matters as the order may specify.

3 Making funds available

(1) A freezing order must include provision as to the meaning (in relation to funds) of making available to or for the benefit of a person.
(2) In particular, an order may provide that the expression includes
    (a) allowing a person to withdraw from an account;
    (b) honouring a cheque payable to a person;
    (c) crediting a person's account with interest;
    (d) releasing documents of title (such as share certificates) held on a person's behalf;
    (e) making available the proceeds of realisation of a person's property;
    (f) making a payment to or for a person's benefit (for instance, under a contract or as a gift or under any enactment such as the enactments relating to social security);
    (g) such other acts as the order may specify.

4 Licences

(1) A freezing order must include
    (a) provision for the granting of licences authorising funds to be made available;
    (b) provision that a prohibition under the order is not to apply if funds are made available in accordance with a licence.
(2) In particular, an order may provide
    (a) that a licence may be granted generally or to a specified person or persons or description of persons;
    (b) that a licence may authorise funds to be made available to or for the benefit of persons generally or a specified person or persons or description of persons;
    (c) that a licence may authorise funds to be made available generally or for specified purposes;
    (d) that a licence may be granted in relation to funds generally or to funds of a specified description;

(e) for a licence to be granted in pursuance of an application or without an application being made;

(f) for the form and manner in which applications for licences are to be made;

(g) for licences to be granted by the Treasury or a person authorised by the Treasury;

(h) for the form in which licences are to be granted;

(i) for licences to be granted subject to conditions;

(j) for licences to be of a defined or indefinite duration;

(k) for the charging of a fee to cover the administrative costs of granting a licence;

(l) for the variation and revocation of licences.

5 Information and documents

(1) A freezing order may include provision that a person

    (a) must provide information if required to do so and it is reasonably needed for the purpose of ascertaining whether an offence under the order has been committed;

    (b) must produce a document if required to do so and it is reasonably needed for that purpose.

(2) In particular, an order may include

    (a) provision that a requirement to provide information or to produce a document may be made by the Treasury or a person authorised by the Treasury;

    (b) provision that information must be provided, and a document must be produced, within a reasonable period specified in the order and at a place specified by the person requiring it;

    (c) provision that the provision of information is not to be taken to breach any restriction on the disclosure of information (however imposed);

    (d) provision restricting the use to which information or a document may be put and the circumstances in which it may be disclosed;

    (e) provision that a requirement to provide information or produce a document does not apply to privileged information or a privileged document;

    (f) provision that information is privileged if the person would be entitled to refuse to provide it on grounds of legal professional privilege in proceedings in the High Court or (in Scotland) on grounds of confidentiality of communications in proceedings in the Court of Session;

    (g) provision that a document is privileged if the person would be entitled to refuse to produce it on grounds of legal professional privilege in proceedings in the High Court or (in Scotland) on grounds of confidentiality of communications in proceedings in the Court of Session;

    (h) provision that information or a document held with the intention of furthering a criminal purpose is not privileged.

6 Disclosure of information

(1) A freezing order may include provision requiring a person to disclose information as mentioned below if the following three conditions are satisfied.

(2) The first condition is that the person required to disclose is specified or falls within a description specified in the order.

(3) The second condition is that the person required to disclose knows or suspects, or has grounds for knowing or suspecting, that a person specified in the freezing order as a person to whom or for whose benefit funds are not to be made available

    (a) is a customer of his or has been a customer of his at any time since the freezing order came into force, or

    (b) is a person with whom he has dealings in the course of his business or has had such dealings at any time since the freezing order came into force.

(4) The third condition is that the information

    (a) on which the knowledge or suspicion of the person required to disclose is based, or

    (b) which gives grounds for his knowledge or suspicion,

came to him in the course of a business in the regulated sector.

(5) The freezing order may require the person required to disclose to make a disclosure to the Treasury of that information as soon as is practicable after it comes to him.

(6) The freezing order may include

    (a) provision that Schedule 3A to the Terrorism Act 2000 (c 11) is to have effect for the purpose of determining what is a business in the regulated sector;

    (b) provision that the disclosure of information is not to be taken to breach any restriction on the disclosure of information (however imposed);

    (c) provision restricting the use to which information may be put and the circumstances in which it may be disclosed by the Treasury;

    (d) provision that the requirement to disclose information does not apply to privileged information;

    (e) provision that information is privileged if the person would be entitled to refuse to disclose it on grounds of legal professional privilege in proceedings in the High Court or (in Scotland) on grounds of confidentiality of communications in proceedings in the Court of Session;

    (f) provision that information held with the intention of furthering a criminal purpose is not privileged.

7 Offences

(1) A freezing order may include any of the provisions set out in this paragraph.

(2) A person commits an offence if he fails to comply with a prohibition imposed by the order.

(3) A person commits an offence if he engages in an activity knowing or intending that it will enable or facilitate the commission by another person of an offence under a provision included under sub-paragraph (2).

(4) A person commits an offence if

    (a) he fails without reasonable excuse to provide information, or to produce a document, in response to a requirement made under the order;

    (b) he provides information, or produces a document, which he knows is false in a material particular in response to such a requirement or with a view to obtaining a licence under the order;

    (c) he recklessly provides information, or produces a document, which is false in a material particular in response to such a requirement or with a view to obtaining a licence under the order;

    (d) he fails without reasonable excuse to disclose information as required by a provision included under paragraph 6.

(5) A person does not commit an offence under a provision included under sub-paragraph (2) or (3) if he proves that he did not know and had no reason to suppose that the person to whom or for whose benefit funds were made available, or were to be made available, was the person (or one of the persons) specified in the freezing order as a person to whom or for whose benefit funds are not to be made available.

(6) A person guilty of an offence under a provision included under sub-paragraph (2) or (3) is liable

    (a) on summary conviction, to imprisonment for a term not exceeding 6 months or to a fine not exceeding the statutory maximum or to both;

    (b) on conviction on indictment, to imprisonment for a term not exceeding 2 years or to a fine or to both.

(7) A person guilty of an offence under a provision included under sub-paragraph (4) is liable on summary conviction to imprisonment for a term not exceeding 6 months or to a fine not exceeding level 5 on the standard scale or to both.

8 Offences: procedure

(1) A freezing order may include any of the provisions set out in this paragraph.

(2) Proceedings for an offence under the order are not to be instituted in England and Wales except by or with the consent of the Treasury or the Director of Public Prosecutions.

(3) Proceedings for an offence under the order are not to be instituted in Northern Ireland except by or with the consent of the Treasury or the Director of Public Prosecutions for Northern Ireland.

(4) Despite anything in section 127(1) of the Magistrates' Courts Act 1980 (c 43) (information to be laid within 6 months of offence) an information relating to an offence under the order which is triable by a magistrates' court in England and Wales may be so tried if it is laid at any time in the period of one year starting with the date of the commission of the offence.

(5) In Scotland summary proceedings for an offence under the order may be commenced at any time in the period of one year starting with the date of the commission of the offence.

(6) In its application to an offence under the order Article 19(1)(a) of the Magistrates' Courts (Northern Ireland) Order 1981 (SI 1981/1675 (NI 26)) (time limit within which complaint charging offence must be made) is to have effect as if the reference to six months were a reference to twelve months.

9 Offences by bodies corporate etc

(1) A freezing order may include any of the provisions set out in this paragraph.

(2) If an offence under the order
  (a) is committed by a body corporate, and
  (b) is proved to have been committed with the consent or connivance of an officer, or to be attributable to any neglect on his part,
he as well as the body corporate is guilty of the offence and liable to be proceeded against and punished accordingly.

(3) These are officers of a body corporate
  (a) a director, manager, secretary or other similar officer of the body;
  (b) any person purporting to act in any such capacity.

(4) If the affairs of a body corporate are managed by its members sub-paragraph (2) applies in relation to the acts and defaults of a member in connection with his functions of management as if he were an officer of the body.

(5) If an offence under the order
  (a) is committed by a Scottish partnership, and
  (b) is proved to have been committed with the consent or connivance of a partner, or to be attributable to any neglect on his part,
he as well as the partnership is guilty of the offence and liable to be proceeded against and punished accordingly.

10 Compensation

(1) A freezing order may include provision for the award of compensation to or on behalf of a person on the grounds that he has suffered loss as a result of
  (a) the order;
  (b) the fact that a licence has not been granted under the order;
  (c) the fact that a licence under the order has been granted on particular terms rather than others;
  (d) the fact that a licence under the order has been varied or revoked.

(2) In particular, the order may include
  (a) provision about the person who may make a claim for an award;
  (b) provision about the person to whom a claim for an award is to be made (which may be provision that it is to be made to the High Court or, in Scotland, the Court of Session);
  (c) provision about the procedure for making and deciding a claim;

(d) provision that no compensation is to be awarded unless the claimant has behaved reasonably (which may include provision requiring him to mitigate his loss, for instance by applying for a licence);

(e) provision that compensation must be awarded in specified circumstances or may be awarded in specified circumstances (which may include provision that the circumstances involve negligence or other fault);

(f) provision about the amount that may be awarded;

(g) provision about who is to pay any compensation awarded (which may include provision that it is to be paid or reimbursed by the Treasury);

(h) provision about how compensation is to be paid (which may include provision for payment to a person other than the claimant).

11 Treasury's duty to give reasons

[(1)][31] A freezing order must include provision that if

(a) a person is specified in the order as a person to whom or for whose benefit funds are not to be made available, and

(b) he makes a written request to the Treasury to give him the reason why he is so specified,

as soon as is practicable the Treasury must give the person the reason in writing.

[(2) Sub-paragraph (1) does not apply if, or to the extent that, particulars of the reason would not be required to be disclosed to the applicant in proceedings to set aside the freezing order.][32]

SCHEDULE 4
EXTENSION OF EXISTING DISCLOSURE POWERS *(omitted)*

SCHEDULE 5   Section 58
PATHOGENS AND TOXINS

VIRUSES

Chikungunya virus
Congo-crimean haemorrhagic fever virus
Dengue fever virus
[Dobrava/Belgrade virus][33]
Eastern equine encephalitis virus
Ebola virus
[Everglades virus][34]
[Getah virus
Guanarito virus][35]
Hantaan virus
[Hendra virus (Equine morbillivirus)
Herpes simiae (B virus)
Influenza viruses (pandemic strains)][36]
Japanese encephalitis virus
Junin virus

---

[31] Number inserted by the Counter-Terrorism Act 2008, s 70.
[32] Inserted by the Counter-Terrorism Act 2008, s 70.
[33] Inserted by SI 2007/929, arts 2, 3.
[34] Inserted by SI 2007/929, arts 2, 3.
[35] Inserted by SI 2007/929, arts 2, 3.
[36] Inserted by SI 2007/929, arts 2, 3.

[Kyasanur Forest virus][37]
Lassa fever virus
[Louping ill virus][38]
Lymphocytic choriomeningitis virus
Machupo virus
Marburg virus
[Mayaro virus
Middleburg virus
Mobala virus][39]
Monkey pox virus
[Murray Valley encephalitis virus
Ndumu virus
Nipah virus
Omsk haemorrhagic fever virus
Polio virus
Powassan virus
Rabies virus][40]
Rift Valley fever virus
[Rocio virus
Sabia virus
Sagiyama virus
Sin Nombre virus
St Louis encephalitis virus][41]
Tick-borne encephalitis virus (Russian Spring-Summer encephalitis virus)
Variola virus
Venezuelan equine encephalitis virus
[West Nile fever virus][42]
Western equine encephalitis virus
Yellow fever virus

RICKETTSIAE

[…][43]
Coxiella burnetii
Rickettsia prowazeki
Rickettsia rickettsii
[Rickettsia typhi (mooseri)][44]

BACTERIA

Bacillus anthracis
Bucella abortus
[Brucella canis][45]
Brucella melitensis

---

[37] Inserted by SI 2007/929, arts 2, 3.
[38] Inserted by SI 2007/929, arts 2, 3.
[39] Inserted by SI 2007/929, arts 2, 3.
[40] Inserted by SI 2007/929, arts 2, 3.
[41] Inserted by SI 2007/929, arts 2, 3.
[42] Inserted by SI 2007/929, art 1.
[43] Repealed by SI 2007/929, arts 2, 4(a).
[44] Inserted by SI 2007/929, arts 2, 4(b).
[45] Inserted by SI 2007/929, arts 2, 5.

Brucella suis
Burkholderia mallei (Pseudomonas mallei)
Burkholderia pseudomallei (Pseudomonas pseudomallei)
Chlamydophila psittaci
Clostridium botulinum
[Clostridium perfringens][46]
[Enterohaemorrhagic Escherichia coli, serotype 0157 and verotoxin producing strains][47]
Francisella tularensis
[Multiple-drug resistant Salmonella paratyphi
Mycobacterium tuberculosis
Salmonella paratyphi A, B, C][48]
Salmonella typhi
[Shigella boydii][49]
Shigella dysenteriae
[Shigella flexneri][50]
Vibrio cholerae
Yersinia pestis

[FUNGI

Cladophialophora bantiana
Cryptococcus neoformans][51]

TOXINS

[Abrin][52]
[…][53]
Botulinum toxins
[Clostridium perfringens epsilon toxin
Clostridium perfringens enterotoxin][54]
Conotoxin
[…][55]
[Modeccin toxin][56]
Ricin
Saxitoxin
Shiga [and shiga–like toxins][57]
[…][58]
[Staphylococcal enterotoxins][59]

---

[46] Inserted by SI 2007/929, arts 2, 5.
[47] Inserted by SI 2007/929, arts 2, 5.
[48] Inserted by SI 2007/929, arts 2, 5.
[49] Inserted by SI 2007/929, arts 2, 5.
[50] Inserted by SI 2007/929, arts 2, 5.
[51] Inserted by SI 2007/929, arts 2, 6.
[52] Repealed by SI 2007/929, arts 2, 7(1), (2).
[53] Repealed by SI 2007/929, arts 2, 7(1), (5).
[54] Substituted, for the entry 'Clostridium perfringens toxin' as originally enacted, by SI 2007/929 arts 2, 7(1), (4).
[55] Repealed by SI 2007/929, arts 2, 7(1), (5).
[56] Inserted by SI 2007/929, arts 2, 7(1), (2).
[57] Substituted by SI 2007/929, arts 2, 7(1), (3).
[58] Repealed by SI 2007/929, arts 2, 7(1), (5).
[59] Inserted by SI 2007/929, arts 2, 7(1), (2).

Tetrodotoxin
[…][60]
[Viscum Album Lectin 1 (Viscumin)
Volkensin toxin][61]

[Notes

1 Any reference in this Schedule to a micro-organism includes:
   (a) intact micro-organisms;
   (b) micro-organisms which have been genetically modified by any means, but retain the ability to cause serious harm to human health;
   (c) any nucleic acid deriving from a micro-organism listed in this Schedule (synthetic or naturally derived, contiguous or fragmented, in host chromosomes or in expression vectors) that can encode infectious or replication competent forms of any of the listed micro-organisms;
   (d) any nucleic acid sequence derived from the micro-organism which when inserted into any other living organism alters or enhances that organism's ability to cause serious harm to human health.

2 Any reference in this Schedule to a toxin includes:
   (a) any nucleic acid sequence coding for the toxin, and
   (b) any genetically modified micro-organism containing any such sequence.

3 Any reference in this Schedule to a toxin excludes any non-toxigenic subunit.][62]

[ANIMAL PATHOGENS

African horse sickness virus
African swine fever virus
Bluetongue virus
Classical swine fever virus
Contagious bovine pleuropneumonia
Foot and mouth disease virus
Goat pox virus
Hendra virus (Equine morbillivirus)
Highly pathogenic avian influenza (HPAI) as defined in Annex I(2) of Council Directive 005/94/EC(a)
Lumpy skin disease virus
Newcastle disease virus
Peste des petits ruminants virus
Rift Valley fever virus
Rabies and rabies-related Lyssaviruses
Rinderpest virus
Sheep pox virus
Swine vesicular disease virus
Vesicular stomatitis virus

Notes

Any reference in this Schedule to a micro-organism includes—
(a) intact micro-organisms;
(b) micro-organisms which have been genetically modified by any means, but retain the ability to cause serious harm to animal health;

---

[60] Repealed by SI 2007/929, arts 2, 7(1), (5).
[61] Inserted by SI 2007/929, arts 2, 7(1), (2).
[62] Substituted by SI 2007/929, arts 2, 8.

(c) any nucleic acid derived from a micro-organism listed in this Schedule (synthetic or naturally derived, contiguous or fragmented, in host chromosomes or in expression vectors) that can encode infectious or replication competent forms of any of the listed micro-organisms;

(d) any nucleic acid sequence derived from the micro-organism which when inserted into any other living organism alters or enhances that organism's ability to cause serious harm to animal health."][63]

SCHEDULE 6
THE PATHOGENS ACCESS APPEAL COMMISSION

Constitution and administration

1 (1) The Commission shall consist of members appointed by the Lord Chancellor.

(2) The Lord Chancellor shall appoint one of the members as chairman.

(3) A member shall hold and vacate office in accordance with the terms of his appointment.

(4) A member may resign at any time by notice in writing to the Lord Chancellor.

2 The Lord Chancellor may appoint officers and servants for the Commission.

3 The Lord Chancellor

(a) may pay sums by way of remuneration, allowances, pensions and gratuities to or in respect of members, officers and servants;

(b) may pay compensation to a person who ceases to be a member of the Commission if the Lord Chancellor thinks it appropriate because of special circumstances; and

(c) may pay sums in respect of expenses of the Commission.

Procedure

4 (1) The Commission shall sit at such times and in such places as the Lord Chancellor may direct [after consulting the following

(a) the Lord Chief Justice of England and Wales;

(b) the Lord President of the Court of Session;

(c) the Lord Chief Justice of Northern Ireland].[64]

(2) The Commission may sit in two or more divisions.

(3) At each sitting of the Commission

(a) three members shall attend;

(b) one of the members shall be a person who holds or has held high judicial office (within the meaning of *the Appellate Jurisdiction Act 1876 (c 59))*[65] *(Part 3 of the Constitutional Reform Act 2005)*[66] *or is or has been a member of the Judicial Committee of the Privy Council*, and

(c) the chairman or another member nominated by him shall preside and report the Commission's decision.

[(4) The Lord Chief Justice may nominate a judicial office holder (as defined in section 109(4) of the Constitutional Reform Act 2005) to exercise his functions under sub-paragraph (1).

(5) The Lord President of the Court of Session may nominate a judge of the Court of Session who is a member of the First or Second Division of the Inner House of that Court to exercise his functions under sub-paragraph (1).

---

[63] Inserted by the Anti-terrorism, Crime and Security Act 2001 (Extension to Animal Pathogens) Order 2007, SI 2007/926, art 2, Schedule.

[64] Inserted by the Constitutional Reform Act 2005, s 15(1), Sch 4, Pt 1, para 300(1), (2),

[65] Repealed by the Constitutional Reform Act 2005, s 145, Sch 17, Pt 2, para 31, not yet in force.

[66] Substituted by the Constitutional Reform Act 2005, s 145, Sch 17, Pt 2, para 31, not yet in force.

(6) The Lord Chief Justice of Northern Ireland may nominate any of the following to exercise his functions under sub-paragraph (1)

    (a) the holder of one of the offices listed in Schedule 1 to the Justice (Northern Ireland) Act 2002;

    (b) a Lord Justice of Appeal (as defined in section 88 of that Act).][67]

5 (1) The Lord Chancellor may make rules

    (a) regulating the exercise of the right of appeal to the Commission;

    (b) prescribing practice and procedure to be followed in relation to proceedings before the Commission;

    (c) providing for proceedings before the Commission to be determined without an oral hearing in specified circumstances;

    (d) making provision about evidence in proceedings before the Commission (including provision about the burden of proof and admissibility of evidence);

    (e) making provision about proof of the Commission's decisions.

(2) In making the rules the Lord Chancellor shall, in particular, have regard to the need to secure

    (a) that decisions which are the subject of appeals are properly reviewed; and

    (b) that information is not disclosed contrary to the public interest.

(3) The rules may, in particular

    (a) provide for full particulars of the reasons for denial of access to be withheld from the applicant and from any person representing him;

    (b) enable the Commission to exclude persons (including representatives) from all or part of proceedings;

    (c) enable the Commission to provide a summary of evidence taken in the absence of a person excluded by virtue of paragraph (b);

    (d) permit preliminary or incidental functions to be discharged by a single member;

    (e) permit proceedings for permission to appeal under section 70(5) to be determined by a single member;

    (f) make provision about the functions of persons appointed under paragraph 6;

    (g) make different provision for different parties or descriptions of party.

(4) Rules under this paragraph

    (a) shall be made by statutory instrument; and

    (b) shall not be made unless a draft of them has been laid before and approved by resolution of each House of Parliament.

(5) In this paragraph a reference to proceedings before the Commission includes a reference to proceedings arising out of proceedings before the Commission.

6 (1) The relevant law officer may appoint a person to represent the interests of an organisation or other applicant in proceedings in relation to which an order has been made by virtue of paragraph 5(3)(b).

(2) The relevant law officer is

    (a) in relation to proceedings in England and Wales, the Attorney General;

    (b) in relation to proceedings in Scotland, the Advocate General for Scotland; and

    (c) in relation to proceedings in Northern Ireland, the *Attorney General for Northern Ireland*[68] (*Advocate General for Northern Ireland*).[69]

(3) A person appointed under this paragraph must

    (a) have a general qualification for the purposes of section 71 of the Courts and Legal Services Act 1990 (c 41) (qualification for legal appointments);

---

[67] Inserted by the Constitutional Reform Act 2005, s 15(1), Sch 4, Pt 1, para 300(1), (3).

[68] Repealed by the Counter-Terrorism Act 2008, s 91(1), (2), not yet in force.

[69] Substituted by the Counter-Terrorism Act 2008, s 91(1), (2), not yet in force.

    (b) be an advocate or a solicitor who has rights of audience in the Court of Session or the High Court of Justiciary by virtue of section 25A of the Solicitors (Scotland) Act 1980 (c 46); or

    (c) be a member of the Bar of Northern Ireland.

(4) A person appointed under this paragraph shall not be responsible to the applicant whose interests he is appointed to represent.

(5) In paragraph 5 of this Schedule a reference to a representative does not include a reference to a person appointed under this paragraph.

SCHEDULE 7
TRANSPORT POLICE AND MOD POLICE: FURTHER PROVISIONS
(omitted)

SCHEDULE 8
REPEALS AND REVOCATION *(omitted)*

Prevention of Terrorism Act 2005

An Act to provide for the making against individuals involved in terrorism-related activity of orders imposing obligations on them for purposes connected with preventing or restricting their further involvement in such activity; to make provision about appeals and other proceedings relating to such orders; and for connected purposes.

(11th March 2005)

Control orders

1 Power to make control orders

(1) In this Act "control order" means an order against an individual that imposes obligations on him for purposes connected with protecting members of the public from a risk of terrorism.

(2) The power to make a control order against an individual shall be exercisable

(a) except in the case of an order imposing obligations that are incompatible with the individual's right to liberty under Article 5 of the Human Rights Convention, by the Secretary of State; and

(b) in the case of an order imposing obligations that are or include derogating obligations, by the court on an application by the Secretary of State.

(3) The obligations that may be imposed by a control order made against an individual are any obligations that the Secretary of State or (as the case may be) the court considers necessary for purposes connected with preventing or restricting involvement by that individual in terrorism-related activity.

(4) Those obligations may include, in particular

(a) a prohibition or restriction on his possession or use of specified articles or substances;

(b) a prohibition or restriction on his use of specified services or specified facilities, or on his carrying on specified activities;

(c) a restriction in respect of his work or other occupation, or in respect of his business;

(d) a restriction on his association or communications with specified persons or with other persons generally;

(e) a restriction in respect of his place of residence or on the persons to whom he gives access to his place of residence;

(f) a prohibition on his being at specified places or within a specified area at specified times or on specified days;

(g) a prohibition or restriction on his movements to, from or within the United Kingdom, a specified part of the United Kingdom or a specified place or area within the United Kingdom;

(h) a requirement on him to comply with such other prohibitions or restrictions on his movements as may be imposed, for a period not exceeding 24 hours, by directions given to him in the specified manner, by a specified person and for the purpose of securing compliance with other obligations imposed by or under the order;

(i) a requirement on him to surrender his passport, or anything in his possession to which a prohibition or restriction imposed by the order relates, to a specified person for a period not exceeding the period for which the order remains in force;

(j) a requirement on him to give access to specified persons to his place of residence or to other premises to which he has power to grant access;

(k) a requirement on him to allow specified persons to search that place or any such premises for the purpose of ascertaining whether obligations imposed by or under the order have been, are being or are about to be contravened;

(l) a requirement on him to allow specified persons, either for that purpose or for the purpose of securing that the order is complied with, to remove anything found in that place or on any such premises and to subject it to tests or to retain it for a period not exceeding the period for which the order remains in force;

(m) a requirement on him to allow himself to be photographed;

(n) a requirement on him to co-operate with specified arrangements for enabling his movements, communications or other activities to be monitored by electronic or other means;

(o) a requirement on him to comply with a demand made in the specified manner to provide information to a specified person in accordance with the demand;

(p) a requirement on him to report to a specified person at specified times and places.

(5) Power by or under a control order to prohibit or restrict the controlled person's movements includes, in particular, power to impose a requirement on him to remain at or within a particular place or area (whether for a particular period or at particular times or generally).

(6) The reference in subsection (4)(n) to co-operating with specified arrangements for monitoring includes a reference to each of the following

(a) submitting to procedures required by the arrangements;

(b) wearing or otherwise using apparatus approved by or in accordance with the arrangements;

(c) maintaining such apparatus in the specified manner;

(d) complying with directions given by persons carrying out functions for the purposes of those arrangements.

(7) The information that the controlled person may be required to provide under a control order includes, in particular, advance information about his proposed movements or other activities.

(8) A control order may provide for a prohibition, restriction or requirement imposed by or under the order to apply only where a specified person has not given his consent or approval to what would otherwise contravene the prohibition, restriction or requirement.

(9) For the purposes of this Act involvement in terrorism-related activity is any one or more of the following

(a) the commission, preparation or instigation of acts of terrorism;

(b) conduct which facilitates the commission, preparation or instigation of such acts, or which is intended to do so;

(c) conduct which gives encouragement to the commission, preparation or instigation of such acts, or which is intended to do so;

(d) conduct which gives support or assistance to individuals who are known or believed [by the individual concerned to be involved in conduct falling within paragraphs (a) to (c);][1]

and for the purposes of this subsection it is immaterial whether the acts of terrorism in question are specific acts of terrorism or acts of terrorism generally.

(10) In this Act

"derogating obligation" means an obligation on an individual which

(a) is incompatible with his right to liberty under Article 5 of the Human Rights Convention; but

(b) is of a description of obligations which, for the purposes of the designation of a designated derogation, is set out in the designation order;

---

[1] Substituted by the Counter-Terrorism Act 2008, s 79(1).

"designated derogation" has the same meaning as in the Human Rights Act 1998 (c 42) (see section 14(1) of that Act);

"designation order", in relation to a designated derogation, means the order under section 14(1) of the Human Rights Act 1998 by which the derogation is designated.

2 Making of non-derogating control orders

(1) The Secretary of State may make a control order against an individual if he

   (a) has reasonable grounds for suspecting that the individual is or has been involved in terrorism-related activity; and

   (b) considers that it is necessary, for purposes connected with protecting members of the public from a risk of terrorism, to make a control order imposing obligations on that individual.

(2) The Secretary of State may make a control order against an individual who is for the time being bound by a control order made by the court only if he does so

   (a) after the court has determined that its order should be revoked; but

   (b) while the effect of the revocation has been postponed for the purpose of giving the Secretary of State an opportunity to decide whether to exercise his own powers to make a control order against the individual.

(3) A control order made by the Secretary of State is called a non-derogating control order.

(4) A non-derogating control order

   (a) has effect for a period of 12 months beginning with the day on which it is made; but

   (b) may be renewed on one or more occasions in accordance with this section.

(5) A non-derogating control order must specify when the period for which it is to have effect will end.

(6) The Secretary of State may renew a non-derogating control order (with or without modifications) for a period of 12 months if he

   (a) considers that it is necessary, for purposes connected with protecting members of the public from a risk of terrorism, for an order imposing obligations on the controlled person to continue in force; and

   (b) considers that the obligations to be imposed by the renewed order are necessary for purposes connected with preventing or restricting involvement by that person in terrorism-related activity.

(7) Where the Secretary of State renews a non-derogating control order, the 12 month period of the renewal begins to run from whichever is the earlier of

   (a) the time when the order would otherwise have ceased to have effect; or

   (b) the beginning of the seventh day after the date of renewal.

(8) The instrument renewing a non-derogating control order must specify when the period for which it is renewed will end.

(9) It shall be immaterial, for the purposes of determining what obligations may be imposed by a control order made by the Secretary of State, whether the involvement in terrorism-related activity to be prevented or restricted by the obligations is connected with matters to which the Secretary of State's grounds for suspicion relate.

3 Supervision by court of making of non-derogating control orders

(1) The Secretary of State must not make a non-derogating control order against an individual except where

   (a) having decided that there are grounds to make such an order against that individual, he has applied to the court for permission to make the order and has been granted that permission;

   (b) the order contains a statement by the Secretary of State that, in his opinion, the urgency of the case requires the order to be made without such permission; or

(c) [...]²

(2) Where the Secretary of State makes an application for permission to make a non-derogating control order against an individual, the application must set out the order for which he seeks permission and

(a) the function of the court is to consider whether the Secretary of State's decision that there are grounds to make that order is obviously flawed;

(b) the court may give that permission unless it determines that the decision is obviously flawed; and

(c) if it gives permission, the court must give directions for a hearing in relation to the order as soon as reasonably practicable after it is made.

(3) Where the Secretary of State makes a non-derogating control order against an individual without the permission of the court

(a) he must immediately refer the order to the court; and

(b) the function of the court on the reference is to consider whether the decision of the Secretary of State to make the order he did was obviously flawed.

(4) The court's consideration on a reference under subsection (3)(a) must begin no more than 7 days after the day on which the control order in question was made.

(5) The court may consider an application for permission under subsection (1)(a) or a reference under subsection (3)(a)

(a) in the absence of the individual in question;

(b) without his having been notified of the application or reference; and

(c) without his having been given an opportunity (if he was aware of the application or reference) of making any representations to the court;

but this subsection is not to be construed as limiting the matters about which rules of court may be made in relation to the consideration of such an application or reference.

(6) On a reference under subsection (3)(a), the court

(a) if it determines that the decision of the Secretary of State to make a non-derogating control order against the controlled person was obviously flawed, must quash the order;

(b) if it determines that that decision was not obviously flawed but that a decision of the Secretary of State to impose a particular obligation by that order was obviously flawed, must quash that obligation and (subject to that) confirm the order and give directions for a hearing in relation to the confirmed order; and

(c) in any other case, must confirm the order and give directions for a hearing in relation to the confirmed order.

(7) The directions given under subsection (2)(c) or (6)(b) or (c) must include arrangements for the individual in question to be given an opportunity [...]³ to make representations about

(a) the directions already given; and

(b) the making of further directions.

[(7A) The individual must be given the opportunity to make those representations

(a) in the case of directions under subsection (2)(c), within 7 days of notice of the terms of the control order being delivered to the individual in accordance with section 7(8);

(b) in the case of directions given under subsection (6)(b) or (c), within 7 days of the court making its determination on the reference.]⁴

(8) On a reference under subsection (3)(a), the court may quash a certificate contained in the order for the purposes of subsection (1)(b) if it determines that the Secretary of State's decision that the certificate should be contained in the order was flawed.

(9) The court must ensure that the controlled person is notified of its decision on a reference under subsection (3)(a).

---

² Repealed by the Counter-Terrorism Act 2008, s 99, Sch 9, Pt 5.
³ Repealed by the Counter-Terrorism Act 2008, ss 80(1), (2), 99, Sch 9, Pt 5.
⁴ Repealed by the Counter-Terrorism Act 2008, s 80(4).

(10) On a hearing in pursuance of directions under subsection (2)(c) or (6)(b) or (c), the function of the court is to determine whether any of the following decisions of the Secretary of State was flawed

    (a) his decision that the requirements of section 2(1)(a) and (b) were satisfied for the making of the order; and

    (b) his decisions on the imposition of each of the obligations imposed by the order.

(11) In determining

    (a) what constitutes a flawed decision for the purposes of subsection (2), (6) or (8), or

    (b) the matters mentioned in subsection (10),

the court must apply the principles applicable on an application for judicial review.

(12) If the court determines, on a hearing in pursuance of directions under subsection (2)(c) or (6)(b) or (c), that a decision of the Secretary of State was flawed, its only powers are

    (a) power to quash the order;

    (b) power to quash one or more obligations imposed by the order; and

    (c) power to give directions to the Secretary of State for the revocation of the order or for the modification of the obligations it imposes.

(13) In every other case the court must decide that the control order is to continue in force.

(14) If requested to do so by the controlled person, the court must discontinue any hearing in pursuance of directions under subsection (2)(c) or (6)(b) or (c).

4 Power of court to make derogating control orders

(1) On an application to the court by the Secretary of State for the making of a control order against an individual, it shall be the duty of the court

    (a) to hold an immediate preliminary hearing to determine whether to make a control order imposing obligations that are or include derogating obligations (called a "derogating control order") against that individual; and

    (b) if it does make such an order against that individual, to give directions for the holding of a full hearing to determine whether to confirm the order (with or without modifications).

(2) The preliminary hearing under subsection (1)(a) may be held

    (a) in the absence of the individual in question;

    (b) without his having had notice of the application for the order; and

    (c) without his having been given an opportunity (if he was aware of the application) of making any representations to the court;

but this subsection is not to be construed as limiting the matters about which rules of court may be made in relation to that hearing.

(3) At the preliminary hearing, the court may make a control order against the individual in question if it appears to the court

    (a) that there is material which (if not disproved) is capable of being relied on by the court as establishing that the individual is or has been involved in terrorism-related activity;

    (b) that there are reasonable grounds for believing that the imposition of obligations on that individual is necessary for purposes connected with protecting members of the public from a risk of terrorism;

    (c) that the risk arises out of, or is associated with, a public emergency in respect of which there is a designated derogation from the whole or a part of Article 5 of the Human Rights Convention; and

    (d) that the obligations that there are reasonable grounds for believing should be imposed on the individual are or include derogating obligations of a description set out for the purposes of the designated derogation in the designation order.

(4) The obligations that may be imposed by a derogating control order in the period between

    (a) the time when the order is made, and

(b) the time when a final determination is made by the court whether to confirm it,

include any obligations which the court has reasonable grounds for considering are necessary as mentioned in section 1(3).

(5) At the full hearing under subsection (1)(b), the court may

(a) confirm the control order made by the court; or

(b) revoke the order;

and where the court revokes the order, it may (if it thinks fit) direct that this Act is to have effect as if the order had been quashed.

(6) In confirming a control order, the court

(a) may modify the obligations imposed by the order; and

(b) where a modification made by the court removes an obligation, may (if it thinks fit) direct that this Act is to have effect as if the removed obligation had been quashed.

(7) At the full hearing, the court may confirm the control order (with or without modifications) only if

(a) it is satisfied, on the balance of probabilities, that the controlled person is an individual who is or has been involved in terrorism-related activity;

(b) it considers that the imposition of obligations on the controlled person is necessary for purposes connected with protecting members of the public from a risk of terrorism;

(c) it appears to the court that the risk is one arising out of, or is associated with, a public emergency in respect of which there is a designated derogation from the whole or a part of Article 5 of the Human Rights Convention; and

(d) the obligations to be imposed by the order or (as the case may be) by the order as modified are or include derogating obligations of a description set out for the purposes of the designated derogation in the designation order.

(8) A derogating control order ceases to have effect at the end of the period of 6 months beginning with the day on which it is made unless

(a) it is previously revoked (whether at the hearing under subsection (1)(b) or otherwise under this Act);

(b) it ceases to have effect under section 6; or

(c) it is renewed.

(9) The court, on an application by the Secretary of State, may renew a derogating control order (with or without modifications) for a period of 6 months from whichever is the earlier of

(a) the time when the order would otherwise have ceased to have effect; and

(b) the beginning of the seventh day after the date of renewal.

(10) The power of the court to renew a derogating control order is exercisable on as many occasions as the court thinks fit; but, on each occasion, it is exercisable only if

(a) the court considers that it is necessary, for purposes connected with protecting members of the public from a risk of terrorism, for a derogating control order to continue in force against the controlled person;

(b) it appears to the court that the risk is one arising out of, or is associated with, a public emergency in respect of which there is a designated derogation from the whole or a part of Article 5 of the Human Rights Convention;

(c) the derogating obligations that the court considers should continue in force are of a description that continues to be set out for the purposes of the designated derogation in the designation order; and

(d) the court considers that the obligations to be imposed by the renewed order are necessary for purposes connected with preventing or restricting involvement by that person in terrorism-related activity.

(11) Where, on an application for the renewal of a derogating control order, it appears to the court

(a) that the proceedings on the application are unlikely to be completed before the time when the order is due to cease to have effect if not renewed, and

    (b) that that is not attributable to an unreasonable delay on the part of the Secretary of State in the making or conduct of the application,

the court may (on one or more occasions) extend the period for which the order is to remain in force for the purpose of keeping it in force until the conclusion of the proceedings.

(12) Where the court exercises its power under subsection (11) and subsequently renews the control order in question, the period of any renewal still runs from the time when the order would have ceased to have effect apart from that subsection.

(13) It shall be immaterial, for the purposes of determining what obligations may be imposed by a control order made by the court, whether the involvement in terrorism-related activity to be prevented or restricted by the obligations is connected with matters in relation to which the requirements of subsection (3)(a) or (7)(a) were satisfied.

5 Arrest and detention pending derogating control order

(1) A constable may arrest and detain an individual if
    (a) the Secretary of State has made an application to the court for a derogating control order to be made against that individual; and
    (b) the constable considers that the individual's arrest and detention is necessary to ensure that he is available to be given notice of the order if it is made.

(2) A constable who has arrested an individual under this section must take him to the designated place that the constable considers most appropriate as soon as practicable after the arrest.

(3) An individual taken to a designated place under this section may be detained there until the end of 48 hours from the time of his arrest.

(4) If the court considers that it is necessary to do so to ensure that the individual in question is available to be given notice of any derogating control order that is made against him, it may, during the 48 hours following his arrest, extend the period for which the individual may be detained under this section by a period of no more than 48 hours.

(5) An individual may not be detained under this section at any time after
    (a) he has become bound by a derogating control order made against him on the Secretary of State's application; or
    (b) the court has dismissed the application.

(6) A person who has the powers of a constable in one part of the United Kingdom may exercise the power of arrest under this section in that part of the United Kingdom or in any other part of the United Kingdom.

(7) An individual detained under this section
    (a) shall be deemed to be in legal custody throughout the period of his detention; and
    (b) after having been taken to a designated place shall be deemed
        (i) in England and Wales, to be in police detention for the purposes of the Police and Criminal Evidence Act 1984 (c 60); and
        (ii) in Northern Ireland, to be in police detention for the purposes of the Police and Criminal Evidence (Northern Ireland) Order 1989 (SI 1989/1341 (NI 12));
    but paragraph (b) has effect subject to subsection (8).

(8) Paragraphs 1(6), 2, 6 to 9 and 16 to 19 of Schedule 8 to the Terrorism Act 2000 (c 11) (powers and safeguards in the case of persons detained under section 41 of that Act) apply to an individual detained under this section as they apply to a person detained under section 41 of that Act, but with the following modifications
    (a) the omission of paragraph 2(2)(b) to (d) (which confers powers on persons specified by the Secretary of State, prison officers and examining officers);
    (b) the omission of paragraph 8(2), (5) and (5A) (which relates to the postponement of a person's rights in England and Wales or Northern Ireland); and

    (c) the omission of paragraphs 16(9) and 17(4) and (4A) (which make similar provision for Scotland).

(9) The power to detain an individual under this section includes power to detain him in a manner that is incompatible with his right to liberty under Article 5 of the Human Rights Convention if, and only if

    (a) there is a designated derogation in respect of the detention of individuals under this section in connection with the making of applications for derogating control orders; and

    (b) that derogation and the designated derogation relating to the power to make the orders applied for are designated in respect of the same public emergency.

(10) In this section "designated place" means any place which the Secretary of State has designated under paragraph 1(1) of Schedule 8 to the Terrorism Act 2000 (c 11) as a place at which persons may be detained under section 41 of that Act.

6 Duration of derogating control orders

(1) A derogating control order has effect at a time only if

    (a) the relevant derogation remains in force at that time; and

    (b) that time is not more than 12 months after

        (i) the making of the order under section 14(1) of the Human Rights Act 1998 (c 42) designating that derogation; or

        (ii) the making by the Secretary of State of an order declaring that it continues to be necessary for him to have power to impose derogating obligations by reference to that derogation.

(2) The power of the Secretary of State to make an order containing a declaration for the purposes of subsection (1)(b)(ii) is exercisable by statutory instrument.

(3) No order may be made by the Secretary of State containing such a declaration unless a draft of it has been laid before Parliament and approved by a resolution of each House.

(4) Subsection (3) does not apply to an order that contains a statement by the Secretary of State that the order needs, by reason of urgency, to be made without the approval required by that subsection.

(5) An order under this section that contains such a statement

    (a) must be laid before Parliament after being made; and

    (b) if not approved by a resolution of each House before the end of 40 days beginning with the day on which the order was made, ceases to have effect at the end of that period.

(6) Where an order ceases to have effect in accordance with subsection (5), that does not

    (a) affect anything previously done in reliance on the order; or

    (b) prevent the Secretary of State from exercising any power of his to make a new order for the purposes of subsection (1)(b)(ii) to the same or similar effect.

(7) In this section

    "40 days" means 40 days computed as provided for in section 7(1) of the Statutory Instruments Act 1946 (c 36);

    "the relevant derogation", in relation to a derogating control order, means the designated derogation by reference to which the derogating obligations imposed by that order were imposed.

7 Modification, notification and proof of orders etc

(1) If while a non-derogating control order is in force the controlled person considers that there has been a change of circumstances affecting the order, he may make an application to the Secretary of State for

    (a) the revocation of the order; or

    (b) the modification of an obligation imposed by the order;

    and it shall be the duty of the Secretary of State to consider the application.

(2) The Secretary of State may, at any time (whether or not in response to an application by the controlled person)

(a) revoke a non-derogating control order;

(b) relax or remove an obligation imposed by such an order;

(c) with the consent of the controlled person, modify the obligations imposed by such an order; or

(d) make to the obligations imposed by such an order any modifications which he considers necessary for purposes connected with preventing or restricting involvement by the controlled person in terrorism-related activity.

(3) The Secretary of State may not make to the obligations imposed by a control order any modification the effect of which is that a non-derogating control order becomes an order imposing a derogating obligation.

(4) An application may be made at any time to the court

(a) by the Secretary of State, or

(b) by the controlled person,

for the revocation of a derogating control order or for the modification of obligations imposed by such an order.

(5) On such an application, the court may modify the obligations imposed by the derogating control order only where

(a) the modification consists in the removal or relaxation of an obligation imposed by the order;

(b) the modification has been agreed to by both the controlled person and the Secretary of State; or

(c) the modification is one which the court considers necessary for purposes connected with preventing or restricting involvement by the controlled person in terrorism-related activity.

(6) The court may not, by any modification of the obligations imposed by a derogating control order, impose any derogating obligation unless

(a) it considers that the modification is necessary for purposes connected with protecting members of the public from a risk of terrorism; and

(b) it appears to the court that the risk is one arising out of, or is associated with, the public emergency in respect of which the designated derogation in question has effect.

(7) If the court at any time determines that a derogating control order needs to be modified so that it no longer imposes derogating obligations, it must revoke the order.

(8) The controlled person is bound by

(a) a control order,

(b) the renewal of a control order, or

(c) a modification by virtue of subsection (2)(d) or (5)(c),

only if a notice setting out the terms of the order, renewal or modification has been delivered to him in person.

(9) For the purpose of delivering a notice under subsection (8) to the controlled person a constable or a person authorised for the purpose by the Secretary of State may (if necessary by force)

(a) enter any premises where he has reasonable grounds for believing that person to be; and

(b) search those premises for him.

(10) Where the Secretary of State revokes a control order or modifies it by virtue of subsection (2)(b) or (c)

(a) he must give notice of the revocation or modification to the controlled person; and

(b) the notice must set out the time from which the revocation or modification takes effect.

(11) A control order, or the renewal, revocation or modification of such an order, may be proved by the production of a document purporting to be certified by the Secretary of State or the court as a true copy of

(a) the order; or

(b) the instrument of renewal, revocation or modification;

but this does not prevent the proof of a control order, or of the renewal, revocation or modification of such an order, in other ways.

[7A Powers of entry and search: absconding

(1) If a constable reasonably suspects that the controlled person has absconded, the constable may enter (if necessary by force) and search premises to which this section applies

(a) for the purpose of determining whether the person has absconded;

(b) if it appears that the person has absconded, for material that may assist in the pursuit and arrest of the controlled person.

(2) The premises to which this section applies are

(a) the controlled person's place of residence;

(b) other premises to which the controlled person is required to grant access in accordance with an obligation imposed by or under the control order;

(c) any premises

(i) to which the controlled person has previously been required to grant access in accordance with an obligation imposed by or under a control order, and

(ii) with which there is reason to believe that the controlled person is or was recently connected.][5]

[7B Powers of entry and search: failure to grant access to premises

(1) This section applies where a constable reasonably suspects that the controlled person is not granting access to premises, as required by an obligation imposed by or under the control order, at a time when the controlled person is required, by an obligation so imposed, to be at those premises.

(2) The constable may enter (if necessary by force) and search the premises

(a) for the purpose of determining whether any of the obligations imposed by or under the control order have been contravened;

(b) if it appears that an obligation has been contravened, for material that may assist in the investigation of the contravention.][6]

[7C Powers of entry and search: monitoring compliance with order

(1) A constable may apply for the issue of a warrant under this section for the purposes of determining whether the controlled person is complying with the obligations imposed by or under a control order.

(2) The application must be made

(a) in England and Wales, to a justice of the peace;

(b) in Scotland, to the sheriff;

(c) in Northern Ireland, to a lay magistrate.

(3) A warrant under this section shall authorise any constable to enter (if necessary by force) and search premises to which this section applies that are specified in the warrant.

(4) The premises to which this section applies are

(a) the controlled person's place of residence;

(b) other premises to which the controlled person is required to grant access in accordance with an obligation imposed by or under the control order;

(c) any premises

---

[5] Inserted by the Counter-Terrorism Act 2008, s 78(1).

[6] Inserted by the Counter-Terrorism Act 2008, s 78(1).

    (i) to which the controlled person has previously been required to grant access in accordance with an obligation imposed by or under a control order, and

    (ii) with which there is reason to believe that the controlled person is or was recently connected.

(5) An application under this section may only be granted if the justice of the peace, the sheriff or the lay magistrate is satisfied that the issue of the warrant is necessary for the purposes of determining whether the controlled person is complying with the obligations imposed by or under the control order.][7]

8 Criminal investigations after making of control order

(1) This section applies where it appears to the Secretary of State

    (a) that the involvement in terrorism-related activity of which an individual is suspected may have involved the commission of an offence relating to terrorism; and

    (b) that the commission of that offence is being or would fall to be investigated by a police force.

(2) Before making, or applying for the making of, a control order against the individual, the Secretary of State must consult the chief officer of the police force about whether there is evidence available that could realistically be used for the purposes of a prosecution of the individual for an offence relating to terrorism.

(3) If a control order is made against the individual the Secretary of State must inform the chief officer of the police force that the control order has been made and that subsection (4) applies.

(4) It shall then be the duty of the chief officer to secure that the investigation of the individual's conduct with a view to his prosecution for an offence relating to terrorism is kept under review throughout the period during which the control order has effect.

(5) In carrying out his functions by virtue of this section the chief officer must consult the relevant prosecuting authority, but only, in the case of the performance of his duty under subsection (4), to the extent that he considers it appropriate to do so.

(6) The requirements of subsection (5) may be satisfied by consultation that took place wholly or partly before the passing of this Act.

(7) In this section

"chief officer"

    (a) in relation to a police force maintained for a police area in England and Wales, means the chief officer of police of that force;

    (b) in relation to a police force maintained under the Police (Scotland) Act 1967 (c 77), means the chief constable of that force;

    (c) in relation to the Police Service of Northern Ireland, means the Chief Constable of that Service;

    (d) in relation to the Serious Organised Crime Agency, means the Director General of that Agency; and

    [(e) in relation to the Scottish Crime and Drug Enforcement Agency, means the Director General of that Agency;][8]

"police force" means

    (a) a police force maintained for a police area in England and Wales;

    (b) a police force maintained under the Police (Scotland) Act 1967;

    (c) the Police Service of Northern Ireland;

    (d) the Serious Organised Crime Agency; or

    [(e) the Scottish Crime and Drug Enforcement Agency;][9]

---

[7] Inserted by the Counter-Terrorism Act 2008, s 78(1).
[8] Substituted by SI 2007/1098, art 6, Schedule, Pt 1 para 5(1), (2)(a)(i).
[9] Substituted by SI 2007/1098, art 6, Schedule, Pt 1 para 5(1), (2)(a)(i).

"relevant prosecuting authority"

  (a) in relation to offences that would be likely to be prosecuted in England and Wales, means the Director of Public Prosecutions;

  (b) in relation to offences that would be likely to be prosecuted in Scotland, means the appropriate procurator fiscal;

  (c) in relation to offences that would be likely to be prosecuted in Northern Ireland, means the Director of Public Prosecutions for Northern Ireland.

(8) [...][10]

(9) [...][11]

9 Offences

(1) A person who, without reasonable excuse, contravenes an obligation imposed on him by a control order is guilty of an offence.

(2) A person is guilty of an offence if

  (a) a control order by which he is bound at a time when he leaves the United Kingdom requires him, whenever he enters the United Kingdom, to report to a specified person that he is or has been the subject of such an order;

  (b) he re-enters the United Kingdom after the order has ceased to have effect;

  (c) the occasion on which he re-enters the United Kingdom is the first occasion on which he does so after leaving while the order was in force; and

  (d) on that occasion he fails, without reasonable excuse, to report to the specified person in the manner that was required by the order.

(3) A person is guilty of an offence if he intentionally obstructs the exercise by any person of a power conferred by section 7(9).

[(3A) A person who intentionally obstructs the exercise by a constable of a power conferred by section 7A or 7B or by a warrant under section 7C commits an offence.][12]

(4) A person guilty of an offence under subsection (1) or (2) shall be liable

  (a) on conviction on indictment, to imprisonment for a term not exceeding 5 years or to a fine, or to both;

  (b) on summary conviction in England and Wales, to imprisonment for a term not exceeding 12 months or to a fine not exceeding the statutory maximum, or to both;

  (c) on summary conviction in Scotland or Northern Ireland, to imprisonment for a term not exceeding 6 months or to a fine not exceeding the statutory maximum, or to both.

(5) In relation to an offence committed before the commencement of section 154(1) of the Criminal Justice Act 2003 (c 44), the reference in subsection (4)(b) to 12 months is to be read as a reference to 6 months.

(6) Where a person is convicted by or before any court of an offence under subsection (1) or (2), it is not to be open to the court, in respect of that offence

  (a) to make an order under section 12(1)(b) of the Powers of Criminal Courts (Sentencing) Act 2000 (c 6) (conditional discharge);

  (b) to make an order under section 228(1) of the Criminal Procedure (Scotland) Act 1995 (c 46) (probation orders); or

  (c) to make an order under Article 4(1)(b) of the Criminal Justice (Northern Ireland) Order 1996 (SI 1996/3160 (NI 24)) (conditional discharge in Northern Ireland).

(7) A person guilty of an offence under subsection (3) [or (3A)][13] shall be liable

  (a) on summary conviction in England and Wales, to imprisonment for a term not exceeding 51 weeks or to a fine not exceeding level 5 on the standard scale, or to both;

---

[10] Repealed by the Counter-Terrorism Act 2008, s 99, Sch 9, Pt 5.
[11] Repealed by SI 2007/1098, art 6, Schedule, Pt 1, para 5(1), (2)(b).
[12] Inserted by the Counter-Terrorism Act 2008, s 78(2)(a).
[13] Inserted by the Counter-Terrorism Act 2008, s 78(2)(b).

(b) on summary conviction in Scotland or Northern Ireland, to imprisonment for a term not exceeding 6 months or to a fine not exceeding level 5 on the standard scale, or to both.

(8) In relation to an offence committed before the commencement of section 281(5) of the Criminal Justice Act 2003, the reference in subsection (7)(a) to 51 weeks is to be read as a reference to 6 months.

(9) [...][14]

(10) In Article 26(2) of the Police and Criminal Evidence (Northern Ireland) Order 1989 (SI 1989/1341 (NI 12)) (offences for which an arrest may be made without a warrant in Northern Ireland), at the end insert

"(o) an offence under section 9(3) of the Prevention of Terrorism Act 2005."

Appeals and other proceedings

10 Appeals relating to non-derogating control orders

(1) Where
  (a) a non-derogating control order has been renewed, or
  (b) an obligation imposed by such an order has been modified without the consent of the controlled person,
the controlled person may appeal to the court against the renewal or modification.

(2) In the case of an appeal against a renewal with modifications, the appeal may include an appeal against some or all of the modifications.

(3) Where an application is made by the controlled person to the Secretary of State for
  (a) the revocation of a non-derogating control order, or
  (b) the modification of an obligation imposed by such an order,
that person may appeal to the court against any decision by the Secretary of State on the application.

(4) The function of the court on an appeal against the renewal of a non-derogating control order, or on an appeal against a decision not to revoke such an order, is to determine whether either or both of the following decisions of the Secretary of State was flawed
  (a) his decision that it is necessary, for purposes connected with protecting members of the public from a risk of terrorism, for an order imposing obligations on the controlled person to continue in force;
  (b) his decision that the obligations to be imposed by the renewed order, or (as the case may be) the obligations imposed by the order to which the application for revocation relates, are necessary for purposes connected with preventing or restricting involvement by that person in terrorism-related activity.

(5) The function of the court on an appeal against a modification of an obligation imposed by a non-derogating control order (whether on a renewal or otherwise), or on an appeal against a decision not to modify such an obligation, is to determine whether the following decision of the Secretary of State was flawed
  (a) in the case of an appeal against a modification, his decision that the modification is necessary for purposes connected with preventing or restricting involvement by the controlled person in terrorism-related activity; and
  (b) in the case of an appeal against a decision on an application for the modification of an obligation, his decision that the obligation continues to be necessary for that purpose.

(6) In determining the matters mentioned in subsections (4) and (5) the court must apply the principles applicable on an application for judicial review.

---

[14] Repealed by the Serious Organised Crime and Police Act 2005, s 174(2), Sch 10, Pt 2.

(7) If the court determines on an appeal under this section that a decision of the Secretary of State was flawed, its only powers are

(a) power to quash the renewal of the order;

(b) power to quash one or more obligations imposed by the order; and

(c) power to give directions to the Secretary of State for the revocation of the order or for the modification of the obligations it imposes.

(8) In every other case, the court must dismiss the appeal.

11 Jurisdiction and appeals in relation to control order decisions etc

(1) Control order decisions and derogation matters are not to be questioned in any legal proceedings other than

(a) proceedings in the court; or

(b) proceedings on appeal from such proceedings.

(2) The court is the appropriate tribunal for the purposes of section 7 of the Human Rights Act 1998 (c 42) in relation to proceedings all or any part of which call a control order decision or derogation matter into question.

(3) No appeal shall lie from any determination of the court in control order proceedings, except on a question of law.

(4) No appeal by any person other than the Secretary of State shall lie from any determination

(a) on an application for permission under section 3(1)(a); or

(b) on a reference under section 3(3)(a).

(5) The Schedule to this Act (which makes provision relating to and for the purposes of control order proceedings and proceedings on appeal from such proceedings) has effect.

(6) In this Act "control order proceedings" means

(a) proceedings on an application for permission under section 3(1)(a);

(b) proceedings on a reference under section 3(3)(a);

(c) proceedings on a hearing in pursuance of directions under section 3(2)(c) or (6)(b) or (c);

(d) proceedings on an application to the court by any person for the making, renewal, modification or revocation of a derogating control order;

(e) proceedings on an application to extend the detention of a person under section 5;

(f) proceedings at or in connection with a hearing to determine whether to confirm a derogating control order (with or without modifications);

(g) proceedings on an appeal under section 10;

(h) proceedings in the court by virtue of subsection (2);

(i) any other proceedings in the court for questioning a control order decision, a derogation matter or the arrest or detention of a person under section 5;

(j) proceedings on an application made by virtue of rules of court under paragraph 5(1) of the Schedule to this Act (application for order requiring anonymity for the controlled person).

(7) In this section "control order decision" means

(a) a decision made by the Secretary of State in exercise or performance of any power or duty of his under any of sections 1 to 8 or for the purposes of or in connection with the exercise or performance of any such power or duty;

(b) a decision by any other person to give a direction, consent or approval, or to issue a demand, for the purposes of any obligation imposed by a control order; or

(c) a decision by any person that is made for the purposes of or in connection with the exercise of his power to give such a direction, consent or approval or to issue such a demand.

(8) In this section "derogation matter" means

(a) a derogation by the United Kingdom from the Human Rights Convention which relates to infringement of a person's right to liberty under Article 5 in consequence of obligations imposed on him by a control order or of his arrest or detention under section 5; or

(b) the designation of such a derogation under section 14(1) of the Human Rights Act 1998 (c 42).

12 Effect of court's decisions on convictions

(1) This section applies where
  (a) a control order, a renewal of a control order or an obligation imposed by a control order is quashed by the court in control order proceedings, or on an appeal from a determination in such proceedings; and
  (b) before it was quashed a person had been convicted by virtue of section 9(1) or (2) of an offence of which he could not have been convicted had the order, renewal or (as the case may be) obligation been quashed before the proceedings for the offence were brought.

(2) The person convicted may appeal against the conviction
  (a) in the case of a conviction on indictment in England and Wales or Northern Ireland, to the Court of Appeal;
  (b) in the case of a conviction on indictment or summary conviction in Scotland, to the High Court of Justiciary;
  (c) in the case of a summary conviction in England and Wales, to the Crown Court; and
  (d) in the case of a summary conviction in Northern Ireland, to the county court.

(3) On an appeal under this section to any court, that court must allow the appeal and quash the conviction.

(4) An appeal under this section to the Court of Appeal against a conviction on indictment
  (a) may be brought irrespective of whether the appellant has previously appealed against his conviction;
  (b) may not be brought more than 28 days after the date of the quashing of the order, renewal or obligation; and
  (c) is to be treated as an appeal under section 1 of the Criminal Appeal Act 1968 (c 19) or, in Northern Ireland, under section 1 of the Criminal Appeal (Northern Ireland) Act 1980 (c 47), but does not require leave in either case.

(5) An appeal under this section to the High Court of Justiciary against a conviction on indictment
  (a) may be brought irrespective of whether the appellant has previously appealed against his conviction;
  (b) may not be brought more than two weeks after the date of the quashing of the order, renewal or obligation; and
  (c) is to be treated as an appeal under section 106 of the Criminal Procedure (Scotland) Act 1995 (c 46) for which leave has been granted.

(6) An appeal under this section to the High Court of Justiciary against a summary conviction
  (a) may be brought irrespective of whether the appellant pleaded guilty;
  (b) may be brought irrespective of whether the appellant has previously appealed against his conviction;
  (c) may not be brought more than two weeks after the date of the quashing of the order, renewal or obligation;
  (d) is to be by note of appeal, which shall state the ground of appeal;
  (e) is to be treated as an appeal for which leave has been granted under Part 10 of the Criminal Procedure (Scotland) Act 1995; and
  (f) must be in accordance with such procedure as the High Court of Justiciary may, by Act of Adjournal, determine.

(7) An appeal under this section to the Crown Court or to the county court in Northern Ireland against a summary conviction
  (a) may be brought irrespective of whether the appellant pleaded guilty;
  (b) may be brought irrespective of whether he has previously appealed against his conviction or made an application in respect of the conviction under section 111 of the Magistrates' Courts Act 1980 (c 43) or Article 146 of the Magistrates' Courts (Northern Ireland) Order 1981 (SI 1981/1675 (NI 26)) (case stated);
  (c) may not be brought more than 21 days after the date of the quashing of the order, renewal or obligation; and

(d) is to be treated as an appeal under section 108(1)(b) of that Act or, in Northern Ireland, under Article 140(1)(b) of that Order.

(8) In section 133(5) of the Criminal Justice Act 1988 (c 33) (compensation for miscarriages of justice), at the end of paragraph (c) insert

"or

(d) on an appeal under section 12 of the Prevention of Terrorism Act 2005."

Supplemental

13 Duration of sections 1 to 9

(1) Except so far as otherwise provided under this section, sections 1 to 9 expire at the end of the period of 12 months beginning with the day on which this Act is passed.

(2) The Secretary of State may, by order made by statutory instrument

(a) repeal sections 1 to 9;

(b) at any time revive those sections for a period not exceeding one year; or

(c) provide that those sections

(i) are not to expire at the time when they would otherwise expire under subsection (1) or in accordance with an order under this subsection; but

(ii) are to continue in force after that time for a period not exceeding one year.

(3) Before making an order under this section the Secretary of State must consult

(a) the person appointed for the purposes of section 14(2);

(b) the Intelligence Services Commissioner; and

(c) the Director-General of the Security Service.

(4) No order may be made by the Secretary of State under this section unless a draft of it has been laid before Parliament and approved by a resolution of each House.

(5) Subsection (4) does not apply to an order that contains a declaration by the Secretary of State that the order needs, by reason of urgency, to be made without the approval required by that subsection.

(6) An order under this section that contains such a declaration

(a) must be laid before Parliament after being made; and

(b) if not approved by a resolution of each House before the end of 40 days beginning with the day on which the order was made, ceases to have effect at the end of that period.

(7) Where an order ceases to have effect in accordance with subsection (6), that does not

(a) affect anything previously done in reliance on the order; or

(b) prevent the making of a new order to the same or similar effect.

(8) Where sections 1 to 9 expire or are repealed at any time by virtue of this section, that does not prevent or otherwise affect

(a) the court's consideration of a reference made before that time under subsection (3)(a) of section 3;

(b) the holding or continuation after that time of any hearing in pursuance of directions under subsection (2)(c) or (6)(b) or (c) of that section;

(c) the holding or continuation after that time of a hearing to determine whether to confirm a derogating control order (with or without modifications); or

(d) the bringing or continuation after that time of any appeal, or further appeal, relating to a decision in any proceedings mentioned in paragraphs (a) to (c) of this subsection;

but proceedings may be begun or continued by virtue of this subsection so far only as they are for the purpose of determining whether a certificate of the Secretary of State, a control order or an obligation imposed by such an order should be quashed or treated as quashed.

(9) Nothing in this Act about the period for which a control order is to have effect or is renewed enables such an order to continue in force after the provision under which it was made or last renewed has expired or been repealed by virtue of this section.

(10) In subsection (6) "40 days" means 40 days computed as provided for in section 7(1) of the Statutory Instruments Act 1946 (c 36).

14 Reporting and review

(1) As soon as reasonably practicable after the end of every relevant 3 month period, the Secretary of State must
   (a) prepare a report about his exercise of the control order powers during that period; and
   (b) lay a copy of that report before Parliament.

(2) The Secretary of State must also appoint a person to review the operation of this Act.

(3) As soon as reasonably practicable after the end of
   (a) the period of 9 months beginning with the day on which this Act is passed, and
   (b) every 12 month period which ends with the first or a subsequent anniversary of the end of the period mentioned in the preceding paragraph and is a period during the whole or a part of which sections 1 to 9 of this Act were in force,
the person so appointed must carry out a review of the operation of this Act during that period.

(4) The person who conducts a review under this section must send the Secretary of State a report on its outcome as soon as reasonably practicable after completing the review.

(5) That report must also contain the opinion of the person making it on
   (a) the implications for the operation of this Act of any proposal made by the Secretary of State for the amendment of the law relating to terrorism; and
   (b) the extent (if any) to which the Secretary of State has made use of his power by virtue of section 3(1)(b) to make non-derogating control orders in urgent cases without the permission of the court.

(6) On receiving a report under subsection (4), the Secretary of State must lay a copy of it before Parliament.

(7) The Secretary of State may pay the expenses of a person appointed to carry out a review and may also pay him such allowances as the Secretary of State determines.

(8) In this section
"control order powers" means
   (a) the powers of the Secretary of State under this Act to make, renew, modify and revoke control orders; and
   (b) his powers to apply to the court for the making, renewal, revocation or modification of derogating control orders;
"relevant 3 month period" means
   (a) the period of 3 months beginning with the passing of this Act;
   (b) a period of 3 months beginning with a time which
     (i) is the beginning of a period for which sections 1 to 9 are revived by an order under section 13; and
     (ii) falls more than 3 months after the time when those sections were last in force before being revived;
   (c) a 3 month period which begins with the end of a previous relevant 3 month period and is a period during the whole or a part of which those sections are in force.

15 General interpretation

(1) In this Act
"act" and "conduct" include omissions and statements;
"act of terrorism" includes anything constituting an action taken for the purposes of terrorism, within the meaning of the Terrorism Act 2000 (c 11) (see section 1(5) of that Act);
"apparatus" includes any equipment, machinery or device and any wire or cable, together with any software used with it;

"article" and "information" include documents and other records, and software;

"contravene" includes fail to comply, and cognate expressions are to be construed accordingly;

"control order" has the meaning given by section 1(1);

"control order proceedings" has the meaning given by section 11(6);

"the controlled person", in relation to a control order, means the individual on whom the order imposes obligations;

"the court"

(a) in relation to proceedings relating to a control order in the case of which the controlled person is a person whose principal place of residence is in Scotland, means the Outer House of the Court of Session;

(b) in relation to proceedings relating to a control order in the case of which the controlled person is a person whose principal place of residence is in Northern Ireland, means the High Court in Northern Ireland; and

(c) in any other case, means the High Court in England and Wales;

"derogating control order" means a control order imposing obligations that are or include derogating obligations;

"derogating obligation", "designated derogation" and "designation order" have the meanings given by section 1(10);

"the Human Rights Convention" means the Convention within the meaning of the Human Rights Act 1998 (c 42) (see section 21(1) of that Act);

"modification" includes omission, addition or alteration, and cognate expressions are to be construed accordingly;

"non-derogating control order" means a control order made by the Secretary of State;

"passport" means

(a) a United Kingdom passport (within the meaning of the Immigration Act 1971 (c 77));

(b) a passport issued by or on behalf of the authorities of a country or territory outside the United Kingdom, or by or on behalf of an international organisation;

(c) a document that can be used (in some or all circumstances) instead of a passport;

"premises" includes any vehicle, vessel, aircraft or hovercraft;

"the public" means the public in the whole or a part of the United Kingdom or the public in another country or territory, or any section of the public;

"specified", in relation to a control order, means specified in that order or falling within a description so specified;

"terrorism" has the same meaning as in the Terrorism Act 2000 (c 11) (see section 1(1) to (4) of that Act);

"terrorism-related activity" and, in relation to such activity, "involvement" are to be construed in accordance with section 1(9).

(2) A power under this Act to quash a control order, the renewal of such an order or an obligation imposed by such an order includes power

(a) in England and Wales or Northern Ireland, to stay the quashing of the order, renewal or obligation pending an appeal, or further appeal, against the decision to quash; and

(b) in Scotland, to determine that the quashing is of no effect pending such an appeal or further appeal.

(3) Every power of the Secretary of State or of the court to revoke a control order or to modify the obligations imposed by such an order

(a) includes power to provide for the revocation or modification to take effect from such time as the Secretary of State or (as the case may be) the court may determine; and

(b) in the case of a revocation by the court (including a revocation in pursuance of section 7(7)) includes power to postpone the effect of the revocation either pending an appeal or for the purpose of giving the Secretary of State an opportunity to decide whether to exercise his own powers to make a control order against the individual in question.

(4) For the purposes of this Act a failure by the Secretary of State to consider an application by the controlled person for

(a) the revocation of a control order, or

(b) the modification of an obligation imposed by such an order,

is to be treated as a decision by the Secretary of State not to revoke or (as the case may be) not to modify the order.

16 Other supplemental provisions

(1) This Act may be cited as the Prevention of Terrorism Act 2005.

(2) The following provisions are repealed

(a) sections 21 to 32 of the Anti-terrorism, Crime and Security Act 2001 (c 24) (suspected international terrorists);

(b) in section 1(4) of the Special Immigration Appeals Commission Act 1997 (c 68), paragraph (b) (which refers to section 30 of the 2001 Act) and the word "or" immediately preceding it;

(c) section 62(15) and (16) of the Nationality, Immigration and Asylum Act 2002 (c 41) and paragraph 30 of Schedule 7 to that Act (which amended sections 23, 24 and 27 of the 2001 Act); and

(d) section 32 of the Asylum and Immigration (Treatment of Claimants, etc) Act 2004 (c 19) (which amended sections 24 and 27 of the 2001 Act).

(3) Subsection (2) comes into force on 14th March 2005.

(4) The repeals made by this Act do not prevent or otherwise affect

(a) the continuation of any appeal to the Special Immigration Appeals Commission under section 25(1) of the Anti-terrorism, Crime and Security Act 2001 that has been brought but not concluded before the commencement of those repeals;

(b) the bringing or continuation of a further appeal relating to a decision of that Commission on such an appeal or on any other appeal brought under section 25(1) of that Act before the commencement of those repeals; or

(c) any proceedings resulting from a decision on a further appeal from such a decision;

but no other proceedings before that Commission under Part 4 of that Act, nor any appeal or further appeal relating to any such other proceedings, may be brought or continued at any time after the commencement of the repeals.

(5) The Secretary of State may enter into such contracts and other arrangements with other persons as he considers appropriate for securing their assistance in connection with any monitoring, by electronic or other means, that he considers needs to be carried out in connection with obligations that have been or may be imposed by or under control orders.

(6) There shall be paid out of money provided by Parliament

(a) any expenditure incurred by the Secretary of State by virtue of this Act; and

(b) any increase attributable to this Act in the sums payable out of such money under any other Act.

(7) This Act extends to Northern Ireland.

(8) Her Majesty may by Order in Council direct that this Act shall extend, with such modifications as appear to Her Majesty to be appropriate, to any of the Channel Islands or the Isle of Man.

SCHEDULE   Section 11

CONTROL ORDER PROCEEDINGS ETC

Introductory

1 (1) In this Schedule "the relevant powers" means the powers to make rules of court for regulating the practice and procedure to be followed in proceedings in the court, the Court of

Appeal or the Inner House of the Court of Session, so far as those powers are exercisable in relation to

(a) control order proceedings; or

(b) relevant appeal proceedings.

(2) In this Schedule "relevant appeal proceedings" means proceedings in the Court of Appeal or Inner House of the Court of Session on an appeal relating to any control order proceedings.

General duty applying to exercise of the relevant powers

2 A person exercising the relevant powers must have regard, in particular, to

(a) the need to secure that the making and renewal of control orders and the imposition and modification of the obligations contained in such orders are properly reviewed; and

(b) the need to secure that disclosures of information are not made where they would be contrary to the public interest.

Initial exercise of relevant powers

3 (1) This paragraph applies

(a) on the first occasion after the passing of this Act on which the relevant powers are exercised in relation to control order proceedings and relevant appeal proceedings in England and Wales; and

(b) on the first occasion after the passing of this Act on which they are so exercised in relation to control order proceedings and relevant appeal proceedings in Northern Ireland.

(2) On each of those occasions

(a) the relevant powers may be exercised by the Lord Chancellor, instead of by the person by whom they are otherwise exercisable; and

(b) the Lord Chancellor is not required, before exercising the powers, to undertake any consultation that would be required in the case of rules made by that person.

(3) The Lord Chancellor must

(a) consult the Lord Chief Justice of England and Wales before making any rules under this paragraph in relation to England and Wales; and

(b) consult the Lord Chief Justice of Northern Ireland before making any rules under this paragraph in relation to Northern Ireland.

(4) The requirements of sub-paragraph (3) may be satisfied by consultation that took place wholly or partly before the passing of this Act.

(5) Rules of court made by the Lord Chancellor by virtue of this paragraph

(a) must be laid before Parliament; and

(b) if not approved by a resolution of each House before the end of 40 days beginning with the day on which they were made, cease to have effect at the end of that period.

(6) Where rules cease to have effect in accordance with sub-paragraph (5)

(a) that does not affect anything previously done in reliance on the rules;

(b) the Lord Chancellor is to have power again to exercise the relevant powers, in relation to the proceedings in question, instead of the person by whom they are otherwise exercisable;

(c) he may exercise them on that occasion without undertaking any consultation that would be required in the case of rules made by that person; and

(d) the rules made by the Lord Chancellor on that occasion may include rules to the same or similar effect.

(7) The following provisions do not apply to rules made by the Lord Chancellor by virtue of this paragraph

(a) section 3(2) of the Civil Procedure Act 1997 (c 12) (negative resolution procedure);

(b) section 56 of the Judicature (Northern Ireland) Act 1978 (c 23) (statutory rules procedure).

(8) In sub-paragraph (5) "40 days" means 40 days computed as provided for in section 7(1) of the Statutory Instruments Act 1946 (c 36).

Special powers to make rules of court

4 (1) Rules of court made in exercise of the relevant powers may, in particular

   (a) make provision about the mode of proof in control order proceedings and about evidence in such proceedings;

   (b) enable or require such proceedings to be determined without a hearing; and

   (c) make provision about legal representation in such proceedings.

(2) Rules of court made in exercise of the relevant powers may also, in particular

   (a) make provision enabling control order proceedings or relevant appeal proceedings to take place without full particulars of the reasons for decisions to which the proceedings relate being given to a relevant party to the proceedings or his legal representative (if he has one);

   (b) make provision enabling the relevant court to conduct proceedings in the absence of any person, including a relevant party to the proceedings and his legal representative (if he has one);

   (c) make provision about the functions in control order proceedings and relevant appeal proceedings of persons appointed under paragraph 7; and

   (d) make provision enabling the relevant court to give a relevant party to control order proceedings or relevant appeal proceedings a summary of evidence taken in his absence.

(3) Rules of court made in exercise of the relevant powers must secure

   (a) that in control order proceedings and relevant appeal proceedings the Secretary of State is required (subject to rules made under the following paragraphs) to disclose all relevant material;

   (b) that the Secretary of State has the opportunity to make an application to the relevant court for permission not to disclose relevant material otherwise than to that court and persons appointed under paragraph 7;

   (c) that such an application is always considered in the absence of every relevant party to the proceedings and of his legal representative (if he has one);

   (d) that the relevant court is required to give permission for material not to be disclosed where it considers that the disclosure of the material would be contrary to the public interest;

   (e) that, where permission is given by the relevant court not to disclose material, it must consider requiring the Secretary of State to provide the relevant party and his legal representative (if he has one) with a summary of the material;

   (f) that the relevant court is required to ensure that such a summary does not contain information or other material the disclosure of which would be contrary to the public interest;

   (g) that provision satisfying the requirements of sub-paragraph (4) applies where the Secretary of State does not have the relevant court's permission to withhold relevant material from a relevant party to the proceedings or his legal representative (if he has one), or is required to provide a summary of such material to that party or his legal representative.

(4) The provision that satisfies the requirements of this sub-paragraph is provision which, in a case where the Secretary of State elects not to disclose the relevant material or (as the case may be) not to provide the summary, authorises the relevant court

   (a) if it considers that the relevant material or anything that is required to be summarised might be of assistance to a relevant party in relation to a matter under consideration by that court, to give directions for securing that the matter is withdrawn from the consideration of that court; and

(b) in any other case, to ensure that the Secretary of State does not rely in the proceeding on the material or (as the case may be) on what is required to be summarised.

(5) In this paragraph "relevant material", in relation to any proceedings, means

(a) any information or other material that is available to the Secretary of State and relevant to the matters under consideration in those proceedings; or

(b) the reasons for decisions to which the proceedings relate.

Application for anonymity for controlled person

5 (1) Rules of court made in exercise of the relevant powers may provide for

(a) the making by the Secretary of State or the controlled person [...]¹⁵ of an application to the court for an order requiring anonymity for that person; and

(b) the making by the court, on such an application, of an order requiring such anonymity; and the provision made by the rules may allow the application and the order to be made irrespective of whether any other control order proceedings have been begun in the court.

(2) Rules of court may provide for the Court of Appeal or the Inner House of the Court of Session to make an order in connection with any relevant appeal proceedings requiring anonymity for the controlled person.

(3) In sub-paragraphs (1) and (2) the references, in relation to a court, to an order requiring anonymity for the controlled person are references to an order by that court which imposes such prohibition or restriction as it thinks fit on the disclosure

(a) by such persons as the court specifies or describes, or

(b) by persons generally,

of the identity of the controlled person or of any information that would tend to identify him.

[(4) In relation to a time before the control order has been made references in this paragraph to "the controlled person" shall be read as references to the person in respect of whom the Secretary of State has made an application to the court for (as the case may be)

(a) permission to make a non-derogating control order under section 3(1)(a), or

(b) the making of a derogating control order under section 4(1).]¹⁶

Use of advisers

6 (1) In any control order proceedings the court may, if it thinks fit

(a) call in aid one or more advisers appointed for the purpose by the Lord Chancellor; and

(b) hear and dispose of the proceedings with the assistance of the adviser or advisers.

[(1A)The Lord Chancellor may appoint an adviser under this paragraph only with the concurrence of the appropriate senior judge.]¹⁷

(2) Rules of court may regulate the use of advisers in accordance with the power conferred by this paragraph.

(3) The Lord Chancellor may, out of money provided by Parliament, pay such remuneration, expenses and allowances to advisers appointed for the purposes of this paragraph as he may determine.

[(4) In this paragraph "the appropriate senior judge" means

(a) in relation to an adviser who may be called in aid wholly or mainly in Scotland, the Lord President of the Court of Session;

---

¹⁵ Repealed by the Counter-Terrorism Act 2008, ss 81(1), (2), 99, Sch 9, Pt 5.

¹⁶ Inserted by the Counter-Terrorism Act 2008, s 81(1), (3).

¹⁷ Inserted by SI 2006/1016, art 2, Sch 1, para 29(1), (2).

      (b) in relation to an adviser who may be called in aid wholly or mainly in Northern Ireland, the Lord Chief Justice of Northern Ireland;

      (c) in any other case, the Lord Chief Justice of England and Wales.

(5) The Lord Chief Justice of England and Wales may nominate a judicial office holder (as defined in section 109(4) of the Constitutional Reform Act 2005) to exercise any of his functions under this paragraph.

(6) The Lord President of the Court of Session may nominate a judge of the Court of Session who is a member of the First or Second Division of the Inner House of that Court to exercise his functions under this paragraph.

(7) The Lord Chief Justice of Northern Ireland may nominate any of the following to exercise his functions under this paragraph

      (a) the holder of one of the offices listed in Schedule 1 to the Justice (Northern Ireland) Act 2002;

      (b) a Lord Justice of Appeal (as defined in section 88 of that Act).][18]

Special representation in control order proceedings

7 (1) The relevant law officer may appoint a person to represent the interests of a relevant party to relevant proceedings in any of those proceedings from which that party and his legal representative (if he has one) are excluded.

(2) In sub-paragraph (1) "relevant proceedings" means

      (a) control order proceedings; or

      (b) proceedings on an appeal or further appeal relating to control order proceedings.

(3) A person may be appointed under this paragraph

      (a) in the case of an appointment by the Attorney General, only if he has a general legal qualification for the purposes of section 71 of the Courts and Legal Services Act 1990 (c 41);

      (b) in the case of an appointment by the Advocate General for Scotland, only if he is a person with appropriate rights of audience in Scotland; and

      (c) in the case of an appointment by the Advocate General for Northern Ireland, only if he is a member of the Bar of Northern Ireland.

(4) In sub-paragraph (3) "person with appropriate rights of audience in Scotland" means

      (a) an advocate; or

      (b) a solicitor with rights of audience by virtue of section 25A of the Solicitors (Scotland) Act 1980 (c 46) in the Court of Session or the High Court of Justiciary.

(5) A person appointed under this paragraph is not to be responsible to the person whose interests he is appointed to represent.

(6) In this paragraph "the relevant law officer" means

      (a) in relation to control order proceedings in England and Wales or proceedings on an appeal or further appeal relating to such proceedings, the Attorney General;

      (b) in relation to proceedings in Scotland or proceedings on an appeal or further appeal relating to such proceedings, the Advocate General for Scotland;

      (c) in relation to proceedings in Northern Ireland or proceedings on an appeal or further appeal relating to such proceedings, the Advocate General for Northern Ireland.

(7) In relation to any time before the coming into force of section 27 of the Justice (Northern Ireland) Act 2002 (c 26), references in this paragraph to the Advocate General for Northern Ireland are to have effect as references to the Attorney General for Northern Ireland.

---

[18] Inserted by SI 2006/1016, art 2, Sch 1, para 29(1), (3).

Effect of court orders

8 (1) Where
   (a) a control order,
   (b) the renewal of such an order, or
   (c) an obligation imposed by such an order,

   is quashed, the order, renewal or (as the case may be) obligation shall be treated for the purposes of section 9(1) and (2) as never having been made or imposed.

   (2) A decision by the court or on appeal from the court
   (a) to quash a control order, the renewal of a control order or an obligation imposed by such an order, or
   (b) to give directions to the Secretary of State in relation to such an order,

   does not prevent the Secretary of State from exercising any power of his to make a new control order to the same or similar effect or from relying, in whole or in part, on the same matters for the purpose of making that new order.

Interception evidence

9 (1) Section 18 of the Regulation of Investigatory Powers Act 2000 (c 23) (exceptions to exclusion of interception matters from legal proceedings) is amended as follows.
   (2) In subsection (1), after paragraph (d) insert
   "(da) any control order proceedings (within the meaning of the Prevention of Terrorism Act 2005) or any proceedings arising out of such proceedings;" .
   (3) In subsection (2) (persons disclosures to whom continue to be prohibited despite section 18), for "paragraph (e) or (f)" substitute "paragraphs (da) to (f)".
   (4) In that subsection, before paragraph (a) insert
   "(za) in the case of any proceedings falling within paragraph (da) to
         (i) a person who, within the meaning of the Schedule to the Prevention of Terrorism Act 2005, is or was a relevant party to the control order proceedings; or
         (ii) any person who for the purposes of any proceedings so falling (but otherwise than by virtue of an appointment under paragraph 7 of that Schedule) represents a person falling within sub-paragraph (i);" .

Allocation to Queen's Bench Division

10 In paragraph 2 of Schedule 1 to the Supreme Court Act 1981 (c 54) (business allocated to Queen's Bench Division), after sub-paragraph (b) insert
   "(ba) all control order proceedings (within the meaning of the Prevention of Terrorism Act 2005);".

Interpretation of Schedule

11 In this Schedule
   "legal representative", in relation to a relevant party to proceedings, does not include a person appointed under paragraph 7 to represent that party's interests;
   "relevant appeal proceedings" has the meaning given by paragraph 1(2);
   "relevant court"
   (a) in relation to control order proceedings, means the court; and
   (b) in relation to relevant appeal proceedings, means the Court of Appeal or the Inner House of the Court of Session;
   "relevant party", in relation to control order proceedings or relevant appeal proceedings, means any party to the proceedings other than the Secretary of State;
   "relevant powers" has the meaning given by paragraph 1(1).

APPENDIX 4

Terrorism Act 2006

An Act to make provision for and about offences relating to conduct carried out, or capable of being carried out, for purposes connected with terrorism; to amend enactments relating to terrorism; to amend the Intelligence Services Act 1994 and the Regulation of Investigatory Powers Act 2000; and for connected purposes.

(30th March 2006)

PART I
OFFENCES

Encouragement etc of terrorism

1 Encouragement of terrorism

(1) This section applies to a statement that is likely to be understood by some or all of the members of the public to whom it is published as a direct or indirect encouragement or other inducement to them to the commission, preparation or instigation of acts of terrorism or Convention offences.

(2) A person commits an offence if

  (a) he publishes a statement to which this section applies or causes another to publish such a statement; and

  (b) at the time he publishes it or causes it to be published, he

    (i) intends members of the public to be directly or indirectly encouraged or otherwise induced by the statement to commit, prepare or instigate acts of terrorism or Convention offences; or

    (ii) is reckless as to whether members of the public will be directly or indirectly encouraged or otherwise induced by the statement to commit, prepare or instigate such acts or offences.

(3) For the purposes of this section, the statements that are likely to be understood by members of the public as indirectly encouraging the commission or preparation of acts of terrorism or Convention offences include every statement which

  (a) glorifies the commission or preparation (whether in the past, in the future or generally) of such acts or offences; and

  (b) is a statement from which those members of the public could reasonably be expected to infer that what is being glorified is being glorified as conduct that should be emulated by them in existing circumstances.

(4) For the purposes of this section the questions how a statement is likely to be understood and what members of the public could reasonably be expected to infer from it must be determined having regard both

  (a) to the contents of the statement as a whole; and

  (b) to the circumstances and manner of its publication.

(5) It is irrelevant for the purposes of subsections (1) to (3)

    (a) whether anything mentioned in those subsections relates to the commission, preparation or instigation of one or more particular acts of terrorism or Convention offences, of acts of terrorism or Convention offences of a particular description or of acts of terrorism or Convention offences generally; and,

    (b) whether any person is in fact encouraged or induced by the statement to commit, prepare or instigate any such act or offence.

(6) In proceedings for an offence under this section against a person in whose case it is not proved that he intended the statement directly or indirectly to encourage or otherwise induce the commission, preparation or instigation of acts of terrorism or Convention offences, it is a defence for him to show

    (a) that the statement neither expressed his views nor had his endorsement (whether by virtue of section 3 or otherwise); and

    (b) that it was clear, in all the circumstances of the statement's publication, that it did not express his views and (apart from the possibility of his having been given and failed to comply with a notice under subsection (3) of that section) did not have his endorsement.

(7) A person guilty of an offence under this section shall be liable

    (a) on conviction on indictment, to imprisonment for a term not exceeding 7 years or to a fine, or to both;

    (b) on summary conviction in England and Wales, to imprisonment for a term not exceeding 12 months or to a fine not exceeding the statutory maximum, or to both;

    (c) on summary conviction in Scotland or Northern Ireland, to imprisonment for a term not exceeding 6 months or to a fine not exceeding the statutory maximum, or to both.

(8) In relation to an offence committed before the commencement of section 154(1) of the Criminal Justice Act 2003 (c 44), the reference in subsection (7)(b) to 12 months is to be read as a reference to 6 months.

2 Dissemination of terrorist publications

(1) A person commits an offence if he engages in conduct falling within subsection (2) and, at the time he does so

    (a) he intends an effect of his conduct to be a direct or indirect encouragement or other inducement to the commission, preparation or instigation of acts of terrorism;

    (b) he intends an effect of his conduct to be the provision of assistance in the commission or preparation of such acts; or

    (c) he is reckless as to whether his conduct has an effect mentioned in paragraph (a) or (b).

(2) For the purposes of this section a person engages in conduct falling within this subsection if he

    (a) distributes or circulates a terrorist publication;

    (b) gives, sells or lends such a publication;

    (c) offers such a publication for sale or loan;

    (d) provides a service to others that enables them to obtain, read, listen to or look at such a publication, or to acquire it by means of a gift, sale or loan;

    (e) transmits the contents of such a publication electronically; or

    (f) has such a publication in his possession with a view to its becoming the subject of conduct falling within any of paragraphs (a) to (e).

(3) For the purposes of this section a publication is a terrorist publication, in relation to conduct falling within subsection (2), if matter contained in it is likely

    (a) to be understood, by some or all of the persons to whom it is or may become available as a consequence of that conduct, as a direct or indirect encouragement or other inducement to them to the commission, preparation or instigation of acts of terrorism; or

(b) to be useful in the commission or preparation of such acts and to be understood, by some or all of those persons, as contained in the publication, or made available to them, wholly or mainly for the purpose of being so useful to them.

(4) For the purposes of this section matter that is likely to be understood by a person as indirectly encouraging the commission or preparation of acts of terrorism includes any matter which

(a) glorifies the commission or preparation (whether in the past, in the future or generally) of such acts; and

(b) is matter from which that person could reasonably be expected to infer that what is being glorified is being glorified as conduct that should be emulated by him in existing circumstances.

(5) For the purposes of this section the question whether a publication is a terrorist publication in relation to particular conduct must be determined

(a) as at the time of that conduct; and

(b) having regard both to the contents of the publication as a whole and to the circumstances in which that conduct occurs.

(6) In subsection (1) references to the effect of a person's conduct in relation to a terrorist publication include references to an effect of the publication on one or more persons to whom it is or may become available as a consequence of that conduct.

(7) It is irrelevant for the purposes of this section whether anything mentioned in subsections (1) to (4) is in relation to the commission, preparation or instigation of one or more particular acts of terrorism, of acts of terrorism of a particular description or of acts of terrorism generally.

(8) For the purposes of this section it is also irrelevant, in relation to matter contained in any article whether any person

(a) is in fact encouraged or induced by that matter to commit, prepare or instigate acts of terrorism; or

(b) in fact makes use of it in the commission or preparation of such acts.

(9) In proceedings for an offence under this section against a person in respect of conduct to which subsection (10) applies, it is a defence for him to show

(a) that the matter by reference to which the publication in question was a terrorist publication neither expressed his views nor had his endorsement (whether by virtue of section 3 or otherwise); and

(b) that it was clear, in all the circumstances of the conduct, that that matter did not express his views and (apart from the possibility of his having been given and failed to comply with a notice under subsection (3) of that section) did not have his endorsement.

(10) This subsection applies to the conduct of a person to the extent that

(a) the publication to which his conduct related contained matter by reference to which it was a terrorist publication by virtue of subsection (3)(a); and

(b) that person is not proved to have engaged in that conduct with the intention specified in subsection (1)(a).

(11) A person guilty of an offence under this section shall be liable

(a) on conviction on indictment, to imprisonment for a term not exceeding 7 years or to a fine, or to both;

(b) on summary conviction in England and Wales, to imprisonment for a term not exceeding 12 months or to a fine not exceeding the statutory maximum, or to both;

(c) on summary conviction in Scotland or Northern Ireland, to imprisonment for a term not exceeding 6 months or to a fine not exceeding the statutory maximum, or to both.

(12) In relation to an offence committed before the commencement of section 154(1) of the Criminal Justice Act 2003 (c 44), the reference in subsection (11)(b) to 12 months is to be read as a reference to 6 months.

(13) In this section

"lend" includes let on hire, and "loan" is to be construed accordingly;

"publication" means an article or record of any description that contains any of the following, or any combination of them

(a) matter to be read;

(b) matter to be listened to;

(c) matter to be looked at or watched.

3 Application of ss 1 and 2 to internet activity etc

(1) This section applies for the purposes of sections 1 and 2 in relation to cases where

(a) a statement is published or caused to be published in the course of, or in connection with, the provision or use of a service provided electronically; or

(b) conduct falling within section 2(2) was in the course of, or in connection with, the provision or use of such a service.

(2) The cases in which the statement, or the article or record to which the conduct relates, is to be regarded as having the endorsement of a person ("the relevant person") at any time include a case in which

(a) a constable has given him a notice under subsection (3);

(b) that time falls more than 2 working days after the day on which the notice was given; and

(c) the relevant person has failed, without reasonable excuse, to comply with the notice.

(3) A notice under this subsection is a notice which

(a) declares that, in the opinion of the constable giving it, the statement or the article or record is unlawfully terrorism-related;

(b) requires the relevant person to secure that the statement or the article or record, so far as it is so related, is not available to the public or is modified so as no longer to be so related;

(c) warns the relevant person that a failure to comply with the notice within 2 working days will result in the statement, or the article or record, being regarded as having his endorsement; and

(d) explains how, under subsection (4), he may become liable by virtue of the notice if the statement, or the article or record, becomes available to the public after he has complied with the notice.

(4) Where

(a) a notice under subsection (3) has been given to the relevant person in respect of a statement, or an article or record, and he has complied with it, but

(b) he subsequently publishes or causes to be published a statement which is, or is for all practical purposes, the same or to the same effect as the statement to which the notice related, or to matter contained in the article or record to which it related, (a "repeat statement");

the requirements of subsection (2)(a) to (c) shall be regarded as satisfied in the case of the repeat statement in relation to the times of its subsequent publication by the relevant person.

(5) In proceedings against a person for an offence under section 1 or 2 the requirements of subsection (2)(a) to (c) are not, in his case, to be regarded as satisfied in relation to any time by virtue of subsection (4) if he shows that he

(a) has, before that time, taken every step he reasonably could to prevent a repeat statement from becoming available to the public and to ascertain whether it does; and

(b) was, at that time, a person to whom subsection (6) applied.

(6) This subsection applies to a person at any time when he

(a) is not aware of the publication of the repeat statement; or

(b) having become aware of its publication, has taken every step that he reasonably could to secure that it either ceased to be available to the public or was modified as mentioned in subsection (3)(b).

(7) For the purposes of this section a statement or an article or record is unlawfully terrorism-related if it constitutes, or if matter contained in the article or record constitutes

    (a) something that is likely to be understood, by any one or more of the persons to whom it has or may become available, as a direct or indirect encouragement or other inducement to the commission, preparation or instigation of acts of terrorism or Convention offences; or

    (b) information which

        (i) is likely to be useful to any one or more of those persons in the commission or preparation of such acts; and

        (ii) is in a form or context in which it is likely to be understood by any one or more of those persons as being wholly or mainly for the purpose of being so useful.

(8) The reference in subsection (7) to something that is likely to be understood as an indirect encouragement to the commission or preparation of acts of terrorism or Convention offences includes anything which is likely to be understood as

    (a) the glorification of the commission or preparation (whether in the past, in the future or generally) of such acts or such offences; and

    (b) a suggestion that what is being glorified is being glorified as conduct that should be emulated in existing circumstances.

(9) In this section "working day" means any day other than

    (a) a Saturday or a Sunday;

    (b) Christmas Day or Good Friday; or

    (c) a day which is a bank holiday under the Banking and Financial Dealings Act 1971 (c 80) in any part of the United Kingdom.

4 Giving of notices under s 3

(1) Except in a case to which any of subsections (2) to (4) applies, a notice under section 3(3) may be given to a person only

    (a) by delivering it to him in person; or

    (b) by sending it to him, by means of a postal service providing for delivery to be recorded, at his last known address.

(2) Such a notice may be given to a body corporate only

    (a) by delivering it to the secretary of that body in person; or

    (b) by sending it to the appropriate person, by means of a postal service providing for delivery to be recorded, at the address of the registered or principal office of the body.

(3) Such a notice may be given to a firm only

    (a) by delivering it to a partner of the firm in person;

    (b) by so delivering it to a person having the control or management of the partnership business; or

    (c) by sending it to the appropriate person, by means of a postal service providing for delivery to be recorded, at the address of the principal office of the partnership.

(4) Such a notice may be given to an unincorporated body or association only

    (a) by delivering it to a member of its governing body in person; or

    (b) by sending it to the appropriate person, by means of a postal service providing for delivery to be recorded, at the address of the principal office of the body or association.

(5) In the case of

    (a) a company registered outside the United Kingdom,

    (b) a firm carrying on business outside the United Kingdom, or

    (c) an unincorporated body or association with offices outside the United Kingdom,

the references in this section to its principal office include references to its principal office within the United Kingdom (if any).

(6) In this section "the appropriate person" means

    (a) in the case of a body corporate, the body itself or its secretary;

(b) in the case of a firm, the firm itself or a partner of the firm or a person having the control or management of the partnership business; and

(c) in the case of an unincorporated body or association, the body or association itself or a member of its governing body.

(7) For the purposes of section 3 the time at which a notice under subsection (3) of that section is to be regarded as given is

(a) where it is delivered to a person, the time at which it is so delivered; and

(b) where it is sent by a postal service providing for delivery to be recorded, the time recorded as the time of its delivery.

(8) In this section "secretary", in relation to a body corporate, means the secretary or other equivalent officer of the body.

Preparation of terrorist acts and terrorist training

5 Preparation of terrorist acts

(1) A person commits an offence if, with the intention of

(a) committing acts of terrorism, or

(b) assisting another to commit such acts,

he engages in any conduct in preparation for giving effect to his intention.

(2) It is irrelevant for the purposes of subsection (1) whether the intention and preparations relate to one or more particular acts of terrorism, acts of terrorism of a particular description or acts of terrorism generally.

(3) A person guilty of an offence under this section shall be liable, on conviction on indictment, to imprisonment for life.

6 Training for terrorism

(1) A person commits an offence if

(a) he provides instruction or training in any of the skills mentioned in subsection (3); and

(b) at the time he provides the instruction or training, he knows that a person receiving it intends to use the skills in which he is being instructed or trained

(i) for or in connection with the commission or preparation of acts of terrorism or Convention offences; or

(ii) for assisting the commission or preparation by others of such acts or offences.

(2) A person commits an offence if

(a) he receives instruction or training in any of the skills mentioned in subsection (3); and

(b) at the time of the instruction or training, he intends to use the skills in which he is being instructed or trained

(i) for or in connection with the commission or preparation of acts of terrorism or Convention offences; or

(ii) for assisting the commission or preparation by others of such acts or offences.

(3) The skills are

(a) the making, handling or use of a noxious substance, or of substances of a description of such substances;

(b) the use of any method or technique for doing anything else that is capable of being done for the purposes of terrorism, in connection with the commission or preparation of an act of terrorism or Convention offence or in connection with assisting the commission or preparation by another of such an act or offence; and

(c) the design or adaptation for the purposes of terrorism, or in connection with the commission or preparation of an act of terrorism or Convention offence, of any method or technique for doing anything.

(4) It is irrelevant for the purposes of subsections (1) and (2)

    (a) whether any instruction or training that is provided is provided to one or more particular persons or generally;

    (b) whether the acts or offences in relation to which a person intends to use skills in which he is instructed or trained consist of one or more particular acts of terrorism or Convention offences, acts of terrorism or Convention offences of a particular description or acts of terrorism or Convention offences generally; and

    (c) whether assistance that a person intends to provide to others is intended to be provided to one or more particular persons or to one or more persons whose identities are not yet known.

(5) A person guilty of an offence under this section shall be liable

    (a) on conviction on indictment, to imprisonment for a term not exceeding 10 years or to a fine, or to both;

    (b) on summary conviction in England and Wales, to imprisonment for a term not exceeding 12 months or to a fine not exceeding the statutory maximum, or to both;

    (c) on summary conviction in Scotland or Northern Ireland, to imprisonment for a term not exceeding 6 months or to a fine not exceeding the statutory maximum, or to both.

(6) In relation to an offence committed before the commencement of section 154(1) of the Criminal Justice Act 2003 (c 44), the reference in subsection (5)(b) to 12 months is to be read as a reference to 6 months.

(7) In this section

"noxious substance" means

    (a) a dangerous substance within the meaning of Part 7 of the Anti-terrorism, Crime and Security Act 2001 (c 24); or

    (b) any other substance which is hazardous or noxious or which may be or become hazardous or noxious only in certain circumstances;

"substance" includes any natural or artificial substance (whatever its origin or method of production and whether in solid or liquid form or in the form of a gas or vapour) and any mixture of substances.

7 Powers of forfeiture in respect of offences under s 6

(1) A court before which a person is convicted of an offence under section 6 may order the forfeiture of anything the court considers to have been in the person's possession for purposes connected with the offence.

(2) Before making an order under subsection (1) in relation to anything the court must give an opportunity of being heard to any person (in addition to the convicted person) who claims to be the owner of that thing or otherwise to have an interest in it.

(3) An order under subsection (1) may not be made so as to come into force at any time before there is no further possibility (disregarding any power to grant permission for the bringing of an appeal out of time) of the order's being varied or set aside on appeal.

(4) Where a court makes an order under subsection (1), it may also make such other provision as appears to it to be necessary for giving effect to the forfeiture.

(5) That provision may include, in particular, provision relating to the retention, handling, destruction or other disposal of what is forfeited.

(6) Provision made by virtue of this section may be varied at any time by the court that made it.

[(7) *The power of forfeiture under this section is in addition to any power of forfeiture under section 23A of the Terrorism Act 2000.*][1]

---

[1] Inserted by the Counter-Terrorism Act 2008, s 38(2), not yet in force.

8 Attendance at a place used for terrorist training

(1) A person commits an offence if
    (a) he attends at any place, whether in the United Kingdom or elsewhere;
    (b) while he is at that place, instruction or training of the type mentioned in section 6(1) of this Act or section 54(1) of the Terrorism Act 2000 (c 11) (weapons training) is provided there;
    (c) that instruction or training is provided there wholly or partly for purposes connected with the commission or preparation of acts of terrorism or Convention offences; and
    (d) the requirements of subsection (2) are satisfied in relation to that person.
(2) The requirements of this subsection are satisfied in relation to a person if
    (a) he knows or believes that instruction or training is being provided there wholly or partly for purposes connected with the commission or preparation of acts of terrorism or Convention offences; or
    (b) a person attending at that place throughout the period of that person's attendance could not reasonably have failed to understand that instruction or training was being provided there wholly or partly for such purposes.
(3) It is immaterial for the purposes of this section
    (a) whether the person concerned receives the instruction or training himself; and
    (b) whether the instruction or training is provided for purposes connected with one or more particular acts of terrorism or Convention offences, acts of terrorism or Convention offences of a particular description or acts of terrorism or Convention offences generally.
(4) A person guilty of an offence under this section shall be liable
    (a) on conviction on indictment, to imprisonment for a term not exceeding 10 years or to a fine, or to both;
    (b) on summary conviction in England and Wales, to imprisonment for a term not exceeding 12 months or to a fine not exceeding the statutory maximum, or to both;
    (c) on summary conviction in Scotland or Northern Ireland, to imprisonment for a term not exceeding 6 months or to a fine not exceeding the statutory maximum, or to both.
(5) In relation to an offence committed before the commencement of section 154(1) of the Criminal Justice Act 2003 (c 44), the reference in subsection (4)(b) to 12 months is to be read as a reference to 6 months.
(6) References in this section to instruction or training being provided include references to its being made available.

Offences involving radioactive devices and materials and nuclear facilities and sites

9 Making and possession of devices or materials

(1) A person commits an offence if
    (a) he makes or has in his possession a radioactive device, or
    (b) he has in his possession radioactive material,
with the intention of using the device or material in the course of or in connection with the commission or preparation of an act of terrorism or for the purposes of terrorism, or of making it available to be so used.
(2) It is irrelevant for the purposes of subsection (1) whether the act of terrorism to which an intention relates is a particular act of terrorism, an act of terrorism of a particular description or an act of terrorism generally.
(3) A person guilty of an offence under this section shall be liable, on conviction on indictment, to imprisonment for life.
(4) In this section
"radioactive device" means
    (a) a nuclear weapon or other nuclear explosive device;

(b) a radioactive material dispersal device;

(c) a radiation-emitting device;

"radioactive material" means nuclear material or any other radioactive substance which

(a) contains nuclides that undergo spontaneous disintegration in a process accompanied by the emission of one or more types of ionising radiation, such as alpha radiation, beta radiation, neutron particles or gamma rays; and

(b) is capable, owing to its radiological or fissile properties, of

(i) causing serious bodily injury to a person;

(ii) causing serious damage to property;

(iii) endangering a person's life; or

(iv) creating a serious risk to the health or safety of the public.

(5) In subsection (4)

"device" includes any of the following, whether or not fixed to land, namely, machinery, equipment, appliances, tanks, containers, pipes and conduits;

"nuclear material" has the same meaning as in the Nuclear Material (Offences) Act 1983 (c 18) (see section 6 of that Act).

10 Misuse of devices or material and misuse and damage of facilities

(1) A person commits an offence if he uses

(a) a radioactive device, or

(b) radioactive material,

in the course of or in connection with the commission of an act of terrorism or for the purposes of terrorism.

(2) A person commits an offence if, in the course of or in connection with the commission of an act of terrorism or for the purposes of terrorism, he uses or damages a nuclear facility in a manner which

(a) causes a release of radioactive material; or

(b) creates or increases a risk that such material will be released.

(3) A person guilty of an offence under this section shall be liable, on conviction on indictment, to imprisonment for life.

(4) In this section

"nuclear facility" means

(a) a nuclear reactor, including a reactor installed in or on any transportation device for use as an energy source in order to propel it or for any other purpose; or

(b) a plant or conveyance being used for the production, storage, processing or transport of radioactive material;

"radioactive device" and "radioactive material" have the same meanings as in section 9.

(5) In subsection (4)

"nuclear reactor" has the same meaning as in the Nuclear Installations Act 1965 (c 57) (see section 26 of that Act);

"transportation device" means any vehicle or any space object (within the meaning of the Outer Space Act 1986 (c 38)).

11 Terrorist threats relating to devices, materials or facilities

(1) A person commits an offence if, in the course of or in connection with the commission of an act of terrorism or for the purposes of terrorism

(a) he makes a demand

(i) for the supply to himself or to another of a radioactive device or of radioactive material;

(ii) for a nuclear facility to be made available to himself or to another; or

(iii) for access to such a facility to be given to himself or to another;

(b) he supports the demand with a threat that he or another will take action if the demand is not met; and

(c) the circumstances and manner of the threat are such that it is reasonable for the person to whom it is made to assume that there is real risk that the threat will be carried out if the demand is not met.

(2) A person also commits an offence if

(a) he makes a threat falling within subsection (3) in the course of or in connection with the commission of an act of terrorism or for the purposes of terrorism; and

(b) the circumstances and manner of the threat are such that it is reasonable for the person to whom it is made to assume that there is real risk that the threat will be carried out, or would be carried out if demands made in association with the threat are not met.

(3) A threat falls within this subsection if it is

(a) a threat to use radioactive material;

(b) a threat to use a radioactive device; or

(c) a threat to use or damage a nuclear facility in a manner that releases radioactive material or creates or increases a risk that such material will be released.

(4) A person guilty of an offence under this section shall be liable, on conviction on indictment, to imprisonment for life.

(5) In this section

"nuclear facility" has the same meaning as in section 10;

"radioactive device" and "radioactive material" have the same meanings as in section 9.

[*11A Forfeiture of devices, materials or facilities*

(1) A court by or before which a person is convicted of an offence under section 9 or 10 may order the forfeiture of any radioactive device or radioactive material, or any nuclear facility, made or used in committing the offence.

(2) A court by or before which a person is convicted of an offence under section 11 may order the forfeiture of any radioactive device or radioactive material, or any nuclear facility, which is the subject of

(a) a demand under subsection (1) of that section, or

(b) a threat falling within subsection (3) of that section.

(3) Before making an order under this section, a court must give an opportunity to be heard to any person, other than the convicted person, who claims to be the owner or otherwise interested in anything which can be forfeited under this section.

(4) An order under this section does not come into force until there is no further possibility of it being varied, or set aside, on appeal (disregarding any power of a court to grant leave to appeal out of time).

(5) Where a court makes an order under this section, it may also make such other provision as appears to it to be necessary for giving effect to the forfeiture, including, in particular, provision relating to the retention, handling, disposal or destruction of what is forfeited.

(6) Provision made by virtue of subsection (5) may be varied at any time by the court that made it.

(7) The power of forfeiture under this section is in addition to any power of forfeiture under section 23A of the Terrorism Act 2000.][2]

12 Trespassing etc on nuclear sites

(1) The Serious Organised Crime and Police Act 2005 (c 15) is amended as follows.

(2) In sections 128(1), (4) and (7) and 129(1), (4) and (6) (trespassing etc on a designated site in England and Wales or Northern Ireland or in Scotland), for "designated", wherever occurring, substitute "protected".

---

[2] Inserted by the Counter-Terrorism Act 2008, s 38(3), not yet in force.

(3) After section 128(1) (sites in England and Wales and Northern Ireland) insert

"(1A) In this section 'protected site' means

    (a) a nuclear site; or

    (b) a designated site.

(1B) In this section 'nuclear site' means

    (a) so much of any premises in respect of which a nuclear site licence (within the meaning of the Nuclear Installations Act 1965) is for the time being in force as lies within the outer perimeter of the protection provided for those premises; and

    (b) so much of any other premises of which premises falling within paragraph (a) form a part as lies within that outer perimeter.

(1C) For this purpose

    (a) the outer perimeter of the protection provided for any premises is the line of the outermost fences, walls or other obstacles provided or relied on for protecting those premises from intruders; and

    (b) that line shall be determined on the assumption that every gate, door or other barrier across a way through a fence, wall or other obstacle is closed."

(4) After section 129(1) (sites in Scotland) insert

"(1A) In this section 'protected Scottish site' means

    (a) a nuclear site in Scotland; or

    (b) a designated Scottish site.

(1B) In this section 'nuclear site' means

    (a) so much of any premises in respect of which a nuclear site licence (within the meaning of the Nuclear Installations Act 1965) is for the time being in force as lies within the outer perimeter of the protection provided for those premises; and

    (b) so much of any other premises of which premises falling within paragraph (a) form a part as lies within that outer perimeter.

(1C) For this purpose

    (a) the outer perimeter of the protection provided for any premises is the line of the outermost fences, walls or other obstacles provided or relied on for protecting those premises from intruders; and

    (b) that line shall be determined on the assumption that every gate, door or other barrier across a way through a fence, wall or other obstacle is closed."

Increases of penalties

13 Maximum penalty for possessing for terrorist purposes *(omitted)*

14 Maximum penalty for certain offences relating to nuclear material *(omitted)*

15 Maximum penalty for contravening notice relating to encrypted information *(omitted)*

Incidental provisions about offences

16 Preparatory hearings in terrorism cases

(1) Section 29 of the Criminal Procedure and Investigations Act 1996 (c 25) (power to order preparatory hearing) is amended as follows.

(2) Before subsection (2) insert

"(1B) An order that a preparatory hearing shall be held must be made by a judge of the Crown Court in every case which (whether or not it falls within subsection (1) or (1A)) is a case in which at least one of the offences charged by the indictment against at least one of the persons charged is a terrorism offence.

(1C) An order that a preparatory hearing shall be held must also be made by a judge of the Crown court in every case which (whether or not it falls within subsection (1) or (1A)) is a case in which

    (a) at least one of the offences charged by the indictment against at least one of the persons charged is an offence carrying a maximum of at least 10 years' imprisonment; and

    (b) it appears to the judge that evidence on the indictment reveals that conduct in respect of which that offence is charged had a terrorist connection."

(3) For subsection (3) (no order in serious and complex fraud cases) substitute

"(3) In a case in which it appears to a judge of the Crown Court that evidence on an indictment reveals a case of fraud of such seriousness or complexity as is mentioned in section 7 of the Criminal Justice Act 1987 (preparatory hearings in cases of serious or complex fraud)

    (a) the judge may make an order for a preparatory hearing under this section only if he is required to do so by subsection (1B) or (1C);

    (b) before making an order in pursuance of either of those subsections, he must determine whether to make an order for a preparatory hearing under that section; and

    (c) he is not required by either of those subsections to make an order for a preparatory hearing under this section if he determines that an order should be made for a preparatory hearing under that section;

and, in a case in which an order is made for a preparatory hearing under that section, requirements imposed by those subsections apply only if that order ceases to have effect."

(4) In subsection (4) (orders to be capable of being made on application or on the judge's own motion), for the words before paragraph (a) substitute

"(4) An order that a preparatory hearing shall be held may be made"

(5) After sub-paragraph (5) insert

"(6) In this section 'terrorism offence' means

    (a) an offence under section 11 or 12 of the Terrorism Act 2000 (c 11) (offences relating to proscribed organisations);

    (b) an offence under any of sections 15 to 18 of that Act (offences relating to terrorist property);

    (c) an offence under section 38B of that Act (failure to disclose information about acts of terrorism);

    (d) an offence under section 54 of that Act (weapons training);

    (e) an offence under any of sections 56 to 59 of that Act (directing terrorism, possessing things and collecting information for the purposes of terrorism and inciting terrorism outside the United Kingdom);

    (f) an offence in respect of which there is jurisdiction by virtue of section 62 of that Act (extra-territorial jurisdiction in respect of certain offences committed outside the United Kingdom for the purposes of terrorism etc);

    (g) an offence under Part 1 of the Terrorism Act 2006 (miscellaneous terrorist related offences);

    (h) conspiring or attempting to commit a terrorism offence;

    (i) incitement to commit a terrorism offence.

(7) For the purposes of this section an offence carries a maximum of at least 10 years' imprisonment if

    (a) it is punishable, on conviction on indictment, with imprisonment; and

    (b) the maximum term of imprisonment that may be imposed on conviction on indictment of that offence is 10 years or more or is imprisonment for life.

(8) For the purposes of this section conduct has a terrorist connection if it is or takes place in the course of an act of terrorism or is for the purposes of terrorism.

(9) In subsection (8) 'terrorism' has the same meaning as in the Terrorism Act 2000 (see section 1 of that Act)."

17 Commission of offences abroad

(1) If
   (a) a person does anything outside the United Kingdom, and
   (b) his action, if done in a part of the United Kingdom, would constitute an offence falling within subsection (2),
   he shall be guilty in that part of the United Kingdom of the offence.

(2) The offences falling within this subsection are
   (a) an offence under section 1 or 6 of this Act so far as it is committed in relation to any statement, instruction or training in relation to which that section has effect by reason of its relevance to the commission, preparation or instigation of one or more Convention offences;
   (b) an offence under any of sections 8 to 11 of this Act;
   (c) an offence under section 11(1) of the Terrorism Act 2000 (c 11) (membership of proscribed organisations);
   (d) an offence under section 54 of that Act (weapons training);
   (e) conspiracy to commit an offence falling within this subsection;
   (f) inciting a person to commit such an offence;
   (g) attempting to commit such an offence;
   (h) aiding, abetting, counselling or procuring the commission of such an offence.

(3) Subsection (1) applies irrespective of whether the person is a British citizen or, in the case of a company, a company incorporated in a part of the United Kingdom.

(4) In the case of an offence falling within subsection (2) which is committed wholly or partly outside the United Kingdom
   (a) proceedings for the offence may be taken at any place in the United Kingdom; and
   (b) the offence may for all incidental purposes be treated as having been committed at any such place.

(5) In section 3(1)(a) and (b) of the Explosive Substances Act 1883 (c 3) (offences committed in preparation for use of explosives with intent to endanger life or property in the United Kingdom or the Republic of Ireland), in each place, for "the Republic of Ireland" substitute "elsewhere".

(6) Subsection (5) does not extend to Scotland except in relation to
   (a) the doing of an act as an act of terrorism or for the purposes of terrorism; or
   (b) the possession or control of a substance for the purposes of terrorism.

18 Liability of company directors etc *(omitted)*

19 Consents to prosecutions

(1) Proceedings for an offence under this Part
   (a) may be instituted in England and Wales only with the consent of the Director of Public Prosecutions; and
   (b) may be instituted in Northern Ireland only with the consent of the Director of Public Prosecutions for Northern Ireland.

(2) But if it appears to the Director of Public Prosecutions or the Director of Public Prosecutions for Northern Ireland that an offence under this Part has been committed [*outside the United Kingdom or*][3] for a purpose wholly or partly connected with the affairs of a country other than the United Kingdom, his consent for the purposes of this section may be given only with the permission
   (a) in the case of the Director of Public Prosecutions, of the Attorney General; and
   (b) in the case of the Director of Public Prosecutions for Northern Ireland, of the Advocate General for Northern Ireland.

---

[3] Inserted by the Counter-Terrorism Act 2003, s 29, not yet in force.

(3) In relation to any time before the coming into force of section 27(1) of the Justice (Northern Ireland) Act 2002 (c 26), the reference in subsection (2)(b) to the Advocate General for Northern Ireland is to be read as a reference to the Attorney General for Northern Ireland.

Interpretation of Part I

20 Interpretation of Part I

(1) Expressions used in this Part and in the Terrorism Act 2000 (c 11) have the same meanings in this Part as in that Act.

(2) In this Part

"act of terrorism" includes anything constituting an action taken for the purposes of terrorism, within the meaning of the Terrorism Act 2000 (see section 1(5) of that Act);

"article" includes anything for storing data;

"Convention offence" means an offence listed in Schedule 1 or an equivalent offence under the law of a country or territory outside the United Kingdom;

"glorification" includes any form of praise or celebration, and cognate expressions are to be construed accordingly;

"public" is to be construed in accordance with subsection (3);

"publish" and cognate expressions are to be construed in accordance with subsection (4);

"record" means a record so far as not comprised in an article, including a temporary record created electronically and existing solely in the course of, and for the purposes of, the transmission of the whole or a part of its contents;

"statement" is to be construed in accordance with subsection (6).

(3) In this Part references to the public
   (a) are references to the public of any part of the United Kingdom or of a country or territory outside the United Kingdom, or any section of the public; and
   (b) except in section 9(4), also include references to a meeting or other group of persons which is open to the public (whether unconditionally or on the making of a payment or the satisfaction of other conditions).

(4) In this Part references to a person's publishing a statement are references to
   (a) his publishing it in any manner to the public;
   (b) his providing electronically any service by means of which the public have access to the statement; or
   (c) his using a service provided to him electronically by another so as to enable or to facilitate access by the public to the statement;
   but this subsection does not apply to the references to a publication in section 2.

(5) In this Part references to providing a service include references to making a facility available; and references to a service provided to a person are to be construed accordingly.

(6) In this Part references to a statement are references to a communication of any description, including a communication without words consisting of sounds or images or both.

(7) In this Part references to conduct that should be emulated in existing circumstances include references to conduct that is illustrative of a type of conduct that should be so emulated.

(8) In this Part references to what is contained in an article or record include references
   (a) to anything that is embodied or stored in or on it; and
   (b) to anything that may be reproduced from it using apparatus designed or adapted for the purpose.

(9) The Secretary of State may by order made by statutory instrument
   (a) modify Schedule 1 so as to add an offence to the offences listed in that Schedule;
   (b) modify that Schedule so as to remove an offence from the offences so listed;
   (c) make supplemental, incidental, consequential or transitional provision in connection with the addition or removal of an offence.

(10) An order under subsection (9) may add an offence in or as regards Scotland to the offences listed in Schedule 1 to the extent only that a provision creating the offence would be outside the legislative competence of the Scottish Parliament.

(11) The Secretary of State must not make an order containing (with or without other provision) any provision authorised by subsection (9) unless a draft of the order has been laid before Parliament and approved by a resolution of each House.

PART II
MISCELLANEOUS PROVISIONS

Proscription of terrorist organisations

21 Grounds of proscription *(omitted)*

22 Name changes by proscribed organisations *(omitted)*

Detention of terrorist suspects

23 Extension of period of detention of terrorist suspects *(omitted)*

24 Grounds for extending detention *(omitted)*

25 Expiry or renewal of extended maximum detention period

(1) This section applies to any time which
  (a) is more than one year after the commencement of section 23; and
  (b) does not fall within a period in relation to which this section is disapplied by an order under subsection (2).

(2) The Secretary of State may by order made by statutory instrument disapply this section in relation to any period of not more than one year beginning with the coming into force of the order.

(3) Schedule 8 to the Terrorism Act 2000 (c 11) has effect in relation to any further extension under paragraph 36 of that Schedule for a period beginning at a time to which this section applies
  (a) as if in sub-paragraph (3)(b) of that paragraph, for "28 days" there were substituted "14 days"; and
  (b) as if that paragraph and paragraph 37 of that Schedule had effect with the further consequential modifications set out in subsection (4).

(4) The further consequential modifications are
  (a) the substitution of the words "a judicial authority" for paragraphs (a) and (b) of sub-paragraph (1A) of paragraph 36;
  (b) the omission of sub-paragraphs (1B) and (7) of that paragraph;
  (c) the omission of the words "or senior judge" wherever occurring in sub-paragraphs (3AA) and (5) of that paragraph and in paragraph 37(2); and
  (d) the omission of the words from "but" onwards in paragraph 36(4).

(5) Where at a time to which this section applies
  (a) a person is being detained by virtue of a further extension under paragraph 36 of Schedule 8 to the Terrorism Act 2000,
  (b) his further detention was authorised (at a time to which this section did not apply) for a period ending more than 14 days after the relevant time, and
  (c) that 14 days has expired,
  the person with custody of that individual must release him immediately.

(6) The Secretary of State must not make an order containing (with or without other provision) any provision disapplying this section in relation to any period unless a draft of the order has been laid before Parliament and approved by a resolution of each House.

(7) In this section "the relevant time" has the same meaning as in paragraph 36 of Schedule 8 to the Terrorism Act 2000.

Searches etc

26 All premises warrants: England and Wales and Northern Ireland

(1) Part 1 of Schedule 5 to the Terrorism Act 2000 (searches etc for the purposes of terrorist investigations in England and Wales and Northern Ireland) is amended as follows.

(2) In paragraph 1 (search warrants authorising entry to specified premises), in sub-paragraph (2)(a), for "the premises specified in the warrant" substitute "premises mentioned in sub-paragraph (2A)".

(3) After sub-paragraph (2) of that paragraph insert

"(2A) The premises referred to in sub-paragraph (2)(a) are

    (a) one or more sets of premises specified in the application (in which case the application is for a 'specific premises warrant'); or

    (b) any premises occupied or controlled by a person specified in the application, including such sets of premises as are so specified (in which case the application is for an 'all premises warrant')."

(4) In sub-paragraph (5) of that paragraph

    (a) in paragraph (b), for "premises specified in the application" substitute "premises to which the application relates";

    (b) in paragraph (c), at the end insert ", and"; and

    (c) after that paragraph insert

"(d) in the case of an application for an all premises warrant, that it is not reasonably practicable to specify in the application all the premises which the person so specified occupies or controls and which might need to be searched."

(5) In paragraph 2 (warrants as to which special conditions are satisfied), in sub-paragraph (1), after "an application" insert "for a specific premises warrant".

(6) After that paragraph insert

"2A (1) This paragraph applies where an application for an all premises warrant is made under paragraph 1 and

    (a) the application is made by a police officer of at least the rank of superintendent, and

    (b) the justice to whom the application is made is not satisfied of the matter referred to in paragraph 1(5)(c).

(2) The justice may grant the application if satisfied of the matters referred to in paragraph 1(5)(a), (b) and (d).

(3) Where a warrant under paragraph 1 is issued by virtue of this paragraph, the powers under paragraph 1(2)(a) and (b) are exercisable only

    (a) in respect of premises which are not residential premises, and

    (b) within the period of 24 hours beginning with the time when the warrant is issued.

(4) For the purpose of sub-paragraph (3) 'residential premises', in relation to a power under paragraph 1(2)(a) or (b), means any premises which the constable exercising the power has reasonable grounds for believing are used wholly or mainly as a dwelling."

(7) In paragraph 11 (applications for search warrants involving excluded or special procedure material), in sub-paragraph (2)(a), for "the premises specified in the warrant" substitute "premises mentioned in sub-paragraph (3A)".

(8) After sub-paragraph (3) of that paragraph insert

"(3A) The premises referred to in sub-paragraph (2)(a) are

    (a) one or more sets of premises specified in the application (in which case the application is for a 'specific premises warrant'); or

    (b) any premises occupied or controlled by a person specified in the application, including such sets of premises as are so specified (in which case the application is for an 'all premises warrant')."

(9) In paragraph 12 (grant of applications where excluded or special procedure material is involved), in each of sub-paragraphs (1) and (2), after "an application" insert "for a specific premises warrant".

(10) After sub-paragraph (2) of that paragraph insert

"(2A) A Circuit judge or a District Judge (Magistrates' Courts) may grant an application for an all premises warrant under paragraph 11 if satisfied

    (a) that an order made under paragraph 5 has not been complied with, and

    (b) that the person specified in the application is also specified in the order.

(2B) A Circuit judge or a District Judge (Magistrates' Courts) may also grant an application for an all premises warrant under paragraph 11 if satisfied that there are reasonable grounds for believing

    (a) that there is material on premises to which the application relates which consists of or includes excluded material or special procedure material but does not include items subject to legal privilege, and

    (b) that the conditions in sub-paragraphs (3) and (4) are met."

(11) In sub-paragraph (4)(b) of that paragraph, for "the premises on which the material is situated" substitute "premises to which the application for the warrant relates".

27 All premises warrants: Scotland *(omitted)*

28 Search, seizure and forfeiture of terrorist publications

(1) If a justice of the peace is satisfied that there are reasonable grounds for suspecting that articles to which this section applies are likely to be found on any premises, he may issue a warrant authorising a constable

    (a) to enter and search the premises; and

    (b) to seize anything found there which the constable has reason to believe is such an article.

(2) This section applies to an article if

    (a) it is likely to be the subject of conduct falling within subsection (2)(a) to (e) of section 2; and

    (b) it would fall for the purposes of that section to be treated, in the context of the conduct to which it is likely to be subject, as a terrorist publication.

(3) A person exercising a power conferred by a warrant under this section may use such force as is reasonable in the circumstances for exercising that power.

(4) An article seized under the authority of a warrant issued under this section

    (a) may be removed by a constable to such place as he thinks fit; and

    (b) must be retained there in the custody of a constable until returned or otherwise disposed of in accordance with this Act.

(5) An article to which this section applies which is seized under the authority of a warrant issued under this section on an information laid by or on behalf of the Director of Public Prosecutions or the Director of Public Prosecutions for Northern Ireland

    (a) shall be liable to forfeiture; and

    (b) if forfeited, may be destroyed or otherwise disposed of by a constable in whatever manner he thinks fit.

(6) In Schedule 1 to the Criminal Justice and Police Act 2001 (c 16) (powers which relate to the seizure of property in bulk)

    (a) in Part 1, at the end insert

        "73H The power of seizure conferred by section 28 of the Terrorism Act 2006."

    (b) in Part 3, at the end insert

        "113 The power of seizure conferred by section 28 of the Terrorism Act 2006."

(7) Nothing in

    (a) the Police (Property) Act 1897 (c 30) (property seized in the investigation of an offence), or

    (b) section 31 of the Police (Northern Ireland) Act 1998 (c 32) (which makes similar provision in Northern Ireland),

applies to an article seized under the authority of a warrant under this section.

(8) Schedule 2 (which makes provision about the forfeiture of articles to which this section applies) has effect.

(9) In this section

"article" has the same meaning as in Part 1 of this Act;

"forfeited" means treated or condemned as forfeited under Schedule 2, and "forfeiture" is to be construed accordingly;

"premises" has the same meaning as in the Police and Criminal Evidence Act 1984 (c 60) (see section 23 of that Act).

(10) In the application of this section to Scotland

    (a) in subsection (1), for the words from the beginning to "satisfied" substitute "If a sheriff, on the application of a procurator fiscal, is satisfied";

    (b) in subsection (5) omit "on an information laid by or on behalf of the Director of Public Prosecutions or the Director of Public Prosecutions for Northern Ireland";

    (c) in subsection (9), for the definition of "'premises'" substitute "'premises' has the same meaning as in the Terrorism Act 2000 (c 11) (see section 121 of that Act)."

29 Power to search vehicles under Schedule 7 to the Terrorism Act 2000

In paragraph 8 of Schedule 7 to the Terrorism Act 2000 (c 11) (search of a person at a port or in the border area to ascertain if he is involved in terrorism), after sub-paragraph (1)(d) insert

    "(e) search a vehicle which is on a ship or aircraft;

    (f) search a vehicle which the examining officer reasonably believes has been, or is about to be, on a ship or aircraft."

30 Extension to internal waters of authorisations to stop and search

(1) The Terrorism Act 2000 is amended as follows.

(2) In section 44 (authorisations for stop and search), after subsection (4) insert

    "(4ZA) The power of a person mentioned in subsection (4) to give an authorisation specifying an area or place so mentioned includes power to give such an authorisation specifying such an area or place together with

        (a) the internal waters adjacent to that area or place; or

        (b) such area of those internal waters as is specified in the authorisation."

(3) After subsection (5) of that section insert

    "(5A) In this section

        'driver', in relation to an aircraft, hovercraft or vessel, means the captain, pilot or other person with control of the aircraft, hovercraft or vessel or any member of its crew and, in relation to a train, includes any member of its crew;

        'internal waters' means waters in the United Kingdom that are not comprised in any police area."

(4) In section 45 (exercise of powers), after subsection (6) insert

    "(7) In this section 'driver' has the same meaning as in section 44."

Other investigatory powers

31 Amendment of the Intelligence Services Act 1994 *(omitted)*

32 Interception warrants *(omitted)*

33 Disclosure notices for the purposes of terrorist investigations

(1) In section 60 of the Serious Organised Crime and Police Act 2005 (c 15) (investigatory powers of DPP etc), in subsection (1), after "applies" insert "or in connection with a terrorist investigation".

(2) After subsection (6) of that section insert

"(7) In this Chapter 'terrorist investigation' means an investigation of—

(a) the commission, preparation or instigation of acts of terrorism,

(b) any act or omission which appears to have been for the purposes of terrorism and which consists in or involves the commission, preparation or instigation of an offence, or

(c) the commission, preparation or instigation of an offence under the Terrorism Act 2000 (c 11) or under Part 1 of the Terrorism Act 2006 other than an offence under section 1 or 2 of that Act."

(3) In section 62 of that Act (disclosure notices), insert

"(1A) If it appears to the Investigating Authority

(a) that any person has information (whether or not contained in a document) which relates to a matter relevant to a terrorist investigation, and

(b) that there are reasonable grounds for believing that information which may be provided by that person in compliance with a disclosure notice is likely to be of substantial value (whether or not by itself) to that investigation,

he may give, or authorise an appropriate person to give, a disclosure notice to that person."

(4) In section 70(1) of that Act (interpretation of Chapter 1)

(a) before the definition of "appropriate person" insert

"'act of terrorism' includes anything constituting an action taken for the purposes of terrorism, within the meaning of the Terrorism Act 2000 (see section 1(5) of that Act);"

(b) after the definition of "document" insert

"'terrorism' has the same meaning as in the Terrorism Act 2000 (see section 1(1) to (4) of that Act);

'terrorist investigation' has the meaning given by section 60(7)."

Definition of terrorism etc

34 Amendment of the definition of "terrorism" etc *(omitted)*

Other amendments

35 Applications for extended detention of seized cash *(omitted)*

PART III
SUPPLEMENTAL PROVISIONS

36 Review of terrorism legislation

(1) The Secretary of State must appoint a person to review the operation of the provisions of the Terrorism Act 2000 and of Part 1 of this Act.

(2) That person may, from time to time, carry out a review of those provisions and, where he does so, must send a report on the outcome of his review to the Secretary of State as soon as reasonably practicable after completing the review.

(3) That person must carry out and report on his first review under this section before the end of the period of 12 months after the laying before Parliament of the last report to be so laid under section 126 of the Terrorism Act 2000 before the commencement of this section.

(4) That person must carry out and report on a review under this section at least once in every twelve month period ending with an anniversary of the end of the twelve month period mentioned in subsection (3).

(5) On receiving a report under this section, the Secretary of State must lay a copy of it before Parliament.

(6) The Secretary of State may, out of money provided by Parliament, pay a person appointed to carry out a review under this section, both his expenses and also such allowances as the Secretary of State determines.

37 Consequential amendments and repeals *(omitted)*

38 Expenses *(omitted)*

39 Short title, commencement and extent *(omitted)*

SCHEDULE 1   Section 20
CONVENTION OFFENCES

Explosives offences

1 (1) Subject to sub-paragraph (3), an offence under any of sections 28 to 30 of the Offences against the Person Act 1861 (c 100) (causing injury by explosions, causing explosions and handling or placing explosives).

 (2) Subject to sub-paragraph (3), an offence under any of the following provisions of the Explosive Substances Act 1883 (c 3)
   (a) section 2 (causing an explosion likely to endanger life);
   (b) section 3 (preparation of explosions);
   (c) section 5 (ancillary offences).

 (3) An offence in or as regards Scotland is a Convention offence by virtue of this paragraph only if it consists in
   (a) the doing of an act as an act of terrorism; or
   (b) an action for the purposes of terrorism.

Biological weapons

2 An offence under section 1 of the Biological Weapons Act 1974 (c 6) (development etc of biological weapons).

Offences against internationally protected persons

3 (1) Subject to sub-paragraph (4), an offence mentioned in section 1(1)(a) of the Internationally Protected Persons Act 1978 (c 17) (attacks against protected persons committed outside the United Kingdom) which is committed (whether in the United Kingdom or elsewhere) in relation to a protected person.

 (2) Subject to sub-paragraph (4), an offence mentioned in section 1(1)(b) of that Act (attacks on relevant premises etc) which is committed (whether in the United Kingdom or elsewhere) in connection with an attack
   (a) on relevant premises or on a vehicle ordinarily used by a protected person, and
   (b) at a time when a protected person is in or on the premises or vehicle.

(3) Subject to sub-paragraph (4), an offence under section 1(3) of that Act (threats etc in relation to protected persons).

(4) An offence in or as regards Scotland is a Convention offence by virtue of this paragraph only if it consists in
   (a) the doing of an act as an act of terrorism; or
   (b) an action for the purposes of terrorism.

(5) Expressions used in this paragraph and section 1 of that Act have the same meanings in this paragraph as in that section.

Hostage-taking

4   An offence under section 1 of the Taking of Hostages Act 1982 (c 28) (hostage-taking).

Hijacking and other offences against aircraft

5   Offences under any of the following provisions of the Aviation Security Act 1982 (c 36)
   (a) section 1 (hijacking);
   (b) section 2 (destroying, damaging or endangering safety of aircraft);
   (c) section 3 (other acts endangering or likely to endanger safety of aircraft);
   (d) section 6(2) (ancillary offences).

Offences involving nuclear material [or nuclear facilities][4]

6   (1) An offence mentioned in section 1(1) [(a) to (d)][5] of the Nuclear Material (Offences) Act 1983 (c 18) (offences in relation to nuclear material committed outside the United Kingdom) which is committed (whether in the United Kingdom or elsewhere) in relation to or by means of nuclear material.
   (2) *An offence under section 2 of that Act (offence involving preparatory acts and threats in relation to nuclear material).*
   (3) *In this paragraph "nuclear material" has the same meaning as in that Act.*[6]
   [(2) *An offence mentioned in section 1(1)(a) or (b) of that Act where the act making the person guilty of the offence (whether done in the United Kingdom or elsewhere)*
      (a) *is directed at a nuclear facility or interferes with the operation of such a facility, and*
      (b) *causes death, injury or damage resulting from the emission of ionising radiation or the release of radioactive material.*
   (3) *An offence under any of the following provisions of that Act*
      (a) *section 1B (offences relating to damage to environment);*
      (b) *section 1C (offences of importing or exporting etc nuclear material: extended jurisdiction);*
      (c) *section 2 (offences involving preparatory acts and threats).*
   (4) *Expressions used in this paragraph and that Act have the same meanings in this paragraph as in that Act.]*[7]

[6A (1) *Any of the following offences under the Customs and Excise Management Act 1979*

---

[4] Inserted by the Criminal Justice and Immigration Act 2008, s 148(1) Sch 26, Pt 2, paras 79(1), (2) not yet in force.

[5] Inserted by the Criminal Justice and Immigration Act 2008, s 148(1) Sch 26, Pt 2, paras 79(1), (3) not yet in force.

[6] Substituted by the Criminal Justice and Immigration Act 2008, s 148(1) Sch 26, Pt 2, paras 71(1), 4 not yet in force.

[7] Substituted by the Criminal Justice and Immigration Act 2008, s 148(1) Sch 26, Pt 2, paras 71(1), 4 not yet in force.

(a) an offence under section 50(2) or (3) (improper importation of goods) in connection with a prohibition or restriction relating to the importation of nuclear material;

(b) an offence under section 68(2) (exportation of prohibited or restricted goods) in connection with a prohibition or restriction relating to the exportation or shipment as stores of nuclear material;

(c) an offence under section 170(1) or (2) (fraudulent evasion of duty etc) in connection with a prohibition or restriction relating to the importation, exportation or shipment as stores of nuclear material.

(2) In this paragraph "nuclear material" has the same meaning as in the Nuclear Material (Offences) Act 1983 (see section 6 of that Act).][8]

Offences under the Aviation and Maritime Security Act 1990 (c 31)

7 Offences under any of the following provisions of the Aviation and Maritime Security Act 1990

(a) section 1 (endangering safety at aerodromes);

(b) section 9 (hijacking of ships);

(c) section 10 (seizing or exercising control of fixed platforms);

(d) section 11 (destroying ships or fixed platforms or endangering their safety);

(e) section 12 (other acts endangering or likely to endanger safe navigation);

(f) section 13 (offences involving threats relating to ships or fixed platforms);

(g) section 14 (ancillary offences).

Offences involving chemical weapons

8 An offence under section 2 of the Chemical Weapons Act 1996 (c 6) (use, development etc of chemical weapons).

Terrorist funds

9 An offence under any of the following provisions of the Terrorism Act 2000 (c 11)

(a) section 15 (terrorist fund-raising);

(b) section 16 (use or possession of terrorist funds);

(c) section 17 (funding arrangements for terrorism);

(d) section 18 (money laundering of terrorist funds).

Directing terrorist organisations

10 An offence under section 56 of the Terrorism Act 2000 (directing a terrorist organisation).

Offences involving nuclear weapons

11 An offence under section 47 of the Anti-terrorism, Crime and Security Act 2001 (c 24) (use, development etc of nuclear weapons).

Conspiracy etc

12 Any of the following offences

(a) conspiracy to commit a Convention offence;

---

[8] Inserted by the Criminal Justice and Immigration Act 2008, s 148(1), Sch 26, Pt 2, para 79(1), (5) not yet in force.

(b) inciting the commission of a Convention offence;

(c) attempting to commit a Convention offence;

(d) aiding, abetting, counselling or procuring the commission of a Convention offence.

SCHEDULE 2   Section 28
SEIZURE AND FORFEITURE OF TERRORIST PUBLICATIONS

Application of Schedule

1 This Schedule applies where an article

   (a) has been seized under the authority of a warrant under section 28; and

   (b) is being retained in the custody of a constable ("the relevant constable").

Notice of seizure

2 (1) The relevant constable must give notice of the article's seizure to

   (a) every person whom he believes to have been the owner of the article, or one of its own-ers, at the time of the seizure; and

   (b) if there is no such person or it is not reasonably practicable to give him notice, every person whom the relevant constable believes to have been an occupier at that time of the premises where the article was seized.

   (2) The notice must set out what has been seized and the grounds for the seizure.

   (3) The notice may be given to a person only by

   (a) delivering it to him personally;

   (b) addressing it to him and leaving it for him at the appropriate address; or

   (c) addressing it to him and sending it to him at that address by post.

   (4) But where it is not practicable to give a notice in accordance with sub-paragraph (3), a notice given by virtue of sub-paragraph (1)(b) to the occupier of the premises where the article was seized may be given by

   (a) addressing it to "the occupier" of those premises, without naming him; and

   (b) leaving it for him at those premises or sending it to him at those premises by post.

   (5) An article may be treated or condemned as forfeited under this Schedule only if

   (a) the requirements of this paragraph have been complied with in the case of that article; or

   (b) it was not reasonably practicable for them to be complied with.

   (6) In this paragraph "the appropriate address", in relation to a person, means

   (a) in the case of a body corporate, its registered or principal office in the United Kingdom;

   (b) in the case of a firm, the principal office of the partnership;

   (c) in the case of an unincorporated body or association, the principal office of the body or association; and

   (d) in any other case, his usual or last known place of residence in the United Kingdom or his last known place of business in the United Kingdom.

   (7) In the case of

   (a) a company registered outside the United Kingdom,

   (b) a firm carrying on business outside the United Kingdom, or

   (c) an unincorporated body or association with offices outside the United Kingdom,

   the references in this paragraph to its principal office include references to its principal office within the United Kingdom (if any).

Notice of claim

3 (1) A person claiming that the seized article is not liable to forfeiture may give notice of his claim to a constable at any police station in the police area in which the premises where the seizure took place are located.

(2) Oral notice is not sufficient for these purposes.

4 (1) A notice of claim may not be given more than one month after
　　(a) the day of the giving of the notice of seizure; or
　　(b) if no such notice has been given, the day of the seizure.

(2) A notice of claim must specify
　　(a) the name and address of the claimant; and
　　(b) in the case of a claimant who is outside the United Kingdom, the name and address of a solicitor in the United Kingdom who is authorised to accept service, and to act, on behalf of the claimant.

(3) Service upon a solicitor so specified is to be taken to be service on the claimant for the purposes of any proceedings by virtue of this Schedule.

(4) In a case in which notice of the seizure was given to different persons on different days, the reference in this paragraph to the day on which that notice was given is a reference
　　(a) in relation to a person to whom notice of the seizure was given, to the day on which that notice was given to that person; and
　　(b) in relation to any other person, to the day on which notice of the seizure was given to the last person to be given such a notice.

Automatic forfeiture in a case where no claim is made

5　The article is to be treated as forfeited if, by the end of the period for the giving of a notice of claim in respect of it
　(a) no such notice has been given; or
　(b) the requirements of paragraphs 3 and 4 have not been complied with in relation to the only notice or notices of claim that have been given.

Forfeiture by the court in other cases

6 (1) Where a notice of claim in respect of an article is duly given in accordance with paragraphs 3 and 4, the relevant constable must decide whether to take proceedings to ask the court to condemn the article as forfeited.

(2) The decision whether to take such proceedings must be made as soon as reasonably practicable after the giving of the notice of claim.

(3) If the relevant constable takes such proceedings and the court
　　(a) finds that the article was liable to forfeiture at the time of its seizure, and
　　(b) is not satisfied that its forfeiture would be inappropriate,
　　the court must condemn the article as forfeited.

(4) If that constable takes such proceedings and the court
　　(a) finds that the article was not liable to forfeiture at the time of its seizure, or
　　(b) is satisfied that its forfeiture would be inappropriate,
　　the court must order the return of the article to the person who appears to the court to be entitled to it.

(5) If the relevant constable decides not to take proceedings for condemnation in a case in which a notice of claim has been given, he must return the article to the person who appears to him to be the owner of the article, or to one of the persons who appear to him to be owners of it.

(6) An article required to be returned in accordance with sub-paragraph (5) must be returned as soon as reasonably practicable after the decision not to take proceedings for condemnation.

Forfeiture proceedings

7 **Proceedings by virtue of this Schedule are civil proceedings and may be instituted**

    (a) in England or Wales, either in the High Court or in a magistrates' court;

    (b) in Scotland, either in the Court of Session or in the sheriff court; and

    (c) in Northern Ireland, either in the High Court or in a court of summary jurisdiction.

8 **Proceedings by virtue of this Schedule in**

    (a) a magistrates' court in England or Wales,

    (b) the sheriff court in Scotland, or

    (c) a court of summary jurisdiction in Northern Ireland,

    may be instituted in that court only if it has jurisdiction in relation to the place where the article to which they relate was seized.

9 (1) In proceedings by virtue of this Schedule that are instituted in England and Wales or Northern Ireland, the claimant or his solicitor must make his oath that, at the time of the seizure, the seized article was, or was to the best of his knowledge and belief, the property of the claimant.

    (2) In any such proceedings instituted in the High Court

        (a) the court may require the claimant to give such security for the costs of the proceedings as may be determined by the court; and

        (b) the claimant must comply with any such requirement.

    (3) If a requirement of this paragraph is not complied with, the court must find against the claimant.

10 (1) In the case of proceedings by virtue of this Schedule that are instituted in a magistrates' court in England or Wales, either party may appeal against the decision of that court to the Crown Court.

    (2) In the case of such proceedings that are instituted in a court of summary jurisdiction in Northern Ireland, either party may appeal against the decision of that court to the county court.

    (3) This paragraph does not affect any right to require the statement of a case for the opinion of the High Court.

11 Where an appeal has been made (whether by case stated or otherwise) against the decision of the court in proceedings by virtue of this Schedule in relation to an article, the article is to be left in the custody of a constable pending the final determination of the matter.

Effect of forfeiture

12 Where an article is treated or condemned as forfeited under this Schedule, the forfeiture is to be treated as having taken effect as from the time of the seizure.

Disposal of unclaimed property

13 (1) This paragraph applies where the article seized under the authority of a warrant under section 28 is required to be returned to a person.

    (2) If

        (a) the article is (without having been returned) still in the custody of a constable after the end of the period of 12 months beginning with the day after the requirement to return it arose, and

        (b) it is not practicable to dispose of the article by returning it immediately to the person to whom it is required to be returned,

    the constable may dispose of it in any manner he thinks fit.

Provisions as to proof

14 In proceedings arising out of the seizure of an article, the fact, form and manner of the seizure is to be taken, without further evidence and unless the contrary is shown, to have been as set forth in the process.

15 In proceedings, the condemnation by a court of an article as forfeited under this Schedule may be proved by the production of either

(a) the order of condemnation; or

(b) a certified copy of the order purporting to be signed by an officer of the court by which the order was made.

Special provisions as to certain claimants

16 (1) This paragraph applies where, at the time of the seizure of the article, it was

(a) the property of a body corporate;

(b) the property of two or more partners; or

(c) the property of more than five persons.

(2) The oath required by paragraph 9, and any other thing required by this Schedule or by rules of court to be done by an owner of the article, may be sworn or done by

(a) a person falling within sub-paragraph (3); or

(b) a person authorised to act on behalf of a person so falling.

(3) The persons falling within this sub-paragraph are

(a) where the owner is a body corporate, the secretary or some duly authorised officer of that body;

(b) where the owners are in partnership, any one or more of the owners;

(c) where there are more than five owners and they are not in partnership, any two or more of the owners acting on behalf of themselves and any of their co-owners who are not acting on their own behalf.

Saving for owner's rights

17 Neither the imposition of a requirement by virtue of this Schedule to return an article to a person nor the return of an article to a person in accordance with such a requirement affects

(a) the rights in relation to that article of any other person; or

(b) the right of any other person to enforce his rights against the person to whom it is returned.

Interpretation of Schedule

18 In this Schedule

"article" has the same meaning as in Part 1 of this Act;

"the court" is to be construed in accordance with paragraph 7.

SCHEDULE 3
REPEALS *(omitted)*

Justice and Security (Northern Ireland) Act 2007

An Act to make provision about justice and security in Northern Ireland.

(24th May 2007)

Trials on indictment without a jury

1 Issue of certificate

(1) This section applies in relation to a person charged with one or more indictable offences ("the defendant").

(2) The Director of Public Prosecutions for Northern Ireland may issue a certificate that any trial on indictment of the defendant (and of any person committed for trial with the defendant) is to be conducted without a jury if
(a) he suspects that any of the following conditions is met, and
(b) he is satisfied that in view of this there is a risk that the administration of justice might be impaired if the trial were to be conducted with a jury.

(3) Condition 1 is that the defendant is, or is an associate (see subsection (9)) of, a person who
(a) is a member of a proscribed organisation (see subsection (10)), or
(b) has at any time been a member of an organisation that was, at that time, a proscribed organisation.

(4) Condition 2 is that
(a) the offence or any of the offences was committed on behalf of a proscribed organisation, or
(b) a proscribed organisation was otherwise involved with, or assisted in, the carrying out of the offence or any of the offences.

(5) Condition 3 is that an attempt has been made to prejudice the investigation or prosecution of the offence or any of the offences and
(a) the attempt was made on behalf of a proscribed organisation, or
(b) a proscribed organisation was otherwise involved with, or assisted in, the attempt.

(6) Condition 4 is that the offence or any of the offences was committed to any extent (whether directly or indirectly) as a result of, in connection with or in response to religious or political hostility of one person or group of persons towards another person or group of persons.

[(6A) *The Director of Public Prosecutions for Northern Ireland may not issue a certificate under subsection (2) if*
(a) the proceedings are taken in Northern Ireland only by virtue of section 28 of the Counter-Terrorism Act 2008, and
(b) it appears to the Director that the only condition that is met is condition 4.][1]

(7) In subsection (6) "religious or political hostility" means hostility based to any extent on
(a) religious belief or political opinion,
(b) supposed religious belief or political opinion, or
(c) the absence or supposed absence of any, or any particular, religious belief or political opinion.

---

[1] Inserted by the Criunter-Terrorism Act 2008, s 100(5), not yet in force.

(8) In subsection (6) the references to persons and groups of persons need not include a reference to the defendant or to any victim of the offence or offences.

(9) For the purposes of this section a person (A) is the associate of another person (B) if

   (a) A is the spouse or a former spouse of B,

   (b) A is the civil partner or a former civil partner of B,

   (c) A and B (whether of different sexes or the same sex) live as partners, or have lived as partners, in an enduring family relationship,

   (d) A is a friend of B, or

   (e) A is a relative of B.

(10) For the purposes of this section an organisation is a proscribed organisation, in relation to any time, if at that time

   (a) it is (or was) proscribed (within the meaning given by section 11(4) of the Terrorism Act 2000 (c 11)), and

   (b) its activities are (or were) connected with the affairs of Northern Ireland.

2 Certificates: supplementary

(1) If a certificate under section 1 is issued in relation to any trial on indictment of a person charged with one or more indictable offences ("the defendant"), it must be lodged with the court before the arraignment of

   (a) the defendant, or

   (b) any person committed for trial on indictment with the defendant.

(2) A certificate lodged under subsection (1) may be modified or withdrawn by giving notice to the court at any time before the arraignment of

   (a) the defendant, or

   (b) any person committed for trial on indictment with the defendant.

(3) In this section "the court" means

   (a) in relation to a time before the committal for trial on indictment of the defendant, the magistrates' court before which any proceedings for the offence or any of the offences mentioned in subsection (1) are being, or have been, conducted;

   (b) otherwise, the Crown Court.

3 Preliminary inquiry

(1) This section applies where a certificate under section 1 has been issued in relation to any trial on indictment of a person charged with one or more indictable offences.

(2) In proceedings before a magistrates' court for the offence or any of the offences, if the prosecution requests the court to conduct a preliminary inquiry into the offence the court must grant the request.

(3) In subsection (2) "preliminary inquiry" means a preliminary inquiry under the Magistrates' Courts (Northern Ireland) Order 1981 (SI 1981/1675 (NI 26)).

(4) Subsection (2)

   (a) applies notwithstanding anything in Article 31 of that Order,

   (b) does not apply in respect of an offence where the court considers that in the interests of justice a preliminary investigation should be conducted into the offence under that Order, and

   (c) does not apply in respect of an extra-territorial offence (as defined in section 1(3) of the Criminal Jurisdiction Act 1975 (c 59)).

4 Court for trial

(1) A trial on indictment in relation to which a certificate under section 1 has been issued is to be held only at the Crown Court sitting in Belfast, unless the Lord Chief Justice of Northern Ireland directs that

(a) the trial,

(b) a part of the trial, or

(c) a class of trials within which the trial falls,

is to be held at the Crown Court sitting elsewhere.

(2) The Lord Chief Justice of Northern Ireland may nominate any of the following to exercise his functions under subsection (1)

(a) the holder of one of the offices listed in Schedule 1 to the Justice (Northern Ireland) Act 2002 (c 26);

(b) a Lord Justice of Appeal (as defined in section 88 of that Act).

(3) If a person is committed for trial on indictment and a certificate under section 1 has been issued in relation to the trial, the person must be committed

(a) to the Crown Court sitting in Belfast, or

(b) where a direction has been given under subsection (1) which concerns the trial, to the Crown Court sitting at the place specified in the direction;

and section 48 of the Judicature (Northern Ireland) Act 1978 (c 23) (committal for trial on indictment) has effect accordingly.

(4) Where

(a) a person is committed for trial on indictment otherwise than to the Crown Court sitting at the relevant venue, and

(b) a certificate under section 1 is subsequently issued in relation to the trial,

the person is to be treated as having been committed for trial to the Crown Court sitting at the relevant venue.

(5) In subsection (4) "the relevant venue", in relation to a trial, means

(a) if the trial falls within a class specified in a direction under subsection (1)(c) (or would fall within such a class had a certificate under section 1 been issued in relation to the trial), the place specified in the direction;

(b) otherwise, Belfast.

(6) Where

(a) a person is committed for trial to the Crown Court sitting in Belfast in accordance with subsection (3) or by virtue of subsection (4), and

(b) a direction is subsequently given under subsection (1), before the commencement of the trial, altering the place of trial,

the person is to be treated as having been committed for trial to the Crown Court sitting at the place specified in the direction.

5 Mode of trial on indictment

(1) The effect of a certificate issued under section 1 is that the trial on indictment of

(a) the person to whom the certificate relates, and

(b) any person committed for trial with that person,

is to be conducted without a jury.

(2) Where a trial is conducted without a jury under this section, the court is to have all the powers, authorities and jurisdiction which the court would have had if the trial had been conducted with a jury (including power to determine any question and to make any finding which would be required to be determined or made by a jury).

(3) Except where the context otherwise requires, any reference in an enactment (including a pro-vision of Northern Ireland legislation) to a jury, the verdict of a jury or the finding of a jury is to be read, in relation to a trial conducted without a jury under this section, as a reference to the court, the verdict of the court or the finding of the court.

(4) No inference may be drawn by the court from the fact that the certificate has been issued in relation to the trial.

(5) Without prejudice to subsection (2), where the court conducting a trial under this section

(a) is not satisfied that a defendant is guilty of an offence for which he is being tried ("the offence charged"), but

(b) is satisfied that he is guilty of another offence of which a jury could have found him guilty on a trial for the offence charged,

the court may convict him of the other offence.

(6) Where a trial is conducted without a jury under this section and the court convicts a defendant (whether or not by virtue of subsection (5)), the court must give a judgment which states the reasons for the conviction at, or as soon as reasonably practicable after, the time of the conviction.

(7) A person convicted of an offence on a trial under this section may, notwithstanding anything in sections 1 and 10(1) of the Criminal Appeal (Northern Ireland) Act 1980 (c 47), appeal to the Court of Appeal under Part 1 of that Act

(a) against his conviction, on any ground, without the leave of the Court of Appeal or a certificate of the judge of the court of trial;

(b) against sentence passed on conviction, without that leave, unless the sentence is fixed by law.

(8) Where a person is convicted of an offence on a trial under this section, the time for giving notice of appeal under section 16(1) of that Act is to run from the date of judgment (if later than the date from which it would run under that subsection).

(9) Article 16(4) of the Criminal Justice (Northern Ireland) Order 2004 (SI 2004/1500 (NI 9)) (leave of judge or Court of Appeal required for prosecution appeal under Part IV of that Order) does not apply in relation to a trial conducted under this section.

6 Rules of court *(omitted)*

7 Limitation on challenge of issue of certificate

(1) No court may entertain proceedings for questioning (whether by way of judicial review or otherwise) any decision or purported decision of the Director of Public Prosecutions for Northern Ireland in relation to the issue of a certificate under section 1, except on the grounds of

(a) dishonesty,

(b) bad faith, or

(c) other exceptional circumstances (including in particular exceptional circumstances relating to lack of jurisdiction or error of law).

(2) Subsection (1) is subject to section 7(1) of the Human Rights Act 1998 (c 42) (claim that public authority has infringed Convention right).

8 Supplementary *(omitted)*

9 Duration of non-jury trial provisions

(1) Sections 1 to 8 (and Schedule 1) ("the non-jury trial provisions") shall expire at the end of the period of two years beginning with the day on which section 1 comes into force ("the effective period").

(2) But the Secretary of State may by order extend, or (on one or more occasions) further extend, the effective period.

(3) An order under subsection (2)

(a) must be made before the time when the effective period would end but for the making of the order, and

(b) shall have the effect of extending, or further extending, that period for the period of two years beginning with that time.

(4) The expiry of the non-jury trial provisions shall not affect their application to a trial on indictment in relation to which

(a) a certificate under section 1 has been issued, and

(b) the indictment has been presented,

before their expiry.

(5) The expiry of section 4 shall not affect the committal of a person for trial in accordance with subsection (3) of that section, or by virtue of subsection (4) or (6) of that section, to the Crown Court sitting in Belfast or elsewhere in a case where the indictment has not been presented before its expiry.

(6) The Secretary of State may by order make any amendments of enactments (including provisions of Northern Ireland legislation) that appear to him to be necessary or expedient in consequence of the expiry of the non-jury trial provisions.

(7) An order under this section

(a) shall be made by statutory instrument, and

(b) may not be made unless a draft has been laid before and approved by resolution of each House of Parliament.

Juries

10–13 *(omitted)*

Human rights commission

14–20 *(omitted)*

Powers

21 Stop and question

(1) A member of Her Majesty's forces on duty or a constable may stop a person for so long as is necessary to question him to ascertain his identity and movements.

(2) A member of Her Majesty's forces on duty may stop a person for so long as is necessary to question him to ascertain

(a) what he knows about a recent explosion or another recent incident endangering life;

(b) what he knows about a person killed or injured in a recent explosion or incident.

(3) A person commits an offence if he

(a) fails to stop when required to do so under this section,

(b) refuses to answer a question addressed to him under this section, or

(c) fails to answer to the best of his knowledge and ability a question addressed to him under this section.

(4) A person guilty of an offence under this section shall be liable on summary conviction to a fine not exceeding level 5 on the standard scale.

(5) A power to stop a person under this section includes a power to stop a vehicle (other than an aircraft which is airborne).

22 Arrest

(1) If a member of Her Majesty's forces on duty reasonably suspects that a person is committing, has committed or is about to commit any offence he may

(a) arrest the person without warrant, and

(b) detain him for a period not exceeding four hours.

(2) A person making an arrest under this section complies with any rule of law requiring him to state the ground of arrest if he states that he is making the arrest as a member of Her Majesty's forces.

(3) For the purpose of arresting a person under this section a member of Her Majesty's forces may enter and search any premises in which he knows, or reasonably suspects, the person to be.

(4) A member of Her Majesty's forces may seize, and detain for a period not exceeding four hours, anything which he reasonably suspects is being, has been or is intended to be used in the commission of an offence under section 31 and 32.

(5) The reference to a rule of law in subsection (2) does not include a rule of law which has effect only by virtue of the Human Rights Act 1998 (c 42).

23 Entry

(1) A member of Her Majesty's forces on duty or a constable may enter any premises if he considers it necessary in the course of operations for the preservation of the peace or the maintenance of order.

(2) A constable may not rely on subsection (1) to enter a building unless
   (a) he has authorisation, or
   (b) it is not reasonably practicable to obtain authorisation.

(3) Authorisation must be
   (a) written authorisation from an officer of the Police Service of Northern Ireland of at least the rank of superintendent, or
   (b) if it is not reasonably practicable to obtain written authorisation, oral authorisation from an officer of the Police Service of Northern Ireland of at least the rank of inspector.

(4) Written authorisation must relate to a specified area of Northern Ireland.

(5) An officer giving oral authorisation shall make a written record as soon as is reasonably practicable.

(6) Where a constable enters a building in reliance on subsection (1) he must ensure that as soon as is reasonably practicable a record is made of
   (a) the address of the building (if known),
   (b) the location of the building,
   (c) the date of entry,
   (d) the time of entry,
   (e) the purpose of entry,
   (f) the police number of each constable entering, and
   (g) the police number and rank of the authorising officer (if any).

(7) A written authorisation, or a record under subsection (5) or (6), must be kept by the person who gave or made it
   (a) while any legal or complaint proceedings to which it might be relevant are pending, and
   (b) in any event, for at least 12 months.

(8) A copy of a written authorisation or of a record under subsection (5) or (6) must be given as soon as is reasonably practicable to the owner or occupier of the premises to which it relates.

(9) A copy of a written authorisation or of a record under subsection (5) or (6) must be given as soon as is reasonably practicable to any person who requests a copy and who has, in the opinion of the person who has the authorisation or record, sufficient reason for the request.

(10) In subsection (7)(a) "complaint proceedings" means proceedings on a complaint made or referred to the Police Ombudsman for Northern Ireland in accordance with the Police (Northern Ireland) Act 1998 (c 32).

24 Search for munitions and transmitters

Schedule 3 (which confers power to search for munitions and transmitters) shall have effect.

25 Search for unlawfully detained persons

(1) A member of Her Majesty's forces on duty who reasonably believes that a person is unlawfully detained in such circumstances that his life is in danger may enter and search any premises for the purpose of ascertaining whether the person is detained there.

(2) A person may enter a dwelling in reliance on subsection (1) only if he is authorised for the purpose by a commissioned officer of Her Majesty's forces.

26 Premises: vehicles, &c

(1) A power under section 24 or 25 to search premises shall, in its application to vehicles (by virtue of section 42), be taken to include
  (a) power to stop a vehicle (other than an aircraft which is airborne), and
  (b) power to take a vehicle or cause it to be taken, where necessary or expedient, to any place for the purpose of carrying out the search.

(2) A person commits an offence if he fails to stop a vehicle when required to do so by virtue of this section.

(3) A person guilty of an offence under subsection (2) shall be liable on summary conviction to
  (a) imprisonment for a term not exceeding six months,
  (b) a fine not exceeding level 5 on the standard scale, or
  (c) both.

(4) In the application to a place or vehicle of a power to search premises under section 24 or 25
  (a) a reference to the address of the premises shall be construed as a reference to the location of the place or vehicle together with its registration number (if any), and
  (b) a reference to the occupier of the premises shall be construed as a reference to the occupier of the place or the person in charge of the vehicle.

(5) Where a search under Schedule 3 is carried out in relation to a vehicle, the person carrying out the search may, if he reasonably believes that it is necessary in order to carry out the search or to prevent it from being frustrated
  (a) require a person in or on the vehicle to remain with it;
  (b) require a person in or on the vehicle to go to and remain at any place to which the vehicle is taken by virtue of subsection (1)(b);
  (c) use reasonable force to secure compliance with a requirement under paragraph (a) or (b) above.

(6) Paragraphs 3(2) and (3), 6 and 7 of Schedule 3 shall apply to a requirement imposed under subsection (5) as they apply to a requirement imposed under that Schedule.

(7) Paragraph 6 of Schedule 3 shall apply in relation to the search of a vehicle which is not habitually stationary only if it is moved for the purpose of the search by virtue of subsection (1)(b); and where that paragraph does apply, the reference to the address of the premises shall be construed as a reference to the location where the vehicle is searched together with its registration number (if any).

27 Examination of documents

(1) A member of Her Majesty's forces who performs a search under sections 24 to 26
  (a) may examine any document or record found in order to ascertain whether it contains information of the kind mentioned in section 58(1)(a) of the Terrorism Act 2000 (c 11) (information likely to be useful for terrorism), and
  (b) if necessary or expedient for the purpose of paragraph (a), may remove the document or record to another place and retain it there until the examination is completed.

(2) Subsection (1) does not permit a person to examine a document or record if he has reasonable cause to believe that it is an item subject to legal privilege (within the meaning of the Police and Criminal Evidence (Northern Ireland) Order 1989 (SI 1989/1341 (NI 12))).

(3) A document or record may not be retained by virtue of subsection (1)(b) for more than 48 hours.

(4) A person who wilfully obstructs a member of Her Majesty's forces in the exercise of a power conferred by this section commits an offence.

(5) A person guilty of an offence under subsection (4) shall be liable
   (a) on conviction on indictment, to imprisonment for a term not exceeding two years, to a fine or to both, or
   (b) on summary conviction, to imprisonment for a term not exceeding six months, to a fine not exceeding the statutory maximum or to both.

28 Examination of documents: procedure

(1) Where a document or record is examined under section 27
   (a) it shall not be photographed or copied, and
   (b) the person who examines it shall make a written record of the examination as soon as is reasonably practicable.

(2) The record shall
   (a) describe the document or record,
   (b) specify the object of the examination,
   (c) state the address of the premises where the document or record was found,
   (d) where the document or record was found in the course of a search of a person, state the person's name,
   (e) where the document or record was found in the course of a search of any premises, state the name of a person appearing to the person making the record to be the occupier of the premises or to have had custody or control of the document or record when it was found,
   (f) where the document or record is removed for examination from the place where it was found, state the date and time when it was removed, and
   (g) where the document or record was examined at the place where it was found, state the date and time of examination.

(3) The record shall identify the person by whom the examination was carried out by reference to his service number, rank and regiment.

(4) Where a person makes a record of a search in accordance with this section, he shall as soon as is reasonably practicable supply a copy
   (a) in a case where the document or record was found in the course of a search of a person, to that person, and
   (b) in a case where the document or record was found in the course of a search of any premises, to a person appearing to the person making the record to be the occupier of the premises or to have had custody or control of the document or record when it was found.

29 Taking possession of land, &c

If the Secretary of State considers it necessary for the preservation of the peace or the maintenance of order, he may authorise a person
(a) to take possession of land or other property;
(b) to take steps to place buildings or other structures in a state of defence;
(c) to detain property or cause it to be destroyed or moved;
(d) to carry out works on land of which possession has been taken by virtue of this section;
(e) to take any other action which interferes with a public right or with a private right of property.

30 Road closure: immediate

(1) If he considers it immediately necessary for the preservation of the peace or the maintenance of order, an officer may
   (a) wholly or partly close a road;
   (b) divert or otherwise interfere with a road or the use of a road;
   (c) prohibit or restrict the exercise of a right of way;
   (d) prohibit or restrict the use of a waterway.
(2) In this section "officer" means
   (a) a member of Her Majesty's forces on duty, or
   (b) a person authorised for the purposes of this section by the Secretary of State.

31 Sections 29 and 30: supplementary

(1) A person commits an offence if he interferes with
   (a) works executed in connection with the exercise of powers conferred by virtue of section 29 or 30, or
   (b) any apparatus, equipment or other thing used in connection with the exercise of those powers.
(2) It is a defence for a person charged with an offence under this section to prove that he had a reasonable excuse for his interference.
(3) A person guilty of an offence under this section shall be liable on summary conviction to
   (a) imprisonment for a term not exceeding six months,
   (b) a fine not exceeding level 5 on the standard scale, or
   (c) both.
(4) An authorisation to exercise powers under section 29 or 30 may authorise
   (a) the exercise of all those powers, or
   (b) the exercise of a specified power or class of powers.
(5) An authorisation to exercise powers under section 29 or 30 may be addressed
   (a) to specified persons, or
   (b) to persons of a specified class.

32 Road closure: by order

(1) If the Secretary of State considers it necessary for the preservation of the peace or the maintenance of order he may by order direct that a specified road
   (a) shall be wholly closed,
   (b) shall be closed to a specified extent, or
   (c) shall be diverted in a specified manner.
(2) A person commits an offence if he interferes with
   (a) road closure works, or
   (b) road closure equipment.
(3) A person commits an offence if
   (a) he executes any bypass works within 200 metres of road closure works,
   (b) he has in his possession or under his control, within 200 metres of road closure works, materials or equipment suitable for executing bypass works, or
   (c) he knowingly permits on land occupied by him the doing or occurrence of anything which is an offence under paragraph (a) or (b).
(4) It is a defence for a person charged with an offence under this section to prove that he had a reasonable excuse for his action, possession, control or permission.
(5) A person guilty of an offence under this section shall be liable on summary conviction to
   (a) imprisonment for a term not exceeding six months,
   (b) a fine not exceeding level 5 on the standard scale, or
   (c) both.

(6) In this section

"bypass works" means works which facilitate the bypassing by vehicles of road closure works,

"road closure equipment" means any apparatus, equipment or other thing used in pursuance of an order under this section in connection with the closure or diversion of a road, and

"road closure works" means works executed in connection with the closure or diversion of a road specified in an order under this section (whether executed in pursuance of the order or in pursuance of power under an enactment to close or divert the road).

(7) An order

(a) may contain savings and transitional provisions,

(b) may make provision generally or for specified purposes only, and

(c) may make different provision for different purposes.

Powers: supplementary

33 Exercise of powers

(1) This section applies for the purposes of sections 21 to 30.

(2) A power conferred on a person

(a) is additional to powers which he has at common law or by virtue of any other enactment, and

(b) shall not be taken to affect those powers or Her Majesty's prerogative.

(3) A constable or member of Her Majesty's forces may if necessary use reasonable force for the purpose of exercising a power conferred on him.

(4) Where anything is seized it may (unless the contrary intention appears) be retained for so long as is necessary in all the circumstances.

(5) A power to search premises conferred by virtue of this Act shall be taken to include power to search a container.

(6) A member of Her Majesty's forces exercising a power when he is not in uniform shall, if requested to do so by a person at or about the time of exercising the power, produce to that person documentary evidence that he is a member of Her Majesty's forces.

34 Code of practice

(1) The Secretary of State may make codes of practice in connection with

(a) the exercise by police officers of a power conferred by this Act, and

(b) the seizure and retention of property found by police officers when exercising powers of search conferred by this Act.

(2) The Secretary of State may make codes of practice in connection with the exercise by members of Her Majesty's forces of a power conferred by this Act.

(3) Where the Secretary of State proposes to issue a code of practice he shall

(a) publish a draft,

(b) consider any representations made to him about the draft, and

(c) if he thinks it appropriate, modify the draft in the light of any representations made to him.

(4) The Secretary of State shall lay a draft of the code before Parliament.

(5) When the Secretary of State has laid a draft code before Parliament he may bring it into operation by order made by statutory instrument.

(6) The Secretary of State may revise the whole or any part of a code of practice issued by him and issue the code as revised; and subsections (3) to (5) shall apply to such a revised code as they apply to an original code.

(7) In this section "police officer" means a member of the Police Service of Northern Ireland or the Police Service of Northern Ireland Reserve.

35 Code: effect

(1) A failure by a police officer to comply with a provision of a code shall not of itself make him liable to criminal or civil proceedings.

(2) A failure by a member of Her Majesty's forces to comply with a provision of a code shall not of itself make him liable to any criminal or civil proceedings other than

(a) proceedings under any provision of the Army Act 1955 (c 18) or the Air Force Act 1955 (c 19) other than section 70 (civil offences), and

(b) proceedings under any provision of the Naval Discipline Act 1957 (c 53) other than section 42 (civil offences).

(3) A code

(a) shall be admissible in evidence in criminal or civil proceedings, and

(b) shall be taken into account by a court or tribunal in any case in which it appears to the court or tribunal to be relevant.

(4) In this section

"criminal proceedings" includes proceedings in Northern Ireland before a court-martial constituted under the Army Act 1955 (c 18), the Air Force Act 1955 (c 19) or the Naval Discipline Act 1957 (c 53) and proceedings in Northern Ireland before the Courts-Martial Appeal Court, and

"police officer" means a member of the Police Service of Northern Ireland or the Police Service of Northern Ireland Reserve.

36 Code: procedure for order *(omitted)*

37 Records

The Chief Constable of the Police Service of Northern Ireland shall make arrangements for securing that a record is made of each exercise by a constable of a power under sections 21 to 26 in so far as

(a) it is reasonably practicable to do so, and

(b) a record is not required to be made under another enactment.

38 Compensation

Schedule 4 (which provides for compensation to be paid for certain action taken under sections 21 to 32) shall have effect.

39 Prosecution

(1) This section applies to an offence under sections 21 to 32, except for an offence under paragraph 12 of Schedule 4.

(2) Proceedings for an offence to which this section applies shall not be instituted without the consent of the Director of Public Prosecutions for Northern Ireland.

(3) But if it appears to the Director of Public Prosecutions for Northern Ireland that an offence to which this section applies has been committed for a purpose wholly or partly connected with the affairs of a country other than the United Kingdom, his consent for the purposes of this section may be given only with the permission of the Advocate General for Northern Ireland.

(4) In relation to any time before the coming into force of section 27(1) of the Justice (Northern Ireland) Act 2002 (c 26), the reference in subsection (3) to the Advocate General for Northern Ireland is to be read as a reference to the Attorney General for Northern Ireland.

40 Review

(1) The Secretary of State shall appoint a person ("the reviewer") to review

(a) the operation of sections 21 to 32, and

    (b) the procedures adopted by the General Officer Commanding Northern Ireland ("GOC") for receiving, investigating and responding to complaints.

(2) The reviewer shall conduct a review as soon as is reasonably practicable after

    (a) 31st July 2008, and

    (b) each subsequent 31st July.

(3) The reviewer shall comply with any request of the Secretary of State to include in a review specified matters (which need not relate to the matters specified in subsection (1)(a) and (b)).

(4) The reviewer shall send the Secretary of State a report of each review.

(5) The Secretary of State shall lay a copy of each report before Parliament.

(6) The reviewer

    (a) shall receive and investigate any representations about the procedures mentioned in sub-section (1)(b),

    (b) may investigate the operation of those procedures in relation to a particular complaint or class of complaints,

    (c) may require GOC to review a particular case or class of cases in which the reviewer considers that any of those procedures have operated inadequately, and

    (d) may make recommendations to GOC about inadequacies in those procedures, including inadequacies in the way in which they operate in relation to a particular complaint or class of complaints.

(7) GOC shall

    (a) provide such information,

    (b) disclose such documents, and

    (c) provide such assistance,

as the Independent Assessor may reasonably require for the purpose of the performance of his functions.

(8) The Secretary of State may pay expenses and allowances to the reviewer, out of money provided by Parliament.

41 Duration

(1) The Secretary of State may by order repeal sections 21 to 40.

(2) An order

    (a) may make provision generally or only for specified purposes,

    (b) may make different provision for different purposes,

    (c) may include incidental, consequential or transitional provision or savings,

    (d) shall be made by statutory instrument, and

    (e) may not be made unless a draft has been laid before and approved by resolution of each House of Parliament.

42 Interpretation

In sections 21 to 38 (and Schedules 3 and 4)

"act" or "action" includes omission,

"dwelling" means

    (a) a building or part of a building used as a dwelling, and

    (b) a vehicle which is habitually stationary and which is used as a dwelling,

"premises" includes any place and in particular includes

    (a) a vehicle,

    (b) an offshore installation within the meaning given in section 44 of the Petroleum Act 1998 (c 17), and

    (c) a tent or moveable structure,

"property" includes property wherever situated and whether real or personal, and things in action and other intangible or incorporeal property, "public place" means a place to which members of the public have or are permitted to have access, whether or not for payment,

"road" has the same meaning as in the Road Traffic Regulation (Northern Ireland) Order 1997 (SI 1997/276 (NI 2)), and includes part of a road, and

"vehicle" includes an aircraft, hovercraft, train or vessel.

Miscellaneous

43–47 *(omitted)*

48 Private Security Industry

(1) This section
 (a) establishes interim arrangements for regulating private security services in Northern Ireland following the expiry of section 106 of, and Schedule 13 to, the Terrorism Act 2000 (c 11) (subsection (2) and Schedule 6), and
 (b) provides for the eventual regulation of those services under the Private Security Industry Act 2001 (c 12) (subsections (3) to (5)).

(2) Schedule 6 (which regulates the private security industry in Northern Ireland until repeal in accordance with subsection (4)(a) below) shall have effect.

(3) For section 26(3) and (4) of the Private Security Industry Act 2001 (extent) substitute
 "(3) This Act extends to
  (a) England and Wales,
  (b) Scotland, and
  (c) Northern Ireland."

(4) An order under section 3(3) of the Private Security Industry Act 2001 (conduct prohibited without a licence) designating an activity in respect of Northern Ireland
 (a) shall include provision repealing Schedule 6 to this Act in so far as it applies to that activity, and
 (b) may include transitional provision or savings.

(5) The amendments of that Act in section 49 below shall have effect.

(6) This section and section 49 shall come into force in accordance with provision made by the Secretary of State by order; and an order
 (a) shall be made by statutory instrument,
 (b) may make provision generally or only for specified purposes,
 (c) may make different provision for different purposes, and
 (d) may include incidental, consequential or transitional provision.

(7) Transitional provision under or by virtue of this section may, in particular
 (a) provide for a licence issued under one provision to have effect, subject to any specified modifications, as if issued under another;
 (b) provide for applications under or by virtue of a provision to be made in advance of its coming into force.

49 Amendments of the Private Security Industry Act 2001 *(omitted)*

Supplemental

50 Repeals and revocations *(omitted)*

51 Financial provisions *(omitted)*

52 Extent *(omitted)*

53 Commencement *(omitted)*

54 Short title *(omitted)*

SCHEDULE 1
TRIALS ON INDICTMENT WITHOUT A JURY: CONSEQUENTIAL
AMENDMENTS *(omitted)*

SCHEDULE 2
RESTRICTIONS ON DISCLOSURE OF JUROR INFORMATION:
FURTHER AMENDMENTS *(omitted)*

SCHEDULE 3   Section 24
MUNITIONS AND TRANSMITTERS: SEARCH AND SEIZURE

Interpretation

1 (1) In this Schedule "officer" means
    (a) a member of Her Majesty's forces on duty, and
    (b) a constable.
  (2) In this Schedule "authorised officer" means
    (a) a member of Her Majesty's forces who is on duty and is authorised by a commissioned officer of those forces, and
    (b) a constable who is authorised by an officer of the Police Service of Northern Ireland of at least the rank of inspector.
  (3) In this Schedule
    (a) "munitions" means
      (i) explosives, firearms and ammunition, and
      (ii) anything used or capable of being used in the manufacture of an explosive, a firearm or ammunition,
    (b) "explosive" means
      (i) an article or substance manufactured for the purpose of producing a practical effect by explosion,
      (ii) materials for making an article or substance within sub-paragraph (i),
      (iii) anything used or intended to be used for causing or assisting in causing an explosion, and
      (iv) a part of anything within sub-paragraph (i) or (ii),
    (c) "firearm" includes an air gun or air pistol,
    (d) "scanning receiver" means apparatus (or a part of apparatus) for wireless telegraphy designed or adapted for the purpose of automatically monitoring selected frequencies, or automatically scanning a selected range of frequencies, so as to enable transmissions on any of those frequencies to be detected or intercepted,
    (e) "transmitter" means apparatus (or a part of apparatus) for wireless telegraphy designed or adapted for emission, as opposed to reception,
    (f) "wireless apparatus" means a scanning receiver or a transmitter, and
    (g) "wireless telegraphy" has the same meaning as in section 116 of the Wireless Telegraphy Act 2006 (c 36).

Entering premises

2 (1) An officer may enter and search any premises for the purpose of ascertaining
    (a) whether there are any munitions unlawfully on the premises, or
    (b) whether there is any wireless apparatus on the premises.

(2) An officer may not enter a dwelling under this paragraph unless he is an authorised officer and he reasonably suspects that the dwelling
    (a) unlawfully contains munitions, or
    (b) contains wireless apparatus.

(3) A constable exercising the power under sub-paragraph (1) may, if necessary, be accompanied by other persons.

3 (1) If the officer carrying out a search of premises under paragraph 2 reasonably believes that it is necessary in order to carry out the search or to prevent it from being frustrated, he may
    (a) require a person who is on the premises when the search begins, or who enters during the search, to remain on the premises;
    (b) require a person mentioned in paragraph (a) to remain in a specified part of the premises;
    (c) require a person mentioned in paragraph (a) to refrain from entering a specified part of the premises;
    (d) require a person mentioned in paragraph (a) to go from one specified part of the premises to another;
    (e) require a person who is not a resident of the premises to refrain from entering them.

(2) A requirement imposed under this paragraph shall cease to have effect after the conclusion of the search in relation to which it was imposed.

(3) Subject to sub-paragraphs (4) and (5), no requirement under this paragraph for the purposes of a search shall be imposed or have effect after the end of the period of four hours beginning with the time when the first (or only) requirement is imposed in relation to the search.

(4) In the case of a search by a constable, an officer of the Police Service of Northern Ireland of at least the rank of superintendent may extend the period mentioned in sub-paragraph (3) in relation to a search by a further period of four hours if he reasonably believes that it is necessary to do so in order to carry out the search or to prevent it from being frustrated.

(5) In the case of a search by a member of Her Majesty's forces, an officer of at least the rank of Major may extend the period mentioned in sub-paragraph (3) in relation to a search by a further period of four hours if he reasonably believes that it is necessary to do so in order to carry out the search or to prevent it from being frustrated.

(6) The power to extend a period conferred by sub-paragraph (4) or (5) may be exercised only once in relation to a particular search.

Stopping and searching persons

4 (1) An officer may
    (a) stop a person in a public place, and
    (b) search him for the purpose of ascertaining whether he has munitions unlawfully with him or wireless apparatus with him.

(2) An officer may search a person
    (a) who is not in a public place, and
    (b) whom the officer reasonably suspects to have munitions unlawfully with him or to have wireless apparatus with him.

(3) A member of Her Majesty's forces may search a person entering or found in a dwelling entered under paragraph 2.

Seizure

5 (1) This paragraph applies where an officer is empowered by virtue of this Schedule or section 25 or 26 to search premises or a person.

(2) The officer may

(a) seize any munitions found in the course of the search (unless it appears to him that the munitions are being, have been and will be used only lawfully), and

(b) retain and, if necessary, destroy them.

(3) The officer may

(a) seize any wireless apparatus found in the course of the search (unless it appears to him that the apparatus is being, has been and will be used only lawfully), and

(b) retain it.

Records

6 (1) Where an officer carries out a search of premises under this Schedule he shall, unless it is not reasonably practicable, make a written record of the search.

(2) The record shall specify

(a) the address of the premises searched,

(b) the date and time of the search,

(c) any damage caused in the course of the search, and

(d) anything seized in the course of the search.

(3) The record shall also include the name (if known) of any person appearing to the officer to be the occupier of the premises searched; but

(a) a person may not be detained in order to discover his name, and

(b) if the officer does not know the name of a person appearing to him to be the occupier of the premises searched, he shall include in the record a note describing him.

(4) The record shall identify the officer

(a) in the case of a constable, by reference to his police number, and

(b) in the case of a member of Her Majesty's forces, by reference to his service number, rank and regiment.

7 (1) Where an officer makes a record of a search in accordance with paragraph 6, he shall supply a copy to any person appearing to him to be the occupier of the premises searched.

(2) The copy shall be supplied immediately or as soon as is reasonably practicable.

Offences

8 (1) A person commits an offence if he

(a) knowingly fails to comply with a requirement imposed under paragraph 3, or

(b) wilfully obstructs, or seeks to frustrate, a search of premises under this Schedule.

(2) A person guilty of an offence under this paragraph shall be liable

(a) on conviction on indictment, to imprisonment for a term not exceeding two years, to a fine or to both, or

(b) on summary conviction, to imprisonment for a term not exceeding six months, to a fine not exceeding the statutory maximum or to both.

9 (1) A person commits an offence if he fails to stop when required to do so under paragraph 4.

(2) A person guilty of an offence under this paragraph shall be liable on summary conviction to a fine not exceeding level 5 on the standard scale.

SCHEDULE 4   Section 38
COMPENSATION

Right to compensation

1 (1) This paragraph applies where under sections 21 to 32

(a) real or personal property is taken, occupied, destroyed or damaged, or

(b) any other act is done which interferes with private rights of property.

(2) Where this paragraph applies in respect of an act taken in relation to any property or rights the Secretary of State shall pay compensation to any person who
   (a) has an estate or interest in the property or is entitled to the rights, and
   (b) suffers loss or damage as a result of the act.

2 No compensation shall be payable unless an application is made to the Secretary of State in such manner as he may specify.

Time limit

3 (1) Subject to sub-paragraphs (2) and (3), an application for compensation in respect of an act must be made within the period of 28 days beginning with the date of the act.
   (2) The Secretary of State may, in response to a request made to him in writing, permit an application to be made
      (a) after the expiry of the period mentioned in sub-paragraph (1), and
      (b) within such longer period, starting from the date of the act and not exceeding six months, as he may specify.
   (3) Where the Secretary of State refuses a request under sub-paragraph (2)
      (a) he shall serve a notice of refusal on the person who made the request,
      (b) that person may, within the period of six weeks beginning with the date of service of the notice, appeal to the county court against the refusal, and
      (c) the county court may exercise the power of the Secretary of State under sub-paragraph (2).

Determination

4 Where the Secretary of State determines an application for compensation he shall serve on the applicant a notice
   (a) stating that he has decided to award compensation and specifying the amount of the award, or
   (b) stating that he has decided to refuse the application.

5 (1) An applicant may appeal to the county court against
      (a) the amount of compensation awarded, or
      (b) the refusal of compensation.
   (2) An appeal must be brought within the period of six weeks beginning with the date of service of the notice under paragraph 4.

6 (1) This paragraph applies where the Secretary of State considers that in the course of an application for compensation the applicant
      (a) knowingly made a false or misleading statement,
      (b) made a statement which he did not believe to be true, or
      (c) knowingly failed to disclose a material fact.
   (2) The Secretary of State may
      (a) refuse to award compensation,
      (b) reduce the amount of compensation which he would otherwise have awarded, or
      (c) withhold all or part of compensation which he has awarded.

7 Where the Secretary of State makes an award of compensation he may make a payment to the applicant in respect of all or part of the costs of the application.

Assignment of right

8 (1) This paragraph applies where
      (a) a person has made an application for compensation, and

    (b) his right to compensation has passed to another person by virtue of an assignment or the operation of law.

(2) The Secretary of State shall treat the person mentioned in sub-paragraph (1)(b) as the applicant.

Offenders

9 (1) This paragraph applies where a person has a right to compensation in respect of an act and

    (a) the act was done in connection with, or revealed evidence of the commission of an offence, and

    (b) proceedings for the offence are brought against the person.

(2) The person's right to compensation shall not be enforceable while the proceedings have not been concluded.

(3) If the person stands convicted of the offence he shall have no right to compensation.

Notices

10 A notice served under paragraph 3(3)(a) or 4 shall contain particulars of the right of appeal under paragraph 3(3)(b) or 5.

11 (1) The Secretary of State may serve a notice under this Schedule on an individual

    (a) by delivering it to him,

    (b) by sending it by post addressed to him at his usual or last-known place of residence or business, or

    (c) by leaving it for him there.

(2) The Secretary of State may serve a notice under this Schedule on a partnership

    (a) by sending it by post to a partner, or to a person having the control or management of the partnership business, at the principal office of the partnership, or

    (b) by addressing it to a partner or to a person mentioned in paragraph (a) and leaving it at that office.

(3) The Secretary of State may serve a notice under this Schedule on a body corporate

    (a) by sending it by post to the secretary or clerk of the body at its registered or principal office, or

    (b) by addressing it to the secretary or clerk of the body and leaving it at that office.

(4) The Secretary of State may serve a notice under this Schedule on any person

    (a) by delivering it to his solicitor,

    (b) by sending it by post to his solicitor at his solicitor's office, or

    (c) by leaving it for his solicitor there.

Offences

12 (1) A person commits an offence if he obtains compensation or increased compensation for himself or another person by deception.

(2) In sub-paragraph (1) "deception" means any deception (whether deliberate or reckless) by words or conduct as to fact or as to law, including a deception as to the present intentions of the person using the deception or any other person.

(3) A person commits an offence if for the purposes of obtaining compensation he

    (a) knowingly makes a false or misleading statement,

    (b) makes a statement which he does not believe to be true, or

    (c) knowingly fails to disclose a material fact.

(4) A person guilty of an offence under this paragraph shall be liable

    (a) on conviction on indictment, to imprisonment for a term not exceeding five years, to a fine or to both, or

    (b) on summary conviction, to imprisonment for a term not exceeding one year, to a fine not exceeding the statutory maximum or to both.

SCHEDULE 5
NORTHERN IRELAND DEPARTMENT WITH POLICING AND JUSTICE FUNCTIONS *(omitted)*

SCHEDULE 6
Section 48

PRIVATE SECURITY INDUSTRY: INTERIM ARRANGEMENTS

Interpretation

1 In this Schedule "security services" means the services of one or more individuals as security guards (whether or not provided together with other services relating to the protection of property or persons).

2 In this Schedule "licence" means a licence under this Schedule.

3 In this Schedule "proscribed organisation" has the meaning given by section 3 of the Terrorism Act 2000 (c 11).

Unlicensed services: offences

4 A person commits an offence if he provides or offers to provide security services for reward unless he

    (a) holds a licence, or

    (b) acts on behalf of someone who holds a licence.

5 (1) A person commits an offence if he publishes or causes to be published an advertisement for the provision for reward of security services by a person who does not hold a licence.

    (2) It is a defence for a person charged with an offence under this paragraph to prove

        (a) that his business is (or includes) publishing advertisements or arranging for their publication,

        (b) that he received the advertisement for publication in the ordinary course of business, and

        (c) that he reasonably believed that the person mentioned in the advertisement as the provider of security services held a licence.

6 (1) A person commits an offence if he pays money, in respect of the provision of security services, to a person who

    (a) does not hold a licence, and

    (b) is not acting on behalf of someone who holds a licence.

    (2) It is a defence for a person charged with an offence under this paragraph to prove that he reasonably believed that the person to whom he paid the money

        (a) held a licence, or

        (b) was acting on behalf of someone who held a licence.

7 (1) A person guilty of an offence under paragraph 4 or 5 shall be liable

    (a) on conviction on indictment, to imprisonment for a term not exceeding five years, to a fine or to both, or

    (b) on summary conviction, to imprisonment for a term not exceeding six months, to a fine not exceeding the statutory maximum or to both.

(2) A person guilty of an offence under paragraph 6 is liable on summary conviction to

    (a) imprisonment for a term not exceeding six months,

    (b) a fine not exceeding level 5 on the standard scale, or

    (c) both.

Application for licence

8 (1) An application for a licence shall be made to the Secretary of State

    (a) in such manner and form as he may specify, and

    (b) accompanied by such information as he may specify.

(2) The Secretary of State may specify information only if it concerns

    (a) the applicant,

    (b) a business involving the provision of security services for reward which is, was or is proposed to be carried on by the applicant,

    (c) a person whom the applicant employs or proposes to employ as a security guard,

    (d) a partner or proposed partner of the applicant (where the applicant is an individual),

    (e) a member or proposed member of the applicant (where the applicant is a partnership),

    (f) an officer or proposed officer of the applicant (where the applicant is a body corporate).

(3) A person commits an offence if in connection with an application for a licence he

    (a) makes a statement which he knows to be false or misleading in a material particular, or

    (b) recklessly makes a statement which is false or misleading in a material particular.

(4) A person guilty of an offence under sub-paragraph (3) shall be liable

    (a) on conviction on indictment, to imprisonment for a term not exceeding two years, to a fine or to both, or

    (b) on summary conviction, to imprisonment for a term not exceeding six months, to a fine not exceeding the statutory maximum or to both.

(5) For the purposes of this paragraph

    (a) a reference to employment or proposed employment by an applicant for a licence shall, where the applicant is a partnership or a member of a partnership, be construed as a reference to employment or proposed employment by the partnership or by any of its partners,

    (b) "officer" includes a director, manager or secretary,

    (c) a person in accordance with whose directions or instructions the directors of a body corporate are accustomed to act shall be treated as an officer of that body, and

    (d) the reference to directions or instructions in paragraph (c) does not include a reference to advice given in a professional capacity.

Issue of licence

9 (1) The Secretary of State shall grant an application for a licence unless satisfied that any of Conditions 1 to 4 applies.

(2) Condition 1 for the refusal of a licence is that a proscribed organisation, or an organisation which appears to the Secretary of State to be closely associated with a proscribed organisation, would be likely to benefit from the licence (whether or not a condition were imposed under paragraph 10).

(3) Condition 2 for the refusal of a licence is that there are reasonable grounds to suspect that any of the following is engaged in criminal activity

    (a) a business involving the provision for reward of security services which is, was or is proposed to be carried on by the applicant,

    (b) a person whom the applicant employs or proposes to employ as a security guard,

(c) a partner or proposed partner of the applicant (where the applicant is an individual),

(d) a member or proposed member of the applicant (where the applicant is a partnership), and

(e) an officer or proposed officer of the applicant (where the applicant is a body corporate).

(4) Condition 3 for the refusal of a licence is that the applicant has persistently failed to comply with the requirements of this Schedule.

(5) Condition 4 for the refusal of a licence is that the applicant has failed to comply with a condition imposed under paragraph 10.

(6) In Condition 1 a reference to a benefit is a reference to any benefit

(a) whether direct or indirect, and

(b) whether financial or not.

(7) Paragraph 8(5) shall have effect for the purposes of Condition 2.

(8) In Condition 3 the reference to this Schedule includes a reference to

(a) Part V of the Northern Ireland (Emergency Provisions) Act 1991 (c 24) (private security services),

(b) Part V of the Northern Ireland (Emergency Provisions) Act 1996 (c 22) (private security services), and

(c) Schedule 13 to the Terrorism Act 2000 (c 11) (Northern Ireland: private security services).

Conditions of licence

10 (1) The Secretary of State may on granting a licence impose a condition if satisfied that it is necessary in order to prevent any of the persons listed in sub-paragraph (2) from benefiting from the licence (within the meaning of paragraph 9(6)).

(2) Those persons are

(a) a proscribed organisation,

(b) an organisation which appears to the Secretary of State to be closely associated with a proscribed organisation, from benefiting from the licence, and

(c) a person who engages in criminal activity.

Refusal of licence

11 If the Secretary of State refuses an application for a licence he shall notify the applicant.

Duration of licence

12 (1) A licence

(a) shall come into force at the beginning of the day on which it is issued, and

(b) subject to sub-paragraph (2), shall expire at the end of the period of 12 months beginning with that day.

(2) Where a licence is issued to a person who already holds a licence, the new licence shall expire at the end of the period of 12 months beginning with the day after the day on which the current licence expires.

(3) The Secretary of State may by order substitute a period exceeding 12 months for the period for the time being specified in sub-paragraphs (1)(b) and (2).

(4) An order under sub-paragraph (3)

(a) may include incidental or transitional provision,

(b) shall be made by statutory instrument, and

(c) shall be laid before Parliament.

Revocation of licence

13 (1) The Secretary of State may revoke a licence if satisfied that
(a) a proscribed organisation, or an organisation which appears to the Secretary of State to be closely associated with a proscribed organisation, would be likely to benefit from the licence remaining in force,
(b) there are reasonable grounds to suspect that any of the persons listed in paragraph 9(3) (taking a reference to the applicant as a reference to the holder of the licence) is engaged in criminal activity,
(c) the holder of the licence has persistently failed to comply with the requirements of this Schedule, or
(d) the holder of the licence has failed to comply with a condition imposed under paragraph 10.
(2) The Secretary of State shall not revoke a licence unless the holder
(a) has been notified of the Secretary of State's intention to revoke the licence, and
(b) has been given a reasonable opportunity to make representations to the Secretary of State.
(3) If the Secretary of State revokes a licence he shall notify the holder immediately.
(4) Paragraph 9(6) and (8) shall apply for the purposes of this paragraph.

Appeal

14 The applicant for a licence may appeal to the High Court if
(a) the application is refused,
(b) a condition is imposed on the grant of a licence, or
(c) the licence is revoked.
15 (1) Where an appeal is brought under paragraph 14, the Secretary of State may issue a certificate that the decision to which the appeal relates
(a) was taken for a purpose specified in sub-paragraph (2), and
(b) was justified by that purpose.
(2) Those purposes are
(a) preventing benefit from accruing to an organisation which was proscribed,
(b) preventing benefit from accruing to an organisation which appeared to the Secretary of State to be closely associated with an organisation which was proscribed, and
(c) preventing benefit from accruing to a person who was engaged in criminal activity.
(3) If he intends to rely on a certificate under this paragraph the Secretary of State shall notify the appellant.
(4) Where the appellant is notified of the Secretary of State's intention to rely on a certificate under this paragraph
(a) he may appeal against the certificate to the Tribunal established under section 91 of the Northern Ireland Act 1998 (c 47), and
(b) sections 90(3) and (4), 91(2) to (9) and 92 of that Act (effect of appeal, procedure, and further appeal) shall apply.
(5) Rules made under section 91 or 92 of that Act which are in force immediately before this paragraph comes into force shall have effect in relation to a certificate under this paragraph
(a) with any necessary modifications, and
(b) subject to any later rules made by virtue of sub-paragraph (4)(b).

Change of personnel

16 Paragraphs 17 and 18 apply to a person who
    (a) holds a licence, or
    (b) has made an application for a licence which has not yet been determined.

17 (1) If a person to whom this paragraph applies proposes to employ a security guard about whom information was not given under paragraph 8, he shall give the Secretary of State such information about the security guard as the Secretary of State may specify.
    (2) The information shall be given not less than 14 days before the employment is to begin.
    (3) For the purposes of this paragraph the provisions of paragraph 8(5) shall have effect in relation to a holder of or an applicant for a licence as they have effect for the purposes of paragraph 8 in relation to an applicant.

18 (1) A person to whom this paragraph applies shall give the Secretary of State such information about a relevant change of personnel as the Secretary of State may specify.
    (2) The information shall be given
        (a) not less than 14 days before the change, or
        (b) if that is not reasonably practicable, as soon as is reasonably practicable.
    (3) A relevant change of personnel is
        (a) where the application for the licence was made by a partnership or a member of a partnership, a change in the members of the partnership, or
        (b) where the application for the licence was made by a body corporate, a change in the officers of the body (within the meaning of paragraph 8).
    (4) But a change of personnel is not relevant if it was mentioned in the information given under paragraph 8.

19 (1) A person commits an offence if he fails to comply with paragraph 17 or 18.
    (2) A person guilty of an offence under this paragraph shall be liable on summary conviction to
        (a) imprisonment for a term not exceeding six months,
        (b) a fine not exceeding level 5 on the standard scale, or
        (c) both.

Records

20 (1) A constable may
    (a) enter premises where a business involving the provision of security services is being carried on, and
    (b) require records kept there of a person employed as a security guard to be produced for the constable's inspection.
    (2) A constable exercising the power under this paragraph
        (a) shall identify himself to a person appearing to be in charge of the premises,
        (b) if the constable is not in uniform, shall produce to that person documentary evidence that he is a constable, and
        (c) may use reasonable force.
    (3) A person commits an offence if he fails to comply with a requirement imposed under sub-paragraph (1)(b).
    (4) But it is a defence for a person charged with an offence under sub-paragraph (3) to show that he had a reasonable excuse for his failure.
    (5) A person guilty of an offence under sub-paragraph (3) shall be liable on summary conviction to
        (a) imprisonment for a term not exceeding six months,
        (b) a fine not exceeding level 5 on the standard scale, or
        (c) both.

21 (1) A person who provides for reward security services commits an offence if he makes or keeps a record of a person employed by him as a security guard which he knows to be false or misleading in a material particular.

   (2) A person guilty of an offence under this paragraph shall be liable

     (a) on conviction on indictment, to imprisonment for a term not exceeding two years, to a fine or to both, or

     (b) on summary conviction, to imprisonment for a term not exceeding six months, to a fine not exceeding the statutory maximum or to both.

Offence: body corporate

22 (1) This paragraph applies where an offence under this Schedule committed by a body corporate is proved

     (a) to have been committed with the consent or connivance of an officer of the body corporate, or

     (b) to be attributable to neglect on the part of an officer of the body corporate.

   (2) The officer, as well as the body corporate, shall be guilty of the offence.

   (3) In this paragraph "officer" includes

     (a) a director, manager or secretary,

     (b) a person purporting to act as a director, manager or secretary, and

     (c) a member of a body corporate the affairs of which are managed by its members.

Notice

23 (1) A notice under this Schedule must be in writing.

   (2) Information required to be given to the Secretary of State under this Schedule

     (a) must be in writing, and

     (b) may be sent to him by post.

   (3) The Secretary of State may serve a notice under this Schedule on an individual

     (a) by delivering it to him,

     (b) by sending it by post addressed to him at his usual or last-known place of residence or business, or

     (c) by leaving it for him there.

   (4) The Secretary of State may serve a notice under this Schedule on a partnership

     (a) by sending it by post to a partner, or to a person having the control or management of the partnership business, at the principal office of the partnership, or

     (b) by addressing it to a partner or to a person mentioned in paragraph (a) and leaving it at that office.

   (5) The Secretary of State may serve a notice under this Schedule on a body corporate

     (a) by sending it by post to the secretary or clerk of the body at its registered or principal office, or

     (b) by addressing it to the secretary or clerk of the body and leaving it at that office.

   (6) The Secretary of State may serve a notice under this Schedule on any person

     (a) by delivering it to his solicitor,

     (b) by sending it by post to his solicitor at his solicitor's office, or

     (c) by leaving it for his solicitor there.

   (7) Sub-paragraphs (3) to (6) do not apply in relation to a notice under paragraph 15.

SCHEDULE 7
REPEALS AND REVOCATIONS *(omitted)*

APPENDIX 6

Counter-Terrorism Act 2008[1]

An Act to confer further powers to gather and share information for counter-terrorism and other purposes; to make further provision about the detention and questioning of terrorist suspects and the prosecution and punishment of terrorist offences; to impose notification requirements on persons convicted of such offences; to confer further powers to act against terrorist financing, money laundering and certain other activities; to provide for review of certain Treasury decisions and about evidence in, and other matters connected with, review proceedings; to amend the law relating to inquiries; to amend the definition of "terrorism"; to amend the enactments relating to terrorist offences, control orders and the forfeiture of terrorist cash; to provide for recovering the costs of policing at certain gas facilities; to amend provisions about the appointment of special advocates in Northern Ireland; and for connected purposes.

(26th November 2008)

PART 1
POWERS TO GATHER AND SHARE INFORMATION

Power to remove documents for examination

1 Power to remove documents for examination

(1) This section applies to a search under any of the following provisions
    (a) section 43(1) of the Terrorism Act 2000 (c 11) (search of suspected terrorist);
    (b) section 43(2) of that Act (search of person arrested under section 41 on suspicion of being a terrorist);
    (c) paragraph 1, 3, 11, 15, 28 or 31 of Schedule 5 to that Act (terrorist investigations);
    (d) section 52(1) or (3)(b) of the Anti-terrorism, Crime and Security Act 2001 (c 24) (search for evidence of commission of weapons-related offences);
    (e) section 7A, 7B or 7C of the Prevention of Terrorism Act 2005 (c 2) (searches in connection with control orders);
    (f) section 28 of the Terrorism Act 2006 (c 11) (search for terrorist publications).

(2) A constable who carries out a search to which this section applies may, for the purpose of ascertaining whether a document is one that may be seized, remove the document to another place for examination and retain it there until the examination is completed.

(3) Where a constable carrying out a search to which this section applies has power to remove a document by virtue of this section, and the document
    (a) consists of information that is stored in electronic form, and
    (b) is accessible from the premises being searched,

---

[1] The majority of this Act is not in force. As at 31 March 2009, the following were in force: ss.19–21, 29, 62–102 (99 in part), sch.1, 7, 8, 9 (in part)—italics are not used.

the constable may require the document to be produced in a form in which it can be taken away, and in which it is visible and legible or from which it can readily be produced in a visible and legible form.

(4) A constable has the same powers of seizure in relation to a document removed under this section as the constable would have if it had not been removed (and if anything discovered on examination after removal had been discovered without it having been removed).

2 Offence of obstruction

(1) A person who wilfully obstructs a constable in the exercise of the power conferred by section 1 commits an offence.

(2) A person guilty of an offence under this section is liable on summary conviction

    (a) in England and Wales, to imprisonment for a term not exceeding 51 weeks or a fine not exceeding level 5 on the standard scale, or both;

    (b) in Scotland, to imprisonment for a term not exceeding twelve months or a fine not exceeding level 5 on the standard scale, or both;

    (c) in Northern Ireland, to imprisonment for a term not exceeding six months or a fine not exceeding level 5 on the standard scale, or both.

(3) In subsection (2)(a) as it applies in relation to an offence committed before section 281(5) of the Criminal Justice Act 2003 (c 44) comes into force, for "51 weeks" substitute "six months".

3 Items subject to legal privilege

(1) Section 1 does not authorise a constable to remove a document if the constable has reasonable cause to believe

    (a) it is an item subject to legal privilege, or

    (b) it has an item subject to legal privilege comprised in it.

(2) Subsection (1)(b) does not prevent the removal of a document if it is not reasonably practicable for the item subject to legal privilege to be separated from the rest of the document without prejudicing any use of the rest of the document that would be lawful if it were subsequently seized.

(3) If, after a document has been removed under section 1, it is discovered that

    (a) it is an item subject to legal privilege, or

    (b) it has an item subject to legal privilege comprised in it,

the document must be returned forthwith.

(4) Subsection (3)(b) does not require the return of a document if it is not reasonably practicable for the item subject to legal privilege to be separated from the rest of the document without prejudicing any use of the rest of the document that would be lawful if it were subsequently seized.

(5) Where an item subject to legal privilege is removed under subsection (2) or retained under subsection (4), it must not be examined or put to any other use except to the extent necessary for facilitating the examination of the rest of the document.

(6) For the purposes of this section "item subject to legal privilege"

    (a) in England and Wales, has the same meaning as in the Police and Criminal Evidence Act 1984 (c 60);

    (b) in Scotland, has the meaning given by section 412 of the Proceeds of Crime Act 2002 (c 29);

    (c) in Northern Ireland, has the same meaning as in the Police and Criminal Evidence (Northern Ireland) Order 1989 (SI 1989/1341 (NI 12)).

4 Record of removal

(1) A constable who removes a document under section 1 must make a written record of the removal.

(2) The record must be made as soon as is reasonably practicable and in any event within the period of 24 hours beginning with the time when the document was removed.

(3) The record must
  (a) describe the document,
  (b) specify the object of the removal,
  (c) where the document was found in the course of a search of a person, state the person's name (if known),
  (d) where the document was found in the course of a search of any premises, state the address of the premises where the document was found,
  (e) where the document was found in the course of a search of any premises, state the name (if known) of
    (i) any person who, when the record is made, appears to the constable to have been the occupier of the premises when the document was found, and
    (ii) any person who, when the record is made, appears to the constable to have had custody or control of the document when it was found, and
  (f) state the date and time when the document was removed.

(4) If, in a case where the document was found in the course of a search of a person, the constable does not know the person's name, the record must include a description of the person.

(5) If, in a case where the document was found in the course of a search of any premises, the constable does not know the name of a person mentioned in subsection (3)(e) but is able to provide a description of that person, the record must include such a description.

(6) The record must identify the constable by reference to the constable's police number.

(7) The following are entitled, on a request made to the constable, to a copy of the record made under this section
  (a) where the document was found in the course of a search of a person, that person; and
  (b) where the document was found in the course of a search of any premises
    (i) the occupier of the premises when it was found, and
    (ii) any person who had custody or control of the document when it was found.

(8) The constable must provide the copy within a reasonable time from the making of the request.

(9) If, in England and Wales or Northern Ireland, the document is found in the course of a search under a warrant, the constable must make an endorsement on the warrant stating that the document has been removed under section 1.

(10) In the application of this section in relation to the search of a vehicle, the reference to the address of the premises is to the location of the vehicle together with its registration number (if any).

5 Retention of documents

(1) A document may not be retained by virtue of section 1 for more than 48 hours without further authorisation.

(2) A constable of at least the rank of chief inspector may authorise the retention of the document for a further period or periods if satisfied that
  (a) the examination of the document is being carried out expeditiously, and
  (b) it is necessary to continue the examination for the purpose of ascertaining whether the document is one that may be seized.

(3) This does not permit the retention of a document after the end of the period of 96 hours beginning with the time when it was removed for examination.

6 Access to documents

(1) Where
  (a) a document is retained by virtue of section 5, and

   (b) a request for access to the document is made to the officer in charge of the investigation by a person within subsection (3),

the officer must grant that person access to the document, under the supervision of a constable, subject to subsection (4).

(2) Where

   (a) a document is retained by virtue of section 5, and

   (b) a request for a copy of the document is made to the officer in charge of the investigation by a person within subsection (3),

that person must be provided with a copy of the document within a reasonable time from the making of the request, subject to subsection (4).

(3) The persons entitled to make a request under subsection (1) or (2) are

   (a) where the document was found in the course of a search of a person, that person,

   (b) where the document was found in the course of a search of any premises

     (i) the occupier of the premises when it was found, and

     (ii) any person who had custody or control of the document when it was found, and

   (c) a person acting on behalf of a person within paragraph (a) or (b).

(4) The officer in charge of the investigation may refuse access to the document, or (as the case may be) refuse to provide a copy of it, if the officer has reasonable grounds for believing that to do so

   (a) would prejudice any investigation for the purposes of which

     (i) the original search was carried out, or

     (ii) the document was removed or is being retained,

   (b) would prejudice the investigation of any offence,

   (c) would prejudice any criminal proceedings that may be brought as the result of an investigation within paragraph (a) or (b), or

   (d) would facilitate the commission of an offence.

(5) In this section

"the officer in charge of the investigation" means the officer in charge of the investigation for the purposes of which the document is being retained; and

"the original search" means the search in the course of which the document was removed.

7 Photographing and copying of documents

(1) Where a document is removed under section 1 it must not be photographed or copied, except that

   (a) a document may be copied for the purpose of providing a copy in response to a request under section 6(2), and

   (b) a document consisting of information stored in electronic form may be copied for the purpose of producing it in a visible and legible form.

(2) Where the original document is returned, any copy under subsection (1)(b) must

   (a) in the case of a copy in electronic form, be destroyed or made inaccessible as soon as is reasonably practicable, and

   (b) in any other case, be returned at the same time as the original document is returned.

(3) The following are entitled, on a request made to the relevant chief officer of police, to a certificate that subsection (2) has been complied with

   (a) where the document was found in the course of a search of a person, that person;

   (b) where the document was found in the course of a search of any premises

     (i) the occupier of the premises when it was found, and

     (ii) any person who had custody or control of the document when it was found.

(4) The certificate must be issued by the relevant chief officer of police, or a person authorised by or on behalf of that chief officer, not later than the end of the period of three months beginning with the day on which the request is made.

(5) For this purpose the relevant chief officer of police is

    (a) where the search was carried out in England or Wales, the chief officer of police in whose area the search was carried out;

    (b) where the search was carried out in Scotland, the chief constable of the police force for the area in which the search was carried out;

    (c) where the search was carried out in Northern Ireland, the Chief Constable of the Police Service of Northern Ireland.

8 Return of documents

(1) Where a document removed under section 1 is required to be returned, it must be returned

    (a) where the document was found in the course of a search of a person, to that person;

    (b) where the document was found in the course of a search of any premises, to the occupier of the premises when it was found.

(2) Subsection (1) does not apply where a person who is required to return the document is satisfied that another person has a better right to it; and in such a case it must be returned

    (a) to that other person, or

    (b) to whoever appears to the person required to return the document to have the best right to it.

(3) Where different persons claim to be entitled to the return of the document, it may be retained for as long as is reasonably necessary for the determination of the person to whom it must be returned.

(4) This section also applies in relation to a copy of a document that is required to be returned at the same time as the original; and in such a case references to the document in paragraphs (a) and (b) of subsection (1) are to the original.

9 Power to remove documents: supplementary provisions

(1) In sections 1 to 8 "document" includes any record and, in particular, includes information stored in electronic form.

(2) In the application of those sections to a search under 52(1) of the Anti-terrorism, Crime and Security Act 2001 (c 24), for references to a constable substitute references to an authorised officer within the meaning of that section.

(3) In the application of those sections in relation to the search of a vehicle references to the occupier of the premises are to the person in charge of the vehicle.

Power to take fingerprints and samples from person subject to control order

10 Power to take fingerprints and samples: England and Wales

(1) In section 61 of the Police and Criminal Evidence Act 1984 (c 60) (fingerprinting), after subsection (6B) insert

    "(6BA) A constable may take a person's fingerprints without the appropriate consent if the person is subject to a control order.".

(2) In section 63 of that Act (other samples), after subsection (3C) insert

    "(3D) A non-intimate sample may also be taken from a person without the appropriate consent if the person is subject to a control order.".

(3) In section 63A of that Act (fingerprints and samples: supplementary provisions)

    (a) in subsection (1) (checking against other fingerprints or samples), after "reported for such an offence" insert "or he is or has been subject to a control order";

    (b) after subsection (6) insert

        "(6A) A constable may require a person who is subject to a control order to attend a police station in order to

(a) have his fingerprints taken in accordance with section 61(6BA);

(b) have a non-intimate sample taken in accordance with section 63(3D).".

(4) In section 64 of that Act (destruction of fingerprints and samples), after subsection (1A) insert

"(1AA) Where fingerprints or samples are taken from a person who is subject to a control order the fingerprints or samples may be retained after they have fulfilled the purposes for which they were taken but shall not be used by any person except as described in subsection (1AB).".

(5) In section 65(1) of that Act (interpretation), at the appropriate places insert

""control order" has the same meaning as in the Prevention of Terrorism Act 2005;";

""person subject to a control order" means a person who has become bound by a control order (see section 7(8) of the Prevention of Terrorism Act 2005) that remains in force;".

(6) The following amendments of that Act are consequential on those above

  (a) in section 61

    (i) in subsection (6C) after "subsection (6A)" insert "or (6BA)";

    (ii) in subsection (7) for "or (6A)" substitute ", (6A) or (6BA)";

    (iii) in subsection (7A) after "subsection (6A)", in both places where it occurs, insert "or (6BA)";

  (b) in section 63 (other samples)

    (i) in subsection (8A) for "or (3C)" substitute ", (3C) or (3D)";

    (ii) in the opening words of subsection (8B) after "police station" insert "or by virtue of subsection (3D) at a place other than a police station";

    (iii) in paragraph (a) of that subsection after "officer" insert ", or, in a subsection (3D) case, a constable,";

  (c) in section 63A(7) after "subsection (4)" insert "or (6A)";

  (d) in section 64(1B) after "subsection (1A)" insert ", (1AA)".

11 Power to take fingerprints and samples: Scotland

(1) This section applies in relation to a person who is subject to a control order in Scotland.

(2) A constable may

  (a) take from the person, or require the person to provide, any relevant physical data,

  (b) with the authority of an officer of a rank no lower than inspector, take from the person any sample mentioned in paragraph (a), (b) or (c) of subsection (6) of section 18 (prints, samples etc in criminal investigations) of the Criminal Procedure (Scotland) Act 1995 (c 46) ("the 1995 Act") by the means specified in that paragraph in relation to the sample,

  (c) take, or direct a police custody and security officer to take, from the person a sample mentioned in subsection (6A) of that section by the means specified in that subsection.

(3) A constable may

  (a) require the person to attend a police station for the purposes of subsection (2), and

  (b) arrest without warrant a person who fails to comply with such a requirement.

(4) A constable may use reasonable force in

  (a) taking any relevant physical data under subsection (2)(a),

  (b) securing compliance with a requirement imposed by the constable under that subsection, or

  (c) taking any sample under subsection (2)(b).

(5) A constable may, with the authority of an officer of a rank no lower than inspector, use reasonable force in taking any sample under subsection (2)(c).

(6) Any relevant physical data or sample obtained under this section, and information derived from it, may be retained but may not be used by any person except

  (a) for the purposes of a terrorist investigation, or

  (b) in the interests of national security.

(7) Subject to subsection (6), any data or sample obtained under this section, or information derived from it, may, in particular, be checked against

(a) other such data, samples or information,

(b) any of the relevant physical data, samples and information to which section 20 of the 1995 Act applies,

(c) any of the fingerprints, samples and information mentioned in section 63A(1)(a) and (b) of the Police and Criminal Evidence Act 1984 (c 60) (checking of fingerprints and samples), and

(d) material to which section 18 of this Act applies (material not subject to existing statutory restrictions).

(8) In this section

"control order" has the same meaning as in the Prevention of Terrorism Act 2005 (c 2);

"person subject to a control order" means a person who has become bound by a control order (see section 7(8) of the Prevention of Terrorism Act 2005) that remains in force;

"relevant physical data" has the same meaning as it has for the purposes of section 18 of the 1995 Act (see subsections (7A) and (7B) of that section);

"terrorist investigation" has the meaning given in section 32 of the Terrorism Act 2000 (c 11).

12 Power to take fingerprints and samples: Northern Ireland

(1) In Article 53(1) of the Police and Criminal Evidence (Northern Ireland) Order 1989 (SI 1989/1341 (NI 12)) (interpretation of Part VI), at the appropriate places insert

""control order" has the same meaning as in the Prevention of Terrorism Act 2005;";

""person subject to a control order" means a person who has become bound by a control order (see section 7(8) of the Prevention of Terrorism Act 2005) that remains in force;".

(2) In Article 61 of that Order (fingerprinting), after paragraph (6B) insert

"(6BA) A constable may take a person's fingerprints without the appropriate consent if the person is subject to a control order.".

(3) In Article 63 of that Order (other samples), after paragraph (3B) insert

"(3C) A non-intimate sample may also be taken from a person without the appropriate consent if the person is subject to a control order.".

(4) In Article 63A of that Order (fingerprints and samples: supplementary provisions)

(a) in paragraph (1) (checking against other fingerprints and samples), after "reported for such an offence" insert "or he is or has been subject to a control order";

(b) after paragraph (6) insert

"(6A) A constable may require a person who is subject to a control order to attend a police station in order to

(a) have his fingerprints taken in accordance with Article 61(6BA);

(b) have a non-intimate sample taken in accordance with Article 63(3C).".

(5) In Article 64 of that Order (destruction of fingerprints and samples), after paragraph (1A) insert

"(1AA) Where fingerprints or samples are taken from a person who is subject to a control order the fingerprints or samples may be retained after they have fulfilled the purposes for which they were taken but shall not be used by any person except as described in paragraph (1AB).".

(6) The following amendments of that Order are consequential on those above

(a) in Article 61

(i) in paragraph (6C) after "paragraph (6A)" insert "or (6BA)";

(ii) in paragraph (7) for "or (6A)" substitute ", (6A) or (6BA)";

(iii) in paragraph (7A) after "paragraph (6A)", in both places where it occurs, insert "or (6BA)";

    (b) in Article 63

        (i)   in paragraph (8A) for "or (3B)" substitute ", (3B) or (3C)";

        (ii) in the opening words of paragraph (8B) after "police station" insert "or by virtue of paragraph (3C) at a place other than a police station";

        (iii) in sub-paragraph (a) of that paragraph after "officer" insert "(or, in a paragraph (3C) case, a constable)";

    (c) in Article 63A(7) after "paragraph (4)" insert "or (6A)";

    (d) in Article 64(1B), after "paragraph (1A)" insert ", (1AA)".

13 Power to take fingerprints and samples: transitional provision

The provisions of

section 10 (power to take fingerprints and samples: England and Wales),

section 11 (power to take fingerprints and samples: Scotland), and

section 12 (power to take fingerprints and samples: Northern Ireland),

have effect from the commencement of the relevant section regardless of when the control order was made.

Retention and use of fingerprints and samples

14 Material subject to the Police and Criminal Evidence Act 1984

(1) The Police and Criminal Evidence Act 1984 (c 60) is amended as follows.

(2) In section 63A(1) (fingerprints, impressions of footwear and samples: what they may be checked against), for paragraphs (a) and (b) substitute

"(a) other fingerprints, impressions of footwear or samples

    (i)   to which the person seeking to check has access and which are held by or on behalf of any one or more relevant law-enforcement authorities or are held in connection with or as a result of an investigation of an offence, or

    (ii) which are held by or on behalf of the Security Service or the Secret Intelligence Service;

(b) information derived from other samples

    (i)   which is contained in records to which the person seeking to check has access and which are held as mentioned in paragraph (a)(i) above, or

    (ii) which is held by or on behalf of the Security Service or the Secret Intelligence Service.".

(3) In section 63A(1ZA) (fingerprints from a person whose identity is unclear: what they may be checked against), for the words from "other fingerprints" to the end, substitute

"other fingerprints

(a) to which the person seeking to check has access and which are held by or on behalf of any one or more relevant law-enforcement authorities or which are held in connection with or as a result of an investigation of an offence, or

(b) which are held by or on behalf of the Security Service or the Secret Intelligence Service.".

(4) In section 64(1A) (purposes for which fingerprints, impressions of footwear or samples may be retained and used), for the words from "except for purposes" to the end substitute "except as described in subsection (1AB)".

(5) After subsection (1AA) of that section (inserted by section 10), insert

"(1AB) The fingerprints, impressions of footwear or samples may be used

    (a) in the interests of national security,

    (b) for purposes related to the prevention or detection of crime, the investigation of an offence or the conduct of a prosecution, or

    (c) for purposes related to the identification of a deceased person or of the person from whom the material came.".

(6) In subsection (1B) of that section, after "(1AA)" (inserted by section 10) insert "or (1AB)".

15 Material subject to the Police and Criminal Evidence (Northern Ireland) Order 1989

(1) The Police and Criminal Evidence (Northern Ireland) Order 1989 (SI 1989/1341 (NI 12)) is amended as follows.

(2) In Article 63A(1) (fingerprints and samples: what they may be checked against), for paragraphs (a) and (b), substitute
"(a) other fingerprints, impressions of footwear or samples
    (i) to which the person seeking to check has access and which are held by or on behalf of any one or more relevant law-enforcement authorities or are held in connection with or as a result of an investigation of an offence, or
    (ii) which are held by or on behalf of the Security Service or the Secret Intelligence Service;
(b) information derived from other samples
    (i) which is contained in records to which the person seeking to check has access and which are held as mentioned in paragraph (a)(i) above, or
    (ii) which is held by or on behalf of the Security Service or the Secret Intelligence Service.".

(3) In Article 63A(1ZA) (fingerprints from a person whose identity is unclear: what they may be checked against), for "other fingerprints" to the end, substitute
"other fingerprints
(a) to which the person seeking to check has access and which are held by or on behalf of any one or more relevant law-enforcement authorities or which are held in connection with or as a result of an investigation of an offence, or
(b) which are held by or on behalf of the Security Service or the Secret Intelligence Service.".

(4) In Article 64(1A) (purposes for which fingerprints or samples may be retained and used), for the words from "except for purposes" to the end substitute "except as described in paragraph (1AB)".

(5) After paragraph (1AA) of that Article (inserted by section 12) insert
"(1AB) The fingerprints, impressions of footwear or samples may be used
    (a) in the interests of national security,
    (b) for purposes related to the prevention or detection of crime, the investigation of an offence or the conduct of a prosecution, or
    (c) for purposes related to the identification of a deceased person or of the person from whom the material came.".

(6) In paragraph (1B) of that Article, after "(1AA)" (inserted by section 12) insert "or (1AB)".

16 Material subject to the Terrorism Act 2000: England and Wales and Northern Ireland

(1) Paragraph 14 of Schedule 8 to the Terrorism Act 2000 (rights of persons detained in England, Wales or Northern Ireland: retention and use of fingerprints and samples etc) is amended as follows.

(2) In sub-paragraph (2) (purposes for which fingerprints and samples may be used) for the words from "or for purposes related" to the end substitute "or as mentioned in sub-paragraph (2A)".

(3) After that sub-paragraph insert
"(2A) The fingerprints or samples may be used
    (a) in the interests of national security,
    (b) for purposes related to the prevention or detection of crime, the investigation of an offence or the conduct of a prosecution, or
    (c) for purposes related to the identification of a deceased person or of the person from whom the material came.".

(4) Omit sub-paragraph (3).

(5) In sub-paragraph (4) (what fingerprints, samples or other information may be checked against), after paragraph (b) insert

"(ba) material to which section 18 of the Counter-Terrorism Act 2008 applies,".

17 Material subject to the Terrorism Act 2000: Scotland

(1) Part 1 of Schedule 8 to the Terrorism Act 2000 (treatment of detained persons) is amended as follows.

(2) In paragraph 20 (persons detained in Scotland: fingerprinting etc), in sub-paragraph (3) (retention and use of physical data or samples), for the words from "except" to the end substitute

"except

(a) for the purposes of a terrorist investigation,

(b) in the interests of national security, or

(c) for purposes related to the prevention or detection of crime, the investigation of an offence or the conduct of a prosecution.".

(3) After paragraph 20, insert

"21 (1) Section 20 of the Criminal Procedure (Scotland) Act 1995 applies to relevant physical data or samples taken from a person detained under Schedule 7 or section 41 at a police station in Scotland with the following modifications.

(2) Omit the references to impressions.

(3) For the words from "against other such data" to the end substitute ", subject to paragraph 20(3) of Schedule 8 to the Terrorism Act 2000, against

(a) other such data, samples and information,

(b) any of the fingerprints, samples and information mentioned in section 63A(1)(a) and (b) of the Police and Criminal Evidence Act 1984 (c 60) (checking of fingerprints and samples), and

(c) material to which section 18 of the Counter-Terrorism Act 2008 applies.".

18 Material not subject to existing statutory restrictions

(1) This section applies to

(a) DNA samples or profiles, or

(b) fingerprints,

that are not held subject to existing statutory restrictions.

(2) Material to which this section applies that is held by a law enforcement authority in England and Wales or Northern Ireland may be retained by that authority and used

(a) in the interests of national security,

(b) for purposes related to the prevention or detection of crime, the investigation of an offence or the conduct of a prosecution, or

(c) for purposes related to the identification of a deceased person or of the person from whom the material came,

if the following condition is met.

(3) The condition is that the material has been

(a) obtained by the authority

(i) pursuant to an authorisation under Part 3 of the Police Act 1997 (c 50) (authorisation of action in respect of property), or

(ii) in the course of surveillance, or use of a covert human intelligence source, authorised under Part 2 of the Regulation of Investigatory Powers Act 2000 (c 23),

(b) supplied to the authority by another law enforcement authority, or

(c) otherwise lawfully obtained or acquired by the authority for any of the purposes mentioned in subsection (2).

(4) In subsection (2)
    (a) the reference to using material includes allowing a check to be made against it, or against information derived from it, or disclosing it to any person;
    (b) the reference to crime includes any conduct that
        (i) constitutes a criminal offence (whether under the law of a part of the United Kingdom or of a country or territory outside the United Kingdom), or
        (ii) is, or corresponds to, conduct that, if it took place in the United Kingdom, would constitute a criminal offence;
    (c) the references to investigation and prosecution include, respectively, the investigation outside the United Kingdom of a crime or suspected crime and a prosecution brought in respect of a crime in a country or territory outside the United Kingdom.
(5) In this section
    "DNA sample" means any material that has come from a human body and consists of or includes human cells;
    "DNA profile" means any information derived from a DNA sample;
    "fingerprints" means a record (in any form and produced by any method) of the skin pattern and other physical characteristics or features of a person's fingers or either of a person's palms;
    "law enforcement authority" means a police force, the Serious Organised Crime Agency or the Commissioners for Her Majesty's Revenue and Customs or an authority having functions under the law of a country or territory outside the United Kingdom
        (a) corresponding to those of a police force, or
        (b) otherwise involving the investigation or prosecution of offences;
    "police force" means any of the following
        (a) the metropolitan police force;
        (b) a police force maintained under section 2 of the Police Act 1996 (c 16) (police forces in England and Wales outside London);
        (c) the City of London police force;
        (d) any police force maintained under or by virtue of section 1 of the Police (Scotland) Act 1967 (c 77);
        (e) the Police Service of Northern Ireland;
        (f) the Police Service of Northern Ireland Reserve;
        (g) the Ministry of Defence Police;
        (h) the Royal Navy Police;
        (i) the Royal Military Police;
        (j) the Royal Air Force Police;
        (k) the British Transport Police.
(6) The following are "the existing statutory restrictions" referred to in subsection (1)
    (a) sections 63A and 64 of the Police and Criminal Evidence Act 1984 (c 60);
    (b) Articles 63A and 64 of the Police and Criminal Evidence (Northern Ireland) Order 1989 (SI 1989/1341 (NI 12));
    (c) paragraph 14 or 20(3) of Schedule 8 to the Terrorism Act 2000 (c 11);
    (d) section 2(2) of the Security Service Act 1989 (c 5);
    (e) section 1(2) of the Intelligence Services Act 1994 (c 13).

Disclosure of information and the intelligence services

19 Disclosure and the intelligence services

(1) A person may disclose information to any of the intelligence services for the purposes of the exercise by that service of any of its functions.
(2) Information obtained by any of the intelligence services in connection with the exercise of any of its functions may be used by that service in connection with the exercise of any of its other functions.

(3) Information obtained by the Security Service for the purposes of any of its functions may be disclosed by it
  (a) for the purpose of the proper discharge of its functions,
  (b) for the purpose of the prevention or detection of serious crime, or
  (c) for the purpose of any criminal proceedings.

(4) Information obtained by the Secret Intelligence Service for the purposes of any of its functions may be disclosed by it
  (a) for the purpose of the proper discharge of its functions,
  (b) in the interests of national security,
  (c) for the purpose of the prevention or detection of serious crime, or
  (d) for the purpose of any criminal proceedings.

(5) Information obtained by GCHQ for the purposes of any of its functions may be disclosed by it
  (a) for the purpose of the proper discharge of its functions, or
  (b) for the purpose of any criminal proceedings.

(6) A disclosure under this section does not breach
  (a) any obligation of confidence owed by the person making the disclosure, or
  (b) any other restriction on the disclosure of information (however imposed).

(7) The provisions of this section are subject to section 20 (savings and other supplementary provisions).

20 Disclosure and the intelligence services: supplementary provisions

(1) The provisions of section 19 (disclosure and use of information) do not affect the duties with respect to the obtaining or disclosure of information imposed
  (a) on the Director-General of the Security Service, by section 2(2) of the Security Service Act 1989;
  (b) on the Chief of the Intelligence Service, by section 2(2) of the Intelligence Services Act 1994;
  (c) on the Director of GCHQ, by section 4(2) of that Act.

(2) Nothing in that section authorises a disclosure that
  (a) contravenes the Data Protection Act 1998 (c 29), or
  (b) is prohibited by Part 1 of the Regulation of Investigatory Powers Act 2000 (c 23).

(3) The provisions of that section are without prejudice to any rule of law authorising the obtaining, use or disclosure of information by any of the intelligence services.

(4) Schedule 1 contains amendments consequential on that section.

21 Disclosure and the intelligence services: interpretation

(1) In sections 19 and 20 "the intelligence services" means the Security Service, the Secret Intelligence Service and GCHQ.

(2) References in section 19 to the functions of those services are
  (a) in the case of the Security Service, to the functions specified in section 1(2) to (4) of the Security Service Act 1989 (c 5);
  (b) in the case of the Secret Intelligence Service, to the functions specified in section 1(1)(a) and (b) of the Intelligence Services Act 1994 (c 13), exercised in accordance with section 1(2) of that Act;
  (c) in the case of GCHQ
    (i) to the functions specified in section 3(1)(a) of that Act, exercised in accordance with section 3(2) of that Act, and
    (ii) to the functions specified in section 3(1)(b) of that Act.

(3) In sections 19, 20 and this section "GCHQ" has the same meaning as in the Intelligence Services Act 1994 (see section 3(3) of that Act).

(4) Section 81(5) of the Regulation of Investigatory Powers Act 2000 (meaning of "prevention" and "detection"), so far as it relates to serious crime, applies for the purposes of section 19 as it applies for the purposes of the provisions of that Act not contained in Chapter 1 of Part 1.

PART II
POST-CHARGE QUESTIONING OF TERRORIST SUSPECTS

22 Post-charge questioning: England and Wales

(1) The following provisions apply in England and Wales.
(2) A judge of the Crown Court may authorise the questioning of a person about an offence
  (a) after the person has been charged with the offence or been officially informed that they may be prosecuted for it, or
  (b) after the person has been sent for trial for the offence,
  if the offence is a terrorism offence or it appears to the judge that the offence has a terrorist connection.
(3) The judge
  (a) must specify the period during which questioning is authorised, and
  (b) may impose such conditions as appear to be necessary in the interests of justice, which may include conditions as to the place where the questioning is to be carried out.
(4) The period during which questioning is authorised
  (a) begins when questioning pursuant to the authorisation begins and runs continuously from that time (whether or not questioning continues), and
  (b) must not exceed 48 hours.
  This is without prejudice to any application for a further authorisation under this section.
(5) Where the person is in prison or otherwise lawfully detained, the judge may authorise the person's removal to another place and detention there for the purpose of being questioned.
(6) A judge must not authorise the questioning of a person under this section unless satisfied
  (a) that further questioning of the person is necessary in the interests of justice,
  (b) that the investigation for the purposes of which the further questioning is proposed is being conducted diligently and expeditiously, and
  (c) that what is authorised will not interfere unduly with the preparation of the person's defence to the charge in question or any other criminal charge.
(7) Codes of practice under section 66 of the Police and Criminal Evidence Act 1984 (c 60) must make provision about the questioning of a person by a constable in accordance with this section.
(8) Nothing in this section prevents codes of practice under that section making other provision for the questioning of a person by a constable about an offence
  (a) after the person has been charged with the offence or been officially informed that they may be prosecuted for it, or
  (b) after the person has been sent for trial for the offence.
(9) In section 34(1) of the Criminal Justice and Public Order Act 1994 (c 33) (effect of accused's failure to mention facts when questioned or charged: circumstances in which the section applies) after paragraph (b) insert
  "; or
  (c) at any time after being charged with the offence, on being questioned under section 22 of the Counter-Terrorism Act 2008 (post-charge questioning), failed to mention any such fact,".
(10) Nothing in section 36 or 37 of that Act (effect of accused's failure or refusal to account for certain matters) is to be read as excluding the operation of those sections in relation to a request made in the course of questioning under this section.

23 Post-charge questioning: Scotland

(1) The following provisions apply in Scotland.

(2) On the application of the prosecutor, a sheriff may authorise the questioning of a person about an offence
  (a) after the person has been charged with the offence, or
  (b) after the person has appeared on petition in respect of the offence,
  if the offence is a terrorism offence or it appears to the sheriff that the offence has a terrorist connection.

(3) The sheriff
  (a) must specify the period during which questioning is authorised, and
  (b) may impose such conditions as appear to be necessary in the interests of justice, which may include conditions as to the place where the questioning is to be carried out.

(4) The period during which questioning is authorised
  (a) begins when questioning pursuant to the authorisation begins and runs continuously from that time (whether or not questioning continues), and
  (b) must not exceed 48 hours.
  This is without prejudice to any application for a further authorisation under this section.

(5) Where the person is in prison or otherwise lawfully detained, the sheriff may authorise the person's removal to another place and detention there for the purpose of being questioned.

(6) A sheriff must not authorise the questioning of a person under this section unless satisfied
  (a) that further questioning of the person is necessary in the interests of justice,
  (b) that the investigation for the purposes of which the further questioning is proposed is being conducted diligently and expeditiously, and
  (c) that what is authorised will not interfere unduly with the preparation of the person's defence to the charge in question or any other criminal charge.

(7) Evidence of any statement obtained from a person as a result of questioning under this section is not inadmissible solely because the questioning occurred after the person had been charged (or had appeared on petition).

(8) In this section "charged" means charged by the police.

24 Post-charge questioning: Northern Ireland

(1) The following provisions apply in Northern Ireland.

(2) A district judge (magistrates' courts) may authorise the questioning of a person about an offence
  (a) after the person has been charged with the offence or been officially informed that they may be prosecuted for it, or
  (b) after the person has been committed for trial for the offence,
  if the offence is a terrorism offence.

(3) The judge
  (a) must specify the period during which questioning is authorised, and
  (b) may impose such conditions as appear to the judge to be necessary in the interests of justice, which may include conditions as to the place where the questioning is to be carried out.

(4) The period during which questioning is authorised
  (a) begins when questioning pursuant to the authorisation begins and runs continuously from that time (whether or not questioning continues), and
  (b) must not exceed 48 hours.
  This is without prejudice to any application for a further authorisation under this section.

(5) Where the person is in prison or otherwise lawfully detained, the judge may authorise the person's removal to another place and detention there for the purpose of being questioned.

(6) A district judge (magistrates' courts) must not authorise the questioning of a person under this section unless satisfied

    (a) that further questioning of the person is necessary in the interests of justice,

    (b) that the investigation for the purposes of which the further questioning is proposed is being conducted diligently and expeditiously, and

    (c) that what is authorised will not interfere unduly with the preparation of the person's defence to the charge in question or any other criminal charge.

(7) Codes of practice under Article 65 of the Police and Criminal Evidence (Northern Ireland) Order 1989 (SI 1989/1341 (NI 12)) must make provision about the questioning of a person by a constable in accordance with this section.

(8) Nothing in this section prevents codes of practice under that Article making other provision for the questioning of a person by a constable about an offence

    (a) after the person has been charged with the offence or been officially informed that they may be prosecuted for it, or

    (b) after the person has been committed for trial for the offence.

(9) In Article 3(1) of the Criminal Evidence (Northern Ireland) Order 1988 (SI 1988/1987 (NI 20)) (effect of accused's failure to mention facts when questioned or charged: circumstances in which the article applies) after sub-paragraph (b) insert

    "; or

    (c) at any time after being charged with the offence, on being questioned under section 24 of the Counter-Terrorism Act 2008 (post-charge questioning), failed to mention any such fact,".

(10) Nothing in Article 5 or 6 of that Order (effect of accused's failure or refusal to account for certain matters) is to be read as excluding the operation of those Articles in relation to a request made in the course of questioning under this section.

25 Recording of interviews

(1) This section applies to any interview of a person by a constable under section 22, 23 or 24 (post-charge questioning).

(2) Any such interview must be video recorded, and the video recording must be with sound.

(3) The Secretary of State must issue a code of practice about the video recording of interviews to which this section applies.

(4) The interview and video recording must be conducted in accordance with that code of practice.

(5) A code of practice under this section

    (a) may make provision in relation to a particular part of the United Kingdom, and

    (b) may make different provision for different parts of the United Kingdom.

26 Issue and revision of code of practice

(1) This section applies to the code of practice under section 25 (recording of interviews).

(2) The Secretary of State must

    (a) publish a draft of the proposed code, and

    (b) consider any representations made about the draft,

    and may modify the draft in the light of the representations made.

(3) The Secretary of State must lay a draft of the code before Parliament.

(4) After laying the draft code before Parliament the Secretary of State may bring it into operation by order.

(5) The order is subject to affirmative resolution procedure.

(6) The Secretary of State may revise a code and issue the revised code, and subsections (2) to (5) apply to a revised code as they apply to an original code.

(7) Failure to observe a provision of a code does not of itself render a constable liable to criminal or civil proceedings.

(8) A code
   (a) is admissible in evidence in criminal and civil proceedings, and
   (b) shall be taken into account by a court or tribunal in any case in which it appears to the court or tribunal to be relevant.

27 Meaning of "terrorism offence"

(1) For the purposes of sections 22 to 24 (post-charge questioning) the following are terrorism offences
   (a) an offence under any of the following provisions of the Terrorism Act 2000 (c 11)
      sections 11 to 13 (offences relating to proscribed organisations),
      sections 15 to 19, 21A and 21D (offences relating to terrorist property),
      sections 38B and 39 (disclosure of and failure to disclose information about terrorism),
      section 54 (weapons training),
      sections 56 to 58A (directing terrorism, possessing things and collecting information for the purposes of terrorism),
      sections 59 to 61 (inciting terrorism outside the United Kingdom),
      paragraph 14 of Schedule 5 (order for explanation of material: false or misleading statements),
      paragraph 1 of Schedule 6 (failure to provide customer information in connection with a terrorist investigation),
      paragraph 18 of Schedule 7 (offences in connection with port and border controls);
   (b) an offence in respect of which there is jurisdiction by virtue of any of sections 62 to 63D of that Act (extra-territorial jurisdiction in respect of certain offences committed outside the United Kingdom for the purposes of terrorism etc);
   (c) an offence under section 113 of the Anti-terrorism, Crime and Security Act 2001 (c 24) (use of noxious substances or things);
   (d) an offence under any of the following provisions of Part 1 of the Terrorism Act 2006 (c 11)
      sections 1 and 2 (encouragement of terrorism),
      sections 5, 6 and 8 (preparation and training for terrorism),
      sections 9, 10 and 11 (offences relating to radioactive devices and material and nuclear facilities);
   (e) an offence in respect of which there is jurisdiction by virtue of section 17 of that Act (extra-territorial jurisdiction in respect of certain offences committed outside the United Kingdom for the purposes of terrorism etc);
   (f) an offence under paragraph 8 or 9 of Schedule 3 to the Justice and Security (Northern Ireland) Act 2007 (c 6) (offences in connection with searches for munitions and transmitters in Northern Ireland).
(2) Any ancillary offence in relation to an offence listed in subsection (1) is a terrorism offence for the purposes of sections 22 to 24.
(3) The Secretary of State may by order amend subsection (1).
(4) Any such order is subject to affirmative resolution procedure.

PART III

PROSECUTION AND PUNISHMENT OF TERRORIST OFFENCES

Jurisdiction

28 Jurisdiction to try offences committed in the UK

(1) Where an offence to which this section applies is committed in the United Kingdom
   (a) proceedings for the offence may be taken at any place in the United Kingdom, and

(b) the offence may for all incidental purposes be treated as having been committed at any such place.

(2) The section applies to
  (a) an offence under any of the following provisions of the Terrorism Act 2000 (c 11)
    sections 11 to 13 (offences relating to proscribed organisations),
    sections 15 to 19, 21A and 21D (offences relating to terrorist property),
    sections 38B and 39 (disclosure of and failure to disclose information about terrorism),
    section 47 (offences relating to stop and search powers),
    section 51 (parking a vehicle in contravention of an authorisation or restriction),
    section 54 (weapons training),
    sections 56 to 58A (directing terrorism and possessing things or collecting information for the purposes of terrorism),
    section 116 (failure to stop a vehicle when required to do so),
    paragraph 1 of Schedule 6 (failure to provide customer information in connection with a terrorist investigation),
    paragraph 18 of Schedule 7 (offences in connection with port and border controls);
  (b) an offence under section 113 of the Anti-terrorism, Crime and Security Act 2001 (c 24) (use of noxious substances or things to cause harm and intimidate);
  (c) an offence under any of the following provisions of the Terrorism Act 2006 (c 11)
    sections 1 and 2 (encouragement of terrorism),
    sections 5, 6 and 8 (preparation and training for terrorism),
    sections 9, 10 and 11 (offences relating to radioactive devices etc).

(3) The Secretary of State may by order amend subsection (2).

(4) Any such order is subject to affirmative resolution procedure.

(5) The power conferred by subsection (3) may be exercised so as to add offences to subsection (2) only if it appears to the Secretary of State necessary to do so for the purpose of dealing with terrorism.

(6) In section 1 of the Justice and Security (Northern Ireland) Act 2007 (c 6) (issue of certificate for trial without a jury), after subsection (6) insert
  "(6A) The Director of Public Prosecutions for Northern Ireland may not issue a certificate under subsection (2) if
    (a) the proceedings are taken in Northern Ireland only by virtue of section 28 of the Counter-Terrorism Act 2008, and
    (b) it appears to the Director that the only condition that is met is condition 4.".

Consent to prosecution

29 Consent to prosecution of offence committed outside UK *(omitted)*

Sentencing

30 Sentences for offences with a terrorist connection: England and Wales

(1) This section applies where a court in England and Wales is considering for the purposes of sentence the seriousness of an offence specified in Schedule 2 (offences where terrorist connection to be considered).

(2) If having regard to the material before it for the purposes of sentencing it appears to the court that the offence has or may have a terrorist connection, the court must determine whether that is the case.

(3) For that purpose the court may hear evidence, and must take account of any representations made by the prosecution and the defence, as in the case of any other matter relevant for the purposes of sentence.

(4) If the court determines that the offence has a terrorist connection, the court
   (a) must treat that fact as an aggravating factor, and
   (b) must state in open court that the offence was so aggravated.

(5) In this section "sentence", in relation to an offence, includes any order made by a court when dealing with a person in respect of the offence.

(6) This section has effect in relation only to offences committed on or after the day it comes into force.

31 Sentences for offences with a terrorist connection: Scotland

(1) This section applies where in Scotland, in relation to an offence specified in Schedule 2 (offences where terrorist connection to be considered)
   (a) it is libelled in an indictment, and
   (b) proved,
   that the offence has been aggravated by reason of having a terrorist connection.

(2) Where this section applies, the court must take the aggravation into account in determining the appropriate sentence.

(3) Where the sentence imposed by the court in respect of the offence is different from that which the court would have imposed if the offence had not been aggravated by reason of having a terrorist connection, the court must state the extent of, and the reasons for, the difference.

(4) For the purposes of this section, evidence from a single source is sufficient to prove that an offence has been aggravated by reason of having a terrorist connection.

(5) This section has effect in relation only to offences committed on or after the day it comes into force.

32 Sentences for offences with a terrorist connection: armed forces *(omitted)*

33 Power to amend list of offences where terrorist connection to be considered

(1) The Secretary of State may by order amend Schedule 2 (offences where terrorist connection to be considered).

(2) Any such order is subject to affirmative resolution procedure.

(3) An order adding an offence to that Schedule applies only in relation to offences committed after the order comes into force.

Forfeiture

34 Forfeiture: terrorist property offences *(omitted)*

35 Forfeiture: other terrorism offences and offences with a terrorist connection *(omitted)*

36 Forfeiture: supplementary provisions *(omitted)*

37 Forfeiture: application of proceeds to compensate victims *(omitted)*

38 Forfeiture: other amendments *(omitted)*

39 Forfeiture: consequential amendments *(omitted)*

PART IV
NOTIFICATION REQUIREMENTS

Introductory

40 Scheme of this Part

(1) This Part imposes notification requirements on persons dealt with in respect of certain offences
  (a) sections 41 to 43 specify the offences to which this Part applies;
  (b) sections 44 to 46 make provision as to the sentences or orders triggering the notification requirements;
  (c) sections 47 to 52 contain the notification requirements; and
  (d) section 53 makes provision as to the period for which the requirements apply.

(2) This Part also provides for
  (a) orders applying the notification requirements to persons dealt with outside the United Kingdom for corresponding foreign offences (see section 57 and Schedule 4); and
  (b) orders imposing restrictions on travel outside the United Kingdom on persons subject to the notification requirements (see section 58 and Schedule 5).

(3) Schedule 6 provides for the application of this Part to service offences and related matters.

Offences to which this Part applies

41 Offences to which this Part applies: terrorism offences

(1) This Part applies to
  (a) an offence under any of the following provisions of the Terrorism Act 2000 (c 11)
    section 11 or 12 (offences relating to proscribed organisations),
    sections 15 to 18 (offences relating to terrorist property),
    section 38B (failure to disclose information about acts of terrorism),
    section 54 (weapons training),
    sections 56 to 61 (directing terrorism, possessing things and collecting information for the purposes of terrorism and inciting terrorism outside the United Kingdom);
  (b) an offence in respect of which there is jurisdiction by virtue of any of sections 62 to 63D of that Act (extra-territorial jurisdiction in respect of certain offences committed outside the United Kingdom for the purposes of terrorism etc);
  (c) an offence under section 113 of the Anti-terrorism, Crime and Security Act 2001 (c 24) (use of noxious substances or things);
  (d) an offence under any of the following provisions of Part 1 of the Terrorism Act 2006 (c 11)
    sections 1 and 2 (encouragement of terrorism),
    sections 5, 6 and 8 (preparation and training for terrorism),
    sections 9, 10 and 11 (offences relating to radioactive devices and material and nuclear facilities);
  (e) an offence in respect of which there is jurisdiction by virtue of section 17 of that Act (extra-territorial jurisdiction in respect of certain offences committed outside the United Kingdom for the purposes of terrorism etc).

(2) This Part also applies to any ancillary offence in relation to an offence listed in subsection (1).

(3) The Secretary of State may by order amend subsection (1).

(4) Any such order is subject to affirmative resolution procedure.

(5) An order adding an offence applies only in relation to offences dealt with after the order comes into force.

(6) An order removing an offence has effect in relation to offences whenever dealt with, whether before or after the order comes into force.

(7) Where an offence is removed from the list, a person subject to the notification requirements by reason of that offence being listed (and who is not otherwise subject to those requirements) ceases to be subject to them when the order comes into force.

42 Offences to which this Part applies: offences having a terrorist connection

(1) This Part applies to
    (a) an offence as to which a court has determined under section 30 (sentences for offences with a terrorist connection: England and Wales) that the offence has a terrorist connection, and
    (b) an offence in relation to which section 31 applies (sentences for offences with terrorist connection: Scotland).

(2) A person to whom the notification requirements apply by virtue of such a determination as is mentioned in subsection (1)(a) may appeal against it to the same court, and subject to the same conditions, as an appeal against sentence.

(3) If the determination is set aside on appeal, the notification requirements are treated as never having applied to that person in respect of the offence.

(4) Where an order is made under section 33 removing an offence from the list in Schedule 2, a person subject to the notification requirements by reason of that offence being so listed (and who is not otherwise subject to those requirements) ceases to be subject to them when the order comes into force.

43 Offences dealt with before commencement

(1) This Part applies to a person dealt with for an offence before the commencement of this Part only if
    (a) the offence is on the commencement of this Part within section 41(1) or (2) (offences to which this Part applies: terrorism offences), and
    (b) immediately before the commencement of this Part the person
        (i) is imprisoned or detained in pursuance of the sentence passed or order made in respect of the offence,
        (ii) would be so imprisoned or detained but for being unlawfully at large, absent without leave, on temporary leave or leave of absence, or on bail pending an appeal, or
        (iii) is on licence, having served the custodial part of a sentence of imprisonment in respect of the offence.

(2) In relation to a person dealt with for an offence before the commencement of this Part
    (a) any reference in this Part to a sentence or order under a specified statutory provision includes a sentence or order under any corresponding earlier statutory provision;
    (b) any reference in this Part to a person being or having been found to be under a disability and to have done the act charged against them in respect of an offence includes a reference to their being or having been found
        (i) unfit to be tried for the offence,
        (ii) insane so that their trial for the offence cannot or could not proceed, or
        (iii) unfit to be tried and to have done the act charged against them in respect of the offence.

Persons to whom the notification requirements apply

44 Persons to whom the notification requirements apply

The notification requirements apply to a person who
(a) is aged 16 or over at the time of being dealt with for an offence to which this Part applies, and
(b) is made subject in respect of the offence to a sentence or order within section 45 (sentences or orders triggering notification requirements).

45 Sentences or orders triggering notification requirements

(1) The notification requirements apply to a person who in England and Wales
  (a) has been convicted of an offence to which this Part applies and sentenced in respect of the offence to
    (i) imprisonment or custody for life,
    (ii) imprisonment or detention in a young offender institution for a term of 12 months or more,
    (iii) imprisonment or detention in a young offender institution for public protection under section 225 of the Criminal Justice Act 2003 (c 44),
    (iv) detention for life or for a period of 12 months or more under section 91 of the Powers of Criminal Courts (Sentencing) Act 2000 (c 6) (offenders under 18 convicted of certain serious offences),
    (v) a detention and training order for a term of 12 months or more under section 100 of that Act (offenders under age of 18),
    (vi) detention for public protection under section 226 of the Criminal Justice Act 2003 (serious offences committed by persons under 18), or
    (vii) detention during Her Majesty's pleasure; or
  (b) has been
    (i) convicted of an offence to which this Part applies carrying a maximum term of imprisonment of 12 months or more,
    (ii) found not guilty by reason of insanity of such an offence, or
    (iii) found to be under a disability and to have done the act charged against them in respect of such an offence,
  and made subject in respect of the offence to a hospital order.

(2) The notification requirements apply to a person who in Scotland
  (a) has been convicted of an offence to which this Part applies and sentenced in respect of the offence to
    (i) imprisonment or detention in a young offenders institution for life,
    (ii) imprisonment or detention in a young offenders institution for a term of 12 months or more,
    (iii) an order for lifelong restriction under section 210F of the Criminal Procedure (Scotland) Act 1995 (c 46),
    (iv) detention without limit of time under section 205(2) of that Act (punishment for murder for offenders under 18), or
    (v) detention for a period of 12 months or more under section 208 of that Act (detention of children convicted on indictment); or
  (b) has been
    (i) convicted of an offence to which this Part applies carrying a maximum term of imprisonment of 12 months or more,
    (ii) acquitted of such an offence on grounds of insanity at the time of the act or omission constituting the offence, or
    (iii) found, following an examination of facts under section 55 of the Criminal Procedure (Scotland) Act 1995 (insanity in bar of trial: examination of facts) in relation to such an offence, to have done the act or omission constituting the offence,
  and made subject in respect of the offence to a hospital order.

(3) The notification requirements apply to a person who in Northern Ireland
  (a) has been convicted of an offence to which this Part applies and sentenced in respect of the offence to
    (i) imprisonment for life,
    (ii) imprisonment or detention in a young offenders centre for a term of 12 months or more,

      (iii) an indeterminate custodial sentence under Article 13 of the Criminal Justice (Northern Ireland) Order 2008 (SI 2008/1216 (NI 1)),

      (iv) an extended custodial sentence under Article 14(5) of that Order (offenders under 21 convicted of certain offences),

      (v) a juvenile justice centre order under Article 39 of the Criminal Justice (Children) (Northern Ireland) Order 1998 (SI 1998/1504 (NI 9)) for a period of 12 months or more,

      (vi) detention during the pleasure of the Secretary of State under Article 45(1) of that Order (punishment of certain grave crimes committed by a child), or

      (vii) detention under Article 45(2) of that Order for a period of 12 months or more (other serious offences committed by a child); or

  (b) has been

      (i) convicted of an offence to which this Part applies carrying a maximum term of imprisonment of 12 months or more,

      (ii) found not guilty by reason of insanity of such an offence, or

      (iii) found to be unfit to be tried and to have done the act charged against them in respect of such an offence,

  and made subject in respect of the offence to a hospital order.

(4) The references in this section to an offence carrying a maximum term of imprisonment of 12 months or more

  (a) are to an offence carrying such a maximum term in the case of a person who has attained the age of 21 (18 in relation to England and Wales), and

  (b) include an offence carrying in the case of such a person a maximum term of life imprisonment and an offence for which in the case of such a person the sentence is fixed by law as life imprisonment.

(5) In relation to any time before the coming into force of section 61 of the Criminal Justice and Court Services Act 2000 (c 43) subsection (4)(a) above has effect with the omission of the words "(18 in relation to England and Wales)".

46 Power to amend specified terms or periods of imprisonment or detention

(1) The Secretary of State may by order amend the provisions of section 45 referring to a specified term or period of imprisonment or detention.

(2) An order reducing a specified term or period has effect only in relation to persons dealt with after the order comes into force.

(3) Where an order increases a specified term or period

  (a) it has effect in relation to persons dealt with at any time, whether before or after the order comes into force, and

  (b) a person who would not have been subject to the notification requirements if the order had been in force when the offence was dealt with (and who is not otherwise subject to those requirements) ceases to be subject to the requirements when the order comes into force.

(4) An order under this section is subject to affirmative resolution procedure.

Notification requirements

47 Initial notification

(1) A person to whom the notification requirements apply must notify the following information to the police within the period of three days beginning with the day on which the person is dealt with in respect of the offence in question.

(2) The information required is
   (a) date of birth;
   (b) national insurance number;
   (c) name on the date on which the person was dealt with in respect of the offence (where the person used one or more other names on that date, each of those names);
   (d) home address on that date;
   (e) name on the date on which notification is made (where the person uses one or more other names on that date, each of those names);
   (f) home address on the date on which notification is made;
   (g) address of any other premises in the United Kingdom at which, at the time the notification is made, the person regularly resides or stays;
   (h) any prescribed information.
(3) In subsection (2) "prescribed" means prescribed by regulations made by the Secretary of State.
Such regulations are subject to affirmative resolution procedure.
(4) In determining the period within which notification is to be made under this section, there shall be disregarded any time when the person is
   (a) remanded in or committed to custody by an order of a court,
   (b) serving a sentence of imprisonment or detention,
   (c) detained in a hospital, or
   (d) detained under the Immigration Acts.
(5) This section does not apply to a person who
   (a) is subject to the notification requirements in respect of another offence (and does not cease to be so subject before the end of the period within which notification is to be made), and
   (b) has complied with this section in respect of that offence.
(6) In the application of this section to a person dealt with for an offence before the commencement of this Part who, immediately before commencement
   (a) would be imprisoned or detained in respect of the offence but for being unlawfully at large, absent without leave, on temporary leave or leave of absence, or on bail pending an appeal, or
   (b) is on licence, having served the custodial part of a sentence of imprisonment in respect of the offence,
the reference in subsection (1) to the day on which the person is dealt with in respect of the offence shall be read as a reference to the commencement of this Part.

48 Notification of changes

(1) A person to whom the notification requirements apply who uses a name that has not previously been notified to the police must notify the police of that name.
(2) If there is a change of the home address of a person to whom the notification requirements apply, the person must notify the police of the new home address.
(3) A person to whom the notification requirements apply who resides or stays at premises in the United Kingdom the address of which has previously not been notified to the police
   (a) for a period of 7 days, or
   (b) for two or more periods, in any period of 12 months, that taken together amount to 7 days,
must notify the police of the address of those premises.
(4) A person to whom the notification requirements apply who is released
   (a) from custody pursuant to an order of a court,
   (b) from imprisonment or detention pursuant to a sentence of a court,

(c) from detention in a hospital, or

(d) from detention under the Immigration Acts,

must notify the police of that fact.

This does not apply if the person is at the same time required to notify the police under section 47 (initial notification).

(5) A person who is required to notify information within section 47(2)(h) (prescribed information) must notify the police of the prescribed details of any prescribed changes in that information.

(6) In subsection (5) "prescribed" means prescribed by regulations made by the Secretary of State.

Such regulations are subject to affirmative resolution procedure.

(7) Notification under this section must be made before the end of the period of three days beginning with the day on which the event in question occurs.

Where subsection (3) applies that is the day with which the period referred to in paragraph (a) or (b) (as the case may be) ends.

(8) In determining the period within which notification is to be made under this section, there shall be disregarded any time when the person is

(a) remanded in or committed to custody by an order of a court,

(b) serving a sentence of imprisonment or detention,

(c) detained in a hospital, or

(d) detained under the Immigration Acts.

(9) References in this section to previous notification are to previous notification by the person under section 47 (initial notification), this section, section 49 (periodic re-notification) or section 56 (notification on return after absence from UK).

(10) Notification under this section must be accompanied by re-notification of the other information mentioned in section 47(2).

49 Periodic re-notification

(1) A person to whom the notification requirements apply must, within the period of one year after last notifying the police in accordance with

(a) section 47 (initial notification),

(b) section 48 (notification of change),

(c) this section, or

(d) section 56 (notification on return after absence from UK),

re-notify to the police the information mentioned in section 47(2).

(2) Subsection (1) does not apply if the period referred to in that subsection ends at a time when the person is

(a) remanded in or committed to custody by an order of a court,

(b) serving a sentence of imprisonment or detention,

(c) detained in a hospital, or

(d) detained under the Immigration Acts.

(3) In that case section 48(4) and (10) (duty to notify of release and to re-notify other information) apply when the person is released.

50 Method of notification and related matters

(1) This section applies to notification under

(a) section 47 (initial notification),

(b) section 48 (notification of change),

(c) section 49 (periodic re-notification), or

(d) section 56 (notification on return after absence from UK).

(2) Notification must be made by the person

(a) attending at a police station in the person's local police area, and

(b) making an oral notification to a police officer or to a person authorised for the purpose by the officer in charge of the station.

(3) A person making a notification under section 48 (notification of change) in relation to premises referred to in subsection (3) of that section may make the notification at a police station that would fall within subsection (2)(a) above if the address of those premises were the person's home address.

(4) The notification must be acknowledged.

(5) The acknowledgement must be in writing, and in such form as the Secretary of State may direct.

(6) The person making the notification must, if requested to do so by the police officer or person to whom the notification is made, allow the officer or person to
   (a) take the person's fingerprints,
   (b) photograph any part of the person, or
   (c) do both these things,
   for the purpose of verifying the person's identity.

(7) In the application of this section to Scotland, references to a police officer are to be read as references to a constable.

51 Meaning of "local police area"

(1) For the purposes of section 50(2) (method of notification) a person's "local police area" means
   (a) the police area in which the person's home address is situated;
   (b) in the absence of a home address, the police area in which the home address last notified is situated;
   (c) in the absence of a home address and of any such notification, the police area in which the court of trial was situated.

(2) In subsection (1)(c) "the court of trial" means
   (a) the court by or before which the conviction or finding was made by virtue of which the notification requirements apply to the person, or
   (b) if that conviction or finding was one substituted on an appeal or reference, the court by or before which the proceedings were taken from which the appeal or reference was brought.

(3) This section and section 50(2) apply in relation to Northern Ireland as if Northern Ireland were a police area.

52 Travel outside the United Kingdom

(1) The Secretary of State may by regulations make provision requiring a person to whom the notification requirements apply who leaves the United Kingdom
   (a) to notify the police of their departure before they leave, and
   (b) to notify the police of their return if they subsequently return to the United Kingdom.

(2) Notification of departure must disclose
   (a) the date on which the person intends to leave the United Kingdom;
   (b) the country (or, if there is more than one, the first country) to which the person will travel;
   (c) the person's point of arrival (determined in accordance with the regulations) in that country;
   (d) any other information required by the regulations.

(3) Notification of return must disclose such information as is required by the regulations about the person's return to the United Kingdom.

(4) Notification under this section must be given in accordance with the regulations.

(5) Regulations under this section are subject to affirmative resolution procedure.

Period for which notification requirements apply

53 Period for which notification requirements apply

(1) The period for which the notification requirements apply is
  (a) 30 years in the case of a person who
    (i) is aged 18 or over at the time of conviction for the offence, and
    (ii) receives in respect of the offence a sentence within subsection (2);
  (b) 15 years in the case of a person who
    (i) is aged 18 or over at the time of conviction for the offence, and
    (ii) receives in respect of the offence a sentence within subsection (3);
  (c) 10 years in any other case.
(2) The sentences in respect of which a 30 year period applies are
  (a) in England and Wales
    (i) imprisonment or custody for life,
    (ii) imprisonment or detention in a young offender institution for a term of 10 years or more,
    (iii) imprisonment or detention in a young offender institution for public protection under section 225 of the Criminal Justice Act 2003 (c 44),
    (iv) detention during Her Majesty's pleasure;
  (b) in Scotland
    (i) imprisonment or detention in a young offenders institution for life,
    (ii) imprisonment or detention in a young offenders institution for a term of 10 years or more,
    (iii) an order for lifelong restriction under section 210F of the Criminal Procedure (Scotland) Act 1995 (c 46);
  (c) in Northern Ireland
    (i) imprisonment for life,
    (ii) imprisonment for a term of 10 years or more,
    (iii) an indeterminate custodial sentence under Article 13 of the Criminal Justice (Northern Ireland) Order 2008 (SI 2008/1216 (NI 1)),
    (iv) an extended custodial sentence for a term of 10 years or more under Article 14(5) of that Order (offenders under 21 convicted of certain offences),
    (v) detention during the pleasure of the Secretary of State under Article 45(1) of the Criminal Justice (Children) (Northern Ireland) Order 1998 (SI 1998/1504 (NI 9)).
(3) The sentences in respect of which a 15 year period applies are
  (a) in England and Wales, imprisonment or detention in a young offender institution for a term of 5 years or more but less than 10 years;
  (b) in Scotland, imprisonment or detention in a young offenders institution for a term of 5 years or more but less than 10 years;
  (c) in Northern Ireland
    (i) imprisonment for a term of 5 years or more but less than 10 years,
    (ii) an extended custodial sentence for a term of 5 years or more but less than 10 years under Article 14(5) of the Criminal Justice (Northern Ireland) Order 2008 (SI 2008/1216 (NI 1)) (offenders under 21 convicted of certain offences).
(4) The period begins with the day on which the person is dealt with for the offence.
(5) If a person who is the subject of a finding within section 45(1)(b)(iii), (2)(b)(iii) or (3)(b)(iii) (finding of disability, etc) is subsequently tried for the offence, the period resulting from that finding ends
  (a) if the person is acquitted, at the conclusion of the trial;
  (b) if the person is convicted, when the person is again dealt with in respect of the offence.

(6) For the purposes of determining the length of the period
- (a) a person who has been sentenced in respect of two or more offences to which this Part applies to consecutive terms of imprisonment is treated as if sentenced, in respect of each of the offences, to a term of imprisonment equal to the aggregate of the terms; and
- (b) a person who has been sentenced in respect of two or more such offences to concurrent terms of imprisonment (X and Y) that overlap for a period (Z) is treated as if sentenced, in respect of each of the offences, to a term of imprisonment equal to X plus Y minus Z.

(7) In determining whether the period has expired, there shall be disregarded any period when the person was
- (a) remanded in or committed to custody by an order of a court,
- (b) serving a sentence of imprisonment or detention,
- (c) detained in a hospital, or
- (d) detained under the Immigration Acts.

Offences in relation to notification

54 Offences relating to notification

(1) A person commits an offence who
- (a) fails without reasonable excuse to comply with
  section 47 (initial notification),
  section 48 (notification of changes),
  section 49 (periodic re-notification),
  section 50(6) (taking of fingerprints or photographs),
  any regulations made under section 52(1) (travel outside United Kingdom), or
  section 56 (notification on return after absence from UK); or
- (b) notifies to the police in purported compliance with
  section 47 (initial notification),
  section 48 (notification of changes),
  section 49 (periodic re-notification),
  any regulations made under section 52(1) (travel outside United Kingdom), or
  section 56 (notification on return after absence from UK),
  any information that the person knows to be false.

(2) A person guilty of an offence under this section is liable
- (a) on summary conviction, to imprisonment for a term not exceeding 12 months or a fine not exceeding the statutory maximum or both;
- (b) on conviction on indictment, to imprisonment for a term not exceeding 5 years or a fine or both.

(3) In the application of subsection (2)(a)
- (a) in England and Wales, in relation to an offence committed before the commencement of section 154(1) of the Criminal Justice Act 2003 (c 44), or
- (b) in Northern Ireland,
  for "12 months" substitute "6 months".

(4) A person
- (a) commits an offence under subsection (1)(a) above on the day on which the person first fails without reasonable excuse to comply with
  section 47 (initial notification),
  section 48 (notification of changes),
  section 49 (periodic re-notification),
  any regulations made under section 52(1) (travel outside United Kingdom), or
  section 56 (notification on return after absence from UK), and

(b) continues to commit it throughout any period during which the failure continues.

But a person must not be prosecuted under subsection (1) more than once in respect of the same failure.

(5) Proceedings for an offence under this section may be commenced in any court having jurisdiction in any place where the person charged with the offence resides or is found.

55 Effect of absence abroad

(1) If a person to whom the notification requirements apply is absent from the United Kingdom for any period the following provisions apply.

(2) During the period of absence the period for which the notification requirements apply continues to run.

(3) The period of absence does not affect the obligation under section 47 (initial notification).

This is subject to subsection (4).

(4) Section 47 does not apply if

    (a) the period of absence begins before the end of the period within which notification must be made under that section, and

    (b) the person's absence results from the person's removal from the United Kingdom.

(5) Section 48 (notification of changes)

    (a) applies in relation to an event that occurs before the period of absence, but

    (b) does not apply in relation to an event that occurs during the period of absence.

Paragraph (a) is subject to subsection (6).

(6) Section 48 does not apply in relation to an event that occurs before the period of absence if

    (a) the period of absence begins before the end of the period within which notification must be made under that section, and

    (b) the person's absence results from the person's removal from the United Kingdom.

(7) Section 49 (periodic re-notification) does not apply if the period referred to in subsection (1) of that section ends during the period of absence.

(8) Section 53(7) (disregard of period of custody etc) applies in relation to the period of absence as if it referred to any period when the person was

    (a) remanded in or committed to custody by an order of a court outside the United Kingdom,

    (b) serving a sentence of imprisonment or detention imposed by such a court,

    (c) detained in a hospital pursuant to an order of such a court that is equivalent to a hospital order, or

    (d) subject to a form of detention outside the United Kingdom that is equivalent to detention under the Immigration Acts.

(9) References in this section and section 56 to a person's removal from the United Kingdom include

    (a) the person's removal from the United Kingdom in accordance with the Immigration Acts,

    (b) the person's extradition from the United Kingdom, or

    (c) the person's transfer from the United Kingdom to another country pursuant to a warrant under section 1 of the Repatriation of Prisoners Act 1984 (c 47).

56 Notification on return after absence from UK

(1) This section applies if, before the end of the period for which the notification requirements apply, a person to whom the requirements apply returns to the United Kingdom after a period of absence and

    (a) the person was not required to make a notification under section 47 (initial notification),

    (b) there has been a change to any of the information last notified to the police in accordance with

        (i) section 47,

        (ii) section 48 (notification of changes),

(iii) section 49 (periodic re-notification), or

(iv) this section, or

(c) the period referred to in section 49(1) (period after which re-notification required) ended during the period of absence.

(2) The person must notify or (as the case may be) re-notify to the police the information mentioned in section 47(2) within the period of three days beginning with the day of return.

(3) In determining the period within which notification is to be made under this section, there shall be disregarded any time when the person is

(a) remanded in or committed to custody by an order of a court,

(b) serving a sentence of imprisonment or detention,

(c) detained in a hospital, or

(d) detained under the Immigration Acts.

(4) This section does not apply if

(a) the person subsequently leaves the United Kingdom,

(b) the period of absence begins before the end of the period within which notification must be made under this section, and

(c) the person's absence results from the person's removal from the United Kingdom.

(5) The obligation under this section does not affect any obligation to notify information under section 52(3) (regulations requiring notification of return etc).

Supplementary provisions

57 Notification orders

Schedule 4 makes provision for notification orders applying the notification requirements of this Part to persons who have been dealt with outside the United Kingdom in respect of a corresponding foreign offence.

58 Foreign travel restriction orders

Schedule 5 makes provision for foreign travel restriction orders prohibiting persons to whom the notification requirements apply from

(a) travelling to a country outside the United Kingdom named or described in the order,

(b) travelling to any country outside the United Kingdom other than a country named or described in the order, or

(c) travelling to any country outside the United Kingdom.

59 Application of Part to service offences and related matters *(omitted)*

60 Minor definitions for Part 4

In this Part

"country" includes a territory;

"detained in a hospital" means detained in a hospital under

(a) Part 3 of the Mental Health Act 1983 (c 20),

(b) Part 6 of the Criminal Procedure (Scotland) Act 1995 (c 46) or the Mental Health (Care and Treatment) (Scotland) Act 2003 (asp 13), or

(c) Part 3 of the Mental Health (Northern Ireland) Order (SI 1986/595 (NI 4));

"home address" means, in relation to a person

(a) the address of the person's sole or main residence in the United Kingdom, or

(b) where the person has no such residence, the address or location of a place in the United Kingdom where the person can regularly be found and, if there is more than one such place, such one of those places as the person may select;

"hospital order" means

    (a) a hospital order within the meaning of the Mental Health Act 1983,

    (b) an order under Part 6 of the Criminal Procedure (Scotland) Act 1995, or

    (c) a hospital order within the meaning of the Mental Health (Northern Ireland) Order 1986 (SI 1986/595 (NI 4));

"passport" means

    (a) a United Kingdom passport within the meaning of the Immigration Act 1971 (c 77), or

    (b) a passport issued by or on behalf of the authorities of a country outside the United Kingdom or by or on behalf of an international organisation,

and includes any document that can be used (in some or all circumstances) instead of a passport;

"photograph" includes any process by means of which an image may be produced;

"release" from imprisonment or detention includes release on licence but not temporary release.

61 References to a person being "dealt with" for an offence

(1) References in this Part to a person being dealt with for or in respect of an offence are to their being sentenced, or made subject to a hospital order, in respect of the offence.

References in this Part to an offence being dealt with are to a person being dealt with in respect of the offence.

(2) Subject to the following provisions of this section, references in this Part to the time at which a person is dealt with for an offence are to the time at which they are first dealt with

    (a) in England and Wales, by a magistrates' court or the Crown Court;

    (b) in Scotland, by a sheriff or by the High Court of Justiciary;

    (c) in Northern Ireland, by the county court.

This is referred to below as "the original decision".

(3) Where the original decision is varied (on appeal or otherwise), then

    (a) if the result is that the conditions for application of the notification requirements to a person in respect of an offence cease to be met (and paragraph (c) below does not apply), the notification requirements are treated as never having applied to that person in respect of that offence;

    (b) if the result is that the conditions for application of the notification requirements to a person in respect of an offence are met where they were not previously met (and paragraph (c) below does not apply)

        (i) the person is treated as dealt with for the offence when the variation takes place, and

        (ii) the notification requirements apply accordingly;

    (c) if

        (i) a conviction of, or finding in relation to, a different offence is substituted, and

        (ii) the conditions for application of the notification requirements were met in respect of the original offence and are also met in respect of the substituted offence,

    the person is treated as if they had been dealt with for the substituted offence at the time of the original decision;

    (d) if the sentence is varied so as to become one by virtue of which the notification requirements would apply for a different period, the period for which those requirements apply shall be determined as if the sentence as varied had been imposed at the time of the original decision;

    (e) in any other case, the variation is disregarded.

(4) For the purposes of

    (a) section 41(5) (effect of order adding offence to list of terrorism offences),

    (b) section 44(a) or paragraph 4(a) of Schedule 6 (persons subject to notification requirements: age when dealt with for offence),

(c) section 46(2) or paragraph 6(2) of Schedule 6 (effect of order reducing term or period triggering notification requirements),

(d) section 53(5)(b) or paragraph 7(5)(b) of Schedule 6 (period for which notification requirements apply: ending of period resulting from finding of disability etc where person subsequently tried), and

(e) paragraph 2(3) of Schedule 5 (conditions for making foreign travel restriction order: behaviour since offence dealt with),

a person is treated as dealt with at the time of the original decision and any subsequent variation of the decision is disregarded.

(5) For the purposes of

(a) section 43(1) and (2) or paragraph 3(1) and (2) of Schedule 6 (application of Part to offences dealt with before commencement), and

(b) paragraph 2(4) of Schedule 5 (conditions for making foreign travel restriction order where offence dealt with before commencement),

a person is dealt with for an offence before the commencement of this Part if the time of the original decision falls before the commencement of this Part.

Where in such a case subsection (3) above applies for the purposes of any provision of this Part, that subsection has effect as if the provisions of this Part had been in force at all material times.

(6) In section 47(6) (adaptation of initial notification requirements in case of offence dealt with before commencement)

(a) the reference in the opening words to an offence dealt with before the commencement of this Part is to an offence where the time of the original decision falls before the commencement of this Part, and

(b) the reference in the closing words to when the offence is dealt with has the same meaning as in subsection (1) of that section.

(7) References in this section to the variation of a decision include any proceedings by which the decision is altered, set aside or quashed, or in which a further decision is come to following the setting aside or quashing of the decision.

PART V
TERRORIST FINANCING AND MONEY LAUNDERING

62 Terrorist financing and money laundering

Schedule 7 makes provision conferring powers on the Treasury to act against terrorist financing, money laundering and certain other activities.

PART VI
FINANCIAL RESTRICTIONS PROCEEDINGS

CHAPTER 1
APPLICATION TO SET ASIDE FINANCIAL RESTRICTIONS DECISION

63 Application to set aside financial restrictions decision

(1) This section applies to any decision of the Treasury in connection with the exercise of any of their functions under

(a) the UN terrorism orders,

(b) Part 2 of the Anti-terrorism, Crime and Security Act 2001 (c 24) (freezing orders), or

    (c) Schedule 7 to this Act (terrorist financing, money laundering and certain other activities: financial restrictions).

(2) Any person affected by the decision may apply to the High Court or, in Scotland, the Court of Session to set aside the decision.

(3) In determining whether the decision should be set aside the court shall apply the principles applicable on an application for judicial review.

(4) If the court decides that a decision should be set aside it may make any such order, or give any such relief, as may be made or given in proceedings for judicial review.

(5) Without prejudice to the generality of subsection (4), if the court sets aside a decision of the Treasury
    (a) to give a direction under any of the UN terrorism orders,
    (b) to make a freezing order under Part 2 of the Anti-terrorism, Crime and Security Act 2001 (c 24), or
    (c) to give a direction or make an order under Schedule 7 to this Act,
the court must quash the relevant direction or order.

(6) This section applies whether the decision of the Treasury was made before or after the commencement of this section.

(7) After the commencement of this section an application to set aside a decision of the Treasury to which this section applies must be made under this section.

(8) This section does not apply to any decision of the Treasury to make an order under paragraph 8 or 28(6) of Schedule 7 to this Act.

64 UN terrorism orders

(1) For the purposes of section 63 the UN terrorism orders are
    (a) the Terrorism (United Nations Measures) Order 2001 (SI 2001/3365);
    (b) the Al-Qa'ida and Taliban (United Nations Measures) Order 2002 (SI 2002/111);
    (c) the Terrorism (United Nations Measures) Order 2006 (SI 2006/2657);
    (d) the Al-Qa'ida and Taliban (United Nations Measures) Order 2006 (SI 2006/2952).

(2) The Treasury may by order amend subsection (1) by
    (a) adding other Orders in Council made under section 1 of the United Nations Act 1946 (c 45),
    (b) providing that a reference to a specified Order in Council is to that order as amended by a further Order in Council (made after the passing of this Act), or
    (c) removing an Order in Council.

(3) An order under subsection (2) is subject to negative resolution procedure.

CHAPTER 2
FINANCIAL RESTRICTIONS PROCEEDINGS

Introductory

65 Financial restrictions proceedings

In this Chapter "financial restrictions proceedings" means proceedings in the High Court or the Court of Session on an application under section 63 or on a claim arising from any matter to which such an application relates.

Rules of court, disclosure and related matters

66 General provisions about rules of court

(1) The following provisions apply to rules of court relating to

(a) financial restrictions proceedings, or

(b) proceedings on an appeal relating to financial restrictions proceedings.

(2) A person making rules of court must have regard to

(a) the need to secure that the decisions that are the subject of the proceedings are properly reviewed; and

(b) the need to secure that disclosures of information are not made where they would be contrary to the public interest.

(3) Rules of court may make provision

(a) about the mode of proof and about evidence in the proceedings;

(b) enabling or requiring the proceedings to be determined without a hearing; and

(c) about legal representation in the proceedings.

(4) Rules of court may make provision

(a) enabling the proceedings to take place without full particulars of the reasons for the decisions to which the proceedings relate being given to a party to the proceedings (or to any legal representative of that party);

(b) enabling the court to conduct proceedings in the absence of any person, including a party to the proceedings (or any legal representative of that party);

(c) about the functions of a person appointed as a special advocate;

(d) enabling the court to give a party to the proceedings a summary of evidence taken in the party's absence.

(5) In this section

(a) references to a party to the proceedings do not include the Treasury;

(b) references to a party's legal representative do not include a person appointed as a special advocate.

(6) Nothing in this section shall be read as restricting the power to make rules of court or the matters to be taken into account when doing so.

67 Rules of court about disclosure

(1) The following provisions apply to rules of court relating to

(a) financial restrictions proceedings, or

(b) proceedings on an appeal relating to financial restrictions proceedings.

(2) Rules of court must secure that the Treasury are required to disclose

(a) material on which they rely,

(b) material which adversely affects their case, and

(c) material which supports the case of a party to the proceedings.

This is subject to the following provisions of this section.

(3) Rules of court must secure

(a) that the Treasury have the opportunity to make an application to the court for permission not to disclose material otherwise than to

(i) the court, and

(ii) any person appointed as a special advocate;

(b) that such an application is always considered in the absence of every party to the proceedings (and every party's legal representative);

(c) that the court is required to give permission for material not to be disclosed if it considers that the disclosure of the material would be contrary to the public interest;

(d) that, if permission is given by the court not to disclose material, it must consider requiring the Treasury to provide a summary of the material to every party to the proceedings (and every party's legal representative);

(e) that the court is required to ensure that such a summary does not contain material the disclosure of which would be contrary to the public interest.

(4) Rules of court must secure that in cases where the Treasury
- (a) do not receive the court's permission to withhold material, but elect not to disclose it, or
- (b) are required to provide a party to the proceedings with a summary of material that is withheld, but elect not to provide the summary,

provision to the following effect applies.

(5) The court must be authorised
- (a) if it considers that the material or anything that is required to be summarised might adversely affect the Treasury's case or support the case of a party to the proceedings, to direct that the Treasury shall not rely on such points in their case, or shall make such concessions or take such other steps, as the court may specify, or
- (b) in any other case, to ensure that the Treasury do not rely on the material or (as the case may be) on that which is required to be summarised.

(6) Nothing in this section, or in rules of court made under it, is to be read as requiring the court to act in a manner inconsistent with Article 6 of the Human Rights Convention.

(7) In this section
- (a) references to a party to the proceedings do not include the Treasury;
- (b) references to a party's legal representative do not include a person appointed as a special advocate; and
- (c) "the Human Rights Convention" means the Convention within the meaning of the Human Rights Act 1998 (c 42) (see section 21(1) of that Act).

68 Appointment of special advocate *(omitted)*

69 Intercept evidence *(omitted)*

70 Qualification of duty to give reasons

In paragraph 11 of Schedule 3 to the Anti-terrorism, Crime and Security Act 2001 (c 24) (Treasury's duty to give reason why person is specified in freezing order), make the existing provision sub-paragraph (1) and after it insert

"(2) Sub-paragraph (1) does not apply if, or to the extent that, particulars of the reason would not be required to be disclosed to the applicant in proceedings to set aside the freezing order."

Supplementary provisions

71 Allocation of proceedings to Queen's Bench Division *(omitted)*

72 Initial exercise of powers by Lord Chancellor *(omitted)*

73 Interpretation

In this Chapter

"financial restrictions proceedings" has the meaning given by section 65;

"rules of court" means rules for regulating the practice and procedure to be followed in the High Court or the Court of Appeal or in the Court of Session;

"special advocate" means a person appointed under section 68.

PART VII
MISCELLANEOUS

Inquiries

74 Inquiries: intercept evidence *(omitted)*

75 Amendment of definition of "terrorism" etc

(1) In the provisions listed below (which define "terrorism", or make similar provision, and require that the use or threat of action is made for the purpose of advancing a political, religious or ideological cause), after "religious" insert ", racial".

(2) The provisions are

    (a) section 1(1)(c) of the Terrorism Act 2000 (c 11),

    (b) section 113A(2) of the Anti-terrorism, Crime and Security Act 2001 (c 24),

    (c) paragraph 4(2)(c) of Schedule 21 to the Criminal Justice Act 2003 (c 44),

    (d) Article 2(3)(c) of the Terrorism (United Nations Measures) Order 2006 (SI 2006/2657),

    (e) Article 4(1)(c) of the Anti-terrorism (Financial and Other Measures) (Overseas Territories) Order 2002 (SI 2002/1822),

    (f) Article 2(1)(a)(iii) of the Terrorism (United Nations Measures) (Overseas Territories) Order 2001 (SI 2001/3366),

    (g) Article 3(1) of the Terrorism (United Nations Measures) (Isle of Man) Order 2001 (SI 2001/3364),

    (h) Article 3(1) of the Terrorism (United Nations Measures) (Channel Islands) Order 2001 (SI 2001/3363).

Terrorist offences

76 Offences relating to information about members of armed forces etc *(omitted)*

77 Terrorist property: disclosure of information about possible offences

(1)–(2) *(omitted)*

(3) After section 22 insert

22A Meaning of "employment

    In sections 19 to 21B

    (a) "employment" means any employment (whether paid or unpaid) and includes

        (i) work under a contract for services or as an office-holder,

        (ii) work experience provided pursuant to a training course or programme or in the course of training for employment, and

        (iii) voluntary work;

    (b) "employer" has a corresponding meaning.".

(4) So far as the amendment in subsection (3) above extends any provision of sections 19 to 21B of the Terrorism Act 2000 involving belief or suspicion to cases to which that provision did not previously apply, that provision applies where the belief or suspicion is held after subsection (3) above comes into force even if based on information that came to the person's attention before that subsection was in force.

In any such case sections 19(2), 21(3) and 21A(4) of that Act (duty to make disclosure as soon as is reasonably practicable) are to be read as requiring the person to act as soon as is reasonably practicable after subsection (3) above comes into force.

Control orders

78 Control orders: powers of entry and search *(omitted)*

79 Control orders: meaning of involvement in terrorism-related activity *(omitted)*

80 Time allowed for representations by controlled person *(omitted)*

81 Application for anonymity for controlled person *(omitted)*

PART VIII
SUPPLEMENTARY PROVISIONS

General definitions

92 Meaning of "terrorism"

In this Act "terrorism" has the same meaning as in the Terrorism Act 2000 (c 11) (see section 1 of that Act).

93 Meaning of offence having a "terrorist connection"

For the purposes of this Act an offence has a terrorist connection if the offence

(a) is, or takes place in the course of, an act of terrorism, or

(b) is committed for the purposes of terrorism.

94 Meaning of "ancillary offence"

(1) In this Act "ancillary offence", in relation to an offence, means any of the following

    (a) aiding, abetting, counselling or procuring the commission of the offence (or, in Scotland, being art and part in the commission of the offence);

    (b) an offence under Part 2 of the Serious Crime Act 2007 (c 27) (encouraging or assisting crime) in relation to the offence (or, in Scotland, inciting a person to commit the offence);

    (c) attempting or conspiring to commit the offence.

(2) In subsection (1)(b) the reference to an offence under Part 2 of the Serious Crime Act 2007 includes, in relation to times before the commencement of that Part, an offence of incitement under the law of England and Wales or Northern Ireland.

95 Meaning of "service court" and "service offence" *(omitted)*

SCHEDULE 1
DISCLOSURE AND THE INTELLIGENCE SERVICES:
CONSEQUENTIAL AMENDMENTS *(omitted)*

SCHEDULE 2 Sections 30, 31, 33, 35 and 42
OFFENCES WHERE TERRORIST CONNECTION TO BE CONSIDERED

Common law offences

Murder.
Manslaughter.
Culpable homicide.
Kidnapping.
Abduction.

Statutory offences

An offence under any of the following sections of the Offences against the Person Act 1861 (c 100)

(a) section 4 (soliciting murder),

(b) section 23 (maliciously administering poison etc so as to endanger life or inflict grievous bodily harm),

(c) section 28 (causing bodily injury by explosives),

(d) section 29 (using explosives etc with intent to do grievous bodily harm),

(e) section 30 (placing explosives with intent to do bodily injury),

(f) section 64 (making or having gunpowder etc with intent to commit or enable any person to commit any felony mentioned in the Act).

An offence under any of the following sections of the Explosive Substances Act 1883 (c 3)

(a) section 2 (causing explosion likely to endanger life or property),

(b) section 3 (attempt to cause explosion or making or keeping explosive with intent to endanger life or property),

(c) section 4 (making or possession of explosive under suspicious circumstances),

(d) section 5 (punishment of accessories).

An offence under section 1 of the Biological Weapons Act 1974 (c 6) (restriction on development etc of certain biological agents and toxins and of biological weapons).

An offence under section 1 of the Taking of Hostages Act 1982 (c 28) (hostage-taking).

An offence under any of the following sections of the Aviation Security Act 1982 (c 36)

(a) section 1 (hijacking),

(b) section 2 (destroying, damaging or endangering safety of aircraft),

(c) section 3 (other acts endangering or likely to endanger safety of aircraft),

(d) section 4 (offences in relation to certain dangerous articles),

(e) section 6(2) (inducing or assisting commission of offence under section 1, 2 or 3 outside the United Kingdom).

An offence under any of the following sections of the Nuclear Material (Offences) Act 1983 (c 18)

(a) section 1B (offences relating to damage to the environment),

(b) section 1C (offences of importing or exporting etc nuclear materials: extended jurisdiction),

(c) section 2 (offences involving preparatory acts and threats), so far as relating to an offence specified in this Schedule.

An offence under any of the following sections of the Aviation and Maritime Security Act 1990 (c 31)

(a) section 1 (endangering safety at aerodromes),

(b) section 9 (hijacking of ships),

(c) section 10 (seizing or exercising control of fixed platforms),

(d) section 11 (destroying ships or fixed platforms or endangering their safety),

(e) section 14(4) (inducing or assisting the commission of an offence outside the United Kingdom), so far as relating to an offence under section 9 or 11 of that Act.

An offence under Part 2 of the Channel Tunnel (Security) Order 1994 (SI 1994/570) (offences against the safety of channel tunnel trains and the tunnel system).

An offence under any of the following sections of the Chemical Weapons Act 1996 (c 6)

(a) section 2 (use etc of chemical weapons),

(b) section 11 (premises or equipment for producing chemical weapons).

An offence under any of the following sections of the Anti-terrorism, Crime and Security Act 2001 (c 24)

(a) section 47 (use etc of nuclear weapons),

(b) section 114 (hoaxes involving noxious substances or things).

Ancillary offences

Any ancillary offence in relation to an offence specified in this Schedule.

SCHEDULE 3
FORFEITURE: CONSEQUENTIAL AMENDMENTS *(omitted)*

SCHEDULE 4   Section 57
NOTIFICATION ORDERS

Introductory

1   A "notification order" is an order applying the notification requirements of this Part to a person who has been dealt with outside the United Kingdom in respect of a corresponding foreign offence.

2 (1) A "corresponding foreign offence" means an act that
    (a) constituted an offence under the law in force in a country outside the United Kingdom, and
    (b) corresponds to an offence to which this Part applies.

  (2) For this purpose an act punishable under the law in force in a country outside the United Kingdom is regarded as constituting an offence under that law however it is described in that law.

  (3) An act corresponds to an offence to which this Part applies if
    (a) it would have constituted an offence to which this Part applies by virtue of section 41 if it had been done in any part of the United Kingdom, or
    (b) it was, or took place in the course of, an act of terrorism or was done for the purposes of terrorism.

  (4) On an application for a notification order the condition in sub-paragraph (3)(a) or (b) is to be taken to be met unless
    (a) the defendant serves on the applicant, not later than rules of court may provide, a notice
      (i) stating that, on the facts as alleged with respect to the act concerned, the condition is not in the defendant's opinion met,
      (ii) showing the defendant's grounds for that opinion, and
      (iii) requiring the applicant to prove that the condition is met; or
    (b) the court permits the defendant to require the applicant to prove that the condition is met without service of such a notice.

  (5) In the application of this paragraph in Scotland, for "defendant" substitute "respondent".

Conditions for making a notification order

3 (1) The conditions for making a notification order in respect of a person are as follows.

  (2) The first condition is that under the law in force in a country outside the United Kingdom
    (a) the person has been convicted of a corresponding foreign offence and has received in respect of the offence a sentence equivalent to a sentence mentioned in section 45(1)(a), (2)(a) or (3)(a), or
    (b) a court exercising jurisdiction under that law has, in respect of a corresponding foreign offence
      (i) convicted the person or made a finding in relation to the person equivalent to a finding mentioned in section 45(1)(b)(ii) or (iii), (2)(b)(ii) or (iii) or (3)(b)(ii) or (iii) (finding of insanity or disability), and
      (ii) made the person subject to an order equivalent to a hospital order.

  (3) This condition is not met if there was a flagrant denial of the person's right to a fair trial.

  (4) The second condition is that
    (a) the sentence was imposed or order made after the commencement of this Part, or
    (b) the sentence was imposed or order made before the commencement of this Part and immediately before that time the person
      (i) was imprisoned or detained in pursuance of the sentence or order,
      (ii) would have been so imprisoned or detained but for being unlawfully at large or otherwise unlawfully absent, lawfully absent on a temporary basis or on bail pending an appeal, or
      (iii) had been released on licence, or was subject to an equivalent form of supervision, having served the whole or part of a sentence of imprisonment for the offence.

(5) The third condition is that the period for which the notification requirements would apply in respect of the offence (in accordance with section 53 as modified by paragraph 8(e)) has not expired.

(6) If on an application for a notification order it is proved that the conditions in sub-paragraphs (2), (4) and (5) are met, the court must make the order.

Application for notification order

4 (1) In England and Wales an application for a notification order in respect of a person may only be made by a chief officer of police.

(2) An application may only be made if
    (a) the person resides in the chief officer's police area, or
    (b) the chief officer believes that the person is in, or is intending to come to, that area.

(3) The application must be made to the High Court.

5 (1) In Scotland an application for a notification order in respect of a person may only be made by a chief constable.

(2) An application may only be made if
    (a) the person resides in the area of the chief constable's police force, or
    (b) the chief constable believes that the person is in, or is intending to come to, that area.

(3) The application must be made to the Court of Session.

6 (1) In Northern Ireland an application for a notification order in respect of a person may only be made by the Chief Constable of the Police Service of Northern Ireland.

(2) An application may only be made if
    (a) the person resides in Northern Ireland, or
    (b) the Chief Constable believes that the person is in, or is intending to come to, Northern Ireland.

(3) The application must be made to the High Court.

Effect of notification order

7 The effect of a notification order is that the notification requirements of this Part apply to the person in respect of whom it is made.

Adaptation of provisions of this Part in relation to foreign proceedings

8 The provisions of this Part have effect with the following adaptations in relation to foreign proceedings and cases where the notification requirements apply because a notification order has been made

    (a) in section 61(1) (references to dealing with an offence) for "being sentenced, or made subject to a hospital order" substitute "being made subject by the foreign court to a sentence or order within paragraph 3(2)(a) or (b) of Schedule 4";

    (b) in section 61(2) (references to time when person dealt with for an offence) for paragraphs (a) to (c) substitute "by the foreign court of first instance";

    (c) for the purposes of section 47 (initial notification) the period within which notification is to be made begins with the date of service of the notification order;

    (d) in section 51 (meaning of "local police area") the reference in subsection (1)(c) to the court of trial shall be read as a reference to the court by which the notification order was made;

    (e) in section 53 (period for which notification requirements apply) a reference to a sentence or order of any description is to be read as a reference to an equivalent sentence or order of the foreign court.

SCHEDULE 5   Section 58
FOREIGN TRAVEL RESTRICTION ORDERS

Introductory

1   A foreign travel restriction order is an order prohibiting the person to whom it applies from
    doing whichever of the following is specified in the order
    (a) travelling to a country outside the United Kingdom named or described in the order;
    (b) travelling to any country outside the United Kingdom other than a country named or
         described in the order;
    (c) travelling to any country outside the United Kingdom.

Conditions for making a foreign travel restriction order

2   (1) The conditions for making a foreign travel restriction order in respect of a person are as
         follows.
    (2) The first condition is that the notification requirements apply to the person.
    (3) The second condition is that the person's behaviour since the person was dealt with for the
         offence by virtue of which those requirements apply makes it necessary for a foreign travel
         restriction order to be made to prevent the person from taking part in terrorism activity
         outside the United Kingdom.
    (4) If the person was dealt with for the offence before the commencement of this Part, the
         condition in sub-paragraph (3) is not met unless the person has acted in that way since the
         commencement of this Part.
    (5) If on an application for a foreign travel restriction order the court is satisfied that the condi-
         tions in sub-paragraphs (2) and (3) are met, it may make a foreign travel restriction order.

Application for foreign travel restriction order

3   (1) In England and Wales an application for a foreign travel restriction order in respect of a
         person may only be made by a chief officer of police.
    (2) An application may only be made if
         (a) the person resides in the chief officer's police area, or
         (b) the chief officer believes that the person is in, or is intending to come to, that area.
    (3) The application must be made by complaint to a magistrates' court whose commission area
         includes any part of the chief officer's police area.
4   (1) In Scotland an application for a foreign travel restriction order in respect of a person may
         only be made by a chief constable.
    (2) An application may only be made if
         (a) the person resides in the area of the chief constable's police force, or
         (b) the chief constable believes that the person is in, or is intending to come to, that area.
    (3) The application must be made by summary application to a sheriff within whose sheriff-
         dom any part of the area of the chief constable's police force lies.
    (4) A record of evidence is to be kept on any such summary application.
    (5) Where the sheriff makes a foreign travel restriction order, the clerk of the court must give a
         copy of the order to the respondent or send a copy to the respondent by registered post or
         the recorded delivery service.
    (6) An acknowledgement or certificate of delivery issued by the Post Office is sufficient
         evidence of the delivery of the copy on the day specified in the acknowledgement or
         certificate.
5   (1) In Northern Ireland an application for a foreign travel restriction order in respect of a per-
         son may only be made by the Chief Constable of the Police Service of Northern Ireland.

(2) An application may only be made if

    (a) the person resides in Northern Ireland, or

    (b) the Chief Constable believes that the person is in, or is intending to come to, Northern Ireland.

(3) The application must be made by complaint under Part 8 of the Magistrates' Courts (Northern Ireland) Order 1981 (SI 1981/1675 (NI 26)) to a court of summary jurisdiction.

Provisions of a foreign travel restriction order

6 (1) A foreign travel restriction order may prohibit the person to whom it applies

    (a) from travelling to any country outside the United Kingdom named or described in the order; or

    (b) from travelling to any country outside the United Kingdom other than a country named or described in the order; or

    (c) from travelling to any country outside the United Kingdom.

(2) The order must only impose such prohibitions as are necessary for the purpose of preventing the person from taking part in terrorism activity outside the United Kingdom.

(3) A foreign travel restriction order containing a prohibition within sub-paragraph (1)(c) must require the person to whom it applies to surrender all that person's passports, at a police station specified in the order

    (a) on or before the date when the prohibition takes effect, or

    (b) within a period specified in the order.

(4) Any passports surrendered must be returned as soon as reasonably practicable after the person ceases to be subject to a foreign travel restriction order containing such a prohibition.

Duration of foreign travel restriction order

7 (1) A foreign travel restriction order has effect for a fixed period of not more than 6 months.

(2) The period must be specified in the order.

(3) A foreign travel restriction order ceases to have effect if a court (whether the same or another court) makes another foreign travel restriction order in relation to the person to whom the earlier order applies.

Variation, renewal or discharge of order

8 (1) In England and Wales an application for an order varying, renewing or discharging a foreign travel restriction order may be made by

    (a) the person subject to the order;

    (b) the chief officer of police on whose application the order was made;

    (c) the chief officer of police for the area in which the person subject to the order resides; or

    (d) a chief officer of police who believes that the person subject to the order is in, or is intending to come to, the officer's police area.

(2) The application must be made by complaint to

    (a) a magistrates' court for the same area as the court that made the order,

    (b) a magistrates' court for the area in which the person subject to the order resides, or

    (c) where the application is made by a chief officer of police, any magistrates' court whose commission area includes any part of that chief officer's police area.

(3) On an application under this paragraph the court may make such order varying, renewing or discharging the foreign travel restriction order as it considers appropriate.

(4) Before doing so it must hear the person making the application and (if they wish to be heard) the other persons mentioned in sub-paragraph (1).

9 (1) In Scotland an application for an order varying, renewing or discharging a foreign travel restriction order may be made by

    (a) the person subject to the order;

    (b) the chief constable on whose application the order was made;

    (c) the chief constable in the area of whose police force the person subject to the order resides; or

    (d) a chief constable who believes that the person subject to the order is in, or is intending to come to, the area of that chief constable's police force.

  (2) The application must be made by summary application

    (a) to the sheriff who made the order, or

    (b) to a sheriff

      (i) within whose sheriffdom the person subject to the order resides, or

      (ii) where the application is made by a chief constable, within whose sheriffdom any part of the area of the chief constable's police force lies.

  (3) A record of evidence is to be kept on any summary application under this paragraph.

  (4) On an application under this paragraph the sheriff may make such order varying, renewing or discharging the foreign travel restriction order as the sheriff considers appropriate.

  (5) Before doing so the sheriff must hear the person making the application and (if they wish to be heard) the other persons mentioned in sub-paragraph (1).

10 (1) In Northern Ireland an application for an order varying, renewing or discharging a foreign travel restriction order may be made by

    (a) the person subject to the order; or

    (b) the Chief Constable of the Police Service of Northern Ireland.

  (2) The application must be made by complaint under Part 8 of the Magistrates' Courts (Northern Ireland) Order 1981 (SI 1981/1675 (NI 26)) to a court of summary jurisdiction for the petty sessions district which includes the area where the person subject to the order resides.

  (3) On an application under this paragraph the court may make such order varying, renewing or discharging the foreign travel restriction order as it considers appropriate.

  (4) It may do so only after hearing the person making the application and (if they wish to be heard) the other person mentioned in sub-paragraph (1).

Provisions of renewed or varied order

11 (1) A foreign travel restriction order may be renewed, or varied so as to impose additional prohibitions, but only if it is necessary to do so for the purpose of preventing the person subject to the order from taking part in terrorism activities outside the United Kingdom.

  (2) Any renewed or varied order must contain only the prohibitions necessary for that purpose.

Appeals

12 (1) In England and Wales

    (a) a person against whom a foreign travel restriction order is made may appeal against the making of the order;

    (b) a person subject to a foreign travel restriction order may appeal against

      (i) an order under paragraph 8 varying or renewing the order, or

      (ii) a refusal to make an order under that paragraph varying or discharging the order.

  (2) The appeal lies to the Crown Court.

  (3) On an appeal under this paragraph the court may make

    (a) such orders as it considers necessary to give effect to its determination of the appeal, and

    (b) such incidental and consequential orders as appear to it to be just.

13 (1) In Scotland an interlocutor of the sheriff granting or refusing a foreign travel restriction order, or an order under paragraph 9 (variation, renewal or discharge of foreign travel restriction order), is appealable.

(2) Where an appeal is taken against such an interlocutor, the interlocutor continues in effect pending disposal of the appeal.

14 (1) In Northern Ireland

(a) a person against whom a foreign travel restriction order is made may appeal against the making of the order;

(b) a person subject to a foreign travel restriction order may appeal against

(i) an order under paragraph 10 varying or renewing the order, or

(ii) a refusal to make an order under that paragraph varying or discharging the order.

(2) The appeal lies to the county court.

(3) On an appeal under this paragraph the court may make

(a) such orders as it considers necessary to give effect to its determination of the appeal, and

(b) such incidental and consequential orders as appear to it to be just.

Breach of foreign travel restriction order an offence

15 (1) A person commits an offence who, without reasonable excuse

(a) does anything they are prohibited from doing by a foreign travel restriction order, or

(b) fails to comply with a requirement imposed on them by such an order.

(2) A person guilty of an offence under this paragraph is liable

(a) on summary conviction, to imprisonment for a term not exceeding 12 months or a fine not exceeding the statutory maximum or both;

(b) on conviction on indictment, to imprisonment for a term not exceeding 5 years or a fine or both.

(3) In the application of sub-paragraph (2)(a)

(a) in England and Wales, in relation to an offence committed before the commencement of section 154(1) of the Criminal Justice Act 2003 (c 44), or

(b) in Northern Ireland,

for "12 months" substitute "6 months".

(4) Where a person is convicted of an offence under this paragraph, it is not open to the court by or before which they are convicted

(a) in England and Wales or Northern Ireland, to make an order for conditional discharge in respect of the offence;

(b) in Scotland, to make a probation order in respect of the offence.

Meaning of "terrorism activity"

16 In this Schedule "terrorism activity" means anything that

(a) if done in any part of the United Kingdom, would constitute an offence to which this Part applies by virtue of section 41, or

(b) is, or takes place in the course of, an act of terrorism or is for the purposes of terrorism.

SCHEDULE 6
NOTIFICATION REQUIREMENTS: APPLICATION TO
SERVICE OFFENCES *(omitted)*

SCHEDULE 7   Section 62
TERRORIST FINANCING AND MONEY LAUNDERING

PART 1
CONDITIONS FOR GIVING A DIRECTION

Conditions for giving a direction

1 (1) The Treasury may give a direction under this Schedule if one or more of the following conditions is met in relation to a country.
  (2) The first condition is that the Financial Action Task Force has advised that measures should be taken in relation to the country because of the risk of terrorist financing or money laundering activities being carried on
      (a) in the country,
      (b) by the government of the country, or
      (c) by persons resident or incorporated in the country.
  (3) The second condition is that the Treasury reasonably believe that there is a risk that terrorist financing or money laundering activities are being carried on
      (a) in the country,
      (b) by the government of the country, or
      (c) by persons resident or incorporated in the country,
      and that this poses a significant risk to the national interests of the United Kingdom.
  (4) The third condition is that the Treasury reasonably believe that
      (a) the development or production of nuclear, radiological, biological or chemical weapons in the country, or
      (b) the doing in the country of anything that facilitates the development or production of any such weapons,
      poses a significant risk to the national interests of the United Kingdom.
  (5) The power to give a direction is not exercisable in relation to an EEA state.

Main definitions

2 (1) "Terrorist financing" means
      (a) the use of funds, or the making available of funds, for the purposes of terrorism, or
      (b) the acquisition, possession, concealment, conversion or transfer of funds that are (directly or indirectly) to be used or made available for those purposes.
  (2) "Money laundering" means an act which falls within section 340(11) of the Proceeds of Crime Act 2002 (c 29).
  (3) "Nuclear weapon" includes a nuclear explosive device that is not intended for use as a weapon.
  (4) "Radiological weapon" means a device designed to cause destruction, damage or injury by means of the radiation produced by the decay of radioactive material.
  (5) "Chemical weapon" means a chemical weapon as defined by section 1(1) of the Chemical Weapons Act 1996 (c 6), other than one whose intended use is only for permitted purposes (as defined by section 1(3) of that Act).
  (6) "Biological weapon" means anything within section 1(1)(a) or (b) of the Biological Weapons Act 1974 (c 6).

PART 2
PERSONS TO WHOM A DIRECTION MAY BE GIVEN

Persons to whom a direction may be given

3 (1) A direction under this Schedule may be given to
    (a) a particular person operating in the financial sector,
    (b) any description of persons operating in that sector, or
    (c) all persons operating in that sector.

  (2) In this Schedule "relevant person", in relation to a direction, means any of the persons to whom the direction is given.

  (3) A direction may make different provision in relation to different descriptions of relevant person.

Persons operating in the financial sector

4 (1) Any reference in this Schedule to a person operating in the financial sector is to a credit or financial institution that—
    (a) is a United Kingdom person, or
    (b) is acting in the course of a business carried on by it in the United Kingdom.

  (2) This is subject to the exceptions in paragraph 6.

Meaning of "credit institution" and "financial institution"

5 (1) "Credit institution" means—
    (a) a credit institution as defined in Article 4(1)(a) of the banking consolidation directive, or
    (b) a branch (within the meaning of Article 4(3) of that directive) located in an EEA state of—
        (i) an institution within sub-paragraph (a), or
        (ii) an equivalent institution whose head office is located in a non-EEA state,
    when it accepts deposits or other repayable funds from the public or grants credits for its own account (within the meaning of the banking consolidation directive).

  (2) "Financial institution" means—
    (a) an undertaking, including a money service business, when it carries out one or more of the activities listed in points 2 to 12 and 14 of Annex 1 to the banking consolidation directive, other than—
        (i) a credit institution;
        (ii) an undertaking whose only listed activity is trading for own account in one or more of the products listed in point 7 of Annex 1 to the banking consolidation directive where the undertaking does not have a customer,
    and for this purpose "customer" means a person who is not a member of the same group as the undertaking;
    (b) an insurance company duly authorised in accordance with the life assurance consolidation directive, when it carries out activities covered by that directive;
    (c) a person whose regular occupation or business is the provision to other persons of an investment service or the performance of an investment activity on a professional basis, when providing or performing investment services or activities (within the meaning of the markets in financial instruments directive), other than a person falling within Article 2 of that directive;
    (d) a collective investment undertaking, when marketing or otherwise offering its units or shares;
    (e) an insurance intermediary as defined in Article 2(5) of Directive 2002/92/EC of the European Parliament and of the Council of 9th December 2002 on insurance mediation (other than a tied insurance intermediary as mentioned in Article 2(7) of that Directive),

when it acts in respect of contracts of long-term insurance within the meaning given by article 3(1) of, and Part II of Schedule 1 to, the Financial Services and Markets Act 2000 (Regulated Activities) Order 2001 (SI 2001/544);

(f) a branch located in an EEA state of—
   (i) a person referred to in any of paragraphs (a) to (e), or
   (ii) a person equivalent to a person within any of those paragraphs whose head office is located in a non-EEA state,
   when carrying out any activity mentioned in that paragraph;

(g) an insurance company (as defined by section 1165(3) of the Companies Act 2006 (c 46));

(h) the National Savings Bank;

(i) the Director of Savings, when money is raised under the auspices of the Director under the National Loans Act 1968 (c 13).

Exceptions

6 (1) For the purposes of this Schedule the following are not regarded as persons operating in the financial sector when carrying out any of the following activities—

(a) a society registered under the Industrial and Provident Societies Act 1965 (c 12), when it—
   (i) issues withdrawable share capital within the limit set by section 6 of that Act (maximum shareholding in society); or
   (ii) accepts deposits from the public within the limit set by section 7(3) of that Act (carrying on of banking by societies);

(b) a society registered under the Industrial and Provident Societies Act (Northern Ireland) 1969 (c 24 (NI)), when it—
   (i) issues withdrawable share capital within the limit set by section 6 of that Act (maximum shareholding in society); or
   (ii) accepts deposits from the public within the limit set by section 7(3) of that Act (carrying on of banking by societies);

(c) a person within any of paragraphs 1 to 23 or 25 to 51 of the Schedule to the Financial Services and Markets Act 2000 (Exemption) Order 2001 (SI 2001/1201), when carrying out an activity in respect of which the person is exempt;

(d) a person who was an exempted person for the purposes of section 45 of the Financial Services Act 1986 (c 60) (miscellaneous exemptions) immediately before its repeal, when exercising the functions specified in that section.

(2) A person who falls within the definition of "credit institution" or "financial institution" solely as a result of engaging in financial activity on an occasional or very limited basis is not regarded for the purposes of this Schedule as operating in the financial sector.

(3) For the purposes of sub-paragraph (2) a person is regarded as engaging in a financial activity on an occasional or very limited basis if—

(a) the person's total annual turnover in respect of the financial activity does not exceed £64,000,

(b) the financial activity is limited in relation to any customer to no more than one transaction exceeding 1,000 euro (whether the transaction is carried out in a single operation or a series of operations which appear to be linked),

(c) the financial activity does not exceed 5% of the person's total annual turnover,

(d) the financial activity is ancillary and directly related to the person's main activity,

(e) the financial activity is not the transmission or remittance of money (or any representation of monetary value) by any means,

(f) the person's main activity is not that of a credit or financial institution, and

(g) the financial activity is provided only to customers of the person's main activity.

Interpretation of this Part

7 In this Part of this Schedule—

"the banking consolidation directive" means Directive 2006/48/EC of the European Parliament and of the Council of 14th June 2006 relating to the taking up and pursuit of the business of credit institutions;

"the life assurance consolidation directive" means Directive 2002/83/EC of the European Parliament and of the Council of 5th November 2002 concerning life assurance;

"the markets in financial instruments directive" means Directive 2004/39/EC of the European Parliament and of the Council of 12th April 2004 on markets in financial instruments.

Power to amend

8 (1) The Treasury may by order amend paragraphs 4 to 7.

(2) Any such order is subject to affirmative resolution procedure.

PART 3
REQUIREMENTS THAT MAY BE IMPOSED BY A DIRECTION

Requirements that may be imposed by a direction

9 (1) A direction under this Schedule may impose requirements in relation to transactions or business relationships with

(a) a person carrying on business in the country;

(b) the government of the country;

(c) a person resident or incorporated in the country.

(2) The direction may impose requirements in relation to

(a) a particular person within sub-paragraph (1),

(b) any description of persons within that sub-paragraph, or

(c) all persons within that sub-paragraph.

(3) In this Schedule "designated person", in relation to a direction, means any of the persons in relation to whom the direction is given.

(4) The kinds of requirement that may be imposed by a direction under this Schedule are specified in

paragraph 10 (customer due diligence);

paragraph 11 (ongoing monitoring);

paragraph 12 (systematic reporting);

paragraph 13 (limiting or ceasing business).

(5) A direction may make different provision

(a) in relation to different descriptions of designated person, and

(b) in relation to different descriptions of transaction or business relationship.

(6) The requirements imposed by a direction must be proportionate having regard to the advice mentioned in paragraph 1(2) or, as the case may be, the risk mentioned in paragraph 1(3) or (4) to the national interests of the United Kingdom.

Customer due diligence

10 (1) A direction may require a relevant person to undertake enhanced customer due diligence measures—

(a) before entering into a transaction or business relationship with a designated person, and

(b) during a business relationship with such a person.

(2) The direction may do either or both of the following—

   (a) impose a general obligation to undertake enhanced customer due diligence measures;

   (b) require a relevant person to undertake specific measures identified or described in the direction.

(3) "Customer due diligence measures" means measures to—

   (a) establish the identity of the designated person,

   (b) obtain information about—

      (i) the designated person and their business, and

      (ii) the source of their funds, and

   (c) assess the risk of the designated person being involved in relevant activities.

(4) In sub-paragraph (3)(c) "relevant activities" means—

   (a) terrorist financing;

   (b) money laundering; or

   (c) the development or production of nuclear, radiological, biological or chemical weapons or the facilitation of that development or production.

(5) A direction may not impose requirements of a kind mentioned in this paragraph on a person who is regarded as operating in the financial sector by virtue only of paragraph 5(2)(g) (certain insurance companies).

Ongoing monitoring

11 (1) A direction may require a relevant person to undertake enhanced ongoing monitoring of any business relationship with a designated person.

(2) The direction may do either or both of the following—

   (a) impose a general obligation to undertake enhanced ongoing monitoring;

   (b) require a relevant person to undertake specific measures identified or described in the direction.

(3) "Ongoing monitoring" of a business relationship means—

   (a) keeping up to date information and documents obtained for the purposes of customer due diligence measures, and

   (b) scrutinising transactions undertaken during the course of the relationship (and, where appropriate, the source of funds for those transactions) to ascertain whether the transactions are consistent with the relevant person's knowledge of the designated person and their business.

(4) A direction may not impose requirements of a kind mentioned in this paragraph on a person who is regarded as operating in the financial sector by virtue only of paragraph 5(2)(g) (certain insurance companies).

Systematic reporting

12 (1) A direction may require a relevant person to provide such information and documents as may be specified in the direction relating to transactions and business relationships with designated persons.

(2) A direction imposing such a requirement must specify how the direction is to be complied with, including—

   (a) the person to whom the information and documents are to be provided, and

   (b) the period within which, or intervals at which, information and documents are to be provided.

(3) The power conferred by this paragraph is not exercisable in relation to information or documents in respect of which a claim to legal professional privilege (in Scotland, to confidentiality of communications) could be maintained in legal proceedings.

(4) The exercise of the power conferred by this paragraph and the provision of information under it is not otherwise subject to any restriction on the disclosure of information, whether imposed by statute or otherwise.

Limiting or ceasing business

13 A direction may require a relevant person not to enter into or continue to participate in—

(a) a specified transaction or business relationship with a designated person,

(b) a specified description of transactions or business relationships with a designated person, or

(c) any transaction or business relationship with a designated person.

PART 4
PROCEDURAL PROVISIONS AND LICENSING

General directions to be given by order

14 (1) A direction given to

(a) a description of persons operating in the financial sector, or

(b) all persons operating in that sector,

must be contained in an order made by the Treasury.

(2) If the order contains requirements of a kind mentioned in paragraph 13 (limiting or ceasing business)

(a) it must be laid before Parliament after being made, and

(b) if not approved by a resolution of each House of Parliament before the end of 28 days beginning with the day on which it is made, it ceases to have effect at the end of that period.

In calculating the period of 28 days, no account is to be taken of any time during which Parliament is dissolved or prorogued or during which both Houses are adjourned for more than 4 days.

(3) An order's ceasing to have effect in accordance with sub-paragraph (2) does not affect anything done under the order.

(4) An order to which sub-paragraph (2) does not apply is subject to negative resolution procedure.

(5) If apart from this sub-paragraph an order under this paragraph would be treated for the purposes of the standing orders of either House of Parliament as a hybrid instrument, it is to proceed in that House as if it were not such an instrument.

Specific directions: notification and duration of directions

15 (1) This paragraph applies in relation to a direction given to a particular person.

(2) The Treasury must give notice of the direction to the person.

(3) The direction (if not previously revoked and whether or not varied) ceases to have effect at the end of the period of one year beginning with the day on which the direction is given.

This is without prejudice to the giving of a further direction.

(4) The Treasury may vary or revoke the direction at any time.

(5) Where the direction is varied or ceases to have effect (whether on revocation or otherwise), the Treasury must give notice of that fact to the person.

General directions: publication and duration of directions

16 (1) This paragraph applies to an order containing directions under paragraph 14 (general directions given by order).

(2) The Treasury must take such steps as they consider appropriate to publicise the making of the order.

(3) An order—

(a) revoking the order, or

(b) varying the order so as to make its provisions less onerous,

is subject to negative resolution procedure.

(4) The order (if not previously revoked and whether or not varied) ceases to have effect at the end of the period of one year beginning with the day on which it was made.

This is without prejudice to the making of a further order.

(5) Where the order is varied or ceases to have effect (whether on revocation or otherwise), the Treasury must take such steps as they consider appropriate to publicise that fact.

Directions limiting or ceasing business: exemption by licence

17 (1) The following provisions apply where a direction contains requirements of a kind mentioned in paragraph 13 (limiting or ceasing business).

(2) The Treasury may grant a licence to exempt acts specified in the licence from those requirements.

(3) A licence may be—

(a) general or granted to a description of persons or to a particular person;

(b) subject to conditions;

(c) of indefinite duration or subject to an expiry date.

(4) The Treasury may vary or revoke a licence at any time.

(5) On the grant, variation or revocation of a licence, the Treasury must—

(a) in the case of a licence granted to a particular person, give notice of the grant, variation or revocation to that person;

(b) in the case of a general licence or a licence granted to a description of persons, take such steps as the Treasury consider appropriate to publicise the grant, variation or revocation of the licence.

PART 5
ENFORCEMENT: INFORMATION POWERS

Enforcement authorities and officers

18 (1) In this Schedule "enforcement authority" means

(a) the Financial Services Authority ("the FSA"),

(b) the Commissioners for Her Majesty's Revenue and Customs ("HMRC"),

(c) the Office of Fair Trading ("the OFT"), or

(d) in relation to credit unions in Northern Ireland, the Department of Enterprise, Trade and Investment in Northern Ireland ("DETINI").

(2) In this Part of this Schedule "enforcement officer" means

(a) an officer of the FSA, including a member of the staff or an agent of the FSA,

(b) an officer of Revenue and Customs,

(c) an officer of the OFT,

(d) an officer of DETINI acting for the purposes of its functions under this Schedule in relation to credit unions in Northern Ireland, or

(e) a local enforcement officer.

(3) A "local enforcement officer" means
    (a) in Great Britain, an officer of a local weights and measures authority;
    (b) in Northern Ireland, an officer of DETINI acting pursuant to arrangements made with the OFT for the purposes of this Schedule.

Power to require information or documents

19 (1) An enforcement officer may by notice to a relevant person require the person
    (a) to provide such information as may be specified in the notice, or
    (b) to produce such documents as may be so specified.

(2) An officer may exercise powers under this paragraph only if the information or documents sought to be obtained as a result are reasonably required in connection with the exercise by the enforcement authority for whom the officer acts of its functions under this Schedule.

(3) Where an officer requires information to be provided or documents produced under this paragraph
    (a) the notice must set out the reasons why the officer requires the information to be provided or the documents produced, and
    (b) the information must be provided or the documents produced
        (i) before the end of such reasonable period as may be specified in the notice; and
        (ii) at such place as may be so specified.

(4) In relation to a document in electronic form the power to require production of it includes a power to require the production of a copy of it in legible form or in a form from which it can readily be produced in visible and legible form.

(5) An enforcement officer may take copies of, or make extracts from, any document produced under this paragraph.

(6) The production of a document does not affect any lien which a person has on the document.

Entry, inspection without a warrant etc

20 (1) Where an enforcement officer has reasonable cause to believe that any premises are being used by a relevant person in connection with the person's business activities, the officer may on producing evidence of authority at any reasonable time
    (a) enter the premises;
    (b) inspect the premises;
    (c) observe the carrying on of business activities by the relevant person;
    (d) inspect any document found on the premises;
    (e) require any person on the premises to provide an explanation of any document or to state where it may be found.

(2) An enforcement officer may take copies of, or make extracts from, any document found under sub-paragraph (1).

(3) An officer may exercise powers under this paragraph only if the information or document sought to be obtained as a result is reasonably required in connection with the exercise by the enforcement authority for whom the officer acts of its functions under this Schedule.

(4) In this paragraph "premises" means any premises other than premises used only as a dwelling.

Entry to premises under warrant

21 (1) A justice may issue a warrant under this paragraph if satisfied on information on oath given by an enforcement officer that there are reasonable grounds for believing that the first, second or third set of conditions is satisfied.

(2) The first set of conditions is

    (a) that there is on the premises specified in the warrant a document in relation to which a requirement could be imposed under paragraph 19(1)(b), and

    (b) that if such a requirement were to be imposed

        (i) it would not be complied with, or

        (ii) the document to which it relates would be removed, tampered with or destroyed.

(3) The second set of conditions is

    (a) that a person on whom a requirement has been imposed under paragraph 19(1)(b) has failed (wholly or in part) to comply with it, and

    (b) that there is on the premises specified in the warrant a document that has been required to be produced.

(4) The third set of conditions is

    (a) that an enforcement officer has been obstructed in the exercise of a power under paragraph 20, and

    (b) that there is on the premises specified in the warrant a document that could be inspected under paragraph 20(1)(d).

(5) A justice may issue a warrant under this paragraph if satisfied on information on oath given by an officer that there are reasonable grounds for suspecting that

    (a) an offence under this Schedule has been, is being or is about to be committed by a relevant person, and

    (b) there is on the premises specified in the warrant a document relevant to whether that offence has been, or is being or is about to be committed.

(6) A warrant issued under this paragraph shall authorise an enforcement officer

    (a) to enter the premises specified in the warrant;

    (b) to search the premises and take possession of anything appearing to be a document specified in the warrant or to take, in relation to any such document, any other steps which may appear to be necessary for preserving it or preventing interference with it;

    (c) to take copies of, or extracts from, any document specified in the warrant;

    (d) to require any person on the premises to provide an explanation of any document appearing to be of the kind specified in the warrant or to state where it may be found;

    (e) to use such force as may reasonably be necessary.

(7) Where a warrant is issued by a justice under sub-paragraph (1) or (5) on the basis of information on oath given by an officer of the FSA, for "an enforcement officer" in sub-paragraph (6) substitute "a constable".

(8) In sub-paragraphs (1), (5) and (7), "justice" means

    (a) in relation to England and Wales, a justice of the peace;

    (b) in relation to Scotland, a justice within the meaning of section 307 of the Criminal Procedure (Scotland) Act 1995 (c 46) (interpretation);

    (c) in relation to Northern Ireland, a lay magistrate.

(9) In the application of this paragraph to Scotland, the references in sub-paragraphs (1), (5) and (7) to information on oath are to be read as references to evidence on oath.

Restrictions on powers

22 (1) This paragraph applies in relation to the powers conferred by

    (a) paragraph 19 (power to require information or documents),

    (b) paragraph 20 (entry, inspection without warrant etc), or

    (c) paragraph 21 (entry to premises under warrant).

(2) Those powers are not exercisable in relation to information or documents in respect of which a claim to legal professional privilege (in Scotland, to confidentiality of communications) could be maintained in legal proceedings.

(3) The exercise of those powers and the provision of information or production of documents under them is not otherwise subject to any restriction on the disclosure of information, whether imposed by statute or otherwise.

Failure to comply with information requirement

23 (1) If on an application made by

(a) an enforcement authority, or

(b) a local weights and measures authority or DETINI pursuant to arrangements made with the OFT

(i) by or on behalf of the authority; or

(ii) by DETINI,

it appears to the court that a person (the "information defaulter") has failed to do something that they were required to do under paragraph 19(1), the court may make an order under this paragraph.

(2) An order under this paragraph may require the information defaulter

(a) to do the thing that they failed to do within such period as may be specified in the order;

(b) otherwise to take such steps to remedy the consequences of the failure as may be so specified.

(3) If the information defaulter is a body corporate, a partnership or an unincorporated body of persons that is not a partnership, the order may require any officer of the body corporate, partnership or body, who is (wholly or partly) responsible for the failure to meet such costs of the application as are specified in the order.

(4) In this paragraph "the court" means

(a) in England and Wales and Northern Ireland, the High Court or the county court;

(b) in Scotland, the Court of Session or the sheriff court.

Powers of local enforcement officers

24 (1) A local enforcement officer may only exercise powers under this Part of this Schedule pursuant to arrangements made with the OFT

(a) by or on behalf of the relevant local weights and measures authority, or

(b) by DETINI.

(2) Anything done or omitted to be done by, or in relation to, a local enforcement officer in the exercise or purported exercise of a power in this Part of this Schedule is treated for all purposes as if done or omitted to be done by, or in relation to, an officer of the OFT.

(3) Sub-paragraph (2) does not apply for the purposes of criminal proceedings brought against the local enforcement officer, the relevant local weights and measures authority, DETINI or the OFT, in respect of anything done or omitted to be done by the officer.

(4) A local enforcement officer must not disclose to any person other than the OFT and the relevant local weights and measures authority or, as the case may be, DETINI information obtained by the officer in the exercise of powers under this Part of this Schedule unless

(a) the officer has the approval of the OFT to do so, or

(b) the officer is under a duty to make the disclosure.

(5) In this paragraph "the relevant local weights and measures authority", in relation to a local enforcement officer, means the authority of which the officer is an officer.

PART 6
ENFORCEMENT: CIVIL PENALTIES

Power to impose civil penalties

25 (1) An enforcement authority may impose a penalty of such amount as it considers appropriate on a person who fails to comply with a requirement imposed
(a) by a direction under this Schedule, or
(b) by a condition of a licence under paragraph 17.
For this purpose "appropriate" means effective, proportionate and dissuasive.

(2) No such penalty is to be imposed if the authority is satisfied that the person took all reasonable steps and exercised all due diligence to ensure that the requirement would be complied with.

(3) In deciding whether to impose a penalty for failure to comply with a requirement, an enforcement authority must consider whether the person followed any relevant guidance which was at the time
(a) issued by a supervisory authority or any other appropriate body,
(b) approved by the Treasury, and
(c) published in a manner approved by the Treasury as suitable in their opinion to bring the guidance to the attention of persons likely to be affected by it.

(4) In sub-paragraph (3) "appropriate body" means a body which regulates or is representative of any trade, profession, business or employment carried on by the person.

(5) A person on whom a penalty is imposed under this paragraph is not liable to be proceeded against for an offence under paragraph 30 in respect of the same failure.

Imposition of penalty by HMRC: procedure and reviews

26 (1) This paragraph applies where HMRC decide to impose a penalty under paragraph 25 on a person.

(2) HMRC must give the person notice of
(a) their decision to impose the penalty and its amount,
(b) the reasons for imposing the penalty,
(c) the right to a review under this paragraph, and
(d) the right to appeal under paragraph 28.

(3) The person may by notice to HMRC require them to review their decision.

(4) A notice requiring a review may not be given after the end of the period of 45 days beginning with the day on which HMRC first gave the person notice under sub-paragraph (2).

(5) On a review under this paragraph, HMRC must either
(a) confirm the decision, or
(b) withdraw or vary the decision and take such further steps (if any) in consequence of the withdrawal or variation as they consider appropriate.

(6) Where HMRC do not, within the period of 45 days beginning with the day the notice under sub-paragraph (3) was given, give notice to the person of their determination of the review, they are to be taken to have confirmed their decision.

Imposition of penalty by other enforcement authority: procedure

27 (1) This paragraph applies if the FSA, the OFT or DETINI ("the authority") proposes to impose a penalty under paragraph 25 on a person.

(2) The authority must give the person notice of
(a) the proposal to impose the penalty and the proposed amount,

(b) the reasons for imposing the penalty, and

(c) the right to make representations to the authority within a specified period (which may not be less than 28 days).

(3) The authority must then decide, within a reasonable period, whether to impose a penalty under paragraph 25 and must give the person notice

(a) if it decides not to impose a penalty, of that decision;

(b) if it decides to impose a penalty, of the following matters

(i) the decision to impose a penalty and the amount,

(ii) the reasons for the decision, and

(iii) the right to appeal under paragraph 28.

Appeal against imposition of civil penalty

28 *(omitted)*

Payment and recovery of civil penalties

29 *(omitted)*

PART 7
ENFORCEMENT: OFFENCES

30–37 *(omitted)*

PART 8
SUPPLEMENTARY AND GENERAL

38–43 *(omitted)*

Meaning of "United Kingdom person"

44 *(omitted)*

Interpretation

45 *(omitted)*

Index of defined expressions

46 *(omitted)*

SCHEDULE 8
OFFENCES RELATING TO INFORMATION ABOUT MEMBERS OF ARMED FORCES ETC: SUPPLEMENTARY PROVISIONS *(omitted)*

SCHEDULE 9
REPEALS AND REVOCATIONS *(omitted)*

Bibliography

These listings concentrate upon post-2000 sources of principal relevance to contemporary anti-terrorism legislation in the United Kingdom. Many more sources and references are contained in the footnotes of individual chapters.

BOOKS AND JOURNALS

Barnum, D., 'Indirect incitement and freedom of speech in Anglo-American law' [2006] *European Human Rights Law Review* 258

Bates, E., 'A "public emergency threatening the life of the nation"?' (2005) 76 *British Yearbook of International Law* 245.

——, 'Anti-terrorism control orders' (2009) 29 *Legal Studies* 99

Bellany, I. (ed), *Terrorism and Weapons of Mass Destruction* (Routledge, Abingdon, 2007)

Bennion, F., 'Is the Real IRA a proscribed organization?' (2004) 168 *Justice of the Peace* 472,

——, 'The Real IRA is proscribed after all' (2004) 168 *Justice of the Peace* 694

Binning, P., 'In safe hands?' Striking the balance between privacy and security—Anti-terrorist finance measures' (2002) 6 *European Human Rights Law Review* 734

Bonner, D., *Executive Measures, Terrorism and National Security* (Ashgate, Aldershot, 2007)

Cabinet Office, *Security in a Global Hub* (London, 2007)

Campbell, C., '"War in terror" and vicarious hegemons' (2005) 54 *International and Comparative Law Quarterly* 321

—— and Connelly, I., 'Making war on terror?' (2006) 69 *Modern Law Review* 935

Chief Surveillance Commissioner, *Report on Two Visits by Sadiq Khan, MP, to Babar Ahmed at HM Prison Woodall* (Cm 7336, London, 2008)

Clarke, R.V. and Newman, G.R., *Outsmarting the Terrorists* (Praeger, Westport, 2006)

Cory Collusion Inquiry Reports, Billy Wright (2003–04 HC 472), Pat Finucane (2003–04 HC 470), Robert Hamill (2003–04 HC 471), Rosemary Nelson (2003–04 HC 473)

Crown Prosecution Service, *Scrutiny of Pre-Charge Detention in Terrorist Cases* (London, 2007)

Delegated Powers and Regulatory Reform Select Committee, *Report on the Anti-terrorism, Crime and Security Bill* (2001–02 HL 45)

Dickson, B., 'Law versus terrorism: can law win?' [2005] *European Human Rights Law Review* 1

Dingley, J. (ed), *Combating Terrorism in Northern Ireland* (Routledge, Abingdon, 2009)

Donohue. L., 'Terrorism and trial by jury' (2007) 59 *Stanford Law Review* 1321

Donohue, L.K., *Counter-Terrorism Law* (Irish Academic Press, Dublin, 2001)

——, *The Cost of Counterterrorism: Power, Politics, and Liberty* (Cambridge University Press, Cambridge, 2008)

Duffy, H., *The 'War on Terror' and the Framework of International Law* (Cambridge University Press, Cambridge, 2005)

Dyzenhaus, D., *The Constitution of Law* (Cambridge University Press, Cambridge, 2006)

Eden, P. and O'Donnell, T., *September 11, 2001: A Turning Point in International and Domestic Law?* (Transnational Publishers, New York, 2005)

Edwards, R.A., 'Stop and search, terrorism and the human rights deficit' (2008) 37 *Common Law World Review* 211

Elagab, O., 'Control of terrorist funds and the banking system' (2006) 21 *Journal of Banking Law & Regulation* 38

European Committee for the Prevention of Torture and Inhuman and Degrading Treatment, Report to the United Kingdom Government on the Visit to the United Kingdom carried out by the European Committee for the Prevention of Torture and Inhuman and Degrading Treatment (Strasbourg, CPT/Inf (2008) 27) and Response of the United Kingdom Government (CPT/Inf (2008) 28)

Feldman, D., 'Proportionality and discrimination in anti-terrorism legislation' (2005) 64 *Cambridge Law Journal* 271

Fenwick, H., 'The Anti-terrorism, Crime and Security Act 2001' (2002) 65 *Modern Law Review* 724

——, *Civil Liberties and Human Rights* (4th edn, Routledge-Cavendish, Abdington, 2007) ch 14

Foster, S., 'Control orders, human rights and the House of Lords' (2007) 171 *Justice of the Peace* 863

Gearty, C., 'Human rights in an age of counter-terrorism' (2005) 58 *Current Legal Problems* 25

——, '11 September 2001, counter-terrorism and the Human Rights Act 1998' (2005) 32 *Journal of Law & Society* 18

Goldstock, R., *Organised Crime in Northern Ireland* (Northern Ireland Office, Belfast, 2004)

Goold, B.J. and Lazarus, L., *Security and Human Rights* (Hart, Oxford, 2007)

Gross, O. and Ní Aoláin, F., *Law in Times of Crisis* (Cambridge University Press, Cambridge, 2006)

Hickman, L., 'Press freedom and new legislation' (2001) 151 *New Law Journal* 716

Hickman, T.R., 'Between human rights and the rule of law' (2005) 68 *Modern Law Review* 655

Hiebert, J.L., 'Parliamentary review of terrorism measures' (2005) 65 *Modern Law Review* 676

HM Treasury, *The Financial Challenge to Crime and Terrorism* (London, 2007)

Home Office, Regulatory Impact Assessments, Anti-terrorism, Crime and Security Bill, Aviation Security, Retention of Communications Data, Security of Nuclear Industry, Security of Pathogens and Toxins, Terrorism Act 2000 Passenger Information, Terrorism Property (London, 2001)

——, Circular 3/2001: *Terrorism Act 2000*

——, Circular 2/2002: *International application of the UK law on corruption*

——, Circular 7/2002: *Guidance for the police and public on the implementation of Section 89; Sections 113–115; Sections 117–120 and Section 121 of the Anti-terrorism, Crime & Security Act 2001. (Part 13 of the Anti-terrorism, Crime & Security Act.)*

——, Circular 16/2002: *Part 6 of the Anti-terrorism, Crime & Security Act 2001—Weapons of Mass Destruction*

——, Circular 24/2002: *A protocol between the Ministry of Defence Police and Home Office Police Forces*

——, Circular 25/2002: *A protocol between British Transport Police and Home Office Police Forces*

——, Circular 30/2002: *Guidance for the police and public on the implementation of Sections 1–3 of the Anti-terrorism, Crime & Security Act 2001*

——, Circular 32/2002: *Section 94 of the Anti-terrorism, Crime & Security Act: Removal of Disguises*

——, Circular 42/2003: *Guidance for the police in the application of 9 of Schedule 8 to the Terrorism Act 2000, subsequent to the ruling of the European Court of Human Rights in the case of Brennan v the United Kingdom*

——, *Counter-Terrorism Powers: Reconciling Security and Liberty in an Open Society* (Cm 6147, London, 2004)

——, *Report of the Official Account of the Bombings in London on the 7th July 2005* (2005–06 HC 1087)

——, Circular 26/2005, *Coordinated Policing Protocol between the Civil Nuclear Constabulary and Home Office Police Forces/Scottish Police Forces*

——, Circular 8/2006, *The Terrorism Act 2006*

——, *Countering International Terrorism* (Cm 6888, London, 2006)

——, *Guidance on Notices Issued under Section 3 of the Terrorism Act 2006* (London, 2006)

——, *Addressing Lessons from the Emergency Response to the 7 July 2005 London Bombings* (London, 2006)

——, *Government Discussion Document Ahead of Proposed Counter Terrorism Bill 2007* (Home Office, London, 2007)

——, *Options for Pre-Charge Detention in Terrorist Cases* (London, 2007)

——, *Possible Measures for Inclusion into a Future Counter-Terrorism Bill* (London, 2007)

——, *Summary of Responses to the Counter-Terrorism Bill Consultation* (Cm 7269, London, 2007)

——, *Terrorist Investigations and the French Examining Magistrates System* (London, 2007)

——, Circular 27/2008: *Authorisation of Stop and Search Powers under Section 44 of the Terrorism Act 2000*

——, *Pursue, Prevent, Protect, Prepare: The United Kingdom's Strategy for Countering International Terrorism* (Cm 7547, London, 2009)

—— and HM Treasury, *Review of Safeguards to Protect the Charitable Sector (England and Wales) from Terrorist Abuse* (<http://www.homeoffice.gov.uk/documents/cons-2007-protecting-charities/>, 2007)

—— and Northern Ireland Office, *Legislation against Terrorism* (Cm 4178, London, 1998)

House of Commons Constitutional Affairs Committee, *The Operation of the Special Immigration Appeals Commission (SIAC) and the Use of Special Advocates* (2004–5 HC 323-I)

—— Defence Select Committee, *The Ministry of Defence Police: Changes in Jurisdiction Proposed under the Anti-terrorism, Crime and Security* Bill 2001 (2001–02 HC 382) and Government Response (2001–02 HC 621)

——, *The Threat from Terrorism* (2001–02 HC 348-I)

House of Commons Home Affairs Committee, *Report on the Anti-terrorism, Crime and Security Bill 2001* (2001–02 HC 351)

——, *Terrorism and Community Relations* (2003–04 HC 165)

——, *Terrorism Detention Powers* (2005–06 HC 910)

——, *The Government's Counter-Terrorism Proposals* (2007–08 HC 43)

—— Library, 01/101: The Anti-terrorism, Crime and Security Bill (Introduction and Summary); 01/94 (Parts VI & VII: Pathogens, Toxins and Weapons of Mass Destruction); 01/96 (Parts IV & V: Immigration, asylum, race and religion); 01/97 (Part X: Police Powers)); 01/98 (Parts III & XI: Disclosure and Retention of Information); 01/99 (Parts I, II, VIII, IX & XIII: Property, Security & Crime); 02/54 The Anti-terrorism, Crime and Security Act 2001:Disclosure of Information; 02/52 Detention of suspected international terrorists - Part 4 of the Anti-terrorism, Crime and Security Act 2001; 05/14 The Prevention of Terrorism Bill; 05/66, The Terrorism Bill ; 05/70 The Terrorism (Northern Ireland) Bill; 08/20 Counter-Terrorism Bill; 08/52 Counter-Terrorism Bill: Committee Stage Report

—— Northern Ireland Affairs Committee, *The Financing of Terrorism in Northern Ireland* (2001–02 HC 978)

——, *Organised Crime in Northern Ireland* (2005–06 HC 886) and Government Reply (2005–06 HC 1642)

——, *Policing and Criminal Justice in Northern Ireland* (2007–08 HC 335)

—— Science and Technology Committee, *The Scientific Response to Terrorism* (2003–04 HC 415) and *Government Reply* (Cm 6108, London, 2004)

——, *UK Transport Security* (2005–06 HC 637)

House of Lords Constitution Committee, *The Prevention of Terrorism Bill* (2004–05 HL 66)

——, *Justice and Security (Northern Ireland) Bill* (2006–07 HL 54)

——, *Counter-Terrorism Bill: The role of ministers, Parliament and the judiciary* (2007–08 HL 167)

Hunt, A., 'The Council of Europe Convention on the Prevention of Terrorism' (2006) 4 *European Public Law* 603

——, 'Criminal prohibitions on direct and indirect encouragement of terrorism' [2007] *Criminal Law Review* 441

Independent Assessor of Military Complaints Procedures in Northern Ireland, Annual Reports (1993–4 HC 369) and onwards

Independent Commissioner for Detained Terrorism Suspects, Annual Reports (Northern Ireland Office, Belfast)

Independent Monitoring Commission, 1st to 20th Reports (2004–08)

Independent Police Complaints Commission, *Stockwell One* (London, 2007) and *Stockwell Two* (London, 2007)

Intelligence and Security Committee, *Inquiry into Intelligence, Assessments and Advice prior to the Terrorist Bombings on Bali 12 October 2002* (Cm 5724, London, 2002)

——, *Inquiry into Intelligence, Report into the London Terrorist Attacks on 7 July 2005* (Cm 6785, London, 2005) and *Government Reply* (Cm 6786, London, 2006)

Jackson, J.D., Quinn, K., and Wolfe, M., *Legislating against Silence* (Northern Ireland Office, Belfast, 2001)

Joint Committee on Human Rights, *Reports on the Anti-terrorism, Crime and Security Bill* (2001–02 HL 37, HC 372) and (2001–02 HL 51, HC 420)

——, *Continuance in Force of Sections 21 to 23 of the Anti-terrorism, Crime and Security Act 2001* (2002–03 HC 462/HL 59)

——, *Statutory Review: Continuance of Pt.IV* (2003–04 HL 38/HC 381)

——, *Review of Counterterrorism Powers* (2003–04 HL 158/HC 713)

——, *Counter-Terrorism Policy and Human Rights: Terrorism Bill and related matters* (2005–06 HL 75, HC 561) and *Government Response* (2005–06 HL 114, HC 888)

——, *Counter-Terrorism Policy and Human Rights: Prosecution and Pre-Charge Detention* (2005–06 HL 240/HC 1576)

——, *The Council of Europe Convention on the Prevention of Terrorism* (2006–07 HL 26/HC 247)

——, *Legislative Scrutiny: Third Progress Report* (2006–07 HL 46/HC 303)

——, *Counter-Terrorism Policy and Human Rights: 28 days, intercept and post-charge questioning* (2006–07 HL 157/HC 394) and *Government Reply* (Cm 7215, London, 2007)

——, *Counter-Terrorism Policy and Human Rights: 42 days* (2007–08 HL 23/HC 156)

——, *Counter-Terrorism Policy and Human Rights: Annual Renewal of 28 days* (2007–08 HL 32/HC 825)

——, *Counter-Terrorism Policy and Human Rights: Counter-Terrorism Bill* (2007–08 HL50/HC199)

——, *Terrorism Policy and Human Rights: Annual Review of Control Orders Legislation* 2008 (2007–08 HL 57/HC 356) and Government Reply (Cm 7368, London, 2008)

——, *Counter-Terrorism Policy and Human Rights: 42 days and public emergencies* (2007–08 HL 116/HC 635)

——, *Government Responses to the Committee's 20th and 21st Reports and other correspondence* (2007–08 HL 127, HC 756)

——, *Counter-Terrorism Policy and Human Rights: Counter-Terrorism Bill* (2007–08 HL 172/HC 1077)

——, *Counter-Terrorism Policy and Human Rights: Counter-Terrorism Bill* (2007–08 HL 50/HC 199) and *Government Reply* (Cm 7344, London, 2008)

——, *Counter-Terrorism Policy and Human Rights, Counter-Terrorism Bill* (2007–08 HL 108/HC 554)

——, *Counter-Terrorism Policy and Human Rights: Annual Renewal of Control Orders Legislation 2009* (2008–09 HL37/HC382)

Jones, A., Bowers, R, and Lodge, H.D., *The Terrorism Act 2006* (Oxford University Press, Oxford, 2006)

JUSTICE, *From Arrest to Charge in 48 Hours* (London, 2007)

Kennison, P. and Loumanksy, A., 'Shoot to kill' (2007) *Crime, Law & Social Change* 151

Leigh, L.H., 'The Terrorism Act 2006—a brief analysis' (2006) 170 *Justice of the Peace* 364

——, 'Arrest: reasonable grounds for suspicion' (2008) 172 *Justice of the Peace* 180

Lennon, G. and Walker, C., 'Hot money in a cold climate' [2008] *Public Law* 37

Lloyd Report, Lord Lloyd and Sir John Kerr, *Inquiry into Legislation against Terrorism* (Cm 3420, London, 1996)

Lord Carlile, *Anti-terrorism, Crime and Security Act 2001 Part IV Section 28*, Reviews 2001–2005 (Home Office, London)

——, *Reports on the Operation in 2001–2005 of Part VII of the Terrorism Act 2000* (Home Office, London)

——, *Proposals by Her Majesty's Government for Changes to the Laws against Terrorism* (Home Office, London, 2005)

——, *Special Report of the Independent Reviewer in relation to Quarterly Reports under section 14(1) of the Prevention of Terrorism Act 2005* (Home Office, London, 2006)

——, *Report on Proposed Measures for Inclusion in a Counter-Terrorism Bill* (Cm 7262, London, 2007)

——, *Report on the Operation in 2001–2008 of the Terrorism Act 2000* (Home Office, London) and *Government replies* (Cm 7133, London, 2007), (Cm 7429, London, 2008)

——, *The Definition of Terrorism* (Cm 7052, London, 2007) and *Government Reply* (Cm 7058, London, 2007)

——, *Reports of the Independent Reviewer pursuant to Section 14(3) of the Prevention of Terrorism Act 2005–2008* (Home Office, London) and *Government replies* (Cm 7194, London, 2007), (Cm 7367, London, 2008)

McCulloch, J. and Pickering, S., 'Suppressing the financing of terrorism' (2005) 45 *British Journal of Criminology* 470

McGoldrick, D., 'Security detention—United Kingdom practice' (2009) 40 *Case Western Reserve Journal of International Law* 507

Metropolitan Police Authority, *Counter-Terrorism: The London Debate* (London, 2007)

Moeckli, D., 'Stop and search under the Terrorism Act' (2007) 70 *Modern Law Review* 659

——, *Human Rights and Non-Discrimination in the 'War on Terror'* (Oxford University Press, Oxford, 2008)

Moran, J., *Policing the Peace in Northern Ireland* (Manchester University Press, Manchester, 2008)

Ni Aolain, F., *The Politics of Force* (Blackstaff, Belfast, 2000)

Northern Ireland Office, *Diplock Review: Report* (Belfast, 2000)

——, *Regulating the Private Security Industry in Northern Ireland* (Belfast, 2006)

——, *Replacement Arrangements for the Diplock Court System* (Belfast, 2006)

Organised Crime Task Force, *Annual Reports and Threat Assessments 2004–2008* (Northern Ireland Office, Belfast)

Police Ombudsman for Northern Ireland, *A Study of the Treatment of Solicitors and Barristers by the Police in Northern Ireland* (Belfast, 2003)

——, *Investigation of Matters relating to the Omagh Bombing on August 15 1998* (Belfast, 2007)

——, *Statement by the Police Ombudsman for Northern Ireland on her investigation into the circumstances surrounding the death of Raymond McCord Jr and related matters* (Belfast, 2007)

Policing Board for Northern Ireland, *Omagh Bomb Investigation* (Belfast, 2008)

Posner, E.A. and Vermeule, A., *Terror in the Balance* (Oxford University Press, Oxford, 2007)

Privy Counsellor Review Committee, *Anti-terrorism, Crime and Security Act 2001, Review, Report* (2003–04 HC 100) ('Newton Report')

Ramraj, V.V., Hor, M., and Roach, K., *Global Anti-terrorism Law and Policy* (Cambridge University Press, Cambridge, 2005)

Roberts, P., 'The presumption of innocence brought home?' (2002) 118 *Law Quarterly Review* 41

Rowe, J.J., 'The Terrorism Act 2000' [2000] *Criminal Law Review* 527

Russell, J., *Charge or release: Terrorism Pre-Charge Detention Comparative Law Study* (Liberty, London, 2007)

Sandhill, A., 'Liberty, fairness and UK control order cases' [2008] *European Human Rights Law Review* 119

Saul, B., 'Speaking of terror' (2005) 28 *University of New South Wales Law Review* 868

——, *Defining Terrorism in International Law* (Oxford University Press, Oxford, 2006)

Schenin, M., *Reports of the Special Rapporteur on the promotion and protection of human rights and fundamental freedoms while countering terrorism* (A/60/370, 2005), (E/CN.4/2006/98, 2005), (A/61/267, 2006), (A/HRC/4/26, 2007), (A/62/263, 2007), (A/HRC/6/17, 2007), (A/63/223, 2008), (A/HRC/10/3. 2009) (United Nations, Geneva)

Smith, I., Owen, T., and Bodnar, A., *Asset Recovery* (Oxford University Press, Oxford, 2007)

Starmer, K., 'Setting the record straight: human rights in an era of international terrorism' [2007] *European Human Rights Law Review* 123

Strawson, J., *Law After Ground Zero* (Glasshouse Press, London, 2002)

Tadros, V., 'Justice and terrorism' (2007) 10 *New Criminal Law Review* 658

——, 'Crime and security' (2008) 71 *Modern Law Review* 940

Tierney, S., 'Determining the state of exception' (2005) 68 *Modern Law Review* 668

Tomkins, A., 'Legislating against terror: The Anti-terrorism, Crime and Security Act 2001' [2002] *Public Law* 205

——, 'Readings of A v Secretary of State for the Home Department' [2005] *Public Law* 259

United Nations Committee against Torture, 4th Report under Article 19 by the United Kingdom of Great Britain and Northern Ireland (CAT/C/67/Add.2, 2004) and Consideration of Reports (CAT/C/CR/33/3, 2004) and Comment by Government (CAT/C/GBR/CO/4/Add.1, 2006)

Vaughan, B. and Kilcommins, S., *Terrorism, Rights and the Rule of Law* (Willan, Cullompton, 2008)

Wadham, J. and Chakrabarti, S., 'Indefinite Detention Without Trial' (2001) 151 *New Law Journal* 1564

Walker, C., 'Biological attack, terrorism and the law' (2004) 17 *Terrorism and Political Violence* 175

——, 'Terrorism and criminal justice' [2004] *Criminal Law Review* 311

——, 'Clamping Down on Terrorism in the United Kingdom' (2006) 4 *Journal of International Criminal Justice* 1137

——, 'Cyber-terrorism: Legal principle and the law in the United Kingdom' (2006) 110 *Penn State Law Review* 625

——, 'Intelligence and Anti-terrorism Legislation in the United Kingdom' (2006) 44 *Crime, Law & Social Change* 387

——, 'Keeping control of terrorists without losing control of constitutionalism' (2007) 59 *Stanford Law Review* 1395

——, 'The legal definition of "Terrorism" in United Kingdom law and beyond' [2007] *Public Law* 331

——, 'The treatment of foreign terror suspects' (2007) 70 *Modern Law Review* 427

——, '"Know thine enemy as thyself": Discerning friend from foe under anti-terrorism laws' (2008) 32 *Melbourne Law Review* 275

——, 'Post-charge questioning of suspects' [2008] *Criminal Law Review* 509

——, 'The governance of the Critical National Infrastructure' [2008] *Public Law* 323

——. and Akdeniz, Y., 'Anti-Terrorism laws and data retention: war is over?' (2003) 54 *Northern Ireland Legal Quarterly* 159

——. and Broderick, J., *The Civil Contingencies Act 2004: Risk, Resilience and the Law in the United Kingdom* (Oxford University Press, Oxford, 2006)

Walsh, D., *Bloody Sunday and the Rule of Law in Northern Ireland* (Gill & MacMillan, Dublin, 2000)

Warbrick, C., 'The principles of the ECHR and the response of states to terrorism' [2002] *European Human Rights Law Review* 287

Whalley, R., *Report of the Independent Reviewer: Justice and Security (Northern Ireland) Act 2007* (Northern Ireland Office, Belfast, 2007)

Wilkinson, P., (ed), *Homeland Security in the UK* (Routledge, Abingdon, 2007)

Zedner, L., 'Securing liberty in the face of terrorism' (2005) 32 *Journal of Law & Society* 507

PARLIAMENTARY PROCESS

Terrorism Act 2000:

House of Commons, First reading: vol 340 col 443 (2 December 1999); Second reading: vol 341 col 152 (14 December 1999); Committee stage: Standing Committee D; Report stage vol 346 col 329 (15 March 2000); Third reading vol 346 col 445 (15 March 2000); Lords amendments vol 353 col 353 (10 July 2000)

House of Lords, First reading: vol 611 col 9 (6 April 2000); Second reading: vol 611 col 1427 (6 April 2000); Committee stage: vol 613 col 214 (16 May 2000); Report stage vol 614 col 159 (20 June 2000); Third reading vol 614 col 1442 (4 July 2000)

Anti-terrorism, Crime and Security Act 2001:

House of Commons, First reading: vol 374 col 571 (12 November 2001); Second reading: vol 375 col 21 (19 November 2001); Committee stage: vol 375 col 342 (21, 26 November 2001); Third reading vol 375 col 801 (26 November 2001); Lords amendments vol 376 col 841 (12, 13 December 2001)

House of Lords, First reading: vol 629 col 130 (26 November 2001); Second reading: vol 629 col 142 (27 November 2001); Committee stage: vol 629 col 301 (28, 29 November, 3, 4 December 2001); Report stage vol 629 col 949 (6, 10 December 2001); Third reading vol 629 col 1238 (11 December 2001); Commons amendments vol 629 col 1420 (13 December 2001)

Prevention of Terrorism Act 2005

House of Commons, First reading: vol 431 col 151 (22 February 2005); Second reading: vol 431 col 333 (23 February 2005); Committee stage: vol 431 col 663 (28 February 2005); Third reading vol 431 col 768 (28 February 2005); Lords amendments vol 431 cols 1573 (9 March 2005), 1761, 1796, 1826, 1854 (10 March 2005)

House of Lords, First reading: vol 670 col 114 (1 March 2005); Second reading: vol 670 col 116 (1 March 2005); Committee stage: vol 670 col 359 (3 March 2005), 482 (7 March 2005); Report vol 670 col 627 (8 March 2005); Third reading vol 670 col 724 (8 March 2005); Commons amendments vol 670 cols 845, 999, 1019, 1032, 1057 (10 March 2005)

Terrorism Act 2006

House of Commons, First reading: vol 437 col 295 (12 October 2005); Second reading: vol 438 col 322 (26 October 2005); Committee stage: vol 438 cols 832, 985 (2, 3 November 2005); Report vol 439 col 325 (9 November 2005); Third reading vol 439 col 492 (10 November 2005); Lords amendments vol 442 col 1427 (15 February 2006), vol 443 col 1664 (16 March 2006)

House of Lords, First reading: vol 675 col 820 (10 November 2005); Second reading: vol 675 col 1384 (21 November 2005); Committee stage: vol 676 cols 421, 485, 609, 1118, 1631, (5, 7, 13, 20 December 2005); Report vol 677 cols 549, 1186 (17 January 2006); Third reading vol 678 col 197 (1 February 2006); Commons amendments vol 679 col 136 (28 February 2006), vol 680 col 241 (22 March 2006)

Terrorism (Northern Ireland) Act 2006
House of Commons, First reading: vol 437 col 169 (11 October 2005); Second reading: vol 438 col 627 (31 October 2005); Committee stage: Standing Committee E (8 November 2005); Report vol 440 col 289 (30 November 2005); Third reading vol 440 col 324 (30 November 2005)
House of Lords, First reading: vol 676 col 307 (1 December 2005); Second reading: vol 676 col 1670 (20 December 2005); Committee stage: vol 677 col 137 (12 January 2006); Report vol 678 col 102 (30 January 2006); Third reading vol 678 col 1078 (14 February 2006)

Justice and Security (Northern Ireland) Act 2007
House of Commons, First reading: vol 453 col 833 (27 November 2006); Second reading: vol 454 col 893 (13 December 2006); Committee stage: Public Bill Committee (16 January 2007); Report vol 456 col 714 (6 February 2007); Third reading vol 456 col 803 (6 February 2007); Lords amendments vol 460 col 321 (10 May 2007)
House of Lords, First reading: vol 689 col 726 (7 February 2007); Second reading: vol 689 col 1024 (20 February 2007); Committee stage: vol 690 cols 99GC, 199GC (19, 21 March 2007); Report vol 691 col 505 (23 April 2007); Third reading vol 691 col 1066 (2 May 2007); Commons amendments vol 692 col 451 (21 May 2007)

Counter-Terrorism Act 2008
House of Commons, First reading: vol 470 col 1652 (24 January 2008); Second reading: vol 474 col 647 (1 April 2008); Committee stage: Public Bill Committee (22 April 2008); Report vol 477 cols 165, 312 (10, 11 June 2008); Third reading vol 477 col 422 (11 June 2008); Lords amendments vol 483 col 240 (19 November 2008)
House of Lords, First reading: vol 702 col 676 (12 June 2008); Second reading: vol 703 col 632 (8 July 2008); Committee stage: vol 704 cols 338, 492, 740, 1048 (9, 13, 15, 21 October 2008); Report vol 705 cols 576, 930 (4, 11 November 2008); Third reading vol 705 col 930 (17 November 2005); Commons amendments vol 705 col 1288 (24 November 2008)

Governmental websites

Bloody Sunday Inquiry	http://www.bloody-sunday-inquiry.org.uk/
Centre for the Protection of the National Infrastructure	http://www.cpni.gov.uk/
Department for Business, Enterprise and Regulatory Reform, Chemical and Biological Weapons	http://www.berr.gov.uk/energy/non-proliferation/cbw/index.html
Department for Business, Enterprise and Regulatory Reform, Nuclear	http://www.berr.gov.uk/energy/non-proliferation/nuclear/index.html
Department for Communities and Local Government, Preventing Extremism	http://www.communities.gov.uk/communities/preventingextremism/
Department for Transport, Transport Security	http://www.dft.gov.uk/pgr/security/
HM Treasury, Financial Sanctions	http://www.hm-treasury.gov.uk/fin_sanctions_index.htm
Home Office, Counter-Terrorism	http://www.homeoffice.gov.uk/counter-terrorism/
Home Office, Office for Security and Counter Terrorism	http://security.homeoffice.gov.uk/
Independent Monitoring Commission	http://www.independentmonitoringcommission.org/

Metropolitan Police Service, Counter Terrorism Command	http://www.met.police.uk/so/counter_terrorism.htm
National Counter Terrorism Security Office	http://www.nactso.gov.uk/index.php
National Extremism Tactical Coordination Unit	http://www.netcu.org.uk/
Northern Ireland Office, Security	http://www.nio.gov.uk/index/key-issues/security.htm
Police Service of Northern Ireland	http://www.psni.police.uk/
Security Service (MI5)	http://www.mi5.gov.uk/
UK Resilience	http://www.cabinetoffice.gov.uk/ukresilience.aspx

Index

Note: in sub-headings 2000 Act refers to Terrorism Act 2000; 2001 Act refers to Anti-terrorism, Crime and Security Act 2001; 2005 Act refers to Prevention of Terrorism Act; 2006 Act refers to Terrorism Act 2006